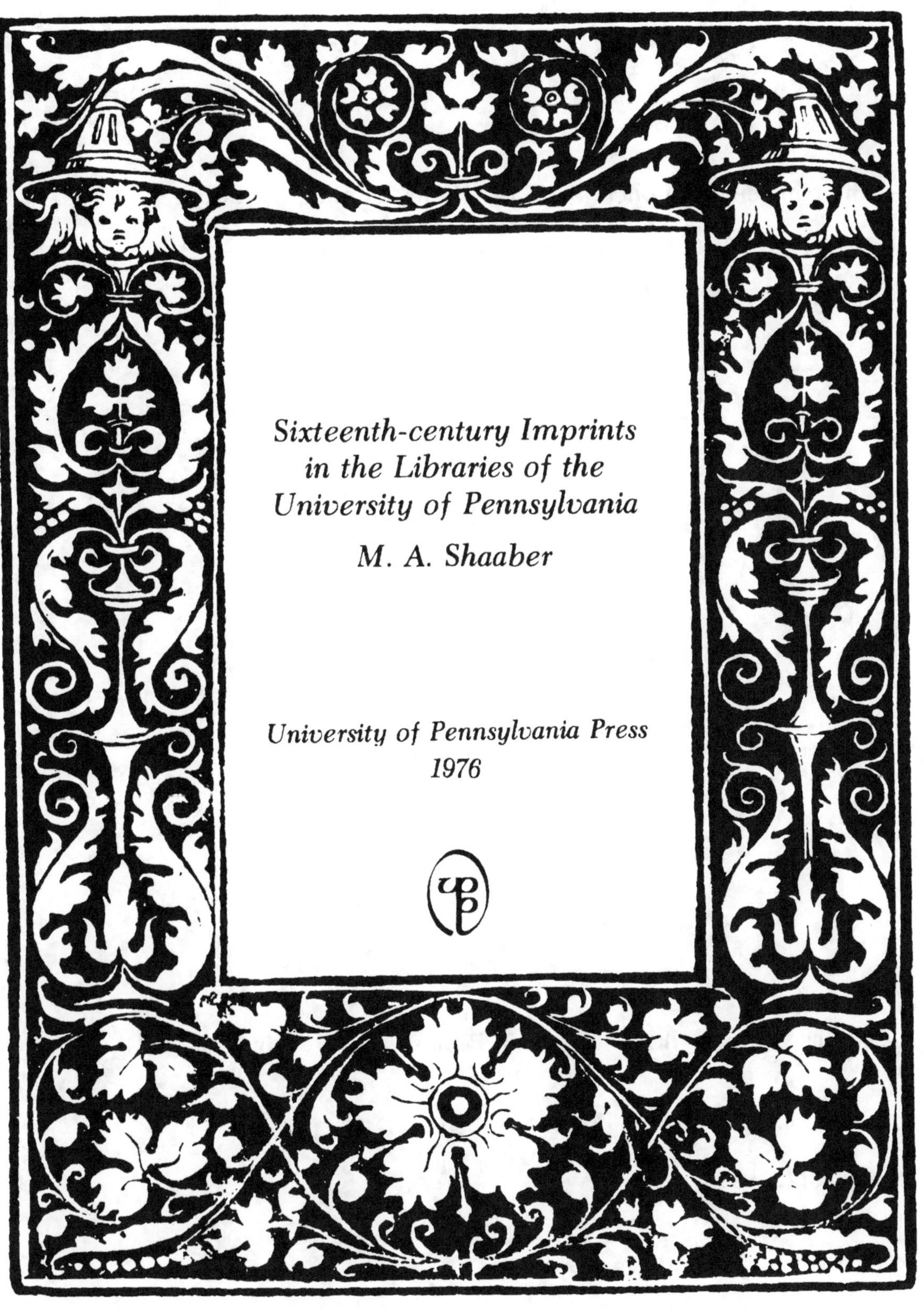

Sixteenth-century Imprints in the Libraries of the University of Pennsylvania

M. A. Shaaber

University of Pennsylvania Press
1976

The Nineteenth Publication in the Haney Foundation Series
University of Pennsylvania

Library of Congress Catalog Card Number: 75-33493

ISBN: 0-8122-7698-1

Printed in the United States of America

PREFACE

This listing of the sixteenth-century books and other printed material in the university's libraries is published as a means of facilitating access to them by isolating them from the many other books with which they are catalogued and by indicating as much of their contents as is possible within the limitations of short-title description. More information about some of them can be found in *Aristotle texts and commentaries to 1700 in the University of Pennsylvania Library: a catalogue* by Lyman W. Riley (Philadelphia, 1961).

The method of description employed, one hopes, needs little explanation. In books with both an imprint and a colophon only so much of the colophon as adds to or varies from the data of the imprint is transcribed; if it adds nothing its presence is merely noted. All data quoted from some part of the book other than the title page are enclosed in parentheses. *B.L.* stands for any kind of non-roman and non-italic type. The page or folio numbers given are those of the first and the last *numbered* page or folio; as a rule no notice is taken of errors or omissions of the numeration. Cross-references are incorporated in the index, through which all joint-authors, translators, editors, etc. can be located.

Occasional reference is made to the following works:

H. M. Adams, *Catalogue of books printed on the continent of Europe, 1501-1600, in Cambridge libraries*, Cambridge, 1967.

Joseph Henry Beale, *A bibliography of early English law books*, Cambridge, Mass., 1926.

Josef Benzing, *Lutherbibliographie: Verzeichnis der gedruckten Schriften Martin Luthers bis zu dessen Tod*, Baden-Baden, 1965 (Bibliotheca bibliographica Aureliana X, XVI, XIX).

George Watson Cole, *A catalogue of books relating to the discovery and early history of North and South America forming a part of the library of E. D. Church*, New York, 1907.

Frank Isaac, *An index to the early printed books in the British Museum, Part II. MDI-MDXX*, London, 1938.

A short-title catalogue of books printed in England, Scotland, & Ireland and of English books printed abroad 1475-1640 compiled by A. W. Pollard & G. R. Redgrave, London, 1926 (Bibliographical Society).

Books domiciled in the Henry C. Lea Library, the Biddle Law Library, the Furness Memorial Library, the Edgar Fahs Smith Memorial Collection, the Yarnall Library of Theology of St. Clement's Church (on deposit), and certain departmental libraries are identified. All others will be found in the Rare Book Collection.

A few books acquired or catalogued too late for inclusion in the main list are added at p. 561.

I am grateful indeed to the many members of the library staff who have, in one way or another, facilitated my work, especially Mrs. Shifra Rin and Dr. William E. Miller, my mentors in Hebrew and Greek respectively, and Mrs. Patricia R. Mack, who supplied with the pen what the typewriter could not supply. The skill with which Miss Elizabeth Webster has prepared the typescript deserves open recognition.

Publication has been assisted by a grant from the Haney Foundation.

M.A.S.

CONTENTS

A

ABD ISU, patriarch. R. D. patriarchae Orientalium Assyriorum de ... Tridentini concilio Approbatio, & professio, et Literae ... Marciantonij Cardinalis Amulij ad legatos ... Concilij Tridentini. MDLXII. Ripae. M D LXII. 4°. A^4. (Lea.) [1

ABDIAS. Abdiae Babyloniae primi episcopi ... de historia certaminis Apostolici, Libri X. Iulio Africano interprete. Matthiae Apostoli, Marci, Clementis, Cypriani, & Apollinarii vitae ... Vita B. Martini Sabariensis ... à Seuero Sulpitio conscripta. ... Marcialis discipuli Domini vita ab Aureliano ... descripta. Martini Turonensis Episcopi fidei Confessio, breuibus scholiis à F. Thoma Beauxamis illustrata. Parisiis, Apud Thomam Belot ... 1571. ... 8°. $\bar{a}^8$ $\bar{e}^8$ $\bar{\imath}^8$ a-z^8 A-I^8 (-I8, *blank*). ff. 1-252. [2

ABDU'L AZIZ IBN UTHMAN AL' QASIBI. ... Alchabitij Opus ad scrutanda Stellarũ Magisteria isagogicũ ... restitutũ ab ... Antonio de Fantis Taruisino. qui ... eiusdẽ Auctoris Libellũ de Planetaꝝ Cõiunctiõibus ... addidit ... cuꝫ ... Ioãnis de Saxonia Cõmentario. 1521 Venetijs In edibus Petri Liechtenstein (*Colophon.*) 4°. B.L. a-h^8. ff. 3-64. [3

ABRAHAM BEN MĒ'IR IBN EZRA. Abraam Iudaei de natiuitatibus ... liber, pristino suo nitore restitutus, per Ioan. Dryandrum ... Colonię apud Eucharium Ceruicornum, Anno 1537 mense Augusto. 4°. A-F^4 G^6. [4

ABRAVANEL, JUDAH. Dialoghi di amore, composti par Leone Medico Hebreo In Vinegia, M. D. LII. (... In casa de' figliuoli di Aldo.) 8°. A-EE^8 FF^4. ff. 3-228. [5

-- -- In Vinegia, M. D. LVIII. (... per Isepo Guiglielmo Vicentino, alle spese però del ... M. Federico Torresano d'Asola. ...) 8°. *Same collation and foliation.* [6

-- -- Philosophie d'amour de M. Leon Hebreu, Traduicte d'Italien en Françoys, par le Seigneur du Parc Champenois. ... A Lyon Chez Guil. Rouille. 1551. (Acheuez d'imprimer le XVII. d'Apuril ...) 8°. a-z^8 A-Y^8. pp. 3-675. [7

-- -- Los dialogos de amor de Mestre Leon Abarbanel ... De nueuo traduzidos en lengua castellana ... En Venetia ... M D LXVIII. 4°. $+^4$ (-+4, *presumably blank*) A-Q^8 (-Q8, *presumably blank*). ff. 1-127. ¶*Translator: Juan Costa.* (Lea.) [8

ABRIL, PEDRO SIMON. La gramatica Griega escrita en lengua Castellana ... En Çaragoça ... en casa de Lorēço i Diego de Robles ermanos. 1586. Vendense ... en casa de Pedro Iuarra ... 8°. A-I^8 K^4 (-K4, *presumably blank*). ff. 1-78. [9

-- La gramatica Griega escrita en lengua Castellana ... En Madrid, por Pedro Madrigal, M.D.LXXXVII. 8°. $+^8$ $++^4$ A-D^8 E-M^4 a-d^4. ff. 1-64. ¶*A different work. Includes the* Table *of Cebes in Greek, Spanish, and Latin.* [10

-- Primera parte de la filosofia llamada la logica ... Impressa en Alcala de Henares, en casa de Iuan Gracian ... 1587. (*Colophon.*) 4°. $¶^4$ $*^4$ A-Cc^4 (-Cc4, *presumably blank*). ff. 2-105. [11

ACCIAJOLI, MADDALENA. Rime Toscane ... Stampata in Firenze, ... Per Francesco Tosi. MDXC. 4°. A-X^4. pp. 5-155. [12

ACCOLTI, BENEDETTO. De bello contra barbaros a Christianis gesto, pro Christi sepulchro & Iudaea recuperandis, ... Libri IIII. Robertus VVinter, Basileae, 1544. (*Colophon.*) 8°. $+^8$ A-Q^8. (Lea.) [13

ACCOLTI, BERNARDO. Verginia. Comedia ... intitolata la Verginia, con un Capitolo della Madonna ... MDXXXV. (Stampata in Vinegia per Nicolo di Aristotile detto Zoppino: MDXXXV.) 8°. A-G^8 (-G8, *presumably blank*). ff. 2-55. (Furness.) [14

ACCOLTIS, FRANCESCO DE, OF AREZZO. [1] Admiranda cõmentaria ... In secunda decretalinꝫ [*sic*] ... (Venetiis per Paganinũ de paganinis Brixiẽsem impressa ... 1511. die .10.

Maij.) fol. B.L. a-r^8 s^{10}. ff. 2-145. [2] ... Comētaria. super titu. de Constitutionibus ꝛ Rescriptis. Cum apostillis. (Venetijs per Paganinum de paganinis Brixiensem. ... 1511. die 7 Maij.) aa-bb^6. ff. 2-12. [3] Tabula ... in commētaria ... super quibusdā titu. decreta ... A^{10}. (Biddle.) [15

-- [Commentaria super corpore juris civilis.] [Lugduni, Vincentius de Portonariis,] 1538 (Ioannes Moylin al's de Cambray ... excudebat.) fol. B.L. [1] Franciscus Aretinus super prima et secunda codicis ... unà cum apostillis Do. Benedicti Vadi. necnon Summarijs per Do. Lucium Paulum Rhosellū Patauinū ... a-n^8. ff. 2-103. [2] ... in secundam digesti veteris. ... a-g^8. ff. 2-56. [3] ... super prima et secunda infortiati. ... aa-zz^8 AA-HH^8. ff. 2-247. [4] ... super prima et secunda digesti noui. ... 3a-3v^8 (-3e2, 3e7) 3x-3y^6. ff. 2-172. [5] Repertorium operum ... A-D^8 E^6 F^4. (Biddle.) [16

-- ... Francisci de Accoltis de Aretio ... commentaria super titulo de Accusa. Inquisisti. ꝛ denuntia. in quinto libro decretali. ... (Impressum venetijs per Paganinum de paganinis Brixiensem ... M.cccccix. die .xxvij. Ianuarij.) fol. B.L. aa-gg^6 hh^8. ff. 2-50. (Biddle.) [17

ACCORAMBONI, FELICE. Felicis Accorombonii ... interpretatio obscuriorum locorum & sententiarum omnium operum Aristotelis ... & omniū ferme controuersiarum ... inter Platonicos, Galenum, & Aristotelem examinatio. ... Et de fluxu & refluxu maris ... tractatus. ... sententiarum Theophrasti in libris de Plantis explanatio; & in librum Galeni de Temperamentis Annotationes. ... Romae, Apud Sanctium, & Soc. M. D. XC. (*Colophon.*) fol. *^{4} A-5L^4 (-5L4, *blank*). pp. 2-822. [18

ACHARISIO, ALBERTO. La grammatica volgare ... In Vinegia M D XXXVIII. (... per Giouan' Antonio de Nicolini da Sabio. Ad instātia di M. Merchiore Sessa. ... Del mese di Febraro.) 8°. A-D^4. [19

-- Vocabolario et grammatica con l'orthographia della lingua volgare ... con l'espositione di molti luoghi di Dante, del Petrarca et del Boccaccio. ... In Venetia alla bottega d'Erasmo di Vicenzo Valgrisio. M D L. (*Colophon.*) 4°. A-ZZ^4 a-11^4. ff. 1-316. [20

ACHILLES TATIUS. Les amours de Clitophon et de Leucippe, escris iadis en Grec, ... & depuis mis en Latin, par L. Annibal Italien, & nouuellement traduits en langage François ... A Paris, A l'Oliuier de l'Huillier ... 1568. ... 8°. ā^4 A-S^8 T^4 (-T4, *presumably blank*). ff. 1-146. [21

-- -- Achille Tatio Alessandrino dell'amore di Leucippe et di Clitophonte Nuouamente tradotto dalla lingua greca. MDLI. (tradotti per Francesc'Angelo Coccio da Iano, et nuouamente stampati da Piero et fratelli de Nicolini da Sabio in Venetia MDL.) 8°. *^{8} A-O^8 P^4. ff. 2-115. [22

-- -- In Venetia, Per Francesco Lorenzini da Turino, M. D. LX. 8°. A-P^8 (-P8, *presumably blank*). ff. 2-113. [23

-- -- In Fiorenza, Per Filippo Giunti, MDIIC. (... 1597.) 8°. †^{4} A-Q^8 R^4. pp. 1-238. [24

ACHILLINI, ALESSANDRO. Alexandri Achillini Bononiensis ... opera omnia ... Cum annotationibus ... Pamphili Montij Bononiensis ... Venetijs apud Hieronymum Scotum. M D XLV. (*Colophon.*) fol. *^{6} A-K^6 L^4 M-KK^6 (-KK6, *presumably blank*). ff. 1-195. [25

-- -- Venetiis, apud Hieronymum Scotum. M D LXVIII. (*Colophon.*) fol. *^{4} A-EE^6. pp. 1-334. [26

ACHILLINI, GIOVANNI FILOTEO. [Viridario de Gioanne Philotheo Achillino Bolognese. ...] (Impresso in Bologna per Hieronymo di Plato Bolognese. nel M.D.XIII. ... a di xxiv di decembre.) 4°. †^{4} (*wanting*) A-Z^4 a-z^4 &^{4} ꝯ^6 (-ꝯ6, *blank*). ff. V-CXCVII *present*. ¶A2-3 *defective*. [27

ACOSTA, CHRISTOBAL. Trattato ... della historia, natura, et virtu delle Droghe Medicinali ... che vengono portati dalle Indie Orientali in Europa ... In Venetia, M D LXXXV. Presso à Francesco Ziletti. 4°. a-d^4 e^6 f^4 A-Ss^4 Tt^6. pp. 1-342. [28

-- Tratado en loor de las mugeres ... In Venetia. M D XCII. Presso Giacomo Cornetti. 4°. π1 *-3*4 (-**1-3) A-Ll4 (-Kk4, Ll4). ff. 1-133. [29

ACOSTA, JOSÉ DE. Iosephi Acosta ... de natura noui orbis libri duo. Et de promulgatione euangelii apud barbaros, siue, de procuranda Indorum salute, libri sex. Coloniae Agrippinae. In officina Birckmannica, Sumptibus Arnoldi Mylij. cIɔ. Iɔ. XCVI. ... 8°. †8 (-†1, *presumably blank*) A-Nn8 Oo4 (-Oo4, *blank*). pp. 1-581. [30

ACOSTA, MANOEL. Rerum a Societate Iesu in Oriente gestarum ad annum ... M.D.LXVIII, commentarius Emanuelis Acostae Lusitani, recognitus, & latinitate donatus. Accessere de Iaponicis rebus epistolarum libri IIII, item recogniti, & in latinum ex Hispanico sermone conuersi. Dilingae Apud Sebaldum Mayer. Anno M.D.LXXI. ... 8°.)(8 A-Ff8. ff. 1-228. (Lea.) [31

ACUÑA, HERNANDO DE. Varias poesias ... En Madrid, en casa de P. Madrigal. 1591. 4°. *-**4 A-3E4. ff. 1-204. [32

ADAMI, FRANCESCO. [1] Francisci Adami ... De Rebus in Ciuitate Firmana gestis Fragmentorum libri duo. Ex Bibliotheca D. Caesaris Ottinelli. Romae. Apud Ascanium & Hieronymum Donangelos. M. D. XCI. (*Colophon.*) 8°. A-P8 (-H1, H8) Q12. ff. 2-122. [2] Caesaris Ottinelli ... de Firmo, Piceni Vrbe nobilissima elogium ... (*Colophon.*) aa-bb8. pp. 3-30. (Lea.) [33

D'ADDA, FERDINANDO. [Ferdinandi Abduensis, Mediolanensis Patritij, ... Oratio qua manifeste declarat, leges plurimum medicinae philosophiaeq; artibus anteferendas esse. Eiusdem Epigrammata nonnulla ...] (Apud Aldi filios. Venetiis, M. D. XLVI.) 8°. A-F8 (-A1). ff. 4-45. [34

ADELPHUS, JOHANNES. Die Türckisch Chronica ... (Getruckt ... in ... Strassburg/ durch Iohannē Knobloch. ... Tausent fünffhundert vñ sechzehen Jare.) fol. A-H6. [35

ADLER, CASPAR. Ein sehr hoch nötige Ermanung/ an das kleine blöde verzagte Christlich heufflein/ das sie ... Gottes ewig Wort frölich bekennen sollen ... Durch M. Casparum Aquilam ... Gedruckt zu Magdeburgk durch Michel Lotther. 1548. 4°. A-E4. [36

-- Der Vier vnd Dreissigst Psalm/ ausgelegt ... Gedruckt zu Wittemberg. jm. xxxiij. jar. (... durch Georgen Rhaw. ...) 4°. A-I4. [37

-- Von Almosen geben/ Ein Sermon/ ... mit D. Mart. Luthers Vorrede. Wittemberg. MDXXXIII. (Gedruckt ... durch Nickel Schirlentz.) 4°. A-H4 I2. [38

-- Wider den spöttischen Lügner vnd vnuerschempten verleumbder D. Islebium Agricolam. Nötige verantwortung/ vnd Ernstliche warnung/ Wider das Interim. Apologia M. Casparis Aquilae ... [Magdeburg, Christian Rödinger,] M.D.XLVIII. 4°. A4 B2. [39

ADOLF VON ANHALT. Handlung des Bischoffs von Merssburg/ mit den zwayen Pfarhern vō Schonbach vñ Bůch ... M.D.XXiij. 4°. A-B4. [40

ADRIAN VI, pope. Hadriani Florentii Traiectensis ... Disputationes in Quartū Sententiarum, praesertim circa Sacramenta ... (Romae ex officina Marcelli Anno. M.D.XXII.) fol. A6 a-z6 A-M6 N4 O6. ff. I-CCXIIII. (Lea.) [41

ADRIANI, GIOVANNI BATTISTA. Istoria de' suoi tempi ... In Firenze, Nella Stamperia de i Giunti. M. D. LXXXIII. (... Del Mese di Settembre. ...) fol. *2 A-L8 M8+1 N-3P8 3Q6. pp. 2-941. [42

-- Oratio ... habita in funere Cosmi Medicis ... Florentiae Ex Officina Iuntarum. M D LXXIIII. (*Colophon.*) 8°. A-E4. [43

ADRICHEM, CHRISTIAEN VAN. Theatrum Terrae Sanctae et biblicarum historicarum ... (Coloniae Agrippinae In Officina Birckmannica, sumptibus Arnoldi Mylij. Anno cIɔ. Iɔ. XCIII.) fol. *6 (*6 + *3 folded sheets*) A-Pp4 (*engraved sheets follow* C4, D3, E3, K1, N2, P2, Q2, R1, S4) Qq6. pp. 1-286. ¶*Engraved t.p.* [44

ADVERTISSEMENTS. Aduertissemens a l'homme Chrestien, pour cognoistre et fuir les modernes heretiques: lesquelz desrobent le Paradis aux ames des fideles, soubz pretexte de la parole de Dieu. ... A Lyon. Pour Michel Ioue ... 1565. 4°. A-D^4 (-D4, *presumably blank*). ff. 3-16. (Lea.) [45

AEGIDIUS ROMANUS. Questiones methaphisicales ... (Venetijs Ĩpresse per Simonē de Luere mandato domini Andree Torresani de Asula 7. octobris. 1501.) fol. B.L. a-e^8. ff. 2-40. [46

AEGIDIUS, PETRUS. Threnodia seu lamentatio ... in obitum Maximiliano Cæsaris Aug. Et in hanc scholia Iacobi Spiegel Selestadieñ. ... (Ex officina Sigismundi Grim̃ Medici, & Marci Vuirsung Augustæ Vindelicorum. M.D.XIX.) 4°. Aa-Cc^4. [47

AELIANUS. Αιλιανου ποικιλης ιστοριας, Βιβλία, ΙΔ'. ... Æliani uariæ Historiæ libri; XIIII. Ex Heraclide de rebus publicis Commentarium. Polemonis Physionomia. Adamantii Physionomia. Melampodis ex Palpitationibus diuinatio. De Neuis. Εν Ρωμη, ἔτει α φ μ έ, μενὶ γαμελιῶνι ... (Romæ [per Antonium Bladum], M.D.XXXXV. Mense Ianuario.) 4°. $*^4$ α-$ω^4$ A-$Δ^4$ 1-3^4 (-33, *presumably blank*). ff. 1-111. [48

-- -- Aeliani de varia historia libri XIIII, ... Iusto Vulteio VVetterano interprete. Item, de politiis, siue rerum publicarum descriptiones, ex Heraclide, eodem interprete. Basileae. (... ex officina Ioannis Oporini, ... M. D. XLVIII. Mense Decembri.) 8°. a-t^8. pp. 3-280. [49

AEPINUS, JOANNES. Bekentnuss vnnd Erklerung auffs interim. ... Gedruckt zu Magdeburgk durch Michael Lotther. (... 1549.) 4°. ✠-✠✠^{4} A-Dd^4. ff. I-CVII. [50

-- -- Bekentniss ... Gedruckt zu Magdeburg durch Christian Rödinger. (*Colophon.*) 4°. *Same collation and foliation.* [51

-- D. Ioannis Æpini liber de Iustificatione hominis. Operibus legis. Fidei iusticia & origine. Fidei discrimine & uirtute. Notis & signis iustificantis fidei & hominum iustificatorum. Imbecillitate & peccatis sanctorum. Discrimine peccatorum. Pręmijs fidei & bonorum operum. ... confutatio argumentorum, quæ ab aduersarijs opponi solent iustificationi fidei. Francoforti ex officina Petri Brubacchij, anno M.D.LI. (*Colophon.*) 8°. A-Z^8 a-c^8 d^4. ff. 2-209. [52

AESCHINES. [1] Λόγοι τουτωνὶ τῶν ῥητόρων. ... Orationes horum rhetorum. Aeschinis. Lysiæ. Alcidamantis. Antisthenis. Demadis. Andocidis. Isæi. Dinarchi. Antiphontis. Lycurgi. Gorgiæ. Lesbonactis. Herodis. Item Aeschinis uita. Lysiæ uita. (Venetiis Apud Aldum, & Andream Socerum mense Aprili. M. D. XIII.) fol. a^{8+1} b-m^8 n^4. pp. 3-197. [2] Λογοι τουτωνι των ρητορων. ... Orationes infrascriptorum rhetorum. Andocidis. ... 3a-$3i^8$ $3k^{10}$. pp. 3-162. [53

-- ... Αισχίνου καὶ Δημοσθένους ... Aeschinis et Demosthenis, orationes inter se contrariæ. ... Argentorati per VVendelinum Rihelium. Anno. M. D. XLV. 8°. α-$ρ^8$ $σ^4$. pp. 1-260. [54

-- -- Due orationi, l'vna di Eschine contra di Tesifonte, l'altra di Demosthene à sua difesa, Di Greco in uolgare nuouamente tradotte per un gentilhuomo Firentino. ... In Vinegia, M. D. LIIII. (... In casa de' figliuoli di Aldo. ...) 8°. A-N^8 O^4 (-O3-4, *presumably blank*). ff. 2-106. [55

AESCHYLUS. Αισχυλου τραγωδιαι εξ. ... Aeschyli tragoediae sex. (Venetiis in aedibus Aldi et Andreae soceri MDXVIII mense Februario.) 8°. a-n^8 o^{10}. ff. 1-113. [56

-- -- Αισχυλου Προμηθευς δεσμωτης, Επτα επι Θηβαις, Περσαι, Αγαμεμνων, Ευμενιδες, Ικετιδες. ... Parisiis Ex officina Adriani Turnebi ... M. D. LII. ... 8°. $α^4$ A-N^8 O^2. pp. 1-211. [57

-- -- Αισχυλου τραγωδιαι ζ ... Aeschyli tragoediae VII. ... Petri Victorii cura et diligentia. [Genevae,] Ex officina Henrici Stephani. M. D. LVII. 4°. a-f^4 g-z^8 A-B^8 C-I^4 (-I4, *blank*). pp. 1-395. ¶*Adams A266.* [58

AESOP. Aesopi Phrygis fabellæ Græce et Latine, Cum alijs opusculis ... Venetiis.

(... apud Petrum & Io. Mariani & Cornelium eorum nepotem Nicolinos Sabienses, impensa Melchioris Sessae. ... M. D. XLIX.) 8°. A-Y^{8} z^{8}. pp. 4-364. ¶*Includes:* Gabriae Graeci fabellae tres & quadraginta ..., Ex Aphthonij exercitamẽtis de fabula ..., De fabula ex imaginibus Philostrati, Homeri Βατραχομυομαχία ..., Musaeus ... de Erò & Leandro, Agapetus de officio regis ..., Hippocratis iusiurandum, Γαλεομυομαχία, ... tragoedia Graeca. [59

-- Fabellae quaedam AEsopi Graecae, ad Puerilem Educationem in Gymnasio Argentoratensi selectae. Argentorati Excudebat Iosias Rihelius. M. D. XCIII. (*Colophon.*) 8°. D-F^{8} (-F8, *presumably blank*). [60

-- Fabularum quae hoc libro continentur interpretes atq3 authores Sunt hi Guilielmus Goudanus Hadrianus Barlandus Erasmus Roterodamus, Aulus Gellius Angelus Politianus Petrus Crinitus Ioannes Antonius Campanus Plinius Secundus Nouocomẽsis Aesopi Vita ex Max. Planude excerpta. In libera Argentina apud Matthiã Schurerium. (... Mense Iunio. ... M.D.XVI.) 4°. π^{4} A-D$^{4 \cdot 8}$ E^{8} (-E8, *presumably blank*). [61

-- Continentur in hoc volumine. AEsopi Phrygis fabulae .CCXIIII. e Graeco in Latinum ... conuersae. Eiusdem fabulae .XXXIII. per Laurentium Vallam ... versae. Eiusdem fabulae .LXIII. a Salone Parmense versu Elego latinitate donatae. Eiusdem item fabulae .XLII. ... ab Auiano tralatae. Laurentii Abstemii Maceratensis Hecatomythium primũ, hoc est Centum fabulae. Eiusdem Hecatomythium secundum ... Eiusdem Libellus de verbis communibus. (Impressum Venetiis in AEdibus Ioannis Tecuini de Tridino ... .MDXIX. Die .VI. Martii. ...) 4°. A^{6} B-P^{8} Q^{10}. [62

-- Aesopi Phrygis vita et fabulae à viris doctiss. ... versae: inter quos L. Valla, A. Gellius, D. Erasmus ... In calce adiectae sunt fabellae tres, ex Politiano, Petro Crinito, Baptista Mantuano. Parisiis ex officina Roberti Stephani ... M.D.XXVII. (... Calend. Iulii.) 8°. A-C^{8} a-h^{8} (-h8, *presumably blank*). ff. 2-24, 1-57. [63

-- Aesopi Phrygis, et aliorum fabulae. ... Apud Seb. Gryphium Lugduni. 1548. (*Colophon*). 8°. a-q^{8} r^{4}. pp. 3-255. ¶*Other authors:* Laurentius Valla, Gulielmus Gudanus, Hadrianus Barlandus, Flavius Avianus, Erasmus, Angelus Politianus, Petrus Crinitus, Ioannes Antonius Campanus, Plinius Secundus Novocomensis, Aulus Gellius, Nicolaus Gerbelius Phorcensis, Laurentius Abstemius. [64

-- -- ... Iconibus illustratae ... Venetiis, Apud Franciscum Zilettum, M D LXXXI. (*Colophon*). 12°. A-N^{12}. pp. 3-295. [65

-- Esbatement moral, des animaux. ... A Anuers, Chez Philippe Galle. (Chez Gerard Smits, pour Philippe Galle.) 4°. A-Kk^{4} (-Ii4, Kk4, *both blank*). plates 1-125. [66

AFFLITTI, MATTEO DEGLI. [Commentarii in constitutiones Siciliae.] Lugduni, apud haeredes Iacobi Giuntae. 1550. fol. B.L. [1] Matthaei ab Afflictis ... in primum librum sacrarum constitutionum regni vtriusq3 Siciliae, Commentarij ... a-z^{8} A-B^{8} C-D^{6}. ff. 3-212. [2] ... in secundum et tertium libros ... Constitutionum ... Commentarij ... a-s^{8} t^{10}. ff. 2-153. [3] Index rerum, verborum, et sententiarum singularium ... A-C^{8} D-E^{6}. (Biddle.) [67

-- [In feuda.] Lugduni, apud haeredes Iacobi Iuntae. 1548 (Excudebant, Petrus Compater, & Blasius Guido. ...) fol. B.L. [1] Mattheus de Afflictis in primum feudorum. A-O^{8} a-b^{8} c^{6}. ff. 2-111. [2] ... in secundum lib. feudo. ... AA-GG^{8} HH^{6} a^{10}. ff. 2-62. [3] ... in tertium librum feudorum. ... A-Z^{8} Aa^{6}. ff. 2-189. [4] Repertorium ... a-h^{8} (-h8, *presumably blank*). (Biddle.) [68

-- Matthaei de Afflictis Parthenopaei ... in vtriusque Sicilae, Neapolisque sanctiones, et constitutiones, nouissima praelectio. Interiecta sunt Io. Anto. Batij erudita adnotamenta. Lugduni, 1556. fol. a-oo^{8} pp^{6} A-DD^{8} EE^{6} 3A-3F^{8}. ff. 2-302, 1-222. (Lea.) [69

AGOSTINO DE MONTALCINO. Lucerna dell'Anima. Somma de' casi di conscienta ... In Venetia, M D LXXXX. Appresso Damian Zenaro. 4°. †-††^{4} A-Xx^{8} Yy^{4} Zz-3A^{8} 3B^{4}. pp. 2-710. (Lea.) [70

AGRICOLA, FRANCISCUS. Ketzerbrunn/ Oder Grundtwurtzel aller Secten. Das ist/ Zwentzig Haupt vñ gewisse vrsachen/ aller jemals gewesener/ vñ jetzo schwebender Ketzereyen. ... Getruckt zu Cölln/ Durch Maternum Cholinum. M. D. LXXXIII. 8°.)^{8}))^{8} ())^{8} ()))^{8} A-

3E^{8}. pp. 1-836. (Lea.) [71

AGRICOLA, GEORGIUS. Georgii Agricolae ... Bermannus, siue de re metallica. ... Lipsiae in officina Valentini Papae. Anno M. D. XLVI. 8°. A-F^{8}. pp. 2-93. (Smith.) [72

-- Georgii Agricolae De mensuris & ponderibus Romanorum atque Graecorum Lib. V De externis mensuris & ponderibus Lib. II Ad ea, quae Andreas Alciatus denuo disputauit ... defensio Lib. I De mensuris, quibus interualla metimur Lib. I De restituendis ponderibus atq3 mensuris Lib. I De precio metallorum & monetis Lib. III Basileae [ex officina Frobeniana] M D L. ... fol. *^{4} a-p^{6} q^{8} r-z^{6} A-D^{6} E-F^{8} (-F8). pp. 1-340. (Smith.) [73

-- Georgii Agricolae De ortu & causis subterraneorum Lib. V De natura eorum quae efflunt ex terra Lib. IIII De natura fossilium Lib. X De ueteribus & nouis metallis Lib. II Bermannus, siue De re metallica Dialogus Lib. I Interpretatio Germanica uocum rei metallicae ... Basileae M D LVIII. ... (... in officina Frobeniana per Hieronymum Frobenium, & Nicolaum Episcopium, Mense Septembri ...) fol. a^{4} A-Oo^{6} Pp^{8} Qq-Ss^{6} Tt^{8} (-Tt2, Tt8, *the latter presumably blank*). pp. 1-470. (Smith.) [74

-- -- Di Giorgio Agricola. De La generatione de le cose, che sotto la terra sono ... Lib. V. De La Natura di quelle cose, che da la terra scorrono. Lib. IIII. De La Natura de le cose Fossili ... Lib. X. De Le Minere antiche e moderne. Lib. II. Il Bermanno ... (In Vinegia, per Michele Tramezzino. M D L.) 8°. a-c^{8} d^{4} A-3M^{8} 3N^{4}. ff. 1-467. (Smith.) [75

-- [Georgii Agricolae de re metallica libri XII ... Eiusdem de animantibus subterraneis liber ...] (Basileae apud Hieronymum Frobenium et Nicolaum Episcopium M.D.LVI mense Martio.) fol. α^{6} (-α1) a-z^{6} (i2 + *folded leaf*) A-Bb^{6}. pp. 1-538. (Smith.) [76

-- Georgii Agricolae Chemnicensis Oratio de bello aduersus Turcam ... Ioannis Baptistae Rasarii de victoria Christianorum ad Echinadas Oratio, cum duabus eâdem de re Ioan. Sturmii epistolis. De Saracenis et Turcis Chronicon VVolfgangi Drechsleri, emendatum & auctum à Georgio Fabricio Chemnicensi ... Edita studio & opera Ioannis Rosini ... M. D. XCIIII. Lipsiae. ... (Imprimebat Michael Lantzenberger. Impensis Henningi Grosii Bibliop. ...) 8°. A-O^{8} (-O8, *presumably blank*). pp. 1-219. (Lea.) [77

-- -- Oration: anred vnd vermanung ... von kriegssrüstung vnd heerzug wider den Türcken/ durch Laurentium Werman auss dem Latein inss Teütsch gebracht. 1531. Gedrückt zu Nüremberg durch Friderich Peypus. 4°. a-c^{4} d^{2} e^{4}. [78

AGRICOLA, JOHANN, ISLEBIUS. Drey hundert Gemeiner Sprichwörter/ der wir Deudschen vns gebrauchen/ ... (Gedruckt zu Zwickaw durch Gabriel Kantz. Anno. M.D.XXIX.) 8°. A-V^{8}. ff. 1-147. [79

-- Das Ander teyl gemeyner Deutscher sprichwortter ... 1529. (Gedruckt zu Haganaw durch Iohannem Secerium/ Ym M.D. vnd xxix. Jare.) 8°. a-b^{8} A-HH^{8}. ff. 2-248. [80

AGRICOLA, RODOLPHUS. Compendiosa librorum Rodolphi Agricolae de inuentione dialectica epitome. Per Iohannem Visorium Coenomanum. Parisiis Apud Simonem Colinaeum. 1534. 8°. a-f^{8}. ff. 2-46. [81

-- Rodolphi Agricolae Phrisii, de inuentione dialectica libri tres, cum scholijs Ioãnis Matthaei Phrissemij. Parisiis Apud Simonem Colinaeum. 1542 (... Quinto Idus Iulij.) 4°. a-z^{8} A-F^{8} G^{6}. ff. 2-445. [82

-- Historia periucunda sanctissime matris Anne. ... carmine heroico: edita. ... (Impressa p Iacobũ Thanner ... Liptzensem. ipse die Seueri Episcopi Anno ... Millesimo quĩgentesimoseptĩo.) 4°. A^{6} B^{4}. [83

AGRIPPA, HENRICUS CORNELIUS. Henrici Cornelii Agrippae ab Nettesheym, ... operum pars posterior. ... Huic accesserunt Epistolarum ad familiares Libri septem, & orationes decem ante hoc seorsim edita. Lugduni. Per Beringos fratres. [c. 1553.] 8°.)(^{8} A-Tt^{8} Vv^{4} A-Gg^{8} (-Gg8, *blank*). pp. 1-1156. (Lea.) [84

-- -- [1] Henrici Cornelii Agrippae ab Nettesheym ... opera, in duos tomos ... digesta ... Lugduni, per Beringos fratres. 8°.)(^{8})(^{4} A-Tt^{8} + 10 *unsigned ll. of tables, some of them folded*. pp. 1-668. [2] ... Operum pars posterior. ... Lugduni, per Beringos fratres. Anno M. DC. *^{8} a-dd^{8} ee^{4} +^{8} A-Z^{8} a-g^{8}. pp. 1-440, 1-480. (Smith.) [85

-- ... Henrici Cornelij Agrippae ab Nettesheym, De Incertitudine & Vanitate Scientiarum, & Artium atq3 excellentia Verbi Dei, Declamatio. ... [Coloniae,] Excudebat Io. Prael. Anno M. D. XXXII. Mense Septembri. 8°. A^8 A-Y^8. pp. 1-350. [86

-- -- Henrici Cornelii Agrippae ab Nettesheym, de incertitudine et vanitate scientiarum declamatio inuectiua ... Lugduni. Anno 1564. 12°. A-Ff^{12}. (Smith.) [87

-- -- Coloniae, Apud Theodorum Baumium ... 1584. 12°. A-Cc^{12}. (Smith.) [88

-- -- Henrie Cornelius Agrippa, of the Vanitie and vncertaintie of Artes and Sciences, Englished by Ia. San. Gent. ... Imprinted at London, by Henry Wykes ... 1569. 4°. B. L. *^{4} A-3B^4 (-3B4, *errata*). ff. 1-187. *S.T.C.* 204. (Furness.) [89

-- Della nobilta et eccellenza delle donne, dalla lingua Francese nella Italiana tradotto. Con vna oratione di M. Alessandro Piccolomini in lode delle medesime. ... In Vinegia appresso Gabriel Giolito de Ferrari. MDXLIX. (*Colophon.*) 8°. A-D^8 E^4. ff. 2-36. [90

-- Henrici Cornelii Agrippae ab Nettesheym ... De occulta philosophia Libri Tres. ... (... M. D. XXXIII. Mense Iulio.) fol. aa^6 a-z^6 A-G^6 (-G6, *blank*; G5 + *3 folded ll.*). pp. II-CCCLXII. ¶*First gathering signed* aaij *&c.* (Smith.) [91

-- -- *Same colophon, collation (-3 folded ll.) and pagination.* ¶*First gathering signed* aaii *&c.* (Smith.) [92

-- Henrici Cornelii Agrippae liber quartus de occulta philosophia, seu de Ceremonijs Magicis. Cui accesserunt Elementa Magica Petri de Abano Philosophi. Impressum Anno M.D. LXVII. 8°. A-L^8. pp. 3-172. (Lea.) [93

AGUSTIN, ANTONIO. Canones paenitentiales cum quibusdam notis Antonii Augustini ... Tarracone apud Philippum Mey CIↃ IↃ XXCII. 4°. ¶^{8} A-K^8 a^{10} b-c^8 aa-ff^8 Aa^6 Bb-Cc^8 (-Cc8, *presumably blank*). pp. 2-153, 2-49, 2-95, 2-41. ¶*Contents:* 1) Paenitentiale Romanum [cum notis], 2) Venerabilis Bedae presbyteri de remediis peccatorum [cum notis], 3) Rabani Mauri ... Paenitentium liber [cum notis], 4) Sancti Gregorii Nysaeni ... epistula canonica ad sanctum Letoium ... [cum notis], 5) Sancti Gregorii Thaumaturgi ... epistulae canonicae canon vltimus [cum notis], 6) Canones paenitentiales Astensis. (Lea.) [94

-- -- Venetiis, Apud Felicem Valgrisium. M D LXXXIIII. (*Colophon.*) 4°. a-b^4 A-Ff^4. pp. 1-229. (Lea.) [95

D'AILLY, PIERRE. De emendatione ecclesiae libellus, a ... Petro de Aliaco Cardinali Cameracensi, patribus olim oblatus in concilio Constantiensi congregatis ... [Basileae, Valentinus Curio, c. 1525.] 4°. A-D^4 E^6. (Lea.) [96

-- Questiones ... super primum tertium et quartum snĩaꝝ. ... Principia quattuor in quattuor libros sētentiaꝝ cū collatiuis questionibus. Theologie laudes vna cum principio ĩ cursum biblie. Questiones in vesperijs et resumpta disputatis. ... (Impresse arte ... Iohis barbier expēsis ... Iohis petit ... [c. 1510]) 8°. B.L. a-c^8 a-z^8 ꝛ^8 ꝯ^8 A-M^8. ff. i-ccxcv. [97

AIX. Statuta Aquensis curiae submissionum, ac forma in ea agendi copiosè tribus libris tractata. Autore Claudio Margaleto ... Impressum Auenione apud Mathaeum Vincentium ... 1559. 4°. a-rr^4 ā-3ā^4 4ā^2. pp. 2-319. [98

ALAMANNI, LUIGI. Opere Toscane ... Sebast. Gryphius excudebat Lugd. 1532 ... (*Colophon.*) 8°. *^{4} a-z^8 A-E^8. pp. 1-435. ¶*Part 1 only.* [99

-- -- M D XXXIII. (In Vineggia per Pietro di Nicolini da Sabbio, Ad instantia di M. Marchio Sessa. ...) 8°. A-S^8 T^4. ff. 2-146. ¶*Part 2 only.* [100

-- -- Venetijs apud haeredes Lucae Antonij Iuntae Anno M. D. XLII. (Stampato ... per Pietro Sceffer Germano Moguntino ... il primo di Luglio. ...) 8°. *^{8} a-z^8 A-D^8 aa-tt^8. pp. 1-431, 2-298. ¶*Additional t.p.* (aa1^r): *Same title, imprint, and colophon.* [101

-- La Auarchide ... In Firenze Nella Stamperia di Filippo Giunti, e Fratelli. MDLXX. (*Colophon.*) 4°. A^4 B-X^8 Y^4 (-Y4, *presumably blank*). pp. 1-325. [102

-- La coltiuatione ... Stampato in Parigi da Ruberto Stephano ... M.D.XLVI. ... 4°. a-t^8 u^2 x^2 *^{2}. ff. 3-154. [103

-- -- In Fiorenza MDXLIX. (... Appresso Bernardo Giunti. ...) 8°. A-N^8. ff. 2-102. [104

ALAMANNI

-- Gyrone il cortese ... Stampato in Parigi da Rinaldo Calderio, & Claudio suo figliuolo. ... (... 1548. ...) 4°. [illegible]^{8} a-y^{8} z^{4}. ff. 1-180. [105

-- -- Girone il cortese ... In Vinegia per Comin da Trino di Monferrato, l'anno M. D. XLIX. (*Colophon.*) 4°. *^{8} A-Z^{8} AA^{2} (-AA2, *blank*). ff. 1-185. [106

ALANTSEE, AMBROSIUS. Tractatus qui intitulatur Fedus christianū. ... (Iohānes Rynmannus Oringensis. impensa sua Augustae Vindelicae impressit ... M.D.iiij. .viij. ydus Augusti.) 4°. B.L. a-c^{6} d^{4} (-d4, *presumably blank*). ¶*Printer: Johann Otmar.* [107

ALBANI, GIOVANNI GIROLAMO. Co. Io. Hieronymi Albani ... libri de potestate papae et Concilii ... Venetiis Apud Cominum de Tridino Montisferrati M D LXI. 4°. a^{4} A-Ii^{4} *^{4}**^{4}. pp. 2-256. (Lea.) [108

ALBER, ERASMUS. [Der Barfuser Muͤnche Eulenspiegel vnd Alcoran. Mit einer Vorrede D. Martini Luth.] (Gedruckt zu Wittemberg/ Durch Hans Lufft. M. D. XLII.) 4°. A-S^{4} T^{2}. ¶*Lacks 8 preliminary ll. (title and preface).* [109

-- Christlicher/ nuͤtzlicher/ vnd nohtwendiger Tractat/ vnd Bericht Von der Kinder Tauff/ wider den Irrthumb vnd falsche Lehre der Schwermer ... Item/ Vom Trost der Eltern/ denen jhre Kindlein vor der Tauff absterben ... Item/ Von des Ananiae Worten zu S. Paulo Acto. 22. ... sampt einer Vorrede vnd Bericht D: Nicolai Selnecceri vom Exorcismo bey der heilig Tauff/ etc. 1591 Notopyrgi ad Menium. 4°. A-I^{4} K^{2}. [110

-- Ein Dialogus/ oder Gespraͤch etlicher Personen vom Interim. Item/ Vom krieg des Antychrists zuͦ Rom/ Bapst Pauli des dritten/ mit hulff Keiser Caroli des Fünfftē/ wider Hertzog Iohañ Friderichen Churfürsten zuͦ Sachssen ꝛc. ... Item/ Von den Zeychen des Iüngsten tags. ... 1548. 4°. A-Q^{4}. [111

-- -- *Another copy.* [112

-- Ehebuͤchlin. Ein schoͤn Lustig Gespraͤch zweyer Weibssbilder ... Getruckt zu Francfurt am Mayn/ 1567. (Getruckt ... bey Martin Lechler/ in verlegung Sigmund Feyrabends vnd Simon Huͤters. ...) 8°. A-G^{8}. ff. 1-47. [113

-- Newe zeittung von Rom/ Woher das Mordbrennen kome? M.D.XLI. 4°. A-B^{4}. [114

-- Widder die verpfluͤchte lerͤ der Carlstader/ vnd alle fuͤrnemste Heubter der Sacramentirer ... 1553. Getrucket zuͦ Newenbrandenburg bei Anthonio vnd Walthero Brenner gebruͤdern/ ... 1556. 4°. *^{4} ❖^{4} ₵^{4} A-Z^{4} a-t^{4} u^{2}. [115

ALBER, MAͦTTHIAS. Ein Summa etlicher Predigen vom Hagel vnd Vnholden/ gethon in der Pfarkirch zuͦ Stuttgarten imm Monat Augusto/ Anno M. D. LXjj. Durch D. Mattheum Alberum/ vnd D. Wilhelmum Bidenbach ... 4°. A-C^{4}. [116

-- Vom Rechten brauch der Ewigen versehung Gottes ... Anno. XXv. (Gedruckt [Reutlingen durch Hans von Erfurt] ... auff den Ersten tag des Herbstmonats ...) 4°. a-c^{4} d^{2}. [117

ALBERGATI, FABIO. Del cardinale ... In Roma, Ad instantia di Gio. Angelo Ruffinelli. Stampato per Guglielmo Facciotto. M.D.XCVIII. 4°. *^{4} A-M^{8} N^{4} a^{4} B^{6}. pp. 2-198. (Lea.) [118

-- Trattato ... del modo di ridurre a pace le inimicitie priuate. ... In Bergamo, MDLXXXVII. Per Comino Ventura, & Compagni. 8°. a-b^{8} A-V^{8} (-V8, *blank*). pp. 1-315. [119

ALBERGATI, VIANEZIO. La pazzia. (Stampata in India Pastinaca, per Messer nō mi biasimate, all'uscire delle Mascare, & delle Pazzie Carnoualesche.) 8°. A-I^{4}. [120

ALBERICO DE ROSATE. Aurea ... Lectura ... super titulo de reg. iur. ... (Impressa Papie ꝑ ... Bernardinū de Garaldis ... Mcccccxv. Die vltimo mensis Maij.) fol. B.L. A^{6} B-N^{4} (-N4, *blank.*) ff. 2-53. (Biddle.) [121

ALBERT OF SAXONY. Acutissime Questiones super libros de Physica auscultatione ... Nicoleti Verniatis Theatini ... contra ꝑuersam Auerrois opinionem de vnitate intellectus: ꝛ de anime felicitate Questiones ... Eiusdem etiam de grauibus ꝛ Leuibus quaestio ... (Venetijs sumptibus heredu ... Octauiani Scoti ... ac Socioꝝ. 2i. Augusti .i5i6.) fol. A-N^{6} O^{4} P-Q^{6}. ff. 2-94. [122

-- Questiões et decisiões physicales insignium virorum: Alberti de Saxonia in Octo libros physicorum. Tres libros de çelo & mundo. Duos lib. de gñaratione & corruptione. Thimonis in Quatuor libros Meteororum. Buridani ī Aristotelis. Tres lib. de anima [& Parva naturalia] ... Recognitae ... iudicio Magistri Georgii Lokert Scoti: a quo sunt tractatus proportionum additi. [Parisiis,] Vaenundantur in aedibus Iodoci Badii Ascensii & Conradi Resch. (... sub Calendas Octobris. M.D.XVIII.) fol. B.L. ā^6 a-z^8 A-C^8 D^6 Aa-Ff^8 Gg-Hh^6 3A^6. ff. I-CCXIIII, I-LX. [123

ALBERTAZZI, GIUSEPPE. Epitome adagiorum ex Grecis Latinisq; scriptoribus excerptorum ... Romae ... Apud Ioannem Osmarinum. M. D. LXXIIII. 12°. A^6 B-O^{12} (-O12, *presumably blank*). pp. 3-12, ff. 13-158. [124

ALBERTI, LEANDRO. [1] Descrittione di tutta Italia ... In Venetia, Appresso Ludouico de gli Auanzi. M.D.LXI. 4°. a-d^8 e^{10} A-Bb^8 3A-3R^8. ff. 1-503. [2] Isole appartenenti alla Italia ... In Venetia, Appresso Lodouico de gli Auanzi. 1561. A-M^8. ff. 2-92. (Lea.) [125

ALBERTI, LEON BATTISTA. De re aedificatoria libri decem ... repurgati, per Eberhardum Tappium Lunensem. Argentorati excudebat M. Iacobus Cammerlander Moguntinus. Anno 1541. 4°. π^6 A-Z^4 a-r^4 s^6. ff. 1-165. (Fine Arts.) [126

-- -- L'architecture et art de bien bastir ... Traduicts ... par deffunct Ian Martin ... A Paris, Par Iaques Keruer ... 1553. (Imprimé ... par Robert Massellin ... le deuxieme iour d'Aoust. ...) fol. ā^8 a-f^6 g^8 h-z^6 A-D^6 E^{6+1} F^{6+2} G^8 H-N^6 O^8. ff. 1-228. [127

-- -- I dieci libri de l'architettura ... de la Latina ne la Volgar Lingua ... tradotti. ... In Vinegia, appresso Vincenzo Vaugris. MDXLVI. 8°. *^{8} **^{4} a-z^8 A-H^8. ff. 1-248. (Fine Arts.) [128

-- -- Los diez Libros de Architectura ... Traduzidos de Latin en Romance. ... [Madrid,] En casa de Alonso Gomez ... 1582. 4°. π^4 A-Z^8 aa^8 bb^2 (-bb^2, *presumably blank*). pp. 1-343. (Fine Arts.) [129

-- Opuscoli morali ... Tradotti ... da M. Cosimo Bartoli. In Venetia, appresso Francesco Franceschi, Sanese. 1568. 4°. A^4 A-Dd^8. pp. 1-426. (Fine Arts.) [130

ALBERTINI, ARNALDO. De agnoscendis assertionibus Catholicis et haereticis tractatus ... Romae, In aedibus Populi Romani. M. D. LXXII. 4°. †^{4} ††^{4} A-M^4 N^2 O-3M^4. ff. 2-216. (Lea.) [131

-- ... ₵ Repetitio noua. siue comētaria rubricę et. c.j. De hereticis li. vj. ... Excudebatur Valentie. Anno ... Milesimo Tricesimo Quarto. (Impressa Valētie: īdustria ... Frācisci romani ... Octauo calēdis septembris. ... M.D.XXXIIII.) fol. B.L. A-Y^8 (-O2) Z^{10}. ff. i-clxv. (Lea.) [132

-- ... Arnaldi Albertini ... tractatus siue q̄stio: de secreto ... 1534 (Impressa Valētie industria ... Francisci Romani ... Anno ... Millesimo quingentesimo tricesimo: quarto.) fol. B.L. A-D^6. ff. IX-XIX. (Lea.) [133

ALBERTINI, FRANCESCO DEGLI. Opusculū ð Mirabilibu ... Vrbis Rome ... (Impressum Romae per Iacobum Mazochium ... M.D.XV. Die .xx. Octob.) 4°. A-Z^4 &^{4} ɔ^4 ꝶ^4 (-ꝶ4, *presumably blank*). ff. 2-105. (Lea.) [134

ALBERTUS MAGNUS. Alberti magni de secretis mulierum libellus cum scholiis. Eiusdem de virtutibus Herbarum, Lapidum, & Animalium ... libellus. Item, de mirabilibus mundi ... Lugduni, 1596. 16°. A-Gg^8 Hh^4 Ii^2. ¶*Additional t.p.* (Y3^r): Albertus Magnus de falconibus, Asturibus & Accipitribus. ... (School of Dentistry.) [135

-- -- ... Adiecimus ... Michaëlis Scoti ... De secretis naturae opusculum. ... Lugduni. Apud Anthonium de Harsy. M. D. XCVIII. 16°. A-Z^8 A^8 B^4 (-B4, *presumably blank*). pp. 3-381. (Smith.) [136

-- [1] Scriptum tertiū ... super tertiū sententiarum. fol. B.L. aA^8 bB^6 cC-eE^8 fF^6 gG-qQ^8 rR-sS^6. [2] Scriptū quartū ... (Impssum Basilee per mgr̄m Iacobū de Pfortzen ... 1506. xv. die Martij.) aa-bb^8 cc-dd^6 ee-hh^8 ii^6 kk^8 ll^6 mm-nn^8 oo^6 pp-qq^8 rr^6 ss-3c^8 3d^6 3e-3g^8 3h^6 3i-3m^8 3n^6 3o-3r^8 3s^6 3t^8 (-3t8, *presumably blank*). (Lea.) [137

ALBERTUS OF ORLAMÜNDE. Alberti magni Philosophia naturalis (Impressum Basilee/ cura ... Michaelis furter: vicesimasecunda die mensis Iunij: Anno ... Millesimo quingentesimosexto.) 4°. B.L. a-g^{8} h^{6} i^{4} (-i4, *presumably blank*). [138

-- -- Alberti magni ... philosophiae naturalis isagoge, siue introductiones. In libros Aristotelis Physicorum. De Coelo & Mundo. De Gene. & corr. Meteororum. De Anima. Craccouiae. In Officina Hieronymi Scharffenbergi. M. D. XLVIII. 8°. A-E^{8} F^{4} G^{8} H^{4} I-O$^{8.8.4}$ P^{4}. [139

ALBERTUS, LAURENTIUS. Absurda Lutheranorum ... Getruckt zů Ingolstatt/ durch Alexander Weyssenhorn. Anno M.D.LXX. 4°. A-G^{4}. [140

-- -- *Another copy.* [141

ALBINO, GIOVANNI. Ioannis Albini Lucani de gestis regum Neapo ab Aragonia qui extant libri quatuor. ... Neapoli apud Iosephum Cachium M. D. LXXXVIIII. (*Colophon.*) 4°. *-**^{4} A-V^{4} A^{4} AA^{2} X-3E^{4}. pp. 1-446. [142

ALBINUS. Αλκινοου ... εις τα του Πλατωνος δογματα εισαγωγη. Alcinoi ... ad Platonis dogmata introductio. Lutetiae apud Michaelem Vascosanum. Mense Decembri. 1532 8°. A-Δ^{8}. [143

-- Alcinoi ... de doctrina Platonis liber. Speusippi ... liber de Platonis definitionibus. Xenocratis ... liber de morte. Basileae 1532. (... per Mich. Isingrinium, mense Augusto ...) 8°. A-H^{8}. pp. 4-126. [144

ALBINUS, JOHANNES. Epithalamion scriptum in nuptiis ... Laurentii Rulichii, et ... Dorotheae ... Guolphgangni Pfentneri ... Viduae. ... Lipsiae Iohannes Rhambau excudebat Anno M.D.LX. 4°. A^{4} B^{2}. [145

ALBRECHT, JOHANN. Christliche vnnd gegrūndte widerlegung/ wider das ... schreiben/ Cyriaci Spangenberg/ so er wider das Ingolstatisch Buch ... Hat lassen aussgehn. Durch M. Ioannem Albertum Vuimpinensem. Getruckt zů Ingolstatt durch Alexander vnd Samuel Weyssenhorn. M.D.LXIII. 4°. *^{4} A-Z^{4} a^{4}. ff. 1-96. ¶a1 *misbound after* a3. [146

ALBUMASAR. Albumasar de magnis ɔiunctionibus: annoꝝ reuolutiōibus: ac eoꝝ profectionibus: octo ɔtinēs tractatus. (Impressum Venetijs: ... expensis Melchiorem Sessa. Per Iacobum pentium de Leucho. ... 1515. Pridie kal'. Iunij.) 4°. B.L. A-L^{8} M^{6}. [147

ALCALÀ DE HENARES. *Collegium Complutense.* Constitutiones Īnsignis Collegij Sancti Illefonsi, ac per inde totius almae Complutensis Academiae. Ab ... Francisco Ximenio Cardinali ... & Archiepiscopo Toletano ... olim sancitae. Compluti Excudebat Andreas ab Angulo. (...1560.) fol. π^{2} A-F^{8} G^{10} (-G10, *presumably blank*). ff. 1-57. (Lea.) [148

ALCIATI, ANDREA. [1] D. Andreae Alciati Mediolanensis lucubrationum in Ius ciuile Tomus tertius. ... Basileae, per Mich. Isingrinium [1549]. fol. 3a-3z^{6} 3A-3V^{6}. f. 3, cols. 8-991. [2] ... Tomus quartus. ... *Same imprint.* Aaaa-Zzzz^{6} AAaa-LLll^{6} MMmm^{8}. cols. 1-820. ¶*Part of a collected edition in 4 volumes.* (Biddle.) [149

-- Aureus Andreae Alciati ... praesumptionum tractatus, Ioannis Nicolai Arelatani ... studio ... auctus additionibus ... Apud Vincentium Portonarium. Lugduni M. D. XXXVIII. ... 8°. a-z^{8} A-S^{8} (-S8). pp. 3-563. [150

-- Andreę Alciati ... De formula Romani Imperij Libellus. ... Dantis Florentini de Monarchia libri tres. Radulphi Carnotensis De translatione Imperij libellus. Chronica M. Iordanis ... Basileae, per Ioannem Oporinum. (... M. D. LIX. Mense Octobri.) 8°. a-t^{8}. pp. 4-297. [151

-- Clarissimi viri D. Andreae Alciati Emblematum libellus , ... & iā recēns per Wolphgangum Hungerum Bauarum, rhythmis Germanicis uersus. Parisiis. Apud Christianum Wechelum ... M.D.XLII. 8°. A-Q^{8}. pp. 2-253. [152

-- -- Francisci Sanctii Brocensis ... comment. in And. Alciati emblemata ... Lugduni, apud Guliel. Rouillium, M. D. LXXIII. ... 8°. A-Nn^{8} Oo^{4}. pp. 3-558. [153

-- -- And. Alciati emblemata ... adiecta sunt epimythia ... Lugduni, apud Guliel. Rouillium. 1588. 16°. A-R^8 (-R8, *presumably blank*). pp. 3-260. [154

-- -- Liuret des Emblemes/ ... mis en rime franco[yse] ... On les vend a Paris/ en la maison de Chrestien Wechel ... M. D. xxxvi. 8°. B.L. A-P^8 Q^4 (-Q4, *presumably blank*). pp. 243-245. ¶A1 *defective*. [155

-- D. And. Alciati Mediolanensis ... In aliquot Titulos Tomi tertij Pandectarum Iuris Ciuilis ... Commentarij ... Lugduni, Apud haeredes Iacobi Giuntae, M. D. L. (... excudebant Godefridus & Marcellus Beringi, fratres, 1551.) 8°. a-t^8 Aa-Cc^8. pp. 3-299. ¶ *Additional t.p.*(Aa1^r): Commentariorum ... Index ... Lugduni, Apud haeredes Iacobi Giuntae, M. D. LI. [156

-- Andreae Alciati in digestorum seu Pandectarum librum XII. qui De rebus creditis primus est, Rubric. Si certum petatur, Commentarius ... [*Device of Vincent de Portinariis.*] Excudebatur Lugduni. M. D. XXXVIII. 8°. a-z^8 (-p3-6) A-B^8 C^4. pp. 5-387. [157

-- D. Andreae Alciati ... Oratio ... in initio praelectionis habita ... Antuerpiae In aedibus Ioannis Steelsij. Anno M.D.XXXV. (Typis Ioannis Graphei.) 8°. A-B^4. [158

ALCOZER, PEDRO DE. Hystoria, o descripcion dela Imperial cibdad de Toledo. ... En Toledo. Por Iuan Ferrer. 1554. ... fol. A-X^6. ff. iij-cxxiiij. (Lea.) [159

-- -- *Another copy* (-X6; K1-N5, O2-P2, T6, X3-5 *defective*). [160

ALEMAN, MATEO. Guzman d'Alfarache. ... Faict François, Par G. Chappuys ... A Paris, Par René Ruelle ... M.DC. ... 12°. $\bar{a}^6$ $\bar{e}^4$ $\bar{\imath}^4$ A-T^{12} V^8 X^1 A-H^{12} I^4. ff. 2-237, 2-100. [161

ALESSANDRO FARNESE, duke of Parma. Sendbrieff des Printzen von Parma an Burgermeister ... der Statt Antorff ... Sampt der ... Antwort der Herren Burgermeister ... Getruckt zu Cölln/ Anno 1584. 4°. A^6. [162

ALESSIO PIEMONTESE. D. Alexii Pedemontani de secretis libri sex ... ex Italico in latinum sermonē nunc primum translati. Per Ioannem Iacobum weckerum ... Basileae anno M. D. LIX. 8°. π^8 a-r^8 s^4 $*^4$ $*^8$ (-*8, *presumably blank*). pp. 2-79. [163

-- -- [The secretes of the reuerende Maister Alexis of Piemount ... Translated out of French into Englishe, by William Warde. Imprinted at London, by Henry Bynneman, for Iohn Wight. ... 1568.] (*Colophon.*) 4°. B.L. $*^6$ (-*1) A-Q^8. ff. 2-117. *S.T.C.* 297. ¶*Lacks t.p., for which the t.p. of* S.T.C. *295 without the last line* (XII. die Mens. Nouemb.) *has been substituted.* *2 *defective.* (Furness.) [164

-- -- The second part of the Secretes of Maister Alexis of Piemont ... newly translated out of French into English ... By Willyam Ward. Printed at London by Rouland Hall, for Nicholas Englande. 1563. 4°. B.L. A^2 A-C^4 D-M^8 N^2. ff. 1-79. *S.T.C.* 301. (Furness.) [165

-- -- The thyrde and last parte of the Secretes of ... Alexis of Piemont ... Englished by Wylliam Warde. Imprinted at London by Henry Denham, for Iohn Wyght. (... 1566.) 4°. B.L. A-B^4 C-L^8 M^4. ff. 1-75. *S.T.C.* 306. (Furness.) [166

-- -- A verye excellent and profitable Booke conteining sixe hundred foure score and odde experienced Medicines ... long tyme practysed of ... Mayster Alexis, which he termeth the fourth and finall booke of his secretes ... Translated out of Italian into Englishe by Richard Androse. ... Imprinted at London by Henry Denham. 1569 (*Colophon.*) 4°. B.L. A^4 a-c^4 B-Z^4. pp. 1-56, 1-64, 1-56. *S.T.C.* 309. (Furness.) [167

ALEXANDER III, pope. Historia di Papa Alessandro' e di Federico Barbarossa Imperatore ... (Stāpata in Vēetia p̱ Alessādro de Viano.) 4°. A^4. ¶*In verse.* [168

ALEXANDER APHRODISIENSIS. Alexandri Aphrodisei ... de anima ad mētem Aristotelis enarratio ... (... impensis heredum ... Octauiani Scoti ... & sociorum ... impraessa Venetiis per Augustinum de Zannis de Portesio ... M.CCCCC.XIIII.) fol. A-C^6. ff. II-XVIII. [169

-- Ἀλεξάνδρου τοῦ ἀφροδισιέως ... ὑπόμνημα. Alexandri aphrodisiensis, in priora analytica Aristotelis, commentaria. (Florentiae per haeredes Philippi Iuntae ... M.D.XXI. Mense Decembri ...) 4°. a-x^8 y^6. ff. 2-173. [170

-- 'Αλεξάνδρου 'Αφροδισιέως ... ὑπομνήματα. Alexandri Aphrodisiei in topica Aristotelis, commentarii. (Venetiis in aedibus Aldi, et Andreae soceri.Mense Septembri. M. D. XIII.) fol. A-R^8 (A1 + 1) S^6 (-S6). pp. 3-281. [171

-- [1] Ἀλεξάνδρου Ἀφροδισιέως ... προβλήματα. (Ἐν τῆ τῶν παρισίων ἐνεχαράχθη Χορηγία καὶ δαπανήμασιν Εμῶνδες Τουσανης, τῆς χήρας Γυναικὸς Κορράδου Νεοβαρίου ... α'φ'μ' [1540] Θαργηλιῶνος μενός.) 8°. α-η^8 θ^{10}. [2] Alexandri Aphrodisiei problemata ... Græcè & Latinè Ioannis Dauioni studio illustrata. ... Parisiis 1541. a-k^8. ff. 2-78. [172

-- -- Problemata Alexandri Aphrodisei. Georgio Valla interprete. Problemata Aristotelis. Theodorus Gaza e graeco transtulit. Problemata Plutarchi per Ioannem petrum Lucensem in latinum conuersa. (Impressum Venetiis per Albertinum Vercellensem. M.CCCCCI. Die .xxvi. Maii.) fol. a-c^8 d-m^6 n^4. ff. ii-lxxxii. [173

-- Alexandri Aphrodisiensis ... quaestiones naturales et morales et de fato, Hieronymo Bagolino Veronensis patre, et Ioanne Baptista filio interpretibus. De Anima Liber primus, Hieronymo Donato ... interprete. De anima Lib. ij. unà cum commentario de Mistione, Angelo Caninio Anglariensi interprete. ... Venetiis apud Hieronymum Scotum. M D XLIX. (*Colophon.*) fol. A-K^6 L^8. ff. 2-67. [174

ALEXANDER OF HALES. Clauis Theologie (Clauis theologie siue Reꝑtoriū ... Petri Keschinger ... in summā ... Alexandri de hales ... per Nicolaum Kessler ciuē Basilieñ. ... elaboratū Anno ... Millesimo quingentesimosecundo.) 4°. B.L. π^4 A-II^8. (Lea.) [175

-- [1] Alexandri de Ales, Angli, ... summae theologiae, Pars Prima. Vniuersum de aeternae Deitatis cognitione, Trinitatisq́ue diuinae manifestatione negotium ... complectens. Venetiis, apud Franciscum Franciscium. MDLXXV. (... MDLXXVI.) fol. a^6 b^4 A-Y^8 Z^6 Aa^4 a^6 B-F^6 G^8. ff. 2-186. [2] ... Pars Secunda. Primam rerum productionem, Angeli, Hominisq́ue creationem, eorundemq́ue casum vel lapsum, ac mala siue peccata inde sequentia mirè dilucidans. ... *Same imprint.* AA-CC^6 Aa-Ll^6 MM-ZZ^8 3A-4F^8. ff. 2-416. [3] ... Pars Tertia. In qua quidquid ad Christi Incarnationem, Conuersationem, Passionem, & Resurrectionem; ad Leges, ad Gratiam, atque Virtutes attinet ... expressum est. ... *Same imprint.* a^6 b^4 a-k^8 L-Z^8 Aa-Oo^8 Pp^6. ff. 2-302. [4] ... Pars Quarta. Sacramentorum ecclesiasticorum institutionem, tum maximè Officii Missae ordinationem ... comprehendens. ... *Same imprint.* *A*^{6} *B*^{4} A-3L^8 3M^{10}. ff. 2-466. (Lea.) [176

ALEXANDER THE GREAT. Alixandre Le Grant. [Paris, Michel Le Noir *or a successor*, c. 1520.] 4°. B.L. A-B^6 C-H$^{4\cdot6}$. [177

ALEXANDER, ANDREAS. Mathemalogiū prime ꝑtis ... suꝑ nouam et veterem loycam Aristotelis. ... (Melchior Lotter Liptzeñ. ... impressit. Anno ... Millesimo quingentesimoquarto. Nonis Marci.) fol. B.L. A-G^6. [178

ALFONCE, JEAN. Les voyages auantureux ... A Rouen, Chez Thomas Mallard ... 1578. (... De l'Imprimerie de George l'Oyselet.) 4°. A-Y^4. ff. 1-64. ¶*Additional t.p.* (S1^r): Les tables de la declinaison ou esloignement ... *Same imprint.* [179

ALFONSO A VERA CRUZ. [1] Rev. Patris Fr. Alphonsi a Vera Cruce Hispani ... speculum coniugiorum ... Nunc primum in Italia Typis excusum. ... Mediolani, Ex Officina Typographica quon. Pacifici Pontij. M. D. XCIX. 4°. *^{6} A-Cc^4 Dd-Oo^8 Pp^6. pp. 1-372. [2] Appendix ad speculum coniugiorum ... *Same imprint.* ✠^{4} A-L^4. pp. 1-88. (Lea.) [180

ALKINDUS. Astrorū iudices Alkind^9 Gaphar de pluuijs imbribus et vētis: ac aeris mutatiōe Venetijs ... 1507. Ex officina Petri Liechtenstein 4°. B.L. a^6 b-c^4. (Smith.) [181

ALLOTT, ROBERT. Wits Theater of the little World. ... Printed by I. R. for N. L. ... 1599. 8°. A^4 B-Mm^8 Nn^4. ff. 2-269. *S.T.C.* 382. ¶A2 *bound in after* A3. (Furness.) [182

ALMODIANO. Almodiano d'incerto autore. In Vinegia [per Girolamo Scoto], M D LVIII. 8°. A-C^4. [183

ALPHABETUM. Alphabetum Graecum ([Parisiis,] In Barranis aedibus. M φ K ά [1521]) 4°. a^4. [184

-- Graecum alphabetum ... Quibus adiectum est Hebraicum alphabetum. ... Venetiis [Haeredes Melchioris Sessae]. 8°. A^8. [185

ALPINO, PROSPERO. Prosperi Alpini de medicina Aegyptiorum, libri quatuor. ... Venetiis, M D XCI. Apud Franciscum de Franciscis Senensem. 4°. a-c^4 A-S^8 T^6 V-Aa^4 Bb^6. ff. 1-150. [186

-- Prosperi Alpini de plantis Aegypti liber. ... Venetiis, M. D. XCII. Apud Franciscum de Franciscis Senensem. 4°. a^4 A-X^4 a-b^4. ff. 1-80. ¶*Additional t.p.* ($Q2^r$): Prosperi Alpini de balsamo, dialogus. ... *Same imprint.* [187

ALTDORF. Solennitas & actus renunciationis, et promotionis, qua in schola et academia Altorfiana Noribergensium primò gradus, & honores Magisterii decernebantur ... M D LXXXI. Noribergae [Katharina Gerlach]. 8°. A-E^8 F^{10}. ff. 3-50. [188

ALTENHEYMER, GEORG. Vocabulorum in Ioannis Coclei Grammaticā Collectaneum ... 1515 (Ioannes Prüss Argētinensis Ciuis ... excripsit ... Septimo Calendas Ianuarias.) 4°. A-Cc^4. ff. I-C. [189

ALTHAMER, ANDREAS. Auslegung der zwo letzten Episteln Iohannis des Theologij ... 1529. (Gedrückt zu Erfford durch Conrad Treffer ...) 8°. A-C^8 D^4. ¶D4 *repaired.* [190

ALTENSTEIG, JOHANN. Dialectica cōgesta et collecta ... ex auctorib⁹ veriorib⁹ ... (expensis ... Ioannis Rynman de Oringau: ꝑ labore ... Henrici Gran in oppido Hagenau excusa sunt. xvij. kal'. Maij ... M.D. supra .xiiij.) 4°. B.L. π^4 a-b^8 c-$s^{4.8}$. [191

-- Vocabularius ... 1515 (... impensa ... Adę Petri de Langendorff ... exaratae ... Basileae. Anno ... Millesimo quingētesimo decimoquarto Mensis ꝟo Decembris, die decimo ...) 4°. A-E^8 F^4 a-$q^{4.8}$ r^8 s^4 t^6 v^8. ff. I-CXVI. [192

-- -- (A Ioāne Prüss Argentinensi ciue ... elaboratam ... Anno ... Millesimo quingentesimo decimo ꝗnto (decimo Calendis Aprilis)) 4°. A^4 aa-ii^4 B^8 C-D^4 E-F^8 G-L^4 M^8 N-$S^{4.4.8}$ T-Y^4 Z^8. ff. I-CXVI. [193

-- Vocabularius Theologie ... (... excusus in officina ... Henrici Gran ... Hagenaw: Impēsis ... Ioānis Rynman ꝺ Oringaw ... M. d. xvij. die .xiij. mensis Decēbris.) fol. B. L. π^4 a^8 b-z^6 A-Z^6. ff. I-CCLXXVII. [194

ALUNNO, FRANCESCO. La fabrica del mondo ... Nella quale si contengono tutte le voci di Dante, del Petrarca, del Boccaccio, & d'altri buoni autori ... In Vinegia M D XLVIII. (Stampata ... per Nicolo de Bascarini ... M. D. XLVI.) fol. $+^6$ a-tt^6 uu^8 A-H^6. ff. 1-259. [195

-- [$*2^r$] Le osseruationi ... sopra il Petrarcha. ... In Vinegia per Pauolo Gherardo M. D. L. (... per Comin da Trino di Monferrato ...) 8°. $*^8$ A-$3V^8$ $3X^2$. ff. 1-527. ¶*Engraved t.p. on* $*1^r$. [196

-- Le ricchezze della lingua vulgare ... In Vinegia. Nel M. D. XXXXIII. (In casa de figliuoli di Aldo. ...) fol. A-DD^8 EE^{10}. ff. 2-225. [197

-- -- In Vinegia, Appresso Giouan Maria Bonelli. M D LV. (*Colophon.*) fol. $*^4$ A-AA^8 BB-CC^6 (-CC6, *presumably blank*). ff. 1-213. [198

ALVAREZ, ANTONIO. [1] Primera parte de la sylua spiritual ... En Salamanca. En casa de Iuan y Andres Renaut ... MDXCIIII. Expensis Ioannis Pulmani ... 4°. $*^8$ A-Ff^8 Gg^{10}. pp. 1-483. [2] Segunda parte ... *Same imprint.* (*Colophon.*) A-Ee^8 ff-gg^8 hh^4 (-hh4, *presumably blank*). pp. 3-427. [199

ALVAROTTI, JACOPO. Iacobus Aluarotus super feudis. ... Lugduni apud Iacobum Giunta. 1545 fol. B.L. a-s^8 t^6. ff. II-CXL. (Biddle.) [200

ALVELD, AUGUSTIN. Eyn gar fruchtbar vñ nutzbarlich buchleyn vō dē Babstlichē stul: vnnd von sant Peter ... 4°. A-B^4 C^6. ¶*Dedication dated St. George's day 1520.* [201

AMADI, ANTONIO MARIA. Di M. Anton Maria Amadi annotationi sopra vna canzon morale ...

In Pado[ua,] Per Lorenzo Pasquatto. M D LXV. 4°. ✠^{4} A-Aa^{4}. pp. 1-181. ¶✠1 *repaired.* [202

AMADIS DE GAULA. *Part 6.* L'historia et gran prodezze in Arme di Don Florisandro ... (In Venetia per Michel Tramezzino. MDL.) 8°. *^{12} A-YY^{8} ZZ^{4}. ff. 1-364. [203

-- *Part 7.* Lisuarte di Grecia ... tradotto ... nell' Italiana lingua. In Venetia, M. D. LXXXI. 8°. †^{4} A-Ll^{8} Mm^{4}. ff. 1-275. [204

-- *Part 9, supplement.* Aggiunta di Amadis di Grecia Intitolata la Terza parte. ... Tradotta nella Italiana. Per M. Mambrino Roseo da Fabriano. In Venetia [per Michele Tramezzino], M. D. XCII. 8°. a^{8} b^{4} A-QQ^{8}. ff. 1-312. [205

-- *Part 10.* La historia de gli ... cauallieri, Don Florisello di Nichea, & Anassartes ... Recata ... da la lingua Spagnuola ne la nostra Italiana. In Venetia, Appresso Camillo, & Franc. Franceschini F. 1565. 8°. *^{8} **^{4} A-OO^{8} PP^{4} A-NN^{8}. ff. 1-298, 1-288. [206

-- -- In Venetia, Appresso Fabio, & Agostino Zopini Fratelli. M. D. LXXXII. 8°. a^{8} A-Oo^{8} A-Cc^{8} DD-NN^{8}. ff. 1-294, 1-287. [207

AMBACH, MELCHIOR. Von Ehbruch vnd huͤrerey/ wie ... Gott dieselbige verpotten vnd alweg gestrafft. ... Item V. ... predige S. Aurelij Augustini/ Verteutscht ... Zu Franckfurt/ truckts Cyriacus Iacob zum Bart. M. D. XLIII. 4°. A-H^{4}. [208

D'AMBRA, FRANCESCO. I Bernardi comedia ... In Fiorenza appresso i Giunti. MDLXIIII. 8°. A-H^{8}. pp. 2-117. [209

-- Il furto comedia ... In Venetia, appresso F. Rampazetti. (... M D LXI.) 12°. A-E^{12}. ff. 2-58. [210

-- -- In Venetia, MDXCVI. Appresso Marc'Antonio Bonibelli. 8°. A-G^{8}. ff. 2-55. [211

AMBROGINI, ANGELO, POLIZIANO. Disertissimi viri Angeli Politiani ... Epistolae Lepidissimae. ... (Impressum Antvverpie Per me Theodoricū Martini. ... M.ccccc.x. iiii. die May.) 4°. a-s$^{8.4}$. [212

-- Angeli Politiani, et aliorum uirorum illustriū, Epistolarum libri duodecim. ... Basileae, anno M.D.XXII. (... apud Andream Cratandrum, mense Februario ...) 8°. a^{4} b-z^{8} A-P^{8} Q^{4}. pp. 1-576. [213

-- -- Illustrium Virorum Epistolę ... cū Syluianis Cōmētariis & Ascēsianis Scholiis ... AEre merent Badio. (... Ad Sextū kalendas Maias. M.D.XXVI.) 4°. aa^{8} a-z^{8} A-P^{8} Q^{4} R^{8}. ff. I-CCCXV. [214

-- Angeli Politiani ... lamia. (Impressum Coloniae apud Nicolaum Caesarium, anno. M.D. XVIII. pridie monas Martias.) 4°. A^{6} B-C^{4}. (Lea.) [215

-- Stanze ... cominciate per la giostra Del Magnifico Giuliano di Piero De Medici. (Stampato per Nicolo Zopino e Vincentio cōpagno nel .M.CCCCC.xxi. adi xxx. de Agosto ...) 8°. A-E^{8} (-E8, *presumably blank*). [216

AMBROSE, S. Des lieplichen lerers ... Sancti Ambrosij buͤchleyn vō priesterlicher wirdigkeyt ... Newlich durch Nicolaum Krumpach verdeutzscht M D XXI. [Erfurt, Mathes Maler.] 4°. A-B^{4}. [218

AMBROSIUS JUTERBOCENSIS. Oratio de ingratitudine cu[c]uli, habita in promotione Magistrorum a D[e]cano Magistro Ambrosio Iuterbocensi. Vitebergae. M. D. XXXVII. 8°. A^{8}. ¶A1-2 *defective.* [219

AMERBACH, VEIT. Antiparadoxa cum duabus orationibus, altera de Laudibus patriae, altera de Ratione studiorum ... Argentorati [Crato Mylius,] M.D.XLI. 8°. A-I^{8}. [220

-- Variorum carminum ... nonnullorumq̄ue aliorum liber. ... Basileae, per Ioannem Oporinum. (... M.D.L. Mense Septembri.) 8°. a-i^{8} (-i8, *presumably blank*). pp. 4-140. [221

AMLING, WOLFGANG. Drey Predigten/ Von der Person/ vnd Ampt Christi ... [Zerbst, Bonaventure Faber,] M. D. Lxxjx. 4°. A-K^4 L^2. [222

AMMIANUS MARCELLINUS. Ammiani Marcellini rerum gestarum libri decem et octo. Apud Seb. Gryphium Lugd. M. D. LII. 16°. a-z^8 A-Z^8 aa^2. pp. 3-716. [224

-- -- Lugduni, Apud Franciscum le Preux. M. DC. 8°. *^{8} a-z^8 A-V^8 X^4. pp. 1-566. ¶*Additional t.p.* (N4^r): Chronologia Marcelliniana ... *Same imprint.* [225

-- -- Ammiano Marcellino delle guerre de Romani. Tradotto per M. Remigio Fiorentino. ... In Vinetia. Appresso Gabriel Giolito di Ferrarii M D L. (*Colophon.*) 8°. *^{8} A-TT^8 VV^4. pp. 1-338. [226

AMMIRATO, SCIPIONE. Delle famiglie nobili Napoletane ... Parte Prima ... In Fiorenza, Appresso Giorgio Marescotti. MDLXXX. fol. ✠^{6} a-g^6 h^8 A-F^6 G^4 H^6 I^4 k-s^6. pp. 1-96, 1-208. [227

-- Discorsi ... sopra Cornelio Tacito ... In Fiorenza, per Filippo Giunti M. D. IIC. ... (*Colophon.*) 4°. †-4†^{4} A-Mm^8 Nn-Qq^4 Rr^6. pp. 1-564. [228

-- Orazione ... al ... sig. nostro Clemente VIII. In Fiorenza, Per Gianantonio Caneo. 1594. ... 4°. A-B^4 C^2. (Lea.) [229

-- Orazione ... alla maesta Cattolica ... Detta Philippica seconda. In Firenze appresso Giorgio Marescotti. MDXCIIII. ... 4°. A-C^4. pp. 3-22. [230

-- [1] Orazioni del Sig. Scipione Ammirato a diuersi principi. Intorno i preparamenti, che s'aurebbono a farsi contra la potenza del Turco. ... In Fiorenza. Per Filippo Giunti. M. D. IIC. 4°. *^{4} Aa-Ii^8 Kk^2. pp. 1-148. [2] Lettere, & Orazioni di Monsignor Bessarione ... Volgarizate dal Signor Filippo Pigafetta. In Firenze, per Filippo Giunti. MDXCIIII. a^8 b^2 A-C^8 D^4 E^2. pp. 1-58. [3] Oratione VII. del Sig. Scipione Ammirato ... In Firenze, per Filippo Giunti. MDXCVI. ... A-C^4 D^2. pp. 3-27. [4] Il rota ouero delle impresse ... *^{2} a-h^8 (-a1) I^4. pp. 3-130. ¶*Lacks the eighth oration.* [231

AMMONIUS HERMEIOU. Αμμωνιου του Ερμειου υπομνημα ... Μαγεντηνου ... εξηγησις ... Ammonii Hermei commentaria in librum peri hermenias. Margentini archiepiscopi Mitylenensis in eundem enarratio. (Venetiis apud Aldum, mense Iunio. .M.DIII.) fol. A-G^8 H^4 I-K^8 Λ^4 M^8 N-O^6 AA-EE^8 FF^6. [232

-- -- Ammonii Hermeae in libros Aristotelis de interpretatione commentarii. Bartholomaeo Syluanio Salonensi Interprete. Venetiis apud Ioan. Gryphium. M D XLIX. 8°. A-F^8 A-T^8. pp. 1-304. [233

-- Ammonius in quinque voces Porphyrii per Pomponium Gauricum Neapolitanum. (Impressum ... Venetiis per Io. Baptistam Sessa. Anno M.CCCCCIIII. XV Cal. Quītil.) fol. a-g^4. [234

-- -- ... Quibus inseruimus textum ipsius Porphyrii ... Venetiis. M. D. XXXIX. (... apud Octauianum Scotum.) fol. A-E^4. ff. 2-20. [235

AMOMO. Rime Toscane d'Amomo per Madama Charlotta d'Hisca. In Vinegia [Bernardino Stagnino]. MDXXXVIII. 8°. A-I^8. [236

AMSDORF, NICOLAUS VON. Antwort/ Glaub vnd Bekentnis auff das schöne vnd liebliche interim. ... [Magdeburg, Michael Lotter,] Anno M. D. XLVIII. 4°. A-E^4. [237

-- Auff Osianders Bekentnis ein Vnterricht vnd zeugnis ... 1552. (Gedruckt zu Magdeburg/ bey Christian Rödinger.) 4°. A-B^4. [238

-- Etliche sprüche aus Doctoris Martini Lutheri schriften/ Darinne er/ als ein Adiaphorist sich mit dem Bapst hat vergleichen wollen. ... 1551. (Am 19 Decembris. 1551) 4°. A^4 B^2. [239

-- Die Hauptartickel durch welche gemaine Christenhait biss her verfürt worden ist. ... [Augsburg, Silvan Otmar,] M. D. XXIII. 4°. a-e^4 f^6. [240

-- Wie sichs mit der ... Hernn Iohans Friderich/ des Eldern/ weiland Hertzogen zu Sachs-sen ... Christlichem abschied zugetragen hat. Sampt einer Leichpredigt ... Anno 1554. ... (Gedruckt zu Ihena/ bey Christian Rödinger. ... 1554.) 4°. A-E^{4}. [241

AMSTERDAM. 1578. Pointen ende articulen van den Satisfactie die van Amstelredamme gheg-heven/ ende gheaccordeert/ etc. Gheprint tot Amstelredam/ by Harman Iansz Muller ... 4°. A^{4} B^{2}. [242

-- Register Van allen den Schouten/ Burghermeesteren/ Schepenen/ XXXvj. Raiden/ ende al-len anderen Regenten der Stede Amstelredamme. Anno/ M.D.XCII 4°. A-E^{4}. pp. 3-39. [243

-- Handt-vesten ende Privilegiē van Amstelredam ... Ghedruct, Anno. cIↄ. cI. IIIC. 4°. A^{4} A-Aa^{4}. pp. 1-192. [244

-- Willekeuren ende Ordonnantien bijden Heeren vanden Gerechte der Stadt Amstelredamme gemaect/ so opde bedelaers/ vagabunden eñ Leprosen ... Ghedruckt T'amsterdam by Barendt Adriaenssz. ... 1597. 4°. A^{4} B^{2}. [245

-- Ordonnantie ende Willekeuren/ by den Heeren vande Gerechte der Stadt Amstelredamme/ ghemaect op tstuck vande Assurantie. Ghedruckt t'Amstelredam/ by Barent Adriaensz. ... 1599. (... M.D.XCVIII.) 4°. A-B^{4}. [246

-- Extract uytet Register vande Willekeuren der Stadt Amsterdamme ... Nopende De Veer-schuijt voerders/ varende op t'Veer tusschen de Steden Amsterdam ende Leyden. Ghedruckt t'Amsterdam/ by Barent Adriaensz/ ... 1600. 4°. A^{4} B^{2}. [247

-- Extract Wttet Register vande Willekeuren der Stadt Amstelredamme ... Nopende Het maecken/ meten/ ende vercoopen vande Catoene Bombazynen ende Trijpen/ etc. Ghedruckt t'Amstelredam/ by Barent Adriaensz ... 1600. 4°. A^{4} (-A1, *presumably blank*). [248

ANABAPTISTS. Ein Göttlich vnnd gründtlich offenbarung: von den warhafftigen widerteuf-fern ... [Augsburg, Philipp Ulhart,] M.D.XXVII. 4°. A-E^{4}. [249

-- Des Münsterischen Königreichs vnd Widertauffs an vnd abgang/ Blůthandel vnd End/ ... M.D.xxxvj. ... 4°. A^{4}. [250

-- Newe Zeytung/ Die Widerteuffer zů Münster belangende. [Augsburg, Heinrich Steiner,] M.D.XXXV. 4°. A^{4}. [251

ANACREON. Ἀνακρέοντος Τηΐου μέλη. Anacreontis Teij odae. Ab Henrico Stephano luce & Latinitate nunc primùm donatae. Lutetiae. Apud Henricum Stephanum. M. D. LIIII. ... 4°. *^{4} A-O^{4}. pp. 2-110. [252

-- Les odes d'Anacreon Teien, traduites de Grec en Francois, Par Remi Belleau de Nogent au Perche, ensemble quelques petites hymnes de son inuention. ... A Paris. Chez André Wechel ... 1556. ... 8°. A-F^{8} G^{4}. pp. 3-103. ¶B4 *bound before* B3, B6 *before* B5. [253

ANANIA, GIANLORENZO. De natura daemonum libri IIII. ... Venetiis [Aldus Manutius se-cundus] M.D. LXXXI. (*Colophon.*) 8°. +^{4} +^{8} A-N^{8} O^{2}. pp. 2-211. (Lea.) [254

ANANIA, JOANNES DE. Consilia ... [*Device of Jacobus Giunta.*] 1540 (Lugduni impressa per Ioannem Moylin alias de Chambray.) fol. B.L. A^{6} a-i^{6} k^{8}. ff. 1-61. (Biddle.) [255

-- Ioannis ab Anania praelectiones in decretalium librum quintum ... Lugduni ... apud Iacobum ac Ioann. Senetonios fratres. ... 1546 (... apud Benedictum Bonnyn ...) fol. B.L. a-z^{8} A-K^{8} L^{6}. ff. 2-270. (Biddle.) [256

ANCONA. Aegidianae constitutiones. Cum additionibus Carpensibus. ... cum Glossis ... Gasparis Caballini de Cingulo ... Venetiis, MDLXXXVIII. fol. a^{8} A-Bb^{8} Cc^{6} Dd^{10}. pp. 1-412. (Lea.) [257

-- Constitutiones, siue statuta magnificae ciuitatis Anconae ... Anconae. Excudebat As-tulfus de Grandis Veronensis. M. D. LXVI. (... M. D. LXVI. Idibus Nouembris.) fol. ✠^{4} A-I^{8}. pp. 2-414. (Lea.) [258

ANDREA, ALESSANDRO. De la guerra de Campaña de Roma, y del reyno de Napoles, En el Pon-tificado de Paulo IIII. Año de M.D.LVI. y LVII. Tres libros ... Impresso en Madrid, en casa de la Viuda de Querino Gerardo. Año de M.D.LXXXIX. ... (*Colophon.*) 4°. ¶[6] A-T[8] V-X[4] Y[2]. pp. 1-320. [259

D'ANDREA, GIOVANNI. [1] Nouella Ioannis andree super tertio decretalium cum apostillis ... (Venetijs per Baptistam de Tortis. M.cccccv. die .xix. aprilis.) fol. B.L. 3a-3v[8] 3x[6]. ff. 2-165. [2] Nouella ... super quarto ꝛ quinto decretalium ... (Venetijs per Baptistam de Tortis. M.ccccc.iiij. die .xv. nouembris.) AA-MM[8] NN[6] OO[4]. ff. 2-105. ¶*Three more parts were published.* (Biddle.) [260

ANDREA, JUAN. Opera chiamata confusione della setta Machumetana, composta in lingua Spagnola, per Giouan Andrea gia Moro & Alfacqui ... Tradotta in Italiano, per Domenico de Gaztelu ... Il mese di Marzo M D XXXVII. (Stampata in Spagna ne la città di Seuiglia ...) 8°. A-I[8] K[4]. ff. 2-74. [261

ANDREAE, JAKOB. Acta Colloquij Montis Belligartensis ... praeside, ... Friderico, comite VVirtembergico ... inter ... D. Iacobum Andreae ... & D. Theodorum Bezam ... Tubingae, Per Georgium Gruppenbachium, anno M.D.LXXXVII. 4°. a-c[4] A-4C[4]. pp. 1-575. [262

-- -- Colloquium Mompelgartense. Gespräch ... Zwischen ... D. Iacobo Andreae ... vnnd D. Theodoro Beza ... Anno 1586. im Mertzen zu Mümpelgart ... Auss dem Latein verdeutscht. Getruckt zu Tübingen/ bey Georg Gruppenbach/ im Jar 1587. 4°.):(-3):([4] 4):([2] A-6H[4] 6I[2]. pp. 1-988. [263

-- Ein Christliche Predig/ über der Leich ... Hansen von Liebenstein ... Getruckt zů Tübingen/ bey Vlrich Morharts Wittib. M. D. LXIIII. (*Colophon.*) 4°. A-G[4] H[2]. ff. 1-27. ¶A1 *defective.* [264

-- Clare vnnd helle Antwort/ auff den ... Gegenbericht/ Iude Iscarioth/ so sich Fridericum Staphylum nennet. ... Getruckt zů Tübingen/ 1561. (... bey Vlrich Morharts Wittib. ...) 4°. A-T[4] V[2]. ff. 1-82. [265

-- Colloquium de Peccato originis. Inter D. Iacobum Andreae, et M. Matthiam Flaccium Illyricum Argentorati Anno 1571. institutum. ... Tubingae, [Georgius Gruppenbach,] M. D. LXXIIII. (*Colophon.*) 4°.)([4] a-g[4] A-G[4] H[2]. pp. 1-56, 1-54. [266

-- Oratio. De disciplina in Academia Tubingensi instauranda et conseruanda. ... Tubingae Excudebat Georgius Gruppenbachius, Anno 1583. 4°. A-C[4]. pp. 1-22. [267

-- Responsio breuis ... contra librum Io: Sturmii Quem Antipappum Quartum imscripsit. ... Dresdae, Anno M. D. LXXXI. (... Excudebat Matteus Stoeckel.) 4°. A-C[4] D[2]. [268

-- Zwo Tröstliche Predigten/ bey der Leich vnd Begrebnis Der ... Frewlin Margaretha/ gebornen Hertzogin zu Braunschweig vnd Lüneburg etc. ... HeinrichsStadt Durch Cunrad Horn/ (... 1580.) 4°. A-L[4]. [269

ANDREAS MONTOPOLITANUS. Vt Numa Romuleum traduxit robur ad aras Sic Leo belligeras traducet ad ociagẽtes [Romae, Joannes Beplin, c. 1515.] 4°. A[6]. ¶A2[r]: Andreę Montopolitani Italię Querella. [270

ANDRELINI, PUBLIO FAUSTO. P. Fausti Andrelini Foroliuiensis ... Epistolę puerbiales & morales ... (Argentorati ex aedibus Mathię Schürerij Selestatini, Kalẽ. Iulij. ... M. D. X.) 4°. b[4] B[4] C[6]. [271

-- -- ... Ex secunda recognitione. (Argentorati ex aedibus Matthiae Schurerij, Selestatini, Mense Aprili. Anno. M. D. XIX.) 4°. Aa-Bb[4] Cc[6]. [272

-- -- ... Ex secunda recognitione. (Argentinae apud Ioan. Prys mense Septem. Anno M. D. XX.) 8°. a-c[8] d[4]. pp. 2-50. [273

-- *Livia.* Publij Fausti Andrelini Foroliuiẽsis ... Amorum Libri Quatuor. ... (Impressum Venetiis per Bernardinum Venetum de Vitalibus ... M.CCCCC.I. mensis Ianuarii ...) 4°. A-M[4]. [274

ANDROUET DE CERCEAU, JACQUES. Petit traitte des cinq ordres de colonnes ... A Paris, Pour Iaques Androuet du Cerceau. 1583. fol. A[2] + 12 *engraved plates.* ¶*A number of unrelated plates bound in.* (Fine Arts.) [275

-- [1] Le premier volume des plus excellents Bastiments de France. ... A Paris, Pour ledit Iacques Androuet, du Cerceau. M. D. LXXVI. fol. A^{8} + 62 *double-page plates.* [2] Le second volume ... *Same imprint.* A^{8} (-A8) + 61 *double-page plates.* (Fine Arts.) [276

ANGELI, NICOLA. Rime amorose di M. Nicola de gli Angioli della Marca. In Bologna, Appresso Giouanni Rossi. MDLXIII. (... alla stampa del Mercurio. ...) 4°. A-F^{4}. [277

ANGELIO, PIETRO. Oratione funerale ... fatta nelle essequie del Sereniss. Cosimo de Medici Gran Duca di Toscana ... tradotta in lingua Fiorentina. In Fiorenza Nella Stamperia de' Giunti. M D LXXIIII. (*Colophon.*) 4°. A-D^{4}. [278

-- Petri Angelii Bargaei poemata omnia ... Item Marii Columnae Quaedam Carmina. Florentiae Apud Iuntas M D LXVIII. ... (*Colophon.*) 8°. *^{8} **^{10} A-Ee^{8}. pp. 2-447. [279

ANGELUCCI, TEODORO. Quod metaphysica sint eadem, quae physica, noua ... sententia. Qua multa obiter obscuriora Aristotelis ... dogmata ... explicantur. ... Venetiis, Apud Franciscum Zilettum. 1584. 4°. a-b^{4} A-Y^{4}. ff. 1-83. [280

ANGELUS DE CLAVASIO. Sūma Angelica: ... cum ... additionibus ... (Venetijs ĩpressa per Alexandrum de paganinis ... M.cccccxi. die .viij. marcij.) 16°. B.L. π^{8} a-z^{16} ʒ^{16} ɔ^{16} ꝶ^{16} A-B^{16} C^{10} a^{10}. ff. 1-458. [281

ANGERIANO, GIROLAMO. Hierony. Angeriani Neapolitani ερωτοπαιγνιον. Eclogae. De obitu Lydae. De vero poeta. De Parthenope. [Neapoli, Caterina Mayr, 1520.] 8°. a-f^{8}. [282

ANGHIERA, PIETRO MARTIRE DE. De orbo nouo ... Decades octo ... restitutae ... industria Richardi Hakluyti Oxoniensis Angli ... Parisiis, Apud Guillelmum Auuray ... M. D. LXXXVII. ... 8°. ā^{8} A-Rr^{8} (Rr8 + *folded map*). pp. 2-605. [283

ANGLES, JOSÉ. [1] Flores theologicarum quaestionum, In Secundum Librum Sententiarum, nunc primùm collecti ... Pars prima. ... Venetiis, Apud Marcum Antonium Zalterium. M D XCV. 8°. †^{8} A-Hh^{8} Ii^{4}. pp. 2-438. [2] ... Pars secunda. ... *Same imprint.* a-aa^{8} bb^{4}. pp. 3-350. (Lea.) [284

-- Flores theologicarum quaestionum, in quartum librum sententiarum. ... Pars prima. Venetiis, Apud Ioannem Baptistam Somaschum. M D LXXXIIII. (... MDLXXXIII.) 8°. *^{4} A-Hh^{8} Ii^{4} A-Ee^{8}. ff. 1-34 [= 222], iiij-viij, 1-205. ¶Hh7^{r}: Flores ... Pars Secunda. ... (Lea.) [285

-- -- [1] ... Pars prima. ... Venetiis, Ex Officina Damiani Zenarij. 1586. 8°. †^{8} A-Z^{8} *^{8}. pp. 2-360. [2] ... Pars secunda. ... Venetiis, Ex officina Damiani Zenarij. M D LXXXVI. A-Y^{8}. pp. 3-326. [3] Tractatus tres de oratione, ieiunio, et eleemosina. (Venetiis. Iacobus Cornettus excudebat, Ad instantiam Damiani Zenarij.) a-p^{8}. pp. 1-162. (Lea.) [286

ANGUILLA, FRANCESCO. Discorso ... sopra quell'oda di Safo, che comincia, Parmi quell' huomo eguale esser à i Dei. Con alcune Rime Amorose ... In Venetia, Appresso Giordano Ziletti, e compagni. M. D. LXXII. 4°. A-K^{4}. pp. 2-80. ¶I3^{r}: Annotationi di Francesco Anguilla. Sopra la traduttione di Vincenzo Obsopeo. K1^{r}: I Macrobi [di Luciano]. [287

ANGUILLARA, GIOVANNI ANDREA DELL'. Edippo tragedia ... In Padoua, Per Lorenzo Pasquatto, M D LXV. 4°. a^{4} A-Q^{4}. ff. 1-63. [288

-- -- In Vinegia, appresso Domenico Farri. M D LXV. 8°. A-H^{8}. ff. 1-62. [289

ANHALT. Kurtze antwort/ Auff etliche neulich wider die Anhaltische Kirchendiener ausgesprengte Schmehecharten. ... 1590. ... (Gedruckt zu Zerbst/ durch Bonauentur Schmid. ...) 4°. A-E^{4} F^{2}. pp. 3-44. [290

ANISIUS, MICHAEL. Siben Catholische Predigen ... wider dess Christlichen Namens Erbfeind dem Tu͏̈rcken/gehalten zu Bamberg/ im 4. vnnd 95. Jar. ... Gedruckt zu Mu͏̈nchen/ bey Adam Berg. ... M. D. XCIX. (*Colophon.*) 4°. (:)^{4} A-Ee^{4} F^{4} (-F4, *presumably blank*). pp. 1-222. [291

ANJOU. [Coustumes, vsages, & communes obseruances du pays d'Anjou ... 1600.] 16°. A-Zz^{8} (-A1). ff. 1-269. (Biddle.) [292

ANSCHLAG. Treffenlicher vnnd Hochnützlicher anschlag/ Bündtnuss vnd verainigung/ durch die ... Hertzogen zů Sachsen/ Marggrauen zů Brandenburg/ vnd Landtgrauen zů Hessen ꝛc. Des Türcken zugs halben fürgenõmen/ bedacht vnd berhatschlagt. ... Der Schlesischen Fürsten vnd Stennd gesandten Instruction vnnd beuelch ... M.D.XLI. (Gedruckt zů Augspurg/ durch Philipp Vlhart.) 4°. A-C⁴. [293

ANSELMO, GIORGIO. Georgij Anselmi Nepotis. Epigrammaton libri septem. (Franciscus Vgoletus & Antonius Viotus Socii imprimebant Parmae mense Septembri. M.D. .XXVI.) 8°. A¹⁰ a-o⁸. [294

ANTIQUARI, JACOPO. Oratio ... pro populo Mediol. [Mediolani, Alexander Minutianus? c. 1510.] 8°. B.L. a⁶ b⁴. [295

ANTONINO, S. Confessionale ... M D XXXXIII. (Stampato in Vinegia per Giouanne Padouano. M D XLIII.) 8°. A-K⁸. ff. 2-78. (Lea.) [296

-- Descerunt. Summa perutilis cõfessionis Descerunt nũcupata ... (impressa Venetiis per Cesarem Arriuabenum Venetum. ... 1522. die 6. mẽsis iunii.) 8°. ✤⁸ A-Z⁸ &⁸ ɔ⁸ ℞⁸ Aa-Bb⁸. ff. I-CCXXIII. [297

-- Opera ... necessaria alla instruttione delli Sacerdoti Idioti. (Stampato in Venetia nella Stamperia di M. Luc'antonio Giunta L'anno M.D.XXXIIII. di Marzo.) 4°. A-X⁴ Y⁶ (-Y1, Y6, *the latter presumably blank*). ff. 2-83. (Lea.) [298

-- [1] ... B. Antonini archiepiscopi Florentini ... summae Sacrae Theologiae, Iuris Pontificij, & Caesarei, prima pars. ... Venetiis, apud Iuntas. M. D. LXXXII. (*Colophon.*) 4°. +⁴ A-Pp⁸. ff. 1-304. [2] Varii indices ... *Same imprint.* a-n⁸ p-u⁸. ff. 2-160. [3] ... Secunda pars ... *Same imprint.* +⁶ A-3A⁸ 3B⁴ (-3B4, *presumably blank*). ff. 1-379. [4] ... Tertia pars. *Same imprint.* +¹⁰ A-3X⁸. ff. 1-538. [5] ... Pars quarta ... Venetiis, Apud Bernardum Iuntam, & Socios. M D LXXI. +⁴ A-3D⁸. ff. 1-397. (Lea.) [299

ANTONIO DE CÓRDOBA. Fratris Antonij Cordubẽsis ... Opus de Indulgentijs ... 1554. (Compluti, Ex officina Ioannis Brocarij. 1554.) 4°. A⁸ b-z⁸ Aa⁸ Bb⁶. ff. 1-190. (Lea.) [300

-- Trattato de casi di conscienza, ... Con vna aggionta di cinquanta due Questioni ... Tradotto di nouo dalla lingua Spagnola nell'Italiana. In Brescia, Presso Pietro Maria Marchetti. 1599. ... 8°. +⁸ A-Gg⁸ (-Gg8, *presumably blank*). ff. 1-239. (Lea.) [301

ANTONIO, ELIO, DE LEBRIXA. Aelius Antonius Nebriss. In vafre dicta Philosophorum. Eiusdem/ Epithalamiũ Lusitaniae principum. Eiusdem/ patriae suae Antiquitas & origo. Eiusdem/ peregrinatio Regis & Reginae ... Petrimartyris ad eundem de Barbariafugata. Eiusdem Antonii ... Responsio. Autor ad suã Grãmatices artem ... Fabiani Nebriss. cũ ipsa Patris arte cõfabulatio. Fabian⁹ idẽ fabulã de duorũ amãtiũ crepidine. ... (Apud. Garnatam mense Nouembri. D.XXXIIII.) 4°. A-C⁸ D⁴. [302

-- [1] Lexicon Latino Catalanum, seu Dictionarium Aelij Antonij Nebrissensis ... ex Catalono in Latinũ sermonem versum. ... Barcinone. Ex officina Claudii Bornatii ... 1560. ... fol. a⁶ (-a6) A-X⁸ A-I⁸ K⁴. ff. 1-168, 1-76. ¶*T.p. repaired.* ²A2, ²G8 *defective.* [2] Onomasticon propriorum nominum ... Barcinone ex officina, Claudij Bornatij. 1563. ... A-Q⁸ (-Q8, *presumably blank*). ff. 2-126. ¶*Additional t.p.* (P6ʳ): Dictionarium medicum ... *1560 Same imprint.* [303

-- Lexicon seu Dict[io]narium Aelii Ant[onii] Nebrissensis ... ex Latino sermone in Cathalanum & Castellanum ... conuersum. ... Adiecimus in fine Valerij Probi ... De litteris Antiquis opusculum ... Barcinone, Apud Antonium Oliuer. Anno M.D.Lxxxvij. (Excudebat ... Iacobus Cendrat ...) fol. ¶⁸ A-Dd⁸ Ee⁴ Aa-Nn⁸ Oo⁴ 3A-3Q⁸ 3R¹⁰. ff. 1-222, 1-108, 2-133. ¶*T.p. torn. Half-title* (3A1): Onomasticon propriorum nominum ... *Additional t.p.* (3Q2): Dictionarium medicum ... Barcinone. Apud Iacobum Cendrat. ... 1585. (Lea.) [304

-- Orationes ad plenum collectę ... quę ꝑ totũ annum ... cantantur. (Compluti in Aedibus Michaelis de Eguia. Anno ... millesimo quingẽtesimo vigesimooctauo tertio idus Iulii.) 8°. a-e⁸ f⁴. [305

-- Aelij Antonij Nebrisseñ. Relectio nona de accentu latino aut latinitate donato ... (Ex impressione hispalensi ... M.d.xiij. decimo calẽdas nouembris.) 4°. B.L. A^{10}. [306

-- AElii Antonii Nebrissensis rerum a Fernando et Elisabe Hispaniar ... Regibus gestarũ Decades duae, Necnõ belli Nauariẽsis libri duo, nũc secũdo editi ... Anno. 1550. (Apud ... Granatam. ...) 8°. A-FF^8. ff. 1-113. [307

ANTONIUS. Hoc volumine continentur. Sententiarum siue capitum, theologicorum praecipue ... Tomi tres, per Antonium & Maximum monachos olim collecti. ... Abbae Maximi ... Aphorismorum ... Centuriae IIII. Theophili sexti Antiochensis episcopi de Deo & fide Christianorum contra Gentes Institutionum libri tres ... Tatiani Assyrij ... Oratio cõtra Graecos. ... Christophorus Froschouerus excudebat Tiguri, Anno M.D. XLVI. fol. *^{6} a-z^6 A-H^6 I^8. pp. 1-385. [308

ANTONIUS DE BURGOS. ... Antonij ó burgos hyspani solẽnis repetitio rubrice de emptio. ⁊ ven. ... (Per me Benedictum hectoris ciuem bononiensem ... impressa fuit. ... i506. Die .4. Iunij.) fol. B.L. A-B^4. [309

ANTWERP. [1] Rechten, Ende Costumen van Antwerpen. Ghedruct tot Ceulen. 1584. 8°. *^{8} **^{8} A-Cc^8. pp. 1-415. [2] Ordonnantie ende Verhael vanden Stijl/ ende Maniere van Procederen/ voor Amptman/ Borghemeester/ ende Schepenen der Stadt van Antwerpen. *Same imprint.* 3A-3D^8. pp. 3-61. (Lea.) [310

-- Antorffischer Empörũg so sich zwischen den Papisten/ vnd den Geusen ... nechst den 13 14. vnd 15. tag Martij zůgetragen/ kurtzer Bericht ⁊c. ... M. D. LXvij. (Getruckt zů Augspurg/ Durch Hans Zimmerman.) 4°. A^4. [311

APHTHONIUS. Aphthonij Sophistae ... progymnasmata. Parisiis Apud Simonem Colinaeum. 1539. 8°. a-c^8. ff. 2-23. [313

-- -- Aphthonii sophistae progymnasmata. Partim à Rodolpho Agricola, partim à Ioanne Maria Catanaeo Latinitate donata. Cum ... Scholijs Reinhardi Lorichij Hadamarij. ... Apud Iacobum Arbillium. M. D. LXXXI. 16°. *^{8} **^{4} A-Ii^8 Kk^4. ff. 1-259. [314

APIAN, PETER. Cosmographia Petri Apiani, per Gemmam Frisium ... aucta, & annotationibus marginalibus illustrata. Additis eiusdem argumenti libelli ipsius Gemmae Frisij. Coloniae Agrippinae, Apud Haeredes Arnoldi Birckmanni. cIↄ Iↄ LXXIV. 4°. A-H^4 (H4 + *folded leaf*) K-S^4. ff. 1-64. [315

-- Inscriptiones sacrosanctae vetustatis ... Petrus Apianus Mathematic⁹ Ingolstadieñ & Barptholomeus Amantius Poẽta ded. Ingolstadii in aedibus P. Apiani. Anno M. D. XXXIIII. fol. Aa-Bb^4 a-c^4 A-Z^4 a-z^4 aa-tt^4. pp. II-CCCCCXII. [316

APOLLINARIUS. Απολιναριου μεταφρασις του Ψαλτηρος, διὸ στίχων ἡρωϊκῶν. Apolinarii interpretatio Psalmorum, versibus Heroicis. Apud Ioannem Bene-natum. Parisiis, M. D. LXXX. (... pridie Kalend. Iunij ...) 8°. ã^8 A-Bb^8 A-Q^8. ff. 1-200, pp. 1-253. [317

APOLLODORUS ATHENIENSIS. Apollodori Atheniensis bibliotheces, siue de Deorum origine, tam graecè, quàm latinè ... libri tres. Benedicto Aegio Spoletino interprete ... Quibus demum additus est Scipionis Tetti ... de Apollodoris ... commentarius. Roma in aedibus Antoni Bladi ... M. D. LV. 8°. A^4 a-k^8 L-M^8 n-z^4 *-3*^{8} *^{8} **^{4}. ff. 1-138. [318

APOLLONIUS PERGAEUS. [1] Apollonii Pergaei conicorum libri quattuor. Vnà cum Pappi Alexandrini lemmatibus, et commentariis Eutocii Ascalonitae. ... Omnia nuper Federicus Commandinus Vrbinas ... è Graeco conuertit, & commentariis illustrauit. ... Bononiae, ex officina Alexandri Benatii. M D LXVI. fol. +^{4} A-Z^4 a-e^4 f^2. ff. 1-114. [2] Sereni Antinsensis ... libri duo. ... *Same imprint.* χ^2 a-i^4. ff. 1-36. [319

APOLLONIUS RHODIUS. [1] Απολλωνιου του Ροδιου Αργοναυτικων βιβλοι ... Item, Apollonii Rhodii Argonauticorum, Carmine Heroico translati per Valentinum Rotmarum Salisburgensem,

Libri IIII. ... Basileae, ... ex officina Henricpetrina. (... CIϽ IϽ LXXII. Mense Martio.) 8°. α-β^8 a-p^8 A-T^8 V^4. pp. 1-236, 1-309. [2] Apollonii Rhodii Argonauticorum ... Libri IIII. ... *Same imprint.* Aa-Tt^8 Vu^4 AA-HH^8. pp. 3-309, 3-127. [320

-- -- Apollonii Rhodii Argonauticorum Libri quatuor ... Ioanne Hartungo interprete. ... Basileae. (... ex officina Ioannis Oporini, ... M.D.L. Mense Februario.) 8°. α-β^8 a-q^8. pp. 2-226. [321

APOSTLES. Canones apostolorum. Veterum conciliorum constitutiones. Decreta pontificium antiquiora. De primatu Romanae ecclesiae. ... Moguntiae Anno M. D. XXV. mense Aprili. ... (Impressum ... in aedibus Ioan. Schoeffer. ...) fol. π^{10} (-π10) A-K$^{4.6}$ L-M^6 N-O^8 P^6 Q-Ff$^{4.6}$ Gg^8. [322

APPEL, PHILIPP. Elegia Epithalamica, in nuptias ... Bernardi Philippi Wolffii à Rosenbach ... Sponsi. ... Barbarae Burresin ... Sponsae. ... Moguntiae, Ex Officina Typographica Henrici Breem 1593. 4°. A-B^4. [323

APPIANUS. Αππιανου Αλεξανδρεως Ρωμαικων ... Appiani Alexandrini Romanarum historiarum Celtica Libyca, vel Carthaginensis Illyrica Syriaca Parthica Mithridatica Ciuilis, quinque libris distincta. ... Lutetiae ... diligentia Caroli Stephani. M. D. LI. fol. A^8 B-Ii^6 Kk^4. pp. 4-393. [324

-- -- *Another copy (variant t.p.:* M. D. L. I.*)* [325

-- -- Αππιανου Αλεξανδρεως Ρωμαικα. ... Henr. Steph. annotationes ... [Genevae,] Excudebat Henricus Stephanus anno M. D. XCII. fol. *-**^{6} (-**6, *blank*) a-4a^6 ā^6 ē^6 ī^6. pp. 1-767, 2-72. [326

-- -- [1] An auncient Historie and exquisite Chronick of the Romanes warres, both Ciuile and Foren. ... With a continuation ... Imprinted at London by Henrie Bynniman. Anno. 1578. 4°. B.L. A^2 B-3E^4 3F^2 *^{4} **^{2}. pp. 3-198. *S.T.C.* 713. ¶*Additional t.pp.:* (3B3^r) A continuation of Appian of Alexandria ... At London, Imprinted by Raulfe Newberry and Henry Bynniman. Anno. 1578. [2] The second part of Appian of Alexandria. ... Translated into English by W: B. *Same imprint.* π^2 ¶^{4} a-oo^4 Pp^4 Qq^2. pp. 2-445. (Furness.) [327

-- -- Appian Alexandrin ... des Guerres des Romains liures xj. traduicts en François par feu Maistre Claude de Seyssel ... A Paris, Pour Guillaume Cauellat ... 1560. (Imprimé ... par Benoist Preuost. 1559.) 8°. aa-bb^8 cc^4 a-z^8 A-KK^8. ff. 1-446. [328

-- -- D'Appian Alexandrin ... des Histoires Romaines, l'Iberique, ou Espagnole: & l'Annibale, ou des exploicts d'Annibal Carthageois en Italie. ... traduict de Grec en François, par Philippe des Auenelles. A Paris, Pour Guillaume Cauellat ... 1560. ... 8°. a-f^8 g^4. ff. 2-51. [329

-- -- Appian Alexandrin ... des guerres des Romains liures XI. traduicts en François par feu Maistre Claude de Seyssel ... Plus y sont adioustez deux liures, traduicts ... par le Seigneur des Auenelles. ... A Paris, Par Pierre du Prē ... M. D. LXIX. (Imprimé ... par Fleury Preuost ...) fol. aa-bb^6 a-z^6 A-Bb^6 Cc^4 a-d^6 e^8. ff. 1-293, 2-32. [330

-- -- [1] Appiano Alessandrino delle guerre ciuili et esterne de Romani ... Aggiuntoui ... un libro del medesimo, delle guerre di Spagna ... M. D. XLV. 8°. a-z^8 A-I^8 K^2. ff. 3-258. [2] Historia delle guerre esterne de' Romani ..., tradotta da Messer Alessandro Braccio... In Vinegia, M. D. XXXXV. (... in casa de' figliuoli di Aldo.) aa-yy^8. ff. 3-175. [3] Libro di Appiano Alessandrino, nel quale si contengono le guerre, che fecero i Romani con li Carthaginesi, et con gli Spagnuoli nella Spagna. Nuouamente tradotto di Greco in uolgare Italiano. ... M. D. XLV. (*Same colophon.*) 3a-3i^4 3k^6 (-3k6). ff. 2-41. [331

-- -- Ciuili. Appiano Alessandrino delle guerre Ciuili de Romani tradotto da. M. Alessandro Braccio ... M. D. XXXVIII. (In Vinegia. Nella case di Pietro di Nicolini da Sabbio. ... Dil Mese d'Aprile.) 8°. A-NN^8 (-NN8, *blank*). ff. 2-287. [332

-- -- Appiano Alessandrino ... Con l'istoria della guerra Illirica, & di quella contra d'Annibale, del medesimo Autore, nuouamente ritrouata in lingua Greca, & tradotta in Italiano dal S. Girolamo Ruscelli. In Venetia, M. D. LXIII. Appresso Domenico, & Gio. Battista Guerra, fratelli. (*Colophon.*) 8°. α-δ^8 A-BB^8. ff. 1-199. [333

-- -- Los triumphos de Appiano (se acabo ... enla ... ciudad ō Valencia a veynte del mes δ Agosto ... Mil D.XXII. por ... Iuan Ioffre ...) fol. B.L. ✠✠✠[6] A-R[8] S[10] (-S10, *presumably blank*). ff. II-CXLIIII. ¶*Engraved t.p. Translator: Juan de Molina.* [334

-- -- Historia de las guerras ciuiles de los Romanos ... Y traduzida de Latin en lengua Castellana, por el Doctor Iayme Bartholome Canonigo ... Impresso en Barcelona, En casa Sebastian de Cormellas al Call, Año. 1592. (*Colophon.*) 4°. *[8] A-Cc[8]. ff. 1-207. [335

APULEIUS, LUCIUS, MADAURENSIS. *Works.* [1] L. Apuleii Madaurensis opera omnia quae exstant ...: Curâ Petri ColuI Brugensis ... Lugduni Batauorum, Ex officina Plantiniana, Apud Franciscum Raphelengium. cIↄ. Iↄ. LXXXVIII. 8°. *[8] **[4] A-Z[8] a-d[8]. pp. 1-431. ¶**1-2 *misbound, in reverse order, after* Tt1, **3-4, *in reverse order, after* Tt3. [2] Petri ColuI ... notae vberiores. *Same imprint.* Aa-Ss[8] Tt[4] a-b[8] c[4]. pp. 3-298. [336

-- -- L. Apuleii Madaurensis operum pars secunda ... Basileae. (Basileae, per Sebastianum Henricpetri: ... cIↄ Iↄ XCVII.) 8°. 3a-4h[8] α-ι[8]. pp. 3-496. (Lea.) [337

-- *Two or more works.* Quae praesenti enchiridio contineantur. .L. Apuleii de Asino aureo libelli. XI. Floridorum libri quattuor. De dogmate Platonis liber unicus. Asclepius, Mercurii Trismegisti dialogus de uoluntate diuina, interprete .L. Apuleio. Eiusdem Trismegisti dialogus de potestate et sapientia dei, interprete Marsilio ficino ... .L. Apuleii orationes duae pro se ipso. (Impressum Florentiae opera et impensa Philippi de Giunta ... Anno ... quingentesimo duodecimo supra Mille, mense Februario) 8°. a-z[8] &[8] A-H[8]. ff. i-ccliii. ¶*Includes* L. Apuleii Madaurensis Cosmographia. [338

-- L. Apuleii Madaurensis philosophi Platonici. Floridorum Libri quattuor De Dogmate Platonis Li. vnus De Philosophia Li. vnus. ... (Argentorati, Ex aedibus Schurerianis, Mense Augusto. M. D. XVI.) 4°. a-f[4.4.8] g[4]. [339

-- L. Apuleii Metamorphoseos, siue lusus Asini libri XI. Floridorū IIII. De Deo Socratis I. De Philosophia I. Asclepius Trismegisti Dialogus eodē Apuleio interprete. Eiusdem Apuleij liber de Dogmatis Platonicis. Eiusdē liber de Mundo ... Isagogicus liber Platonicae philosophiae per Alcinoū philosophum, graece impressus. ... (Venetiis in aedibus Aldi, et Andreae soceri mense Maio M.D.XXI.) 8°. a-z[8] A-K[8] 1-3[8] 4[4]. ff. 2-266. [340

-- *Separate works.* Apuleius Platonicus, de viribus herbarum ... Parisiis Apud Petrum Drouart ... 1543 8°. A-H[4]. ff. 2-32. ¶H4 *repaired.* [341

-- Apuleio dell'asino d'oro. Tradotto per Messer Agnolo Firenzuola ... In Vinegia appresso Gabriel Giolito de Ferrari. MDL. (*Colophon.*) 12°. A-L[12] (-M10-12, *blank*). ff. 2-142. [342

-- -- In Vinegia appresso Gabriel Giolito de' Ferrari. MDLXVII. 8°. *[6] A-X[8] Y[6]. pp. 1-346. [343

AQUILARI, FRANCESCO. Francisci Aquilarii Vulcanus, Siue carmen de duobus incendijs, quae Venetiis euenerunt anno ... CIↃ. IↃ. LXXIIII. Venetiis, Ex Officina Dominici Guerraei, & Io. Baptistae, fratrum. CIↃ. IↃ. LXXIIII. 4°. A[4]. [344

AQUILEIA. Concilium prouinciale Aquileiense primum. Celebratum Anno Domini 1596. Vtini, Apud Io. Baptistam Natolinum. 1598. (*Colophon.*) 4°. A-R[4]. ff. 2-66. (Lea.) [345

ARAGON, PEDRO DE. R.P.F. Petri de Arragon ... In Secundum Secundae D. Thomae ... Commentaria, de iustitia et iure. ... Venetiis, M D XCV. Apud Societatem Minimam. fol. a-b[8] A-Q[8] R-T[6] V-Z[4] Aa-3E[8] 3F[6]. pp. 1-827. (Lea.) [346

D'ARAGONA, TULLIA. Dialogo ... della infinita di amore. ... In Vinegia Appresso Gabriel Giolito de Ferrari. MDXLVII. (*Colophon.*) 8°. A-V[4]. ff. 2-79. [347

ARATUS. Αρατου Σολεως φαινομενα και διοσημεῖα. Θεωνος σχολια. Λεοντιου μηχανικου περὶ ἀρατείας σφαίρας. ... Parisiis M. D. LIX. Apud Guil. Morelium ... 4°. *[2] A-Q[4] R[2] (R2 + *folded sheet*). pp. 1-132. [348

-- -- Arati Solensis phænomena, et prognostica, Interpretibus, M. Tullio Cicerone. Rufo Festo Auieno, Germanico Cæsare, vna cum eius commentarijs. C. Iulii Hygini astronomicon. ... Parisiis, M. D. LIX. Apud Guil. Morelium ... (... Cal. August.) 4°. *[4] A-C[4] D[2] E-V[4] a-f[4] g-h[2] (h2 + *folded sheet*). pp. 1-155, 1-56. [349

-- Hug. Grotii Bataui syntagma Arateorum ... Ex Officinâ Plantinianâ, apud Christophorum Raphelengium ... cIↃ. IↃc. 4°. $*^4$ $**^2$ A-E^4 F^2 A-D^4 E^2 a-m^4 (a4 + *folded leaf*) Aa-Cc^4 α-π^4. pp. 1-42, 1-36, 1-94, 1-24, 1-128. [350

D'ARBRES, JEAN. Compendiaria Ioannis Arborei Laudunensis in dialectica elementa introductio ... Parisiis Apud Simonem Colinaeum. 1539. 8°. A^8 b-k^8. ff. 1-70. [351

ARCANGELO DA BORGONOVO. Dechiaratione sopra il nome di Giesu. Secondo gli Hebrei cabalisti, Greci, Caldei, Persi, & Latini. ... In Ferrara appresso Francesco Rossi 1557. (*Colophon.*) 8°. $✠^4$ A-HH^8 Ii^4. ff. 1-250. [352

ARCHINTO, FILIPPO. Christianum de fide, et sacramentis, edictum. Romae. Antonius Bladus imprimebat. M. D. XXXXV. 4°. aa^4 A-M^4. pp. 1-94. (Lea.) [353

ARCOLANI, GIOVANNI. Practica ... particularium morborum omnium ... Venetiis apud Iuntas M D LVII. (*Colophon.*) fol. $✠^6$ (-✠2-5) A-AA^8 (-F4-5, Q4-5) BB^{10} (-BB10, *presumably blank*). ff. 1-201. ¶BB8-9 *defective.* (School of Dentistry.) [354

ARCUAS, JOANNES FRANCISCUS. Io. Frãcisci Arcuantis Sutrini ... ad Iulium. .II. Pont. Max. Oratio. [Romae, Eucharius Silber, 1503?] 4°. π^4. [355

ARENA, ANTONIO DE. Antonius de Arena, Prouincialis, de bragardissima villa de Soleriis. ... Parisiis, Ex Typographia Nicolai Bonfonij ... 1584. 8°. A-F^8. [356

ARETINO, PIETRO. Il Genesi ... con la visione di Noe ne la quale vede i misterii del Testamento Vecchio e del Nuouo ... M D XXXVIIII. 8°. A-P^8. pp. 3-239. [357

-- Quattro comedie del diuino Pietro Aretino. Cioè Il Marescalco La Cortegiana La Talanta. L'Hipocrito. ... [London, John Wolfe,] MDLXXXVIII. 8°. A-Oo^8. ff. 2-285. *S.T.C.* 19911. [358

-- I quattro libri de la humanita di Christo. .. M D XXXIX. (Impresso in Venetia per Francesco Marcolini da Forli il mese di Agosto ...) 8°. A-P^8. ff. 2-119. [359

-- Ragionamento nel quale M. Pietro Aretino figura quattro suoi amici. ... (Stampata in Nouara nel MDXXXVIII) 8°. π^4 a-r^4 s^6. [360

AREZZO. Constitutiones, et decreta publicata in synodo Dioecesana Arretina, quam Petrus Vsimbardius Episcopus Arretij habuit. ... CIↃ. IↃ. XCVII. Florentiae, In Officina Michaelangeli Sermartellij. MDXCVIII. (*Colophon.*) 4°. $†^4$ A-Ii^4. pp. 1-252. (Lea.) [361

ARGENTI, AGOSTINO. [1] Caualerie della citta di Ferrara. Che contengono il castello di Gorgoferusa. Il monte di Feronia. Et il tempio d'amore. [Ferrara, Francesco Rossi, 1566.] 4°. π^2 A-O^4. ff. 2-55. ¶*Additional t.pp.:* ($A1^r$) Il castello di Gorgoferusa et il monte di Feronia. Ne' quali si contengono le cose d'arme fatte in Ferrara nel Carneuale del M D LXI. ... M. D. LXVI. [2] Il tempio d'amore nel quale si contengono le cose d'arme fatte in Ferrara nelle nozze del Duca Alfonso et della Regina Barbara d'Austria. M. D. LXVI. $✠^4$ A-Z^4 ✠-$✠✠^4$. pp. 1-181. [362

ARIOSTO, LODOVICO. [Comedie.] In Vinegia appresso Gabriel Giolito de' Ferrari. ... 12°. [1] Comedie di M. Lodouico Ariosto, cioè, I Suppositi ... ricorretto, per Thomaso Porcacchi. ... M D LXII. A-C^{12} D^6. ff. 2-41. [2] La cassaria. ... M D LX. A-D^{12} E^6. ff. 2-34. [3] La lena ... MDLXII. A-B^{12} C^6. ff. 2-30. [4] Il negromante ... MDLXII. A-C^{12}. ff. 3-36. [5] Scolastica ... MDLXII. A-D^{12}. ff. 2-48. [363

-- -- *Another copy of* La lena. [364

-- Cassaria. Comedia ... intitolata Cassaria. (Stampata in Vineggia per Francesco Bindoni & Mapheo Pasini compagni. ... MDXXXVII. Del mese di Aprile.) 8°. A-D^8. ff. II-XXXII. [365

-- -- M D XXXVIII. (Stampata in Vinegia per Nicolo di Aristotile di Ferrara detto Zoppino. ...) 8°. A-D^8 E^4. ff. 3-36. [366

-- -- (Stampata in Vinegia per Agostino de Bendoni ... M.D.XXXXII. Del mese de Luio.) 8°. A-B^8 E^4. ff. 3-36. [367

-- -- La cassaria, comedia ... riformata, et ridotta in versi. ... In Vinegia Appresso Gabriel Giolito de Ferrari. MDXLVI. (*Colophon.*) 8°. A-G^{8}. ff. 2-56. [368

-- Herbolato ... Nel quale figura Mastro Antonio Faentino, che parla della nobiltà dell' huomo, et dell'arte della Medicina ... M. D. XLV. (In Vinegia per Giouann'Antonio, & Pietro fratelli de Nicolini da Sabio. ...) 8°. A-D^{4}. [369

-- -- In Ferrara, Appresso Vittorio Baldini, MDLXXXI. ... 8°. A-B^{8}. pp. 3-32. [370

-- La lena, comedia ... M D XXXVII. (In Vinegia Per Nicolo d'Aristotile detto Zoppino. ...) 8°. A-D^{8}. [371

-- Il negromante. Comedia ... M D XXXVIII. (In Vinegia per Nicolo d'Aristotile detto Zoppino. ...) 8°. A-D^{8} E^{4}. [372

-- [1] Orlando furioso ... Con alcune stanze del S. Aluigi Gonzaga in lode del medesimo. ... In Venetia appresso Gabriel Gioli di Ferrarii M. D. XLIIII. (*Colophon.*) 4°. A-II^{8} KK^{4}. ff. 4-260. [2] Espositione de tutti i vocaboli et luoghi difficili ... *Same imprint.* *^{8} **-6*^{4}. [373

-- -- ... con alcune stanze, et cinque canti d'vn nuouo libro del medesimo ... In Vinegia appresso Gabriel Giolito de Ferrari. M D LIIII. (*Colophon.*) 8°. *^{8} A-QQ^{8} RR^{4}. ff. 1-9, pp. 10-588. ¶*Additional t.pp.* (LL4^{r}): Cinque canti di vn nuouo libro ... In Vinetia appresso Gabriel Giolito di Ferrarii e fratelli. 1553. (PP3^{r}) Espositione di tutti i vocaboli et luoghi difficili ... In Vinegia appresso Gabriel Giolito de Ferrari e fratelli. M D LIIII. [374

-- -- [1] [Orlando furioso. ... Le Annotationi, gli Auuertimenti, et le Dichiaratione di Girolamo Ruscelli, La Vita dell'Autore, descritta dal Signor Giouambattista Pigna ... In Vinegia, Appresso Vicenzo Valgrisi ... M D LVI.] 4°. *-**^{4} (*wanting*) 3*^{4} A-Z^{8} a-k^{8} l-n^{4} o^{2}. pp. 2-556. [2] Annotationi, et auuertimenti, di Girolamo Ruscelli ... *Same imprint.* a-l^{4} (-l4) M-O^{4} P^{2}(*wanting*). [375

-- -- In Lione, Appresso Bastiano di Bartholomeo Honorati, M. D. LVI. (Stampato ... per Iacopo Fabro.) 4°. A-Ll^{8} (-Ii8, *blank*) Mm^{4}. pp. 3-508. ¶*Additional t.pp.:* (Ff1^{r}) Gli cinque canti di vn nuouo libro ... *Same imprint.* (Kk1^{r}) Le sposizione di tutti i vocaboli et luoghi difficili ... *Same imprint.* [376

-- -- ... Con li Discorsi si Girolamo Ruscelli ... In Venetia, Appresso Vincenzo Valgrisio. 1570. 12°. A-Z^{12} a-z^{12} Aa-Bb^{12}. pp. 4-1151. ¶*Additional t.p.* (x1^{r}): I cinque canti ... *Same imprint.* [377

-- -- ... reuisto ..., sopra le correttioni di Ieronimo Ruscelli. ... In Lyone, appresso Gugliel. Rouillio. 1570. 12°. A-3C^{12} (-3C12, *blank*). pp. 2-1148. [378

-- -- ... Con le Annotationi, gli Auuertimenti, & le Dichiarationi di Ieronimo Ruscelli. La Vita dell'Autore descritta dal Signor Giouan Battista Pigna. ... La dichiaratione di tutti le Istorie, & Fauole toccate ..., fatte da M. Nicolo Eugenico. ... Li Cinque Canti del medesimo Autore. .. In Venetia. Appresso gli Heredi di Vincenzo Valgrisi. M. D. LXXX. 4°. *^{8} A-VV^{8} (-VV8, *blank*). pp. 1-654. [379

-- -- In Venetia, M.D.LXXXVII. Appresso Felice Valgrisi. (*Colophon.*) *Same collation and pagination.* [380

-- -- ... Con nuoui Argomenti di M. Lodouico Dolce: Con la vita dell'Auttore di M. Simon Fornari: ... Le nuoue Allegorie, & Annotationi di M. Tomaso Porcacchi ... In Venetia, Appresso Giouanni Alberti. M.D.XCVIII. (*Colophon.*) 4°. a^{8} A-RR^{8} Ss^{12}. [381

-- -- *Canto I. Bergamasco dialect.* Orlandi Furius De Misser Lodouic Ferraris Nouament compost in buna lingua da Berghem ... indrizat dal Gobo da Venesia a M. Pasqui. ... (Stampata in Venetia per Agustino Bindoni. ... 1550.) 8°. A-B^{4}. [382

-- -- *French.* Roland furieux ... traduict en prose Françoyse ... On les vend a Paris ... par Guillaume le Bret. 1545. 8°. ā^{8} a-z^{8} A-Cc^{8}. ff. 1-391. [383

-- -- Cinq discours de cinq chants nouueau ... Traduictz nouuellement en François par Gabriel Chappuys Tourangeau. A Lyon, par Barthelemi Honorati. M. D. LXXXII. ... (... par Basile Bouquet. ...) 8°. A-F^{8} G^{4}. pp. 4-102. [384

-- -- *Spanish.* Orlando furioso ... traduzido en Romance Castellan por don Ieronymo de Vrrea. (Imprimiose enla ... villa de Anuers en casa de Martin Nucio y acabose a XXV dias de Agosto. De. M. D. XLIX. años.) 4°. A-Ii^{8} Kk^{4} Ll^{2}. ff. 4-260. [385

-- -- A Lyon en casa de Gulielmo Rouille. 1550. (Imprimiose ... en casa de Mathias Bonhomme.) 4°. A-Dd^{8} Ee^{4}. pp. 5-436. [386

-- -- Impresso en Venecia por Gabriel Giolito de Ferrarii y sus hermanos. M D LIII. (... Acabose a xx dias andados del mes de Henero ...) 4°. π^{4} A-II^{8} KK^{10} *-5*^{8} 6*^{2}. pp. 1-529. ¶*Additional t.p.* (*1^{r}): Exposicion de todos los lugares difficultosos ... *Same imprint.* [387

-- -- [Orlando furioso ... Bilbao, en case de Mathias Mares. 1583.] 4°. π^{8} (-π1-6) A-Oo^{8}. ff. 1-302. [388

-- -- *Selections.* Bellezze del furioso ... Scielta da Oratio Toscanella. ... In Venetia, Appresso Pietro de i Franceschi, & nepoti. M. D. LXXIIII. (*Colophon.*) 4°. *^{6} A-3A^{4} 3B^{6}. pp. 1-327. ¶*Additional t.p.* (Tt2^{r}): I luoghi communi di tutta l'opera ... *Same imprint.* *3-4 *misbound after* *6. [389

-- Rime ... In Vinegia M. D. LII. (... M. D. LIIII.) 8°. A-G^{8}. ff. 2-55. [390

-- Le satire ... volgare in terza rima, di nuouo stampate, del mese di Luio. M D XXXVII. (... in Vinegia. ...) 8°. A-D^{8}. [391

-- Scolastica comedia ... [Venezia, Giovanni Griffio, 1547.] 8°. A-N^{4}. [392

-- I suppositi. Comedia ... intitulata li suppositi. (Stampata in Vineggia per Agostino de Bindoni. ... M.D.XXXXII.) 8°. A-D^{8}. ff. 2-32. [393

-- -- La comedie des supposez, ... en Italien & Françoys. ... A Paris, Par Estienne Groulleau ... 1552. 8°. A-L^{8} (-L8, *presumably blank*). ff. 2-87. [394

ARISTEAS. Aristea de settantadue interpreti ... tradotto per M. Lodouico Domenichi. In Fiorenza. Appresso Lorenzo Torrentino. MDL. ... (... a IIII di Gennaio. ...) 8°. A-I^{8} (-I8, *presumably blank*). pp. 1-142. [395

ARISTIPPIA. Comedia chiamata Aristippia. (Stampata in Roma [per Francesco Minizio Calvo] nel mese d'Agosto del .M.D.XXIIII.) 12°. A-F^{6}. ff. II-XXXIIII. [396

-- -- MDXXX (Stampata in Vinegia per Nicolo d'Aristotile detto Zoppino. ...) 8°. A-D^{8}. ff. 2-32. [397

ARISTOPHANES. Αριστοφανους ... κωμῳδίαι ἕνδεκα. Aristophanis facetissimi comoediae vndecim. ... Parisiis. Apud Christianum Wechelum ... M. D. XL. 4°. a-z^{4} &^{4} Aa^{4} Bb^{6} Cc-Zz^{4} &&^{4} AA-II^{4} KK^{6} LL-YY^{4}. pp. 3-567. ¶*A separate t.p. before each play except the first.* [398

-- -- (Venetiis in ædibus Bartholomæi Zanetti Casterzagensis, sumptibus uero D. Melchionis Sessa. Anno. MDXXXVIII. Mense Septembri.) 8°. A-MM^{8}. [399

-- -- Venetiis. M D XLII. (... apud Ioannem Farreum, & fratres. ...) 8°. A-MM^{8}. [400

-- -- Basileæ, M. D. XLII. (... apud haeredes Cratandri, Mense Martio ...) 8°. a-z^{8} A-M^{8}. pp. 3-559. [401

-- -- Αριστοφανους κωμωδιαι εννεα ... Aristophanis comoediae nouem cum commentariis antiquis ... Basileae, in officina Frobeniana an. M D XLVII (*Colophon.*) fol. ✠^{6} a-z^{6} A-Aa^{6} Bb^{4} Cc-Dd^{6}. pp. 1-571. [402

-- -- Aristophanii ... Comoediæ vndecim, è græco in latinum, ad verbũ, translatæ; Andrea Diuo Iustinopolitano interprete ... Venetijs. M D XXXVIII. (... apud D. Iacob a Burgofrancho Papiensem, mense Iunio. ...) 8°. A-CC^{8} DD^{4} EE-KK^{8}. ff. 2-260. [403

-- -- Le comedie del facetissimo Aristofane, Tradutte di Greco in lingua commune d'Italia, per Bartolomio & Pietro Rositini de Prat' Alboino. ... In Venegia. Apresso Vicenzo Vaugris ... M. D. XLV. 8°. a-z^{8} A-P^{8}. ff. 2-304. [404

-- Αριστοφανους ... Βάτραχοι. Aristophanis ... Ranæ. (Ἐτυγώθη παρ' Ἰωάννη τῷ Φροβενίῳ ... Ἀ. φ. κ. δ. [1524.]) 4°. a-i^{4}. [405

-- Ἀριστοφάνους ... Πλοῦτος. Aristophanis ... Plutus, iam nunc per Carolum Girardum Bituricum & Latinus factus, & Commentarijs ... illustratus. Editio prima. ... Parisiis, Apud Mathurinum Dupuys ... M.D.XLIX. (Imprimebat Christianus Wechelus sibi, et Mathurino Dupuys ...) 4°. A-Cc^{4} Dd^{6}. pp. 4-214. [406

ARISTOTLE. *Works*. *Greek*. Ἀριστοτέλους ἅπαντα. Aristotelis ... opera ... Basileae, per Io. Beb. et Mich. Ising. anno M. D. XXXIX. (... μηνὶ Μαιμακτηριῶνι.) fol. a^8 a-oo^8 pp^4 α^4 A-EE^8. pp. 2-598, 2-447. [407

-- -- Basileae, per Io. Beb. et Mich. Ising. anno M. D. L. (... μηνὶ Μουνυχιῶνι.) fol. a^8 a^6 b-z^8 Aa-Nn^8 A^{10} B-Bb^8 Cc-Dd^6. pp. 2-572, 1-425. [408

-- -- [1] Αριστοτελους ... τομος. α'. Aristotelis omnem logicam, rhetoricam, et poeticam disciplinam continens, tomus I. Venetiis. (... apud Aldi filios, expensis ... Federici de Turrisanis eorum auunculi. M. D. LI.) 8°. $*^{10}$ a-dd^8 ee^4 ff-uu^8. pp. 1-679. [2] Αριστοτελους ... τόμος β'. Aristotelis de physica auscultatione, de coelo, de mundo ... de generatione et corruptione, et meteorologicam disciplinam continens tomus II. Venetiis, M D LI. *Same colophon.* $*^8$ A-Ω^8 α-γ^8 δ^6. pp. 1-438. [3] Αριστοτελους ... τόμος III. Aristotelis de historia animalium disciplinam et ... agnatos libros continens tomus III. Venetiis, M. D. LIII. (Apud Aldi filios. Expensis ... Federici de Turrisanis ... M. D. LII.) *-$**^8$ 3A-$3Z^8$ 3a-$3z^8$ AAa-MMm^8. pp. 1-948. [4] Αριστοτελους ... τόμος IIII. Aristotelis problemata cum Alex. Aphrodis. probl. et mechanica, et metaphysices disciplinam continens tomus IIII. Venetiis, MDLII. *Same colophon.* $**^8$ 4A-$4Z^8$ 4a-$4p^{8}$. pp. 1-607. [5] Αριστοτελους ... τόμος ε'. Aristotelis moralia magna, et moralia Eudem. et moralia Nicomach. et rei familiaris, ciuilisque disciplinam continens tomus V. Venetiis M.D.LII. (... apud Aldi filios. Expensis ... Federici de Turrisanis ... M. D. LII.) $*^8$ $**^4$ AA-ZZ^8 aa-rr^8 ss^4. pp. 1-646. [409

-- -- *Another copy of tome III.* [410

-- -- [1] Αριστοτελους τα ευρισκομενα. Aristotelis opera quae exstant. ... Opera & studio Friderici Sylburgii Veterensis. Francofurdi Apud Andreae Wecheli heredes, Claudium Marnium, & Ioannem Aubrium, MDLXXXVII. ... 4°.):(^{4} A-D^4 E^2 $+^2$ a-$3y^4$. pp. 4-444, 1-542. ¶*Additional t.p.* (+1^r): Αριστοτελους οργανον. ... Francofurdi Apud heredes Andreae Wecheli, MDLXXXV. 3y2-3 *misbound, in reverse order, after* +1. [2] Αριστοτελους ... Artis Rhetoricae libri III. Rhetorices ad Alexandrum lib. I. De arte Poetica liber I. ... Francofurti Apud heredes Andreae Wecheli MDLXXXIIII. A-Vv^4. pp. 3-341. [3] Αριστοτελους ... ethicorum, siue de moribus, ad Nicomachum Libri Decem: Opera ... Petri Victorij emendati. ... *Same imprint.* [:]^4 A-Z^4 a-f^4. pp. 1-232. [4] Αριστοτελους .... Ethicorum magnorũ libri 2. Ethicorũ Eudemiorum 1. 7. De virtutibus & vitijs 1. 1. Theophrasti characteres Ethici. Alexandri Aphrodis. Quod virtus non sufficiat ad beattitudinem. ... *Same imprint.* (:)^2 A-Ss^4 Tt^2. pp. 1-332. [5] Αριστοτελους ... polliticorum et Oeconomicorum libri ... Francofurdi Apud Andreę Wecheli heredes, Claudium Marnium, & Ioann. Aubrium, MDLXXXVII. (:)^4 a-zz^4 $3a^2$. pp. 1-370. [6] Αριστοτελους ... de animalium historia libri X. Addita e Theophrasto Collectanea quaedam de animalibus ... *Same imprint.* $+^2$ a-$3o^4$ $3p^2$. pp. 1-484. [7] Αριστοτελους ... De animalium partibus, lib. IIII De animalium ingressu, lib. I De animalium motu, lib. I De animaliũ generatione, lib. V De Spiritu, lib. I: qui spurius esse creditur. ... Francofurdi Apud heredes Andreae Wecheli, MDLXXXV. $+^2$ A-$3E^4$ $3F^2$. pp. 1-412. [8] Αριστοτελους .... Physicae auscultationis lib. 8. De Coelo 4. De Gener. & Corruptione 2. Meteorologicorum 4. De Mundo 1. De Anima 3. De Sensu & sensilibus, lib. 1. De Memoria & reminiscentia 1. De Somno & vigilia 1. De Insomniis 1. De Diuinatione per somnum 1. De Iuuentute, senectute, vita & morte 1. De Respiratione 1. De Longitudine & breuitate vitae 1. ... Francofurti Apud haeredes Andreae Wecheli, Claud. Marnium, & Ioan. Aubrium. MDXCVI. (*Colophon.*) A-Bb^4 Cc^2 a-n^4 o^2 aa-gg^4 hh^2 Aa-Qq^4 Rr^2 A-D^4 AA-KK^4 3A-$3O^4$. pp. 3-204, 1-108, 1-60, 1-132, 1-31, 1-78, 1-111. [9] Αριστοτελους και Θεοφραστου .... metaphysica. ... Francofurdi Apud heredes Andreae Wecheli, MDLXXXV. $*^2$ A-Rr^4. pp. 1-318. ¶Rr2-3 *misbound, in reverse order, after* *1. [10] Αριστοτελους ... Varia opuscula. De Xenophanis, Zenonis, & Gorgiae dogmat. De lineis insecabilibus. Mechanica problemata. De audibilibus. De mirabilibus auditis. Ventorũ situs & nomina. Physiognomonica. De coloribus. De plantis libri duo. ... inserta sunt Sotionis & Athenaei collectanea ... Item Polemonis & Adamantii Physiognomonica: cum lib. Melampodis De palpitationibus & lib. De naeuis oleaceis. ... Francofurdi Apud Andreae Wecheli heredes, Ioann. Aubrium, & Claudium Marnium, MDLXXXVII. π^2 AA-ZZ^4 Aa-Ddd^4. pp. 1-398. [11] Αριστοτελους, Αλεξανδρου τε και Κασιου Προβλήματα ... Aristotelis, Alexandri, et Casssii problemata, cum Theophrasteorum quorundam collectaneis. ... Francofurdi Apud heredes Andreae Wecheli, MDLXXXV. (*Colophon.*) $+^4$ A-$3Q^4$. pp. 1-493. [411

-- -- *Another copy of* [1] *(lacking the preliminaries), of* [2], *and of* [9]. [412

-- -- *Greek & Latin.* [1] Αριστοτελους ... τα σωζομενα. Operum Aristotelis ... noua editio, Graecè & Latinè. Lugduni, Apud Iacobum Bubonium. M. D. XC. (Exucdebat Guillelmus Laemarius ... Kal. Martii.) fol. (.˙.)^{10} a-z^{6} Aa-3Q^{6} 3R^{4}. pp. 1-755. [2] Operum Aristotelis tomus II. ... Lugduni, Apud Guillelmum Laemarium. M. D. XC. (*Colophon.*) π^{2} A-3C^{6} 3D-3E^{4} *^{4} ¶-4¶^{6}. pp. 1-595. [413

-- -- *Latin.* [1] Aristotelis ... opera ... omnia ... Item Io. Lodouici Viuis Valentini, de libris Aristotelicis censura ... De uita Aristotelis, ... commentatio ... per Philippum Melanchthonem. Basileae [per Joannem Oporinum] M. D. XXXVIII. fol. α^{6} a-z^{6} A-Z^{6} aa-zz^{6} AA-BB^{4}. pp. 1-843. [2] Operum Aristotelis ... tomus secundus. *Same imprint.* (... Mense Septembri.) β^{4} a-z^{6} A-Gg^{6} Hh^{4} (-Hh4, *blank*). pp. 1-640. ¶*Vol. 3 lacking.* [414

-- -- [1] Aristotelis ... opera ... omnia ... in Tres Tomos digesta. ... Item, supra censuram Io. Lodouici Viuis Valentini de Libros Aristotelicis, & Philippi Melanchthonis Commentationem, ... adiecta ... fuit ... Dissertatio ... Basileae, ex officina Ioan. Oporini, Anno 1548. fol. α-β^{6} a-r^{6} s^{4}. pp. 1-211. [2] Operum Aristotelis tomus secundus ... Basileae, M. D. XLVIII. αα^{4} Aa-Zz^{6} AA-3I^{6} 3K^{4}. pp. 1-667. ¶*Tome 3 lacking.* [415

-- -- *Another copy of* [2]. [416

-- -- [1] Secundum volumen. Aristotelis ... de rhetorica, et poetica libri. Cum Auerrois Cordubensis ... paraphrasibus ... Venetiis apud Iuntas .M D L. (*Colophon.*) fol. **^{4} AA-GG^{8} HH^{10} II-LL^{8} MM^{4}. ff. 1-94. [2] Tertium volumen. ... libri moralem ... philosophiam complectentes. Cum Auerrois ... expositione, et in Platonis libros de republica paraphrasi ... *Same imprint & colophon.* *^{10} 3A-3Z^{8} 3&^{8}. ff. 1-192. [3] Quartum volumen. Aristotelis ... de physico auditu libri octo, cum Auerrois ... commentariis. ... *Same imprint & colophon.* *^{2} a-cc^{8}. ff. 2-207. ¶*Parts of an edition in 11 vols.* [417

-- -- [Omnia opera.] Venetiis MDLX. (... Apud Cominum de Tridino Montisferrati. ...) 8°. [1] Omnia opera Aristotelis Stagiritae omnia, quae extant, opera ... Auerrois Cordubensis ... Commentarii. ... Marci Antonii Zimarae ... solutiones ... +^{8} *^{8} A-Xx^{8} Yy^{4}. ff. 2-356. [2] Posteriora Tomus secundus operum Aristotelis ... *^{8} A-Ll^{8}. ff. 2-270. [3] Rhet. et mor. Tomus tertius ... *^{8} **^{4} A-X^{8} Z^{8} &^{8} Aa-3T^{8}. ff. 1-520. [4] Physica Quartus tomus ... a^{12} B-Xx^{8} Yy^{4}. ff. 1-356. [5] De coelo Tomus Quintus ... A-Ss^{8}. ff. 2-328. [6] Meteorolo. Tomus sextus ... A^{12} B-Oo^{8}. ff. 5-295. [7] De anima. Tomus septimus ... A-Pp^{8} Qq^{4}. ff. 2-307. [8] Metaphy. Tomus octauus ... A^{12} B-3D^{8} 3E^{4}. ff. 5-404. [9] Colliget Tomus Nonus in quo magni Auerrois ... septem libri Colliget ... *A^{8} B-3A^{8} 3B^{4}. ff. 2-380. [10] Dest. destr. Tomus decimus operum. In quo magni commen. Auer. disputationes quae destructio destructionum Algazelis dicuntur, cum expositione ... Augustini Suessani continentur. Et translatione Calo Calonymos ... *^{4} A-Yy^{8}. ff. 1-360. [11] Spur. & cont. Tomus undecimus operum. In quo libelli quidam spurii Aris. ascripti continentur. ... *^{4} A-Dd^{8} Ee^{4}. ff. 1-220. [418

-- -- [Opera.] Venetiis apud Iunctas. M. D. LXII. 8°. [1] Primum Volumen. Aristotelis Stagiritae Organum. Auerrois Cordubensis in eo commentaria ... Leui Gersonidis ... annotationes. Arabum quorundam Quaesita & Epistolae. ... Bernardini Tomitani Patauini ... Animaduersiones quaedam, & Contradictionum Solutiones. ... ✠^{8} A-N^{8} O^{4} A-X^{8}. ff. 2-106, 1-168. [2] Primi Voluminis Pars .II. Aristotelis Stagiritae Posteriorum Resolutiorum Libri Duo. Cum Auerrois ... commentariis, triplici interpretatione distinctis. Bermardini Tomitani ... Animaduersiones & Contradictionum Solutiones ... ✠^{8} A-4B^{8}. ff. 2-568. ¶*Lacks Tomitano's* Animadversiones *&c.* [3] Primi Voluminis Pars .III. Aristotelis Stagiritae Topicorum, atq3 Elenchorum Libri. Cum Auerrois ... expositione Abramo de Balmes, & Mantino interpretibus. ... A-Y^{8}. ff. 2-176. [4] Secundum Volumen. Aristotelis de rhetorica, et poetica libri, Cum Auerrois ... paraphrasibus ... (... apud haeredes Lucaeantonij Iunctę. ...) ✠^{4} A-EE^{8} FF^{4}. ff. 2-228. [5] Tertium Volumen. Aristotelis Stagiritae libri Moralem, totam Philosophiam complectentes, cum Auerrois ... in moralia Nicomachia expositione, Et in Platonis Libros de Republica Paraphrasi ... ✠-✠✠^{8} A-ZZ^{8} 3A^{4}. ff. 2-372. [6] Quartum Volumen Aristotelis de physico auditu libri octo. Cum Auerrois ... commentariis. ... Marci Antonij Zimarae Contradictionum ... Solutiomes. ... (... apud haeredes Lucae Antonij Iunctę. ...) ✠^{4} A-3R^{8} 3S^{4}. ff. 2-508. [7] Quintum Volumen. Aristotelis de coelo, De Generatione & Corruptione, Meteorologicorum, De Plantis cum Auerrois ... commentariis. M. A. Zimarae Contradictionum Solutiones ... ✤^{4} A-3Q^8 3R^4. ff. 2-499. [8] Sextum Volumen. Aristotelis libri omnes, Ad Animalium cognitionem attinentes. Cum Auerrois ... commentariis. M. A. Zimarae Contradictionum Solutiones ... ✤^{8} ✤✤^{4} A-CC^8 DD^4. ff. 1-212. [9] Aristotelis de anima libri tres, Cum Auerrois commentariis et Antiqua tralatione ... His accessit ... noua tralatio, ... Michaele Sophiano interprete. Adiecimus etiam Marci Antonii Passeri Ianuae disputationem ... [et Zimarae solutiones.] †^{8} A-FF^8. ff. 2-228. [10] Sexti Voluminis Pars II. Aristotelis libri reliqui, ad Animalium cognitionem attinentes, qui vulgõ Parua Naturalia nuncupantur. Cum Auerrois ... paraphrasibus ... (... apud haeredes Lucaeantonij Iunctae. ...) A^8 b-u^8. ff. 4-139. [11] Septimum Volumen. Aristotelis Stagiritae Extra. ordinem. Naturalium varij Libri. ... Aristoteli ascripti Alexandri problematum libri duo. ... *Same colophon.* ✤^{4} A-DD^8 EE^4. ff. 1-220. [12] Octauum Volumen. Aristotelis metaphysicorum libri XIIII. Cum Auerrois ... commentariis, et epitome. Theophrasti Metaphysicorum Liber. Marci Antonij Zomarae Contradictionum Solutiones ... *Same colophon.* †^{4} A-3G^8. ff. 2-424. [13] Nonum Volumen. Auerrois Cordubensis Sermo de Substantia Orbis. Destructio destructionum Philosophię Algazelis. De Animae beatitudine, seu epistola de Intellectu. ... M. Antonij Zimarae ... Contradictionum Solutiones. *Same colophon.* A-V^8. ff. 2-159. [14] Decimum Volumen. Auerrois Cordubensis colliget libri VII. Cantica item Auicennae cum ... Auerrois commentariis, M. A. Zimarae Contradictionum Solutiones ... ✤^{8} A-QQ^8. ff. 2-312. [15] Aristotelis omnia quae extant Opera. ... Auerrois ... commentarij. ... Marciantonii Zimarae ... Contradictionum Solutiones ... Barnardini Tomitani ... Contradictionum Solutiones ... Tabulam vero M. A. Zimarae huic adiunximus operi ... (... Impressa in officina haeredum Lucęantonij Iunctę. ...) ✤^{8} ✤✤^{4} A-3F^8. ff. 2-415. ¶*Additional t.p.* (A1^r): Marci Antonii Zimarae ... Tabula ... *Same imprint.* [419

-- -- *Another copy of* [9] *and* [11]. [420

-- -- [1] Aristotelis Stagiritae tripartitae philosophiae opera omnia ... Basileae, per Ioannem Heruagium, Anno M.D.LXIII. fol. α†-β†^{6} a-z^6 A-C^6. cols. 1-620. [2] Pars secunda operum Aristotelis ... Basileae ex officina Heruagiana. M.D.LXIII. α*^{4} a-v^6 x^4 y^6. cols. 1-516. [3] Pars tertia ... *Same imprint.* α^6 a-z^6 A-Ff^6. cols. 1-1248. [4] Pars quarta ..., uarias continens ... quaestiones, & tanquam exercitationes. *Same imprint.* αα*^{4} a-k^6 l^4 m-p^6 q^4 r^6 (-r6, *presumably blank*). cols. 1-256. [421

-- -- [1] Aristotelis ... opera ... Lugduni, Apud Ioannem Frellonium, M. D. LXIII. (... Excudebat Symphorianus Barbierus.) fol. α-β^8 a-z^8 A-F^8 G-H^6 a-m^8. cols. 1-976. [2] Aristotelis ... operum Tomus Secundus. Lugduni, Apud Ioannem Frellonium. (*Same colophon.*) aa-zz^8 Aa-Zz^8 AA-DD^8. cols. 1-1578. [422

-- -- [Opera.] Venetiis apud Iuntas. ... 8°. [1] Primum Volumen. ... M. D. LXXIIII. ✤^{8} A-N^8 O^4 A-X^8. ff. 2-106, 1-168. [2] Primi Voluminis Pars .II. ... M. D. LXXIIII. ✤^{4} A-4B^8 a-q^8. ff. 2-568, 2-128. [3] Primi Voluminis Pars III. ... M. D. LXXIIII. A-Y^8. pp. 2-176. [4] Bernardini Tomitani ... Animaduersiones aliquot In Primum Librum Posteriorum Resolutorium. ... M. D. LXXIIII. (... M D LXXV.) A-S^8 T^4 V^8 X^4. pp. 4-160. [5] Michaelis Pselli metaphrasis libri secundi posteriorum analyticorum Aristotelis. Emmanuele Margunio Cretense interprete. ... M. D. LXXIIII. A-D^8. pp. 3-32. [6] Secundum Volumen. ... M. D. LXXIIII. (*Colophon.*) A-EE^8 FF^4. ff. 2-228. [7] Tertium Volumen. ... M. D. LXXIIII. ✤-✤✤^{8} A-ZZ^8 3A^4. ff. 1-372. [8] Quartum Volumen ... M. D. LXXIIII. (... M D LXXII.) ✤^{4} A-3R^8 3S^4. ff. 2-508. [9] Quintum Volumen ... M. D. LXXIIII. ✤^{4} A-3Q^8 3R^4. ff. 2-499. [10] Sextum Volumen. ... M. D. LXXIIII. ✤^{8} ✤✤^{4} A-CC^8 DD^4. ff. 1-212. [11] Aristotelis de anima libri tres. ... M. D. LXXIIII. †^{8} A-FF^8. ff. 2-228. [12] Sexti Voluminis. Pars II. ... M. D. LXXIIII. (*Colophon.*) A^8 b-u^8. ff. 4-139. [13] Septimum Volumen. ... M. D. LXXIII. (*Colophon.*) ✤^{4} A-DD^8 EE^4. ff. 1-220. [14] Octauum Volumen. ... M. D. LXXIIII. †^{4} A-3G^8. ff. 2-424. [15] Nonum Volumen. ... M. D. LXXIII. (*Colophon.*) A-V^8. ff. 2-159. [16] Decimum Volumen. ... M. D. LXXIIII. A^4 A-QQ^8. ff. 1-312. [17] Aristotelis omnia quae extant Opera. ... MDLXXV. (... M. D. LXXVI.) ✤^{8} ✤✤^{4}. [18] Marci Antonii Zimarae ... Tabula ... M. D. LXXVI. A-3F^8. ff. 2-415. [423

-- -- Index rerum omnium quae in Aristotelis operibus continentur ... Lugduni, Apud Ioannam Iacobi Iuntae f. (... Excudebat Basileus Bouquetius. 1579.) 16°. a-z^8 A-Z^8 aa-hh^8. ¶*Part of an edition of the works in 8 volumes.* [424

-- -- [1] Aristotelis Stagiritae ... operum omnium pars prima, quam logicam, Seu organum appellant: cui addidimus Argumenta, ac potius paraphrases, & Annotationes ex Boethi,

Ammonij, Simplicij, Io. Grammat. & Alexandri sententia ... Ex Ioan. Marinelli scriptis. ... Venetiis, Apud Ioachimum Bruniolum M D LXXXIIII. (... Ex Officina Nicolai Moretti. ...) 16°. a-b^8 C-3O^8 (-3O8, *presumably blank*). pp. 3-32, 1-879. [2] Aristotelis Stagiritae rhetoricorum Ad Theodect. Libri III. Quos Carolus Sigonius, & M. Anton. Maioragius vertebat. De Rhetorica ad Alexan. lib. De Arte Poetica liber. Pars secunda. ... Venetiis, MDLXXXV. (... Apud Nicolaum Morettum. M D LXXXIIII.) A-3E^8 3F^4. pp. 3-799. [3] Aristotelis Stagiritae physicorum libri VIII. Omniaq; Opera, quae ad Naturalem Philosophiam spectare videntur. Pars tertia. Summae ... explanationesque ex Simplicio, Ioan. Gram. & Auerroe. Curtii Marinelli Solutiones Quaestionum ... *Same imprint and colophon.* A-3H^8 3K-3R^8 (-3R8, *blank*). pp. 2-989. [4] Aristotelis Stagiritae Libri Omnes, Quibus Historia ... animalium, atque etiam plantarum naturae breuis descriptio, pertractantur. Pars quarta. ... *Same imprint and colophon.* 3A-5G^8 (-5G8, *blank*). pp. 3-842. [5] Aristotelis Stagiritae Libri omnes, Quibus tota Moralis Philosophia ... continentur. Pars quinta. ... *Same imprint.* A-3K^8. pp. 2-894. [6] Aristotelis ... Problematum Sectiones duae de quadraginta. Quaestiones Mechanicae. De miraculis naturae. Physionomica. De lineis insectabilibus. haec & alia ... Quibus Alexandri Aphrodysaei Problematum libri adiecti fuere. Pars sexta. ... Venetiis, Apud Ioachimum Bruniolum. 1585. A-Yy^8 Zz^4. pp. 2-728. [7] Aristotelis Stagiritae metaphysicorum libri XIIII. Theophrasti Metaphysicorum Liber. De causis Liber. Pars septima ... Curtij Marinelli, Argumenta ... Venetiis, Apud Ioachimum Bruniolum M D LXXXV. A-Xx^8. pp. 3-703. [8] Index rerum omnium, quae in Aristotelis operibus continentur ... Venetiis, M D LXXXV. (... Apud Nicolaum Morettum. ...) A-Z^8 A-I^8 KK^8 Ll-3H^8 (-3H8, *blank*). [425

-- -- [1] Aristotelis operum, quotquot extant, Latina Editio ... Francofurti, Apud Andreae Wecheli heredes, Claudium Marnium, & Ioan. Aubrium. M D XCIII. 8°.):(-2):(^{8} A-HH^8 II^2. pp. 3-473. ¶*Additional t.p.* (A1^r): Aristotelis I tomus logicus ... *Same imprint.* [2] Aristotelis II tomus logicus ... *Same imprint.* 4A-4P^8. pp. 3-218. ¶*The first volume of an edition in 4 volumes.* [426

-- *Two or more works. Greek.* Aristotelis, et Xenophontis Ethica, Politica, & Oeconimica. Cum alijs aliquot ex Plutarcho, Proclo, Alexandro Aphrodesiensi Cōmentationibus. Basileae. Apud Ioan. Vualder. 8°. a^8 a-z^8 A-P^8. pp. 2-606. [427

-- -- *Another copy* (-a8, P8, *both blank*). [428

-- Ἀριστοτέλους Φυσικῆς ἀκροάσεως, βιβλία Θ. ... Aristotelis De Physica auscultatiōe, lib. 8. De Coelo 4. De Gener. & Corruptione 2. Meteorologicorum 4. De Mundo 1. De Anima 3. De Sensu & sensibilibus, lib. 1. De Memoria & reminiscentia 1. De somno & vigilia 1. De Insomniis 1. De Diuinatione per somnum 1. De Iuuentute, senectute, vita & morte 1. De Respiratione 1. De Lōgitudine & breuitate vitae, 1. ... Francofurti Ex Typographia Andreae Wecheli. M. D. LXXVII. (*Colophons.*) 4°. A-Y^4 Z^2 a-m^4 n^2 aa-gg^4 Aa-Oo^4 Pp^2 A-II^4 3A-3L^4 3M^2. pp. 3-180, 1-99, 1-52, 1-115, 1-24, 1-69, 1-92. [429

-- -- *Another copy.* [430

-- *Latin.* Expositiones textuales dubio𝔷 ... in libros de Celo ⁊ mūdo. Generatione ⁊ corruptōne. Metherologo𝔷. ac Paruo𝔷 naturaliū Aristotelis. ... ex ... cōmentarijs ... Thome Aq̄natis ... transsumpte ... (... in Officina Quentell Colonie ... ĩpressa [post 1500].) fol. B.L. aa-ff^6 gg^4 hh-mm^6 nn^4 oo-qq^6 rr^4 ss-zz^6 A-C^6 D^4 E-G^6 H^4 I-K^6 L^4 M-N^6 O^4 P^8. ff. i-xlix, i-xxxv, j-xlviij, i-xxxix, j-xxiiij, j-x. [431

-- Quae in hoc uolumine continentur Vitae Aristotelis ... Praedicabilia prophyrii [*sic*]. Praedicamenta Aristotelis. Sex principia Giberti poretani interp̄te Hermolao barbaro. Libri duo periherminias Arist. Liber priorum arist. Libri duo posteriorum arist. Physicorum libri octo. Metaphysicae libri duodecim. De coelo & mundo libri tres. De anima libri tres. Aethicorū libri decem interprete Io. Argiropilo. Politicorum libri octo. Economicorum liber unus. Libellus de moribus interprete Leonardo aretino. Magnorum moralium Georgio ualla interprete. ... (Venetiis a Philippo pincio Impressa: sumptibus dñi Benedicti Fontana. ... M.cccccv. die .xii. Septembris.) fol. a-z^8 &^{8} ꝯ^8 ℞^{8} A-S^8 T^6. [432

-- Habentur hoc volumine haec Theodoro Gaza interprete. Aristotelis de natura animalium. lib. ix. Eiusdem de partibus animalium. lib. iiii. Eiusdem de generatione animalium. lib. y. Theophrasti de historia plantarum. lib. ix. ... Eiusdem de causis plantarum. lib. yi. Aristotelis problemata ... Alexādri Aphrodisiensis ꝓblemata ... (Venetiis In AEdibus Aldi, & Andreae Asulani Socieri Mense Februario. M.D.xiii.) fol. a^{12} b-n^8 o-p^6 q-z^8 A-M^8 N^6 O-P^8. ff. 1-273. [433

-- Contenta. Politicorum libri Octo. Comentarii. Economicorum Duo. Commentarii. Hecatonomiarum [Fabri Stapulensis] Septem. Economiarū publ. Vnus. Explanationis Leonardi in oeconomia Duo. Venundātur [Parisiis] a Ponceto le preux ... (M D XV.) fol. a^4 a-z^6 &^{6} (-&6, *presumably blank*). ff. II-CXLIII. [434

-- Introductio Physica. [a1^r] Ex physiologia Aristotelis, libri duodetriginta. 1 De auscultatione naturali octo, 2 De coelo quatuor, 5 De anima tres, Ioanne Argyropylo interprete. 3 De generatione & corruptione duo, 4 Meteorologicorum quatuor, 6 De sensu & sensili vnus, 7 De memoria & reminiscentia vnus, 8 De somno & vigilia vnus, 9 De insomnijs vnus, 10 De diuinatione in somno vnus, 11 De longitudine & breuitate vitae vnus, 12 De iuuentute & senectute & vita & morte & respiratione vnus, Francisco Vatablo interprete. ... (Parisiis in aedibus Henrici Stephani. Mense Augusto. M.D.XVIII.) fol. π^2 a-z^8 A-L^8 M-N^6 O-T^8 V^6 (-V6, *presumably blank*). ff. 2-336. [435

-- -- *Another copy* (-π^2). [436

-- Aristotelis ... Libri De Coelo .IIII. Argiropilo De Generatione. II. Nypho Meteororum .IIII. Boetio interprete Adiectis Eckij Commentarijs. ... (Excusa in officina Sigismundi Grim̄ ... & Marci Vuyrsung Augustę Vindelicoℛ. ... M.D.XIX. Decimo quinto Kaleñ. Iun.) fol. a-x^6. ff. II-CXXV. [437

-- -- *Another copy*. [438

-- Aristotelis ... De anima Libri III. Per Argyropilum De sensu & sensato Liber I De memoria ⁊ reminiscentia I De somno & vigilia I De longitudine & breuitate vitae Ex antiqua traductione. Adiectis Eckij Commentarijs. ... (Excusa in officina Sigismundi Grym̄ ... & Marci Wirsung Augustae Vindelicorum. Decimosexto Cal. Apriles. ... M.D.XX.) fol. A-H^6 I^4 K-N^6 O^4. ff. II-LXXIX. [439

-- ... Summa philosophie naturalis ... Pauli Veneti ... cum textu a Ioanne Argiropylo e greco in latinam conuerso. Adiecta sunt etiam ex Columella capita aliquot de Minimo ac Maximo naturali. ... Naturalis Auscultationis Libri ... Ex Aristotele. De physico auditu octo. De celo et mundo quatuor. De generatione et corruptione duo. De teorologicorum [*sic*] quatuor. De anima tres. [Metaphysica.] 1523 Simon Vincētius. (Lugduni impressa ... in edibus ... Antonij du Ry Anno ... millesimo quingentesimo. xxv. die vero .vj. Mensis Septembris.) fol. B.L. AA^6 a-kK^8 lL^4. ff. j-clxxvj, j-lxxxiiij. [440

-- In hoc volumine haec continentur. Aristotelis De historia animalium libri IX. De partibus animalium & earum causis libri IIII. De generatione animalium libri V. Theodoro Gaza interprete. De communi animalium gressu liber I. De communi animalium motu liber I. Petro Alcyonio interprete. ... Parisiis. Ex officina Simonis Colinaei. 1524. (*Colophon.*) fol. Aa-Ee^8 Ff^6 a-l^8 m^6 n^8 [illegible]^8 aa^6 bb-ee^8 ff^{10} 3[illegible]^6 3a-3h^8 4a^8 4b^6. ff. 1-101, 1-42, 1-53, 1-13. [441

-- In hoc libro contenta. Politicorum libri Octo. Commentarij. Oeconomicorum Duo. Commentarij. Hecatonomiarum Septem [Fabri Stapulensis]. Oeconomiarum publ. Vnus. Explanationis Leonardi in oeconomica. Duo. Parisiis Ex officina Simonis Colinaei. 1526. (... pridie Calen. Maii.) fol. A^6 a-z^8 &^{10} (-&10, *presumably blank*). ff. 1-193. [442

-- Ethica & Poli. Aristo. cū com. Auer. Aristote. Stagyrite Ethicorum Lib. x. cū Auer. corduben. ... commentarijs. Item ... Politicoruʒ. lib. viij. ac Oeconomicorū Lib. ij. Leonardo aretino interprete. ... Venundantur Lugduni apud Scipionē de Gabiano ... (Impressum ... cura Iacobi Myt. Anno ... Millesimo trigesimo .xviij. Ianuarij. ...) 8°. B.L. A-GG^8. ff. ij-ccxxxviij. ¶GG8 *defective*. [443

-- ... Aristote. Stagyrite Libri tres de anima ... Eiusdēqʒ Parua naturalia: cuʒ Auer. cordubē. fidiss. interprete: ac apostillis M. Anto. Zimare ... Venūdantur Lugduni apud Scipionē de Gabiano ... (... per ... Iacobū myt impressus. ... M.D.xxx. die .xxj. aprilis.) 8°. B.L. a^8 B-V^8 X^6. ff. ij-clxvj. [444

-- Aristotelis Stagyritae libri quatuor de coelo et mundo, subnexis eius duobus illis de generatione & corrup. ... ac Auerro. ... interprete: necnon eiusdem opusculum de substātia orbis ..., cum apostillis. M. Ant. Z. ... Lugduni apud Iacob. Giunctam. 1542. (... apud Theobaldum Paganum. ...) 8°. A-QQ^8 RR^4 SS^8. ff. 2-324. [445

-- In hoc libro contenta. Politicorum libri Octo. Commentarij. Oeconomicorum Duo. Commentarij. Hecatonomiarum Septem. Oeconomiarum publ. Vnus. Explanationis Leonardi in oeconomica. Duo. Parisiis Ex officina Simonis Colinaei. 1543 fol. [illegible]^6 a-z^8 &^{8} aa^6. ff. 1-191. [446

-- [1] Physicorum Aristotelis, seu, de naturali auscultatione, libri octo. Ioanne Argyropylo Byzantio Interprete. Lugduni, Apud Theobaldum Paganum. M.D. XLVI. 8°. a-n^8 o^4. pp. 3-215. [2] Aristotelis de coelo libri quatuor. Ioanne Argyropilo Byzantio interprete. *Same imprint.* aa-gg^8 hh^2. pp. 3-115. [3] Aristotelis de generatione et corruptione libri duo. Francisco Vatablo interprete. *Same imprint.* 3a-3d^8 3e^2. pp. 3-67. [4] Meteorologicorum Aristotelis libri quatuor. Francisco Vatablo interprete. *Same imprint.* 4A-4H^8 4I^4. pp. 3-136. [5] Aristotelis de anima libri tres. Ioanne Argyropylo Byzantio interprete. *Same imprint.* 5A-5F^8. pp. 3-91. [447

-- [1] Aristotelis et Theophrasti historiae. ... Lugduni, Apud Gulielmum Gazeium, M. D. LII. ... (... Excudebat Nicolaus Bacquenoius ...) 8°. α-ε^8 a-z^8 A-I^8. pp. 1-495. [2] Theophrasti ... de historia plantarum ... *Same imprint.* a-c^8 d^4 aa-zz^8 AA-CC^8 (-CC8, *presumably blank*). pp. 1-399. ¶*Includes:* De historia animalium, De partibus animalium, De generatione animalium, De communi animalium gressu, De communi animalium motu. *Translators: Theodorus Gaza, Petrus Alcyonius.* [448

-- Aristotelis ... Politicorum siue de Republica libri octo Leonardo Aretino interprete cum D. Thomae Aquinatis explanatione ... D. Thomae de regimine principum libri quatuor ... Oeconomica etiam ex antiqua interpretatione ... Iul. Martiani Rotae labore ... Venetiis apud Iuntas M D LVIII (... MDLVII. Mense Septembri.) fol. ✠^{8} a-x^8 A-B^8 C-D^6 (-D6, *presumably blank*). ff. 1-168, 1-27. [449

-- Aristotelis ars rhetorica ab Antonio Riccobono Rhodigino ... latine conuersa. Eiusdem Riccoboni explicationum liber ... Aristotelis ars poetica ab eodem in latinam linguam versa. Cum eiusdem de re Comica disputatione. ... Venetiis, Apud Paulum Meiettum, Bibliopolam Patauinum, 1579. 8°. a-b^8 A-Ff^8. pp. 1-457. ¶*Additional t.p.* (Aa1^r): Aristotelis ars poetica ... *Same imprint.* [450

-- [1] Aristotelis Stagiritae ... philosophiae naturalis libri omnes, Ioanne Argyropylo Byzantio, et Francisco Vatablo Interpretibus. ... Coloniae Agrippinae, Apud haeredes Arnoldi Birckmanni. Anno cIↃ. IↃ. LXXX. (... Typis Godefridi Kempensis.) 4°. *^{4} **^{2} A-Rr^4. pp. 2-320. [2] ... Tomus alter ... *Same imprint.* (... Typis Godefridi Kempensis. Anno 1579.) A-3D^4 (-3D4, *presumably blank*). pp. 4-398. ¶3D3 *defective.* [451

-- Aristotelis Physica ... Ioannis Demerlierij ... argumentis illustrata. Parisiis, Ex officina Iacobi du Puys ... 1580. ... 4°. ã^4 a-aa^8 bb^4 A-Ee^8. ff. 1-419. ¶*Includes:* De coelo, De mundo, De ortu et interitu, Meteorologica, De anima, Parva naturalia. *Translators: Joachim Périon, Nicolas de Grouchy, Guillaume Budé.* [452

-- *Italian.* Col nome de Dio il segreto de segreti, le Moralita, & la Phisionomia d'Aristotile, ... Fatti nuouamente volgari, per Giouanni Manente. (Stampata in Vinegia per Zuan Tacuino da Trino ... M. D. XXXVIII. Adi dodese Luio.) 4°. *^{4} A-FF^4. ff. I-CXII. [453

-- Rettorica, et poetica d'Aristotile Tradotte di Greco In Lingua Vulgare Fiorentina da Bernardo Segni ... In Firenze appresso Lorenzo Torrentino ... MD XLIX. ... 4°. [illegible]^6 A-ZZ^4 3A^6. pp. 1-355. [454

-- -- In Vinegia M D LI. (Stampata ... per Bartholomeo detto l'Imperador, & Francesco suo genero. ...) 8°. a-z^8 A-E^8 F^4 (-F3-4, *presumably blank*). ff. 2-209. [455

-- *Spanish.* La philosofia moral del Aristotel: es a saber Ethicas: Polithicas: y Economicas: En Romançe. (... impressos enla ... ciudad de çaragoça/ por ... Gorge coci Aleman: a .xxj. del mayo: del año de mill y quinientos y nueue.) fol. B.L. a^4 b-i^8 k^{10} A-M^6. ¶*Translator: Charles, prince of Viana.* [456

-- *Analytica posteriora. Latin.* Aristotelis ... Libri ... posteriorū resulotiuorū ... ab Ioāne Argyropylo Byzantio ... Latio donati ... (Lipsiae ex aedibus Valentini Schumañ Anni dñi Millesimo quingentesimo vndeuigesimo.) fol. A-E^6. [457

-- -- Apolinaris sup posteriora. ... Expositio in Primum Posteriorum Aristotelis librum. Cum Questionibus eiusdem per .V.P. Ioannem Romberch de kyrspe ... recognita ... (Venetijs mandato ... Luceantonij de Giunta Florentini. ... 1520. Die .2. Mensis Augusti.) fol. B.L. ✠^{8} A-O^8 P^{10}. ff. 2-84. [458

-- -- Paulus venetus super libris posteriorum ... recognita: per magistrū Augustinum Montifalconiū: vtroq3 textu scil3 Boetij ꝛ Argiropoli īterposito ... (Venetijs mandato ... Luceantonij de Giunta Florentini ... 1521. die .26. Martij.) fol. B.L. ✠^{8} a-n^8 o-p^6 (-p6, *presumably blank*). ff. 1-115. [459

-- -- Suessa. super poste^ra ... Eutychi Augustini Nyphi ... Suessani Cōmentaria in libris Posteriorum Aristotelis. ... (Venetijs ęre ... heredum .q. D. Octauiani Scoti ... ac socioꝝ impressa ... 1526. Die ꝟo .4. Mensis Decembris.) fol. ✠⁴ a⁶ b⁴ c-o⁶ p⁴ (-p4, *presumably blank*). ff. 1-85. [460

-- Posteriora Egidii. Egidij Romani ... in Libros Posteriorum Aristotelis ... cōmentaria. Cum duplici textus translatione. antiqua. scilicet ꝛ Ioannis Argyropili ... M D XXX (Impressum ꝟo Venetijs ... sumptib⁹ heredu3 ... Octauiani Scoti ... ac socioꝝ. ... Die ꝟo .XXV. Augusti.) fol. B.L. a-s⁸ t¹⁰. ff. 2-147. [461

-- -- Eustratii episcopi Nicaeni commentaria in secundum librum posteriorum resolutiuorum Aristotelis. ... Andrea Gratiolo Tusculano ex Benaco interprete. ... Venetijs Apud Hieronymum Scotum. 1542 (*Colophon.*) fol. A⁴ B-N⁶ O⁴ P-R⁶. pp. 3-195. [462

-- -- Augustinus Suessanus super posteriora ... Venetiis Apud Octauinaum Scotum. D. AmaDei, 1544 fol. B.L. ✠⁴ ✠✠² (-✠✠2) a⁶ b⁴ c-n⁶ o⁸. ff. 1-85. [463

-- -- Venetijs Apud Octauianum Scotum. D. AmaDei. M. D. XLVIII. fol. *⁴ a-g⁶ h⁴ i-n⁶ o⁸. ff. 1-80. [464

-- -- Commentaria Ioannis Grammatici Alexandrei cognomento Philoponi in libros posteriorum Aristotelis. ... per ... Theodosium collata. ... Venetiis apud Hieronymum Scotum. 1548 (*Colophon.*) fol. A-Q⁴. ff. 2-64. [465

-- -- Expositio Ioannis grammatici ... in libros analyticos Aristotelis Posteriores ... a Martiano Rota ... collata ... Venetiis, Ex Officina Valgrisiana. M. D. LIX. (*Colophon.*) fol. A-K⁶. pp. 6-118. [466

-- *Analytica priora. Latin.* Reuerendi ... Egidij Romani in libros Priorum analecticorum Aristotelis Expositio ꝛ interpretatio ... Questiones item Marsilij in eosdem. Questio Ioannisantonij Scotij de potissima demonstratione. Laurentianus Florentinus in librum Aristotelis de elocutione. (Venetijs impensis Heredum ... Octauiani Scoti ... ꝛ sociorum. Die .5. Iunij. 1516.) fol. B.L. Aa-Kk⁸ Ll⁶ A-E⁸ 3a¹⁰. ff. 2-86, 1-40, 1-10. [467

-- -- Ioannis grammatici Alexandrei cognomente Philoponi in libros priorum Resolutiuorum ... commentariae annotationes/ ex colloquijs Ammonij Hermeae ... Guilelmo Dorotheo Veneto interprete. ... Venetijs Apud Hieronymum Scotum. 1541. fol. B.L. ✠² A-O⁶ P⁴. ff. 1-87. [468

-- -- ... Lucillo Philalthaeo interprete. ... Venetiis apud Hieronymum Scotum 1548 (*Colophon.*) fol. A-O⁶. ff. 2-84. [469

-- -- Aristotelis priora analytica seu resolutoria Io. Francisco Burana Veronensi in Latinum sermonem versa, commentariis ... illustrara. ... Hieronymi Bagolini Veronensis ... Annotationes. ... Venetiis apud Hieronymum Scotum 1550 (*Colophon.*) fol. *⁴ A-M⁸ N⁶ a-d⁴ e⁶ (-e6, *presumably blank*). ff. 1-103, 1-21. [470

-- -- Alexandri Aphrodisiensis Super Priora resolutoria Aristotelis ... Explanatio: a Ioanne Bernardo Feliciano in latinum conuersa ... Venetiis apud Hieronymum Scotum. M D LX. (*Colophon.*) fol. A-P⁶ Q-R⁴. pp. 3-8, cols. 9-440. [471

-- -- Ioannis grammatici cognomento Philoponi in duos priores analyticos Aristotelis libros commentarii ... ab Alexandro Iustiniano Chio ... conuersi ... Venetiis, Ex Officina Valgrisiana. M. D. LX. fol. π^2 A-N⁶. pp. 1-156. [472

-- -- Io. Francisci Buranae Veronensis ... Commentaria ...Venetiis, apud Hieronymum Scotum. M D LXVII. (*Colophon.*) fol. *⁴ A-R⁸. pp. 1-271. [473

-- *Categoriae. Latin.* Textus veteris artis .s. Isagogarum Porphirii. predicamētorū Aristotleis simul cu3 duobus libris perihermenias eiusdem. Item Exercitata ... collecta ... per ... Iohannē parreudt ... (Imp̄ssa ꝑ ... Henricū Gran in ... oppido Hagenawe. expēsis ... Ioh̄is Rynman ... M.d.j. vltīo die Augusti.) 4°. B.L. a-p⁸ q¹⁰. [474

-- -- Textus Predicamētorum Aristotelis (... Impressaq3 Liptzig ꝑ ... Martinū Lantzberg Anno ... octauo sesquimillesimum 1 Die vero .1. mensis Agusti.) fol. B.L. A-C⁶. [475

-- -- Commētaria scd̄m doctrinam magni Alberti in totam logicā Aristotelis ... precessum gymnasij Coloniensis qd̄ bursam Laurentij vocant cōtinentia. ... (In officina quondam ... Henrici Quentell Coloniēsis ciuis ... anno ... Millesimo quingētesimoquarto rursus Impressi vltima die mēsis Iulij ...) fol. B.L. AA-DD⁶ EE⁴ FF-LL⁶ MM⁴ NN-RR⁶ SS⁴ TT-YY⁶. [476

-- -- Reuerendi ... Thome de Vio Caietani ... in Predicabilia Porphyrij: ₹ Aristotelis Predicamēta: ac Posteriorum analecticorum libros. Et super tractatum de ente ₹ essentia Diui Thome Aquinatis Cōmētaria ... Et tractatus eiusdeʒ de Analogia ... (Venetijs Impensis ... Luceantonij de giunta florentini. die .9. mensis Iulij. 1519.) fol. B.L. A-S^8 T-V^6. ff. 2-154. [477

-- -- Burleus in artem veterem Gualterij Burlei Anglici ... in ysagogas Porphyrij: Gilbertuʒ Poretanum: ₹ artem veterem Aristotelis ... cōmentaria: cum duplici textus translatione: antiqua scilʒ ₹ Ioānis Argyropili ... Venetiis M D XLI (... expensis heredum Luceantonij Iunte Florentini ... 1541. die .2. Martij.) fol. B.L. ♣^{6} a-m^8. ff. 1-95. [478

-- -- Hammonii Hermeae in praedicamenta Aristotelis commentarii, per Bartholomaeum Syluanium Salonensen ... conuersi ... Venetijs apud Hieronymum Scotum. M. D. XLI. (*Colophon.*) fol. A-P^4. pp. 3-117. [479

-- -- Ammonii Hermei commentaria in librum Porphyri de quinque uocibus, & in Aristotelis Praedicamenta, ac Perihermenias ... Petrus Rosetinus [emendavit] ... Venetijs Ioan. Gryphius excudebat. MDLV. (*Colophon.*) fol. a^4 A-H^6 *^{4} A-F^6 G^4 a^6 b^4. ff. 1-13. cols. 1-128, 1-154. [480

-- -- Simplicii ... Commentationes ... in praedicamenta Aristotelis. ... Venetiis, apud Hieronymum Scotum. M D LXVII. (... M D LXVIII.) fol. A-O^6 P^8. pp. 3-183. [481

-- -- Thomae de Vio Caietani ... In Praedicabilia Porphyrii praedicamenta, & libros Posteriorum Analyticorum Aristotelis ... commentaria ... Venetiis, apud haeredem Hieronymi Scoti, M D LXXV. (*Colophon.*) fol. *^{2} A-M^8 N^{10}. pp. 1-212. ¶N3-10 *defective.* [482

-- *De anima. Greek.* Ιωαννου γραμματικου ... υπομνημα ... Ioannis grammatici Philoponi comentaria in libros de anima Aristotelis. ... M D XXXV. (Venetiis in aedibus Bartholomaei Zanetti Casterzagensis, aere ... Ioannis Francisci Trincaueli. ... Mense Nouembri.) fol. *^{2} A-S^8. [483

-- -- *Latin.* Aristotelis tres de anima libri per Ioannem Argyropylum e greco in latinum traducti. ... (Impressum Venetiis per Iacobum de Pentio de Leuco. x. kl'. nouembris.) 4°. a-g^4 h^6. [484

-- -- Summi Philosophoꝝ principis Aristotelis libri tres de historia Anime ... (Impressum Liptzk per Iacobum Thanner Herbipolenseʒ. Anno ... Millesimoquingentesimotertio.) fol. B.L. A-B^6 F^8 (-F8, *presumably blank*). [485

-- -- [A1^r] Gaietanus super libros de anima. Eiusdeʒ qōnes de sensu agente: ₹ de sensibilibus cōmunibus: ac de ītellectu. Iteʒ de substātia orbis Ioānis de gandauo cum questionibus eiusdem. (Venetijs per Gregoriuʒ de gregorijs. Cal'. Ian. Mcccccv.) fol. B.L. π^2 A-T^6 (-T6, *blank*). ff. 2-113. [486

-- -- Aristotelis ... de anima libri tres ... Gentiano Herueto Aurelio interprete. Item, In eosdem libros, Ioannis Grammatici Philoponi Commentarius, ab eodem versus. Lugduni 1544. ... apud AEgidium & Iacobum Huguetan, fratres. fol. A-R^6 S-T^4. [487

-- -- Ioannis Alexandrei philosophi in tres libros de anima Aristotelis breues annotationes, ex dissertationibus Ammonii Hermei ... Venetiis apud Hieronymum Scotum. 1547. (*Colophon.*) fol. A-Q^6 R^4. ff. 2-100. ¶*Translator: Matthaeus à Bove.* [488

-- -- D. Thomae Aquinatis in tres libros de anima Aristotelis expositio. Cum duplici Textus translatione, antiqua scilicet & Argyropyli ... Quaestiones Magistri Dominici de Flandria ... Venetiis Apud Hieronymum Scotum. 1550 (*Colophon.*) fol. *^{6} A-O^6. ff. 1-84. [489

-- -- Nicolai Tignosii Fulginatis, In Libros Aristotelis de Anima commentarii ... Ex Bibliotheca Medicea. 1551. (Florentiae excudebat Laurentius Torrentinus ... V. Non. Iul. ...) fol. a-z^6 Aa-Oo^6 Pp-Qq^4. pp. 3-460. [490

-- -- Aristotelis de animo libri tres, Ioachimo Perionio ... interprete. Eiusdem Perionij ... Obseruationes. ... Basileae, per Ioannem Oporinum. (... M.D.LIII. Mense Ianuario.) 8°. A-I^8. pp. 3-129. [491

-- -- Aristotelis de Animo Libri III. Ioachimo Perionio interprete: per Nicolaum Grouchium correcti & emendati. Parisiis, Ex officina Gabrielis Buon ... 1560. 4°. A-F^8. ff. 2-48. [492

-- -- Parisiis, Apud Thomam Brumennium ... 1560. 4°. A-F^8. ff. 2-48. [493

-- -- Coloniae, Apud Maternum Cholinum. M. D. LXIIII. 4°. A-M^4. pp. 3-96. [494

-- -- *Another copy.* [495

-- -- Eruditissimae dilucidationes trium librorum Aristotelis, qui de anima inscribuntur; Necnon Comentariorum S. Doct. Aquinatis in eosdem; Cum textu duplici, translationis scilicet antiquae, & Ioachimi Perionij ... Authore ... Vincentio Quintiano Brixiensi ... Eiusdem Authoris ... Appendix, de potentijs, de passionibus, deque moralibus virtutibus Animae. ... Bononiae, Typis Alexandri Benacij ... Die Sancti Dominici. M. D. LXXV. ... 4°. +^{4} +-4+^{4} A-Nn^4 Oo^6 Pp-3Z^4 4A^6. ff. 1-286. [496

-- -- Aristotelis de Animo Libri III. Ioachimo Perionio interprete: per Nicolaum Grouchium correcti ... Parisiis, Ex officina Gabrielis Buon ... 1577. 4°. A-F^8. ff. 2-48. [497

-- -- D. Thomae Aquinatis in tres libros Aristotelis de anima ... expositio. ... Venetiis, Apud Haeredem Hieronymi Scoti. M D LXXXVII. (... M D LXXXVI.) fol. *^{6} A-K^8 L-N^6. pp. 1-183. [498

-- -- *Summaries.* Paraphrasi sopra i tre libri dell'anima d'Aristotile, del R. D. Angelico Buonriccio ... In Venetia, appresso Andrea Arriuabene. 1565. 8°. a^6 A-V^8 X^2. ff. 2-163. [499

-- *De audibilibus. Greek.* Εκ των Αριστοτελους και Θεοφραστου. Aristotelis et Theophrasti scripta quaedam ... Ex officina Henrici Stephani Parisiensis ... M. D. LVII. 8°. a^4 b-k^8 l^4. pp. 17-168. [500

-- *De coelo. Greek.* Σιμπλικιου υπομνηματα ... Simplicii commentarii in quatuor Aristotelis libros de coelo, cum textu ... (Venetiis in Aedibus Aldi Romani, & Andreae Asulani Soceri, M. D. XXVI. Mense Ianuario.) fol. *^{4} A-K^8 L^4 M-Q^8 R^6 S-X^8 Y^{10}. ff. 1-178. [501

-- -- *Latin.* Haec, volumine hoc continetur. Interpretamēto ... Thomae Aquinatis in libros de coelo ⁊ mūdo Aristotelis ānotationibus textuū ⁊ cōmētorū Auerroys ... cum additiōibus Petri aluerniatis. Textus Aristotelicus cuȝ duplici translatiōe antiqua vȝ et Ioannis Argyropyli ... Fratris Hieronymi Sauonarolae Ferrariēsis tractatus: ī quo diuidūtur oēs sciāe ... (... Venetijs impressa per Simonē de Luere Impēsa ... Alexādri Calcedonij ciuis Pisaurensis. 19. Maij. 1506.) fol. B.L. ✠^{6} A-P^6 Q^4. ff. 2-94. [502

-- -- S. Tho. de celo ⁊ mundo. ... (... Venetiis impressa per d. Lucantonium de giunta florentinum. 4. decembris. 1516.) fol. B.L. ✠^{6} A-L^8 M^6. ff. 1-94. [503

-- -- Suessanus de celo et mundo. Aristotelis ... de celo ⁊ mūdo Libri quatuor e greco in latinum ab Augustino Nipho ... Suessano cōuersi ... (... excussa ... Venetijs/ per heredes .q. Dñi Octauiani Scoti ... ac sociorum. ... M.D.XXV. Die vero .X. mensis Nouembris.) fol. B.L. ✠^{6} A-T^8 V^{10}. ff. 1-162. [504

-- -- Simplicii ... commentaria in quatuor libros de celo Aristotelis. Guillermo Morbeto interprete. ... Venetiis. M. D. XL. (...apud Hieronymum Scotum.) fol. B.L. A^4 B-V^6 X^4 (-X4, *presumably blank*). ff. 2-118. [505

-- -- Aristotelis ... de coelo libri IIII. Ex Graeco iuxta tralationem veterem ... recogniti. À D. Thoma Aquinate ... commentarijs illustrati. ... Petri Aluerniatis ... expositio. ... Venetijs apud Hieronymum Scotum. 1545. (*Colophon.*) fol. *^{4} A-P^6 Q^4. ff. 1-94. [506

-- -- Simplicii ... commentaria in quatuor libros de coelo ... Venetiis apud Hieronymum Scotum. 1548 (*Colophon.*) fol. A-R^6 S^8. ff. 2-110. [507

-- -- Aristotelis ... de Coelo & Mundo libri quatuor, e Graeco in Latinum ab Augustino Nipho ... conuersi ... Venetiis apud Hieronymum Scotum. M D XLIX. fol. ✠^{6} A-V^8 (-V8, *presumably blank*). ff. 1-159. [508

-- -- Aristotelis De Coelo libri quatuor: Ioachimo Perionio interprete. Eiusdem Perionij ... Obseruationes. ... Basileae, per Ioannem Oporinum. (... M.D.LIII. Mense Februario.) 8°. Aa^4 Aa-Kk^8 Ll^4. pp. 1-149. [509

-- -- Aristotelis De Caelo Libri IIII. Ioachimo Perionio interprete: per Nicolaum Grouchium correcti & emendati. Parisiis, Ex officina Gabrielis Buon ... 1560. 4°. A-G^8 H^6. ff. 2-62. [510

-- -- Coloniae, Apud Maternum Cholinum. M. D. LXIIII. 4°. A-O^4 P^6. pp. 3-124. [511

-- -- *Another copy.* [512

-- -- S. Thomae Aquinatis in libros Aristotelis de coelo, et mundo commentaria: Quae .. absoluit Petrus de Aluernia: Cum duplici textus tralatione, Antiqua videlicet, & Io. Argyropoli ... Venetiis, apud Iuntas anno. M D LXIIII. (... Impressum per Dominicum Nicolinum ...) fol. $*^8$ a-m^8. ff. 1-95. [513

-- -- Aristotelis De Caelo Libri IIII. Ioachimo Perionio interprete: per Nicolaum Grouchium correcti ... Parisiis, Ex officina Thomae Brumennij ... 1567. 4°. A-G^8 H^6. ff. 3-64. [514

-- -- Parisiis, Ex officina Gabrielis Buon ... 1573. 4°. A-G^8 H^6. ff. 3-64. [515

-- -- Themistii ... paraphrasis In Libros Quatuor Aristotelis de Coelo ... Moyse Alatino Hebraeo Spoletino ... Interprete. ... Venetiis, apud Simonem Galignanum de Karera, M D LXXIIII. (... Apud Georgium Angelerium ...) fol. a^4 A-P^4 Q^6. ff. 1-66. [516

-- -- *Italian.* Aristotile de celo et mondo Tradotto di Greco in Volgare Italiano. Per Antonio Bruccioli. Impresso in Venetia, per Bartholomeo Imperatore. Nel 1552. (... per Bartholomeo detto l'Imperadore et Francesco suo genero.) 8°. $*^4$ A-O^8 (-O2, O7) P^4. ff. 1-123. [517

-- *De coloribus (suppositious). Greek & Latin.* De coloribus libellus, à Simone Portio Neapolitano Latinitate donatus, & commentarijs illustratus ... Florentiae Ex officina Laurentii Torrentini. M D XLVIII. ... 4°. A-Bb^4. pp. 5-197. [518

-- -- *Another copy, with additional errata on* $Bb4^v$. [519

-- *De generatione et corruptione. Greek & Latin.* Commentarii Collegii Conimbricensis Societatis Iesu. In libros de generatione et corruptione Aristotelis Stagiritae. Hac secunda editione Graeci contextus Latino è regione respondentis accessione auctiores. ... Moguntiae In officina Typographica Ioannis Albini. Anno cIↃ. IↃ. IC. 4°. (a)-$(b)^4$ A-$4A^4$. pp. 1-524. [520

-- -- *Latin.* Cōmentaria ... Egidij Romani in libros de generatiōe ꝛ corruptiōe Aristotelis cū textu ... Questiones quoqȝ ... Marsilii Inguē in prefatos libros ... Item questiones ... Alberti de saxonia in eosdē libros ... (Impressum Venetijs per Gregoriū de gregorijs .x. cal'. Decembris . M. D. v.) fol. B. L. AA-FF^8 GG^{12} HH-TT^8. ff. 2-155. [521

-- -- Aristotelis de generatione ꝛ corruptione liber Augustino nipho ... suessano interprete ꝛ expositore. ... (Imp̄ssum Venetijs mandato ... hęredū ... Octauiani Scoti ... Anno ... Sexto supra millesimuȝ sexiesqȝ centesimum. Per Bonetū Locatellum ... Pridie kalendas Octobres.) fol. B. L. A-G^8 H-K^6. ff. 2-74. [522

-- -- Ioannis grammatici Philoponi Alexandrei, Commentaria in libros de generatione & corruptione Aristotelis: ex colloquiis Ammonii Hermeae ... congesta. Hieronymo Bagolino Veronensi interprete. ... Venetijs apud Hieronymum Scotum. 1540. fol. B. L. $[*]^4$ A-G^6 H-I^4. ff. 1-50. [523

-- -- Sancti Thomae ... In libris de generatione & corruptione Aristotelis ... Expositio ... Cum duplici Textuum translatione, Antiqua scilicet, & Petri Alcyonii ... Venetiis apud Octauianum Scotum D. Amadei F. M D XLIX. fol. aa^4 A-H^6. ff. 1-48. [524

-- -- Aristotelis De Ortu & interitu libri duo: Ioachimo Perionio interprete. Eiusdem Perionij ... Obseruationes. ... Basileae, per Ioannem Oporinum. (... M. D. LIII. Mense Februario.) 8°. AA^4 AA-EE^8 FF^6. pp. 1-182. [525

-- -- S. Thomae Aquinatis In Libro Aristotelis de generatione et corruptione ... Commentaria, Cum Duplici Textus tralatione, antiqua uidelicet & noua Francisci Vatabli ... De mistione etiam elementorum ... Opus ... ex Opusculis eiusdem S. Thomae excerptum ... Venetiis apud Hieronymum Scotum. M D LV. (*Colophon.*) fol. $*^4$ A-D^8 E^6 (-E6, *presumably blank*). ff. 1-37. [526

-- -- Aristotelis de ortu & interitu Libri duo. Ioachimo Perionio interprete: per Nicolaum Grouchium correcti & emendati. Parisiis, Ex officina Gabrielis Buon ... 1560. 4°. A-I^4. ff. 2-36. [527

-- -- Coloniae Apud Maternum Cholinum. 1564. 4°. A-I^4. pp. 3-17 [= 71]. [528

-- -- *Another copy.* [529

-- -- Io. grammatici, cognomento Philoponi, In Aristotelis libros de Generatione, & Corruptione explicatio: Andrea Syluio, Brugensi, interprete. ... Venetiis, Apud Vincentium Valgrisium. M D LXIIII. (*Colophon.*) fol. A^2 A-G^6 H^4. pp. 1-90. [530

-- -- Aristotelis de ortu & interitu Libri duo, Ioachimo Perionio interprete: per Nicolaum Grouchium correcti ... Parisiis, Ex officina Thomae Brumennij ... 1567. 4°. A-I^4. ff. 2-36. [531

-- -- Parisiis, Ex officina Gabrielis Buon ... 1577. 4°. A-D^8 E^4. ff. 2-36. [532

-- -- Aristotelis de generatione, et interitu liber primus, A Flaminio Nobilio in Latinam linguam conuersus, et ... Explanatione ... illustratus. ... Patauii, Apud Petrum Paulum Tozzium, & Ioannem Speronium Socios. M. D. XCVI. fol. A-AA^4 BB^6. ff. 1-98. [533

-- -- -- Aristotelis de generatione, et interitu. Liber secundus. A Flaminio Nobilio Lucense ... conuersus. ... Venetiis, Apud Petrum Paulum Tozzium, & Ioannem Speronium socios. M D XCVIII. fol. a^2 A-F^4 G^2. ff. 1-26. [534

-- *De interpretatione. Greek & Latin.* Ammonii Hermeae ... in Aristotelis ... librum περὶ ἑρμηνείας, hoc est, de interpretatione Commentaria, cum duplici textu Graeco & Latino: quae omnia latina effecit Bartholomaeus Syluanus Salonensis. His accessit Magentini Mitilanensis compendiosa in eundem ... librum expositio, Hieronymo Leustrio Veronensi interprete. ... Parisiis, Apud Iacobum Keruer ... 1544. (*Colophon.*) fol. a^4 A-M^6 N^4. ff. 2-75. [535

-- -- *Latin.* Luculentissimi Ioannis Arborei Laudunensis in librum περὶ ἑρμηνέιας Aristotelis cõmentarij. Parisiis Apud Simonem Colinaeũ 1535. 8°. a-m^8 n^4. ff. 2-100. [536

-- -- Perihermenias Aristotelis Libri duo. Parisiis. Apud Prigentium Caluarin ... 1537. 8°. A-B^8. ff. 2-16. ¶*Translator: A. M. S. Boethius.* [537

-- -- Aristotelis περὶ ἑρμηνείας Lib. Anitio Mãlio Seuerino Boetio interprete: Paraphrasi Michaelis Psellis ... illustratus. Parisiis apud Ioannem Lodoicum Tiletanum ... M. D. XXXIX. 4°. a-n^4. ff. III-LII. [538

-- -- Aristotelis Perihermenias hoc est de interpretatione Liber: a ... Augustino Nipho ... intèrpretatus ꝛ expositus. ... Venetiis. Apud Octauianum Scotum. D. Amadei. F. 1543. (*Colophon.*) fol. B.L. a-d^6 e-f^4. ff. 2-32. [539

-- -- Magentini in Aristotelis librum de interpretatione explanatio Ioanne Baptista Rasario interprete. Venetijs apud Hieronymum Scotum. M. D. XXXXV. (*Colophon.*) 4°. A-I^4 K^6. ff. 2-41. [540

-- -- Hieronymi Balduini è Montearduo ... expositio in libellum Porphyrii de quinque uocibus ... Eiusdem commentaria in libros Aristotelis de interpretatione ... Expositio item in primum posteriorum analyticorum Aristotelis, & magnam in eo Auerrois commentationem ... His accessit quaesita aliquot eiusdem authoris, & logica, & naturalia ... Venetiis, M D LXIII. (... Ioan. Gryphius Excudebat. ...) fol. A^6 A-Ss^6 Tt^4. ff. 2-250. [541

-- -- Breuissimae in Aristotelis περι ερμηνειας libros methodi ... Vnâ cum ... Annotationibus ... Alfonso Baroccio Ferrariensi auctore. ... Venetiis, Ex Officina Dominici Guerrei, & Io. Baptistae fratrum. M. D. LXIX. fol. A-L^4. pp. 6-87. [542

-- *De mundo. Greek & Latin.* Aristoteles De Mundo, Graece: Cum duplici interpretatione Latinâ, prior quidem L. ApuleI; alterâ verò Guilielmi Budaei. Cum Scholiis & Castigationibus Bonauenturae Vulcanii ... Accessit seorsim Gregorii Cyprii Encomium Maris Graecè ... Et Pauli Silentiari Iambica. Lugduni Batauorum, Ex officina Plantiniana, Apud Franciscum Raphelengium. cIↃ. IↃ. XCI. 8°. *^{8} A-T^8. pp. 1-297. ¶*Lacks the* Encomium maris *and the* Iambica. *T.p. defaced.* [543

-- -- *Latin.* Aristotelis ... de Mundo Libellus Gulielmo Budaeo interprete. Philonis Iudaei itidem de Mundo Libellus ... Parisiis. Apud Prigentium Caluarin ... 1537. 8°. A-E^8. ff. 2-40. [544

-- -- Aristotelis de mũdo seu de cosmographia liber unus ..., Andrea à Lacuna Secobiẽsi interprete ... Luciani dialogus tragopodagra nominatus ... Per eiusdem ... latinitate donatus. (Compluti excudebat Ioannes Brocarius. ... M.D.xxxviii. Die uero decimaquarta, mensis Nouēbris.) 8°. a-e^8 f^6. ff. ij-xlviij. [545

-- -- Aristotelis Liber de Mundo ..., Gulielmo Budaeo interprete. Parisiis, Ex officina Gabrielis Buon ... 1560. 4°. A-B^8. ff. 2-16. [546

-- -- Coloniae, Apud Maternum Cholinum M. D. LXIIII. 4°. A-D^4. pp. 3-32. [547

-- -- *Another copy.* [548

-- -- Parisiis, Ex officina Thomae Brumennij ... 1567. 4°. A-B^8. ff. 2-16. [549

-- -- Parisiis, Ex officina Gabrielis Buon ... 1577. 4°. A-B^8. ff. 2-16. [550

-- *De partibus animalium. Greek.* Αριστοτελους περὶ ζώων μορίων, Βιβλία δ'. Aristotelis de partibus Animalium Libri quatuor. Parisiis, Excudebat Christianus Wechelus ... M.D.XLVIII. 4°. A-Π^4. pp. 3-132. ¶ Z 3-4 *misbound after* Π2. [551

-- *De virtutibus. Greek & Latin.* Aristotelis de virtutibus libellus ... per Simonem Grynaeum latinitate donatus. ... Venetiis M D XLV. (... apud Cominum de Tridino ...) 8°. a^8 B-C^8. pp. 4-40. [552

-- *Economica. Greek & Latin.* Aristotelis Stagiritae Oeconomicorum, seu de Re Familiari Libri duo. Bernardino Donato Veronensi interprete. ... Venetiis Apud Hieronymum Scotum. 1540 8°. A-C^8 α-γ^8 δ^4. pp. 1-41, ff. 1-26. [553

-- -- *Latin.* Oeconomicorum Aristotelis libelli cum cōmentariis Leonardi Aretini. (Impressus Senis per Symeoneȝ Nicolai Nardi ... M.D.VIII. Calendis Februarii. Michael angelus me composuit) 4°. a-c^8. [554

-- -- Oecologiū ex duobus Aristotelis Oeconomicorū libellis accumulatū. Cōclusiōes centū et q̄ttuor: ac noue traductiōis Textū/ duplici cū Regesto. complectēs. ... ([Lipsiae,] p̲ Vuolfganguȝ Stockel. Monacensem ... imp̄ssum. Anno ... Millesimoquingentesimo vndecimo.) fol. B.L. a-h^6 k^4 l^6 (-16, *presumably blank*). ff. ij-xlviij. [555

-- -- Oeconimica Aristotelis a Bernardino Baldino versibus ... Latine expressa. Mediolani Apud Iac. Mariam Metium. M. D. LXXVIII. 4°. A-C^4 D^6. pp. 1-31. [556

-- *Ethica Nicomachea. Greek.* Ευστρατιου ... υπομνηματα ... Eustratii et aliorum ... Peripateticorum commentaria in libros decem Aristotelis de moribus ad Nicomachum, vna cum textu ... (Venetiis, in aedibus haeredum Aldi Manutii, at Andreae Asulani soceri, mense Iulio. M. D. XXXVI.) fol. [*]^2 α-ψ^8 ω^6. ff. 1-189. [557

-- -- Αριστοτελους ἠθικῶν Νικομαχείων. Βιβλία δέκα. Aristotelis de morib. ad Nicomachum filium libri decem. Florentiae apud Iunctas MDXLVII. (...apud Bernardum Iunctam ...) 4°. 4α-4θ^8 4ι^6. ff. 2-68. [558

-- -- Argentorati per Vuendelinum Rihelium, anno M. D. XLIX. 8°. π^8 A-V^8 X^6. ff. 1-166. [559

-- -- Parisiis, M.D.LIIII. Apud Adr. Turnebum ... (... Id. Aug. ...) 4°. a^6 A-Aa^4 Bb^6. pp. 1-201. [560

-- -- Florentiae apud Iuntas MDLX. (*Colophon.*) 4°. 4α-4θ^8 4ι^6 4*^{4}. ff. 2-69. [561

-- -- Parisiis, M.D.LX. Apud Guil. Morelium ... 4°. a^6 A^4 B^6 C-H^4 I^6 K-R^4 S-Z$^{4.6}$. pp. 1-204. [562

-- -- Argentorati Excudebat Iosias Rihelius. M. D. LXIII. 8°. π^8 (-π2-7, *the last blank*) a-y^8. ff. 1-154. [563

-- -- *Greek & Latin.* Αριστοτελους ηθικων Νικομαχειων βιβλια δεκα. Aristotelis de moribus ad Nicomachum, Lib. X. ... Parisiis M. D. LV. Apud Adrianum Turnebum ... (Excudebat ... Guil. Morelius. ... XII. Cal. Martias.) fol. *^{2} A-V^6 X^8 (-X8, *presumably blank*). pp. 1-253. [564

-- -- *Another copy.* [565

-- -- Αριστοτελους ηθικων Νικομαχειων βιβλία δέκα. Aristotelis de moribus ad Nicomachum libri decem. ... Heidelbergae. M. D. LX. (Excudebat Lodouicus Lucius ... Mense Septembri.) 8°. a-z^8 A-M^8 N^4 O^2. pp. 1-567. [566

-- -- Aristotelis Stagiritae De Moribus ad Nicomachum Libri decem. In quibus Latina Graecis, Dionysio Lambino interprete, eregionè respondent. ... Annotationibus Lambini, nouisq̃3 [Theodori] Zuingeri Scholijs illustrantur. ... Adiecta sunt Fragmenta quaedam Pythagoreorum ..., ex emendatione & uersione Gul. Canteri. ... Basileae, Per Ioannem Oporinum, et Eusebium Episcopium: M. D. LXVI. (... Mense Augusto.) 4°. α-β^4 a-z^4 A-Ss^4 Tt^6. pp. 9-15, 2-487. [567

-- -- Αριστοτελους ηθικων Νικομαχειων βιβλία δέκα. ... Basileae, per Paulum Quecum. M.D.LXVII. (... Sumptibus Ioannis Oporini ... Mense Martio.) 8°. α^4 a-z^8 A-M^8 N-O^4. pp. 1-571. [568

-- -- Basileae, ex officina Oporiniana. (... 1573. Mense Ianuario.) 8°. *Same collation and pagination.* [569

-- -- Petri Victorii commentarii in X. libros Aristotelis De Moribus ad Nicomachum. ... Florentiae ex officina Iunctarum CIↃ IↃ LXXXIIII. (... Ex Typographia Philippi, & Iacobi Iunctae, & Fratrum. ...) fol. *^{6} A-3I^6. pp. 1-616. [570

-- -- Aristotelis ethicorum, siue de moribus, ad Nicomachum libri decem. Adiecta ad contextum Graecum interpretatione Latina Dionysii Lambini ... opera Matthiae Bergii ... 1591. Francofurti Apud her. And. Wecheli, Claud. Marn. & Io. Aubr. ... 8°. A-Hh^8 Ii^4. pp. 3-502. [571

-- -- Αριστοτελους ηθικων Νικομαχειων βιβλια δεκα. Aristotelis ethicorum ad Nicomachum Libri Decem, ab Antonio Riccobono Latine conuersi: ... Marco Cornelio ... cum Commentariis dicati. ... Francofurti Apud heredes And. Wecheli; Claudium Marnium, & Ioan. Aubrium. M D XCVI. ... 8°. A-Zz^8 AA-EE^8 FF^2. pp. 3-818. [572

-- -- *Latin.* Ethica seu moralia Aristotelis ex traductione Ioannis Argyropyli ab Egidio Delpho singulorum capitũ argumentis prenotata: & ab Iodoco Badio Ascẽsio Indice & annotatiunculis illustrata. [*Device of Denis Roce.*] Venundantur parrhisius ... 8°. A-Y^8 &^{8}. ff. ii-clix. [573

-- -- Contenta Decem librorum Moraliũ Aristotelis, tres conuersiones Prima Argyropili Byzantij, secunda Leonardi Aretini, tertia vero Antiqua ... I. Fab. introductio in Ethicen. Magna moralia Aristo. Georgio Valla interprete. Leonardi Aretini dialogus de moribus. ... Parisiis Ex officina Simonis Colinaei. 1527 (... 1528. die 3 Mensis Iulij.) fol. a-n^8 o^{10} p-q^8 r^6 s^4 A-I^8 K-L^6. ff. 3-140, 1-83. [574

-- -- S. Tho. super Ethica. Sancti ... Thome Aquinatis in decem Libros Ethicorum Aristotelis ... Cõmentaria/ cum triplex Textus trãslatione. Antiqua. v3. Leonardi Aretini/ necnon Ioãnis Argyropili ... MDXXXI (Impressaq3 Venetijs ... expensis ... heredum ... Octauiani Scoti ... ac sociorum. ... Die ?o .15. Mensis Februarij.) fol. B.L. π^2 a-v^8 x^6. ff. 1-166. [575

-- -- Aristotelis Stagiritae ... ethicorum ad Nicomachum libri decem, Ioanne Argiropylo Byzantio interprete, ... & cum Donati Acciaioli Florentini ... commentariis ... editi. Venetiis in officina Lucaeantonii Iuntae. M. D. XXXV. (... Mense Februario.) fol. *^{6} A-KK^6 LL^8. ff. 2-205. [576

-- -- Ethicorum Aristotelis ... libri decẽ ad Nicomachũ, ex traductione ... Ioannis Argyropili Byzãtij: ... Iacobi Fabri Stapulẽsis Commẽtario elucidati ... Adiectus est Leonardi Aretini de moribus Dialogus ... Impressum Lugduni M. D. XXXV. (... typis Benedicti Bonnyn. Nomine verò Iacobi Giunta.) 8°. a-z^8 A-X^8. ff. 2-352. [577

-- -- Aristotelis ... moralia Nicomachia cum Eustratii Aspasii, Michaelis Ephesii, ... aliorum Graecorum explanationibus. ... a Ioanne Bernardo Feliciano Latinitate donata. ... Apud haeredes Lucaeantonij Iuntae Florentini Venetiis M. D. XLI. (... mense Nouembri.) fol. *-**^{8} a-kk^8 ll-mm^6 (-mm6, *blank*). pp. 1-548. [578

-- -- Aristotelis Stagiritae ethicorum ad Nicomachum libri decem. Raphaelis Volaterrani argumenta in eosdem. Ioanne Bernardo Feliciano interprete. Venetijs apud Hieronymum Scotum. 1542. 8°. a-z^8 &^{4}. ff. 2-187. [579

-- -- Contenta Decem librorũ Moralium Aristotelis, tres conuersiones: Prima Argyropyli Byzantij, secũda Leonardi Aretini, tertia verò Antiqua ... I. Fabri introductio in Ethicen. Magna Moralia Aristot. Georgio Valla interprete. Leonardi Aretini dialogus de moribus. ... Parisiis Ex officina Simonis Colinaei. 1542 (... 6. Calend. Nouembr.) fol. a-n^8 o^{10} p-q^8 r^6 s^4 A-I^8 K-L^6. ff. 2-140, 1-83. [580

-- -- Aristotelis ethicorum, siue de moribus, ad Nicomachum filium libri decem ... à Ioachimo Perionio Cormoeriaceno latinitate donati ... Epitomen, Hermolao Barbaro ... autore

... Lugduni, Apud Guliel. Rouillium ... M. D. XLVIII. (... excudebant Philibertus Rolletus, et Bartholomaeus Fraenus, impensis ... Gulielmi Rouillii, & Antonii Constantini.) 8°. †^{8} A-V^8. pp. 1-299. [581

-- -- Aristotelis ad Nicomachum filium, de Moribus ...Libri decem ... Basileae, per Ioannem Oporinum. (... M.D.LII. Mense Nouembri.) 8°. α^8 a-y^8 z^4 (-z4, *presumably blank*). pp. 1-319. [582

-- -- Aristotelis ... Ethicorum ad Nicomachum libri decem. Ioanne Argyropylo Byzantio interprete ... Cum Donati Acciaioli Florentini ... Commentarijs ... Lugduni, apud Ioan. Frellonium. 1553 (... excudebat Petrus Fradin ...) 8°. α^8 β^4 a-z^8 A-LL^8 MM^4. pp. 1-919. [583

-- -- Aristotelis Ethicorum, siue de moribus, ad Nicomachum filium, Libri decem, à Ioachimo Perionio primùm conuersi, ac Nicolai Grouchij opera ... emendatiores ... editi. Eorundem Aristotelis librorum Compendium, per Hermolaum Barbarum. Item aliud in eosdem Compendium ac σύνοψις, à Cuthberto Tonstallo editum. ... Basileae, per Ioannem Oporinum. (... M.D.LV. Mense Martio.) 8°. a^{10} a-z^8 A-H^8 I^4. pp. 4-467. [584

-- -- Aristotelis ethicorum ... libri decem ... Lugduni, Apud Guliel. Rouillium ... M. D. LVI. 8°. †^{8} A-V^8. pp. 1-299. [585

-- -- Aristotelis de moribus ad Nicomachum libri decem. ... e Graeco et Latinè ... à Dionysio Lambino expressi. Eiusdem Dionys. Lambini ... annotationes ... Venetiis, Ex Officina Erasmiana, apud Vincentium Valgrisium. CIↃ IↃ LVIII. 8°. *^{8} A-Z^8 a-e^8. pp. 1-401. [586

-- -- Aristotelis ad Nicomachum filium de moribus, ... Libri decem, Ioachimo Perionio interprete, per Nicolaum Gruchium correcti & emendati. ... Parisiis, Ex officina Simônis Caluarini ... 1562. 4°. ā^4 ē^4 A-Q^8 R^6. ff. 1-134. [587

-- -- Aristotelis de moribus ad Nicomachum libri decem. ... Dionys. Lambini ... annotationes ... Duaci, Ex officina Ioannis Bogardi ... M.D.LXXV. ... 4°. A-Oo^4. ff. 1-143. [588

-- -- Ethicorum Aristotelis ... libri decem, ad Nicomachum ... Ioanne Argyropylo ..., & Dionysio Lambino interpretibus cum Donati Acciaioli Florentini ... Commentarijs, & Raphaelis Volateran. ... argumentis ... Venetiis, M D LXXVI. Apud Ioannem Antonium Bertanum. (*Colophon.*) fol. a-b^6 c^8 A-Mm^6. ff. 1-203. [589

-- -- Aristotelis ... Ethicorum ad Nicomachum libri decem. Ioanne Argyropylo Byzantio interprete ... Cum Donati Acciaioli ... Commentarijs ... Geneuae, apud Iacobum Stoer, M. D. XIIC. α^8 β^4 a-z^8 A-LL^8 MM^4. pp. 1-919. [590

-- -- De moribus libri decem iis, qui Aristotelis Ad Nicomachum inscribuntur, ordine perpetuo, atque sententia respondentes. ... Auctore Laelio Peregrino Somninate ... Romae, Apud Aloysium Zannettum. M. DC. ... (*Colophon.*) 4°. *^{4} A-3C^4. pp. 1-380. [591

-- -- *Italian.* L'ethica d'Aristotile tradotta in lingua vulgare Fiorentina et comentata per Bernardo Segni. In Firenze M D L. (Stampato ... appresso Lorenzo Torrentino ... del mese d'Agosto ...) 4°. a-z^8 A-Zz^8 AA^4. pp. 3-547. [592

-- -- In Vinegia M D LI. (Stampato ... appresso Bartolomeo detto l'Imperadore, & Francesco suo genero. ...) 8°. a-z^8 A-V^8 X^4. ff. 2-158. ¶a1 *defective.* [593

-- -- *Summaries.* Artificialis introductio [Jodoci Clichtovii] per modum Epitomatis [Jacobi Fabri Stapulensis]/ in decem libros Ethicorum Aristotelis ... (... absoluta est in Alma Parhisiorum academia per Henricum Stephanum ... 1506 vicesimatertia februarij.) fol. a-f^8 g-h^6. ff. 2-60. [594

-- [a1^v] Iacobi Stapulēsis Introductio in Ethicen Aristotelis ... (Presens Artificialis Introductio ... suum finem assecuta est In alma Parisiorum academia. 1510) fol. B.L. a^8. ¶a1^r: Virtutis querimonia ex Baptista Mantuano. [595

-- -- L'ethica d'Aristotile ridotta in compendio da Ser Brunetto Latini. Et altre Tradutioni, & scritti di quei tempi. ... In Lione, per Giouanni de Tornes. M. D. LXVIII. 4°. ¶^{4} A-Y^4 Z^6. pp. 1-185. [596

-- -- [1] L'ethica di Aristotile a Nicomacho, Ridutta in modo di Parafrasi dal Reuerendo M. Antonio Scaino ... In Roma, Appresso Gioseppe de gli Angeli. M D LXXIIII. (*Colophon.*) 4°. a-c^4 A-O^8. pp. 2-218. [2] Annotationi et resolutioni di varii dubbi ... *Same imprint.* †-††^{4} A-X^4 Y^6. pp. 1-179. [597

-- *Historia animalium.* Aristotelis liber, qui decimus historiarum inscribitur, nunc primum Latitinus [*sic*] factus à Iulio Caesare Scaligero ... & Commentariis illustratus. Lugduni, Apud Antonium de Harsy, M.D.LXXXIV. 8°. A-I^{8}. pp. 4-144. [598

-- -- *Another copy.* [599

-- *Mechanica. Greek and Latin.* Aristotelis mechanica Graeca, emendata, Latina facta, & Commentariis illustrata. Ab Henrico Monantholio ... Parisiis, Apud Ieremiam Perier ... M.D.XCIX. ... 4°. ā^{4} ē^{4} ī^{4} ō^{4} ū^{4} A-Cc^{4} Dd^{2}. pp. 1-211. [600

-- -- *Summary.* Alexandri Piccolominei in mechanicas quaestiones Aristotelis, paraphrasis ... Eiusdem commentarium de certitudine Mathematicarum disciplinarum ... M.D.XLVII. (Excussum Romae apud Antonium Bladum Asulanum. Tertio Noñ. Ianuarii. ...) 4°. A-EE^{4} FF^{2}. ff. I-CX. [601

-- *Metaphysica. Greek & Latin.* Commentariorum P. Fonsecae ... in libros metaphysicorum Aristotelis Stagiritae. Tomus primus. ... Lugduni, sumptibus Sib. á Porta. M.D.LXXXV. 8°. +^{8} ++^{4} A-Zz^{8} 3A^{4}. pp. 2-724. [602

-- -- *Latin.* Commentaria ... Ioannis Scoti in .12. li. Metaphysicę Aristotelis: Scripta ... ab ... Antonio Andreę: cuȝ duplici textu: Argiropili .s. ⁊ Boecij ... Necnō opusculum ... Io. Sco. conclusiones CCCLXXVIII. cōplectēs ... (Venetijs per Simonem de Luere: expensis .d. Andree Torresani de Asula .6. Maij. 1503.) fol. B.L. a-z^{8} ⁊^{8} ɔ^{10} ɥ^{10} A^{8} B^{6} (-ɥ10, *blank*, B6, *presumably blank*). ff. 2-211, 2-13. [603

-- -- Contenta. Continetur hic Aristotelis ... opus metaphysicū a ... Bessarione Cardinale Niceno latinitate ... donatum ... cum adiecto in xij primos libros Argyropyli Byzantij interpretamēto ... Theophrasti metaphysicorum liber I Item metaphysica introductio ... Venale habetur [Parisiis] ... apud Henricum Stephanum ... MDXV. vicesima die mensis Octobris. (*Colophon.*) fol. a-p^{8} q^{4} r-t^{8} v-x^{6}. ff. 2-160. [604

-- -- Bessarionis cardinalis Niceni... metaphysicorum Aristotelis XIIII librorum tralatio. (Venetiis in aedibus Aldi, et Andreae soceri mense Septembri M.D. XVI.) fol. aa^{8} b-f^{8} g^{6}. ff. 2-55. ¶*Published with* Bessarionis ... in calumniatorē Platonis libri quatuor... [605

-- -- Aristo. Stagyri. Lib. Metaphysi. XII. cū singulaꝝ Epitomatis ...: Auerroeqȝ ... ac. M. A. Z. apostillis: necnō duob⁹ aliis lib. quos Aristotelē redolere ... (... Papieqȝ ... impressos per ... Iacob de Burgofrāco. Anno ... Millesimo quingentesimo vigesimoprimo. Tertio Calendis. Aprilis.) 8°. B.L. aa-zz^{8} ⁊⁊^{8} ɔɔ^{8} ɥɥ^{8} 3a-3q^{8} 3r^{4} (-3r4, *presumably blank*). ff. 2-339. [606

-- -- Venūdantur Lugduni apud Scipionē de Gabiano ... (... impressos per ... Iacobum myt Anno ... Millesimo quingētesimo vigesimo nono. Decimanona Octobris.) 8°. B.L. aa-zz^{8} ⁊⁊^{8} ɔɔ^{8} ɥɥ^{8} 3q-3i^{8} 3k^{4}. ff. ij-cclxxxiiij. [607

-- -- Alexandri Aphrodisiei commentaria in duodecim Aristotelis libros de prima Philosophia, interprete Ioāne Genesio Sepulueda Cordubensi ... Parisiis Apud Simonem Colinaeum. M.D.XXXVI. (... ex officina chalcographica Ludouici Cyanei ... mense Aprili.) fol. Aa^{10} a-z^{8} Λ^{8} B^{10}. pp. 1-402. [608

-- -- Venetijs apud Hieronymum Scotum. M. D. XXXXIIII. (*Colophon.*) fol. ❦^{4} a-z^{6} &^{6} ɔ^{6} ꝶ^{6} aa-ee^{6} ff^{8} (-ff8, *blank*) ff. 1-193. [609

-- -- Aristotelis Stagiritae metaphysicorum Libri XIIII. Cum Scholiis ... Auerrois Cordubensis Digressiones omnes ... Contradictiones ac solutiones ... absolutae per ... Marcum Antonium Zimaram ... Lugduni, Apud Theobaldum Paganum, M. D. XLVII. 8°. a-z^{8} A-B^{8}. pp. 3-400. [610

-- -- Alexandri Aphrodisiei commentaria in ... libros de prima Philosophia ... Venetiis apud Hieronymum Scotum. 1551 (*Colophon.*) fol. A-CC^{6} (-CC6, *presumably blank*). ff. 2-155. ¶*The register calls for 4 preliminary ll.* [611

-- -- Aristotelis metaphysicorum, vt vocant libri tredecim ...: Ioachimo Perionio ... interprete ... Lugduni, Apud Antonium Vincentium, 1560. (... Excudebat Symphorianus Barbierus.) 8°. a-u^{8} (-u8, *presumably blank*). pp. 3-317. [612

-- -- Aristotelis Stagiritae metaphysicorum libri XIIII. Theophrasti Metaphysicorum Liber. De causis liber. Pars septima ac suprema. Curtij Marinelli Argumenta ... solutionesq; quaestionum ... Venetiis, M D LXXXV. 16°. A-Xx^{8}. pp. 3-703. ¶*Variant of part* [7] *of* A425. (Smith.) [613

-- -- *Summary*. Paraphrasis in XIIII. Aristot. libros de prima philosophia cum adnotationibus et quaestionibus ... Antonio Scayno Salodiensi auctore ... Romae Apud Bartholomaeum Grassium. M. D. LXXXVII. ... fol. a^4 b^6 A-$3B^6$ $3C^4$. pp. 1-582. [614

-- *Meteorologica*. *Greek*. Aristotelis ... Μετεωρολογικῶν βιβλία. Δ. ... Antuerpiae, Ex Officina Ioannis Loei. Anno M. D. XLVI. 8°. A-K^8 L^4. [615

-- -- *Greek & Latin*. [1] Ολυμπιοδωρου ... ὑπομνήματα. Ἰωάννου γραμματικοῦ ... σχόλια ... Olympiodori ... in meteora Aristotelis commentarii. Ioannis grammatici ... scholia in primum meteorum ... Venetiis. M. D. LI. (... apud Aldi filios, expensis ... Federici de Turrisanis ...) fol. A-L^6 M^8 N-R^6 S^4. ff. 3-108. [2] Olympiodori ... commentarii. Ioannis grammatici ...scholia ... Ioanne Baptista Camotio ... interprete. ... *Same imprint and colophon*. π^4 A-Y^6 Z^8. ff. 1-139. [616

-- -- Francisci Vicomercati Mediolanensis in quatuor libros ... meteorologicorum commentarii. Et eorundem librorum e Graeco in Latinum per eundem conuersio. ... Lutetiae Parisiorum, apud Vascosanum. M. D. LVI. ... fol. A-Ii^6 *A-L^6*. pp. 1-372, 1-130. [617

-- -- Venetiis, M D LXV. Ex officina Dominici Guerrei, et Io. Baptistae fratrum. (*Colophon*.) fol. $*^6$ A-Mm^6 Nn^8. ff. 2-217. [618

-- -- Aristotelis meteorologicorum lib. I Graece et Latinè ... scholiis ... illustratus. Argentorati excudebat Iosias Rihelius. M. D. LXVI. 8°. A-H^8. ff. 1-61. (Smith.) [619

-- -- *Latin*. Meteorologia Aristotelis, Eleganti Iacobi Fabri Stapulensis Paraphrasi explanata. Cōmentarioq3 Ioannis Coclaei Norici declarata ... (Impressa Norinbergae. In officina Friderici Peypuss. ... M.ccccc.xii. Tertio Idus. Nouembris.) 4°. A^6 B^4 C^8 Γ^4 E-$K^{6.6.4}$ L-$Q^{6.4}$ R^4 S-T^6 (-T6, *presumably blank*). ff. IIII-XCIIII. [620

-- -- Libri Meteororum Aristo. cū com. Auer. Aristote. Stagyrite Meteororum Libri quatuor: cum Auer. cordubensis ... commentarijs ... Venūdantur Lugduni apud Scipionē de Gabiano ... (... impressum per ... Iacobum Myt. ... M. D.xxx. die .xxij. Aprilis.) 8°. B.L. a^8 BB-II^8 KK^6. ff. ij-lxxviij. [621

-- -- *Another copy*. [622

-- -- S. Tho. super meteo. Habes ... libros Meteororu3 cum duplici Interpretatione antiqua ꝑ Francisci vatabli: Expositore diuo Thoma Aquinate ... M D XXXVII (Venetijs in officina Luceantonij Iunte Florentini ... mense Iulio.) fol. B.L. A-B^6 A-L^6 M^4 (-M4, *presumably blank*). ff. 1-69. [623

-- -- Augustini Niphi ... in libris Aristotelis meteorologicis commentaria ... Venetiis M. D. XLVII (... apud Hieronymum Scotum. 1551) fol. A^6 B^8 A-Z^6 Aa-Bb^4. ff. 1-146. [624

-- -- Aristotelis Meteorologicorum libri quatuor: Ioachimo Perionio interprete. Eiusdem Perionij ... Obseruationes. ... Basileae, per Ioannem Oporinum. (... M. D.LIII. Mense Februario.) 8°. aA^4 aA-lL^8 mM^4. pp. 1-156. [625

-- -- Aristotelis Meteorologicorum libri quatuor, Ioachimo Perionio interprete: per Nicolaum Grouchium correcti & emendati. Parisiis, Ex officina Gabrielis Buon ... 1560. 4°. A-H^8 I^6. ff. 2-70. [626

-- -- Coloniae, Apud Maternum Cholinum, M. D. LXIIII. 4°. A-Q^4 R^6. pp. 3-140. [627

-- -- *Another copy*. [628

-- -- Parisiis, Ex officina Thomae Brumennij ... 1567. 4°. A-H^8 I^6. ff. 2-70. [629

-- -- Parisiis, Ex officina Gabrielis Buon ... 1571. 4°. A-H^8 I^6. ff. 2-70. [630

-- -- *Italian*. Opera nuoua laquale tratta della filosofia naturale, chiamata la Metaura d'Aristotile; chiosata da San Thomaso d'Aquino ... In Vinegia per Comin da Trino, l'anno M. D. LIIII. 8°. $*^4$ A-L^8 M^4. ff. 1-92. [631

-- *Organon*. *Greek*. Οργανον του Αριστοτελους. ... Aristotelis Organum, ac primum Aristotelicorum operum uolumen ... (Venetiis in aedibus Bartholomaei Zanetti Casterzagensis, aere uero, & diligētia Ioannis Francisci Trincaueli. ... M D XXXVI. Mēse Augusti.) 8°. a-ll^8 mm^{10}. [632

-- -- Οργανον ὀργάνων ... Basileae apud Isingriniū, M. D. XLXIX [*sic*]. 8°. a-z^8 A-Aa^8. pp. 2-745. [633

-- -- *Greek & Latin.* Αριστοτέλους οργανον. Aristotelis organum Graecolatinum, ... conuersum & emendatum ... opera Iohannis Spondani. ... Basileae, ex officina Oporiniana. 1583. (... Mense Ianuario.) 8°. α^8 a-z^8 A-$3A^8$ $3B^{10}$. pp. 1-1133. [634

-- -- Αριστοτέλους ὄργανον. Aristotelis ... Organum, Hoc est libri omnes ad Logicam pertinentes, Graecè & Latinè. Iul. Pacius recensuit: e Graeca ... conuertit ... Morgiis, Excudebat Guillelmus Laimarius, M. D. LXXXIIII. ... 4°. $¶^4$ A-$3F^8$. pp. 3-831. [635

-- -- [1] Quaestionum et commentariorum in organon Aristotelis, pars prima. in qua et textus Graecus integer quaestionibus accommodatus est, & ... in Latinam linguam conuersus ... Industria & studio Guilielmi Hildenii. Berlini sumptibus ac typis autoris. ... M. D. LXXXV . ... 4°. $(*)^4$ A-Vu^4. pp. 1-342. [2] Quaestionum et commentariorum ... pars altera ... *Same imprint.* $(:)^4$ A-Z^4 Aa-Zz^4 AA-$3I^4$. pp. 1-683. [3] ... pars tertia ... Berlini ... M. D. LXXXV. $(:)^4$ A-$3V^4$. pp. 1-526. [636

-- -- [1] ... Aristotelis ... Organum ... Editio Secunda ... Francofurti Apud Heredes Andreae Wecheli, Claudium Marnium, & Iohan. Aubrium. Anno cIↄ Iↄ XCVII. ... 4°. $*^8$ A-$3K^8$ $*^4$. pp. 3-895. [2] Iul. Pacii a Beriga ... Commentarius Analyticus. ... *Same imprint.* A-$3X^4$. pp. 2-436. [637

-- -- *Latin.* Interpretatio scholastica noue logice Aristotelis ... cōmentarijs. principijs tū ... Thome Aq̄natis cōformiter extat cōgesta. ac ꝑ ... exercitiū magistroꝝ Agrippinēsis ... emēdata. ... (Impressa Colonie in officina ... Liberorum quondā Henrici Quentell. Anno ... quingētesimoq̄nto supra mille. pridie kalendarum Nouembrium.) fol. B.L. A-E^6 F^4 G-I^6 K^4 L-N^6 O^4 P-R^6 S^4 T-Y^6 Z^4 Aa-Cc^6 Dd^4 Ee-Ii^6 Kk-$Nn^{4.6}$ Pp^4 Aa-Cc^6 Dd^4 Ee-Hh^6 Ii-$Pp^{6.4}$. ff. i-CCvij. [638

-- -- Libri logicorum in officina Henrici .S. secunda recognitione ([$k6^v$] ... Septembris. III. [$P6^v$] Parisijs ... M.D.X. quarta Aprilis.) fol. a-i^8 k^6 1-z^8 A-M^8 N-P^6. ff. 2-296. ¶i4 *misbound before* i3, i6 *before* i5. [639

-- -- Questiones magistri Bartoli castrensis habitae pro totius logice prohemio. Questiones eiusdem in predicamenta Aristotelis disputatae secūduȝ opinionem Thome Scoti et Ochaȝ textu ex traslatione Argiropili inserto. Canones triumphi numerorum ab eodē Bartolo ... (Impressum ... in ... ciuitate toleti āno ... millesimo quingētesimodecimo tertio octaua die octobris per Ioanem de villaq̄ram ... impēsis alfonsi de castro bibliopole complutensis accademie ... correctum ... per ginesiū marti valētinensem ...) fol. B.L. a^8 b-k^6 m-r^6. ff. II-XCIII. [640

-- -- Aristotelis Stragyrite [*sic*] Dialectica: cū quīque vocibus Porphyrii Phenicis: Argyropilo traductore: a Ioanne Eckio ... explanatione declarata ... (Excusa in officina Millerana Augustae Vindelicorū ad .V. Cal'. Maias. ... M.D.XVII.) fol. A-O^6 P^8 a-z^6 Aa-Gg^6 Hh^4 Ii^6 V^4 (-V4, *presumably blank*). ff. III-XCII, I-CLXXXIX. [641

-- -- Logica Aristotelis ex tertia recognitione. ... Parisiis Ex officina Simonis Colinaei. 1531 fol. a-z^8 A-L^8 (-L8). ff. 2-271. [642

-- -- [1] Aristotelis Stagiritae organum, seu libri ad dialecticam attinentes ... Venetiis apud Ioan. Gryphium. M D XLVII. (*Colophon.*) 8°. a-n^8 o^{10}. ff. 2-114. [2] Aristotelis Stagiritae organum, hoc est Libri ad Logicam attinentes, Boethio Seuerino interprete. ... *Same imprint and colophon.* A-T^8 V^4. ff. 2-156. [643

-- -- [1] Aristotelis logica ... Lutetiae, Ex officina Michaëlis Vascosani ... M. D. LVI. ... 4°. A-D^4. ff. 2-16. [2] Aristotelis categoriae, Ioachimo Perionio interprete: per Nicolaum Grouchium correctae & emendatae. *Same imprint.* A-F^4. ff. 2-23. [3] Aristotelis de interpretatione liber, Ioachimo Perionio interprete, per N. Gruchium correctus & emendatus. Lutetiae. Apud Michaelem Vascosanum ... M. D. LVI. A-D^4. ff. 2-16. [4] Aristotelis priorum analyticorum ... libri II. Firmino Durio interprete, per N. Gruchium correcti & emendati. Lutetiae, Apud Vascosanum ... M. D. LVIII. A-S^4. ff. 2-71. [5] Aristotelis de demonstratione ... libri duo, Nicolao Gruchio Rotomagensi interprete. Lutetiae. Ex officina typographica Michaëlis Vascosani ... M. D. LVII. ... a-b^4 A-O^4 P^6. ff. 1-62. [6] Aristotelis topicorum libri VIII. Ioachimo Perionio interprete, per N. Gruchium correcti & emendati. Lutetiae, Apud Michaëlem Vascosanum ... M. D. LVII. a-Bb^4. ff. 2-100. [7] Aristotelis ... de reprehensionibus sophistarum liber vnus. Nicolao Gruchio ... interprete. *Same imprint as* [1]. A-I^4 K^6. ff. 2-42. [644

-- -- [Organon.] Lugduni, apud Theobaldum Paganum. 1557. (*Colophon.*) 8°. [1] Aristotelis Stagiritae organum ... Boëthio Seuerino interprete ... A-D^8 F^4. pp. 3-71. [2] Peri Hermenias ... AA-BB^8. pp. 3-31. [3] Priorum analyticorum ... libri duo ... 3A-$3H^8$.

pp. 2-128. [4] Posteriorum analyticorum ... libri duo ... 4A-4E^8 4F^4. pp. 2-88. [5] Topicorum ... Libri octo ... 5A-5P^8. pp. 2-239. [645

-- -- Aristotelis logica, ab eruditissimis hominibus conuersa, Et à Nicolao Grouchio correcta atque emendata ... Lugduni, Apud Antonium Vincentium, 1560. (... Excudebat Symphorianus Barbierus.) 8°. a-z^8 A-Q^8. pp. 2-621. [646

-- -- Aristotelis Stagiritae organum, seu libri ad logicam attinentes, Seuerino Boetho Interprete ... Venetiis Apud Ioannem Bonadeum. M D LXIIII. (*Colophon.*) 8°. A-Zz^8 (-Zz8, *presumably blank*). ff. 2-366. [647

-- -- D. Francisci Toleti ... commentaria, vnà cum Quaestionibus, in vniuersam Aristotelis logicam. ... Coloniae Agrippinae, Apud Haeredes Arnoldi Birckmanni. Anno. M. D LXXV. ... 4°. *^{4} A-3Q^4 3R^2. ff. 1-250. [648

-- -- Venetiis, Apud Hieronymum Polum. M D LXXIX. 4°. a^2 A-S^8 T^4 V-Gg^8 Hh^{10} *^{4}. ff. 2-246. [649

-- -- Aristotelis Logica ab Ioachimo Perionio ... conuersa, & per Nicolaum Gruchium correcta & emendata. Firminus verò Durius suae interpretationi manum extremam nuper addidit. ... Parisiis, Ex Typographia Dionysij à Prato ... 1582. 4°. ā^4 ē^4 A-Aa^8 Bb^4 Cc-Tt^8 Vu^6. ff. 1-338. [650

-- -- Porphyrii Phoenicis isagoge id est, introductio in Dialecticen. Item Aristotelis Stagiritae ... opera omnia, quae pertinent ad inuentionem & iudicationem Dialecticae. Partim Argyropolo Bizantino, partim Boethio Seuerino interprete. ... Coloniae. Apud Maternum Cholinum. M. D. LXXXVI. ... 4°. a-z^4 (-i^4) A-Qq^4. pp. 3-495. [651

-- -- Aristotelis Stagiritae ... organum ... Venetiis, M D XCIIII. Apud Minimam Societatem. (... Apud Florauantem Pratum. ...) 16°. A-Rr^8. pp. 4-637. [652

-- -- D. Francisci Toleti ... commentaria, vnà cum Quaestionibus, in vniuersam Aristotelis logicam. ... Coloniae Agrippinae, In officina Birckmannica, sumptibus Arnoldi Mylij. Anno cIↄ. Iↄ. XCVI. ... (... Typis Godefridi Kempensis. ... Mense. Ianuario.) 4°. *^{4} A-3M^4. pp. 1-454. ¶*1 *defective.* [653

-- -- *Summary.* [1] Γεωργίου ... Παχυμέρους ἐπιτομὴ τῆς Ἀριστοτέλους λογικῆς. Parisiis Apud Vascosanum ... M.D.XLVIII. ... 8°. A-I^8. ff. 2-71. [2] Georgii Pachymerii in vniuersam Aristotelis disserendi artem epitome. Ioanne Baptisto Rasario interprete. Parisiis, Apud M. Vascosanum ... M. D. XLVIII. ... A-K^8. ff. 3-80. [654

-- *Parva naturalia. Greek & Latin.* Aristotelis ... libelli duo, unus de longitudine & breuitate uitae, alter de diuinatione per somnum, à Christophoro Hegēdorphino ... in latinam uersi, & scholijs ... illustrati. ... Basileae apud Brptholomaeum [*sic*] Vvesthemerum et Nicolaum Brylingerum. Anno M. D. XXXVI. 8°. [A]^1 B-G^8. pp. 1-93. ¶[A]1 *may be all that is present of a gathering of four or eight leaves.* [655

-- -- *Latin.* Aristotelis ... parua naturalia ... Omnia in latinum conuersa & ... explicata. à .N. Leonico Thomaeo. ... (... ex Impressione repesentauerunt Bernardinus & Mattheus fratres Vitales Veneti ... M.D.XXIII. Mense Iunii ...) fol. AA-BB^6 a-z^8 &^{8} ↄ^8 ℞^{8} A-F^8 ✚^{4} (-F8, ✚4, *presumably blank*). ff. I-CCXLV. [656

-- -- Aristotelis libelli, qui parua naturalia vulgo appellantur. Ioachimo Perionio interprete: per Nicolaum Grouchium correcti & emendati. Parisiis, Ex officina Gabrielis Buon ... 1560. 4°. A^4 B-I^8 K^4. ff. 5-72. [657

-- -- Coloniae, Apud Maternum Cholinum M. D. LXIIII. 4°. A-S^4. pp. 1-135. [658

-- -- *Another copy.* [659

-- -- Parisiis, Ex officina Thomae Brumennij ... 1567. 4°. A^4 B-I^8 K^4. ff. 5-72. [660

-- -- Alexandri Aphrodisiensis ... In Aristotelis Opusculum de Sensibus atque his quae cadunt in sensum ... Commentarium ... Lucillo Philalthaeo interprete. Michaelis Ephesii scolia in Aristotelis libros aliquot ... Venetiis, apud haeredem Hieronymi Scoti, M D LXXIII. (*Colophon.*) fol. A-I^4. pp. 3-70. ¶I1 *misbound after* I3. [661

-- -- Aristotelis libelli, qui parua naturalia vulgo appellantur. ... Parisiis, Ex officina Gabrielis Buon ... 1577. 4°. A-H^8 I^6. ff. 5-72. [662

-- *Peplus (supposititious).* Aristotelis Stagiritae, pepli fragmentum, siue Heroum Homericorum epitaphia ... Latinè versa ... per Gulielmum Canterum. ... Ausonii Epitaphia Heroum ... Editio secunda ... Antuerpiae, Ex officina Christophori Plantini. cIↄ.Iↄ.LXXI. 8°. A-C^8 D^4. pp. 3-31. [663

-- *Physica. Greek.* Σιμπλικιου υπομνηματα ... Simplicii commentarii in octo Aristotelis physicae auscultationis libros cum ipso Aristotelis textu. ... (Venetiis in Aedibus Aldi, & Andreae Asulani Soceri Mense Octobri. M. D. XXVI.) fol. *^{4} a-z^8 &^{8} aa-gg^8 hh^{10} ii-pp^8 qq^{10}. ff. 1-322. [664

-- -- *Another copy.* [665

-- -- Αριστοτελους φυσικῆς ἀκροάσεως βιβλία θ Aristotelis Naturalis auscultationis libri octo. Excudebat Christianus Wechelus ... M.D.XXXII. 4°. A-AA^4. pp. 3-191. [666

-- -- Ιωαννου γραμματικου υπομνημα ... Ioannis grammatici in primos quatuor Aristotelis de naturali auscultatione libros comentaria. ... M D XXXV. (Venetiis in aedibus Bartholomaei Zanetti Casterzagensis, aere ... Ioannis Francisci Trincaueli. ... Mense Septembri.) fol. [*]^2 a-l^8 m^{10} n-t^8 v^4. ¶r4, r5 *reversed.* [667

-- -- Αριστοτελους φυσικῆς ἀκροάσεως βιβλία ὀκτώ. Aristotelis naturalis auscultationis libri octo ... Venetiis. (... apud Ioan. Ant. & Petrum fratres de Nicolinis de Sabio, Sumptu Melchioris Sessę. M. D. XLVI.) 8°. A-P^8 Q^4. ff. 5-123. [668

-- -- Αριστοτελους φυσικης ακροασεως βιβλία θ. Aristotelis commentationum De natura, Libri VIII. ... Parisiis, M.D.LVI. Apud Guil. Morelium ... 4°. A-Z^4. pp. 3-182. [669

-- -- *Greek & Latin.* Francisci Vicomercati Mediolanensis in octo libros Aristotelis De Naturali Auscultatione Commentarij. Et eorundem librorum è Graeco in Latinum per eundem conuersio. ... Venetiis, M D LXVII. Ex officina Dominici Guerrei, et Io. Baptistae fratrum. fol. *^{4} A-EE^8. ff. 2-223. [670

-- -- *Latin.* Egidij Romani in libros de physico auditu Aristotelis cõmentaria ... Eiusdeȝ questio de gradibus formaꝝ. ... (Venetijs im̄pssus mãdato ... Heredũ ... Octauiani Scoti ... ꝑ Bonetuȝ Locatellum ... i2°. kal. Octobr. i502.) fol. B.L. A-AA^8 BB^6 CC-DD^8. ff. 2-2i4. [671

-- -- Gualteri Burlei in physicaȝ Aristotelis. expositio ⁊ questiones: ac etiam questio de primo ⁊ vltimo ĩstanti ... (Im̄pssi Venetijs mãdato ... heredũ ... Ocauiani [*sic*] scoti ... Correcti ... per ... Mattheuȝ Siculũ ... Im̄pssi arte ... Boneti locatelli ... i508. die ꝟo .27. mẽsis Iulij.) fol. B.L. π^2 a-z^8 ⁊^{8} ↄ^8 ꝶ^8 aa-bb^8 cc^{10} dd^6 (-dd6, *presumably blank*). ff. 1-239. [672

-- -- [1] Accipe ... Aristotelẽ ... ac eius ... ĩterpretẽ Auerroeȝ ... fol. B.L. a-y^8 z^{10}. ff. 2-106. [2] Marci Antonii zimare ... Questio de primo cognito. Eiusdem solutiones contradictionum in dictis Auerrois. ... (Venetijs per heredes ... Octauiani Scoti ... ⁊ socios ... i5i6. Die .4. Iunij.) AA-DD^8 EE^4. pp. 2-36. [673

-- -- Aristotelis ... acroases physicae libri .VIII. Ioan. Argyropilo interprete, adiectis Ioan. Eckii adnotationibus & commentarijs ... (In Augusta Vindelica, in Sigismundi Grim̄ ... & Marci Vuirsung officina, Mense Iunio. ... M.D.XVIII.) fol. a-s^6 t^4. ff. I-CXI. [674

-- -- Libri octo physicoꝝ Aristotilis per Ioannem Argyropylũ e graeco in latinũ traducti. ... (Impressum Craccouię, in ędibus ... Ioannis Haller ... 1519.) 4°. A-B^8 C^4 D-F^8 G-I^4 K^8 L-R^4 S-T^8 V-X^4 Y^6. [675

-- -- Ioannis grammatici cognomento Philoponi ... commentaria in primos quatuor Aristotelis de naturali auscultatione libros. ... Guilelmo Dorotheo Veneto ... interprete. ... Venetiis. MDXXXIX. (Impressum ... per Brandinum ⁊ Octauianum Scotum. ...) fol. B.L. π^2 a-o^6 A-H^6. ff. 1-84, 1-48. [676

-- -- Aristotelis Stagiritae de Physico Auditu Libri Octo ... Auerrois Cordubensis Digressiones oẽs in eosdem. Accesserunt contradictiones ac solutiones ... absolute per ... Marcum Antonium Zimarram ... Venetijs apud Hieronymum Scotum. 1540. 8°. a-z^8 &^{8} ↄ^8 ꝶ^8 aa-bb^8 cc^4. pp. 9-468. [677

-- -- Augustini Niphi ... Suessani Expositio super octo Aristotelis ... libros de Physico auditu: Cum duplici textus tralatione, Antiqua videlicet, & Noua eius ... Auerrois etiam Cordubensis ... Prooemium, ac Commentaria ... Venetiis. Apud Hieronymum Scotum. M D LVIII (*Colophon.*) fol. *^{6} **^{4} 3*-4*^{2} A-Rr^8 Ss^6. pp. 1-651. [678

-- -- Aristotelis physicorum Libri Quatuor, cum Ioannis grammatici, cognomento Philoponi, commentariis. Quos ... restituit Ioannes Baptista Rasarius, Nouariensis ... Venetiis, Apud Hieronymum Scotum. M D LVIII. (*Colophon.*) fol. *^{2} A-Q^{8} R^{4}. pp. 2-262. [679

-- -- S. Thomae Aquinatis In octo Physicorum Aristotelis commentaria ... Cum duplici textus tralatione, antiqua, & Argyropoli ... Roberti Linconiensis in eodem Summa. Sancti Thomę libelli ad negocium Physicum spectantes ... ac Thomae de Vio Caietani Quaestiones duae ... Venetiis, Apud Hieronymum Scotum M D LVIII. (*Colophon.*) fol. *-**^{4} A-Hh^{6}. ff. 1-186. [680

-- -- Aristotelis de Natura, aut de Rerum principiis lib. VIII. Ioachimo Perionio interprete, & per Nicolaum Grouchium correcti & emendati. Accessit ... argumentū in vniuersam tractationē scientię naturalis, ... studio Matthaei Prigillani Bellouaci. Parisiis, Ex officina Gabrielis Buon ... 1560. 4°. A^{4} A^{4} B-P^{8}. ff. 2-120. ¶^{2}A1 *misbound after* A1. [681

-- -- Coloniae, Apud Maternum Cholinum. M. D. LXIIII. ... 4°. a^{4} A-Z^{4} a-f^{4}. pp. 1-231. [682

-- -- Aristotelis Stagiritae ... de physico auditu libri octo. ... Auerrois ... Quaestiones ... Marciantonii Zimarae ... Solutiones ... Patauii, Ex Officina Laurentij Pasquati. M D LXIIII. (*Colophon.*) 8°. A-Ee^{8}. ff. 2-223. [683

-- -- Aristotelis de Natura, aut de Rerum principiis lib. VIII. ... Parisiis, Ex officina Thomae Brumennij ... 1567. 4°. A^{4} A^{4} B-P^{8}. ff. 2-120. [684

-- -- Parisiis, Ex officina Gabrielis Buon ... 1577. 4°. A^{4} A-O^{8} P^{4}. ff. 3-120. [685

-- -- Francisci Vicomercati Mediolanensis in octo libros Aristotelis De Naturali Auscultatione Commentarij. ... Et eorundem librorum ... per eundem conuersio. Venetiis. Apud haeredem Hyeronymi Scoti. MDLXXXIIII. (*Colophon.*) fol. A-S^{8} T^{4}. pp. 3-294. [686

-- -- Gualteri Burlaei ... super Aristotelis libros, de physica auscultatione ... commentaria. Cum noua veterique Interpretatione. Venetiis, Apud Michaelem Berniam Bononiensem M D LXXXIX. (... Apud Dominicum de Farris. Ad instantiam Michaelis Berniae ...) fol. †^{6} (-†6) ††^{8} A-Zz^{6} 3A^{4}. cols. 1-1116. [687

-- -- *Summaries.* Epitomata noua: que vulgo Reparationes dicūtur Lectionū et exercitioꝝ libroꝝ physice Aristotelis in vniuersitate Coloniēsi legi consuetorū ... M.ccccc.viij. (... opa ꝛ impensis ... Liberoꝝ Quētell ... impressa. ... Idib⁹ Aprilis.) 4°. B.L. a-g^{6} h^{4} i-q^{6} r^{4} s-z^{6} aa-ff$^{6.4}$ A-B^{6} C^{4} D-G^{6} H^{4} I-M^{6} N^{4} O-T^{6} V-Z$^{4.6}$ (-Z6, *presumably blank*). [688

-- Textus philosophie naturalis [*Device of Jehan Petit.*] (... [Parisiis,] impressus per magistrum Thomam duguernier [1519 *or earlier*].) 8°. B.L. a-m^{8} n^{4}. ¶a2^{r}: Incipit textus abbreuiatus Aristotelis ... a magistro. Thoma bricot ... compilatus ... [689

-- -- Georgii Pachimerii ... Cōpendiariae institutiones, in Phisicam Aristotelis, ... Latinitati donatae, Nicolao Lundano Naupliense Franc. f. interprete. Patauii Iacobus Fabrianus. M. D. L. ... 8°. A-L^{4}. ff. 2-44. [690

-- -- Aristotelis de rerum principiis libri IIII. antehac in epitomen contracti ... Authore Gerardo Matthisio Geldriensi. ... Coloniae, Excudebat Petrus Horst Anno 1570. 8°. A-Dd^{8} (A8 + *folded leaf*) Ee^{2}. pp. 3-434. [691

-- *Physiognomia (suppositious). Latin.* Liber Aristotelis de physiognomia ... (Impressum Lipsigk per Baccalaureū Vuolffgangum Monacensem. ... 1517.) 4°. B.L. A-B^{6}. ¶*Translator: Bartholomaeus of Messina.* [692

-- -- Physiognomonica Aristotelis Latina facta, a Iodoco Willichio Reselliano. Addita est eiusdem interpretis oratio in laudem Physiognomoniae. (Excusum Vitebergae, in officina Nicolai Schirlentz. Anno M. D. XXXVIII.) 8°. A^{8} B^{4} C-E^{8}. [693

-- *Poetica. Greek & Latin.* Francisci Robortelli Vtinensis in librum Aristotelis de arte poetica explicationes. ... Florentiae In Officina Laurentii Torrentini ... MDXLVIII. ... (... Mense Octobri ...) fol. ✠^{6} A-Dd^{6} aa^{4} bb-dd^{6} ee-gg^{4}. pp. 1-322, 1-64. ¶aa1^{r}: ... Paraphrasis in librum Horatii ... de arte poetica ... [694

-- -- Vincentii Madii Brixiani et Bartholomaei Lombardi Veronensis in Aristotelis librum de poetica communes explanationes ... Eiusdem [Madii] de Ridiculis: Et in Horatii librum de arte Poetica interpretatio. ... Venetiis, in officina Erasmiana Vincentij Valgrisij .M D L. (*Colophon.*) fol. *^{6} †^{6} A-Hh^{6}. pp. 1-369. [695

-- -- Petri Victorii Commentarii in primum librum Aristotelis De Arte Poetarum. ... Secunda editio. Florentiae In officina Iuntarum, Bernardi Filiorum. MDLXXIII. ... (*Colophon.*) fol. a⁶ b⁴ A-Bb⁶ Cc⁴ Dd⁶. pp. 2-308. [696

-- -- *Greek & Italian.* Poetica d'Aristotele vulgarizzata et sposta Per Lodouico Casteluetro. Stampata in Vienna d'Austria, per Gaspar Stainhofer ... M. D. LXX. 4°. A-5F⁴. ff. 1-385. [697

-- -- Stampata in Basilea ad instanza di Pietro de Sedabonis ... M D LXXVI. 4°.)(-2)(⁴ A-Zz⁴ AA-ZZ⁴ AAa-ZZz⁴ AAA-CCC⁴. pp. 1-699. [698

-- -- *Italian.* Il libro della poetica d'Aristotele. Tradotto di Greca lingua in volgare, da M. Alessandro Piccolomini. Con vna sua epistola ... del modo del tradurre. In Siena. Per Luca Bonetti ... 1572. ... 4°. ✠⁴ A-G⁴. pp. 1-55. [699

-- -- Annotationi di M. Alessandro Piccolomini, nel libro della Poetica d'Aristotele; con la traduttione del medesimo Libro, in lingua Volgare. ... In Vinegia, Presso Giouanni Guarisco, & Compagni. (... M. D. LXXV.) 4°. +⁴ ++⁸ A-Cc⁸ Dd⁴. pp. 1-422. [700

-- *Politica. Greek.* Ἀριστοτέλους πολιτικῶν βιβλ. ὀκτώ. Aristotelis De optimo statu Reipub. Libri octo. ... Parisiis, M, D. LVI. Apud Guil. Morelium ... (*Colophon.*) 4°. *⁴ A⁴ B-C⁸ D¹² E⁸ F¹⁰ G⁸ H⁶ I-T⁴ V⁶ X-Y⁴ Z². pp. 1-240. ¶*Adams A1911.* [701

-- -- *Greek & Latin.* Petri Victorii commentarii in VIII. libros Aristotelis de optimo statu ciuitatis. ... Florentiae, apud Iuntas. CIↃ IↃ LXXVI. (... Mense Augusto. ...) fol. +⁸ A-Zz⁸. pp. 1-698. [702

-- -- Aristotelis politicorum libri octo ex Dion. Lambini & P. Victorii interpretationib. puriss. Graecolatini Theod. Zuingeri Argumentis atq3 Scholiis ... Victorii Commentarijs ... declarati. Pythagoreorum ueterum Fragmenta Politica, à Io. Spondano conuersa ... Basileae Eusebii Episcopii opera ac impensa. CIↃ IↃ XCII. fol. α⁶ β⁴ a-z⁶ A-Gg⁶. pp. 2-623. [703

-- -- In Politica, hoc est in ciuiles libros Aristotelis Antonii Montecatini Ferrariensis progymnasmata. ... Ferrariae, CIↃ IↃ XXCVII. Excudebat Victorius Baldinus ... (*Colophon.*) fol. a² b-p⁴ A-3S⁴ A-G⁴ H². pp. 1-59, 1-509. ¶*Book I only.* [704

-- -- *Latin.* Dissertissimi ... Ferdinādi Rhoensis ... cōmentarii in politicorum libros cu3 tribus eiusde3 ... repetitionibus ab ... martino de Frias ... recogniti ... (... Salmantice impressi in officina ... Ioannis de porres ac eiusdem ⁊ ... Ioannis de zaraus impēsis. ... M.d.ij. iiij. kalendas martias ...) fol. B.L. a⁸ b-z⁶ ⁊⁶ ꝯ⁶ ꝶ⁶ A-C⁶ aa-bb⁶ χ⁹ ²χ⁶. ff. II-CLXXVI, I-XII. [705

-- -- Aristotelis Stagiritae politicorum ad Nicomachum lib. primus Raphaelis Volaterrani argumenta in eosdem. Leonardo Aretino interprete. Venetijs Apud Hieronymum Scotum. 1542. (... 1543.) 8°. A-Z⁸ aa⁸ bb⁴. ff. 2-195. [706

-- -- Aristotelis de republica, qui politicorum dicuntur, libri VIII. à Ioachimo Perionio ... latinitate donati ... Accesserūt eiusdem Perionij ... Obseruationes ... Basileae. (... sumptibus Ioannis Oporini, ... M.D.XLIIII. Mense Februario.) 8°. *⁸ a-z⁸ A-T⁸. pp. 3-600. [707

-- -- Aristotelis de Republica libri VIII. interprete & enarratore Io. Genesio Sepulueda Cordubensis. ... Parisiis Apud Vascosanum ... M. D. XLVIII. ... 4°. A⁴ a-z⁴ A-TT⁴. ff. 2-259. [708

-- -- Aristotelis de republica, qui politicorum dicuntur, libri VIII. ... Basileae per Ioan. Oporinum. (... M. D. XLIX. Mense Martio.) 8°. α⁸ A-Dd⁸ Ee⁶. pp. 1-409. [709

-- -- Donati Acciaioli in Aristotelis Libros Octo Politicorum commentarii ... Venetijs, apud Vincentium Valgrisium, M D LXVI. (*Colophon.*) 8°. +⁸ A-Mm⁸ (-Mm8, *blank*). ff. 9-278. ¶+1 *defective.* [710

-- -- Aristotelis de reip. bene administrandae ratione, libri octo, a Dionys. Lambino Monstroliensi ... Latini facti ... Lutetiae, Apud Iacobum du Puys ... M. D. LXXX. ... 4°. ā⁴ ē⁴ A-Rr⁴ (-Rr4, *blank*). ff. 1-158. [711

-- -- Aristotelis politicorum, hoc est ciuilium librorum secundus, ab Antonio Montecatino In Latinam Linguam conuersus ... Cum alijs quibusdam ... Ferrariae Apud Benedictum Mammarellum. M.D.XCIIII. fol. +⁴ A-T⁶ V-X⁴ X⁶ Y-Oo⁶ Pp⁴ Qq² Qq-3B⁶ 3C⁸ 3D-3M⁶ 3N-3O⁴ 3P² 3Q-3R⁶ 3S⁸ 3T-3Y⁶·⁴ (-3Y4, *presumably blank*). pp. 1-766. ¶*Additional t.pp.:* (X1ʳ) Platonis

... de republica vel de iusto Libri decem ... Antonii Montecatini ... Partitiones, & veluti Paraphrasis quaedam ... *Same imprint.* (Qq1r) Platonis ... de legibus vel de legumlatione Libri duodecim cum Epinomide ... Antonii Montecatini epitome ... *Same imprint.* (3P1r) Quinque veterum rerumpublicarum, Hippodamiae, Laconicae, Creticae, Carthaginiensis, Atheniensis ... antiqua fragmenta. ... *Same imprint.* [712

-- -- *English.* Aristotles politiques, or discourses of gouernment. Translated out of Greeke into French ... By Loys Le Roy, called Regius. Translated out of French into English. At London printed by Adam Islip. ... 1598. fol. A^6 (-A1, *presumably blank*) B-Nn^6. pp. 1-393. *S.T.C.* 760. [713

-- -- *French.* Les politiques d'Aristote ... Traduictes de Grec en Francois ... Par Loys le Roy, dict Regius, de Costentin. ... A Paris, Par Michel de Vascosan ... M. D. LXVIII. ... 4°. $ā^4$ $ē^6$ A-Z^4 a-z^4 Aa-Zz^4 AA-ZZ^4 AAa-ZZz^4 3A-$3C^4$ $3D^6$. pp. 1-949. [714

-- -- A Paris, Par Michel de Vascosan ... M. D. LXXVI. ... fol. a^6 b^4 a-z^6 A-P^6 a-b^6 c-d^4 (-d4, *presumably blank*). pp. 1-454. ¶a1, c4, d1-3 *repaired.* [715

-- -- *Italian.* Trattato dei gouerni di Aristotile Tradotto di Greco in lingua uulgare Fiorentina da Bernardo Segni ... In Firenze appresso Lorenzo Torrentino ... MDXLIX. 4°. A-$3I^4$. pp. 3-420. [716

-- -- In Vinegia M D LI. (Stampato ... per Bartholomeo detto l'Imperador, & Francesco suo genero. ...) 8°. a-z^8 A-H^8 (-H8, *blank*). ff. 2-230. [717

-- -- *Spanish.* Los ocho libros de republica del Filosofo Aristoteles, traduzidos originalmēte de lengua Griega en Castellana por Pedro Simon Abril ... Vendense en Çaragoça en casa de Luis Ganareo ... En Çaragoça ... impressos En casa de Lorenço, i Diego de Robles Hermanos Año .M.D.LXXXIIII. (*Colophon.*) 8°. $¶^6$ A-Kk^8 Ll^2. ff. 1-268. [718

-- -- *Selections.* Polilogium: ex Aristotelis octo Politicorū libris ... Lipsi imp̄ssit Vuolfgang⁹ Monaceñ. ... (Anno ... Millesimoquingētesimo decimotertio. Die vero .xvj. Mensis Aprilis.) fol. B.L. A-E^6 F^4 G-P^6 Q^4 χ^6. ff. ij-lxxxviij. (Lea.) [719

-- -- *Summaries.* Epythomata in octo libris Politicorum Arist. per fratreȝ Chrisostomum Iauellum canapicium ... digesta ... Venetiis MDXXXVI ... (... per Stephanum de Sabio. ... Mensis Maij.) 4°. B.L. A-S^8 T^6. ff. 2-150. [720

-- -- La politica di Aristotile ridotta in modo di parafrasi Dal Reuerendo M. Antonio Scaino da Salo. Con alcune Annotationi & dubbi. E sei Discorsi sopra diuerse materie ciuili. ... In Roma, Nelle case del Popolo Romano. M D LXXVIII. (*Colophon.*) 4°. +-$++^4$ A-$3O^4$ $3P^6$ a-r^4 (-r4, *presumably blank*). ff. 1-232, 2-67. ¶*Additional t.p.* (a1r): Sei discorsi ... *Same imprint.* [721

-- *Problemata (supposititious). Latin.* Problemata Aristotelis cū duplici trāslatiōe antiqua vȝ. ꝛ noua .s. Theodori gaze. cū expōne Petri Aponi. Tabulum sôm magistrū Petrū de tussignano ... Problemata Alexandri aphrodisei. Problemata Plutarchi. ... (... ipressa Venetijs ꝑ Gregoriuȝ de gregorijs. ... i505. Tertio calendas sextiles.) fol. B.L. aa^{10} bb^8 cc^4 a-z^8 $ꝛ^8$ $ɔ^8$ $ꝭ^8$ A-L^8. ff. 2-22, 1-296. [722

-- -- In hoc libro cōtinentur problemmata. Aristotelis ... [Parisiis, Jehan Petit.] 8°. B.L. a-e^8 f^4. [723

-- -- Venundantur ab Iohanne petit ... (Impressa ... Parrisijs Opera ... Andree boucard. Impensis vero Iohannis petit ... 1520. Ad kal'. Iul.) fol. B.L. aa-cc^8 a-z^8 $ꝛ^8$ $ɔ^8$ $ꝭ^8$ A-H^8 I-K^6 (-K6, *presumably blank*). ff. i-cclxxxiiij. [724

-- -- Problematum Aristotelis sectiones duædequadraginta. Problematum Alexandri Aphrodisiei libri duo. Theodore Gaza interprete. ... Basileae, [per Andream Cratandrum,] M. D. XXXVII. fol. A-E^6 a-o^6 p^8. ff. 2-92. [725

-- -- Problemata Aristotelis ac philosophorum medicorumq́ȝ complurium ... Marci Antonii Zimaræ Sanctipetrinatis Problemata his addita, unà cum trecentis Aristotelis & Auerrois Propositionibus ... Item Alexandri Aphrodisei, super Quæstionibus nonnullis Physicis, Solutionum Liber, Angelo Politiano interprete. (Francoforti ex officina Petri Brubachij, Anno M. D. XLVIII.) 8°. A-V^8 (-V8, *blank*). pp. 6-316. [726

-- -- Parisiis. Apud Gulielmum Cauellat ... M. D. LIII. (Excudebat Martinus Iuuenis ... Nonis April. ...) 16°. A-R^8 S^6. ff. 2-141. [727

-- -- Venetiis, Apud Dominicum Farreum. 1580. 16°. A-Y⁸. ff. 2-156. [728

-- -- *French.* Problemes d'Aristote et autres filozofes ... Auec ceux de Marc Antoine Zimara. Item, Les solutions d'Alexandre Aphrodisee, sus plusieurs questions Physicales. A Lion par Ian de Tournes. M. D. LIIII. ... 8°. A⁴ a-q⁸. pp. 1-252. [729

-- -- *German.* Ein schöner Tractat/ mancherley Frag/ Menschlicher vñ Thyerlicher natur vnnd geschicklichkait zů Latein genant Problemata Arestotilis/ Galieni/ vnd ander natürlicher ... Philosophi. M. D. XXXI. 4°. A-C⁴ D⁶. [730

-- -- Problemata Aristotelis. Mancherley zweyfelhafftiger Fragen ... Dess ... Aristotelis/ vnd vil anderer ... Naturerkündiger ... Getruckt zu Franckfurt am Mayn/ Anno 1568. (... durch Iohannem Wolffium ...) 8°. A-T⁸. [731

-- *Rhetorica. Greek.* Αριστοτελους τεχνης ρητορικης βιβλια γ. Aristotelis de arte rhetorica libri tres. Basileae in officina Frobeniana an. MDXXIX (... per Hieronymum Frobenium et Ioannem Heruagium ... mense Augusto.) 4°. α-ν⁴ ο-φ⁴. pp. 3-156. [732

-- -- Αριστοτελους τέχνης ρêτορικῆς βιβλία τρία. Aristotelis de arte Rhetorica libri tres. Parisiis Ex officina Christiani Wecheli. M.D.XXXVIII. 8°. a-n⁸ o⁴. pp. 3-216. [733

-- -- *Another copy.* [734

-- -- Εις την Αριστοτελους ρητορικην υπομνημα ανωνυμον. ... Parisiis per Conradum Neobarium ... 1539. fol. a-c⁶ d-f⁴ g-i⁶ k-m⁴ n-o⁶ p-r⁴ s². ff. 4-80. [735

-- -- Αριστοτέλους τέχνης ῥητορικῆς βιβλία γ'. Aristotelis de arte rhetorica libri tres. Basileae apud Isingriniū, M. D. XLVI. 8°. A-O⁸. pp. 4-240. [736

-- -- Petri Victorii commentarii in tres libros Aristotelis de arte dicendi. ... Florentiae In officina Bernardi Iunctæ. M.D.XLVIII. (... Editum idibus Septembribus. ...) fol. ☞⁸ A-3K⁶ (-KK6, *presumably blank*). pp. 2-637. [737

-- -- Basileae. (... ex officina Ioannis Oporini M.D.XLIX. Mense Martio.) fol. a⁶ A-Oo⁶. cols. 1-871. [738

-- -- Florentiæ. Ex officina Iunctarum. An. CIↃ IↃ LXXIX. ... fol. *⁶ **⁴ A-3S⁶ 3T⁸ (-3T8). pp. 1-756. [739

-- -- *Greek & Latin.* Martini Borrhai Stugardiani in tres Aristotelis de Arte dicendi libros Commentaria. Hermolai Barbari, eorundem versio, cum Graeco textu ... Basileae. (... ex officina Iacobi Parci, impensis Ioannis Oporini, ... M.D.LI. Mense Septembri) fol. α⁶ A-Z⁴ a-z⁴ AA-GG⁴ HH⁶ II-KK⁴. pp. 1-436. [740

-- -- Aristotelis Rhetoricorum libri III. in Latinum sermonem conuersi, & Scholis ... explicati à Ioanne Sturmio. ... Argentinae Excudebat Theodosius Rihelius. (... M. D. LXX.) 8°. .§.⁸ A-3H⁸. ff. 2-429. [741

-- -- Aristotelis ... De Arte Rhetorica Libri Tres, cum M. Antonii Maioragii commentariis. Additis nuper Græco textu ad ipsius Maioragii versionem, & Petri Victorii sententiam emendato: ... per Fabium Paulinum Vtinensem ... Venetiis, Apud Franciscum de Franciscis Senensem, M D XCI. (*Colophon.*) fol. +⁸ ++⁴ A-Aa⁸ Bb-2°Bb⁶ Cc-Kk⁸ Ll⁶ Mm-Nn⁸. ff. 2-270. [742

-- -- *Latin.* Aristotelis rhetoricorum ad Theodecten, Georgio Trapezuntio interprete, libri III. Eiusdem rhetorices ad Alexandrum, à Francisco Philelpho in latinū versæ liber I. ... Parisiis Apud Simonem Colinæum 1540 (*Colophon.*) 8°. a-s⁸. ff. 3-142. [743

-- -- Rhetoricorum Aristotelis libri tres, interprete Hermolao Barbaro P. V. Commentaria in eosdem Danielis Barbari. Pauli Gerardi opera. ... M. D. XXXXIIII. (Venetiis apud Cominum de Tridino Montisferrati ...) 4°. ✠⁴ A-BB⁸ CC⁶. ff. 1-202. [744

-- -- Danielis Barbari in tres libros rhetoricorum Aristotelis commentaria. Lugduni apud Seb. Gryphium, 1544. 8°. a-z⁸ A-K⁸. pp. 3-524. [745

-- -- Aristotelis Stagiritae, rhetoricorum libri III. Quos M. Antonius Maioragius vertebat. Venetiis per Ioannem Patauinum. (... M. D. LII.) 8°. A-O⁸. pp. 3-221. [746

-- -- Aristotelis de arte rhetorica Libri Tres. Carolo Sigonio Interprete. Bononiae, Ex Officina Alexandri Benatii. MDLXV. 4°. A-Bb⁴ (-Bb4, *presumably blank*). pp. 4-197. [747

-- -- Venetiis, Ex Officina Stellæ Iordani Ziletti. M D LXVI. 8°. a⁴ A-Q⁸ R⁴. pp. 2-262. [748

-- -- M. Antonii Maioragii in tres Aristotelis libros, De Arte Rhetorica, quos ipse Latinos fecit, Explanationes. ... Venetiis, Apud Franciscum Franciscium Senensem. M. D. LXXII. fol. *^{8} A-Ee^{8} Ff^{10} Gg-Hh^{8}. ff. 1-8, pp. 9-458. [749

-- -- Aristotelis rhetoricorum libri. duo M. Antonio Mureto Interprete. Romae, Apud Bartholomaeum Grassum. M. D. LXXXV. (... Excudebat Franciscus Zanettus. ...) 8°. †^{4} A-L^{8} M^{4}. pp. 1-180. [750

-- -- *Italian.* Tradottione antica de la rettorica d'Aristotile, nuouamente trouata. In Padoua ... (Stampata ... per M. Giacomo Fabriano L'Anno M. D. XLVIII.) 8°. a^{8} A-Z^{8}. ff. 1-184. [751

-- -- Rettorica d'Aristotile fatta in lingua Toscana dal Commendatore Annibal Caro. ... In Venetia, Al segno della Salamandra, M D LXX. 4°. a^{4} A-LL^{4}. pp. 2-270. [752

-- -- I tre libri della retorica d'Aristotele a Theodette; tradotti in lingua volgare, Da M. Alessandro Piccolomini. ... In Venetia, MDLXXI. Appresso Francesco de' Franceschi Sanese. (*Colophon.*). 4°. *^{4} **^{2} A-Nn^{4} Oo^{2}. pp. 2-292. [753

-- -- *Commentary.* Εις την Αριστοτελους ρητορικην υπομνημα ανωνυμον. Parisiis per Conradum Neobarium ... 1539. fol. a-c^{6} d-f^{4} g^{6} h-m^{4} n-o^{6} p-r^{4} s^{2}. ff. 4-80. [754

-- -- *Summaries.* Copiosissima Parafrase, Di M. Alessandro Piccolomini: Nel primo libro della Retorica d'Aristotele. ... Venetia per Giouanni Varisco, e compagni. M D LXV. (*Colophon.*) 4°. a^{4} A-Rr^{4} Ss^{6}. pp. 1-331. [755

-- -- Piena, et larga Parafrase; di M. Alessandro Piccolomini; nel secondo libro Della Retorica d'Aristotele à Theodette. ... In Venetia, Appresso Gio. Francesco Camotio ... M D LXIX. 4°. *^{4} A-3S^{4}. pp. 1-507. [756

-- -- Piena, et larga parafrase, di M. Alessandro Piccolomini, nel terzo libro della retorica d'Aristotele, à Theodette. ... In Venetia, Per Giouanni Varisco, & compagni. M D LXXII. 4°. *^{4} A-4D^{4} (-4D4, *presumably blank*). pp. 1-582. [757

-- -- Antonii Riccoboni paraphrasis in rhetoricam Aristotelis ... Francofurdi, Apud Andreæ Wecheli heredes, Claudium Marnium, & Ioannem Aubrium, anno MDLXXXVIII. ... 8°. a-y^{8} z^{2}. pp. 9-354. [758

-- -- Piena, et larga Parafrase; di M. Alessandro Piccolomini; nel secondo libro Della Retorica d'Aristotele à Theodette. ... In Venetia, Appresso gli Heredi di Giouanni Varisco. (... M. D. XCII.) 4°. ✠^{4} A-Ii^{8}. pp. 1-503. [759

-- *Secreta secretorum (suppositious). Latin.* Aristotelis ... secretum secretorum ... De regum regimine: De sanitatis conseruatione. De physionomia. Eiusdem de signis tempestatum uentorum & aquarum. Eiusdem de mineralibus Alexandri Aphrodisei ... de intellectu. Auerrois ... de anime beatitudine. Alexandri Achillini bononiensis de Vniuersalibus. Alexandri macedonis ... de mirabilibus Indiæ ... (... impressus Bononiæ Impēsis Benedicti Hectoris. ... i50i. 26 octob. ...) fol. B.L. a-f^{6}. ff. 2-36. [760

-- -- *German.* Das aller edlest vñ bewertest Regiment der gesundtheit ... Aristotelis. ... Auss Arabischer Sprach durch Mayster Philipsen/ dem Bischoff von Valentia ... In das Latein verwandelt/ Nachmals auss dem latein in das Teutsch gebracht/ Bey Doctor Iohann Lorchner zů Spalt ... Durch Iohann Besolt in Truck verordnet. M.D.XXX. (Gedruckt zů Augspurg durch Heynrich Stayner/ Am .28. Decembris ...) 4°. A-M^{4} (-A4) N^{2}. ff. I-XLVI. [761

-- *Sophistici elenchi. Latin.* Super Elenchis Augustini Niphi ... Suessani in libros de Sophisticis Elenchis Aristotelis expositiones. Cum Textu ... ab ipso auctore interpretato. ... Venetiis Apud Octauianum Scotum. D. Amadei. F. 1542 (*Colophon.*) fol. B.L. A-F^{6} G^{4} H-L^{6} M-N^{4}. ff. 2-72. [762

-- -- Annotationes Alexandri Aphrodisiensis ... in librum elenchorum ... Aristotelis ... Guilelmo Dorotheo Veneto interprete. ... Parisiis Imprimebat Simon Colinæus sibi & Ioanni Roigny. 1542. fol. A-H^{6}. ff. 2-47. [763

-- *Theologia (suppositious). Latin.* Sapientissimi Philosophi Aristotelis stagiritae. Theologia siue mistica Phylosophia secundu3 Aegyptios ... (Excussum in ... Roma apud Iacobum Mazochium ... M.D.XIX. kl' Iunii.) 4°. B.L. A-I^{4} k^{4} a-z^{4}. ff. 1-92. [764

-- -- Libri quatuordecim qui Aristotelis esse dicuntur, de secretiore parte diuinæ sapientiæ secundum Ægyptios. ... Opus ... recognitum & illustratum scholiis ... per Iacobum

Carpentarium, Claromontanum Bellouacum. Parisiis, Ex officina Iacobi du Puys ... 1571. ... 4°. ā⁴ A-L⁴ M² N-Pp⁴ ā⁴ ē⁴ ī². ff. 2-150. [765

-- *Topica. Latin.* Aristotelis ... Topica inuentio in octo secta Libros/ a ... Augustino Nipho ... interpetrata atq3 exposita ... Venetiis. M.D.XXXV. ... (... Apud Octauianum Scotum.) fol. B.L. a-x⁶ A-C⁶ D-E⁴. ff. 2-152. [766

-- -- Alexandri Aphrodisei ... in octo libros topicorum ... Aristotelis Commentatio ... Guilelmo Dorotheo Veneto interprete. ... Venetijs Apud Hieronymum Scotum. 1541. (*Colophon.*) fol. B.L. A-Q⁶ R-S⁴ (-S4, *presumably blank*). ff. 3-103. [767

-- *Selections.* Auctoritates aristotelis Senece Boetii/ Platonis/ Apulei/ Affricani Empedoclis Porphirii et Gilberti porritani (Impressū p Iohāne petit .xx. Anno dñi millesimo quingentesimosexto. Die vero mensis Ianuarii.) 8°. B.L. [a]⁸ b-h⁸ i⁴. ff. 2-68. [768

-- -- Autoritates Aristotelis ... insup ꝛ platonis Boetij Senece Apulei Aphricani Porphyrij Auerroys Gilberti Porritani ... (Impressum est in publica Calchographia Liberorū ... Henrici Quentel. Anno ... Nono supra Millesimum quingentesimum.) 4°. B.L. A-F⁶·⁴ G-K⁶. f. 4 (A5). [769

-- Aristotelis sententiae omnes vndiquaque selectissimae ... His accesserunt & aliæ ex variis Senecæ, Boëtij, & Apuleij libellis sententiæ ... Parisiis. Apud Hieronymum de Marnef ... 1560. 16°. A-O⁸. pp. 3-219. [770

-- Thesauri Aristotelis Stagiritae libri XIIII. commentariis illustrati. ... Autore Petro Sainctfleur Monspeliensi. ... Parisiis, Apud Martinum Iuuenem ... 1562. ... 16°. *-**⁸ a-z⁸ A-Mm⁸. ff. 2-463. [771

-- Florum illustriorum Aristotelis ex vniuersa eius philosophia collectorum ... libri tres. Per Iacobum Bouchereau Parisinum. Parisiis, Apud Hieronymum de Marnef, & Gulielmum Cauellat ... 1575. 16°. †⁸ A-Yy⁸. ff. 1-354. [772

-- *Summaries.* Textus octo Phisicorū Aristotelis/ Necnō libroꝝ naturalium/ cū sex eiusdē Metaphysices/ pm traditionē seu abbreuiationē .M. Thome Bricot ... Nup ab Orontio Fine Delphinate ... reuisus ... [Parisiis] Venundantur a Reginaldo Chaudiere. (Impressum ... Apud Michaelem Lesclencher ... Anno ... Millesimo quingētesimo decimo septimo. Octobris die .vij.) 8°. B.L. a⁸ B-X⁸ y⁴. [773

-- In hoc opere cōtinenter totius Philosophie naturalis Paraphrases ... Introductio in libros physicoꝝ Paraphrasis octo physicoꝝ Aristotelis ... Ex officina Henrici Stephani. (Impressum in alma Parhisiorū achademia ... 1510 Vicesima secunda octobris) fol. B.L. a-z⁸ A-K⁸ L⁴. ff. 2-270. [774

-- -- Totius naturalis philosophiae Aristotelis paraphrases per Iacobum Fabrum Stapulensem recognitæ ... & scholijs ...Iudoci Clichthouei illustratæ ... Friburgi Brisgoiae, excudebat Ioannes Faber Emmeus Iuliacensis Anno M. D. XL. (*Colophon.*) fol. a⁶ A-XX⁶ YY⁸. ff. I-CCLXXII. [775

-- Librorum Aristotelis. Physica auscultatione, De [*vinculum*] Generatione & corruptione, Longitudine & breuitate uitæ, Vita & morte animalium, Anima, compendium, per Ioannem Lonicerum. ... Marpurgi, in officina Christiani Egenolphi, Anno M. D. XL. (*Colophon.*) 4°. A-Z⁴ a-k⁴. ff. 2-130. [776

-- Compendio de toda la Philosophia Natural de Aristoteles, traduzido en metro Castellano ...: por vn Collegial en el Collegio de nuestra Señora la Real de Hirach. Fue Impresso en ... Stella, por Adrian de Anuerez. M. D. XLVII. 4°. A-G⁸ (-G8, *presumably blank*). [777

-- In Aristotelis vniuersam naturalem philosophiam ... Theodori Metochitæ Paraphrasis ... Basileæ, per Nicolaum Bryling. M. D. LXII. 4°. *⁴ a-z⁴ A-Zz⁴ AA-RR⁴ A-C⁴. pp. 1-675. [778

-- Themistii ... paraphrasis in Aristotelis posteriora, & physica. In libros item de anima, memoria et reminiscentia, somno et vigilia, insomniis, & diuinatione per somnum. Hermolao Barbaro ... Interprete. ... Additoq; ... contradictionibus ac solutionibus Marci Antonii Zimarræ in dictis eiusdem Themistii ... Venetijs Apud Hieronymum Scotum. 1542 fol. ✠-✠✠⁴ a-i⁴ k-z⁶ ꝛ⁶ ꝯ⁶ ꝶ⁶ aa-ff⁶ gg-hh⁴. pp. 1-363. ¶y4 *misbound before* y3. [779

-- Epitome philosophiae naturalis, ex Aristotelis ... libris ... excerpta ... Per Georgium Lieblerum ... Basileae, per Ioannem Oporinum. (... M.D.LXVI. Mense Maio.) 8°. α⁸ β⁴ a-u⁸ x⁴. pp. 1-302. [780

-- Somma della filosofia d'Aristotele, e prima della dialettica. Raccolta da M. Lodouico Dolce. ... In Venetia appresso Gio. Battista, & Marchiò Sessa, & fratelli. (*Colophon.*) 8°. $*^4$ a-q^8 r^4 A-N^8 O^4. ff. 1-132, 2-104. ¶*Additional t.pp.:* (h6^r) Abbreuiatione della moral filosofia di Aristotele ... In Venetia. (A1^r) Somma di tutta la natural filosofia ... In Venetia. [781

-- -- *Another copy.* [782

ARISTOXENUS. Aristoxeni ... harmonicorum elementorum libri III. Cl. Ptolemæi Harmonicorum, seu de Musica lib. III. Aristotelis de obiecto Auditus fragmentum ex Porphyrij commentarijs. Omnia ... latine conscripta & edita ab Ant. Gogauino Grauiensi. ... Venetijs, Apud Vincentium Valgrisium, M D LXII. 4°. A-V^4. pp. 7-160. ¶*Apparently lacks 4 ll. (one of them blank) at the end.* [783

ARLENIUS, ARNOLDUS, PERAXYLUS. Lexicon Graecolatinum ... Venetiis apud Alexandrum Bruciolum, & Fratres eius. M. D. XLVI. (... M. D. XLV.) fol. π^4 a-$4d^6$ $4e^4$ α-η^6 θ^8. ¶*Additional t.p.* (α1^r): Farrago libellorum ... Cyrilli opusculum de dictionibus, quæ accentu uariant significatum. Ammonius de similitudine ac differentia dictionum. De re militari ueterum, & nominibus præfectorum libellus. Orbicii de ordinibus exercitus. In quibus dictionibus addatur, uel abiicitur, ex Choerobosco ... De proprietate linguæ Græcæ, ex Ioanne Grammatico, Plutarcho & Corintho. De passionibus dictionum, ex Tryphone Grammatico. ... [784

ARLES Y ANDOSILLA, MARTINEZ DE. Tractatus De Superstitionibus, contra maleficia seu sortilegia quae hodie vigent in orbe terrarum ... Romæ, Apud Vincentium Luchinum. 1559. (Romae apud Vincentium Lucrinum 1560) 8°. a-h^8 I^8. ff. 1-71. (Lea.) [785

ARNAUD, ANDRÉ. Ioci. G. du V. ... Auenioni, ex typograph. Iacobi Bramereau. 1600. ... 12°. A-I^{12} K^6. pp. 1-216. [786

ARNAULD, ANTOINE. L'antiespagnol, Oder Ausfuͤhrliche Erklerunge/ Wie der Koͤnig auss Spanien sich ... ein Protector vber das gewaltige Frantzoͤsische Koͤnigreich nennet ... Trewlich auss Frantzoͤsischer Sprache/ durch einen natuͤrlichen Castilianern/ verdeudscht. Gedruckt ausserhalb Madrill/ Durch Giovan Spinardum/ in Basilisco [= Basel, Samuel Apiarius] ... 1590. 4°. A-E^4. ¶*Translator: Johann Fischart.* [787

-- Philippica ... nomine Universitatis Parisiensis actricis, in Jesuitas reos. ... Ex Gallico Latina facta. Anno cIↄ Iↄ XCIV. 8°. A-G^8. pp. 3-112. [788

ARNIGIO, BARTOLOMMEO. Prima canzone ..., Nellaquale si celebra la ... Vittoria della Christiana Lega in Mare contra l'Armata Turchesca. In Venetia, appresso Giorgio Angelieri. M.D.LXXII. 4°. A^4. [789

ARNOBIUS AFER. Arnobii disputationum aduersus gentes libri septem ... Theodori Canteri Vltraiectini ... Notæ ... Antuerpiæ, Ex officina Christophori Plantini. M. D. LXXXII. 8°. A-S^8 (-S8, *blank*). pp. 3-285. [790

ARNOLD, RICHARD. In this boke is conteined yͤ names of the baylyfs Custose mayers and sherefs of yͤ cyte of london ... [Southwark, Peter Treveris, 1521.] fol. B.L. A^4 (-A1) B^8 C^4 B^4 C-E^8 F-Q^4 R^8 S-V^6 (-V6, *presumably blank*). *S.T.C.* 783. (Biddle.) [791

ARNOLDUS DE TUNGRIS. Ein Grundtlich vnd lieplich vnderweisung/ Wie man die heiligen im himel ... anruffen soll. 1536. ... (Gedruckt zu Leiptzick ... Melchior Lotter.) 4°. A-H^4. [792

ARNOLFINI, BARTOLOMMEO. Oratio habita ad ... Leonē X. Pont. Max. per ... Bartholomeū Arnolphū ... pro publica obedientia Senatus populiq3 Luceñ. noīe. [Romae, Marcellus Silber, c. 1513.] 4°. π^4. [793

ARRIANUS, FLAVIUS. Αρριανου περι Αλεξανδρου αναβασεως. Arriani de ascensu Alexandri. ... MDXXXV (Venetiis in ædibus Bartholomæi Zanetti Casterzagensis, ære uero, & diligentia Ioannis Francisci Trincaueli. ... Mēse Septēbri.) 8°. $*^4$ α-ω^8 αα-$\eta\eta^8$. [794

-- -- Αρριανου περι Αλεξανδρου αναβασεως ιστοριων βιβλία ὀκτώ. Arriani de expeditione siue rebus gestis Alexandri ... libri octo ... Basileae. (Ἐτυπώθη ... ἀναλώμασι Ῥοβέρτου τοῦ Χειμερινοῦ, ἔτει τῷ ... χιλιοστῷ πεντακοσιοστῷ τριακοστῷ ἐννατῳ [1539], μουνυχιῶνος μήνός.) 8°. α^8 a-z^8 A-R^8. [795

-- -- Αρριανου περι αναβασεως Αλεξάνδρου, ἱστοριῶν Βιβλία ῆ. Arriani (qui alter Xenophon vocatus fuit) de expedit. Alex. magni, Historiarum Libri VIII. Ex Bonauent. Vulcanii Brug. noua interpretatione. ... Alexandri vita, ex Plut. Eiusdem libri II, de fortuna vel virtute Alexandri. [Genevae,] Anno M. D. LXXV. Excudebat Henr. Stephanus ... fol. $*^6$ A-Q^6 R^4 a-g^6. pp. 1-198, 1-68. [796

-- -- Arriani historia De Rebus gestis Alexandri Macedonis e greco nuper traducta. fol. a-b^6 c-e^4 f-l^6 m^4 n^6 aa-bb^6 A^{4+2}. ¶*Translator: Charolus Valgulinus Brixianus.* [797

-- -- Les faicts & cõquestes d'Alexandre le grand ... Traduicts nouuellement de Grec en François par Cl. Vuitart ... A Paris, De l'Imprimerie de Federic Morel ... M. D. LXXXI. ... 4°. $\bar{a}^4$ $\bar{e}^2$ a-z^4 A-Z^4 &^{4}. pp. 1-361. [798

-- Arriani Nicomediensis de Epicteti philosophi ... dissertationibus Libri IIII ... Iacobo Scheggio ... Tubingensi interprete. Accessit Epicteti enchiridion, Angelo Politiano interprete. Græca etiam Latinis adiunximus ... Basileae, per Ioannem Oporinum. (... M.D.LIIII. Mense Martio.) 4°. α^4 a-z^4 A-Aa^4 A-Ff^4. pp. 1-371, 1-231. (Lea.) [799

-- Αρριανου περι πλους ευξεινου γοντου. ... Arriani & Hannonis periplus. Plutarchus de fluminibus & montibus. Strabonis epitome. Basileae anno M. D. XXXIII. (Ετυπώθη ... παρ' Ἱερωνύμῳ Φρωβενίῳ καὶ Νικολάῳ τῷ Ἐπισκοπίῳ ...) 4°. α-β^4 a-z^4 A-C^4. pp. 1-205. [800

ARS. Ars notariatus 8°. B.L. a^8 b^4. [801

ARSENIOS, archbishop of Malvasia. Σχολια των πανυ δοκιμων εις ἑπτὰ τραγωδίας του Ευριπιδου ... Scholia in septem Euripidis tragoedias ex antiquis exemplarib. ab Arsenio archiepiscopo Monembasiæ collecta ... Basileae, per Ioannem Heruagium. 1544. (... μεταγειτνιῶνος μενὸς.) 8°. $+^4$ A-Ω^8 (-A8) Αα-$\Lambda\lambda^8$ $M\mu^4$. pp. 17-580. [802

ARSENIUS, ARISTOBULUS. [1] Αποφθέγματα φιλοσόφων ... συλλεγέντα, παρὰ Αρσενίου ... Præclara dicta Philosophorum, Imperatorum, Oratorumq3, & Poetarum, ab Arsenio ... collecta. [Romae, Zacharias Kallierges, c. 1519.] 8°. α-ξ^8 o^4. [2] Γέρας εἰμ' ὀνομάσειας σπάνιον τῶν σπουδαίων, ὀυκ ἂν ἁμάρτοις δηλαδὴ, τῆς Αληθείας φίλε. 8°. α-γ^8 δ^6. [803

ARTEMIDORUS DALDIANUS. Artemidori Daldiani ... De somniorum interpretatione, libri Quinq3, Iam primum à Iano Cornario ... latina lingua conscripti. Basileae anno M.D.XXXIX. (Basileæ per Hieronymũ Frobenium & Nicolaum Episcopiũ, mense septembri, Anno 1539.) 8°. a-z^8 A-G^8. pp. 4-479. ¶*T.p. slightly defective.* (Lea.) [804

-- -- Les iugemens astronomiques des songes: par Artemidorus ... Plus le liure d'Auguste Niphus, des Diuinations & Augures: par Antoine de Moulin Masconnois. A Rouen, Chez Thomas Mallard ... [1584]. 16°. A-S^8. ff. 2-89, 2-49. ¶*Translator: Charles Fontaine.* [805

-- -- Artemidoro Daldiano ... dell'interpretatione de' sogni. Nuouamente di Greco in volgare, tradotto per Pietro Lauro Modonese. ... In Vinegia appresso Gabriel Giolito de' Ferrari. M D LVIII. (*Colophon.*) 8°. $*^8$ A-S^8 T^4. ff. 1-147. (Lea.) [806

ARTICULI. Articuli ad narrationes nouas pertim. formati. Londini in aedibus Roberti Redman. Anno. M.D.XXXIX. 8°. A-D^8. *S.T.C.* 818. (Biddle.) [807

-- Articuli fidei. (Rothomagi impressus. Impensis Raulini gaultier ... [c. 1510.]) 16°. B.L. $[A]^8$ B^4. [808

ARTIKEL. Die Artikel vnd bewerung derselbigen/ so die Prelaten/ Ebt/ Stifft vnd Cloͤster haben eyngelegt/ in Lutherischen sachen ... M.D.XXiiij. 4°. A-C^4 D^2. [809

ARTZNEI. Artzney Buchlein/ wider allerlei kranckeyten vnd gebrechen der tzeen/ getzogen auss dem Galeno ... vnd andern mehr der Artzney Doctorn ... M. D. XXX. (Gedruckt tzu Leyptzigk durch Michael Blum. ...) 8°. A-C^8. (School of Dentistry.) [810

ASCHAM, ROGER. ... Rogeri Aschami ... Familiarum Epistolarum libri tres ... Addita sunt ... Rogeri Aschami Poemata. Omnia ... collecta operâ & studio E. G. Adiecta est ... eiusdem E. G. Oratio, de vita & obitu Rogeri Aschami ... Londini, In officina Typographica Ar. Hatfield pro Francisco Coldocke. 1590 (... 1589.) 8°. A-Mm8. pp. 1-540. *S.T.C.* 829. ¶*Additional t.p.* (Dd8r): Ioannis Sturmii, Hieronymi Osorii, aliorumque epistolæ ... 1589. [811

ASCONIUS PEDIANUS. Asconii Pediani explanatio In Ciceronis orationes in C. Verrem, In orationem pro C. Cornelio, In orationem contra competitores, In orationem pro M. Scauro, In orationem contra L. Pisonem, In orationem pro Milone. Scholia Pauli Manutii. ... Venetiis, [Aldine press,] M. D. LXIII. (*Colophon.*) 8°. A8 AA4 B-O8. ff. 1-104. [812

-- -- Q. Asco. Pediani in Ciceronis orationes commentarii atq; Georgius Trapezuntius, de artificio Ciceronianæ orationis. Pro .Q. Ligurio ... (Florentiæ, per hæredes Philippi Iuntæ Florentini. M.D.XIX. ...) 8°. A-F8 g-r8. ff. 2-128. [813

ASIANI, GASPARO. La pronuba comedia ... In Mantoua per Francesco Osanna ... MDLXXXVIII. 8°. A-G8. pp. 3-110. [814

ASINARI, FEDERICO. La Gismonda tragedia del Signor Torquato Tasso ... A Paris, Chez Pierre Cheuillot ... 1587. 8°. ã8 A-E8. ff. 1-40. [815

-- -- Il Tancredi tragedia del Signor Conte di Camerano dal Sig. Gherardo Borgogni di nuouo posta in luce. ... In Bergamo, Per Comino Ventura. MDLXXXVIII. 4°. a4 A-F8 G4. ff. 1-51. [816

ASOLA, GIOVANNI MATTEO. [1] [Cantus ...] 4°. A12 (-A1, A12). pp. 1-20 *present.* [2] Altus Missae octonis compositae tonis ... Per R.D. Io: Matthæum Asulam Veronensem, edite. Cum quatuor vocibus. Venetiis Apud Iacobum Vincentium, & Riciardum Amadinum, socios. M D LXXXVI. C12. pp. 1-22. [3] [Bassus ...] D12 (-D1-3, D10-12). pp. 5-16 *present.* (Music.) [817

-- [1] Officium maioris hebdomadæ ... quatuor paribus decantanda vocibus. ... Tenor. Venetiis apud Riciardum Amadinum. MDXCV. 4°. E-H4. pp. 1-30. [2] ... Bassus. *Same imprint.* 4°. N-Q4. pp. 1-30. (Music.) [818

ASSARACO SARRACHO, ANDREA. Historiae nouae ac veteres: ab nouiss. Francisci Sfortiae temporibus ... hoc dialogo elegiaco compraehenduntur. (Impressum Mediolani in officina libraria Gotardi Pontici ... M.D.XVI. die .xxiiii. Decembris.) fol. A-G8 (-A1, *presumably blank*) H6 I-M8 N10 O8. ff. IIII-CIIII. [819

ASSER, JOANNES. [Alfredi regis res gestae. London, John Day, 1574.] fol. A4 (-A1) ¶2 (-¶2, *blank*) A-F4. pp. 1-40. *S.T.C.* 863. [820

ASSISI. [1] [Magnifice Ciuitatis Asisij Statutorum. Liber primus de regimine Reipublica ...] (Perusiae. In aedibus Hieronymi Chartularii.) fol. ✠6 (-✠1, ✠6, *the latter presumably blank;* ✠2-5 *bound after* M6) A-M6. ff. [I]-LXXII. ¶A1, A2 *defective and mounted.* [2] ... Statutorum Liber Secundus de Ciuilibus causis. ... (Perusiae, In Aedibus Hieronymi Chartularij. M.D.XLI.) AA-DD6. ff. 1-23. [3] Tabula Tertij Libri Statutorum ... Asisij De criminalibus causis. (... opus perfectum extitit Perusie per Hieronymum Francisci Baldasarris de carthuarijs. MDXLIII. Die .xj. Augusti.) 3A6 3B4 3C-3D6 3E4. ff. 1-26. [4] Tabula Quarti Libri Statutoru3 ... Asisij De extraordinarijs. (... Die .ix. Septemb. 1543.) π2 4A-4B6 4C8. ff. 1-19. [5] Tabula Quinti Libri ... De dãnis datis. (... Die .xvij. Nouemb. 1543.) π2 5A-5C6 5D4. ff. 1-22. (Lea.) [821

ASTESANUS DE AST. Summa Astensis. ℭ ... fratris Astesani de ast. ... Sũma de casib9 ... octo librorum volumina duabus partibus condistincta habens. ... Venundãtur Lugduni a Stephano gueynard: als pinet ... (sumptibus ... Stephani gueynard als pinet. Opera ... Guilhelmi huyon imp̃ssoris ... Anno dñi. M.cccccxix. Die ꝟo. iiij. Maij.) fol. a-z8 A-B8 C4 aa-zz8 AA-LL8. ff. iij-cciij, i-ccxxxviij. (Lea.) [822

ASTI. [1] ... Hec sunt capitula statuta & ordinamenta Composita ... per ... Dños Antonium de moriena. Philippum de uiallo legũ doctores. Antonium alamannum Iuris peritum. Loisium pellatam. Andreonum ricium. Roban donum ottinum. Gasparonum alionum. Manuelem serrariū. & Antonium paterium ciues Astenses ... (Impressus ... Ast per Franciscum Garonum de liburno ... 1534. Die. 16. Mensis May.) fol. A^8 (-A6; A3 *duplicated*) B-M^8 N-O^9. ff. 1-109. [2] Statuta Reuarum Ciuitatis Ast. (Impressum Ast per Franciscum Garonum de Liburno. ... M.D.XXXIII. Die. vi. Augusti.) A^8 B^6 C^4 (-C2, C3). ff. 2-18. (Lea.) [823

-- *Diocese.* Decreti della prima sinodo diocesana Astense ... In Asti, Per Giouanni, & Virgilio Giangrandi Fratelli. M. D. LXXXIX. (*Colophon.*) 4°. $++^4$ A-N^4. pp. 1-102. [824

-- Decreta edita, et promulgata In Synodo Dioecesana Astensi secunda. ... Astæ, Apud Virgilium de Zangrandis. M. D. XCI. 4°. π^2 A^6 B^8. pp. 1-26. [825

ATANAGI, DIONIGI. De le lettere di tredici huomini illustri libri tredici. ... In Venetia, L'anno M D LIIII. 8°. a^8 A-Fe^8 Ff^4. ff. 1-228. [826

-- -- Lettere di XIII. huomini illustri. ... In Venetia Per Comin da Trino di Monferrato. M D LXI. (*Colophon.*) 8°. A-$3C^8$. pp. 1-768. [827

-- De le lettere facete, et piaceuoli di diuersi grandi huomini ... libro primo. Raccolte per M. Dionigi Atanagi ... In Venetia, appresso Bolognino Zaltieri, M D LXI. (*Colophon.*) 8°. $*^8$ A-KK^8. pp. 1-527. [828

-- -- In Venetia, Appresso Fabio, & Agostino Zopini, Fratelli. M D LXXXII. 8°. $*^6$ A-Z^8 Aa^{10}. pp. 1-384. [829

-- [1] De le rime di diuersi nobili poeti Toscani, Raccolte da M. Dionigi Atanagi, libro primo. ... In Venetia. Appresso Lodouico Auanzo. M. D. LXV. 8°. a-b^8 A-Kk^8 Ll^4. ff. 1-236. [2] ... libro secondo. ... *Same imprint.* 8°. a^8 A-Mm^8 Nn^4. ff. 1-248. [830

-- [1] Rime di diuersi ... autori, In morte della Signora Irene delle Signore di Spilimbergo. ... In Venetia, appresso Domenico, & Gio. Battista Guerra, fratelli, 1561. 8°. A^8 Aa^4 B-L^8 M-N^6. pp. 2-179. ¶A1-3 *defective.* [2] Diuersorum praestantium poetarum carmina in obitu Irenes Spilimbergiae. Venetiis, M D LXI. 8°. a-d^8. pp. 6-57. [831

ATHENAEUS. Αθηναιου δειπνοσοφιστων βιβλια πεντεκαιδεκα. Athenaei deipnosophistarum libri XV. Isaacus Casaubonus recensuit ... Adiecti sunt eiusdem Casauboni in eundem scriptorem Animaduersionum libri XV. Addita est & Iacobi Dalechampii Cadomensis, Latina interpretatio. [Heidelbergae,] Apud Hieronymum Commelinum. Anno M.D.XCVII. fol. π^2 *-$4*^6$ a-$3m^6$ $3n^4$ (-3n4, *blank*). pp. 1-702. [832

-- -- Athenaei dipnosophistarum siue Coenæ sapientum Libri XV. Natale de Comitibus Veneto ... è Græca in Latinam linguam uertente. ... Venetiis apud Andream Arriuabenum ... M D L V I. fol. $*^6$ A-AA^6. pp. 1-288. (Lea.) [833

ATHANASIUS, S. Subnotata hic continentur Magni Athanasij in psalmos opusculum. Enchiridion Epicteti stoici. Basilij oratio de inuidia. Plutarchus de differētia inter odiū & inuidiā. Tabula Cebetis Thebani. ([Argentorati,] Mathias Schürerius ... ex officina sua impressoria ... emisit. Die viij. Iunij. Anno M.D.VIII.) 4°. A^8 B-C^4 D^6 E-G^4 H^6 I^4. ¶H4ᵛ: Basilij epistola: De vita solitaria ... [834

ATTENDOLO, GIOVANNI BATTISTA. Oratione ... Nell'essequie di Carlo d'Austria Principe di Spagna ... Con alcune rime di Diuersi in morte del medesimo, & di Carlo V. In Napoli, appresso Gioseppo Cacchi. 1571. 4° A-I^4. ff. 1-31. [835

ATTILA. La guerra d'Atila flagello di Dio. Tratta dallo Archiuo dei Prencipi D'Esti. (In Ferrara Per Francesco de' Rossi da Valenza. M. D. LXVIII.) 4°. [A]-Ii^4. ff. 3-127. [836

AUBERT, JACQUES. Iacobi Auberti Vindonis de metallorum ortu & causis contra Chemistas ... explicatio. Lugduni. Apud Iohannem Berion. 1575. 8°. A-D^8 E^4. pp. 3-69. (Smith.) [837

AUGSBURG. *Official publications.* Aussschreiben an die Römisch Kaiserlich vnd Künigkliche Maiestaten ... Von Burgermaister vnnd Ratgeben des ... Statt Augspurg/ Abthüung der Päpstischen Mess/ vnd annderer ergerlichen Ceremonien vnd Missbreüch belangende. 4°. A-C^4 D^6. ¶*Dated 17 January 1537.* [838

-- Warhaffte verantwurtung ... vō ... Christoffen Bischoffen zů Augspurg/ ... vff der Burgermaister vñ Ratgeben daselbst vnerfindtlich schmach gedicht ... 4°. a-e^4. ¶*Dated 26 February 1537.* [839

-- Ains Erbern Rats/ der Stat Augspurg/ Zucht vnd Pollicey Ordnung. M.D.XXXVII. 4°. a-d^4. [840

-- Reuerendissimi principis ... Othonis Cardinalis & Episcopi Augustani ... uera confutatio, responsio, & excusatio aduersus falsas & calumniosas nouitates, nuper ... diuulgatas. M.D.LVI. ... 4°. A-C^4. [841

-- -- Des Hochwürdigsten Fürsten ... Otho Cardinals/ vnd Bischouen zu Augspurg ... warhaffte ablainung ... wider die erdichten/ vnwarhafftige newe Zeytungen/ newlich ... aussgebrayt. M.D.LVI. ... 4°. A-D^4. [842

-- Publication/ dern in der Calender sach/ am ... Kayserlichen Camergericht zů Speyer ... für einen E. Raht der Statt Augspurg ... 1584. 4°. A^6 B^4. [843

-- Berůff So ein E. Raht der Statt Augspurg den 14. Iunij Anno 1584. auff den Plaͤtzen der Statt thůn vnd Publicieren lassen. 1584. 4°. A^4 B^2. [844

-- Abtruck der anzeyg vn̄ Protestation ... zů Augspurg in den Kirchen Augspurgischer Confession verlesen worden. 1584. 4°. A^8. [845

-- Gegründte Christliche Antwort der jetzigen Euangelischen Predicanten in der Statt Augspurg. Auff Doctor Georgen Müllers ... Send vnd Trostbrieff. ... Getruckt zů Augspurg/ durch Valentin Schoͤnigk ... M. D. LXXXVI. 4°. A-F^4 G^2 H^4. [846

-- Der Herren Pfleger vnd Geheimen Rath des ... Reichstatt Augspurg. Warhaffter gegenbericht/ der Augspurgischen Haͤndel vnd gegründte widertreybung D. Georg Müllers ... Famos gedichts. Getruckt zů Augspurg/ durch Valentin Schoͤnigk ... 1587. 4°. A-Cc^4. [847

-- -- *Another copy.* [848

-- Eines Ersamen Rahts der Statt Augspurg Hochzeyt Ordnung. M. D. XCIX. Getruckt zu Augspurg/ Durch Valentin Schoͤnigk ... 4°. A-D^4. [849

-- *Gymnasium S.J.* Catalogus librorum qui hoc extremo anno, M. D. IC. et deinceps sequenti, Augustæ, in Societatis Iesu gymnasio, explicabuntur. Dilingae, Apud Ioannem Mayer. s. sh. 44.5 × 30.5 cm. [8492

-- *Synod.* Acta et statuta. Synodi dioecesanæ Augustensis. ... Ingolstadii ex officina typographica Alexandri Vueissenhorn. Anno. M. D. XLIX. (... Mense Ianuario.) fol. A-H^4 (-H4, *presumably blank*). [850

-- Von dem new gebornen Abgott zu Babel. ... An die Kauffleut gen Augspůrg geschriebenn. ... 1550. 4°. π^4. [851

AUGSBURG CONFESSION. Kirchenordnung: Wie es ... zu Witteberg vnd in etlichen Chur vnd Fuͤrstenthum/ Herrschafften vnd Stedte der Augsburgischen Confession verwand/ gehalten wird. Witteberg: Gedruckt durch Hans Lufft. 1559. 4°. A-Z^4 a-n^4. ff. 2-144. [852

-- [1] Concordia Christliche/ Widerholete einmuͤtige Bekentnuͤs nachbenanter Churfuͤrsten/ Fuͤrsten vnd Stende Augspurgischer Confession ... Tübingen 1580. (... bey Georgen Gruppenbach. Anno M.D.LXXXI.) fol. a-b^4)(^{6} A-C^6 D^2 E-Z^6 a-c^6 d^8 e^6 f-g^4 h-v^6 x^2 y-z^6 AA-KK^6 LL^8 Lll-Nnn^6 Ooo^4. ff. 1-353. ¶*Additional t.p.* ($g1^r$): Gründtliche/ lautere/ Richtige/ vnd endtliche widerholung vnd erklaͤrung etlicher Artickel Augspurgischer Confession ... Tübingen 1580. [2] Vorzeichnuͤs der Zeugnissen heiliger Schrifft/ vnd der alten reinen Kirchenlehrer. ... Tübingen. 1580. A-C^6 D^8 (-D8, *presumably blank*). pp. 1-48. [853

AUGURELLO, GIOVANNI AURELIO. I. Aurelius Augurellus. (Venetiis in aedibus Aldi mense Aprili. M. D. V.) 8°. a-q^8. [854

-- Ioannis Aurelii Augurelli P. Ariminensis Chrysopoeiae libri .III. et Geronticon liber primus. (Impressit Simon Luerensis ... Venetiis ... M.D.XV.) 4°. a-n^4 o^6. (Smith.)[855

AUGUSTINE, S. Quattuor diui Augustini Libri, de Doctrina Christiana ... (Impressi ... Lipsi in officina Melchiaris Lotteri, Mense Maio, Anno &c, xv,) fol. A-H^6 I^4 K^6 (-K6, *presumably blank*). [856

-- D. Aurelii Augustini ... de Fide & operibus liber unus. Parisiis. Vænit apud Ioannem Roigny ... 1534. 16°. Aa-Gg^8. ff. 3-52. [857

-- D. Aurelii Augustini ... de Natura & Gratia, liber unus. Parisiis. Væmit apud Ioannem Roigny ... 1534. 16°. aa-hh⁸ i⁸ kk². ff. 2-67. [858

-- D. Aurelii Augustini ... de prædestinatione sanctorum liber primus. (Parisiis. Væmit apud Ioannem Roigny ... 1534.) 16°. a*-o*⁸ p*⁴. ff. 2-115. [859

-- Diui Aurelii Augustini ... de Spiritu & Litera, liber vnus. Venundantur apud Ambrosium Girault ... Parisiis. 1534. 16°. a-i⁸ k². ff. 2-71. [860

-- D. Aurelii Augustini enchiridion ad Laurentium, Siue summa et praecipua totius Christianæ religionis capita. ... commentariis illustratus. Per Lamb. Danaeum. ... [Genevae,] Apud Eustathium Vignon. M. D. LXXIX. 8°. *-**⁸ a-z⁸ A-V⁸ X⁴. ff. 1-332. [861

-- Liber epistolarum beati Augustini ... Venundatur [Parisiis] ab Ioanne Paruo & Iodoco Badio Ascensio. (... MDXV. ad decimūquartū Calendas Iulias.) fol. ā⁸ a-z⁸ A-I⁸ K⁶ a-d⁸. ff. I-CCLXII. [862

-- Diui Aurelii Augustini ... principia rhetorices. Parisiis Apud Simonem Colinæum. 1534 8°. a⁸ b⁴. ff. 3-12. [863

-- In hoc volumine continentur infrascripta. Regula beati Augustini episcopi. Constitutiones fratrum ordinis predicatorum [*and other documents*]. ... Impresse hec oīa sub ... frē Vincentio Bandello de Castronouo ... Mcccccv. die .x. Mensis Maij. ([x8ᵛ] Impressum Mediolani per Ioannem Angelū Scinzenzeler sub impensis Ioannis Iacobi & fratrum de lignano. ... M.ccccc.v. die x. Maij. [²e10ᵛ] Impressum Mediolani per Ioannem de Castelliono. ... M.ccccc.v. Die .viij. Mensis. Maij.) 4°. B.L. ♣⁶ a-s⁴ t⁸ v⁴ x⁸ y⁴ z⁶ &⁴ ɔ⁴ ꝶ⁴ Aa⁶ aa-bb⁴ cc⁶ A-B⁴ C-H⁸ I¹⁰ a-d⁸ e¹⁰⁺¹. ff. 1-48, 1-14, 1-64. [864

-- Sermones sancti Augustini ad heremitas. [*Device of Denis Roce.*] (Parisius impressi ... .1501. die vero .15 Februarii.) 8°. B.L. a-o⁸. [865

AUGUSTINIANS. Schlusse der Augustiner Veter yn yhrer versamlung tzu Wittenberg ... [1522.] 4°. π². [866

AURBACH, JOHANNES DE. Processus Iuris ... Iohannis de Aurbach vna cum lectura expositionibusq3 ... Iohannis de Eberhausen ... (Impssus Lipsi per ... wolfgangū Monacensem Anno ... Millesimo q̃ngentesimo duodecimo.) fol. B.L. A-D⁶ E⁴ F-H⁶ I⁴ K-Q⁶ R⁴ S-X⁶ Y-Z⁴ Aa⁶. ff. 2-j34. (Lea.) [867

AURELIUS, CORNELIUS. Batauia, siue de ... insulæ quam Rhenus on Hollandia facit situ, descriptione & laudibus; aduersus Gerardum Nouiomagum, Libri duo ... Bonauenturæ Vulcani operâ ... edita. Antuerpiæ, Apud Christophorum Plantinum. cIↄ. Iↄ. LXXXVI. 8°. *⁸ A-H⁸ I⁴. pp. 1-135. ¶*Includes:* 1) Aloisii Marliani De Batauiæ laudibus ... Epistola, 2) Cornelii Aurelii Epistolæ aliquot, 3) Eiusdem Diadema Imperatorium ..., 4) Ex Gerardi Nouiomagi Geldenhaurij Batauia. [868

AURELIUS VICTOR, SEXTUS. Il libro de gli huomini illustri di Gaio Plinio Cecilio, ridotto in lingua volgare. Le vite d'Alessandro, di M. Antonio, di Catone Vticese, di Cesare, & d'Ottauiano, aggiunteui per M. Dionigi Atanagi. ... In Venetia, M D LXII. Appresso Domenico Guerra, & Gio. Battista suo fratello. 8°. A-Aa⁸ Bb⁴. pp. 2-375. [869

AURIA, GIUSEPPE. Iosephi. Auriae Neapolitani oratio. De Vitæ Humanæ Fragilitate. ... Altera editio. Romæ, Apud Dominicum Basam. M. D. LXXXVIII. ... 4°. A-B⁴. pp. 4-16. [870

AUSONIUS, DECIUS MAGNUS. Ausonius. (Venetiis in aedibus Aldi et Andreae soceri mense Nouembri M. D. XVII.) 8°. a-n⁸ o⁴. ff. 2-107. [871

-- [1] D. Magni Ausonii Burdig. ... opera a Iosepho Scaligero, & Elia Vineto denuo recognita ... [Genevae,] Typis Iacobi Stoer M. D. XCV. 16°. ¶-¶¶⁸ a-g⁸. pp. 1-350. [2] Iosephi Scaligeri ... Ausoniarum lectionum libri duo. Adiectis præterea, Doctissimorum id genus authorum: vtpote Adriani Turnebi, Hadriani Iunij, Guilelmi Cāteri, Iusti Lypsij, & Eliæ Vineti notis. Excudebat Iacobus Stoer, M. D. XCV. 16°. A-Q⁸ R⁴. pp. 3-247. [872

AUSTRIA. *Ferdinand, archduke.* Des durchleüchtigen ... Ertzhertzog Ferdinanden vrteyl/ zwischeṇ dem Regiment ... in Osterreych so wider dasselb Regiment gestanden seind. Getruckt zů Freyburg [1522]. 4°. a⁴. [873

-- *Ferdinand, king of Hungary and Bohemia.* [Proclamation concerning laborers in the vineyards, with countersignatures.] Geben in ... Wienn/ am letzten tag des Monats Martij. Anno ꝛc. jm Sibenundtzwaintzigisten. ... s.sh. 33 × 45 cm. [874

-- Die New Pollicey vnd Ordnūg der Hanndtwercher vnd dienstuolck der Niderosterreichischen Lannde. fol. A-C^4 (-C4, *presumably blank*). ¶*Dated 1 April 1527.* [875

-- [Mandate forbidding the export of grain in order to sustain the fighting against the Turks and to combat inflation, with countersignatures.] Geben in ... Wienn/ am zwenundzwaintzigisten tag des Monats Aprilis. Anno ꝛc. jm Sibenundtzwaintzigisten ... s.sh. 32.5 × 43 cm. [876

-- [Mandate restricting the internment of beggars and other idlers, with countersignatures.] Geben in ... Wienn am fünfftzehendten tag des Monats Apprilis. Anno ꝛc. im Achtvndzwaintzigisten ... s.sh. 32 × 43.5 cm. [877

-- [Proclamation extending fiefs by one year, with countersignatures and seal.] Geben in ... Wienn/ am̄ Zwaintzigisten tag/ des Monats Decembris: Anno ꝛc. im̄ Achtundzwaintzigisten ... s.sh. 32.5 × 43.5 cm. [878

-- *Ferdinand, king of the Romans.* [Proclamation announcing a cessation of hostilities, preliminary to a meeting in Altenburg.] Geben in ... Wieñ/ am Zwenundzwaintzigisten tag des Monats Ianuarij. Anno ꝛc. jm Drewunddreyssigisten ... s.sh. 32.5 × 44.5 cm. ¶*Slightly defective.* [879

-- [Mandate against the use of firearms, especially by the common people and peasants, with stamped signature.] Geben in ... Wienn/ am Vierundtzwaintzigisten tag des Monats Nouembris. Anno ꝛc, jm Drewunddreissigisten ... s.sh. 57.5 × 34.5 cm. [880

-- [Order restraining his subjects in Austria from allowing their hounds to roam in game preserves, with countersignatures.] Geben in ... Wienn am dreyzehenden tag May Anno ꝛc. jm Neünunduiertzigisten ... s.sh. 31 × 43 com. [881

-- [Instructions to the clergy for the filling of vacancies in parishes, with stamped signature, countersignatures, and seal.] Geben in ... Wienn/ den Dreyssigisten tag des Monats Maij/ Anno ꝛc. im Einvndfünfftzigisten ... s.sh. 34.5 × 47.5 cm. ¶*Worn at the folds.* [882

-- [Mandate prohibiting the export of grain to halt rising prices.] Geben in ... Wienn am Zwenvndzwayntzigisten tag Septembris/ Anno ꝛc. im Ainssvndfünfftizigisten ... s.sh. 31 × 41 cm. [883

-- [Proclamation against depriving the clergy of their possessions and income, with countersignatures.] Geben in ... Wienn/ am Dreiundzwaintzigisten tag Februarij. Anno ꝛc. im Zwayvndfünfftzigisten ... s.sh. 31 × 42 cm. ¶*Slightly defective.* [884

-- [Proclamation forbidding the export of horses useful for the army, with stamped signature and countersignatures.] Geben in ... Wieñ/ den Zwenvndzwaintzigisten tag Septembris/ Anno ꝛc. im Zwayvndfünfftzigisten ... s.sh. 32 × 43.5 cm. [885

-- [Proclamation prohibiting poaching, with stamped signature and countersignatures.] Geben in ... Wieñ/ am Dreyzehenden tag des Monats Octobris/ Anno ꝛc. im Zwayvndfünffzigisten ... s.sh. 36 × 48 cm. [886

-- [Proclamation forbidding the misappropriation of ecclesiastical property, with stamped signature and countersignatures.] Geben in vnserm Schloss Ebersdorff den Letsten tag Octobris/ Anno ꝛc. im zwayvndfünfftzigisten ... s.sh. 35.5 × 47.5 cm. [887

-- [Proclamation restricting the holding of markets on Sundays and holy days, with stamped signature and countersignatures.] Geben in ... Wienn/ den Dreyzehenden tag Martzii Anno/ ꝛc. im Viervndfünfftzigisten ... s.sh. 31 × 43 cm. [888

-- Reformation vnnd ernewerung der Lanndtgerichts ordnung so weilendt Kaiser Maximilian ... im Ertzhertzogthumb Osterreych vnnder der Enns aufgericht hat. ... Gedruckt zu Wienn durch Iohannem Singriener 1555. fol. A-B^4 (-B4, *presumbaly blank*). [889

-- [Proclamation prescribing penalties for poachers, with countersignatures and seal.] Geben inn ... Augspurg/ den zwenvndzwaintzigisten tag Iunii/ ... Fünfftzehenhundert/ vnd im fünffvndfünfftzigisten ... s.sh. 32 × 44 cm. [890

-- [Mandate prohibiting the export of oats without permission, with countersignatures.] Geben in ... Wienn/ am dreyzehenden tag May/ Anno/ ꝛc. im Siebenundfünfftzigisten ... s.sh. 32.5 × 43 cm. [891

-- GerichtsProcess vnd ordnung des Landssrechtens des ... Ertzhertzogthumbs Osterreich vnnder der Enns. ... Gedruckt zů Wienn durch Hans Singreiner/ Anno M. D. LIX. (*Colophon.*) fol. A-L⁴. ff. I-XXXIX. (Biddle.) [892

-- [Law restraining blasphemy, drunkenness, gluttony, games, adultery, wanton intercourse, vanity of dress, extravagant weddings, usury, &c., with countersignatures and seal.] Geben in ... Wienn/ den Fünfften tag Inauarij/ Anno ꝛc. im Sechtzigisten ... s.sh. 43 × 59 cm. [893

-- Römischer ... Küniglicher Mayestat ... Ordnung vnnd Reformation güter Pollicey. ... Anno 1552. ... Gedruckht zů Wienn in Osterreich/ durch Iohannem Syngriener. Anno M. D. LX. fol. A-I⁴ K⁶. ff. I-XI. (Biddle.) [894

-- *Ferdinand, Roman emperor.* [Mandate prohibiting crimes and abuses of mercenaries, with stamped signature and countersignature.] Geben in ... Wienn/ den Fünffzehenden tag May/ ꝛc. im Ainvndsechtzigisten ... s.sh. 34.5 × 54.5 cm. [895

-- [Prohibition of entry into Vienna of persons from places where inhabitants have died within 30 days from the plague.] Geben in ... Wienn den Ersten tag Augusti/ Anno/ ꝛc. im Ainvndsechtzigisten ... s.sh. 32.5 × 44.5 cm. [896

-- [Mandate forbidding the exportation of grain.] Geben in ... Wienn den Andern tag Ianuarij Anno ꝛc. im Zwayvndsechtzigisten ... s.sh. 33 × 43 cm. [897

-- [Proclamation restricting the purchase of meat in Vienna by non-residents.] Geben in ... Wienn den Sechsten tag Martij/ Anno/ ꝛc. im Zwayundsechtzigisten ... s.sh. 33 × 44 cm. [898

-- [Prohibition of entry into Vienna of persons from infected places, with countersignature.] Geben in ... Wienn den Achtvndzwaintzigisten tag des Monats Augusti/ im Fünfzehenhundertisten/ vnd Zwayvndsechtzigisten [Jahr] ... s.sh. 37 × 54 cm. ¶*Defective.* [899

-- [Mandate against devalued coins.] Geben in ... Wienn am Sibenden tag Octobris/ Anno ꝛc. Zwayundsechtzigisten ... s.sh. 33 × 47.5 cm. [900

-- [Mandate prohibiting the sale or purchase of ecclesiastical property, with stamped signature, countersignature, and seal.] Geben in ... Ynsprugg/ den Sybendentag des Monats Martij. Anno ꝛc. im Dreyvndsechtzigisten ... s.sh. 32.5 × 47.5 cm. [901

-- [Renewal of the mandate on the sale and export of tallow, with countersignature.] Geben in ... Wienn/ den Andern tag Nouembris/ Anno ꝛc. im Dreyundsechtzigisten ... s.sh. 36 × 50.5 cm. [902

-- *Karl, archduke.* [Proclamation prohibiting the sale of cattle abroad.] Geben in ... Wienn am zwenundzwaintzigisten tag Decembris/ Anno/ ꝛc. im Vierundsechtzigisten. s.sh. 33 × 44.5 cm. [903

-- *Maximilian II, Roman emperor.* [Renewal of his father's mandate against the abuses of mercenaries, with countersignatures.] Geben in ... Wienn/ den Vierundzwaintzigisten tag des Monats May/ Anno ꝛc. im Fünffundsechtzigisten ... s.sh. 37 × 50 cm. [904

-- [Proclamation against the withholding of bread from the poor.] Geben in ... Wienn den vierten tag Februarij/ Año ꝛc. im Sibenzigisten ... s.sh. 33 × 41 cm. [905

-- -- *Another copy.* [906

-- [Mandate suspending duties and taxes on grain, flour, and bread to help the poor during the famine.] Geben in ... Wienn am Neunvndzwaintzigisten tag Aprilis. Anno/ ꝛc. im Sibentzigisten ... s.sh. 32 × 41 cm. [907

-- [Mandate renewing the regulation of the export and sale of tallow, with countersignatures and seal.] Geben in ... Wienn den zwelfften tag Iulij/ Anno/ ꝛc. im Sibentzigisten ... s.sh. 32 × 41.5 cm. [908

-- -- *Variant* (Geben in ... Winn.) [909

-- [Proclamation deprecating the rising cost of grain, to the detriment of the poor, with countersignatures.] Geben in ... Wien/ den Sechtzehenden tag Iulij/ Anno ꝛc. im Sibentzigisten ... s.sh. 38.5 × 54 cm. [910

-- [Mandate suspending fairs and church festivities during the plague and prohibiting visits to fairs outside the country.] Geben in ... Corneuburg am zwaintzigisten tag Septembris/ Anno/ ꝛc. im Sibentzigisten ... s.sh. 32 × 41 cm. [911

-- [Order suspending all types of levies on the importation of grain.] Geben in ... Corneuburg am andern tag Nouembris/ Anno ꝛc. im Sibenzigisten ... s.sh. 33 × 40.5 cm. [912

-- [Mandate forbidding the hoarding of grain, with countersignatures.] Geben in ... Corneuburg/ den sechsten tag dits Monats Nouembris Anno/ ꝛc. im Sibentzigisten ... s.sh. 32.5 × 40.5 cm. [913

-- [Mandate on the care of roads.] Geben in ... Corneuburg/ den Achzehenden tag Decembris Anno ꝛc. im Sibenzigisten ... s.sh. 33.5 × 47 cm. [914

-- [Proclamation deploring the high cost of grain and bread, to the detriment of the poor.] Geben in ... Wienn am zwainzigisten tag Aprilis/ Anno/ ꝛc. im Ainvndsibentzigisten ... s.sh. 38 × 53.5 cm. [915

-- [Mandate regulating the immigration of foreign, suspect, and unemployed persons, their registration, and their elimination if necessary, with countersignatures.] Geben in ... Wienn am zwainzigisten tag May/ Anno/ ꝛc. im Ainvndsibentzigisten ... s.sh. 32 × 42.5 cm. [916

-- [Proclamation setting prices for meat.] Geben in ... Wienn/ den Achten tag May/ Anno ꝛc. im Zwaivndsibentzigisten ... s.sh. 31.5 × 44 cm. [917

-- [Order regulating the importation of firewood into Vienna for the purpose of controling the price.] Geben in ... Wienn/ am Zwenundzwaintzigisten tag Octobris/ Anno ꝛc. im Vierundsibentzigisten ... s.sh. 38 × 53.5 cm. [918

-- -- *Another copy.* [919

-- *Rudolf II, Roman emperor.* [Renewal of the proclamation of Maximilian II restricting travel in areas visited by the plague, with countersignatures.] Geben in ... Wienn/ am Viervndzwaintzigisten Tag Octobris/ Anno ꝛc. im Sibenvndsibentzigisten ... s.sh. 32 × 43 cm. [920

-- [Restatement of mandates issued by the emperors Ferdinand and Maximilian II requiring produce for home use to be sold in the regular markets so as to stem inflation.] Geben in ... Wienn/ am Achtvndzwaintzigisten tag Octobris/ Anno/ ꝛc. im Neunvndsibentzigisten ... s.sh. 31 × 43.5 cm. [921

-- [Regulations of the sale of oats, barley, malt, lentils, etc., with countersignatures.] Geben in ... Wienn den Sechsten Tag Augusti, Anno etc. im ZwayvndAchtzigisten ... s.sh. 31 × 41 cm. [922

-- [Regulations for the control of vagabonds who endanger the security of the people, prescribing supervision, prosecution, registration of strangers, inspection of inns, etc., with countersignatures.] Geben/ in ... Wienn/ den ersten Tag Marti Anno im Vierundachttzigisten ... s.sh. 43.5 × 57 cm. ¶*Worn at the folds.* [923

-- [Regulations of the sale and export of grain, livestock, salt, linen, flax, etc., with countersignatures.] Geben in ... Wienn/ den Vierzehenden tag Iunij Anno ꝛc. im Fünffundachtzigisten ... s.sh. 37 × 49 cm. [924

-- [Reaffirmation of a mandate of 30 January 1581 regulating the sale of livestock and the butchers' trade, with countersignatures and seal.] Geben in ... Wienn den vierzehenden tag Iunij/ Anno ꝛc. im Fünffondachtzigisten ... s.sh. 37 × 49 cm. [925

-- [Restatement of two earlier mandates against mercenaries and vagabonds.] Geben in ... Wienn/ den Acten tag Iunij/ Anno/ ꝛc. im ZwayndNeüntzigisten [*sic*] ... s.sh. 31.5 × 43 cm. [926

-- [Regulations of the trade in food and wine to restrain abuses detrimental to the poor, with countersignatures.] Geben in ... Wienn/ den Zweintzigisten tag Februarij/ Anno/ ꝛc. im Viervndneüntzigisten ... s.sh. 44.5 × 57 cm. [927

-- -- *Another copy.* [928

-- [Mandate on the improvement of roads.] Geben in ... Wienn/ den Zwölfften tag Martij/ Anno/ ꝛc. im ViervndNeuntzigisten ... s.sh. 38.5 × 54.5 cm. [929

-- [Mandate interdicting luxury, gluttony, blasphemy, music, dancing, drunkenness, etc. in view of the renewed Turkish threat, and ordering various measures for a mobilization.] Geben in ... Wienn den Dritten tag Augusti/ Anno/ ꝛc. im ViervnndNeüntzigisten ... s.sh. 62.5 × 59.5 cm. ¶*Worn at the folds.* [930

-- [Call for provisions for the army defending Hungary against the Turks, with countersignatures and seal.] Geben in ... Wienn den Siben vnd zwaintzigisten tag Augusti/ Anno/ ꝛc. im VierunndNeüntzigisten ... s.sh. 32 × 41.5 cm. [931

-- [Order for mobilization following the fall of Raab to the Turks, with countersignatures.] Geben in ... Wienn/ den Sibenden Nouembris/ Anno/ ꝛc. im ViervndNeüntzigisten ... s.sh. 42 × 55.5 cm. [932

-- [Mandate requiring provisions for the war against the Turks, with countersignatures.] Geben in ... Wienn/ den Sibenden Tag Iunij/ Anno/ ꝛc. im SechssvndNeüntzigisten ... s.sh. 38.5 × 53.5 cm. [933

-- [Reaffirmation of an earlier mandate on the moral behavior of the people, requiring proper care of wounded soldiers in hospitals, help from doctors and apothecaries, supplying of medicine etc., and the use of private houses in places without hospitals, with countersignatures.] Geben in ... Wienn/ den ersten Tag Iulij/ Anno/ ꝛc. im SechssvndNeüntzigisten ... s.sh. 43.5 × 58.5 cm. [934

-- [Mandate prohibiting the sale of grain which might fall into the hands of the Turks, with countersignatures.] Geben in ... Wienn den Viervndzwaintzigisten tag Iulij/ Anno/ ꝛc. im SechssvndNeüntzigisten ... s.sh. 32 × 43 cm. [935

-- [Renewal of the mandate against the sale of grain which might fall into the hands of the Turks, with countersignatures.] Geben in ... Wienn den Vierundzwaintzigisten tag Ianuarij/ Anno/ ꝛc. im Sibenundneuntzigisten ... s.sh. 32 × 42.5 cm. [936

-- [Proclamation against the rebellious peasants in Mannhartzperg and the Wiennerwaldt, with countersignatures.] Geben in ... Wienn/ den Sechsten Tag Februarij/ Anno/ ꝛc. SibenvndNeüntzigisten ... s.sh. 39 × 51 cm. [937

-- [Mandate on the sale and export of horses through illegal channels to avoid the payment of taxes, with countersignatures.] Geben in ... Wienn/ den Zwayvndzwaintzigisten Ianuarij/ Anno/ ꝛc. AchtvnndNeüntzig ... s.sh. 44 × 68 cm. [938

-- [Mandate on the sale and the price of firewood, with countersignatures and seal.] Geben in ... Wienn/ den Zehenden Februarij, Anno/ ꝛc. AchtvndNeüntzig ... s.sh. 44 × 59.5 cm. [939

-- -- *Another copy (defective).* [940

-- [Order to mobilize a regiment in Langen, Entzerstorff, Marcheck, and surrounding villages and to supply it with provisions, with countersignatures and seal.] Geben in ... Wienn/ den Zwaintzigisten Tag Maij/ Anno ꝛc. AchtvndNeuntzig ... s.sh. 33 × 42 cm. [941

-- -- *Another copy.* [942

-- [Mandate setting a ceiling on the price of cattle, which has risen because of the war against the Turks.] Geben in ... Wienn/ den Zwaintzigisten Augusti/ Anno/ ꝛc. AchtvndNeüntzig ... s.sh. 32 × 42 cm. [943

-- [Mandate restricting travel and ordering the slaughter of infected cattle for the purpose of controling the spread of the infection, with countersignatures and seal.] Geben in ... Wienn/ den Viertzehenden tag Decembris/ Anno/ ꝛc. AchtvndNeüntzig ... s.sh. 32 × 42.5 cm. [944

-- -- *Another copy.* [945

-- [Mandate restraining the abuses of mercenaries, with countersignatures.] Geben in ... Wienn den Zehenden Tag Iunij/ Anno im Sechtzehenhundertisten ... s.sh. 32 × 42 cm. [946

-- *Landtag.* Der Niderösterreychischen Erblanndt sambt der Fürstlichen Graffschafft Görtz

Aufgerichte vergleichung vnd Anlag des werdts ... Zů Prag beslossen worden/ der Aindlfften tag des Monnats Ianuarij. Anno zc. xlij. fol. π^4. [947

-- *History.* Verteutschte Capitulation des Anstanndts. (Geben zů Megier/ den .XXX. tag Decembris. Anno domini zc. jm Zwayunddreissigisten.) s.sh. 59.5 × 39 cm. ¶*Defective.* [948

AUTHORITATES. Autoritates notabiles De castitate et moribus ... 16°. B.L. A-B^4. ¶A1, B4 *defective.* [949

AVERROES. Auerrois Cordubensis epithoma Totius Metaphysices Aristotelis. Prohemium duodecimi libri Metaphysices. Eiusdem paraphrases In Libris quatuor de Coelo. & duobus de Generatione & corruptione Aristotelis. ... Venetijs apud Hieronymum Scotum. 1542. (*Colophon.*) 8°. A-Z^8 aa-dd^8. pp. 3-430. [950

AVILA Y ZUÑIGA, LUIS DE. ... D. Ludouici ab Auila et Zunniga ... Commentariorum de bello Germanico, à Carolo V. ... gesto, libri duo à Gulielmo Malinæo Brugensi latinè redditi ... Antuerpiæ, In ædibus Ioan. Steelsij. M.D.L. ... 8°. A^8 (+ *folding map*) B-T^8 (+ *folding maps following* E4 *and* Q1). ff. 2-144. (Lea.) [951

-- -- Brieue commentario ... del MDXLVI. et MDXLVII. Tradotto di Spagnuolo in lingua Toscana. ... In Venetia Nel M D XLVIII. (*Colophon.*) 8°. A-N^8. ff. 3-103. [952

AVISO. Vltimo auiso de vna littera venuta dall'armata Christiana, alli 3. di Settembre 1572. ... In Roma, Appresso Giouanni Osmarino. Et in Bologna, per Alessandro Benacci. M. D. LXXII. 4°. A^4. [953

AYRAULT, PIERRE. Des procez faicts au cadauer, aux cendres, a la memoire, aux bestes brutes, choses inanimées, & aux contumax: Liure IIII. de l'Ordre, Formalité & Instruction Iudiciaire ... A Angers, Par Anthoine Hernault ... M. D. XCI. 4°. $¶^4$ A-Q^4 R^2 (-R2, *presumably blank*). ff. 1-65. (Lea.) [954

AZO, PORTIUS. De præscriptionibus, quae cum iure ciuili, tum pontificio continentur tractatus ... à diuersis editi. ... Coloniae Agrippinae Apud Ioannem Birckmannum & Theodorum Baumium, ... 1568. ... 8°.)$(^{8} $*^8$ A-Bb^8. pp. 1-397. ¶*Additional authors:* Dynus Muxellanus, Henricus de Sugusio Hostiensis, Gulielmus Durandus, Constantius Rogerius, Johannes Oldendorp. [955

-- Sũma Azonis. ... 1530 Constantin Fradin (Lugd. impressa per Antoniũ du Ry. ... die .xj. mensis Decembris.) 4°. B.L. A^8 B^6 a-z^8 $\&^8$ o^8 ꝝ^8 A-V^8 X^6. ff. j-ccclxxiij. (Biddle.) [956

AZPILCUETA, MARTIN AB. Apologia libri de reditibus ecclesiasticis ... Antuerpiæ, Ex officina Christophori Plantini ... M. D. LXXIIII. 4°. A-Q^8 A^8. pp. 1-222, 1-12. [957

-- Commentaria in septem distinctiones de pænitentia ... Romae, ... M.D.LXXXI. Ex Typographia Georgij Ferrarij. (... In Aedibus Accoltianis. ...) 4°. $+^4$ A-Bb^8 a-ee^8 ff-ll^4. ff. 3-220, 1-219. (Lea.) [958

-- De anno iobeleo et tota indulgentiarum materia, Commentarius, Quem Martinus Azpilcueta Nauarrus conscripsit In §. Leuitico, cap. Quis aliquando de penit. distint. 1. Quo in commentario explicantur quinque Extrauagantes de pęn. et remis. Huic accessit, breuis quaedam eius anni explicatio contexta a D. Stephano Nottio ... Constitutiones etiam summorum Pontificum. ... Mediolani, Apud Pacificum Pontium. M. D. LXXIII. 8°. $*^8$ A-R^8 S^4. pp. 1-261. (Lea.) [959

-- Enchiridion, siue manuale confessariorum et pænitentium ... Venetiis, MDLXXXIIII. Apud Franciscum Zilettum, De consensu Auctoris, & Georgij Ferrarij ... 4°. $+^8$ A-$3V^8$ $3X^{10}$. pp. 2-1010. (Lea.) [960

B

B., C. Nuoua canzone nella felicissima vittoria Christiana contra infideli, Del Sig. C. B. Fiorentino. In Venetia, M D LXXI. 4°. A^4. [1

B., D. R. Differentiae aliquot iuris ciuilis et Saxonici, iam tertio auctæ ... per ... D. R. B. Coloniae Agrippinae, Apud Ioannem Birckmannum & Theodorum Baumium. Anno 1573. ... 8°. $*^8$ $**^4$ A-P^8 Q^4. pp. 1-247. (Biddle.) [2

B., H. A. Informatio iuris, In causa poenali ... Rechtliches Bedencken/ In Malefitzsachen; Ob drey Weiber/ der Zauberey halben angegeben/ in Gefängliche Verhafft angenommen/ vnd Peinlich befragt werden können/ oder nicht? Per H. A. B. V. I. D. Franckf. bey Christ. Egen. Erben. M. D. XC. 8°. A-H^8 I^4. ff. 2-68. [3

BACCILLIERI, TIBERIO. Tiberij Bacilerij Bononiensis Lectura in Quattuor Libros Aristotelis ⁊ Auerrois de celo ⁊ mundo ... (Impssum Papie p magrm Iacob de Burgofrãco ... M.cccccix. die vij. Iulij.) fol. B.L. A-L^6 M^8. ff. 2-72. [4

-- Tiberij Bacilerij Bononiensis Lectura in tres libros de anima ⁊ parua naturalia: Et in tractatum Auerrois de substantia orbis: Necnon ⁊ in duo de generatione ⁊ corruptione volumina ... (Papie Impressi per Iacob de paucisdrapis de Burgofrãco. ... 1508. die .24. Mensis Iulij.) fol. B.L. A-V^6. ff. 2-117. [5

-- Tiberij Bacilerij ... Lectura in vniuersaȝ Aristotelis ⁊ Auer. Dyalecticam facultatẽ ... (Papie p Iacob de burgofrãcho. Impẽsis Aloysij comẽsis ac Bartholomei bergomẽsis sociol. ... 1512. die .5. Maii.) fol. B.L. a-r^6 s^4 A-B^6 C-D^4. ff. 2-106, 2-19. [6

BACHMANN, PAUL. Wider die Natterzungen/ Honsprechen vnd Lestermeuler/ ... Dobey ein Antwort auff Constantini Donation/ welche der Luther spöttlich nennet den Vohen Artickel des ... Bebstlichen glaubens. Durch Herrn Paulum Abt zur Aldten Czellen. ... 1538. (Gedruckt zu Dressden durch Wolffgang Stöckel.) 4°. a-f^4. [7

BACON, ROGER. [Le miroir d'alchimie.] A Lyon, Par Macé Bonhomme, 1557 ... 16°. [1] Le miroir d'alquimie de Rogier Bacon ... Traduict de Latin en François, par vn gentilhomme du D'aulphiné. ... A-H^8 I^4. pp. 2-134. [2] Roger Bachon de l'admirable pouuoir et puissance de l'art, & de nature ... Traduit en François par Iaques Girard de Tournus. a-f^8. pp. 2-95. [3] L'elixir des philosophes ... attribué au Pape Iean XXII ... a-n^8. pp. 2-205. [4] Des choses merueilleuses en nature ... Traduit en François par Iaques Girard de Turnus. a-m^8. pp. 2-191. [8

BACQUET, JEAN. Trois premiers traictez ... des droicts du domaine, de la couronne de France. Auec l'establissement et iurisdiction de la Chambre du Tresor. ... A Paris, Chez Sebastien Niuelle ... M. D. LXXVII. ... 4°. $ā^4$ $ē^4$ $ī^4$ $ō^4$ $ū^4$ A-Zz^4 AA-CC^4. ff. 2-194. ¶CC^4 *defective.* [9

BADER, JOHANN. Brůderliche warnung für dem newen Abgöttischen orden der Widertäuffer ... [Strassburg, Wolfgang Köpfel,] M. D. XXVII. ... 8°. A-O^8 P^4. [10

BADOARO, PIETRO. Orationi ciuili ... In Venetia, M. D. XCIII. Appresso Gio. Battista Ciotti Senese ... 4°. a^4 A-Ii^4. ff. 2-127. [11

BADUEL, CLAUDE. Cl. Baduelli oratio funebris in funere Flotetae Sarrasiae habita. ... Lugduni, Apud Steph. Doletum. 1542. 4°. A-D^4. pp. 3-31. [12

BADWEILER, JOHANN BAPTISTA. Caluinisch Badstůbl/ Das ist: Ein kurtzer ... Bericht/ was massen die Casimirische/ Schweitzerische/ vnd Nauarrische/ Teutsche vnnd Frantzösische Caluinisten den grossen Schandfleck/ welchen sie im Frantzösischen Krieg/ Anno 87. daruon getragen/ gern wolten abwaschen ... (Gedruckt zu München/ bey Adam Berg [1588].) 4°. A-M^4. [13

BÃR, LUDWIG. Ludouici Beri ... ad Quæstionem ei propositam, Vtrum uidelicet tempore pestis

... ad uitandam mortem ... fugere interdum liceat ... Responsio. Basileae, per Ioannem Oporinum. (... M. D. LI. Mense Aprili.) 4°. A-C^{4} (-C4, *presumably blank*). pp. 4-21. [14

BAERLAND, ADRIAN VAN. Rerum gestarum a Brabantiae ducibus historia ... vsq; in annum vigesimum sextum, supra M.D. ... Catalogus insignium oppidorum Germaniæ inferioris. ... Antuerpiæ, Excudebat Ioannes Grauius ... 1551. 8°. a^{4} A-N^{8} O^{4}. ff. 1-108. (Lea.) [15

-- -- Ducum Brabantiae chronica ... Item Brabantiados Poema Melchioris Barlaeii Iconibus nunc primùm illustrata, Ære ac studio Ioan. Bapt. VrientI: Operâ quoque ... AntonI de Succa. ... Antuerpiæ, in officina Plantiniana, Apud Ioannem Moretum. ... CIↃ. IↃC. fol. *-**^{4} (**4 + *engraved double leaf*) A-Ff^{4} Gg^{6} (-Gg6, *blank*). pp. 2-192. [16

BAERLAND, MICHIEL VAN. Carmen in Honorem ... Philiberti a Borsalia. Cum ... In publico juridicæ facultatis collegio propugnaret ... Lugduni Batavorum, Ex officina Ioannis Paetsij, & Ioannis Balduini. 1596. 4°. A^{4}. [17

BAFFI, BARTOLOMMEO. Oratio Bartholomaei Baphii Lucinianensis ... habita in ... Concilio Tridentino ... secunda Dominica aduentus Domini ... M. D. LXII. Brixiae apud Ludouicum Sabiensem, expensis Philippi de Salis. 4°. A^{6} (-A6, *presumably blank*). (Lea.) [18

BAGNOLINI, GIROLAMO. Opereta molto dignissima qual tratta de gli mirabel fatti de un caualléro detto Tebaldo Ferrarese contra de uno altro detto Gurato ꝑ amor del Filissetta ... in ... rima ... cōposta ... (Stampata per Paulo danza. A di. XXVI. Mazo. M.D.XXII. In Venesia.) 4°. A-F^{4}. [19

BAÏF, LAZARE DE. Lazari Bayfii annotationes in legem II De captiuis & postliminio reuersis, in quibus tractatur De re nauali ... Eiusdem Annotationes in tractatum De auro & argento legato ... Item Antonii Thylesii De coloribus libellus ... Basileae anno M D XXXVII (... apud Hier. Frobenium et Nic. Episcopium ...) 4°. a-r^{4} s^{6} t-z^{4} A-E^{4} F^{6} G-M^{4} N-Q$^{6.4}$. pp. 9-323. ¶P3, P4 *transposed in binding.* [20

-- Lazari Bayfii ... annotationum in L. Vestis, ff. de auro & argento leg. seu de re uestiaria, liber ... Basileae apud Ioannem Bebelium an. M. D. XXVI. mense Martio. 4°. *^{4} a-i^{4}. pp. 1-64. [21

-- De re nauali libellus, ... ex Bayfij uigilijs excerptus ... Lugduni apud hæredes Simonis Vincentii M.D.XXXVII. 8°. a-d^{8} e^{4} f^{8}. pp. 3-72. [22

-- De re vestiaria libellus, ex Bayfio excerptus ... Secunda editio. Parisiis, Ex officina Rob. Stephani M.D.XXXVI. (... III. Non. Maii.) 8°. A-E^{8}. pp. 3-68. [23

-- -- Lugduni apud hæredes Simonis Vincentii M. D. XXXVI. (Excudebant ... Melchior et Gaspar Trechsel fratres. ...) 8°. a-d^{8} e^{4}. pp. 2-62. [24

-- De vasculis libellus, adulescentulorum causa ex Bayfio decerptus ... Parisiis. Ex officina Rob. Stephani. M.D.XXXVI. (... XV. Cal. Iunii.) 8°. A-D^{8}. pp. 3-56. [25

-- -- Lugduni, apud hæredes Simonis Vincentii M. D. XXXVI. (Excudebant ... Melchior et Gaspar Trechsel fratres. ...) 8°. a-c^{8} d^{4}. pp. 3-50. [26

BALBI, GIOVANNI FRANCESCO. Tractatus praescriptionibus ... Eiusdem repetitio L. Celsus. D. de vsucapionibus. ... Coloniae Agrippinae, Apud Ioannem Gymnicum ... M. D. LXXXX. 8°. A-Zz^{8} 3A-3B^{4}. pp. 1-708. [27

BALBI, SCIPIONE. Nuptiae ill. Herculis Esten. Et Diuæ Reneæ ... (Impressum Bononiæ per Io. Baptistã Phaelem M.DXXIX.) 4°. A^{6}. [28

BALDI, BERNARDINO. Il lauro Scherzo giouenile ... In Pauia, per li Bartoli, MDC ... 12°. A-H^{12}. pp. 3-168. [29

-- Versi e prose, ... In Venetia, Appresso Francesco de' Franceschi Senese. 1590. 4°. a^{6} B-O^{4} P^{4+2} Q-4H^{4}. pp. 9-614. ¶*The two leaves added to sig.* P *are misbound between* a3 *and* a4. [30

BALDINI, BACCIO. Discorso dell' essenza del fato, e delle forze sue sopra le cose del mondo ... In Fiorenza, Nella Stamperia di Bartolomeo Sermartelli. MDLXXVIII. fol. A-D^{4} E^{6}. pp. 3-42. [31

-- Discorso sopra la mascherata della geneologia degl'iddei de' Gentili. ... In Firenze Appresso i Giunti. MDLXV. ... (... 1566.) 4°. A-Q^{4}. pp. 6-130. ¶A1 *defective and repaired.* [32

-- Orazione fatta nella Accademia Fiorentina, In lode del ... Sig. Cosimo Medici Gran Duca di Toscana ... In Firenze. Nella Stamperia di Bartolomeo Sermartelli. MDLXXIIII. 4°. A-D^{4}. [33

-- Vita di Cosimo Medici, primo gran duca di Toscana. ... In Firenze, Nella Stamperia di Bartolomeo Sermartelli. MDLXXVIII. fol. *^{4} a-l^{4} A-H^{4}. pp. 1-88, 1-62. [34

BALDINI, BERNARDINO. Bernardini Baldini dialogi duo, in quorum altero agitur de multitudine rerum ... in altero uerò de materia omnium disciplinarum ... disputatur. Mediolani Apud Antonium de Antonijs. M D LVIII. (... Imprimebant Metij fratres. ...) 8°. A-D^{8} E^{6} a-l^{8}. ff. 2-37, 1-88. [35

BALDINI, VITTORIO. Tre discorsi volgari. L'vno di quel ch'è col mezo d'amore. L'altro dell'amore del Petrarca ... Il terzo della compassione. ... In Ferarra, M D LXXXV. Appresso Vittorio Baldini ... 8°. A^{4} B-G^{8}. pp. 13-103. [36

BALDUINI, GIROLAMO. Quesita logicalia ... expositio Super Prohemium Epitomatum Logicalium Auerr. Cordubensis ... Ponderationes, Declarationes, Et Annotationes Vicentii Colle Sarnensis ... M.D.L.XI. Descripsit Matthias Cancer Neapoli. fol. π^{2} A-F^{4}. ff. 1-24. [37

BALE, JOHN. Illustrium Maioris Britanniae scriptorum ... Summariū ... ad annum domini. M. D. XLVIII. ... Excudebatur ... anno ... quadragesimo octauo supra millesimum & quingentesimum, pridie Calendas Augusti. ([Excusumque fuit Gippeswici in Anglia per Ioannem Ouerton ...]) 8°. A^{4} ❧^{4} ❧2^{4} A-3S^{4} (-Q^{4}, Z^{4}, 3F-3G^{4}, 3P-3Q^{4}, 3S4, *the last blank*). ff. 2-255. *S.T.C.* 1295. ¶*T.p. mounted;* A4 *defective.* [38

BALLATA. Ballata del Paradiso. (Se vēdano al pōte de Rialto da Comino libraro.) 8°. A^{4}. [39

BALLINO, GIULIO. Tre canzoni sopra la guerra Turchesca ... (In Venetia, Appresso Domenico, & Gio. Battista Guerra, fratelli. MDLXXI.) 4°. A-B^{4}. [40

BALTNER, THEOBALD. Der krieg zwischenn dem ... propheten Sophi/ Tůrcken/ vnd dem Soldan ... Im Jar M.CCCCC. vnd Xvij. (Finis. Theobaldus Baltner.) 4°. π^{4}. [41

BAMBERG. *Wigand von Redwitz, bishop.* Acht Erklerung vnnd verruffung wider Marggraf Albrechtē zu Brandenburg den Iůngern. Von wegen vnd auff eruolgen der ... Herren Weygarden Bischouen zu Bamberg. Herren Melchiorn Bischouen zu Wirtzburg/ vnnd Hertzogen zu Francken. Auch Ains Erbern Raths der Stadt Nůrmberg. M. D. LIII. 4°. A-C^{4} D^{2}. [42

BANCROFT, RICHARD. A suruay of the pretended Holy Discipline ... Imprinted at London by Iohn Wolfe. 1593. 4°. *^{4} A-3M^{4}. pp. 1-464. *S.T.C.* 1352. (Yarnall.) [42a

BANDELLO, MATTEO. XVIII. histoires tragiques, Extraictes des oeuures Italiennes de Bandel, & mises en langue Françoise. Les six premieres, par Pierre Boisteau, surnommé Launay, natif de Bretaigne. Les douze suiuans, par Franc. de Belle-Forest, Comingeois. A Lyon, par Iean Martin. M. D. LXIIII. 8°. A-3I^{8} (-3I8, *presumably blank*). ff. 6-436. (Furness.) [43

-- Le troisiesme tome des histoires tragiques, extraictes des oeuures Italiennes de Bandel, Contenant dix-huit Histoires, traduites & enrichies outre l'inuention de l'Auteur: Par François de Belle-Forest Comingeois. A Paris, Chez Iean de Bourdeaux, ... 1582. (Acheué d'imprimer le premier iour de Septembre. 1582.) 8°. *^{8} a-z^{8} A-Tt^{8}. ff. 1-514. (Furness.) [44

-- Le quatriesme tome des histoires tragiques, partie extraites des oeuures Italiennes de Bandel, & partie de l'inuention de l'Autheur François. Contenant vingt-six Histoires ... Par François de Belle-forest Comingeois. A Lyon, par Ierosmo Farine. M. D. LXXXVIII. 8°. a-z^{8} A-Ii^{8} (-Ii8, *end of table*). pp. 3-875. (Furness.) [45

-- Le cinquiesme liure des histoires tragiques ... par François de Belleforest Comingeois. A Lyon, par Benoist Rigaud. 8°. A-Pp^{8}. pp. 3-606. ¶*Foot of t.p. repaired; part of imprint wanting?* (Furness.) [46

-- Le sixiesme tome des histoires tragiques ... Par Françoys de Belle-forest Comingeois. ... A Lyon, pour Cesar Farine. 1585. 8°. a-z^{8} A-Hh^{8} (-Hh8, *presumably blank*). pp. 2-840. (Furness.) [47

-- Le septiesme tome des histoires tragiques ... Par F. de Belleforest Commingeois. A Lyon, Par Benoist Rigaud, 1595. (A Lyon, De l'Imprimerie de Pierre Dauphin. 1595.) 8°. ā^{8} a-z^{8} Aa-3C^{8}. ff. 2-386. (Furness.) [48

-- Dernier volume des nouuelles de Bandel, Traduites d'Italien en François ... A Lyon, Par Alexandre Marsilij. 1577. (De l'imprimerie de Antoine Blanc.) 16°. *^{8} A-X^{8} Y^{4}. ff. 1-172. ¶*Translator: Jean de Tournes.* [49

-- La quarta parte de le Nouelle del Bandello nuouamente composte ... In Lione, Appresso Alessandro Marsilij. M.D.LXXIII. ... (Stampato ... per Pietro Roussino. ...) 8°. *^{8} a-x^{8} y^{4}. ff. 1-171. [50

BANGE, JOHANN. Thüringische Chronick oder Geschichtbuch ... Gedruckt zu Muͤlhausen/ durch Andream Hantzsch/ Anno 1599. 4°. A-3K^{4}. ff. 1-212. ¶3I^{4} *misbound after* 3K4. [51

BARBA, POMPEO DELLA. Spositione d'vn sonetto Platonico ... doue si tratta de la immortalità de l'anima secondo Aristotile, e secondo Platone. In Fiorenza [per Lorenzo Torrentino,] MDLIIII. ... 8°. a-g^{8}. pp. 3-107. [52

BARBA, SIMONE DELLA. Nuoua spositione del sonetto che comincia In nobil sangue uita humile, e' queta ... In Firenze [per Lorenzo Torrentino] MDLIIII. 8°. a-c^{8}. pp. 3-44. [53

BARBARO, DANIELE. Della eloquenza, dialogo ... Nuouamente mandato in luce da Girolamo Ruscelli. ... In Venetia, Appresso Vicenzo Valgrisio. M D LVII. 4°. a^{4} b^{2} A-M^{4}. pp. 1-85. [54

-- La pratica della perspettiua ... In Venetia, Appresso Camillo, & Rutilio Borgominiari fratelli ... M D LXVIII. (... M D LXVIIII.) fol. A-O^{4} P^{6} Q-Aa^{4} Bb^{6}. pp. 4-195. (Fine Arts.) [55

BARBARO, ERMOLAO. Cōpendium ethicorum librorum ... Parisiis. Apud Ioannem Roigny ... 1546. 8°. A-D^{8}. ff. 2-31. [56

-- Hermolai Barbari ... compendium scientiae Naturalis, ex Aristotele. ... [Parisiis,] Apud Ioannem Roigny ... 1547. 8°. A-H^{8} (-H8, *blank*). ff. 3-57. [57

-- -- Naturalis scientiae totius compendium ... D. Conradi Gesneri ... studio purgatum. Cui accessit, Hieronymi Wildenbergij Aurimontani in uniuersam Aristotelis Physicam Epitome ... Basileae. (... ex officina Ioannis Oporini, ... M.D.XLVIII. Mense Decembri.) 8°. α^{4} A-S^{8} T^{4}. pp. 1-267. [58

BARBARO, FRANCESCO. Prudentissimi et graui documenti circa la elettion della moglie ... In Vinegia appresso Gabriel Giolito de Ferrari MDXLVIII. 8°. A-G^{8} H^{10}. ff. 5-62. [59

BARBATIA, ANDREA DE. [Commentaria in decretalia.] (Impressa in oppido Tridini ... Impensis ... Ioannis de ferrarijs al's de Iolitis: ac dñi Girardi de Zeijs ꝑdicti loci. ... Mcccccxvij. ...) fol. B.L. [1] Andree Barbatie sicculi ... in primum decretaliū ... cōmētaria ... (... die .xxvj. Mensis Iunij.) a-z^{8} ꝛ^{8} ɔ^{8} ꝶ^{8} A-G^{8} H^{10}. ff. II-CCLXXIIII. [2] Repertorium ... super prima parte ꝑncipali primi decretalium. a-d^{8} e^{6}. ff. II-XXXVIII. [3] Secunda primi partis ... super primo decretaliuꝫ. (... die .xxvij. Mensis Aprilis.) aa-xx^{8} yy^{6}. ff. II-CLXXIII. [4] Repertorium ... aa^{8} bb^{10}. ff. II-XVIII. [5] ... in ꝺm decretalium ... cōmentaria ... (die .xxvij. Mensis Marcij.) A-X^{8} Y^{10}. ff. II-CLXXVIII. [6] Repertoriuꝫ ... ī primā partē principalē secūdi decretalium. AA-BB^{6}. ff. II-XI. [7] Secunda secunde partis ... super secundo decretalium. (... die .xxv. Mensis februarij.) a-v^{8} x^{10}. ff. II-CLXX. [8] Repertorium ... A-B^{8} (-B8, *blank*). ff. II-XV (A2-B7). [9] ... in tertium decretaliū ... cōmentaria. (... die .xxviij. Mensis Ianuarij.) a-z^{8} ꝛ^{8} ɔ^{8} ꝶ^{8} A^{10}. ff. II-CCXXVII. [10] Repertorium ... Aa-Bb^{6}. ff. II-XII. (Biddle.) [60

BARBATIA

-- [Consilia.] Venetijs Impressa per Philippum Pincium mantuanuȝ. Mcccccxvj. ...) fol. B.L. [1] Consilioꝝ quatuor ... volumina ... Andree Barbatie siculi ... (... tertio. Maij.) π^{12} aa-ss^{8} tt^{10} (-tt10, *presumably blank*). ff. 1-153. [2] Tabula secunde partis consiliorum ... (... die .xxvij. Iunij.) π^{12} 3A-3R^{8} 3S-3T^{6}. ff. 1-147. (Biddle.) [61

-- Andree siculi barbacie ... lectura ... in clementinaruȝ compillationem ... Addito ... repertorio: labore ... egidij Daurigny bellouaci ... (Papie īpressa per ... Bernardinū de garaldis ... M.ccccc.xviij. die .xv. mensis Septembris.) fol. B.L. A^{4} b^{4} a-y^{4}. ff. j-lxxxviij. (Biddle.) [62

-- Solemnis ... repetitio .c. Raynaldus. de testamētis. dicta Ioānina ... (Impressa Papie ꝑ ... Iacob de paucisdrapis de burgofrancho. ... 1507. die .3. Iulij.) fol. B.L. a-g^{6} h-i^{4} A^{6} B^{4}. ff. 2-49. (Biddle.) [63

BARBO, PAOLO, DE SONCINO. Pauli Soncinatis ... quæstiones Metaphysicales ... Lugduni, apud Carolum Pesnot. M. D. LXXIX. fol. *-**^{8} a-z^{6} A-F^{6} G^{8}. pp. 1-363. [64

BARBUO, SCIPIONE. Sommario delle vite de' duchi di Milano ... In Vinetia Appresso Francesco Ziletti MDLXXXIV. fol. π^{2} A-D^{4}. ff. 2-11. ¶*Engraved t.p.* [65

BARDI, GIROLAMO. Dichiaratione di tutte le istorie, che si contengono ne i quadri posti nouamente nelle Sale dello Scrutinio, & del Gran Consiglio, del Palagio Ducale della ... Republica di Vinegia ... In Venetia, Appresso Felice Valgrisio. 1587. 8°. †^{8} A-H^{8}. ff. 1-64. [66

BARET, JOHN. An aluearie or Quadruple Dictionarie, containing foure sundrie tongues: namelie, English, Latine, Greeke, and French. ... [London: Henry Denham, 1580.] fol. A^{8} (-A1, *blank*) B-Y^{6} Aa-Yy^{6} 3A-3N^{6} 3O^{4} 4A-4E^{4} 4D^{4} 4G-4S^{4} 4T^{6} (-4T5 *colophon*, -4T6 *blank*). *S.T.C.* 1411. (Furness.) [67

BARGAGLI, GIROLAMO. Dialogo de giuochi che nella vegghie Sanesi si vsano di fare. Del Materiale Intronato. ... In Venetia, MDLXXIIII. (... Appresso Gio. Antonio Bertano. ...) 8°. A-S^{8}. pp. 17-228. [68

-- -- In Venetia, appresso Giouan. Griffio. M D XCII. (*Colophon.*) 8°. *^{8} A-R^{8} S^{4}. pp. 1-280. [69

-- La Pellegrina commedia ... In Siena, Nella Stamperia di Luca Bonetti. M.D.LXXXIX. 4°. A-T^{4}. pp. 3-152. [70

-- La prima parte dell'imprese ... In Siena Appresso Luca Bonetti. M.D.LXXVIII. 4°. A-O^{4} (-A3, A4) P^{2}. pp. 3-116. [71

-- I trattenimenti ... doue ... rappresentati sono Honesti; & dilettcuoli Giuochi; narrate Nouelle; e cantate alcune amorose Canzonette. ... In Venetia, Appresso Bernardo Giunti, M D XCII. 4°. *^{4} A-Nn^{4}. pp. 1-286. [72

BARLAAM. Histoire de Barlaam et de Iosaphat, roy des Indes, composee par sainct Iean Damascene, et traduicte par F. Iean de Billy ... A Paris, Chez Guillaume Chaudiere ... M.D.LXXVIII. ... 8°. A-Aa^{8}. ff. 2-189. [73

BARNAUD, NICOLAS. Le secret des finances de France, Descouuert, & departi en trois liures par N. Froumenteau ... Premier liure ... cIↄ. Iↄ. LXXXI. 8°. *-3*^{8} 4*^{4} A-I^{8} K^{4}. pp. 1-152. [2] Le second liure ... cIↄ.Iↄ.LXXXI. 8°. b-z^{8} A-F^{8} G^{4}. pp. 3-472. [3] Le troisiesme liure ... cIↄ.Iↄ.LXXXI. 8°. †^{4} AA-3D^{8} 3E^{2}. pp. 1-439. [74

BARNES, ROBERT. Vitae Romanorum pontificum, quos Papas uocamus, ... collectæ, per D. Robertum Barns ... Eiusdem sententiae, siue præcipui Christianæ religionis articuli ... Basileae [1536?]. 8°. α^{8} β^{4} a-z^{8} A-B^{8} C^{4} D^{8} E^{4}. pp. 1-406. [75

BARO, EGUINAIRE. Eguinarii Baronis ... ad Obertum Ortensium, de Beneficiis, Commentarii, Methodo in eundem subiecti. Lugduni apud Seb. Gryphium, M. D. XLIX. 4°. a-s^{4} t^{6}. pp. 3-154. [76

-- -- Methodus ad Obertum Ortensium, de beneficiis ... Lugduni apud Seb. Gryphium, M. D. XLIX. 4°. a-r^{4}. pp. 3-132. [77

BARONIO, CESARE. Il compendio de gli annali ecclesiastici ... In Roma, Per gli Heredi di Giouanni Gigliotto. M. D. XC. 4°. A^4 A-$3B^4$ ✠-5✠^{4}. pp. 2-376. [78

BAROZZI, FRANCESCO. Francisci Barocii ... opusculum, in quo vna Oratio, & duæ Quęstiones: altera de certitudine, & altera de medietate Mathematicarum continentur. Patauii, E. G. P. M. D. LX. 4°. A-K^4. ff. 2-40. [79

BAROZZI, GIROLAMO. Regola delli cinque ordini d'architettura di M. Iacomo Barozzio da Vignola. [Venetiis,] Bolognini Zaltierii formis. M. D. LXX. fol. *engr. t.p. + 32 plates.* (Fine Arts.) [80

BARREIROS, GASPAR. Censura, In quendam auctorem, qui sub falsa inscriptione Berosi Chaldaei circunfertur. Gaspare Varrerio auctore. Romæ, M.D.LXV. 4°. π^2 A-I^4 K^2 (-K2). pp. 1-73. ¶π2 *misbound after* A1. [81

BARTHOLOMAEUS ANGLICUS. Batman vppon Bartholome, his Booke De Proprietatibus Rerum ... 1582. London Imprinted by Thomas East ... (*Colophon.*) fol. π^2 ¶$¶^6$ $¶^6$ B-$4C^6$. ff. 1-426. *S.T.C.* 1538. ¶C1 *bound after* C2. (Furness.) [82

-- -- Libro de proprietatibus en romance. ... (... trasladado de latin en romance. Por ... Vicente de burgos/ ... ynpreso enla ... ciudad de Toledo/ en casa de Gaspar de auila .../ a costa ... del ... varon Ioan thomas fabio milanes vezino de Segouia. Acabo se a diez dias del mes de Iulio/ del año de mil ꝫ quiniẽtos veynte y nueue años.) fol. B.L. A^6 A-Y^8 a-v^8 x^4. [83

BARTHOLOMAEUS COLONIENSIS. Dialogus mythologicus ... (Viennæ Pannoniæ in ædibus Hieronymi Vietoris, & Ioannis Singrenii. Pridie Nonas Octob. ... M.CCCCC.XII.) 8°. A^8 B-D^4. [84

BARTHOLOMAEUS ARNOLDI DE USINGEN. Compendiū Natural' phie Opa ... Bartholomei de vsingen. ... (Impressum Erphordie per wolffgangum Schencken) 4°. B.L. A-$F^{4.6}$ G^4 H-$O^{4.6}$ P^6 (-P6, *presumably blank*). [85

-- Libellus F. Bartholomei de Vsingen ... de falsis prophetis ... De recta et mūda p̄dicatiōe euāgelij ... De Celibatu sacerdotum Noue legis ... Responsio ad Sermonē Langi de Matrimonio sacerdotali ... Cōtra factionē Luttheranā. Erphurdie. 1525. 4°. B.L. A-K^4. [86

-- Exercitium Phisicorū ... (Impressum Erphordie p̄ me wolffgangum Schencken [c. 1505.]) 4°. B.L. A-$Y^{6.4}$ Z^6 $ꝛ^4$ $ꝯ^4$. ¶T3-4 *misbound after* S2. [87

-- Libellus Fratris Bartholomei de Vsingen ... De tribus necessario requisitis ad vitā christianam que sunt gratia/ fides et opera Contra Lutheranos/ Hussopycardos. Herbipoli. 1526. (Balthassar Muller Impressor.) 4°. A-G^4 H^6. [88

-- Regule congruitatis et Figure constructionis ... Lipsi impressit Vuolfgangus Monacensis ... (... Anno ... supra millesimūquingentesimū duodecimo. Die .vij. mēsis decembris finitum.) 4°. A-D^6. [89

-- -- (Impressum Cracouie per Florianum, in Expensis domini Marci Bibliopoli. Anno ... Millesimo Quingentesimo Vigesimo secundo.) 4°. B.L. a-d^4 e^6. [90

BARTOLI, COSIMO. Cosimo Bartoli ... del modo di misurare le distantie, le superficie ... Secondo le uere regole d'Euclide ... In Venetia, Per Francesco Franceschi Sanese. 1564. (*Colophon.*) 4°. A^4 A-Z^4 (V4 + *folded leaf*, X2 + *folded leaf*) Aa-Nn^4. ff. 1-141. [91

-- Discorsi historici vniuersali ... In Genoua [per Antonio Roccatagliata,] M. D. L. XXXII. (*Colophon.*) 4°. *^{4} A-Xx^4 (-Xx4, *presumably blank*). pp. 1-350. [92

-- Ragionamenti accademici ... sopra alcuni luoghi difficili di Dante. ... In Venetia, Appresso Francesco de Franceschi Senese. 1567. 4°. *^{6} A-S^4 T^6. ff. 1-77. [93

BARTOLINI, RICCARDO. Ad diuum Maximilianum Cæsarem Augustum ... de bello Norico Austriados Libri duodecim. (Argentorati, Ex Aedibus Matthiæ Schurerij, Mense Februario ... M. D. XVI. Ductu Leonhardi, & Lucæ Alantseæ fratrum.) 4°. π^8 A-$K^{8.4}$ L-$Q^{8.8.4}$ R-T^8 V^4 X-Aa^8 Bb^6. ¶*In verse.* [94

-- Ricchardi Bartholini ... de conuentu Augusteñ concinna descriptio rebus etiā externaꝝ gentium quę interim gestę sunt ... [Augustae, Silvanus Otmar,] M.D.XVIII. 4°. A-D^4. [95

-- Richardi Bartolini Perusini Oratio, ad Imp. Cæs. Maximilianū Aug. ac ... Germaniaꝝ Principes, de expeditione contra Turcas suscipienda. ... MDXVIII (In excusoria Sigismundi Grim̄ Medici, & Marci Vuirsung officina Augustæ Vindelicoꝝ ... duodecimo Kalen̄. Octobres.) 4°. a-c^4. [96

BASADONA, GIOVANNI. Ioannis Basadona ... de ueriori Mortalium Fine ac foelicitate. Dyalogus primus. Eiusdem de intellectuali Natura Dei ac diuina Sapientia. Dyalogus secundus. Eiusdem de singularium ac rerum omnium Cognitione ab Intellectu diuino. Dyalogus tertius. Eiusdem de admirabili Dei Prouidentia & Mortalium Cura. Dyalogus quartus. Eiusdem de diuina electorum Prædestinatione. Dyalogus quintus. (Venetiis ī ædibus Ioannis Tacuini mense Augusto ... M.D.XVIII.) 4°. a^4 A-V^4 X^6 (-X6, *blank*). [97

BASCAPÉ, CARLO. De vita et rebus gestis Caroli ... archiepiscopi Mediolani Libri Septem. Carolo a Basilicapetri ... auctore. ... Ingolstadii ex officina typographica Dauidis Sartorii ... M. D. XCII. 4°. (:)^4 (+^{2}(:)4 + *blank*) A-Z^4 a-z^4 Aa^2 (+ Errata). pp. 1-371. (Lea.) [98

BASEL. *University. Faculty of Law.* D.O.M.A. Disputatio de Possessione Acquirenda, Retinenda & Amittenda: Quam ... habebit Franciscus Meynsma ... Basileae, Typis Leonhardi Ostenij. Anno cIↃ.IↃ.XCII. 4°. A^4. [99

BASIL, S. Opera magni Basilij: Per Raphaelem Volaterranum Nup. in latinum conuersa ... (Impressum Romę apud Iacobum Mazochium ... M.D.XV. Die .XV. Mensis Septembris. ...) fol. a-z^6 &^{6} ꝯ^6 ꝝ^6 A-C^6. ff. II-CLXXIII. [100

-- -- D. Basilii ... opera ... Monodia Gregorij Nazianzeni. Interpretes: Iohannes Argyropilus. Georgius Trapezuntius. Raphaēl Volaterranus. Ruffinus presbyter. Colonię, ex officina Eucharij, anno 1531 (... impendio .M. Godefridi Hittorpij ... Mense Februario.) fol. A^8 a-z^6 Aa-Gg^6 Hh^8. pp. 1-375. [101

-- Diui Basilii Magni de Instituenda studiorum ratione, & legendis profanorum scriptorum libris ... Parisiis, Ex Typographia Dionysij à Prato ... 1568. 4°. A-B^4 C^2. ff. 2-10. [102

-- Basilij Magni de legendis antiquoꝝ libris opusculum ... (Impressum Argentine Anno ... Millesimoquīgētesimo septimo Die vero lune ante purificationis Marie per ... Matthiam Hupfuff.) 4°. B.L. A-B^4. [103

-- Hexameron Magni Basilii per Ioannem Argyropolum e greco in latinuȝ conuersum. ... (Impressum Romę apud Iacobum Mazochium ... M.D.XV. Die .XII. Mensis Septembris.) fol. aa-gg^6 hh^4. ff. II-XLV. [104

-- Orationes due Elegantissime. vna Basilij ... de Inuidia Altera Pluthargchi cheronei de discrimine Inuidie et odij. (Impressum Liptzigk per Iacobum Thanner herbipolensem. Anno ... Millesimo quingentesimoseptimo. Die vero duodecima mensis Iulij.) 4°. B.L. a^6 b^4. ¶*Translator of Basil: Nicolò Perotti.* [105

BASIL I, emperor. [1] Βασιλειου του Ρωμαιων βασιλεως κεφαλαια παραινετικὰ ξς' ... Basilii Romanorum imp. Exhortationum capita LXVI. ... Lutetiæ, Apud Federicum Morellum ... M.D.LXXXIIII. ... 4°. A-Δ^4 E^2. ff. 2-17. [2] Basilii ... exhortationum capita sexaginta sex ... nunc primum Latinitate donato ... *Same imprint.* A-D^4. ff. 2-16. [106

BASSANO DA ZARA, LUIGI. I costumi, et i modi particolari de la vita de Turchi ... M. D. XLV. (Stampato in Roma per Antonio Blado Asolano. ...) 8°. a^4 A-H^8. ff. 1-62. [107

BASSE, NIKOLAUS. [1] Collectio in vnum corpus, omnium librorum ... qui in nundinis Francofurtensibus ab anno 1564. vsque ad nundinas Autumnales anni 1592 ... venales extiterunt: desumpta ex omnibus Catalogis VVillerianis singularum nundinarum ... Francofurti. Ex officina Typographica Nicolai Bassæi. M. D. XCII. (*Colophon.*) 4°. (:)-2(:)^4 A-4K^4 4L^2. pp. 1-636. [2] Catalogi librorum Germanicorum ... Secunda pars. ... Gedruckt zu Franckfort am Mayn/ bey Nicolao Bassæo. M. D. XCII. A-3A^4. pp. 3-372. [3] Collectio in vnum corpus, librorum Italice, Hispanice, et Gallice ... Pars tertia. ... A Francfort sur le Maine: par Nicolas Basse. M D XCII. ***-2***^{4} A-H^4. pp. 1-62. [108

BATRACHIUS, HIERONYMUS. Oratio. Absque Græcarum literarum cognitione nullam ex liberalibus artibus maiorumûe Gentium disciplinis recte addisci posse ... Per Hieronymum Batrachium Augustanum ephebum etiamnû. M.D.XLII. (Augustæ Vindelicorum, excudebat Philippus Vlhardus.) 8°. A-B^8. [109

BATTIFERRA DEGLI AMMANNATI, LAURA. Il primo libro dell'opere Toscane ... In Firenze appresso i Giunti M D L X. (*Colophon.*) 4°. A^6 B-P^4 Q^2. pp. 9-122. [110

BAUDIUS, DOMINIQUE. Dominici Baudii Insulensis Carmina ... Lugduni Batauorum, Ex officina Ioannes Paetsij. M.D.LXXXVII. 8°. A-G^8 (-G8, *blank*). pp. 3-108. [111

BAUERN. Das hond zwen schweytzer bauren gemacht. Für war sy hond es wol betracht. (M.D.XXI.) 4°. A^6. ¶*In verse.* [112

BAUMAN, JOHANN. Tractatus de sequestris ... Francofurti, Apud heredes Andreæ Wecheli, Claudium Marnium, & Ioannem Aubrium. Anno MDXCVII. 8°.)(^{8} (-)(8, *presumably blank*) A-H^8 I^2. pp. 1-118. (Biddle.) [113

BAUMANN, HANS. Newe Zeittung. Ware vnd gründtliche anzeigung vnd bericht/ in was gestalt/ auch wenn/ wie vnd wo/ Hertzog Iohann Friedrich/ gewessner Churfürst zu Sachssen/ von der Röm. Keis. vnd Kön. Maie. neben Hertzog Moritz zu Sachssen ꝛc. ... Erlegt vnd gefangen worden ist. ... 1547. (Gedrückt zu Leipzig durch Valentin Bapst.) 4°. A-B^4. [114

-- Ein Schöner Newes Lied/ von Carolo dem Fünfften ... Römischen Kaiser/ vnd Philipsen weylendt Landtgrafen zů Hessen/ sambt andern ... Potentaten dess vnglückhafftigen Schmalckaldischen bundts verwandten ... Im M.D.XLVII. Jare. In der weiss wie die schlacht von Pauia gesungen wirt. M. D. XLVII. 4°. A-B^4. [115

-- Wie/ vnd in welcher gestalt/ der Römischen Kayserlichen Mayestat/ Landtgraff Philips von Hessen/ auff den neüntzehenden tag Iunij/ zů Hall in Sachsen den füssfall gethon. Anno M. D. XLVII. (Hans Bawmañ Bůchtrucker gesell/ yetzo dess Duco de Alba trabant.) 4°. a^4. [116

BAUMGARTNER, AUGUSTIN. Oratio habita ab oratore ... Alberti ducis Bauariae in generali Congregatione ... Concilii Tridentini, ... die XXVII. Iunii. M D LXII. Vna cum responsione Sanctæ Synodi. Pataui Apud Laurentium Pasquatium & Socios. M D LXII. 4°. A^4 B^2. (Lea.) [117

BAVARIA. *Official publications.* Die Ordnung vber gemeiner Landtschafft in Bairn aufgerichte Hanndtüesst. Tausent funffhundert vnd jm sechzehenden jar. au Ingolstat beslossen. fol. A^6. [118

-- Erclärung der Landsfreihait in Obern vnnd Vadern Bairn widerumb verneut Im funfftzehenhundert Drei und funfftzigsten Jar. 1553. (Gedruckt zu München [durch Andreas Schobser].) fol. A^8 A-D^6 E^4. ff. I-XXVIII. [119

-- *Laws &c.* Dy new erclerūg der landssfreyhait des ... Furstenthumbs obern vnd Nidern Bairn. Anno funffzehenhundert vnd jm Sechzehenden auf den viervndzweintzigsten tag des monats Aprilis zu Ingelstat aufgericht. (Getruckt durch herr Iohann Weyssenburger jn demselben jar/ jn ... Landsshůt/ am Abendt Petri vnd Pauli ...) fol. A-C^6. ¶*On the t.p. and on* A2^r *the words* vier *and* Aprilis *are pasted on.* [120

-- Das bůch der gemeinen lanndpot. Landsordnung. Satzung/ vnd Gebreuch/ des Fursten-thombs/ in Obereñ/ vnd Niderñ Bairn/ im funftzehenhundert vnnd Sechtzehendem Jar aufgericht. [München, Johann Schobser, 1516.] fol. a-b^6 A-D^6 E^8 F-K^6 L^8. ff. ij-lxvij. [121

-- Gerichtsordnung Im Fürstenthumb Obern vnd Nidern Bayrn Anno M.D.XX. Auffgericht ... nach gedruckt/ Anno M.D.LXXXVIII. [München, Adam Berg.] fol. A-B^8 A-M^6 N-O^8. ff. i-lxxxvij. [122

-- Reformation Der Bayrischen Landrecht ... Im Fünffzehenhundert vnd Achtzehenden Jar auffgericht. ... nachgedruckt. Anno M.D.LXXXVIII. [München, Adam Berg.] fol. a-b^6 A-Cc^6 Dd^8. ff. i-clxviiii. [123

-- Ernewerte Mandata vnnd Landtgebott/ Dess ... Herrn Maximilian Pfaltzgraue bey Rheyn ... Gedruckt zu München/ durch Nicolaum Henricum. M. D. XCVIII. fol. A-B^8. pp. I-XXIX. [124

BAVARIA

-- Ain laijsche/ anzaigung/ So allen Landsässen/ vnd denen/ die ... oberkhait haben ... zů dienst/ vnd guetem/ in druckh/ geben worden. ... (Gedruckht zů München/ durch .A. Schobsser [1531].) fol. A-C^6. [125

BAZZANO, GIOVANNI GUGLIELMO. La Cliitia ... In Trino. Appresso Gio. Francesco Giolito de' Ferrari. 1571. 4°. A-G^4. [126

BEALE, ROBERT. [1] Rerum Hispanicarum scriptores aliquot ... Ex Bibliotheca ... Roberti Beli Angli. ... Tomus prior. Francofurti, Ex officina typographica Andreæ Wecheli, M D LXXIX. (*Colophon.*) fol.)(^{6} a-z^6 A-Z^6 Aa-Dd^6 Ee^8 Ff-Zz^6 AA-ZZ^6 AAa-PPp^6 QQq^8 (-QQq8, *presumably blank*). pp. 1-1258. ¶*Additional t.p.* (Ee7^r): Rerum Hispanicarum scriptorum tomus posterior ... Francofurti ad Moenum, apud And. Wechelum, M D LXXIX. *Authors:* Marius Aretius, Joannes episcopus Gerundensis, Rodericus archiepiscopus Toletanus, Rodericus Santius, Joannes Vasaeus Brugensis, Alfonsus à Carthagena, Michael Ritius, Franciscus Tarapha, Lucius Marineus Siculus, Laurentius Valla, Ælius Antonius Nebrissensis, Damianus à Goes. [2] De rebus gestis a Francisco Ximenio Cisnerio ... libri octo, authore Aluaro Gomecio: qui sunt rerum Hispanicarum Tomus III. ... quibus inscriptiones aliquot Tarraconenses ex historia Hispanica Ludouici Pontis adiunctæ sunt. Omnia studio Ioan. Sambuci Pannonii ... Francofurti Apud Andream Wechelum, M. D. LXXX. ¶^{4} A-Y^6 Z^4 &^{4}. pp. 1-271. [127

-- -- *Another copy, lacking tome III.* (Lea.) [128

BEAUCAIRE DE PEGUILLON, FRANÇOIS. Francisci Belcarii Peguilionis ... oratio de victoria, qua Carolus IX. Galliarum rex Francisci Lotharingi Guisae ducis, necnon et Annæ Monmorencii ... rebelles causam religionis prætexentes ingenti clade superauit. Habita est Tridenti ... Quarto Idus Ianuarii. M. D. LXIII. Brixiæ, Apud Damianum Turlinum. Ad instantiam Io: Baptistæ Bozolæ. Anno M. D. LXIII. (*Colophon.*) 4°. A^4 B^6. (Lea.) [129

BEAUNE, RENAUD DE. Declamation ou harangue faicte aux Estats tenus à Bloys. Par Monsieur l'Archeuesque de Bourges ... A Lyon, Par Iean Pillehotte. 1589. ... 8°. A-I^4. pp. 4-69. [130

BEAZIANO, AGOSTINO. De le cose volgari et latine dal Beatiano. ... (Impressum Venetijs per Bartholomęum de Zanettis de Brixia3 ... M. D. XXXVIII Die decima Octob.) 8°. A-F^8 G^4 H-N^8. [131

-- Le rime volgari del Beatiano. ... In Vinetia appresso Gabriel Giolito di Ferrarii e fratelli. 1551. 8°. π^2 (-π2) A-F^8 (-A2) G^4. [132

BEBEL, HEINRICH. [Bebeliana opuscula ... necnon & adolescentie labores, librique facetiorum cum multis additionibus.] (Parrhysiis ex ædibus Nicolai de Pratis. Mense Iulii Anno. M.D.XVI.) 4°. A-B^4 (-A1) C^6 D-R$^{4.8}$. [133

-- Ars uersificandi et carminum condendorum cum quantitatibus syllaborum ... (Tubingæ in ædibus Thomæ Anshelmi Badensis ... M.D.XI. mense Octobri.) 4°. a-h^4 i^6. [134

-- [a1^r] Commētaria epistolarum conficiendarum ... (Phorce in ædibus Thomę Anshelmi Badensis ... M.D.X. mense Martio.) 4°. A-C^4 D^6 a^8 b-d^4 e^8 f-h^4 i^8 k-l^4 m^8 n-o^4 p^8 q-t^4 u^8 x-z^4 aa^4 bb^8 cc-ff^4 gg^8 hh-ii^4 kk^8. ff. I-CLXV. ¶*Additional t.p.* (A1): Index seu ... Registrum Commentariorum Bebelianorum factus a Sebastiano zuifuldensi ... [135

-- -- (Tubingæ in ædibus Thomæ Anshelmi Badensis ... M.D.XI. Mense Iulio) 4°. a-v$^{8.4.4.4}$ x^8 y-z^4 A^4 B^8 C-E^4 F^8 G-H^4 I^6 A-C^4 D^6. ff. I-CLVII. ¶*Additional t.p.* (^{2}A1^r): Index ... [136

-- -- (Argentinæ [per Mathiam Schürer] Mense Februario. M. D. XVI.) 4°. [A]-B^4 C^6 a-h$^{4.8}$ i^4 k-r$^{4.8}$ s^4 t-y$^{4.8}$ z^4 Aa-Bb^8 Cc-Dd^4 Ee^8 Ff^4. ff. I-CLXVIII. [137

-- Triumphus Veneris ..., cum commentario Ioannis Altenstaig Mindelheimensis. (Argentinę [Matthias Schürer]. ix. Calen. Septem. ... M.D.XV.) 4°. A^6 A^8 B-Y$^{4.4.8}$. ff. IIII-CXVIII. [138

BECCADELLI, ANTONIO, PANORMITA. Antonii Panormitae de dictis et factis Alphonsi regis Aragonum libri quatuor: Commentarium in eosdem Aeneæ Syluij ... Adiecta sunt singulis libris

Scholia per D. Iacobum Spiegelium. Basileae Ex officina Heruagiana. Anno. M.D.XXXVIII. (*Colophon.*) 4°. a-z^4 A-N^4 O^6. pp. 1-278. ¶a1, O5 *defective.* [139

BECHLER, HANS. Eyn Gesprech eynes Fuchs/ vnnd wolffs ... wo vnd wye die beyde parthey den Wintter sich halten/ vnnd nerenn wo̊llen. M. D. XXiiij. (Gedycht durch Hanns Bechler von Scholbrunnen.) 4°. A^4 B^2. [140

BECKER, KONRAD. Propositiones de quibus disputabit Magister Cunradus Becker Brunsuicensis ... VVitebergae. Anno 1556. ... (... ex officina typographica Viti Creutzer.) 8°. A-B^8. [141

BECKER, PETER. Latinae phrasis elegantiæ ex potissimis authoribus conscriptæ. Per Petrum Artopæum. Vitebergæ. 1534. (... apud Petrum Seitzen. ...) 8°. A-Ee^8. ff. 2-209. [142

BECON, THOMAS. The Reliques of Rome, contayning all such matters of Religion as haue in times past bene brought into the Church by the Pope and his adherentes ... 1563. ... Imprinted at London, by Iohn Day ... (... September .30. ...) 8°. B.L. ℭ^8 [illegible]^8 A^8 B^4 C-Y^8 2A-2N^8. ff. 2-266. *S.T.C.* 1755. (Furness.) [143

BEDE. [Opera.] Basileae, per Ioannem Heruagium, Anno M.D.LXIII. fol. [1] Opera Bedae venerabilis ... α-λ^6 μ^4 ν^6 A-Z^6 aa-ff^6. cols. 1-542. [2] Secundus tomus operum Venerabilis Bedæ ... a-z^6 A-E^6 F^4 G^6. pp. 1-353. [3] Tertius tomus ... a-z^6 A-D^6 E^4 F^6. cols. 1-674. [4] Quartus tomus ... *A^8 A-3F^6 3G^8. cols. 1-26, 1-1280. [5] Quintus tomus ... α-δ^6 ε^8 a-z^6 A-Z^6 Aa^4 Bb^6. cols. 1-122, 1-1138. [6] Sextus tomus ... †a-†b^6 Aa-Zzz^6 AAa-BBb^6 CCc^8 (-CCc8, *blank*). cols. 1-42, 1-1179. [7] Septimus tomus ... a-z^6 A-E^6. cols. 1-664. [8] Octauus tomus ... a-z^6 A-Z^6 Aa^4 Bb^6. cols. 1-1138. [144

-- Homiliae venerabilis Bedae ..., hyemales, quadragesimales, de tempore item & sanctis ... Coloniæ Ioannes Gymnicus excudebat. Anno M.D.XLI. 8°. *^{8} A-Xx^8. pp. 1-699. [145

-- Repertoriū siue tabula generalis authoritatū Aristotelis & philosophorum cum cōmento per modum alphabeti. (... impresse rursus parisijs in officina Ascensiana ... duodecimo Calendas maias Anni Millesimi quingentesimidecimi.) 4°. B.L. a-f^8 g^4. [146

-- -- Axiomata philosophica, Venerabilis Bedæ ... ex Aristotele & aliis ... Philosophis ... collecta ... Opusculum ... editum Studio M. Ioannis Kroeselii Vilseccensis ... Ingolstadii, Ex Officina Typographica VVolfgangi Ederi, Anno cIↄ Iↄ XXCIII. ... 8°. A-M^8. pp. 1-185. [147

BEEKE, HERMANN VAN. Elucidarius Carminum et Historiarū vel Vocabularius poeticus, continēs fabulas. historias. prouincias. vrbes. insulas. fluuies. et montes illustres. ... (Impressum Dauentrie Per me Iacobum De Breda ... M.ccccc.v.) 4°. B.L. A-H$^{8\cdot4}$ I^6 K^4. [147a

-- -- Elucidarius ... Item vocabula et interpretationes Grecorū & Hebraicoꝝ: vnacū vocabulis cōmunibus Sarracenoꝝ in latinū translatis ... Anno .M.D.XIIII. (Excussum Argētine per Renatum Beck ... M.D.xiij) 4°. B.L. A-K$^{8\cdot4\cdot4}$ L^8. [148

-- -- Elucidarius poeticus ... Anno M. D. XXV. (Coloniæ apud Eucharium Ceruicornum, impensa ... Godefridi Hittorpij ... nonis Iulij.) 8°. a-l^8 m^6. [149

-- -- Elucidario poetico. ... di Latino tradotto in volgare da M. Oratio Toscanella. In Venetia, Appresso Giacomo Cornetti 1585. 8°. A-R^8 (-R8, *presumably blank*). pp. 3-286. [149a

BEELZEBUB. Beelzebub an die Heilige Bepstliche Kirche. MDXXXVII 4°. A^4. [150

BEGNO, SIMON DE. Simo. Begnii ... Oratio ī Sexta Lateranā. Cōcilii Sessione. Quinto Kalen̄. Maias habita. M.D.xiii. [Romae, Marcellus Silber, 1513.] 4°. A-B^4. ¶A1^v, *l. 9 begins:* tulos præseserat. (Lea.) [151

-- -- [Romae, Marcellus Silber, 1513.] 4°. A-B^4. ¶A1^v, *l. 9 begins:* los præseserat. (Lea.) [152

BEGRIFF. Ain kurtzer begriff in eyl gefasst/ was gstalt vn̄ maynūg der ... Herr Maximilian Ro̊mischer Kůnig ... gehandelt ... (gedruckt zů der zeit des ... Reichstags zů Costentz Anno ... Fůnftzehenhundert vnd im Sibenden ꝛc.) 4°. A^8 B^6. [153

BEJA, LUIS DE. Responsiones casuum conscientiae, qui omnibus curatis, ac Poenitentiarijs ... coram ... Card. Palæoto Archiepisc. Bonon. proponuntur. Per ... Lodouicum de Beia Palæstrelum Lusitanum ... Huic postrema impressioni additi sunt duo ... tractatus. Alter quidem de contractibus liuellarijs. Alter verò de venditione rerum fructuosarum ad terminum. Venetiis, M D XCI. Apud Iacobum Cornettum. 8°. *-3*^{8} A-Ee^{8} (-Ee8, *presumably blank*). pp. 1-446. (Lea.) [154

BELLARMINO, ROBERTO. Roberti Bellarmini Politiani ... de translatione imperii Romani a Graecis ad Francos, libri tres, Aduersus Matthiam Flaccium Illyricum. Coloniae Agrippinae Apud Ioannem Gymnicum ... M. D. XCIX. 8°. A-P^{8} Q^{4}. pp. 3-245. [155

-- [1] Disputationes Roberti Bellarmini ... de controuersiis Christianae fidei ... Ingolstadii, ex officina typographica Dauidis Sartorii. ... M. D. LXXXVI. fol. *^{4} **^{8} A-K^{6} L^{4} M-Z^{6} a-b^{6} c^{4} d-z^{6} Aa^{6} Bb-Cc^{4} Dd-3K^{6} 3L-3M^{4} 3N-3R^{6} 3S^{4} 3T-4H^{6} 4I^{4} 4K-4L^{6}. cols. 1-2274. [2] Disputationum ... tomus secundus ... Ingolstadii, ex officina typographica Dauidis Sartorii. ... M. D. LXXXVIII. *-**^{6} A-L^{6} M^{4} N-S^{6} T^{8} V-Cc^{6} Dd^{4} Ee-Nn^{6} Oo-Pp^{4} Qq-Zz^{6} AA-HH^{6}. cols. 1-1741. (Yarnall.) [155a

-- Roberti Bellarmini ... iudicium, De Libro, quam Lutherani vocant Concordiae. Coloniae Agrippinae, Apud Ioannem Gymnicum ... M. D. XCIX. 8°. A-F^{8}. pp. 3-94. [156

BELLEAU, REMI. Sylua, cui titulus Veritas Fugiens, Ex R. Bellaquei Gallicis versibus Latina facta, A Florente Christiano Aurelio. ... Lutetiae, Ex officina Roberti Stephani ... M. D. LXI. 4°. A^{4} C^{2}. [157

BELLEMÈRE, GILLES DE. [Praelectiones in decretalia.] Lugduni ... apud Senneton. fratres. ... fol. [1] Aegidii Bellemeræ ... in Primam Primi Decre. Lib. partē Prælectiones ... 1548 (*Colophon.*) a^{2} a-z^{8} A-I^{8} K-L^{6} A^{10}. ff. 1-268. [2] ... in Secūdam Primi Decre. Lib. partē Prælectiones ... 1548 (*Colophon.*) Aa-Zz^{8} AA-FF^{8} GG^{6} aa-bb^{8}. ff. 2-238. [3] ... in tertiam Primi Decre. Lib. partē Prælectiones ... 1548 3a-3x^{8} Aaa-Bbb^{6}. ff. 3-168. [4] ... in Primam Secundi Decret. Lib. partem Prælectiones ... 1549 a-x^{8} z^{8} A-F^{8} G^{6}. ff. 3-230. [5] ... in Secundam Secundi Decret. Lib. partem Prælectiones ... 1549 (*Colophon.*) aa-zz^{8} AA-EE^{8} FF^{6} Aa^{8} Bb^{10}. ff. 2-230. [6] ... in Tertiā Secundi Decret. Lib. partē Pręlectiones ... 1549 (*Colophon.*) 3a-3z^{8} 3A-3D^{8}. ff. 2-199. (Biddle.) [158

-- [Remisorius.] Lugduni ... apud Sennetonios fratres. M D L. ... (*Colophon.*) fol. [1] Aegidii Bellemerae ... remisorius, qui primus est tomus ... ad Commentaria in Gratiani Decreta ... a-z^{8} A-G^{8} aa-bb^{8}. ff. 2-240. [2] ... Remisorius, qui secundus est tomus Commentariorum ... A-GG^{8} a^{10}. ff. 2-239. [3] Remisorius, qui posterior est tomus Commentariorum ... 3a-3q^{8} A^{10}. ff. 2-128. (Biddle.) [159

BELLENTANI, GIOVANNI FRANCESCO. La fauola di Pyti Et Quella di Peristera insieme con quella di Anaxarete ... In Bologna per Anselmo Giaccarello. M. D. L. 8°. A-G^{8} (-G8, *presumably blank*). ff. 2-55. [160

BELLEPERCHE, PIERRE DE. Petri de Bella Perthica ... Lectura ... super Prima parte Codicis ... Iustiniani: vna cum ... apostillis ... Prostat Parrhisijs apud Galleotum du pre ... ([H8^{r}] Anno ... millesimo ꝗngentesimo decimo nono. Die vero .iiij. Martij. [yy5^{v}] ... die vero quarta Iulij.) fol. B.L. π^{2} a-z^{8} A-H^{8} aa-vv^{8} xx-yy^{6}. ff. I-CCCCVII. ¶aa1^{r}: Lectura ... suꝑ Secunda parte Codicis ... (Biddle.) [161

BELLÈRE, JEAN. Bonne responce a tous propos ... Traduit d'Italien en nostre vulgaire Francois. A Paris. Pour la vefue Iean Bonfons ... [c. 1570.] 16°. A-I^{8}. [162

BELLEVUE, ARMAND DE. Declaratio difficilium terminorum theologiae, philosophiae atq. logicae D. Armandi Bellouisii ... Venetiis, ∞.D.XXCVI. Apud Aldum. 8°. a^{4} b-d^{8} A-Z^{8} Aa^{4}. pp. 2-374. [163

BELLEWE, RICHARD. Les ans du roy Richard le second ... 1585. ... At London, imprinted by Robert Robinson ... 8°. B.L. ₵^{4} A-X^{8} Y^{4} Aa^{4} (-Aa4). pp. 2-326. *S.T.C.* 1848. (Biddle.) [164

BELLI, SILVIO. Siluio Belli Vicentino della proportione, et proportionalita Communi Passioni del Quanto. Libri tre. ... In Venetia, alla Elefanta. M D LXXIII. 4°. *^{4} A-K^{4}. ff. 1-40. [165

BELLI, VALERIO. Madrigali ... In Venetia presso Gio.bat. Ciotti 1599 12°. A-D^{12}. ff. 2-47. [166

BELLO, FRANCESCO. El Beco comedia de Francesco Belo Romano. (Stampata in Roma per Antonio Blado d'Asula ... .M.D.XXX.VIII.) 4°. A-D^{4}. [167

BELLOY, PIERRE DE. Conference des edicts de pacification des troubles esmeus au Royaume de France, pour le faict de la Religion; & Traittez ou Reglement faicts par les Rois Charles IX. & Henri III. & de la Declaration d'iceux du Roy Henri IIII. ... A Paris, Chez P. L'huillier, & Iamet Mettayer ... M. DC. ... (Acheué d'imprimer pour la premiere fois, le huictiesme iour de Mars ...) 8°. *^{8} a-xx^{8}. ff. 1-326. [168

-- Examen du discours publie contre la maison royalle de France ... Par vn Catholique, Apostolique, Romain, mais bon François ... Imprimé Nouuellement. 1587. 8°. ã^{8} A-Z^{8}. ff. 2-355. [169

-- Memoires, et recueil de l'origine, alliances, & succession de la Royale famille de Bourbon ... A La Rochelle, Par P. Haultin. 1587. 8°. A-Bb^{8} (-Bb8, *presumably blank*). pp. 3-398. [170

BELLUCCI, FILIPPO. Itinerarium Philippi Bellucii (Romae Per Ludouicum Henricum Vicentinum impressum) 4°. a-d^{4} (-d4, *blank*). [171

BELON, PIERRE. Petri Bellonii Cenomani de admirabili operum antiquorum et rerum suspiciendarum præstantia Liber primus. De medicato funere, seu cadauere condito, & lugubri defunctorum eiulatione. Liber secundus. De medicamentis nonnullis, seruandi cadaueris vim obtinentibus. Liber tertius. ... Parisiis. In Bibliotheca Egidii Corrozet ... 1553. ... 4°. a^{4} ẽ^{4} A-O^{4} P^{2}. ff. 1-54. [172

-- L'histoire de la nature des oyseaux, auec leurs descriptions, & naïf portraicts ... A Paris, On les vend ... en la boutique de Gilles Corrozet ... 1555. ... (Imprime ... par Benoist Preuost ...) fol. ã^{6} ẽ^{4} ĩ^{4} a-f^{6} g^{4} h-m^{6} n^{4} o-t^{6} v^{4} x-z^{6} A-E^{6} F^{4} G-I^{6} K-L^{4} (-L4, *blank*). pp. 1-381. ¶*Additional t.pp.:* (h1) Le second liure de la nature des oyseaux ... (r2) Le troisiesme liure ... (v1) Le quatriesme liure ... (x1) Le cinqiesme liure ... (B1) Le sixiesme liure ... (G1) Le septiesme liure ... *Each with imprint:* A Paris, ... en la boutique de Gilles Corrozet. 1555. ... [173

-- Les obseruationes de plusieurs singularitez ... trouées en Grece, Asie, Iudée , Egypte, Arabie, & autres pays estranges, redigées en trois liures ... A Paris, Chez Guillaume Cauellat ... 1555. ... (Imprimé ... par Benoist Preuost ...: Pour Gilles Corrozet, & Guillaume Cauellat ... Acheué d'imprimer le douziesme iour de Mars, mil cinq cens cinquante trois.) 4°. ã^{4} ẽ^{4} ĩ^{4} a-z^{4} A-Gg^{4}. ff. 1-211. ¶*Additional t.p.* (V2^{r}): Le tiers liure ... *Same imprint.* [174

BELVISO, JACOBUS DE. Practica iudiciaria Iac. de bel. visu. ... [Lugduni,] 1543 8°. B.L. Aa^{8} Bb^{4} A-O^{8}. ff. j-cxij. (Biddle.) [175

BEMBO, PIETRO. Petri Bembi ... opera ... Basileae, [Michael Isingrin,] 1556. 8°. A-Qq^{8}. pp. 12-624. ¶*The first volume of an edition in three volumes.* [176

-- -- Petri Bembi insignia, quotquot extant, opuscula. ... [Basileae, per Thomam Guarinum, 1567.] 8°. 3A-3Q^{8} (-3Q8, *blank*). pp. 4-230. ¶*The 3d volume of an edition of the works in 3 volumes. T.p. mounted and repaired, with pen-drawn imprint:* Florentiæ. Apud Iohannem Giuntam 1548. [177

-- [1] Petri Bembi ad Nicolaum Teupolum de Guido Vbaldo Feretrio deque Elisabetha Gonzagia Vrbini ducibus liber. (Venetijs per Io. Anto. eiusq; fratres Sabios. Ann. M.D.XXX.) 4°. A-G^{8} (-A1, G8, *both blank*). [2] Petri Bembi de Aetna ... liber. *Same colophon.* Aa-Bb^{8} (-Aa1, *blank*). [3]Petri Bembi ... de Virgilii Culice et Terentii fabulis liber. *Same colophon.* a-d^{8} e^{4}. [4] Io. Francisci Pici ad Petrum Bembum de imitatione libellus. *Same colophon.* aa-cc^{8} (-cc8, *blank*). [178

-- -- Petri Bembi opuscula aliquot ... Apud Gryphium Lugduni, 1532 8°. a-r^{8}. pp. 3-271. ¶*Includes also:* Responsio ad eundem [libellum Pici], Benacus, Epigramma pro ara Coryciana, Epistolae aliquot. [179

-- Gli Asolani di Messer Pietro Bembo. (Impressi in Venetia nelle Case d'Aldo Romano nel anno .MDV. del mese di Marzo ...) 4°. a-m^8 n^2. [180

-- -- (Impressi in Vinegia nelle Case d'Aldo Romano & d'Andrea Asolano suo suocero nel anno M. D. XV. del Mese di Maggio.) 8°. a-p^8 q^{10}. ff. 2-129. [181

-- -- In Venegia per Comin de Trino di Monferrato M. D. XLIIII. (*Colophon.*) 8°. A-N^8 O^4. ff. 2-107. ¶A1^v: Edition seconda. [182

-- -- In Venetia M. D. XLVI. (... per Bartholomeo detto l'Imperador, et Francesco suo genero. ...) 8°. A-N^8. ff. 2-104. ¶A1^v: Edition seconda. [183

-- -- Les Azolains de ... Pierre Bembo de la nature D'amour. Traduictz d'Italien en François par Iean Martin ... A Paris, pour Galiot du Pré ... 1576. 16°. A-Ll^8 (-Ll8, *presumably blank*). ff. 2-271. [184

-- Carmina quinque illustrium poetarum ... Additis nonnullis M. Antonii Flaminii libellis ... Florentiae. Apud Laurentium Torrentinum MDLII. ... 8°. A-T^8 V^2. pp. 3-308. ¶*Additional authors: Andrea Navagero, Baldassare Castiglione, Giovanni Cotta, Marco Antonio Flaminio.* [185

-- -- Venetiis, Presb. Hieronymus Lilius, & socij excudebant. M. D. LVIII. (*Colophon.*) 8°. A-Z^8. ff. 2-183. [186

-- Della historia Vinitiana ... Libri XII. ... In Vinegia M. D. LII. (... Appresso Gualtero Scotto. ...) 4°. *^{8} **^{10} A-Y^8 Z^4. ff. 1-179. [187

-- -- Petri Bembi ... historiae Venetae libri XII. ... Venetiis M.D.LI. (... apud Aldi filios. ...) fol. *^{4} A-Z^4 a-z^4 Aa-Ee^4. ff. 1-203. [188

-- [A2^v] Petri Bembi epistolarum Leonis decimi ... nomine scriptarum libri sexdecim ... (Impressi Venetiis ab Ioanne Patauino & Venturino de Roffinellis. Decimo Cal. Sextileis Cola Bruno procurante [1535]. ...) fol. A-HH^6 (-HH6, *blank*). [189

-- -- ... Placuit præterea eiusdem autoris epistolas aliquot ... adnectere. Videlicet Ad Longolium III, Ad Budæum II, Ad Erasmum I. Lugduni, Apud hæredes Simonis Vincentij. (Dionysius ab Harsio excudebat ... M.D.XXXVIII.) 8°. a-z^8 A-D^8. pp. 3-432. ¶*Includes* Benacus. (Yarnall.) [189a

-- -- M. D. XXXIX (Basileae per Hier. Frobenium & Nic. Episcopium, ... Mense Martio.) 8°. A-Yy^8 Zz^4. pp. 3-711. (Lea.) [190

-- [Lettere.] In Venetia, M D LX. (... appresso F. Sansouino, et compagni. ...) 8°. [1] Delle lettere di M. Pietro Bembo ... Primo volume. ... Corretto da Francesco Sansouino. ... *^{8} (-*8, *blank*) A-T^8 V^4. ff. 1-155. [2] ... Secondo volume. *^{8} a-u^8. ff. 1-158. [3] ... Terzo volume. ... *^{8} A-Bb^8. ff. 1-200. [4] ... Quarto volume. ... *^{4} A-P^8 Q^4. ff. 1-123. [191

-- Prose di Monsignor Bembo M D XXXIX. 8°. A-N^8 O^{12}. ff. II-CXV. ¶A1^v: Edition seconda. [192

-- -- In Vinegia M. D. XLVI. 8°. A-O^8. ff. 2-112. ¶A1^v: Edition seconda. [193

-- -- In Vinegia M D XLVII. 8°. A-O^8. ff. 2-112. ¶A1^v: Edition seconda. [194

-- [A1^v] Prose di. M. Pietro Bembo nellequali si ragiona della volgar lingua ... (Impresse in Vinegia per Giouan Tacuino, nel mese di Settembre del M. D. XXV. ...) fol. A-Q^6 (-Q6, *presumably blank*). ff. I-XCIIII. [195

-- -- *Another copy.* [196

-- [A2^v] Rime di M. Pietro Bembo. (Stampate in Vinegia per Maestro Giouan Antonio & Fratelli da Sabbio. ... M.D.XXX.) 4°. A-D^8 E^{10} A-C^4 (-A1, C4, *presumably blank*). [197

-- -- Delle rime di M. Pietro Bembo.Seconda impressione. (Stampate in Vinegia per Giouann' Antonio de Nicolini da Sabio. ... MDXXXV.) 4°. A-F^8 G^{10}. ¶*Title on* A1^v. [198

-- -- Le rime ... In Venetia, Per Giordano Ziletti ... M. D. LXII. 8°. A-G^8 H^2. ff. 2-48. ¶*Additional t.p.* (G1^r): Stanze ... *Same imprint.* [199

-- -- Delle rime ... In Venetia, M D LXXXVI. Appresso Pietro Marinelli. (*Colophon.*) 12°. A-F^{12}. ff. 3-79. [200

BENCI, FRANCESCO. Francisci Bencii ab Aqua Pendente ... oratio in. funere. Antonii. Carafae cardinalis ... Romæ Apud Franciscum Zannettum. C'Ↄ. IↃ. XCI Mense Aprili. 4°. A-F^4. pp. 3-48. (Lea.) [201

-- [1] Francisci Bencii ..., Orationes & Carmina, cum disputationes de stylo et scriptione. Editio Tertia. ... Ingolstadii, Excudebat Adam Sartorius, Anno M. D. IC. 8°. A-Z^8 a-e^8 f^4. pp. 1-449. [2] Francisci Bencii ... carminum libri quatuor ... *Same imprint.* A-Y^8 Z^4. pp. 1-349. [202

-- Francisci Bencii ... Quinque Martyres. Coloniae Agrippinae, In officina Birckmannica, sumptibus Arnoldi Mylij. Anno M. D. XCIV. ... (... Excudebat Godefridus Kempensis. ... Mense Maio.) 12°. A-H^{12} I^8. pp. 3-209. (Lea.) [203

BENDINELLI, ANTONIO. Oratione ... recitata nel mortorio di Carlo quinto imperadore. In Lucca per Vincenzo Busdragho. MDLVIIII. 4°. A-C^4. pp. 3-22. [204

BENE, SENUCCIO DEL. Il solenne triompho fatto in Roma, quando ... Francesco Petrarcha, fu laureato, et coronato Poeta ... Stãpato In Padoua per Giacopo Fabriano. M.D.XLIX. (*Colophon.*) 8°. A-C^4. [205

BENEDETTI, PIETRO. Discorso della dignità delle leggi, Rispetto à tutte l'altre Scienze ... In Bologna, Per Alessandro Benaccio. 1570. ... 4°. A-M^4 N^2. ff. 2-50. [206

BENEDICT, S. [*Head-title*] Regola del santissimo Benedetto padre de' monaci. (In Firenze. Appresso Filippo Giunti. M. D. IIC.) 8°. A-I^8 (-A1, I8, *the latter presumably blank*). pp. 3-135. (Yarnall.) [206a

BENEDICTI, JEAN. Abregé de la somme des pechez ... Enrichi d'vn petit traité des vices et vertus ... A Liege, De l'Imprimerie Christian Ouvverx ... M. D. XCV. Aux depens de Iacques Gregoire ... 4°. †-5†^{4} 6†^{2} A-3L^4 3M^2. pp. 1-442. (Lea.) [206b

BENEDICTUS, ZACHARIAS. Elegia in obitum ... Antonii Suriano Venetorum patriarchae per monachum Carthusien. aedita. (Exarata in Carthusiana Eremo Sancti Andreæ de littore Venetis. XIII. calen. Iunias. M.D.VIII.) 4°. A^4. [207

BENI, PAOLO. Pauli Benii Eugubini disputatio; in qua ostenditur praestare Comoediam atque Tragoediam metrorum vinculis soluere ... Patauii, Apud Franciscum Bolzetam. An: CIↃ IↃC. Ex Typographia Laurentij Pasquati. ... (*Colophon.*) 4°. a^4 A-G^4. ff. 1-28. [208

-- Risposta alle considerationi o dubbi dell' ... Dottor Malacreta ... Sopra il Pastor fido ... In Padoua, M. D C. Appresso Francesco Bolzetta. (... nella Stãperia del Pasquato. ...) 4°. A^6 A-R^4. pp. 1-144. [209

BENINCASA, CORNELIO. Cornelii Benincasii Perusini ... Tractatus. De paupertate ac eius priuilegiis ... (Impressum Perusiæ ex Typis Andreæ Brixiani. M. D. LXII.) 8°. A-GG^8. ff. 2-240. [210

BENIVIENI, ANTONIO. Vita di Piero Vettori, L'antico ... In Fiorenza, Nella Stamperia de'Giunti. MDLXXXIII. ... (*Colophon.*) 4°. ¶^{2} A-H^4 I^6. pp. 1-80. [211

BENIVIENI, GIROLAMO. Amore ... Et una Caccia de Amore ... & cinq; Capituli, Sopra el timore, zelosia, speranza, amore, & uno Trionpho del mondo, Composti per il Conte Matteo Maria Boiardo ... (Stampata nella ... Citta di Venetia p̱ Nicolo Zopino e Vincentio compagno. Nel .M.ccccc.XXIII. adi .XXX. de Luio ...) 8°. A-P^8. ¶*Includes works by Egidio da Viterbo, Girolamo Cartulario, Domenico Baglioni.* [212

-- -- (In Vinegia per Vettor. q. Piero Rauano della Serena & Cõpagni ... M.D.XXXII. Del mese di Luio.) 8°. A-F^8. [213

-- Opere ... Con vna Canzona dello Amor celeste & diuino, col Commento dello ... S. Conte Giouãni Pici Mirãdolano ... Et altre Frottole de diuersi Auttori. (Stampato in Venetia per Nicolo Zopino e Vincentio compagno nel M.CCCCC.XXII, Adi .XII. de Aprile ...) 8°. A-Z^8 &^{8} AA-BB^8. ff. 2-302. [214

BENJAMIN OF TUDELA. Itinerarium ... Ex Hebraico Latinum factum Bened. Aria Montano interprete. Antuerpiæ, Ex officina Christophori Plantini ... M. D. LXXV. (*Colophon.*) 8°. A-H^{8}. pp. 3-114. (Lea.) [215

BENTIVOGLIO, ERCOLE. I fantasmi comedia ... In Vinegia Appresso Gabriel Giolito de Ferrari. MDXLVII. (*Colophon.*) 8°. A-E^{8}. ff. 2-38. [216

-- Il geloso comedia ... In Vinegia Appresso Gabriel Giolito de Ferrari. MDXLV. (*Colophon.*) 8°. A-D^{8} E^{12}. ff. 2-43. [217

-- -- In Vinegia appresso Gabriel Giolito de' Ferrari. M D LX. 12°. A-C^{12} D^{6}. ff. 4-41. [218

BENTZ, MICHAEL. Rettung Der wolgegründten vrsachen des abtrettens von dem Secten/ zu der alten ... Catholischen Kirchen. ... M. D. LXIX. (Gedruckt zu München bey Adam Berg.) 4°. A-3K^{4}. ff. 2-222. [219

BENTZIUS, JOANNES. Thesaurus elocutionis oratoriæ Græcolatinus Nouus ... Basileae Ex Officina Heruagiana, per Eusebium Episcopium Anno cIↃ Io XXCI. (*Colophon.*) fol. α-β^{4} a-z^{6} A-I^{6} K^{4} L^{6} M^{8}. cols. 1-772. [220

BENVOGLIENTI, FABIO. Discorso ... Sopra la materia de gliaffetti, Per dichiarazione del secondo libro della Retorica d'Aristotile. In Siena Appresso Luca Bonetti. 1578. 4°. A-B^{4}. pp. 3-15. [221

BENZONI, GIROLAMO. [1] Historia Indiae occidentalis ... Hieronymo Benzone Italo, & Ioanne Lerio Burgundo ... autoribus. ... Vrbani Caluetonis & G. M. studio conuersi ... [Genevae] Excudebat Eustathius Vignon. M. D. LXXXVI. 8°. **^{8} ¶¶^{8} a-z^{8} A-H^{8}. pp. 1-480. [2] Historia nauigationis in Brasiliam ... *Same imprint.* 8°. *-4*^{8} A-Y^{8} (M1 + *folded leaf*) Z^{4} a^{8}. pp. 1-341. [222

BEOLCO, ANGELO. Anconitana comedia del ... tasco Ruzante ... In Vineggia appresso Stephano di Alesi ... MDLI. (... Appresso Bartholomeo Cesano. ...) 8°. A-K^{4}. ff. 2-39. [223

-- -- In Vinegia, appresso Domenico de Farri. M. D. LXI. (*Colophon.*) 8°. A-E^{8}. pp. 3-77. [224

-- Due dialoghi di Ruzzante in lingua rustica ... In Vinegia appresso Stefano de Alessi ... 1551. (... per Bartholomeo Cesano ...) 8°. A-E^{4}. ff. 2-20. [225

-- Fiorina comedia del ... Ruzzante ... In Vinegia, appresso Domenico de Farri. M. D. LXI. 8°. A-D^{4}. ff. 2-15. [226

-- Moschetta comedia del ... Ruzzante ... In Venetia appresso Stephano di Alessi ... MDLI. (... Appresso Bartholomeo Cesano. ...) 8°. a-g^{4}. [227

-- -- In Vinegia, appresso Dominico de Farri. M. D. LXI. (*Colophon.*) 8°. A-G^{4}. pp. 3-56. [228

-- Piouana comedia, ouero noella del tasco di Ruzante. ... In Vinegia appresso Gabriel Giolito de Ferrari MDXLVIII. (*Colophon.*) 8°. A-G^{8} (-G7-8, *presumably blank*). ff. 4-54. [229

-- Vaccaria comedia del ... Ruzzante ... In Vinegia, appresso Domenico de Farri. M. D. LXI. 8°. A-E^{8}. pp. 3-102. [230

BERARDUCCIO, MAURO ANTONIO. Summa corona confessorum ... ex varijs Doctoribus collecta ... Neapoli, Ex Officina Saluiana 1581. (... Apud Horatium Saluianum ...) 8°. A-B^{8} B-FF^{8}. pp. 1-445. (Lea.) [231

BÉRAULD, NICOLAS. Oratio de pace restituta, et foedera sancto apud Cameracum ... Antuerpie excusum, per me Henricum Petri Middelburgensem ... [1529.] 8°. A^{4}. [232

BERGAMO. Ordo Per Magnificam Ciuitatem Bergomi recens statutus, ... De Notariorum mercede pro publicorum instrumentorum traditione & exhibitione ... Venetiis, M. D. LXVII. Ex officina Dominici Guerrei, & Io. Baptistæ fratrum. 4°. A-H^{4}. pp. 3-63. (Lea.) [232a

-- Copia delle stupende z horribile cose che ne bolchi di Bergamo sono a questi giorni apparse. 4°. B.L. a^2. ¶a2^v: Data in Castella de Villa chiara adi. xxiii. di Dicēbre. M.ccccc.xvii. [233

BERICHT. Ain beschaidner historischer/ vnschmählicher Bericht/ an alle Churfürsten/ Fürsten vnd Stennde dess Reichs. Von des Pabstum̄s auf vnd abnemen/ desselben geschicklichhait/ vnnd was endtlich darauss folgen mag. ... 4°. A-K^4. [234

-- Grüntdlicher bericht aus heiligen schrifft/ wie ferne man den Oberherrn/ gehorsam schüldig ... Anno. 1552. 4°. A-C^4. [235

-- Kurtzer Bericht/ von gemeinem kalender ... Auss anlass der Päpstlichen newlich aussgegangenen Kalenders Reformation/ Gestelt in Fürstlicher/ Pfaltzgräuischer Schul zu Newstadt an der Hardt. Gedruckt ... zu Newstadt an der Hardt/ durch Matthæum Harnisch. M. D. LXXXIII. 8°. A-D^4, E^2. pp. 1-32. [236

BERLAND, MICHEL. Sommaire des loix statuts et ordonnances Royaulx ... A Paris Pour Poncet le Preux ... 1548. 8°. A-Z^8 &^{4}. [237

BERN. Ratschlag/ halltender Disputation zů Bernn. [1528.] 4°. π^4. [238

-- Gemayn Reformation: vnd verbesserung der ... Gotsdiensten/ vn̄ Ceremonien ... durch ... Radt/ der stat Bern in ůchtland/ aussgreütet seind ... [Augsburg, Philipp Ulhart, 1528.] 4°. A^4 B^2. [239

-- De quattuor heresiarchis ordinis Predicatorū de Obseruātia nuncupatorū, apud Suitenses in ciuitate Bernensi cōbustis, ... M D IX ... 4°. A-E^4. (Lea.) [240

-- -- De quattuor heresiarchis ordinis Prædicatorum de Obseruantia nuncupatorum/ apud Suitenses in ciuitate Bernensi cōbustis. ... M. D. IX. ... 4°. A-D^8. (Lea.) [241

-- Warhafftige vnnd Erschrockenlich: Newe Zeittung/ Von dem grossen vnd gewaltigen zůlauff/ dess Wasserfluss/ der Statt Bern ... Geschehen den 30 vnd 31 tag Octobris/ diss 1567 Jars. Getruckt zů Augspurg/ Durch Hans Zimmerman. 4°. A^4. [242

-- *Synod.* Acta synodi Bernensis. ... Simone Sultzæro interprete. (Basilaeae apud And. Cratand. Anno M. D. XXXII.) 4°. a^6 b-i^4. [243

BERNAERTS, JAN. Iohannis BernartI de Vtilitate legendæ Historiæ libri duo. Antuerpiae, Ex officina Plantiniana, Apud Viduam, & Iannem Moretum. M. D. XCIII. (*Colophon.*) 8°. *^{8} A-L^8 (-L8, *blank*). pp. 1-161. [244

BERNARD OF CLAIRVAUX. Diui bernardi abbatis ad sororem modus bene viuendi in christianā religionem. (Impressum Venetijs per Petrum de Quarengijs Bergomēseȝ. Mcccccij. Die .iij. Octobris.) 8°. B.L. A^8 b-k^8. [245

-- -- (Impressi ... Venetiis per Cęsarem arriuabenum uenetum Anno ... milesimo quingentesimo decimo octauo die ultimo septembris.) 8°. A-L^8. ff. II-LXXXVII. [246

-- Liber florum Beati Bernardi abbatis Clareuallensis. M.D.XIX. (Impressum ... In officina Sigismundi Grim̄ ... atqȝ Marci Vuirsung. Augustæ Vindelicorum. 9. cal'. decem. ...) 4°. ℭ^6 A-YY^4 ZZ^6. ff. I-CLXXXV. [247

-- Diui Bernardi abbatis meditationes ... Ac alia quædam eiusdem, et aliorum pia opuscula. ... Venetijs apud Bernardinū de Bindonis. M. D. XXXXIII. (*Colophon.*) 16°. A-PP^8 QQ^6. ff. 2-310. ¶*Includes:* 1) Meditationes diui Anselmi, 2) Precationesqȝ ... eiusdē, 3) Dialogus sanctæ Catherinæ Senensis ..., 4) Tractatus uitę spiritualis diui Vincentij ..., 5) Sermo Petri Damiani Cardinalis, 6) Enchiridion uitæ spiritualis ... authoris ignoti, 7) Exercitium uitæ & passionis domini ad modum rosarij distinctum, 8) Diuæ Brigidæ orationes quindecim de passione domini. [248

BERNARD, ÉTIENNE. Harangue prononcee deuant le roy, seant en ses Estats generaux tenus à Bloys ... A Lyon, Par Iean Pillehotte. 1589. ... 8°. A-D^4. pp. 3-32. [249

BERNARDI, ANTONIO. Antonii Bernardi Mirandulani ... disputationes. ... Basileae, per Henricum Petri, et Nicolaum Bryling. Anno 1562. fol. α^6 β^4 a-z^6 A-Mm^6. pp. 2-694. [250

BERNARDINI, PAULINO. Concordia ecclesiastica contra tutti gli heretici ... Discorso sopra la uita et dottrina Lutherana, per il medesimo authore tradotto. In Fiorenza MDLII. 8°. A-Bb^8. pp. 3-394. (Lea.) [251

BERNARDINO, S. Legēda de Sancto Bernardino. (In Venetia stampata per Simone de Luere ... Adi .xvi. Luio. M.D.XIII.) 4°. A-E^4. ff. 1-20. [252

BERNARDUS COMENSIS. Lucerna inquisitorum haereticae prauitatis ... Mediolani apud Valerium & Hieronymum fratres Metios ann. S. M. D. LXVI. 8°. A-N^8 A-C^8 D^2. ff. 2-102, 1-25. (Lea.) [253

-- -- *Another copy.* (Lea.) [254

-- -- Lucerna inquisitorum haereticae prauitatis ...: Et eiusdem Tractatus De strigibus Cum annotationibus Francisci Pegnae ... Additi sunt ... duo Tractatus Ioannis Gersoni, vnus de Protestatione circa materiam fidei, alter de Signis pertinaciæ haereticæ prauitatis. Romae, ... Ex Officina Bartholomæi Grassi. CIↃ. IↃ. LXXXIV. (... Excudebat Vincentius Accoltus. ...) 4°. $†^4$ A-Z^4 a-b^4 c^6. pp. 1-184. (Lea.) [255

BERNHARDI, JOHANN. Ioannis Velcurionis commentarii in vniuersam physicam Aristotelis ... Tubingae, ex officina typographica viduae Vlrici Morhardi. Anno M.D.LX. 8°. A-Z^8 a-s^8. ff. 1-293. [256

-- -- Ioannis Velcurionis commentariorum libri IIII. ... Londini, Impensis Georg. Bishop. 1588 16°. $*^8$ A-Y^8 Aa-Nn^8. pp. 1-527. *S.T.C.* 24632. [257

BERNI, FRANCESCO. Dialogo contra i poeti del Bernia .... [Venezia,] M.D.XXXX. 8°. A-B^8. ff. 2-14, pp. 15-16. [258

-- Il primo libro dell'opere burlesche, di M. Francesco Berni. Di Messer Gio. della Casa, del Varchi, del Mauro, di M. Bino, del Molza, del Dolce, & del Firenzuola. ... In Venetia, per Dominico Giglio. (*Colophon.*) 8°. A-I^8 AA-SS^8. ff. 2-222. ¶*Dedication dated 20 December 1564.* [259

-- Tutte le opere del Bernia in terza rima ... M.D.XXXX. 8°. A-X^8. ff. 2-168. [260

BERÒ, AGOSTINO. [Commentarii.] Lugduni [Hugo à Porta] ... M. D. LI. (Excudebat Nicolaus Baccaneus.) fol. B.L. [1] Augustini Beroii ... in primam partem libri primi Decretalium Commentarii. ... a-k^8 l^4. ff. 3-84. [2]... in secundam partem libri Primi Decretalium Commentarij ... AA-KK^8 LL^6. ff. 2-86. [3] ... in primam partem libri Secundi Decretalium Commentarij. ... aa-nn^8 oo-pp^6. ff. 2-115. [4] ... in secundam partem libri Secundi ... A-V^8 X^4. ff. 2-163. [5] ... in librum tertium Decretalium Commentarij. ... Aa-Xx^8 Yy^{10}. ff. 2-177. [6] ... in quintum librum Decretalium Commentarij. ... 3A-$3I^8$ $3K^{10}$. ff. 2-81. [7] Repertorium commentariorum Augustini Beroii. ... Ioanne Thomasio authore. ... a-n^8 o^4. (Biddle.) [261

-- Augustini Beroii Bononiensis ... quaestiones familiares ... Lugduni, Apud Hæredes Iacobi Iuntæ. M. D. LI. 8°. a-x^8 y^4. ff. 2-149. [262

BEROALDO, FILIPPO. *Two or more works.* Philippi Beroaldi Carmen Lugubre Epigrammata: ac Ludicra quædam facilioris musæ carmina ... (Ex ædibus Ascensianis. Ad calendas Martias. MDVIII.) 4°. AA^8 BB^4 CC-DD^8 $*^4$. ¶$*1^r$: L. Celii Lactãtii Firmiani pia Nenia ... $*4^r$: Finis ad idus Martias M.D.Viij. ... [263

-- Orationes et Carmina Baroaldi. (Impressæ uero Bononiæ anno .M.CCCCCII. die ultimo Iulii.) 4°. A-S^4. [264

-- Orationes Prelectiones Præfationes & quædam Mithicæ Historiæ Philippi Beroaldi. Item Plusculæ Angeli Politiani. Hermolai Barbari. Atq3 vna Iasonis Maini Oratio. Quibus addi possunt varia eiusdem Philippi Beroaldi opuscula cum epigrãmatis & eorum cõmentariis. ... venũdãtur Parrhisiis In Aedibus Ascensianis: & sub Pelicano [per fratres de Marnef.] (Ad Idus Decembris M.DVIII.) 4°. a-g^8 h^4 i^8 k^4 $3A^6$. ff. II-LXXVIII. [265

-- Varia Philippi Beroaldi Opuscula. Libellus de septem sapientium sententiis. Symbola Pythagoræ moraliter explicata. De optimo statu Et de felicitate. Declamatio Phlosophi [*sic*] medici & oratoris. Declamatio Ebriosi scortatoris & aleatoris. Oratio aũt prouerbialis cęteris apposita est. ... venundantur Parrisiis in vico sancti Iacobi sub Leone argẽteo [per Joannem Parvum]: Et sub Pelicano [per fratres de Marnef] et in ædibus Ascensianis. (Impressa sunt ... In Aedibus Ascensianis ... M.D.VIII. Ad Calendas Ianuarias.) 4°. A^8 B^4 C^8 $D\text{-}E^6$ $F\text{-}G^8$ H^4 A^6 B^4 C^6. ff. III-LVI. [266

-- Varia Philippi Beroaldi opuscula ... (Basileæ exarata [per Joannem Frobenium] ... M.D.XIII) 4°. $A\text{-}T^8$ V^4 X^6. ff. 2-162. ¶*Contents: those of the* Orationes *of 1508*, Lactantii Pia Naenia, *those of the* Varia opuscula *of 1508*, Opusculum de terræmotu & pestilentia, Annotationes in Galenum. [267

-- *Separate works*. Annotationes ... in commentarios Seruij Virgiliani commentatoris ... (Phorce mense Aprili M.D.X.) 4°. $a\text{-}b^4$ c^8 d^4. [268

-- [Carmen lugubre Philippi Beroaldi de dominice passionis die.] (Impressum est autem Parrhisiis opera ... & impendio ipsius Ascensii ad nonas Iulias anni, NDIII [*sic*].) 4°. a^8 (-a1) b^6. ff. II-XIIII. ¶a2 *defective*. [269

-- Declamatio lepidissima Ebriosi Scortatoris Aleatoris de viciositate Disceptantium ... (Impressum Parisius ... Per Anthonium Bõnemere ꝑ dyonisio Roce ... Anno Dñi. Millesimo Quingentesimo Viij. Die Vero Vltima Mẽsis Martij.) 4°. $a\text{-}b^6$. [270

-- -- Ein künstlich hőflich Declamation vnd hefftiger wortkampff ... dreyer Brůder ... Namlich eins Sauffers/ Hůrers/ vnd Spilers ... verteütscht [durch Sebastian Franck]. Anno. 1531. (Gedrůckt zů Nůrmberg durch Friderich Peypus. ...) 4°. $a\text{-}d^4$. [271

-- -- (Gedruckt zů Augspurg durch Hainrich Stainer/ Anno D.M XXXIX. Jar.) 4°. $A\text{-}E^4$. [272

-- [$A3^r$] Symbola Pythagorae ... moraliter explicata. (Impressum Bononiæ a Benedicto Hectoris. ... M.D Tertio. Pridie Dominicũ Natalem.) 4°. $A\text{-}C^8$ D^4. [273

BEROSUS. Berosus Babilonicus De his quæ præcesserunt inundationem terrarum. ... (Impressum ... Parrhisiis ... per Ioannem Marchant Impensis Godofredi de Marnef. ... .1510. Septimo Idus Maias.) 4°. $*^4$ a^8 b^4 $c\text{-}d^8$. ff. 2-28. [274

-- -- Berosi sacerdotis Chaldaici, antiquitatum Italiae ac totius orbis libri quinque, Commentarijs Ioannis Annij Viterbensis ... illustrati ... Antuerpiæ, In ædibus Ioan. Steelsii. M. D. LII. ... (Typis Ioan. Graphei.) 8°. $*\text{-}3*^8$ $A\text{-}3C^8$ $3D^4$. pp. 2-748. [275

-- La antichità di Beroso Caldeo sacerdote, Et d'altri Scrittori, cosi Hebrei, come Greci, et Latini, che trattano delle stesse materie. Tradotte ... da M. Francesco Sansouino. ... In Vinegia, Presso Altobello Salicato. 1583. ... 4°. $+^8$ $A\text{-}O^8$. ff. 1-104. [276

BERSMAN, GREGOR. Auctariorum ... libri duo. ... 1581 Lipsiæ. (... imprimebat Ioannes Steinman ...) 8°. $A\text{-}D^8$ (-D8, *presumably blank*). pp. 1-58. [277

-- Indicium luctus publici, propter obitum Ioachimi Ernesti Prin. Anhaltini ... Seruestæ excudebat Bonauentura Faber. Anno 1586. 4°. A^4. [278

-- Lacrymæ et luctus in funere ... Ioachimi Ernesti, Pr. Anhaltini ... M.D.LXXXVII. ... (Seruestae Excudebat Bonauentura Faber. Anno 1587.) 4°. $A\text{-}B^4$. ¶*In verse*. [279

-- Oratio funebris ad celebrandam memoriam obitus ... quo vitam ... clausit ... Ioachimus Ernestus Pr. Anhaltinus ... Seruestæ excudebat Bonauentura Faber. Anno M. D. LXXXVII. 4°. $A\text{-}B^4$. [280

-- Poemata ... Lipsiae. ... (... Imprimebat Ioannes Steinman. Typis Voegelianis. Anno M. D. LXXVI.) 8°. $A\text{-}Y^8$. pp. 1-333. [281

-- Pons sublicius Anhaldinus. ... Carmen ἐγκωμιαστικὸν. ... Seruestæ Bonauentura Faber excudebat, Anno M. D. LXXXIIII. 4°. $A\text{-}B^4$. [282

BERSUIRE, PIERRE. Reductorii moralis Petri Berchorii Pictauiensis ... Libri Quattuordecim ... Venetiis, apud hæredem Hieronymi Scoti, M D LXXV. (*Colophon*.) fol. $*^4$ $A\text{-}Vu^8$ Xx^6. pp. 2-698. [283

BERTACHINI, GIOVANNI. [1] Secunda pars Reportorij Ioan. Bertachini. (Lugduni ex officina Sebastiani Gryphii Germani.) fol. B.L. ^{8} (- 8) $aa\text{-}zz^8$ $AA\text{-}OO^8$ $PP\text{-}QQ^6$. ff. 1-308. [2] ... tertia pars. Repertorium ... Excudebatur Lugduni anno M. D. XXXII. (... apud Sebastianum Gryphiũ Germanum.) fol. B.L. $3a\text{-}3z^8$ $Aa\text{-}Pp^8$ Qq^6. ff. 1-310. (Biddle.) [284

-- Quarta pars repertorii ... opera & labore Do. Ioan. Thierry Lingonensis ... cumulata ... Lugduni, 1552. (... excudebat Bartholomaeus Fraenus ...) fol. B.L. $+^4$ 4a-4z^8 4A-4G^8. ff. 1-240. [285

BERTHOLD OF RATISBON. [horologium deuotiōis circa vitam christi. Parisiis, Antonius Chappiel pro Dionysio Roce, c. 1504.] 16°. B.L. [A]^8 (-A1) B-F^8 G^4. [286

BERTRAND, PIERRE. Libellus dñi Bertrandi aduersus magistrum Petrum de cugneriis. (Impressus parrhisiis pro Iohanne Petit ... Anno domini millesimo quingentesimo decimotertio pridie Kalendas Ianuarias.) 8°. B.L. a-e^8 (-e8, *presumably blank*). (Lea.) [287

BÉRULLE, PIERRE DE. Traicté Des Energumènes, Suiuy d'vn discours sur la possession de Marthe Brossier: Contre les calomnies d'vn Medicin de Paris. Par Leon d'Alexis. A Troyes, 1599. 4°. A-X^4. ff. 2-83. ¶*Additional t.p.* (X4): Discours De la possession de Marthe Brossier. Contre les calomnies d'vn Medecin de Paris. ... Par Leon d'Alexis. A Troyes. 1599. *The* Discours, *however, is wanting, as apparently also in some other copies.* (Lea.) [288

BESANÇON. Statuta synodalia ecclesiae Bisuntinæ ... Lugduni, apud Gulielmum Rouillium. 1560. 4°. a-z^4 (-n^4) A-P^4 Q^2. pp. 3-304. [289

-- -- Lugduni, Apud Guliel. Rouillium ... M. D. LXXV. ... 4°. +-++^{4} a-z^4 A-Dd^4 (-Dd4, *presumably blank*). ff. 1-194. (Lea.) [289a

BESSELMEYER, SEBASTIAN. Warhafftiger Bericht/ des Magdeburgischenn Kriegs ... oͤrdentlicher vnd grűntlicher verfasset/ denn zuuor mit vnfleiss/ zu Basel ym drucke ist ausgangen. ... 4°. A-I^4. [290

BETTI, BENEDETTO. Orazione funerale ... recitata nelle Esequie del Sereniss. Cosimo Medici Gran Duca di Toscana ... In Fiorenza Appresso i Giunti MDLXXIIII. ... 4°. A-D^4. [291

BETUSSI, GIUSEPPE. Il rauerta dialogo ... nel quale si ragiona d'amore ... In Vinegia appresso Gabriel Giolito de' Ferrari. M D LXII. 8°. A-M^8 N^4. pp. 3-199. [292

BEURER, JOHANN JAKOB. Synopsis historiarum, et methodus noua: ... libris Duobus. ... Editio secunda ... 1599. Hanouiae Apud Guilielmum Antonium. 8°. A-L^8 M^4. pp. 4-183. [293

BEUST, JOACHIM VON. Christiados libellus ... ita vt quatuor iam sit instructus exornatusque Linguis, Latina videlicet, Græca, Ebræa & Germanica. ... VVitebergae anno M. D. LXXII. (... Excudebat Ioannes Crato ...) 8°. A-P^8. pp. 2-232. [294

BEUTER, PEDRO ANTONIO. Cronica generale d'Hispagna, et del regno di Valenza. ... nuouamente tradotta in lingua Italiana dal S. Alfonso d'Vlloa. ... In Vinegia appresso Gabriel Giolito de' Ferrari. M D LVI. (*Colophon.*) 8°. *-4*^{8} 5*^{6} A-KK^8 LL^4. pp. 1-533. [295

BEUTHER, ABRAHAM. ... Εναγισματα electoralia Saxonica, Consecrata memoriæ ... Augusti, Sax. ducis ... Lipsiæ, Iohannes Beyer imprimebat, Anno 1586. (*Colophon.*) 4°. A-C^4 D^2. [296

BEUTHER, MICHAEL. Michaelis Beutheri Carolopolitae commentariorum de rebus in Europa et aliis ... regnis, eodem Carolo V. Imperatore gestis Libri VIII ... Matthæo Delio Hamburgense interprete. ... Argentinæ Excudebat Theodosius Rihelius, Anno M. D. LXVIII. fol.)(^{6} a-ff^4. ff. 1-115. [297

BEYER, HARTMANN. Pro ficticio missae sacrificio Argumenta erronea Sophistarum Pontificiorum, cum Refutationibus eorundem. ... Andreas Epitimus. ... M. D. LI. (Magdeburgi per Christianum Rhodium.) 8°. A-F^8 (-F8, *presumably blank*). [298

-- Quaestiones nouae, in libellum de Sphæra Iohannis de Sacro Busto, ... collectæ ab Ariele Bicardo. 1549. Francoforti ex Officina Petri Brubachij. 8°. A^4 B-L^8 M^4. ff. 2-84. [299

BÈZE, THÉODORE DE. De haereticis a ciuili Magistratu puniendis Libellus, aduersus Martini

Belli farraginem, & nouorum Academicorum sectam [Genevae,] Oliua Roberti Stephani. M. D. LIIII. 8°. a-r^{8}. pp. 3-171. (Lea.) [300

-- [1] Histoire ecclesiastique des eglises reformees au royaume de France ... Deuisee en trois tomes ... A Geneue, De l'Imprimerie de Iean Remy. 1580. 8°. [*]-**^{6} a-3k^{8} 3l^{4} 3m^{8} 3n^{4}. pp. 1-901. [2] Deuxiesme volume de l'histoire ecclesiastique ... *Same imprint.* 8°. A^{8} A-3F^{8} 3G^{2} 3H^{8} 3I^{2}. pp. 1-836. [3] Troisiesme volume ... *Same imprint.* 8°. *^{4} A^{4} Aa-3G^{8} 3H^{4} A^{4} B^{2}. pp. 1-480. [301

-- Theodori Bezae Vezelii poemata. Lutetiae. Ex officina Conradi Badij sub prelo Ascensiana ... M. D. XLVIII. ... (... Roberto Stephano ... et sibi Conradus Badius excudebat, Idibus Iulii. ...) 8°. a-f^{8} g^{2}. pp. 3-100. (Lea.) [302

-- Tractatio de polygamia, in qua et Ochini apostatæ pro polygamia, et Montanistarum ac aliorum aduersus repetitas nuptias argumenta refutantur ... Ex Theodori Bezae Vezelii prælectionibus in priorem ad Corinthios Epistolam. Geneuæ, apud Eustathium Vignon. M. D. LXXIII. 8°. a-q^{8} r^{2}. pp. 3-260. [303

-- -- Geneuæ, apud Eustathium Vignon. M. D. LXXXVII. 8°. a-r^{8}. pp. 3-256. [304

-- Tractatio de repudiis et diuortiis ... ex Th. Bezae Vezelii praelectionibus in priorem ad Corinthios Epistolam. Geneuæ. Apud Eustathium Vignon. M. D. LXXIII. 8°. a-t^{8} v^{2}. pp. 3-293. [305

BIANCHI, FILIPPO. Trattato De gli Huomini illustri di Bologna ... Raccolto per Bartolomeo di Galeotti Bolognese. In Ferrara, Appresso Vittorio Baldini. M. D. XC. ... 4°. A-R^{4}. pp. 3-135. [306

-- -- *Another copy.* [307

BIBAUCUS, GUILIELMUS. Reuerendi patris Guilielmi Bibauci ... sacræ conciones. His additæ sunt orationes nonnullę ... Iodoci Hessi ... Item Poemation eiusdem de ordinis Carthusiani origine ... [Erfordiae, per Melchiorem Sachse,] Anno. M.D.XXXIX. 4°. a-c^{4} A-Z^{4} a-aa^{4} bb^{6}. [308

BIBLE. *Latin.* [1] Biblie iampridem renouate pars prima: cōplectēs pentateuchū: vna cū glosa ordinaria: et litterali moraliq3 expositione Nicolai de lyra: necnō additiōibus Burgēsis: ac replicis Thoringi ... fol. B.L. a-z$^{8.6}$ A-C^{6} D-Z$^{8.6}$ aa-ff$^{8.6}$ gg-hh^{8} (-hh8, *presumably blank*). ff. 2-377. [2] Secunda pars huius operis ... Super libros [*vinculum*] Iosue Iudicum Ruth Regum Paralipomenon Esdre Neemie Tobie Iudith Hester a-d^{8} e-f^{6} g-r^{8} s^{6} t^{8} v-x^{6} y-z^{8} A^{8} B-N$^{8.6}$ O-P^{8} (-b1-2, b7-8) Q-S^{6} T-V^{8}. ff. 2-327. [3] Tertia pars ... Super libros [*vinculum*] Iob Psalterium Prouerbiorum Ecclesiasten Cantica canticorum Sapientie Ecclesiasticum a-z^{8} A-Z^{8} aa-qq$^{8.6}$ rr^{6}. ff. 2-439. [4] Quarta pars ... Super libros [*vinculum*] Esaie Hieremie Threnorum Baruch Ezechielis Danielis Osee Amos Abdie Ione Michee Naum Abachuc Sophonie Aggei Zacharie Malachie Machabeorum a-z$^{8.6}$ A-Z$^{6.8}$ aa-xx$^{8.6}$ yy^{10}. ff. 2-478. [5] Quinta pars ... Sup libros [*vinculum*] Matthie Marci Luce Iohānis a-z$^{8.6}$ A-L$^{6.8}$ M^{6}. ff. 2-244. [6] Sexta pars Sup Epl'as ad [*vinculum*] Romanos Corinthios Galathas Ephesios Philippenses Colossenses Thessalonicenses Timotheum Titum Philemonem Hebreos Actus apostolorū Sup Canōica [*vinculum*] Iacobi Petri Iohānis Iude Apocalypsim (Cura ⁊ impensis ... Iohannis de Amerbach. Iohānis petri ᵭ Langendorff et Iohānis frōben ᵭ Hāmelburg ... industria ipsius Iohānis frōben ... Basilee impressum: Anno ... Millesimoquingentesimosecūdo. idibus Maijs explicit.) a-z$^{8.6}$ A-R$^{6.8}$. ff. 2-280. (Yarnall.) [308a

-- Biblia sacra Vtriusq3 Testamēti ... (Nurembergę per Foedericu3 Peypus. Sumptu ... Ioannis Koberger Nurembergēsis. Anno ... Millesimo quingentesimo vicesimotertio: Mense Augusto.) fol. B.L. π^{4} a-z^{6} A-Z^{6} A-C^{6}. ff. j-cclxxvj. [309

-- Biblia ... Lutetiae. Ex officina Roberti Stephani ... M. D. XLV. ... 4°. *^{8} **^{4} a-t^{8} v^{4} aa-xx^{8} yy^{4} 3a-3o^{8} 3p^{4} A-S^{8} T^{12} V-Y^{8} Z^{4} AA-RR^{8} SS^{4} TT-VV^{8} XX-ZZ^{4}. ff. 1-156, 1-172, 1-116, 1-180, 1-128. [310

-- Biblia sacra .... Lugduni, Apud Hæredes Iacobi Guinctæ. M. D. LI. 8°. *^{8} A-3B^{8} (-3B8, *presumably blank*). ff. 2-560. [311

-- Biblia Veteris ac Noui Testamenti, ... S. Pagnini ac Fr. Vatabli opera ita ex Hebræis Græcisq; fontibus expressa ... Basileae per Thomam Guarinum, M. D. LXIIII. ([Qq4^{r}] ...

Calend. Martii.) fol. α^{6} β^{4} a-z^{6} A-OO^{6} PP^{4} Aa-Pp^{6} Qq^{8} Rr-Vu^{6} Xx-Yy^{8}. pp. 1-727, 2-266. [312

-- Biblia sacrosancta Veteris ac Noui Testamenti Adiectis ... scholijs ... Auctore Isidoro Clario, Brixiano ... ex secunda eius recognitione. Deputatorum Concilij Tridentini seruata censura. Venetiis, apud Iunctas M D LX IIII. (... MDLVII. Mensis Iulij.) fol. π^{2} A-3R^{8} 3S^{10} 4A-4B^{8}. ff. 2-514, 1-15. (Lea.) [313

-- Biblia, Ad vetustissima exemplaria nunc recens castigata, Romæq; reuisa. ... Venetiis, Ex Officina Iuntarum. M D LXXIX. (*Colophon.*) 8°. ✠^{8} A-4A^{8} 4B^{4}. ff. 1-552. [314

-- [1] [Testamenti Veteris ... libri Canonici ... Latini ... facti ... ab Immanuele Tremellio & Francisco Iunio: accesserunt libri ... Apocryphi ... adjunximus novi Testamenti libros ... Londini, Excudebat Henricus Middletonus, impensis G.B. M.D.LXXX.] 4°. ¶^{8} (-¶1, ¶8, *the latter blank*) A-N^{8} O^{6}. pp. 2-219. [2] Bibliorum pars secunda, id est libri historici ... Londini, Typis Henrici Middletoni. M.D.LXXIX. Aa-Ss^{8} Tt^{6}. pp. 4-299. [3] Bibliorum pars tertia, id est, quinque libri Poetici ... *Same imprint.* 3A-3P^{8} 3Q^{6}. pp. 3-251. [4] Bibliorum pars quarta, id est, prophetici libri omnes ... *Same imprint.* 4A-4Z^{8} 4&^{8} 4$^{9\,4}$ (-4^{9}4, *blank*). pp. 4-390. [5] Libri apocryphi ... *Same imprint.* 5A-5M^{8}. pp. 3-192. [6] Iesu Christi D.N. Nouum Testamentum ... Londini, Excudebat T.V. Typographus, impensis G.B. M. D. LXXX. *^{2} A-L^{8} M^{10}. pp. 1-191. *S.T.C.* 2056.2. [315

-- [1] ... Secunda cura Francisci Junii. Genevæ, apud Ioan. Tornæsium, impensis And. Wecheli hæredum, Claudii Marnii, & Ioannis Aubrii. M. D. XC. 4°. &^{6} a-o^{8} p^{2}. pp. 1-228. [2] *Same imprint.* A^{4} A-R^{8}. pp. 1-271. [3] Francofurdi apud Andreæ Wecheli hæredes, Claudium Marnium, & Ioannem Aubrium. M. D. XC. A^{4} aa-nn^{8} oo^{6}. pp. 1-219. [4] *Geneva imprint.* A^{2} AA-XX^{8} YY^{4}. pp. 1-342. [5] *Frankfurt imprint.* A^{4} 3a-3i^{8} 3k^{10}. pp. 1-162. [6] D. N. Jesu Christi Testamentum Novum ... E Græco archetypo, Latino sermone redditum, Theodoro Beza interprete ... Cui ex adverso additur ejusdem novi Testamenti ex vetustissima tralatione Syra, Latina translatio Immanuelis Tremelii ... Franciscus Junius recensuit ... *Geneva imprint.* 4°. A^{4} Aa-Zz^{8} aA-gG^{8} hH^{10}. pp. 1-500. [316

-- *Danish.* [1] Biblia/ Det er den gantske Hellige Scrifft/ vdsoet paa Danske. ... Prentit i Kϕbenhaffn/ aff Ludowick Dietz. M. D. L. fol. B.L. 3A^{6} (-3A3, 6) A-P^{6} (-P6, *blank*) a-z^{6} Aaa-Fff^{6} Ggg^{4} (-Ggg4, *blank*). ff. [I]-LXXXIX, II-CLXXVII. [2] Alle Propheterne fordantskede. ... M. D. L. Aa-Za^{6} 3a-3c^{6} 3d^{4}. ff. II-XCVIII, II-LXII. [3] Det ny Testamente paa Danske. ... M. D. L. A-T^{6} V^{4} (-T6, V4). ff. II-XCI *present.* ¶*At the beginning and the end, many leaves are worn and more or less defective.* [317

-- *Dutch.* Biblia sacra Dat is De geheele Heylighe Schrifture bedeylt int Oudt eñ Nieu Testament. ... t'Antwerpen By Ian Moerentorf. Anno M. D. XCIX. ... (Typis Danielis Vervliet, & Henrici Swingelij.) fol. *^{4} A-3X^{6} 3Y^{8} A-Q^{6} R^{10}. ¶*Engraved t.p.* [318

-- *English.* [1] Biblia The Byble: that is the holy Scrypture of the Olde and New Testament, faythfully translated in to Englyshe. M. D. XXXV. ... fol. ✠^{8} a-p^{6}. ff. i-xc. [2] The seconde parte of the olde Testament. ... aa-vv^{6} Aa-Hh^{6} Ii^{4}. ff. ij-cxx, i-lij. [3] All the Prophetes in Englishe. ... 3A-3R^{6}. ff. ij-cij. [4] Apocripha ... A-O^{6}. ff. ij-lxxxi. [5] The new testament. ... (... fynished the fourth daye of October.) AA-TT^{6} (TT5 + *folded map*; -TT6, *blank*). ff. ij-cxiij. *S.T.C.* 2063. ¶✠^{8}, a1, *map in facsimile. Translator: Miles Coverdale.* [319

-- The Byble/ which is all the holy Scripture: In whych are contayned the Olde and Newe Testament truly and purely translated into Englysh by Thomas Matthew. ... [Antwerp, for Richard Grafton & Edward Whitchurch,] M, D, XXXVII, ... (*Colophon.*) fol. B.L. *^{6} **^{8} 3*^{6} a-Hh^{8} AA-LL^{8} MM^{6} 3A-3I^{8} 3K^{10} A-O^{8}. ff. ij-Ccxlvij, j-xciiij, ij-lxxj, ij-Cxi. *S.T.C.* 2066. [320

-- [1] The most sacred Bible, Whiche is the holy scripture, conteyning the old and new testament, translated in to English, and newly recognised ... by Rychard Tauerner. ... Prynted at London ... by Iohn Byddell, for Thomas Barthlet. ... M. D. XXXIX. fol. ☞^{4} ☞☞^{6} 3☞^{6} A-Oo^{6} Pp^{8} AA-OO^{6} PP^{8} 3A-3M^{6} 3N^{4}. ff. II-CCCXXX, II-LXXXXI, I-LXXV. [2] The New Testament ... Prynted ... M.D.XXXIX. A-I^{6} L-Q^{6} R^{8}. ff. II-CI. *S.T.C.* 2067. ¶☞^{4}, 3G1, 3G6, ^{2}R7-8 *in facsimile; some leaves repaired.* [321

-- The Byble in Englyshe, that is to saye the contẽt of al the holy scripture, both of ẏ^{e} olde, and newe testamẽt, with a prologe therinto made by ... Thomas archbysshop of Canterbury. ... Prynted by Edward whytchurche ... M.D.xl. (... ffynisshed in Apryll ...) fol.

B.L. *^{6} +^{4} a-k^{8} l^{4} A-P^{8} Q^{4} (-Q4, *blank*) AA-PP^{8} QQ-RR^{6} 3A-3K^{8} Aa-Nn^{8}. ff. ij-lxxxiiij, ii-cxxiij, ii-cxxxii, ii-lxxx, ij-ciiii. *S.T.C.* 2070. ¶*Great Bible version.* [322

-- [1] The Byble in Englyshe of the largest and greatest volume ... Printed by Edwarde Whitchurch ... 1541. fol. B.L. *^{6} a-i^{8}. ff. i-lxxij. [2] The seconde parte of the Byble ... A-N^{8} O^{4}. ff. ii-cviij. [3] The thirde parte of the Bible ... AA-OO^{8} PP^{4}. ff. ii-cxvi. [4] The .iiij. parte of the Byble ... 3A-3H^{8} 3I^{6}. ff. ii-lxxij. [5] The newe Testamēt in englyshe ... (... ffynyshed in Nouember. Anno. M.CCCCC.XL.) Aa-Kk^{8} Ll-Mm^{6} (-Mm6). ff. ii-lxxxix. *S.T.C.* 2072. ¶*Some leaves mounted. Great Bible version.* [323

-- [1] [The Byble, that is to say all the holy Scripture: In whych are cōtayned the Olde and New Testamente, truly ⁊ purely trāslated into English ... Imprinted at London by Ihon Daye ... and William Seres ... xvii. day of August. M.D.XLIX.] fol. B.L. AA-BB^{6} (-AA^{6}, BB1) CC^{8} (-CC8) D-R^{6} (-D1) S^{4}. ff. i-lxxxvi. [2] The seconde parte of the Byble ... 1549. Aa-Tt^{6}. ff. ij-cxiij. [3] The thyrd part of the Bible ... M.D.xlix. AA-GG^{6} HH^{8} II-ZZ^{6} AAa^{8}. ff. ii-cxlv. [4] The volume of the bokes called Apocripha ... Aaa-Mmm^{6} Nnn^{4}. ff. ij-lxxvi. [5] The newe Testament ... Printed ... M.D.XLIX. A-T^{6} V^{8}. ff. ij-cxxiij. *S.T.C.* 2077. ¶*Matthew version.* [324

-- [1] The Bible and Holy Scriptures conteyned in the Olde and Newe Testament. Translated according to the Ebrue and Greke, and conferred With the best translations in diuers langages. ... At Geneua. Printed by Rouland Hall. M.D.LX. 4°. ***^{4} a-z^{4} (v2 + *double-page map*) A-Zz^{4} (C3 + *folded map*) &^{6} 3A-5B^{4} (3T2 + *double-page map*). ff. 1-474. [2] The Newe Testament ... *Same imprint.* AA-ZZ^{4} (AA1 + *double-page map*, SS1 + *double-page map*) AAa-LLl^{4}. ff. 2-128. *S.T.C.* 2093. ¶*Geneva version. The authenticity of* 4P2-3 *and* FFf2-LLl3 *is uncertain.* [325

-- -- *Another copy* (-Ll2, Ll4, *map following* C3, *half of maps following* v2, 3T2, SS1). [326

-- -- *Another copy of the New Testament.* [327

-- The. holie. Bible. conteynyng the olde Testament and the newe. (Imprinted at London ... by Richarde Iugge ... [1568.]) fol. B.L. π^{8} *$^{10+1}$ *^{6} A-Q^{8} A-Y^{8} Z^{10} A-E^{8} F^{6} G-Aa^{8} Bb^{12} A-O^{8} P^{6} A-T^{8} V^{6} (-V6, *blank*). ff. j-Cxxviij, ij-clxxxv, ii-CCiiij, ij-cxviij, ii-clix. *S.T.C.* 2099. ¶*Bishops' Bible.* [328

-- -- *Another copy: t.p. defective, mounted, and colored; preliminaries bound in a different order.* (Yarnall.) [328a

-- [The holie Bible. Imprinted at London in Powles churcheyarde by Richard Iugge [1572].] fol. B.L. π^{8} (-π1, π3) *^{8} ℭ^{10} A-Kk^{8} Ll^{6} 3A-3Z^{8} 3&^{6} 4A-4M^{8} 4N^{10} A-R^{8} R^{8} (-R8) S^{4} (-S3-4). *S.T.C.* 2107. ¶*Bishops' version.* π^{2} *damaged and mounted. Lacks inserted map.* (Furness.) [329

-- [1] The Bible. Translated according to the Ebrew and Greeke, and conferred with the best translations in diuers languages. ... Imprinted at London by Christopher Barker ... (... 1578.) fol. B.L. (*.*)^{6} a-d^{6} e^{4} A-3Q^{6} 3R^{4} A-N^{6}. ff. 1-376, 1-76. ¶a1^{r}: Proper Lessons to be read for the first lesson ... b4^{r}: The booke of Common prayer ... [2] The Nevve Testament ... Imprinted at London by Christopher Barker ... 1578. (*Colophon.*) χ^{2} Aa-Tt^{6} *^{6} **^{4}. ff. 1-113. *S.T.C.* 2123. ¶*Geneva version.* [330

-- [1] The Bible and Holy Scriptures conteined in the Olde and Newe Testament. ... Printed in Edinbrugh Be Alexander Arbuthnet ... 1579. fol. (.˙.)^{10} (-(.˙.)2-4) a-r^{6} s^{6+1} t-4p^{6} (-4p6). ff. 1-503. [2] The Newe Testament ... At Edinburgh. Printed by Thomas Bassandyne. M.D.LXXVI. ... A-Y^{6} (-V4, X3-4, Y^{6}) Z^{8} (-Z1, Z4-8). ff. 1-125. *S.T.C.* 2125. ¶*Geneva version.* (.˙.)1, 5-10, Z2-3 *in facsimile; many margins repaired.* [331

-- [1] [The Bible ... with ... annotations ... And also a most profitable Concordance ... Imprinted at London by Christopher Barker ... 1581.] (*Colophon.*) 4°. B.L. π^{2} (*wanting*) A-3H^{8} (-Yy6) 3I^{2} *^{4} 3K-3Y^{8} 3Z^{10} A-L^{8} M^{4}. ff. 1-554. *S.T.C.* 2131. ¶*Additional t.pp.:* (*1) The Newe Testament ... Imprint[ed at London by] Christo[pher Barker ...] ... [1581. ...] (^{2}A1) Tvvo right profitable and fruitfull Concordances ... Imprinted at London [by Christopher Barker ...] ¶*1 *badly and* ^{2}A1 *slightly mutilated. For* Yy6 *another printing of the last leaf of Malachi has been substituted.* [2] The whole booke of Psalmes, collected into English meter by T. Sternhold, I. Hopkins, and others ... At London Printed by Iohn Daye ... 1581. ... 4°. B.L. A^{4} B-H^{8} (-H4-8). pp. 1-98. *S.T.C.* 2458. ¶*Geneva version.* [332

-- -- *Another copy.* ¶*Lacks* π^2. *Some running-titles trimmed. Without* The whole booke of Psalmes. (Furness.) [333

-- [1] The Bible. Translated according to the Ebrew and Greeke, and conferred with the best translations in diuers languages. Imprinted at London, by Christopher Barker ... 1583. fol. B.L. A-C^6 (-A1, *blank*, A6) D^4 A-4V^6. ff. 1-532. ¶*Additional t.pp.:* (Xx5^r) The Psalter, or Psalmes of Dauid ... Anno Do. 1583. (4E1^r) The bookes called Apocrypha ... Anno. 1583. [2] The Nevve Testament ... *Same imprint.* A-Z^6 *^{6} (*wanting*) **^{4} (*wanting*). ff. 1-137. *S.T.C.* 2136. ¶*Geneva version.* [334

-- [1] The Bible, that is, The holy Scriptures conteined in the Olde and Newe Testament ... Imprinted at London by the Deputies of Christopher Barker ... 1599. ... 4°. ¶^{4} A-Z^8 &^{6} Aa-Qq^8. ff. 1-190, 2-127. ¶1^r: *t.p. within border;* ¶2^r: *t.p. above.* [2] The New testament ... *Same imprint.* (*Colophon.*) 3A-3Q^8 (-3Q8) 3R^4. ff. 3-121. *S.T.C.* 2174. ¶*Geneva version. Probably printed after 1599 at Amsterdam.* [3] The booke of Psalmes: collected into English Meeter, by Thomas Sternehold, Iohn Hopkins, and others ... 4°. A-G^8. pp. 1-93. [335

-- -- *Same imprint, colophon, collation, and foliation. S.T.C.* 2179. ¶*With* Book of Psalms *dated 1636.* (Furness.) [336

-- *French.* [1] La saincte Bible en Francoys ... En Anuers/ par Martin Lempereur. An. M. D. ? .xxxiiij. ... fol. π^6 [device]^8 *^{6} A-Z^8 a-i^8 k^{10} l-z^8 Aa-Bb^8 Cc^{10}. ff. j-ccxcvj. [2] Le nouueau Testament ... [device]^8 AA-MM^8 NN^6 (-NN6). ff. j-ci. ¶*Translator: Jacques Lefèvre d'Étaples.* [337

-- La Bible, qui est toute la saincte escriture ... [Genève,] De l'imprimerie de Iean Crespin. M. D. LIII. 8°. a-z^8 A-X^8 AA-LL^8 *^{8}. ff. 2-351, pp. 1-175. [338

-- *German.* [1] Biblia Das ist: Die gantze heilige Schrifft: Deudsch. D. Mar. Luth. ... Wittemberg. Gedruckt durch Hans Lufft. 1565. (... 1564.) fol.)(^{8} A-Z^6 a-z^6 Aa-Ii^6 Kk^8. ff. 1-338. [2] Propheten alle Deudsch. ... *Same imprint.* A-Z^6 a-z^6 Aa-Rr^6 Ss^4. ff. 2-382. [339

-- [1] Biblia Das ist/ Alle Bᵉucher Alts vnnd Neüws Testaments/ ... verteütschet. ... 4°. **^{8} 3a-3b^8 a-z^8 A-N^8. ff. 1-288. ¶*Lowest fourth of t.p. wanting.* [2] Das ander teil dess alten Testaments mit sampt dem Neuwen. (Getruckt zů Zürych bey Christoffel Froschower/ ... M. D. LXX.) aa-zz^8 Aa-Ll^8. ff. 2-271. [340

-- *Greek.* Της θειας γραφης ... Diuinae sacripturae, Veteris ac Noui Testamenti, omnia ... Basileae, per Ioan. Heruagium, M D XLV. Mense Martio. (*Colophon.*) fol. *^{4} a-z^6 A-Z^6 Aa-Ss^6 Tt^4 Vv-Zz^6 AA-MM^6 NN^4. pp. 2-969. ¶*T.p. defective.* [341

-- *Spanish.* La Biblia, que es, los sacros libros del Vieio y Nueuo Testamento. Trasladada en Español. ... [Device of Thomas Guarinus of Basel.] M.D.LXIX. (... en Septiembre.) 4°. π^2 (-π2, *blank*) †^{8} *$_*$*^{6} A-Yy^8 AA-RR^8 a-q^8. cols. 3-1438, 1-544, 3-508. ¶*The t.p. is variant A of Darlow & Moule (8472). Lacks 4 ll. at the end. Translator: Cassiodoro de Reina. A copy of a 1619 ed. of* The booke of Psalmes (S.T.C. *2564*) *is bound in.* (Yarnall.) [341a

-- *Old Testament. Polyglot.* Biblia sacra, Ebraice, Chaldaice, Græce, Latine, Germanice, Saxonice, Studio & Labore Eliæ Hutteri Germani. Noribergæ. ... M. D. XCIX. fol. (*)^4 (-(*)4, *blank*) A-V^6 W-Z^6 Aa-4V^6 4X-4Z^8. ¶*Ends with* Deuteronomy. [342

-- *Hebrew & Latin.* מקדש י״י En tibi lector Hebraica Biblia, latina planeq; noua Sebast. Munsteri tralatione ... in hac secunda editione ... Basileae 1546. (... ex officin Michaelis Isingrinii & Henrici Petri, ...) fol. α-β^6 γ^8 a-z^6 A-Z^6 Aa-Zz^6 AAa-ZZz^6 AAA-ZZZ^6 Aaaa-Rrrr^6 Ssss^4 Tttt^6 (-Tttt6). pp. 2-1601. ¶*Additional t.p.* (Rr1): Veteris instrumenti tomus secundus ... Qq6 *mounted.* (Lea.) [343

-- *Hebrew.* [חמשה חומשי תורה] [Venice, Daniel Bomberg, 1521.] 4°. 1-17^8 (-11-2, 22-7) 18^4 19^8 20^{10} 21-34^8 35^6 36-49^8 50^{10} 51-54^8 55^4 56-57^8 58^{10} 59-66^8 67^6 (-676). ¶13-8 *misbound after* 38. [344

-- [1] ... מקדש י״י. עשרים וארבעה ספרי המכתב הקדוש ע ... Hebraica Biblia Latina planeque noua Sebast. Munsteri tralatione ... Basileae 1534 (... ex officina Bebeliana, impendiis Michaelis Isingrinii et Henrici Petri. ...) fol. α-β^6 a-z^6 A-Pp^6. ff. 2-365. [2] ... Veteris instrumenti tomus secundus ... Basileae M. D. XXXV. (... ex officina

Bebeliana, impendiis Michaëlis Isingrinij & Henrici Petri. ...) fol. α^4 AA-ZZ^6 aa-3z^6 3A-3C^6. ff. 336-795. [345

-- חמשה חמשי תורה. [Antwerp, Christopher Plantin, 1573-1574.] 8°. א-ת^8 אא^8 בב^8 גג^4 cols. 2-3, ff. 4-389. [346

-- דרך הקדש. Hoc est via sancta ... siue Biblia sacra eleganti et maiuscula characterum forma ... Authore Elia Huttero. ... Hamburgi. Impressa Typis Elianis, per Iohannem Saxonem. Anno M. D. LXXXVII. fol. (.)^6 ()^4 A-Z^4 AA^4 BB-TT^6 VV^8 XX-ZZZ^6 AA-ZZ^6 AAA-ZZZ^6 3A-3Z^6 AAAA^4. pp. 2-1572. [347

-- *Job.* Il libro di Iob, tradotto dalla Ebraica uerita, in lingua Italiana ... per Antonio Bruciolo. M D XXXIIII. (Stampato in Vinegia per Aurelio Pincio Veneto, fece stampare Antonio Brucioli ... del mese di Ottubrio.) 8°. π^2 A-PP^4. ff. 1-144. [348

-- *Proverbs. Italian.* Annotationi Di Antonio Brucioli, sopra i Prouerbi di Salomo, Tradotti per esso, dalla Ebraica uerita, in lingua Toscana. In Venetia M D XXXIII. (Stampate ... per Aurelio Pincio Venetiano del mese d'Ottobre. ...) 8°. ✠^{4} A-OO^4. ff. 1-148. [349

-- *Latin.* Prouerbia Salomonis iuxta Hębraicam ueritatem, per Philippum Melanchthonē reddita ... M.D.XXXVI. (Augustę Vindelicorum, per Alexandrum Vueyssenhorn.) 8°. A-G^8. [350

-- *Psalms. Polyglot.* Quincuplex Psaltęrium. Gallicum. Romanum. Hebraicum. Vetus. Conciliatū. (... ex ... Henrici Stephani officina ... emissū ... 1509 pridie Calēdas Augusti ...) fol. a^2 a^4 b-y^8 A-F^8 G^{10} H-O^8 P^4. ff. 5-292. ¶Iacobi Fabri Stapuleñ. præfatio. [351

-- Psalterium, Hebręum, Gręcū, Arabicū, & Chaldęū, cū tribus latinis īterp̄tatōibus & glossis. (Impressit ... Petrus Paulus Porrus, genuæ in ædibus Nicolai Iustiniani Pauli ... anno ... millesimo quingentesimosextodecimo mense. VIIIIbri.) fol. A^{10} B-Z^8 &^{8} ɔ^6. ¶*Editor: Augustinus Justinianus.* [352

-- *Latin.* Psalteriū Beati Brunonis ...: a Iohāne Cochleo ... restitutum ... Lipsiae. ... M. D. XXXIII. ... (Excusum ... per Nicolaum Fabrū ...) 4°. †^{22} A-Z$^{4.4.8}$ a-z$^{4.4.8}$ Aa-Zz$^{4.4.8}$ AA-BB^8 CC^6. [353

-- Psalmi aliquot ex Dauide ... versibus redditi, a Bernardo Holtorpio Hagensi. Anno M.D.LVIII. Mense Augusto. Francoforti ad Oderam per Iohan. Eichorn. 8°. A-B^8 C^4. [354

-- *English.* The whole booke of Psalmes, collected into Englishe Metre by T. Sternhold, W. Whitingham, I. Hopkins, and others: Conferred with the Hebrue, with apt Notes to sing them withall. ... At London, Printed by Iohn Daye ... 1583. 4°. B.L. A^4 B-Cc^8. pp. 1-384. ¶*Imperfect, lacking all after* Cc8. *After* Cc8 *two ll. of a 17th-century printing containing Ps.* Cxlviii-CL *and other matter have been added. Some ll. damaged and repaired. Seems to differ from the 1583 printings listed in the* S.T.C. (Furness.) [355

-- *Ps. lxiii.* Der sechs vnd dreyssigst psalm Dauid eynen Christlichen menschen zu leren vnd trösten ... Martinus Luther. Wittemberg [durch Melchior Lotter den J.]. M.D.XXiiij. 4°. a-c^4. [356

-- *Ps. ciii.* Der 103. Psalm ... In gesangs weiss. Mer drey schöner Geistlicher Lieder. ... (Gedruckt zu Nürnberg/ durch Friderich Gutknecht [c. 1555].) 8°. A^4. [357

-- *Ps. cxlvii-cil.* Die letztē drey Psalmen von Orgelen/ Pauckē/ Glocken vnd dergleychen eūsserlichen Gotssdienst/ ob vnd wie Got darynnen gelobt wyrdt/ Verdeūtscht durch Wentzesslaum Linck ... M D.XXIII. Zwickaw. (Gedruckt ... durch Iörg Gastel ...) 4°. A-C^4. [358

-- *Apocrypha.* Tomus quintus in quo continentur omnes libri Veteris Instrumenti qui sunt extra canonem Hebraicum, perperam Apocryphi ... Commentarijs Chuonradi Pellicani Rubeaquensis expositi. Chrsitophorus Froschouerus excudebat Tiguri mense Martio, anno M. D. XXXV. fol. *-**^{6} a-z^6 A-Ll^6. ff. 1-342. ¶*Part of an edition in 7 vols.* [359

-- *Ecclesiasticus.* Iesus Syrach zu Wittemberg verdeudscht. Martinus Luth. 1533. (Gedruckt durch Melcher Sachssen.) 8°. A-G^8. [360

-- *Maccabees.* Das buch von den Maccabeern ... Verdeudscht zu Wittemberg. D. Mart. Luth. M.D.XXXIII. (Gedruckt zu Wittemberg/ durch Hans Lufft. ...) 8°. a^8 A-L^8. [361

-- *New Testament. Greek.* Η Καινη Διαθηκη. Εν λευκετία τῶν παρησιων, παρα

Σίμωνι τῷ Κολιναίῳ, δεκεμβρίου μηνὸς δευτέρᾳ φθίνοντος ..., α. φ. λ. δ. [1534.] 8°. [a]^{2} b-g^{8} h^{2} i-z^{8} A-K^{8} L^{4} M-N^{8} O^{4} P^{8} Q^{6} R-X^{8} Y^{4} Z-BB^{8} CC^{6} DD^{8} EE^{2} FF-GG^{8} HH^{10} II^{8} KK^{10}. ff. 1-414. [362

-- [1] Της καινης διαθηκης απαντα. Nouum Testamentum. ... Lutetiae. Ex officina Roberti Stephani ... M. D. XLVI. (... VII. Id. Nouemb.) 16°. a-z^{8} A-K^{8}. pp. 3-528. [2] Αι του αγιου Παυλου εριστολαι. ... aa-yy^{8} zz^{6}. pp. 3-361. [363

-- -- Lutetiae, Ex officina Roberti Stephani ... M. D. L. (... XVII. Cal. Iul.) fol. *-**^{8} a-q^{8} r^{6} A-M^{8} N^{6}. pp. 2-272, 3-202. [364

-- Της καινης διαθηκης απαντα. [Antwerp, Christopher Plantin, 1573.] 8°. α-υ^{8}. pp. 1-207. [365

-- Η καινη διαθηκη. Nouum Testamentum. ... interpretationes margini adscripsit Henricus Stephanus. ... [Genevae, Henricus Stephanus?] Anno M. D. LXXXVII. 16°. A-C^{8} a-z^{8} A-F^{8} Aa-Xx^{8} (-Xx8, *blank*). ff. 2-230, 2-167. [366

-- *Greek & Latin.* Nouum instrumentū omne, diligenter ab Erasmo Roterodamo recognitum & emendatum ... Apud ... Basileam. ... (... in ædibus Ioannis Frobenij Hammelburgensis Mense Februario. Anno. M.D.XVI. ...) fol. 3a^{6} 3b^{8} A-DD^{6} a-h^{6} i^{8} k-s^{6} t^{6+1} u-mm^{6} nn^{8} oo-zz^{6} Aa-Ee^{6} Ff^{8}. pp. 2-324, 2-672. [367

-- Nouum Testamentum Graece et Latine, studio et industria Des. Erasmi Roterodami accurate editum ... Lipsiae. In officina Voegeliana. Anno M. D. LXIII. 8°. a-z^{8} A-Ff^{8} Gg^{4}. pp. 1-779. [368

-- [Novum Testamentum Graecum, cum interpretatione Latina Benedicti Ariae Montani. Antverpiae, Christophorus Plantin, post 1571.] 8°. A-Vu^{8} (-A1, *t.p.*). pp. 4-681. (Lea.) [369

-- Iesu Christi domini nostri Nouum Testamentum, siue Nouum foedus, Cuius Græco contextui respondent interpretationes duæ: vna, vetus: altera, Theodori Bezæ. ... [Genevae] Sumptibus haered. Eust. Vignon. M. D. XCVIII. fol. ¶^{4} (-¶4, *blank*) a-b^{6} A-5A^{6} 5B^{8} 5C-5D^{6}. pp. 2-577, 1-563. [370

-- *Latin.* Noui testamenti aeditio postrema, per D. Erasmum Roterodamum, cum Scripturæ Concordantijs. ... capitum Argumenta, Elegiaco Carmine, per Rodolphum Gualterum. Impressum Francoforti ad Menum, per Vuigandum Han. M. D. LX. 8°. †^{8} (-†2) *^{8} A-Z^{8} a-z^{8} Aa-Bb^{8}. ff. 1-367. [371

-- -- Tiguri in officina Froschouiana, Anno M. D. LXIII. 8°. Aa^{8} a-z^{8} A-F^{8} aa-bb^{8} cc^{4}. ff. 1-320. [372

-- Nouum Iesu Christi Testamentum. Antuerpiae, Ex officina Christophori Plantini. M. D. LXIIII. (... XI. Kalend. Ianuarii.) 16°. a-z^{8} A-S^{8}. ff. 2-316. [373

-- *Latin & English.* The newe Testament in Englyshe and Latyn accordyng to the translacyon of doctour Erasmus of Roterodam. Anno. M.CCCCC.XXXVIII. ... Printed in Fletestrete by Robert Redman ... (*Colophon.*) 4°. B.L. π^{4} A-NN^{8} OO^{4} PP^{8} QQ^{4}. ff. iij-CC.CXXXXij. *S.T.C.* 2815. ¶*Additional t.p.* (A1^{r}): The newe Testament ... Anno Dñi. 1538. π^{4}, QQ^{4} *in facsimile; some leaves repaired.* [374

-- The newe testament both Latine and Englyshe ... Faythfully translated by Miles Couerdale. Anno. M.CCCCC.XXXVIII. ... Printed in Southwarke by Iames Nicolson. ... 4°. ✠^{6} A-Vv^{8}. ff. 2-344. *S.T.C.* 2816. [375

-- *English.* The newe Testament/ dylygently corrected and compared with the Greke by Willyam Tindale: and fynesshed ... A. M. D. ꝛ xxxiiij. in the moneth of Nouember. 8°. *-**^{8} A-Z^{8} a-z^{8} Aa-Ee^{8}. ff. i-ccccii. *S.T.C.* 2826. ¶*Additional t.p.* (A1^{r}): The newe Testament, Imprinted at Anwerp by Marten Emperowr. Anno. M.D.xxxiiij. [376

-- The Nevve Testament of our Lord Iesus Christ. ... At Geneua Printed By Conrad Badius. M. D. LVII. (... this X. of Iune.) 8°. *^{8} **^{4} a-z^{8} A-Ll^{8}. ff. 1-455. *S.T.C.* 2871. ¶*Translator: presumably William Whittingham.* [377

-- [The Newe Testament of our Sauiour Iesus Christe ... (Imprinted at London ... by Richard Iugge ... [1566?])] 4°. B.L. ☛^{8} (*wanting*) ℭ^{10} (*wanting*) A-Pp^{8} (-A1, Pp^{8}) Qq^{4} (*wanting*). *S.T.C.* 2873. ¶*Translator: William Tyndale.* [378

-- The Nevv Testament of our Lord Iesus Christ translated Out Of Greeke By Theod. Beza ...

Englished by L. Tomson. Imprinted at London by Christopher Barker ... 1576. ... (*Colophon.*) 8°. ♠^{2} †^{8} ♣^{8} *^{8} A-3L^{8} 3M^{4} 3N-3O^{8}. ff. 1-460. *S.T.C.* 2878. [379

-- The New Testament of Iesus Christ, translated faithfully into English, out of the authentical Latin ... In the English College of Rhemes. ... Printed at Rhemes, by Iohn Fogny. 1582. ... 4°. a-c^{4} d^{2} A-5D^{4} 5E^{2}. pp. 1-745. *S.T.C.* 2884. [380

-- The text of the New Testament of Iesus Christ, translated out of the vulgar Latine by the Papists of the traiterous Seminarie at Rhemes, With Arguments ... and Annotations ... VVhereunto is added the Translation out of the Original Greeke, commonly vsed in the Church of England, with A Confutation of all such arguments, glosses, and Annotations As Conteine Manifest impietie, of heresie, treason and slander ... By William Fulke ... Imprinted at London by the Deputies of Christopher Barker ... 1589. fol. *^{4} A-4V^{6} 4X^{4}. ff. 1-496. *S.T.C.* 2888. [381

-- *German.* Das New Testament/ durch ... Hieronymum Emser trewlich verdeutscht ... Gedrückt zur Neyss/ durch Iohann Creutziger/ In vorlegung des ... Herrn Wilhelm Bischoffs zu Olmutz etc. ... M. D. LXXI. (*Colophon.*) 8°. a-b^{8} c^{4} A-3I^{8} 3K^{4} (-3I8, 3K4, *the latter presumably blank*). pp. 1-881. [382

-- *Syriac.* דיתיקא חדתא. [Antwerp, Christopher Plantin, 1574.] 8°. A-H^{8}. pp. 1-121. [383

-- *Gospels. Latin.* Commentarii initiatorii in quatuor euangelia. ... Iacobo Fabro Stapulensi authore. (Basileae, ex aedibus Andreae Cratandri, mense Martio, anno M D XXIII.) fol. a-z^{6} A-Yy^{6} Zz^{8}. ff. 1-410. [384

-- *English & Old English.* The gospels of the fower Euangelistes translated in the olde Saxons tyme out of Latin into the vulgare toung of the Saxons ... At London. Printed by Iohn Daye ... 1571. ... (*Colophon.*) 4°. A^{4} ¶^{2} B-Y^{4} Aa-Yy^{4} AA-HH^{4}. pp. 2-408. *S.T.C.* 2961. ¶*The English text in the Bishops' version.* [385

-- *Revelation.* Apocalipsis idest reuelatio Iesu christi ... (impressum est in ... Parisiorum gymnasio per Iohannem barbier ... pro Iohāne paruo. Anno ... millesimo quingentesimo decimo quinto. sole vero Iunij vicesimā claudēteꝫ.) 8°. B.L. AA-BB^{8} CC^{4}. [386

-- *Concordances.* Concordantiæ Bibliorum vtriusque Testamenti ... Antuerpiae, ex officina viduae et haeredum Ioannis Stelsii. Anno M.D.LXVII. ... (... ecxudebat [*sic*] Amatus Tauernerius anno M. D. LXVI.) fol. a-zz^{8} A-Y^{8} Z^{4}. ¶*By Robert Estienne. T.p. repaired.* [387

-- Concordantiæ bibliorum vtriusque Testamenti, Veteris et noui ... Antuerpiæ, Ex officina Christophori Plantini, M. D. LXXXV. (*Colophon.*) 4°. A-Z^{8} a-z^{8} AA-SS^{8} TT^{10}. [388

-- *Glossary.* Bibliorum phrasis sanctae ... Haganoæ, ex officina Iohan. Sec. An. M. D. XXVIII. (... Mense Augusto.) 8°. A-BB^{8}. ff. 1-191. [389

BIBLIANDER, THEODOR. Ad illustrissimos Germaniae principes ... Oratio Theodori Bibliandri: de restituenda pace in Germanico Imperio ... Basileae, per Ioannem Oporinum. 4°. a-l^{4} (-l4, *blank*). pp. 4-83. ¶*Dated 3 August 1553.* [390

-- De ratione comuni omnium linguarum & literarū commentarius ... Tiguri apud Christoph. Frosch. an. M.D.XLVIII. 4°. α^{4} a-z^{4} A-E^{4} F^{6}. pp. 1-235. [391

BIDELLI, GIULIO. Diuerse rime ... MDLI. (In Vinegia per Francesco Marcolini ...) 8°. A-D^{8} (-D8, *presumably blank*). [392

BIEL, GABRIEL. Gabriel in secundū librum sententiaꝝ. fol. B.L. a^{8} b-v^{6} x^{8} (-x8). ¶*Part of* Collectorium super IV libros sententiarum (Augustae, Iohannes Otmar pro Friderico Meynberger). [393

-- -- [1] Inuentarium seu Repertorium generale ... contentorū in quattuor collectorijs ... Gabrielis byel: super quattuor libros sententiarum. fol. B.L. ♣a^{10}. [2] Gabriel super primo sententiarum (in ... Lugduneñ. emporio arte ... Iohānis Cleyn alemāni impressum [1519].) a^{8} b-o^{6} p^{8}. [3] Gabriel in secundum librum sententiarum. aa^{8} bb-oo^{6} ♣aa^{8}. [394

-- -- [1] Gabriel Biel in tertium librum Sententiarum. ... Simon Vincentius, 1526 fol. B.L. A-M^{8} N^{6} †A^{8} (-†A8, *presumably blank*). [2] Gabriel Biel in quartum librum Sententiarum. ... Simon Vincentius. 1526 (Impressus est ... in ... ciuitate Lugduñ. per ... Iacobum Myt Sumptu ... Symonis vincentij ... M.cccccxxvij.) AA-VV^{8} XX^{6} yy^{4}. (Lea.) [395

-- -- Commentarius in tertium librum sententiarum Magistri Gabrielis Biel ... Brixiae apud Thomam Bozolam. M. D. LXXIIII. 4°. †-††^{8} Aa-3A^{8} 3B^{6}. pp. 1-392. ¶*Published with commentaries on books I-II, IV.* [396

-- Gabrielis Biel ... sacri canonis misse tam mystica q̄3 litteralis expositio ... (in officina ... Iacobi Pfortzensis ... excusa Basilee. Anno dn̄i millesimo quingentesimo decimoquinto/ sub Kalendas Nouembres.) fol. B.L. a^{8} b-z^{6} A-K^{6} L^{8} M-X^{6} 1-2^{8} (-14-5). ff. II-CCLXVIII. (Lea.) [397

-- -- *Another copy (lacking* 23-4*).* [398

-- -- Sacri canonis missae ... expositio ... addita fuit ... sanctiss. Altaris Sacrificij expositio, Autore Zacharia Andriano Brix. ... Brixiae apud Thomam Bozzolam. M. D. LXXVI. (*Colophon.*). 4°. ✠^{8} 1-3^{8} A-3R^{8} 3S^{4} (-3S4, *presumably blank*). pp. 1-1013. (Yarnall.) [398a

-- Sermones ... de festiuitatibus ... virginis marie (Impensis ... Ioannis Rynman de Oringaw ... in officina ... Henrici Gran in oppido ... Hagenaw Ciuis ... M.d.x. impressi, die .x. Iulij finiunt ...) 4°. B.L. nn-pp^{8} qq^{6} rr-ss^{8} tt^{6} vv-zz^{8} ꝛꝛ^{8} ꝯꝯ^{8} ꝝꝝ^{8} 3a-3d^{8} 3e^{6} 3f^{8} (-3f8, *blank*). ff. CCXCVII- CCCCXLVII. ¶*Additional t.p.* (yy1^{r}): Sermões de Sanctis ... [399

-- Gabrielis Byel Suppleme̅tū in octo & viginti Distinctiones vltimas Quarti Magistri Senten. [per D.] Vuendelinū Stambachum Butzb[achen]sem ... collectum ... [Ve̜nunda]tur apud Conradum Resch ... ([prelo quidem & industria Iodoci Badii Ascensii, ... impendio Conradi Resch, Bibliopolarum Parrhisiis iuratarum, nuper impressum ... ad Idus Ianuarias ... .M.D.XXI.]) fol. a-z^{8} A-N^{8}. ff. II-CCLXXXVIII. ¶*Lacks index* (O-P^{8} Q-R^{6}); *t.p. repaired.* (Lea.) [400

-- ... Gabrielis Biel ... Tractatus de potestate ꝛ vtilitate monetarū. [Oppenheimii, Jacobus Kōbel, 1516.] 4°. a-b^{4}. [401

BIESIUS, NICOLAUS. Nicolai Biesii Gandauensis, de natura, lib. V. Antuerpiæ, Apud Philippum Nutium. M. D. LXXIII. ... 8°. *^{8} **^{4} A-Y^{8} Z^{4}. ff. 1-180. [402

BIGI, LUIGI. In Christi Vitam Epigrammaton Libellus (Impressum Mediolani per Ioannem Angelū scinze̅zeler ... M.ccccxiii. die, xvii. decembris.) 4°. A-D^{8} E^{4+1}. [403

-- Lodouici Bigi Pictorii Ferrariensis Opusculorum Christianorum, libri tres ... Pontii Paulini Carmen Iambicum Christianā pietatem commendans. ... (stamneis calamis Arge̅toraci ... exscripta sunt [per Matthiam. Schürer]. Decimo sexto K. Februar. ... M.D.VIIII.) 4°. A^{4} B^{8} C-D^{4} E^{8} F-L$^{4\cdot4\cdot8}$ M^{8} (-M8, *blank*). ff. II-LX. [404

BILDNIS. Bildnüs vnd Abcontrafactur: etlicher Vornemer Gelerten Menner ... Dressden. Gedruckt durch Gimel Bergen. Anno 1588. (*Colophon.*) 4°. A-P^{4}. [405

BILLERBEG, FRANCISCUS DE. Epistola Constantinopoli recens scripta. De præsenti Turcici imperii statu, & Gubernatoribus præcipuis, & de Bello Persico. Item confessio fidei, quam Gennadius, patriarcha Constantinopol. post captam primùm à Turcis vrbem, Mahometi II. imp. flagitanti exhibuit. Et De Tartaris quædam. Anno M. D. LXXXII. 4°. A-D^{4} E^{2}. ¶A2^{r}: Franciscus de Billerbeg Dauidi Chytræo S. D. (Lea.) [406

BINSFELD, PETER. Tractatus de confessionibus maleficorum & Sagarum, an, et quanta fides ijs adhibenda sit. ... Augustae Treuirorum Excudebat Henricus Bock, Anno M D LXXXIX. ... 8°. (:)^{8} A-N^{8} O^{4} (-O4, *presumably blank*). pp. 2-196. (Lea.) [407

BINWALD, DAVID. De videndi ratione ac modo disputatio ... Lipsiæ anno M. D. LXX. 8°. A-B^{8} (-B8).. (Smith.) [408

BIONDO, FLAVIO. Roma trionfante di Biondo da Forli, Tradotta ... per Lucio Fauno di latino in buona lingua volgare. ... (In Venetia, per Michiele Tramezzino. Nel M D XXXXVIII.) 8°. A-C^{8} a-zz^{8}. ff. 1-368. [409

BIONDO, MICHEL ANGELO. Angoscia la prima furia del mondo. ... Dalla Casuppula del Biondo. (In Vinegia per Giouann'Antonio, e Pietro fratelli de Nicolini de Sabio. Nell'anno. M D XXXXII. del Mese di Marzo.) 8°. A-E^{8} F^{4}. [410

-- Doglia la seconda furia del mondo. ... M D XLII. Dalla Casuppula del Biondo. (In Vinegia per Giouann'Antonio, e Pietro fratelli, de Nicolini da Sabio. ...) 8°. A-E^8. [411

BIRCK, SIXT. De vera nobilitate orationes duae ... autore Bonagarso Pistoriense ... Tota rei actio in ludi formam redacta per Xystum Betuleium Augustanum ... M.D.XL. (Augustae Vindelicorum apud Philippum Vlhardum. ...) 8°. A-E^8. ¶E3^r: Dionysii Halicarnassei præcepta de oratione Nuptiali eodem interprete. [412

-- Iudith drama comicotragicum. ... Xysto Betuleio Augustano Autore. (Augustae Vindelicorum Philippus Vlhardus excudebat [1539].) 8°. A-K^8. [413

-- Susanna comoedia tragica. Per Xystum Betulium Augustanum. Coloniae Ioannes Gymnicus excudebat. Anno M. D. XXXXI. 8°. A-F^8. [414

BIRCK, THOMAS. Comoedia. Dariñen den Gottsuergessnen Doppelspilern/ ... vñ ... die Würffel vnnd Karten ... erklårt ... Getruckt zu Tübingen/ bey Georgen Gruppenbach ... 1590. 4°.):(-2):(^{4} 3):(^{2} A-V^4 X^2. pp. 1-164. [415

BIRINGUCCIO, VANNUCCIO. Pirotechnia. Li diece libri della pirotechnia ... M D L. (In Vinegia, per Giouan Padoano, a instantia di Curtio di Nauò. ...) 4°. ✠^{8} A-X^8. ff. 1-157. (Smith.) [416

-- -- M D LVIII. (In Vinegia Per Comin da Trino di Monferrato. M D LIX.) 4°. *^{8} A-X^8. ff. 1-168. ¶X8 *defaced.* (Smith.) [417

-- -- Pirotechnia del S. Vannuccio Biringuccio ... In Venetia Appresso P. Gironimo Giglio, e compagni. M. D. LIX. 8°. a-xx^8. ff. 2-345. (Smith.) [418

-- -- La pyrotechnie, ou art du feu ... traduite d'Italien en Francois, par feu maistre Iaques Vincent. ... A Paris, Chez Claude Fremy ... 1556. 4°. *^{4} a-z^4 A-Kk^4 Ll^6. ff. 1-230. (Smith.) [419

BISCHOFF, JOHANN. Ein schön new lustigs Keyserbůchlein/ in drey theyl getheylt. ... Durch M. Iohan Episcopium, von Würtzburg. [Rothenburg, Zacharias Gros, in verlegung Iohann Bischoffs, 1569.] 8°.)(^{8} A-Z^8 a^8 b^4 (-b4, *colophon*). ¶*In verse.* [420

BLANCAS, JERONIMO. Aragonensium rerum commentarii. Hieron. Blanca, Cæsaraugustano, ... auctore. ... Cæsaraugustæ. Apud Laurentium Robles, & Didacum fratres ... ∞DXXCIIX. fol. ✠^{6} *^{4} A-Tt^6 Vu^8 Xx^4 (-Xx4, *blank*) Y^6 Zz^6 3A^6 3B^8. pp. 1-519. (Lea.) [421

BLANCHELLUS, MENGHUS. Menghi Fauentini ... expositiones questionesqȝ super summulis ... Pauli Veneti: vna cū ... additionibus Iacobi Ritij Aretini: ⁊ Manfredi de Medicis. ... Venetiis M D XLII (Venetijs apud heredes Luce antonij Iunte [Florentini] ... mense Martio.) fol. B.L. a^6 A-O^8 P^6 Q-T^8 V^{10} X-Y^8 Z^6 AA-DD^8 EE^{10} (-EE10, *presumably blank*). ff. 1-132 *present.* ¶EE9 *defective.* [422

BLOCHINGER, MATTHIAS. Klag an künigkliche Maiestat Vngern vñ Behem wiđ ainen Lutherischen münch prediger ordēs über viertzig artickel von jm geprediget ... Wittemberg. [Augsburg, Melchior Ramminger, 1523.] 4°. A-C^4. [423

BOAISTUAU, PIERRE. Histoires prodigieuses, extraictes de plusieurs fameux Autheurs, Grecs & Latins, sacres & Prophanes, diuisees en deux Tomes. Le premier mis en lumiere par P. Boistuau ... Le second par Claude de Tesserant, & augmenté de dix histoires par François de Belle-Forest ... A Paris, Chez Iean de Bordeaux ... 1574. ... 8°. ã^8 A-3E^8. ff. 1-396. ¶*Additional t.p.* (Ee1^r): Le second tome, contenant vingtquatre histoires prodigieuses. Scauoir est, Quatorze par Claude de Tesserā ..., & dix ... par François de Belleforest ... *Same imprint.* (Acheué d'imprimer le quinziesme iour de Feurier ...) (Furness.) [424

-- -- Historias. Prodigiosas y marauillosas ... Escriptas en lengua Francesa, por Pedro Bouistau, Claudio Tesserant, y Francisco Beleforest. Traduzidas en romance Castellano, por Andrea Pescioni, vezino de Seuilla. ... En Medina del Campo Por Francisco del Canto. A costa de Benito Boyer ... M. D. LXXXVI. 8°. (?)^8 A-3D^8 3E^4 (-3E4). ff. 1-390. ¶(?)1-2 *defective.* [425

-- Le theatre du monde, ou il est faict vn ample discours des miseres Humaines. ... nouuellement traduict en Aleman ... Ein schawplatz oder spiegel der Welt ... Coloniae, Apud Ioannem Gymnicum. M. D. LXXIIII. ... 8°. 3^4 A-Y^8 Z^4 &^{2}. ff. 2-182. ¶*Parallel French and German texts.* [426

BOATTO, ANTONIO. Le Theuolane de Boatto academico Desioso ... In Vinegia M.D.XLII. (... stampati ... per Venturino di Roffinelli ...) 8°. A-B^8 C^4. ff. 1-15. [427

BOBALJEVIĆ, SABO MISETIĆ. Rime amorose, e pastorali, et satire, Del Mag. Sauino de Bobali Sordo, Gentil'huomo Raguseo. ... In Venetia. CIↃ IↃ XXCIX. Presso Aldo. 4°. *^{4} A-Y^4. pp. 2-171. [428

BOCCACCIO, GIOVANNI. *Ameto.* Ameto di Messere Giouanni Boccaccio. Con le osseruationi in uolgare grãmatica sopra esso di Hieronimo Claricio (Impresso in Milano nella officina Minutiana a ispese di Andrea Caluo A Di. X. de Giugnio. M. D. XX.) 4°. AA^6 [a]^4 b-c^4 A-Z^4 &^{4} ɔ^4 ℞^{4}. ff. V-ciiii. ¶[a]^4 *bound before* AA1. [429

-- -- Ameto del Boccacio. (Impresso in Fiorenza per gli heredi di Philippo de Giunta. ... M D XXI. adi .xx. Febraio.) 8°. a-n^8. ff. 2-94. [430

-- -- Ameto ouer comedia delle nimphe Fiorentine ... (Stampata nella ... citta di Venetia per Nicolo Zopino e Vicentio compagno. nel .M.D.XXIIII. adi xx. de Decembrio. ...) 8°. A-M^8. ff. 2-95. [431

-- -- (Stampata in Vinegia per Gregorio de Gregori nel M.D.XXVI. del mese de Maggio.) 8° A-M^8. ff. 2-95. [432

-- -- Ameto del Boccaccio. (Impresso in Firenze per gli heredi di Philippo de Giunta ... M.D.XXIX. adi .xxix. di Maggio.) 8°. a-n^8. ff. 2-102. [433

-- -- Ameto comedia delle ninfe Fiorentine, ... con la dichiaratione de'luoghi difficili di M. Francesco Sansouino. ... In Venetia, M D XCII. Presso Gio. Battista Bonfadino. 12°. A-L^{12}. pp. 3-260. [434

-- *Amorosa Fiametta.* Fiammetta del Boccaccio. (Stampata in Firenze per Philippo di Giũta ... M.D.XVII Del mese Daprile ...) 8°. a-o^8 (-o8, *presumably blank*). ff. 2-110. [435

-- -- Fiammetta amorosa ... M.D.XXVII. (Stampata in Vinegia per Francesco Bindoni, & Mapheo Pasini, compagni ... Adi .XX. del mese di Febraro.) 8°. A-L^8. [436

-- -- L'amorosa Fiammetta ... In Vinegia appresso Gabriel Giolito de' Ferrari. M D LXII. 12°. A-I^{12} K^6. pp. 3-228. [437

-- -- L'amor[osa] Fiamme[tta] ... In Venetia Appresso Fabio, & Agostin Zoppini Fratelli. MDLXXXIIII. 12°. A-I^{12} K^6. pp. 3-219. ¶A1 *defective.* [438

-- -- In Venetia appresso i Gioliti. M D LXXXV. (*Colophon.*) 8°. A-N^8 O^4. ff. 2-107. [439

-- *Amorosa visione.* Amorosa visione Di M. Giouan Boccaccio ... Apologia di Gieronimo Claricio Immol. contra Detrattori della Poesia del Boccaccio. Osseruationi di uolgar grammatica del Boccaccio. M D XXXI. (In Vinegia per Nicolo d'Aristotile detto Zoppino. ...) 8°. A-P^8 (-P8, *presumably blank*). [440

-- -- In Vinegia appresso Gabriel Giolito de' Ferrari. M D LVIII. (... MDXLIX.) 8°. A-K^8. ff. 2-78. [441

-- *Compendium Romanae historiae (spurious).* Ioannis Boccatii. Die Gantz Rœmisch histori ... Ein ... Oration M. T. Ciceronis/ für M. Marcellum ... Alles zůsamen bracht/ vnd verteũtscht/ durch Christophorum Brunonem von Hyrtzweil ... Getruckt zů Augspurg/ bey Hainrich Stayner/ im̃ M.D.XXXXII. Jar. (... am xij. tag Iunij ...) fol. A^4 B-E^6. ff. I-XXIII. [442

-- *Corbaccio.* Laberinto d'amore di .M. Giouanni Boccaccio con una Epistola à Messer Pino de Rossi confortatoria del medesimo autore. (Im̃psso in Firenze [per Filippo di Giunta] ... M.D.XVI.) 8°. A-I^8. ff. 2-72. [443

-- -- (Im̃psso in Firenze ... M.D.XXV.) 8°. A-I^8. ff. 2-72. [444

-- -- Laberinto d'amore di M. Giouanni Boccaccio ... In Vinegia Appresso Gabriel Giolito de Ferrari. MDXLV. 8°. A-G^8 H^4. ff. 2-56. [445

-- -- Il Corbaccio, altrimenti laberinto d'amore ..., di nouo corretto da M. Lodouico Dolce ... In Vinegia appresso Gabriel Giolito de Ferrari e fratelli. MDLI. 12°. A-D^{12} E^6. ff. 2-51. [446

-- -- Laberinto d'amore ... In Venetia, Appresso Fabio, & Agostin Zoppini Fratelli. MDLXXXIIII. 12°. A-E^{12}. pp. 3-113. [447

-- *De casibus virorum illustrium*. Ioannis Bocatii de Certaldo ... de casibus virorum illustrium libri nouem. ... opera Hieronymi Ziegleri Rotenburgensis repurgatus ... Augustæ Vindelicorum. ... M.D.XLIIII. (... Philippus Vlhardus excudebat. Mense Maio. ...) fol. α-γ^4 A-Z^4 a-k^4 l^6. ff. 1-273. [448

-- -- The tragedies, gathered by Ihon Bochas, of all such Princes as fell from theyr estates ... Translated into Englysh by Iohn Lidgate ... Imprinted at London, by Iohn Wayland ... [1554.] fol. ¶^{6} A-Y^6 Z^4 ꝛ^6 W^6 *^{6} +^{6} ₵^{6} Aa-Ff^6 Gg^4 (-Gg4). ff. i-clxiii, i-xxxvii. *S.T.C.* 3178. [449

-- -- Traite des mesaduentures de personnages signalez. Traduict du Latin de Iean Boccace, & reduict en neuf liures: par Cl. Witart ... A Paris, Chez Nicolas Eue ... 1578. ... 8°. ã^4 a-z^8 A-V^8 X^4. pp. 1-696. [450

-- -- I casi de gli huomini illustri ... tradotti, & ampliati per M. Giuseppe Betussi da Bassano ... In Vinegia al segno del pozzo MD L I (... per Pietro & Giouan Maria fratelli de i Nicolini da Sabbio ... à tredici d'Agosto.) 8°. A-KK^8 LL^4 *^{8}. ff. 9-264. [451

-- *De claris mulieribus*. Boccace des dames de renom, Nouuellement traduict d'Italien en Langue Françoys. ... A Lyon chez Guil. Rouille ... 1551 8°. a-z^8 A^8 (-A8). pp. 3-384. ¶*Translator: Denis Sauvage.* [452

-- -- Lopera de misser Giouanni Boccacio de mulieribus claris. ... (Stampado in Venetia per maistro Zuanne de Trino: chiamato Tacuino: ... m.d.yi. adi vi. de marzo ...) 4°. a^6 b-c^8 (-b8) D-T^8 V^4. ¶*Translator: Vincenzo Bagli.* M4 *misbound after* M2, M6 *after* M3. [453

-- -- Libro di M. Giouanni Boccaccio Delle Donne Illustri. Tradotto di Latino in Volgare per M. Guiseppe Betussi, con vna giunta fatta dal medesimo, D'Altre Donne Famose. E vn' altra nuoua giunta fatta per M. Francesco Serdonati ... In Fiorenza, Per Filippo Giunti. M D XCVI. ... (*Colophon.*) 8°. †-††^{8} A-Tt^8 Vu-Xx^4 Yy-3A^8 (-3A7-8, *presumably blank*). pp. 1-676. [454

-- *Genealogia deorum*. Genealogie Iohannis Boccacij ... Eiusdēq3 de mōtib. & siluis ... nominib. ... Parrhisiis ... impressi ... (... opera et expensis Dionisii roce Lodouici hornken & sociorum eius vicesima secunda die Augusti anno ... millesimo quingentesimo vndecimo.) fol. a^4 b-t^8 v^{10}. ff. vi-CLXII. [455

-- -- Ioannis Bocatii περι γενεαλογιας deorum, libri quindecim, cum annotationibus Iacobi Micylli. Eiusdem de montium, syluarum ... nominibus, Liber I. ... Basileae apud Io. Heruagium mense Septembri anno M. D. XXXII. (*Colophon.*) fol. aa-ee^6 ff^4 a-z^6 A-S^6 T^8. pp. 1-504. [456

-- -- Geneologia de gli dei. I quindeci libri di M. Giouanni Boccaccio ... Tradotti et adornati per Messer Giuseppe Betussi da Bassano. ... In Vinegia al segno del pozzo MDXLVII (Stampato ... per Comino da Trino di Monferrato. ...) 4°. *^{8} A-PP^8. ff. 1-286. [457

-- -- Della geneologia de gli dei ... In Venetia, Appresso Francesco Lorenzini da Turino. M D LXIIII. 4°. *^{8} b^8 c^4 A-KK^8. ff. 2-263. [458

-- -- In Venetia, Appresso Marc'Antonio Zaltieri. 1588. 4°. *^{8} b^8 c^4 A-Kk^8 Ll^4. ff. 1-268. [459

-- *De montibus*. Opera dell'huomo dotto et Famoso Giouan Boccaccio ... dalla lingua latina nel thosco idioma per Meser Nicolo Liburnio nouamente trallatata. Doue per ordine d'Alphabeto si tratta diffusamente delli monti; selue: boschi: fonti: laghi: fiumi: stagni: paludi golfi: & mari: Dell'uniuerso mondo ... 4°. ☞^{2} A-H^8 I^6. ff. I-LXX. [460

-- *Decamerone*. Il decamerone di M. Giouanni Boccaccio. (Impresso in Vinegia per Gregorio de Gregori il mese di Maggio dell'anno M.D.XVI.) 8°. A-X^8 AA-XX^8 3A^8 3B^{12} ✠^{8} (-✠8, *blank*). ff. I-CCCIII. [461

-- -- Il decamerone ... con tre nouelle aggiunte. (Impresso in Vinegia nelle Case d'Aldo Romano, & d'Andrea Asolano suo suocero ... M.D.XXII. Del mese di Nouembre.) 8°. a-z^{8} A-N^{8} O^{10} P-Q^{8} F^{4} S^{8}. ff. 2-317. [462

-- -- Il decamerone ... In Venetia M. D. XLV. (... Appresso di Agostino Bendone ...) 8°. A-3M^{8}. ff. 2-453. [463

-- -- Il decamerone ... Nuouamente alla sua vera lettione ridotto da M. Lod. Dolce. ... In Vinegia appresso Gabriel Giolito de Ferrari, et fratelli. M D LII. (*Colophon.*) 12°. *^{12} A-PP^{12} (-PP12, *presumably blank*). pp. 1-848. ¶*Additional t.p.* (NN4^{r}): Dichiaratione di M. Francesco Sansouino di tutti vocaboli, detti, prouerbij, e luogi difficili ... *Same imprint.* [464

-- -- Il decamerone ... Aggiuntee le annotationi di tutti quei luoghi, che ... da Monsig. Bembo ... sonó stati nelle sue prose allegati. In Lione, appresso Gulielmo Rouillio. 1555. ... 16°. a-z^{8} A-Oo^{8}. pp. 3-932. [465

-- -- Il decameron ... Emendato secondo l'ordine del Sacro Conc. di Trento ... In Fiorenza Nella Stamperia de i Giunti MDLXXIII. (*Colophon.*) 4°. *-4*^{4} a-z^{8} Aa-Nn^{8} Oo^{2}. pp. 1-578. [466

-- -- Il Decameron ... alla sua vera lezione ridotto dal Caualier Lionardo Saluiati ... Seconda editione. In Firenze. Del mese d'Ottobre. Nella stamperia de' Giunti. M.D.LXXXII. (*Colophon.*) 4°. *-**^{8} a-nn^{8} oo^{6} pp-ss^{8} tt^{6}. pp. 1-585. [467

-- -- ... Quarta editione. In Firenze. Del mese di Febbraio. Nella stamperia de' Giunti. M.D.LXXXVII. (*Colophon.*) *Same collation and pagination.* [468

-- -- Il decamerone ... Di nuouo riformato da M. Luigi Groto cieco d'Adria ... Con le Dichiarationi Auertimenti, & vn Vocabolario fatto da M. Girolamo Ruscelli. ... In Venetia, M D LXXXVIII. Appresso Fabio, & Agostino Zoppini Fratelli, Et Onofrio Fari Compagni. (*Colophon.*) 4°. *^{4} A-Mm^{8} Nn^{2} Oo-Rr^{8} Ss^{4} (-Ss4, *presumably blank*). pp. 1-564. [469

-- -- Centum Nouella Iohannis Boccatij. Hundert neuwer historien ... M. D. XXXV. (Zů Strassburg durch verlegung Iohannis Albrechts getruckt bey M. Iacob Cammerlandern.) fol. π^{4} A-Z^{6} a-m^{6} n^{8}. ff. j-ccxviij. [470

-- -- *Selections.* Mythica Historia Ioannis Boccacij: ꝑ Philippũ Beraaldũ de Italico in latinum translata. In qua ostendit exemplo ... ob mores beluinos Cymonis dicti ... (Impressuȝ Liptzk ꝑ Iacobũ Tanner. 1505) 4°. B.L. A^{6} B^{4}. [471

-- *Dialogo d'amore (suppositious).* Dialogo d'amore di M. Giouanni Boccaccio. ... Tradotte di Latino in volgare, da M. Angelo Ambrosini. ... In Venetia, Appresso Fabio, & Agostin Zoppini Fratelli. M D LXXXIIII. (*Colophon.*) 12°. A-B^{12} C^{6}. ff. 3-26. [472

-- *Filocolo.* Il Philopono di Messer Giouanni Boccaccio ... da Messer Tizzone Gaetano di Pofi riuisto. ... (Impressa in uinegia da me Iacobo da lecco ... 1527. & .6. di settembre.) 8°. A-Z^{8} a-u^{8} x^{12}. pp. 1-702. [473

-- -- Il Philocopo ... (Stampata in Venegia, per Bernardino di Bindoni, Milanese. ... M D XXXVIII.) 8°. A-Z^{8} a-u^{8} x^{12} (-x12, *blank*). *Same pagination.* [474

-- -- Il Filocopo ... Di nuouo riueduto ... da M. Francesco Sansouino. ... In Venetia Appresso Francesco Lorenzini. M. D. LXIIII. 8°. A-3A^{8} 3B^{4}. ff. 2-390. [475

-- -- In Venetia, MDLXXV. Appresso Giouan Antonio Bertano. 8°. A-3A^{8} 3B^{4}. ff. 2-293. [476

-- -- Le Philocope ... Traduict d'Italien en Francois, par Adrien seuin ... A Paris Chez la veuue Maurice de la Porte ... 1555. 8°. ā^{8} A-GG^{8} (-GG8, *presumably blank*). pp. 3-7, ff. 1-240. [477

-- *Urbano (suppositious).* Vrbano di M. Giouan Boccaccio. ... di nuoua reuista da Nicolao Granucci Lucchese. ... In Lucca per Vincentio Busdrago. MDLXII. 8°. A-E^{8}. pp. 3-80. [478

BOCCADIFERRO, LUIGI. Ludouici Buccaferrei Bononiensis ... in duos libros Aristotelis de generatione et corruptione ... commentaria. A Ioanne Carolo Saraceno ... repurgata. ... Venetiis, Apud Franciscum de Franciscis Senensem MDLXXI. fol. π^{2} a-g^{6} h^{4} A-Ss^{6} Tt^{4}. ff. 1-248. [479

-- Ludouici Buccaferrei ... Lectiones, In quartum Mateororum Aristotelis Librum ... Venetijs, Apud Franciscum de Franciscis Senensem. M D LXIII. (*Colophon.*) fol. $*^6$ $**^4$ $A\text{-}X^6$ (-X6, *blank*). ff. 1-249. [480

-- Ludouici Buccaferei ... lectiones super primum librum meteorologicorum Aristotelis ... Venetiis Ex officina Ioan. Baptistæ Somaschi. M D LXV. (*Colophon.*) fol. $*\text{-}**^6$ $A\text{-}S^6$. ff. 2-108. [481

-- Domini Ludouici Buccaferrei ... lectiones super tres libros de anima Arist. ... Venetiis, Ex officina Ioan. Baptistæ Somaschi & fratres. M D LXVI. (*Colophon.*) fol. a^4 b^6 $A\text{-}Nn^4$ (-Nn4, *blank*). ff. 2-143. [482

BOCCAFUOCO, CONSTANTIO. Conciliatio dilucida omnium controuersiarum, quæ in doctrina ... S. Thomæ, & ... Ioannis Scoti passim leguntur. ... Auctore ... Constantio Sarnano ... Romae, Apud Dominicum Basam. M. D. LXXXIX. 4°. $*^4$ $A\text{-}Kk^4$ Ll^6. pp. 1-255. [483

-- Expositiones quaestionum ... Ioannis Duns Scoti, in vniuersalia Porphyrii. Ab ... Constantio Sarnano ... collecta. ... Venetijs, apud Franciscum Franciscium, 1591. 8°. $a\text{-}b^8$ c^4 $A\text{-}Ll^8$. pp. 1-534. [484

BOCER, JOHANN. De origine et rebus gestis, ducum Megapolensium. Libri tres ... Lipsiae in officina Valentini Papae. Anno M. D. LVI. 8°. $A\text{-}H^8$ I^4 (-I4, *presumably blank*). ¶*In verse.* [485

BOCKEL, JOHANN. Oratio funebris de ... Iulio duce Brunouicens. et Lunæburg. ... Helmaestadii Excudebat Iacobus Lucius, Anno M. D. LXXXIX. 4°. $A\text{-}C^4$. [486

BODEKER, JOHANN. Carmen panegyricum de Iohanne Baptista ... Lubecae Typis suis recens excudebat Iohannes Balhorn ... M. D. LI. 4°. A^4. [487

BODENSTEIN, ANDREAS, of Karlstadt. Appellation: Andres Bodenstein võ Carolstad zu dem ... gemeynẽ Cõcilio Christlicher vorstendiger vorsamelung. Vuittemberg [Melchior Lotter junior, 1520]. 4°. A^6. [488

-- De coelibatu, monachatu, et viduitate. ... [Basileae, Andreas Cratander,] Anno M. D. XXI. 4°. $a\text{-}d^4$. [489

-- Ain frage ob auch yemant moͤge selig werden on die fürbit Marie. ... Anno. M. D. xxiiij. Wittenberg. [Augsburg, Philipp Ulhart, 1524.] 4°. $A\text{-}B^4$. [490

-- Missiue von der aller hochsten tugent gelassenhait. ... [Augsburg, Sigmund Grim & Marcus Wirsung, 1519.] 4°. $A\text{-}B^4$. [491

-- Ob man mit heyligen schrifft erweysen müge/ das Christus mit leyb/ bluͦt vnd sele im Sacrament sey. ... [Basel, Thomas Wolff,] M. D. XXIIII. 4°. $A\text{-}E^4$ F^6. [492

-- Andree Bodenstains von Carolstat Predig zuͦ Wittenberg. Von empfahung des hailigen Sacraments. [Augsburg, Silvan Otmar,] M.D.XXII. 4°. $a\text{-}b^4$. [493

-- Sendbrief D. An. Boden. von Carolstat meldende seiner Wirtschafft. ... Wittemberg [Augsburg, Melchior Ramminger, 1522.] 4°. A^4. [494

-- Vrsachen das Andreas Carolstat ain zeyt stillgeschwigen. Vonn rechter vnbetrüglicher berüffung. [Augsburg, Simprecht Ruff,] M,D.XXiiij. 4°. $A\text{-}C^4$. [495

-- Verba Dei Quanto candore & q̃ȝ syncere prædicari, quantaqȝ solicitudine vniuersi debeant addiscere. ... Cõtra D. Ioannẽ Eckiũ ... Vuittenbergæ, apud Melchiorem Lottherum iuniorem, Anno M.D.XX. 4°. $A\text{-}G^4$. ff. II-XXVII. [496

-- Von abtuhung der Bylder/ Vnd das keyn Betdler vnther den Christen seyn sollen. ... (Gedruckt tzu Wittenberg Nickell Schyrlentz ... Tausent funff hundert vñ tzway vnd tzwentzigsten Jar.) 4°. $A\text{-}E^4$. [497

-- Von Bepstlicher heylickeit ... Wuittemberg [Melchior Lotter junior, 1520]. 4°. $A\text{-}F^4$ G^6. ¶G6 *defective.* [498

-- Von dem Newen vnd Alten Testament. ... [Augsburg, Philipp Ulhart,] M. D. XXV. 4°. $A\text{-}C^4$ D^2 E^4. [499

-- Von den empfahern zaychen/ vnd zůsag des hailigen sacraments flaisch vñ blůts Christi. 4°. A-C4. [500

-- Von gelubden vnterrichtung ... (Gedruckt zu Wittembergk [durch Nickel Schirlentz] ... Tausent funff hundert vnnd ayn vnnd zwentzigsten iar) 4°. A-H4. [501

-- Von geweychtem Wasser vnd Saltz: Do. Andreas Carlstat Wider den vnuerdienten Gardian Franciscus Seyler. (Getruckt [zu Strassburg durch Martin Flach] ... M D XX.) 4°. A-D4 (-D4, *presumably blank*). [502

-- Von manigfeltigkait des ainfeltigen ainigen willen Gottes. Was sũnd sey. Andreas Bodenstain von Carolstat/ ain newer Lay. [Augsburg, Silvan Otmar,] Anno. M.D.XXIIII. 4°. A-G4 H6 (-H6, *presumably blank*). [503

-- Von vormugen des Ablas. wider bruder Franciscus Seyler ... (Gedruckt zu Wittenbergk durch Iohan. Grunenberg. 1520.) 4°. A-B4. [504

-- Welche bucher Biblisch seint. ... Vuittembergk. ([Melchior Lotter junior] ... M.D.XX.) 4°. A-C4. [505

-- Wider die alte vñ newe Papistische Messen. ... [Basel, Thomas Wolff,] M. D. XXIIII. 4°. [A]4. [506

BODERIUS, THOMAS. De ratione & vsu dierum criticorum opus ... Cui accessit Hermes Trismegistus de decubitu informorum ... Parisiis, Apud Andream Wechelum ... M. D. LV. (*Colophon.*) 4°. a-o4. ff. 2-56. [507

BODIN, JEAN. De la demonomanie des sorciers. ... A Paris, Chez Iacques du Puys ... M. D. LXXX. ... 4°. ã4 ẽ4 ĩ4 õ2 A-3S4. ff. 1-252. (Lea.) [508

-- -- Io. Bodini Andegauensis de Magorum Dęmonomania libri IV. Basileae Per Thomam Guarinum M D LXXXI. 4°.):(4 *-**4 ***4 a-z4 A-Pp4. pp. 2-488. (Lea.) [509

-- -- *Another copy.* (Lea.) [510

-- -- *Another copy, with a different setting of sig.*):(, *here signed*)(. Io. Bodini Andegauensis de magorum daemonomania libri IV. Nunc primum e Gallico in Latinum translati Per Lotarium Philoponum. Basileae Per Thomam Guarinum, M. D. LXXXI. [511

-- [1] Les six liures de la republique ... A Paris. Chez Iacques du Puys ... 1583. ... 8°. ã8 ẽ4 a-zz8 A-Z8. pp. 1-1060. [2] Apologie de Rene Herpin pour la republique de I. Bodin. A Paris. Chez Iacques du Puys ... M.D.LXXXI. 8°. A-E8 F4. ff. 2-44. [512

-- -- Ioannis Bodini Andegauensis de republica libri sex, Latine ab authore redditi ... [Parisiis,] Apud Iacobum Du-puys, Anno 1591. 8°. ¶8 a-z8 A-G8 H1 *present.* pp. 1-482. ¶*Three books only.* [513

-- Io. Bodini paradoxon, quod nec virtus vlla in mediocritate, nec summum bonum in virtutis actione consistere possit. ... Parisiis, Excudebat Dionysius Duvallius ... M. D. LXXXXVI. 8°. A-F8 G2. pp. 3-100. [514

BOECE, HECTOR. Scotorum Historiæ ... Quæ omnia impressa quidem sunt Iodoci Badii Ascensii typis & opera: impensis ... Hectoris Boethii Deidonani: a quo sunt & condita & edita [1527]. fol. ã8 ẽ8 ĩ8 õ8 ũ10 AA-BB8 CC6 a-z8 A-Z8. ff. III-XXI, I-CCCLXVIII. ¶Z8 *defective.* [515

BOEHME, MICHAEL. Vita Alberti III. animosii, ducis Saxoniæ ... Accessit oratio de ... Duce Augusto Saxoniæ Electore, &c. ... 1586. Lipsiæ ... (... Typis Georgij Defneri. ...) 4°? A-X4. pp. 1-156. [516

BOEMUS, JOANNES. ... Liber Heroicus de Musicæ laudibus. Carmen Sapphicum/ de laude & situ Vlmæ ... Oratiunculæ item Metricæ sex ... Quæstio quædam Theologica ... Elegiæ duæ ... Cum multis alijs Epigrãmatib9 (In officina excusoria Ioannis Miller Augustæ Vindelicorum: quartadecima die mensis Decembris ... M.D.XV.) 4°. a-d4 e6 (-e3-4, *supplied photographically*). [517

-- Mores, leges, et ritus omnium gentium ex multis ... scriptoribus ... Parisiis Apud Hieronymum de Marnef ... 1561. 16°. A-AA8. ff. 2-178. [518

-- -- Gli costumi le leggi, et l'vsanze di tutte le genti, raccolte qui insieme da molti Illustri scrittori ... tradotti per il Fauno in questa nostra lingua uolgare. In Questi tre Libri si contiene. l'Africa, l'Asia, l'Europa. In Venetia, Nel MDXLIX. ... (Stampata ... per Michele Tramezino, ... Del mese di Marzo.) 8°. ✠^{8} A-Z^8 (-Z8, *presumably blank*). (Lea.) [519

BOETHIUS, ANICIUS MANLIUS SEVERINUS. Duplex cõmentatio ... ĩ Boetium (seu Boethum mauis) de consolatione philosophica ⁊ de disciplina scholastica. Ea videlicet que diuo Thome aquinati ascribitur: ⁊ que ab Ascensio recentius est emissa. Vna cum libello de moribus in mensa ... a Sulpitio verulano edito. (Impressum Mediolani per zanotum de Castelliono Impensis ... Io. Iacobi ⁊ Fratrũ de Legnano. ... Mcccccxij. Die vero octauo Mensis Octobris.) fol. B.L. A-P^8 Q^6 a-b^8 c^{10} (-c10, *presumably blank*). [520

-- -- Seuerini Boetii de philosophiae consolatione eiusdem de scholastica disciplina. ([Venetiis,] Alexander Paganinus [c. 1515].) 24°. A-I^8. ff. 2-72. (Lea.) [521

-- -- Boetio Seuerino di consolatione Philosophica uolgare ... (Stampato in Vinegia per Marchio Sessa ... MDXXXI. nel mese di Dicembrio.) 8°. A-O^8. ff. 2-104. ¶*Translator: Anselmo Tanzo.* [522

-- -- Boezio Seuerino della consolazione della filosofia. Tradotto di lingua Latina, in uolgare Fiorentino, da Benedetto Varchi. ... In Venetia, Ad instantia de i Giunti di Fiorenza. MDLXII. 8°. A^{12} B-N^8 (-N8, *presumably blank*). ff. 3-103. [523

-- -- In Fiorenza. Appresso Giorgio Marescotti 1584. 12°. A^6 B-K^{12} L-M^6 (-M6, *presumably blank*). pp. 1-211. [524

-- Anitii Manlii Seuerini Boethi ... dialectica, ... à Martiano Rota restituta ... Ioan. Gryphius Venetiis excudebat. ... MDXLIX. (*Colophon.*) fol. *^{4} A-LL^4 MM^6 (-MM6, *presumably blank*). pp. 1-279. [525

BOHEMIA. Confessio fidei ac religionis, baronum ac nobilium regni Bohoemiæ, ... Romanorum, Bohoemiæ &c. Regi, Viennæ Austriæ, sub anno Domini 1535 oblata. ... (Witebergae in officina Georgii Rhavv.) 4°. A-L^4. ff. 2-34. ¶*Includes:* Praefatio Doctoris Martini Lutheri. [526

BOHEMIAN BRETHREN. Bekāntnuss/ Des Heiligen Christlichen Glaubens/ aller dreyer Stānde des Kōnigreichs Behmen ... Gedruckt ... M. D. XCV. 8°. A-E^8 F^4 (-F4, *presumably blank*). pp. 1-62. ¶*Translator: Heinrich von Kurzbach.* [527

BOHIER, NICOLAS. Consuetudines Bituricẽses præsidatuum ... à Domino Nicolao Boerio ... decisæ. Aurelianenses præsidatuum, à Pyrrho Englebermeo ... enucleatæ. Turonenses præsidatuũ, à Ioanne Sainson ... Parisiis, Apud Ioannem Foigny ... 1543 ... (*Colophon.*) 4°. π^1 a-z^8 A-S^8 T^{10} aa-bb^8 (-aa1). ff. j-cccxxxiij. ¶T10^v: *device of Galliot du Pré.* [528

-- -- [1] Consuetudines infrascriptarum ciuitatum, et prouinciarum. ... Francofurti, Ex officina Typographica Nicolai Bassæi. M. D. LXXV. (*Colophon.*) fol.)(^{4} A-K^6 L-M^4 N-O^6. pp. 1-137. [2] Consuetudines Aurelianae ciuitatis ... *Same imprint.*)(^{4} a-o^6 p^4 Aa-Yy^6. pp. 1-127, ff. 128-145, pp. 1-245. [529

-- Dn. Nic. Boerii decisionum aurearum, in sacro Burdegalens. senatu ... Pars prima. ... Venetiis, M D LXIII. 4°. a-c^8 d^4 A-3N^8 3O^4. pp. 2-949. (Biddle.) [530

-- -- Decisiones Burdigalenses Nicol. Boerii ... Eiusdem item Tractatus de vita & statu Eremitarum, Additiones in tract. Io. Montani de authorit. magni Concilij. ... Boerij Consilia, Tractatus de Seditiosis & De custodia clauium portarum ciuitatis. Lugduni, apud Caesarem Farinam. M D LXVI. fol. *a*^{4} a-z^6 A-Zz^6 AA-FF^6 GG^4 HH-LL^6 MM^4. pp. 2-908. [531

-- Questio de custodia clauium portarum ciuitatũ: castrorum: ⁊ aliorum locorum fortilitiorum ... [*Privilege to Simon Vincent of Lyon dated 3 June 1512.*] 4°. B.L. A-B^8 C^4 (-C4, *presumably blank*). ff. ii-xix. (Biddle.) [532

-- Solẽnis repetitio famose .l. cõsentaneũ .C. quomodo ⁊ qñ iudex. ... [Lugduni, Simon Vincent, 1512.] 4°. B.L. a-d^8 e^6. ff. ii-xxxviij. (Biddle.) [533

BOIARDO, MATTEO MARIA. Orlando inamorato composto gia dal Signor Matteo Maria Boiardo conte di Scandiano, et rifatto ... da M. Francesco Berni. ... Stampato In Milano nelle case di Andrea Caluo. M.D.XXXXII. 4°. π^4 A-KK^8 (-KK7-8, *presumably blank*). ff. 1-262. [534

-- -- ... seconda editione ... M D XLV. (Stampati ... In Venetia per li heredi di Lucantonio Giunta ... Nel mese di Giugnio.) 4°. A-FF^8 GG^6. ff. 2-238. [535

BOISSARD, JEAN JACQUES. Vitæ et icones sultanorum Turcicorum, principum Persarum aliorumq3 illustrium Heroum Heroinarumq3 ab Osmane usq3 ad Mahometem II. ... Omnia ... incisa ... per Theodorū de Bry ... Francf. ad moen. A° M.D.XCVI. 4°. A-Zz^4. pp. 1-356. ¶*Engraved t.p.* [536

BOLLO, PIERRE DE. [1] Oeconomia canonica de sacrorum catholicæ Christi familiæ Ministrorum officio & conseruanda vbique maiorum Ecclesiastica disciplina ... Lugduni, sumptibus Petri Landry. M.D.LXXXVIII. ... 8°. *-$5*^4$ a-z^4 A-Zz^4 AA-CC^4. pp. 1-552. [2] Authentica probatio sacrosancti missæ sacrificii. ... *Same imprint.* $+^4$ A-CC^4. pp. 1-204. (Lea.) [536a

BOLOGNA. *Collections of laws.* Statuta criminalia communis Bononiae ab originali in Bononiensi archiuo publico existente sumpta ... (Bononiæ Impressa Impensis Heredum Benedicti quondam Hectoris de Faellis ... M.D.XXV. Nonis Maii.) fol. A-P^6 Q^4 AA-CC^8 (-CC8, *presumably blank*). ff. 2-94. (Lea.) [537

-- Statuta ciuilia Ciuitatis Bononiæ ... (Ioannes Baptista Phaellus ... Bononiæ typis suis formauit, impensis ... Hippolyti Fronto, Anno ... Millesimo Quingētesimo Trigesimo secundo Kal. Iuniis.) fol. a-p^6 q^8 A-LL^6 MM^8. ff. I-CCXI. (Lea.) [538

-- [1] Statutorum inclytae ciuitatis studiorumque matris Bononiæ. Cum scholiis D. Annibalis Monterenti ... Tomus Primus. Bononiae, Typis Ioannis Rubei. 1561. ... (*Colophon.*) fol. π^4 A-PP^6. pp. 1-455. [2] Sanctionum, ac prouisionum inclytae ciuitatis ... Bononiae, cum ... scholiis ... Annibalis Monterentii. Tomus Secundus. Bononiae, Apud Ioannem Rossium ... MDLXIX. ... (*Colophon.*) fol. π^2 a-ff^6. pp. 1-344. [3] Sanctionum, ac prouisionum inclytae ciuitatis ... Bononiae ... Tomus Tertius. Bononiae, Apud Ioannem Rossium ... MDLXXIIII. ... (... MDLXXVII.) fol. $✠^6$ A-BB^6 CC^4 (-CC4, *presumably blank*). pp. 1-288. [4] Lib. VI. A^6 B-M^4 N^2. pp. 1-103. [5] Liber VII. A-I^6. pp. 1-108. [6] De vendit. & alienationib. bon fum. a^6 b^2. pp. 1-7. [7] Bulla Prima Iulii secundi. A^6 B^4. pp. 1-20. ¶*A copy of* Scholia ... Monterentii ... ad nonnullas pactorum formulas instrumentis inserendas *is bound in between* [6] *and* [7]. (Lea.) [539

-- *Separate laws, ordinances, &c.* Bando della Quaresima publicato ... Febraro M D LXI. In Bologna per Alessandro Benaccio. 4°. π^2. [540

-- Bando delli cartelli publicato ... alli XI. Marzo. MDLXIIII. In Bologna, Per Alessandro Benaccio. 4°. π^2. [541

-- Bando sopra gli archebusetti prohibiti, et libelli famosi con la insertione della Bolla de N.S. Papa Pio Quarto sopra detti archebusetti ... Publicatto ... alli xxvii. Aprille. MDLXIIII. In Bologna. Per Alessandro Benaccio. M D LXIIII. 4°. π^4. [542

-- Bando che non si possa dar ne pigliar denari per andar a soldo. Publicato in Bologna alli XXIII. Marzo. M D LXV. (Per Alessandro Benaccio.) s.sh. 19 × 31 cm. [543

-- Bando dell'armi del ... Cardinale il Sig. Francesco Crasso. Publicato ... li 2. di Maggio. MDLXV. In Bologna per Alessandro Benaccio. 4°. π^2. [544

-- Sopra le licenze d'arme. Publicato alli VIIII. Febraro. MDLXVI. In Bologna per Alessandro Benaccio. 4°. π^2. [545

-- Bando sopra le arme et altri capi Publicato ... alli X. & XIII. Aprile MDLXVI. In Bologna, Per Alessandro Benaccio. MDLXVI. 4°. A^4. [546

-- Bando sopra il denonciare tutti li trasgressi, & eccessi de gli Ebrei. Publicato in Bologna adi xxiii. Nouemb. 1566 ... In Bologna, Per Alessandro Benacci. 4°. A^4. [547

-- Bando sopra il denontiare li frumenti de cittadini che si trouano in contado. ... Publicato ... Alli 29. Nouembre, & reiterato alli 3. Decembre. M D LXVII. In Bologna, Per Alessandro Benaci. MDLXVII. 4°. π^2. [548

-- Constitutio ab ... Ioanne Baptista Doria Bonon. Gubernatore, edita ... Super literis cambii, scriptis priuatis, et eorum vsu. Bononiae, Ex officina Alexandri Benatij. M.D.LXVII. 4°. A^4. ¶*Dated* X. Kal. Decemb. [549

-- Bando sopra le prouocationi, cartelli, disfide, ò altre Scritture per combattere, ò Questioni. Publicato in Bologna il di 21. di Maggio. MDLXVIII. (In Bologna per Alessandro Benacci. ...) s.sh. 31 × 21.5 cm. [550

-- Prohibitione d'ogni sorte d'arme per la citta eccetto che della Spada sola ... Publicata ... alli VII. Luglio. MDLXVIII. (In Bologna, per Alessandro Benazzi. ...) 4°. π^2 ($\pi 1^r$ *and* $\pi 2^v$ *blank*). [551

-- Dicchiaratione del portare dell'Arme, & Lanterne. Publicata alli xii. & reiterata alli xiii di Nouembre. M D LXVIII. (In Bologna per Alessandro Benacci.) 4°. π^2 ($\pi 1^r$ *and* $\pi 2^v$ *blank*). [552

-- Decreta, et constitutiones ... Io. Baptistae Doria ... Bononiæ Gubernatoris, Super Procuratoribus, & Notariis Ciuitatis Bon. Bononiae Apud Ioannem Rossium ... 1568. ... 4°. A-C^4. (Lea.) [553

-- Bando sopra gli Archibugi da Ruota, & da Fuoco Publicato ... alli xiiii d'Aprile 1569. (In Bologna per Alessandro Benacci. ...) 4°. π^2 ($\pi 1^r$ *and* $\pi 2^v$ *blank*). [554

-- Bandi dell'illustris. ... Cardinale Sfortia di Bologna ... In Cesena, Appresso Bartholameo Rauerii. M D LXX. fol. A^8. (Lea.) [555

-- Bando Sopra quelli che vendono Olio à minuto ... Publicato ... alli di Marzo MDLXXVII. (In Bologna per Alessandro Benacci.) 4°. π^2 ($\pi 1^r$ *and* $\pi 2^v$ *blank*). [556

-- Confirmatione de bandi. Rinouationi delle Sicurtà di non offendere. Riuocationi delle Licenze dell'Armi. Prohibitioni de Pugnali lunghi, & corti, & Archibugi. ... Publicata ... alli 16. & reiterata alli 18. di Genaro. 1578. In Bologna per Alessandro Benacci. MDLXXVIII. 4°. π^2. [557

-- Bando Sopra la Reuocatione delle licenze d'Armi ... Publicato ... l'ultimo d'Aprile 1578. In Bologna, per Alessandro Benacci. 4°. A^2. [558

-- Bando Per l'osseruanza delle Feste, e Giorni di Mercato, e di non Sonare, Ballare, e giocchare ne le Feste. Publicato ... alli 3. d'Agosto. 1579. 4°. π^2 ($\pi 1^r$ *and* $\pi 2^v$ *blank*). [559

-- Bando generale dell' ... Sig. Pietro Donato cardinal Cesi legato di Bologna. Publicato ... alli 22. di Settembre. 1580. In Bologna per Alessandro Benacci. ... M D LXXX. 4°. A-C^4 D^6 (-D6, *presumably blank*). [560

-- Tariffe della gabella grossa di Bologna. In Bologna, Per Alessandro Benacci. MDLXXX. fol. A^2 B-M^4 N^2. ff. 2-47. [561

-- Prohibitione del portare gli archibugi ... Publicata ... alli X. & reiterata alli XII. di Giugno. M D LXXXI. In Bologna, Per Alessandro Benacci. ... 4°. π^2. [562

-- Bando che si nettino, et conseruino nette le strade. ... Publicato in Bologna alli 2. & 15. d'Ottobre. M D LXXXII. In Bologna per Alessandro Benacci. s.sh. 32 × 24 cm. [563

-- Bando sopra la poluere Da Arcobuso, & Salnitro. Publicato in Bologna alli 19. & reiterata alli 20. d'Agosto. 1583. (In Bologna per Alessandro Benacci.) s.sh. 34 × 26.5 cm. [564

-- Capitoli e conuentioni de ... il Duca di Ferrara, il Duca di Mantoua, e la ... Contessa della Mirandola Intorno alli Bāditi, malfattori, et altri scelerati ... publicati per opera dello ... Legato di Bologna ... notificati in Bologna alli 29. & 30. di Giugno. M D LXXXV. In Bologna, per Alessandro Benacci. 4°. A^4. [565

-- Bando Sopra la Caccia, & cōtro quelli, che danno la pasta à pesci, con la reuocatione delle licenze. Publicato ... alli 7. d'Aprile 1592. (In Bologna, Per Vittorio Benacci.) 4°. π^2 ($\pi 1^r$ *and* $\pi 2^v$ *blank*). [566

-- Bando Del denonciare il siglio, & altra grassa buona per far candele. Publicato ... alli 10. d'Aprile 1592. (In Bologna, Per Vittorio Benacci.) 4°. π^2 ($\pi 1^r$ *and* $\pi 2^v$ *blank*). [567

-- Reformatio constitutionis Sfortianæ de, et super modo protocollandi, & præsentandi ... 1595. fol. π^2. [568

-- *Rota*. Constitutiones Rotae Bononien. nouissime reformatae ... æditæ Anno. M D LX. Bononiæ apud Alexandrum Benacium. 4°. π^2 A-P^4 Q^2. pp. 1-111. [569

-- Decisiones causarum Rotae Bononiensis, Per ... Petrum de Benintendis Cæsenatum ... recollectæ ... Cum summariis, et indice ... D. Ioan. Baptistæ Ziletti Veneti. Venetiis, M D LXXXIII. 8°. a-c^8 A-V^8 X^4 (-X4). ff. 2-162. [570

-- Constitutiones almi rotæ Bononiæ auditorii cum syndicatus decretis. ... Bononiæ apud Alexandrum Benatium ... M D LXXXVI. ... 4°. $[\dagger]^2$ A-T^4 V^6 X^4 Y^6 (-Y6, *presumably blank*). pp. 1-162. ¶*Additional t.p.* ($P4^r$): Nouæ reformationes priorum constitutionum ... Bononiæ, Apud Alexandrum Benatium. (Lea.) [570a

-- *Senate*. Decretum Senatus Bononiensis, in quo priuilegia, et immunitates Germanicae Nationi, Bononiense Gymnasium adeunti conceduntur, S.D.N. Gregorii XIII. Pont. Max. auctoritate confirmatum. Bononiae, Apud Ioannem Rossium. MDLXXVI. 4°. A^4. [571

-- Senatus consultum ... Quadraginta virorum reformatorum status libertatis Ciuit. Bononiæ Super concernentibus ius Congrui ... promulgatum ... M D LXXXVI. Bononiae, Typis Benatianis ... 1587. 4°. A-B^4. pp. 3-16. [572

-- *Accademia degli Gelati*. [1] Ricreationi amorose de gli academici Gelati di Bologna. 12°. A-D^{12}. pp. 3-96. ¶*Engraved t.p.* [2] Psafone trattato d'amore del medesimo Caliginoso Gelato Melchiorre Zoppio ... In Bologna, per Gio. Rossi MDXC. ... (*Colophon.*) 12°. A-L^{12}. pp. 3-260. [573

-- Rime de gli academici Gelati: di Bologna. (In Bologna, Presso gli Heredi di Gio. Rossi. MDXCVII. ...) 12°. $\dagger^2$ A-H^{12} (-H11-12, *presumably blank*). pp. 2-186. ¶*Engraved t.p.* [574

-- *Compagnia della carità de' poveri*. Statuti della Compagnia Della Carità de' poueri Carcerati della Città di Bologna, fatti l'Anno ... 1595. ... Per Rogito di Ser Francesco Barbadoro li 2. di Giugno di detto Anno. In Bologna, Per Vittorio Benacci. ... 4°. A-C^4. pp. 3-24. (Lea.) [575

-- *Compagnia de' fabbri*. Statuti, et ordinationi dell'honoranda Compagnia de' Fabbri dell'inclita città di Bologna. ... In Bologna, Per Giouanni Rossi MDLXXIX. ... fol. $*^4$ A-H^4. pp. 1-59. (Lea.) [576

-- *Fratres Minores de Observantia*. Statuti della prouincia di Bologna de i frati minori osseruanti ... publicati ... il di xxij. di Nouembre. MDLXXXI. In Bologna ... 4°. A-F^4. pp. 3-48. (Lea.) [576a

-- *Monte di pietà*. Sommario, Che contiene breuemente la sostanza delli Statuti del sacro Monte di Pietà. 4°. π^2. (Lea.) [577

-- Capitoli con il Monte della Pieta della Citta di Bologna per lofficio del Massarolo. (Stampato in Bologna per Bartholomeo da Parma. Nel M.D.XLVIII.) 4°. B.L. A^4. [578

-- *Societas mercatorum*. Statuti della Honoranda Vniuersita' de Mercatanti della Inclita Città di Bologna Riformati l'Anno M. D. L. Per Anselmo Giaccarello. (In Bologna ... A di. XVII. Nouembre.) fol. $\dagger^4$ A-X^6. ff. 2-126. [579

-- Prouisioni et ordinationi Nuouamente fatte al foro de Mercanti ... In Bologna per Alessandro Benacci. ... M D LXXXIII. fol. A-B^4 C^2. ff. 2-10. [580

-- Additioni allo statuto del foro de Mercanti, sotto la rubrica dell'appellationi ... (In Bologna per Alessandro Benacci. M D LXXXIX.) fol. A-B^2. [581

-- Dichiarationi, o additioni fatte ad alcuni statuti del foro delli mercanti ... (In Bologna, Per Giouanni Rossi. M D LXXX. Et ristampate, per Alessandro Benacci. M D LXXXIX. ...) fol. A^6. pp. 1-11. [582

-- *Universitas juristarum*. Statuta et priuilegia almae vniuersitatis iuristarum gymnasii Bononiensis. Bononiae, Apud Alexandrum Benacium. 1561. (... Mense Aprilis. ...) fol. $*^6$ A-N^4 O^2. pp. 1-109. [583

-- *Diocese*. Constitutiones Synodales Bononien. M. D. XXXV. (Impressum Bononiæ ... per

Vincentium Bonardum Parmeñ. et Marcũ Antonium de Carpo socios. ... M.XXXV. Die. III. Augusti.) 8°. A-N^{8} +^{4}. ff. 2-103. (Lea.) [584

-- *History*. Alle Bellisime, Et Honoratissime Gentildonne Bolognesi. 8°. A-D^{4} E^{8} (-E8, *presumably blank*). [585

BOLOGNETTI, FRANCESCO. Il Constante ... In Venetia, Per Domenico Nicolino. MDLXV. 8°. A-CC^{8} (-CC8, *presumably blank*). pp. 3-410. [586

BOLOGNETTI, GIOVANNI. Ioannis Bolognetti Bononien. ... Super Prima & Secunda Parte Codicis repetitiones ... Neapoli. Apud Raymundum De Amato. .M.D.LIIII. fol. A-Z^{6} aa-hh^{6} ii^{8}. ff. 2-194. ¶*Part of a series of 4 volumes.* (Biddle.) [587

BOLZANIO, URBANO. Vrbani Bellunensis ... institutionũ in linguam Græcam grammaticarum, libri duo. ... Basileae In officina Ioannis Valderi Anno M.D.XXXV. ... (... mense Septembri ...) 4°. a-z^{4} A-Oo^{4}. pp. 1-472. [588

BOMBAST, THEOPHRAST, VON HOHENHEIM. [Werke.] Getruckt zu Basel/ durch Conrad Waldkirch. 4°. [1] Erster Theil Der Bůcher vnd Schrifften ... Philippi Theophrasti Bombast von Hohenheim/ Paracelsi genannt: ... an tag geben: Durch Iohannem Huserum Brisgoium ... Anno M. D. LXXXIX. A^{4} B^{6} a-z^{4} A-Z^{4} *-6*^{4} 7*^{6}. pp. 1-426. [2] Ander Theil ... M. D. LXXXIX. Aa-Zz^{4} AA-3D^{4}. pp. 1-342. [3] Dritter Theil ... M. D. LXXXIX. Aaa-Zzz^{4} AAa-ZZz^{4} AAA-XXX^{4} (-XXX4, *presumably blank*). pp. 1-420. [4] Vierdter Theil ... M. D. LXXXIX. Aaaa-Zzzz^{4} (-Aaaa2-3) AAAa-ZZzz^{4} AAAa-SSSs^{4} TTTt^{6}. pp. 9-417. [5] Fünffter Theil ... M. D. LXXXIX. ***5)^{4} a5)-z5)^{4} A5)-N5)^{4} O5)$^{4+1}$ P5)-R5)^{4} S5)^{6} T5)-Z5)^{4} a5)-g5)^{4} A5)-Z5)^{4} (Y5)4 + *folded leaf*) a5)-d5)^{4} e5)^{6} f5)-l5)^{4}. pp. 1-332, 3-228. [6] Sechster Theil ... M. D. XC. a6)-z6)^{4} A6)-Z6)^{4} aa6)-ff6)^{4} gg6)^{6} hh6)^{4} ii6)^{6} kk6)-mm6)^{4}. pp. 1-440. [7] Siebender Theil ... M. D. XC. a7)^{6} a7)-z7)^{4} A7)-Z7)^{4} aa7)-kk7)^{4}. pp. 1-439. [8] Achter Theil ... M. D. XC. *8)^{6} a8)-z8)^{4} A8)-X8)^{4} Y8)^{6} **^{4} Z8)^{4} aa8)-gg8)^{4}. pp. 1-428. [9] Zehender Theil ... M. D. XCI. *10)^{4} a10)-h10)^{4} i10)$^{4+1}$ k10)-z10)^{4} A10)-Z10)^{4} aa10)-oo10)^{4} pp10)^{6} *a*10)-*z*10)^{4} *A*10)-*K*10)^{4} *L*10)^{6} *10)^{4} Aa10)-Mm10)^{4} Nn10)^{6}. pp. 1-491, 3-275, 5-106. ¶*The ninth part of this set, dated 1603, belongs to another edition.* (Smith.) [589

-- [1] Archidoxa ... zwölff bůcher/ darin alle gehaimnůss der natur eröffnet ... Auch noch vier andere Bůchlein/ so darzu gethan worden ... Von D. Iohanne Alberto Wimpinæo ... Gedruckt zu Můnchen/ bey Adam Berg. Anno M.D.LXX. ... 4°. ●^{4} *^{4} A-Z^{4} a-g^{4}. [2] ... etliche Tractetlein zur Archidoxa gehörig. ... *Same imprint.* A-I^{4} (-I4, *presumably blank*). (Smith.) [590

-- -- Archidoxorum ... de secretis naturae mysteriis libri decem ... His accesserunt libri De Tinctura Physicorum. De Præparationibus. De Vexationibus Alchemistarum. De Cementis metallorum, & De Gradationibus eorundem. ... per Gerardum Dorn è Germanico sermone Latinitati ... donata. Basileae per Petrum Pernam M. D. LXX. 8°. +^{8} a-z^{8} A-G^{8}. pp. 1-460. (Smith.) [591

-- Astronomica et astrologica, ... Opuscula aliquot ... Getruckt zu Cöln/ bey Arnoldi Byrckmans Erben/ Anno 1567. (... truckts Gerhart Vierendunck ...) 4°. ✠^{4} A^{6} B-Hh^{4}. pp. 1-235. [592

-- Aureoli Theophrasti Paracelsi De summis Naturæ mysteriis Commentarij tres, à Gerardo Dorn conuersi ... Basileae, ex officina Pernæa per Conr. Waldkirch, CIↃ IↃ XXCIV. 8°.)(^{8} a-k^{8} (g8 + *folded leaf*). pp. 1-173. (Smith.) [593

-- ... Aureoli Theophrasti Paracelsi ... de Tartaro libri septem ... Opera ... Adami a Bodenstein ... editi ... Basileae, Per Petrum Pernam. 1570. 8°. *^{8} a-z^{8} A-F^{8}. pp. 1-151 [= 451]. (Smith.) [594

-- ... Theophrasti Paracelsi ab Hohenheim ... Libri quatuor De uita longa. Diligentia ... Adami à Bodenstein recogniti ... Anno M. D. LX. 8°. a-f^{8} g^{2}. pp. 1-78. (Smith.) [595

-- Theophrasti Paracelsi philosophiae et medicinae vtriusque vniuersa, compendium ... Auctore Leone Suauio ... Parisiis In ædibus Rovillii ... (... Cal. Ianuar. Ann. M.D.LXVII.) 8°. A-Zz^{4} &&^{4} *-3*^{4} *^{4}. pp. 3-376. (Smith.) [596

-- Philosophiae magnae, ... Aure[o]li Theophrasti von Hohenhaim/ Paracelsi genandt/ ꝛc.

Tractatus aliquot ... Getruckt zu Cöln/ bey Arnoldi Byrckmans Erben Anno 1567. (... truckts Gerhart Vierendunck ...) 4°. A-Ii^4. pp. 1-247. ¶*T.p. defective.* [597

BONARDO, GIOVANNI MARIA. La minera del mondo ... In Venetia, Appresso Fabio, & Agostin Zoppini Fratelli. M. D. LXXXV. (*Colophon.*) 8°. a^8 A-O^8. ff. 1-112. [598

BONAVENTURE, S. Diui Bonauenturae ... In Quartum Librum Sententiarum Elaborata Dilucidatio. ... Recognoscente R.P.M. Angelo Rocch. ... Venetiis. M D LXXX. (*Colophon.*) 8°. +^{8} A-4L^8. ff. 1-640. (Lea.) [599

-- [1] Seraphici doctoris S. Patris Ioannis Eustachii Bonauenturae ... Opusculorum Theologicorum. Tomus primus. ... Venetiis. Apud hæredem Hyeronimi Scotti. M.D.LXXXIIII. (... M D LXXXIII.) fol. +^{8} ++^{6} +^{8} 4+^{6} A-Gg^8 Hh^6. pp. 1-489. [2] ... Tomus secundus. ... Venetiis, apud hæredem Hyeronimi Scotti. M.D.LXXXIIII. (*Colophon.*) fol. +^{4} A-Rr^8 Ss^6 (-Ss6, *presumably blank*). pp. 1-650. (Lea.) [600

-- Der spygel der tzucht ... des heiligen Bonauenture ... (Vordeutzscht vnd vollendet ... durch einenn bruder prediger ordens/ des klosters tzu Leyptzk/ ... M.ccccc. vñ .x. Am tage Agathe ... Gedruckt tzu Leyptzk durch Melcher Lotter.) 4°. B.L. A^4 B-C^6 D^4 E-G^6 H^4 I-L^6 M^4 N-S^6. ff. i-xcv. ¶*Sig.* G *misbound after sig.* H. [601

BONETTI, EMILIO. Canzone ... nel ... natale del ... Primogenito del ... Don Ferdinando Medici Granduca III. di Toscana, & ... sua Consorte ... In Siena, Nella Stamperia di Luca Bonetti. M.D.XC. ... 4°. A^8. pp. 3-15. [602

BONFINI, ANTONIO. Dess Aller Mechtigsten Künigreichs inn Vngern/ warhafftige Chronick ... durch Hieronimum Boner ... inn ... Tütsch bracht ... Zů Basel by Růprecht Winther/ im Jar M. D. XLV. ... (Gedruckt inn ... Bern inn Vchtlandt/ Bey Mathia Apiario/ inn kosten ... Růprechten Winther ... vnd vollendet auff den fünfften tag Martij.) fol. *^{6} A-X^6 a-z^6 Aa-Ss^6 Tt^8. ff. I-CCCLXXX. [603

BONGO, PIETRO. [1] Mysticae numerorum significationis liber ... Bergomi CIↃ IↃ XXCV. Typis Comini Venturæ, & Socij. Sumptibus ... Francisci Franc. Senensis. fol. a^6 b-c^4 A-V^6 X^4 (-X4, *presumably blank*) a^8. pp. 1-245. [2] ... Pars altera ... *Same imprint.* fol. π^2 A-P^6 (-P6, *presumably blank*). pp. 1-177. [604

BONI, PIETRO ANTONIO. Petri Boni Ferrariensis, margarita nouella de lapide philosophorum, Denuò per Ianum Lacinium correcta ... Venetiis, Apud Aldum. M. D. XLV. (... M. D. XXXXVI.) 8°. *-**^{8} 3*^{4} A-CC^8 (-V-CC^8) DD^{10} (-DD1). ff. 1-152 *present.* (Smith.) [605

BONN, HERMANN. Clariss. imperialis Vrbis Lubeci chronicorum libri tres ... à Doct. Iustino Goblero Goarino ... in Latinum uersi ... Vnà cum orationibus duabus eiusdem D. Iustini Gobleri in obitum ... Erici Senioris Ducis Brunsuicensis, &c. ... Basileae. (... in officina Barth. Vuesthemeri, sumptib. uero Ioannis Oporini ... M. D. XLIII. Mense Augusto.) 8°. α^8 b-o^8 p^4. pp. 2-193. (Lea.) [606

BONNONTIO, ONOFRIO. Rimario ... (In Cremona per Vincenzo Conti. M. D. LVI.) 8°. *^{4} A-EE^4. ff. 1-105. [607

BONOMI, GIOVANNI FRANCESCO. Io. Francisci Bonhomii Cremonensis ... Borromeis. Mediolani, Apud Iacobum Picaleam. M. D. LXXXIX. ... 4°. [A]^4 B-P^4 Q^6. pp. 1-122. [608

BONSI, LELIO. Cinque lezzioni di M. Lelio Bonsi Lette da Lui publicamente nella Accademia Fiorentina Aggiuntoui vn breue Trattato della Cometa E nella fine vn Sermone sopra l'Eucarestia ... In Fiorenza Appresso i Giunti MDLX. ... (*Colophon.*) 8°. *^{4} A-N^8 O-P^4. ff. 1-112. [609

BORDONE, PLACIDO. Ad Vrbem in Mortem Iulii Secundi Pontificis Maximi ... [Romae, Jacobus Mazochius, c. 1513.] 4°. π^4. [610

BORDONI, GERONIMO. Supplicatione in vn syluiculo poema Latino in verso heroico, & in vna vulgare epistola fatta in nome del ... Citta ... Roma, & seco Italia, ... Inuiata al Inuittissimo ... Carlo .V. ... [Roma, Antonio Blado, c. 1536.] 4°. A-E^4. [611

BOREGK, MARTIN. Behmische Chronica ... Erster Theil. ... Gedruckt zu Wittemberg/ durch Zacharias Krafft. Im Jhar/ M. D. LXXXVII. fol. (*)^6 A-Cc^6 Dd^4 Dd-3L^6 3M^4. pp. 2-691. ¶*Additional t.p.* (^{2}Dd1^r): ... Der ander Theil. *Same imprint.* [612

BORGHESI, DIOMEDE. [1] Del quarto volume delle rime ... Parte vna. ... Al Signore Scipione della Staffa. ... In Perugia: Appresso Valente Panizzi ... M. D. LXX. 4°. a^4 A-F^4 b-c^4. ff. 1-24. [2] Del quarto volume delle rime ... Parte vna. Al S. Lodouico Senso. ... *Same imprint.* 4°. A-G^4. ff. 1-20. [613

BORGHINI, RAFFAELLO. L'amante furioso comedia ... In Fiorenza, Appresso Giorgio Marescotti 1583. ... 12°. *^{6} A-G^{12} H^6. pp. 1-175. [614

-- La donna costante comedia ... In Fiorenza, Appresso Giorgio Marescotti. MDLXXXII. (*Colophon.*) 12°. A-G^{12}. pp. 3-166. [615

BORGHINI, VINCENZO MARIA. Annotationi et discorsi sopra alcuni luoghi Del Decameron, Di M. Giouanni Boccacci ... In Fiorenza Nella Stamperia de i Giunti MDLXXIIII. (*Colophon.*) 4°. *^{4} Aa-Dd^4 A-S^4 T^8. pp. 1-142. ¶*Additional authors: Pier Francesco Cambi, Sebastiano Antinori.* [616

-- -- *Another copy.* [617

-- -- *Another copy* (-*1, *4, T1, T8, *the last blank*). [618

-- [1] Discorsi ... Parte Prima. ... In Fiorenza. Nella Stamperia di Filippo, e Iacopo Giunti, e Fratelli. MDLXXXIIII. (*Colophon.*) 4°. †^{4} A-Pp^4 Qq-Rr^8 Ss-Tt^2 (*consisting of folded plates*) 3A-3M^8 3N^4. pp. 2-205, ff. 206-221, pp. 313-476. [2] ... Parte Seconda. ... M D LXXXV. (*Colophon.*) 4°. π^2 (π2 + *folded leaf*) A-G^4 GH^2 I-Vu^4 ††^{2} 3A-4K^4 A-G^4. pp. 1-598. ¶*Additional t.p.* (††1^r): Trattato della chiesa e vescoui Fiorentini, di Don Vincenzio Borghini. ... In Fiorenza, Nella Stamperia de'Giunti. M D LXXXV. ... [619

BORGOGNI, GHERARDO. [1] Le Muse Toscani di diuersi nobilissimi ingegni dal Sig. Gherardo Borgogni ... raccolte ... In Bergamo, cIↄ Iↄ XCIIII. Per Comin Ventura. 8°. π^8 A-I^8. ff. 1-72. [2] [Rime] Del Sig. Gherardo Borgogni A-H^8. ff. 1-64. [620

BORNATO, GREGORIO. De libero hominis arbitrio. ... Brixiae, Apud Iacobum Britannicum. 1571. 8°. A-K^8. ff. 2-80. [621

BORRA, LUIGI. L'amorose rime ... (Stampato In Milano in casa di Gio. Antonio de Castiglioni ad instantia di Messer Andrea Calui L'anno M. D. XLII. Adi xxij di Decembre.) 4°. π^4 A-G^8 H^6. [622

BORRO, GIROLAMO. Hieronymus Borrius Arretinus De Motu Grauium, & Leuium ... Florentiae, In Officina Georgii Marescotti. MDLXXVI. (*Colophon.*) 4°. †^{4} A^6 B-Pp^4. pp. 1-272. [623

-- Hieronymus Borrius Arretinus, de peripatetica docendi atque addiscendi Methodo ... Florentiae. Apud Bartholomæum Sermartellium. MDLXXXIIII. (*Colophon.*) 8°. A^8 A-G^8 H^4. pp. 1-107. [624

BORROMEO, ANTONIO. Clypeus Virginis ... (Venetijs Ex officina Petri Liechtenstein. .1508.) 4°. B.L. a^6. [625

BOSCAN, JUAN. Las obras de Boscan y algunas de Garcilasso dela Vega ... Año M. D. XLVII. ([Roma] Estampado por M. Antonio de Salamanca ...) 8°. A-Ll^8 (-Ll8, *presumably blank*). ff. 2-271. [626

-- -- En Leon, Empremidas por Iuan Frellon, M. D. XLIX. 12°. †^{12} a-z^{12} A-I^{12} (-I12). pp. 1-766. [627

-- -- En Anuers, En casa de Pedro Bellero. Año. M. D. LXXVI. ... (... Typis Gerardi Smits. ...) 12°. A^6 B-Y^{12} Z^6 (-Z6, *presumably blank*). ff. 1-257. [628

BOSIO, GIACOMO. Dell'istoria della sacra religione et ill^{ma} militia di San Giouanni Gierosolimitano ... parte Secōda. In Roma nella stamperia Apost. Vaticana ... 1594. (*Colophon.*) fol. ♣^{6} A-3D^{6} 3E^{8}. pp. 1-591. ¶*Engraved t.p. Part of a made-up set: vol. 1, 1621; vol. 3, 1602.* (Lea.) [629

BOSSO, MATTEO. Contenta. Matthaei Bossi Veronensis ... de Veris & salutaribus animi gaudijs, Dialogus ... Eiusdem de Instituendo Sapientia animo, siue de vero Sapientiæ cultu Libri octo. Eiusdem de Tolerandis aduersis Libri duo. Eiusdem de Gerendo magistratu iustitiaq; colenda Opusculū. Eiusdem de Immoderato mulierum cultu Repræhensoria ad Bessarionem cohortatio. ... (Argentorati in ædibus Matthæi Schūrerij ... mense Octobri ... M.D.VIII.) 4°. a^{8} b-c^{4} d-g$^{8.4}$ h^{6} i^{4} k^{8} B^{8} C^{4} D-E^{8} F-G^{4} H-N$^{8.4}$ O^{4} P-Q^{8} R^{4} S^{6} T^{8} V^{4} X-Y^{8} Z^{6} &^{8}. [630

BOTHO, KONRAD. Chronica Der Sachsen vnd Nidersachsen. ... Durch M. Iohannem Pomarium ... Mit einer Vorrede D. Sigfridi Sacci ... M. D. LXXXVIII. ... Gedruckt zu Wittenbergk Durch Zacharias Krafft/ In vorlegung Iohan Francken. fol.):(^{6} A-Z^{6} (M6 + *folded leaf*, N5 + *folded leaf*) a-z^{6} Aa-3B^{6}. pp. 1-826. [631

-- Sächsisch Chronicon. ... biss vff den Monat Maium ... 1596. ... Durch Mattheum Dresserum ... Gedruckt zu Wittembergk bey M. Iohan Krafft/ In verlegung Iohan Francken Buchführer zu Magdeburgk. fol.)o(^{6} A-3T^{6} (L6 + *folded leaf*) 3V^{4} 3X-3Y^{6}. pp. 1-788. [632

BOTTAZZO, GIOVANNI JACOPO. Dialogi maritimi ... Et alcune rime maritime di M. Nicolo Franco, et d'altri diuersi spiriti, dell'Accademia de gli Argonauti. ... In Mantoua per Iacopo Ruffinelli ... M D XLVII. (*Colophon.*) 8°. A-TT^{4}. ff. 2-168. [633

BOTERO, GIOVANNI. Dell'vffitio del cardinale libri II. ... In Roma, per Nicolò Mutij 1599. ... Ad instanza di M. Vincenzo Pelagallo. (*Colophon.*) 8°. a^{8} A-K^{8} L^{12}. pp. 1-184. [634

-- Raison et gouuernement d'estat, en dix liures. ... Traduicts ... par Gabriel Chappuys ... *Italian & French.* A Paris, Chez Guillaume Chaudiere ... M. D. XCIX. ... 8 . ā^{8} ē^{8} ī^{4} A-Xx^{8}. ff. 1-347. [635

BOUCHER, JEAN. De iusta Henrici tertii abdicatione e Francorum Regno, libri quatuor. ... Lugduni, apud Ioannem Pillehotte, ... M. D. XCI. ... 8°. +^{8} A-Hh^{8} Ii^{4}. pp. 1-460. (Lea.) [636

BOUCHER, NICOLAS. Nicolai Bocherii Rhemi apologia aduersus Audomari Talæi explicationem in primum Aristotelis Ethicum librum ... In Rhemorum Academia, Excudebat Ioannes Fognæus in officina Calcographica N. Bacnetij ... 1562. 4°. A-T^{4}. pp. 1-144. [637

BOUCHET, JEAN. Les anciennes et modernes Genealogies des roys de France/ ... auec leurs Epitaphes et effigies ... On les vend a Paris ... par Arnoul ꝛ Charles les angeliers freres. (... Lan mil cinq cens. xxxix.) 8°. B.L. A-T^{8} V^{6}. ff. ii-c.xliii. [638

-- Les Annales d'Aquitaine. ... A Poictiers, Par Enguilbert de Marnef. ... M. D. LVII. fol. ✠ -2✠^{6} 3✠^{6} A-ZZ^{6} 3a-3r^{6}. ff. 1-378. [639

BOUELLES, CHARLES DE. Caroli Bouilli Samarobrini liber de differentia vulgariū linguarū, & Gallici sermonis varietate. ... Parisiis. Ex officina Roberti Stephani. M.D.XXXIII. (... Pridie Non. Febr.) 4°. A-F^{8} G^{6}. pp. 3-107. [640

-- Quę hoc volumine continētur. Liber de intellectu. Liber de sensu. Liber de nichilo. Ars oppositorum. Liber de generatione. Liber de sapiente. Liber de duodecim numeris Epistole complures. Insuꝑ mathematicū opus quadripartitū ... (... emissum ex officina Henrici Stephani Impensis eiusdem et Ioannis parui ... 1510. Primo Cal. Februarij. Parisiis) fol. a-b^{8} c^{4} d-h^{8} i^{6} k^{2} l-z^{8} A-C^{8}. ff. 2-196. [641

BOURBON, NICOLAS. Nicolai Borbonii Vandoperani Lingonensis nugarum libri octo. ... Apud Seb. Gryphium Lugduni, 1538. 8°. a-z^{8} A-M^{8}. pp. 2-504. [642

BOURCHIER, THOMAS. Historia Ecclesiastica, de martyrio fratrum Ordinis Minorum Diui Francisci, de obseruantia, qui partim in Anglia sub Henrico IIX. Rege, partim in Belgio sub

[Princ]ipe Auriaco, partim & in Hybernia tempore Elizabethæ regnante Reginæ, passi sunt. ... Ingolstadii ex Officina VVolfgangi Ederi. Anno 1583. 12°. A-Q^{12}(-Q11-12, *presumably blank*). ff. 1-178. ¶*T.p. repaired.* (Lea.) [643

BOURDIGNÉ, JEAN DE. [Hystoire agrégatiue des annales et cronicques d'Aniou ...] (... imprimees a Paris par Anthoyne couteau ... Pour ... Charles de boigne/ et Clement alexandre ... Demourans a Angiers. ... au moys de Ianuier. Lan Mil cinq cens .xxix.) fol. ā^{4} (-ā1) A-MM^{6} (-MM6). ff. i-CC.vij. [644

BOURLÉ, JACQUES. Regrets sur la mort hastiue du ... roy de France, Charles de Valois, Neufiesme ... A Paris, Chez Iean Hulpeau ... 1574. 8°. A-B^{4}. ff. 2-8. [645

BOUSSARD, GEOFFROY. De cōtinentia sacerdotū. Sub hęc questione noua. Vtrū Papa possit cū sacerdote dispensare vt nubat. (Impressum oppido Nůrmbergeñ. per ... Ioannem Weyssenburger. presbiterum. Anno. Millesimoquingentesimodecimo. Die vero xviij. mensis Iunij.) 4°. B.L. a-b^{6} c^{4}. (Lea.) [646

-- -- *Another copy.* [647

BOZIO, TOMASO. De antiquo et nouo Italiae statu libri quatuor. Aduersus Macchiauellum ... Romae, Apud Guglielmum Facciottum. M.D.XCVI. Ad Instantiam Bartholomæi Grassi. ... (*Colophon.*) 4°. a-d^{4} e^{6} A-Qq^{4}. pp. 1-294. [648

-- De robore bellico diuturnis et amplis Catholicorum regnis liber vnus. Aduersus Macchiauellum. ... Romae, Ex Typographia Bartholomæi Bonfadini. M. D. XCIII. ... 4°. *^{6} **^{4} A-N^{4} O^{6}. pp. 1-101. [649

BOZZA, FRANCESCO. Fedra, tragedia ... In Vinegia, appresso Gabriel Giolito de' Ferrari. M D LXXVIII. 8°. A-H^{8}. ff. 7-64. [650

BRACELLI, JACOPO. Iacobi Bracelli Genuensis ... Libri quinq3. Item Iohannis Iouiani Pontani, de bello Neapolitano, Libri sex. Vna cum Historiæ Encomio ..., Andrea Alciato Authore. Haganoæ per Iohannem Secerium, Anno M.D.XXX. (... Mense Septembri.) 4°. a^{4} A-KK^{4}. [651

BRACESCO, GIOVANNI. De alchemia dialogi II. Quorum prior, Genuinam librorū Gebri sententiam ... retegit ... Alter Raimundi Lullij Maioricani, Mysteria in lucem producit. ... Norimbergæ apud Iohan. Petreium, Anno M.D.XLVIII. 4°. A-Q^{4}. [652

-- La espositione di Geber philosopho di misser Giouanni bracescho da Iorci noui ... In Vinetia Appresso Gabriel Giolito di Ferrarii. M D XLIIII. (*Colophon.*) 8°. A-K^{8} L^{4}. ff. 9-83. (Smith.) [653

-- -- *Another copy* (-K1, L4). (Smith.) [654

-- -- In Vinegia appresso Gabriel Giolito de' Ferrari. M D LXII. 8°. A-K^{8}. pp. 3-180. (Smith.) [655

BRACK, WENCESLAUS. Vocabularius rerum. [(Impressum Argentine per Martinum Flach. ... .M·d·xij.)] 4°. a-i$^{8.4.4}$ k^{8} (-k8). ff. I-LIII *present.* [655a

BRACTON, HENRY DE. Henrici de Bracton de Legibus & consuetudinibus Angliæ Libri quinq; ... Londini. Apud Richardum Tottellum, ... 1569. ... 4°. 1¶-3.¶^{4} A-5S^{4} 5T^{6}. ff. 2-444. *S.T.C.* 3475. (Biddle.) [656

-- -- *Another copy.* (Lea.) [657

BRANCACCIO, LELIO. Il Brancatio, della vera disciplina, et arte militare Sopra i Comentari di Giulio Cesare ... In Venetia, Appresso Vittorio Baldini. M D LXXXII. (*Colophon.*) fol. A-B^{4} C^{2} D-H^{4} I^{6} K-Aa^{4} BB^{6}. pp. 3-203. [658

BRANDENBURG. *Casimir, margrave.* Ettlich artickel So der ... Fürst Casimir⁹ zů brandenburg ... darzů verordnet ... Zů Onnoltzbach Am sampstag nach michaelis Anno 1524 4°. A^{4}. [659

-- *Joachim II, elector.* Des Durchleuchtigen ... Marggraue Ioachim des iüngern/ etc. schrifft. wie die Türcken yn Osterreych geschlagen sind. 8°. [A]^{8}. ¶*Dated* am Abend Matthei. Anno ꝛc. 32. [660

-- *Albrecht Alcibiades, margrave.* Des Durchleuchtigen ... Herrn Albrechten/ Marggraffen zu Brandenburg/ des jüngern ... gemein Ausschreiben vnd vrsachen dieser fürgenommen Expedition. Anno 1552. 4°. A-B⁴ C². [661

-- Der Durchleuchtigen ... Herrn Albrechts des Jüngern Marggrauen zu Brandenburg ... Ander-er/ vnd ferner warhafftiger bericht/ an die Frenckischen Grauen ... 4°. A-K⁴. ¶*Dated 12 January 1554.* [662

-- [1] Des durchleüchtigen ... Albrechts des jüngern/ Marggrafens zů Brandenburg ... erclārung vnd bericht: welcher gestalt sein F.G. von wegen erlaubter defension vñ natürlicher gegenwehr/ dazů dieselbig von den ... Bischofen zů Bamberg vnd Würtzburg/ Weigand Redwitzer vnd Melchior Zobel ... in die vermainte Acht erkant ... fol. a-o⁶ p⁴. pp. 3-175. [2] Etzliche beigetruckte ... Aussschreiben ... A-H⁶ I⁴ K⁶. pp. 3-111. [3] ... Wilhelmen von Grumpachs ... Klagschrifft ... Aa-Hh⁶. pp. 3-94. ¶*Last document dated 8 January 1556.* [663

-- *Georg Friedrich, margrave.* [1] Triplicæ Meines ... Herrn Marggraf Georg Friderich zu Brandenburg/ Contra Ein Erbarn Rath zu Nürmberg ... In puncto der Nürmbergischen Exception & respectivè Replic vnd Duplicschrifft. Product. Spiræ 14. Novemb. Anno 1572. 1. fol. Aa-3A⁶. ff. 2-144. [2] Duplicæ et respective triplicæ, Meins ... Herren/ Marggraf Georg Friderichs zu Brandenburg/ ꝛc. Contra Ein Erbarn Rath der Statt Nürnberg. ... Producirt Spiræ, 19. Novembris/ Anno 1572. 2. fol. aa-zz⁶ 3A-3g⁶ 3H⁸. ff. 2-187. [3] Duplicæ Meins ... Herren/ Marggraf Georg Friderichs zu Brandenburg/ ꝛc. Contra Ein Erbarn Rath der Statt Nürnberg. ... Producirt Spiræ, 19. Novembris/ Anno 1572. 3. fol. 3a-3m⁶ 3n⁸. ff. 2-79. [4] Conclusiones Meins ... Herren/ Marggraf Georg Friderichs zu Brandenburg/ ꝛc. Contra Herrn Burgermeister vnd Rath der Statt Nürnberg. ... Producirt Spiræ, 25. Maij/ Anno 1574. fol. A-I⁶ K⁸. ff. 2-60. [664

-- *Church.* Grüntliche anzeigung was die Theologen des Churfürstenthumbs der Marck zu Brandenburgk von der Christlichen Euangelischen Lehr halten/ lerhen vnd bekennen. Auch warinne Andreas Osiander wider solche Lehr vnrecht lerhet ... Gedruckt zu Franckfordt an der Oder/ durch Iohannem Eichhorn ... 1552. 4°. A-P⁴. [665

-- Widerlegung der Opinion oder bekentnus/ Osiandri/ welche er nennet Von dem einigen mitler Ihesu Christo/ vnd der rechtfertigung des glaubens/ von F.G. Marggraff Iohansen zu Brandeburgk etc. Theologen ... Gedruckt zu Franckfurt an der Oder durch Iohann Eichorn/ Anno M. D. LII. 4°. A-F⁴. [666

-- Kirchen Ordnung In ... der Marggrauen zu Brandenburg/ Vnd eins Erbarn Raths der Stadt Nürmberg Oberkeyt vnd Gebieten/ wie man sich ... halten solle. ... Zu Nürnberg/ bey Christoff Heussler. 1.5.6.4. fol. A-G⁶ H-I⁴ K⁶ L⁴ (-L4, *presumably blank*). ff. I-LVII. [667

BRANDOLINI, RAFFAELLO. [a2ʳ] Raphaelis Brandolini Lippi Iunioris Parētalia Oratio de obitu Dominici Ruuere ... Romæ ... habita. M.D.I. [Romae, Eucharius Silber.] 4°. a¹⁰. [668

BRANT, SEBASTIAN. Der Richterlich Clagspiegel. ... Wie man setzen vnnd formieren sol nach ordnung der rechten/ ein jede Clag/ Antwort/ vñ aussprechene/ Vrteilen. ... Durch Doctorem Sebastianum Brand ... M. D. LIII. (Getruckt zů Strassburg/ durch Wendel Rihel vnd Georgen Messerschmidt/ den vij. Augusti ...) fol. Aa-Yy⁶ Zz⁴ AA⁶. ff. I-CXXXV. (Biddle.) [669

-- Sōnia domini Sebastani Brant ... 4°. B.L. [A]⁶. [A5]ʳ: in ... opus Rabani mauri ... de laudibus crucis ... cōmendacō Sebastiani brant. [670

BRANTEGHEM, WILLEM VAN. Iesu Christi vita, iuxta quatuor Euangelistarū enarrationes, artificio graphices ... picta, vna cum totius anni Euangelijs ac Epistolis. 8°. A-T⁸. pp. 3-296. [671

BRASSICANUS, JOANNES. Grammaticæ Institutiones ... (... Industria & impensa ... Ade Petri de Langendorff ... exaratæ ... Basileæ. Anno ... Millesimo quingentesimo decimoquarto. Mensis ꝯo Augusti, die quarto ...) 4°. A⁴ B⁶ a-e⁴ f-i⁸·⁴ k-t⁴·⁸ v⁴ x⁶. ff. I-CXIIII. [672

BRAUN, GEORG. Le vere imagini et descritioni delle piu nobilli citta del mondo. Venetijs apud Donatum Bertellũ ... M. D. LXIX. fol. *engraved t.p.* + 21 *double-page plates*. (Fine Arts.) [673

BRAUN, GEORG, & FRANZ HOGENBERG. [De praecipuis totius vniuersi vrbibus liber secundus.] fol. π^2 $(-\pi 1)$ $(?)\text{-}4(?)^2$ + 16 *double-page plates (out of 59) with letterpress on the first recto of each sheet* + $\dagger\text{-}3\dagger^2$ $(-3\dagger^2)$. ¶*The collation agrees with that of editions printed at Cologne in 1582 and 1588.* (Fine Arts.) [674

BRAUN, KONRAD. De seditionibus libri sex ... Ioannis Cochlaei ... de seditiosis appendix triplex ... Ex officina Francisci Behem ... Moguntiæ apud S. Victorem. M. D. L. (*Colophon.*) fol. a♣^{6} b♣^{4} A-Z^6 a-f^6 g^4. pp. 1-355. [675

-- Kurtzer ausszug etlicher Capitulen/ von der hailigen Catholischen Kirchen Authoritet vnd gwalt ... in Lateinischer sprach geschriben/ gezogen/ vnnd durch jn/ den Authorem verteutschet. Anno &c. 1555 ... M. D. LIX. (Gedruckt zu Dilingen durch Sebaldum Mayer.) fol. a^4 A-X^6. ff. I-CXXIIII. [676

-- D. Conradi Bruni ... opera tria ... De legationibus libri quinque ... De caeremoniis libri sex ... De imaginibus liber vnus ... Ex officina Francisci Behem ... Moguntiæ apud S. Victorem. M. D. XLVIII. (... Mense Augusto ...) fol. *^{6} ✱^{4} A-V^6 X^8 *^{6} A^4 A-S^6 T^4 *^{6} A^4 B-O^6. pp. 1-242, 1-223, 1-154. [677

BREIDBACH, JOHANN TOLMER. Carmen panegyricon De ædificatione scholæ Bonon. ... Bononiae. Ex officina Ioan. Rubrii ... [1560.] 4°. A^4. [678

BREITKOPF, GREGOR. Paruorũlogicalium opusculũ de suppositione ... (Impressum Liptzigk per me Iacobum Thanner herbipolensem. Anno. 1.50.7.) 4°. B.L. A-D^6. [679

BRENZ, JOHANN. Breuis et pia explicatio in librum Iosuę. Autore Ioanne Brentio. Halae Sueuorum Per Petrum Frentium. Anno 1549. (*Colophon.*) 8°. A-V^8 X^4. [680

-- MDXXVI Clare vnd Christliche antwortung etlicher ... predicanten so zů Hall in Schwaben versam̃let gewesst/ auff doctor Iohañ Oecolampadi biechlin ... über die wort dess nachtmals dess herren verteütscht Durch S. K. ... 4°. A-H^4 I^2 K^4 (-K4, *presumably blank*). ¶*Dated 21 October 1526.* [681

-- De maiestate Domini nostri Iesu Christi ..., et de vera præsentia Corporis & Sanguinis eius in Coena. In hoc scripto respondetur Petro Martyri, & Henrico Bullingero, Cingliani dogmatis de Coena Dominica propugnatoribus. ... Francoforti apud Petrum Brubachium ... 1562. mense Septembri, 4°. A-Z^4 a^4 b^2. pp. 4-181. [682

-- Des Ernwirdigen Herrn Iohannis Brentij Declaratio von Osiandri Disputatio ... Wittemberg. 1553. 4°. A^6. [683

-- ... Epistola Ioannis Brentij, de libro, quem Petrus à Soto scripsit aduersus Prolegomena Brentij. M.D.LVII. 4°. A-D^4. [684

-- Der erst Theil des Testaments Herrn Ioannis Brentij. Betreffendt sein Confession vnnd Predigampt ... Getruckt zů Tübingen [durch Ulrich Morharts Witwe]/ M. D. LXX. 4°. a-b^4. ff. 1-7. [685

-- Esaias propheta, commentariis explicatus ... Francoforti ex officina typographica Petri Brubachii, anno ... millesimo quingentesimo quinquageșimo, mense vero Sept. fol. π^6 A-Z^6 a-z^6 AA-ZZ^6 aa-xx^6. pp. 1-1079. [686

-- Ordenliche beschreibung deren ding/ so in namen des ... Herrn Christoffen Hertzog zů Wirtemberg vnd Teckh ... auff dem Concilio zů Triende/ durch seine gesandten gehandelt seind. ... [Tübingen, Ulrich Morhart, 1552.] 8°. A-K^8 L^4. ff. II-LXXXIIII. [687

-- Türcken Biechlein. wie sich Prediger vnd Laien halten sollen/ so der Türck das Teutsche land überfallen wurde. ... M. D. xxxvij. 4°. A-B^4. [688

-- Von Bůndtnůs Aydschweren vnnd Verträg: Ob die zuhalten sein vnnd wie weit. ... [c. 1560.] 4°. π^4. [689

-- Von Gehorsam der vnderthon/ gegen jrer oberkait. Geprediget durch Iohannẽ Brentz zů Schwebischen Hall. [Hagenau, Johann Setzer,] M.D.XXV. 4°. A-B^4. [690

-- Wie man sich Christlich zu dem sterben bereiten sol. ... Auff drey Sermon gestellet. ... Gedruckt zu Wittemberg durch Hans Lufft. M.D.XXXII. 8°. A-E^{8}. [691

BRESCIA. *Accademia degli Occulti*. Rime de gli academici occulti con le loro imprese et discorsi. In Brescia. MDLXVIII. (... appresso Vincenzo di Sabbio. ...) 4°. *^{6} A-HH^{4} II^{6} KK^{4} LL^{2}. ff. 1-126. ¶*Engraved t.p.* [692

BRETON, ROBERT. Roberti Britanni Attrebatensis orationes duae, ... altera de Pace, altera de Philosophia. Parisiis In officina Christiani Wecheli. M. D. XXXVIII. 8°. A-C^{8}. [693

-- Ratio conscribendarum epistolarū in unoquoque genere ... Parisiis. Apud Lud. Grandinum ... 1545. ... (... mense Martio. ...) 8°. a-e^{8} (-e8, *presumably blank*). ff. 2-39. [694

BREUNLE, MORITZ. Eyn kurtz Formular vnd kantzley bůchleyn ... 1529. (Gedrůckt zu Leypsigk durch Iacob Thanner ...) 8°. A-L^{8}. ff. 2-84. [695

BRICOT, THOMAS. Textus logices bricot [Parisiis, Durand Gerlier, post 1500.] 8°. B.L. [a]^{8} b-s^{8}. [696

BRIDGES, JOHN. A defence of the gouernment established in the Church of Englande for ecclesiasticall matters. ... At London, Printed by Iohn Windet, for Thomas Chard. 1587. 4°. ¶^{4} ¶¶^{2} A-Aa^{8} Bb^{6} Cc-3Y^{8} 4A-4G^{8} 4H^{4} 4I-4T^{8} 4V^{6}. pp. 2-1401. *S.T.C.* 3734. [697

BRIENEN, CASPAR. Poemation Ad ... Iacobum Brouchovium Cum ... Theses Iuridicas ... Publicè assereret Ludg. Bat. Ex officinâ Thomae Basson. cIↃ. IↃ. IIIC. 4°. A^{4}. (Lea.) [698

BRIESSMANN, JOHANN. Ein Sermon gepredigt zu Künigssberg in Preüssenn ... Von anfechtung des Glaubens vnd der Hoffnung. 1524 4°. [A]-B^{4}. [699

BRISSAC, CHARLES DE COSSE, comte de. Harangue pronocee deuant le roy, seant en ses Estats generaux, tenuz à Bloys ... A Lyon, Par Iean Pillehotte. 1589. ... 8°. A-D^{4}. pp. 3-[30]. [700

BRISSON, BARNABÉ. De regio Persarum principatu libri tres: Ex aduersariis ... Barnabæ Brissonii ... Editio altera ... [Heidelbergae,] Ex typographeio Hieronymi Commelini, ... MDXCV. 8°. †^{6} A-Z^{8} Aa^{6}. pp. 1-378. [701

-- Obseruationum diuini et humani iuris liber I. ... Parisiis. In Ædibus Rouillij ... 1564. ... 8°. *^{8} A-O^{8} P^{4}. pp. 1-229. [702

-- Discours sur la mort de Monsieur le President Brisson. Ensemble les Arrests donnez à l'encontre des assassinateurs. A Paris. Par Claude de Montr'oeil, & Iean Richer. 1595. ... 8°. ã^{4} A-G^{4}. pp. 1-53. [703

BRITONIO, GIROLAMO. Del Britonio i cantici, et i ragionamenti; et quelli del pontefice ... In Vinegia per Baldassar Constantini. M D L. 8°. A-NN^{8} OO^{4}. ff. 6-290. [704

-- Opera volgare ... intitolata gelosia del sole. (Impresso in Napoli: della Stampa di Maestro Sigismondo Mair Alamano: del Mese dAprile. M D XIX.) 4°. A-DD^{8} (-A1, *presumably blank*). ff. iii-ccxiiii. [705

BRITTANY. Coustumes generalles des pays et duche de Bretaigne ... publiees ... en la congregation & assemblee des troys Estatz ... au moys Doctobre, Lan mil cinq cens trenteneuf. ... On les uend a Rennes & a Nantes pour Philippes Bourgoignon ... 1540 (*Colophon.*) 4°. B.L. A^{4} A-C^{4} B-Z^{4} ꝛ^{6} a-p^{4} q^{6}. ff. i-lxvi. [706

-- Instructions ꝛ articles pour labbreuiation des proces ... Faict a Vennes le parlement y tenant le .v. iour Doctobre mil cinq cens quarante. On les vend a Rennes chiez Thomas Mestrard ... 4°. π^{4}. [707

-- Ordōnāces royaulx sur le faict de la Iustice ... en ce pays ꝛ Duche de Bretaigne ... publiees en la court de parlemēt tenu a nātes/ le dernier Iour de septēbre Lā m.d.xxxix. Imprime a Rennes par Iehan georget ... pour Thomas mestrard ... 4°. A-H^{4}. [708

BRITTON, JOHN. ¶ : Britton. ... (Imprynted at London ... by me Robert Redman ...

[1540.]) 8°. B.L. ✠[6] A-X[8] AA-PP[8] QQ[4]. ff. I-CC.lxxxvii. *S.T.C.* 3803. (Biddle.) [709

BROCARDUS DE MONTE SION. Veridica Terre Sancte: Regionūq3 finitimarum: ac in eis mirabilium Descriptio. ... (Impressum Venetijs in Edibus Ioannis Tacuini de Tridino Anno. M.D.XIX. die. iiij. mensis Aprilis.) 8°. B.L. A-M[8]. (Lea.) [710

BROMYARD, JOHN DE. [1] Summa prædicantium ... Prima Pars. ... Venetiis, M D LXXXVI. Apud Dominicum Nicolinum. (... M D LXXXV.) 4°. †[8] ††[4] a-b[8] c[2] A-3L[8] 3M[10]. ff. 1-466. [2] Summa prædicantium ... Secunda Pars. ... *Same imprint.* (... M D LXXXV.) †[8] a[6] b[8] c[4] A-3O[8]. ff. 1-480. [711

BROOK, SIR ROBERT. [1] 1576. La Graunde Abridgement ... In ædibus Richardi Tottell Duodecimo die Octobris. 1576. ... 4°. B.L. ¢[4] A-XX[8] (-XX8). ff. 1-351. [2] 1576. La Secounde part du Graunde Abridgement. *Same imprint.* (*Colophon.*) A-SS[8]. ff. 2-328. *S.T.C.* 3828. (Biddle.) [712

BROSSIER, SIMON. Philosophiae naturalis totius epitome, ex uniuersis Physicis Aristotelis decerptum. ... Vnà cum Hieronymi Rupei Metinensis Lucubrationibus ... Basileae M. D. XXXVIII. (... per Thomam Platterum ... Mense Martio.) 8°. a[8] A-N[8]. pp. 1-180. [713

BROTUFF, ERNST. Historia. Von dem ... Herrn Heinrichen des j. ... Rᵒͤmischen Keysern ... (Gedruckt zu Leipzig/ durch Iacobum Berwaldt ...) 4°. A-G[4]. ¶*Dedication dated 14 September 1556.* [714

BRUGORA, GALEAZZO. Galeatii Brugorae patricii Mediolanen. ... oratio, habita Tridenti in Concilio Patrum, nomine ... Marchonis Piscariæ, Regis Catholici Oratoris, die lunæ. XVI. Martij. M D LXII. Ripae. M D LXII. 4°. A[4]. (Lea.) [715

BRULEFER, STEPHANUS. [1] ... Fratris Stephani Brulefer ... in quatuor diui ... Bonauenture sententiarum libros interpretatio subtilissima. Interpretatio libri primi. ... fol. B.L. A-T[6] V-X[4]. ff. II-CXXII. [2] Magistri Stephani Brulefer In Secundum Sententiarum librum sancti Bonauenture. ... AA-HH[6] II[4]. ff. II-LII. [3] ... In Tertium Sententiarum librum ... 3A-3I[6]. ff. II-LIIII. [4] ... In Quartum Sententiarum librum ... 4A-4B[6] 4C[8] 4D-4H[6]. ff. II-L. [5] Fratris Stephani Brulefer ... Formalitatu3 Textus Vna cu3 ipsius commento ... (Venetijs per Lazarum Soardis ... Die vltima Iulij. 1504.) a-e[6] f-g[4]. ff. II-XXXVIII. [716

BRUN, BLASIUS. Ein Lob Spruch/ Von den ... Thaten vnd herkomen/ des ... Herren Wilhelm/ Printz zu Vranien/ etc. Vnd der ... Frewlin Anna, Hertzogin zu Sachssen/ etc. Als Brawt vnd Breutigam zu ehren ... M. D. LXI. (Gedruckt zu Nᵘͤrenberg/ Bey Valentin Newber.) 4°. A-B[4] (-B4, *presumably blank*). ¶*In verse.* [717

BRUNETTO, ORAZIO. Lettere ... [Venezia,] M D XLVIII 8°. *A*[12] A-KK[8]. ff. 9-261. [718

BRUNFELS, OTTO. Confutatio sophistices & Quæstionū curiosarum, ex Origene, Cypriano, Naziãzeno, Cyrillo Chrysostomo, Hieronymo, Ambrosio, Augustino, Athanasio, Lactantio ... Selestadij apud Lazarum Schūrerium. (... Mense Maio. M.D.XX.) 4°. a-e[4]. [719

-- De disciplina et institutione puerorum, ... paraenesis. Parisiis ex officina Roberti Stephani ... M.D.XXVI. (X. Calen. Decemb.) 8°. a[8] b[4]. ff. 2-12. [720

-- -- Apud Seb. Gryphium Lugduni, 1538. 8°. a[8] b[4]. pp. 3-23. [721

-- Loci omnium ferme Capitū Euangelij secundum Mathæum. Marcum. Lucam. Ioannem. Actorum item Apostolicorum. Argentorati apud Ioannem Schotum. Anno. 1534. (... mense Ianuario ...) 8°. A-T[8] V[4]. [722

-- Vereum [*sic*] Dei multo magis expedit audire, quam missam ... Christus in parabolis quare locutus sit. Euangeliorum ratio, & authoritas. ... [Argentinae, Johannes Schott, 1524.] 4°. a-d[4] e[6] (-e6, *presumably blank*). [723

BRUNI, DOMENICO. Opera ... Intitolata difese delle donne ... In Firenze M. D. LII. (... Appresso i Giunti. ...) 8°. A-L[8]. ff. 2-86. [724

BRUNI, FRANCESCO. Tractatus de indiciis, et tortura ... Item & D. Guidonis de Suzaria Mantuani. Et D. Baldi de Periglis Perusini. Cum additionibus D. Ludouici Bolognini Bononieñ. ... Venetiis. M. D. XLIX. (... in ædibus Francisci Bindoni, & Maphei Pasini, Mense Octobrii. ...) 8°. a^{8} b^{4} A-M^{8}. ff. 1-99. (Lea.) [725

BRUNI, GIOVANNI. Le cose volgari de Ioã bruno Ariminense. Cioe Sonetti. clxiii. Canzone. iiii. Capiltoli. xvi. Barzellete. xxiii. Stantie (Stampato in Venetia per Georgio de Rusconi Milanese. M.D.XVII. Adi .XII. de Febraro.) 8°. A^{8} A-M^{8}. [726

BRUNI, LEONARDO, ARETINO. La historia vniuersale de suoi tempi ... Con la giunta delle cose fatte ... fino all' Anno M D LX. ... In Venetia. (... appresso Fran. Sansouino. M D LXI.) 4°. $*^{6}$ A^{4} B-HH^{8}. ff. 1-236. [727

-- Libro della guerra de Ghotti composto da Misser Leonardo Aretino in lingua latina e fatto uulgare da Lodouico Petroni caualiere Senese ... (Impresso in Firenze per li heredi di Philippo di Giunta ... M.D.XXVI. di Settembre ...) 8°. A-L^{8} (-L8, *presumably blank*). ff. 2-87. [728

-- Libro intitolato aquila volante, di Latino in uolgar lingua dal ... messer Leonardo Aretino tradotto. Nel qual si contiene del principio del mondo, di molte ... historie & fauole di Saturno & Gioue: delle gran guerre fatte in da Greci, da Troian: & da Romani fin al tempo di Nerone. ... In Venetia per Melchior Sessa. (... per Pietro, & Zuanmaria fratello de Nicolini da Sabbio: ad instantia de Marchio Sessa ... M.D.XLIX.) 8°. a^{8} b^{4} A-CC^{8} DD^{4}. ff. 2-211. [729

-- Leonardi Aretini rerum suo tempore in Italia gestarum commentarius. Eiusdem De rebus Græcis Liber. Lugduni apud Seb. Gryphium, 1539. 4°. a-b^{4} A-O^{4} P^{6}. pp. 1-123. [730

BRUNI, MATTEO. Tractatus ... de cessione bonorum ... Secunda editio. ... Venetiis, Apud Hæredes Aloysij Valuassoris, & Ioannem Dominicum Michaelem. M D LXXV. 4°. a-e^{4} f^{6} A-Pp^{4}. ff. 2-152. [731

BRUNO, S. Sermo de scō brunone ... [Coloniae, c. 1530.] 16°. a-e^{4}. [732

BRUNO, CHRISTOPH. Etliche Historien vnnd fabulen gantz lustig zů lesen ... zůsamenn getragenn/ vnnd inn das Teuͤtsche gebracht/ Durch Christophorum Brunonem ... M.D.XLI. (Gedruckt zů Augspurg durch Hainrich Stayner/ am xiiij. tage Martij ...) 4°. A-M^{4} N^{2}. ff. I-XLV. [733

BRUNSWICK (city). *Rat.* Ein vermeint vngegruͤnd/ vnerfindlich schreiben/ so deñ Rath zu Braunschweig/ wider ... Balthasern von Stechaw/ grosse Vogt zu Wulffenbuͤttel/ an die heimuerordenten Hoffrethe daselbst ausgehen lassen/ Vnd sein des Vogts ... gegenbericht ... Wulffenbuͤttel. 1540. (Gedruckt ... durch Henningk Růdem.) 4°. A-C^{4}. [734

-- Warhafftige vorantwortunge vnd ablenunge eins Erbarn Raths der Stadt Braunschweig/ wieder Hertzog Heinrichs zu Braunschweig vnd Luͤnenburg etc. vngnedig vnerfintlich ausschreiben ... [1540.] 4°. A-D^{4} F^{4}. [735

-- -- *Another copy.* [736

-- Eins Erbarn Raths der Stadt Braunsweig/ andere warhafftige ... vorantwurtung vnnd gegenbericht/ widder Hertzog Heinrichs zu Braunsweig vnnd Lunenburg ꝛc. ... gedichte ... 4°. A-S^{4}. ¶*Dated 16 March 1541.* [737

-- -- *Another copy.* [738

-- Warhafftiger bestendiger/ gegrünter gegenbericht/ des Erbarn Raths/ der Stadt Braunschweig ... Wieder das ... schreiben/ so Baltasar von Stechaw/ Grossevoget zu Wulffenbuͤttel ... gestellet ... 4°. A-F^{4}. [739

-- Der Stadt Braunschweig Ordnunge/ auff die zierunge vnd kleidunge/ vnd auff die vorloͤbnusse vnd Hochzeite ... [Magdeburg, Wolfgang Kirchner] im Fuͤnfftzehenhundert Drey vnd Siebentzigsten Jare/ Donnerstags nach dem Sontage Reminiscere. 4°. a-i^{4} (-i4, *presumably blank*). ff. 2-33. [740

-- -- ... im Fuͤnfftzehenhundert Neun vnd Siebentzigsten Jare/ Donnerstags nach Lichtmessen. (Gedruckt zu Magdeburgk/ durch Wolffgang Kirchner ...) 4°. a-i^{4}. ff. 2-32. [741

-- Der Stadt Braunschweig Ordnunge/ jre Christliche Religion/ auch allerhandt Criminal/ Straff vnd Policey sachen betreffendt. ... im Fuͤnfftzehenhundert Neun vnd Siebentzigsten Jare/ Donnerstags nach Lichtmessen. (Gedruckt zu Magdeburgk/ durch Wolffgang Kirchner ...) 4°. A-Q^4. ff. 2-58. [742

-- Offentliche widersprechung/ Der lesterlich ... Famosschrifft/ so Nicodemus Frischlinus, wider einen Erb: Rath/ der Stadt Braunschweigk/ vnd ... M. Michaëlem Mascum ... ausgehen lassen etc. 1590. ... 4°. A-B^4. [743

BRUNSWICK (duchy). *Heinrich der Jüngere, duke.* Des durchleuchtigen ... Herrn Heinrichs des juͤngern/ Hertzogs zu Braunschweig vnd Luͤneburg ꝛc. An S.F.B. gemeine Landschafft ausgegangen warhafftige summarien/ anzeige vnd beweisung ... (Gedruckt zu Wulffenbuͤttel durch Henningk Ruͤdem.) 4°. A^4 B^2 C^4. ¶*Dated 1540.* [744

-- Ergangene schrifften zwischen des ... Herrn Heinrichs des Iuͤngern/ Hertzogen zu Braunschweig vnd Luͤneburg/ etc. Hoffrethen/ vnd ... Ernesten/ Hertzogen zu Braunschweig vnd Luͤneburg etc. Der stadt Braunschweig ... Mit was vngrunde/ der Churfuͤrst zu Sachsen vnd Landgrafe zu Hessen/ ... jnn jrem ... ausschreiben ... bericht gethan haben. (Gedruckt zu Wulffenbuͤttel durch Henningk Ruͤdem. Anno M. D. xl.) 4°. A-I^4 (H4 + *folded leaf*). [745

-- ... Des ... Herrn Heinrichs des Iuͤngern Hertzogen zu Braunschweig vnd Luͤneburg etc. ... antwort/ Auff des Landgrauen zu Hessen (wie er sich nennet) ... verantwortung ... (Gedruckt zu Wulffenbuͤttel durch Henningk Ruͤdem. M.D.XLI.) 4°. A-S^4. [746

-- Anderer bestendiger warhafftiger ergruͤnter bericht/ des ... Herrn Heinrichs des Iuͤngern/ Hertzogs zu Braunschweig vnd Luͤneburg etc. Gegen S.F.G. vngetrewen Vnterthanen des Raths zu Braunschweig ... verantwortung ... (Gedruckt zu Wulffenbuͤttel durch Henningk Ruͤdem. M. D. XLI.) 4°. A-G^4. [747

-- -- *Another copy.* [748

-- Furtrag/ Supplication/ Bit vnd Erbieten/ so der ... Herr Heinrich der Iuͤnger Hertzog zu Braunschweig vnd Luͤneburg etc. vor der Roͤm. Kay. May. ... wider beide Chur vnd Fuͤrsten/ Sachssen vnd Hessen/ gethan vnd vbergeben hat. ... (Gedruckt zu Wulffenbuͤttel durch Henningk Ruͤdem. M.D.XLI.) 4°. A^4 (-A4, *presumably blank*). [749

-- Antwort so Hertzog Heinrich zu Braunschweig vnd Luͤneburg etc. auff ein vermeinte Supplication des mortbrennens halben ... Actum decima Iunij. Anno M.D.XLI. 4°. A-E^4. [750

-- -- Hertzog Heinrichs von Braunschweig Antwort/ Der Keiserlichen Maiestat/ auff die vbergebene Supplication/ der Mordbrenner halben/ gegeben. [Wolfenbüttel, Henning Rüdem,] M. D. XLI. 4°. a-c^4 d^2. [751

-- [Erhebliche, ergrünte, warhafftige, Göttliche vnd Christliche Quadruplicae, wider des ... Kirchenraubers ... der sich Hansen Fridrichen, Hertzogen zu Sachssen nennt, ... Lesterbuch.] (Gedruckt zu Wulffenbuͤttel durch Henningk Ruͤdem. M. D. XLI.) 4°. A-V^4 (-A1). [752

-- [Proclamation convening the Landstag to provide assistance against the Turks.] Datum Wulffenbuͤttel den andern Monats Maij/ Anno etc. Lvij. s.sh. 32 × 21 cm. [753

-- Vnser von Gottes Gnaden Heinrichen vnd Wilhelmen der Iüngern/ Gebrüder/ Hertzogen zu Braunschweig vnd Lünenburg Hoffgerichts Ordnung ... Wittenberg. 1564. (Gedruckt ... durch Georgen Rhawen Erben.) 4°. A-P^4. [754

-- Ein kurtz vnderricht/ Wie/ vnd in was gestalt sich alle Priester im Fuͤrstenthumb Braunschweig sollen halten/ in ausspendung vnd verreichung des ... Sacraments ... Wulffenbuͤttel [durch Konrad Horn?] ... M. D. LXVII. 4°. A-B^4. [755

-- *Appendix.* Warhafftige Contrafactur Hertzog Heinrichs des Iuͤngern von Braunschweig/ vnd seine Geselschafft. ... [Wittenberg, Georg Rhau, c. 1541.] 4°. A-C^4. ¶*In verse.* [756

-- Ein lustig gesprech der Teuffel vnd etlicher Kriegssleut/ Von der flucht des grossen Scharrhansen H. Heinrichs von Braunschweig. Anno M.D.XLII. 4°. A-B^4. [757

-- Alle vnd yede geschicht vnd handlung/ was anfaͤnglich Heinrich/ der sich nennet den Iüngern von Braunschweyg ... Vnd dagegen was ... vor Röm. Kay. May. vnd gemainen Reichstaͤnden/ zuͦ Speyr Anno 1544. ... fürbracht haben. M.D.XLIIII. 4°. A-Z^4 a-b^4 c^2. pp. I-CLXXXIX. [758

-- -- *Another copy* (-c²). [759

-- *Julius, duke.* Kirchenordnung Vnnser ... Iulij/ Hertzogen zu Braunschweig vnd Lüneburg/ ꝛc. ... Gedruckt zu Wolffenbüttel/ durch Cunrad Horn. M. D. LXIX. (*Colophon.*) 4°.)(^{4} ()^4 A-O^4 a-z^4 Aa-3L^4. pp. 1-442. [760

-- Hoffgerichts Ordnung: Des ... Herrn Iuliussen/ Hertzogs zu Braunschweig/ vnd Lüneburgk/ etc. Auffs new verbessert ... Gedruckt in der Heinrichstadt/ bey der ... Vestung Wolffenbüttel/ durch Conradt Horn. M. D. LXXI. 4°. a-b^4 A-X^4 Y^2. ff. 1-80. [761

-- [Order to local authorities to give publicity to the mandate attached.] Datum Heinrichstadt/ bey vnser Vhestung Wolffenbuttel/ am xxviij. Iulij. Anno/ etc. Lxxiij. s.sh. 31 × 20 cm. [762

-- [Unused form requiring the delivery of all sheep, young and old.] Datum Heinrichstadt bey vnserm Hofflager den 4. Aprilis/ Anno etc. 83. s.sh. 33.5 × 20.5 cm. [763

BRUSCH, CASPAR. Magni operis de omnibus Germaniæ episcopatibus epitomes: tomus primus. ... 1549. (Noribergæ apud Io. Montan. & Vlricũ Neuberum.) 8°. A-Hh^8 Ii^4. ff. 1-233. [764

-- Monasteriorum Germaniæ Præcipuorum ac maxime illustrium: Centuria Prima. In qua Origines, Annales ac celebriora cuiusq3 Monumenta, bona fide recensentur. ... Ingolstadii apud Alexandrum & Samuelem [V]ueyssenhornios fratres. M. D. LI. (... Mense Maio ...) fol. *^{6} ℞^{6} A-Z^6 a-l^6. ff. 1-191. ¶*A few worm-holes in t.p. repaired.* (Lea.) [765

BRUSONI, LUCIO DOMIZIO. L. Domitii Brusonii Contursini Lucani facetiarum exemplorumq. libri VII. (Impressum Romæ per Iacobũ Mazochiũ ... XV. Kal'. Septē. 1518) fol. A^8 B-I^6 K^8 L-Z^6 a-m^6 n^8. ff. II-CCXXI. [766

-- -- ... editum, opera ac studio Conradi Lycosthenis Rubeaquensis. Basileae, ex officina Nicolai Brylingeri [1559]. 4°. ()^4 ()^4 a-z^4 A-Qq^4. pp. 1-494. [767

-- -- Lugduni, Apud Antonium Vincentium, 1562. (... Excudebat Symphorianus Barbierus.) 8°. *^{8} a-z^8 A-H^8 I^4. pp. 1-499. [768

BUCCELLI, ENRICO. Dialogus cui titulus est religio ... (Ioannes Baptista Phaellus Bononiensis Lucæ impressit ... M.D.XXXIX. Cal. Aprilis.) 4°. A-C^4 D^{10}. [769

-- Henrici Buccellii Lucensis Iureconsulti, in Constantini Imp. Donationem, Iuris Vtriusq3 praxis. (Ioannes Baptista Phaellus Bononien. Lucæ impressit Cal. Aprilis. ... M. D. XXXIX.) 4°. A-G^8 H-I^6. [770

-- Henrici Buccellii Lucensis paratasis. Id est ꝑ testes Approbatio, De Amore, et Timore Dei. (Io. Baptista Phaellus Bononieñ. Lucæ impressit ... M.D.XXXIX. Calendis Martiis.) 4°. A-E^8 F^{12}. [771

BUCER, MARTIN. Martini Buceri Scripta Anglicana fere omnia ... A Con. Huberto ... collecta. ... Adiuncta est historia de Obitu Buceri: quæq3 illi & Paulo Fagio post mortem & indigna & digna contigêre. Basileae ex Petri Pernae officina M D LXXVII. fol. α-β^6 a-z^6 A-H^6 I^4 K-3H^6. pp. 3-959. (Yarnall.) [771a

BUCHANAN, GEORGE. Baptistes, siue calumnia, tragoedia ... Francofurti, Apud Andream Wechelum. M.D.LXXIX. 8°. A-D^8. [772

-- Paraphrasis psalmorum Dauidis poetica ... Eiusdem Buchanani tragoedia quæ inscribitur Iepthes. Antuerpiae, Ex officina Christophori Plantini. cIↄ. Iↄ. LXVI. ... 16°. a-v^8. pp. 4-318. [773

-- Rerum Scoticarum historia libri XX. descripta ... Accessit De iure regni apud Scotos Dialogus ... 1594. Francofurti ad Moenum. (... apud Ioannem Feyrabend, impensis hæredum Sigismundi Feyrabendij. ...) 8°. (:)^4 A-Z^8 Aa-Zz^8 AA-HH^8 II^4 (-II4, *presumably blank*). pp. 1-767. (Lea.) [774

BUCHOLTZER, ABRAHAM. Abrahami Bucholzeri index chronologicus, Curâ secundâ Gottfridi Bucholzeri ... vsq; ad finem anni 1598. ... continuatus. ... Gorlicii Excusus typis & sumptib. Iohannis Rhambæ. M. D. XCIX. 8°. (*)^8 (**)^8 A-3N^8. pp. 2-832. [775

BUCHSTAB, JOHANN. Dass die Biblischen geschrifften müssen eyn geystliche vsslegung han ... durch Ioan. bchůstab võ Winterthůr. ... [Strassburg, Johann Grieninger, c. 1527.] 4°. A-D^4 E^6 (-E6, *presumably blank*). [776

-- Eygentliche vnd Grundtliche kunstschafft auss Gőtlicher Biblischer geschrifft/ dass M. Vlrich zwinglein/ eyn falscher Prophet ... ist ... [Strassburg, Johann Grieninger,] M.D.XXviij. 4°. a-f^4 g^6. [777

-- Vier artickel (einem jetlichen Cristenlichē menschen not zethůn vnd zehalten) ... [c. 1528.] 4°. A-D^4. [778

BUDÉ, GUILLAUME. Gulielmi Budaei ... altera aeditio annotationum in pandectas. [Parisiis,] Venundatur Badio. 1532 (... ad viii. Caled. Maias. M.D.XXXII.) fol. ā^4 A-H^8 I^6. ff. I-LXX. [779

-- Annotationes ... in quatuor et viginti pandectarum libros ... ab Iodoco Badio Ascensio [Parisiis] impressæ. Anno. 1532. mense Augusto. fol. ā^8 A-X^8 Y^{10}. ff. I-CLXXVIII. [780

-- Commentarii linguae Graecae ... Basileae, anno M. D. XXX. (... in aedibus Io. Bebelii, mense Martio. ...) fol. α-δ^6 ε^4 a-z^6 A-Nn^6 Oo^4. cols. 1-1424. [781

-- Guillielmi Budaei Parisiensis ... libri V. de Asse, & partib. eius ... M. D. XXII. (Venetiis in aedibus Aldi, et Andreae Asulani soceri mense Septembri ...) 4°. aa^8 bb^4 a-t^8 u^6 A-N^8. ff. 1-262. [782

-- -- De asse et partibus eius Libri quinq3 ... Vænundantur in ædibus Ascēsianis. ... (... ad Idus Ianua. ... M.D.XXVII.) fol. ā$^{8+2}$ a-z^8 A-C^8. ff. I-CCVIII. [783

-- -- Coloniae, Opera & impēsa Ioānis Soteris. Anno M D XXVIII. Mense Augusto. 8°. aa^8 bb^6 a-z^8 A-V^8. pp. 2-679. [784

-- Gulielmi Budæi Parisiensis, de Contemptu rerum fortuitarum Libri Tres ... [Parisiis,] Vænundantur in officina Ascensiana. (... Cal. April. 1528.) 4°. a-k^8. ff. II-LXXV. [785

-- G. Budæi ... de transitu Hellenismi ad Christianismum, Libri tres. Parisiis. Ex officina Rob. Stephani. M. D. XXXV. ... (... III. Non. Mart.) fol. a^6 A-Q^8 R^6. ff. 2-132. [786

-- Epistolae ... Posteriores. Venundantur Iodoco Badio ... [(Sub Prelo Ascensiano Mense Martio. 1522)] 4°. A-G^8 H^{10} I^8 αa-εe^8 (-εe8, *colophon*). ff. 2-74, 1-39. [787

BUDEL, RENER. De monetis, et re numaria, libri duo ... Coloniae Agrippinae, apud Ioannem Gymnicum ... M. D. LXXXXI. ... 4°. +^{6} ++-3+^{4} ā^4 ē^4 ī^4 ō^4 ū^4 &^{4} A-T^4 V^2 A^4 b-o^4 Aa-4I^4 4K^2. pp. 2-798. ¶*Additional t.pp.*: (^{2}A1^r) ... Liber Secundus. ... *Same imprint.* (Aa1^r) De monetis, et re numaria, varii tractatus ... *Same imprint.* [788

BŮCHLEIN. Diss biechlin sagt von den falschen Kamisierern die sich auss thůnd vil gůts mit fasten/ peten/ messe lessen für andere ... Anno. ꝛc. M.D.XXiij. 4°. A^4 B^2 (-B2, *presumably blank*). [789

-- In dissem biechlin vindet man wie man eynem yeglichen Teütschen Fürsten vnd Herren schryben sol ... (Getruckt zů Strassburg von Mathis hůpfuff ... M.ccccc. vnd .iiij. Iar.) 4°. A^6. [790

BŮCHNER, NICOLAUS. Was die Recht war Apostolisch heylig Mess seye ... Geprediget ... M. D. XLVIII. ... (Gedruckt zů Tůbingen durch Vlrich Morhart.) 4°. *^{4} A-O^4. [791

BŮTNER, WOLFGANG. Dialectica Das ist: Disputier Kunst. ... M. D. XCVI. Gedruckt zu Leipzig/ In vorlegung Iacob Apels Buchhändlers. (Gedruckt ... durch Zachariam Berwald.) 8°. A-T^8. [792

BUFALINI, FRANCESCA TURINA. Rime spirituali sopra i misterii del ... rosario ... In Roma Presso a Domenico Gigliotti. M. D. XCV. 4°. *^{4} A-X^4. pp. 1-172. [793

BUGENHAGEN, JOHANN. Ein Schrifft ... Von der jtzigen Kriegsrüstung. Witteberg. Gedruckt durch Hans Lufft. 1546. 4°. A-B^4. [794

-- Eyn Sendbrieff widder den newen yrrthumb bey dem Sacrament des leybs vnd blutts vnsers Herrn ... Wittemberg. 1525. (Gedruckt ... durch Ioseph Klug.) 4°. A-B^4. [795

-- Ein vnderricht deren/ so in kranckheyten vnd tods nöten ligen/ Vnd von dem heyligen Sacrament ... [Nürnberg, Friedrich Peypus,] M. D. XXVII. 4°. A^4. [796

-- Wie es vns zu Wittemberg in der Stadt gegangen ist/ in diesem vergangen Krieg ... Warhafftige Historia M. D. XLVII. (Gedruckt zu Wittemberg/ Durch Veit Creutzer. ...) 4°. A-E^4 F^2 G^4. [797

-- Zwo wunderbarlich Hystorien/ zu bestetigung der lere des Euangelij. Iohann Pomer. Philipp. Melanchthon. 4°. A^4. [798

BUGNYON, PHILIBERT. Commentaire sur les ordonnances faictes par le Roy Charles neufiesme en sa ville de Moulins au mois de Feurier, l'an mil cinq cens soixante six. ... A Lyon, par Claude Rauot. M. D. LXVII. ... 8°. *^{8} A-S^8 (-S8, *presumably blank*). pp. 1-285. [799

BULLINGER, HEINRICH. Antiquissima fides et vera religio. ... Apodixis, ... è Germanico in Latinam linguam traducta, per Diethelmum Cellariū Tigurinum. ... (Tiguri apud Christ. Froschouerum, mense Aug. Anno M. D. XLIIII.) 8°. A-I^8. ff. 1-66. [800

-- De origine erroris libri duo ... Tiguri in officina Froschouiana [1539]. 4°. *^{4} a-z^4 A-Q^4 R^6. ff. 1-161. [801

-- Tractatio verborum Domini, in domo Patris mei mansiones multæ sunt ... Tiguri excudebat Froschouerus, Anno M.D.LXI. 8°. a-e^8 f^4. ff. 2-41. [802

-- Der Widertöufferen vrsprung/ fürgang/ Secten ... Getruckt zů Zürych by Christoffel Froschower/ im̄ Ienner/ Anno M.D.LXI. 4°. aa-bb^4 cc^6 a-z^4 A-Mm^4 (-Mm4, *presumably blank*). ff. 1-231. [803

BUNDERE, JAN VAN DER. Compendium concertationis, huius seculi sapientium ac theologorum, sup̱ erroribus moderni tēporis, editum ... Venetijs ad signum spei. 1552 8°. A-Gg^8. ff. 113-240. (Lea.) [804

-- Detectio nugarum Lutheri, cum declaratione veritatis Catholicae ... Louanij Ex officina Bartholomei Grauij 1551. ... (... impensis Martini Rotarij. ... 6. Idus Octob.) 8°. A-O^8 P^4 (-P4, *blank*). ff. 1-107. [805

BUONACCORSI, BIAGIO. Diario de successi ... Seguiti in Italia, & particolarmente in Fiorenza dall'anno 1498 in sino all'anno 1512 ... Con La Vita Del Magnifico Lorenzo De' Medici ... Scritta da Niccolò Valori ... In Fiorenza Appresso i Giunti 1568. ... (*Colophon.*) 4°. π^2 A-AA^4 a-f^4 g^2. pp. 2-184. [806

BUONACCORSO, UBERTO DE. ... Vberti de Buonacurso ... opus quod præludia & exceptiones appellauit ... Vna cum ... additionibus ... Antonij de Tremolis e castro corduarū Albigesij oriundi. ... 1533 (impressa Lugduni per Ioan. Crespinum. ... 1533.) 8°. B.L. a-t^8. ff. j-cxliiij. (Lea.) [807

BUONACOSSA, IPPOLITO. Rime ... (In Ferrara Per Francesco Rosso da Valenza alli. xvi. Aprille M.D.XLV.) 4°. [A]^4 B-E^4 F^6 A-C^4 (-C4, *presumably blank*). [808

BUONAMICI, FRANCESCO. Discorsi poetici nella Accademia Fiorentina In difesa d'Aristotile. ... In Fiorenza Appresso Giorgio Marescotti. MDXCVII. 4°. a^4 A-T^4 V^2. pp. 1-155. [809

BUONANNI, VINCENZO. Discorso ... sopra la prima cantica del ... Theologo Dante d'Alighieri ... In Fiorenza Nella Stamperia di Bartolomeo Sermartelli. M D LXXII. (*Colophon.*) 4°. a^4 A-Ee^4 Ff^6. pp. 1-230. [810

BUONAROTTI, MICHELANGELO. Esequie del diuino Michelagnolo Buonarroti Celebrate in Firenze dall'Accademia de Pittori, Scultori, & Architettori. ... 28. Giugno MDLXIIII. In Firenze Appresso i Giunti 1564. ... (*Colophon.*) 4°. A-E^4 F^2. [811

BUONINSEGNI, PIETRO. Historia Fiorentina ... In Fiorenza, Appresso Giorgio Marescotti, M. D. LXXXI. (... M D LXXIX.) 4°. ÷^{4} (-÷1, *presumably blank*) a^8 b^{10} (-b10, *presumably blank*) A-3F^8 (-3F8, *presumably blank*). pp. 1-829. (Lea.) [812

BURATELLI, GABRIELE. Præcipuarum controuersiarum Arist. et Platonis conciliatio ... Venetijs, Apud Franciscum, Gasparem Bindonum, & Fratres. 1573. 8°. *-3*^{8} a^{4} A-Ii^{8} KK^{4}. ff. 2-268. [813

BURCH, LAMBERT VAN DE. Sabaudorum ducum principumq. historiæ gentilitiæ libri duo [Lugduni Batavorum,] Ex officina Plantiniana, Apud Christophorum Raphelengium ... cIↃ. IↃ. IC. 4°. *-**^{4} (**1 + *folded leaf*, **3 + 2 *folded leaves*, **4 + *folded leaf*) A-Z^{4} a-i^{4} k^{2} 3*^{2}. pp. 1-255. ¶3*^{2} *misbound, in reverse order, after* k1. [814

BURCHARD VON URSPERG. Conradi a Liechthenauu ... chronicum ... a Nino Assyriorum rege vsque ad tempora Friderici II. Imp. ... Paraleipomena rerum memorabilium, a Friderico II. vsque ad Carolum V. ... Basileae apud Petrum Pernam, M.D. LXIX. (... mense Augusto ...) fol. M̄^{6} a-z^{6} A-Q^{6} R^{8} S^{6}. pp. 1-483. (Lea.) [815

BURCHARD, GEORG. XIIII. Vrsachen. Die billich jederman bewegen sollen/ den Ehestand lieb vnd hoch zu haben vnd achten ... durch: Georgium Spalatinum ... (Gedruckt zů Nůrmberg/ durch Hans Koler.) 8°. A^{8} B^{4}. [816

BURCHIELLO, GIOVANNI DI DOMENICO. Rime del Burchiello Fiorentino Comentate del Doni. ... In Vicenza, Per gli Heredi di Perin Libraro. 1597 ... 8°. A-T^{8}. pp. 1-261. [817

BURENIUS, ARNOLD. Causæ cur scholae philosophicae praefecti in Academia Rostochiana, in disciplina resarcienda elaborarint ... VVitebergæ excudebant hæredes Petri Seitzij. Anno M.D.LVI. 4°. A-D^{4}. A2^{r}-B1^{v}: Philippus Melanthon piis lectoribus S. D. [818

BURGO, JOHN DE. Pupilla oculi. De septem sacramentorū administratione: de decem preceptis decalogi ... (opa lĩrarioq3 p̄lo Io. Knoblouchij: impēsis ꝓ Pauli Goetz ... Bibliopole Argētini ... Nonis septēbrib⁹. M.d.xiiij.) 4°. B.L. A^{8} b-x^{8} y^{4} z^{8} ꝛ^{8}. ff. ij-clxx. (Yarnall.) [819

-- -- 1516. (sumptib3 ... Ioannis Knoblouchi/ & Pauli Gŏtz ... Argeñ. p̄lo Ioannis Schotti ... M. D. xvij. Kal' Martij.) 4°. B.L. A-X^{8} Y^{4} Z^{8} ꝛ^{8} (-ꝛ8, *blank*). ff. II-Clxx. ¶E3-6, L1-3, L5-8 *defective*. [819a

BURGOS, JUAN BAUTISTA. Ioan. Baptistae Burgos ... concio Euangelica ad Patres Concilii Tridentini, habita Dominica tertia Aduentus Domini, Anno M. D. LXII. De quattuor extirpandarum omnium hæresum præcipuis remediis. Patauii Apud Christophorum Gryphium, M D LXIII. 4°. A^{4} B^{2}. (Lea.) [820

BURLAT, HUGUES. Astutiarum vulpeculæ Domini vineam demolientis, declaratio ... Lutetiæ, Apud Ioannem Macæum ... 1578. ... (... Excudebat Carolus Rogerius ...) 8°. ā^{8} A-F^{8} G^{4}. ff. 1-49. (Lea.) [821

BUSBECQ, OGIER GHISLAIN DE. Itinera Constantinopolitanum et Amasianum ab Augerio Gislenio Busbequio ... Eiusdem Busbequii de re militari contra Turcam instituenda consilium. Altera editio. Antuerpiæ, Ex officina Christophori Plantini. cIↃ.IↃ.LXXXII. 8°. A-H^{8}. pp. 3-127. [822

-- Augerii Gislenii Busbequii D. legationis Turcicæ Epistolæ quatuor. ... Francofurti Apud heredes Andreæ Wecheli, Claud. Marnium & Ioann. Aubrium. M. D. XCV. 8°. A-Aa^{8}. pp. 3-360. [823

BUSCHE, ALEXANDER VAN DEN. The Orator: Handling a hundred seuerall Discourses, in forme of Declamations: Some of the Arguments being drawne from Titus Liuius ... Written in French by Alexander Siluayn, and Englished by L. P. London Printed by Adam Islip. 1596. 4°. A^{4} (-A1, *presumably blank*) B-Ee^{8} Ff^{4}. pp. 1-436. *S.T.C.* 4182. (Furness.) [824

BUSCHE, HERMANN VON DEM. De saluberrimo fructuosissimoq3 diui virginis Marie Psalterio. triplex Hecatostichō Hermanni Buschij monasteriensis. cum quibusdam alijs carminibus. Ma. Diui Cipriani ... de ligno salutifere crucis carmen heroicū Claudiani ... inuocatio ad Christum pro Theodosio celare Augusto. [Coloniae, haeredes Henrici Quentel, c. 1508.] 4°. A-B^{6}. [825

BUSMANN, JOHANN. Expostulatio cum obstinatis Papistis, quod sacri Euangelij doctrinam non recipiunt ... (Hannouerae per Henningum Rudenum, Anno. 1544.) 4°. A-D⁴. [826

BUSTETER, HANS. Ernstlicher Bericht/ wie sich ain Frume Oberkayt Vor/ In/ vnd Nach/ den gefärlichsten Kriegssnöten/ ... zů ... Sig/ loblichen vben/ vñ halten sol ... vss Ritterlichen geschichten beschriben. M. D. XXXII. Jar. (Gedruckt jn ... Augspurg/ durch Hainrichen Stayner/ am 17. tag May. ...) 4°. $A\text{-}G^4\ H^2$. ff. II-XXVI. [827

BUSTI, BERNARDINO DE. Defensorium Montispietatis Contra figmenta omnia emule falsitatis. (Ex officina ... Henrici Gran ciuis Hagenaweñ. Impensis ... Ioannis Rynman de Oringaw ... 1513. In vigilia Natiuitatꝫ ... ꝟginis Marie ...) fol. B.L. $a\text{-}b^8\ c^6\ d^8\ e^6\ f\text{-}g^8$. (Lea.) [828

BUTRIO, ANTONIO DE. Consilia ... consilium ... Hieronymi de Tortis in fauorem ... populi Florentiæ datum. [*Device of Jacobus Giunta.*] 1541 (Lugduni per Ioannem Dominicum Guarnerium.) fol. B.L. ☙² $A\text{-}F^6$. ff. 2-35. (Biddle.) [829

-- -- Consilia seu responsa ... Gasparis Caballini ... scolijs illustrata. Accessit Hieron. de Tortis ... Consilium ... Venetiis, Apud Christophorum Zanettum, 1575. 4°. †-††⁴ A-RR⁴. pp. 1-320. (Biddle.) [830

BUTURINUS MANCASOLA, FAUSTINUS. De genere vestimentorum hendacasyllabi. (Romę quinto Calendas Aprilis M.D.XXV.) 8°. $A\text{-}C^4\ D^2$. [831

C

CABALLUS, SERAPHINUS. De Christo iudice laetis animis expectando oratio ... in Dominica prima Aduentus. 1562. Ad ... Tridentinum Concilium. ... (Brixiæ, Apud Damianum Turlinum ... Imprimebatur. Ad instantiam Ioan. Baptistæ Bozolæ. Anno M. D. LXIII.) 4°. A-B^4. (Lea.) [1

CABURACCI, FRANCESCO. Trattato ... Doue si dimostra il ... modo di fare le Imprese, Con vn breue discorso in difesa dell'Orlando Furioso di M. Lodouico Ariosto. In Bologna, Per Gio. Rossi MDLXXX. ... 4°. $†^4$ A-L^4. pp. 5-94. [2

CACHERANO D'OZZASCO, OTTAVIANO. Decisiones sacri Senatus Pedemontani ... Venetiis, Apud Bartholomæum Rubinum. M D LXX. (*Colophon.*) 4°. a-e^8 f^4 A-$3A^8$. pp. 1-733, 1-15. ¶*Additional t.p.* (Zz8): Disputatio an principi Christiano fas sit, pro sui suorumque bonorum tutella foedus inire, ac amicitia infidelibus iungi, ab eiusq̃3 auxilium aduersus alios Principes Christianos petere. Octauiano Osasco ... Autore. (Lea.) [3

CAELIUS, MICHAEL. Newer jrthumb vnd schwermerey vom Sacrament: Sampt etzlicher lügen/ so Georg Witzel gepredigt ... Wittemberg. M.D.XXXIIII. (Gedruckt ... durch Georgen Rhaw.) 4°. a-f^4 A^2 B-L^4 M^2 N^4. [4

CAEPOLLA, BARTOLOMMEO. Dom. Bartholomei. Cepollae Veronensis commentaria in tit. ff. De ædilitio edicto ... Lugduni, Apud Hæredes Iacobi Giuntæ. M. D. L. 4°. a-z^8 A-D^8. ff. 2-186. (Biddle.) [5

-- Consilia ... [*Device of Jacobus Giunta.*] ... 1541 (Lugduni apud Ioannem Dominicum Guarnerium.) fol. B.L. a^6 A-H^8 I-K^6. ff. 1-75. (Biddle.) [6

-- Consi. Cepo. Consilia Criminalis ... 1531 (Impressa Lugduni opera ... Antonij du Ry Ac impensis ... Iacobi de Giuncta Florentini. ... M.cccccxxx. Die vero penultima mensis Februarij.) 8°. B.L. A^{12} a-v^8 x^{12}. ff. j-clxxij. (Lea.) [7

-- Tractatus de seruitutibus ... Accessit ... D. Martini Laudensis I.C. Repetitio ad 1. Seruitutes 14. ff. de Seruitutibus. Item D. Ioannis Superioris I.C. in singulas leges quæ sunt sub titulo ff. de Seruitutibus, Commentarij ... Coloniae Agrippinae, Apud Ioannem Gymnicum ... M. D. LXXIX. ... 8°. †-$5†^8$ A-$3G^8$. pp. 2-841. [8

-- Varii tractatus, ac repetitiones ... cum cautelis eiusdem, ac Thomae Ferratii Brixiani. ... Venetiis, Ex officina Francisci Laurentini, de Turino, D. M. LXIII. 4°. a-d^8 A-MM^8 NN^{10}. ff. 1-290. (Biddle.) [9

CAESAR, CAIUS JULIUS. C. Iulii Caesaris commentarii. ... Parisiis Apud Ioannem Lodoicum ... 1539. 8°. α-$δ^8$ (-β8, δ8) a-ii^8 kk^6 ll-nn^8. pp. 1-524. ¶*Includes:* 1) A. Hircii aut Oppii commentariorum de bello Alexandrino liber quartus, 2) ... commentariorum de bello Africo liber Quintus, 3) ... commentariorum de bello Hispanensi liber sextus. [10

-- -- Lugduni, Apud Steph. Doletum. 1543. 8°. A-D^8 a-oo^8. pp. 1-524. [11

-- -- C. Iulii Caesaris commentariorum libri VIII. quibus adiecimus ... D. Henrici Glareani ... annotationes. ... Basileae per Nicolaum Bryling. Anno, M. D. XLVIII. 8°. a-b^8 a-z^8 A-Z^8 A-C^8. pp. 1-741. [12

-- -- Hoc volumine continentur. Commentariorum de bello Gallico libri VIII, De bello ciuili Pompeiano libri III, De bello Alexandrino liber I, De bello Africano liber I, De bello Hispaniensi liber I. ... Cum correctionibus Pauli Manutii. Venetiis, M. D. LIX. (apud Paulum Manutium, Aldi F. ...) 8°. a-b^8 A-Rr^8. ff. 1-318. [13

-- -- [1] Commentaires de Iules Cesar, de la guerre de Gaule. Traduictz par feu Robert Gaguin. Reueuz ... par Antoine du Moulin, Masconnois. A Lyon, Par Iean de Tournes. M.D.XLV. 16°. aa-cc^8 (+ 2 *folded ll.*) a-z^8 A-H^8. pp. 1-496. [2] Commentaires de Iules Cesar ... Traduictz par ... Estienne de Laigue, dit Beaunois. Tome II. A Lyon, Par Iean de Tournes. 1545. $*^4$ A-Z^8 Aa-Hh^8 Ii^4. pp. 1-503. [14

-- -- A Paris On les vend chez Oudin Petit ... 1546 (Imprimé ... par Pierre Gaultier. ...) 16°. ❧^{8} ℭ^8 ¶¶^{8} a-z^8 &^{8} A-Ff^8. ff. 2-423. [15

-- -- A Lyon, Par Ian de Tournes. 1555. 16°. A-C^8 a-hh^8 ii^4 *^{4} A-Z^8 aa-hh^8. pp. 1-503, 1-496. [16

-- -- Commentarii di .C. Iul. Cesare tradotti in volgare per Agostino Ortica della Porta Genouese. (Stampato in Venetia per Iacopo penzio da Lecho nel .M.ccccc.xvii. adi .iiii. de Feuraro.) 16°. ✠^{8} A-OO^8 (-OO8, *presumably blank*). ff. 2-295. [17

-- -- ([Toscolano,] P. Alex. Pag. Benacenses. F. Bena. .V. .V.) 8°. ✠^{8} A-II^8 kk^8 (-kk8, *presumably blank*). ff. 1-262. [18

-- -- I commentarii ... Nuouamente tradotti da M. Francesco Baldelli ... In Vinegia appresso Gabriel Giolito de' Ferrari. M D LVIII. (... M D L VII.) 8°. *-**^{8} 3*^{6} 4*-5*^{2} A-3B^8 (I2 + 2, Y7 + 2, EE2 + 2) 3C^4. pp. 1-773. [19

-- -- Libro delos comentarios de Gayo Iulio Cesar delas guerres dela Gallia, Africa, y España tambien dela ciuil traduzido en Español ... En Paris. Vendese ... enla ciudad de Anueres ..., y en Paris ... M. D. XLIX. *(Device of Arnold Birckman.)* 8°. 3a^8 3b-3c^4 aa-bb^8 a-z^8 A-X^8. ff. 1-343. ¶*Translator: Diego Lopez de Toledo.* [20

CAESARIUS, JOANNES. Dialectica Ioannis Cæsarii ..., nunc recens Hermanni Raijani Vuelsdalij ... Scholijs illustrata, & ... emendata. Accessit huic Ioannis Murmelii Isagoge in decem Aristotelis Prædicamenta. Coloniae Excudebat Petrus Horst, Anno 1559. 8°. *^{8} A-Dd^8. [21

-- -- Venetiis, Apud Nicolaum Beuilacquam Tridentinum. M. D. LXIII. 8°. A-Y^8 Z^4. ff. 9-189. [22

CAFARO, GIROLAMO. Hieronymi Caphari Salernitani de conscribendis epistolis deque orthographia opus ... Apud Cortonam. M. D. XLVI. (Imp̄ssum ... ꝑ Ant. & Nic. sociū ... Pridie Calen. Martias.) 8°. A-K^8 L^4. ff. 3-84. [23

CAGLI. Statuta ordinationes atque decreta ciuitatis Sancti Angeli papalis alias Callii. ... Pisauri, Apud Hieronymum Concordiam. M. D. LXXXIX. (*Colophon.*) fol. A^6 B-Zz^4 3A^2 ✠^{4} ✠✠^{2} (-✠✠2) +^{6}. ff. 3-180. (Lea.) [24

CAGNOLI, GIROLAMO. Dn. Hieronymi Cagnoli Vercellensis ... Commentarij in Titulum ff. de Regulis Iuris ... Coloniae Agrippinae, Apud Ioannem Gymnicum ... M. D. LXXXV. 8°. †^{4} A-3E^8 3F^4. pp. 1-771. (Biddle.) [25

-- [1] ... Hieronymi Cagnoli ... In Constitutiones & Leges Primi Secundi Quinti, & Duodecimi Pandectarum ... enarrationum Liber primus ... Venetiis apud Hieronymum Scotum, M D LIIII. (... M D LIII) fol. A-B^6 C^4 A-R^8 S-T^6. ff. 1-147. [2] Secunda editio ... in Iustiniani Codicem enarrationes ... Tomus secundus. Venetiis apud Hieronymum Scotum. M D LIII a^6 B-F^6 G^4 A-P^6 Q^8. ff. 2-40, 1-98. (Biddle.) [26

CAGNOZZO, GIOVANNI. Summa Summarum quae Tabiena reformata dicitur. (Bononie īpressa in edibus Benedicti Hectoris ... 1520. die. 21. Aprilis.) 4°. B.L. a-3Q^8 3o^8. ff. 2-526. (Lea.) [27

CALAIS. Gewiss vnd Warhafftige Zeitung/ was sich mit der ... Stadt ... Cales ... zugetragen hat mit dem ... Herrn Alberten ... Ertzhertzogen zu Oesterreich ... Auss Niderlaͤndischer spraach vertiert in Hochteutsch/ Durch Conrad Loͤw. Erstlich zu Antorff gedruckt/ vnd jetzt Coͤlln bey Willhelm von Luͤtzenkirchen ... M.D.XCVI. 4°. A^4. [28

CALCAGNO, LORENZO. Consilia Do. Laurentii Calcanei. [*Device of Jacobus Giunti.*] ... 1534 (Excu. Lugduni: typis Nicolai Parui: ⁊ Hectoris Penet. ...) fol. B.L. AA-BB^6 A-Y^8. ff. 1-176. (Biddle.) [29

CALDERINI, GIOVANNI. Ioannis Calderini consilia. quibus contexta ... sunt respōsa Gasparis ipsius Autoris filij, Dominici à S. Geminiano, Francisci de Rampon. Laurentij à pino, Angeli à Perusio, Petri ab Ancharano, Francisci de Horsa, Floriani à Sancto Petro ... Lugduni, Apud Hæredes Iacobi Giuntae. 1550 fol. B.L. a-g^8 h^6 i^4. ff. 2-62. (Biddle.) [30

-- Tractatus nouus aureus et solemnis de haereticis. ... Cui adiecta est noua forma procedendi contra de hæresi inquisitos ... Venetiis, ad Candentis Salamandræ insigne, M D LXXI. 4°. A-N^8 O^4 (-O4, *presumably blank*). ff. 2-98. (Lea.) [31

CALDRUSIUS, HENNINGUS. De vita et passione Sanctissime Agnetis ... decantatio. (Impressum Erphordie ꝑ Matheum Maler [c. 1515.]) 4°. A-B^6. [32

CALEPINO, AMBROGIO. Ambrosius Calepinus Bergomates ... Dictionū latinarum e greco pariter diriuātiū ... (Impressum Argentorati. Opa Ioānis Grüninger. V. Idus Martij. Anno ... Millesimo q̄ngentesimodecimo. tertio) fol. B.L. A-B^8 C-F^6 G-Z^8 a-l^8 m^6 n^8 o^6 p^8 q-s^6 t^8 v-y^6. ff. II-CCCXVI. [33

-- En tibi opt. lector: dictionarium linguae Latinæ autore primo Ambrosio Calepino, postea autem à multis ... eruditis uiris ... emendatum & locupletatum ... Accedit quoque huc onomasticon propriorum Nominum per D. Conradum Gesnerum ... collectum ... Basileae. (... ex officina Hieronymi Curionis, impensis Henrichi Petri, mense Martio, anno M. D. LI.) fol. †^{4} a-z^8 Aa-Zz^8 AA-ZZ^8 ††^{4} A-Z^8 A*^{8} B*^{10} (-B*10, *presumably blank*). ¶*Additional t.p.* (††1): Onomasticon Propriorum Nominum ... (Lea.) [34

-- Ambrosii Calepini dictionarium ... Adiunctæ sunt præterea singulis vocibus Latinis Italicæ, Gallicæ, & Hispanicæ, interpretationes, cum selectiorum Adagiorum ... Præterea subiuncta sunt, Pauli Manutij Aldi F. Additamenta ... Lutetiæ, Apud Ioannem Macæum ... M.D.LXX. fol. A^2 a-z^8 A-3D^8 3E-3F^6 MM^8 *^{6}. pp. 1-1190, ff. 273-280. [35

-- -- Ambrosii Calepini dictionarium linguarum septem ... Onomasticum uerò, hoc est, proprium nominum ... catalogum ... Basileæ, ex officina Henricpetrina. (... CIↃ. IↃ. LXXV. mense Martio.) fol. *^{4} a-c^6 a-z^8 A-Z^8 Aa-Zz^8 AA-ZZ^8 AAa-MMm^8 NNn^6 A-X^8 Y^{10}. pp. 1-1674, 3-355. [36

-- -- Basileae, ex officina Henricpetrina. (... CIↃ. IↃ. LXXIX. mense Martio.) *Same collation and pagination.* [37

-- -- 1580. Lugduni, Apud Guilielmum Rouillum ... fol. ❦^{2} a-z^8 A-3R^8 (-3R8, *presumably blank*). pp. 1-1374. [38

CALLIMACHUS. Callimachi Cyrenæi Hymni (cum suis scholiis Græcis) & Epigrammata. Eiusdem poematium De coma Berenices, à Catullo versum. Nicodemi Frischlini Balingensis interpretationes ... Henrici Stephani partim Emendationes partim Annotationes ... [Genevae,] Excudebat Henricus Stephanus, anno M. D. LXXVII. 4°. ¶-¶¶^{4} a-i^4 aa-rr^4 (-rr4, *blank*). pp. 1-72, 2-134. [39

CALMO, ANDREA. Le bizzarre, faconde, et ingeniose rime pescatorie ... Et il Commento di due Sonetti del Petrarcha ... In Vinegia Appresso Iouambattista Bertacagno ... M D LIII. 8°. A-F^8 G^4. pp. 3-104. [40

-- Le giocose moderne et facetissime egloghe pastorali ... In Vinegia, Appresso Iouambattista Bertacagno ... M D LIII. (*Colophon.*) 8°. A-G^8 H^4. pp. 3-119. [41

-- [Lettere.] In Venetia. MDLXIII. (... per Giouanni Bonadio & Domenico F. & C. ...) 8°. [1] Lettere di M. Andrea Calmo ... Libro primo. A-E^8 F^4. ff. 2-44. [2] ... Libro secondo. A-G^8. ff. 2-55. [3] ... Libro terzo. A-H^8 I^4. ff. 2-66. [42

-- -- In Vinegia, M.D.LXXX. 8°. [1] Delle lettere di M. Andrea Calmo, libro primo. ... A-E^8 F^4. ff. 3-43. [2] ... libro secondo. ... A-G^8. ff. 4-56. [3] ... libro terzo. ... A-H^8 I^4. ff. 3-65. [4] Residuo delle lettere ... libro quarto. ... A-K^8. ff. 5-79. [43

-- La piaceuole, et giocosa comedia ... intitolata il saltuzza. ... In Vinegia appresso Stefano de Alessi ... 1551 (... appresso Bartholomeo Cesano. ...) 8°. A-H^4. ff. 2-32. [44

-- Il residuo delle lettere facete, et piaceuolissime amoròse. ... In Vinegia, per Domenico Farri. 8°. A-L^8. ff. 5-87. [45

-- Rhodiana comedia ... Composta per ... Ruzzante. In Vinegia, appresso Domenico de Farri. M. D. LXI. 8°. A-G^8 H^4. pp. 3-119. [46

-- Il rimanente de le piaceuole, et ingeniose littere ... dechiarati per Messer Andrea Calmo. In Vinegia, appresso Stephano di Alessi ... M D LVII. (*Colophon.*) 8°. A-F^{8} G^{4}. ff. 2-51. [47

CALVETE DE ESTRELLA, CHRISTOVAL. El felicissimo viaie del ... Principe Don Phelippe, Hijo d'el Emperador Don Carlos Quinto ..., desde España à sus tierras dela baxa Alemaña ... En Anuers, en casa de Martin Nucio. Año de M.D.LII. (... Acabose à veynte y cinco de Mayo ...) fol. ✠^{8} A-3N^{6}. ff. 2-335. [48

CALVIN, JEAN. Ioannis Caluini ... epistolarum et responsorum Editio secunda ... Eiusdem I. Caluini vita a Theodoro Beza ... descripta. ... Lausannae, Excudebat Franciscus le Preux ... Sumptibus Io. de Serens. CIↃ IↃ LXXVI. 8°. A-D^{8} a-z^{8} A-X^{8} Y^{4}. pp. 1-693. [49

-- Foure sermons ... With a briefe exposition of the LXXXVII. Psalme. Translated out of Frenche into Englishe by Iohn Fielde. Imprinted at London for Thomas Man ... 1579. (Imprinted ... by Thomas Dawson ...) 4°. ☞^{4} *$_{*}$*^{2} A-G^{8} H^{4}. ff. 1-79. *S.T.C.* 4439. (Yarnall.) [49a

-- D. Ioannis Caluini ... institutio Christianae religionis ... Additi sunt postea duo Indices ab Augustino Morlorato collecti ... Et haec quidem concinnabat hoc anno N. Collado ... Lausannae, Excudebat Franciscus le Preux ... cIↄ cI LXXVI. 8°. *-**^{8} a-z^{8} A-Ll^{8}. ff. 1-380. (Lea.) [50

-- -- [Institucion de la Religion Christiana, ... traduzida en Romance Castellano, Por Cypriano De Valera. [Londres,] En casa de Ricardo del Campo. 1597.] 4°. *^{8} (-*1, *blank*, *2) A-3T^{8} 3V^{6} 4a-4c^{8} 4d^{2}. pp. 1-1032. *S.T.C.* 4426. (Yarnall.) [50a

-- Thirteene sermons ..., Entreating of the Free Election of God in Iacob, and of reprobation in Esau. ... Translated into Englishe by Iohn Fielde ... Imprinted at London for Thomas and Tobie Cooke. 1579. (Imprinted ... by Thomas Dawson ...) 4°. A-B^{4} B-Z^{8}. ff. 2-176. *S.T.C.* 4457. (Yarnall.) [50b

-- Two and twentie Sermons ... In which ... is ... handled, the hundredth and nineteenth Psalme ... Translated out of French into Englishe by T. S. Imprinted at London for Iohn Harison and Thomas Man. 1580. (Imprinted ... by Thomas Dawson ...) 4°. ☞^{4} A-Z^{8} Aa^{6}. ff. 2-190. *S.T.C.* 4460. ¶*Translator: Thomas Stocker.* (Yarnall.) [50c

CAMALDULENSES. Priuilegia summorum pontificum Congregationis Sacrae Eremi, & S. Michaelis de Muriano, Ord. Camaldulensium concessa, & Communicata. ... Venetijs, Apud Goergium Angelerium. 1597. ... 4°. [a]^{4} b^{4} b^{4} A-Cc^{4} Dd^{6} Ee-Ff^{4}. pp. 1-238. (Lea.) [51

CAMBANIS, VITALIS DE. Tractatus in clausulas, et conclusiones vtriusque iuris, Auctoribus Vitali Cambano, et Celso Hugone Cabilionense ... Venetiis, Apud Iacobum Vitalem. M D LXXV. (*Colophon.*) 4°. a-d^{8} A-Yy^{8}. pp. 1-720. [52

CAMBI, PIERFRANCESCO. Orazione funerale ... delle lodi del Caualier Lionardo Saluiati ... In Firenze Per Anton Padouani. 1590. 4°. A-D^{4} E^{2}. pp. 3-34. [53

CAMBINI, ANDREA. Commentario ... della origine de Turchi, et imperio della casa Ottomanna. [Venezia,] MDXXXVIII. 8°. A-I^{8}. ff. 2-72. [54

CAMBRAI. Acta & decreta Synodi dioecesanae Cameracensis ... M.D.L. mense Octob. ... Parisiis, Ex typographia Matthæi Dauidis. 1551. (... decimosexto Calend. Maii.) 4°. ā^{8} ē^{4} a-m^{8} n^{4} o^{6}. pp. 1-209. [55

CAMDEN, WILLIAM. Britannia siue florentissimorum regnorum, Angliæ, Scotiæ, Hiberniae ... Chorographica descriptio. Nunc denuò recognita, & ... adaucta. Londini, Per Radulphum Newbery. ... 1587 8°. A-Vv^{8} (-Vv8, *blank*). pp. 1-698. *S.T.C.* 4504. ¶*Additional t.p.* (Oo1^{r}): Hiberniae, et insularum Britanniae adiacentium descriptio. ... *Same imprint.* (Furness.) [56

-- -- ... Nunc quartò recognita, & ... adaucta. Londini impensis Georg. Bishop. 1594. 4°. A-3A^{8} 3B^{4} (-3B4, *blank*). pp. 1-717. *S.T.C.* 4506. (Furness.) [57

CAMERARIO, BARTOLOMMEO. Bartholomei Camerarii Beneuentani, de purgatorio igne dialogi duo.

Romæ apud Antonium Bladum ... M. D. LVII. (*Colophon.*) 4°. A-L^4. ff. 3-44. (Lea.) [58

-- Repetitio legis imperialem de prohib. feud. alien. per fede. ... Romae apud Hipp. Saluianum. M. D. LVIII. fol. A-S^6 T-V^4. ff. II-CVIII. ¶A1 *defaced.* (Biddle.) [59

CAMERARIUS, JOACHIM. Capita pietatis et religionis Christianae, versibus Graecis comprehensa ad institutionem puerilem, cum interpretatione Latina. ... Ὑποθῆκαι Salomonis, vt vitentur confortia prauorum, de Teutonicis uersibus [Martini Lutheri] translatæ in Græcos & Latinos ... Preces Christianae expositæ uersibus heroicis, à Ioanne Stigelio. Lipsiae per haeredes Valentini Papae. Anno M. D. LXIIII. 8°. A-E^8. [60

-- Commentarii explicationum in reliquos quatuor M. T. Ciceronis Tusculanarum Quæstionum libros ... Basileae, apud Ioannem Oporinum. (... MDXLIII. Mense Martio.) 4°. α-γ^4 A-M^4. pp. 2-91. [61

-- Commentariorum in M. T. Ciceronis Tusculanam primam, siue de Morte ... Libri duo. ... Eiusdem ... super Apollonij Tyanei de Imitatione ... Epistola, Responsum, ad Ioannem Oporinum. ... Basileae, M. D. XXXVIII. (... in officina Roberti VVinter ... Mense Martio.) 4°. α-β^4 a-z^4 A-S^4 (-S4, *presumably blank*). pp. 2-277. [62

-- Commentatio explicationum omnium tragoediarum Sophoclis, cum exemplo duplicis conuersionis ... Basileae, per Ioannem Oporinum. (... M.D.LVI. mense Augusto.) 8°. a-z^8 A-L^8 M^4. pp. 4-515. [63

-- Ioachimi Camerarii Bapenbergensis epistolarum familiarium libri VI. ... Francofurti Apud hæredes Andr. Wecheli, M. D. LXXXIII. 8°. (:)^8 a-z^8 A-L^8 M^{10}. pp. 1-562. [64

-- Ethicorum Aristotelis Nicomachiorum explicatio ... Francofurti Apud Andream Wechelum. M.D.LXXVIII. ... (*Colophon.*) 4°. ã^6 a-z^4 A-Ss^4 Tt^6. pp. 2-494. [65

-- Libellus continens eclogas et alia quaedam poēmatia ... Lipsiæ Anno M. D. LXVIII. (Excudebat Iohannes Rhamba impensis M. Ernesti Võegelini. ...) 8°. A-I^8 K^4 (-K4, *presumably blank*). pp. 1-141. [66

-- Libellus Nouus, epistolas et alia quædam monumenta doctorum ... complectens. ... Editus studio Ioachimi Camerarij Pabeperg. Lipsiæ Iohannes Rhamba exprimebat ... M.D.LXVIII. ... 8°. A-X^8 (-X8, *presumably blank*). [67

-- Tertius libellus Epistolarum H. Eobani Hessi et aliorum quorundam virorum ... Editus autore Ioachimo Camerario Pabeperg. Lipsiae anno M. D. LXI. (... in officina M. Ernesti Voegelini Constantiensis. ...) 8°. A-T^8. [68

CAMERARIUS, JOACHIM, junior. [1] Hortus medicus et philosophicus: in quo plurimarum stirpium breues descriptiones, nouæ icones ... continentur. ... Item sylua Hercynia: siue catalogus plantarum ... Hercyniæ Syluæ ... conscriptus ... à Ioanne Thalio Medico Northusano. ... Francofurti ad Moenum M. D. LXXXVIII. ... (Impressum ... apud Iohannem Feyerabend, impensis Sigismundi Feyerabendij,Heinrici Dackij, & Petri Fischeri. ...) 4°. A-B^4 a-z^4 pp. 1-184. [2] Sylua Hercynia ... *Same imprint and colophon.* A-R^4 (-R4, *blank*). pp. 3-133. [3] Icones ... praecipuarum stirpium ... Impressum Francofurti ad Moenum. M. D. LXXXVIII. (*Colophon.*) Aa-Hh^4 (-Hh4, *blank*). [69

CAMERATA, GIROLAMO. [1] Trattato dell'honor vero, et del vero dishonore. ... In Bologna, Per Alessandro Benacci. MDLXVII. ... 4°. π^2 A-G^4. ff. 1-28. [2] Questioni doue si tratta chi piu meriti honore o' la donna, o' l'huomo ... *Same imprint.* A-F^4. ff. 2-24. [3] Questione doue si tratta chi meriti piu honore o il soldato, o il Letterato ... *Same imprint.* Aa-Ff^4 Gg^2. ff. 28-50. [4] Questione doue si tratta, chi meriti piu honore o' il leggista, o' l'artista. ... *Same imprint.* 3A-3G^4. ff. 52-78. [70

CAMERS, JOHANN. Annotationum/ in Lucium Florum/ Ioannis Camertis ... libellus. ... (Impressũ Viennæ Austriæ, in ædibus Hieronymi Vietoris. & Ioan. Singrenii sociorũ/ ductu Leonardi, & Lucæ Alantsee fratrũ. Idibus Septēb. An. M.D.XI.) 4°. A-G^6 H^8. [71

CAMILLI, CAMILLO. [1] Imprese illustri di diuersi, co i discorsi di Camillo Camilli, et con le figure ... di Girolamo Porro Padouano ... Parte Prima ... In Venetia Appresso Francesco Ziletti. MDLXXXVI. 4°. a^4 A-L^8 M^4. pp. 1-182. [2] ... Parte seconda. ...

Same imprint. A-F⁸. pp. 4-95. [3] ... Parte Terza. *Same imprint.* A-C⁸ D⁴. pp. 3-56. ¶*Engraved t.pp.* [72

CAMILLO, GIULIO. [1] Opere ... In Vinegia appresso Gabriel Giolito de' Ferrari. M D LX. 12°. A-N¹². pp. 3-311. [2] Il secondo tomo dell'opere ... *Same imprint.* A-I¹² K⁶. pp. 3-227. [73

-- Due trattati ...: l'vno delle materie, che possono uenir sotto lo stile dell'eloquente: l'altro della imitatione. ... (In Venetia Nella stamparia de Farri, del XLIIII.) 4°. A-M⁴. ff. 2-48. [74

CAMMERLANDER, JAKOB. Practica der Pfaffen. Anfangk vnnd aussganck dess gantzen Bapstumbs/ auss alten Practicken vnd Propheceyen ... (Gedruckt [zu Strassburg] auff dem Campoflor [durch Jakob Cammerlander]. Kalen. Vndecembres [c. 1544].) 4°. A-F⁴. [75

CAMOSIO, GIOVANNI BATTISTA. Ioannis Baptistae Camotii oratio de antiquitate literarum ... Romae, Apud Hæredes Antonij Bladij ... M. D. LXXV. 4°. A-B⁴. [76

CAMPANA, CESARE. Arbori delle famiglie lequali hanno signoreggiato con diuersi titoli in Mantoua ... In Mantoua, per Francesco Osanna ... MDXC. (*Colophon.*) 4°. A⁴ A-Q⁴ (+ *folded leaves following* B2, F3, H3, I2). pp. 2-78, 4-45. ¶*Additional t.p.* (L2ʳ): Arbori delle tre famiglie Aledrama, Paleologa e Gonzaga ... In Mantoua, Per Francesco Osanna ...[77

-- Compendio historico, delle guerre vltimamente successe tra Christiani, & Turchi, & tra Turchi, & Persani: ... sino al presente Anno M D XCVII. ... In Vinegia, Presso Altobello Salicato & Giacomo Vincenti, compagni. M D XCVII. 4°. *⁴ A-Q⁴ (A4 + *folded leaf*) R². ff. 1-65. [78

CAMPANA, FRANCESCO. Ad Adrianum sextum pontificem max. oratio panegyrica ... (Papiæ cussa, apud Iacob de Burgofranco M.D.XXIII. X. Cal. Februarii.) 4°. AA-CC⁴. [79

-- Francisci Campani Quæstio Virgiliana, Per quam ... Poeta negligentiæ, quam Tucca, & Varus, ac cæteri hactenus obiecerunt, absoluitur ... Mediolani apud Caluum M.D.XXXX. 4°. A⁶ B-H⁴. ff. I-XXVII. [80

CAMPANO, GIOVANNI ANTONIO. L'historie et vite di Braccio Fortebracci detto da Montone, et di Nicolo Piccinino Perugini. Scritte in Latino, quella da Gio. Antonio Campano, & questa da Giouambattista Poggio Fiorentino, & tradotte in uolgare da M. Pompeo Pellini Perugino. ... Mandate pur'hora in luce da Luciano Pasino. In Vinegia, appresso Francesco Ziletti. 1572. (... M D LXXI.) 4°. A-B⁴ A-Zz⁴ 3A². ff. 2-172. [81

CAMPEGGI. Transumptum priuilegiorum, concessionum, immunitatum, Et indultorum, auctoritate Apostolica, Et Imperiali concessorum ... Comitibus de Campegijs, Nobilibus Bonon. Bononiae, Apud Ioan. Rossium. 1587. ... 4°. A-D⁴. pp. 3-31. [82

CAMPEGGI, CAMILLO. De mundi fallaciis atque ruina oratio. ... in Dominica I. Aduentus Domini. 1561. Ad ... Patres ... Tridentini Concilij. ... Brixiae Ad instantiam Io: Baptistæ Bozolæ. M. D. LXIII. 4°. A⁴. (Lea.) [83

CAMPEGGI, LORENZO. Constitutiones ad remouendos abusus, & ordinatio ad cleri uitam reformandā per ... Laurentiū ... Cardinalem, & ... Legatum, nuper Ratisponæ edita. Coloniae? 1524?] 8°. B.L. a⁸. (Lea.) [84

-- -- Furstlicher durchleichtikait [Erzherzog Ferdinands] General verkhündt vnd gepots brieff betreffendt den Christlichen verstandt/ des sich etlich Fürsten auff dem tag zů Regenspurg mit einander vergleicht. Ordnung vnd Reformation ... durch Bāpstlicher heiligkait Legatē ꝛc. zu Regenspurg auffgericht. [Wien, Johann Singriener, 1524.] 4°. A-D⁴. [85

CAMPEN, CLAUDIUS. Claudii Campensis medici, in librum Aristotelis de Memoria & Recordatione commentarij: quibus opinio Aristotelis refutatur. ... Parisiis. Apud Sebastianum Niuellium ... 1556. 8°. A-E⁸ (-E7-8, *blank*). ff. 3-38. [86

CAMUS, CHARLES. Caroli Camusij Diuionensis ..., De iis quæ ad Tutorum excusationes pertinent ad Herenn. Modestin, libellus. ... Parisiis. Apud Galeotum à Prato ... 1552. (... excudebat Matthæus Dauid, 19. Calend. Septemb. ...) 4°. A-F^8. pp. 3-94. [87

CANALI, MATTEO DE. Oratio cinerum. Mathias de Canali Ferrariensis ... Cardinali Agrigentino. [Romae, Johannes Besicken.] 4°. A^4. ¶*Dedication dated 1503.* [88

CANCIONERO. [Cancionero de Romances. ... En Anuers. En casa de Martin Nucio ... M.D.L.V.] 12°. A-Bb^{12} (-A1, A2, A3, P3, P10). ff. 6-300. [89

CANISIO, EGIDIO. Oratio prima Synodi Lateranensis habita per Egidium Viterbiensem ... (Romæ impressa ... per Ioannem Bepliñ. Alemanum [1512].) 4°. A^4 B^6. [90

-- -- [Romae, Joannes Beplin, 1513.] 4°. $[A]^4$ B^6. (Lea.) [91

CANISIUS, PETRUS, S. Summa doctrinae Christianæ per quæstiones ... conscripta ... Antuerpiæ, Ex officina Christophori Plantini. M. D. LXIX. ... (... V. Idus Martii.) 16°. A-Y^8 (-Y8, *presumably blank*). pp. 7-330. (Yarnall.) [91a

CANO, FRANCISCO MELCHER. ... Melchioris Cani ... De locis Theologicis Libri duodecim. ... Salmanticae, Excudebat Mathias Gastius, ... M. D. LXIII. ... (*Colophon.*) fol. π^2 A-Tt^6 Vv^8 $*^6$ $**^8$. pp. 1-518. (Lea.) [92

-- Relectio de poenitentia habita in Academia Salmanticensi, anno. M. D. XLVIII. ... Salmanticae. Excudebat Andreas de Portonariis. M. D. L. (*Colophon.*) 4°. a-v^8. ff. 2-159. (Lea.) [93

-- -- ... Compluti. Ex officina Petri à Robles, & Francisci à Cormellas. ... Veneunt in ædibus Ludouici Gutierrez Bibliopolæ. 1563. fol. A^4 B-I^6. ff. 2-54. (Lea.) [94

-- Relectio de sacramentis in genere habita in Academia Salmanticensi anno 1547. ... Salmanticae. Excudebat Andreas de Portonarijs. M. D. L. 4°. A-G^8. ff. 2-54. (Lea.) [95

-- -- Compluti. Excudebant Petrus à Robles, & Franciscus à Cormellas. 1563. (... Impensis Ludouici Gutierrez bibliopolæ.) fol. A-B^6 C^8. (Lea.) [96

CANONS. Çanones apostolorum. Veterum conciliorum constitutiones. Decreta pontificum antiquiora. ... Moguntiae anno M. D. XXV. Mense Aprili. ... (Impressum ... in aedibus Ioan. Schoeffer. ...) fol. π^{10} A-$K^{4.6}$ L-M^6 N-O^8 Q-$Ff^{4.6}$ Gg^8. [97

CANTALICIO, GIOVANNI BATTISTA. Cantalycii, Pinnensis atque Adriensis episcopi, de Parthenope bis recepta, Gonsaluia. Libri quattuor. ... (Argentorati, Ex ædibus Schürerianis. Mense Iunio, Anno. M. D. XIII.) 4°. π^6 A-$H^{8.4}$ I^8 K^6. [98

CANTER, WILLEM. Gulielmi Canter Vltraiectini nouarum lectionum libri quatuor. ... Basileae, per Ioannem Oporinum. (... M. D. LXIIII. Mense Maio.) 8°. a-p^8. pp. 4-273. [99

-- -- [1] ... nouarum lectionum libri octo. Editio tertia ... Eiusdem De ratione emendandi Græcos auctores syntagma ... Antwerpiæ, Ex officina Christophori Plantini ... M. D. LXXI. 8°. A-Z^8 a-g^8 h^4. pp. 3-478. [2] ... Syntagma ... *Same imprint.* a-d^8. pp. 4-64. [100

CAPECE, ANTONIO. [1] Inuestitura feudalis ... Antonii Capycii ... Neapoli. Apud Iosephum Cacchium, & Socium. ... M. D. LXX. (... Apud Iohannem de Boy. 1569.) fol. A-T^6 V^8 X-Z^6 &^{4}. pp. 13-287. [2] Repetitio l. imperialem de prohib. feud. alienat. per Feder. ... Neapoli. Apud Iosephum Cachium, & Socios. ... M.D.LXIX. (*Colophon.*) A^4 B-F^6 (-F6, *presumably blank*). pp. 1-58. (Lea.) [101

CAPECE, SCIPIONE. Scipionis Capicii de principiis rerum libri duo. Eiusdem de vate maximo libri tres. Venetiis, M. D. XLVI. (Apud Aldi filios. ...) 8°. A-H^8. ff. 4-61. ¶*In verse.* [102

CAPELLA, GALEAZZO FLAVIO. L'anthropologia ... M. D. XXXIII. (In Venetia nelle case delli heredi d'Aldo Romano, & d'Andrea d'Asola ... del mese di Genaro.) 8°. A-I^8 K^4. ff. 3-74. [103

-- Galeatii Capellae de rebus nuper in Italia gestis, libri octo. ... Norimbergæ apud Io. Petreium, Anno M.D.XXXII. 4°. a-t^4. ff. 3-75. [104

-- Commentarii ... delle cose fatte per la restitutione di Francesco Sforza Secondo Duca di Milano. Tradotte di Latino in lingua Toscana per M. Francesco Philipopoli Fiorentino. ... Venetiis. Apud Ioannem Giolitum, de Ferrariis. M.D.XXXIX. (... del Mese d'Ottobre ...) 4°. *^{4} A-Y^4. ff. II-LXXXVI. [105

CAPELLA, MARTIANUS MINEIUS FELIX. Martiani Minei Felicis Capellæ Carthaginiensis ... satyricon, in quo De nuptiis Philologiæ & Mercurij libri duo, & De septem artibus liberalibus libri singulares. ... Notis ... Hug. Grotii illustrati. [Lugduni Batavorum,] Ex Officinâ Plantinianâ, Apud Christophorum Raphelengium ... cIↄ. Iↄ. IC. 8°. *^{8} **^{4} †^{4} A-X^8 A^8 (A1+1) B-E^8 (-E8, *blank*). pp. 1-336. [106

CAPELLO, GIROLAMO. De disciplinis ingenuis ... Libri sex. ... Pataui, Laurentius Pasquatus Excudebat, MDLXX. 4°. *^{4} b-t^4. pp. 1-140. [107

CAPELLONI, LORENZO. Ragionamenti varii ... sopra essempii ... In Genoua, Appresso Marc' Antonio Bellone. MDLXXVI. (*Colophon.*) 4°. a^4 A-AA^4 b-d^4. pp. 1-192. [108

-- Vita del prencipe Andrea Doria ... In Vinetia appresso Gabriel Giolito di Ferrarii MDLXVIIII. 4°. *^{8} (-*8) **^{4} (-**4) A-M^8 (-M8, *presumably blank*). pp. 1-188. ¶*T.p. mounted.* [109

CAPILUPI, IPPOLITO, et al. Capiluporum carmina (Romae, Ex Typographia Hæredum Io. Llioti. CIↄ Iↄ XC. ...) 4°. †^{6} A-3B^4 3C^6. pp. 1-394. ¶*Authors: Ippolito, Lelio, Camillo, Alphonso, Giulio Capilupi.* (Lea.) [110

-- -- *Another copy.* [111

CAPITO, WOLFGANG FABRICIUS. Appellation der Eelichen Priester/ von der vermayntẽ Excõmunication/ ... Wilhelmen Bischoffen zů Strassburg. ... M.D.xxiiij. 4°. A-B^4. [112

-- Das die Pfaffhait schuldig sey Burgerlichen Ayd zuthůn. ... M.D.XXV. 4°. A^6. [113

-- Was man halten/ vnnd Antwurtten soll/ vonder spaltung zwischen Martin Luther/ vnnd Andres Carolstadt. ... 4°. A-B^4. [114

CAPORALI, CESARE. Rime piaceuoli de Cesare Caporali, del Mauro, et d'altri Auttori. ... In Venetia, Presso Gio. Battista Bonfadini, 1587. 12°. A-N^{12}. pp. 3-307. [115

-- -- ... Accresciute in questa quarta impressione di molte Rime ... Del Sig. Torq. Tasso, & di diuersi nobiliss. Ingegni. ... In Venetia, Appresso Giacomo Cornetti. 1588. 12°. A-N^{12} (-A6, A7). pp. 3-307. [116

-- -- In Piacenza, Appresso Giouanni Bazachi. 1596. ... (... 1597. ...) 12°. A-M^{12} (-M12, *presumably blank*). ff. 2-143. [117

CAPORELLA, PIETRO PAOLO. Quaestio de matrimonio ... Reginæ Angeliæ nunq̃ȝ incudine ... Ioannis Scoti antehac uersata ... (Impressum Neapoli per Ioannē Sulczbachiũ, & Antonium de Iubenis ... M.D.XXXI. Die Secunda Septembris) 4°. A-L^4. [118

CAPPELLO, BERNARDO. Rime ... In Venetia, M D LX. Appresso Domenico, et Gio. Battista Guerra, fratelli. (*Colophon.*) 4°. *-**^{4} A-Qq^4 Rr^2. pp. 1-275. [119

CAPPELLO, CARLO. Epitome apostolicarum constitutionum, In Creta Insula, per Carolum Capellium Venetum repertarum, & é Greco in Latinum translatarum. Adiecta sunt ... quaedam Apostolicorum discipulorum, Dionysii Areopagitæ, Ignatij, & Polycarpi Testimonia. Et per oppositum ... Carolstadij & Munceri gesta & euentus. ... Ingolstadii excudebat Alexander Vueissenhorn. ... M. D. XLVI. (*Colophon.*) 4°. A-F^4. ff. 1-23. [120

CAPRA, BENEDETTO. Comsilia D. Benedicti Capræ & Ludouici de Bologninis. ... Lugduni, Apud Hæredes Iacobi Iunctæ. 1556 (... excudebat Matthias Bonhomme. ...) fol. B.L. a-z^6 A-Q^6 R^4 (-R4, *presumably blank*). ff. 2-210. (Biddle.) [121

CAPRA, GIULIO. Iulii Caprae Vicentini ... in xlj. Digestorum, seu Pandectarum ... librum Paraphrasis. Basileae, apud Petrum Pernam. M. D. LX. fol. *^{8} A-PP^6 QQ^8. cols. 1-940. (Biddle.) [122

CARACCIOLO, ROBERTO. Spechio de la fede Vulgare ... (stato produtto in luce in la Cita Venetia. Stampato per ... Piero de Quarengis Bergomascho del .M.D.XVII. Adi ultimo Setembrio.) fol. A-Z^6 &^{6} ɔ^6 ꝶ^6. ff. III-CLV. [123

CARADOC OF LLANCARFAN. The historie of Cambria, now called Wales ... translated into English by H. Lhoyd Gentleman: Corrected, augmented, and continued ... by Dauid Powel ... (1584 Imprinted at London by Rafe Newberie and Henrie Denham. ...) 4°. B.L. ¶^{8} A^8 B^4 C-Ee^8 Ff-Gg^4 (-Gg4, *blank*). pp. 1-401. *S.T.C.* 4606. [124

CARAVITA, PROSPERO. Prosperi Carauitæ Ebolitani ... Commentaria. Super ritibus magæ curiæ vicariae regni Neapolis. ... His adiunximus commentaria dominorum, Annibalis Troysij Cauensis, & Ioannis Francisci Scaglioni, super eisdem Ritibus. ... Venetiis, M. D. LXXXVI. Apud Valerium Bonellum. Expensis Iacobi Anielli Mariæ, Bibliopolæ Neapolitani. (*Colophon.*) fol. †-3†^{6} 4†^{8} A-Hh^6 Ii^4 Kk-Qq^6. ff. 1-231. (Lea.) [125

CARBONE DE CORTACCIARO, LODOVICO. [1] De pacificatione et dilectione inimicorum iniuriarumque remissione. ... Florentiae Apud Bartholomaeum Sermartellium. MDLXXXIII. 8°. †^{8} ††^{4} A-Aa^8. pp. 1-369. [2] De amore et concordia fraterna. ... *Same imprint.* *^{4} a-h^8 i^4. pp. 1-121. ¶*2 *misbound before* *1; i1 *before* *2; i2-3 *after* *2; i4 *after* *4. (Lea.) [126

CARDANO, GIROLAMO. Hieronymi Cardani Mediolanensis ... de rerum varietate libri XVII. ... Basileæ, anno M.D.LVII. (... per Henrichum Petri ...) fol. ❦^{6} A-Z^6 a-z^6 aA-pP^6 qQ^4. pp. 1-707. (Lea.) [127

-- -- Basileæ, anno M. D. LVII. (... per Henrichum Petri ...) 8°. aa-bb^8 A-Z^8 a-z^8 aA^{8+1} bB^{8+2} cC-dD^8 (dD2 + 2 ll., *misbound after* bB4) eE-zZ^8 AA-KK^8. pp. 1-1195. [128

-- Hieronym[i] Cardani medici Mediolanensis, de subtilitate libri XXI. ... Parisiis, Ex officina Michaëlis Fezandat, & Roberti GranIon ... 1550. 8°. Aa-Cc^8 (-Cc8, *presumably blank*) a-z^8 A-Q^8. ff. 1-312. ¶*T.p. repaired.* (Lea.) [129

-- -- Lugduni, Apud Gulielmum Rouillium ... 1550. (... excudebat Philibertus Rolletius.) †-††^{8} *-**^{8} a-z^8 A-Q^8 (-Q8, *blank*). pp. 1-621. (Smith.) [130

-- -- Lugduni, Apud Guliel. Rouillium. 1554. 8°. α-δ^8 ε^4 a-z^8 A-Ee^8. pp. 1-813. ¶*Sig.* δ *misbound between* α *and* β. [131

-- -- Les liures de Hierosme Cardanus ... intitulez de la Subtilité ... Traduits de Latin en François par Richard le Blanc. ... A Paris, Pour Pierre Cauelat ... 1584. 8°. *^{4} ā^4 ē^8 ī^8 ō^8 ū^4 a-z^8 A-Oo^8 (-Oo8, *blank*). ff. 1-478. (Smith.) [132

CARDENUS, MATTHAEUS. Artis rhetoricae ... introductio ... Prostant Coloniæ apud Lambertum Syluium. Anno M. D. LIII. 8°. A^4 B-F^8 G^4. [133

CARDOSO, JERÓNIMO. [1] Dictionarium Latinolusitanicum et ... Lusitanicolatinum ... Recognita ... per Sebast. Stokhamerum Germanum ... Conimbricæ. Excussit Ioannes Barrerius ... 1588. ... (... Nonis Ianuarij. ...) 4°. A^2 A-O^8 P^6 Q-Hh^8 Ii^{10} A-M^8. ff. 1-266, 1-84. [2] Dictionarium aliud: de propriis nominibus ... Collegit ... Sebastianus Stochamerus ... Comimbricæ [*sic*]. Apud Ioannem Barrerium. Prid. Id. Decemb. 1587. A-F^8 G^6 (-G6, *presumably blank*). [134

CARIERO, ALESSANDRO. Apologia ... Contra le imputationi Del Sig. Belissario Bulgarini Sanese. Palinodia del medesimo Cariero, nella quale si dimostra l'eccellenza del Poema di Dante. ... In Padoua, Presso Paulo Meietto. MDLXXXIII. 4°. π^2 a-i^4 B-N^4. ff. 1-34, pp. 1-95. [135

-- Brieue, ed ingegnoso discorso ... Contro all' opera di Dante. In Padoua Per Paolo Mejetti. 1582. 4°. [A]^1 B-N^4. ff. 1-4, pp. 9-95. [136

-- Possint ne Arte simplicia ueraq̄3 Metalla gigni. ... disputatio. Pataui L[aurentius]. P[asquatus]. Excude. 4°. a^4 A-H^4. ff. 1-32. ¶*Dedication dated 1579.* (Smith.) [137

CARINTHIA

CARINTHIA. Des Ertzhertzogthumbs Khärndten/ aufgerichte Müllner/ Pecke/ Gewicht/ Ellen/ vnnd Mass/ Ordnung. Anno M. D. LXII. (Gedruckt zu Wienn in Ostereich/ durch Michael Zimmerman ...) fol. A-G^4 H^2. (Biddle.) [138

-- Des Ertzhertzogthumbs Khärndten New aufgerichte Landtssrechts ordnung/ Im ain tausend fünffhundert vnd Sibenvndsibentzigisten Jer. ... Gedruckt zu Grätz/ durch Zachariam Bartsch. M. D. LXXVIII. fol. A^4 B-F^6. ff. 1-29. (Biddle.) [139

-- Des Ertzhertzogthumbs Khärndten New aufgerichte Landtgerichtsordnung ... Gedruckt zu Grätz/ durch Zachariam Bartsch. M. D. LXXVIII. fol. A-D^6 E^4. ff. 1-24. (Biddle.) [140

-- -- *Another copy* (-E4, *blank*). [141

-- Des Ertzhertzogthumbs zu Khärndten new aufgerichte Zehendordnung ... Gedruckt in ... Grätz durch Zachariam Bartsch ... M. D. LXXVII. fol. A^2 B^4 C^6. ff. I-X. (Biddle.) [142

-- [1] Des Ertzhertzogthumbs Khärndten verbesserte vnd New aufgerichte Policey ordnung/ Im ain tausend fünffhundert vnd Sibenvndsibentzigisten Jar. ... Gedruckt zu Grätz/ durch Zachariam Bartsch. M. D. LXXVIII. fol. A-L^6 M^4. ff. 1-63. [2] Auf der ... Ertzherzogen Carls zu Osterreich ꝛc. Consens ... sein volgende articl der Policei angehengt worden. *Same imprint.* a^6 b^8. ff. 1-12. (Biddle.) [143

-- -- *Another copy.* [144

-- *Ferdinand, Roman emperor.* [Prohibition of the export or transit shipment of grain, with countersignatures and seal.] Geben in ... Wienn am Fünffundzwaintzigisten tag Octobris etc. Anno etc. Neunundfünfftzigisten ... s.sh. 32.5 × 43 cm. [145

-- [Mandate prohibiting abuses and crimes of mercenaries, with stamped signature and countersignatures.] Geben in ... Wienn/ den letsten tag Nouembris. Anno/ ꝛc. im Sechtzigisten ... s.sh. 32 × 43.5 cm. [146

CARION, JOHANN. Bedeütnuss vnd Offenbarung warer hymlischer Influentz ... von Jarn zů Jarn werende/ Biss man schreybt 1550. Jar ... M. D. XXXIIII. 4°. A-G^4. [147

-- -- Bedeutnus ... Von dem 1540 jar zů jaren werende/ biss man schreybt 1550. jar ... (Gedruckt zů Nürnberg durch Georg Wachter [1539].) 4°. A-D^4. [148

-- Chronicon Carionis expositum et auctum ... ab exordio Mundi vsqꝫ ad Carolum Quintum Imperatorem. A Philippo Melanthone et Caspare Peucero. Adiecta est narratio historica de electione & coronatione Caroli V. Imperatoris. ... Witebergæ excudebat Iohannes Crato, anno M. D. LXXII. (*Colophon.*) fol. a^8 (-a8) b^6 (+ *folding table*) c-d^6 e^4 A-$3X^6$. pp. 1-746. ¶*T.p. repaired.* (Lea.) [149

-- -- Tertia pars chronici Carionis, a Carolo magno, vbi Philippus Melanthon desiit, vsque ad Fridericum Secundum. Exposita & aucta a Casparo Peucero. VVitebergæ Apud Clementem Schleich & Antonium Schön. Anno M. D. LXXVII. 8°. A-Ee^8 Ff^4. ff. 331-575. [150

-- -- Quarta pars chronici Carionis a Friderico secundo vsq; ad Carolum Quintum. Expositus et auctus a Casparo Peucero. ... VVitebergæ Excudebat Matthæus VVelack. Anno M. D. LXXX. (*Colophon.*) 8°. A-Ll^8 Mm^4 (Mm4 + *folded leaf*) a-h^8. ff. 2-262. [151

-- -- Chronicon Carionis expositum et auctum ... a Philippo Melanthone & Casparo Peucero. ... Francofurti ad Moenum, apud Ioannem Feyrabendt. M. D. XCIIII. (... Impensis Sigismundi Feyrabendij.) 8°. A-Oo^8 Pp^2 Qq-Zz^8 AA-ZZ^8 AAa-ZZz^8 AAA-BBB^8 CCC^4. pp. 3-1377. ¶*Additional t.p.* ($Qq1^r$): Tertia pars chronici Carionis ... Francofurti ad Moenum. M. D. XCIIII. [152

-- -- Chronica Carionis ... vermeerdert ende gebetert/ Door Philippum Melanthonem ende Casparum Peucerum. ... ouerghesett ... door W. V. N. Tot Dordrecht. Ghedruckt by Ian Canin ... 1586. ... fol. $*^2$ A-$3C^8$ A-B^8 C-D^6 (-D6, *presumably blank*). pp. 1-784. ¶*Translator: Willem van Zuylen van Nyevelt.* [153

CARLES, LANCELOT DE. Lanciloti Carlei Regiensis episcopi, de Francisci Lotharingi Guisii ducis postremis dictis et factis, ad regem epistola, ex Gallico sermone in Latinum conuersa. Per Ioannem Veterem. Brixiae Ad instantiam Io: Baptistæ Bozolæ. M. D. LXIII. (... apud Ludouicum Sabiensem.) 4°. A-B^4. (Lea.) [154

CARMINA. Carmina quinque Hetruscorum poetarum ... Florentiae Apud Iuntas MDLXII. ... (*Colophon.*) 8°. A^4 B-M^8. pp. 2-173. ¶*Francesco Vinta, Fabio Segni, Francesco Berni, Benedetto Accolti, Benedetto Varchi.* [155

-- Complurium eruditorum uatum carmina, ad ... D. Blasium Hölcelium ... Augustę Vindelicorum/ in ... principum conuentu/ impressa. M.D.XVIII. 4°. [A]-G^4 H^6. [156

-- Illustrium aliquot Germanorum carminum liber. De ... Christianorum laniena ab ... Galliæ Tyrannis ... Anno ... M.D.LXXII. Vna cum Epicedijs & Epitaphijs ... Herois D. Casparis Collignij Comitis ... Quibus addidimus ... Foedus Henrici cum Turca: & Conditiones Caroli IX. Polonis oblatas ... Vilnæ M. D. LXXIII. 4°. a-e^4. pp. 3-39. [157

CARNIOLA. [Landshandvest dess ... Hertzogthums Crain ...] (Gedruckt zu Grätz/ durch Hansen Schmid. ... M. D. XCVIII.) fol. A-N^6 O^8 (!)3. ff. 1-86. ¶*Lacks 4 preliminary ll. and one, perhaps more, at the end.* [158

-- *Ferdinand, Roman emperor.* [Levy of six patzen to support the infantry.] Geben in ... Wienn/ am funfften tag des Monats Aprilis/ Anno ꝛc. im AinvndSechtzigisten ... s.sh. 33.5 × 44 cm. [159

CARO, ANNIBALE. Apologia de gli academici di Banchi di Roma, contra M. Lodouico Castelueтro da Modena. In forma d'uno Spaccio di Maestro Pasquino. ... In difesa de la seguente Canzone del Commendatore Annibal Caro. ... (In Parma, in casa di Seth Viotto, del mese di Nouembre, l'anno M D LVIII.) 4°. A-Z^4 a-i^4 k^6 l-m^4. pp. 3-268. [160

-- -- In Parma, appresso Seth Viotto. 1573. 8°. $†^8$ A-P^8. ff. 2-120. ¶*Additional t.p.* ($A1^r$): Spaccio di Maestro Pasquino Romano ... In Parma, appresso di Seth Viotto. 1572. [161

-- [1] De le lettere familiari ... volumo primo. ... In Venetia, Appresso Aldo Manutio. ∞ D LXXIV. 4°. π^2 A-Oo^4. pp. 2-296. [2] ... volumo secondo. ... In Venetia, Appresso Aldo Manutio. M. D. LXXV. $†^6$ Aa-$4I^4$ $4K^2$. pp. 2-444 *present.* ¶†3-4 *bound after* 4K2. 4K2 *defective.* [162

-- Ragione d'alcuni cose segnate nella canzone d'Annibal Caro. ... In Parma. Appresso Seth Viotto. 1573. (*Colohpon.*) 8°. $†^4$ A-Y^8 Z^4. ff. 1-180. [163

-- Rime ... In Venetia. Appresso Aldo Manutio. M D LXIX. 4°. $*^4$ B-O^4 P^{4+1}. pp. 1-103. [164

-- -- *Another copy* (P^4). [165

CAROSO, MARCO FABRIZIO. [1] Il ballarino ... con l'Intauolatura di Liuto nella Sonata di ciascun Ballo ... In Venetia, Appresso Francesco Ziletti. M D LXXXI. 4°. A-F^4. ff. 2-16. [2] Trattato secondo del ballarino ... *Same imprint.* a-z^4 Aa-Zz^4. ff. 3-184. [166

CARRAFA, FERRANTE. L'Austria dell' ... S. Ferrante Carrafa marchese di S. Lucido ... In Napoli. M D LXXIII. Appresso Gioseppe Cacchij, dell'Aquila. (*Colophon.*) 4°. A^4 Aa^2 A-H^4 I^2 A-V^4 X^6 Y-Aa^4 BB-MM^4 NN^{6+1} OO-RR^4 SS^6 TT-VV^4. ff. 2-41, 2-167. ¶X3-4 *misbound after* X6. [167

CARRANTUS, PETRUS MATTHAEUS. Petrimathaei Carranti Cotignolani: Ludouici Sphortiae captiuitas ... [Bononiae, 1507.] 4°. A^8 B^6 C^2. [168

CARRANZA Y MIRANDA, BARTOLOMÉ. Comentarios ... sobre el catechismo Christiano ... En Anuers, En casa de Martin Nucio. Año M. D. LVIII. ... fol. $*^8$ A-$4B^6$ $4C^8$. ff. 1-433. ¶*Hole in t.p.* A *misbound after* B, C *after* D. (Lea.) [169

-- Controuersia de necessaria residentia personali Episcoporum, & aliorum inferiorum Pastorum, Tridenti explicata ... Lugduni. M D L. 8°. A-L^8 M^6. pp. 3-189. (Lea.) [170

-- Summa omnium conciliorum, a Sancto Petro vsque ad Pium quartum Pontificem ... Antuerpiæ, In ædibus Viduæ & Hæredum Ioan. Stelsii. Anno M. D. LXIX. ... (Typis Ioan. Graphei.) 8°. A-$3B^8$ $3C^4$. ff. 1-380. (Lea.) [171

CARRARA. Albericus Cibo princ. primus. Statuta Carrariæ (Lucae Apud Vincentium Busdrachium. M.D.LXXIIII.) fol. a^4 A-Mm^4 Nn^6 (-Nn6, *presumably blank*). pp. 2-282. (Lea.) [172

CARRETTO, GALEOTTO, marchese del. Noze de Psyche & Cupidine celebrate ... [Milano, Alessandro Minuziano, c. 1520.] 8°. A-F^8 G^6. [173

-- La Sophonisba tragedia ... In Vinegia Appresso Gabriel Giolito de Ferrari. MDXLVI. 8°. A-F^8 G^4. ff. 2-52. [174

CARRILLO, LUCAS. Arte poetica Española ... por Iuan Diaz Rengifo natural de Auila ... En Salamanca, en casa de Miguel Serrano de Vargas, Año 1592. (*Colophon.*) 4°. π^4 $*^2$ A-Rr^4 Ss^2 a-e^4. pp. 1-324, 1-40. [175

CARTARI, GIOVANNI LODOVICO. Ioannis Ludouici Chartarii Bononiensis ... conciliationes ... omnium Controuersiarum Super Libros Posteriorum Aristot. ... Bononiæ, Apud Faustum Bonardum. 1590. ... 8°. †-††^{8} A-Z^8 Aa^4. ff. 1-188. ¶†1 *defective.* [176

-- Ioannis Ludouici Cartarii Bonon. ... de immortalitate, Atq; Pluralitate Animae Secundum Aristotelem. ... Bononiæ, Apud Faustum Bonardum. 1587. ... 8°. $*^8$ $**^4$ A-P^8 Q^4 R^8 S^4. ff. 2-124. [177

-- De primis principis vniuersam Logicam constituentibus quæstiones ... Bononiae, Apud Io. Rossium. MDLXXXVII. 8°. †-††^{8} A-O^8. pp. 1-223. [178

-- Lectiones super Arist. prooemio Lib. de physico auditu ... Perusiae. In AEdibus Valentis Pannitij ... M. D. LXXII. 4°. a-b^4 A-Hh^4. ff. 2-124. [179

CARTARI, VINCENZO. Il Flauio intorno a i fasti volgari. In Vinegia, Appresso Gualtero Scotto. M D LIII. (*Colophon.*) 8°. $*^8$ $**^4$ A-Z^8 a-d^8 e^4. pp. 1-438. [180

-- Le imagini con la spositione de i dei de gliantichi. ... In Venetia per Francesco Marcolini. M D LVI. ... (... il mese di Ottobre. ...) 4°. A^4 a-z^4 AA-GG^4 HH^2. ff. 2-4, pp. 1-CXXII. [181

-- -- Le imagini de i dei de gli antichi ... In Lione Apresso Bartholomeo Honorati ... 1581. 8°. *-3$*^8$ 4$*^4$ a-z^8 A-G^8. pp. 1-474. [182

-- -- Imagines deorum qui ab antiquis colebantur. ... Latino sermone ab Antonio Verderio ... expressæ ... Lugduni, apud Barptolemæum Honoratum. M. D. LXXXI. ... (... Excudebat Guichardus Iullieron ... mense Sextilis ...) 4°. $*^4$ A-$3F^4$. pp. 1-359. [183

CARTHUSIANS. Anagraphe de origine Carthusiani ordinis, versibus hexametris descripta in minore claustro Cartusiæ Parisiensis. Parisiis, Apud Guilielmum Chaudiere ... M. D. LXXVIII. ... 4°. A-D^4 (-D4, *presumably blank*). ff. 2-15. [184

-- -- Description de l'origine et premiere fondation de l'ordre sacré des Chartreux, naifuement pourtraicte au Cloistre des Chartreux de Paris. Traduicte par ... François Iary ... A Paris, Chez Guillaume Chaudiere ... M. D. LXXVIII. ... 4°. a-h^4. ff. 2-32. [185

-- Statuta ordinis carthusiensis a domino Guigone priore cartusie edita. (impressa Basilee arte ... iohannis amorbachij ac collegarū suorum: impensis domus montis sancti iohannis baptiste/ prope friburgum: Anno domini quingentesimo decimo/ supra millesimum ad .18. calendas februarias.) fol. B.L. A^8 (-A1) B-D^6 a^8 b^6 c^8 d^6 e-g^8 h-m^6 n-p^8 q-s^6 t-v^8 x-y^6 z^8 a^8 b-h^6 i-k^8 A^{10} b-h^6 i^8. ff. 1-50. (Lea.) [186

-- -- *Another copy* (-^{3}i7-8). (Yarnall.) [186a

CARVALLO VILLAS BOAS, MARTIN DE. Volume primero del espeio de principes y ministros. ... En Milan, En casa de los herederos de Paçifico Pōçio ... 4°. A^4 A-T^4 T-Nn^4. pp. 1-276. ¶*Dedication dated 15 October 1598.* [187

CASA, GIOVANNI DELLA. Le Galatee, ... mis en François, Latin, & Espagnol par diuers auteurs. ... [Genève] Par Iean de Tournes. M. D. XCVIII. 16°. A^2 A-Z^8 a-e^8 f^6. pp. 1-459. [188

-- Ioannis Casæ Latina monimenta. ... Florentiae, In Officina Iuntarum Bernardi filiorum ... Nonis Sept. 1567. (*Colophon.*) 4°. a-b^4 A-EE^4. pp. 2-210. [189

-- Rime, et prose ... Impresse in Vinegia, per Nicolo Beuilacqua, nel mese d'Ottobre. M. D. LVIII. (... ad instantia di M. Erasmo Gemini ...) 4°. a^4 b^2 A-X^4 Y^2. pp. 1-170. [190

CASAS, BARTOLOME DE LAS. Aqui se cõtienẽ treynta proposiciones muy juridicas: en las quales ... se tocã muchas cosas perteneciẽtes al derecho q̃ la yglesia y los principes christianos tienen/ o puedẽ tener sobre los infieles ... 1552. (Impresso en seuilla en casa de sebastiã trugillo.) 4°. B.L. a^{10}. [191

-- Aqui se contiene vna disputa/ o controuersia: entre el Obispo dõ fray Bartholome de las Casas/ ... y el doctor Gines de Sepulueda ... q̃ las conquistas delas Indias contra los Indios eran licitas ... 1552. (Fue impressa ... enla ... ciudad de Seuilla: en casa de Sebastian Trugillo ... Acabosse a .x. dias del mes de Setiembre. ...) 4°. B.L. a-g^8 h^6. ¶*E. D. Church 91.* [192

-- Aqui se cõtienẽ vnos auisos y reglas para los confessores q̃ oyeren confessiones delos Españoles que son/ o han sido en cargo a los Indios delas Indias del mar Oceano ... (Fue impressa ... enla ... ciudad de Seuilla/ en casa de Sebastian Trugillo ... Acabosse a .xx. dias del mes de Setiembre. Año de mil ⁊ quinientos ⁊ cincuenta y dos.) 4°. B.L. a^{10}. [193

-- Breuissima relacion de la destruycíon de las Indias ... 1552. (Fue impressa ... enla ... ciudad de Seuilla en casa de Sebastian Trugillo ...) 4°. B.L. a-e^8 f^{10} g^4 (-f9-10, g^4). [194

-- -- Narratio regionum Indicarum per Hispanos quosdam deuastatarum ... Francofurti, Sumptibus Theodori de Bry, & Ioannis Saurii typis. Anno M. D. XCVIII. 4°.)(^{4} A-S^4. pp. 1-141. [195

-- -- Tyrannies et cruautez des Espagnols ... traduictes par Iaques de Miggrode ... A Anuers, Chez François de Rauelenghien ... M. D. LXXIX. 8°. *^{8} A-L^8 M^4. pp. 1-184. [196

-- -- A Paris, Par Guillaume Iulien ... M.D.LXXXII. ... 8°. *^{8} A-L^8 M^4. pp. 1-184. [197

-- -- Histoire admirable des horribles insolences, crauatez, & tyrannies exercees par les Espagnols ... M. D. LXXXII. 8°. *^{8} A-O^8 (-O8, *presumably blank*). pp. 1-222. [198

-- -- The Spanish Colonie, or Briefe Chronicle of the Acts and gestes of the Spaniardes in the West Indies ... translated into english, by M.M.S. Imprinted at London for William Brome. 1583. (Imprinted ... by Thomas Dawson ...) 4°. B.L. ¶-¶¶^{4} A-Q^4 R^2. *S.T.C.* 4739. [199

-- Entre los remedios q̃ dõ fray Bartolome delas casas ... refirio por mandado del Emperador rey nr̃o senor: ... para reformaciõ delas Indias. ... (Fue impressa ... en la ... ciudad de Seuilla/ en las casas de Iacome Crõberger. Acabose a diez ⁊ siete dias del mes do Agosto/ año de mill ⁊ quinientos ⁊ cinquenta y dos años.) 4°. B.L. a-f^8 g^6. [200

-- Este es vn tratado q̃ ... Bartholome de las Casas ... compuso/ por comissíon del Consejo Real delas Indias: sobre la materia de los yndios que se han hecho en ellas esclauos. ... 1552. (Fue impressa ... enla ... ciudad de Seuilla/ en casa de Sebastian Trugillo ... Acabosse a doze dias del mes de Setiembre. ...) 4°. B.L. a-c^8 d^{12}. [201

-- Kurtze Erklärung Der Fůrnembsten Thaten/ so durch die Spanier beschehen in etlicher Orten der neuwen Welt ... [Frankfurt, J. T. de Bry,] M. D. XCIX. 4°. a-d^4. ¶*15 numbered plates with letterpress.* b1 *defective.* [202

-- Principia quedã ex quibus procedendum est in disputatione ad manifestandam et defendendam iusticiam Yndorum (Impressum Hispali in edib⁹ Sebastiani Trugilli.) 4°. B.L. A^{10} [203

-- Tratado cõprobatorio del Imperio soberano y principado vniuersal que los Reyes de Castilla y Leon tienen sobre las Indias ... 1552. (Fue impressa ... en la ... ciudad ꝺ Seuilla en casa ꝺ Sebastiã Trugillo ... Acabosse a ocho dias ꝺl mes de Enero. Año. 1553.) 4°. B.L. a-k^8. [204

CASAS, CRISTÓBAL DE LAS. Vocabulario de las dos lenguas Toscana y Castellana ... Vendense en Casa de Francisco de Aguilar ... en Seuilla. 1570 (Impresso ... en casa de Alonso Escriuano ...) 4°. ✠^{4} A-Gg^8 Hh^4. ff. 13-247. [205

-- -- ... Et accresciuto da Camillo Camilli ... En Venetia, Vendese en casa de Damian Zenaro ... M. D. LXXXVII. (Impresso ... en casa de Gio. Antonio Bertano ...) 8°. a-c^8 A-Cc^8 Dd^4. pp. 1-437. [206

-- -- En Venetia, Vendese en casa de Damian Zenaro ... M. D. XCI. (Impresso ... en casa de Gio. Antonio Bertano ...) 8°. a-c^{8} A-Cc^{8} Dd^{4} (-Dd4, *presumably blank*). pp. 1-437. [207

-- -- [In Venetia M.D.C. Appresso Olivier Alberti.] 8°. a-c^{8} (-a1) A-Dd^{8} (-Dd8). pp. 1-415. [208

CASE, JOHN. Sphæra ciuitatis, authore Magistro Iohanne Caso Oxoniensi ... Oxoniæ, Excudebat Iosephus Barnesius, 1588. 4°. ¶-¶¶^{8} 3¶^{2} A-3A^{8}. pp. 1-740. *S.T.C.* 4761. [209

-- Thesaurus oeconomiæ, seu commentarius in oeconomica Aristotelis ... Oxoniæ, Ex officina Typographica Iosephi Barnesij, & veneunt Londini in Coemiterio D. Pauli, ad insigne Bibl. [per Ioannam Broome] 1597. 4°. ¶^{4} ¶¶^{2} (¶¶2 + *folded leaf*) A-R^{8} S-T^{4}. pp. 1-277. *S.T.C.* 4765. [210

CASELIUS, JOANNES. Επιταφιος ... Iulio, Duci Brunsuig. & Lunæburg. ... Helmaestadii Excudebat Iacobus Lucius. Anno cIↄ. Iↄ. XIC. 4°. A-F^{4}. [211

CASIO DE' MEDICI, GIROLAMO. Hieronimo Casio de Medici ... Bolognese Alla. S. de'l. N.S. Clemene [*sic*] VII. P.M. ... 8°. π^{8}. ¶*In verse.* [212

-- Capitoli quatro et tre sonetti dil Casio ... 8°. a^{8}. [213

CASONE, GIROLAMO. Rime ... In Venetia, Appresso Gio. Battista Ciotti. 1598. ... 12°. A^{6} B^{12}. ff. 2-18. [214

CASONI, GUIDO. Della magia d'amore, ... Dialogo Primo. ... In Venetia, Appresso Fabio, & Agostin Zoppini Fratelli. MDXCII. (... 1591.) 4°. a^{4} b^{6} A-O^{4}. ff. 1-56. [215

CASOPERO, GIANO TESEO. Iani Thesei Casoperi Psychronæi amorum Libri quattuor ... (Venetijs per Bernardinum de Vitalibus Venetum ... M.D.XXXV. Mense Iunij.) 8°. a-h^{8}. [216

CASPARIUS, CASPAR. Princeps Auriacus, siue libertas defensa: tragoedia noua. ... Delphis, Ex officinâ Brunonis Schinckelij. cIↄ Iↄ IIC. 8°. *^{4} A-F^{4}. pp. 1-46. [217

CASSANDER, GEORGIUS. Liturgica de ritu et ordine Dominicae Coenae celebrandæ, quam celebrationem Græci Liturgian, Latini Missam appellarunt ... Coloniae, Apud hæredes Arnoldi Birckmanni. Anno 1558. 8°. *a*^{8} A-N^{8}. ff. 1-104. (Lea.) [218

CASSIANUS, JOANNES. D. Cassiani Constantinopolitani Diaconi, de Lib. Arbitrio Collatio. (Haganoæ, per Iohan. Secerium Mense Martio. Anno M.D.XXVIII.) 4°. A-H^{4}. [219

CASSIODORUS, MAGNUS AURELIUS. Antiqua regum Italiæ Gothicæ gentis Rescripta, ex. 12. libris Epistolarum Cassiodori ad Eutharicū, per Iohannem Cochlæum ... excerpta. [Lipsiae, Nicolaus Schmidt,] M. D. XXIX. 8°. A-M^{8} N^{4} (-N4, *blank*). ff. 1-93. [220

-- L'histoire ecclesiastique nommée Tripartite, diuisée en douze liures ... traduite de Latin en François, par Loys Cyaneus. A Paris, Chez Gilles Gorbin ... 1568. ... fol. ¶^{4} a-z^{4} A-I^{4} K^{2}. pp. 1-251. (Lea.) [221

-- Magni Aurelii Cassiodori variarum libri XII item de anima liber vnus ... in lucem dati a Mariangelo Accursio. ... M.D.XXXIII (Augustae Vindelic. ex aedibus Henrici Silicei mense Maio ...) fol. A-Z^{6} a-d^{6} e^{8}. pp. 1-327. [222

CASSOLA, LUIGI. Madrigali ... In Vinegia Appresso Gabriel Giolito de Ferrari MDXLV. (*Colophon.*) 8°. A-I^{8} K^{10}. pp. 3-156. [223

CASTALDI, RISTORO. Restauri Castaldi Perusini ... Tractatus de Imperatore ... (Romae in Lucem missum, Antonij Bladi Asulani cura ... M. D. XL.) fol. a^{8} A-TT^{6} VV^{4} a^{6} b-c^{4} d^{2}. ff. I-CCLV. [224

CASTELLANI, GIULIO. Ad Cosmum Medicem ... De Humano Intellectu libri tres. Bononiæ apud Alexandrum Benaccium. M D LXI. 4°. +-++^{4} A-V^{4} X^{2}. ff. 1-77. [225

CASTELLANI, VINCENZO. Vincentii Castellani Forosemproniensis de officio regis libri IIII. ... Marpurgi, Apud Paulum Egenolphum. M. D. XCVII. 8°. †[8] A-Mm[8] (-Mm8, *presumably blank*) ††[8] (-††8, *presumably blank*). pp. 1-558. [226

CASTELLENSE, ADRIANO. Hadrianus ... card. Botoien. de sermone Latino, et modis Latinè loquendi. Eiusdem uenatio ad Ascanium Cardinalem. Item iter Iulij II. ... Coloniae Agrippinae, Apud Ioannem Gymnicum, ... M.D.LXXVIII. 8°. A-Ee[8]. pp. 1-429. [227

-- De vera philosophia ex quatuor doctoribus ecclesiae. (Impressum Romę per Magistrum Iacobum Mazochium ... M.D.xiiii. ...) 4°. A[4] A[4] B-K[8]. [228

CASTELLETTI, CHRISTOFORO. I torti amorosi comedia ... In Venetia, Appresso Gio. Battista Sessa & Fratelli. 1581. 12°. A-H[12] (-H12, *presumably blank*). pp. 3-190. [229

CASTELLINI, JACOPO. Gallinacea farsa ... In Fiorenza Appresso L. Torrentino MDLXII. 8°. A-C[8]. pp. 8-48. [230

CASTELVETRO, LODOVICO. Correttione d'alcune cose del dialogo delle lingue di Benedetto Varchi, et vna giunta al primo libro delle Prose di M. Pietro Bembo doue si ragiona della vulgar lingua ... Stampata in Basilæa ... M. D. LXXII. 4°. **[4] a-z[4] A-Q[4]. pp. 1-290. [231

-- Giunta fatta al ragionamento degli articoli et de verbi di Messer Pietro Bembo. ... (In Modona, Per gli Heredi di Cornelio Gadaldino. M D LXIII.) 4°. [a][2] b-d[4] A-X[4] Y[6]. ff. 1-90. [232

-- Ragione d'alcune cose segnate nella canzone d'Annibal Caro venite al'ombra de gran gigli d'oro. [Modena, Antonio Gadaldino, 1559.] 4°. ✠[4] A-Ff[4]. ff. 1-116. [233

CASTIGLIONE, BALDASSARE. Il libro del cortegiano del Conte Baldesar Castiglione. ... (In Venetia nelle case d'Aldo Romano, & d'Andrea d'Asola suo Socero ... M. D. XXVIII. del mese d'Aprile.) fol. *[4] a-o[8] p[6]. [234

-- -- M D XLI. (In Vinegia ... In casa de' figliuoli di Aldo.) 8°. A-BB[8]. ff. 1-195. [235

-- -- Il Cortegiano ... In Vinegia Appresso Gabriel Giolito de Ferrari. MDXLVI. (*Colophon.*) 8°. A-Bb[8] Cc[4]. ff. 6-204. [236

-- -- Il libro del cortegiano ... M. D. XLVII. (In Vinegia ... In casa de' figliuoli di Aldo.) 8°. A-CC[8]. ff. 1-195. [237

-- -- Il cortegiano ... In Vinegia. MDLII. (... Per Domenico Giglio. ...) 12°. ✠[6] A-Q[12]. ff. 1-192. [238

-- -- In Venetia, Per Comin da Trino. M D LXXIII. 8°. a[12] b[8] A-DD[8] EE[4]. ff. 3-220. [239

-- -- Le parfait courtisan du Comte Baltasar Castillonnois, Es deux langues ... De la traduction de Gabriel Chappuys Tourangeau. A Lion, par Iean Huguetan. M.D.LXXXV. (Acheué d'Imprimer le dernier de Iuillet ... Imprimé par Claude Bourcicaud. ...) 8°. *[8] **[6] a-z[8] A-S[8] T[10] V[8]. pp. 1-660. ¶T5-6 *follow* **3 *(as imposed?)*. [240

-- -- A Paris, Par Nicolas Bonfons ... 1585. (*Colophon.*) 8°. ā[8] ē[8] a-z[8] A-V[8]. pp. 1-678. [240a

CASTIGLIONE, GIUSEPPE. Iosephi Castalionis pro studiis humanitatis oratio. Romae, Apud Aloysium Zannettum. 1594. ... 4°. A[4]. [241

CASTILE. Leyes del estillo. Y declaraciones sobre las leyes del fuero. (Fueron impressas ... enla ... ciudad de Toldedo: por Iuan Varela de Salamanca: año de mill ⁊ quiniẽtos ⁊ onze años. A dezioch dias de Febrero.) fol. B.L. a-d[6] e[4]. (Lea.) [242

-- -- [Salamanca, Juan de Junta, c. 1540.] fol. B.L. a-c[8] d[6]. ff. II-XXX. (Lea.) [242a

-- Ordenãças reales de Castilla. ... (Fue impresso ... enla ... ciudad de Toledo. En casa de Iuan de Ayala. A costa de Diego lopez ... Acabose a seys dias del mes de Iulio. Año de mil ⁊ quinientos ⁊ quarenta y nueue años.) fol. B.L. π[2] a-p[8]. ff. j-c.xx. (Lea.) [243

-- -- Sub Philippo. II. Hisp. Rege. Ordenanças reales de Castilla ... Nueuamẽte glossadas, y enmẽdadas ... Por el doctor Diego Perez de Salamanca ... Salamanticæ, Excudebat Ioannes Maria à Terranoua. M. D. LX. Expensis Ioannis Moreni ... (... M.D.LIX.) fol. π^2 A-3B^8 3C-3D^6 a^8 ¶a^8 b^8 c^6. ff. 1-2, cols. 3-1572. ¶*Additional t.p.* (a1): Index ... Salmanticæ, Excudebat Ioannes Maria à Terranoua. M. D. LX. (Lea.) [244

-- Quaderno delas leyes y nueuas decisiones: ... las quales se ymprimierõ por mandado del Rey hecha enla cibdad de Toro a catorze dias del mes de Marco de mill y quinientos y cinco años. ... [Toledo, Juan Varela.] fol. B.L. a^8. (Lea.) [245

-- *Alfonso X, king.* [Fuero real de España.] (Salmanticae Excudebat Ioannes Baptista à Terranoua. ... 1569.) fol. ¶^{4} (-¶1) ††^{8} A-Kk^8. ff. 1-263. [246

CASTILLA, FRANCISCO DE. [1] Theorica de virtudes en coplas/ y con cõmento. ... Y otras obras ... 4°. B.L. A-H^8 I^6. ff. ij-lxx. [2] Pratica delas virtudes delos buenos Reyes Despaña ... (Fue impresso ... enla ... ciudad de Caragoça por Agostin millan ... M.D.L.II.) A-C^8 D^{10} E^4. ff. iij-xxxiiij. [247

CASTILLEJO, CHRISTOVAL DE. Las obras ... En Anuers. En casa de Martin Nutio. 1598. ... 12°. A^{16} B-Hh^{12}. ff. 3-372. [248

CASTILLO, JULIÁN DE. Historia de los reyes Godos que vinieron dela Scitia de Europa, contra el Imperio Romano, y a España: y la succession dellos hasta ... Philippe segundo ... Impressa en Burgos, por Philippe de Iunta. 1582. (*Colophon.*) fol. ¶^{10} A-T^8 V^6 *^{10} (-*10, *presumably blank*). ff. j-clviij. [249

CASTRO, ALFONSO DE. Opera Alphonsi a Castro Zamorensi, ... videlicet Aduersus omnes hæreses Lib. quatuordecim. De iusta punitione hæreticorum Lib. tres. De potestate legis poenalis Lib. duo. ... Parisiis, Apud Sebastianum Niuellium ... M. D. LXXI. fol. A^8 B-E^6 A-Zz^6 AA-ZZ^6 3A-3L^6 3M^4 (-3M4, *presumably blank*). cols. 1-1932. (Lea.) [250

-- F. Alfonsi de Castro ... aduersus omnes hæreses Libri quatuordecim. ... Venetiis M. D. XLVI. Ad signum spei. 8°. a-c^8 d^4 A-4H^8. pp. 1-1231. (Lea.) [251

-- Fr. Alfonsi A Castro ... De iusta Hæreticorum punitione Libri tres. ... Antuerpiæ In ædibus Viduæ & Hæredum Ioan. Stelsii. M. D. LXVIII. ... 8°. a-b^8 A-YY^8 ZZ^4. ff. 1-361. (Lea.) [252

CATALONIA. [Constitutions.] En Barcelona. (Foren estampadas ... en la ciutat de Barcelona, en casa de Hubert Gotart ...) fol. [1] Constitutions y altres drets de Cathalunya ... volum primer. ... ¶-¶¶^{8} ¶¶¶^{10} A-Nn^8 Oo^4 Pp^8 Qq^{10}. pp. 1-584. [2] Pragmaticas, y altres drets de Cathalunya ... volum segon. ... Any M.D.LXXXVIIII. ... π^2 A-D^8 E^{10} F-K^8 L^{10}. pp. 1-171. [3] Constitutions, y altres drets de Cathalunya ... volum tercer. ... Any M.D.LXXXVIIII. π^2 A-D^8 E^4. pp. 1-72. (Lea.) [253

-- La sentencia reyal donada ꝑ ... Rey don Ferrando segõ enla primera cort de Barçelona: ... en virtut ðl poder donat ala magestat per la d:ta cort sobre les differencies de part a part deuallants per causa deles turbacions passades. (Acaben ... en ... Barcelona ꝑ Pere mõpezat a despeses de Latzer milla ... A. vi. dies del mes de Agost del Any. M.D.xxxx.) fol. B.L. A^6 B^4 a^6 b^8 A^6. (Lea.) [254

-- Constitucions fetes ꝑ ... don Ferrando Rey de Argao ... enla quĩta cort de Cathalunya ... En lany Mil cinch cents e deu. (Acabẽ ... Per Iaume de Vingles: a despẽsas de mestre Latzar milla ... A. xxvj. del mes de Ianer Lan mil cinch cents etrenta e sis.) fol. B.L. a-b^6 c^8 A^6 B^8. (Lea.) [255

-- Pragmatica sãcio feta per ... don ferrando Rey de arago ... ([$\pi 2^v$] Estampat en Barcelõa per Carles a moros En despesa de mestre Lazer milla ... a vi. ð Mar. Any. Mil.D. y xiii. ...) fol. B.L. π^2 a-b^6. ¶*Additioanl t.p.* (a1): Constituciõs fetes perla ... Reyna dona Germana ... (Lea.) [256

-- Constitucions fetes per la ... magestat ð dõ Carles ... Mil.D.xx. ... (Acaben ... per Carles amoros prouensal. A despeses de mestre Lazar Milla ... enla ... Ciutat de Barcelona ... acabada de estampar lo primer dia del mes de Abril del any ... Mil.D.xx. ...) fol. B.L. a-c^8. (Lea.) [257

-- Carolus imperator Romanorum. M.D.xxviij. fol. B.L. π^2 A^6 b-c^6. ¶*Additional t.p.* (A1): Costitucions fetes p̲ la ... Magestat del Emperador Don Carles ... en lany. M.D.xxx.iiij. ... (... Estampats [en Barcelona] ... per Carles amoros prouensal/ a despeses δ Mestre Lazer milla ...: a. x. del mes de Setẽbre δl any. ... M.D.xxxiiij. ...) (Lea.) [258

-- Constitucions fetes per la ... Magestat del Emperador don Carles ... En lany: Mil.D.xxxvij. (Estampats per Iaume Cortrey ... A. xxiij. de Iuny. de. M.D.liij. anys. ...) fol. B.L. A-B^6. ¶*Additional t.p.* (B5): Pragmatica sanctio feta per la ... Magestat δl Emperador don Carles ... a. vij. dies del mes δ Març δl Any. M.D.xxxix. (Lea.) [259

-- Constitucions fetes p̲ la ... Magestat del Emperador don Carles ... Any. M.D. XXXXII. (Estampats per Carles Amoros: enla ... ciutat de Barcelona: ... Fonch acabada a. xxv. del mes de Febrer Any ... M.D.xliij.) fol. B.L. A-B^8 C^6 D^4. ff. II-XXVI. (Lea.) [260

-- Constitucions fetes per ... don Phelip princep deles Asturies ... Enlo any M.D.xlvij. (stampats per Pere Mompezat enla ... ciutat de Barcelona a. xiij de Abril. M.D.xxxxviij. A despeses de Iaume Cortey ...) fol. B.L. $✠^4$ A-D^8 E^{10}. ff. I-XLI. (Lea.) [261

-- Constitucions fetes perlo ... dõ Phelip Princep δles Asturies ... Enlo any M.D.L.iij. (Acabense .. Enla ... Ciutat de Barcelona. A. xxviij. de Març de. M.D.liij. Enla Imprenta de Iaume Cortey ...) fol. B.L. π^2 A-B^8. ff. j-xvj. (Lea.) [262

CATANEO, DANESE. Dell'amor di Marfisa tredici canti ... In Venetia, Appresso Francesco de Franceschi Senese. M D LXII. 4°. a^2 A-M^4 N^6. pp. 1-106. [263

CATANEO, GIROLAMO. Libro nuouo di fortificare ... In Brescia presso Thomaso Bozzola. M D LXVII. (... per Vincenzo di Sabbio ... M. D. LXVI.) 4°. $*^4$ A-D^4 E-Y^2 Z^4 AA-HH^2 II^4 KK^2 (KK2 + *folded leaf*). ff. 1-78. (Fine Arts.) [264

-- Vita del ... Papa Pio quinto. ... Con vna raccolta di lettere di Pio V. ... Et i nomi delle Galee, et de capitani, cosi Christiani, come Turchi, che si trouarono alla battaglia nauale. In Mantoua, per Francesco Osanna. 1587. ... (*Colophon.*) 4°. $*^4$ $**^4$ A-Hh^4. pp. 1-246. (Lea.) [265

-- -- In Roma, ... M. D. LXXXVII. (... Per Alessandro Gardano & Francesco Coattino. ...) 8°. †-†††^{8} A-Z^8. pp. 1-367. (Lea.) [266

CATENA, PIETRO. Vniuersa loca in logicam Aristotelis in mathematicas disciplinas hoc nouum opus declarat. ... Venetiis in oficina Francisci Marcolini. M D LVI. 4°. A-O^4. pp. 3-110. [267

CATHERINE OF SIENA, S. Dialogo de la seraphica vergine santa Catharina da Siena ... (impresso in Venetia per Marchio Sessa. ... M.D.XXXX. Adi .xxix. Aprile. ...) 8°. a-d^8 A-EE^8. ff. 1-224. [268

-- Lettere deuotissime ... In Venetia, ... al segno della Speranza. MDLXII. 4°. a^4 A-N^4 O-$3F^8$ $3G^{10}$ (-3G10, *presumably blank*). ff. 1-373. [269

CATO, DIONYSIUS. Contenta in hoc opere sunt hæc. Catonis pręcepta moralia recognita atqȝ interpretata ab Erasmo Roterodamo. Mimi Publiani. Septem sapientũ illustres sententie. Institutio hominis Christiani uersibus hexametris. per Erasmum Roterodamum. Isocratis Paręnesis ad Demoniacũ Rudolpho Agricola interprete. recognita per Martinũ Dorpiũ. Epicteti Stoici Enchiridion. Plutarchi libellus de odio & inuidia. ... (Argentorati, ex ædibus Schurerianis Mense Martio. M. D. XVI.) 4°. π^4 A^4 B^8 C-D^4 E^8 F^4 G^8 H-I^4 K^8. [270

-- -- Disticha de moribus nomine Catonis inscripta, Cum Latina & Gallica interpretatione. ... Dicta [septem] Sapientum, cum ... interpretatione. A Lyon, Par Pierre Chapperon. 1578. 8°. a-i^8. pp. 3-134. [271

CATO, MARCUS PORCIUS. Libri de re rustica M. Catonis lib. I. M. Terentii Varronis lib. III. L. Iunii Moderati Columellae lib. XII. ... Palladii lib. XIIII. ... Georgij Alexandrini enarrationes ... (Venetiis in aedibus Aldi, et Andreae soceri mense Maio M.D.XIIII.) 8°. $*^8$ aa-bb^8 cc^{10} a-h^8 i^4 k-z^8 A-Q^8. ff. 1-308. [272

-- -- Libri de re rustica a Nicolao Angelio ... recogniti ... Additis ... commentarijs

Iunij Pompo. Fortunati ... cum adnotationibus Philippi Beroaldi. ... (Florentiæ per heredes Philippi Iuntæ. ... M.D.XXI. Die .XXVIII. Mensis Septembris.) 4°. AA⁸ BB¹² a-z⁸ &⁸ ɔ⁸ ꝶ⁸ Aa⁸ Bb⁶ A¹⁰ B-O⁸ P¹². ff. 1-218, 1-125. [273

-- -- Libri de re rustica ... Parisiis apud Ioannem paruum ... (Impressum ... prælo Antonii Augerelli, Impensis autem Ioannis Parui, & Galeoti à Prato. Mense Februario. Anno M. D. XXXIII.) fol. A⁶ B⁸ C⁸ a⁶ a-z⁸ A-G⁸ H¹⁰. pp. 1-506. [274

-- -- ... Basileae ex officina Ioan. Heruag. anno M.D.XXXV. (... mense Iulio.) 4°. aa-nn⁴ a-z⁴ A-Zz⁴ AA-EE⁴. ff. 1-295. [275

-- Methodus rustica Catonis atq. Varronis Præceptis aphoristicis per Locos communes digestis à Theodoro Zuingero ... Basileæ Petri Pernae opera atque impensa. ... 8°. α⁸ β⁴ A-I⁸ K⁴ a-z⁸ (-K4, *blank*). pp. 2-494. ¶*Preface dated* Kl. Augusti *1576*. [276

CATTANI, FRANCESCO, DA DIACCETO. Opera omnia ... Basileae, M. D. LXIII. (... per Henrichum Petri, & Petrum Pernam ...) fol. ✱⁴ ✱⁴ A-Hh⁶ α-β⁶ γ⁴ δ⁶. pp. 3-371. [277

-- Discorso dell'autorita del papa Sopra Concilio. ... In Fiorenza appresso i Giunti. MDLXII. 8°. A-C⁸. pp. 5-46. [278

-- Discorso ... Sopra la superstizzione dell'arte magica. ... In Fiorenza Appresso Valente Panizzi & Marco Peri C. M D LXVII. 4°. A-K⁴. ff. 1-36. [279

-- L'essamerone ... In Fiorenza, appresso Lorenzo Torrentino ... MDLXIII. 4°. †⁴ A-Zz⁴. ff. 1-180. [280

CATULLUS, GAIUS VALERIUS. Catullus. Tibullus. Propertius. (Venetiis in aedibus Aldi, et Andreae soceri mense Martio. M. D. XV.) 8°. A-D⁸ E¹⁰ AA-DD⁸ EE⁴ a-i⁸. ff. 2-148. [281

-- -- (Impressum Venetiis per Melchiorem Sessam, ... M.D.XXXI. Die .XX. Septembris.) 8°. A-S⁸. ff. 2-142. [282

-- -- ... His accesserunt Corn. Galli fragmenta. Lugduni, apud haeredes Seb. Gryphii, M. D. LXI. 16°. a-x⁸ y⁴ (-y4, *presumably blank*). pp. 3-342. [283

-- -- [1] Catulli, Tibulli, PropertI noua editio. Iosephus Scaliger ... recensuit. ... Lutetiae, Apud Mamertum Patissonium, in officina Rob. Stephani. M.D.LXXVII. ... 8°. ā⁸ A-R⁸ S². pp. 1-174. ¶ā1 *defective*. [2] Iosephi Scaligeri ... castigationes ... *Same imprint*. a-r⁸. pp. 3-252. [284

CAUCUS, ANTONIUS. Antonii Cauci, patricii Veneti ... oratio habita in secunda Sessione ... Concilij Triden. ... die XXVI. Februarii, anno M. D. LXII. Brixiae, Ad instantiam Ioannis Baptistæ Bozolæ. M. D. LXIIII. (... Apud Ludouicum Sabiensem.) 4°. A⁴. (Lea.) [285

CAUMONT, JEAN DE. Aduertissement des aduertissemens, Au peuple treschrestien. ... M.D.LXXXVII. 8°. A-D⁴. pp. 2-32. [286

CAVAGNOLO, ROLANDO. [1] Rolandi Cauagnolii ... Obseruationum, & Declarationum ad Antiqua Decreta Montisferrati Ciuilia. Libri duo ... In vrbe Casalis. Bernardus Grassus ... Excudebat. ... M.D.XCV. (*Colophon*.) fol. †⁶ ¶⁶ a-f⁶ g¹⁰ A-Ff⁶ Gg⁸. pp. 1-364. [2] ... Liber secundus. *Same imprint and colophon*. A-E⁶ F⁴ G-N⁶ O⁴. pp. 3-160. (Lea.) [287

CAVALCA, DOMENICO. Libro titulato Spechio di Croce ... in lingua fiorentina ridutto. ... (Impresso in Venetia ... Stāpato ꝑ Maestro Māfrino bon de Monfera del .M.CCCCCXV.) 4°. A-Q⁴. [288

-- -- *Another copy* (-F-H⁴). [289

CAVALCANTI, BARTOLOMMEO. [1] Giudicio sopra la tragedia di Canace, et Macareo. ... con la Tragedia appresso. In Venetia, MDLXVI. 8°. A-G⁸. ff. 2-54. [2] Canace tragedia di M. Sperone Speroni ... *Same imprint*. A-E⁸. ff. 2-48. [290

-- La retorica ... In Vinegia appresso Gabriel Giolito de' Ferrari. M D LIX. fol. ✱-✱✱⁶ 3✱⁴ A-3A⁶. pp. 1-563. [291

-- -- In Venetia. Appresso Camillo, e Francesco Franceschini fratelli, M D LXXIIII. 4°. ✱⁴ A-Nn⁸. pp. 1-571. [292

-- [1] Trattati ouero discorsi ... sopra gli ottimi reggimenti delle republiche antiche et moderne. Con un discorso di M. Sebastiano Erizo gentil'huomo Vinitiano de Gouerni Ciuili ... In Venetia MDLXXI. (... Appresso Iacopo Sansouino il Giouane. M D LXX.) 4°. +^{4} A-Y^4. ff. 1-86. [2] Discorso de i gouerni ciuili ... A-C^4 D^2. ff. 2-14. [293

CAVALLERINI, ANTONIO. Il conte di Modona tragedia ... In Modona. Nella Stamperia di Paolo Gadaldino. ... 4°. A-N^4. ff. 2-51. [294

-- Ino tragedia ... In Modona. Nella Stamperia di Paolo Gadaldino. ... 4°. A-O^4. ff. 2-55. ¶A2-4 *bound in reverse order. Dedication dated 1583.* [295

CAVICEO, GIACOMO. Libro del Peregrino ... con la vita dello Auctore. ... (Stampato in Venetia per Bernardino de Lisona Vercellese. M.D.XX. Adi .IX. Marzo.) 4°. A^8 B^4 C-V^8 X^4 (-X4, *presumably blank*). [296

-- -- Dialogue treselegant intitule le Peregrin/ traictant de lhonneste ꝛ pudicq amour ... traduict de vulgaire Italien en langue Frãcoyse/ ꝑ maistre Frãcoys dassy ...ꝛ corrige oultre sa premiere impressiõ/ par Iehã martin ... On les vend a Paris ... par maistre Pierre vidoue. 1540. 8°. B.L. ℭ^8 ℭ^4 A-V^8 x-z^8 AA-SS^8. ff. i-cccxxvii. [297

CAVITELLI, LODOVICO. Lodouici Cauitelli ... annales. ... vsq; ad ... 1583. ... Cremonae M.D.LXXXVIII. Apud Christophorũ Draconium. ... 4°. *^{8} A-3H^8 b-h^4 (-h4, *blank*). ff. 2-431. [298

CAVRETTO, PIETRO. De miseria humana, Petri Haedi Fortunaensis libri quinque. In Academia Veneta, M D LVIII. (*Colophon*) 4°. A-R^4. ff. 1-64. [299

CAYET, PIERRE VICTOR PALMA. Paradigmata de quatuor linguis orientalibus præcipuis, Arabica, Armena, Syra, Æthiopica. ... Parisiis, M.D.XCVI. E Typographia Steph. Preuosteau, hæredis Guil. Morelij ... Pro ipso Authore. ... 4°. *^{4} A^8 B-Aa^4 Bb^2. ff. 1-8, pp. 9-196. [300

CAZZA, GIOVANNI AGOSTINO. Le rime spirituali ... In Nouara appresso Francesco & Giacomo Sesalli. M.D.LII. 8°. A-O^8 P^4. ff. 2-104. [301

CEBES. Κεβητος Θηβαιου πιναξ. Cebetis Thebani tabula. (Hagnoæ in ædibus Thomæ Anshelmi, Mense Ianuario [c. 1520].) 8°. a-b^8. ¶*Title mounted.* [302

-- -- Le tableau de Cebes de Thebes ... exposé en Rythme Francoyse. ... 1543. A Paris. On les uend ... en la boutique de Gilles Corrozet. (Imprimé ... par Denys Ianot ...) 8°. A-H^8 (-H7-8, *presumably blank*). ¶E6^v: La Volupté vaĩcue. F6^v: Sensuyuent plusieurs emblemes. [303

-- -- Cebete Thebano, che in vna tauola dipinta philosophicamente mostra le qualita de la vita humana. Dialogo ridotto di Greco in volgare. ... M D XXXVIIII. (Impresso in Venetia per Francesco Marcolini da Furli ... Il mese di Settembre.) 8°. A-C^4. ff. 2-11. ¶*Translator: Francesco Angelo Coccio.* [304

CECCARELLI, ALFONSO. Dell'historia di Casa Monaldesca ... In Ascoli, Appresso Gioseppe de gl'Angeli. M D LXXX. (*Colophon.*) 4°. A-Ff^4 Gg^6. pp. 1-222. [305

CECCHERELLI, ALESSANDRO. Delle attioni, et sentenze del S. Alessandro de' Medici primo duca di Fiorenza, ragionamento ... In Vinegia appresso Gabriel Giolito de' Ferrari. M D LXIIII. 4°. *^{4} B-P^4. ff. 5-59. [306

CECCHI, GIANMARIA. [Comedie.] In Venetia, Appresso Bernardo Giunti. M D LXXXV. 8°. [1] Comedie di M. Gianmaria Cecchi Fiorentino. Libri primo. ... +^{4} A-E^8. ff. 1-40. [2] La moglie ... A-E^8. ff. 2-40. [3] Il corredo ... A-E^8 F^2 (-F2, *blank*). ff. 2-41. [4] La stiaua ... A-D^8. ff. 2-31. [5] Il donzello ... A-E^8 F^4. ff. 2-43. [6] Gli incantesimi ... A-D^8. ff. 2-31. [7] Lo spirito ... A-D^8 E^4. ff. 2-35. [307

-- I dissimili comedia ... In Vinegia appresso Gabriel Giolito de Ferrari e fratelli. M D L. (*Colophon.*) 12°. A-D^{12}. ff. 4-45. [308

CECCHI

-- [1] L'esaltazione della croce con i suoi intermedi ... In Firenze, Appresso Michelagnolo di Bart. Sermartelli. MDLXXXXII. ... (... Nella Stamperia di Bartolomeo Sermartelli. l'Anno 1586.) 8°. a^4 $B-H^8$. pp. 17-127. [2] Descrizione dell'apparato, e de gl'Intermedi ... In Firenze, Per Michelagnolo di Bartolommeo Sermartelli. MDXCII. A^8 $B-C^4$. pp. 3-31. [309

-- Gl'incantesimi comedia di Gio. Maria Cerchi [*sic*] Fiorentino. ... In Vinegia appresso Gabriel Giolito de Ferrari e fratelli. M D L. (*Colophon.*) 12°. $A-C^{12}$ D^6. ff. 2-42. [310

CECCO D'ASCOLI. Lo illustro poeta Cecho Dascholi: con comẽto ... (Impresso in Milano per Iohanne Angelo Scinzenziler. ... Mccccc.xiiii. A di .xvii. de Nouembre.) 4°. $A-H^8$ I^{10} (-I5-6). ff. II-LxxIIII. [311

CEDRENUS, GEORGIUS. Georgii Cedreni annales, siue historiae ab exordio mundi ad Isacium Comnenum usque Compendium: ... Græcè & Latinè editi: Guilielmo Xylandro Augustano interprete ... Basileae, per Ioan. Oporinum, et Episcopios fratres [1566]. fol. α^4 $a-z^6$ $A-Z^6$ $Aa-Kk^6$ Ll^8 $Mm-Pp^2$ $Qq*^2$ $Qq**^2$ $Rr-Ss^6$ Tt^8. pp. 1-662, cols. 663-714. (Lea.) [312

CEI, FRANCESCO. Sonecti. capituli. canzone. sextine. stanze. et. strambocti. ... in laude di Clitia. (Impresso in Firenze per Philippo di Giunta ... M.CCCCC.III.) 8°. π^4 $a-g^8$ h^2. [313

-- -- (Impresso in Milano per Rocho ꝛ Fratello da Valle ad Instantia de Miser Nicolo da Gorgonzola ... M.ccccc.xx. adi .xxx. de Marzo.) 8°. B.L. $A-G^8$ (-A1, A8). [314

CELADONI, ALESSIO. Alexij Celadeni Episcopi Gallipolitani oratio ad sacrum Cardinalium senatum ingressurum ad nouum Pont. eligendum. [Romae, Joannes Besicken, 1503?] 4°. B.L. a^6. [315

CELESTINA. Celestina. Tragicomedia de Calisto y Melibea. ... [Anveres] En la officina Plantiniana. 1599. 16°. $A-T^8$ V^4. pp. 3-311. [316

-- Celestine ... On les vend a Paris ... M.D.XLII. (Imprime ... per Nicolas Barbou ...) 8°. B.L. A^4 $B-Y^8$ (-B1) Z^4. [317

-- La Celestine ... repurgee ... par Iacques de Lauardin ... A Paris, Par Nicolas Bonfons ... [c. 1578.] 16°. π^4 $A-Nn^8$. ff. 1-273. [318

-- Celestina tragicomedia de Calisto et Melibea nouamente Tradotta de lingua Castigliana in Italiana idioma ... (Stampata in Vinegia per Francesco Caron Nel anno ... M.D.XXV. Nel mese di Nouẽbre.) 8°. $A-P^8$. ff. Ix-CXIX. [319

-- -- *Another copy* (-P8, *blank*). (Lea.) [320

-- ([Venezia,] stampata per Gicuann'antonio e Pietro de Nicolini da Sabio M. D. XLI. De mese di Mazzo.) 8°. $A-O^8$. ff. II-CXII. [321

-- In Vinetia, M D XLIII. (Stampata ... per Bernardino de Bendoni. ...) 8°. $A-P^8$ (-C8, D^8, P8, *the last presumably blank*). ff.II-CXIX. [322

CELICHIUS, ANDREAS. Kurtze/ deutliche vnd richtige Fragestücke/ Von der Himmelfart vnsers Herrn ... Gedruckt zu Magdeburg/ durch Wolffgang Kirchner. Anno M. D. LXXV. 4°. $A-M^4$. [323

CELLINI, BENVENUTO. Due trattati vno intorno alle otto principali arti dell'oreficeria. L'altro in materia dell'Arte della Scultura ... In Fiorenza Per Valente Panizzij, & Marco Peri. M D LXVIII. (*Colophon.*) 4°. A^6 (-A6, *blank*) $B-S^4$. ff. 1-47. [324

CELSI, MINO. Mini Celsi Senensis De Haereticis capitali supplicio non afficiendis. Adiunctæ sunt eiusdem argumenti Theodori Bezae & Andreae Duditii Epistolæ duæ contrariæ. ... cIo Io LXXXIIII. 8°.):(^{8} $A-Z^8$ $a-l^8$ m^4. ff. 1-260. (Lea.) [325

CELTIS, CONRAD. Conradi Celtis Protucij ... libri Odaꝝ quatuor, cum Epodo, & sæculari carmine ... (Argentorati, ex officina Schüreriana, ductu Leonhardi & Lucę Alantsee fratrum, ann. M.D.XIII. mense Maio.) 4°. a^8 b^6 $A-M^{8.4}$ $N-O^8$. [326

CENEAU, ROBERT. Complainte ou response catholique contre la defense et le defenseur de la cause des tenebrions heretiques de ce temps, par ... R. Coenalis ... Et depuis traduite de latin en francoys. A Paris, Par Guillaume Iulien ... 1558. ... 8°. A-E^8 F^4. ff. 2-44. [327

-- Opus quadripartitum super compescenda hereticorum petulantia, authore Roberto præsulo Arboricensi ... Parisiis, Apud Iacobum Keruer ... 1557. ... 8°. AA^8 A-Dd^8 Ee^4. ff. 2-239. (Lea.) [328

-- Pro tuendo sacro coelibatu axioma catholicum: authore ... Roberto, Arboricensi Præsule ... Parisiis Apud Ioannem Roigny ... 1545. 8°. a-n^8. pp. 3-208. ¶n8^v: Finis, *but other copies include* o^8. (Lea.) [329

CENTIO, ALESSANDRO. Il padre afflitto, commedia ... In Macerata. Appresso Sebastiano Martellini. M.D.LXXVIII. 8°. A-L^8. ff. 2-87. [330

CENTORIO DEGLI HORTENSI, ASCANIO. Le amorose rime ... M. D. LIII. (In Venetia Per Matthio Pagan ... Il XXVIII. de Giugno. ...) 8°. A-N^4 O^2. ff. 1-47. [331

-- -- In Melano Appresso di Giouan' Antonio de gli Antonij. M D LIX. (... Imprimeuano i fratelli da Meda. ...) 8°. A-D^8 E^4. ff. 1-23. [332

-- I cinque libri de l'auuertimenti, ordini, gride, et editti: fatti, et osseruati in Milano, ne' tempi sospettosi della peste; ne gli anni MDLXXVI. et LXXVII. ... In Vinegia, appresso Giouanni, e Gio. Paolo Gioliti de' Ferrari, MDLXXIX. 4°. a-b^4 c^6 A-Ee^8 Ff^4. pp. 1-454. (Lea.) [333

-- Commentarii della guerra di Transiluania ... In Vinegia appresso Gabriel Giolito de' Ferrari. MDLXV 4°. *^{4} **-3*^{8} A-Q^8 R^6. pp. 1-265. [334

CEPORINUS, JACOBUS. Compendium grammaticae Graecae ... Hesiodi Georgicon ... Epigrammata quaedam lepidiora ... Tiguri apud Christophorum Froschouerum. Anno M.D.XXXIX. 8°. A-L^8 M^4 N^8. pp. 2-197. [335

CERDÁN DE TALLADA, TOMÁS. Visita de la carcel, y de los presos; en la qual se tratan largamente sus cosas, y casos de prision, assi en causas ciuiles, como criminales; segun el derecho Diuino, Natural, Canonico, Ciuil, y leyes de Partida, y Fueros de los reynos de Aragon, y de Valencia. ... En Valencia, en casa de Pedro de Huete, Año. M. D. Lxxiiij. (*Colophon.*) 4°. ❦-2❦^{4} A-Kk^4. pp. 1-242. (Lea.) [336

CEREDI, GIUSEPPE. Tre discorsi sopra il modo d'alzar acque da' luoghi bassi. ... In Parma, Appresso Seth Viotti. 1567 4°. a^4 b^6 A-D^8 E^{12} (E3, E4, E7, E9 *are folded leaves*) F^8. pp. 1-100. [337

CERUTI, FEDERICO. Ad Ludouicum Beuilaqua Lazisium ... carmen. Veronæ, Apud Hieronymum Discipulum, M D LXXXVI. 4°. A^4. [338

CERVONI, GIOVANNI. Giouanni Ceruoni da Colle sopra il sonetto del Petrarca Amor, fortuna, & la mia mente schiua, letto publicamente nell'Accademia Fiorentina. In Firenze. M D L. (... appresso Lorenzo Torrentino à di. XXVI. di Giugno ...) 8°. A-B^8 C^4. pp. 3-32. [339

CESALPINO, ANDREA. Andreæ Cæsalpini Aretini, Quæstionum Peripateticarum Lib. V. ... Dæmonum inuestigatio Peripatetica. ... Secunda editio. Quæstionum Medicarum Libri II. De Medicament. facultatibus Lib. II. ... Nunc primum editi. Venetiis, Apud Iuntas. M D XCIII. ... 4°. †-††^{4} a^8 b^4 A-Nn^8 Oo^4. ff. 2-291. [340

CESARI, CESARE DE. Cleopatra tragedia ... In Venetia Appresso Giouan. Griffio. M D LII. 8°. A-F^8 (-F8, *blank*). ff. 5-46. [341

-- Romilda tragedia ... (In Venetia per Francesco Bindoni, et Mapheo Pasini. ... M D LI.) 8°. *^{4} A-G^4. ff. 1-28. [342

-- Scilla. Tragedia ... In Venetia Appresso Giouan. Griffio. M D LII. 8°. A-F^8 G^4. ff. 5-51. [343

CESARINI, GABRIELE. Oratio funebris ... habita, dum ... Alexandro Farnesio Romano Parmae et Placentiae duci III. Iusta funebria ... persoluerentur. ... Romæ Apud Antonium Zannettum. M.D.XCIII. ... 4°. A-B⁴. [344

CESENA. Statuta ciuitatis Cæsenæ cum additionibus, ac reformationibus ... Caesenae. Apud Bartholomaeum Rauerium. ... M D LXXXIX. (... CIↃ IↃ XC.) fol. π^2 a-c^4 A-NN^6 OO^4 A^4 B^2. pp. 1-419, 1-12. (Lea.) [345

CEVA, GIOVANNI ANDREA. Lettione ... Nella quale tolta occasione da vn Sonetto del Petrarca, con dimostratione naturali si discorre dell'humana felicità, e de' mezi di conseguirla. ... In Genoua, Appresso Girolamo Bartoli, 1588. 4°. A-C^4 D^2. [346

CEVERIO DE VERA, JUAN. Viaie de la Tierra Santa, y descripcion de Ierusalen, ... con relacion de cosas merauillosas, assi de las prouincias de Leuante, como de las Indias de Occidente ... en Pamplona, por Mathias Mares. A costa de Hernando de Espinal ... 1598. (... a veynte dias del mes de Mayo ...) 8°. π^8 A-R^8. ff. 1-137. [347

CHACÓN, PEDRO. Petrus Ciacconius Toletanus de Triclinio Romano Fului Vrsini Appendix Romæ In Ædibus S.P.Q.R. M.D.L.XXXVIII apud Georgium Ferrarium ... 8°. a^8 A-N^8 (-N8, *blank*). pp. 1-192. [348

CHAERICUS, JACOBUS. Teutsches Keysertumb. Das ist: Ein gründlicher Bericht/ wie das Römische Keyserthumb ... Auff den Sechsischen Stam gebracht/ die falsche Meinung Roberti Bellarmini ... zuwiderlegen ... Anno 1594. (Gedruckt zu Mülhausen/ durch Andream Hantzsch.) 4°. a-$4a^4$ A-YY^4. ff. 1-179. [349

CHAMPIER, SYMPHORIEN. Index librorum qui in hoc volumine continent̃ Mirabiliũ diuinoꝝ humanorũq; volumina quattuor. ... (Impressa Lugð. per Iacobum mareschal. ... M.cccccxvij. xxij. mensis Augusti.) 4°. B.L. A^6 B^4 a-g^8 aa-ee^8 ff^4 3a-$4b^8$ $4c^4$ $4d^6$ (-4d6, *presumably blank*). ff. j-lvi, ij-xliiij, ij-xxiiij, ij-xxv. (Lea.) [350

CHARLEMAGNE. Caroli imperatoris illius magni, et D. Albini, de Rhetorica & Virtutibus disputatio, per Menradum Moltherum restituta. Parisiis Apud Simonē Colinaeũ 1529 8°. a-f^8. ff. 2-48. [351

CHARLES II, emperor. Liber precationum, quas Carolus Caluus imperator ... sibi ... mandauit. ... Ingolstadii, Ex Typographia Dauidis Sartorii, Anno M. D. LXXXIII. 8°. *-$**^8$ $3*^4$ A-L^8. pp. 1-175. [352

CHARLES V, emperor. Pro diuo Carolo ... quinto Romanorum Imperatore ... Apologetici libri duo nuper ex Hispanis allati ... (Excusa sunt ... Moguntiae in aedibus Ioannis Schoeffer Nonis Septemb. anno M.D.XXVII. ...) 4°. A^6 (-A3-4) B-Z^4 a-c^4 d^6 (-d4). pp. 1-218. [353

-- -- In ... oppido Antuerpiae apud Godfridum Dumæum. Anno. M.D.XXVII. 8°. A-G^8 H^4. (Lea.) [354

-- Von Kayserlicher Maiestat einreytten/ auff den Reychstag gen Augspurg/ Beschehen am fünffzehenden tag Iunij/ im 1530. Jar. [Augsburg, Philipp Ulhart, 1530.] 4°. A^4. [355

CHARLES DE GUISE, cardinal of Lorraine. Conspiratio pontificia Des Cardinals Von Lotaring Römische Practicken/ von austilgung der Ketzer in Deudschlande/ wie sie den Frantzösischen Gesandten in Polen vortrawlichen zugeschrieben worden. ... im Ianuario/ Anno 1573. Gedruckt Anno 1573. (Verdeudscht den 8. Februarij Anno 1573.) 4°. A-B^4. (Lea.) [356

CHAROPUS, ANDREAS. Elegia Valedictoria, ad Fratrem Paulum Matzium sponsum, celebrantem diem suum nuptialem, scripta ab Andrea Charopo ... in Italiani vnà cum ... Iohanne Baptista Sandeccero, Paulo Reuchelio & Andrea Eberstorfero ... Paduam versiis discedente, anno M. D. LXX. Viennæ Austriæ, Ex officina Typographica Casparis Stainhoferi. 4°. A^4. [357

CHARTIER, ALAIN. Les oeuures ... On les vend a Paris ... 1529 (Imprimees ... ꝑ maistre Pierre vidoue, ... pour Galliot du pre ...) 8°. aa^8 bb^4 a-z^8 $\&^8$ A-X^8. ff. [i]-ccclxvi. [358

CHASSANION, JEAN. Histoire des Albigeois ... recueilli fidelement de deux vieux exemplaires ecris à la main ... [Genève,] Chez Pierre de Sainctandré. M. D. XCV. 8°. A-Q^{8}. pp. 3-252. [359

CHASSENEUX, BARTHÉLEMY DE. [*1^{r}] Consuetudines ducatus Burgundiae ... (Lugduni a Dionysio de Harsy ... excusa. Anno ... quinto et tricesimo vltra sesquimillesimum, mense Iulio.) fol. B.L. Aa-Ii^{6} Kk^{4} *^{4} a-z^{6} A-Z^{6} aa-tt^{6}. ff. 1-398. ¶Aa1-Kk4: Repertorium in commentaria ... super Cōsuetudinibus Burgūdiæ ac totius penè Galliæ ... Lugduni, apud haeredes Simonis Vincentii. M. D. XXXV. ... (*Colophon.*) (Lea.) [360

-- -- Consuetudines ducatus Burgundiae, ferēque totius Galliae. Commentariis ... illustratæ ... Lugduni, Apud Antonium Vincentium. M.D.LII. (... Excudebat Michael Syluius. ...) fol. aa-hh^{8} a-z^{8} A-Aa^{8} Bb^{10} (-Bb10, *presumably blank*). cols. 1-1528. [361

-- -- 1590. Francofurti, Ex officina Martini Lechleri, Impensis Sigismundi Feyrabend. (*Colophon.*) fol. aa^{6} A-3V^{6}. cols. 1-1438. (Lea.) [362

-- [1] Bartholomæi Chassenei ... responsa, seu (si mauis) consilia caussarum patronis ... Quæ ... ab ... Hugone Darlay Ledouensi Sequano ... redacta sunt. Lugduni, Apud Hæredes Iacobi Giuntæ. 1551 (*Colophon.*) fol. B.L. A-AA^{6} BB^{4}. ff. 2-147. [2] Index rerum, ac verborum ... Lugduni. Apud Hæredes Iacobi Giuntæ. 1550 a-b^{6} c^{4}. (Biddle.) [363

CHAUCER, GEOFFREY. [The workes of Geffray Chaucer ... Printed by Wyllyam Bonham ... 1542.] fol. B.L. A^{4} (-A1-3) B-Yy^{6} AA-TT^{6} (-Qq^{6}, Ss2, RR2, TT6, *in place of which* A4 *is bound in*). ff. i-ccclxxx *present*. *S.T.C.* 5069. (Furness.) [364

-- -- The woorkes of Geffery Chaucer ...: with the siege and destruccion of ... Thebes, compiled by Ihon Lidgate ... (Imprinted at London, by Ihon Kyngston, for Ihon Wight ... 1561.) fol. B.L. [illegible]^{4} A-V^{6} Aa-Pp^{6} Q-T^{6} V-X^{8} Y-Z^{6} 3A-3T^{6} 3V^{8}. ff. j-ccclxxviij. *S.T.C.* 5076. [365

CHAUMEAU, JEAN. Histoire de Berry ... A Lyon, par Antoine Gryphius, 1566. ... fol. *^{4} a-y^{6} (t3 + *folded leaf*, t5 + *folded leaf*) z^{8} A-F^{6} G^{8} (-G8) *-**^{6}. pp. 1-365. [366

CHAUNCY, MAURICE. Historia aliquot nostri saeculi Martyrum ... Anno M. D. L. (Moguntiæ apud S. Victorem excudebat Franciscus Behem. ...) 4°. a-b^{4} B-S^{4}. ff. I-LXV. [367

CHAVEZ, JERÓNIMO DE. Chronographia o reportorio delos tiempos el mas copioso y preciso ... (Fue impresso ... en la ... ciudad ō Seuilla, por Christoual aluarez. ... Acabose a veynte y ocho dias del mes se Agosto, del año de mill y quinientos y cincuēta. ...) 4°. B.L. †^{8} a-z^{8} A-B^{8} C^{6}. ff. j-ccvj. [368

CHEKE, SIR JOHN. Historia uera: de uita, obitu, sepultura, accusatione hæreseos, condemnatione, exhumatione, combustione, honorificaq̄ȝ tandem restitutione ... Martini Buceri & Pauli Fagii ... Item historia Catharinae Vermiliae ... 1562. (Excusum Argentinae apud Paulum Machæropoeum, sumptibus Iohannis Oporini, Anno M. D. LXI.) 8°. a^{8} B-O^{8} P^{12} A-Ee^{8} (-Ee8, *presumably blank*). ff. 2-215. ¶*Additional authors: Nicholas Carre, Walter Haddon, Matthew Parker, George Acworth, James Pilkington, James Calfhill. Editor: Conrad Hubert.* (Lea.) [369

CHEMNITZ, MARTIN. D. Martini Kemnicii, Bericht vom newen Bäptischen Gregoriano calendario ... Gedruckt Anno 1584. 4°. A^{4}. [370

CHERUBINO DE SPOLETO. Sermones quadragesimales ... Venetiis ... (Impressum Venetiis Per Georgium Arriuabenū ... Mcccccii. Die. xx. Octobris.) 8°. B.L. π^{4} a-z^{8} ⁊^{8} ꝯ^{8} ꝶ^{8} A-Z^{8} aa-oo^{8} pp^{6}. ff. 1-510. (Lea.) [371

-- -- *Another copy.* [372

CHIEREGATO, FRANCESCO. Francisci Chæregati ... Oratoris apostolici Orō habita Nurībergæ in senatu Principum Germaniæ .xiij. Cal'. Decēbris, M.D.XXII. 4°. A-B^{4}. [373

CHOLIÈRES, NICOLAS DE. Les neuf matinees du Seigneur de Cholieres. ... A Paris, Chez Iean Richer ... 1586. ... 12°. ā^{12} A-V^{12} X^{6}. ff. 1-246. [374

CHRISTIAN, ANDREAS. Oratio de vita et morte ... Guilielmi, Landgravii Hassiæ ... Herbornæ Typis Christophori Coruini, cIↄ Iↄ xcII. 4°. A-D^4 E^6. pp. 3-42. [375

CHRISTIANI, FRANCESCO. Rime di diuersi ecc. autori, in vita, e in morte dell'ill. S. Liuia Col. ... (Stampato in Roma per Antonio Barrè, Ad instantia di M. Francesco Christiani, l'anno 1555.) 8°. A-MM^4 NN^6. ff. 2-137. [376

CHRISTOFORO ARMENO. Peregrinaggio di tre giouani figliuoli del re di Serendippo. Per opera di M. Christoforo Armeno dalla Persiana nell'Italiana lingua trapportato. ... (In Venetia per Michele Tramezzino, MDLVII.) 8°. *^{8} (-*8, *blank*) A-K^8 L^4. ff. 1-83. [377

CHRONICA. Chronica New/ Manicherlay historien/ vnd besondere geschicht/ viler jar/ nach der Geburt Iesu Christi ... begreiffend/ ... Vnd biss in das jar M.CCCCC. vnd XXX. erlengert. ... [Augsburg, Philip Ulhart, 1531?] 4°. A-K^4 L^2. [378

-- Chronica ... von der geburt Christi/ biss auff das M.D. vñ .xxxj. Jar ... (Getruckt zů Augspurg/ durch Philip Vlhart ...) 4°. A-T^4 V^2. [379

CHRONOLOGIA. Chronologia ecclesiastica, seriem temporum continens quib. Pont. Max. Caesares, Catholici scriptores, ac haeresiarchae vixerunt. ... Bononiae, Apud Societatem Typographiæ Bonon. MDLXXX. ... 4°. A-D^4 E^2. [380

CHRYSOLORAS, MANUEL. Ερωτήματα του Χρυσολωρα. ... Erotemata Chrysoloræ. De anomalis uerbis. De formatione temporum ex libro Chalcondylæ. Quartus Gazæ de Constructione. De Encleticis. Sententiæ monostichi ex uarijs poetis. Cato. Erotemata Guarini. (Venetiis in aedibus Aldi et Andreae soceri mense Nouembri M.D.XVII.) 8°. a-s^8 t^4 v-z^8 A-C^8 D^4. pp. 2-415. ¶*Greek texts.* [381

-- Emanuelis Chrysoloræ, Byzantini, ... integræ Grammatices ... Albano Torino Vitudurensi interprete. ... M D XXXIII. 8°. A-G^8. [382

CHRYSOSTOM, JOHN, S. Sancti Ioannis Chrysostomi de virginitate liber, a Iulio Pogiano conuersus. Romae, M. D. LXII. Apud Paulum Manutium, Aldi F. 4°. a-b^4 A-Q^4. ff. 1-64. [383

-- [1] Πατρος ημων Ιωαννου του Χρυσοστομου ... ἑρμηνεία ἐις τὰς του αγιου παυλου επιστολας. S. Ioannis Chrysostomi ... Expositio in Diui Pauli epistolas. ... D. Ioannis Apocalypsis cum Commentario Andreæ Cæsariensis Latine reddito Theodori Peltani opera. [Heidelbergae,] Apud Hieronymum Commelinum ... CIↃ IↃ XCVI. fol. (:)^2 MM-ZZ^6 Aa-Zz^6 3a-3z^6 3A-3Z^6 aAa-cCc^6 dDd^4. pp. 961-1975. [2] ... Andreae archiepiscopi Cæsareæ Cappadociæ ... commentarius. ... Fridericus Sylburgius ... Notis ... illustrauit. E Typographeo Hieronymi Commelini, cIↄ Iↄ XCVI.):(^{4} A-S^4 (-S4, *blank*). pp. 1-141. [384

-- Io. Frob. studioso lectoris. D. Tria noua dabit hic libellus, Epistolam Erasmi, de modestia profitendi linguas. Libellum ... D. Ioannis Chrysostomi Græcũ, de Babyla martyre. Epistolam Erasmi Roterodami in tyrologum quendam ... calumniatorē. ... Basileae an. M.D.XXVII. (... apud Ioan. Frob. Mense Augusto. ...) α-ι^8 (-α2). [385

-- *Homilia in Genesin XVI.* Discours de l'arbre de science, a sçauoir si Adam a eu la cognoissance du bien & du mal deuant que d'en gouster du fruict ... Traduict nouuellement par Fed. Morel ... sur l'original Grec de S. Iean Bouche d'or ... A Paris, Chez Federic Morel ... M. D. XCVI. 8°. A-B^4. pp. 3-14. [386

CHYTRAEUS, DAVID. Anni proximè elapsi M. D. XCIX. Euentus aliquot memorabiles annotati a Dauide Chytræo. M. DC. 8°. A-C^8 D^4. [387

-- Dauidis Chytræi chronicon Saxoniæ & vicinarum aliquot Gentium ... Lipsiæ Impensis Henningi Grosii ... (... Imprimebat Michael Lantzenberger ... M. D. XCIII.) fol.):(^{6})?(^{4} A-4O^6. pp. I-XVIII, 1-969. (Lea.) [388

-- De ratione discendi, et ordine studiorum ... rectè instituendo. ... Witebergæ. Anno M.D.LXIIII. 8°. A-P^8 A-E^8 (-A1) F^6. ff. 1-13. [389

-- Dauidis Chytræi oratio de statu ecclesiarum hoc tempore in Graecia, Asia, Africa, Vngaria, Boëmia, &c. et epistolae aliquot Patriarchæ Constantinopolitani, & aliorum ... VVitebergae Typis Zachariæ Lehmanni Anno M. D. LXXXII. 8°. A-L^8. [390

-- Dauidis Chytræi orationum illustrium tomus vnus ... Argentorati, typis Iosiæ Rihelij, Anno M DC. 8°. A-Z^8. pp. 1-353. (Lea.) [391

CHYTRAEUS, NATHAN. De philosophica animi tranquillitate, seu in Horatii odam libri secundi XVI, Prælectiones aliquot ... Rostochii Typis Stephani Myliandri cIↄ. Iↄ. XCII. 4°. A-F^4. [392

-- ἤθη καὶ πάθη, Seu de affectibus mouendis, Aristotelis ex II. rhetoricorum doctrina ... explicata ... Herbornæ, Excudebat Christophorus Coruinus, M.D.LXXXVI. 8°. a-k^8. pp. 1-152. [393

-- Nathanis Chytræi. In Sallustii Iugurtham prolegomena ... Rostochii Typis Stephani Myliandri. Anno CIↃ IↃ XXCVI. 8°. A-C^8. [394

CICERO, MARCUS TULLIUS. M. Tullii Ciceronis orationes. Parisiis. Ex officina Roberti Stephani. M.D.XXXIX. (... Idib. Augusti.) fol. aa-$3q^8$ 3r-$3s^6$ (-3s6, *presumably blank*). pp. 3-340. ¶*The second of a 5-volume* Opera. [395

-- [1] M. Tullii Ciceronis opera omnia, quae exstant, a Dionysio Lambino Monstroliensi ... emendata, & aucta ... Eiusdem ... annotationes ... Lutetiæ, Apud Bernardum Turrisanum ... M. D. LXVI. ... fol. $*^8$ a-aa^8. pp. 1-384. [2] Tomus secundus operum M. Tullii Ciceronis ... Lutetiæ, Apud Bernardum Turrisanum ... 1565. ... aa-$3z^8$ Aaa-Ggg^8 Hhh^2. pp. 3-852. [3] Tomus tertius ... *Same imprint as tome I.* A-Ll^8 Mm-Nn^6. pp. 3-566. [4] Tomus quartus ... *Same imprint.* (... Excudebat Floricus Prævotius anno CIↃ IↃ LXVI. Mense Februario, sumtibus Iac. à Puteo, Bern. Turrisani, Ph. Galt. Rouillij.) AA-$3P^8$ $3Q^{10}$. pp. 3-627. [396

-- Epistolarum M. T. Ciceronis ad familiareis, libri XVI. Eiusdem epistolarum ad M. Brutum, liber singularis. Eiusdem epistolarum, quæ non exstant, fragmenta. Ex Dionis. Lambini emendatione. ... Argentorati Impensis Iosiæ Rihelij, & Iacobi Dupuys. M. D. LXXXI. 8°. Aa-Zz^8 aa-tt^8 vv^4. ff. 2-290. ¶*Vol. 6 of a 9-volume ed. of the works.* [397

-- *Two or more works.* Hoc in volumine infrascripta opuscula continentur. Marci Tullii Ciceronis ... oratio pro Milone ... Compendium Rhetorices/ ex Tulliano thesauro diductum ... per Iacobum Locher Philomusum ... Aptissima syntaxis de cōponenda orōne funebri Viti Vuerleri ode ... (Impressum Augustę a Syluano Otmar ..., impensis ... Erhardi Sampachii ... Anno &c̄ Decimo septimo Mense Nouembri.) 4°. a^6 b-$g^{4.4.8}$ h-i^4 k^6. [398

-- M. T. Ciceronis de partitione oratoria Dialogus. M. T. Ciceronis de optimo genere oratoꝝ et Cthesiphontis et Eschinis caussa libellus. ... (Lipsiæ-ex ædibus Lottherianis Anno ... supra Millesimū quingentesimū decimoseptimo.) fol. A^6 B-C^4 D^6. [399

-- -- Ex officina Melchioris Lottheri. (Lipsiæ ... Anno ... Millesimū quingentesimū vigesimo.) fol. A^6 B-C^4 D^6. [400

-- In hoc volumine haec continentur. Rhetoricorum ad C. Herennium lib. IIII. M.T. Ciceronis de inuentione lib. II. Eiusdem de oratore ad Quintum fratrem lib. III. Eiusdem de claris oratoribus, ꝗ dicitur Brutus: lib. I. Eiusdem Orator ad Brutum lib. I. Eiusdem Topica ad Trebatium lib. I. Eiusdem oratoriæ partitiones lib. I. Eiusdem de optimo genere oratorum præfatio quædam. ... (Venetiis in aedibus Aldi, et Andreae soceri mense Octobri M. D. XXI.) 4°. *-$**^8$ a-k^8 l^4 m-z^8 A-G^8 H^{10}. ff. 1-245. [401

-- -- *Another copy.* [402

-- -- ... emendati à Ioan. Sturmio. ... (Argentorati per Vuendelinum Rihelium. Mense Iulio. Anno M. D. XL.) 4°. α^8 a-k^8 l^4 m-z^8 A-H^8 I^{10}. ff. 1-245. [403

-- Di Marco Tullio Cicerone de gli vffici. Della amicitia. Della vecchiezza. Le paradosse. Tradotte per vn nobile Vinitiano. ... (Impresse in Vinegia per Bernardino di Vitale Vinitiano il mese di Marzo ... M.D.XXVIII.) 4°. π^4 a-z^4 A-O^4. [404

-- M. T. Ciceronis libri III. de officiis ... De amicitia liber: de senectute: paradoxis atque de somnio Scipionis ... Ioachimi Camerarii ... Annotationes ... D. Erasmi Roterodami, Philippi Melanchthonis, Aldi Manutij, Barptholomæi Latomi, Wuolfgangi Anemoetij, passim etiam Conradi Coclenij Scholia ... Ioannis Metzleri Commentariola in Catonem Maiorem ... Dialogus Anemoetij ... Basileae [per Joannem Froben, c. 1540]. 8°. a-z^8 (-a8, z8). pp. 2-347. [405

-- Oraison que feit Marc Tulle Ciceron, opinant pour les Prouinces Consulaires. Le premier liure des Epistres que Ciceron escrit à son frere Quinte. L'epistre que Cicerō escrit à Octauius ... Imprimé à Paris par Simon de Colines. 1544. 8°. a-g^8. ff. 2-56. [406

-- [1] M. Tullii Ciceronis de philosophia, prima pars ... Cum scholijs, & coniecturis Pauli Manutij. ... M. D. XLVI. (Apud Aldi filios. Venetiis ...) 8°. a-u^8 aa-oo^8. ff. 1-251. ¶*Additional t.p.* (aa1^r): Tusculanarum quaestionum ... libri V. Cum scholijs Pauli Manutij. ... *Same imprint & colophon.* [2] ... volumen secundum ... *Same imprint & colophon.* A-EE^8. ff. 2-213. [407

-- Libros de Marco Tulio Ciceron, en que tracta Delos Officios, dela Amicicia, y Dela Senectud. Con la Economica de Xenophon, traduzidos de Latin en Romance Castellano, por Francisco Thamara ... Añadieronse ... los Paradoxos, y el Sueño de Scipion, traduzidos por Iuan Iaraua. En Anuers, En casa de Iuan Steelsio [1546]. (Fue impresso en Emberes en casa de Iuan Lacio.) 8°. A-Ii^8 (-Ii8, *presumably blank*). ff. 1-237. ¶A1 *defective.*[408

-- [1] M. Tulli Ciceronis de philosophia, prima pars, Academicarum quæstionum ... [libri ii] De finibus bonorum & malorum libri V. Tusculanarum quæstionum libri V. Cum scholiis Pauli Manutii. ... Venetiis, [Aldine press,] M. D. LX. 8°. a-rr^8 ss^4 tt^8. ff. 3-286. [2] M. Ciceronis de philosophia volumen secundum. De natura deorum, De diuinatione, De fato, De legibus, De uniuersitate, Arati uersus in latinum conuersi, Q. Ciceronis de petitione consulatus. ... *Same imprint.* A-II^8 Kk-Mm^8 Mm^8 Nn^4. ff. 4-258. [409

-- Opere morali ... Tradotti da M. Federico Vendramino ... Allequali opere s'è aggiunto il Sogno di Scipione. ... corretti da M. Lodouico Dolce ... In Vinegia appresso Gabriel Giolito de' Ferrari. M D LXIIII. 8°. *^{8} **^{6} A-AA^8. pp. 1-381. [410

-- -- M. Tullii Ciceronis de philosophia, prima pars ... Cum scholiis Pauli Manutii. ... Venetiis, [Aldine press,] M. D. LXV. 8°. a-tt^8. ff. 3-286. [411

-- M. T. Ciceronis librorum philosophicorum volumen I. Post Naugerianam & Victorianam correctionem, emendatum à Ioan. Sturmio. ... M. D. LXXIIII. (Impressum Argentorati, apud Iosiam Rihelium ...) 8°. a^8 a-z^8 A-N^8 O^4. ff. 1-251. [412

-- M. Tullii Ciceronis academicarum quæstionum lib. I. Eiusdem, de fato. Cum Commentariis ... Adriani Turnebi ... Heidelbergæ, Apud Ieronymum Comelinum. M. D. XCIIII. 8°. A-G^8. pp. 3-103. [413

-- *Academica.* Marci Tullii Ciceronis academicarum quæstionum lib. I. In eundē commentarius, Adriano Turnebo auctore. Parisiis, M.D.LIII. Apud Adrianum Turnebum ... (... Cal. August. ...) 4°. *^{2} A-E^4 F^2. pp. 1-41. [414

-- *Brutus.* Sebastiani Corradi commentarius, in quo M. T. Ciceronis de Claris Oratoribus liber, qui dicitur Brutus, ... explicantur. Florentiæ apud Laurentium Torrentinum ... MDLII. ... fol. *^{6} a-z^6 A-S^6 T^4 V^6 (-V6, *blank*). pp. 1-457. [415

-- *Cato major.* M. T. Ciceronis Cato maior, seu de Senectute dialogus ... Cum annotationibus Erasmi, Betuleij, ac Balduini ... Parisiis. Prostant exemplaria apud Thomam Richardum ... 1565 4°. a-g^4. ff. 3-28. [416

-- *De divinatione.* M. Tullij Ciceronis ... de diuinatione Libri duo. (Impressorū Lipsick per ... Vuolffgangum Monacensem. ... j.j5.4. [=1514.]) fol. B.L. a-b^6 C-I^6. [417

-- -- Marc Tulle Cicero de Diuination, nagueres translaté de Latin en Frāçois, par Robert du Souchey. On les vend a Paris ... [par Pierre Gromors.] 16°. A-G^8 H^4 I-Q^8. ff. 2-124. ¶*Privilege dated 1545.* [418

-- *De legibus.* Marci Tullij Ciceronis Tres libros de legibus ... Melchiar Lottherus ... imp̄ssit. ... M.d.xiiij. ... Lipsi ... fol. A-D^6. [419

-- *De natura deorum.* De natura deorum. Tres Ciceronis de Natura deorū libri ... [Lipsiae, Wolfgang Stōckel, 1506-1510.] fol. B.L. A-I^6 K^4 L^6. [420

-- *De officiis.* Marci Tullij Ciceronis ... Officiorum Liber ... (... diligētia Iacobi Thāners Liptzeñ ciuis: anno decimo supra millesimūquīgētesimū exaratos. ...) fol. A-H^6 I^4 K^6. [421

-- -- Marci Tullij Ciceronis ... Officiorum liber ... (... diligētia Iacobi Thanners Liptzen. ciuis. Anno decimoquinto supra millesimū quingētesimū exaratos.) fol. B.L. A-F$^{6.4}$ H-K^6. [422

-- -- M. T. Ciceronis de officiis libri tres, Commentarijs illustrati à Martino Henrico Saganensi ... Vitaebergae Excusi in officina Simonis Gronenbergij. ... M. D. LXXXII. 8°. A^8 a-c^8 A-$3P^8$. pp. 1-975. [423

-- -- Officia Ciceronis ... vertaelt in nederlantscher spraken door Dierick Coornhert. Tot Haerlem, By Ian van Zuren. 1561. ... 8°. $*^8$ A-S^8. ff. 1-142. [424

-- -- Les offices ... Traduyctes de Latin en Francoys ... A Paris. 1538. On les vend ... par Denys Ianot ... 8°. A-N^8 O^4 P-T^8 V^4. ff. 2-147. [425

-- -- Tulles des offices ⁊ operations humaynes ... On les vend ... par Phelippe le Noir ... (Imprime a Paris par Philippe le Noir ... [1544 *or earlier*].) 8°. B.L. a-r^8. [426

-- *De oratore.* M. Tull. Ciceronis de oratore Dialogi tres, à Philippo Melāchthone ... enarratione illustrati. Parisiis Ex officina Simonis Colinæi, 1537 (*Colophon.*) 8°. a-c^8 a-t^8. ff. 1-152. ¶^{2}a1 *defective.* [427

-- -- M. T. Ciceronis de Oratore ad Quintum fratrem Dialogi tres, Iacobi Lodoici Strebaei, Leodegarij à Quercu, & cuiusdam incerti authoris commentariis, itémque scholiis Philippi Melanchthonis ... illustrati. Parisiis, Apud Thomam Richardum ... 1557. ... (... 1555.) 4°. a-z^4 A-Zz^4 AA-FF^4 GG^6. ff. 5-304. [428

-- -- Il dialogo dell'oratore di Cicerone. Tradotto per M. Lodouico Dolce. ... In Vinegia Appresso Gabriel Giolito de Ferrari. MDXLVII. (*Colophon.*) 8°. *-$**^8$ A-Y^8. ff. 1-176. [429

-- *Epistolae: collections.* M. T. Ciceronis epistolarum ad Atticum, ad Brutum, ad Quintum fratrem, libri XX. ... M.D.XXI. ... (Venetiis in aedibus Aldi, et Andreae soceri. Mense Ianuario. ...) 8°. AA-BB^8 a-ss^8 tt^4 (-tt4). ff. 1-331. [430

-- M. Tullii Ciceronis epistolae ad Atticum, ad M. Brutum, ad Quintū fratrem ... Paulus Manutius Aldi f. Venetiis, M. D. XL. (Apud Aldi filios. ... Mense Augusto.) 8°. A-VV^8 3A-$3C^8$. ff. 1-331. ¶*Additional t.p.* (3A1^r): Pauli Manutii ... scholia ... *Same imprint.* (*Colophon.*) [431

-- [M. T. Ciceronis Epistolæ Ad Atticum Brutum & Q. Fratrem. ... Apud Seb. Gryphium Lugduni. 1551.] 16°. a-z^8 (-a1) A-Z^8 aa-ff^8 (-ff8, *blank*). pp. 3-784. [432

-- Epistolæ Marci Tul. Ciceronis, ad Atticum, Brutum, & Q. Fratrem. ... Ex castigatione Ioannis Boulierij. Lugduni, Apud Antonium Vincentium. 1562 ... (... Excudebat Symphorianus Barbierus.) 8°. a-pp^8 qq^2. pp. 3-610. [433

-- *Epistolae ad Atticum.* Le pistole di Cicerone ad Attcio, fatte volgari da M. Matteo Senarega. ... In Vinegia. M. D. LV. ... (... in casa de' figliuoli di Aldo. ...) 8°. A-Z^8 a-dd^8. ff. 2-399. [434

-- *Ad familiares.* M. Tullii Ciceronis epistolae familiares. Pauli Manutii annotationes ... Venetiis, [Aldine press,] M. D. LXV. (*Colophon.*) 8°. A-ZZ^8 aa^4. ff. 1-315. [435

-- -- ... D. Lambini annotationes ... Item Pauli Manutii annotationes ... Londini, Excudebat Robertus Robinsonus, Impensis. R. D. ... 1595. 8°. A-Ii^8. pp. 1-478. *S.T.C.* 5300.1. [436

-- -- Les epistres familiaires de Marc Tulle Cicero ... traduictes de Latin en Francoys, par Etienne Dolet ... On les vend à Paris, ... par Guillaume le Bret ... 1549. (Imprimées ... par Maurice Menier. ...) 16°. a-z^8 (-z6-8) A-P^8 (-A1-3, F3-8, G1-2, P8, *the last presumably blank*). ff. 2-302. [437

-- -- Les epistres familiaires de Marc Tulle Cicero ... Latin et Francoys, respondant l'vn à l'autre: Le Françoys traduit par Estienne Dolet, natif d'Orleans. A Lyon, Par Guillaume Rouille. M. D. LXI. (Imprimé ... par Françoys Gaillard. ...) 16°. a-z^8 A-R^8 S^6. pp. 3-649. [438

-- -- Le epistole famigliari di Cicerone, tradotte ... M. D. XLV. (In Vinegia, nelle case de figliuoli di Aldo. ...) 8°. A-SS^8 TT^6 (-TT6, *presumably blank*). ff. 5-333. ¶*Translator: Guido Loglio.* [439

-- -- Epistole di Marco Tullio Cicerone dette le familiari, Già dal Fausto recate in Italiano ... In Vinegia, ... Appresso Vicenzo Valgrisi. MDLV. 8°. $*^4$ A-Xx^8 Yy^4. pp. 1-707. [440

-- -- Le epistole famigliari di Cicerone, Da M. Aldo Manutio tradotte ... In Vinegia, Presso Altobello Salicato, M D LXXIII. (*Colophon.*) 8°. A-Rr^8 (-Rr8, *presumably blank*). ff. 3-318. [441

-- -- Los deziseis libros de las epistolas, o cartas de M. Tulio Ciceron, vulgarmente llamadas familiares, traduzidas ... por el Dotor Pedro Simon Abril ... En Barcelona, En la Emprenta de Iayme Cendras. Año M. DC. (*Colophon.*) 8°. ¶^{8} A-3H^8. ff. 1-431. [442

-- *Orationes*. [1] M. Tullii Ciceronis orationum pars I. Corrigente Paulo Manutio, Aldi filio. Venetiis, M. D. XLVI. (... apud Aldi filios. ...) 8°. A-PP^8 QQ^4. ff. 1-303. [2] M. Tullii Ciceronis orationum pars II. ... *Same imprint*. (Apud Aldi filios. ... Mense Maii.) aa-uu^8 xx^{10} yy-zz^8 AA-LL^8 MM^{10}. ff. 4-281. ¶*The third volume is wanting*. [443

-- [1] M. Tullii Ciceronis orationum. Pars I. Corrigente Paulo Manutio, Aldi filio. Venetiis, M. D. L. (... apud Aldi filios. ...) 8°. A-PP^8 QQ^4. ff. 1-303. [2] M. Tullii Ciceronis orationum pars III. ... Venetiis, M. D. L. (Apud Aldi filios. ... Mense Iulio.) 3a-3z^8 3A-3M^8. ff. 3-271. [444

-- M. Tullii Ciceronis orationum pars II. Cum correctionibus Pauli Manutij. Venetiis, [Aldine press,] M D LXV. (... M. D. LIX.) 8°. aa-zz^8 Aa-Oo^8 Pp^4. ff. 1-295. ¶*The t.p. comes from a copy of another edition*. [445

-- M. Tullii Ciceronis orationum pars tertia, Post Pauli Manutij & aliorum ... correctiones, emendata, & Scholijs ... illustrata. Antuerpiae, In AEdibus viduæ & hæredum Ioannis Stelsij. 1567. 16°. AA-3R^8 3S^6. ff. 2-327. ¶ZZ2-3 *defective*. [446

-- Les oraisons de M. T. Cicero traduictes de Latin en François, par Estienne le blanc ... A Paris. Par Iehan Ruelle ... 1559 16°. A-V^8 X^4. pp. 3-325. [447

-- [1] Le orationi di Marco Tullio Cicerone, tradotte da M. Lodouico Dolce prima parte. ... In Vinegia appresso Gabriel Giolito de' Ferrari. M D LXII. (*Colophon.*) 4°. *^{10} A-Z^8 AA^{10}. pp. 1-385. [2] Le orationi ... seconda parte. ... *Same imprint*. (*Colophon.*) **^{4} aa-yy^8. pp. 1-352. [3] Le orationi ... terza parte. ... *Same imprint*. 3*^{4} 3a-3y^8. pp. 1-352. [448

-- *De provinciis consularibus*. M. T. Ciceronis de Prouinciis Consularibus Oratio. Parisiis, Apud Thomam Richardum ... 1555. 4°. A-C^4. ff. 2-12. [449

-- *In Catilinam*. Quatro ... orationes de M. T. Ciceron, contra Catilina, trasladadas en lengua Española, Por el Doctor Andres de Laguna ... En Anuers, En casa de Christoual Plantin ... 1557. ... 8°. A-M^8. ff. 1-88. [450

-- *In Verrem*. I sette libri di Marco Tullio Cicerone contra Gaio Verre, tradotti dal Latino nella lingua uolgare da M. Gioseffo Tramezzino. ... (In Venetia per Michele Tramezzino. M D LIIII.) 8°. *^{8} A-RR^8 SS^4. ff. 2-319. [451

-- *In Pisonem*. Marci Tullij Ciceronis in Lu. Pisonem Oratio. ... Lipsiae Ex aedibus Lottherianis (... Anno ... supra Millesimū quingentesimum decimosexto.) fol. A-D$^{6\cdot 4}$. [452

-- *Philippica*. Cōmentarii Philippicarum cum Annotationibus Philippi Beroaldi. (Impressum ... Bononiæ per Benedictum Hectoris ... MCCCCCI. Die uero .xxiii. Decembris.) fol. A-R^6 S^4. ff. 2-105. [453

-- *Pro Flacco*. Marci Tullij Ciceronis pro .L. Flacco Oratio. ... ([Lipsiae,] Ex officina Melchiaris Lottheri Anno ... Millesimo quingētesimo decimosexto.) fol. A-C^6. [454

-- *Pro Ligario*. Marci Tullij Ciceronis pro .Q. Ligario Oratio. ... (Ex officina Melchiaris Lottheri Anno ... Millesimo quīgentesimo decimosexto.) fol. A-B^4. [455

-- -- *Another copy*. [456

-- *Pro M. Caelio*. M. T. Ciceronis pro Marco Cælio Oratio. Parisiis, Apud Thomam Richardum ... 1549. 4°. A-C^4 D^6. ff. 2-17. [457

-- *Pro Milone*. M. Tul. Ciceronis oratio pro T. An. Milone cum enarratione Iacobi Cruquii ... 4°. A-P^4. pp. 4-119. ¶*T.p. defective: probably a copy of the Plantin ed. of 1582*. [458

-- *Paradoxa*. Paradoxa. ... jetzo in teutsche sprach transsferiert ... M. D. XXXVIII.

(Getruckt in ... Augspurg/ durch Alexander Weissenhorn.) fol. π^2 A-C^4. ff. I-XII. ¶*Translator: Simon Schaidenreisser.* [459

-- *Rhetorical works.* Rhetorica di Marco Tullio Cicerone, Tradotta di latino in lingua Toscana, per Antonio Brucioli ... In Venetia per Gabriel Iolito di Ferrarii M. D. XLII. (*Colophon.*) 8°. A-K^8 L^4. ff. 2-84. [460

-- M. Tulii Ciceronis rhetoricorum ad Herennium libri IIII. ... Rhetoricorum de inuentione libri II. ... In Rhetorica ad Herennium, Hieronymi Capiduri Parentini commentaria, Gyberti Longolij Annotationes, Claudij Pontani scholia, Petri Victorij castigatio, Marini Becichemi Scodrensis castigationes. In Rhetorica de Inuentione, M. Fabij Victorini ... commentariorum libri duo: Marini Becichemi ... castigationes. Venetijs apud Hieronymum Scotum. M D XLVI. (*Colophon.*) fol. *^{6} A-Z^6 AA-BB^4. ff. 1-142. [461

-- M. T. Cic. rhetoricorum ad C. Herennium libri quatuor. Eiusdem de inuentione libri duo. Ex Petri Victorij, ac Pauli Manutij castigationibus. Apud Seb. Gryphium Lugduni. 1546. 16°. a-x^8 y^4. pp. 3-342. [462

-- -- Apud Seb. Gryphium Lugduni. 1555. 16°. *Same collation and pagination.* [463

-- M. T. Ciceronis rhetoricorum ad C. Herennium Libri IIII. Eiusdem de Inuentione Libri II. Post Naugerianam et Victorianam correctionem emendati à Ioan. Sturmio. ... M. D. LXVIII. (Argentorati per Iosiam Rihelium, ... Mense Maio.) 8°. α^8 β^4 A-R^8. pp. 1-262. [464

-- La topica di Cicerone, col comento. ... tradotta da M. Simon de la Barba da Pescia ... In Vinegia appresso Gabriel Giolito de' Ferrari. M D LVI. (*Colophon.*) 8°. *-**^{8} A-P^8 Q^4. pp. 1-245. [465

-- -- *Another copy.* [466

-- [1] Rhetoricorum ad C. Herennium libri IIII. incerto auctore. Ciceronis De inuentione libri II. Topica ad Trebatium, Oratoriæ partitiones. Cum annotationibus Dionysii Lambini ... Ex bibliotheca Aldina. Venetiis, M. D. LXIX. 8°. *-3*^{8} A-Z^8. ff. 1-184. [2] Annotationes, seu emendationum rationes Dionisii Lambini ... *Same imprint.* A-E^8 (-E8, *blank*). ff. 2-38. [467

-- [1] Rhetoricorum ad Herennium libri quatuor. M. T. Ciceronis de inuentione libri duo. ... Lugduni, apud Antonium Gryphium. M. D. LXXXV. 16°. a-y^8. pp. 3-340. [2] M. Tullii Ciceronis rhetoricorum posterior tomus. *Same imprint.* aa-zz^8 AA-TT^8 VV^4. pp. 3-631. [468

-- *Somnium Scipionis.* Somnium Scipionis, ex libro sexto de Republica Marci Tullij Ciceronis, Elia Vineto Santone interprete. Burdigalæ, Apud Simonem Millangium ... 1579. 4°. A-P^4. [469

-- -- Il sogno di Scipione. di Marco tullio Cicerone ... tradotto in lingua toscana per Antonio Brucioli. [Venezia, Lucantonio Giunta, c. 1539.] 8°. [A]^4 B-D^4 E^6. [470

-- *Tusculanae quaestiones.* Tusculanae q̃stiones ... (Impressæq3 Venetiis ... per Benedictum Augustinumq3 Bindonos ... MDXXV. Die .X. Nouembris.) fol. aa^6 A-N^8 O-P^{10}. ff. I-CXXIIII. [471

-- -- M. T. Ciceronis Tusculanae quaestiones, per D. Erasmum Roterodamum ... emendatæ, & scholiis illustratæ. Parisiis. Ex officina Roberti Stephani. M.D.XXXVII. 8°. a-o^8. pp. 3-223. [472

-- -- Tusculanarum quaestionum Ciceronis ... libri V. Cum Scholijs Pauli Manutij. Venetiis, Apud hæredes Melchioris Sessæ. M. D. LXXVI. (*Colophon.*) 8°. A-P^8 (-P8, *presumably blank*). ff. 2-114. [473

-- -- Le Tusculane di M. Tullio Cicerone recate in Italiano. ... In Vinegia. Appresso Vicenzo Vaugris ... M. D. XLIIII. 8°. A-R^8 s^8. ff. 2-144. ¶*Translator: Sebastiano Fausto da Longiano.* [474

-- *Selections.* M. Tullii Ciceronis sententiæ Illustriores, Apophthegmata item, & Parabola siue Similia ... Authore, Petro Lagnerio Compendiensi. Venetiis ad Signum Spei. 1548. 16°. A-T^8 V^6 (-V2, V5). pp. 3-306 *present.* [475

-- Synonyma ... Ciceronis. Victurii ... una cũ Stephani Flisci synonymis utriusq3 linguæ

... oratio ... Frācisci Mutinēsis/ de poeticæ excellētia. ([Impressum Viennę Austrię Per Hieronymū Vietorem & Ioannem Singreniū, socioꝝ. Expensis vero Leonardi & Lucę Alantsę. fratrū. Kal'. Ianuarij. ... M.D.XIII.]) 4°. A-I^{4} K-L^{8} M^{4} N^{8} O^{6} (-O6). [476

CIGOGNA, GIOVANNI MATTEO. Il primo libro del trattato militare ... In Venetia, Appresso Camillo Castelli. M D LXXXIII. (*Colophon.*) 4°. *^{6} A-P^{4} Q^{6}. ff. 1-65. [477

CIMINELLI, SERAFINO, AQUILANO. Opere del Facūdissimo Seraphino Aquilano ... impresse per compassione dele incorrectione de glialtri. ... laudarai la diligentia de Francesco Flauio Die .xx. Aprilis. M.ccccc.xvi. ... 12°. B.L. a-i^{12} k^{6}. [478

-- -- Opere dello elegante Poeta Seraphino Aquillano. ... (Stampato in Venetia per Marchio Sessa & Piero de Rauani compagni. ... M.D.XIX. A di .XV. de Octobrio.) 4°. A-M^{4}. [479

-- -- (In Vinegia. Appresso di Agostino Bindoni ... 1557.) 8°. A-R^{8} S^{12}. ff. 2-128. [480

CINO DA PISTOIA. Delle rime Toscane dell' ... Sig. Cino Sigibaldi da Pistoia. Raccolte ... dal R.P. Faustino Tasso ... Libro Primo. In Venetia, Presso Gio. Domenico Imberti. MDLXXXIX. 4°. †-3†^{4} A-P^{4} Q^{2}. pp. 1-124. [481

CIPELLARIO, BERNARDINO. Panegyricus D. Antonini Martyris ... A Fran. Bernardino Cypell: buxetano ... (Impressum Mediolani per Magistrū Ioannem de Castelliono ipsius Authoris sumptibus. Quarto Caleñ. Iulij. M.D.XXI.) 4°. A-P^{4}. ff. iii-lx. [482

CIRCIGNANI, NICCOLÒ. [1] Ecclesiae Anglicanae trophæa Siue Sanctoꝝ Martyrum, qui pro Christo Catholicæꝗ fidei Veritate asserenda, ... mortem in Anglia subierunt, Passiones Romæ in Collegio Anglico per Nicolaum Circinianum depictæ; nuper autem Per Io. Bap. de Cauallerijs æneis typis repræsentatæ. ... M.D.LXXXIIII. Romæ ex officina Bartholomæi Grassi. fol. *36 engraved plates, including t.p.* [2] Descriptiones quaedam illius inhumanæ et multiplicis persecutionis, Quam in Anglia propter fidem sustinent Catholicè Christiani. (Romæ, Apud Franciscum Zannettum. 1584.) *5 engraved plates.* [483

-- Ecclesiae militantis triumphi siue Deo amabilium martyrum gloriosa pro Christi fide Certamina: prout opera RR Patrum Societatis Iesu Collegij Germanici et Hungarici ... Nicolai Circiniani pictoris manu uisuntur depicta, ... a Ioanne Bap.^{ta} de Caualleriis, æneis typis accurate expressa ... M.D.LXXXV. ... Romæ ex officina Bartholomæi Grassi. fol. *Engraved t.p. + 31 numbered and 4 unnumbered plates.* [484

CIRILLO, BERNARDINO. Annali della città dell'Aquila, con l'historie del suo tempo ... In Roma, appresso Guilio Accolto. 1570. 4°. a-b^{4} A-II^{4} KK^{6} LL^{4}. ff. 1-134. [485

CIRNI, ANTON FRANCESCO. Comentarii ..., ne quali si descriue la guerra ultima di Francia ... In Roma, Appresso Giulio Accolto, M D LXVII. 4°. A-LL^{4} MM^{4+2}. ff. 2-132. [486

-- Successi della armata della maestà Catolico Destinata all'impresa di Tripoli di Barberia, Della presa delle Gerbe, e progressi dell'armata Turchesca, ... Aggiuntoui il disegno con la descrittion dell'Isola. In Vinegia per Giouanni Bariletto. M D LI. (*Colophon.*) 8°. *^{8} A-F^{8} (-F8, *presumably blank*). ff. 1-44. (Lea.) [487

CISNER, NICOLAUS. Oratio ... in funere ... Hermanni Ludouici Palatini Rheni ... Parisiis, Apud Andream Wechelum ... 1557. 4°. A-B^{4} C^{2}. ¶A2 *misbound before* A1, A4 *before* A3. [488

-- Visitation abschiede: Aller Vnd jeder des hochlöblichen Keyserlichen Chammergerichts ... Visitationen publicierter Abschiedten ... Getruckt zu Franckfurt am Mayn/ Anno 1570. (... bey Martin Lechler/ in verlegung Hieronymi Feyerabends ...) fol. ^{4} A-N^{6}. ff. I-LXXII. (Lea.) [489

CITOLINI, ALESSANDRO. La lettera ... in difesa della lingua uolgare ... Con vna lettera di Girolamo Ruscelli. al Mutio, in difesa dell'uso delle Signorie. ... In Vinegia [appresso Andrea Arrivabene] al segno del pozzo. M. D. LI. (... il mese di Setembre. ...) 8°. π^{4} A-D^{8}. ff. 1-31. ¶*Lacks the letter of Ruscelli.* [490

-- La tipocosmia ... In Venetia Appresso Vincenzo Valgrisi. M. D. LXI. 8°. *^{8} (-*8, *blank*) A-Ll^{8} Mm^{4}. pp. 1-552. [491

CITTÀ DI CASTELLO. Reformatio ciuitatis Castelli, super modo actitandi in causis Ciuilibus, ac Mercede Notariorum & Procuratorum ... Perusiae, Apud Petrumiacchum Petrutium. 1579. (*Colophon.*) 4°. A-H^4 I^6. pp. 4-74. (Lea.) [492

CITTADINI, ANTONIO. Antonii Cittadini Fauentini Auscultationes in Posteriora Aristotelis Analytica. ... (Im̄pessum Fauentiæ per Ioannem mariam de Simonettis Cremonē. ... M.D.XXVIII. Die .VIII. Maii.) fol. a-h^6 i-k^4 (-k4, *presumably blank*). ff. II-LIIII. [493

CITTADINI, CELSO. Rime Platoniche ... Venetia, Ad instantia di Gio. Martinelli. 1585. (*Colophon.*) 8°. a^8 A-K^8 L^4. ff. 1-84. [494

CITTADINI, PAOLO. Tractatus iuris patronatus et summaria distinctionū: ac questionū causarū decreti. (Im̄pssus Argentine ... 1.5.0.6. Finitus ī vigilia Iohannis baptiste. ꝑ Iohannē Reinhart. al's groninger.) 4°. B.L. A^6 B-K^8 L^6 M^8 N-Q$^{8.6}$ R-T^8. [495

CLAMORINUS, BARTHOLOMAEUS. Oratio funebris Historica ... de ... obitu ... Ducis Christiani Electoris Saxoniæ, 25. Septemb. 1591. Historiche Grabschrifft ... Dressden. Bey Gimel Bergen. 4°. A-E^4 F^2. [496

CLAUDIANUS, CLAUDIUS. Cl. Claudiani opera ... (Venetiis in aedibus Aldi et Andreae Asulani soceri, mense Martio M. D. XXIII.) 8°. a-y^8. ff. 2-176. [497

-- -- *Another copy.* [498

CLEMANGIIS, NICOLAUS DE. Nicolai de Clamēgiis, de lapsu & reparatione iusticiæ libellus. Eiusdem disputatio super materia cōcilii generalis. Item libellus apostolorum nationis Gallicanæ, cū cōstitutione sacri cōcilii Basilien. & Arresto curiæ Parlamēti, super annatis nō soluēdis. [Basileae, Andreas Cratander, 1519?] 4°. A-Q^4 R^6. pp. 1-131. (Lea.) [499

CLEMENS ROMANUS. Κλημεντος επισκοπου Ῥώμης, περὶ των πράξεων ... ἁγίου Πέτρου ἐπιτομή ... Clementis Romani episcopi, de rebus gestis ... sancti Petri epitome ... Eiusdem Clementis vita. ... Parisiis M. D. LV. Apud Adr. Turnebum ... (... Cal. Februar. ...) 4°. *^{2} A-M^4 N^2. pp. 1-98. [500

-- -- ... Eiusdem Clementis vita ... Ioachimo Perionio ... interprete. ... Parisiis, M. D. LV. Apud Guilielmum Morelium. ... (*Colophon.*) 4°. *^{2} A-Q^4. pp. 1-128. [501

-- Diui Clementis recognitionum libri X. .., Rufino Torano Aquileiense interprete. Cui accessit non poenitenda epistolarum pars uetustissimorū Episcoporum ... In ... Basilea. ... (... apud Ioan. Bebelium an. XXVI. mense Augusto.) fol. α^4 a-y^4 A-M^4. pp. 2-174, 2-82. [502

-- -- *Another copy.* (Lea.) [503

CLEMENT VII, pope. Newe zeytung des einzugs so der Babst zu Marsilien in Franckreich gethan/ aus etlichen Frantzōsischen brieffen in Deutsche sprach ... gezogen. [Nuremberg, Johann Stuchs, 1533.] 4°. π^4. [504

CLEOFILO, FRANCESCO OTTAVIO. Octauii Cleophili Fanensis Opera nunq́ʒ alias impressa. Anthropotheomachia. Historia de bello Fanensi. Et quędam alia. (Imprimebat Fani Hieronymus Soncinus ... M.D.XVI. Die .xxix. Mensis. Ianuarij.) 8°. A-E^4 a-i^4 K-L^4. [505

-- Octauius Cleophilus Phanensis ... de coetu poetarum. ... (Basileae apud Ioannem Frobenium. Mense Februario. An. M. D. XVIII.) 4°. A-D^4. pp. 3-30. [506

CLEYNAERTS, NICLAES. Institutiones ac meditationes in Græcam linguam, N. Clenardo authore, cum Scholiis & Praxi P. Antesignani Rapistagnensis. ... Parisiis, Apud Andream Wechelum. M. D. LXVI. (*Colophon.*) 4°. α-ν^4 ξ^2 A-Z^4 a-z^4 Aa-Ff^4. pp. 1-414. [507

-- -- Institutiones linguae Graecae ... Editio quinta. Coloniae, Ex officina Theodori Graminæi. M.D.LXIX. 8°. *^{8} A-Z^8 a-l^8 (-l7, l8). pp. 1-508 *present.* [508

-- Nicolai Clenardi peregrinationum ac de rebus Machometicis epistolae ... Louanii, Apud Petrum Phalesium, anno M. D. L. ... 8°. A-E^8 F^4. ff. 1-41. [509

-- לוחות הדקדוק Tabulae in grammaticam Hebraeam ... A Iohanne Isaac ... correctæ ... Coloniae, In Officina Birckmannica. M. D. LXXXI. (... Typis hæred. Iac. Soteris. ...) 8°. A-L^8. ff. 2-84. [510

CLICHTOVE, JOSSE. AntiLutherus Iudoci Clichtouei Neoportuensis. ... Anno. M. D. XXV. (apud ... Coloniensis Academiæ gymnasium. In officina ... Petri Quentell. Anno ... uicesimoquīto, supra millesimum & quingentesimum, sexto Kalendas Martias.) 4°. π^{12} a-z^4 A-Z^4 aa-hh^4 (-hh4, *presumably blank*). ff. I-CCXV. (Lea.) [511

-- In hoc opusculo agitur. De laudibus sancti Ludouici: regis Franciæ. De laudibus ... virginis & martyris Ceciliæ. (Completum in alma Parisiorum academia ... per Henricū Stephanū ... Anno ... decimosexto supra millesimum & quingentesimum: die vero Ianuarij decima.) 4°. a-g^8 h^6 i^4. ff. 2-65. [512

-- De vera nobilitate opusculum ... Ex secunda recognitione. 1520 Venale habetur Parisijs, in officina Simonis Colinæi ... (... die vero Martij. 15.) 4°. a-g^8 h^6 (-h6, *blank*). ff. 2-60. [513

-- Dogma Moralium Philosophorum ... collectum. (Argentorat. ex aedibus Schurerianis mense Iulio. Anno. M. D. XII.) 4°. A^8 B^4 C^8 D^6. ff. III-XXV. [514

-- Fundamentum logicae. Introductio in terminorum cognitionem, in libros Logicorū Aristotelis, ... vna cū Ioannis Cæsarij Commentarijs. Parisiis. Apud Petrum gromorsum. 1535. 8°. A-C^8. pp. ij-xlvij. [515

-- -- Parisiis. Ex officina Christiani Wecheli ... M.D.XXXVIII. 8°. A-D^8. pp. 2-63. [516

-- Introductiones artificiales in Logicā Iacobi Fabri Stapulensis, per Iudocū Clichtoueum Neoportuēsem collectæ ... Iudoci item Clichtouei in Terminorum Cognitionem Introductio, cum altera de Artium diuisione ... Lugduni Apud hæredes Simonis Vincentii. M. D. XL. (... per Dionysium Harsium ...) 8°. a-z^8 A-L^8 M^4. ff. 2-274. [517

COCCINIUS, MICHAEL. Opusculum Michaelis Coccinij Tübingensis alias Kōchlin dicti. De imperij a Grecis ad Germanos tralatione. ... Item de Francoꝝ origine ... Apologiæ duæ ... (Ioannes Grüninger imprimebat Argeñ.) 4°. A-D^8. ¶*Dedication dated* iiij. nonas Martij ... M.D.vi. [518

-- Opuscūlū ... De rebus gestis in Italia: a mense Maio: anni vndecimi ... Supra millesimū quingentesimū vsq3 ad Kalendas Maij: Anni .xij. sequentis. ... fol. B.L. A-B^6. [519

COCHLAEUS, JOHANNES. Ad Paulum III. Pont. Max. congratulatio ... super eius electione ... M. D. XXXV. (Lipsiæ excudebat Michaēl Blum. ...) 4°. A-D^4. [520

-- An die Herrenn/ Schulteis vnnd Radt zu Bern/ widder yhre vermainte Reformation. Doct. Io. Cocleus M.D.xxviij. (Gedruckt zu Dressden durch Wolffgang Stöckel.) 4°. a-b^4 c^2 d-e^4. [521

-- Annotationes et antitheses ... In quædam scripta, & Propositiones Collocutorum Vuittenbergensium. ... Ingolstadii excudebat Alexander Vueissenhorn. ... M. D. XLVI. 4°. AA-GG^4 aa-cc^4. ff. 2-27, 1-11. [522

-- Articuli CCCCC. Martini Lutheri. Ex sermonibus eius Sex & Triginta. Quibus singulatim responsum est ... [Coloniae, Petrus Quentell,] An. M. D. XXVI. 4°. B.L. A-Q^4 R^6. [523

-- Auff den Tewtschen Auszug vbers Decret/ von vnbenanten leuthen gemacht. Antwortt D. Io. Cocleus. Gedrugkt zu Dressden durch Wolffgang Stöckel. M. D. XXX. 4°. a-e^4. [524

-- -- In obscuros viros, qui decretorum volumen infami compendio Theutonice corruperunt, Expostulatio ... Augustæ. M. D. XXX. 4°. A-D^4. [525

-- Bockspiel Martini Luthers ... (Aussgangen zu Mentz/ bey Peter Jordan/ Am xv. tag Julij. M.D.XXXI.) 8°. A-F^4. [526

-- Catalogus breuis eorum quæ contra nouas Sectas scripsit Ioannes Cochlæus. ... Per Franciscum Behem apud S. Victorem prope Moguntiam ... M. D. XLVIII. 8°. A-B^8. [527

-- Confutatio XCI. articulorum: e tribus Martini Lutheri Teuthonicis sermonibus excerptorum ... (Coloniæ in officina ... Petri Quentell. Anno. M.D.XXV.) 4°. A-C^4 D^6. (Lea.) [528

-- -- *Another copy.* [529

-- Consyderatio Iohannis Cochlæi, de futuro Concordiæ in Religione Tractatu, Vuormatiæ habendo. ... M. D. XLV. (Ingolstadij Excudebat Alexander Vueyssenhorn. Mense Ianuario ...) 4°. A-F^4 G^2. [530

-- De animarum purgatorio Igne Epitome, Cōtra nouas sestas [*sic*] quæ Purgatorium negant ... Ingolstadij Ex officina Typographica Alexandri Vueissenhorn. M D. XLIIII. 4°. A-F^4. (Lea.) [531

-- De baptismo paruulorum liber vnus ... Aduersus assertionem Marti. Lutheri. (Excusum Argentine impensis & opera ... Ioannis Grieninger ... in die Sanctę Appolonię Anno ... Millesimo Quingentesimo vicesimo tercio.) 4°. A-N^4 O^6. ff. II-LVII. [532

-- De Canonicæ scripturę & Catholicæ Ecclesiæ Authoritate, ad Henricum Bullingerū ... Libellus. M.D.XLIII. (Ingolstadii in officina Alexandri Vueissenhorn.) 4°. A-M^4. [533

-- De imaginibus fragmentum Libri Vnius. ... Anno M. D. XLVII. [Ingolstadii, Alexander Weissenhorn?] 8°. A-B^8. [534

-- De libero arbitrio hominis, aduersus locos cōmunes Philippi Melanchthonis, libri duo ... [Tubingae, Ulrich Morhart,] Anno. M. D. XXV. 8°. A-O^8 P^{10}. (Yarnall.) [534a

-- De matrimonio ... Regis Angliæ, Henrici Octaui, Congratulatio disputatoria ... 1535. (Lipsiæ excudebat Michaël Blum Mense Februario. ...) 4°. A-N^4 O^2. [535

-- -- *Another copy.* (Yarnall.) [535a

-- De nouis ex Hebraeo Translationibus sacræ scripturæ, Disceptatio ... Ingolstadii, Ex officina Alexandri Vueissenhorn. M. D. XLIIII. 8°. A-I^8 K^4. [536

-- De Petro et Roma aduersus Velenū Lutheranum, libri quatuor, ... (Coloniæ in officina ... Petri Quentell. Anno .M.D.XXV. Mense Februario.) 4°. [A]^4 B-Q^4. pp. 2-119. [537

-- -- *Variant with imprint:* Anno. M. D. XXV. (Lea.) [538

-- Defensio ceremoniarum Ecclesiæ aduersus errores & calumnias Trium librorum D. Ambrosij Moibani Vratislauiae Concionantis. ... Ingolstadij ex officina Alexandri Vueissenhorn. M. D. XLIIII. 8°. A-K^8. [539

-- Dialogus de bello contra Turcas, in Antilogias Lutheri ... XV. Contradictiones, ex duobus primis Quaternionibus Libri Lutherici de bello, contra Turcas. M. D. XXIX. (Excusum Lipsiæ, in Officina Valentini Schumāni, pridie Calendas Iulias. ...) 8°. a^8 B-I^8 K^4 L^8 (-L8, *presumably blank*). ff. II-LXXXII. [540

-- XXi. Artickel der Widderteuffer zu Munster ... widerlegt ... M. D. XXXIIII. (Gedruckt zu Dressden durch Wolffgang Stöckel Mense Martio ...) 4°. A-C^4. [541

-- Fidelis et pacifica commonitio ... contrà Infidelem & seditiosam Cōmonitionem Mart. Lutheri ad Germanos. M. D. XXXI. (Excusa est ... Lipsiæ per Valentinum Schumañ ...) 8°. A-B^8. [542

-- Grāmatica ... Rudimenta ... Anno .M.D.XIIII. (Excusum Argentinę per Renatum Beck ... M.D.X.III.) 4°. π^4 a-b^4 c-d^6 e^4 f-l$^{8.4.4}$ m^8 n^4 o^8 p^8. ff. I-LXXXII. [543

-- Hertzog Georgens zu Sachssen ... entschuldigung/ wider Martin Luthers ... verlogenne brieff vnd Verantwortung. Zu Dressden. M. D. XXXiij. ... (Gedruckt zu Leyptzigk/ durch Michael Blum.) 4°. A-I^4 K^2 L^4. [544

-- Historia Ioannis Cochlæi de actis et scriptis Martini Lutheri Saxonis, Chronographicè ex ordine ab Anno Domini M.D.XVII. vsq3 ad Annum M.D.XLV Inclusiuè ... Coloniæ, Apud Theodorum Baumium ... M. D LXVIII. 8°. α-γ^8 A-Z^8 a-t^8 v^4. pp. 1-48, ff. 49-363. (Lea.)[545

-- -- *Another copy.* (Yarnall.) [545a

-- [1] Historiae Hussitarum libri duodecim ... duo de septem sacramentis et de cæremoniis ecclesiæ tractatus duorum Bohemorum, Io. Rokyzanæ, & Io. Przibram: Cum Philippica Septima Io. Cochlæi, De publica Caroli V. Imperatoris Ordinatione, quæ uulgo interim dicitur. ... Apud S. Victorem prope Moguntiam, ex officina Francisci Behem ... M. D. XLIX. (*Colophon.*) fol. a*-b*^{6} c*^{4} A-Yy^6 Zz^4 3A-3C^6 3D^8. pp. 1-599. [2] Commentaria Ioannis Cochlaei, de actis et scriptis Martini Lutheri ... *Same imprint.* (... Mense Septembri ...) a✠^{6} b*^{6} c♣^{6} A-Dd^6 Ee^8. pp. 1-339. (Lea.) [546

-- -- *Another copy.* [547

-- In Causa Religionis miscellaneorum libri tres ... Ingolstadii excudebat Alexander Vueissenhorn. ... M. D. XLV. 4°. A-B^4 C^2 a-z^4 Aa-3C^4 3D^2. ff. 1-194. [548

-- -- *Another copy.* [549

-- In primum Musculi Anticochlaeum Replica breuis ... In epilogo adiecta est breuis responsio in Antibolen Bullingeri. Addita est appendix gemina in librum Buceri, quem in Bart. Latomum ædidit. ... M. D. XLV. (Impressum Ingolstadij excudebat Alexander Vueissenhorn. ...) 4°. A-M^4. ff. 2-48. [550

-- In quatuor Andraeae Osiandri Coniecturas de fine Mundi, uelitatio ... M.D.XLV. (Ingolstadij Excudebat Alexander Vueysenhorn. Mense Ianuario ...) 4°. A-I^4. [551

-- Ioannis Caluini in acta synodi Tridentinæ Censura, & eiusdem Breuis Confutatio ... Elenchus Capitulorum e Sex Libris D. Conradi Bruni, De Concilio Vniuersali. Apud S. Victorem prope Moguntiam, ex officina Francisci Behem ... M. D. XLVIII. 16°. A-E^8. [552

-- Ein nötig vnd Christlich Bedencken/ auff des Luthers Artickeln/ die man Gemeynem Concilio fürtragen sol. M. D. XXXVIII. Gedruckt zu Leipzig durch Nicolaum Wolrab. 4°. A-M^4. [553

-- -- Necessaria et catholica consyderatio super Lutheri articulis, quos uelit Concilio Generali proponi. ... Ingolstadii excudebat Alexander Vueissenhorn. M. D. XLVI. 4°. A^4 a-i^4 k^2 l-m^4. ff. 1-41. [554

-- -- Responce aux articles, que Martin Luther vouloit estre proposez par ceux de sa secte, au Concile general. ... tournée de Latin en François, par Gabriel du Preau ... A Paris, Chez Estienne Petit & Michel Iulien ... 1563. ... 8°. *^{8} A^4 B-L^8. ff. 1-88. [555

-- Philippicæ quatuor ... in Apologiam Philippi Melanchthonis ... Lipsiae. M. D. XXXIIII. (... excudebat Nicolaus Faber, mense Iunio ...) 4°. ☞^{6} A-T^4 V^2 X^4. [556

-- Philippica quinta. In tres libellos Philippi Melanchthonis. ... Imgolstadij ex officina Alexandri Vueissenhorn. M.D.XLIII. 4°. A-N^4 O^2. [557

-- Philippica sexta. ... Cum adiunctis Tractatulis Tribus Quorum. I. est Michaelis Vehe ... II. Arnoldi Vuesaliensis ... III. Eiusdem Io. Cochlæi. De uera Ecclesia Christi. Contra Philippi Melan. Responsionem pro Bucero ... Ingolstadij ex officina Alexandri Vueissenhorn. M.D.XLIIII. ... 4°. A-Q^4. [558

-- Pia exhortatio Romae ad Germaniam, suam in fide filiam ... (Excusum Tubingæ. Anno .M.D.XXV. Mense Februario.) 8°. A-E^8 F^4 G^{10}. [559

-- Replica breuis ... aduersus prolixam Responsionem Henrici Bullingeri De scripturæ & Ecclesiæ authoritate. Ingolstadij, apud Alexandrum Vueissenhorn. M. D. XLIIII. 4°. A-E^4 F^2 G^4. [560

-- -- Ein kurtze Replica Auff die langen Antwort Heyntzen Bullingers/ von der heyligen Schrifft vnnd der kirchen Authoritet. ... Gedruckt zů Ingolstadt durch Alexander Weyssenhorn. Anno. M. D. XLIIII. 4°. [A]^2 B-F^4. [561

-- Septiceps Lutherus, vbiq3 sibi, suis scriptis, cõtrari9, in Visitationẽ Saxonicã, ꝑ D.D. Ioã. Coclęũ, ędìtus (Lipsiæ Impressit Valentinus Schumañ, ... M. D. XXIX. X. Maias Calendas.) 4°. (^{6} A-Q^4. [562

-- -- Parisiis, Apud Nicolaum Chesneau ... 1564. 8°. a^8 b^4 A-R^8 T^4. ff. 1-136. [563

-- Sieben Köpffe Martini Luthers Vom Hochwürdigen Sacraments des Altars ... (Gedruckt zu Leypsig durch Valten Schuman im. xxix. Jhar.) 4°. A-E^4 F^2 G^4. [564

-- -- Sieben kopff Martin Luthers ... M. D. XXXi. [Gedrugkt zu Dressden durch Wolffgang Stöckel. ...) 4°. A-F^4. [565

-- Sieben kopffe Martin Luthers/ von sieben sachen des Christlichen glaubens ... 1529 (Gedrugkt zu Dressden durch Wolffgang Stöckel. ...) 4°. a-b^4 c^2 d-e^4. [566

-- Speculum antiquae deuotionis circa missam ... ... Apud S. Victorem extra muros Moguntiæ, ex officina Francisci Behem. M. D. XLIX. (... Mense Februario.) fol. ❦ a^8 A-X^6. pp. 1-251. [567

-- Velitatio ... in apologiam Philippi Melanchthonis. M.D.XXXIIII. (Excusum Lipsię, apud Michaēlem Blum. ...) 4°. A-E⁴. [568

-- Verthedigung vnsers Priesterthumbs vnd opffers im Newen Testament wider zwů Predig Wolfgang Meusslins .. [Ingolstadt, Alexander Weissenhorn,] M. D. XLIIII. 4°. A-O⁴. [569

-- Vita Theoderici regis quondam Ostrogothorum & Italiæ. Querela item de reipublicæ statu sub Iustiniano Imp. I. ... Ex officina Alexandri Vueissenhorn ... Ingolstadiensis M. D. XLIIII. ... 4°. Aa-Pp⁴. (Lea.) [570

-- Vom vermögen vnd Gewalt eines gemeynen Concilij ... Gedruckt zu Leiptzigk/ Durch Nickel Wolrab. 1537. (*Colophon.*) 8°. A-E⁸. [571

-- Von altem gebrauch des Bettens in Crichlicher [*sic*] Kirchen zehen Vnderschaid. Getruckt zů Ingolstadt durch Alexander Weissenhorn. M. D. XLIIII. 4°. A-K⁴. [572

-- Von Christglaubigen Selen im fegfewr ... ... Zu Cöln/ im Jar .M.D.xxvi. (*Colophon.*) 8°. A-K⁴. [573

-- Zwey kurtze Tractätlein Vom Fegfewr der Seelen/ wider die newen Secten/ so dasselbe verneinen. Erstlich beschriben durch weylandt ... Ioannem Cochleum ... vnd jetzo mit Dolmetschung dess ersten ... in Truck gefertigt: Durch Iohann Christoff Hueber. ... Getruckt zů Ingolstadt/ bey Dauid Sartorio. Anno M. D. LXXXIII. 8°. A-Q⁸ R⁴. ff. 1-124. ¶*Half-title* (I1ʳ): Von Christglaubigen Seelen im Fegfeur ... Zů Cöln/ im Jar 1526. [574

COCLES, BARTHOLOMAEUS. La geomantia ... nuouissimamente tradotta ... In Vinegia, per Giouita Rapirio. M D L. (... appresso Bartholomeo Cesano M D LII.) 8°. A-L⁸. ff. 2-88. [575

-- Barptolomaei Coclitis Bononiensis ... Physiognomiæ & Chiromantiæ Compendium. Argentorati anno M. D. XXXIIII. (Argentinae apud Ioannem Albrecht. ...) 8°. A-N⁸ O⁴ (-O4, *presumably blank*). (Lea.) [576

COELESTINUS, CLAUDIUS. De his quę mundo mirabiliter eueniunt: vbi de sensuum erroribus, & potentijs animę, ac de influentijs cælorum, ... opusculum. De mirabili potestate artis et naturae, vbi de philosophorum lapide, F. Rogerij Bachonis Anglici, libellus. ... Orontius F. Delph. ... recognoscebat ... Lutetiæ Parisiorum. Apud Simonem Colinæum. 1542. 4°. ?⁴ a-i⁴. ff. 1-36. ¶*Lacks the second part.* [577

COELESTINUS, JOHANN FRIEDRICH. Von Buchhendlern/ Buchdruckern vnd Buchfürern: Ob Sie auch one sünde ... Vnchristliche/ Ketzerische/ Bepstische/ Vnzüchtige ... Bücher drucken ... mögen ... [Regensburg, Johann Burger,] 1569. 8°. A-E⁸ F⁴. [578

COIMBRA. *Collegium Societatis Jesu.* Commentarii Collegii Conimbricensis Societatis Iesu in libros Aristotelis, qui parua naturalia appellantur. ... Olisipone, Ex officina Simonis Lopesij, Anno M.D.XCIII. 4°. A-N⁴. pp. 2-104. [579

-- Commentarii ... In libros meteororum Aristotelis ... Olisipone, Ex officina Simonis Lopesij. Anno M.D.XCIII. 4°. A-S⁴. pp. 3-143. [580

-- Commentarii ... In quatuor libros de coelo Aristotelis ... Olisipone. Ex officina Simonis Lopesij. Anno M.D.LXXXXIII. 4°. π⁴ A-3I⁴ 3K⁴. pp. 1-447. [581

-- In libros ethicorum Aristotelis ad Nicomachum, aliquot Conimbricensis cursus disputationes ... Olisipone. Ex officina Simonis Lopesij. Anno M.D.XCIII. 4°. A-M⁴. pp. 3-95. [582

COLALDI, AGOSTINO. Rime de diuersi autori all' ... P.F. Iacomo Clauerio ... reuiste ... per Agostino Colaldi da Ciuita Ducal In Viterbo ... 4°. A-K⁴ K⁴ A-B⁴. [583

COLER, MARTIN. De alimentis libri tres ... Quibus præmissi sunt ... Bartoli de Saxoferrato & Ioannis Baptistae Pontani ... eadem de re tractatus ... 1596 Lipsiae, ... Sumtibus Andreæ Hoffmanni Bibliop. VVitteb. 4°.)?(⁸ A-3Q⁸ 3R⁶ 3S-3Y⁴ (-3Y3-4). pp. 1-995. (Biddle.) [584

COLERUS, JOHANN. Calendarium Oeconomicum & perpetuum. ... Zu Wittemberg bey Christoff Axin/ vnd Paul Hellwign. ... (... M. D. XCII.) 4°. A-Y⁴. [585

COLIGNY, GASPARD DE CHÂTILLON, amiral de. Epicedion ... Casparis Castilionæi, amirallii Galliae, Parisiis, hoc anno 1572. die 24. Augusti ... perfidia & immanitate trucidati. ... 8°. A^4. [586

COLLE. Constitutiones synodales, et decreta condita. A ... Vsimbardo Vsumbardio Episcopo Collense Primo in Dioecesana Synodo. Habita ... die 16.17.18 Mensis Iunii 1594. Florentiae, Apud Michaelangelum Sermartellium. B.F. M.D. XCV. (*Colophon.*) 4°. $\dagger^2$ A-Mm^4 Nn-Oo^2. pp. 1-276. (Lea.) [587

COLLENUCCIO, PANDOLFO. Compendio delle historie del regno di Napoli ... In Venetia. M.D.XXXXI. ... (... per Michele Tramezino ... d'il mese di Luglio.) 8°. A-BB^8. ff. 1-196. [588

-- -- [1] Compendio ... Con la giunta delle cose notabile successe per tutto l'anno M D LXII. ... In Napoli Appresso Gio. Maria Scotto. M D LXIII. 8°. a-g^8 h^4 A-VV^8. ff. 1-344. [2] Secondo volume dell'historia del regno di Napoli ... *Same imprint.* a-c^8 d^4 a-tt^8 uu^4. ff. 1-340. [3] Nomi delle prouintie, citta, terre, e castella, del Regno di Napoli. ... *Same imprint.* A-D^8. (Lea.) [589

-- Opera noua ... Intitulata Philotimo. ... (Impresso in Venetia per Iacobo pintio de Lecho ad instantia de Nicolo ditto Zopino ⁊ Vincenzo suo compagno. Nel anno .M.D.XVII. Adi vltima del mese de Agosto.) 8°. B.L. a-e^4. [590

-- Specchio di Esopo. (In Vinegia, per Ioan. Ant. & Pietro fratelli, di Nicolini da Sabio, ad instantia de M. Mattio Pagan. Nel M. D. XLIIII.) 8°. A-D^4. [591

COLLUTHUS. Origo & Exitus belli Troiani. Κολουθου Λυκοπολιτου Θηβαιου, Ἑλένης αρπαγή. Τρυφιοδωρου ποιητου Αιγυπτιου, Ιλίου ἅλωσις. Coluthi Thebæi, Helenæ raptus. Tryphiodori Ægyp. Ilij excidium. Omnia versione Latina & expositione M. Neandri illustrata. [Genevae,] παρὰ Ε. Οὐϊγνῶνι. ϥ φ' π' [1580]. 16°. a-e^8. pp. 3-79. [592

COLOGNE. Abdruck vnd gemeiner begriff der Pollicey/ Ordnungen/ Plebisciten/ vnnd Statuten der ... Stadt Coͤllen etc. M. D. LXII. fol. $*^4$ A-F^4 G^2 H^4 I-K^2 L^4 M^2 N-P^4. ff. j-lj. [593

-- Folgen die statuta vnd concordata der ... Statt Coͤlln ... 4°. A-Z^4 Aa^2 A-Y^4 Z^2. pp. 1-186, 1-177. [594

-- -- *Another copy.* [595

-- *University. Faculty of Law.* Volumen praecipuarum iuris materiarum in certas theses distributarum ... apud Coloniam Vbiorum Collegij disputationibus collectum. ... De quibus praesentibus successiue D. Ioanne Michaelis Cronenburgero, D. Ioanne Hollandt, ac D. VVinoldo Kiuer ... disputatum fuit. Coloniae Agrippinae excudebat Petrus Keschedt ... 1596. 4°. A-Z^4 $\dagger^4$ A-$3I^4$. ¶*Presumably the general t.p.* ($\dagger 1^r$) *of this collection though not bound at the beginning. There is a catchword on* $\dagger 4^v$. *The collection consists of 78 theses disputed from 9 September 1593 to 9 May 1596, each consisting of four leaves with a separate t.p. The order of printing does not correspond to that of the dates given.* [596

-- *Adolf III von Schauenburg, archbishop-elector.* Adolphus Dei gratia Sanctæ Coloniensis Ecclesiæ Archiepiscopus ... [order forbidding clerical marriages]. Datum ... Anno Domini, millesimo, quingentesimo, quadragesimo octauo, die secunda mensis Octobris. [Coloniae, Jaspar Gennepaeus.] s.sh. 29 × 19 cm. [597

-- Adolphus ... Coloniensis Ecclesiæ Archiepiscopus ... [order prohibiting the administration of communion to vagrant monks]. Datum ... Anno domini Millesimo, quingentesimo, quadragesimo octauo, die secunda Mensis Octobris. [Coloniae, Jaspar Gennepaeus] s.sh. 29 × 19 cm. ¶*Printed with C597 on conjugate leaves.* [598

-- *Johann Gebhard von Mansfeld, archbishop-elector.* BergkOrdenung sampt eyner neuwen Bergkfreiheit ... Iohans Gebharten/ Erwoͤlten zu Ertzbischoffen zu Coͤllen ... zu Coͤllen bey Iaspar Gennep/ M. D. LIX. fol. $[A]^4$ B-M^4 [A]-B^4. ¶*Additional t.p.* ($^2[A]1^r$): Bergkfreiheit ... *Same imprint.* (Biddle.) [599

-- *Gebhardt Truchsess von Waldburg, archbishop-elector.* Ausschreiben Vnd Gruͤndlicher warhaffter Bericht Vnser Gebhardts/ ... Ertzbischoffs zu Coͤlln ... Warumb wir vns mit etlichen Soldaten/ zu beschützen vnserer land/ Leuth/ vnd eigenen Person ... zubegeben genottrangt ... M. D. LXXXIII. 4°. a-f^4 g^6 A-Ee^4 (-Ee4, *presumably blank*). pp. 1-221. [600

-- -- Ausschreiben vnd ... Bericht: Vnser Gebhards ... 4°. A-Z^{4} a-g^{4}. [601

-- Warnungs Schrifft: Vnser Gebharts ... Ertz Bischoff zu Cöllen vnd Churfürsten ... wider die vermeinte ... Newe Wahl/ eines andern Ertz Bischoffs vnd Churfürsten zu Cöllen ... Geschehen den 15. Maij ... 1583. M. D. LXXXIII. (Gedruckt zu Erffurd/ durch Esaiam Mechlern ...) 4°. A^{4}. [602

-- [1] Zwo Protestationschrifften Vnser Gebhards ... Ertzbischoffen zu Cölln ... Deren die Erste/ wider die vermeynte Visitation de Anno 85. ... M. D. LXXXVI. 4°. A-O^{4}. [2] Protestationschrifft ... Wider den zu Worms angestelten vermeinten Deputation Tag. ... M. D. LXXXVI. A-B^{4} C^{2}. (Lea.) [603

-- *Province.* [1] Canones Concilii Prouincialis Coloniensis ... Anno 1536. Quibus adiectus est Enchiridion Christianæ institutionis. ... Impress. Colo. anno. XXXVIII. (Ex ædibus Quentelianis ... M.D.XXXVIII.) fol. a^{6} b^{4} A-H$^{6.4}$ I-L^{6} M^{4} N^{6} O^{4} P-Q^{6} R^{4} S^{6} T^{4} V^{6} X^{4} Y-Z^{6} AA^{4} BB-NN^{6} OO^{4} PP-QQ^{6} RR^{4} SS-ZZ^{6} 3A-3H^{6} 3I^{4} 3K-3M^{6}. [2] Formula ad quam visitatio intra Diocoesim Coloniensem exigetur. Adijciuntur ... Canonum ferme omnium Argumenta Concilij ... (Coloniæ in officina Quenteliana. Anno M. D. XXXVI.) A-B^{6} (-B6, *presumably blank*). (Yarnall.) [604

-- -- *Another copy.* (Yarnall.) [604a

-- -- *Variant: 2d colophon dated* M. D. XXXVII. (Lea.) [604b

-- Canones concilii prouincialis Coloniensis ... anno M D XXXVI. ... Item enchiridion Christianae institutionis ... in secunda hac nostra operis editione ... Veronae, apud Antonium Putelletum. M D XLIII. (*Colophon.*) 4°. A^{8} ✠^{8} ✠✠^{4} B-OO^{8} PP^{4} QQ^{8} RR^{4}. ff. 2-8, 9-299. ¶*Additional t.pp.:* (✠1^{r}) Formula adquam visitatio ... exigetur. ... Veronæ Apud Antonium Putelletum. M D XLII. (G1^{r}) Institutio compendiaria doctrinae Christianae ... Veronae. Apud Antonium Putelletum. M D XLIII. (Yarnall.) [604c

-- Canones ... Quibus nuperrimè hæc addita sunt: Reformatio Cleri ad correctionem vitæ & morum, ac ad remouendas abusus, Per ... D. Laurentium ... Legatum Ratisponæ edita. Statuta Synodalia ... D. Valentini, Episcopi Hildesemensis. Formula viuendi Canonicorum, Vicariorum, & aliorum presbyterorum secularium. Parisiis, Apud Iacobum Bogardum ... 1545. 8°. ¢^{8} a-m^{8}. ff. 1-96. (Lea.) [605

-- -- [*Variant*] Parisiis, Prostant apud Galeotum Pratensem ... 1545. (Lea.) [606

-- Enchiridion Christianae institutionis in Concilio Prouinciali Coloniensi editum ... Venetijs, apud Ioannem Francesium. 1543 [(... apud Cominum de Tridino Monferrati ...)] 8°. *-3*^{8} a-z^{8} &^{8} Aa-Ll1^{8} (-Ee-Ll1^{8}). ff. 1-224 *present.* (Yarnall.) [606a

-- -- Parisiis, Prostant apud Galeotum Pratensem ... 1545. 8°. ¢¢^{8} ¢¢^{10} A-RR^{8} SS^{4}. ff. 1-322. (Lea.) [607

COLOMBO, FERNANDO. Historie Del S.D. Fernando Colombo; Nelle quali s'ha particolare ... de' fatti dell'Ammiraglio D. Christoforo Colombo ... In Venetia. M D LXXI. Appresso Francesco de' Franceschi Sanese. 8°. a-b^{8} c^{4} A-Hh^{8}. ff. 1-247. [608

COLOMBO, REALDO. Realdi Columbi Cremonensis ... De re Anatomica libri XV. Parisiis, Apud Ægidium Gillium ... 1562. 8°. ã^{8} A-Gg^{8} Hh-Ii^{4}. pp. 1-495. [609

COLONNA, GIORGIO. Canzone ... nell'allegrezza della liberatione del mal contagioso della citta di Venetia. In Venetia, M. D. LXXVII. 4°. A^{4}. [610

COLONNA, GUIDO DELLA. Cronica Troyana ... En Medina. Por Francisco del Canto. M. D. Lxxxvij. A costa de Benito Boyer ... (*Colophon.*) fol. A-R^{8}. ff. 3-136. ¶*Translator: Pedro Lôpez de Ayala.* [611

COLONNA, MARC'ANTONIO MARSILI. M. Antonii Marsilii Columnae Bononiensis ... hydragiologia Siue De Aqua Benedicta. ... Romæ, Typis Bartholomæi Bonfadini. M D LXXXVI. ... (*Colophon.*) 4°. *-6*^{4} A-3X^{4} a-f^{4}. pp. 1-537. [612

COLONNA, STEFANO. I sonetti, le canzoni, et i triomphi di M. Laura in risposta di M. Francesco Petrarcha per le sue rime in vita, et dopo la morte di lei Peruenuti alle mani del

... M. Stephano Colonna, Gentil'huomo Romano ... A san Luca al segno del Diamante. M. D. LII. (In Vinegia per Comin da Trino di Monferrato ...) 8°. A-Z^8. ff. 2-173. [613

-- -- *Another copy* (Z7 *defective*). [614

COLONNA, VITTORIA. Rime de la diua Vetuoria Colonna ... In Venetia M D XXXX (Stampati ... per Comin de Trino ad instantia de Nicolo d'Aristotile, detto Zoppino. ...) 8°. A-G^8. ff. 2-53. [615

-- -- Rime della S. Vittoria Colonna ... In Vinegia appresso Gabriel Giolito de' Ferrari. M D LIX. (... M D LX.) 12°. A-F^{12}. pp. 3-134. [616

-- Le rime spirituali ... In Vinegia; appresso Vincenzo Valgrisi: MDXLVI. 4°. A-M^4 *^{2}. ff. 2-48. [617

-- -- In Vinegia, ... appresso Vincenzo Valgrisi: M.D.XLVIII. 4°. A-P^4. pp. 3-120. [618

COLORNI, ABRAHAM. [Scotographia ouero, scienza di scriuere oscuro ... Opera di Abram Colorni Heb: Mant: ... In Praga presso Giouani Sciuman, M.D.XCIII.] obl. 12°. A-Q^6 (-A^6) R^{6+1} A-Y^6 Z^{6+1} A^6 w^6 (w6 + 4 *folded ll.*) ff. 1-93. [619

COLUMNA, PETRUS, GALATINUS. Opus ... de arcanis catholice ueritatis, contra obstinatissimam Iudęorū ... ꝑfidiam: ex Talmud ... excerptum: & quadruplici linguarum genere ... congestum. ... (Impressum uero Orthonæ maris, ... per Hieronymum Suncinum: ... M.D.XVIII. quintodecimo kalendas martias.) fol. a-z^6 &^{6} ɔ^6 ꝶ^6 A-CC^6. ff. II-CCCXI. ¶*Lowest third of t.p. wanting.* [620

COMEDIA. Comedia Intitolata sine nomine ... In Fiorenza Nella Stamperia de' Giunti, MDLXXIIII. (*Colophon.*) 8°. A-E^8. pp. 7-76. [621

COMINES, PHILIPPE DE. Philippi Cominei Gründtliche Beschreibung allerlei ... Hãndel/ so sich bey Regierung der ... Herren Ludwigen des Eylfften/ Kônigs von Franckreich ... haben verlauffen vnd zugetragen. Mit einer Vorrede ... Durch Michaelem Beuther ... Getruckt zů Strassburg durch Iosiam Rihel. M D. LXXX. fol. A^4 B-Hh^6. pp. 1-333. ¶*Translator: Caspar Hedio.* [622

COMMENDONE, LEONARDO. Oratio ... cōgratulatoria ad ... Venetoꝝ Prīcipē Dn̄m. .D. Leonardū Lauretanū: habita publice Ven̄. Die .28. Nouēb. IDI. (Impressum Venetiis ꝑ Bernardinū Venetū de Vitalibus. Die primo Decembris .M.ccccc.I.) 4°. A^4. [623

COMPARINI, LORENZO. Due comedie di Lorenzo Comparini Fiorentino. Cioè il pellegrino, et il ladro ... In Vinegia appresso Gabriel Giolito de Ferrari et fratelli. MDLIIII. (*Colophon.*) 12°. A-H^{12} H^4. ff. 5-98. [624

COMPONIMENTO. Componimento di parlamenti, formulario nuouo, che insegna ... à dittar lettere Messiue, & responsiue ... In Venetia, Per gli Heredi di Luigi Valuassori, & Gio. Domenico Michieli. 1584. (... 1583.) 8°. A-E^8. [625

CONESTAGGIO, GIROLAMO. Dell'vnione del regno di Portogallo. Alla Corona di Castiglia. Istoria del Sig. Ieronimo de Franchi Conestaggio ... In Genoua. Appresso Girolamo Bartoli, 1585. 4°. A^4 A^8 A-Kk^8. ff. 1-264. (Lea.) [626

-- -- *Another copy.* (Lea.) [627

-- -- Historien Der Kônigkreich/ Hispannien/ Portugal vnd Aphrica ... Auss dem Italianischen/ durch Albrecht Fůrsten in das Hochteutsch gebracht. M. D. LXXXIX. ... (Gedruckt in ... Mũnchen/ bey Adam Berg. ... Den 26. Iulij. ...) fol. A-B^4 a-c^6 A-Mm^6 Nn-Oo^4. ff. 1-126. [628

CONFESSIONARIO. Confessionario breue y muy puechoso ... 8°. B.L. A-B^8. (Lea.) [629

CONJURATIO. Coniuratio malignoꝝ spirituū in corporibus hoīum existentiū ... [Romae, post 1500.] 8°. π^8. (Lea.) [630

CONNAT, FRANÇOIS DE. Francisci Connani, Parisiensis, ... Commentariorum Iuris Ciuilis libri X. argumentis ... per ... Franciscum Hotomanum exornati ... Bartholomaei Faii præfatio ... Basileae apud Nic. Episcop. iuniorem, M. D. LVII. (... mense Martio ...) fol. α-β6 a-z6 A-Zz6 AA-3M6. pp. 1-1128. (Biddle.) [631

CONRADINUS, HENNINGUS. Lacrymae Dauidis regis in morte Absolonis. f. ... VVitebergae excudebat Laurentius Schuenck. 1560. 8°. A-B8. [632

CONSILIA. [1] Consilia feudalia ... Alberti Bruni, Bartholomei Socini, Iasonis Mayni, Martini Laudens. Ioannis Campezii, Ioannis Calderini, Ioannis Neuizani, Ioannis de Ligna. Ioan. de Coconato, Bap. de S. Blasio, Io. Bar. de Sca. Astẽ. Io. Iaco. de Leonar. Ioannis Claudii, Ioan. à S. Iulia, Ioan. Anto. à Ferrar. Fran. & Ia. de Alua. Nicolai de Agatiis, Hierony. Schurpf, Sigismundi Loffre. & Gulielmi à Perno. ... Lugduni, Apud hęredes Iacobi Iuntę, M. D. LIII. fol. B.L. A-KK8 LL4. ff. 2-68. [2] Index in consilia feudalia. ... *Same imprint.* a-g8 h6. (Biddle.) [633

CONSOLATO. Libro del consolato ... con la gionta delle ordinationi sopra legni Armati, e Sicurta, e Cerca lentrate, & vscite. ... In venetia al signo della Torre. M D XLIX. (Stampato ... per Giouanni Padoano Ad instantia de Giuan Battista Pedrezzano. ...) 4°. a10 A-V8 X6 (-X6, *presumably blank*). ff. I-CLXV. (Biddle.) [634

-- Libro del consolato de' marinari, Nelquale si comprendono tutti gli statuti, & ordini disposti da gli antichi per ogni caso di Mercantia, ò di Nauigare, cosi à beneficio de' Marinari, come de' Marcanti, & Patron de' Nauilijj. Con l'aggiunta delle Ordinationi sopra l'Armate di Mare, sicurtà, entrate, & vscite. In Venetia, Per Francesco Lorenzini, M D LXIIII. 4°. a8 A-P8. ff. 1-117. ¶a2r: Giouan Battista Pedrezano salute. A1r: Nuouamente di lingua Spagnuola nella nostra Italiana tradotto ... (Lea.) [635

-- Il Consolato del mare ... In Venetia, Appresso Daniel Zanetti, & compagni. M. D. LXXVI. 4°. a8 A-P8. pp. 1-230. (Lea.) [636

CONSTANCE. Benedictionale ecclesiae, et diocoesis Constantiensis. Continens ecclesiasticas certarum rerum benedictiones, exorcismos, & Cantica nonnulla. ... Constantiae, Per Nicolaum Kalt ... M. D. XCVII. 4°. a-ll4. pp. 1-168. (Yarnall.) [636a

-- Constitutiones et decreta synodalia ciuitatis et dioecesis Constantieñ. ... M.D.LXVII. statuta ..., præsidente ... Marco Sitico ... Episcopo Constantieñ. ... (Diligae, apud Sebaldum Mayer. M. D. LXIX.) 4°. *-**4 A-Z4 a-z4 Aa-Zz4 aa-cc4 dd2. ff. 1-288. (Lea.) [637

CONSTANTINE I, emperor. Donationis, quæ Constantini dicitur priuilegium: Bartolomeo Pincerno de monte arduo ... interprete. Laurentii Vallæ ... contra ipsum, ut falso creditum & ementitum priuilegiũ declamatio: cũ Vlrichi Hutteni ... præfatione. Nicolaus de Cusa ... de donatione Constantini. Antoninus archiepiscopus Florentinus, de eadem re. R.P.D. Hieronymus Paulus Catthalanus ... de eadem donatione. [Basileae, Andreas Cratander, 1520.] 8°. A-I8 K4. (Lea.) [638

-- -- *Another copy.* [639

CONSTANTINE VII, emperor. Sapientissimi Regis Constantini Porphyrogennetæ de thematibus, Siue De Agminibus militaribus per Imperium Orientale distributis, Liber ... Ex Bibliotheca & Versione Bonauenturæ Vulcanii ... Ex officina Plantiniana, Apud Franciscum Raphelengium, cIↄ. Io. LXXXVIII. 8°. *4 A-C8 a-c8 d4. pp. 1-42, 2-34. [640

-- Libri VIII. βασιλικων διατάξεων, id est, Imperialium Constitutionum, in quibus continetur totum Ius Ciuile, à Constantino Porphyrogenneta in LX. libros redactum, Gentiano Herueto interprete. Lutetiæ Parisiorum Apud Arnulphum L'angelier ... 1557. ... (... excudebat Matthæus Dauid ... Idibus Aprilis.) fol. *4 a-z6 A-F6 G4. pp. 2-356. [641

CONSTANTINOPLE. Abschrifft ains bryeffs von Constantinopel/ Auss wëlchem man zů vernemen hat/ wëlcher gestalt der Gross Tůrck seine Priester vnd Doctores hat lassen ũbringen ... M D XXXIX. (Getruckt zů Augspurg durch Melchior Ramĩnger.) 4°. A4. ¶*Translated from the Italian.* [642

-- Dernieres Nouuelles De Constantinople, faisans mẽtion d'vn grand & merueilleux accident ... A Paris. Par Federic Morel ... 1575. ... 8°. A4. [643

CONSTANTIUS, ANTONIUS. In hoc uolumine contenta hæc sunt Antonii Constantii epigrammatum libellus [*and other works*]. ... (Hoc Soncinus opus Fanestri impressit in urbe ... Mille & quingentis annis ... atq3 duobus: Et quarta octobris ...) 4°. π^2 a-b^8 c-n^4 o^8. ¶n1^r: Iacobi Constantii epigrammata quædam Eiusdem epicedion in Thadæam matrem. [644

CONSTANTIUS, JACOBUS. Iacobi Constantii Fanensis. Collectaneorum Hecatostys Prima ... In Ibin Ouidii Sarritiones annotationum ultra centum. In Eiusdem methamorphoses assumenta: annotationum supra ter centum. Impressa Fani ab Hieronymo Soncino. (... Sexto idus Iulias. MDVIII.) 4°. π^6 A-L^8 M^6. [645

CONTARINI, FRANCESCO. La fida ninfa Fauola Pastorale ... In Venetia, Appresso Giacomo Vincenti. M. D. XCVIII. 8°. a^8 A-K^8 L^4 (-L4, *presumably blank*). ff. 1-83. [646

CONTARINI, GASPARO. Gasparis Contareni ... de Elementis & eorum mixtionibus libri quinque. ... Scipionis Capitij de principiis rerum poēma. ... Parisiis, Apud Andream Wechelum. 1564. 8°. A-R^8. ff. 2-128. [647

-- La republica, e i magistrati di Vinegia, ... nuouamente fatti uolgari. ... In Vinegia, appresso Girolamo Scottò. M.D.XLIIII. (*Colophon.*) 8°. A-I^8. ff. II-LXX. [648

-- -- The commonwealth and Gouernment of Venice. ... translated out of Italian into English, by Lewes Lewkenor Esquire. ... VVith sundry other Collections, annexed by the Translator ... With a short Chronicle ... of the liues and raignes of the Venetian Dukes ... London Imprinted by Iohn Windet for Edmund Mattes ... 1599. 4°. ❦^{4} A-Gg^4. *S.T.C.* 5642. (Furness.) [649

CONTARINI, GIOVANNI PIETRO. Ioan. Petri Contareni Veneti historiae de bello nuper Venetiis a Selimo II. Turcarum imperatore illato, liber vnus. Ex Italico sermone in latinum conuersus, a Ioan. Nicolao Stupano ... Basileæ per Petrum Pernam, Anno M.D.LXXIII. 4°. *^{4} **^{2} A-S^4 T^2 (T2 + *folded leaf*). pp. 1-147. ¶**2 *bound, in reverse order, after* T1. [650

CONTARINI, LUIGI. [1] Il vago, e diletteuo[le] giardino ... Et in questa terza editione ... emendato. In Vicenza, Appresso gli Heredi di Perin Libraro. 1597. 8°. ✠^{6} A-Hh^8 Ii^4 Kk-Mm^8 Nn^4. pp. 1-504. ¶✠1 *defective.* [2] Aggiunta Al vago, e dilletteuole giardino ... In Vicenza, Appresso gli Heredi di Perin Libraro. M D XCVI. ... A^4 ††^{8} A-P^8 Q^{4+1}. ff. 1-124. [651

CONTI, ANTONIO MARIA DE'. M. Antonii Maioragii, commentarius in dialogum De Partitione Oratoria M. Tullij Ciceronis. Opera ... Io. Petri Ayroldi Marcellini Mediolanensis ... in propriam faciem versus ... Venetiis, M D LXXXVII. Apud Franciscum Franciscium Senensem. (... apud Nicolaum Morettum. M. D. LXXXVI.) 4°. *-**^{4} A-Xx^4 Yy^6 (-Yy6, *presumably blank*) a-e^4. ff. 1-181. [652

-- M. Antonii Maioragii, commentarius in dialogum, seu lib. primum de oratore Ad Q. Fratrem M. Tullij Ciceronis. ... Io. Petri Ayroldi Marcellini Mediolanensis ... industria in lucem prolatus. ... Venetiis, M D LXXXVII. Apud Franciscum Franciscium Senensem. 4°. *^{4} A-Ss^4 a-c^4. pp. 1-7, ff. 5-165. [653

-- M. Antonii Maioragii Orationes, & Præfationes omnes; Nunc primum à Io. Petro Ayroldo ... edita: Vna cum Dialogo ipsius Maioragij de eloquentia ... Venetiis, Apud Angelum Bonfadium M D LXXXII. 4°. *^{6} A-$3D^4$ $3E^6$. ff. 1-210. [654

-- Antonii Comitis pro Decreto ... Alphonsi Auali Istonii Marchionis, & ... Senatus Mediolanensis, in Aleatores Oratio. ... Mediolani [Andrea Calvo,] M.D.XXXXI. 4°. A-D^4. [655

CONTI, ASCANIO. Ascanii Comitis Spolentini ... Præfationes Sex in omnes Aristotelis libros Philosophiæ Naturalis ... Venetiis, Apud Gratiosum Perchacinum, MDLXX. 4°. A-Dd^4 Ee^2. ff. 2-102. [656

CONTI, GIUSTO DE'. Rime ... intitolato la bella mano. ... M. D. XXXI. (Stampata in Vinegia per maestro Bernardino di Vidali ... A di XX. del mese di Settembrio.) 8°. a-r^4 s^2. ff. 2-66. [657

CONTI, NATALE. Commentarii Hieronymi Comitis Alexandrini de ... Turcarum bello, in Insulam

Melitam gesto, Anno M. D. LXV. Noribergæ Excudebant Vlricus Neuberus, & Theodoricus Gerlatzen. M. D. LXVI. 8°. a-b^8 A-I^8. ff. 1-71. ¶*Additional t.p.* (H7^r): Insulæ Melitae descriptio ... F. Ioan. Quintini ... M.D.LXVI. [658

-- Ναταλιος των Κομιτων του Ενετου περὶ ὥρων βιβλίον ἕν. Natalis Comitum Veneti de horis liber unus. Eiusdem de anno libri quatuor. Myrmicomyamachiae libri quatuor. Amatoriarum Elegiarum libri duo. Eiusdem Elegiæ sex. Impressum Venetijs, per Fratres de Nicolinis de Sabio ... MDL. mense Septembri. (*Colophon.*) 8°. A-T^8 V^{10}. ff. 2-160. [659

CONTILE, LUCA. Comedia del Contile chiamata la Cesarea Gonzaga. ... (In Milano per Francesco Marchesino. Il Di .X. D'ottobre. 1550.) 4°. π^2 A-P^4. ff. 2-50. [660

-- La nice ..., Breuemente comentata dal Signor Caualiero Vendramini. (In Milano Per Valerio, & Girolamo fratelli da Meda. Adi 6. del mese de Luglio, MDLI.) 4°. A-H^4 I^2. ff. I-XXX. [661

-- [1] Il primo volume delle lettere ... In Venetia. M D LXIIII. 8°. *^{8} A-Y^8. ff. 1-176. [2] Il secondo volume delle lettere ... In V[enetia.] M D [LXIIII.] *^{8} **^{4} a-z^8 Aa-Ee^8. ff. 1-222. ¶*1-2 *defective.* [662

-- Le rime ..., con discorsi, et argomenti di M. Francesco Patritio, et M. Antonio Borghesi. ... In Venetia, appresso Francesco Sansouino, et compagni. MDLX. (*Colophon.*) 8°. *^{4} A-N^8 O^4. ff. 1-108. [663

CONTINUATIO. [Continuatio cantionum sacrarum ... de fetis praecipuis anni ... Cantus. Norimbergae, Katharina Gerlach, 1588.] 4°. a-o^4 (-a^4). (Music.) [664

CONTRERAS, ALFONSO. Oratio ad patres in ... Synodo Tridentina. ... Habita ... Domimica [*sic*] II. Qaadragesimæ. [*sic*] M D LXIII. Ad Ecclesiæ reformationem persuadendam. Birxiae [*sic*] Ad instantiam Io: Baptistæ Bozolæ. M. D. LXIII. (... Apud Ludouicum Sabiensem. ...) 4°. A-B^4. (Lea.) [665

CONVENTI, STEFANO. Ad reuerendissi.^{um} Ioannem Baptistam Campegium ... De Intrinsecis Corporum Coelestium principijs, Sectionæs Duæ. Bononiæ, apud Alexandrum Benacium. M. D. LXI. 8°. π^4 A-M^8 N^4. ff. 1-97. [666

COOPER, THOMAS. [Thesaurus linguae Romanæ & Britannicæ ... Accessit dictionarium historicum et poeticum propria vocabula ... Excusum Londini in aedibus quondam Bertheleti ... per Henricum VVykes. ... 1565. 16. Martij.] fol. (*)^6 (-(*)1-3, (*)6, *the last blank*) A-6S^6 A-R^6 (-R6, *presumably blank*). *S.T.C.* 5686. [667

-- -- Impressum Londini. 1573. fol. ¶^{6} (-¶1, *presumably blank*) A-Y^6 Aa-Yy^6 3A-3Y^6 4A-4Y^6 5A-5Y^6 6A-6V^6 7D-7O^6 7P-7Q^4. *S.T.C.* 5687. (Furness.) [668

-- -- Thesaurus ... toties aucta Eliotæ Bibliotheca opera & industria Thomæ Cooperi Magdalensis. ... Impressum Londini. 1578. fol. ¶^{6} (-¶1, *blank*) A-Y^6 Aa-Yy^6 3A-3Y^6 4A-4Y^6 5A-5Y^6 6A-6V^6 7D-7O^6 7P-7Q^4 (-7Q4, *presumably blank*). *S.T.C.* 5688. [669

COPERNICUS, NICOLAUS. Nicolai Copernici Torinensis de reuolutionibus orbium coelestium, Libri VI. ... Item, de libris reuolutionum Nicolai Copernici Narratio prima, per M. Georgium Ioachimum Rheticum ... scripta. ... Basileae, ex officina Henricpetrina [September 1566]. fol. π^6 a-z^4 A-Ff^4 Gg^6 (-Dd-Ff^4, Gg1-5). ff. 1-196 *present.* ¶*With variant setting of* D2-3. [670

COPIA. Copia delle lettere venute de diuersi Paesi. Per le quali se intende il successo della guerra contra il Turco ... In Pauia ... [c. 1570.] 8°. A^4. [671

COPPETTA DE BECCUTI, FRANCESCO. Rime ... In Venetia, Appresso Domenico, & Gio. Battista Guerra, fratelli. M D LXXX. 8°. A-N^8 (-N8, *presumably blank*). pp. 1-188. [672

COPTIUS, FRANCISCUS. Francisci Coptii Narniensis ad Caesarem oratio pro Christiana repu. de concordia principum aduersus Turcas. (Impressum Romæ ... per Magistrum Marcellum [Silber] die octaua Augusti. M.D.xxiii.) 4°. A-C^4. [673

COPUS, MARTINUS. Das Spissglas Antimonium oder Stibium genandt ... D. Martini Copi ... Anno M. D. LXIX. 4°. A-G^4. (Smith.) [674

CORAS, JEAN DE. Ioannis Corasii ... de iuris arte libellus ... Coloniae, Apud Maternum Cholinum. 1563. 8°. $*^8$ a-z^8 A^8. pp. 1-366. [675

-- Ioannis Corasii Tolosatis ... in titulum ff. de seruitutibus, commentarii, hac secunda editione ... purgati ... Lugduni, Apud Guliel. Rouillium ... M. D. LII. ... (... excudebat Philibertus Rolletius.) 8°. a-z^8 A-F^8. pp. 3-439. (Biddle.) [676

-- Ioannis Corasii ... in vniuersam sacerdotiorum materiam ... paraphrasis ... Parrisiis Apud Arnoldum l'Angelier ... 1549. (Excudebat Franciscus Girault ...) 8°. a^4 A-Q^8. ff. 1-114. [677

CORDIER, MATHURIN. De syllabarū quãtitate, regulae speciales, quas Despauterius in carmen nõ redegit. ... Parisiis, Væneunt apud Simonem Colinæum. 1540. 8°. a-d^8. [678

CORDUS, EURICIUS. Opera poetica ... 1564 Franc. Apud Haered. Chr. Egen. 8°. A-Z^8 a-o^8. pp. 2-286. [679

CORDUS, VALERIUS. Valerii Cordi Simesusii de halosantho seu spermate ceti vulgo dicto, liber ... Tiguri [Jacobus Gesner,] M.D.LXVI. 8°. α-$ε^8$. ff. 2-37. (Smith.) [680

CORIO, BERNARDINO. L'historia di Milano volgarmente scritta ... Con le vite insiemi di tutti gli Imperatori ... In Vinegia, per Giouan Maria Bonelli, M D LIIII. (*Colophon.*) 4°. 1^6 2-4^8 5^4 a-z^8 A-QQ^8 RR^4 SS-ZZ^8 $3A^{10}$ (-3A10, *presumably blank*). ff. 1-557. [681

-- -- ... Con vn breue sommario di Thomaso Porcacchi ... della cose successe fino a questi tempi ... In Vinegia presso Giorgio de' Caualli, M D LXV. 4°. †-5$†^4$ A-$6Z^4$ a-r^4. pp. 1-1262. (Lea.) [682

CORNAGIA, BERNARDO. Vita sancti Benedicti. ... [post 1500?] 4°. A-B^8 C^4. ¶*In verse.* [683

CORNARIUS, JANUS. Iani Cornarii ... Zuiccauiensis, De Conuiuiorum ueterū Græcorum, & hoc tempere Germanorum ritibus, moribus ac sermonibus: item de Amoris præstantia, & de Platonis ac Xenophontis dissensione, Libellus. Item, Platonis ... Symposium, eodē Iano Cornario interprete. Et, Xenophontis ... Symposium, ab eodem latinè conscriptum. Basileae. (... ex officina Ioannis Oporini, Anno M.D.XLVIII Mense Septembri.) 8°. a-m^8 n^4. pp. 3-198. [684

CORNAZZANO, ANTONIO. Cornazano de re militari ... (In Vinegia. Nelle case di Pietro di Nicolini da Sabbio. ... M. D. XXXVI. del mese di Marzo.) 8°. A-Z^8. ff. 3-183. [685

-- Opera Noua ... ĩ terza rima: laq̄l tratta. De modo regēdi. De motu Fortũe. De ĩtegritate rei Militaris: ⁊ qui in re militari Imperatores excelluerint. ... (Impressa in Venetia per Nicolo Zoppino & Vincentio compagni. ... M.D.XVIII. Adi .XIII. del mese de Septembre.) 8°. A-C^8 D^6 E-H^8 I^{10}. [686

-- Antonii Cornazani placentini ... quod de prouerbiorum origine inscribitur ... (Impressum Ml'i per Petrũmartirem de mantegatiis ... M.ccccciii. die ultimo septēbris.) 4°. $π^2$ a-f^8 g^4 h^6. ff. i-lvii. [687

-- Soneti e Canzone ... (Stampata in ... Vinetia per ... Manfredo de Monteferato. M.CCCCCIII. adi .X. Febraro.) 8°. a-b^8. [688

-- La Vita ⁊ Passione de Christo: Composta ... in Terza Rima ... (Stampata in Venetia per Nicolo dicto Zopino: & Vincentio compagni. ... M.D.XVIII. Adi .V. del mese de Septembre.) 8°. A-G^8 H^4. [689

CORNEJO, PEDRO. Della historia de Fiandra, di Pietro Cornelio libri X. ... Nouamente Tradotta di Spagnuolo in lingua Italiana da Camillo Camilli. ... In Brescia, appresso Pietro Maria Marchetti. M. D. LXXXIII. (... per Vincenzo Sabbio, ad instanza di Pietro Maria Marchetti. M. D. LXXXII.) 4°. $♣^4$ A-Ff^4 Gg^2. pp. 1-233. (Lea.) [690

CORNEO, PIERFILIPPO. Aurea ... commentaria ... in sextũ librum Codicis Cum additionibus ... Lanceloti Decij ... autẽ ... Henrici Ferrandat Niuernensis ... (Impressa lugduni in edibus ... Ioannis de Ionuelle. alias piston. ... Sumptib⁹ ... Vincentij de portonaris ...

Anno ... millesimo quĩgentesimo decimo nono. die xviij. mensis Maij.) fol. B.L. a^8 $b\text{-}z^6$ $A\text{-}F^6$ Aa^6 Bb^4. ff. II-CLXXV. (Biddle.) [691

-- [Consilia.] (Impresse perusij ... impensis ... Petripauli ac Iulijcesaris ... filioꝝ ... diligentia Frãcisci baldasaris ...) fol. B.L. [1] Tabula Primi uoluminis ɔsilioꝝ ... (... Mccccci. die .x. Martij.) A^{10} $a\text{-}z^8$ ⁊^{8} ɔ^8 ꝝ^8 $aa\text{-}oo^8$ pp^{10}. ff. 2-329. [2] Tabula Secundi uoluminis ɔsilioꝝ ... AA^8 BB^6. [3] Secundum uolumen cõsilioꝝ ... (... Mccccci. die .vij. Septembris) $A\text{-}MM^8$ NN^{10}. ff. 2-289. [4] Tabula tertii uoluminis ... AA^8 BB^{10}. [5] Tertium volumen ... (M.cccccij. die .xiiij. Aprilis.) $3a\text{-}3z^8$ 3⁊^{8} 3ɔ^8 3ꝝ^8 $3A\text{-}3Q^8$ $3R^6$. ff. 2-341. [6] Quartum Volumen ... (... M.cccccij. die .xxvij. octobris.) $4a\text{-}4z^8$ 4⁊^{8} 4ɔ^8 4ꝝ^8 $4A\text{-}4M^8$ $4N\text{-}4O^6$. ff. 2-315. [7] Tabula Quarti uoluminis ... $4A^8$ $4B^{10}$. (Biddle.) [692

CORRADO, MATTEO. Speculum cõfesorum & lumẽ conscientie continens plenã normã cõfitẽdi & examinãdi ... editũ ꝑ ... Matheum Corradonũ de Cilentio. ... (Venetiis per Alexander de Vianis Venetian. M.D.LIIII.) 8°. $A\text{-}G^8$ (-G8, *presumably blank*). ff. 2-55. (Lea.) [693

CORREGIA, NICCOLÒ DA. Opere ... intitulate la Psyche & la Aurora. ... (Impressa in Venetia ꝑ Georgio de Rusconi Milanese. ... M.ccccc.xy. Adi .xx. Decembrio.) 8°. $A\text{-}M^4$. ¶G4^r: Fabula di Cephalo ... [694

CORROZET, GILLES. Les antiquitez croniques et singularitez de Paris ... augmentees; Par N. B. Parisien. A Paris, Par Galiot Corrozet ... 1586. ... (... De l'Imprimerie de Nicolas Bonfons ...) 8°. ã^8 *^{8} $A\text{-}Cc^8$ Dd^4. ff. 212. ¶*Lacks part 2.* [695

-- Icones historiarum Veteris Testamenti ... Lugduni, Apud Ioannem Frellonium, 1547. (*Colophon.*) 4°. $A\text{-}N^4$. [696

-- -- The images of the Old Testament, Lately expressed, set forthe in Ynglishe and French ... Printed at Lyons, by Iohan Frellon, ... 1549. 4°. $A\text{-}N^4$. *S.T.C.* 3045. [697

-- Les propos memorables des Nobles & illustres hõmes de la Chrestienté. ... A Paris, Par Nicolas Bõfons ... 16°. $A\text{-}T^8$. ff. 2-145. [698

CORSETTI, ANTONIO. Repertorium Antonii corseti in Abbatem (Impressuȝ Mediolani ꝑ magistrum Iohãnẽ Angelũ Scinzenzeler Ad ĩpẽsis Magistri Iohãnis de Lignano. ... Mccccci. die .xviiij. mensis Octob.) fol. B.L. $A\text{-}Z^8$ ⁊^{8} ɔ^8 ꝝ^8 $A\text{-}F^8$ $G\text{-}H^6$. (Biddle.) [699

CORSI, PIETRO. Ad humani generis seruatorem in vrbis Romae excidio P. Cursii ciuis Rom. deploratio. Parisiis ex officina Roberti Stephani ... M.D.XXVIII. (... mense Maio.) 8°. A^{10}. [700

-- Petri Cursii ciuis Ro. defensio pro Italia ad Erasmum Roterodamum. (Impressum Romæ apud Antoniũ Bladum de Asula. ... M.D.XXXV.) 4°. $A\text{-}I^4$ k^4 (-k4, *blank*). [701

-- Cursii panegyris de foedere inter Iulium .II. Pont: Max: et Hispan. regem. 4°. π^4. ¶*Preface dated* ꝑdie kal'. Nouẽ. M.D.XI. *In verse.* [702

CORSO, ANTON' GIACOMO. Le rime ... A San Luca al segno della Cognitione. (In Vinegia per Comin da Trino di Monferrato L'anno M. D. L.) 8°. $A\text{-}K^8$. ff. 2-76. [703

CORSO, RINALDO. Fondamenti del parlar Thoscano. ... In Venetia [per Melchiore Sessa, c. 1550]. 8°. $A\text{-}N^8$. ff. 2-104. [704

-- -- In Roma per Antonio Blado. 1564. 8°. $A\text{-}N^8$. pp. 3-207. [705

CORTESE, ISABELLA. I secreti ... In Venetia, Appresso Giouanni Bariletto. 1574. (*Colophon.*) 8°. †^{8} $A\text{-}N^8$. pp. 1-207. (Smith.) [706

CORTI, FRANCESCHINO. [1] Do. Francischini Curtii iunioris repertorium. M.D.XXXIIII. fol. B.L. $A\text{-}C^6$ D^4. [2] Consilia ... M. D. XXXIIII. (sumptibus ... Vincentij de Portonarijs de Tridino de monte Ferrato: ac Iacobi Giunte Florentini. Excusa fuere Lugduni apud Ioannem Moylin al's de Cambray.) $a\text{-}q^6$ $A\text{-}X^6$. ff. 2-95, 1-125. (Biddle.) [707

-- Francischinus Curtius iunior de feudis. [*Device of Jacobus Giunti.*] 1534 (Excu. Lugduni typis Nicolai Parui ⁊ Hectoris Penet.) fol. B.L. ^{6} $a\text{-}h^6$. ff. 1-47. (Biddle.) [708

-- ... Francischini Curtij Iunioris Tractatus Feudalis ... Lugduni apud haeredes Iacobi Giunta. M. D. XLVII. (... Excudebant Petrus Compater, & Blasius Guido. ...) 8°. a-z⁸ A-M⁸ N¹⁰. pp. 2-525. (Biddle.) [709

CORTI, FRANCESCO. Consilia francisci curtii ... (... per Andream Torresanum de Asula ... Venetijs ... Impressum. ... Mcccccij. Die .xv. Martij.) fol. B.L. 3a-3v⁸ 3x¹⁰ 3y⁸ 3z¹⁰. ff. 2-186. (Biddle.) [710

CORVINUS, ANTONIUS. Ludus Syluani Hessi in defectionem Georgij Vuicelij ad Papistas. Cum Præfatione Iusti Ionæ. ... Vitenbergae. 1534. (Excusum ... per Nicolaum Schirlentz.) 4°. A-E⁴. [711

CORVINUS, ELIAS. Eliæ Coruini Ioachimici poëmatum libri duo. ... 1568. (Lipsiæ excudebat Ioannes Rhamba. Typis Voegelianis.) 8°. A-P⁸. pp. 3-279. [712

CORVINUS, LAURENTIUS. Latinum ideoma ... (Impressum Liptzk per Melchiorem Lotter. ... M.ccccc.viiij.) 4°. B.L. A⁸ B⁶. [713

COSIN, RICHARD. [1] An apologie for sundrie proceedings by Iurisdiction Ecclesiasticall ... Imprinted at London by the Deputies of Christopher Barker ... 1593. 4°. A-V⁴. pp. 1-130. [2] The second part of an apologie ... Imprinted at London by the Deputies of Christopher Barker ... Aa-Tt⁴. pp. 1-140. [3] The third part ... *Same imprint.* [A]² B-Kk⁴. pp. 1-256. *S.T.C.* 5821. ¶Ii1ᵛ: Quæstionis: nunquid per ius Diuinum, Magistratui liceat, a Reo Iusiurandum exigere? ... Theologica Determinatio: ... Per Lancelotum Andrevvs ... (Biddle.) [714

-- -- *Another copy* (-A⁴; *possibly S.T.C.* 5822). [715

COSMIO, FILOTERO. Clarice comedia ... In Venetia, Appresso Domenico Imberti. M. D. XC. 12°. A-H¹². ff. 2-75. [716

COUSTEAU, PIERRE. Petri Costalii de pace carmen. Parisiis, Apud Annetum Briere ... 1559. 4°. A-B⁴ (-B4, *blank*). [717

-- Le pegme de Pierre Coustau, auec les Narrations Philosophiques, Mis de Latin en Françoys par Lanteaume de Romieu Gentilhome d'Arles. A Lyon, par Macé Bonhome ... M. D. LX. ... (*Colophon.*) 8°. A-CC⁸ DD⁴. pp. 3-416. [718

COVARRUVIAS À LEYVA, DIEGO. [1] Didaci Couarruuias a Leyua Toletani ... Opera omnia ... tomus primus. Venetiis, Apud Hæredem Hieronymi Scoti, M D LXXXI. fol. *-**⁶ ***⁸ A-3K⁶ 3L⁴ (-3L4, *presumably blank*). pp. 1-678. [2] ... Operum Tomus Secundus. *Same imprint.* A⁸ B-3C⁶ 3D⁸. pp. 1-593. (Lea.) [719

COVERDALE, MILES. Certain most godly, fruitful, and comfortable letters of such true Saintes and holy Martyrs of God, as in the late bloodye persecution ... gaue their lyues for the defence of Christes holy gospel ... Imprinted at London by Iohn Day, ... 1564. ... (*Colophon.*) 4°. B.L. A⁴ B-Y⁸ Aa-Xx⁸ Yy⁶ ☞Y⁶. pp. 2-689. *S.T.C.* 5886. [720

-- A Christian exhortacion vnto customable Swearers. ... Imprinted at London by Iohn Awdeley. 1575 (*Colophon.*) 8°. B.L. A-D⁸ (-D8, *presumably blank*). *S.T.C.* 1286. [721

CRAMER, DANIEL. Danielis Crameri isagoge In metaphysicam Aristotelis ... Hanouiæ Apud Guilielmum Antonium, MDXCIIII. 8°. A-P⁸. pp. 3-235. ¶A1 *defective.* [722

-- Tyrocinium apologeticum Danielis Crameri, Pro Præceptore suo Dn. D. Polycarpo Lysero, ad vindicandam Historiam Iesuitici ordinis, ab Eliâ Hasenmullero conscriptam: Solidè oppositum futili Apologiæ Iesuiticæ, à Petro Steuarcio Leodio ... 1594. VVitebergae, Typis M. Georgij Mullerj. Sumptibus Andreæ Hoffmanni. 4°.)(⁴ A-L⁴. pp. 1-88. [723

CRANTZ, ALBERT. Dennmärckische Chronick/ Alberti Krantzij von Hamburg. Newlich durch Henrich von Eppendorff verteütschet. ... Zů Strassburg bey Hans Schotten. M. D. xlv. (... vff den .iij. des Hornungs. ...) fol. A⁴ a-vv⁶ (-vv6, *presumably blank*). pp. j-diiij. [724

-- Alberti Crantzii ... metropolis, siue historiae ecclesiasticae Saxoniae libri XII. ... Coloniae, in ędibus Quentelianis. Anno M. D. XCVI. ... 8°. †a-†e^8 †f^4 a-3i^8. pp. 1-854. [725

-- [a1^r] Saxonia Alberti Krantz Coloniae impressa [per Johannem Soter] MDXX. (... mense Maio ...) fol. π^8 a^8 b-z^6 A-S^6. ¶*Half-title* (π1): Saxonia. [726

-- -- ... Cum praefatione Nicolai Cisneri ... Francofurti ad Moenum apud A. Wechelum, M. D. LXXX. (*Colophon.*) fol. ā^6 ē^6 a-z^6 A-H^6 I-K^4. pp. 1-354. [727

-- [a1^r] Wandalia Alberti Krantz Coloniae impressa MDXVIIII. (Mense Aprili. ... Iohannes Soter alias Heil ex Bentzheim, & Socij impresserunt.) fol. π^6 a^8 b-s^6 t-v^8 A-T^6. ¶*Additional t.p.* (π1): Wandalia in qua de Wandalorum populis ... Coloniae Agrippinae ... MDXVIIII. Mense Septembri. [728

-- -- Francofurti, Ex officina typographica Andreæ Wecheli, M. D. LXXX. (*Colophon.*) fol. Aa-3G^6 3H^4. pp. 1-338. [729

-- [1] Vandaliæ & Saxoniæ Alberti Cranzii continuatio. Ab anno Christi 1500. ... Per studiosum quendam historiarum instituta. Accessit metropolis seu episcoporum ... Catalogus ... Cum Præfatione Dauidis Chytræi ... VVittebergæ Typis hæredum Iohannis Cratonis Anno M. D. LXXXVI. fol. A^8 B^{6+2} C-Ff^6. pp. 5 [=2]-338. [2] Dauidis Chytraei prooemium metropolis. ... Anno M. D. LXXXV. a-d^6. pp. 3-48. [730

CRASTONUS, JOANNES. Dictionarium Graecum, ultra Ferrariensem æditionem locupletatum ... Cyrilli opusculum, de dictionibus, quæ accentu uariant significatum. Ammonius de similitudine ac differentia dictionū. De re militari ueterum, & nominibus præfectorū, libellus græcus, incerto autore. Orbicii, de ordinibus exercitus. ... Dictionarium, quo latina græcis exponuntur. Basileae. An. M. D. XIX. (... apud Andream Cartandrum. Mense Martio. ...) fol. a-z^6 Aa-Bb^6 Cc^8 A-C^6 D^8 E-Q^6. ff. 2-168, 1-95. [731

CRATEPOIL, PETER. Catalogus academiarum, id est, celebrium vniuersitatum orbis Christiani ... Operâ F. Petri M. Cratepolei ... Coloniae Agrippinae, Apud God[ef]ridum Kempensem. Anno M.D.XCIII. (*Colophon.*) 8°. A-G^8 H^4 (-H4, *presumably blank*). pp. 3-167. ¶*T.p. defective.* [732

-- Speculum humanæ vitæ, hoc est: de virtutibus, vitiis, eorumque remediis libellus. Auctore Fr. Petro Opmersensi Cratepolio ... Coloniae Apud Ioannem â Mertzenich. Anno M. D. C. 8°. A-Q^8. pp. 3-237. (Lea.) [733

CRAVETTA, AYMO. [1] Aymonis Crauettae a Sauiliano ... Consiliorum, siue Responsorum, tomus tertius ... 1589. Francofurdi Apud Ioan. Wechelum, impensis Sigismundi Feyrabendii. fol. π^2 A-3C^6 3D^4. pp. 1-595. [2] ... tomus quartus. ... *Same imprint.* (*Colophon.*) a^4 A-Pp^6 Qq^8. pp. 1-470. (Lea.) [734

-- Tractatus de antiquitatibus temporum ... Lugduni, Apud Hæredes Iacobi Iuntæ, 1559. (Excudebat Hector Penet.) 8°. a-z^8 A-V^8. ff. 1-309. [735

CREMA. Municipalia Cremae. (Excudebat Venetiis Aurelius Pincius Venetus. Anno. M. D. XXXVI.) fol. ✠^{10} A^4 B-R^8 S^{10} (-S10, *presumably blank*). ff. 1-140. ¶✠10^v: Municipalium Cremae liber primus extraordinariorum incipit. (Lea.) [736

CREMONA. Prouisiones Victualium ... ciuitatis Cremonę nouiter reformate. Cremonae apud Vincentium Conctum MDLXIII. (*Colophon.*) 4°. A-C^4. pp. 4-21. [737

-- Statuta ciuitatis Cremonae ... Cremonæ, ... M. D. LXXVIII. (... Apud Christophorum Draconium ... & Petrum Bozolam, socios. ...) fol. *^{6} A-Gg^6 Hh^4. pp. 1-311. (Lea.) [738

-- *Compagnia di Santa Maria di Misericordia.* Capitoli, regole, Ordini, Priuilegij, & Indulgenze della Cōpagnia di Sta Maria di Misericordia ... In Cremona, Appresso Christoforo Draconi, 1599. ... 4°. A-E^4. pp. 3-39. [739

CREMONA TERZANI, GIOVANNI FRANCESCO. Oratio ad ... Gregorium ... papam XIV. pro ... duce Ferrariæ Alfonso II. Estensi ... Romæ, IX. Kal. Martij. M. D. XCI. ... Romae, Ex Typographia Vincentij Accolti ... 4°. A^6. [740

CRENNE, HÉLISENNE DE. Les Angoysses Dolouréuses qui procedent Damours: composees par Dame Helisenne. Premiere Partie. De Crenne. [1539.] 8°. A-H^8 AA-II^8 3A-3D^8 3E^2 a^8. ¶*Additional t.pp.:* (AA1^r) La seconde partie des Angoysses douloureuses ... (3A1^r) La tierce partie ... [741

-- -- [1541.] 8°. A-H^8 (-A1, C4-5) I^4 AA-II^8 kk^2 3A-3D^8 3E^6. [742

CRESCENZI, PIETRO DE. De omnibus agriculturæ partibus, & de Plantarum animaliumq; natura & utilitate lib. XII. ... Per ... Petrum Crescentiensem ... Basileæ per Henrichum Petri. (... mense Martio, anno M. D. XLVIII.) fol. a^6 A-Kk^6. pp. 1-385. [743

-- Pietro Crescentio d'agricoltura. ... In Venetia. M D XLII. (Stampato ... per Bernardino Bindoni. ...) 8°. A-ZZ^8 ❦^{8}. [744

-- -- In Venetia. (... per li heredi di Ioanne Padouano. M. D. LIII.) 8°. A-TT^8 VV^6. ff. 2-335. [745

-- -- Pietro Crescentio tradotto ... per M. Francesco Sansouino nel quale si trattano le cose della villa ... In Venetia Apresso Francesco Rampazetto M D LXIIII. (*Colophon.*) 8°. *^{8} A-3O^8 (-3O8, *presumably blank*). ff. 1-481. ¶*T.p. repaired.* [746

CRESPIN, JEAN. Acta martyrum, eorum videlicet, qui hoc seculo in Gallia, Germania, Anglia, Flandria, Italia, constans dederunt nomen Euangelio, idque sanguine suo obsignarunt: ab Wicleffo & Husso ad huncvsque diem. ... Apud Io. Crispinum. Anno M. D. LVI. (... Geneuae ... Cal. Martii.) 8°. *^{8} a-z^8 A-C^8 aa-rr^8. pp. 1-279. (Lea.) [747

-- -- Actiones et Monimenta Martyrum ... Geneuæ, Ioannes Crispinus. M. D. LX. 4°. α-β^8 γ^2 A^4 B-V^8 X^4 Y-Ss^8. ff. 1-321. (Lea.) [748

-- -- *Another copy.* (Lea.) [749

CRIGINGER, JOHANN. Die Historia vom Reichen man vnd armen Lazaro ... Mit Zweien schönen Vorreden/ D. Wolffgangi Pfentnerj ... M. D. LV. ... (Gedruckt zu Dressden durch Matthes Stöckel ...) 4°. A-Y^4 Z^2 a^4. ¶*Play in verse.* [750

CRINITO, PIETRO. Petri Criniti ... de Honesta disciplina libri XXV. De poëtis Latinis eiusdem libri V. Poëmatum quoq3 illius libri II. ... Basileae excudebat Henricus Petrus. (... mense Augusto, anno M. D. XXXII.) 4°. a-g^4 h^2 A-Zz^4 AA-ZZ^4 Aaa-Ddd^4. pp. 1-575. [751

CRISPUS, JOHANNES. Ioannis Crispi ... ad Pont. Romanum, & Christianos Principes epistola. 4°. A-B^4. ¶B3^v: Datæ Cal. Decemb. ... M. D. XXXVII. (Lea.) [752

CROLLEUS, DAVID. Carmen de agno Paschali. ... Rostochii. Ex Officina Ludouici Ditij. M.D.LVIII. 8°. A-B^8. [753

CROMER, MARTIN. De falsa Lutheranorum, siue euangelicorum nostri temporis, et vera Christi religione libri duo ... Parisiis, Apud Gulielmum Guillard & Almaricum Warancore ... 1561 8°. ā^4 A-Q^8 R^4. ff. 1-125. [754

-- Martini Cromeri de origine et rebus gestis Polonorum libri XXX. ... Funebris eiusdem autoris Oratio, Sigismundo Regis uitam ... complexa ... Accessit iudicium Francisci Robortelli Vtinensis, de authore & libro. ... Basileae, ex officina Oporiniana. 1568. (... mense Augusto.) fol. α^6 a-z^6 A-V^6 X^8. pp. 2-468. [755

CROMPTON, RICHARD. L'authoritie et iurisdiction des courts de la maiestie de la Roygne ... Londini. In ædibus Caroli Yetsweirti ... 1594. (*Colophon.*) 4°. B.L. A-B^4 C-GG^8 HH^4. ff. 1-232. *S.T.C.* 6050. ¶*T.p. mounted.* (Biddle.) [756

CRONBERG, HARTMUTH VON. Ein Sendbrieff an Bapst Adrianum/ darynn ... angezaygt würt ein sicherer haylsamer weg zů aussreüttūg aller Ketzereyen/ vnd zů haylsamer rettung gantzer Christenhait von des Türcken tyranney. ... Wittemberg [Lukas Cranach & Christian Doering]. M.D.xxiij. 4°. A^4 B^2. [757

CROTTI, ELIO GIULIO. Aelii Iulii Crotti Cremonensis opuscula. ... Ferrariae Excudebat

Valens Panicius Mantuanus ... MDLXIIII. (... Dominico Mammarellio auspice) 8°. A-V^{8}. pp. 1-304. [758

CRUSIUS, MARTINUS. Germano-Græcicæ libri sex: In quorum prioribus tribus, Orationes: in reliquis Carmina, Græca & Latina, continentur. Ob Græcæ linguæ studium ... editi. ... Basileæ, per Leonardum Ostenium, Sebastiani Henricpetri impensa [1585]. fol. (:)^{8} a-z^{6} A-F^{6} G^{4} H^{6}. pp. 1-355. (Lea.) [759

-- Martini Crusii ... libri duo ad Nicodemum Frischlinum ... I. Animaduersionum in Grammaticen eius Latinam: II. Ad eiusdem strigilim Grammaticam, antistrigilis. ... M. D. LXXXVI. (Argentorati Excudebat Iosias Rihelius ...) 8°. a^{8} b^{2} A-Aa^{8} Bb^{6}. pp. 1-366. [760

-- Martini Crusii ... Oratio de Illustris. Principe Eberhardo Barbato, primo VVirtembergensi Duce. ... 'Tybingæ Typis Georgij Gruppenbachij, M. D. XCIII. 4°. A-H^{4} I^{2}. pp. 2-38. ¶*Half-title* (F1^{r}): Eadem Epitaphia musicis modis quinarum vocum, ab ... Zacharia Schæffero ... composita. [761

-- Martini Crusii ... orationes Scholasticæ tres. ... Tubingæ, Typis Cellianis. Anno M. D. XCIX. 4°. A-K^{4}. ff. 1-36. [762

-- Turcograeciae libri octo ... Basileae, per Leonardum Ostenium, Sebastiani Henricpetri impensa. (... M.D.LXXXXIIII.) fol. *^{6} †^{4} α-β^{6} a-r^{6} s^{4} t-y^{6} z^{8} A-I^{6} K^{8} L-X^{6} Y^{4} Aa^{6} Bb^{4}. pp. 2-557. [763

CRUZ, LUIZ DE LA. Interpretatio poetica Latine in centum quinquaginta psalmos. Autore Ludouico Crucio Olysipponensi ... Madriti, Ex officina Ludouici Sanchez. Anno M.D.C. (*Colophon.*) 16°. ¶^{8} A-T^{8}. pp. 1-299. [764

CUESTION. Libro llamado q̃stion de amor. (Fue imprimido ... enla ... ciudad de Seuilla por Iacobo cromberguer ... Acabose a quatro dias δl mes δ Iunio. Año ... de mil ⁊ quiniẽtos ⁊ veynte ⁊ vn años.) fol. B.L. a-e^{8} f^{6}. [765

-- -- Question de amor nueuamente impresso. En Caragoça, Año de 1548. (... en casa de George coci/ por Pedro Bernuz. Acabo se a diez dias del mes de Março ...) 4°. B.L. a-g^{8} h^{10}. ff. ij-lxvj. [766

-- -- [1] Question de amor, y carcel de amor. En Anuers, En casa de Martino Nucio ... M. D. XCVIII. 12°. A-I^{12} K^{4}. pp. 3-221. [2] Carcel de amor, del cumplimiento de Nicolas Nuñez. *Same imprint.* A-F^{12} G^{2}. pp. 3-135. [767

CULMANN, LEONHARD. Iungen Gesellen/ Iunckfrawen vnd Witwen ... wie sie sich in ehlichen stand richten sollen ... M.D.LXVII. (Gedruckt zu Nuͤrnberg/ bey Christoff Heussler) 8°. A-C^{8}. [768

-- Praeparatio et instructio ad crucem, tentationem & mortem, deq́ȝ sub cruce, tentatione & morte consolatio Christiana. ... Norimbergae Apud Gabriel Hayn, Iohannis Petrei Generum. Anno M. D. LII. 8°. A-I^{8}. [769

CUMELIUS, PETRUS. Oratio, ad ... patres ... Concilii Tridentini: habita ... In Festo omnium Sanctorum: ... M. D. LXIII. Brixiae: Ad instantiam Io: Baptistæ Bozole. M. D. LXIII. (... apud Ludouicum Sabiensem.) 4°. A^{6}. (Lea.) [770

CUPERS, RUDOLF. Tractatus de sacrosancta vniuersali ecclesia ... Venetiis, Apud Dominicum de Farris. M D LXXXVIII. 4°. †^{4} a-i^{4} A-Vu^{4}. pp. 1-342. (Lea.) [771

CURA. Cura clericalis ... vna cuȝ abbreuiatione compoti ([Rothomagi,] Pro radulfo gaultier [c. 1510].) 16°. B.L. [a]-b^{8}. [772

CUREUS, JOACHIMUS. Gentis Silesiæ annales ... Witebergæ M.D.LXXI. (... excudebat Iohannes Crato ...) fol.)(^{6} 3A-3C^{6} A-Kk^{6}. pp. 1-393. [773

CURIONE, CELIO SECUNDO. Pasquillus ecstaticus ... cum aliquot aliis ... Dialogis. ... Geneuae per Ioan. Girardum. M.D.XLIIII. 8°. A-R^{8}. pp. 1-257. [774

-- -- Der verzucket Pasquinus/ Auss Welscher sprach inn das Teütsch gebracht . M.D.XLIII. (Getruckt zů Rom/ auff anhalten Maister Pasquini.) 8°. A-K^{8}. [775

CURTIUS RUFUS, QUINTUS. The Historie of Quintus Curtius, conteyning the Actes of the great Alexander. Translated out of Latin into English by Iohn Brende. London Printed by Abell Ieffes ... 1592. 8°. B.L. A-Oo^{8} Pp^{4} (-Pp^{4}). ff. 2-203 *present*. *S.T.C.* 6146. [776

-- -- Quinte curse. ... Contenant les belliqueux faitz darmes/ ... de guerre du ... roy Alexandre le grãt. Translate de latin en francoys ... Nouuellement imprime a Paris. On les vend ... chez Iacques Keruer ... (imprime ... par Iacques le messier le penultime iour doctobre mil cinq cens trente quatre.) fol. B.L. ã^{6} A-S^{6}. ff. i-cviii. [777

-- -- Quinto Curtio (Impresso in Florentia per li heredi di Philippo di Giunta ... M.D.XXX. di Nouembrio. ...) 8°. A-Z^{8} &^{8} ɔ^{8} ℞^{8} A-B^{8}. ff. 2-222. [778

-- -- Quinto Curtio da P. Candido ... tradotto ... (In Vineggia per Vettor. q. Piero Rauano, della Serena & Compagni ... M.D.XXXI. del mese di Agosto.) 8°. a-z^{8} &^{8} ɔ^{4}. ff. 2-196. ¶ɔ4 *defective*. [779

-- -- Q. Curtio de' fatti d'Alessandro magno ... tradotto per M. Tomaso Porcacchi ... In Vinegia appresso Gabriel Giolito de' Ferrari. M D LVIIII. (*Colophon.*) 4°. *-4*^{8} 5*^{4} A-P^{8} Q^{6} (-Q6, *presumably blank*). pp. 1-249. [780

CUSA, NICOLAUS DE. D. Nicolai de Cusa cardinalis ... opera. ... Basileæ ex officina Henricpetrina. (... mense Augusto, anno M.D.LXV.) fol. a-d^{8} e^{6} †^{10} A-V^{8} X^{6} Y^{4} Aa-3N^{8} 3O^{6} 3P^{4} AAa-OOo^{8} PPp^{10}. pp. 1-1176. ¶*Half-titles:* (Aa1^{r}) Tomus secundus. Nicolai de Cusa ... (AAa1^{r}) Tomus tertius. ... [781

CUSPINIAN, JOHANNES. Ein ausserlessne Chronicka von C. Iulio Cesare dem ersten/ biss auff Carolum quintum ... Strassburg. M.D.XLI. (Getruckt ... bei Crafft Myller ...) fol. π^{6})(^{4} A-Z^{6} aa-ff^{6} gg^{8} Aa-Yy^{6}. pp. j-dcxxxviij, j-cclviij. ¶*Translator: Caspar Hedio.* [782

-- Wo vnd wie Ro. Kay. Maiestat vnd die kunig von Hungern. Poln. vñ Peham zusamen kumen vnd zu wienn eingeritten sendt. [Wien, Johann Singriener, 1515.] 4°. a-b^{4}. [783

CUYCK, HENDRIK VAN. Speculum concubinariorum sacerdotum, monarchorum ac clericorum. Authore Henrico Cuyckio ... Coloniae Apud Bernardum Gualtheri, Anno M. D. XCIX. 8°. †^{8} ††^{4} A-I^{8} K^{4}. pp. 2-148. (Lea.) [784

CYMBER, ODELO, CUSANUS. Epistola Vdelonis Cymbri Cusani de exustione librorum Lutheri, & Monachorum Dominicanæ factionis nequitia ... [Basileae, Valentinus Curio, c. 1522.] 4°. A-B^{4}. [785

CYPRIAN, S. Diui Caecilii Cypriani ... opera ... repurgata, per Des. Erasmum Roterod. Basileae, ex officina Frobeniana anno M. D. XXX. (... mense Ianuario.) fol. a^{8} (-a2-8) b-z^{6} A-V^{6} X^{8} Y^{6} Z^{4} A^{6} B^{8}. pp. 1-527. ¶*T.p. defaced.* [786

-- -- D. Cæcilius Cyprianus ope veterum librorum repurgatus ... Gul. Morelii diligentia ... Parisiis, M. D. LXIIII. Apud Gul. Morellium ... fol. [1]^{4} (-11, *blank*) 2-3^{6} 4-5^{4} A-Z^{6} a-q^{6} r-x^{4} y^{6}. pp. 1-483. [787

-- -- ... Opera ... Adnotationes Iacobi Pamelij ... Editio altera ... Parisiis, Apud Sebastianum Niuellium ... M. D. LXXIIII. fol. a-f^{6} g-h^{10} A-S^{6} T^{8} V-Ll^{6} Mm^{8} Nn-3C^{6} 3D-3E^{8}. pp. 3-607. [788

-- Orazione di San Cipriano. Et il Vangelo di San Giouanni. 16°. A^{8}. ¶A2^{r}: Questa orazione fece Santo Cipriano con la qual si caccia via ogni maligno spirito, ... & ogni forza del diauolo. [789

CYRIL, S., of THESSALONICA. Spiegel/ der Natürlichen Weysshait/ durch den alten ... Bischof Cyrillum ... beschriben/ yetzund von newem inn Teütsche Reymen ... Gemacht durch Danieln Holtzman ... 1571 (Getruckt in ... Augspurg/ bey Philipp Vlhart.) 4°. A-Z^{4} Aa-Zz^{4} AA-ZZ^{4} aa-hh^{4}. ff. 1-302. [790

CZECANOWSKI, SYLVESTER. De corruptis moribus vtriusque partis, Pontificiorum uidelicet, & Euangelicorum, dialogus ... Authore Syluestro Czecanouio. ... [Francofurti, c. 1560.] 4°. A-Q^{4}. [791

D

DAGONNEAU, JEAN. Legende de domp Claude de Guise, abbe de Cluny. Contenant ses faits & gestes ... M. D. LXXXI. 8°. $*^8$ $**^2$ A-Q^8. pp. 1-256. (Lea.) [1

DAMHOUDER, JOSSE. Practique iudiciaire es causes ciuiles ... Composée en Latin ... En Anuers. Chez Iean Bellere ... M. D. LXXII. ... (De l'Imprimerie de Gerard Smits ...) fol. $*$-$3*^6$ $4*^4$ A-Gg^6. pp. 2-331. (Biddle.) [2

DAMIANI, GIANO. Iani Damiani Senensis ad Leonem X. Pont. Max. de expeditione in Turcas Elegeia, cū ... epigrammatibus. Epistola Pisonis ad Io. Coritium, de conflictu Polonorum & Lituanorum cum Moscouitis. Henricus Penia ... de gestis Sophi contra Turcas. Epistola Sigismundi Poloniæ Regis ad Leonem X. Pont. Max. de uictoria contra Schismaticos Moscouios ... Erasmi Roterodami epistola ad Leonem X. Pont. Max. de laudibus illius, & noua Hieronymianorum operum æditione. Eiusdem ad ... D. Grimannum ... Cardinalem Epistola. Eiusdem ad ... Raphaelem Rearium ... Cardinalem Epistola. Eiusdem ad ... Martinum Dorpium Hollandum Epistola Apologetica de suarum lucubrationum æditione. Eiusdē in laudē urbis Selestadij Panegyricū Carmē Basileae apud Ioannem Frobenium. (... mense Augusto. M.D.XV.) 4°. A-O^4. [3

DAMIANO DA ODEMIRA. [Libro da imparare giocare a scachi ...] [c. 1530.] 8°. A-H^8 (-A1). [4

DANEAU, LAMBERT. De veneficis, quos olim sortilegos, nunc autem vulgò Sortiarios vocant, dialogus ... [Genevae,] Apud Eustathium Vignon. Anno M. D. LXXIIII. 8°. A-H^8. pp. 3-127. [5

-- -- Coloniae Agrippinae. Apud Ioannem Gymnicum ... M. D. LXXV. 8°. A-G^8 H^4 (-H4, *blank*). pp. 3-118. (Lea.) [6

DANÈS, PIERRE. Apologia/ Darin Kͤnigklicher Maiestat zu Franckreich gut gerͤcht vertheydingt vnnd verantwort wͤrt/ von einem seiner getrewen/ widder der Kaiserlichen ... verleumbdung/ damit yrer Maie. zugemessen/ sie habe des Tͤrcken kriegvolck/ die Christenheyt anzugreiffen/ vnnd zubekriegen/ bewegt. Anno 1552. 4°. A-D^4 E^2. [7

-- Oratio ... Tridenti, in congregatione Præsulum, VII. Iulij habita. Romæ M. D. XLVI. 4°. A^4. [8

DANIELLO, BERNARDINO. La poetica ... (In Vinegia per Giouan'Antonio di Nicolini da Sabio ... M D XXXVI.) 4°. A-Q^4 R^6. pp. 4-136. ¶*Title on* A1^v. [9

DANTE ALIGHIERI. *Convito.* Lo amoroso Cōuiuio di Dante: con la additione ... (Stampata in venetia per Zuane Antonio: & Fradelli da Sabio: Ad instantia de Nicolo e Dominico dal Iesus fradelli. ... M.D.XXI. Del Mese di Ottubrio.) 8°. a^8 a-t^8. ff. 1-151. [10

-- -- MDXXIX. (Impresso in Vinegia per Nicolo di Aristotile detto Zoppino ...) 8°. $*^8$ A-O^8 P^{12}. ff. 1-124. [11

-- -- (Impresso in Vinegia per Marchio Sessa ... MDXXXI.) 8°. $*^8$ A-O^8. ff. 1-112. [12

-- *De vulgari eloquentia.* Dantis Aligerii ... de vulgari eloquentia libri duo. ... Ex libris Corbinelli: Eiusdémque Adnotationibus illustrati. ... Parisiis, Apud Io. Corbon ... 1577. ... 8°. $ā^4$ A-E^8 F^4 G-K^8 (-G4) L^4. pp. 1-81, 3-56. [13

-- -- Dante de la vωlgare elωquenzia. ... (Stampata in Vicenza, per Tωlωmeω Ianiculω da Bressa ... MDXXIX. Del Mese di Genarω.) fol. a-b^8 c^6 d^4. [14

-- *Divina comedia.* [Le terze rime di Dante.] (Venetiis in aedib. Aldi. ... men. Aug. M.DII.) 8°. a-z^8 (-a1) A-G^8 H^4. ¶*For the missing t.p. a leaf with the title* Terze rime di Dante Alighieri *has been substituted.* H4^v *blank.* [15

-- -- *Another copy* (-a^8, *with the printer's device on* H4^v). [16

-- -- Le terze rime di Dante. [Lione, Balthazar de Gabiano, c. 1503.] 8°. a-z^8 A-F^8 G^{12}. [17

-- -- [Commedia di Dante insieme con vno dialogo circa el sito forma et misure dello Inferno. (Impresso in Firenze per opera e spesa di Philippo di Giunta fiorentino ... MDVI a di XX dagosto.)] 8°. a^{6} (-a1, a6) b-z^{8} (-m1, *for which the corresponding leaf of the Lyon 1503 edition, signed* liii, *has been substituted*) &^{8} A-F^{8} G^{10}. ¶*Lacks the dialog* (H-P^{8}). [18

-- -- Dante col sito, et forma dell'Inferno. ([Toscolano,] P. Alex. Pag. Benacenses. .f. Bena. .V. .V.) 8°. a-z^{8} A-H^{8} (-H8, *presumably blank*). [19

-- -- *Another copy.* [20

-- -- Danthe alighieri Fiorentino historiado. ... (Impressa in Venetia per Bartholomeo de Zanni da Portese. Del .M.D.VII. A di .xvii. de Zugno.) fol. aa^{10} a-z^{8} &^{8} ɔ^{8} ℞^{8} A-H^{8} I^{10} K-L^{8}. ff. I-CCXCVIII. ¶*With the commentary of Christoforo Landino.* [21

-- -- Opere del diuino poeta Danthe con suoi comenti ... (Impresse in Venetia per Miser Bernardino stagnino da Trino de monferra. Del .M.CCCCC.XII. Adi .XXIIII. Nouembris.) 4°. AA^{12} a-z^{8} ꝛ^{8} aa-zz^{8} ꝛꝛ^{8} ɔɔ^{8} 44^{8} A-E^{8}. ff. 3-441. ¶*Commentator: Christoforo Landino.* [22

-- -- Dante. (Impresso in Vinegia nelle Case d'Aldo & d'Andrea di Asola suo suocero nell' anno M.D.XV. Del mese di Agosto.) 8°. π^{2} a-z^{8} A-H^{8}. ff. 2-244. ¶π2^{r}: Dante col sito, et forma dell'Inferno ... [23

-- -- *Another copy* (-π1). [24

-- -- Dante col sito, et forma dell'Inferno. [Venezia, Alessandro de Paganinis, c. 1516.] 24°. A-DD^{8} EE^{4}. ff. 2-202. [25

-- -- [Opere del Diuino Poeta Danthe con suoi comenti ...] (Impressa in Venetia per Miser Bernardino stagnino da Trino de monferra. Del .M.CCCCC.XX. A di .XXVIII. Marzo.) 4°. AA^{12} *(wanting)* a-z^{8} ꝛ^{8} aa-zz^{8} ꝛꝛ^{8} ɔɔ^{8} 44^{8} A-E^{8}. ff. 3-440. ¶*For the* AA *gathering,* AA-BB^{8} a1 *from a copy of the edition of 1536 have been substituted.* [26

-- -- *Another copy, lacking all before* a1. [27

-- -- Comedia di Danthe Alighieri ... cō l'espositione di Christophoro lādino ... M D XXIX (Stāpato in Venetia per Iacob del Burgofrāco, Pauese. Ad instantia del ... messere Lucantonio giūta, Fiorētino. ... A di .XXIII. di Genaro.) fol. AA-BB^{6} a-z^{8} &^{8} ɔ^{8} ℞^{8} A-L^{8} (-L8, *blank*). ff. I-CCXCV. [28

-- -- Comedia del diuino poeta Danthe Alighieri, con la ... spositione di Christophoro Landino ... M D XXXVI In Vinegia ad instantia di M. Gioanni Giolitto da Trino. (... per M. Bernardino Stagnino.) 4°. ✢✢^{12} AA-BB^{8} A-Z^{8} &^{8} AA-ZZ^{8} ꝛꝛ^{8} ɔɔ^{8} 44^{8} A-E^{8}. ff. 2-440. [29

-- -- La comedia di Dante Alighieri con la noua espositione di Alessandro Vellutello (Impressa in Vinegia per Francesco Marcolini ad instantia di Alessandro Vellutello del mese di Gugno lanno MDXLIIII.) 4°. AA-BB^{8} CC^{10} A-Z^{8} AB-AZ^{8} BC-BI^{8} (-BI8, *blank*). [30

-- -- Lo'nferno e'l Purgatorio e'l Paradiso dal Diuino Poeta Dante Alaghieri. In Venetia al segno de la Speranza. 1545. 18°. A-Z$^{8.10}$ &^{10}. ff. 2-216. [31

-- -- Il Dante ... In Lione, per Giouan di Tournes. M.D.XXXXVII. 16°. a-z^{8} A-L^{8} (-L8, *blank*). pp. 3-539. [32

-- -- Dante con nuoue, et vtili ispositioni. ... In Lyone, appresso Guglielmo Rouillio. 1551 ... 16°. a-z^{8} A-S^{8} (-S8, *presumably blank*). pp. 2-644. [33

-- -- *Variant.* In Lyone, appresso Guglielmo Rouillio. 1552 ... 16°. a-z^{8} A-S^{8}. pp. 2-644. [34

-- -- Dante con ... annotationi. ... In Venetia, per Giouann'Antonio Morando. M D LIIII. 8°. A-MM^{8} NN^{4}. ff. 2-278. [35

-- -- La diuina comedia ... In Vinegia appresso Gabriel Giolito de Ferrari, et fratelli. M D LV. (... M D LIIII.) 12°. *^{12} **^{6} A-BB^{12}. pp. 2-598. [36

-- -- Dante con l'espositione di Christoforo Landino, et di Alessandro Vellutello ... riueduto ... per Francesco Sansouino Fiorentino. In Venetia, Appresso Giouambattista, Marchiò Sessa, & fratelli. 1564. (... Appresso Domenico Nicolini, Per Giouambattista, Marchio Sessa, & Fratelli. ...) fol. *^{8} **^{6} 3*^{4} +^{10} A-V^{8} X^{12} Y-3C^{8}. ff. 1-392. [37

-- -- Dante con l'espositione di M. Bernardino Daniello da Lucca ... In Venetia, appresso Pietro da Fino, M D LXVIII. 4°. $*^6$ A-4Y^4. pp. 1-727. [38

-- -- La diuina comedia ... In Vinegia, appresso Domenico Farri. M D LXIX. (*Colophon.*) 12°. a^{12} b^6 A-BB^{12}. pp. 2-598. [39

-- -- Dante con ... ispositioni. In Lione, Appresso Guglielmo Rouillio. 1571. 16°. A-Rr^8 pp. 3-627. [40

-- -- *Variant.* In Lione, Appresso Guglielmo Rouillio. 1575. 16°. A-Rr^8. pp. 3-627. [41

-- -- La diuina comedia ... In Vinegia, Appresso Dominico Farri. M D LXXVIII. 12°. a^{12} (-a7-12) b^6 (-b1-5) A-Bb^{12} (-Bb12). pp. 2-598. [42

-- -- Dante con l'espositione di Christoforo Landino, et di Alessandro Vellutello ... riueduto ... per Francesco Sansouino ... In Venetia, Appresso Giouambattista, Marchiò Sessa, & Fratelli. 1578. (... Appresso gli Heredi di Francesco Rampazetto. Ad instantia di ... Sessa ...) fol. a^8 b^6 c^4 d^{10} A-V^8 X^{12} Y-$3C^8$. ff. 1-392. [43

-- -- La diuina commedia ... ridotta a miglior lezione dagli Accademici della Crusca. ... In Firenze per Domenico Manzani 1595 ... (*Colophon.*) 8°. $†^8$ (†8 + *folded leaf*) A-F^8 G^6 H-Nn^8. pp. 1-493. [44

-- -- Dante con l'espositione di Christoforo Landino, et di Alessandro Vellutello ... riueduto ... per Francesco Sansouino ... In Venetia, Appresso Gio. Battista, & Gio. Bernardo Sessa, fratelli. 1596. (... Appresso Domenico Nicolini. Ad instanza di ... Sessa ...) fol. a^8 b^6 c^4 d^{10} A-V^8 X^{12} Y-$3C^8$. ff. 1-392. [45

DANTZ, JOHANNES. [1] Tabulae simplicium medicamentorum ... Basileae apud Henrichum Petrum (... mense Augusto, anno M. D. XLIII.) fol. a-b^6 A-G^6 H-I^4 Aa-Cc^6 Dd^4 Ee^6. pp. 2-155. ¶*Additional t.pp.:* ($A1^r$) Tabula simplicium ... Basileae. (*Colophon.*) ($Aa1^r$) Pro artis medicae opera exercentibus index simplicium ... Basileae. [2] De simplicium medicamentorum facultatibus ... Basileae. AA-FF^6 GG-HH^4. pp. 3-85. (Smith.) [46

DASYPODIUS, PETRUS. [Dictionarium Latino Germanicum et vice versa Germanicolatinum ... M. D. LIX.] (Argentorati Excudebat Iosias Rihelius, Anno M. D. LIX.) 8°. a^4 ($-a^4$) A-Mm^8 Nn^4 a-v^8 x^6. [47

-- Dictionarium voces ... in autoribus latinæ linguæ probatis, ac uulgò receptis occurrentes Germanicè explicans ... M. D. XXXV. (Argentorati, expensis ... Vendelini Rihelij ... Mense uero Martio.) 4°. π^4 a-z^4 A-Ll^4. [48

-- Λεξικον Graecolatinum ... Impressum Argentorati in Officina Vuendelini Rihelij. Mense Martio. Anno M. D. XXXIX. ... (*Colophon.*) 8°. α^4 β-γ^8 d-z^8 A-O^8 P^4. ff. 3-295. [49

DAUL, FLORIAN. Tantzteuffel: Das ist/ wider den leichtfertigen/ vnuerschempten Welt tantz ... Franckfurt am Mayn/ Anno 1569. (Gedruckt ... bey Martin Lechler/ in verlegung Simon Hůters. ...) 8°. A-P^8 Q^4 (-Q4, *presumably blank*). ff. 1-113. [50

DAUPHINÉ. Libertates per ... principes delphinos viennenses delphinalibus subditis concesse ... Impensis Francisci Pichati et Bartholomei Bertoleti grationopolitanoruȝ ciuium. Venales habentur ... grationopoli ... apud Franciscum pichatuȝ: et ... apud Bartholomeum Bertoletum. fol. B.L. π^4 a-l^8 aa-bb^8 cc^6 dd-ee^8 (-ee8, *blank*) A^2. ff. I-LXXXVII, I-XXXVII. ¶*Latest date given: 4 March 1508.* [51

DAVIDICO, LORENZO. Compendium cuius titulus est thesaurus animae in Dominicam precationem ... (Terminatum Romæ in officina Antonii Bladi ... Die 13. Mensis Martii, ... M. D. LI.) 8°. A-Q^8 R^4. ff. 9-132. (Lea.) [52

DAYMA, JOANNES. Cõcordata inter ... Papam Leonem decimum, et ... Regem Franciscum ... primũ in suprema Parlamenti curia Parisius vigesimasecũda mẽsis Martij. Anno ... Millesimo Quingẽtesimo decimoseptimo ... registrata ... Vna cum Ioãnis Dayma Baionẽsis ... commentariolis ... 1535 (Lugduniqȝ ... excusa in edibus ... Iacobi Myt ... Expensis vero Guilelmi de Guelques.) 8°. B.L. aa^8 a-z^8 A-G^8 $Ꞇ^8$. ff. j-ccxl. (Lea.) [53

DAZZI, ANDREA. Andreae Dactii ... poemata. Florentiae apud Laurentium Torrentinum. M D XLIX. ... 8°. a-u^8. pp. 3-320. [54

DECEMBRIO, ANGELO. Politiæ literariae ... libri septem ... Augustæ Vindelicorum Henricus Steynerus excudebat. Anno M. D. XXXX. (... Mense Ianuario, die uero XII.) fol. π^{6} A-Z^{6} a-c^{6} d^{8}. ff. I-CLXIII. [55

DECIMATOR, HEINRICH. [1] Secunda pars syluae vocabulorum et phrasium: continens nomina propria Deorum, Dearumque gentilium, virorum & mulierum, vrbium, regionum, ... atque id genus alia ... ... 1591. ... Francofordi, Apud Ioan. Wechelum, impensis Henningi Grosii, Bibliop. Lipsensis. 8°. *^{8} A-Vu^{8} Xx^{4}. [2] Tertia pars Syluæ ... 1596 Lipsiæ. ... (... Excudebat Michael Lantzenbergerus, Sumptibus ... Heningi Grosij ...) (.)^{8} (.)^{4} A-3V^{8}. pp. 1-1047. [56

DECIO, ANTONIO. Acripanda tragedia ... In Firenze, Nella Stamperia del Sermartelli 1592. (*Colophon.*) 4°. †^{2} A-T^{4} V^{2}. pp. 1-155. [57

DECIO, FILIPPO. [1] Cōsiliorum Decij .iij. Volu. ... [*Device of Vincentius de Portonariis.*] 1533 (... excusum ... Lugdun̄ Typis ... Ioānnis [*sic*] Mareschal. ... vj. idus Ianuarij.) fol. B.L. A-P^{6} Q^{4}. ff. 2-87. [2] Consilia ... Quartum volumen ... 1536 (... excusum: Lugduni typis ... Ioānis Moylin al's de Chambray.) a^{8} b-t^{6} v^{2}. ff. 88-194. [3] Consiliorum ... quintum volu. ... 1536 A-G^{8}. ff. 2-49. (Biddle.) [58

-- ... Philippi Decij Mediolan̄. scripta siue lectura super titulo de regulis iuris .ff. ... cū ... apostillis ac ēt Repertorio dn̄i Hieronymi Chuchalon Hispani ... MDXX ... (Impressa Mediola. per Ioannē Angelum Scinzenzeler Impensis ... Io. Iacobi ⁊ fratrum de Lignano ... .1520. die .16. nouembris.) fol. B.L. A^{6} B-C^{4} D-I^{6} K^{8} L-M^{6} N^{2}. ff. II-LVII. ¶A1, N2 *defective*; N2 *misbound after* A1. (Biddle.) [59

-- -- ... vnâque recens analyticis adnotationibus D. Gabrielis Saraynae ... Lugduni, ex officina Iuntarum. M. D. XIIC. 8°. aa-bb^{8} cc^{4} a-z^{8} A^{8} B^{4}. pp. 1-389. (Lea.) [60

-- Philippus Decius Mediolanensis super decretalibus. [*Device of Vincentius de Portonariis.*] ... 1536 (Imprimebatur Lugduni per Ioannem Moylin al's de Chambray.) fol. B.L. a-z^{8} A-M^{8} N^{6}. ff. 2-268. (Biddle.) [61

DECIO, LANCELOTTO. Lanciloti Decij Mediolanensis Lectura ... super Prima parte .ff. veteris ... M D XXIII (Venetijs a Philippo pincio Mantuano Impressa. ... Die .xvij. Nouembris.) fol. B.L. A-D^{6}. ff. II-XXIIII. (Biddle.) [62

DECLAMATIONE. Declamatione tutta hiperbolica contra vna donna crudele. ... In Venetia, per Plinio Pietrasanta. M D LV. 4°. A-C^{4}. pp. 1-22. [63

DEDEKIND, FRIEDRICH. Grobianus. De morum simplicitate, libri duo. ... Franc. Apud Chr. Egen. (M.D.XLIX.) 8°. A-F^{8}. [64

DEE, JOHN. Monas hieroglyphica ... Guliel. Silvius ... Excud. Antuerpiæ, 1564. (... Calend. Aprilis. ...) 4°. A-G^{4}. ff. 2-28. [65

DEFENSIO. Defensio veritatis contra impugnatores Venundant̄ Parisiis ... apud Gaufridū de marnef ... 8°. B.L. A-D^{8} E^{4}. ff. ii-xxxvi. [66

DELBENE, ALPHONSE. Coppie des lettres escrites a d'Epernon, par Monsieur l'Abbé d'Elbene. (A Paris, Pour Gerard Vedie ...) 8°. A-C^{4}. pp. 2-21. ¶*Imprimatur dated 19 September 1589.* [67

DELFINI, CESARE. Cesaris Petrimichaelis Dolphini ... Matris Virginis Mariados tripartita series. Venetijs apud Cominum de Tridino Montisferrati. M D LII. 4°. a-h^{4} M^{4} B^{2}. [68

DELFINO, DOMENICO. Sommario di tutte le scienze ... In Venetia appresso i Gioliti. M D LXXXV. 8°. *-3*^{8} 4*^{4} A-Y^{8} Z^{4}. pp. 1-360. [69

DELFINO, PIETRO. Petri Delphini Veneti ... Epistolarum Volumen. (Impressum Venetiis arte ... Bernardini Benalii ... M.D.XXIIII. Die prima Martii.) fol. a-z^{8} &^{8} ɔ^{8} ℞^{8} A-Z^{8}. ¶a1^{v}: Iacobus Brixianus ... lectori Salutem. (Lea.) [70

DELRIO, MARTINO ANTONIO. [1] Martini Antonii Delrii ... syntagma tragoediae Latinae ...

Antuerpiae, Ex officina Plantiniana, Apud Viduam, & Ioannem Moretum. M. D. XCIII. ... 4°. $*-**^4$ $A-Y^4$ Z^6. pp. 1-188. [2] ... Syntagmatis tragoediae Latinae Pars secunda. *Same imprint.* $A-Z^4$ $a-p^4$ q^6. pp. 3-315. [3] Syntagmatis tragici Pars vltima ... Antuerpiae, Ex officina Plantiniana, Apud Viduam, & Ioannem Moretum. M. D. XCIIII. (... M. D. XCV.) $A-Z^4$ $a-Zz^4$ $AA-MM^4$ NN^6 $OO-YY^4$. pp. 3-559. [71

DEMETRIUS CYDONIUS. Τοῦ κυδωνίου περί τοῦ καταφρονεῖν τόν θάνατον. Ἑρμείου ... διασυρμός τῶν ἔξω φιλοσόφων. Cydonij de contemnenda morte Oratio. Hermiae ... irrisio gentilium philosophorum. ... cùm Grecè, tum Latinè, Raphaelis Seileri Augustani ... opera ac uersione in lucem prolata. Basileae, per Ioannem Oporinum. (... M.D.LIII. Mense Martio.) 8°. $a-l^8$. pp. 4-172. [72

DEMETRIUS PHALAREUS. Demetrij Phalerei de elocutione Liber, à Stanislao Ilouio Polono Latinitate donatus, & Annotationibus illustratus. Item, Dionysii Halicarnassei quædam Opuscula, eodem interprete ... Adiecimus eadem & Græcè ... Basileae, per Ioannem Oporinum. (... M. D. LVII. Mense Martio.) 8°. $a-q^8$ r^4. pp. 4-262. [73

-- -- Petri Victorii commentarii in librum Demetrii Phalerei de Elocutione ... Florentiae apud Philippum Iuntam. MDXCIIII. (*Colophon.*) fol. a^6 b^4 $A-Y^6$ Z^4 AA^6. pp. 2-268. [74

DEMOSTHENES. [1] Demosthenis ... Opera ... omnia, unà cum Vlpiani rhetoris commentariis, ... conuersa, per Hieronymum VVolfium Oetingensem ... Basileae, per Ioannem Oporinum [c. 1549]. fol. $\alpha-\beta^4$ $a-s^4$ $AA-3L^4$ $3M^6$ $A-Z^4$ $\&*^4$. pp. 1-144, 3-283, 3-192. [2] Vlpiani rhetoris Enarrationes ... Basileae. $\alpha-\delta^4$ $a-ff^4$ gg^6 $AA-ZZ^4$ $Aa-Ll^4$. cols. 3-486, pp. 4-266, cols. 268-273. [75

-- *Two or more works.* Δημοσθενους Ἀθηναιου ... Ολυνθιακος λογος πρωτος. 8°. $\alpha-\lambda^4$. [76

-- Demosthenis orationes Philippicæ quatuor latinæ factæ. Interprete Christophoro Hegendorfino. Accessit et secunda Olynthiaca ... Græca ipsa ad calcem subiecta sunt ... Anno. XXXV. (Haganoae excudebat Petrus Brubachius anno M.D.XXXV. Mense Martio.) 8°. π^{12} $A-E^8$ $[F]^8$. [77

-- Cinque orationi di Demosthene, et vna di Eschine, tradotte di lingua Greca in Italiana ... In Venetia, [Aldine Press,] M.D.LVII. ... 8°. $A-II^8$. ff. 2-254. ¶*Translator: Girolamo Ferro.* [78

-- Demosthenis orationes Olynthiacæ tres, & quatuor Philippicæ, cum quibusdam alijs ... in vsum adolescentum ... editæ. Argentorati, Excudebat Theodosius Rihelius. 8°. $A-N^8$ O^6 (-O6, *presumably blank*). ff. 2-109. [79

-- Orationi di Demostene, et Eschine, Tradotto ... di Lingua Greca in Italiana. In Venetia. Appresso Giorgio Angelieri. M. D. XCVII. 8°. $A-II^8$ (-II8, *blank*). ff. 2-254. ¶*For the most part a reissue of the Aldine edition of 1557.* [80

-- *De symmoriis.* Demosthenis oratio de classibus, siue περι συμμοριων, Latina facta per Ioannem Lonicerum. Philosophiae encomium per eundem. ... Basileae [Robertus Winter,] 1537. 8°. $a-c^8$ d^4. pp. 5-14 [=41]. [81

-- *Philippica.* Demosthenis orationes quatuor contra Philippum. A Paulo Manutio latinitate donatæ. Venetiis, M. D. XLIX. Apud Aldi filios. 4°. $A-N^4$. [82

-- -- Le vndici Filippiche di Demosthene con vna lettera di Filippo a gl'Atheniesi. Dichiarate in lingua Toscana per M. Felice Figliucci Senese. In Roma Appresso Vincenzo Valgrisi M. D. L. ... 8°. $*^4$ $A-R^8$ S^4. ff. 1-119. [83

DENCK, JOHANN. Vom gsatz gottes. Wie das Gsatz auffgehaben sey: vnd doch erfüllet werden můss. Hanns Denck. [Strassburg, Johann Prüss, 1526.] 4°. $A-B^4$ C^2 D^4. [83a

DENIS LE CHARTREUX. D. Dionysii Carthusiani contra Alchoranum & sectam Machometicam libri quinque. ... Eiusdem De instituendo bello aduersus Turcas, & de generali celebrando Concilio. Contra vitia superstitionum. ... Coloniae apud Petrum Quentel. Anno XXXIII. 8°. AA^8 $A-Nn^8$ Oo^{10} $Pp-Qq^8$. pp. 2-628. [84

-- -- Alchoran. Das ist/ des Mahometischen Gesatzbůchs/ vnd Türckischen Aberglaubens ynnhalt/ vnnd ablenung. ... Zů Strasszburg bey Hans Schotten. M. D. XL. fol. $A-H^4$. [85

DENIS LE CHARTREUX

-- D. Dionysii Carthusiani de quatuor hominis nouissimis ... Editio prima Coloniæ Anno 1532. (... Iohannes Dorstius excudebat. ...) 8°. A^8 a-q^8. ff. i-cxxviij. [86

-- D. Dionysij Carthusiani in euangelium Ioãnis enarratio ... Parisiis, Apud Audoẽnum Paruum ... 1545. 8°. B^4 a-z^8 A-M^8 N^4. ff. 1-275. [87

-- D. Dionysij Carthusiani in euangelium Matthæi enarratio ... Parisiis, Apud Audoẽnum Paruum ... 1545. (Typis Renati Aprilis ...) 8°. ₵^{8} A-Gg^8 Hh^4. ff. 1-244. [88

-- D. Dionysii Carthusiani in omnes beati Pauli Epistolas Commentaria. ... Parisiis, Apud Ioannem Roigny ... 1542. (... excudebat Carola Guillard ...) 8°. AA^8 BB^4 a-z^8 A-Y^8 Z^4. ff. 1-363. [89

-- D. Dionysii Carthusiani, in quatuor euangelistas enarrationes ... Coloniæ Petrus Quentell suis impensis excudebat, anno M.D.XXXIII. Mense Septembri. (*Colophon.*) fol. A-B^4 A-Z^6 a-g^6 h^8 i-qq^6 rr-ss^4. ff. II-CCCLXXXIII. [90

DENISSE, NICOLAS. Diuinis humanisq3 dignũ conspectibus ... opus super quattuor nouissimis cui Speculũ mortaliũ titulus prefertur A ... nicholas denijse ... editum. ... impensis ... Henrici Eckert de hõberch Antuerpie ... impressioni traditũ. ... anno Millesimo quingentesimo decimo octauo. (... decimo nono. Die vero .viij. mẽsis februarij) 8°. B.L. A-Z^8 A-C^8 (-C8, *presumably blank*). ¶*Sig.* ^{2}B *misbound before* ^{2}A. [91

DENMARK. *Frederick II, king.* Vnser von Gottes gnaden Friederichen des andern zu Denmarcken/ Norwegen ... Kõnig/ Vnd ... Iohansen des Eltern/ vnd Adolffen Erben zu Norwegen ... Landtgerichts Ordnung ... Gedrückt zu Hamburg/ durch Nicolaum Wegener. M. D. LXXIII. 4°. A-S^4 (-I4). [92

DESAINLIENS, CLAUDE. A Dictionarie French and English: ... Gathered and set forth by Claudius Hollyband. ... Imprinted at London by T. O. for Thomas Woodcock. 1593. 4°. A^4 B-Ii^8 Kk^2. *S.T.C.* 6737. (Furness.) [93

DESCOUSU, CELSE HUGUES. Las leyes de todos los reynos de Castilla: abreuiadas ... en forma de Reportorio ... por Hugo de Celso ... M.D.xl. ... (Fue impresso en ... Alcala de Henares en casa de Iuan de brocar: a veynte dias del mes de Nouembre ...) fol. B.L. AA^8 a-z^8 A-X^8. ff. j-ccclij. (Lea.) [94

-- Tractatus clausularum. Celsi Hugonis dissuti ... (Venetijs vero per Alexandrum ac fratres de Bindonis ... ĩpressus. Sumptibus ... Ioannis baptiste de Pederçanis brixiensis. ... 1522. Die vero 27. mensis Septembris.) 12°. B.L. a-h^{12} A^{12}. ff. 2-96. (Lea.) [95

DES FREUX, ANDRÉ. Epigrammata in Hæreticos. Authore Andrea Frusio Societatis Iesu. Mussiponti, Ex officina Martini Mercatoris ... 1587. 12°. A-E^{12}. (Lea.) [96

DESPORTES, PHILIPPE. Les oeuures de Philippes des Portes. ... A Lyon, Par les heritiers de Benoist Rigaud. M.D.XCIX. 12°. $ã^4$ A-Ff^{12} Gg^8. pp. 1-706. [97

-- Imitations de quelques chans de l'Arioste, par diuers poetes François ... A Paris, Pour Lucas Breyer ... M.D.LXXII. ... 8°. A-I^8. ff. 2-72. ¶*Additional authors: Mellin de Saint-Gelais, Jean-Antoine de Baïf, Louis d'Orleans.* [98

DEXIPPUS. Dexippi ... in defensionem Prædicamẽtorum Aristotelis aduersus Plotinũ ... Quæstionum libri III. ... Ioanne Bernardo Feliciano authore. Parisiis Apud Vascosanum ... M. D. XLI. 8°. A-F^8. ff. 2-48. [99

DIALECTICA. Dialectica prodidagmata ad adeundum Aristotelem ... necessaria. ... Væneunt sub signo S. Martini via ad diuum Iacobum [per Vivantium Gaultherot]. 1545 ... (Excudebat Benedictus Preuost ...) 8°. A-H^8 I^4. [100

DIALOGI. Dialogi duo rerum verborumque lepore, et copia insignes: quorum prior, continet colloquium inter Deum & Euam (vt ferunt) eiusq́; liberos, posterior Salomonis & Marcolphi ... decertationem proponit. Quibus accessit ... CisioIanus vetus & nouus ... Argentinæ [1525?]. 8°. A-C^8. [101

DIALOGUE. Dialogue du royaume, Auquel est discouru des vices & vertues des Roys, & de leur

Establissement ... A Paris, Chez Didier Millot ... M. D. LXXXIX. ... 8°. A-R^4 S^2. pp. 3-142. [102

DIALOGUS. Dialogus libertatis ecclesiastice defensorius cum Imperatorum sanctionibus ... (Impressum Oppenheim [per Jacobum Köbel]. ... 15.16.) 4°. π^4 A-C^4. [103

-- Dialogus nouus et mire festiuus, ex quorundam virorum salibus cribratus ... 4°. A-C^4. ¶A2^r: Interlocutores. M. Ortuinus. M. Lupoldus. M. Gingolphus. Erasmus. Reuchlin. Faber Stapulensis. [104

-- Dialogus Oder gesprech wider ein vermeinte vngeschickte Expostulation oder Straffschrifft Satane des Fürsten dieser welt/ mit Hertzogen Heinrichen zu Braunschweig/ aus beuelch des Landgrauen zu Hessen gehalten. M. D. XLI. 4°. A-E^4. [105

-- Ain gůtter grober dyalogus Teütsch/ zwyschen zwayen gůten gesellen/ mit namen Hans Schöpfer/ Peter Schabēhůt/ bayd von Basel ... [Strassburg, Reinhard Beck, 1521.] 4°. A-B^4. [106

-- Ain schöner dialogus oder gesprech/ so ain Prediger mūnch Bembus genant/ vnd ain Burger Silenus/ vnd sein Narr mit ainander habent. [1522.] 4°. [A]^4. [107

-- Ain schöner Dialogus zwischen ainem Priester vñ Ritter/ von ainer steür/ über die gaistlichem etwan in Frãckreich angelegt/ gehalten. 4°. a-c^4. [108

DIAZ, NICOLAS. Tratado del iuyzio final ... Impresso en Valladolid por Diego Fernandez de Cordoua y Ouiedo ... A costa de Iuan Boyer ... M. D. LXXXVIII. 4°. A^4 A-Kk^8 LL^2 (-LL2, *presumably blank*). ff. 1-264. [109

DIAZ, RODRIGO, DE BIVAR. Chronica del famoso Cauallero Cid Ruy Diez campeador. ... En Burgos. En la Imprimeria de Philippe de Iunta y Iuan Baptista Varesio. 1593. (*Colophon.*) fol. ¶-¶¶^{8} 3¶^{6} A-V^8 (-V8, *blank*). pp. 1-317. [110

-- -- *Another copy, lacking* ¶1-2. [111

DIAZ DE LUCO, JUAN BERNARDO. Practica criminalis canonica, omnia propemodum quæ a clero committi possunt flagitia, una cum poenis eorumdem ... complectens. ... Venetiis Ex officina Erasmiana apud Vincentium Vaugris ... M. D. XLIII. 8°. *^{8} a-x^8 y^4. ff. 1-172. (Lea.) [112

-- -- Venetiis, Apud Dominicum, & Cornelium de Nicholinis. M D LX. 8°. A-R^8 S^4. (Lea.) [113

-- -- Singularis et excellentissima practica criminalis canonica ... Recognita ... locupletata ... a Doctore Ignatio Lopez de Salzedo ... Compluti. Excudebat Ioannes Gracian ... 1587. ... (... Kalend. Septembris.) fol. π^2 A-Ii^8 Kk^6 ¶^{8} §^{8}. ff. 1-522. (Lea.) [114

DIAZ DE MONTALVO, ALFONSO. Por mãdado delos ... principes rey don Fernãdo ⁊ reyna doña Ysabel ... Compusto este libro de leyes el doctor Alfonso diaz de montaluo ... (emprimido enla ... cibdad de Salamanca por Laurencio de leon de dey: año de mill ⁊ quinientos: ⁊ treze años: acabo se a veynte ⁊ cinco dias ó Iunio.) fol. B.L. a^8 (-a6) b-p^8. ff. [j]-cxix. ¶*Sig.* a *remargined.* (Lea.) [115

DICTIONARIOLUM. Dictionariolum Latinogræcogallicum. ... Auec les mots Francois, selon l'ordre des Lettres, ... tournez en Latin. ... Parisiis, Apud Nicolaum Chesneau ... M. D. LXXIII. ... 8°. A-Ff^8 Gg^2 a-o^8 p^4 q^2. ¶*Additional t.p.* (a1^r): Les mots Francois ... tournez en Latin. ... A Paris, Chez Nicolas Chesneau ... M. D. LXXII. ... [116

DICTIONARIUM. Dictionarium historicum, geographicum, poeticum ... [Genevae,] Apud Iacobum Stoer, M. D. XC. fol. ¶^{4} A-3K^8 3L^4. ff. 1-352. (Lea.) [117

DICTYS CRETENSIS. Les histoires de Dictis Cretensien, traitant des guerres de Troye ... Interpretées en François. Par Ian de la Lande ... A Paris. Pour Vincent Sertenas ... 1556. (... imprimez par Estienne Groulleau, le vingte septiesme iour de Feburier ...) 8°. ã^8 A-R^8 S^{10} (-S10, *presumably blank*). ff. 1-145. [118

DICTYS CRETENSIS

-- -- Ditte Candiano della guerra Troiana. Darete Frygio della rouina Troiana. Declamatione di Libanio ... Mirsilio Lesbio dell'origine d'Italia, è de Tirreni. Archiloco de tempi. Beroso Babilonio dell'antichità. Manethone de i Re d'Egitto. Metasthene Persiano del giudicio de tempi, & annuali historie de Persani. Quinto Fabio Pittore dell'Aurea età, è dell'origine di Roma. Caio Sempronio della diuisione d'Italia, & origine di Roma. ... In Vinegia. Appresso Vincenzo Vaugris ... M. D. XLIII. 8°. *^{8} A-Q^8 R^4. ff. 1-132. [119

-- -- Ditte Candiotto et Darete Frigio della guerra Troiana, tradotti per Thomaso Porcacchi da Castiglione Arretino ... In Vinetia appresso Gabriel Giolito di Ferrarii MDLXX. 4°. a-d^4 A-X^4 Y^6. pp. 1-180. [120

-- -- Warhafftige Histori vnd beschreibung/ von dem Troianischen krieg/ vnd zerstörung der Stat Troie/ Durch ... Dictyn Cretensem/ vn̄ Darem Phrygium ... durch Marcum Tatium &c. Auss dē Latein ins Teütsch verwandelt ... M.D.XL. (Gedruckt ... inn der ... Statt Augspurg durch Haynrich Stayner/ Am xxiiij tag Aprilis ...) fol. a-b^6 A-N^6 O^4. ff. II-LxxxII. [121

-- -- *Another copy.* [122

DIDYMUS CHALCENTERUS. [1]Σκολια ... εις την του Ομηρου Ιλιαδα, και εις την Οδυσσεα. Interpretationes ... in Homeri Iliada, nec non in Odyssea. 8°. a-z^8 A-R^8. ff. 2-319. [2] ... Porphyrij ... homericarum quæstionum liber. Eiusdem de Nympharum antro in Odyssea, opusculum. (Venetiis in aedibus Aldi, et Andreae soceri mense Maio. M.D.XXI.) a-e^8 f^4. [123

DIEPOLD, JOHANN. Ain Nutzliche Sermon ... von der rechte Euangelische mess. ... [Augsburg, Heinrich Steiner,] M.D.XXij. 4°. A^4 B^2. [124

DIETENBERGER, JOHANN. Ioannis Dytenbergii ... cōtra temerarium Martini Lutheri, de uotis monasticis iudicium, libri duo ... Coloniæ. Expensis ... Petri Quentell. Anno. M. D. XXV. Mense Iunio. 8°. a-p^8 q^4 A-T^8 (-T8) a^8 b^4. ff. 2-272 *present.* ¶*Additional t.p.* (A1^r): ... de uotis monasticis liber secundus ... M. D. XXV. [125

-- -- Doctor Ioannes Dietenberger. wider. CXXXIX schlussrede Mar. Luthers/ von gelübdniss vn̄ geistlichē leben der klosterlüt ... vertütscht durch Io. Cochleū ... (Getruckt zů Strassburg vō Iohanne Grieninger vff sant Thomas abent. Anno. 1523.) 4°. A-G^4. ¶*The text is actually that of Cochlaeus' translation of part of Bishop Fisher's confutation of Luther (cf.* F104*).* [126

-- -- Grundt vn̄ vrsach/ aus ð heyligē schrifft/ wie vnbillich vn̄ vnredlich/ das heylig lobsangk Marie Salue regina ... in etlichē Stetten wirt vnderlassen/ verspott vnd abgestellt. ... Anno M. D. xxvj. 8°. a-h^4. [127

-- -- Grundt vnnd vrsach ... 8°. A-H^4. [128

-- Postill oder Ausslegung der Epistelen vn̄ Euangelien auff alle Sontag vnd etliche Feirtag des gantzen iars ... In Cöln am Rhein/ durch die Erben des erbarn Iohan Quentels/ Anno 1555. 4°. A^4 a-3b^4. ff. ij-vij, 8-192. [129

DIETRICH, VEIT. Agend Bůchlein für die Pfar-Herren auff dem Land. (Gedruckt zu Nürmberg/ durch Iohan vom Berg/ vnd Vlrich Neuber ... 1543.) 4°. a-z^4 A-B^4. [130

-- -- M. D. LIII. (Gedruckt zu Nürnberg/ durch Iohan̄ vom Berg/ vnd Vlrich Newber.) 4°. π^4 A^4 a-z^4 A-F^4. (Yarnall.) [130a

-- -- Nürmberg. M. D. LXXXVI. (Gedruckt ... durch Nicolaum Knorrn. ...) 4°. a-y^4. (Yarnall.) [130b

-- Gründtlicher vnterricht vom Sacrament des Altars ... 1543. (Gedruckt zu Nürmberg/ durch Iohan vom Berg/ vnd Vlrich Neuber ...) 4°. A-M^4. [131

-- Ain Sermon von dem fůsswaschen. Gepredigt zu Nürmberg ... 1543. [Nürnberg, Johann vom Berg & Ulrich Neuber.] 4°. A-C^4. [132

-- Summaria vber die gantze Bibel ... Item/ Vnterschied des alten vnd newen Testaments. Fürneme vnterschied zwischen reiner Christlicher Lehre des Euangelij/ vnd die Abgöttischen Papisten lehre. Christlicher ... vnterricht/ von vergebung der sünde vnd seligkeyt/ Durch

Philip. Melanch. Kurtzer begriff vnd inhalt der gantzen heyligen Schrifft ... durch Iohannem Brentium. ... Nürnberg. M. D. LIX. (Gedruckt ... durch Iohañ vom Berg/ vnd Vlrich Newber.) fol. a-dd^6 ee^8 A-Dd^6 Ee-Ff^8 (-Ff8). ¶a^6, b1-3 *repaired.* [133

DIGGES, LEONARD. An Arithmeticall Militare Treatise, named stratioticos ... Long since attēpted by Leonard Digges Gentleman, Augmented, digested, and lately finished, by Thomas Digges, his Sonne. ... At London: Printed by Henrie Bynneman. ... 1579. (*Colophon.*) 4°. B.L. A^4 a^4 B-Z^4 (Y4 + 2 *folded leaves*) &^{4}. pp. 2-191. *S.T.C.* 6848. [134

-- A geometrical practical treatize named pantometria ... Containing rules manifolde for mensuration ... First published by Thomas Digges ... At London Printed by Abell Ieffes. Anno. 1591. fol. [A]^4 (-[A]1, *blank*) B-Cc^4. pp. 1-195. *S.T.C.* 6859. [135

DILBAUM, SAMUEL. Marsilianische Historia. Summarischer bericht/ dessen/ so sich mit/ vnd von wegen der Statt Marsilia/ inn disem noch wehrenden Krieg/ zwischen Heinrico dem IIII. .../ Kȍnig inn Franckreich vnd Nauarra/ auch Philippo dem Kȍnig in Hispania/ zugetragen ... Beschriben vnd zu Augspurg inn den Truckh verordnet/ durch Samuelem Dilbaum ... M. D. XCVI. 4°. A^4 B^2. [136

DINNER, CONRAD. De ortu, vita, et rebus gestis ... Georgii Ludouici à Seinsheim senioris ... historicae Expositionis Libri Quinque Impressi, ... M D XC. fol. a^6 b-c^4 A-3A^4 3B^6. pp. 1-387. [137

DIODORUS SICULUS. Διοδωρου Σικελιωτου ιστοριων βιβλια ... Diodori Siculi hiatoriarum libri aliquot, qui extant, opera & studio Vincentii Obsopoei in lucem editi. ... Basileae. (Ετυπωθη ... ἐπιμελέια μὲν Ιωάννου Ὀπωρινοῦ, ἀναλώμασι δὲ Ρὸβέρτου Χειμερινοῦ, ἔτει ... α φ λ θ [1539]. βοηδρομιῳνος μενὸς.) 4°. Aα^6 a-z^4 A-Nn^4 Oo^6. pp. 2-481. [138

-- -- Diodorus Siculus [*signum Francisci Regnault*] Venundantur Parisius in vico Sancti Iacobi sub signo Diui Claudii 4°. a-v$^{8.4}$ x^6 y^4. ff. II-CXXIII. ¶*Translator: Poggio Bracciolini.* (Lea.) [139

-- -- Diodori Siculi bibliothecae historicae libri XVII. Lugduni, apud haered. Seb. Gryphii, 1559. 16°. a-z^8 A-Z^8 aa-zz^8 AA^8 BB^4. pp. 2-1127. [140

-- -- Diodori Siculi bibliothecæ historicæ libri XV. ... Sebastiano Castalione totius operis correctore, partim interprete. Interiecta verò est, Dictys Cretensis & Daretis Phrygii de bello Troiano historia, & Tryphiodori Aegyptij, Ilij excidium, Gulielmo Xylandro interprete, ad supplendam lacunam quinqȝ librorum ... Basileæ (... ex officina Henricpetrina, ... CIↃ. I.Ↄ LXXIIX. mense Martio.) fol. a^4):(^{4} b-c^6 A-N^8 O^{12} P-Vu^8 Xx^6 Yy^8. pp. 1-715. [141

-- -- Histoire de Diodore Sicilien traduite de Grec en Francois. Les premiers liures par M. Robert Macault ... Et les autres ... Par M. Iacques Amyot ... Reueuē & enrichie de ... Annotations ..., par M. Loys le Roy, Dit Regius. A Paris, Chez Gilles Beys ... M. D. LXXXV. fol. ā^6 ē^6 A-3O^6. pp. 2-686. [142

-- -- [1] Historia ouero libraria historica di Diodoro Siciliano ... Tradotto di Greco in Latino da diuersi auttori, & nella nostra lingua da M. Francesco Baldelli. ... In Vinegia appresso Gabriel Giolito de' Ferrari. M D LXXV. 4°. *-**^{4} a-c^8 d^6 A-3Q^8 3R^4. pp. 1-1000. [2] La seconda parte della libraria historica ... *Same imprint.* *-**^{8} a-y^8 z^4. pp. 7-357. [143

-- -- *Selections.* Diodori Siculi ... libri duo: Primus. De Philippi Regis Macedoniae: Aliorumqȝ quorundam Illustrium Ducum: Alter de Alexandri Filij rebus gestis. Vtrunqȝ Latinitate donauit Angelus Cospus Bononiensis. Alexandri regis vita: quam Graece scriptam a Ioanne Monacho Angelus Cospus vertit in nostram linguam. (Impressum Venetiis per Georgium de Rusconibus Mediolanēsem. ... M.D.XVIII. Die .XXII. Maii.) fol. AA^4 A-I^6 K^4. ff. I-LVII. [144

-- -- L'histoire des successeurs de Alexandre le Grand, extraicte de Diodore Sicilien, & quelques peu de vies escriptes par Plutharque, Translatée par Messire Claude de Seyssel ... Imprimé a Paris par Pierre Gaultier pour Iehan Barbé & Claude Garamont. 1545. 16°. a-z^8 A-R^8. ff. 2-307. [145

DIODORUS SICULUS

-- -- Diodoro Siculo delle antiche historie fauolose. ... In Vinegia appresso Gabriel Giolito de Ferrari. MDXLVII. (*Colophon.*) 8°. *8 A-O8 P10. ff. 2-119. [146

DIOGENES. Dolium Diogenis Strepitu suo collaborans Dynastis Christianis, bellum in Turcas parantibus. Anno M. D. XCIIII. 8°. A10. [147

DIOGENES LAERTIUS. Διογενους Λαερτίου ... βιβλία Ι. Diogenis Laertii de vitis, dogmatis & apophthegmatis eorum qui in philosophia claruerunt, libri X. ... Cum annotationibus Henr. Stephani. Pythag. philosophorum fragmneta. Cum Latina interpretatione. Anno M. D. LXX, [Genevae,] Excudebat Henricus Stephanus. 8°. a4 a-z8 A-H8 aa-bb8 cc4 A-Dd8. pp. 3-8, 1-494, 1-40, 2-432. [148

-- -- Diogenis Laertii de vita et moribus philosophorum libri X. ... Apud Seb. Gryphium Lugduni, 1546. 8°. a-z8 A-G8 H4. pp. 3-468. ¶*Translator: Ambrogio Traversari.* [149

-- -- ... restituti ... opera Ioannis Sambuci ... Antuerpiae, Ex officina Christophori Plantini, cIↄ Iↄ LXVI. ... 8°. A-Z8 a-f8. pp. 3-[456]. [150

-- -- Le vite degli illustri filosofi di Diogene Laertio, Da'l Greco Idiomate ridutte ne la lingua commune d'Italia. ... In Vinegia. Appresso Vicenzo Vaugris ... M. D. XLV. 8°. *8 a-z8 A-H8 I4. ff. 1-251. ¶z8 *misbound before* y1. *Translators: Bartolommeo and Pietro Rositini.* [151

DIOMEDES. Diomedis grammatici opus, ab Iohanne Caesario ... emendatum, scholijsq́; illustratum ... Item Donati de octo orationis partibus, & Barbarismo libellus ... Coloniae, per Iohannem Soterem Anno, MDXXXVI. (... Calendis April.) 8°. A8 a-y8. ff. 1-176. ¶A1 *defective.* [152

DION CASSIUS. Dion Historien Grec, des faictz & gestes insignes des Romains ... Premierement traduict de Grec en Italien, par messire Nicolas Leonicene, Ferrarois: & depuis de Italien en vulgaire Francois, par Claude Deroziers, de Bourges en Berry. ... Nouuellement imprimé à Paris, pour Arnoul & Charles les Angeliers ... M. D. XLII. (*Colophon.*) fol. ã4 a-z8 Aa-Ll8 Mm10. ff. I-CCLXXXI. [153

-- -- Dione Historico delle Guerre & Fatti de Romani: Tradotto di Greco in lingua uulgare, per M. Nicolo Leoniceno. ... M D XXXIII. (Impresso in Vinegia per Nicolo d'Aristotile di Ferrara detto Zoppino ... del mese di Marzo.) 4°. *6 A-LL8 MM10. ff. I-CCLXXXII. [154

-- -- Dione Cassio Niceo historico Greco de' fatti de' Romani dalla guerra Di Candia ... Tradotto di Greco in Latino per Guglielmo Xilandro d'Augusta, e nouamente nella nostra lingua ridotto per M. Francesco Baldelli. Con la vita dell' auttore, descritta per Thomaso Porcacchi ... In Venetia appresso i Gioliti. M D LXXXV. 4°. a4 +4 *-4*8 5*2 A-3F8 3G6. pp. 1-843. [155

-- -- *Epitome.* Εκ των Διωνος του Νικαεως Ρωμαϊκῶν ἱστοριῶν ... Dionis Nicaei rerum Romanarum à Pompeio Magno ad Alexādrum Mamææ, Epitome authore Ioanne Xiphilino. ... Lutetiae, Ex officina Roberti Stephani ... M. D. LI. 4°. a-z4 A-Y4. pp. 3-357. [156

-- -- Epitome della historia Romana di Dione Niceo di XXV. imper. Romani ... tradotto per M. Francesco Baldelli ... In Venetia appresso i Gioliti. M D LXXXV. 4°. *10 A-Z8. pp. 1-367. [157

-- -- *Selections.* In hoc volumine haec continentur. Neruæ & Traiani, atqȝ Adriani Cæsarum uitæ ex Dione, Georgio Merula interprete. Aelius Spartianus. Iulius Capitolinus. Lampridius. Flauius Vopiscus. Trebellius Pollio. Vulcatius Gallicanus. Ab Ioanne Baptista Egnatio Veneto ... castigati. Heliogabali prīcipis ad meretrices ... oratio. Eiusdem Io. Baptistæ Egnatij de Cæsaribus libri tres ... Eiusdem in Spartiani, Lampridijq́; uitas, & reliquorum annotationes. Aristidis Smyrnæi oratio de laudibus urbis Romæ à Scipione Carteromacho in latinum uersa. ... Cōflagratio Veseui montis ex Dione, Georgio Merula interprete. (Venetiis in aedibus Aldi, et Andreae soceri, mense Augsuto. M. D. XIX.) 8°. *8 a-zz8 A-G8. ff. 1-422. [158

DIONYSIUS THE AREOPAGITE. Dionysii Areopagitae opera omnia quae extant. ... Scholia incerti auctoris in librum De Ecclesiastica Hierarchia. Quæ omnia ... à Ioachimo Perionio ... conuersa sunt. ... Lutetiae Parisiorum, ex officina typographica Michaëlis Vascosani ... M. D. LVI. ... fol. *6 A-O6. ff. 1-84. [159

-- -- Γεωργιου του Παχυμερη παραφρασις ... Georgii Pachymeræ paraphrasis in omnia Dionysij Areopagitæ ... opera quæ extant. ... Parisiis. M.D.LXI. Excudebat Guil. Morelius ... (*Colophon.*) 8°. *⁶ A-Z⁸ a-d⁸ e⁶. pp. 1-444. [160

-- Dionysii Areopagitæ ... Libri duo, alter de Mystica Theologia, alter de Diuinis nominibus: Marsilio Ficino et interprete et explanatore. *Greek & Latin.* ... Venetiis. MDXXXVIII. (... in ædibus Bartholomæi de Zanettis Casterzagensis. ... M D XXXIX. Mense Ianuario.) 8°. a-z⁸ A-H⁸ I⁴. ff. 2-251. [161

-- Preclarum opusculũ Dyonisii Areopagite De diuinis nominibus Marsilio Ficino interprete ... (Impressum Venetiis ... 1501. quarto nonas aprilis. Impensa Petri Liechteusteyn [*sic*] Coloniensis arte ... Iacobi de Leucho.) 4°. A-N⁶ O-P⁸. ff. 2-94. [162

-- D. Dionysii Areopagitae De mystica Theologia lib. I. Graece Ioan. Sarraceno Ambrosio Camaldul. Marsilio Ficino Interpret. ... Ioan. Eckius Commentarios adiecit ... (... excusum ... Augustę Vindelicorũ, in officina Ioannis Miller, Die XXV. Mens. Maij. ... M. D. XIX.) fol. A-E⁶ F⁸. [163

DIONYSIUS OF HALICARNASSUS. Dionysii Halicarnassei Antiquitatum Rom. Libri XI. Ab Æmilio Porto ... Latinè redditi. [Lugduni,] Ex officina Antonij de Harsy, Anno 1590. 16°. ¶-¶¶⁸ A-3Z⁸ 4Z⁴. pp. 1-1082. [164

DIONYSIUS PERIEGETES. Διονυσιου Αλεξανδρεως τῆς οἰκουμένης περιήγησις ... Dionysii Alexandrini de situ orbis libellus, Eustathii Thessalonicensis archiepiscopi commentariis illustratus. ... Lutetiae, Ex officina Rob. Stephani ... M. D. XLVII. ... 4°. A-Y⁴ Z⁶. pp. 3-158. [165

-- -- Denys Alexandrin, de la situation du monde. Nouuellement traduict de Grec en François, & illustré de Commentaires ... Par Benigne Saumaize. ... A Paris, Chez Adrian Perier ... M.D.XCVII. ... 12°. ã⁸ A-K¹² L⁴. ff. 1-124. [166

DIOSCURIDES. Dioscoridis libri octo Graece et Latine. ... Parisiis, Apud Petrum Haultinum ... 1549 ... (Excudebat Benedictus Preuost ... mense Augusto ...) 8°. aa-bb⁸ cc⁴ a-z⁸ A-Cc⁸. ff. 1-392. ¶*Translator: Joannes Ruellius.* [167

DIRECTORIUM. Directoriũ cõcubinariorũ ... (Impressum ... Agrippine al's Colonie ... M.ccccc.viij. Et iã denuo ibidẽ anno seq̄uti .M.D.ix. in officina litteraria ... liberoꝝ Quẽtell) 4°. B.L. A-H⁶·⁶·⁶·⁴. ff. Primũ-xxxj. [168

-- -- Tractatꝰ fructuosi. Directorium concubinariorum. Iam tertio Coloniæ impressum ... Purgatorium detractorum. Iam denuo impressum ... Stimulus veneficiatorum. denuo iam impressus ... Stupor collatorũ bñficiorũ. iam primũ in lucem æditus. Opusculum de feris dũ per easdẽ proximus damnificatur, iam denuo impressum. ... (Coloniæ. Anno. M. D. XXVI.) 4°. A-Rr⁴. ff. II-CLI. [169

DISPUTATION. Des newen Bischofs zu der Lochaw disputation mit Doctor Ochssenfart vor dem Bischoff von Meyssen zů der Lochaw geschehen In Saxen Im M. D. vnnd XXij. Jar. 4°. A⁴ B². [170

-- Eyn trostliche disputation/ ... den glawben vnd die lieb betreffend/ Vnd wie eyner den andern Christenlich vnterweisen soll/ gãtz nützlich zu den artickeln D. Vrbani Regij vnd Gretzingers. Wittemberg. 1524. 8°. A-G⁸ H⁴. [171

DISTELMAIR, CONRAD. Ain trewe ermanung/ das ain yeder Christ selbs zů seiner seelhait sehe ... [Augsburg, Heinrich Steiner,] 1523. 4°. A-B⁴. [172

DITMAR. Chronici Ditmari episcopi Mersepurgii, libri VII. ... Accessere de vita & familia Ditmari, ... item de veteribus Mysniæ Marchionibus ... expositiones: Auctore Reinero Reineccio Steinhemio. Francofurti ad Moenum Ex officina Typographica Andreæ Wecheli, M D LXXX. fol. ã⁶ A-I⁶ K⁸ L⁴. pp. 1-123. (Lea.) [173

DIVIZIO DA BIBBIENA, BERNARDO. Comedia di Bernardo Diuitio da Bibiena intitolata Calandra. (Stampata in Roma [per Francesco Minizio Calvo] nellanno M.D.XXIIII.) 12°. A-H⁶ (-H6, *presumably blank*). ff. II-XLVII. [174

DIVIZIO DA BIBBIENA

-- -- Calandra comedia di M. Bernardo da Bibiena ... In Fiorenza, MDLVIII. (... Appresso i Giunti. M D LIX.) 8°. A-E^{8} F^{4}. ff. 2-42. [175

-- -- In Venetia, Per gli heredi di Bortolamio Rubin. M D LXXXVI. 12°. A-D^{12}. ff. 2-47. [176

DOCTRINAL. Le doctrinal de la religion et foy catholique. ... A Paris, Par Guillaume Nyuerd ... 8°. A^{8} B-H^{4} (-H4, *presumably blank*). ff. 2-34. ¶*Privilege dated 26 March 1560.* [177

DOES, JORIS VAN DER. Georgii Dousæ, de itinere suo Constantinopolitano, Epistola. ... [Lugduni Batavorum,] Ex Officina Plantiniana, Apud Christophorum Raphelengium ... cIↄ. Iↄ. IC. 8°. A-I^{8}. pp. 3-141. [178

DOLCE, LODOVICO. L'Achille et l'Enea di Messer Lodouico Dolce. ... Aggiuntoui ... vna oratione del S. Andrea Menechini Sopra le lodi della Poesia, & de' Fautori delle Virtù. In Vinegia appresso Gabriel Giolito de' Ferrari. M D LXXII. 4°. a^{6} a-b^{4} A-LL^{8} a-e^{4}. pp. 1-544. ¶*Additional t.p.* (^{3}a1^{r}): Delle lodi della poesia, d'Omero, et di Virgilio. ... *Same imprint.* [179

-- Il capitano comedia ... Con alcune stanze del medesimo nella fauola d'Adone. ... In Vinegia Appresso Gabriel Giolito de Ferrari. MDXLV. (*Colophon.*) 8°. A-F^{8} G^{10}. ff. 2-57. [180

-- -- In Vinegia Appresso Gabriel Giolito de Ferrari. MDXLVII. (*Colophon.*) 8°. A-F^{8} G^{10} (-G10, *presumably blank*). ff. 3-55. [181

-- Dialogo della institution delle donne ... In Vinegia Appresso Gabriel Giolito de Ferrari. MDXLVII. (*Colophon.*) 8°. A-L^{8}. ff. 2-84. [182

-- Dialogo della pittura ... intitolato l'Aretino. ... In Vinegia appresso Gabriel Giolito de' Ferrari. M D LVII. 8°. A-G^{8} H^{4}. ff. 2-60. (Fine Arts.) [183

-- Dialogo ..., Nel quale si ragiona del modo di accrescere e conseruar la memoria. ... In Venetia. (... appresso Gio. Battista, et Marchio Sessa fratelli. MDLXII.) 8°. *^{4} A-P^{8}. ff. 3-119. [184

-- -- In Vinegia. Per gli Heredi di Marchiò Sessa. 1575. (... appresso Enea de Alaris.) 8°. A-P^{8}. ff. 3-118. [185

-- -- In Venetia, Appresso Giouanbattista Sessa, & fratelli. M. D. LXXXVI. 8°. A-P^{8}. ff. 2-118. [186

-- Dialogo ..., nel quale si ragiona delle qualità, diuersità, & proprietà de i colori. ... In Venetia appresso Gio. Battista, Marchio Sessa, et fratelli. (... 1565.) 8°. A-L^{8}. ff. 4-87. [187

-- -- *Another copy.* [188

-- Didone, tragedia ... In Vinegia, M. D. XLVII. (... in casa de' figliuoli di Aldo ...) 8°. A-D^{8} E^{10}. ff. 2-42. [189

-- Fabritia. Comedia ... [Venice, Aldine Press,] M D XXXXIX. 8°. A-G^{8} H^{4}. ff. 2-60. [190

-- -- In Vinegia appresso Gabriel Giolito de' Ferrari. M D LX. 12°. A-E^{12} (-A12) F^{6} (-F6, *presumably blank*). ff. 2-65. [191

-- Giocasta. Tragedia ... In Vinegia, M.D.XLIX. (... appresso i figliuoli d'Aldo ... Il mese di Marzo.) 8°. A-G^{8}. ff. 2-54. [192

-- La Hecuba tragedia ..., tratta da Euripide. ... In Venetia Appresso Gabriel Gioli di Ferrarij. M.D.XLIII. (... Dil mese di Luglio.) 8°. A-F^{8}. ff. 3-47. [193

-- -- In Vinegia appresso Gabriel Giolito de Ferrari. MDXLIX. (*Colophon.*) 12°. A-D^{12}. ff. 4-48. [194

-- Ifigenia. Tragedia ... In Vinegia appresso Gabriel Giolito de Ferrari e fratelli. MDLI. (*Colophon.*) 12°. A-D^{12} E^{6}. ff. 2-51. [195

-- -- In Venetia, appresso Domenico Farri. M D LXVI. 8°. A-G^{8}. ff. 2-56. [196

-- Lettere di diuersi eccellentiss. huomini ... In Vinegia appresso Gabriel Giolito de' Ferrari. MDLIX. (*Colophon.*) 8°. A-HH^8 II^4. pp. 3-488. ¶*Edited by Dolce.* [197

-- Libri tre ...; ne i quali si tratta delle diuerse sorti delle Gemme, che produce la Natura ... In Venetia appresso Gio. Battista, Marchio Sessa, et Fratelli. (... M D LXV.) 8°. A-M^8 N^4. ff. 2-99. [198

-- Marianna, Tragedia ... Con alcune rime e versi Del Detto. ... In Vinegia appresso Gabriel Giolito de' Ferrari. MDLXV. 8°. A-K^8. pp. 3-147. [199

-- Il marito comedia ... In Vinegia Appresso Gabriel Giolito de Ferrari. MDXLVII. 8°. A-C^8 D^4. ff. 5-28. [200

-- La Medea tragedia ... In Vinegia appresso Gabriel Giolito de' Ferrari. M D LVIII. 8°. A-F^8. ff. 2-40. [201

-- Le osseruationi del Dolce. ... in questa seconda editione ... In Vinegia appresso Gabriel Giolito de Ferrari, et fratelli. M D LII. (*Colophon.*) 12°. A-K^{12} (-K11-12, *blank*). pp. 3-230. [202

-- -- I quattro libri delle osseruationi ... Sesta editione. ... In Pesaro Appresso gli Heredi di Bartolomeo Cesano, & Guid'vbaldo Bicillo da Vrbino Compagni. l'Anno MDLXI.) 8°. A-M^8. pp. 3-190. [203

-- Il Palmerino ... In Venetia, appresso Gio. Battista Sessa, et fratelli. M D LXI. (*Colophon.*) 4°. A-Q^8 R^{10}. ff. 3-137. [204

-- Paraphrasi nella sesta satira di Giuuenale ... Dialogo in cui si parla di che qualita si dee tor moglie ... Lo epithalamio di Ca=| Catullo [*sic*] nelle nozze di Peleo & di Theti. M D XXXVIII. (In Venegia per Curtio nauo e Fratelli.) 8°. A-O^4 P^6. [205

-- Il primo libro di Sacripante ... (Impresso in Vinegia per Francesco Bindoni e Mapheo Pasini il Mese di Giugno l'Anno MDXXXVI.) 4°. A^6 B-T^4. [206

-- Il ragazzo. Comedia ... In Vineggia M D LIX. (... Per Francesco detto lo Imperador. ...) 8°. A-G^8. ff. 2-55. [207

-- Rime di diuersi, et eccellenti autori. ... In Vinegia appresso Gabriel Giolito de' Ferrari, et fratelli. M D LVI. 12°. $*^{12}$ $**^6$ A-CC^{12}. pp. 3-86, 1-624. ¶*Edited by Dolce.* [208

-- -- *Another copy.* [209

-- -- Il primo volume delle rime scelte da diuersi autori ... In Vinegia appresso Gabriel Giolito de' Ferrari M D LXV. 12°. *Same collation.* pp. 1-624. [210

-- Il ruffiano comedia ... Tratta del Rudente di Plauto. ... In Venetia, Per gli heredi di Bortolamio Rubin. M D LXXXVII. 12°. A-D^{12}. ff. 2-48. [211

-- Stanze di diuersi illustri poeti. Nuouamente raccolte da M. Lodouico Dolce ... In Vinegia appresso Gabriel Giolito de' Ferrari, et fratelli. MDLVI. 12°. *-$**^{12}$ *(wanting)* A-X^{12}. pp. 6-502. [212

-- Thyeste tragedia ..., tratta da Seneca. ... In Venetia Appresso Gabriel Gioli di Ferrarij. M. D. XLIII. (... Del mese di Settembre.) 8°. A-D^8. ff. 3-32. [213

-- Le tragedie di M. Lodouico Dolce cioe, Giocasta, Didone, Thieste, Medea, Ifigenia, Hecuba ... In Venetia, appresso Domenico Farri. M D LXVI. 8°. A-G^8 (-G6-8, *blank*). ff. 3-53. ¶Giocasta *only*. [214

-- Le Troiane tragedia ... In Vinegia appresso Gabriel Giolito de' Ferrari. M D LXVII. 8°. A-I^8 (-I8). pp. 8-141. [215

-- Vita dell' ... imperador Carlo Quinto ... In Vinegia appresso Gabriel Giolito de' Ferrari, M D LXI. 4°. $*^6$ A-L^8 M^4. pp. 1-168. [216

DOMENICHI, LUIGI. Dialoghi ... In Vinegia appresso Gabriel Giolito de' Ferrari. MDLXII. 8°. $*^8$ $**^{10}$ A-BB^8. pp. 1-399. [217

-- Le due cortigiane, comedia ... In Fiorenza, a stanza di Giorgio Mariscotti; M D LXIII. (... appresso i figliuoli di Lorenzo Torrentino ...) 8°. A-E^8 F^4. pp. 3-88. [218

-- -- In Venetia, Appresso Francesco Franceschini. 1567. (*Colophon.*) 8°. A-E^8 F^4. ff. 2-44. [219

-- Facetie motti, et burle di diuersi signori ... raccolte per M. Lodouico Domenichi ... Con vna nuoua aggiunta di Motti, raccolti da Thomaso Porcacchi ... (Stampato ... Vinegia Per Alessandro de Viano ... M. D. LXVIII.) 8°. *-**^{6} A-Ii^8 (-Ii8, *presumably blank*). pp. 1-509. [220

-- Historia varia ... In Vinegia appresso Gabriel Giolito de' Ferrari. M D LXV. 8°. *-3*^{8} A-3F^8. pp. 1-830. [221

-- La nobilta delle donne ... In Vinetia appresso Gabriel Giolito di Ferrarii MDXLIX. (*Colophon.*) 8°. *$^{8+1}$ A-LL^8 MM^4. ff. 1-272. [222

-- -- In Vinetia appresso Gabriel Giolito di Ferrarii e fratelli. 1551. (*Colophon.*) 8°. *^{8} A-LL^8 MM^4. ff. 2-8, 1-275. [223

-- -- *Another copy (with a duplicate of sig.* K *bound in after* V8*).* [224

-- Progne, tragedia ... In Fiorenza appresso i Giunti; MDLXI. (*Colophon.*) 8°. A-D^8 E^2. pp. 9-68. [225

-- Rime ... In Vinegia appresso Gabriel Giolito de Ferrari M D XLIIII. (*Colophon.*) 8°. A-N^8. ff. 5-104. [226

-- Rime diuerse di molti eccellentiss. autori ... Libro primo ... In Vinetia appresso Gabriel Giolito di Ferrarii. MDXLVI (*Colophon.*) 8°. A-Bb^8. pp. 3-374. ¶*Edited by Domenichi.* A1 *repaired.* [227

-- -- In Vinetia appresso Gabriel Giolito di Ferrarii MDXLIX. 8°. A-Bb^8. pp. 4-374. [228

DOMENICO DA SAN GEMIGNANO. ... Dominici de sancto geminano cōmētaria ... in Decretū ... (... per Lucam antoniuȝ de giunta florentinum Venetijs impressa: ... Kl'. Februarij ... Mcccccciij.) fol. B.L. a-u^8 x^6 A-BB^8 CC-DD^{10}. ff. 2-166, 1-211. (Biddle.) [229

DOMODOSSOLA. ... Statuta curiae matarellae Domus Ossulae ... Mediolani, Ex Officina Typographica Pacifici Pontij. M. D. LXXXVII. fol. π^2 A-E^4. pp. 2-40. (Lea.) [230

DONATO, BERNARDINO. [1] De Platonicae atque Aristotelicæ Philosophiæ differentia, Libellus. ... Venetiis Apud Hieronymum Scotum. 1540. 8°. a-d^8 e^4. pp. 3-71. [2] Γεωργίου τοῦ Γεμιστοῦ τοῦ καὶ Πλήθωνος περὶ ὧν Ἀριστοτέλης πρὸς Πλάτωνα διαφέρεται. 8°. α-γ^8. ff. 1-23. [231

DONATUS, AELIUS. Partes orationis ... (Explicit donatus. Imprime a Caen par Laurens hostingue pour Michel angier ... [c. 1515.]) 16°. B.L. A^8. [232

DONER, LORENZ. Eine Warhafftige historia geschehen zu Stasfard/ im iar/ MDXXXIIII. am abend der geburt Christi. Wittemberg/ gedruckt Nickel Schirlentz 1535. 4°. A^4. [233

DONI, ANTON FRANCESCO. L'asinesca gloria dell' Inasinito academico Pellegrino. In Vinegia nell'Academia Pellegrina per Francesco Marcolini. M D L III. (*Colophon.*) 8°. A-B^8 C^6. pp. 3-44. [234

-- [1] Il cancellieri del Doni, libro della memoria, doue si tratta per paragone della prudenza de gli antichi, con la sapienza de moderni ... In Vinegia appresso Gabriel Giolito de' Ferrari. M D LXII. 4°. A-G^4. pp. 3-56. [2] Il cancellieri del Doni, libro dell'eloquenza ... *Same imprint.* A-H^4. pp. 3-64. [235

-- Dichiaratione del Doni, sopra il XIII. cap. dell'Apocalisse, contro a gli heretici ... In Vinegia appresso Gabriel Giolito de' Ferrari. M D LXII. 4°. A-C^4 D^2. pp. 3-27. [236

-- Disegno del Doni ... ne quali si tratta della scoltura et pittura ... In Vinetia Appresso Gabriel Giolito di Ferrarii M D XLIX. (*Colophon.*) 8°. A-H^8. ff. 2-63. [237

-- Inferni del Doni academico pellegrino. Libro secondo de mondi In Vinegia per Francesco Marcolini nel MDLIII. (*Colophon.*) 4°. A-FF^4. pp. 3-224. ¶*Additional t.pp.:* (F1^r) Inferni del Doni. Secondo inferno del Perduto academico peregrino. (K1^r) ... Terzo inferno del Pazzo academico peregrino. (O1^r) ... Quarto inferno del Sauio academico peregrino.

(S1r) ... Quinto inferno dell'Ardito academico peregrino. (Y1r) ... Sesto inferno dello Smarrito academico peregrino. (CC1r) ... Settimo inferno dell'Ostinato academico peregrino. *Each with imprint:* In Vinegia nell'Academia Peregrina per Francesco Marcolini. M D L III. [238

-- [I marmi.] In Vinegia per Francesco Marcolini MDLII. (*Colophon.*) 4°. [1] I marmi del Doni, academico Peregrino. A-X4. pp. 3-167. [2] La seconda parte de marmi ... Aa-Pp4. pp. 3-119. [3] La terza parte ... a4 B-X4. pp. 3-166. [4] La quarta parte ... AA-MM4. pp. 3-93. [239

-- I mondi del Doni, libro primo. In Vinegia Per Francesco Marcolini ... M D LII. (... del Mese d'Aprile ...) 4°. a4 A-HH4. ff. 2-120. ¶*Additional t.pp.* (A1r, P3r): L'Academia Peregrina e i mondi sopra le medaglie del Doni. ... In Vinegia nell' Academia P. MDLII. [240

-- -- Les mondes, celestes, terrestres et infernaux. ... Tirez des oeuures de Doni Fiorentino, per Gabriel Chappuis Tourangeau. A Lyon, pour Barthelemy Honorati. 1578. ... (Imprimé ... par Guichard Ielayron ...) 8°. *8 a-z8 A-F8 G4. pp. 1-464. [241

-- Pistolotti amorosi del Doni, con alcune altre lettere d'amore di diuersi autori ... In Vinegia appresso Gabriel Giolito de Ferrari e fratelli M D LII. (*Colophon.*) 8°. *8 A-M8 (-M8, *blank*). ff. 1-95. [242

-- La seconda libraria del Doni. ... In Vinegia M D LV. ... (... perr Francesco Marcolini. ...) 8°. A-L8. pp. 3-167. [243

-- Le ville del Doni. ... In Bologna, Appresso Alessandre Benacci. M D LXVI. 8°. A-B8 C4. ff. 2-19. [244

-- La zucca del Doni ... In Venetia, Appresso Fran. Rampazetto, ad instantia di Gio. Battista, & Marcio Sessa fratelli. (... M D LXV.) 8°. *8 A-Qq8 Rr4. ff. 1-316. [245

DORÉ, PIERRE. Le College de sapience ... Auec le Dialogue de la Foy ... imprimé a Paris, par Anthoine Bonnemere ... 1539. ... 8°. A-Z8 a-m8 n4. ff. ii-cvi. [246

DORFFMAN, HANS. Vber dise nachkom̄enden Schlussreden wellend wir der pfarrer zů S. martin zů Chur ... M.D.XXVI. ... 4°. π4. [247

DRACONITES, JOHANNES. Eyn Christlicher Sendebrieff an die Miltenberger. Ioannes Carlstat. Vuittemberg M.D.XXiiij. (Gedruckt ... durch Nickel Schyrlentz. ...) 4°. A-B4 C2. [248

-- -- Ain Christlicher Sendbrieff ... Vuittemberg M. D. xxiiij. [Augsburg, Philipp Ulhart.] 4°. A-B4. [249

-- Epistel an die Gemeyne zů Miltenberg den abschyed des Pfarhers daselbst betreffendt/ So alle priester vnuerjagt/ auss der Stat flohen. ... [Augsburg, Melchior Ramminger,] M D XXiij ... 4°. A-C4. [250

-- Eine OsterPredigt Von der Aufferstehung: Iesu Christi. ... M.D.L. ([Lübeck,] Gedruckt durch Georgen Richolff ...) fol. ✠2 A6. [251

-- Eine Predigt von des Weibes Samen: Vber der Tauffe des Leuiten vnd Rabi Isaac vnd seines Sones Iacob ... M. D. L. ([Lübeck,] Gedruckt durch Georgen Richolff ...) fol. A6. [252

-- Vom Breutgam Iesu Christo. ... (Gedruckt zu Hamburg durch Ioachim Lew.) fol. *2 A4. [253

-- Vom Dürchbrecher Iesu Christo. ... M. D. L. ([Lübeck,] Gedruckt durch Georgen Richolff. ...) fol. A4. [254

-- Vom einigen Hirtten Iesu Christo. ... M. D. LI. ([Lübeck,] Gedruckt durch Georgen Richolff ...) fol. ✠2 A6. [255

-- Vom Ewigen Fewer des Altars. ... M. D. L. ([Lübeck,] Gedruckt durch Georgen Richolff ...) fol. ✠2 A4. [256

-- Vom Gerechten den aller welt ende loben: Iesu Christo. ... (... gedruckt zu Rostock [durch Ludwig Dietz] M.D.Liiij.) fol. A2 B4. [257

DRACONITES

-- Vom Gnedigen Wortt vnsers Gottes. ... (Geschrieben ... 1. Septemb. M.D.Lij. ... Gedruckt zu Rostock durch Ludowig Dietz.) fol. A^6. [258

-- Vom hern Zebaoth Des alle land voll sind: Iesu Christo. ... M. D. LI. ([Lübeck,] Gedruckt durch Georgen Richolff ...) fol. π^2 A^6. [259

-- Vom Konig Dauid Iesu Christo. ... M.D.L. ([Lübeck,] Gedruckt durch Georgen Richolff ...) fol. A^4. [260

-- Vom Menschen Der odem in der nasen hat: Iesu Christo. ... (... gedruckt zu Rostock M.D.Lij.) fol. A^2 B^4. [261

-- Vom Schuldopffer Vnd DanckOpffer. ... M.D.XLIX. ([Lübeck,] Gedruckt durch Georgen Richolff xxvij. Octobris ...) fol. A^6. [262

-- Vom Starcken Heiland: Iesu Christo. ... M. D. L. ([Lübeck,] Gedruckt durch Georg Richolff. ...) fol. A^6. [263

-- Vom Streitbarn Helden Gideon. ... M. D. L. ([Lübeck,] Gedruckt durch Georgen Richolff ...) fol. $*^2$ A^6 A^4. [264

-- Vom Werckmeister Iesu Christo. ... M. D. L. ([Lübeck,] Durch Georgen Richolff ...) fol. $*^2$ A^4. [265

-- Vom zarten Reis Des hohen Cederbawms: Iesu Christo. ... M. D. LI. ([Lübeck,] Gedruckt durch Georgen Richolff. ...) fol. ✤² A^4. [266

-- Von deinen Man Vnd Hern Iesu Christo. ... (... gedruckt zu Rostock [durch Ludwig Dietz] M. D. LII.) fol. A-B^4. [267

-- Von dem Erloͤser Der Gefangen Zion. ... M.D.L. ([Lübeck,] Gedruckt durch Georgen Richolff ...) fol. $*^2$ A^4. [268

-- Von dem Fels Iesu Christo. ... M.D.L. ([Lübeck,] Gedruckt durch Georgen Richolff ...) fol. $\dagger^2$ A^4. [269

-- Von dem Geist Der gnaden vnd des gebettes: Iesu Christi. ... M. D. L. (Geschrieben ... XII. Iunii M.D.L. ... Gedruckt [zu Lübeck] durch Iohan BalHorn.) fol. ƒ² A^6. [270

-- Von dem guten Hirten: Des Euangelion Ioan. x. ... ... (Gedruckt zu Lübeck durch Ioan BalHorn. M.D.L.) fol. BB^4 CC^2. [271

-- Von dem Heiligen Vnter Dir: Iesu Christo. ... [Lübeck, Georg Richolff,] M.D.L. fol. A^4. [272

-- Von dem Knecht Gottes Dauid aller einigen Koͤnig Hirtten vnd Ewigen Fuͤrsten: Iesu Christo. ... M. D. L. ([Lübeck,] Gedruckt durch Georg Richolff ...) fol. ❧² A^6. [273

-- Von dem Konig Den alle koͤnige anbetten werden: Iesu Christo. ... M.D.XLIX. ([Lübeck,] Gedruckt durch Georgen Richolff ...) fol. ʃ² A^4. [274

-- Von dem Konig Vber Alle Land: Iesu Christo. ... M.D.L. ([Lübeck,] Gedruckt durch Georgen Richolff ...) fol. ✤² A^4 B^6. ¶*Additional t.p.* ($B1^r$): Eine Dreifaltige Predigt Des Engel Gabriels. Luce. j. ... M.D.L. [275

-- Von dem Man Der Linwad anhat vnd einen Schreibzeug an der seitten. ... (Geschrieben ... 3. Iunij. M.D.L. [Lübeck, Johann Ballhorn.]) fol.)o(^{2} A^6 (-A6, *presumably blank*). [276

-- Von dem Newen Testament Gottes. ... (Geschrieben ... 3. Ianua. M.D.L. ... [Lübeck,] Gedruckt durch Iohann Balhorn.) fol. ❦ 2 A^6. [277

-- Von dem Richter vnter allen voͤlckern: Iesu Christo. ... [Lübeck, Georg Richolff,] M. D. LI. fol. ƒ² A^6. [278

-- Von dem Schild Dauid Christi aller Christen. ... M.D.L. ([Lübeck,] Gedruckt durch Georgen Richolff ...) fol. $*^2$ A^6. [279

-- Von dem Stein Onhende vom Berge gerissen: Iesu Christo. ... M.D.L. ([Lübeck,] Gedruckt durch Georgen Richolff ...) fol. $*^2$ A-B^4. [280

-- Von dem Stuel Im Himel darauff einer sitzt Gestalt wie ein mensch. (... gedruckt zu Rostock [durch Ludwig Dietz] M. D. Lv.) fol. $[A]^2$ $B-C^4$. [281

-- Von dem Zweige Des Hern: Iesu Christo. ... (Geschrieben zu Lübeck. M.D.XLIX. Gedruckt durch Ioan Balhorn.) fol. A^2. [282

-- Von den Heilanden Der Prophet Obadia. ... M.D.L. ([Lübeck,] Gedruckt durch Georgen Richolff ...) fol. $✠^2$ $A-B^4$. [283

-- Von den Newen Himel vnd Erden. ... M.D.L. ([Lübeck,] Gedruckt durch Georgen Richolff ...) fol. A^6. [284

-- Von der Auffart Iesu Christi. ... (Geschrieben ... X. Ianua. M. D. L. ... [Lübeck,] Gedruckt durch Iohan Balhorn.) fol. aa^2 bb^2. [285

-- Von der Eherne Schlangen die Mose auffricht Zum FürBild des Creützes Iesu Christi. ... M. D. LI. ([Lübeck,] Gedruckt durch Georgen Richolff ...) fol. $✠^2$ $A-B^4$ C^2. [286

-- Von der Iüden Füersten Vnd Hern: Iesu Christo. ... M. D. L. ([Lübeck,] Gedruckt durch Georgen Richolff ...) fol. f^2 A^6. [287

-- Von der Sindflüt Vnd dem Casten Noah. ... M.D.XLIX. ([Lübeck,] Gedruckt durch Georgen Richolff ...) fol. $✠^2$ A^4. [288

-- Von der Sonnen Der Gerechtickeit: Iesu Christo: ... M.D.XLIX. ([Lübeck,] Gedruckt durch Georgen Richolff ...) fol. $*^2$ A^4. [289

-- Von der Stat Vnser Gottes. ... (Geschrieben ... 28. Mar. 1550. ... [Lübeck,] Gedruckt durch Ioann Balhorn.) fol. A^6. [290

-- Von der Weihe Aarons vnd seiner Söne. ... M.D.L. ([Lübeck,] Gedruckt durch Georgen Richolff ...) fol. $✠^2$ A^4. [291

-- Von des Menschen Sone: Iesu Christo. ... M.D.L. ([Lübeck,] Gedruckt durch Georgen Richolff ...) fol. $A-B^4$. [292

-- Von des Weibes Samen: Iesu Christo. ... M. D. L. ([Lübeck,] Gedruckt durch Georgen Richolff ...) fol. $✠^4$ $A-C^4$. [293

-- Von ewerm Gott Iesu Christo. ... [Lübeck, Georg Richolff,] M.D.L. fol. A^6. [294

DRAMATA. [1] Dramata sacra, comoediae atque tragoediæ aliquot è Veteri Testamento desumptæ ... Basileae. 8°. $*^8$ $a-z^8$ $A-L^8$. pp. 2-561. [2] Dramatum Sacrorum ... tomus secundus. (Basileae ex officina Ioannis Oporini, ... M. D. XLVII. Mense Martio.) $aa-zz^8$ $3A-3L^8$. pp. 3-542. ¶*Includes:* Hieronymus Zieglerus, Protoplastus, Isaaci immolatio, Nomothesia, Samson, Heli sive Paedonothia; Xystus Betuleius, Eva, Sapientia Salomonis, Judith, Susanna, Beel, unà cum Draconis historia (Latinè reddita per Martinum Ostermincherum), Zorobabel (per Ioannem Entomius Latinis numeris reddita); Cornelius Crocus, Josephus; Andrea Dietherus, Josephus; Jacobus Zovitius, Ruth; Joannes Lorichius, Jobus; Thomas Naogeorgus, Hamanus. [295

DRASCOVICH, GIORGIO. Oratio habita ... in Generali Congregatione Die XXIIII. Februarij. M. D. LXII. Vna cum responsione ... Synodi. Ripae: ad instantiam Baptistæ Bozolæ 1562. 4°. A^4. (Lea.) [296

DRESDEN. Vrgichten Zweyer zu Dresen gerechtfertigter Vbeltheter/ von Welche wegen der Churfürst Augustus/ bei Iohan Friderich zu Sachsen/ Wilhelm von Grumbach vñ Wilhelm vom Stein gefenglich zunemen/ Schrifftlich angehalten. ... Auch/ Des ... Fürsten Iohans Friderich ... entschüldigung/ etc. M.D.LXVII. 4°. $A-F^4$. [297

DRESSER, MATTHÄUS. De cancellarii munere et dignitate ... oratio ... [Lipsiae,] M. D. XCIIII. Michael Lantzenberger imprimebat. 4°. $A-C^4$ D^2. [298

DRUSIUS, JOHANNES. I. Drusii quaestionum ac responsionum liber. In quo varia scripturæ loca explicantur aut emendantur. ... In Academia Lugdunensi. M. D. LXXXIII. 8°. $A-D^8$ E^4. pp. 3-72. [299

DU BARTAS, GUILLAUME SALUSTE, sieur. Guilielmi Salustii Bartassii hebdomas A Gabriele

Lermæo latinitate donata. ... Londini Apud Robertum Dexter ... 1591. 12°. A^6 (-A6) A-I^{12} K^6 (-K6, *presumably blank*). ff. 1-112. *S.T.C.* 21656. [300

DU BEC-CRESPIN, JEAN. The historie of the great emperour Tamerlan. Drawen from the auncient Monuments of the Arabians, by Messire Iean du Bec, Abbot of Mortimer. Newly translated out of French into English ... by H. M. London Printed for William Ponsonby. 1597. 4°. A-R^8 (-R8, *presumably blank*). pp. 1-265. *S.T.C.* 7263. (Furness.) [301

DU BELLAY, GUILLAUME. Gemein abschrifft der werbnug [*sic*] Durch Kȏniglich Maiestat auss Franckreich/ vnd der selbigen Sȏnen bottschafft ... 4°. A^4 B^2. ¶Credentz *dated 1 June 1536.* [302

-- Tre libri della disciplina militare tradotti nella lingua Italiana. ... (In Venetia per Michele Tramezzino. M D L.) 16°. A-B^8 A-DD^8. ff. 1-216. [303

DU BELLAY, JEAN. Oraison escripte suyuant lintention du Roy treschrestien, aux ... Seigneurs, & a tous les estas du sainct Empire assemblez en la ville de Spire. A Paris De limprimerie de Robert Estienne ... M.D.XLIIII. 4°. A-G^4 H^6. [304

DU BELLAY, JOACHIM. Ioachimi Bellaii Andini poematum libri quatuor ... Parisiis, Apud Federicum Morellum ... M. D. LVIII. ... 4°. A-P^4 Q^2. ff. 2-62. [305

DU BELLAY, MARTIN. Les memoires ... ausquels l'autheur a inseré trois livres & quelques fragmens des Ogdoades de Mess. Guillaume du Bellay ... son frere. ... A Paris, A l'Olivier de P. L'Huillier ... 1571. ... 8°. $\bar{a}^8$ a-z^8 A-Qq^8. ff. 1-289. [306

DU BOIS, JACQUES. Methodus sex librorum Galeni in differentiis & causis morborum & symptomatum, in tabellas sex ordine suo coniecta ... De signis omnibus medicis, ... commentarius ... per Iacobum Syluium Medicum. Parisiis, Apud AEgidium Gorbinum ... 1561. 8°. $\bar{a}^8$ B-N^8. ff. 2-103. [307

DUBRAVIUS, JOANNES. Historiæ Regni Boiemiæ ... Libri XXXIII. ... M.D.LII. (Impressum ... Prostannæ, in Officina Ioannis Guntheri, vigesimo sexto die Martij ...) fol. ✠^{4} A-Ll^6 Mm^4. ff. II-CCVIII. [308

DUCCHI, GREGORIO. La Scacheide ... In Vicenza, Appresso Perin Libraro & Giorgio Greco compagni. 1586. 4°. $*^6$ A-Ff^4 Gg^6 (-Gg6, *presumably blank*). ff. 1-120. [309

DUCCI, LORENZO. Oratione funerale ... Nell'Essequie di Torquato Tasso. In Ferrara, 1600. Per Vittorio Baldini ... 4°. A^{10}. [310

DU CHALARD, JOACHIM. Sommaire exposition des ordonnances du Roy Charles IX. Sur les plaintes des trois Estats ... tenuz à Orleans, l'an M.D.LX. ... A Lyon, par Benoist Rigaud. 1582. 8°. a-v^8. ff. 1-132. [311

DUCHER, GILBERT. Gilberti Ducherii Vultonis Aquapersani epigrammaton libri duo. Apud Seb. Gryphium Lugduni, 1538. 8°. a-k^8 l^4. pp. 3-167. ¶*Sig.* b *misbound after sig.* c. [312

DUCHESNE, JOSEPH. Le grand miroir du monde. ... A Lyon, Pour Barthelemi Honorat. M.D.LXXXVII. 4°. ¶^{4} $*^4$ a-z^4 A-C^4. pp. 1-206. [313

DUCHESNE, LÉGER. In M. T. Ciceronis libellum de optimo genere oratorum annotatiunculæ Per Leodegarium à Quercu Rothomageum. Parisiis. Ex officina Prigentii Caluarini ... 1538. 8°. A^4. [314

-- In tristissimum Adriani Turnebi ... obitum, Epicedion, Auctore Leodegario à Quercu. Parisiis, Apud Federicum Morellum ... M. D. LXV. 4°. A^2 B^4 C^2. ¶*Includes poems by Jean Passerat, Alphonse Delbene, and Nicolas Vergèce.* [315

-- Leodegarii a Quercu votum, pro ... Galliarum rege Henrico, pridie quam moreretur. Eiusdem de eodem Epitaphium. Parisiis, Apud Federicum Morellum ... M. D. LVIIII. 4°. π^2. [316

DU CLERC, JACQUES. Colloque familier, du vray, pudic & syncere amour, concilié entre deux amans. Traduict de Latin en François ... A Lyon, par Iean de Tournes. M. D. XLVI. 16°. A-R^{8}. pp. 1-241. [317

DUDITH, ANDREAS. Orationes duae in ... Concilio Tridentino habita ... M D LXII. Brixiæ, apud Damianum Turlinum, M D LXII. (*Colophon.*) 4°. A-D^{4}. (Lea.) [318

DÜRER, ALBRECHT. Alberti Dureri ... de vrbibus, arcibus, castellisque condendis, ac muniendis rationes aliquot ... è lingua Germanica in Latinam traductæ. Parisiis, Ex officina Christiani Wecheli ... M.D.XXXV. fol. a-d^{6,4} (-c6) e^{6} f^{4+1} g^{4} h^{4+1} (*folded leaves inserted after* a6, b1, b3, d1, d3, f2, g2, g4, h2, h4). (Fine Arts.) [319

DUMAS, ANTOINE ROBERT. Epythomata grammatice ... [Rothomagi,] Venalis habeť ... in officina Raulini gaultier [c. 1513]. 16°. B.L. A-C^{8}. [320

DU MONIN, JEAN-ÉDOUARD. L'vranologie, ou le ciel ... A Paris, Chez Guilhaume Iulien ... 1583. ... 16°. ā^{8} ē^{4} ī^{4} A^{8} B^{4} C-X^{8} Y^{4} Z^{8} Aa-Kk^{8} Ll^{4} Mm^{8} (-Mm8, *errata*). ff. 1-209. [321

DU MOULIN, CHARLES. Commentarius ad edictum Henrici secundi contra paruas Datas & abusus curiæ Romanæ, & in antiqua edicta & Senatusconsulta Francię contra Annatarum ... Authore Carolo Molinaeo ... Lugduni, Apud Antonium Vincentium. M D. LII. 4°. †^{4} A-KK^{4}. pp. 1-245. (Lea.) [322

-- Tractatus de euictionibus Gasparis Caballini ... Eiusdem libellus de Aedilicijs actionibus. ... Secunda editio. ... Venetiis, Apud Iordanum Zilettum. M. D. LXXIII. 8°. A-Ff^{8}. pp. 10-344. [323

DUNGERSHEYM, HIERONYMUS. Anntwurt Hieronimi Tungersshaim von Ochsenfart auf Iorgen schonigen von Eylenburg zů schreiben. [Leipzig, Wolfgang Stoeckel.] (Geben jm M D XXiij. Jare.) 4°. A^{4}. [324

-- Confutatio: apologetici cuiusdā sacre scripture falso inscripti ... edita. ... Lipsi impressit Vuolfgangus Monaceñ. ... j5j4. (... vicesimotertia die Mensis Marcij.) 4°. A-Z^{6}. ff. ij-c.xxvij. [325

-- Etliche buchlin ... wider den Luther der titel balde hernoch folgen. 4°. [A]^{2}. [1] Erzeigung der falscheit des vnchristlichen Lutherischen coments vber das sibende Capitel δ ersten Epistel an dē Chorintherñ ... A^{2} B-T^{4}. ff. 3-73. [2] Abschlack des anschlages Martini Luthers vom brennen/ zu lateyn vri ... (Gedruckt zu Leyptzick/ durch Valentinū Schumañ/ ... D. M. xxx.) A-G^{4}. ff. 2-27. [3] Wore widerlegung ... Des falschen buchleins Martini Luthers von beyden gestald des Hochwirdigsten Sacraments. (*Colophon.*) A-Bb^{4}. ff. 2-100. [4] Bekentnis des glaubens Doct. Mart. Luthers. mit kurtzē glossen ... (*Colophon.*) A-B^{4}. ff. 2-8. [5] Dadelung des obgesatzten bekentnus ... (*Colophon.*) A-I^{4} K^{2} L^{4}. ff. 2-42. [6] Wider Martinum Luther samt den widerdeufferñ ... A-F^{4} (-F4). ff. 2-23. [7] Fur/ vnd wider den vntterricht des Luthers ... A-B^{4}. ff. 2-8. [8] Wyder den Sermon des Luthers von der sunde in den heyligengeyst. A-C^{4} D^{2} E^{4} (-E4). ff. 2-17. [9] Etliche spruche/ aus den der Luther von eygenem bekentnus verdůmet wirth. A-E^{4} (-E4). ff. 2-19. [10] [Von worheyt des fegfeurs wyder den Luther ...] (Geendet zu Leyptzk durch Valten Schumañ. ... M. D. xxxi.) A-I^{4} (-A1) K^{2} L^{4}. ff. 2-42. [326

DUNS SCOTUS, JOANNES. En lector candide Disputationes Collationales ... (... Lugduniꝗ excusuꝫ in edibus Iacobi Myt: sumptu ... Iacobi .q. Frācisci de Giūta ⁊ socij florētini ... Anno ... ꝙngētesimovigesimo supra millesimū kal'. aꝑlis.) 8°. B.L. A-H^{8} I^{2}. ff. 2-64. [327

-- [1] Fratris Ioannis Duns Scoti ... In Quartum Lib. Sententiarum Perutiles Quæstiones, plurimis Annotationibus exornatæ, in opus Quolibetorum, Collationum, ac Epitomatum, eiusdem Doctoris ... Venetiis, M D XCVIII. Apud hæredes Melchioris Sessæ. fol. π^{1} A-Gg^{6} Hh^{4}. ff. 1-184. [2] Resolutiones quæstionum ... in librum IIII. sententiarum ... a R.P. Melchiore Flauio ... illustratæ. A-D^{8} E^{4}. ff. 1-36. [3] ... Quæstiones Quodlibetales. A-K^{6} L^{4}. ff. 1-63. [4] ... Collationes, seu Disputationes. A-D^{6} E^{8}. ff. 1-31. [5] Quaestionum F. Ioan. Scoti ... In libros Sententiarum Epitome ... auctore F. Antonio de Fantis ... A-M^{8} N^{4}. [6] Tabula generalis super scriptum Oxoniense ... a-c^{8} d^{4}. ¶*The second vol. of an edition in 2 vols.* (Lea.) [328

-- Questiones quolibetales ex quattuor Sentētiarū voluminibus ... a ... Anto. de Fautis Taruisino pristino nitori restituti ... (Lugduni impresse per ... Iacobum Myt. Anno ... quingētesimo vigesimo supra millesimuȝ kal'. aprilis.) 8°. B.L. AAa-RRr^{8} S^{2}. ff. 2-136. [329

-- Questiones ... Super Libros priorum. Eiusdem questiones super Libros posteriorum. (Impresse Venetijs a Philippo pincio Mantuano. ... 1512. die .9. Octobris ...) fol. B.L. a-g^{8}. ff. 2-54. [330

-- Questiones Scoti Super Vniuersalia Porphy. necnon Aristotelis Predicamenta ac Peryarmenias. Item super libros Elenchorum. Et Antonii Andree suꝑ libro Sex principioꝝ. Item qōnes Ioannis Angelici super questiones vniuersales eiusdem Scoti. (Impresse Venetijs ꝑ Philippum pinciuȝ Mantuanū. ... 1512. die .9. Augusti. ... 1511. die .1. Decembris.) fol. B.L. A-G^{8} H-O^{6} P^{4}. ff. 4-101. [331

DU PERAC, ÉTIENNE. I vestigi dell'antichità di Roma ... ritratti in perspettiua ... In Roma appresso Lorenzo della Vaccharia ... MDLXXV. obl. fol. *engraved t.p. + 39 plates.* (Fine Arts.) [332

-- -- *Another copy.* [333

DU PINET, ANTIONE. Taxe des parties casuelles de la boutique du pape, En Latin & en François ... Par A. D. P. A Lyon [par Jean Saugrain]. 1564. 8°. A-L^{8} M^{6}. pp. 3-173. ¶*Many margins damaged.* (Lea.) [334

DUPRAT, ANTOINE. Oratio habita Bonōie corā Leone .X. Pont. max. ī frequēti Cardinaliū Concilio ... a ... Antonio Prato magno Gallie Cancellario Tertio Idus Decēbris. M.D.XVI. 4°. A^{4}. [Romae, Jacobus Mazochius.] (Lea.) [335

DU PRÉAU, GABRIEL. De vitis, sectis, et dogmatibus omnium haereticorum ... elenchus alphabeticus ... Per Gabrielem Prateolum Marcossium ... Coloniæ, Apud Geruuinum Calenium, & hæredes Ioannis Quentel, Anno M. D. LXIX. ... fol. a^{6} b-k^{4} A-3S^{4} (-3S4, *blank*). pp. 1-509. (Lea.) [336

DUPUYHERBAULT, GABRIEL. Tractat Herrn Gabriel Putherbeien von Thuron/ ꝛc. Von verbot vnnd auffhebung deren Bücher vnd Schrifften/ so ... nit mögen gelesen oder behalten werden. ... Erstlich ... im Latein beschrieben/ Diser zeit ... in das hoch Teutsch ... transsferiert ... M. D. LXXXI. (Getruckt zu München/ bey Adam Berg. ...) 8°. A-X^{8} Y^{4}. ff. 2-170. [337

DU PUYS, NICOLAS . N. Bonespei trecensis libellus de lepidis grauium diuinorūqȝ virorum epistolis ... Venendantur parisijs ... [per Dionysium Roce]. 4°. A^{8}. [338

DURANDUS, GUILIELMUS, À SANCTO PORCIANO. D. Durandi a sancto Portiano super sententias theologicas Petri Lombardi commentariorum Libri quatuor, per fratrem Iacobum Albertum Castrensem ... recogniti. Venundantur Parisiis apud Ioannem Roigny ... 1539 fol. aa-bb^{8} cc-dd^{6} a-z^{8} A-R^{8} S^{6}. ff. 1-324. (Yarnall.) [339

-- -- ... Per Nicolaum à Martimbos ... recogniti. ... Parisiis, Apud Carolam Guillard, viduam Claudij Cheuallonij ... & Gulielmum Desbois ... 1550. fol. *a-*c^{8} *d^{6} a-y^{8} z^{6} A-Y^{8} Z^{6} Aa^{6} (-Aa6, *presumably blank*). ff. 1-364. (Lea.) [340

-- -- ... in Petri Lombardi Sententias Theologicas Commentariorum libri IIII. ... Venetiis, MDLXXI. Ex Typographia Guerræa. fol. *A-*C^{8} *D^{10} A-3F^{8} 3G^{10}. ff. 1-423. [341

DURAND, GUILLAUME, bishop of Mende. Rationale diuinorum officiorum a R. D. Gulielmo Durando ... concinnatum ... Adiectum fuit praetereà aliud Diuinorum officiorum Rationale ab Ioanne Beletho ... Lugduni, Apud Hæredes Iacobi Iuntæ, 1565. 8°. α-ε^{8} ξ^{4} a-z^{8} A-Z^{8} AA-BB^{8} CC^{4}. ff. 1-569. (Lea.) [342

-- [1] Speculum iuris ... Cum Io. And. Baldi de Vbaldis, aliorumq. ... Iurisc. Theorematibus. ... Pars prima. Venetiis, M D LXXXV. fol. *^{4} a-h^{6} i^{4} A-Y^{8}. pp. 1-352. [2] Speculum iuris ... pars secunda. Venetiis, M D LXXXV. Aa-3M^{8} 3N^{10}. pp. 355-930. [3] Speculum iuris ... pars III. et IIII. Venetiis, M D LXXXV. a-z^{8} aa-ii^{8} kk^{6}. pp. 3-522. (Lea.) [343

-- -- [1] D. G. Durandi ... speculum iuris, cum Ioan. Andreae, Baldi, reliquorumque ... I.V. doctorum visionibus ... Auctore Alexandro de Neuo. Addidimus eiusdem Gul. Durandi Aureum Repertorium ... Pars Prima & Secunda. Francofurti Sumtibus heredum Andreæ Wecheli, & Ioannis Gymnici. MDXCII. fol.)(^{4} A-Ee^6 Ff^4 a-zz^6 3a^8. pp. 1-344, 3-567. [2] ... Pars Tertia & Quarta. *Same imprint.* AA-SSs^6 TTt^8 AAA-OOO^6. pp. 3-506, 1-87. (Yarnall.) [343a

DURANS, JOHANNES DILECTUS, DE GUALDO. De arte testandi, et cautelis vltimarum voluntatum tractatus. ... ... Venetiis Apud Georgium de Caballis. M D LXVIII. 8°. A-D^8 A-S^8. pp. 1-287. (Lea.) [344

DURANTI, JEAN-ÉTIENNE. Ioannis Stephani Duranti ... de ritibus ecclesiae Catholicae libri tres. ... Romæ Ex Typographia Vaticana. M. D. XCI. (*Colophon.*) fol. *^{4} A-Ff^6 a^6 b^8. pp. 2-347. (Yarnall.) [344a

DURET, JEAN. Commentaires et annotations sur l'Edict & Ordonnance du Roy, pour le bien & authorité de Iustice, & des Officiers de sa Majesté. ... A Lyon, par Benoist Rigaud. M.D.LXXIII. ... 8°. A-F^8. ff. 2-48. [345

DU RIVAIL, AYMAR. Aymari Riuallii Allobrogis ... Ciuilis historiæ Iuris, siue in XII. Tab. Leges cōmentariorū libri quinq3. Historiæ item Iuris Pont. liber Singularis. Moguntiae anno M. D. XXVII. ... (... apud Ioannem Schoeffer mense Martio ...) 8°. π^8 A-R^8 S^{10}. pp. 1-291. [346

DU SOUHAIT, FRANÇOIS. Beauté et amour. Pastorelle. Par le S. Du Souhait, gentilhomme Champenois. A Paris, Chez Iacques Rezé ... 1599. ... 12°. A-B^{12}. ff. 3-23. [347

-- Les diuers souhaits d'amour ... A Paris, Chez Iacques Rezé ... 1599. ... 12°. ā^6 A-B^{12}. ff. 2-22. [348

-- Les neuf muses Francoises. ... A Paris, Chez Iacques Rezé ... 1599. ... (Acheué d'imprimer le 12. Februier.) 12°. A^{12} B^6. ff. 1-15. [349

-- Le plaidoye et iugement des trois graces Françoises. ... A Paris, Chez Iacques Rezé ... 1599. ... 12°. A-B^{12} C^6. ff. 3-27. [350

-- Tragedie de Radegonde duchesse de Bourgongne. ... A Paris, Chez Iacques Rezè ... 1599. ... 12°. A-B^{12} C^6. ff. 2-33. [351

DU TILLET, JEAN. Recueil des roys de France ... Plus, Vne Chronique abbregée ... A Paris, Chez Iaques du Puys ... M. D. LXXX. ... fol. A^6 A-Dd^6 Ee^4 Ff-Pp^6 Qq^4 Rr^8 A^6 B^8 aa-rr^6 ss^8 (-ss8). pp. 1-471, ff. 4-113. ¶*Additional t.p.* (Ff1^r): Recueil des rangs des grands de France ... 1579. [352

DU VERDIER, ANTOINE. La bibliotheque d'Antoine du Verdier, seigneur de Vaupriuas, Contenant le Catalogue de tous ceux qui ont escrit, ou traduict en François ... A Lyon, par Barthelemy Honorat. M. D. LXXXV. ... (Acheué d'Imprimer le 15. de Decembre 1584. ... par Iean d'Ogerolles.) fol. *-**^{6} 3*^{2} a-z^6 A-Zz^6 AA-ZZ^6 AAa-LLl^6 MMm^4 (-MMm4, *presumably blank*). pp. iij-xxviij, 1-1233. [353

-- Les omonimes, satire des moeurs corrompues de ce siecle. ... A Lyon, Par Antoine Gryphius. 1572. ... (... De l'imprimerie de Pierre Roussin. ...) 4°. A-C^4. ff. 2-12. [354

DU VERDIER, CLAUDE. In auctores pene omnes, antiquos potissimum, censio ... Claud. Verderio Anton. fil. auctore. Lugduni, Apud Bartholomæum Honoratum ... M. D. LXXXVI. 4°. A-AA^4 (-AA4, *presumably blank*). pp. 3-187. [355

E

EBER, PAUL. Calendarium historicum ... Vitebergæ excusum in officina Hæredum Georgij Rhauu. M. D. LIX. (*Colophon.*) 8°. A-Ii^8 Kk^4. pp. 2-432. [1

-- -- VVitebergæ Excudebant Hæredes Ioannis Cratonis, anno M. D. LXXIX. 4°. A-E^4 F^6 G-3N^4 3O^6. pp. 1-413. [2

-- Vocabula rei numariae ponderum et mensurarum Græca, Latina, Ebraica ...: collecta ex Budaei, Ioachimi Camerarii, et Philip. Melanth. annotationibus. Additae sunt appellationes quadrupedum [*&c.*] ... Collecta a Paulo Ebero et Casparo Peucero. ... Lipsiae in officina Voegeliana. Anno M. D. LXIIII. 8°. A-O^8. [3

EBERLEIN, JOHANN. Der Clocker thurn bin ich genant Vñ meld hie ő võ gũntzburg schand ... [Tũbingen, Ulrich Morhard.] (Datum in einem dorff zwůundsibentzig meyll von Niclas port jm xxiij. jare.) 4°. A-B^4. [4

-- Der denck Spiegel eines Christẽlichẽ lẽbẽs 8°. A^8 B^4. [5

-- Ain fraintlich trostliche vermanung an alle frummen Christen/ zů Augspurg Am Leech/ Darin̄ auch angezaygt wũrt/ wazů der Doc. Martini Luther von Gott gesandt sey. ... Wittemberg. 4°. A-B^4. [6

-- Der Frommen pfaffen trost. Ain ... vnderricht vnd antwurt vff der syben trostlosen pfaffen clage Newlich durch die Fũnfzehen Bundsgnossen beschriben ... [Bamberg, Georg Erlinger, 1523.] 4°. A-B^4. [7

-- Wie gar gfarlich sey. So Ain Priester kain Eeweyb hat. ... Anno. 1522. 4°. a-b^4 c^2. [8

-- Ein zuversichtig ermanung an die ... herren obern vnd vnderthon gemainer Eydgnoschafft (Genant Schwytzer) das sy trewlich helffen handthaben Ewangelische leer vnd frumme christen. Der .XIII. bundtsgnoss [Basel, Pamphilus Gengenbach, 1521.] 4°. a^4. [9

ECK, JOHANN. Ad D. Pauli Ricii Israelitæ de anima coeli examina. ... amica responsio. [Augsburg, Sigmund Grim & Marcus Wirsung, 1519.] 4°. A-B^4. [10

-- Ad Generosum D. Maximilianum ex baronibus Zeuenbergijs ... defensio aduersus inuectiones Ritianas ... [Augsburg, Johann Miller, 1519.] 4°. A-C^4. [11

-- Ad inuictissimum Poloniae regem Sigismundum, de sacrificio Missæ Contra Lutheranos, libri duo. ... M. D. XXVI. 8°. A-P^8 Q^4 R^8. pp. 1-247. [12

-- Apologia pro ... principibus Catholicis, ac alijs ordinibus Imperij aduersus mucores & calumnias Buceri, super actis Comitiorum Ratisponæ. Apologia pro ... Caspare Contareno. ... Ingolstadij Baioariæ excusa [per Alexandrum Weissenhorn]. M. D. XLII. 4°. A-Z^4 a-o^4 p^2 q^4. ff. I-CLVI. [13

-- -- Antuerpiæ apud Io. Steelsium An. 1542. 8°. A-Z^8 &^{8}. ff. 3-192. (Lea.) [14

-- Bursa pauonis logices exercitamẽta Appellata parua logicalia. ... (Impssuȝ Argẽtine ꝑ Matthiã Hupfuff Anno M.d.vij.) 4°. B.L. A-D$^{8.4}$ E^4 F^8 G-H^4 I^8 K^6. [15

-- Christenliche vnderricht ... wider die Angemassten setzer vnnd angeber/ vermainter Newer Kirchen Ordnung/ Iũngst in der obern Marggraffschafft vñ Nẽrmberger gebiet ... Aussgangen. ... Getruckt zů Ingolstat Durch Georgem krapffen Im .M.D.XXXiij. Jar am andren tag des hẽrbstmonats. (*Colophon.*) fol. A-O$^{6.4}$ P-Q^6. ff. 2-82. [16

-- De non tollendis Christi & sanctorum Imaginibus, contra hæresim Fælicianam sub Carolo magno damnatam, & iam sub Carolo .v. renascentẽ decisio. [Ingolstadii, 1522.] 4°. a-b^4 c^6. ¶*Margins of t.p. cropped.* (Lea.) [17

-- Defensio Ioan. Eckii contra amarulentas D. Andreae Bodenstein Carolstatini ... inuectiones ... (Excusum in Augusta [per Sigmundum Grim & Marcum Wirsung] ... M. D. XVIII. Die .xiiij. Mensis Augusti.) 4°. A-D^4. [18

-- Disputatio et excusatio ... Aduersus crimĩatiões .F. Martini Lutter ... [Lipsiae, Martinus Landsberg, 1519.] 4°. A^4. [19

-- Disputatio Ioan. Eckij ... Viennæ Pannoniæ habita cū epistola ed ... Episcopum Eistettensem. Oratio Ioannis Eckij ... nomine vniuersitatis Ingoldstadieñ. habita. Oratio iucunda & faceta Ioan. Eckij Triuij quęrelam aduersus bonarum artium odores explicans. ... (Augustæ ex officina Millerana VI. Cal'. Feb. ... M.D.XVII. ...) 4°. A-F^4 G^6. [20

-- Elementarius Dialectice ... (Impressum Augustæ Vindelicorum in officina Millerana. pridie idus Februarias. Anno. M.D.XVII.) 4°. A^8 B-D^6. [21

-- Enchiridion locorum communium aduersus Lutteranos. ... Ab autore quarto recognitū ... Ingolstadii [Georgius & Petrus Apianus]. (... M. D. XXVII. Mense Februario.) 8°. A-I^8 K^6. [22

-- -- *Another copy.* (Lea.) [23

-- -- Tubingae. (Excusum ... per Hulderichum Morhardum. An. M.D.XXVII. Mense Martio.) 8°. AA-KK^8 LL^6. (Lea.) [24

-- -- ... quinto recognitum ... M. D. XXIX. (... mense Ianuario.) 8°. π^8 a-$aa^{8.4}$ bb^4. ff. 1-146. [25

-- -- ... Interiecta sunt ... stellulis ... per ... F. Tilmannum Sibergensem ... Anno M. D. XXXII. (Coloniæ apud Heronem Alopecium: ære ... Petri Quentel ...) 8°. A-L^8 M^{12}. (Lea.) [26

-- -- Antuerpiæ in ædibus Ioan. Steelsii. Anno M.D.XXXV. Mense Augusto. (... typis vero Ioan. Graphei ...) 8°. A-O^8 P^4 Q-S^8. [27

-- -- Enchiridion locorum communium aduersus Lutherum & alios hostes ecclesiæ. ... M. D. XLIX. (Ingolstadii in officina Alexandri Vueissenhorn.) 8°. A-$Z^{8.4}$ a-$x^{4.8}$. ff. 1-253. (Yarnall.) [27a

-- -- Lugduni, Apud Theobaldum Paganum. 1549. 8°. a-z^8 A-F^8. pp. 3-457. (Lea.) [28

-- Epistola Iohan. Eckii ... de ratione studiorum suorū, scripta Anno M. D. XXXVIII. nunc uero primum ædita. Alia epistola. De obitu Ioan. Eckii ..., aduersus calumniā Viti Theodorici ... Autore Erasmo Vuolphio. Ingolstadij Excudebat Alexander Vueissenhorn Anno M. D. XLIII. 4°. A-C^4. [29

-- Epistola Ioh. Eccii ... quę docebit quā uera sit Epistola quā e Lipsia VVittembergam scripsit, qua se inuitū ait suscepisse munus legationis aduersus Lutherū. [Wittenberg, Johannes Rhau, 1520.] 4°. π^2. [30

-- Homiliarum siue sermonum ... aduersum quoscunqȝ nostri temporis hæreticos, super Euangelia de tempore ab Aduentu usqȝ ad Pascha, tomus .I. ... Anno M. D. XXXIIII. Mense Martio. 8°. aA^8 a-xx^8. pp. 1-703. (Lea.) [31

-- Ioan. Eckii ... in summulas Petri Hispani ... explanatio ... (Augustæ Vindelicorum ex officina Millerana mense Maio M. D. XVI. ...) fol. B.L. A-S^6 T-V^4. FF. II-CXI. (Lea.) [32

-- Oratio funebris habita ... in exequiali pompa ... Henrici Episcopi Augustensis. M D. XVII. ... (Impressum Augustę in officina Syluani Otmari ... [1517.]) 4°. A-C^4. [33

-- ... Ioannis Eckii ... Orationes quatuor ... (Augustæ ex officina excusoria M. Ioan. Otmar. XXIIII. die mens. Decembris. ... M.D.XIII.) 4°. a^8 b^4 c^6. [34

-- Audi lector Ioannis Eckij ... orationes ... tres ... De nobilitate literis exornāda, & laude Marchionū Brandenburgensiū. Oratio .I. De fidei Christianæ amplitudine vltra reliquas infideliū sectas. Oratio .II. De Germania exculta cōtra Grillos. Oratio .III. ... (Augustæ ex officina excusoria Millerana. V. die Mensis Decēbris. ... D.D.D.XV.) 4°. A-E^4 F^6. [35

-- [1] Postilla Catholica Euangeliorum de Tempore totius Anni. Das ist: Catholische Postill ... im Teutschen trewlich gebessert ... Der Erste Theil ... Getruckt zu Ingolstatt durch Wolfgang Eder. ... M.D.LXXXIII. ... fol. $)(^8$ A-II^6 KK^4. pp. 1-390. [2] ... Der Ander Theil ... *Same imprint.* (*Colophon.*) ☞^{6} A-Qq^6. pp. 1-463. [3] Postilla Catholica Euangeliorum de Sanctis totius Anni. ... Der erste Theyl dess andern tomi ... *Same imprint.* †-$††^4$ A-P^6 Q-R^4. pp. 1-195. [4] ... Der ander Theyl ... *Same imprint.* (*Colophon.*) AA-$3I^6$ 3K-$3L^4$. pp. 1-395. [36

-- Prima pars operum Iohan. Eckii contra Ludderum. ... M. D. XXX. ... (Excusum ... Augustæ Vindelicorum, in Alexandri Vueissenhorn ... officina. Impensis ... Georgij Krapff ciuis Ingolstadij ...) fol. π^{6} A-Z^{6} a-o^{6}. ff. I-CCXXI. ¶*Four more parts were published.* [37

-- Sperendam esse in breui victoriam aduersus Turcam, ... Homiliæ V. ex Byblia desumptæ. ... (Augustæ Vindelicorum, per Alexandrum Vueissenhorn. M.D.XXXII.) 4°. A-G^{4}. [38

ECKARDT, GEORG. Sechzehen Predig/ von der waren vnnd falschen Kirchen ... Item zehen Predig/ wider die jrthumb der Schwenckfeldischen/ Widertauffer vnd Sacramenthierer. Dessgleichen zehen Predig/ wider die fürnembste Hauptlaster ... Durch M. Georgium Ecardum ... M. D. LXII. (Gedruckt zu Nürnberg/ durch Christoff Heussler.) 8°. A-Z^{8} a-y^{8}. [39

ECKSTEIN, UTZ. Der Bawren Reichsstag vnd Concilium. ... (M.D. XXXjX.) 4°. A-P^{4} (-P4, *presumably blank*). [40

-- Dialogus. Ein hüpsche disputation/ Die Christus hat mit Adā thō ... [c. 1526.] 8°. a-e^{8}. [41

EDER, GEORG. Catalogus Rectorum & Illustrium virorum Archigymnasii Viennensis ... Viennæ Austriæ. (... excudebat Raphael Hofhalter, Anno 1559.) 4°. *^{4} A-P^{4}. pp. 1-106. [42

-- Ein Christliche ... Warnungschrifft An den vierten stand der ... Stätt ... in Oesterreich vnder vnd ob der Enns ... Ingolstatt. Anno M. D. Lxxx. (Getruckt ... durch Dauidem Sartorium.) 4°. A-G^{4} H^{6}. [43

-- Euangelische inquisition Wahrer and falscher Religion. ... Getruckt zů Diligen/ durch Sebaldum Mayer. M. D. LXXIII. 4°. *-**^{4} ♣-4♣^{4} A-3L^{4}. ff. 1-227. [44

-- Das guldene Flüss Christlicher Gemain vnd Gesellschaft/ das ist/ ain allgemaine richtige Form der ersten ... Kirchen ... Getruckt zů Ingolstatt/ durch Dauidem Sartorium. Anno M.D.LXXIX. 4°.)(-2)(^{4} A-Z^{4} a-nn^{4} oo^{2}. pp. 1-473. [45

-- Malleus hæreticorum, de variis falsorum dogmatum notis, atque censuris, libri duo. ... Siue methodus contra sectas, ad arguendos et conuincendos Hæreticos ... Ingolstadii Apud Dauidem Sartorium. Anno M. D. LXXX. 8°. *-5*^{8} A-Z^{8} aa-ii^{8}. pp. 1-510. (Lea.) [46

-- -- Ingolstadij Apud Dauidem Sartorium. Anno M. D. LXXXI. 8°. *-5*^{8} A-Z^{8} aa-ll^{8}. pp. 1-542. (Lea.) [47

-- Matæologia hæreticorum siue summa hæreticarum fabularum, ... Babylonia siue confusio hæresum ... Ingolstadij, Apud Dauidem Sartorium. Anno M. D. LXXXI. 8°. α-γ^{8} A-T^{8}. pp. 1-296. (Lea.) [48

EGENOLFF, CHRISTIAN. [Chronic von an vñ abgang aller Welt wesenn. ...] (Getruckt zu Franckfurt am Meyn/ Bei Christian Egenolff. ... M.D.XXXiij.) 4°. A-Z^{4} a-k^{4}. ff. I-CXXVIII. ¶*Lacks 4 preliminary leaves.* [49

EGNAZIO, GIOVANNI BATTISTA. Ioannis Baptistae Egnatii ... de exemplis Illustrium Virorum Venetæ ciuitatis atque aliarum Gentium. ... Venetijs, apud Nicolaum Tridentinum. M D LIIII. (*Colophon.*) 4°. *^{4} A-Z^{4} a-q^{4}. pp. 1-309. (Lea.) [50

-- Ioannis Baptistae Egnatii Veneti oratio habita in funere ... Nicolai Vrsini Nolae Petilianique principis. [Venetiis, Gregorius de Gregoriis de Forlivio, 1509.] 4°. a-b^{8} c^{10} (-c10, *blank*). [51

EID. Vom eydt: da bissher so lang von gezancket ist/ zeugnuss der schrifft: Auch wie Iohannes Huss/ ... den spruch Christi: Ihr solt nit schweren/ verstanden hab/ aus dem heyligen Chrysostomo/ zanck weitter zů uermeiden/ dem vnerfarnen zůnutz ... M. D. XXXI. 4°. A^{4} B^{2}. [52

EISENGREIN, MARTIN. Acht Predigen vber den Sontag Septuagesima: ... Getruckt zů Ingolstatt/ bey Dauid Sartorio. M. D. LXXVIII. 4°. A^{6} A-Pp^{4} Qq^{2}. ff. 1-154. [53

-- Beschaydne ... erklärung dreyer Hauptarticul Christlicher lehr. ... Gedruckt zů Ingolstatt/ durch Alexander Weissenhorn. Anno M.D.LXVIII. 4°. *^{4} *^{4} A-Z^{4} a-z^{4} Aa-3H^{4}. ff. 1-307. [54

-- Confessionale, in quo vniuersa materia de confessione peccatorum apud Catholicos vsitata per Quæstiones explicatur ... Ingolstadii Ex Typographia Dauidis Sartorij. cIↄ. Iↄ. LXXVII. 12°. a-b^{12} A-R^{12}. ff. 1-203. (Lea.) [55

-- Vnser liebe Fraw zů Alten Oetting. Das ist/ Von der Vralten H. Capellen vnser Lieben Frawen vnd dem Für. Stifft S. Philip vnnd Iacob zů Altē Oetting ... Getruckt zů Ingolstat/ [durch Alexander Weissenhorn] M.D.LXXI. 8°. $(:)^6$ $():()^8$ A-Z^8 Aa^4 (-Aa4, *presumably blank*). ff. 1-188. [56

EISENGREIN, WILHELM. Catalogus testium veritatis ... omnium orthodoxæ matris eccelsiæ Doctorum ... qui adulterina Ecclesiæ dogmata ... impugnarunt ... Dilingæ excudebat Sebaldus Mayer. ... M. D. LXV. 4°. A-Z^4 a-z^4 Aa-Hh^4 (-Hh4, *blank*). ff. 1-211. ¶*Lacks* Ii-Ll^4 *(index?)*. [57

-- Chronologicarum rerum ... vrbis Spiræ, Nemetum Augustæ ... Libri xvi. ... (Dilingæ, Excudebat Sebaldus Mayer. Anno M.D.LXIIII.) 8°. A-Z^8 a-o^8 p^4. ff. 3-298. [58

-- [1] Guilielmi Eysengreinei de Nemeto Spirensis. Centenarij XVI. continentes descriptionem rerum memorabilium, in Orthodoxa ... Christi Ecclesia gestarum ... Aduersus nouam historiam ecclesiasticam, quam Matthias Flacius Illyricus, & eius Collegæ ... ædiderunt. Centenarius I. ... Ingolstadii apud Alexandrum & Samuelem VVeissenhornios fratres. M. D. LXVI. fol. A-Z^4 a-z^4 Aa-Mm^4. ff. I-CCXXIIII. [2] Centenarius II. ... M. D. LXVIII. (Monachi Anno 1568.) A-Dd^6. pp. 2-319. [59

EITZEN, PAUL VON. Ethicæ doctrinæ libri quatuor, conscripti ... a D. Paulo ab Eitzen Hamburgensi. VVitebergæ Excusi typis Iohannis Schvvertelij. Anno M.D.LXXI. 8°. A-Yy^8 Zz^4 (-Zz4, *presumably blank*). [60

ELEGIA. Elegia funesta Nepharij sceleris heretici [Device of Gilles de Gourmont, Paris, c. 1520.] 4°. a^6 b^4. [61

EMDEN. Protocol. Dath is/ Alle handelinge des Gesprecks tho Embden in Oistfriesslandt mit den Wedderdöperen/ de sick Flaminge nömen/ geholden/ angefangen den 27. Februarij Anno 1578. ... Mit einer vorrede ... Iohans Graffen vnde Heren tho Oistfriesslandt ... Gedrucket in ... Embden by Goossen Goebens. 1579. (Volendet ... den 16. Martij. ...) 4°.)$(^8$ A-$3B^8$ $3C^2$ $3D^8$. ff. 1-386. [62

EMILIO, PAOLO. [Historia.] Basileæ, per Sixtum Henricpetri. M. D. LXIX. fol. [1] Historiae iam denuo emendatae Pauli Aemylii Veronensis, de rebus gestis Francorum ... Libri x. ... α^8 A-$3C^6$ $3D^4$. pp. 1-593. [2] Arnoldi Ferroni ... de Rebus Gestis Gallorum libri IX. ... α^4 a-z^6 A-L^8 M^4. pp. 1-414. [3] Paralipomena Gallicanæ historiæ ... Per Ioannem Thomam Freigium. a-c^6 d^8. pp. 3-50. [4] Ioannis Tilii Chronicon de Regibus Francorum ... $+^4$ A-G^6. (Lea.) [63

EMSER, HIERONYMUS. Annotationes Hieronimi Emsers/ vber Luthers Newe Testamēt ytzt tzum vierden mal vbersehen ... (Gedruckt zu Leypsig durch Valten Schuman ... M.D.XXIX.) 8°. A^4 A-Y^8 (-Y8, *presumably blank*). ff. I-CLXXIIII. [64

-- De disputatione Lipsicensi, quantum ad Boemos obiter deflexa est. Epistola Hieronymi Emser. Ad ægocerotem Emserianum Martini Lutheri additio. ... [Augustae, Johannes Miller, 1519.] 4°. B.L. a-d^4. [65

-- Opuscula Hieronymi Empser ... (Augustæ ex ædibus Siluani Otmar. ... M.D.XIX. Die .xii. Octobris.) 4°. A-D^4. [66

-- Wyder den falschgenāten Ecclesiasten/ vñ warhafftigen Ertzketzer Martinum Luter Emsser getrawe vñ nawe vorwarnung ... (Gedruckt tzu Leyptzck durch Martinum Herbipolensem im M.D. vnd xxiij Jar) 4°. A-R^4. [67

ENCINAS, FRANCISCO DE. Historia uera de morte sancti uiri Ioannis Diazij Hispani, quem eius frater germanus Alphonsus Diazius ... nefariè interfecit: per Claudium Senarclæum. Cum præfatione D. Martini Buceri ... [Basileae,] M. D. XLVI. 8°. α-γ^8 a-m^8 n^4. pp. 1-178. ¶m2^r: Christianae religionis Summa: ... Ioanne Diazio Hispano autore. (Lea.) [68

ENDORF, HIERONYMUS VON. Ain Christliche vermanūg an Ro. K. M. vñ die stend des hayligen Reychs ꝛc. Einsehen zů haben gemayner Christenhayt abnemens. [Augsburg, Alexander Weissenhorn,] M. D. XXV. 4°. A^4. [69

ENGEL, ANDREAS. Annales Marchiae Brandenburgicæ. Das ist Ordentliche Verzeichnus ... der ... Mårckischen Jahrgeschichten vnd Historien ... Durch M. Andream Angelum, Struthiomontanum. Am Ende ... ein bedencken der Theologen zu Franckfurt an der Oder/ von den Besessenen zu Spandaw ... M. D. XCVIII. ... In verlegung Iohan Hartman/ Buchführer in Franckfurt an der Oder. (Gedruckt durch Friederich Hartman ...) fol.)(^{6} A-T^6 V^8 X-Ll^6 Mm^{4+2} (Mm 3 + *folded leaf*) Nn^4 (Nn4 + *folded leaf*) Oo-Rr^6 Ss^4. pp. 1-453. [70

-- Calvinischer Betlersmantel ... Durch M. Andream Angelum ... 1598. 4°. A-H^4 I^2. pp. 1-60. [71

ENGELBERT. Engelberti Abbatis Admontensis ... de Ortu & fine Romani Imperij Liber. Cum Gasparis Bruschii ... Præfatione. Accessit eiusdem Bruschij Hodoeporicon Bauaricum ... Basileae, per Ioannem Oporinum. (... M. D. LIII. mense Iulio.) 8°. a-k^8 l^4. pp. 4-165. [72

ENGERD, JOHANN. Congratulatio inscripta ... Michaeli Clör Neunstadiano Franco ... cùm ... artium liberalium Magister ac Philosophiæ Doctor publicè ... crearetur: autoribus M. Ioanne Engerdo ... M. Martino Haimburgio ... Emerico Kratzero ... Euchario Sangio ... Sebastiano Weinningo ... Ingolstadii, Ex Officina VVeissenhorniana, apud Vuolfgangum Ederum. 1578. 4°. A^6. [73

ENGELHART, LEONHARD. Lachrymæ ad tumulum ... Sebastiani Coccyi ... effusæ: Cùm obiisset Bebenhusij, Die 28. Septemb. Anno 1562. Tubingæ. 4°. A-C^4. [74

ENGLAND. *Statutes*. [Antiqua statuta.] (Londoñ ... per Richardū Pynson ... Anno ... Millesimo q̊ngētesimo. xiiij. decimo sexto idus Marcius.) 12°. A^6 A^{10} A-N^{12}. ff. i-C.liiij. *S.T.C.* 9267. (Biddle.) [75

-- [The great Charter called in Latyn Magna Carta: with diuers olde statutes ...] (... translated out of Latyn and Frenshe into Englysshe By George Ferrerȝ. Imprynted at London ... by Thomas Petyt. M.D.XLij. ...) 8°. B.L. ✠^{4} (-✠1) A-Dd^8 (-Dd8, *presuambly blank*). ff. i-ccix. *S.T.C.* 9276. (Biddle.) [76

-- Magna charta, cum statutis quæ Antiqua vocantur ... [Londini,] apud Richardum Totelum, 12. Iun. 1556. ... 8°. B.L. ✠^{8} A-X^8 Y^4. ff. 1-170. *S.T.C.* 9278. ¶*The first part only*. (Biddle.) [77

-- Magna Charta, cum statutis, tum antiquis, tum recentibus ... tipis ædita, per Richardum Tottell. ... 1576. ... (... the 8. day of March.) 8°. ₵^{8} A-Hh^8. ff. 2-247. *S.T.C.* 9280. (Biddle.) [78

-- -- tipis ædita, per Richardum Tottill. ... 1587. ... (*Colophon.*) 8°. ¶^{8} A-Hh^8 Ii^4 (-Ii4, *presumably blank*). ff. 2-250. *S.T.C.* 9282. (Biddle.) [79

-- -- *Another copy (interleaved and heavily annotated).* [79a

-- Institutions or principall groundes of the Lawes, and statutes of England ... Imprinted at London ... by Richard Tottell. 8°. B.L. A-H^8 I^4. ff. iii-lxvi. ¶*J. H. Beale T281.* (Biddle.) [80

-- In this volume are conteined the statutes made ... from the time of kyng Henry the thirde, vnto the fyrste yere of the reigne of ... king Henry the .viii. Anno .M.D.XLIII. (Londini in officina Thomæ Bertheleti ...) fol. B.L. A^8 A-I^8 A-D^6 E-Y^8 A-G^8 Hh-Qq^8 Rr-Tt^6 a-f^8 g-i^6. ff. I-LXIX. *S.T.C.* 9301. (Biddle.) [81

-- The second Volume, conteininge those Statutes which haue beene made in the time of ... Kinge Henry the eight ... 1575. Imprinted at London ... by Thomas Marshe. fol. B.L. A^8 A-H^6 I^4 A-D^6 E^4 A-D^6 E^8 A-D^6 E^4 A^4 C^6 A-G^6 A-C^6 D^8 A-G^6 H^4 A-C^6 D^8 A-E^6 A-M^6 A-L^6 M^4 A-G^6 H-I^4 A-D^6 E-F^4 A-F^6. *S.T.C.* 9304. ¶*Additional t.pp.:* (^{7}A1^r) Anno XXV. Henrici Octaui. ... Excudebat Londini, Anno .M.D.LXII. (^{9}A1^r) Anno XXVII. ... Imprinted at London ... by Thomas Powell ... 1562. (^{12}A1^r) Anno XXXII. ... Anno MDXL. (^{15}A1^r) Henry the eyght ... beganne this thirde Session of his ... parliament ... Londini in ædibus Thomæ Bertheleti ... M.D.XLIIII. (... the IX. daye of Aprill ...) (Biddle.) [82

-- A colleccion of all the statutes (from the begynning of Magna Carta vnto the yere ... (1557.) ... Whereunto be addyd the collection of the statutes, made in the fourth and fifth yeres of the reignes of king Philip and Quene Mary, and also ... in the first yere of ... Queene Elizabeth. ... In ædibus Richardi Tottelli, 1559 ... (Imprinted at London ... the .ix. daye of Nouēber ...) 4°. B.L. ¶^{6} A-4C^8 4D^4. ff. 1-580. *S.T.C.* 9307. (Biddle.) [83

-- -- A collection ... And also the statutes made in the first, and fifth yeare of the raigne of ... Queene Elizabeth. ... In ædibus Richardi Tottelli Anno. 1566. Octobris vltimo. ... (Imprinted at London ...) 4°. B.L. ¶^{6} A-3V^8 3X-3Y^4 3Z-4I^8 4K^4 (-4K4, *presumably blank*). ff. 1-618. *S.T.C.* 9308.1. (Biddle.) [84

-- -- A collection ... vnto this present yere ... 1572. In ædibus Richardi Tottelli. An. 1572. vicesimo quarto. Ianuarij. ... (Imprynted at London ...) 4°. B.L. ¶^{8} A-4O^8. ff. 1-664. *S.T.C.* 9311. (Biddle.) [85

-- The whole volume of statutes at large ... At London Printed for Christopher Barker ... 1587. ... fol. B.L. *^{8} (-*1, *presumably blank*) +^{6} A-V^8 Aa-Ii^8 Kk^4 Ll-Vv^8 3A-3V^8 4A-4E^8 4F^6 A-V^8 AA-VV^8 3A-3I^8 3K^2 (-3K2). pp. 1-1043, 1-786. *S.T.C.* 9316. (Biddle.) [86

-- A Collection in English, of the Statutes now in force ... Imprinted at London by Thomas Wight, and Bonham Norton. ... 1598. ... fol. B.L. A-C^8 D^6 A-3Z^8 A-B^6 C-D^4 4A^8 4B^6. ff. 1-552. *S.T.C.* 9321. (Biddle.) [87

-- The greate abbrydgement of all ẏͤ statutes of Englande/ vntyll the .xxx. yere of the reygne of ... kynge Henry the eyght. ... (Imprynted at London ... by me Roberte Redman ... [1540.]) 8°. B.L. ❧^{8} A-3F^8. ff. j-CCCCxv. *S.T.C.* 9522. (Biddle.) [88

-- -- The great Abredgement ... with the abredgemētes of the statutes made in the .xxxiij. yere of the reygne of ... kynge Hēry the eyght. ... (Imprynted at London ... by Thomas Petyt. ... M.D.XLij. 8°. B.L. ✠^{8} A-Y^8 Aa-Ss^8 Tt^{10} A^8 B-D^8. ff. j-CCC.xxi, j-xxx. *S.T.C.* 9523. (Biddle.) [89

-- The newe greate abredgement ... [*6 words canceled by overprinting:*] Excusum Londini in officina Thomae Gaultier ... 1551. (Imprinted at London ... by Wyllyam Powel ...) 8°. B.L. *^{8} A-3D^8. ff. i-ccc.lxxxi. *S.T.C.* 9526. (Biddle.) [90

-- An Abstract of all the penal Statutes ... Moreouer, the Authoritie and duetie of all Iustices of Peace, Sherifes, Coroners, Eschetors, Maiors, Bailiffes ... Collected by Ferdinando Pulton ... Imprinted at London by Christopher Barker ... Anno. 1581. Septembris. 30. ... (*Colophon.*) 4°. B.L. A-Y^8 Z^{10} AA-3A^8. ff. 1-368. *S.T.C.* 9529. (Biddle.) [91

-- -- Imprinted at London by the Deputies of Christopher Barker ... 1592. ... (*Colophon.*) 4°. B.L. A-3A^8. ff. 1-368. *S.T.C.* 9531. (Biddle.) [92

-- *Year books.* [Regis Edwardi Tertii a primo ad decimum (inclusiue) anni ... opera & impensis Richardi Tottelli. ... 1562. ...] (*Colophon.*) fol. B.L. A-3Z^4 (-A1) A-3T^4 3V^6. ff. ij-Dxlij. *S.T.C.* 9551. (Biddle.) [93

-- -- 1596 Anni decem priores, regis Edwardi tertii ... Londini In Ædibus Ianæ Yetsweirt relictæ Caroli Yetsweirt ... fol. B.L. A-3V^6 3X-3Y^4. ff. 2-404. *S.T.C.* 9552. (Biddle.) [94

-- De termino Hillarii. Anno .xvii. Edwardi tertii. [London, Richard Tottel, 1561.] fol. B.L. A-V^4. ff. i-lxxx. *S.T.C.* 9556. (Biddle.) [95

-- -- [London, Richard Tottel, 1584.] fol. B.L. A-V^4. ff. j-lxxx. *S.T.C.* 9557. (Biddle.) [96

-- -- *Another copy.* (Biddle.) [97

-- -- *Another copy.* (Biddle.) [98

-- De termino Hillarii. Anno .xviii. Edwardi tertii. [London, Richard Tottel, 1561.] fol. B.L. A-P^4. ff. i-lix. *S.T.C.* 9559. (Biddle.) [99

-- -- [London, Richard Tottel, 1584.] fol. B.L. A-P^4. ff. i-lix. *S.T.C.* 9560. (Biddle.) [100

-- -- *Another copy.* (Biddle.) [101

-- De termino Hillarii anno regni regis Edwardi tertii .xxi. (Imprinted at London ... by Richard Tottyll. the .xii. daye of Maye ... 1561. ...) fol. B.L. A-O^4 P^6. ff. i-lxij. *S.T.C.* 9563. (Biddle.) [102

-- -- (Imprinted at London ... by Richard Tottyll. the .xij. day of May ... 1584.) fol. B.L. A-O^4 P^6. ff. 1-xlii [= lxii]. *S.T.C.* 9564. (Biddle.) [103

-- -- *Another copy.* (Biddle.) [104

-- De termino Hillarii/ Anno regni regis Edwardi tertii post conquestum vicesimo secundo. (Impress. Londini in edibus Thome Bertheleti ... 1532. mense Nouembr̄.) fol. B.L. A-M^6 N^4 O-R^6. ff. i-C. *S.T.C.* 9565. ¶D3^r: De termino sancti Michaelis/ Anno ... vicesimo tertio. D5^v: De termino Hillarii/ Anno ... vicesimo quarto. G1^v: De termino Hillarii/ Anno ... vicesimo quinto. K1^r: De termino Hillarii/ Anno ... vicesimo sexto. O1^r: De termino Pasche/ anno ... vicesimo septimo. Q2^r: De termino sancti Hillarii anno ... .xxviii. (Biddle.) [105

-- -- fol. B.L. A-T^4 A-Q^4. ff. j-lxxix, xxxviij-c. *S.T.C.* 9566. ¶F1^r: De termino Michaelis anno ... vicesimo tertio. F3^r: ... anno ... vicesimo quarto (Imprinted at London ... by Rychard Tottell, the seconde day of Ianuarye. An. 1567. ...) T4^v: ... anno ... vicesimo quinto (*Same colophon.*) ^{2}E2^r: ... anno ... vicesimo sexto. (*Same colophon.*) ^{2}K4^r: ... anno ... vicesimo septimo. ^{2}O1^r: ... anno ... xxviii. (Imprinted at London ... by Rychard Tottel, the xxiii. daye of Ianuarye. An. 1567) (Biddle.) [106

-- -- (Imprinted at London ... by Richard Tottyl. ... 1585) fol. B.L. A-V^4 A-Q^4. ff. 1-C. *S.T.C.* 9567. (Biddle.) [107

-- De termino Hillarii anno regni regis Edwardi tertii .xxix. (Imprinted at London ... by Richard Tottyll. ... 1561.) fol. B.L. A-L^4 M^6. ff. i-xlix. *S.T.C.* 9571. (Biddle.) [108

-- -- (Imprinted at London ... by Richad [*sic*] Tottyl. 1585.) fol. B.L. A-L^4 M^6. *S.T.C.* 9572. (Biddle.) [109

-- -- *Another copy.* (Biddle.) [110

-- De termino Hillarii Anno regni Regis Edwardi tercii, post conquestum tricesimo. (Imprentyd at London by me Robert Redman [c. 1533].) fol. B.L. A-B^6 C^4 D^6 E^4 F-G^6 H^4. ff. i-xlii. *S.T.C.* 9573. (Biddle.) [111

-- -- (Imprinted at London ... by Richard Tottyll. ... 1561.) fol. B.L. A-H^4. ff. i-xxxii. *S.T.C.* 9574. (Biddle.) [112

-- -- (Imprinted at London ... by Richard Tottell. ... 1585.) fol. B.L. A-H^4. ff. i-xxxii. *S.T.C.* 9575. (Biddle.) [113

-- -- *Another copy.* (Biddle.) [114

-- De termino Hillarii anno regni regis Edwardi tertii .xxxviii. (Imprinted at London ... by Richard Tottyll. ... 1561.) fol. B.L. A-H^4 I^6. ff. i-xxxvii. *S.T.C.* 9577. (Biddle.) [115

-- -- (Imprinted at London ... by Richard Tottel. ... 1585) fol. B.L. A-H^4 I^6. ff. j-xxxvij. *S.T.C.* 9578. (Biddle.) [116

-- -- *Another copy.* (Biddle.) [117

-- De termino Hillarii anno regni regis Edwardi tertii post conquestum .xxxix. (Imprinted at London ... by Richard Tottyll. ... 1561. ...) fol. B.L. A-H^4 I^6. ff. i-xxxviij. *S.T.C.* 9580. (Biddle.) [118

-- -- (Imprinted at London ... by Richard Tottill. ... 1585.) fol. B.L. A-H^4 I^6. ff. i-xxxviii. *S.T.C.* 9581. (Biddle.) [119

-- -- *Another copy.* (Biddle.) [120

-- Regis ... Edwardi tertii a quadragesimo ad quinquagesimum, anni ... 1555. Londini in ædibus Richardi Tottelli. ... (... the .xiii. daye of Ianuarye ... 1556.) fol. B.L. A^6 B-3Z^4 A-T^4 V^6 (-V6, *presumably blank*). ff. ii-xlix, ii-xxxi, i-xxvi, i-xxxvi, ii-xlvj, ii-xxviii, ii-xxxiiij, ii-xxvi, i-xxxiiij, j-xxvii, i-xxvij. *S.T.C.* 9582. (Biddle.) [121

-- -- 1565. Londini in ædibus Richardi Tottelli. ... (... the xv. daye of August ...) fol. B.L. *Same collation and foliation.* *S.T.C.* 9583. (Biddle.) [122

-- -- 1576. Londini in ædibus Richardi Tottelli. ... fol. B.L. *Same collation and foliation.* *S.T.C.* 9584. (Biddle.) [123

-- -- Londini in ædibus Thomæ Wight ... 1600. fol. B.L. A-3O^{6} A-D^{6} E^{2}. ff. 2-49, 2-31, 1-26, 1-36, 2-46, 2-28, 2-34, 2-26, 1-34, 1-27, 1-27. *S.T.C.* 9585. (Biddle.) [124

-- Le liuer des Assises & plees del Corone ... en temps le Roy Edwarde le tierce ... Londini in ædibus Richardi Tottelli. ... 1580. ... (... the xvj. day of Marche. ...) fol. B.L. A^{4} A-H^{4} A-4L^{4} 4M^{6} ¶^{4} ¶¶^{6}. ff. I-CCCxxvi. *S.T.C.* 9601. (Biddle.) [125

-- -- 1581. Londini in Edibus Richardi Totteli. ... (... the .xvi. daye of Ianuary. ...) fol. B.L. *Same collation and foliation.* (Biddle.) [126

-- In hoc volumine continentur omnes anni Regis Henrici quarti ... impressi opera & impensis Richardi Tottelli. 1562. ... (Imprinted at London ... the .ii. daye of Ianuary ... 1563.) fol. B.L. A-4M^{4} 4N^{6} (-4N6, *presumably blank*). ff. i-vi, j-xxv, i-xjx, j-iiij, j-iiij, j-ix, i-xlvi, j-xxiiii, i-viii, i-ix, i-xcv, ij-xxvi, i-xvij, i-xl. *S.T.C.* 9608. (Biddle.) [127

-- -- impressi opera & impensis Richardi Tottelli. 1575. (... 1576.) fol. B.L. A-4N^{6}. ff. i-CCCxxviii. *S.T.C.* 9609. (Biddle.) [128

-- In hoc volumine continentur aliquot anni Regis Henrici quinti ... 1563. mensis Ianuarii secundo. In ædibus Richardi Tottelli ... (Imprinted at London ... the .xv. daye of Ianuary ...) fol. B.L. A-G^{4} A-C^{4} D^{2} A-I^{4}. ff. i-xiiii, i-xii, i-xiij, l-ix, i-xi, i-xv. *S.T.C.* 9614. (Biddle.) [129

-- -- 1563. Mensis Ianuarij secundo. In ædibus Richardi Tottelli. ... (Imprynted at London ... 1570.) fol. B.L. *Same collation and foliation (except that* ^{3}A1 *is not numbered).* *S.T.C.* 9615. (Biddle.) [130

-- De termimo [*sic*] Michaelis anno regni Regis Henrici sexti primo. (Imprinted at London ... by Rychard Tottyl. Anno 1584. ...) fol. B.L. A-B^{4}. ff. i-viii. *S.T.C.* 9623. (Biddle.) [131

-- De termino sancti Michaelis. Anno regni Regis Henrici Sexti .ii. ([Londini,] Impressum ... ꝑ Richardū Pynson ... [c. 1510.]) fol. B.L. A-B^{6} C^{4}. ff. .i-xvi. *S.T.C.* 9624. (Biddle.) [132

-- -- (Imprinted at London ... by Rychard Tottyl. Anno 1584. ...) fol. B.L. A-B^{6} C^{4}. ff. i-xvi. *S.T.C.* 9630. (Biddle.) [133

-- De termino Michaelis anno iij. regni Regis Henrici vj. (Imprinted at London ... by Ry-charde Tottell. 1582. ...) fol. B.L. A-O^{4}. ff. i-lvi. *S.T.C.* 9636. (Biddle.) [134

-- De termino Michaelis anno iiij. regni Regis Henrici vj. (Imprinted at London ... by Rycharde Tottell. 1582. ...) fol. B.L. A-H^{4}. ff. i-xxxii. *S.T.C.* 9641. (Biddle.) [135

-- De termino Michaelis anno Regni Regis Henrici sexti septimo. (Imprinted at London ... by Rychard Tottyl. Anno 1584. ...) fol. A-V^{4} X^{2}. ff. i-xlv, l-xxxvii. *S.T.C.* 9647. ¶M2^{r}: De termino Michaelis anno ... octauo. (Biddle.) [136

-- De termino Pasche anno regni regis Henrici sexti nono. (Imprynted at London ... by Rychard Tottyl. Anno. 1570. ...) fol. B.L. A^{6} B-D^{4} E^{6} F-Q^{4} (-Q4, *presumably blank*). ff. l-lxvii. *S.T.C.* 9655. (Biddle.) [137

-- De termino Michaelis Anno decimo Henrici sexti. (Imprinted at London ... by Richarde Tottyll. 1587.) fol. B.L. A-E^{4} F^{6}. ff. 1-26. *S.T.C.* 9663. (Biddle.) [138

-- De Termino Michaelis An. xi. H. vi. (Imprynted at London by me Robert Redman ... [c. 1527.]) fol. B.L. A-O$^{6.4}$. ff. i-lxii. *S.T.C.* 9664. (Biddle.) [139

-- -- (Imprinted at London ... by Rychard Tottell, the xij. day of Iune. 1582. ...) fol. B.L. A-O^{4}. ff. i-lvi. *S.T.C.* 9668. (Biddle.) [140

-- De termīo Michaelis. Anno. xii. Henrici sexti. ([Londini,] Impress. per Richardum Pynsonum ... [c. 1520.]) fol. B.L. A-B^{4}. *S.T.C.* 9669. (Biddle.) [141

-- -- (Imprinted at London ... By Rychard Tottel the vi. day of December ... 1574. ...) fol. B.L. A-B^{4}. ff. i-viii. *S.T.C.* 9672. (Biddle.) [142

-- Anno quartodecimo Henrici Sexti. ([Londini,] Impressus per me VVilhelmum Meddelton [c. 1540].) fol. B.L. A-D$^{6.4}$ E^{6}. ff. i-xxvii. *S.T.C.* 9676. (Biddle.) [143

-- -- (Imprinted at London ... By Rychard Tottel the vi. day of December ... 1574. ...) fol. B.L. A-E^{4} F^{6}. ff. i-xxvi. *S.T.C.* 9679. (Biddle.) [144

-- De termino Paschae anno xviij. regni Regis Henrici sexti. ([Londini,] Imprinted by Rycharde Tottel [c. 1562]. ...) fol. B.L. A-G^{4} H^{6}. ff. j-xxxiiii. *S.T.C.* 9684. (Biddle.) [145

-- De termino Michaelis anno XIX. regni regis Henrici sexti. (Imprinted at London ... by Richard Tottill ... 1567.) fol. B.L. A-V^{4}. ff. i-lxxx. *S.T.C.* 9689. (Biddle.) [146

-- De termino Michls. Anno xxj. H. vi. ([London,] Imprynted by my Robert Redman. ... [c. 1550.]) fol. B.L. A-F$^{6.6.4}$ G^{6} H^{4} I-L^{6} M^{4} (-M4, *presumably blank*). ff. i-lxiij. *S.T.C.* 9699. (Biddle.) [147

-- -- (Imprinted at London ... by Richard Tottill. ... [c. 1555.]) fol. B.L. A-N^{4} O^{6}. ff. i-lviii. *S.T.C.* 9700. (Biddle.) [148

-- -- (Imprinted at London ... by Richard Tottill ... 1567.) fol. B.L. A-N^{4} O^{6}. ff. i-lviij. *S.T.C.* 9701. (Biddle.) [149

-- -- (Imprinted at London ... By Rychard Tottel the 10. day of Nouember ... 1575.) fol. B.L. A-N^{4} O^{6}. ff. i-lviii. *S.T.C.* 9702. (Biddle.) [150

-- De Termino sancti Michaelis Anno regni Regis Henrici sexti vicesimo Secundo. ([London,] Enprented by my Robert Redman [c. 1530]. ...) fol. B.L. A-I$^{6.6.4}$ K-M^{6}. ff. ij-lxvi. *S.T.C.* 9705. (Biddle.) [151

-- -- (Imprinted at London ... by Richard Tottill [c. 1550]. ...) fol. B.L. A-P^{4}. ff. i-lx. *S.T.C.* 9706. (Biddle.) [152

-- -- (Imprinted at London ... by Richard Tottill ... 1567.) fol. B.L. A-F^{4}. ff. ii-lx. *S.T.C.* 9707. (Biddle.) [153

-- -- (Imprinted at London ... By Rychard Tottel the 18. day of October ... 1575.) fol. B.L. A-P^{4}. ff. ii-lx. *S.T.C.* 9708. (Biddle.) [154

-- De Termino Michaelis An. xxvii. H. vi. (Imprynted by me Robert Redman [c. 1530.]) fol. B.L. A-C^{4}. ff. i-xii. *S.T.C.* 9711. (Biddle.) [155

-- -- (Imprinted at London ... by Richard Tottel [c. 1550] ...) fol. B.L. A-B^{4} C^{2}. ff. ii-x. *S.T.C.* 9712. (Biddle.) [156

-- -- (Imprinted at London ... By Rychard Tottel the xxix. day of Marche ... 1575. ...) fol. B.L. A-B^{4} C^{2}. ff. i-x. *S.T.C.* 9715. (Biddle.) [157

-- De Termino sancti Michaelis Anno regni Regis Henrici Sexti post conquestum vicesimo octauo. (Imprinted at London by me Robert Redman [c. 1530] ...) fol. B.L. A^{6} B^{4} C^{6}. ff. ii-xii. *S.T.C.* 9717. (Biddle.) [158

-- -- (Imprinted at London ... by Richard Tottle, the .xxx. day of Ianuarie ... 1556. ...) fol. B.L. A-B^{4} C^{6}. ff. j-xiii. *S.T.C.* 9718. (Biddle.) [159

-- -- (Imprinted at London ... By Rychard Tottel the vij. day of Aprell ... 1575.) fol. B.L. A-B^{4} C^{6}. ff. i-xiii. *S.T.C.* 9720. (Biddle.) [160

-- De termino Michaelis Anno. xxx. H. vi. (Imprynted at London ... by Wyllyam Myddylton [c. 1540].) fol. B.L. A-D^{4}. ff. i-xvi. *S.T.C.* 9722. ¶B4^{v}: De termino sancti Michaelis Anno ... tricesimo primo. (Biddle.) [161

-- -- (Imprinted at London ... by Richard Tottel, Anno .1556. ...) fol. B.L. A-D^{4}. ff. i-xvj. *S.T.C.* 9723. (Biddle.) [162

-- -- (Imprinted at London ... By Rychard Tottel the 10. day of Nouember ... 1575. ...) fol. B.L. A-D^{4}. ff. i-xvii. *S.T.C.* 9725. (Biddle.) [163

-- De termino Trinitatis anno trisesimo Secundo Henrici Sexti. (Imprinted at London ... by

Richard Tottel, Anno .1556. ...) fol. B.L. A-G^{4} H^{6}. ff. i-xxxiiii. *S.T.C.* 9728. (Biddle.) [164

-- -- (Imprinted at London ... By Rycharde Tottel. Anno .1576. ...) fol. B.L. A-G^{4} H^{6}. ff. i-xxxiiii. *S.T.C.* 9730. (Biddle.) [165

-- De termino Hillarii anno xxxiii. regni regis Henrici .vi. (Imprinted at London ... by Richard Tottel, the .vi. day of Marche. Anno .1556. ...) fol. B.L. A-O^{4}. ff. i-lvi. *S.T.C.* 9734. (Biddle.) [166

-- -- (Imprinted at London ... by Richard Tottell. ẏᵉ vi. day of March. 1556. ...) fol. B.L. A-O^{4}. ff. j-lvi. *J. H. Beale R186.* (Biddle.) [167

-- -- (Imprinted at London ... By Rychard Tottel the 14. daye of Maye ... 1575. ...) fol. B.L. A-O^{4}. ff. i-lvi. *S.T.C.* 9736. (Biddle.) [168

-- De termino Michaelis anno. XXXIIII. regni regis Henrici sexti. (Imprinted at London ... by Richard Tottel, the .vi. day of Marche. Anno .1556.) fol. B.L. A-M^{4} N^{6}. ff. i-liii. *S.T.C.* 9739. (Biddle.) [169

-- -- (Imprinted at London ... by Richard Tottel ẏᵉ .vi. of March, Anno .1556. ...) fol. B.L. A-M^{4} N^{6}. ff. i-liii. *S.T.C.* 9740. (Biddle.) [170

-- -- (Imprinted at London ... By Rychard Tottel the xiij. day of Aprell ... 1575.) fol. B.L. A-M^{4} N^{6}. ff. i-liii. *S.T.C.* 9741. (Biddle.) [171

-- De termino Michaelis anno XXXV. regni regis Henrici .vi. (Imprinted at London ... by Richard Tottel, Anno .1556.) fol. B.L. A-Q^{4}. ff. i-lxiii. *S.T.C.* 9746. (Biddle.)[172

-- -- (Imprinted at London ... by Richard Tottell. 1556.) fol. B.L. A-Q^{4}. ff. i-lxiii. *S.T.C.* 9747. (Biddle.) [173

-- -- (Imprinted at London ... By Rychard Tottel the 21. daye of Iune ... 1575.) fol. B.L. A-Q^{4}. ff. i-lxiii. *S.T.C.* 9748. (Biddle.) [174

-- Anno tricesimo sexto Henrici sexti. (Imprinted at London ... by Richard Tottle, Anno .1557. ...) fol. B.L. A-G^{4} H^{6}. ff. i-xxxiiii. *S.T.C.* 9752. (Biddle.) [175

-- -- (Imprinted at London ... By Rychard Tottel the 24. day of Nouember ... 1575. ...) fol. B.L. A-G^{4} H^{6}. ff. i-xxxiiii. *S.T.C.* 9754. (Biddle.) [176

-- De termino Michaelis. anno. xxxvii. Henrici sexti. (Imprinted at London ... by Richard Tottill [c. 1566].) fol. B.L. A-H^{4} I^{6}. ff. j-xxxiiii. *S.T.C.* 9757. (Biddle.) [177

-- -- (Imprinted at London ... By Rychard Tottel the 2. daye of Iune ... 1575. ...) fol. B.L. A-H^{4} I^{6}. ff. 1-xxxviii. *S.T.C.* 9759. (Biddle.) [178

-- De termino Michaelis. anno XXXVIII. regni regis Henrici .vi. (Imprinted at London ... by Richard Tottel, Anno .1556. ...) fol. B.L. A-K^{4}. ff. i-xxxviii. *S.T.C.* 9761. (Biddle.) [179

-- -- (Imprinted at London ... by Rychard Tottel, An. 1566. ...) fol. B.L. A-K^{4}. ff. ii-xxxviii. *S.T.C.* 9762. (Biddle.) [180

-- -- (Imprinted at London ... By Rychard Tottel the v. daye of Maye ... 1575. ...) fol. B.L. A-K^{4}. ff. ii-xl. *S.T.C.* 9763. (Biddle.) [181

-- De termino Michaelis anno xxxix. Henrici sexti. (Imprinted at London ... by Richard Tottle, Anno .1557. ...) fol. B.L. A-N^{4}. ff. i-li. *S.T.C.* 9766. (Biddle.) [182

-- -- (Imprinted at London ... By Rychard Tottel the 14. day of December ... 1575. ...) fol. B.L. A-N^{4}. ff. 1-li. *S.T.C.* 9768. (Biddle.) [183

-- Les ans ou Reports del raigne du Roye Edward le quart ... Londini In ædibus Thomæ Wight & Bonhami Norton. 1599. ... fol. B.L. A-5A^{6} A-F^{6} G^{4}. ff. 1-10, 1-29, 1-28, 1-44, 1-8, 1-12, 1-32, 1-25, 1-5, 1-53, 1-19, 1-11, 1-21, 1-10, 1-8, 1-33, 1-12, 1-8, 1-30, 1-10, 1-19, 1-84, 1-51. *S.T.C.* 9769. (Biddle.) [184

-- De termino Michaelis anno primo Edwardi quarti. (Imprinted at London ... by Richard Tottel, Anno .1556. ...) fol. B.L. A^{4} B^{6}. ff. i-x. *S.T.C.* 9775. (Biddle.) [185

-- -- (Imprinted at London ... by Richard Tottill. Anno .1556.) fol. B.L. A^{4} B^{6}. ff. i-x. *S.T.C.* 9776. (Biddle.) [186

-- -- (Imprinted at London ... by Rychard Tottel. 1582. ...) fol. B.L. A^4 B^6. ff. 1-x. *S.T.C.* 9778. (Biddle.) [187

-- De termino Pasche anno secundo. Edwardi quarti. (Imprinted at London ... by Richard Tottell. Anno .1566. ...) fol. B.L. A-G^4. ff. 1-xxvii. *S.T.C.* 9782. (Biddle.) [188

-- -- (Imprinted at London ... by Rycharde Tottel. 1584. ...) fol. B.L. A-F^4 G^6 (-G6, *presumably blank*). ff. 1-xxviii. *S.T.C.* 9783.1. (Biddle.) [189

-- De termino Trinitatis anno .III. Edwardi quarti. (Imprinted at London ... by Richard Tottell. ... 1558. ...) fol. B.L. A-G^4. ff. i-xxviij. *S.T.C.* 9786. (Biddle.) [190

-- -- (Imprinted at London ... by Richard Tottill. Anno .1566 ...) fol. B.L. A-G^4. ff. 1-xxviii. *S.T.C.* 9788. (Biddle.) [191

-- -- (Imprinted at London ... by Rycharde Tottel. 1583. ...) fol. B.L. A-G^4. ff. 1-xxviii. *S.T.C.* 9789. (Biddle.) [192

-- De termino Pasche, anno .IIII. Edwardi quarti. (Imprinted at London ... by Richard Tottell. Anno .1558. ...) fol. B.L. A-L^4. *S.T.C.* 9792. (Biddle.) [193

-- -- (Imprinted at London ... by Richard Tottill. Anno. 1558 ...) fol. B.L. A-L^4. ff. 1-xliiii. *S.T.C.* 9794. (Biddle.) [194

-- -- (Imprinted at London ... by Rycharde Tottel. 1583. ...) fol. B.L. A-L^4. ff. 1-xliiii. *S.T.C.* 9795. (Biddle.) [195

-- De termino Pasche anno .V. Edwardi quarti. (Imprinted at London ... by Richard Tottle. Anno .1557. ...) fol. B.L. A-B^4. ff. i-viii. *S.T.C.* 9799. (Biddle.) [196

-- -- (Imprinted at London ... by Richard Tottell. 1566. ...) fol. B.L. A-B^4. ff. i-viii. *S.T.C.* 9800. (Biddle.) [197

-- -- (Imprinted at London ... by Richard Tottill. Anno. 1566 ...) fol. B.L. A-B^4. ff. 1-vi. *S.T.C.* 9801. (Biddle.) [198

-- -- (Imprinted at London ... by Rycharde Tottel. 1584. ...) fol. B.L. A-B^4. ff. 1-viii. *S.T.C.* 9802. (Biddle.) [199

-- En cest volume est conteinus le longe Report de Anno quinto Edwardi quarti ... In ædibus Richardi Tottelli. ... (Imprinted at London ... 1587.) fol. B.L. $¶^4$ A-NN^4. ff. 1-142. *S.T.C.* 9803. (Biddle.) [200

-- De termino Michaelis anno vj. Edwardi quarti. (Imprinted at London ... by Rycharde Tottell. 1556. ...) fol. B.L. A-C^4. ff. 1-xii. *S.T.C.* 9808. (Biddle.) [201

-- -- (Imprinted at London ... by Richard Tottell. Anno .1557. ...) fol. B.L. A-C^4. ff. i-xii. *S.T.C.* 9809. (Biddle.) [202

-- -- (Imprinted at London ... by Rychard Tottel ... 1572. ...) fol. B.L. A-C^4. ff. i-xii. *S.T.C.* 9811. (Biddle.) [203

-- De termino Pasche anno VII. Edwardi quarti. (Imprinted at London ... by Richard Tottill. ye. last day of April ... 1567) fol. B.L. A-H^4. ff. ij-xxxii. *S.T.C.* 9816. (Biddle.) [204

-- -- (Imprinted at London ... by Richard Tottill, ye. last day of April ... 1567) fol. B.L. A-H^4. ff. 1-xxxii. *S.T.C.* 9817. (Biddle.) [205

-- De termino Pasche anno viii regni Edwardi quarti. (Imprinted at London ... by Richard Tottel, Anno .1556. ...) fol. B.L. A-E^4 F^6 (-F6, *presumably blank*). ff. i-xxv. *S.T.C.* 9822. (Biddle.) [206

-- -- (Imprinted at London ... by Richard Tottill. Anno .1556. ...) fol. B.L. A-E^4 F^6. ff. ii-xxv. *S.T.C.* 9824. (Biddle.) [207

-- -- (Imprinted at London ... by Rycharde Tottel. 1582. ...) fol. B.L. A-E^4 F^6. ff. i-xxv. *S.T.C.* 9824.1. (Biddle.) [208

-- De termino Pasche anno ix. regni regis Edwardi quarti. (Imprinted at London ... by Richard Tottell. the .viii. daye of Februarie ... 1556. ...) fol. B.L. A-M^4 N^6 (-N6, *presumably blank*). ff. i-liij. *S.T.C.* 9829. (Biddle.) [209

-- -- (Imprinted at London ... by Rychard Tottel ... 1572. the .24. of Iuly. ...) fol. B.L. A-M^4 N^6. ff. i-liii. *S.T.C.* 9830. (Biddle.) [210

-- -- (Imprinted at London ... by Rychard Tottel, the vj. day of Iune. 1582. ...) fol. B.L. A-M^4 N^6. ff. 1-liii. *S.T.C.* 9831. (Biddle.) [211

-- De termino Pasche anno X. Edwardi quarti. (Imprinted at London ... by Richard Tottell. 1566. ...) fol. B.L. A-N^4. ff. i-xix, 1-xi, i-xxi. *S.T.C.* 9834. ¶D1^r: De Termino Michaelis Anno ab incohacione regni Henrici sexti. xlix. et recaptionis regie potestatis primo. (*Colophon.*) E4^r: De termino Trinitatis anno XI. regni regis Edwardi quarti. (*Colophon.*) H3^r: De termino Pasche anno XII. regni regis Edwardi quarti. (Biddle.) [212

-- -- (Imprinted at London ... by Rychard Tottyl. Anno 1584. ...) fol. B.L. A-N^4. ff. 1-xix, i-xi, 1-xxi. *S.T.C.* 9835.2. (Biddle.) [213

-- De termĩo Michaelis Anno .xiii. E. iiii. ([Londini,] Impressus per Richardum Pynson ...) fol. B.L. A^6 B^4. ff. i-x. *S.T.C.* 9840.1. (Biddle.) [214

-- -- (Imprinted at London ... by Richard Tottill. y^e .xvi. day of August ... 1566.) fol. B.L. A^6 B^4. ff. i-x. *S.T.C.* 9842. (Biddle.) [215

-- -- (Imprinted at London ... by Rychard Tottel, the xij. day of Iune. 1582. ...) fol. B.L. A^6 B^4. ff. i-x. *S.T.C.* 9844. (Biddle.) [216

-- De termino Michaelis anno .XIIII. regni regis Edwardi quarti. (Imprinted at London ... by Richard Tottell [c. 1552]. ...) fol. B.L. A-B^4. ff. 1-viii. *S.T.C.* 9847. (Biddle.) [217

-- -- (Imprinted at London ... by Rychard Tottel ... 1572.) fol. B.L. A-B^4. ff. 1-viii. *S.T.C.* 9849. (Biddle.) [218

-- -- (Imprinted at London ... by Rychard Tottel, the xij. day of Iune. 1582. ...) fol. B.L. A-B^4. ff. 1-viii. *S.T.C.* 9850. (Biddle.) [219

-- De termino Michaelis anno XV. regni regis Edwardi quarti. (Imprinted at London ... by Richarde Tottel, the .ii. daye of Februarye ... 1556. ...) fol. B.L. A-G^4 H^6 (-H6, *presumably blank*). ff. i-xxxiii. *S.T.C.* 9853. (Biddle.) [220

-- -- (Imprinted at London ... by Rychard Tottel ... 1572.) fol. B.L. A-G^4 H^6. ff. 1-xxxiii. *S.T.C.* 9854. (Biddle.) [221

-- -- (Imprinted at London ... by Rychard Tottel, the xij. day of Iune. 1582. ...) fol. B.L. A-G^4 H^6. ff. j-xxxiii. *S.T.C.* 9855. (Biddle.) [222

-- De termino Pasche anno XVI. Edwardi quarti. (Imprinted at London ... by Richard Tottell. Anno .1556. ...) fol. B.L. A-C^4. ff. i-xii. *S.T.C.* 9857. (Biddle.) [223

-- -- (Imprinted at London ... by Richard Tottill. Anno .1556. ...) fol. B.L. A-C^4. ff. i-xii. *S.T.C.* 9858. (Biddle.) [224

-- -- (Imprinted at London ... by Rycharde Tottel. 1583. ...) fol. B.L. A-C^4. ff. 1-xii. *S.T.C.* 9860. (Biddle.) [225

-- De termino Pasche anno .XVII. Edwardi quarti. (Imprinted at London ... by Richard Tottel. Anno .1557.) fol. B.L. A-B^4. ff. i-viii. *J. H. Beale R334.* (Biddle.) [226

-- -- (Imprinted at London ... by Richard Tottel, Anno .1557. ...) fol. B.L. A-B^4. ff. i-viii. *J. H. Beale R336.* (Biddle.) [227

-- -- (Imprinted at London ... by Rychard Tottel ... 1572. ...) fol. B.L. A-B^4. ff. 1-viii. *S.T.C.* 9864. (Biddle.) [228

-- -- (Imprinted at London ... by Rycharde Tottel. 1583. ...) fol. B.L. A-B^4. ff. 1-viii. *S.T.C.* 9864.1. (Biddle.) [229

-- De termino Pasche anno XVIII. regni regis Edwardi quarti. (Imprinted at London ... by Richard Tottell. ...) fol. B.L. A-F^4 G^6. ff. ii-xxix. *S.T.C.* 9867. (Biddle.) [230

-- -- (Imprinted at London ... by Rychard Tottel ... 1572. ...) fol. B.L. A-F^4 G^6. ff. i-xxx. *S.T.C.* 9869. (Biddle.) [231

-- -- (Imprinted at London ... by Rycharde Tottell. 1582. ...) fol. B.L. A-F^4 G^6. ff. i-xxx. *S.T.C.* 9870. (Biddle.) [232

-- De termino Michaelis anno xix. Edwardi quarti. (Imprinted at London ... by Richard Tottel, Anno .1556. ...) fol. B.L. A^4 B^6. ff. ij-x. *S.T.C.* 9873. (Biddle.) [233

-- -- (imprinted at London ... by Richard Tottill. Anno .1556. ...) fol. B.L. A^4 B^6. ff. ii-x. *S.T.C.* 9875. (Biddle.) [234

-- -- (Imprinted at London ... by Rycharde Tottell. 1556. ...) fol. B.L. A^4 B^6. ff. ii-x. *J. H. Beale R350.* (Biddle.) [235

-- De termino Pasche anno. XX. regni Regis Edwardi quarti. (Imprinted at London ... by Richard Tottill. Anno .1556. ...) fol. B.L. A-E^4. ff. 1-xix. *S.T.C.* 9880. (Biddle.) [236

-- -- (Imprinted at London ... by Richard Tottell [c. 1570]. ...) fol. B.L. A-E^4. ff. i-xix. *S.T.C.* 9881. (Biddle.) [237

-- -- (Imprinted at London ... by Rycharde Tottyll. 1582.) fol. B.L. A-E^4. ff. i-xix. *S.T.C.* 9882. (Biddle.) [238

-- De termino Pasche anno xxi. Edwardi quarti. (Imprinted at London ... by Richard Tottill. Anno .1566 ...) fol. B.L. A-X^4. ff. 1-lxxxiiii. *S.T.C.* 9887. (Biddle.) [239

-- -- (Imprinted at London ... by Rycharde Tottel. Anno 1584. ...) fol. B.L. A-X^4. ff. 1-lxxxiii. *S.T.C.* 9887.1. (Biddle.) [240

-- De termino Pasche. anno. XXII. regni regis Edwardi quarti. (Imprinted at London ... by Richard Tottell. the .viii. daye of Februarie ... 1556. ...) fol. B.L. A-N^4. ff. i-li. *S.T.C.* 9892. (Biddle.) [241

-- -- (Imprinted at London ... by Richard Tottle. 1572.) fol. B.L. A-N^4. ff. i-li. *S.T.C.* 9893. (Biddle.) [242

-- -- (Imprinted at London ... by Rycharde Tottel ... 1578.) fol. B.L. A-N^4. ff. i-li. *S.T.C.* 9894. (Biddle.) [243

-- -- *Another copy.* (Biddle.) [244

-- De termino Trinitatis anno .I. regni regis Edwardi quinti. (Imprinted at London ... by Richard Tottell. the .xii. daye of September ... 1559. ...) fol. B.L. A-B^4. *S.T.C.* 9898. (Biddle.) [245

-- -- (Imprinted at London ... by Richard Tottyll. ... the .12. day of September. ... 1559. ...) fol. B.L. A-B^4. *S.T.C.* 9899. (Biddle.) [246

-- -- (Imprinted at London ... by Richard Tottill. Anno. 1568 ...) fol. B.L. A-B^4. ff. i-viii. *S.T.C.* 9900 . (Biddle.) [247

-- -- (Imprinted at London ... by Richard Tottyl. ... 1585. ...) fol. B.L. A-B^4. ff. j-viii. *S.T.C.* 9902. (Biddle.) [248

-- Anni, regum, Edwardi quinti, Richardi tertii, Henrici septimi, et Henrici octaui ... Londini In ædibus Ianæ Yetsweirt. ... 1597. fol. B.L. A-3T^6. *Pagination hopelessly confused. S.T.C.* 9903. (Biddle.) [249

-- De termino Michaelis anno primo Richardi tertii. (Imprinted at London ... by Richard Tottell [c. 1556]. ...) fol. B.L. A^4. ff. i-iiii. *S.T.C.* 9907. (Biddle.) [250

-- -- (Imprinted at London ... by Richard Tottyll [c. 1560]. ...) fol. B.L. A^4. ff. j-iiij. *S.T.C.* 9908. (Biddle.) [251

-- -- (Imprynted at London ... by Rychard Tottel. Anno .1568.) fol. B.L. A^4. ff. i-iiii. *S.T.C.* 9909. (Biddle.) [252

-- -- (Imprinted at London ... by Richarde Tottyll. 1587.) fol. B.L. A^4 A-D^4 E^6. ff. 1-4, 1-22. *S.T.C.* 9912. ¶^{2}A1^r: De termino Michaelis, anno secundo Richardi tercij. (Biddle.) [253

-- Incipit Annus secundus Richardi tertij. (Imprinted at London ... by Richard Tottell [c. 1558]. ...) fol. B.L. A-D^4 E^6. ff. i-xxii. *S.T.C.* 9914. (Biddle.) [254

-- -- (Imprinted at London ... by Richard Tottyll [c. 1558]. ...) fol. B.L. A-D^4 E^6. ff. i-xxii. *S.T.C.* 9915. (Biddle.) [255

-- -- (Imprynted at London ... by Rychard Tottel. Anno. 1568.) fol. B.L. A-D^4 E^6. ff. 1-xxii. *S.T.C.* 9916. (Biddle.) [256

-- Anni regis Henrici septimi. ... 1555. Londini in ædibus Richardi Totteli. ... (... 1567) fol. B.L. A^6 B-Z^4 ꝛ^4 AA-3Z^4 a-v^4 x^6 aa-mm^4 nn^6. ff. ii-xli *embracing 18 separate series of numbers.* *S.T.C.* 9924. (Biddle.) [257

-- -- In hoc volumine continentur omnes Anni ... Londini in Ædibus Richardi Tottelli. 1580. ... (*Colophon.*) fol. B.L. A^6 B-Z^4 ꝛ^4 AA-3Z^4 A-V^4 X^6 Aa-Mm^4 Nn^6. *Same foliation (with insignificant variations).* *S.T.C.* 9925. (Biddle.) [258

-- -- Londini, in Ædibus Richardj Tottelli. 1585. ... (... 1583.) fol. B.L. *Same collation and foliation.* *S.T.C.* 9926. (Biddle.) [259

-- De termino Trinitatis anno regni Regis Henrici octaui XII. (Imprinted at London ... by Rycharde Tottel. 1556. ...) fol. B.L. A-D^4 A-H^4. ff. i-xvi, i-xxxi. *S.T.C.* 9937. ¶C3^v: De termino Michaelis anno ... XIII. ^{2}A1^r: De termino Michaelis anno ... XIIII. (Biddle.) [260

-- -- (Imprinted at London ... by Rycharde Tottyll. ... 1560. ...) fol. B.L. A-D^4 A-H^4. ff. i-xvi, i-xxxi. *S.T.C.* 9938. ¶A1^r: fo.i. (Biddle.) [261

-- -- *Same colophon, collation, and foliation.* ¶A1^r: Fo.i. (Biddle.) [262

-- -- (Imprynted at London ... by Rychard Tottel. Anno. 1569. ...) fol. B.L. A-D^4 A-H^4. ff. i-xvi, i-xxxi. *S.T.C.* 9941. (Biddle.) [263

-- De termino Michaelis Anno .xviii. regni regis Henrici octaui. (Imprinted at London ... by Richard Tottil. ...) fol. B.L. A-C^4 D^2. ff. 1-xiiii. *J. H. Beale R431.* ¶B2^r: De termino Pasche. Anno ... xix. (Biddle.) [264

-- -- (Imprinted at London ... by Rycharde Tottel. 1556. ...) fol. B.L. A-B^4 C^6. ff. ii-xiiii. *S.T.C.* 9948. (Biddle.) [265

-- -- (Imprinted at London ... by Richard Tottell. 1566. ...) fol. B.L. A-C^4 D^2. ff. 1-xiiii. *S.T.C.* 9949. (Biddle.) [266

-- -- (Imprynted at London ... by Rychard Tottel. Anno. 1569. ...) fol. A-B^4 C^6. ff. ii-xiiii. *S.T.C.* 9951. (Biddle.) [267

-- De termino Pasche. anno. XXVI. regni regis Henrici octaui. (Imprinted at London ... by Richard Tottell. the .iiii. daye of February ... 1556. ...) fol. B.L. A^4 B^6. ff. i-x. *S.T.C.* 9956. (Biddle.) [268

-- -- (Imprinted at London ... by Rychard Tottel. 1556. ...) fol. B.L. A^4 B^6. ff. 1-x. *S.T.C.* 9957. (Biddle.) [269

-- -- (Imprinted at London ... by Rychard Tottell. 1566. ...) fol. B.L. A^4 B^6. ff. 1-x. *S.T.C.* 9958. (Biddle.) [270

-- -- (Imprynted at London ... by Rychard Tottel. Anno. 1569. ...) fol. B.L. A^4 B^6. ff. i-x. *S.T.C.* 9960. (Biddle.) [271

-- De termino Pasche. Anno regni regis Henrici octaui .XXVII. (Imprinted at London ... by Richard Tottell. the .viii. daye of February ... 1556. ...) fol. B.L. A-G^4 H^2. ff. i-xxx. *S.T.C.* 9963. (Biddle.) [272

-- -- (Imprinted at London ... by Rychard Tottel. Anno. 1569. ...) fol. B.L. A-F^4 G^6. ff. i-xxx. *S.T.C.* 9965. (Biddle.) [273

-- -- (Imprinted at London ... by Rycharde Tottel. 1583. ...) fol. B.L. A-F^4 G^6. ff. 1-xxx. *S.T.C.* 9967. (Biddle.) [274

ENGLAND, CHURCH of. Articles to be enquired of in the visitatiō, in the First yeere of the Raign of ... Elizabeth ... of England ... Queene ... Anno Dom. 1559. (Imprinted at London by the Assignement of Robert Barker ... 1600.) 4°. B.L. A-B^4 (-B4, *presumably blank*). *S.T.C.* 10133. ¶B2, B3 *defective.* [275

-- [The book of common prayer. London: Christopher Barker, c. 1584.] 4°. ¶*An imperfect copy consisting of* B4-B8, C-Y^8 (-T6-T8) Aa-Ii^8 Kk^4 *Perhaps S.T.C.* 16309. (Furness.) [276

ENNIUS, QUINTUS. Q. EnnI ... annalium libb. XIIX Quae apud varios Auctores superant, fragmenta: conlecta ... ab Paullo G.F.P.N. Merula ... Lugduni Batavorum, Ex officina Ioannis Paetsij, & Ludovici Elzevirij. Anno cIↃ IↃ xcv. (... Typis Ioannis Balduini. ...) 4°. a-g[4] A-4N[4]. pp. γ-ϛ, I-IↃCXXXII. [277

ENNIUS, SIMON. Sententiae aliquot ex Iesu Syrach excerptæ, & in carmen redactæ ... Item. Oratio ... ad Deum, cum Somnio ... Viennæ Austriæ Hæredes Singrenij excudebant. 4°. A-B[8]. ¶*Last poem dated 8 February 1548.* [278

ENTZELT, CHRISTOPH. De re metallica ... libri III. Autore Christophoro Encelio Saluelden-si. ... Franc. Apud Chr. Egenolphum [1551]. 8°. α[8] A-F[8] (F6 + *folded leaf*, F8 + *folded leaf*) G[8] (G2 + *folded leaf*) H-R[8]. pp. 1-271. [279

EOBANUS, HELIUS, HESSUS. Operum ... farragines duae ... Halae Sueuorum [Petrus Brubach,] anno XXXIX. 8°. A[8] a-z[8] A-V[8] A-Q[8]. ff. 3-340, 2-128. [280

-- De tuenda bona valetudine, libellus ..., Commentarijs ... illustratus, à Ioanne Placotomo ... Franc. Apud Chr. Egen. (... Mense Martio. M.D.LI.) 8°. A-O[8] P[4]. ff. 2-114. (Smith.) [281

-- Eobani Hessi Elegia, recens scripta de Columnia. (Martiburgi Calendis Maij. M D XXXVIII.) 4°. A[6]. [282

-- Helii Eobani Hessi ... Operum Flores ... selecti, Opera Christophori Aulaei ... Accesserunt eiusdem Aulaei Christianae precationes, Elegiaco carmine redditæ. ... Franc. Apud Chr. Egenolphum. (... 1551.) 8°. A-L[8] M[4]. [283

-- Vrbs Noriberga Illustrata carmine Heroico, ... Anno M. D. XXXII. ... [Norembergae,] . Excusum per Io. Petreium. 4°. a-h[4]. [284

EPHESUS. *Synod.* Τα πρακτικα της οικουμενικης τριτης συνοδου ... Acta oecumenicae tertiae synodi Ephesi habitæ ... Græce ... Heidelbergæ, E Typographeio Hieronymi Commelini, CIↃ IↃ XCI. fol. (:)[4] A-Cc[6] Dd-Ee[4] Ff[6]. pp. 1-319. [285

EPICTETUS. Epicteti enchiridion ... Item Cebetis Thebani tabula ... *Greek & Latin.* Antuerpiæ, Ex Officina Christophori Plantini ... M. D. LXXVIII. 16°. A-E[8] F[4]. pp. 3-87. ¶*T.p. repaired.* [286

-- -- Thesaurus philosophiæ moralis, Quo continentur, Græcè & Latinè, Epicteti Enchiridion, Cebetis Thebani Tabula. Theophrasti Characteres. Pythagoreorum Fragmenta, Cantero, & Spondano interpres. CIↃ. IↃ. XXCIX. Apud Ioan. Tornaesium. ... Lugd. 16°. *[8] A-N[8]. pp. 1-208. [287

-- -- La morale filosofia Breuemente descritta per due filosofi; Epitteto Stoico, Aristotele Peripatetico ... Et il trattato di Plutarco dell'amor de'Genitori uerso i Figliuoli. ... di Greco ridotte in Volgare da M. Giulio Ballino. In Venetia, Per Gio. Andrea Valuassori. M D LXIIII. 8°. A-M[8] N[4] (-N4, *presumably blank*). pp. 3-167. [288

-- -- Arte di corregger la vita humana, scritta da Epitteto ..., Et commentata da Simplicio. Tradotta da M. Matteo Franceschi ... In Venetia, Appresso Francesco Ziletti. 1583. 8°. a[8] b[4] A-Bb[8] Cc[4]. ff. 1-202. [289

EPICURO, MARCO ANTONIO. Dialogo di tre ciechi di M. Epicuro Characciolo ... M. D. XXXI. (Stampato in Vinegia per Marchio Sessa ... Adi. V. Decembrio.) 8°. A-F[4] (-F4, *presumably blank*). [290

-- -- Cecaria. Tragicomedia del Epicuro Napolitano ... M D XXXV. (Stampata in Vinegia per Nicolo d'Aristotile detto Zoppino del mese di Genaro. ...) 8°. A-D[8]. [291

-- -- In Vinegia appreso Gabriel Giolito de Ferrari e fratelli. M D LIII. (*Colophon.*) 12°. A-B[12] C[6]. ff. 2-29. [292

EPIGRAMMATA. Epigrammata. Selectorum e Graecis scriptoribus Epigrammatum Centuriæ duæ. Tiguri apud Frosch. (... M. D. XLVIII.) 8°. a-f[8]. pp. 3-95. ¶*Editor: Rudolf Walther.* [293

EPIPHANIUS. D. Epiphanii ... contra octoaginta hæreses opus, Panarium, siue Arcula, aut

Capsula Medica appellatum ... Iano Cornario ... interprete. Vnà cum alijs eiusdem D. Epiphanij operibus ... Basileæ, ex officina Heruagiana, per Eusebium Episcopium, anno M. D. LXXVIII. fol. a-z^6 A-P^6. pp. 1-430. (Lea.) [294

-- Oratio ... de fide Catholica, & Apostolica Ecclesia, Per Vitum Amerpachium in Latinum conuersa, & quibusdam Annotationibus enarrata. Augustae Rheticæ Philippus Vlhardus excudebat. 8°. A-E^8. ¶*Preface dated* postrid. feriarum S. Trinitatis ... 1548. [295

EPISTOLAE. Clarorum virorum epistolae latinæ græcæ & hebraicæ uariis temporibus missæ ad Ioannem Reuchlin Phorcensem ... (Tubingæ per Thomam Anshelmum Bedensem, Mense Martio, Anno M.D.XIIII.) 4°. a^2 b-g$^{4\cdot 8}$ h-i^4 k^6. [296

-- Duo volumina epistolarum obscurorum virorum ... Francoforti ad Moenum. 1581. 8°. A-Aa^8 Bb^4. ¶*Additional t.p.* (Z4^r): Conciliabulum theologistarum aduersus Germaniæ, & bonarum literarum studiosos, Coloniæ celebratum, 16. Kalend. Maij, postquàm I. Hohenstratus deiectus est ab officio Prioratus, & ab officio inquisitoris. ... [297

-- Epistolae aliquot illustres ..., extra bibliorum canonem licet, ... ab ipso scilicet Christo, Paulo, Apostolorū discipulis, atq; aliquot alijs Apostolicis uiris ... M. D. XXIX. (Augustæ Vindelicorum per Alexandrum Weyssenhorn ... Mense Septmebri.) 8°. A-N^8 O^{10} (-O10, *presumably blank*). ff. 2-113. [298

-- Epistolae clarorum virorum selectae ... Coloniae Agrippinae, Apud Ioannem Gymnicum ... M. D. LXXXXVI. 8°. *^{4} A-T^8 V-X^4. pp. 1-320. [299

EQUICOLA, MARIO. Chronica di Mantua (M.D.XXI. .X. del mese di Iuglio.) 4°. A-Z^8 &^{8} ɔ^8 ℞^{8} ⁂^{4} Aa-Cc^8 Dd^4. [300

-- Institutioni ... al comporre in ogni sorte di Rima della lingua volgare, con vno ... Discorso della Pittura, & con molte segrete allegorie circa le Muse & la Poesia. In Milano l'Anno M. D. XLI. 4°. A-E^4 F^6. [301

-- Libro di natura d'amore ... MDXXVI. (Stampato in Vinegia per Gioanniantonio & Fratelli de Sabbio. ...) 8°. A-CC^8 DD^4. ff. 2-203. [302

-- -- M.D.XXXI. (Stampato nella ... Citta di Vinegia ... per Francesco di Alessandro Bindoni, & Mapheo Pasini cōpagni. ... 1531. del mese di Marzo.) 8°. A-EE^8 (-EE8, *presumably blank*). ff. 2-223. [303

ERASMUS, DESIDERIUS. ... Adagiorum chiliades Des. Erasmi Roterodami ... Basileae ex officina Frobeniana an. M. D. XXXIX. (... per Hieronymum Frobenium, & Nicolaum Episcopium, Mense Martio ...) fol. aa-ff^6 a-z^6 A-3T^6 3V^8. cols. 1-96, pp. 2-1071. [304

-- -- *Another copy*. (Lea.) [305

-- -- Adagiorum opus ... Lugduni apud Sebastianum Gryphium, M. D. L. (*Colophon.*) fol. aa-ee^8 a-z^8 A-O^8 P-Q^6 (-Q6, *presumably blank*). cols. 5-1226. [306

-- -- Adagiorum chiliades ... quatuor cum sesquicenturia ... Basileae M. D. LIX. (... in officina Frobeniana per Hieronymum Frobenium, & Nicolaum Episcopium, Mense Martio ...) fol. aa-hh^6 ii^4 a-z^6 A-3T^6 3V^8. pp. 1-1071. [307

-- -- Adagiorum ... Chiliades quatuor cum sesquicenturia ... secundum Concilij Tridentini decretum expurgatæ ... Quibus adiectae sunt Henrici Stephani Animaduersiones ... His ... accesserunt: ... Hadriani Iunij centuriæ octo cum dimidia. Ioan. Alexandri Brassicani prouerbiorum σύμμικτα, cum appendice Symbolorum Pythagoræ ex Iamblico. Io. Vlpij Adagiorum Epitome. Gilberti Cognati Adagiorum συλλογή. Specimen adagior. per Iunium, Cantherum, & Giselinum. Melchioris Neipij adagia. Item adagia quædam collecta ex Cælio Rhodigino. Polydoro Virgilio. Petro Godofredo. Carolo Bouillo. M. Anto. Mureto. Io. Hartungo. Adria. Turnebo. Gulielmo Gentio Nouiomago. Parisiis, Apud Michaelem Sonnium ... M.D.LXXII. ... (Cudebat ... Ioannes Charron ..., quinto Calendas Decembris, anno Domini Millesimo quingentesimo septuagesimo.) fol. ā^6 ē^6 ī^6 ō^6 ū^4 a-z^6 Aa-Zz^6 AA-KK^6. cols. 1-1359. [308

-- -- Des. Erasmi Roterodami adagiorum chiliades quatuor cum sesquicenturia ... Basileae, ex officina Episcopiana, per Eusebium Episcopium & Nicolai Fr. hæredes. M. D. LXXIIII. (... Mense Augusto.) fol. *^{6} β-θ^6 ι^{10} a-z^6 A-Zz^6 AA-ZZz^6 3A-3M^6 3N^8. pp. 1-852, cols. 1-96, pp. 97-647. ¶*1 *defective*. [309

-- *Annotationes in Novum Testamentum.* Herr Erasmus võ Roterdam verteutschte ausslegung vber sant Hieronymus Allegation/ was guts die Philosophi in der heyligen schrifft schaffen. Vnd vber diss wort Christi Matthei am .xvj. Capitel ... Auch vber disse wort Ioannis. Luce am dritten Capitel ... M. D. xxj. 4°. A^4. [310

-- Antibarbarorum D. Erasmi Roterodami, liber unus ... (Coloniae ... M. D. XX.) 8°. a-h^4 I^6 K-L^4 M^6 N^4 O^6. [311

-- Apophthegmatum ex optimis ... scriptoribus, per Des. Erasmum Roterodamum collectorum, libri octo. Basileae MDL (... per Hier. Frobenium et Nic. Episcopium. ... mense Augusto.) 8°. aa^8 a-z^8 A-Dd^8. pp. 1-750. [312

-- -- Les troys derniers liuures des apohthegmes [*sic*] ... recuillies par Erasme. Mises de nouueau en Françoys ... A Paris. Pour Iean Longis ... 1553. 8°. $\bar{a}^8$ A-AA^8 (-AA8, *presumably blank*). ff. 1-191. [313

-- Colloquia Erasmi. ... verdeütscht ... Durch Iustum Alberti ... M.D.XXXXV. (Gedruckt ... in ... Augspurg/ durch Haynrich Stayner/ am v. tag Decembris ...) fol. a^6 A-N^6 O^8. ff. I-LXXXVI. [314

-- D. Erasmi Roterodami opus de conscribendis epistolis ... Basileae per Nicolaum Brylingerum. Anno M. D. XXXXIII. 8°. a-z^8 A-B^8 (-A8, *blank*). pp. 1-326. [315

-- -- [1] D. Erasmi Roterodami opus de conscribendis epistolis ... Coloniae Excudebat Petrus Horst. Anno, 1557. 8°. Aa^8 Aa-Zz^8 Aa^8 BB-DD^8. pp. 1-429. [2] De conscribendis epistolis. Ioannis Ludouici Viuis Valentini Libellus uerè aureus. D. Erasmi Roterodami Compendium ... Conradi Celtis Methodus. Christophori Hegendorphini Methodus. ... *Same imprint.* A-K^8. ff. 2-75. [316

-- Des. Erasmi Roterodami de duplici copia verborum ac Rerum Commentarij duo ... Addita sunt ... commentaria M. Veltkirchij ... Coloniæ Martinus Gymnicus excudebat, Anno M.D.XLVIII. 8°. A-Ee^8. pp. 3-348. [317

-- D. Erasmi Roterodami de immensa Dei misericordia, concio. Virginis et martyris comparatio per eundem. Væneunt Antuerpiæ apud Ioannem Gymnicum, Anno. M. D. XL. 8°. A-H^8. [318

-- De interdicto esu carniũ, deq; similibus hominum cõstitutionibus ... epistola apologetica Eras. Rot. (Apud ... Coloniam Io. Soter excudebat anno MDXXII. mense Nouemb.) 8°. a-c^8 d^6. (Lea.) [319

-- De libero arbitrio διατριβή siue Collatio. Desiderij Erasmi Roterod. ... Basileæ apud Ioannem Frobenium, Anno M. D. XXIIII. Mense Septembri. (*Colophon.*) 8°. a-f^8. [320

-- De octo orationis partium constructione libellus ... Erasmi Roterodamo autore. An. M. D. XVII. (Basileæ, In officina Adæ Petri, Mense Augusto. ...) 4°. A^4 b-c^4. ¶*By William Lily, revised by Erasmus.* [321

-- Erasmi Roterodami De ratione studij ac legendi interpretandiqȝ autores libellus ... Officium discipulorũ ex Quintiliano. Qui primo legendi ex Eodem. Erasmi Concio de puero Iesu ... Eiusdem expostulatio Iesu ad mortales. Eiusdem carmina scholaria. ... (Argentorat. Ex ædibus Schũrerianis Mense Iulio. Anno M.D.XII.) 4°. A-D^4. [322

-- Des. Erasmi Rot. ecclesiastae siue de ratione concionandi libri quatuor ... Basileae in officina Frobeniana anno MDXXXV ... a^4 b-i^6 k^4 l-z^6 A-L^6 M^4 N-P^6 Q^8 (-Q8, *presumably blank*). pp. 1-444. [323

-- Enarratio in Psalmum I. Ein fast nutzlich Ausslegũg des ersten Psalmẽ ... Durch D. Erasmum von Roterdam beschriben. (Getruckt zů Strassburg durch den Erasmẽ Ioannẽ Knoblouch ... M. CCCCC. Vnd XX.) 4°. A-I^4. ff. iij-xxxvj. ¶*Translator: Leo Juda.* [324

-- *Epistolae.* Opus epistolarum ... Basileae ex officina Frobeniana anno M. D. XXIX. (... apud Hieronymum Forbenium et Ioannem Heruagium et Nicolaum Episcopium) fol. π^4 a-z^6 A-$3O^6$ $3P^8$. pp. 1-1010. [325

-- -- D. Erasmi Rot. epistolae breuiores aliquot, ... selectæ, per Ioan. Pedium Tethingerum ... Friburgi Brisgoiae, Stephanus Melechus Grauius excudebat, Anno M. D. XLIII. 8°. a-y^8. ff. 2-167. [326

-- Hyperaspistes diatribae aduersus Seruum Arbitriũ Martini Lutheri, per D. Erasmum Roterodamum. (Anno M. D. XXVI.) 8°. A-O^8 P^6. [327

-- Institutio Principis Christiani ... per Erasmum Roterodamum, cum alijs nonnullis ... Apud ... Basileam. ([O4^v] ... apud Ioannem Frobenium Mense Aprili. M. D. XVI. [BB4^v] ... Mense Maio. ...) 4°. a-p^4 q^6 A-BB^4. ¶*Includes:* Erasmi Roterodami ad Philippum panegyricus; Erasmi Roterodami ad Paludanum epistola; Libellus Plutarchi ... docens quo pacto dignosci possit adulator ab amico ... Erasmo interprete; Quo pacto quis efficiat vt ex inimicis capiat vtilitatem Plutarchi Chaeronensis Erasmo Roterodamo interprete; In principe requiri doctrinam, Plutarchi commentarium, Erasmo Roterodamo interprete; Cum principibus maxime philosophum debere disputari, Plutarchi, Erasmo Roterodamo interprete. (Lea.) [328

-- D. Erasmi Roterodami liber de sarcienda ecclesiæ concordia ... Parisiis, Venit apud Ioannem Roigny ... 8°. A-G^8. pp. 3-110. [329

-- Lingua ... Cui accessit Plutarchi Chaeronei De immodica uerecundia libellus. Lugduni apud Seb. Gryphium, 1538. 8°. a-p^8. pp. 2-234. [330

-- D. Erasmi Roterodami ... Lucubrationes ... In libera Argentina [per Matthiam Schürer, 1515]. 4°. π^4 A-O$^{8.4}$ P^8 Q-R^4 S-V^8 X-Y^4 Z^8 Aa^4 Bb^8 (-Bb2-8). pp. 1-285. (Lea.) [331

-- Modus orandi Deum ... (Norembergae apud Ioannem Petreium excudebatur, Anno M. D. XXV. Mense Februario.) 8°. a-e^8 f^4 (-f4, *presumably blank*). (Lea.) [332

-- -- Antuerpiae Apud Michaelem Hillenium in Rapo. An. M.D.XXV. 8°. a-e^8. [333

-- Ioan. Frobenius lectori S.D. Habes iterum Moriæ encomium ..., unà cum Listerij commentarijs, & alijs complusculis libellis ... Apud ... Basileam M. D. XXI. (... mense Octobri ...) 8°. a-z^8 A-B^8 C^4 D^8. pp. 4-419. ¶*Includes also:* Ludus L. Annei Senecæ, De morte Claudij Cæsaris, ... cũ Scholijs Beati Rhenani; Synesius Cyrenensis de laudibus caluitij, Ioãne Phrea Britanno interprete, cum scholijs Beati Rhenani; Epistola apologetica Erasmi Roterodami, ad Martinũ Dorpium ... [334

-- -- Moriae encomium ... Gerardi Listrij Commentarijs illustratum. Coloniae apud Iohan. Soterẽ. Anno M. D. XXXIIII. 8°. A-O^8 (-O8, *presumably blank*). pp. 4-214. [335

-- -- The praise of Folie. Moriæ encomium a booke made in latyne by that great clerke Erasmus Roterodame. Englished by sir Thomas Chaloner knight. Anno M. D. XLIX. 4°. A^4 A-T^4 (-T4 *colophon:* Imprinted at London ... in the house of Thomas Berthelet. ... M. D. LXIX [*sic*].). *S.T.C.* 10501. (Furness.) [336

-- -- La moria d'Erasmo nouamente in volgare tradotta. In Venetia. L'anno M. D. XXXIX. (Stampata ... per Giouanni dalla Chiesa Pauese ... Il mese di Febraio.) 8°. A-X^4. ff. 2-82. [337

-- -- Das Theũr vnd Künstlich Bůchlin Morie Encomion ... von Erasmo Roterodamo ... Alles zum tail verteũscht/ zum tail beschrieben/ durch Sebastianum Francken von Wörd. ... [*Device of Hans Varnier of Ulm.*] 4°. A-Z^4 a-y^4. ff. 2-170. [338

-- Paraclesis, id est, adhortatio ad ... Christianæ philosophiæ studium ... Parisiis. Ex officina Roberti Stephani M. D. XXIX. 8°. a^8. ff. 2-8. [339

-- *Paraphrases.* Tomus secundus continens paraphrasim ... In omneis epistolas apostolicas ... [*Device of Johann Froben.*] (Apud ... Basileam an. M. D. XXIII.) fol. a-z^6 A-P^6. pp. 2-454. [340

-- -- [1] Tomus primus paraphraseon ... in Nouum Testamentum, videlicet in quatuor Euangelia, & Acta apostolorum ...Basileae in officina Frob. M. D. XXXV fol. α^8 a-p^6. pp. 1-177. [2] In euangelium Marci paraphrasis ... *Same imprint.* A^6 a-l^6 m^4. pp. 1-139. [3] In euangelium Lucae paraphrasis ... *Same imprint.* Aa-Yy^6. pp. 3-264. [4] ... paraphrasis in euangelium secundum Ioannem ... Basileae, anno MDXXXV. aa-pp^6 qq^8. pp. 4-194. [5] In acta apostolorum paraphrasis ... *Same imprint as* [1]. (*Colophon.*) A-K^6 L^4. pp. 4-126. [6] Tomus secundus continens paraphrasim ... In omneis epistolas apostolicas ... (Basileæ in officina Frobeniana, per Hieronymum Frobenium & Nicolaum Episcopium M. D. XXXII) a-z^6 A-O^6. pp. 3-442. [341

-- -- Tomus secundus continens paraphrasim ... In omneis epistolas apostolicas ... Basileae in officina Frobeniana an. M. D. XXXIX. (... per Hieronymum Frobenium & Nicolaum Episcopium Anno M. D. XL.) 8°. a-z^8 A-Mm^8. pp. 3-926. [342

-- -- [1] The first tome or volume of the Paraphrase of Erasmus vpon the newe testamente. Enpriented at London ... by Edwarde Whitchurche the last daie of Ianuarie. ... 1548. fol. B.L. a^8 B^8 ₵^{4} A-R^6 S^8 ₵^{2} ₵^{6} Aa-Pp^6 Qq^4 ₵^{6} (.˙.)^8 a^6 B-D^6 e-ff^6 Gg-Hh^6 ii^8 ₵^{2} ()^6 A-S^6 T^{10}

$\complement^{2}$ A-O^{6} P^{4} (-P4, *presumably blank*). ff. ii-cxxi, i-xciii, ii-cxciiii, ii-cxiiii, ii-lxxxvii. [2] The seconde tome ... Imprinted at London ... by Edwarde Whitchurche, the xvi. daye of August ... 1549. ✠-✠✠^{6} $\complement^{4}$ A-G^{6} H^{2} Aa-Kk^{6} Ll^{4} aa-cc^{6} dd^{4} $\complement^{6}$ (-$\complement$6, *presumably blank*) AA-BB^{6} CC^{4} (-CC4, *presumably blank*) 3A^{6} 3B^{4} 4a^{6} 4b^{4} AAAa-BBBb^{6} (-BBBb6, *presumably blank*) 4A-4E^{6} 4F^{4} 5A-5D^{6} 5E^{4} (-5E4, *presumably blank*) *^{2} $\complement^{6}$ $\complement$B-$\complement$H^{6} $\complement$I^{8} $\complement\complement$A-$\complement\complement$F^{6} $\complement\complement$G^{4}. ff. j-xliiij, i-lxiiii, ij-xxi, ii-xv, iii-x, ii-x, j-xi, i-xxxiii, ii-xxvii, ii-liiii, i-xl. *S.T.C.* 2854. (Yarnall.) [342a

-- -- [The first tome or volume of the Paraphrases of Erasmus vpon the newe Testament. London, Edward Whitchurch, 1551-1552.] fol. B.L. $\complement\complement^{8}$ (-$\complement\complement$1^{r}, *the verso pasted down*) A-4G^{8}. ff. i-cccccccviii. *S.T.C.* 2866. ¶*Lacks the t.p. and presumably the dedication to Edward VI.* [343

-- Epistola nuncupatoria ad Carolum Cæsarem. Exhortatio ad studium Euangelicæ lectionis. Paraphrasis in Euangeliũ Matthæi, per D. Erasmum Rot. nunc denuo recognita. Epistola ad R.D. Matthæum Card. Sedun. [Basileae, Joannes Froben, 1522.] 8°. a-z^{8} &^{8} A^{8}. ¶n8 *defective.* [344

-- -- Paraphrasis in euangelium Matthaei, ... Epistola nuncupatoria ad Carolum Cæsarem. Exhortatio ad studiũ Euãgelicæ lectionis. Epistola ad R.D. Matthæum Card. Sedun. Moguntiae an. M. D. XXII. 8°. A-B^{8} a-z^{8}. pp. 1-367. (Yarnall.) [344a

-- D. Erasmi Roterodami Paraphrasis in Euangelium secundum Ioannem ..., nunc primum excusa. Basileae in officina Frobeniana. Ann. M. D. XXIII. ... (*Colophon.*) 8°. a-z^{8} A-D^{8}. ff. 2-202. (Yarnall.) [344b

-- Paraphrasis ... in omnes epistolas apostolicas ... Antuerpiae. Apud Ioannem Steelsium ... M.D.XL. 8°. A-QQ^{8} RR^{4}. ff. 2-312. (Yarnall.) [344c

-- Parabolae siue similia ... Accesserunt annotationes ..., authore D. Ioanne Artopæo Spirense. Friburgi Brisgoiæ, Stephanus Grauius excudebat. Anno M. D. LI. (*Colophon.*) 8°. A-O^{8}. pp. 3-198. [345

-- Querela pacis vndique gentium eiectæ profligatæ que. ... [c. 1530.] 8°. A-B^{8} C^{10} (-C10, *possibly blank*). ff. 2-23. [346

-- -- Das Kristlich büchlein hern Erasmus Roterdamus genañt/ die Klage des Frids ... Durch Georgium Spalatinum verteütscht. (Gedruckt in ... Augspurg/ Durch Sigismunden Grym̄ Doctor/ vnd Marxen Wirsung. ... M.D.XXj.) 4°. A-I^{4} (-I4, *presumably blank*). [347

-- Spongia Erasmi aduersus aspergines Hutteni. (Basileae per Io. Frobenium, An. M. D. XXIII.) 8°. a-g^{8} h^{4}. ¶*Adams E837.* [348

ERASTUS, THOMAS. De astrologia diuinatrice epistolae ... in lucem æditæ, opera & studio Ioannis Iacobi Grynaei. ... Basileæ, per Petrum Pernam. M.D.LXXX. 4°. α^{4} A-Hh^{4}. pp. 2-236. [349

-- De cometis dissertationes nouae ... Thom. Erasti, Andr. Dudithij, Marc. Squarcialupi, Simon. Grynaei. [Basileae,] Ex officina Leonardi Ostenij, sumptibus Petri Pernæ. M. D. LXXX. 4°. *^{4} α-γ^{4} A-Y^{4} a-l^{4}. pp. 1-196, 3-88. [350

ERCILLA, ALONSO DE. Primera, [se]gunda, y tercera Partes de la Araucana ... En Madrid, En casa del Licēciado Castro Año de 1597. A costa de Iuan de Montoya. 8°. §-4§^{8} A-3M^{8} 3N^{4} (-3N4, *presumably blank*). ff. 1-445. ¶*T.p. defective. Additional t.pp.:* (Bb5^{r}) Segunda parte de la Araucana ... *Same imprint.* (Zz6^{r}) Tercera parte ... *Same imprint.* [351

ERCKER, LAZARUS. Beschreibung/ Allerfurnemisten Mineralischen Ertzt vnnd Bergkwercks arten ... Gedruckt zu Franckfurt am Mayn/ durch Iohan Feyerabendt. 1598. (*Colophon.*) fol.)(^{4} A-Z^{4} a-k^{4} l^{6} (-l6, *blank*). ff. 1-134. (Smith.) [352

ERCOLANI, FRANCESCO. Quis teneatur probare negatiuam, et quibus modis negatiua probetur tractatus Francisci Herculani Perusini ... Florentiae Apud filios Laurentii Torrentini ... MDLXIIII. 8°. ❧^{8} A-Q^{8} pp. 1-255. [353

-- Tractatus Francisci Herculani Perusini ... De cautione de non offendendo. ... Venetiis, Apud Hæredes Aloysij Valuassoris, & Io. Dominicum Michaelem. M. D. LXXX. (*Colophon.*) 8°. a-d^{8} A-V^{8}. ff. 1-159. [354

ERFURT. Der Stadt Erffurdt ernewerte Policey vnd andere Ordnung ... M. D. LXXXIII. (Gedruckt zu Erffurdt/ durch Melchior Sachssen.) 4°. A-R⁴. ¶*Index begins on* R2ᵛ. [355

-- -- *Same date, colophon, and collation.* A4 *blank; index begins on* R3ᵛ. [356

-- Wiewol alle Vnordnung vnd vnnötige Verschwendung der Gaben Gottes an im selbst sündlich ... Publicatum den 13. Aprilis Anno 1598. s.sh. 20.5 × 29 cm. [357

ERHARD, CHRISTOPH. Catholisches Sendtschreiben ... Oder Zehen ... Vrsachen ... Warumben sich ein rechter Christ durchauss dess Wörtleins Römisch nit schämen ... Getruckt zu Ingolstat/ durch Wolffgang Eder. Anno M.D.LXXXVIII. 4°. A-D⁴ E². pp. 2-13. [358

-- Der Lutheraner Zweyffelsknopff: Mit ... Erweyssung/ dass Luther vnd sein Anhang/ vnserm Herren Iesu Christo vnd den lieben Aposteln/ ... zuwider lehren ... Getruckt zu Ingolstatt/ durch Wolffgang Eder. Anno M. D. LXXXVI. 4°. A-I⁴. pp. 1-69. [359

ERIZZO, SEBASTIANO. Espositione ... Nelle tre canzoni di M. Francesco Petrarca, Chiamate le tre sorelle. Nuouamente mandata in luce da M. Lodouico Dolce. In Venetia Appresso Andrea Arriuabene. MDLXII. (... per Bernardino Fasani. M D LXI.) 4°. *⁴ (-*2-3) A-N⁴. ff. 1-51. [360

-- Le sei giornate ... mandate in luce da M. Lodouico Dolce ... In Venetia appresso Giouan Varisco, e compagni. M D LXVII. (*Colophon.*) 4°. *⁴ *⁴ A-Y⁴ Z⁶. ff. 2-93. [361

ERNHOFFER, SIGMUND. Der Euangelische WetterHan: Das ist: Vergleiche Reden/ Martini Lutheri/ Von den fürnembsten Artickeln Christlicher Religion. ... M.D.LXXXVII. (Getruckt zu Ingolstat/ bey Wolffgang Eder.) 8°. A-Y⁸ (-Y8, *presumably blank*). pp. 1-321. [362

-- Warhaffte Augenscheinliche vñ wolgegründte Schutzschrifft dess gemehrten vnd verbesserten kleinen Catechismi D. Martini Lutheri ... Wider Wilhelm Zimmermann ... vnd Iacob Heerbrandt ... Getruckt zu Ingolstat/ durch Wolfgang Eder/ Anno M.D.LXXXIIX. (*Colophon.*) 8°. A-L⁸ M⁴. pp. 1-173. [363

ERTLIN, JOHANN. Ein Catholische Leichpredig/ Bey der ... Begräbnus ... Herrn Iacob Feuchten Episcopi Naturensis ... Ingolstatt In der Weyssenhornischen Truckerey durch Wolffgang Eder. Anno cIↄ. cI. xxc. 4°. A-K⁴. pp. 1-70. [364

ERYTHROPEL, RUPERT. Weckglock/ darinnen die schlaffende Teutschen wider die wachende Türcken auffgewecket worden. ... Gedruckt zu Franckfurt am Mayn/ durch Iohann Spies ... M.D.XCV. (*Colophon.*) 4°. a-c⁴ A-3I⁴ 3K². pp. 1-444. [365

-- -- *Another copy.* [366

ESANATOGLIA. Statuta decreta, et reformationes: Coeteráq; iura municipalia Terræ Sanctæ Anatholiae ... Antonius Gioiosus ... Camerini Imprimebat ... M. D. LII. (*Colophon.*) fol. ✠⁶ A-H⁶ I⁴. pp. 1-103. (Lea.) [367

ESPINOSA DE LOS MONTEROS, TOMÁS DE. Heroicos hechos, y vidas de varones yllustres ... Refumidas en breue Cōpendio por ... Fray Thomas de Spinosa ... En Paris, Por Françisco de Prado ... 1576. 4°. A-O⁴. ff. 1-52. [368

ESTIENNE, CHARLES. De dissectione partium corporis humani libri tres ... Vnà cum figuris, & incisionum declarationibus, à Stephano Riuerio Chirurgo cōpositis. ... Parisiis. Apud Simonem Colinæum. 1545. fol. *-**⁶ A-Z⁸ AA⁶. pp. 1-375. [369

-- De re hortēsi libellus ... Parisiis. Ex officina Roberti Stephani. M.D.XXXVI. (... VI. Cal. April.) 8°. a-g⁸. pp. 6-96. [370

-- -- Lugduni apud hæredes Simonis Vincentii M. D. XXXVI. (Excudebant ... Melchior et Gaspar Trechsel fratres. ...) 8°. a-f⁸ g⁴. pp. 5-88. [371

-- Dictionarium historicum ac poeticum ... Lutetiae. Apud Ioannem Macæum ... 1561. ... 4°. ❧² a-z⁴ A-Zz⁴ AA-LL⁴ MM². ff. 1-326. [372

-- Paradoxes, ce sont propos contre la commune opinion: debatuz, en forme de Declamations forēses ... A Paris, Par Charles Estienne ... M. D. LIII. ... 16°. A-K⁸. pp. 3-158. [373

-- Seminariū siue plantarium earum arborum, quæ post hortos conferi solent ... (Excudebat Rob. Stephanus Parisiis, ann. M.D.XXXVI. XII. Cal. Iulii.) 8°. A-H^8. pp. 3-107. [374

-- Thesaurus M. Tullii Ciceronis. Parisiis. Apud Carolum Stephanum ... M. D. LVI. ... (... IIII. Cal. Nouemb.) fol. $ā^4$ (-ā4, *blank*) a-$3z^6$ A-$3R^6$ $3S^4$. pp. 2-1591. [375

ESTIENNE, HENRI. Ad M. Ter. Varronis assertiones analogiæ sermonis Latini, appendix Henrici Stephani. Item, Iulii Caes. Scaligeri de eadem Disputatio doctissima. Loci Varronis quamplurimi emendati. Excudebat Henricus Stephanus anno M.D.XCI. 8°. $¶^2$ A-L^8 M-N^4 O^2. pp. 2-196. [376

-- Henrici Stephani annotationes in Sophoclem & Euripidem ... Eiusdem Tractatus de orthographia quorundam vocabulorum Sophocli cum cæteris tragicis communium. Eiusdem Dissertatio de Sophoclea imitatione Homeri. [Genevae, Henricus Stephanus,] Anno M. D. LXVIII. 8°. $*^8$ a-n^8. pp. 1-207. [377

-- Catharinæ Mediceæ reginae matris, vitæ, actorum, & consiliorum, quibus vniuersum regni Gallici statum turbare conata est, stupenda eâque vera enarratio. M. D. LXXV. 8°. A-G^8 H^4. pp. 3-116. [378

-- Comicorum Graecorum sententiae, id est γνωμαι, Latinis versibus ab Henrico Stephano redditæ ... Anno M. D. LXIX Excudebat Henr. Steph. 32°. ¶-$¶¶^8$ a-r^8 s^4 t^8 v^4 x-rr^8. pp. 3-633. (Lea.) [379

-- -- *Another copy.* [380

-- De abusu linguae Græcæ, in quibusdam vocibus quas Latina vsurpat, admonitio ... [Genevae,] Anno M. D. LXIII, Excudebat Henricus Stephanus. 8°. π^2 a-f^8 g^6. pp. 1-107. [381

-- De Latinitate falso suspecta, Expostulatio ... Eiusdem de Plauti Latinitate Dissertatio ... [Genevae,] Anno M. D. LXXVI. Excudebat Henricus Stephanus. 8°. $*^8$ A-Bb^8. pp. 2-400. [382

-- De Lipsii latinitate (vt ipsimet antiquarii antiquarium Lipsii stylum indigitant) palæstra I, Henr. Stephani, Parisiensis: nec Lipsiomimi, nec Lipsiomomi, nec Lipsiocolacis: multóque minus Lipsiomastigis. ... Francfordii, Anno M.C.XCV. ... 8°. *-$**^8$ A-Mm^8. pp. 3-29, 1-560. [383

-- Henrici Stephani epistola ad Iacobum Dalechampium. Cui subiuncta sunt carmina super obitu Petri Victorii. 4°. A-B^4. [384

-- Epistolia, dialogi breues, oratiunculæ, poematia, Ex variis vtriusque linguæ scriptoribus. ... [Genevae,] Anno M. D. LXXVII. Excudebat Henr. Stephanus. 8°. a^2 b-s^8 t^2 aa-gg^8 hh^4. pp. 2-276, 1-120. [385

-- L'introduction au traitté de la conformité des merueilles anciennes auec les modernes. Ou, traitté preparatif à l'Apologie pour Herodote. ... A Strasbourg, Par Pierre Estiart. M.D.LXVII. 16°. *-$**^8$ a-z^8 A-V^8 X^4. pp. 1-654. [386

-- -- [A Lyon, Par Benoist Rigaud. CIↃ. IↃ. XCII.] 8°. $*^8$ (-*1) $**^8$ a-z^8 A-Q^8. pp. 1-593. ¶*Possibly a copy of the 1591 ed. with identical collation.* (Lea.) [387

-- Nizoliodidascalus, Siue, Monitor Ciceronianorum Nizolianorum, Dialogus ... [Genevae,] Excudebat Henricus Stephanus, Anno M. D. LXXVIII. 8°. A^4 B-N^8 O^4. pp. 2-200. [388

-- Οι της ηρωικης ποιήσεως ... ποιηταί ... Poetae Graeci principes heroici carminis, & alii nonnulli. Homerus, Hesiodus, Orpheus, Callim, Aratus, Nicand, Theocrit. Moschus, Bion, Dionysius Coluthus, Tryphiodorus, Musæus Theognis, Phocylides, Pythagoræ aurea carmina. Fragmanta aliorum. ... Anno M. D. LXVI. Excudebat Henricus Stephanus ... fol. $*^6$ $**^4$ A-D^8 E^4 a-bb^8 cc^6 Aa^{10} Bb-Yy^8 Zz^6 Zzz^4 (-Zzz4, *blank*) a-g^4 AA-$3R^6$ 3S-$3T^4$ (-3T4, *blank*). pp. 3-20, III-LXXII, 1-781, I-LVII, 1-489. [389

-- Parodiæ morales H. Stephani, In poetarum vet. sententias celebriores, totidē versibus Gr. ab eo redditas. ... [Genevae,] Anno M. D. LXXV, Excudebat Henricus Stephanus. 8°. $*^8$ a-i^8 k^4 A-M^8. pp. 2-150, 1-187. [390

-- Principum monitrix musa. siue, De Principatu bene instituendo & administrando Poema. ... Eiusdem poematium, ... cauete vobis principes. Eiusdem libellus ... de Aristotelicae Ethices differentia ab historica & poetica. ... Basileae, Anno M.D.LXXXX. 8°.)(^{8} a-z^8 A-F^8. pp. 1-464. [391

-- Pseudocicero, dialogus ... [Genevae,] Anno M. D. LXXVII. Excudebat Henr. Stephanus. 8°. *^{2} a-n^{8} o-p^{4} q^{2}. pp. 1-228. [392

-- -- *Another copy.* [393

-- [1] Θησαυρος της Ελληνικης γλωσσης, thesaurus Graecae linguae ... [Genevae,] Anno M. D. LXXII, excudebat Henr. Stephanus. fol. a^{4} b^{6} A^{6} B^{4} *^{6} a^{4} b-4f^{6} 4g-4h^{4} 4i-4m^{6} 4n-4o^{4} (-4o4, *presumably blank*). pp. 2-20, II-XX, cols. V-XXIIII, 1-1946. [2] Thesauri linguæ Græcæ ... tomus II. *^{4} A^{4} B-G^{6} H-K^{4} L-R^{6} S-T^{4} V-3Y^{6} 3Z-4G^{4} (-4G4, *blank*). cols. V-XII, 1-1700. [3] ... Tomus III. Aa-Gg^{4} Hh^{6} Ii^{4} Kk-3C^{6} 3D^{4} 3E-3G^{6} 3H^{4} 3I^{6} 3K-3M^{4} 3N-5I^{6} 5K^{8}. cols. 5-1793. [4] ... Tomus IIII. 4A-4C^{4} 4D-5F^{6} 5G^{4} 5H-5M^{6} 5N-5O^{4}. cols. 1-834. [5] Glossaria duo, à situ vetustatis eruta: ad vtriusque linguae cognitionem & locupletationem perutilia. Item, de Atticae linguæ seu dialecti idiomatis, comment. ... Anno M. D. LXXIII, excudebat Henr. Stephanus. ... *^{4} a-i^{6} k^{4} l-n^{6} o^{4} p-z^{6} A-C^{6} D^{4} ¶^{4} A-T^{6} V^{4} α^{4} *α^{4} β^{4} γ-ι^{6} κ^{8} λ-4α^{6} 3β^{6} 4γ^{6} Ααα-Ιιι^{6} (-Ιιι6, *blank*). cols. 2-666, pp. 13-247, cols. 5-1746, 1-212. [394

-- Traicté de la conformité du langage François auec le Grec ... Auec vne preface remonstrant quelque partie du desordre & abus qui se commet auiourdhuy en l'vsage de la langue Françoise. ... A Paris. Par Robert Estienne ... M. D. LXIX. 8°. *^{8} **^{10} a-k^{8} l^{6}. pp. 2-171. [395

ESTIENNE, ROBERT. Dictionaire Francoislatin, contenant les motz & manieres de parler Francois, tournez en Latin. A Paris. De l'imprimerie de Robert Estienne. M.D.XXXIX. ... (... M. D. XL. XII. Cal. Mart.) fol. a-z^{8} A-K^{8}. pp. 3-523 [=527]. (Lea.) [396

-- Dictionarium Latinogallicum ... Lutetiae, Ex officina Rob. Stephani ... M. D. XLIIII. (... M. D. XLV. VIII. Id. Febr.) fol. A-YY^{8} ZZ^{6}. pp. 3-731. (Lea.) [397

-- -- Lutetiae, Apud Carolum Stephanum ... M. D. LII. ... (... Idib. Iul.) fol. a-zz^{8} A-TT^{8} VV-XX^{6} (-XX6, *blank*). pp. 5-1430. [398

-- -- Lutetiae, Apud Iacobum du Puys ... M. D. LXI. ... (Excudebatur ... apud Carolum Stephanum ... Non. Febr.) fol. a-zz^{8} A-TT^{8} VV-XX^{6} (-XX6, *blank*). pp. 5-1430. [399

-- [Dictionarium, seu thesaurus Latinae linguae ... expurgatus ... per Marium Nizolium Brixellensem ... Venetiis ex Sirenis officina MDLI.] (... apud hæredes Petri Rauani et socios Mense Octobri. M D L.) fol. A-Vu^{8}. ¶*Vol. 3 only.* [400

-- Hebræa, Chaldæa, Graeca et Latina nomina ... quæ in Bibliis leguntur, restituta, cum Latina interpretatione. ... Parisiis Ex officina Roberti Stephani. M. D. XXXVII. (... IIII. Cal. Octob.) 8°. a-z^{8} A-L^{8}. pp. 5-542. ¶*Adams S1824.* [401

ESZTERGOM. Grüdliche vnd warhafftige Anzeygung/ wie das Kőniglich Schloss Gran/ in Hungern/ von den Türcken belegert/ beschossen/ vnd eingenomen ist. 1543. 4°. [A]^{4}. [402

EUCLID. Euclidis Megarensis ... Elementorum geometricorum libri XV. Cum expositione Theonis in priores XIII à Bartholomæo Zamberto Veneto latinitate donata, Campani in omnes, & Hypsiclis Alexandrini in duos postremos. ... Basileae, per Ioannem Heruagium, & Bernhardum Brand, Anno M.D.LVIII. (... mense Martio.) fol. †^{4} (-†2-4) a-z^{6} Aa-Zz^{6} AA-CC^{6}. pp. 2-587. [403

-- -- Les six premiers liures des elemens d'Euclide: Traduicts & commentez par I. Errard de Bar-le-duc ... A Paris, Chez Guillaume Auuray ... M.D.XCVIII. ... 8°. ā^{4} A-E^{8} F-G^{4}. ff. 1-48. [404

-- -- De gli elementi d'Euclide libri quindici. Con gli scholii antichi. Tradotti ... da M. Federico Commandino ... In Vrbino, appresso Domenico Frisolino. M. D. LXXV. ... (... in casa di Federico Commandino ...) fol. [*]^{2} **^{4} 3*^{2} A-3Z^{4} 4A^{2}. ff. 1-278. [405

-- Euclide Megarense ... solo introduttore delle scientie mathematice. ... rassettato ... per ... Nicolò Tartalea Brisciano. ... Secondo le due tradottioni. ... In Venetia, Appresso gli Heredi di Troian Nauo ... M D LXXXVI. 4°. A-Qq^{8}. ff. 3-315. [406

-- La perspectiua, y especularia de Euclides. Traduzidas en vulgar Castellano ... Por Pedro Ambrosio Onderiz ... En Madrid. En casa de la viuda de Alonso Gomez. Año. M.D.LXXXV. (... M.D.LXXXIIII.) 4°. †^{6} A-P^{4}. ff. 1-60. ¶*Additional t.p.* (L1^{r}): La especularia ... En Madrid. En casa de la viuda de Alonso Gomez Año. M.D.LXXXIIII. [407

EUGENIUS PISAURENSIS. Oratio ... ad ... Synodum Tridentinam habita. In Dominica tertia Aduentus Domini. M. D. LXI. Brixiæ, Apud Damianum Turlinum ... imprimebatur. Ad instantiam Io. Babtistæ Bozolæ. Anno M. D. LXIII. (*Colophon.*) 4°. A^{4}. (Lea.) [408

EUGIPPIUS. [1] D. Eugyppii abbatis Aphricani thesaurorum ex D. Augustini operibus ... selectorum, tomus primus, ... cura Ioannis Herold Acropolitæ ... æditus. *Greek*. Basileae. (... per Robertum VVinter ... M. D. XLII. Mense Augusto.) fol. Aα^{6} (-Aα2-4) ¶^{6} §^{6} *^{8} a-t^{6} u^{4}. ff. 1-116. [2] ... tomus secundus ... (... Mense Septembri.) Aa^{6} (-Aa2-4) ξ^{6} <^{8} α^{8} A-R^{6} S^{4} T^{6}. ff. 1-115. ¶*T.pp. defaced.* [409

EULENSPIEGEL, TYL. Noctuae speculum. Omnes res memorabiles, variasque et admirables, Tyli Saxonici machinationes complectens, ... ex idiomate Germanico latinitate donatum ... Authore Aegidio Periandro, Bruxellensi, Brabantino. ... Francofurti ad Moenum. M. D. LXVII. [(Apud Goergium Coruinum sumptibus Sigismundi Feyrabent & Simonis Huteri.)] 8°. A-Z^{8} a-d^{8} (-d8). ff. 2-210. [410

EURIPIDES. Ευριπιδου τραγῳδίαι ἑπτακαίδεκα ... Euripidis tragoedia septendecim ... (Venetiis apud Aldum mense Februario .M.D.III.) 8°. A-Γ^{8} Δ^{4} E-H^{8} Θ^{6} I-Λ^{8} M^{6} N-Ξ^{8} O^{10} Π-P^{8} Σ^{10} T-Y^{8} Φ^{6} X-Ω^{8} AA-BB^{8} ΓΓ^{6} ΔΔ-ZZ^{8} HH^{6} ΘΘ-II^{8} KK^{10} χ^{4} ΛΛ^{8} MM^{10} NN-PP^{8} ΣΣ^{10} TT^{8} YY^{6} ΦΦ-XX^{8} ΨΨ^{4} ΩΩ^{8} 3A-3B^{8} 3Γ^{6} 3Δ-3Z^{8} 3H^{6} 3Θ-3K^{8} 3Λ^{4}. [411

-- -- Ευριπιδου τραγωδιαι οκτωκαίδεκα ... Euripidis tragoediae octodecim ... Basileæ apud Ioan. Heruagium anno, M.D.XXXVII, mense Martio. (*Greek colophon.*) 8°. α^{6} a-ii^{8} (-ii7, *blank*) Aa-Zz^{8}. [412

-- -- Basileæ per Ioannem Heruagium. Anno M.D.LI. Mense Septembri. 8°. *^{8} a-zz^{8} Aa-Ll^{8}. [413

-- -- Ευριπιδου τραγωδιαι ιθ. Euripidis tragoediæ XIX. ... opera Gulielmi Canteri Vltraiectini. Antvverpiae, Ex officina Christophori Plantini ... M.D.LXXI. 16°. *-**^{8} A-Z^{8} a-z^{8} Aa-Gg^{8}. pp. 1-809. [414

-- -- Euripides ... in Latinum sermonem conuersus, adiecto e regionè textu Græco: cum annotationibus ...: autore Gasparo Stiblino. Accesserunt, Iacobi Micylli, De Euripidis uita ...: item, De Tragoedia & eius partibus προλεγόμηνα quædam. Item, Ioannis Brodaei Turonensis Annotationes ... Basileae, per Ioannem Oporinum. (... M.D.LXII. Mense Martio.) fol. a-z^{6} A-Ss^{6} Tt^{8} (-Tt8, *blank*). pp. 4-667, coll. 668-845. [415

-- -- [1] Ευριπιδης. Euripidis tragoediæ XIX. Accedit nunc recens vigesimæ, cui Danae nomen, initium ... Graece iunctim & Latine. Latinam interpretationem M. Æmilius Portus ... correxit & expoliuit ... Carminum ratio ex Gul. Cantero ... obseruata, additis eiusdem ... Notis. Heidelbergæ, typis Hieronymi Commelini, Anno cIↄ Iↄ XCVII. 8°. (:)^{4} A-3D^{8}. pp. 2-800. [2] Ευριπιδου τραγωδιων τμῆμα δευτερον. Euripidis tragoediarum Pars altera. a-z^{8} aa-ss^{8} tt^{2} A-G^{8} H^{4}. pp. 2-659, 1-119. [416

-- Εὐριπίδου τραγῳδίαι δύο ... Euripidis tragoediae duae, Hecuba & Iphigenia in Aulide, Latinæ factæ, Des. Erasmo Roterodamo interprete. Apud ... Basileam. An. M. D. XXIIII. ... (... apud Ioannem Frobenium. Mense Februario. ...) 4°. a-r^{8} s^{6}. [417

-- -- Hecuba, & Iphigenia in Aulide Euripidis tragoediæ in latinum tralatæ Erasmo Roterodamo interprete. Eiusdem Ode de laudibus Britanniæ ... Eiusdem Ode de senectutis incommodis. (Venetiis in aedibus Aldi mense Decembri M. D. VII.) 8°. π^{8} a-i^{8}. [418

-- Ευριπιδου Ηλεκτρα. Euripidis Electra ... Adiecta est eadem Latinè ad uerbum reddita ... M. D. XLVI. 8°. A-H^{8}. [419

EUSEBIUS PAMPHILI. Ecclesiasticae historicae autores. ... Basileae M D LVII. (... per Hier. Frobenium et Nic. Episcopium, mense Martio, anno M. D. LVII.) fol. α^{4} a-z^{6} A-Xx^{6} Yy^{8} a-c^{6} d^{8} (-d8, *presumably blank*). pp. 1-819. ¶*Authors: Eusebius Pamphili, Rufinus, Socrates Scholasticus, Theodoretus, Sozomenos, Theodorus Lector, Evagrius Scholasticus, S. Dorotheus. Translators: Wolfgang Musculus, Joachim Camerarius.* (Lea.) [420

-- Ευσεβιου του Παμφιλου ευαγγελικης αποδειξεως βιβλια δεκα. Eusebii Pamphilii Euangelicæ demonstrationis Lib. X. ... *Greek*. Lutetiae. In officina Rob. Stephani ... M.D.XLV. ... (... M.D.XLVI, Cal. April.) fol. Aa-Zz^{6} AAa-CCc^{6} DDd^{4}. pp. 3-138. [421

-- -- *Another copy.* ¶*Aa1 precedes the* Evangelica praeparatio (E424) *with which this is bound.* (Lea.) [422

-- Ευσεβιου του Παμφιλου ευαγγελικης προπαρασκευης βιβ. πεντεκαιδεκα. Eusebii Pamphili Euangelicæ præparationis Lib. XV. ... *Greek.* Lutetiae. Ex officina Rob. Stephani ... M. D. XLIIII. ... fol. a-z^{6} aa-ss^{6} tt^{4}. pp. 3-498. [423

-- -- *Another copy* (-a1). (Lea.) [424

EUSTACHI, BARTOLOMMEO. [1] Bartholomaei Eustachii ... opuscula anatomica. ... Venetiis, M D LXIIII. [*stamped*:] Vincentius Luchinus excudebat. 4°. *^{6} α-β^{8} ϰ^{4} *^{4} *(wanting)* A-Ii^{4} (-A-C^{4}) Kk^{2} Ll-Ss^{4}. pp. 25-323 *present.* [2] Bartholomaei Eustachii ... libellus de dentibus. ... Venetiis, M D LXIII. a-h^{4} I-N^{4}. pp. 1-35. [3] Annotationes horum opusculorum ... A-V^{4} X^{2}. (School of Dentistry.) [425

EUSTATHIUS ANTECESSOR. De varia temporum in iure ciuili obseruatione, Eustathij ... Libellus. Item: leges Rhodiorum nauales, militares et Georgicæ Iustiniani ... Opera & studio Simonis Schardii I.C. *Greek and Latin.* Basileae, per Ioannem Oporinum. (... M.D.LXI. mense Augusto.) 8°. α^{8} a-s^{8}. pp. 17-292. [426

EUSTATHIUS MACREMBOLITA. Gli amori d'Ismenio composti per Eustathio philosopho et di Greco tradotti per Lelio Carani. In Fiorenza M D L. (Stampati ... appresso Lorenzo Torrentino ... à di xx del mese di Settembre ...) 8°. A-P^{8} Q^{4}. pp. 3-247. [427

-- -- In Venetia, appresso Domenico, & Gio. Battista Guerra, fratelli, M. D. LX. (*Colophon.*) 8°. A-M^{8} N^{4}. pp. 2-100. [428

EVANGELIA. [Euangelia dominicorum et festorum dierum musicis ... comprehensa & ornata ... Nürnberg, Johannes Montanus & Vlrich Neuber, 1554.] [1] Bassus in quinto tomo euangeliorum. obl. 4°. A-O^{4}. [2] Bassus in sexto tomo euangeliorum. A-O^{4}. [429

EXORCISMI. Exorcismi contra Demoniacos diuersorum sanctorum approbati: cum Benedictionibus necessariis: ac cum Cathecumino ⁊ Baptismo (Venetijs per Simonem de Luere. 1513.) 8°. B.L. a-n^{8}. ff. 2-104. (Lea.) [430

EXORCISMO. Exorcismo Mirabile da distare ogni sorte de maleficij: ⁊ da caciare li demonij: ... per vn deuoto Religioso composto ... M.D.XXXII. (Impressum Venetiis per Bernardinum de Vianis de Lexona Vercellēsem ... Die. VI. Nouēbris. ...) 8°. A-C^{8} D^{4}. (Lea.) [431

EXERCITIUM. Exercitiū grāmaticale puerorum per dietas distributum. (Impressus de nouo ... Finit ... M.v^{c} ij. ante festum sancti Ambrosij.) 4°. B.L. a-b^{8} c^{4} d-e^{8} f^{4} g-i^{8} k^{4} l-m^{8} n-v$^{4.8}$ (-v8, *presumably blank*). [432

EYB, ALBRECHT VON. Spiegel der sitten. im latein genañt Speculum morū. ... Dabey auch nachuolgklich Comedien Plauti in Menechino et Bachide vnd Philegenia Vgolini. ... (... in ... Augspurg. durch ... Iohañ Ryñman von Oͤringen ... In dem jar ... tausent fünf hundert vnd aylff jar. Am abent Mathei ...) fol. ₵^{6} A-M$^{8.6}$ N^{6} O^{8} P-V$^{8.6}$ X^{6} Y-Z$^{8.6}$ aa-bb$^{8.6}$ cc^{8} dd^{10}. ff. i-cxci. [433

EYMERICUS, NICOLAUS. [1] Directorium inquisitorum ... cum commentariis Francisci Pegñæ ... In hac postrema editione ... locupletatum. Romae, in aedibus Populi Romani Apud Georgium Ferrarium. MDLXXXVII. (*Colophon.*) fol. †-††^{8} A-Xx^{8} Yy-Zz^{10}. pp. 3-687. [2] Litterae apostolicae diuersorum Romanorum pontificum ... vsque ad hæc tempora MDLXXXVII. *Same imprint and colophon.* *^{4} A-K^{8}. pp. 1-155. (Lea.) [434

EYTZINGER, MICHAEL. [Michaelis Aitsingeri Austriaci Pentaplus regnorum mundi. Antuerpiae ex officina Christophori Plantini, 1579.] 4°. A^{6} (-A1) B-O^{4} A-F^{4} (F3 + 2 *folded leaves*; -F4). pp. 1-110. [435

F

FABER, TOBIAS. Ain Sermon Thobie Fabri ... Im Jar M D XXIII. 4°. A-B^4. [1

FABRI, JOHANN, of Heilbrunn. Antwort/ Auff das vnnütz/ vnrain/ jrrig geschwetz Mathie Flaccij Illyrici/ so er geschribē wider das büchlein/ genant Rechter weg. ... M. D. LVIII. (Gedruckt zu Dilingen durch Sebaldum Mayer.) 4°. a-b^4 A-Rr^4. ff. 1-160. [2

-- Ein ernstliche Christliche ermanung an das Edel Bayerland/ wider das Lasterbůch/ so ein Sectmaister ... hin vnnd her aussgebrait hat. ... 4°. *-**^{4} A-Nn^4 Oo^6 (-Oo6). ff. I-CLI. [3

-- Der recht Weg: Welche weg oder strass/ der glaubig wandeln oder geen soll/ dass er komme zů der ewigen rhů vnd friden ... M. D. LVII. (Gedruckt zu Dilingen durch Sebaldum Mayer. ...) 4°. ✠-3✠^{4} A-Z^4 a-l^4. ff. 1-135. [4

-- Ein sehr schöner Bericht/ vnd Christenlicher grundt/ von haltung des Conciliums/ so zů Triendt ... angefangen. Durch ... F. Iohannem Cussium/ den mañ nennt Fabri ... Anno M. D. LI. (Gedruckt zů Dillingen/ durch Sebaldum Mayer.) 4°. π^4 A-E^4 F^2. [5

-- Was die Euangelisch Mess sey/ Grundeliche vnd Christenliche anzaigung ... Getruckt zů Dilingen durch Sebaldum Mayer. M. D. LXIX. 8°. A-Z^8 a-i^8. ff. I-CCXL. [6

FABRI, JOHANNES, bishop of Vienna. Antilogiarum Martini Lutheri Babylonia, ex eiusdem libris, per D. Ioannem Fabri excerpta. M. D. XXX. (Excusum Augustæ Vindelicorum in officina Alexandri Weyssenhorn.) 4°. A-H^4. ff. 1-19. [7

-- Malleus ... in hæresim Lutheranā ... M D XXIIII. (Coloniæ apud Ioannem Soterem, expensis ... Petri Quentel.) fol. Aa-Bb^6 a-y$^{6.4}$ z^6 A-M$^{4.6}$. ff. I-CXXVI. [8

-- Ioannis Fabri ... opus aduersus noua quaedam et a Christiana religione prorsus aliena dogmata Martini Lutheri ... (Impressum Romæ ... per Marcellum Silber al's Franck. ... M.D.XXII. In uigilia Assumptionis ... uirginis Marię ...) fol. A^4 B-3C^6. (Lea.) [9

-- Sermones consolatorii ... super immanissimi Turcorum Tyranni altera imminenti obsidione ... vrbis Viennensis. ... M.D.XXXII. Viennæ Austriæ in ædibus Ioannis Singrenij. (... ultima die Mensis Septembris. ...) 4°. a-z^4 A-I^4 K^6. ff. 3-134. [10

-- -- *Another copy.* [11

-- Sermones ... de sacrosancto Eucharistiæ Sacramento. Apud Friburgum Brisgaudiae. Anno M. D. XXIX. (... Ioannes Faber Emmeus Iuliacensis excudebat.) 4°. a-l^4 m^6. [12

-- D. Iohannis Fabri ... Sermones fructuosissimi ... Item, Oratio funebris in laudem D. Margaretæ, Ducissæ Austriæ, &c̄. & quædā alia, quæ ad honorē ... Iob cōscripta sunt [ab Orthuino Gratio] ... Anno M. D. XXXVII. (Impressum ... Coloniæ in officina ... Petri Quentel ... Mense Februario.) fol. A^4 A-BB^6 CC-DD^4. ff. II-CXLVII. [13

-- Wie sich Iohannis Husss/ der Pickarder/ vnd Ioannis vō wessalia/ Leren vnd buecher mit Martino Luther vergleichen. ... (Gedruckt tzu Leyptzck/ durch Valten Schumañ ... 1528.) 4°. A-I^4. (Lea.) [14

FABRICIUS, ANDREAS. Harmonia confessionae Augustanae, doctrinae euangelicae consensum declarans. Adiunctum est Caroli Quinti ... iudicium. ... Editio secunda ... Coloniae. Apud Maternum Cholinum. M. D. LXXXVII. ... fol. a^6 A-Vu^6. pp. 1-515. [15

FABRICIUS, GEORG. Georgii Fabricii Chemnicensis, De re Poëtica Libri VII. Lipsiæ ... (... imprimebat Iohannes Steinman typis Voegelianis. Anno M. D. LXXIIII.) 8°. A-Z^8 a-z^8 Aa-Gg^8. pp. 3-815. [16

-- -- 8°. A-Z^8 (-A1) a-p^8 Q-T^8 v-z^8 AA-CC^8 DD^4. pp. 3-764. ¶*Sigg. T and ^{2}T transposed in binding.* [17

-- Georgii Fabricii ... elegantiarum poëticarum ex Ouidio, Tibullo, Propertio, similitudinum et comparationum ex ijsdem, epitomes de prosodia Libellus. Lipsiae ... (... in Officina Voegeliana.) 8°. A-I^8 K^{10}. pp. 1-162. ¶*T.p. repaired.* [18

-- Georgii Fabricij ... odarum libri tres. Ad Deum Omnipotentem. Basileae, ex officina Ioannis Oporini, Anno M.D.LII. (... Mense Martio.) 8°. a-m^{8}. pp. 1-174. ¶*Includes:* M. Antonii Flaminii de rebus Diuinis Carmina, Petrus Victorius Reginaldo Polo ..., Reginaldus Polus ... Petro Victorio. [19

-- Georgii Fabricii ... Partitionum Grammaticarum, quæ Tabulis delineatæ sunt, libri III. ... Basileae, per Ioannem Oporinum [1560 *or later*]. fol. α^{8} β^{4} A-P^{6} Q^{8}. pp. 1-195. [20

-- Poetæ historici item Germani aliquot celebres, singulis Distichis descripti. ... Authoribus Gerardo Fausto. Georgio Fabricio. Eõbano Hesso. Antonio Carchesio. Antonio Vicedomino. Argentorati apud Ioannem Schottum ... M. D. XLVI. 4°. a-e^{4}. [21

-- Georgii Fabricii ... Rerum Misnicarum libri VII. ... Lipsiæ Curante Ernesto Voegelino [1569]. 4°. A-Y^{8} (B1 + *folded leaf*) Z^{4} Aa-Cc^{8}. pp. 1-352. [22

-- Georgii Fabricii ... Virorum illustrium seu Historiæ Sacræ libri X. ... Lipsiae. ... (... Imprimebat Iohannes Steinman. Typis Voegelianis. Anno M. D. LXXI.) 8°. A-Z^{8} a^{8}. pp. 1-329. (Lea.) [23

FABRICIUS, HIERONYMUS. Hieronymi Fabricii ab Aquapendente de visione voce auditu Venetiis Per Franciscum bolzettam 1600 ([R3^{v}] Patauii, Ex officina Laurentij Pasquati ...) fol. *^{6} A-R^{4} ❡^{6} A-I^{4} K^{6} ✠^{4} A-E^{4}. pp. 1-133, 1-83, 2-38. ¶*Engraved t.p.* [24

FABRICIUS, THEODORUS. Theodori Fabritii institutiones in linguam sanctã ... Coloniæ apud Io. Soterẽ. Anno MDXXVIII. 4°. π^{2} a-k^{4} l^{6}. ff. IX-XCI. [25

FABYAN, ROBERT. [1] The Chronicle of Fabian, whiche he nameth the concordaunce of histories, ... continued from the beginnyng of Kyng Henry the seuenth, to thende of Queene Mary. 1559. Mense Aprilis. Imprinted at London, by Ihon Kyngston. fol. B.L. A-B^{6} a-z^{6} A-G^{6} H^{4}. pp. 1-369. [2] The seconde volume of Fabians Chronicle ... aa-zz^{6} AA-3B^{6} (-3B6, *blank*). pp. 1-571. *S.T.C.* 10664. [26

FACETUS. Liber Faceti docẽs mores hominũ ... (Impressa Colonie per Martinũ de werdena ... Anno dñi Millesimo Quingẽtesimonono. sequẽti die post Nicolai.) 4°. B.L. A-B^{6} C^{4}. [27

-- Facetus in latein durch Sebastianum Brant geteutschet. (Impressus Maguntie per Fridericum hewman ... 1509.) 4°. aa-cc^{4}. ¶*Latin and German texts.* [28

FAERNO, GABRIELE. Gabrielis Faerni Emendationes. In sex fabulas Terentij. ... Florentiae Apud Iuntas. M. D. LXV. (*Colophon.*) 8°. a-q^{8} (-q8, *presumably blank*). pp. 3-251. [29

FALCO, BENEDETTO DI. Rimario del Falco ... (Stampata in Napoli per Matthio Canze da Brescia, e ad instantia de ... Antonio Iouino & Francesco Vitolo Librari Napoletani, compagni M.D.XXXV. adi .8. del Mese de Giuglio.) 4°. a-z^{8} &^{8} ꝯ^{8} ℞^{8} A-K^{8} L^{6}. [30

FALETI, GIROLAMO. Delle guerre di Alamagna ... In Vinegia appresso Gabriel Giolito de Ferrari e fratelli M D LII. 8°. A-BB^{8} CC^{6}. pp. 17-389. ¶*Apparently other copies include* CC7-8, *^{4}. (Lea.) [31

FALLOPIO, GABRIELE. Gabrielis Falloppii Mutinensis ... opera ... omnia, in vnum congesta ... Francofurti Apud hæredes Andreæ Wecheli, MDLXXXIIII. fol. *^{6} a-z^{6} A-Zz^{6} AA^{6} BB^{4} CC-DD^{6} EE^{4}. pp. 1-848. [32

-- Gabrielis Fallopii ... De simplicibus medicamentis purgantibus, Tractatus ... Ab ... Andrea Marcolino Fanestri ... collectus ... Venetiis, Ad Insigne Stellæ Iordani Ziletti. MDLXV. (*Colophon.*) 4°. *-3*^{4} A-Kk^{4} Ll^{2}. pp. 1-263. [33

-- Kunstbůch: Dess ... Herrn Gabrielis Fallopij ... in Frantzösischer sprach/ durch Christophorum Landrinum aussgangen ... in Teũtsche sprach verfertiget/ durch: Hieremiam Martium ... M.D.XCVII. (Getruckt zu Augspurg/ bey Michael Manger.) 8°. a^{8} A-Ii^{8}. pp. 1-466. (Smith.) [34

FALUGI, GIOVANNI. Morte del ... Signor Giouanni de Medici ... M D XXXII (In Venetia per Aurelio Pincio Venetian. ... Del Mese di Settembre.) 8°. A-F^{8} (-F7-8, *blank*). ¶*In verse. Colophon pasted on.* [35

FAUCHET, CLAUDE. Recueil de l'origine de la langue et poesie Françoise, ryme et romans. Plus les noms et sommaire des oeuures de CXXVII. poetes François, viuant auant l'an M. CCC. A Paris, Par Mamert Patisson ... au logis de Robert Estienne. M.D.LXXXI. ... 4°. ā^4 A-Z^4 a-c^4 d^2. pp. 1-209. ¶d2 *defective.* [36

-- Recueil des antiquitez Gauloises et Françoises. A Paris. Chez Iacques du Puys ... M. D. LXXIX. ... 4°. *^{4} A-Ii^4 Kk^2. ff. 1-139. [37

FAUNO, LUCIO. Lucio Fauno. Delle antichita della citta di Roma ... (In Venetia per Michele Tramezzino. M D LIII.) 8°. A^8 B^4 (-B4) a-z^8. ff. 1-160. [38

FAURE, JEAN, DE ROUSSINES. Ioannis Fabri ... in Iustiniani Imperatoris Codicem, Breuiarium ... Access[it] tractatus Do. Bartholi de insignibus & armis, & repetitio in materia torturarum seu quæstionum. Lugduni, M.D.L. (... Balthazares Arnolletus Excudebat ...) fol. aa^8 bb^6 A-P^8 Q^{10}. pp. 1-256. ¶aa1 *slightly defective.* (Biddle.) [39

-- Ioannis Fabri commen. in quatuor lib. insti. ... Lugduni, Apud Hæredes Iacobi Giuntæ. 1549 (... impressa apud Iacobum Berion.) fol. B.L. a-q^8 r^{10} A^8 B^6. ff. 2-138. (Biddle.) [40

FAUSTO, SEBASTIANO. Dialogo del Fausto da Longiano, del modo de lo tradurre d'vna in altra lingua segondo le regole mostrate da Cicerone ... In Vinegia M D LVI. (... per Gio. Griffio. Ad instanza di Lodouico delli Auanzi ...) 8°. A-G^8 (-G8, *presumably blank*). ff. 2-54. [41

-- Il gentil'huomo del Fausto da Longiano. In Vinegia M D XLIIII. 8°. A-K^4. [42

-- -- *Another copy.* [43

-- Vita et gesti d'Ezzelino terzo da Romano ... Autore Pietro Gerardo Padouano suo contemporaneo. ... In Vinegia M. D. LII. (... per Comin da Trino, di Monferrato. ...) 8°. A-O^8. ff. 2-110. [44

-- -- *Another copy* (-O8, *blank*). [45

FAVONIO, PIETRO. Sermo ... habita ad ... Synodum Tridentinam in die Pentecostes ... M. D. LXII. Brixiæ Apud Damianum Turlinum ... Imprimebatur. Ad instantiam Ioannis Baptistæ Bozolæ. Anno M. D. LXII. 4°. A^4. (Lea.) [46

FAZELLI, TOMMASO. Rerum Sicularum scriptores ex recentioribus præcipui, in vnum corpus ... congesti ... Francofurti ad Moenum, apud And. Wechelum. M. D. LXXIX. fol. (:)^4 A-3Q^6 (-3Q6, *presumably blank*). pp. 1-705. ¶*Authors: Thomas Fazellus, Marius Aretius, Dominicus Marius Nigrus, Michael Ritius, Hugo Falcandus, Gervasius Tornacaeus.* (Lea.) [47

FEDINI, GIOVANNI. Le due Persilie commedia ... In Firenze. Nella Stamperia de'Giunti. MDLXXXIII. ... (*Colophon.*) 8°. A-G^8. pp. 1-96. [48

FENAROLO, LODOVICO. Il Sergio comedia ... In Venetia, Appresso Bolognino Zaltieri. M D L XVIII. 8°. A-I^8. ff. 2-72. [49

FERDINAND I, emperor. Coronatio Ferdinandi regis inuictissimi [1527.] 4°. A-B^4. [50

FERENTILLI, AGOSTINO. Discorso vniuersale ... Nel quale discorrendosi per le sei età & le quattro Monarchie ... sino all'anno M D LXIX. In Vinetia appresso Gabriel Giolito di Ferrarii M D LXXIIII. 4°. *-**^{4} A-O^8 P^4 a^4 b-d^8. pp. 1-231. ¶*Additional t.p.* (a1^r): La creatione del mondo, descritta da Filone Hebreo, et tradotto da M. Agostino Ferentilli. ... *Same imprint.* [51

-- Primo volume della scielta di stanze Di diuersi Autori Toscani, raccolte da M. Agostino Ferentilli ... In Venetia, appresso gli heredi di Marchiò Sessa. M. D. LXXI. 12°. *^{12} A-Z^{12}. pp. 2-548. [52

-- -- In Venetia, Appresso gli Heredi di Marchio Sessa. M D LXXXIIII. (... Appresso gli heredi di Pietro Dehuchino. ...) 12°. †^{12} A-Z^{12}. pp. 2-551. [53

FERNAND, CHARLES. De animi Trãquillitate Libri duo. ... Venundantur parrhisiis in ædibus

Ioannis parui & Iodoci Badii Ascensii. (... MDXII. ad Idus Nouemb. ...) 4°. Aa^6 A-H^8 I^{10}. ff. I-LXXIII. [54

-- Epistolę Caroli Phernandi. ... [Parisiis,] Venundantur in ędibus Ascensianis ... 4°. A-$D^{8.4}$. ¶*Preface dated* ad Sextum idus aprilis. M.D.VI. [55

FERNANDEZ, TELLUS. Prima pars commentariorum in primas triginta et Octo leges Tauri ... In hac secunda editione locupletatum ... Madrid, apud Ludouicum Sanchez. Anno 1595. fol. π^2 $¶^6$ $¶¶^8$ A-Gg^8 Hh^6 (-Hh6, *presumably blank*). ff. 1-245. (Biddle.) [56

FERNANDEZ DE SANTA ELLA, RODRIGO. Vocabularium ecclesiasticum ... Stellæ excudebat Michael de Eguia. Anno. M. D. XLVI. (... mense Maio.) 4°. B.L. A-X^8 Y^{10}. [57

FERRANTE, CESARE. Caesaris Ferrantii Suessani ... oratio ad patres Concilii Tridentini, habita in festo D. Ioannis Apostoli & Euangelistæ, anno ... M. D. LXII. Brixiæ Apud Damianum Turlinum. Anno. M. D. LXII. 4°. A^6. (Lea.) [58

FERRARA. Statuta vrbis Ferrariae nuper reformata. ... M. D. LXVII. (Ferrariae Excudebat Franciscus Rubeus de Valentia. M. D. LXVI.) fol. $*^4$ $+^6$ A-$3D^6$ $3E^8$ $*$-$**^6$. ff. 1-307. (Lea.) [59

-- Grida, Capitoli, & Ordini sopra il guadare il Pò, nelle sue escrescenze. (Stampata per Vittorio Baldini ... Adi 3. Marzo. M. D. XCVIII.) fol. A^6. (Lea.) [60

-- Gride, bandi, ordini, decreti, editti, Constitutioni, Dichiarationi, & Gratie Ordinate ... dell' ... Card. Aldobrandino ... In Ferrara, Per Vittorio Baldini ... M.D.XCVIII. fol. π^1 A-D^6 E^4 A^8 A^4 B^6. pp. 1-55, 1-15, 1-19. [61

-- *Diocese.* Ordinationi generali per le chiese Della Città, & Diocese di Ferrara. ... In Ferrara, Appresso Benedetto Mammarello. M D XCIII. 8°. A-B^8 C^6. pp. 3-40. [62

-- Decreta edita, et promulgata In Synodo Dioesesana Ferrariensi Habita. ... M.D.XCIX. ... Ferrariae, M. D. XCIX. Apud Victorium Baldinum ... (*Colophon.*) 8°. A-Dd^8 Ee^4. pp. 3-406. (Lea.) [63

FERRARI, GIOVANNI FRANCESCO. Le rime burlesche ... In Venetia, Appresso gli Heredi di Marchiò Sessa. M D LXX. 8°. $*^4$ A-O^8 P^{10}. ff. 1-121. [64

FERRARIUS MONTANUS, JOANNES. Ioannis Ferrarij Montanij, de Republica bene instituenda, Parænesis ... Basileae, per Ioannem Oporinum. (... M. D. LVI. Mense Augusto.) fol. α^4 A-Aa^4. pp. 2-178. [65

FERREIRA, ANTONIO. Poemas Lusitanos ... Em Liboa. Impresso ... Por Pedre Crasbeeck. M. D. XCVIII. ... A custa de Esteuão Lopez ... 4°. $¶^4$ A-Z^8 a-g^8 h^4. ff. 1-240. [66

FERRER, MIGUEL. Methodus siue Ordo procedendi Iudiciarius iuxta stylum & foros Regni Aragonum ... Cæsaraugustæ. In ædibus Petri Bernuz. M. D. LIIII. (... tertiodecimo Calendas Augusti.) 4°. B.L. A^8 a-k^8 l^{10}. ff. 1-81. (Lea.) [67

FERRERI, ZACCARIA. De reformatione ecclesiae. Suasoria. ... (Venetijs per Io. Antonium & fratres de Sabio.) 4°. A-C^4. ¶*Dated* pridie Cal'. Septembres. M.D.XXII. [68

FERRETTI, GIOVANNI BATTISTA. Primum volumen consiliorum, ac responsorum ... Venetiis MDLVII (... Aurelius Pincius excudebat.) fol. B.L. A-X^8 Y^4. ff. 1-171. (Biddle.) [69

FEUCHT, JAKOB. Ein Catholische Communion Predig. ... Gedruckt zu Bamberg/ durch Iohañ Wagner. 1575. 8°. $+^8$ $§^8$ A-I^8. pp. 1-143. [70

-- Ein Catholische Messpredig : Darinnen ... erwisen wirdt: Dass die heilig Mess ein Opffer sey. ... Getruckt zů Dilingen/ durch Sebaldum Mayer. 1575. 8°. A-I^8 (-I8, *presumably blank*). pp. 1-123. [71

-- Neun vnd dreissig Catholische Predigen ... Gedruckt zu Cöln/ durch Gerwinum Calenium/ vnd die Erben Iohan Quentels. ... M. D. LXXVIII. ... 4°. A-$4R^4$ $4S^2$. pp. 5-691. [72

FIAMMA, GABRIELLO. Rime spirituali ... In Vinegia, M D LXX. Presso a Francesco de' Franceschi Senese. (*Colophon.*) 8°. a^{10} A-Mm^8 (-Mm8, *presumably blank*). pp. 1-519. [73

FICINO, MARSIGLIO. [1] Marsilii Ficini Florentini ... opera ... omnia, ... in duos Tomos digesta ... Vnâ cum gnomologia, hoc est, sententiarum ex iisdem operibus collectarum farragine ... adiecta. ... Basileae. Anno M. D. LXI. fol. a^4 a^6 b^8 A-$3Q^8$ $3R^{10}$. pp. 1-1012. [2] Tomus secundus ... operum ... Basileæ. (... Per Henricum Petri, mense Martio. Anno M.D.LXI.) $+^4$ AA-ZZ^8 AAa-ZZz^8 AaA-NnN^8 OoO^4 PpP^8. pp. 1013-1979. [3] Sententiae ... ex Marsilij Ficini ... operibus collectæ ... Per Adamum Henricum Petri. ... Basileae. Anno M. D. LXI. α-$β^6$ $γ^8$. ¶*In both volumes the word* Basileae *on the t.p. has been covered by a paste-on.* (Lea.) [74

-- *Commentaria in Platonem.* Le Commentaire de Marsille Ficin, Florentin: sur le banquet d'Amour de Platon: faict Francois par Symon Siluius, dit I. De la Haye ... On les vend a Poictiers, a l'enseigne du Pelican [par Jean & Enguilbert de Marnef]. M. D. XLVI. (Acheué d'Imprimer, le xvi. Feurier, M. D. XLV. auant Pasques.) 8°. a-o^8 p^{10}. ff. I-CXIIII. [75

-- -- Marsilio Ficino sopra lo amore o ver' convito di Platone. In Firênze per Nêri Dortelâta ... Novêmbre M.D.XXXXIIII. (*Colophon.*) 8°. a^4 A-S^8 T^4. pp. 1-251. [76

-- De la religion Chrestienne ... Auec La harangue de la dignité de l'homme, Par Iean Picus ... traduit de Latin en François par Guy le Feure de la Boderie ... A Paris, Chez Gilles Bēs ... 1578. ... 8°. a^8 a-z^8 A-D^8 E^4. pp. 1-439. [77

-- Marsilius Ficinus Florentinus De triplici vita. [c. 1506.] 4°. a-l^8 m-n^6. [78

-- Marsilii Ficini Florentini ... de vita libri tres. ... Parisiis, Apud Viuantium Gaultherot ... 1547 8°. A-S^8. pp. 2-288. (Lea.) [79

-- -- Les trois liures de la vie ... traduit en François. Par Guy le Feure de la Boderie ... A Paris, Pour Abel l'Angelier ... M. D. LXXXII. ... (Acheué d'Imprimer le tresiesme iour de Nouembre, par Pierre le Voirrier ... 1581.) 8°. $\bar{a}^8$ $\bar{e}^8$ B-Cc^8. ff. 1-198. [80

FICKLER, JOHANN BAPTIST. Richtschnur Rechter Lehr. Darbey der Gemeine Mann/ vnd das einfeltig Christenvͤlcklein ... erkennen kan/ welches der rechte Glaub/ vnd Religion ... in vnser Teutsch getreulich verwendet. Gedruckt zu Mͤnchen/ bey Adam Berg. M. D. XCVII. ... 4°. A-H^4. [81

FIGLIUCCI, FELICE. Di Felice Figliucci Senese, de la filosofia morale libri dieci. Sopra li dieci libri de l'ethica d'Aristotile. ... In Roma Appresso Vincenzo Valgrisi. ... (... MDLI.) 4°. $*^4$ A-$3X^4$. pp. 1-504. [82

-- -- In Vinegia, per Giouanmaria Bonelli. M D LII. (*Colophon.*) 8°. a-z^8 A-XX^8 YY^4 (-YY4, *presumably blank*). ff. 2-520. [83

FILELFO, FRANCESCO. Franciscus Philelphus ... Francisco barbaro ... Salutem dicit ... (Epistolio ... Francisci Philelphi. adiunctis aliquot illustris viri Epl'is. ... Colonie agrippine Anno sesquimillesimo sexto ad finem Haprilis.) 4°. B.L. A^6 B-$I^{4.8}$ K^6. ff. [i]-lx. ¶K4 *misbound after* K2. C7-8 *defective.* [84

-- -- Francisci Philelfi epistolae ... Item Angeli Politiani epistolæ quædam familiares ... (Argentorati, Ex Aedibus Schurerianis, Mense Maio. Ann. M. D. XIIII.) 4°. $π^6$ A-$F^{8.4.4}$ G^8 H^4 I^8 K^4 L^6 (-L6, *presumably blank*). ff. I-LXI. [85

-- -- M.D.XIX. ... Item Epistole L. Annei Senece ad Apostolum Paulum/ ꝛ rursus Pauli ad Senecam ... (Auguste Vindelicoꝝ: in edibus Siluani Otmar excusum ... M.D.xix. Die vero tricesima Mensis Iulij.) 4°. B.L. $π^6$ a-b^4 c-d^8 e-g^4 h^8 i^4 k^6. ff. [I]-LIIII. [86

FILICAJA, LODOVICO DA. Leggenda ouero vita del dispregiator del mondo, Christifero Santo Francesco composta in ottaue rime ... In Venetia al segno della speranza 1549. 4°. A-K^8. ff. 2-79. [87

FILLON, ARTHUR. Speculum curatorum vna cum cōfessionali ac tractatu de misterio misse ... [Parisiis,] Venūdatur a Iohāne paruo ... [c. 1510.] 16°. B.L. A-D^8 E^4. [88

FILOSSENO, MARCELLO. Sylue de Marcello Philoxeno Taruisino ... (Stampati in Venetia per Marchio Sessa & Piero di Rauani bersano compagni. Nel .M.D.XVI. adi .x. Nouēbrio.) 8°. a-s^8 A-R^8 S^4. ¶A1^r: *title repeated.* [89

FINCEL, JOB. Oratio de vita et obitu ... Poëtæ Ioannis Stigelii ... Ienæ excudebat Donatus Ritzenhayn. Anno 1563. 8°. A-F^8. [90

FINDLING, JOHANN. Adhortatoria Epistola ad Martinum Luther, ut cesset maledictis bonos persequi, & Ecclesiam Dei turbare. ... [Ingolstadii, Andreas Lutz, 1521.] 4°. a-c^4. [91

FINÉ, ORONCE. Orontij Finæi Delphinatis ... In eos quos de Mundi sphæra conscripsit libros, ac in Planetarum theoricas, Canonum Astronicorum libri II. Lutetiae, Apud Michaëlem Vascosanum ... 1553. ... 4°. A-O^4 P^6. ff. 2-62. [92

FIORAVANTI, FLAVIO. De capricci medicinali ... libri quattro. ... In Venetia, Appresso Lodouico Auanzo. 1573. 8°. a-c^8 A-Nn^8 Oo^4. ff. 1-283. (Smith.) [93

FIORAVANTI, LIONARDO. Il tesoro della vita humana ... In Venetia, Appresso gli Heredi di Melchior Sessa. MDLXXXII. 8°. a-d^8 A-Ss^8 (-Ss8, *blank*). ff. 1-327. (Smith.) [94

FIRENZUOLA, AGNOLO. I lucidi comedia ... In Firenze M. D. LII. (... apresso i Giunti. ...) 8°. A-E^8 F^4. ff. 3-44. [95

-- Prose ... In Fiorenza, appresso i Giunti. MDLXII. (*Colophon.*) 8°. A^4 B-Z^8 AA-BB^4. pp. 2-369. [96

-- Le rime ... In Fiorenza, MDXLIX. (... appresso Bernardo Giunti. ...) 8°. A-R^8. ff. 2-135. [97

-- La trinutia comedia ... In Fiorenza, MDXLIX. (... appresso Bernardo Giunti. ...) 8°. A-E^8 F^4. ff. 2-44. [98

FIRMI. [1] Statuta Firmanoꝝ ... (Impressum Venetiis auspiciis ... Marci martelli ... in calcographia ... Nicholai de Brentis: & Alexandri de Bãdonis. ... M.D.VII. Die. xvii. Martii.) fol. ✠^{6} a-q^8 r-s^6. ff. I-CXLII. [2] Ordinamenta & consuetudo maris edita per consules ciuitatis Trani. A^4. ff. II [=I]-IIII. (Lea.) [99

-- -- Firmi Apud Sertorium de Montibus impressa ... 1589. (*Colophon.*) fol. *A*^{6} A-Q^6 R-S^8. pp. 1-224. [100

FIRMICUS MATERNUS, JULIUS. Iulii Firmici Materni iunioris Siculi ... Astronomicω̃n Libri VIII, per Nicolaum Prucknerum ... mendis uindicati. His accesserunt, Claudii Ptolemaei ... ἀχοτελεσμάτων, quod Quadripartitum uocant, Lib. IIII. De inerrantium stellarum significationibus, Lib. I. Centiloquium eiusdem. ... Hermetis ... centum Aphoris. Lib. I. Bethem Centiloquium. Eiusdem de Horis Planetarum Liber alius. Almanzoris ... Propositiones ... Zahelis Arabis de Electionibus Lib. I. Messahalah de ratione Circuli & Stellarum ... Lib. I. Omar de Natiuitatibus Lib. III. Marci Manilii ... Astronomicω̃n Lib. V. Postremô, Othonis Brunfelsii de Diffinitionibus & terminis Astrologiæ libellus isagogicus. Basileae, per Ioannem Heruagium, ... M.D.LI. Mense Aprili. (*Colophon.*) fol. α^6 a-t^6 u^8 A-T^6. pp. 2-244, 1-227. [101

FISCHART, JOHANN. Der Barfuͤsser Secten vnd Kuttenstreit. [c. 1574.] s.sh. 75 × 39.5 cm. (Lea.) [101a

FISHER, JOHN. Assertiones Lutheranae confutatio ... Per ... Ioannẽ Roffensem Episcopũ ... Anno M D XXV. (Coloniæ, Impensis ... Petri Quentel. ...) 4°. A-C^4 a-zz^4 Aa-Zz^4. pp. I-D.LII. [102

-- -- Parisiis [apud] Petrum drouart ... M. D. XLV. 8°. a-z^8 A-Y^8. ff. 2-359. ¶*T.p. defective.* (Lea.) [103

-- -- Von dem ... bischoff Io. võ Roffen vss Engelland/ seines ... bůchs zwen artickel verteutscht võ Doctor Io. Cochleus ... 1524. (Getruckt zů Strassburg võ Iohanne Grienĩger vff Sant Laurentzen abent. ...) 4°. A-G^4 H^6. [104

-- De veritate corporis et sanguinis Christi in eucharistia, per ... D. Iohãnem Roffensem Episcopum, aduersus Iohannem Oecolampadium. Coloniæ, ... M.D.XXVII. Aeditio prima. (Excusum ... per ... Petrum Quentell ... Mense Martio.) 4°. [A]^4 B-D^4 a-z^4 A-3D^4 3E^6. ff. 2-297. [105

-- Sacri sacerdotii defensio contra Lutherum, per ... Ioannem Roffen. Episcopum ... Antuerpiae Apud Ioannem Steelsium ... M.D.XXXVII. 8°. A-F^8 G^4. ff. 2-51. (Yarnall.) [105a

FITZHERBERT, SIR ANTHONY. Diuersite de courtz et lour iurisdiccions ... (Impressum Londini ... M.CCCCC.xliii. Per me Wyllyam Myddylton.) 8°. B.L. A-B^8 C^4. *S.T.C.* 10952. (Biddle.) [106

-- La nouuelle Natura breuiū du Iudge ... Anthonie Fitzherbert ... auecques vn Table ... compose per Guiliaulme Rastell ... Londini in ædibus Richardi Tottelli. ... 1567. ... 8°. B.L. A-D^8 A-Ll^8 (-L18, *presumably blank*). ff. 2-271. *S.T.C.* 10962. (Biddle.) [107

-- -- Londini, In Edibus Thomæ Wight, & Bonhami Norton. ... 1598. ... 8°. B.L. A-D^8 A-Ll^8 (-L18, *presuambly blank*). ff. 1-271. *S.T.C.* 10964. (Biddle.) [108

-- The nevve boke of iustices of peace ... translated out of Frēch into Englishe ... 1554. ... (Imprinted at London ... by Richarde Tottyll, the vii. day of February ... 1560.) 8°. B.L. A-Y^8. ff. 2-173. *S.T.C.* 10976. (Biddle.) [109

-- Loffice Et aucthoritie de Iustices de peace, in part collect per ... A. Fitzherbert, et ore enlarge per Richard Crompton ... 1583. ... Imprinted at London by Richarde Tottill. ... 4°. B.L. A^4 A-B^8 C^6 A-Bb^8 Cc^6. ff. 1-206. *S.T.C.* 10978. (Biddle.) [110

-- -- 1587. ... At London by Richard Tottell. 4°. B.L. $¶^8$ A^4 A-Aa^8 BB-KK^8 LL^4. ff. 1-268. *S.T.C.* 10980. (Biddle.) [111

-- -- 1593. ... Imprinted at London by Richard Tottell. 4°. B.L. $¶^4$ C^6 A-Hh^8 Ii^4. ff. 1-252. *S.T.C.* 10981. (Biddle.) [112

-- -- *Another copy* (-¶4). [113

-- In this Booke is conteyned the offyce of Shyryffes, Baylyffes of lybertyes, Escheatours, Constables, and Coroners ... (Imprinted at London ... by Iohn King.) 8°. B.L. A-K^8. *S.T.C.* 10984.1. (Biddle.) [114

-- -- 1562. Imprinted at London ... by Richard Tottle. 8°. B.L. A-I^8 k^8 (-k8, *presumably blank*). *S.T.C.* 10991.5. (Biddle.) [115

-- -- 1573. (Imprinted at London/ by Iohn Allde. ...) 8°. A-G^8. ¶*J. H. Beale T303a.* (Biddle.) [116

FLACIUS, MATTHIAS, ILLYRICUS. Antidotum auff Osiandri gifftiges Schmeckbier/ Durch Matt. Fla. Illyri. vnd Nico. Gallum. ... (Gedruckt zu Magdeburg bey Christian Rödinger.) 4°. A-B^4 C^2. [117

-- Apologia ... auff zwo vnchristliche Schrifften Iusti Menij ... Ihenae [durch Thomas Rebart?]. Anno M. D. LVIII. 4°. A^6 B-R^4 S^2. [118

-- Argumenta psalmorum sexaginta, distributis ordine Versuum Sententijs ... Philippus Melanchthon [praefatur]. Francoforti ex Officina Petri Brubachij, anno M. D. L. 8°. A-R^8. pp. 1-255. [119

-- Beweisung/ das Osiander helt vnd leret/ das die Gottheit eben also in den rechtgleubigen wone/ wie in der menscheit Christi selbst. ... (Gedruckt zu Magdeburg bey Christian Rödinger. Prima Ianuarij Anno 1553.) 4°. A^4. [120

-- Catalogus testium veritatis, qui ante nostram ætatem reclamarunt Papæ. ... Cum Præfatione Mathiæ Flacii Illyrici ... Basileae, per Ioannem Oporinum. (... per Michaelem Martinum Stellam ... M.D.LVI. Mense Martio.) 8°. α^8 a-z^8 A-$3A^8$ $3B^4$. pp. 2-1095. [121

-- Cleri fletus. Est deploratio perditae maliciae Clericorum ... 1550. (Impressum Magdeburgi per Michaelem Lottherum.) 8°. A^8. [122

-- Das alle Verfolger der Kirchen Christi zu Magdeburgk/ Christi des Herrn selbs verfolger sindt. ... ... (Gedruckt zu Magdeburgk/ durch Michael Lotther. Anno 1551. mense Iulio.) 4°. A-B^4. (Lea.) [123

-- De Iesu, nomine Christi Seruatoris nostri proprio, contra Osiandrum. ... VVittebergæ ex officina Iohannis Cratonis. Anno M. D. LII. 4°. A-B^4 D^6. [124

-- De translatione imperii Romani ad Germanos. Item de electione episcoporum, quòd æquè ad plebem pertineat. ... Accessit ... liber Lupoldi Babembergensis de iuribus Imperij & Regni Rom. Basileae 1566. (Apud Petrum Pernam) 8°. π^{12} *-**^{8} ***^{4} a-r^8 *^{4} b-z^8 &^{8} †^{8}. pp. 1-271, 17-398. [125

-- Eine entschůldigung ... an einen Pfarherr. Item desselben/ was da sey die Kirchen verlassen odder nicht verlassen. Item zween Trewme Philippi. ... M.D.XLIX. 4°. A-B^4. [126

-- Ermanung an alle Stende der Christlichen kirchen in Preussen Osianders lere halben. Durch Matthium Flacium Illyricum. vnd Nicolaum Gallum. ... (Gedruckt zu Madgeburg bey Christian Rödinger.) 4°. A-B^4 C^2. [127

-- Eine Erschreckliche Historia von einem/ den die feinde des Euangelij inn welsch Land gezwungen haben/ den erkanten Christum zuvorleugnen. ... Anno 1549. 4°. A-D^4. ¶*Francesco Spira.* [128

-- Eine freidige vermanung/ zu klarem vnd öffentlichem bekentnis Ihesu Christi/ wider die Adiaphoristische/ Dauidianische/ vnd Epicurische klugheit ... Gestelt durch Ciuilium einen Italiener. Verdeudscht auss dem welschen. ... 1550. (Gedruckt zu Magdeburgk durch Michael Lotther/ den 4. Octobris. ...) 4°. A-C^4. [129

-- Ein geistlicher trost dieser betrübten Magdeburgischen Kirchen Christi ... 4°. A^4 B^2. [130

-- Gründliche verlegung aller schedlichen Schwermereyen des Stenckfelds ... M.D.LVII. 8°. A-Z^8 a-z^8 AA^4. [131

-- Gründliche verlegung aller Sophisterey/ so Iuncker Issleb/ D. Interim/ Morus/ Pfeffinger/ D. Geitz in seinem gründlichen bericht vnd jhre gesellen ... gebrauchen. ... 4°. A-L^4 M^2. [132

-- Kurtze antvort ... auff der Hoch verkertenn angeschlagne Schmach Zettel. ... 4°. A^4 B^2. [133

-- Kurtze vnd klare erzelung der argument Osiandri mit jhrer verlegung ... von der gerechtigkeit des glaubens. ... (Gedruckt zu Magdeburg/ bey Christian Rödinger. Anno M. D. LII. j. Septemb.) 4°. A-F^4. [134

-- Ein rechter lesteriger Rabsakes brieff/ geschrieben von einem Bischoff an einem Christlichen Fürsten/ in welchem er ihn vermanet das er sol von der erkanten warheit Christi zu dem Antichrist abfallen ... Anno 1549. 4°. A-C^4. ¶*Preface by Flacius.* (Yarnall.) [134a

-- Ein Sendbrieff/ P. Aesquillij von dem tode Pauli des dritten Babsts dieses namens/ Item Was jhm nach seinem tode begegnet ist. ... (Impressum ex alio iam alibi impresso exemplari, quod erat uersum ex latino Placentiæ excuso [1549].) 4°. A-D^4 (-D4, *presumably blank*). (Lea.) [135

-- -- *Another copy.* [136

-- Varia doctorū piorumque virorum, De corrupto Ecclesiæ statu, Poemata, Ante nostram ætatem cōscripta ... Cum præfatione Mathiæ Flacii Illyrici. Basileae, per Ludouicum Luciam. (... M.D.LVII. Mense Martio.) 8°. a-z^8 A-H^8. pp. 4-494. [137

-- Verlegung des Bekentnis Osiandri von der Rechtfertigung der armen sünder durch die wesentliche Gerechtigkeit ... Gottes allein. ... Mit vnterschreibung Nicolai Gallj ... (Gedruckt zu Magdeburgk bey Christian Rödinger. 1552.) 4°. a-c^4 A-P^4 Q^2. [138

-- -- (Gedruckt zu Magdeburg/ bey Christian Rödinger. 1552.) 4°. a-b^4 A-Q^4. [139

-- Verlegung des vnwarhafftigen vngegründten berichts Hansen Funckens/ von der Osiandrischen schwermerey. ... [Magdeburg? 1554.] 4°. A-C^4 D^2. [140

-- Ein vermanung zur bestendigkeit/ in bekentnis der warheit/ Creutz/ vnd Gebett ... (Gedrückt zu Magdeburgk durch Michael Lotther [1549?].) 4°. A-H^4. [141

-- Von dem Concilio zu Trient. ... Matth. Flacius Illyricus. Nicolaus Gallus. ... 1563. (Gedruckt zu Regenspurg durch Heinrichen Geissler.) 4°. A-O^4. [142

-- Von der Gerechtigkeit wider Osiandrum ... (Gedruckt zu Magdeburg/ bey Christian Rödinger. Anno M.D.LII. XXIIII. Septembris.) 4°. A-E^4 F^2. [143

-- Von einigkeit vnd vneinigkeit der Euangelischen vnd Papisten gegen einander ... 4°. A-B^4. ¶B4 *defective.* [144

-- Wider Das interim. Papistische Mess/ Canonem/ vnd Meister Eissleuben ... (Anno. 1549.) 4°. A-D^4. [145

-- Widder den ausszug des Leipsischen Interims ... (Gedruckt zu Magdeburg bey Christian Roͤdinger/ Anno M. D. xlix.) 4°. A-B^4. [146

-- Wider den Euangelisten des heiligen Chorrocks/ D. Geitz Maior. ... Basel. Anno 1552. 4°. A-C^4. [147

-- Wider den Schnoͤden Teuffel ... das ist wider das newe interim/ Durch Carolum Azariam Gotsburgensem. ... M.D.XLIX. 4°. A-C^4. [148

-- Wider die Goͤtter in Preussen. ... 4°. A-C^4 D^2. [149

-- Wider die newe ketzerey der Dikaeusisten ... (Gedruckt zu Magdeburg/ bey Christian Roͤdinger.) 4°. A-C^4. [150

-- Widder die vnchristlicheͤ Vermanungschrifft/ des Bisthumbs zu Naumburg ... (Gedruckt zu Magdeburg bey Christian Roͤdinger. M. D. L.) 4°. A^4 B^2. [151

-- Widder die vermeinte gewalt/ vnd Primat des Babstes ... (Gedruckt zu Magdeburg/ bey Christian Roͤdinger [1549].) 4°. A-D^4 E^2. [152

-- Widder drei Gottislesterische vnnd Sophistische Argumenta des Funckens ... 8°. A^8. [153

-- Widderlegung des Catechismi des Laruen Bischoffes von Sidon ... 1550. (Getruͤckt zu Magdeburg.) 4°. A-E^4 F^2. [154

-- Widerlegung/ Eines Kleinen Deutschen/ Caluinischen Catechismi ... Item/ Beweisung/ Das auch die vnwirdigen den waren Leib vnd Blut Iesu Christi im Abendmahl empfahen/ Wider ein Schwenckfeldisch Buͤchlein ... (Zu Regenspurg druckts Heinrich Geissler [1563].) 4°. A-I^4. [155

-- Zwo fuͤrnemliche gruͦnde Osiandri verlegt/ zu einem Schmeckbier. ... s.sh. 24 × 30.5 cm. [156

FLAMINIUS, LUCIUS. [*Caption* a2^v) Lutij flaminij. S. oratio de summo bono ... [c. 1505.] 8°. a-g^8 h^6 a-b^8. ¶^{2}a1^r: Lucii Flaminii. Siculi epigrãmatũ Libellus. [157

FLANDERS. [1] Dits die excellente cronike vã vlaenderẽ ... Gheprent Tantwerpen/ by my Willem Vorsterman. (... Anno. M.CCCCC. ende. xxxi. Ende es voleyndt den. xi.sten dach der maent Iulij.) fol. B.L. ✠^{6} a-z^6 ꝛ^6 ꝯ^6 A-BB^6. ff. i-CCC. [2] Vanden ... Princhе Carolus/ Keyser vã Roomen/ Coninck vã Spaengien ... A-F^6 G^8 H^2 (+ *folding leaf, damaged*) I-L^6. (Lea.) [158

-- Warhafftige Zeyttung von einer grossen Niderlage/ so am 13. Iulij in Flandern/ nicht ferne von Dumkirche geschehen ist. Aus einem Brieffe/ welchen ein Kauffman zu Antorff ... geschrieben. 1558. 4°. A^2. [159

FLEETWOOD, WILLIAM. Annalium tam Regum Edwardi quinti, Richardi tertij, & Henrici septimi, quàm Henrici octaui ... Elenchus. ... [Londini,] In Ædibus Richardi Tottelli, 1579. ... (... the x. day of September ...) 8°. B.L. ¶^{4} A-AA^8 BB^4. *S.T.C.* 11034. (Biddle.) [160

FLOCCUS, ANDREAS DOMINICUS. L. Fenestellae de magistratibus Sacerdotijsq́; Romanorum libellus ... Pomponii Laeti itidem de magistratibus & sacerdotijs, præterea de diuersis legibus Romano. Valerii Probi grammatici de literis antiquis opusculum. Basileae apud Thomam Volfium. An. M. D. XXXV. Mense Augusto. (*Colophon.*) 8°. A-L^8. [161

-- -- Venetiis, Apud Fabii, & August. Zoppinos, Fratres, M. D. LXXXIII. (*Colophon.*) 12°. A-F^{12}. pp. 3-143. [162

-- Andreæ Dominici Flocci, Fiorentini, de Potestatibus Romanorum, lib. II. ... restituti, studio ac industria Egidii Wiitsii, I.C. Brugens. Pomponij Læti, Raphaelis Volaterrani, & Henrici Bebelij, eiusdem argumenti libelli ... Antuerpiæ. Ex officina Christophori Plantini ... M. D. LXI. ... (... vicesimaseptima Ian. ...) 8°. A-M^8. ff. 1-85. [163

FLORENCE. *Laws, ordinances, &c., in chronological order by date of enactment.* Statuti, e Riforma della gabella de Beni in Pagamento del Contado. Cauati del quarto Libro delli Statuti di Fiorenza. In Fiorenza, Appresso Giorgio Marescotti. MDLXXV. 4°. A^2. (Lea.) [164

-- Legge, et deliberatione ... Sopra le Monete Fatta il di 4. d'Agosto MDXXXI. In Fiorenza appresso i Giunti 1561. 4°. A^4. (Lea.) [165

-- -- *Another copy.* (Lea.) [166

-- Legge, et deliberatione ... Sopra le Monete Fatta il di 5. di Marzo MDXXXIIII. In Fiorenza appresso Giunti 1561. 4°. A^4. (Lea.) [167

-- -- In Fiorenza, Appresso Giorgio Marescotti. MDLXXV. 4°. A^4. (Lea.) [168

-- Prouisione ... Fatta ... In fauore di chi ammaza Sbanditi. Publicata sotto di 30. di Luglio, 1535. In Fiorenza, Nella Stamperia di lor'Altezze. 1571. 4°. π^2. (Lea.) [169

-- Bando sopra e banditi, Publicato a dì 16. di Marzo. 1537. In Fiorenza, Appresso Giorgio Marescotti. 4°. A^2. (Lea.) [170

-- Bando dell' arme Mandato adi 28. di Maggio MDXXXIX. In Fiorenza, Appresso Giorgio Marescotti. 4°. A^2. (Lea.) [171

-- Legge sopra gli stupri, violentie, incesti, sacrilegii, coiti, nefarii, assassinamenti, Et Furti. A di 9. di Febraio. 1542. In Fiorenza, Appresso i Giunti. 4°. π^2. (Lea.) [172

-- Legge sopra i precetti, et regole da osseruarsi per li esattori fiscali nel riscuotere, Fatta il dì 22. Dicembre 1543. In Fiorenza, Appresso Giorgio Marescotti 4°. A^4. (Lea.) [173

-- Prouisioni, et deliberationi fatte negl'infrascritti tempi ... Per conto della Seta. ([$A1^v$] il di 22. di Febraio, MDXLV. [$A3^r$] el di XV. di Febraio. MDXLVI.) In Fiorenza, Appresso Giorgio Marescotti. 4°. A^4. (Lea.) [174

-- Deliberatione fatta per li signori conseruadori Dell'arte della Lana Sotto di 1. di Marzo. 1545. In Fiorenza Appresso i Giunti. 4°. A^4. (Lea.) [175

-- Bando sopra i tiralori, et battilori Publicato il dì 6. dì Marzo. 1545. In Fiorenza, Appresso Giorgio Marescotti. 4°. A^2. (Lea.) [176

-- Legge fatta ... Sopra gli Scrocchi, & altri Contratti illeciti. Ostenuta ... el dì 14. d'Aprile. 1545. Nuouamente ristampata. In Fiorenza, Nella Stamperia Ducale. Appresso Giorgio Marescotti. M D LXXIIII. 4°. π^2. (Lea.) [177

-- Prouisione et ordine ... Circa l'offitio & autorita delli operai. Sopra alli monasterij. Ostenuta, & passata ... Il dì 17. d'Aprile 1545. In Fiorenza Appresso i Giunti. 4°. A^4. (Lea.) [178

-- -- In Fiorenza appresso i Giunti. 1563. 4°. $[A]^4$. (Lea.) [179

-- Prouisione circa il pagare le spese fatte in vn luogo a Soldati Fanterie & genti d'arme & al Commessario quando occorre che vadino di luogo a luogo. Publicata ... sotto di 10. Ottobre. 1545. In Fiorenza appresso i Giunti. 4°. π^2. (Lea.) [180

-- Legge sopra l'osseruanza et approuatione delli statuti. Delle Comunita di fuori e del tenere i Rettori e Birri & Famigli ne loro Palazzi, & che detti famigli non si possino partire. Adi 27. di Luglio. 1546. In Firenze. Appresso i Giunti. 4°. A^4. (Lea.) [181

-- Prouisione sopra l'essentione delle gabelle annullate Publicato il dì 19. d'Ottobre 1546. In Fiorenza, Appresso Giorgio Marescotti 4°. A^4. (Lea.) [182

-- Gratie fatte ... Alli Cittadini & altri habitori della sua Città di Pisa: Publicato in quella sotto di xxiiij. di Nouembre MDXLVI. In Fiorenza Appresso i Giunti. 4°. A^4. (Lea.) [183

-- Deliberatione de ... XVI. reformatori delle esentioni, ... Sopra i Bestiami, & altre Grascie, da trarsi per i distrettualigià esenti, de' Cõtadi di Firenze, di Pisa, & d'Arezzo, & per le Grascie da mettersi per li già detti nel Contado di Firenze. Il di 20. d'Aprile, 1547. In Firenze Appresso i Giunti. 4°. A^4. (Lea.) [184

-- Bando et deliberatione ... Sopra gl'Archibusi, & Scoppi da Ruota. Publicato il di 2. di Giugno. 1547. In Fiorenza, Appresso Giorgio Marescotti. MDLXXIII. 4°. A^2. (Lea.) [185

-- Legge ... Come s'intendino rotte l'offese Pubblicata a di 2. di Agosto M DXLVII. In Fiorenza Nella Stamperia de'Giunti. 4°. A^2. (Lea.) [186

-- Bando ... Per quelli, che hauessero parlato a' Banditi. Publicato il dì 27. Settembre, 1547. In Fiorenza Appresso i Giunti 1567. 4°. π^2. (Lea.) [187

-- -- Nuouamente Ristampata. In Fiorenza. Appresso Giorgio Marescotti. MDLXXIII. 4°. A^2. (Lea.) [188

-- Legge ... fatta sotto di 15. di Ottobre 1547. Sopra le Tenute e beni in Pagamento. In Fiorenza, appresso i Giunti 1562. 4°. A^2. (Lea.) [189

-- Bando sopra i zingani, et zingane. Mandato adi 3. di Nouembre. 1547. In Fiorenza Appresso i Giunti. 4°. π^2. (Lea.) [190

-- Deliberatione fatta ... sopra le cose di Pisa. Et publicato sotto il di 20 di Dicembre 1547. In Fiorenza, Nella Stamperia de'Giunti. 4°. A-B^4 (-B4, *presumably blank*). (Lea.) [191

-- Deliberatione ... Circa il procedere ne Malefitij & degl'Affronti Publicata l'Anno MDXLVII. In Fiorenza Appresso i Giunti. 4°. π^2. (Lea.) [192

-- -- In Fiorenza, Appresso Giorgio Marescotti. 1577. 4°. A^2. (Lea.) [193

-- Deliberatione ... In beneficio delle pouere Persone. Fatta il di 8 di Febraio MDXLVIII. In Fiorenza appresso i Giunti 1561. 4°. π^2. (Lea.) [194

-- -- Nuouamente Ristampate. In Fiorenza. Appresso Giorgio Marescotti. MDLXXIII. 4°. A^4. (Lea.) [195

-- Legge ... Fatta il di xi. di Marzo. 1548. Contra a quelli che machinassino auuerso la persona, o Stato di S. E. o de Sua ... Figliuoli, o descendenti. In Fiorenza, MDXLVIII. (... appresso Bernardo Giunti.) 4°. A-D^4. (Lea.) [196

-- Deliberatione fatta ... Sopra le cose de Pisa Per conto delle mulcte, & condennationi pecuniarie, & debiti publici, & priuati. Publicata addi 26. Marzo. 1548. In Fiorenza, Appresso i Giunti. 4°. A^4. (Lea.) [197

-- Deliberatione fatta ... el di 26. di Maggio 1548 Sopra le Tenute e beni in Pagamento. ... In Fiorenza appresso i Giunti MDLXII. 4°. A^4. [198

-- Legge ... Del modo di ammettere il beneficio della Pace publicata il di 8. d'Agosto. 1548. Insieme con la legge del 1514. del modo di procedere nelle cause delle Tregue é Paci Rotte. Et delle proroghe da farsi delle instantie di detti cause. In Fiorenza Appresso i Giunti. 4°. A^4 B^2 (-B2, *presumably blank*). (Lea.) [199

-- Legge ... Del modo del congregare e sua Magistrati, Passata ... il dì xvii. di Gennaio 1549. In Fiorenza, Appresso Giorgio Marescotti. MDLXXV. 4°. A^4 B^2. [200

-- Bando sopra li archibusi a ruota, et altre armi prohibite, Mandato à di 3. di Settembre. 1549. In Fiorenza, Nella Stamperia di Giorgio Marescotti. 4°. A^2. (Lea.) [201

-- Legge fatta ... Sopra l'unione de Magistrati de'Capitani di Parte, & delli Officiali di Torre. Passata ... el di XVIII. di Settembre, MDXLIX. Nuouamente ristampata con vna aggiunta nel fine. In Fiorenza appresso i Giunti MDLX. 4°. A-E^4 F^6. (Lea.) [202

-- -- In Fiorenza, Appresso Giorgio Marescotti. MDLXXVI. 4°. A-D^4. [203

-- Deliberatione ... Sopra la Cognitione de Contratti illeciti. Fatta il dì xxi. di Febraio. MDL. Nuouamente ristampata. In Fiorenza, Nella Stamperia Ducale, Appresso Giorgio Marescotti. MDLXXIIII. 4°. A^2. (Lea.) [204

-- Deliberatione ... Sopra la Gabella delle bestie Mulini Caualline, & Asinine. Fata il di 5. di Marzo. 1550. In Fiorenza Appresso i Giunti. 4°. A^4. (Lea.) [205

-- Bando degl' archibusi a ruota grandi Publicato il dì 8. di Marzo 1550. In Fiorenza, Appresso Giorgio Marescotti. 1577. 4°. A^2. (Lea.) [206

-- Deliberatione fatta per li ... signori conseruadori. Dell'arte della Lana. Sotto di 28. di Marzo. 1550. In Fiorenza Appresso i Giunti. 4°. A^4. (Lea.) [207

-- Bando ... Sopra le Sete. Publicato ... il dì 29. di Marzo 1550. In Fiorenza, Nella Stamperia di Giorgio Marescotti. 4°. A^2. (Lea.) [208

-- Bando sopra le scommesse Mandato a di 6. di Giugno. 1550. In Fiorenza, Appresso i Giunti. 4°. π^2. (Lea.) [209

-- Legge ... Sopra le Donationi. Publicato il di cinque di Gennaio MDLI. ... In Firenze appresso i Giunti 1566. 4°. π^2. (Lea.) [210

-- -- *Another copy.* (Lea.) [211

-- -- In Fiorenza, Appresso Giorgio Marescotti. MDLXXIIII. 4°. A^2. (Lea.) [212

-- Deliberatione fatta ... Sopra l'ordine da tenersi nelle Rassegne da farsi delli descritti nelle ... militie & altro. Il di 21. Gennaio 1551. In Fiorenza Appresso i Giunti. 4° π^2. (Lea.) [213

-- Deliberatione fatta ... sopra le cose di Pisa, & publicata sotto di primo di Maggio, MDLI. In Firenze appresso i Giunti 1566. 4°. A^8. (Lea.) [214

-- Prouuisione contro a quelli Del Dominio Che piglieranno soldo de Altro Principe, Fatta il di 8. di Maggio, M D LI. In Fiorenza Nella Stamperia de'Giunti. 4°. A^2. (Lea.) [215

-- Decreto ... Sopra li pagamenti della valuta de' Fiorini, ò Ducati per conto di Liuelli, Affitti, Censi, & altre Prestationi. Pubblicato il di x. di Giugno. MDLII. In Fiorenza, Appresso Giorgio Marescotti. 4°. A^2. (Lea.) [216

-- Deliberatione ... Sopra la gabella della carne da macellarsi per vso delle Proprie famiglie. Fatta el di 25. d'Agosto. M.D.LII. In Fiorenza, Nella Stamperia di Giorgio Marescotti. 4°. a^2. (Lea.) [217

-- Legge prima ... sopra la Gabella delle farine passata ... el di. VII. d'Ottobre. M D L I I. 4°. A^8. pp. 1-15. ¶*Marginal note on* $A7^r$ *begins:* E prouisto | altrimẽti ... (Lea.) [218

-- -- *Another issue.* ¶*Note begins:* E prouisto al|trimenti ... [219

-- Prouisione che'l premio di chi ammazza banditi che non si paghi à chi non domanda in tra l'anno. A di 23. di Gennaio. 1553. In Fiorenza, Nella Stamperia di Giorgio Marescotti. 4°. A^2. (Lea.) [220

-- Legge ... in benefitio del monasterio delle Conuertite, & della Spedale dell'innocenti. Passata ... el di 19. di Settembre. 1553. In Fiorenza appresso i Giunti. 4°. A^4. (Lea.) [221

-- Bando che non si faccino Ragunate, ne si corra alle Quistioni. Publicato adi 13. di Nouembre. 1553. In Firenze Appresso i Giunti. 4°. π^2. (Lea.) [222

-- Legge seconda ... sopra la gabella della macine passata ... el di. IX. di Decembre. MDLIII. ... 4°. A^8 B^{10}. pp. 1-30. (Lea.) [223

-- Sommario delle riforme, leggi, et Ordini dell'vfizio de Cinque Conseruadori del contado, & distretto di Firenze l'anno M D LIII. In Fiorenza Nella Stamperia de'Giunti. 4°. A-B^4. (Lea.) [224

-- Legge ... Sopra la extintione & liberatione della decima, & arbitrio della sua Città & Contado di Firenze publicata ... El di 5. di Maggio 1554. In Fiorenza, Appresso i Giunti. 4°. A^4. (Lea.) [225

-- Bando per conto delle frombe, et scaglie. Publicato adi 25. di Ottobre. 1554. In Firenze. Appresso i Giunti. 4°. π^2. (Lea.) [226

-- Bando sopra i colombi Publicato adi 23. di Genaio. 1555. In Fiorenza, Nella Stamperia di Giorgio Marescotti. 4°. π^2. (Lea.) [227

-- Deliberatione sopra le monete forestiere prohibite, Publicata adi 28. di Febbraio 1555. In Fiorenza, Nella Stamperia di Giorgio Marescotti. 4°. A^2. (Lea.) [228

-- Bando delli ... signori di zecca ... Sopra la prohibitione delli Scudi, & Monete, e altro. Bandito adi 4. di Marzo 1555 ... In Fiorenza, Appresso Giorgio Marescotti. 4°. A^4. (Lea.) [229

-- Partito ... De 14. di Maggio. 1555. Sopra la Gabella della Farina. In Fiorenza, Appresso Giorgio Marescotti. MDLXXV. 4°. A^2. (Lea.) [230

-- Bando degl'archibusetti Publicato il di XXVIII. di Nouembre 1555. In Fiorenza, Appresso Giorgio Marescotti. 1577. 4°. π^2. (Lea.) [231

-- Bando sopra li scudi ducali Fiorentini, Publicato il di 23. dì Gennaio. 1556. In Fiorenza, Appresso Giorgio Marescotti. 4°. A^2. (Lea.) [232

-- MDLVI. Legge, et nuoua prouisione ... Contro li Sicarij, et qualunque per danari, ò per amicitia à requisitione d'altri offendere il prossimo, passata ... sotto di 18. di Giugno. 1556. In Fiorenza, Appresso Giorgio Marescotti. MDLXXIIII. 4°. A^4. (Lea.) [233

-- Bando sopra la valuta dello scudo Fiorentino et delli altri non prohibite. Publicato ... il di 25. di Luglio. MDLVI. In Fiorenza Appresso i Giunti. 4°. π^2. (Lea.) [234

-- Legge ... Sopra la Gabella della Carne, Passata ... sotto di 26. di Marzo MDLVII. In Fiorenza Nella stamperia d'i Giunti 4°. A-D^4 E^2. (Lea.) [235

-- -- In Firenze MDLVII. 4°. A-D^4 E^6. [236

-- Deliberatione ... Fatta Adi primo di Giugno, MDLVII. In Fauore de' Lotti publicati piu fa nella Città di Firenze. Nuouamente Ristampata. In Fiorenza, Nella Stamperia di Lor' Altezze. Appresso Giorgio Marescotti. 1572. 4°. A^4. (Lea.) [237

-- Bando et deliberatione ... Sopra le Monasterij di Monache della città di Fiorenza, & suo Ducale Dominio. Publicato addi 11. d'Ottobre. 1557. Nuouamente Ristampato. In Fiorenza Nella Stamperia de'Giunti. 1574. 4°. π^2. (Lea.) [238

-- Bando delle monete forestiere et oro di bassa legha. Nuouamente Ristampata. (Bandito ... 27. Nouembre. 1557.) In Fiorenza, Nella Stamperia Ducale, Appresso Giorgio Marescotti. MDLXXV. 4°. π^2. (Lea.) [239

-- Legge come le meretrici si cancellino dell'vfitio. Pubblicato a di 10. di Febbraio. 1558. In Fiorenza, Appresso Giorgio Marescotti. MDLXXV. 4°. A^2. [240

-- Deliberatione ... Fatta il di 21. di Marzo 1558. Sopra la quinta parte delle condennationi da pagarsi al Fisco secondo la riforma del Monte. In Fiorenza, Appresso Giorgio Marescotti. 4°. A^2. (Lea.) [241

-- Decreto contra à contumaci. Deliberato a di xvi. di Settembre, ... M D LVIII. In Fiorenza Nella stamperia de'Giunti. 4°. A^2. (Lea.) [242

-- -- In Fiorenza, Nella Stamperia di Giorgio Marescotti. 4°. A^2. (Lea.) [243

-- Legge delle meretrici del comperare da loro. Pubblicato il 1. d'Ottobre, 1558. In Fiorenza, Appresso Giorgio Marescotti. MDLXXV. 4°. A^2. (Lea.) [244

-- Legge ... Contro a quelli che vseranno forza, & violenza a femina, o maschio per desiderio carnale. Bandito a di 2. di Dicembre MDLVIII. In Fiorenza, Nella stamperia di lor' Altezze. MDLXXI. 4°. π^2. (Lea.) [245

-- Bando che non si dia impedimento A li Birri della Mercatantia Publicato il di xiii di Giugno. 1559 In Fiorenza Nella stamperia de'Giunti. 4°. π^2. (Lea.) [246

-- Bando della gabella delle bestie. Publicato sotto di 18. di Nouembre 1559. In Fiorenza Nella stamperia de'Giunti. 4°. π^2. (Lea.) [247

-- -- *Another copy*. (Lea.) [248

-- Ordine et prohibitione ... Che non si metta in nel Dominio Fiorentino Cuoiami Vaccini, & Bufolini, conci fra le cento miglia presso della Città di Fiorenza, o Pisa. 1559. In Firenze Appresso i Giunti. 4°. π^2. (Lea.) [249

-- Bando ordinato secondo la riforma fatta da' riformatori della grascia. Et mandato alla entrata de' Maestri. Nuouamente Ristampato. (Bandito ... 29. de Gennaio 1560.) In Fiorenza. Appresso Giorgio Marescotti. MDLXXIII. 4°. A^6. (Lea.) [250

-- Reformatione del gouerno della citta e stato di Siena. Fermata ... Il di primo Febraio M D LX. In Fiorenza, Appresso i Giunti. 4°. A-B^4 C^2 (-C2, *presumably blank*). (Lea.) [251

-- Ordinatione ... della iurisditione, & dominio Fiorentino, per li quattro Vicariati del contado, & Podesterie, & luoghi in quelli compresi. Adi XXIIII d'Aprile. MDLX. In Fiorenza. Appresso i Giunti. 4°. π^2. (Lea.) [252

-- Legge & Prouisione ... Sopra Il Bisogno delli Poueri Pupilli. (Datum ... XIX. Iulii. MDLX.) In Fiorenza appresso i Giunti 1562. 4°. A^4. (Lea.) [253

-- Forma, regola, et ordini, da osseruarsi da i rettori del dominio Fiorentino, & loro Vfitiali, & da i Cancellieri de' Magistrati intorno alle Cancellature de' condennati, & confinati. Cap. xxxvi. Publicato alli xxii. di Nouembre MDLX. In Fiorenza, Appresso Giorgio

Marescotti. 4°. A^2. (Lea.) [254

-- Bando ... Mandato ... dalli Mag. S. Commess. e vfficiali de fossi della citta e Contado di Pisa. Sotto di XXXI. di Gennaio MDLXI. In Fiorenza nella Stamperia de'Giunti 1574. 4°. π^4. (Lea.) [255

-- Bando sopra il giuoco della palla da maglio. Publicato adi 17. di Maggio. 1561. In Firenze Appresso i Giunti. 4°. π^2. (Lea.) [256

-- Nuoua legge sopra le habitationi Delle Meretrici, che fussero vicine ai Monasterij di Monache ... Fermata ... il di xxix. di Luglio MDLXI. In Fiorenza appresso i Giunti 1561. 4°. π^2. (Lea.) [257

-- Legge Sopra la interpretatione, et vigore de Rescritti di S. Eccl. Illust. & delle lettere, & Decreti de Sua Magistrati. Passata ... il di. XXIX. di Luglio M. D. LXI. In Firenze. 4°. π^2. (Lea.) [258

-- Deliberatione, sopra la gabella della carne. Fatta ... il di 23. di Settembre 1561. In Fiorenza, Nella Stamperia di Giorgio Marescotti. 4°. A^2. (Lea.) [259

-- Additioni, et limitationi, sopra alcuni capitoli et bandi della gabella della carne. Fatta Adi XIIII. d'Ottobre. MDLXI. Nuouamente Ristampate. In Fiorenza, Nella Stamperia Ducale. Appresso Giorgio Marescotti. M D LXXIIII. 4°. A^4 (-A4, *presumably blank*). (Lea.) [260

-- Nuoua riforma sopra delli capitoli, et bandi, Della Gabella della Farina. Et di piu Aggiuntoui alcune cose a'detti Capitoli. Fatta Adi XXIIII. d'Ottobre. MDLXI. Nuouamente Ristampata. In Fiorenza, Nella Stamperia Ducale, Appresso Giorgio Marescotti. MDLXXIIII. 4°. A^4. (Lea.) [261

-- Fiera da farsi nella citta di Pisa Due volte l'Anno con sue franchigie, & esentioni ... In Fiorenza appresso i Giunti 1561. 4°. A^4. (Lea.) [262

-- Bando contro a chi fa danno ne legnami, Publicato a dì 18. di Febraio. 1562. In Fiorenza, Nella Stamperia di Giorgio Marescotti. 4°. A^2. (Lea.) [263

-- Legge et prouisione sopra i pagamenti delle tasse De Testamenti, Codicilli, Donationi, causa mortis, & altre vltime volonti, da pagarsi all'Opera di Santa Maria del Fiore ... Publicata il Dì 10. di Marzo. 1562. In Fiorenza, Nella Stamperia de'Giunti. 4°. A^4. (Lea.) [264

-- Bando ... sopra i messi cauallari et birri. Publicato sotto il dì 4. d'Aprile 1562. ... In Firenze Appresso i Giunti. M. D. LXII. 4°. π^2. (Lea.) [265

-- Bando ... Sopra i Legati ad pias Causas. Pubblicato il dì 22. d'Aprile. MDLXII. In Fiorenza, Appresso Giorgio Marescotti. MDLXXV. 4°. A^2. (Lea.) [266

-- Bando ... Sopra la ricognitione Delle transgressioni di chi hauessi mal'amministrato le cose publiche di Capitanati, Vicariati, Potesterie, Comuni, & luoghi del ... stato della Città di Fiorenza, Publicato il di VI. di Maggio MDLXII. In Fiorenza Appresso i Giunti. 4°. π^2. (Lea.) [267

-- Bando, & Legge ... sopra l'Extrattione de Grani, Biade, & altre Grascie, del suo Ducale Stato, Publicato l'Anno. M.D.LXII. Alli. IIII. di Luglio. 4°. π^4. (Lea.) [268

-- -- Publicato l'Anno. 1563. alli di Luglio. 4°. π^4. (Lea.) [269

-- Legge Delle scommesse che si farrano à mastio, ò femina, & loro cognitione, & giudice. Fermata questo di xi. di Febraio. 1563. ... In Firenze Appresso i Giunti. 1563. 4°. A^4. (Lea.) [270

-- -- In Fiorenza, Appresso Giorgio Marescotti. MDLXXVI. 4°. A^4. (Lea.) [271

-- Dichiarationi et limitationi ... Alla Legge, & ordinatione, sopra i pagamenti delle tasse de' Testamenti. Publicate il di 7. di Giugno 1563. In Fiorenza appresso i Giunti 1568. 4°. π^2. (Lea.) [272

-- Prouisione et ordine ... Sopra alli Monasterii. In Fiorenza appresso i Giunti. 1563. 4°. π^4. (Lea.) [273

-- Bando ... Sopra la comparitione & rappresentatione de Banditi Confinati & condennati. Publicato a di 13. d'Aprile 1564. Nuouamente Ristampato. In Fiorenza, Nella Stamperia Ducale, Appresso Giorgio Marescotti. MDLXXV. 4°. π^2. (Lea.) [274

-- Confirmatione et approuatione Della legge del 1529. Circa i Ribelli. Publicato il di 7. di Maggio. M D LXIIII. Nuouamente Ristampata. In Fiorenza, Nella Stamperia Ducale, Appresso Giorgio Marescotti. MDLXXV. 4°. π^2. (Lea.) [275

-- Bando, et legge, nuouamente fatto, contro a quelli, che incettano Grani, & Biade, publicato l'Anno. 1564. Alli. 5. di Luglio. 4°. π^4. (Lea.) [276

-- Bando per la prohibitione del portare arme in hasta. Publicato il di IIII. di Settembre M. D. LXIIII. In Fiorenza, Nella stamperia di lor'Altezze. 4°. π^2. (Lea.) [277

-- Prouisione, sopra le gabelle della farina, et carne, Fatta ... il dì 17. di Nouembre. 1564. In Fiorenza, Nella Stamperia di Giorgio Marescotti. 4°. A^2. (Lea.) [278

-- Prouisione ... Sopra la materia della falsità di Testimoni Ottenuta il dì 5. di Marzo 1565. In Fiorenza, Nella Stamperia di Giorgio Marescotti. 4°. A^2. (Lea.) [279

-- Dichiarationi, et limitationi, Fatte dalli ... Riformatori dell'Opera di Santa Maria del Fiore ..., Alla Legge, & ordinatione, sopra i pagamenti delle Tasse de'Testamenti. Publicato il di 7. di Giugno. 1565. Nuouamente Ristampate. In Fiorenza, Nella Stamperia Ducale, Appresso Giorgio Marescotti. MDLXXIIII. 4°. A^2. (Lea.) [280

-- Bando et nuoua publicatione di piu ordini della grascia, Che comprendono tutto el Dominio. Nuouamente Ristampato. (Bandito ... il di. XIII. di Giugno. M.D.L.X.V.) In Fiorenza. Appresso Giorgio Marescotti. MDLXXIII. 4°. A^4. (Lea.) [281

-- Riforma delli statuti De gli Vficiali de Pupilli, fatta il di 20. di Agosto 1565. Con l'aggiunte sino al presente anno 1575. ... In Fiorenza. Appresso i Giunti. 1575. 4°. A-G^4 H^2. (Lea.) [282

-- Capitoli, ordini priuilegii della militia, et bande di S. E. illust. di nuouo ampliati. ... Il di primo di Maggio. 1566. ... In Fiorenza nella Stamperia Ducale. 1566. ... 4°. A-D^4. pp. 2-31. (Lea.) [283

-- -- Capitoli ordini, e priuilegii Fatti ... alle militie ... In Fiorenza. ... Appresso Giorgio Marescotti. MDLXXII. 4°. A-D^4. pp.2-32. [284

-- Capitoli, et Priuilegii concessi, & Stabiliti ... alla sua Militia de Caualli armati alla Leggiera. Il di primo di Maggio. 1566. In Firenze alla Stampa Ducale. MDLXVI. ... 4°. A^4 B^2. (Lea.) [285

-- Prouisione ... Sopra la vendita de macelli, in alcuni luoghi, & della tassa, de particulari della gabella della carne, de 5. denari per libra. Passata ... Sotto di. 7. di Maggio. 1566. In Firenze. Appresso i Giunti. 4°. π^2. (Lea.) [286

-- Bando sopra li stamaiuoli, Lanini, & Filatrici. Deliberato ... il dì 18. di Luglio. 1566. Nuouamente Ristampato. In Fiorenza, Appresso Giorgio Marescotti. MDLXXIIII. 4°. π^2. (Lea.) [287

-- Bando ... Sopra le Cose di Pisa. In Firenze Appresso i Giunti 1566. 4°. A^2. (Lea.) [288

-- Decreto sopra la nuoua militia d'huomini d'arme Ordinata ... 1567. Il dì 15. di Marzo. In Fiorenza, Appresso Giorgio Marescotti. 4°. A^2. (Lea.) [289

-- Bando dell'arme publicato ... Il di 7. d'Aprile, MDLXVII. Et nuouamente Ristampato. In Fiorenza, Nella Stamperia di lor'Altezze. Appresso Giorgio Marescotti. 1571. 4°. A^2. (Lea.) [290

-- Bando de pregi della paglia, et fieno. Pubblicato il di 26. di Giugno. 1567. In Fiorenza Nella stampera [*sic*] de'i Giunt. 4°. A^2. (Lea.) [291

-- Bando, & Legge da osseruarsi delli infrascritti. Ottonai, Calderai, Fabbri, Magnani, Ferraiuoli, Ferrauecchi, Stagnaiuoli, & altri sottoposti all'Arte & vniuersità de' Fabbricanti. Publicato l'Anno 1567. In Fiorenza Appresso i Giunti 1567. 4°. π^2. (Lea.) [292

-- -- In Fiorenza, Appresso Giorgio Marescotti, MDLXXIIII. 4°. π^2. (Lea.) [293

-- Bando ... Contro à quelli che tagliano legnami ne'beni d'altrui. Rinouato il dì 24. di Gennaio M D LXVIII. In Fiorenza Appresso i Giunti. M. D. LXVIII. 4°. π^2. (Lea.) [294

-- Capitoli della nuoua militia marittima. ... Il di 8. di Febraio 1568. In Fiorenza Nella stamperia de'Giunti M D LXXII. 4°. A^2. (Lea.) [295

-- Bando de' riscontri delle polize della gabella della farina, Rinouato, & di nuouo Publicato il dì 12. di Marzo MDLXVIII. Nuouamente Ristampato. In Fiorenza, Nella Stamperia Ducale, Appresso Giorgio Marescotti. MDLXXV. 4°. A^2. (Lea.) [296

-- Nuoua prouisione Sopra l'vna, & l'altra Gabella Macine, & Carne della Città di Fiorenza. Passata ... Sotto dì 6. d'Aprile. 1568. Nuouamente Ristampata. In Fiorenza, Appresso Giorgio Marescotti. MDLXXIIII. 4°. π^2. (Lea.) [297

-- Deliberatione sopra le sicurta Da pigliarsi per i Magistrati, & Rettori, da quelli, che incolpati d'alcuno demerito debbono da loro essere relassati à sodamento, Fatta a dì primo di Maggio. MDLXVIII. In Fiorenza, Nella Stamperia Ducale, Appresso Giorgio Marescotti. 4°. A^2. (Lea.) [298

-- -- In Fiorenza Nella Stamperia de'Giunti. 4°. A^2. (Lea.) [299

-- Decreto Attenente alli Rettori del Dominio che condenneranno in pena, ò bando della vita, ò di Rebelli stabilito per il supremo Magistrato. Il dì xviiii. di Maggio. M.D.LXVIII. Nuouamente Ristampato. In Fiorenza. Nella Stamperia di Lor'Altezze. Appresso Giorgio Marescotti. 1572. 4°. A^2. (Lea.) [300

-- Capitoli et priuilegii delli huomini d'arme ... (Il dì xxv. di Giugno. 1568.) In Fiorenza nella Stampa Ducale 1569. ... 4°. A^6. (Lea.) [301

-- Statuto et nuoua prouisione in fauore delle donne Che vorranno obligarsi per Contratto. Fermata il dì 30. di Luglio. MDLXVIII. Nuouamente Ristampata. In Fiorenza, Appresso Giorgio Marescotti. MDLXXVI. 4°. π^2. (Lea.) [302

-- Deliberatione ... Dell'obligo di quelli, che vorrano participare delle offese, paci, Et tregue rotte, Fatta il di 6. d'Agosto. M D LXVIII. In Fiorenza Nella stamperia de'Giunti. 4°. A^2. (Lea.) [303

-- Deliberazione in augmento della gabella Delle Bestie. Publicata questo di quattro di Dicembre 1568. In Firenze appresso i Giunti 1568. 4°. π^2. (Lea.) [304

-- Prouisione sopra il coiame da Suola concio fuor dello stato di Fiorenza & il modo da conciarsi in detto stato. ... publicata questo di. vii. di Dicembre MDLXVIII. In Fiorenza, Appresso i Giunti. 1568. 4°. π^2. (Lea.) [305

-- Decreto ... Sopra l'augmento d'vn soldo per lira, del quinto delle condennationi, secondo la legge dellotto in benefitio della Platta della Militia de i Caualli armati alla Leggiera, Fatto il di 20. di Dicembre MDLXVIII. Nuouamente Ristampato. In Fiorenza, Nella Stamperia Ducale, Appresso Giorgio Marescotti. MDLXXIIII. 4°. A^2. (Lea.) [306

-- Bando Sopra la Proibitione del comperare cose rubate. (Bandito ... questo dì 10. d'Aprile. 1569.) In Fiorenza, Appresso Giorgio Marescotti. MDLXXV. 4°. A^2. (Lea.) [307

-- Bando delle monete Fiorentine tose. Nuouamente Ristampato. (Bandito ... questo di 6. di Luglio. MDLXIX.) In Fiorenza, Nella Stamperia Ducale, Appresso Giorgio Marescotti. MDLXXIIII. 4°. π^2. (Lea.) [308

-- Bando generale sopra l'estrattione de grani, biade farine, et castagne, & altre Grascie, Rinouato questo dì .27. d'Agosto. 1569. In Fiorenza. Appresso i Giunti. 4°. π^2. (Lea.) [309

-- Bando ... Che nō si possa tenere Otri da Olio pieni, ne voti come in detto bando si cōtiene publicato sotto di d'Agosto 1569. In Fiorenza. Appresso i Giunti. 4°. π^2. (Lea.) [310

-- Bando ... Sopra l'ordine, & modo da tenersi del macellare Vacche, Publicato ... il dì 10. di Settembre. 1569. In Fiorenza. Appresso Giorgio Marescotti. MDLXXV. 4°. A^2. (Lea.) [311

-- Bando dell'additione et augmento della pena alla prohibita et generale Estratione de' Grani, & Grascie. Fermato questo di primo di Febbraio. 1570. In Fiorenza Nella Stampa di loro Altezze. ... M. D. L. XX. 4°. A^2. (Lea.) [312

-- *Undated laws*. Statuto dell'arte di Por San Piero circa l'entrature. In Fiorenza Nella Stamperia de'Giunti. 4°. π^4. (Lea.) [313

-- Il bando delle cose et compositioni appartenente all'arte delli speciali. [Firenze, post 1547.] s.sh. 48 × 24.5 cm. (Smith.) [314

-- Bando ... Sopra la Bestemmia. Nuouamente Ristampato. In Fiorenza. Appresso Giorgio Marescotti. MDLXXIII. 4°. A^4. (Lea.) [315

-- *Ordine de Cavalieri di Santo Stefano.* ... Dichiarationi, Statuti, Reformationi, & Additioni del Capitolo Generale dell' anno 1571. Fatte ... Il di xiij. di Settembre 1571. In Fiorenza Appresso Filippo Giunti, e Fratelli, l'anno 1571. ... 4°. A-B^4. (Lea.) [316

-- Statuti capitoli et constitutioni del Ordine de Caualieri di Santo Stephano ... In Fiorenza, Appresso Lorenzo Torrentino ... M D LXII. (*Colophon.*) fol. a^4 A-L^4 Aa^6. pp. 1-86. [317

-- Statuti, e constitutioni ... In Firenze Nella Stamperia di Filippo Giunti, e Fratelli, 1571. (*Colophon.*) 4°. $*^8$ A-M^8. pp. 1-189. (Lea.) [318

-- -- Statuti, capitoli, et constitutioni ... In Fiorenza, Nella Stamperia di Filippo Giunti. M D XCV. (*Colophon.*) 4°. $*^8$ A-M^8 N^{8+1}. pp. 4-200. [319

-- *Council.* Statuta Concilij Florentini. (impresse in ... Vrbe Florentiæ ... Per Hæredes Philippi Iuntæ. ... M.D.xviij. Die uero. XXIII. Maij.) 4°. A^4 a-h^8 i^4. ff. 2-68. (Lea.) [320

-- -- Florentiæ Apud Bartholomæum Sermartellium MDLXIIII. (*Colophon.*) 4°. a^4 b^8 A-H^8. pp. 1-126. (Lea.) [321

-- *Diocese.* Dioecesana synodus Florentiæ celebrato tertio Nin. Maias MDLXIX. ... Florentiæ, Apud Bartholomæum Sermartellium. MDLXIX. 4°. A-G^4 H^2. pp. 1-45. (Lea.) [322

-- Decreta prouincialis synodi Florentinae, Præsidente in ea ... D. Antonio Altouita Archiepiscopo. ... Florentiae, Apud Bartholomæum Sermartellium. MDLXXIIII. (*Colophon.*) 4°. *-$**^4$ A-R^4 S^2. pp. 1-139. (Lea.) [323

-- *History.* Le dieci mascharate delle bufole Mandate In Firenze il giorno di Carnouale L' anno 1565. ... In Fiorenza appresso i Giunti. MDLXVI. 8°. A-C^8 (-A5-8) D^4. pp. 2-56. [324

FLORES, JUAN DE. L'histoire d'Aurelio & Isabelle ... mise en Español & François. ... En Anuers Chez Iehan VVithaye ... M.D.LVI. 12°. A-H^{12}. [325

-- -- Amorosa historia de Isabella et Aurelio, da M. Lelio Aletiphilo di lingua Castigliana in Italico idioma tradotta. MDXXIX. (Stampata in Vinegia per Melchiore Sessa. ... Dil mese di Settembre.) 8°. A-I^4 (-C1, C4). [326

-- -- In Vinegia appresso Gabriel Giolito de Ferrari MDXLVIII. (*Colophon.*) 8°. A-E^8. ff. 3-40. [327

FLORIMONTE, GALEAZZO. Ragionamenti di M. Agostino da Sessa ... sopra l'etica d'Arist. Raccolti dal Reuer. ... Galazzo Florimontio ... In Parma appresso Seth Viotti. M D L II. 8°. a^8 A-N^8 O^4. ff. 1-107. [328

-- -- Ragionamenti di Mons. Galeazzo Florimonte ... In Venetia, Appresso Domenico Nicolini. M D LXVII. (*Colophon.*) 4°. $*^4$ A-Xx^4 Yy^2. ff. 1-177. [329

FLORIO, JOHN. Florio His firste Fruites: which yeelde familiar speech, merie Prouerbes, wittie Sentences, and golden sayings. ... Imprinted ... by Thomas Dawson, for Thomas Woodcocke. (Di Londra á di. 10. Agosto. 1578. ...) 4°. *-$3*^4$ A-Y^4 Aa-Tt^4 (-Tt4, *presumably blank*). *S.T.C.* 11096. ¶A2-A4 *bound in reverse order.* (Furness.) [330

-- Florios second frutes ... To which is annexed his Gardine Of Recreation yeelding six thousand Italian Prouerbs. London Printed for Thomas Woodcock ... 1591. (Finito di stampare ... l'vltimo di Aprile. 1591.) 4°. A^4 $*^2$ B-$2D^4$ A-Aa^4 (-Aa4, *presumably blank*). pp. 2-217. *S.T.C.* 11097. ¶*Additional t.p.* (^{2}A1): Giardino di ricreatione ... sei mila Prouerbij, e piaceuoli riboboli Italiani ... In Londra. Appresso Thomaso Woodcock. CIↃ IↃ XCI. (Furness.) [331

-- A worlde of Wordes, Or Most copious, and exact Dictionarie in Italian and English ... Printed at London, by Arnold Hatfield for Edw. Blount. 1598 (*Colophon.*) fol. a^6 b^4 A-Pp^6 Qq^4 (-a1, Qq4, *presumably blank*). pp. 1-462. *S.T.C.* 11098. (Furness.) [332

FLORUS, LUCIUS ANNAEUS. Lucii Flori libri historiarum quatuor a Cuspiniano castigati ... (Impressum Vienne p Ioānem Winter. 1511. 12. kalen. Augus.) 4°. π^{6} a-g^{4} H-I^{4} k-l^{4} m^{6}. [333

-- -- Compendio de las catorze decadas de Tito Liuio Paduano, ... escrito en Latin por Lucio Floro, y al presente traduzido en lengua Castellana. En Argentina en casa de Augustin Frisio, Año de M. D. L. (*Colophon.*) 8°. A-V^{8} X^{6}. ff. II-CLXVI. [334

FOGLIETTA, UBERTO. Vberti Folietae clarorum Ligurum elogia. ... Romae, Apud heredes Antonii Bladii ... M.D.LXXIII. 4°. A-Ii^{4} KK^{4} Ll^{6}. pp. 1-265. [335

-- Vberti Folietae de . lingua . Latinae vsu . et . praestantia libri . tres ... (Romae, Apud Iosephum de Angelis, M D LXXIIII.) 4°. A-Cc^{4} (-Cc4, *presumably blank*). pp. 3-205. ¶A1, A2 *defective.* [336

-- Vberto Foglietta, delle cose della republica di Genoua ... In Milano, Per Gio. Antonio de gli Antonij. M D LXXV. 8°. †^{6} A-L^{8} M^{2}. pp. 1-180. (Lea.) [337

-- Vberti Folietae ... Historiæ Genuensium Libri XII. ... Genuæ, Apud Hieronymum Bartolum, MDLXXXV. ... fol. †^{6} A^{8} A-Oo^{8} Pp^{10} Qq^{6} Rr^{2}. ff. 1-314. (Lea.) [338

FOLCO, GIULIO. Effetti mirabili de la limosina et sentenze degne di memoria, appertenenti ad essa. ... In Roma, Appresso Francesco Zanetti. 1586. 8°. a-b^{8} c^{4} A-N^{8} O^{4}. pp. 1-216. (Lea.) [339

FOLENGO, TEOFILO. Chaos del tri per vno ... (Stampata in Vinegia per Giouanni Antonio, & Fratelli da Sabbio. Ad instantia de Nicolo Garanta, adi. Primo Zener. M.D.XXVII.) 8°. a^{4} B^{4} c-z^{4} &^{4} A-G^{4}. [340

-- La humanita del figliuoli di Dio In ottaua rima ... (In Venegia nella Officina di Aurelio Pincio Venetiano. A'di .xiiii. di Agosto. M D XXXIII) 4°. ✠^{4} a-z^{8} &^{8}. ff. I-CXCI. [341

-- Macaronicorum poema. ... Venetiis, Apud Petrus Boselli. M D LV. (*Colophon.*) 12°. A-Y^{12} Z^{6}. ff. 4-266. [342

-- Opus Marlini Cocaii poetae Mantuani Macaronicorum. ... Venetijs, Apud Iacobum Simbenium. 1572. (... Apud Horatium de Gobbis. M. D. LXXX.) 12°. A-Z^{12} (-Z12, *blank*). pp. 2-540. [343

-- -- Venetiis, Apud Horatium de Gobbis. 1581. (... M. D. LXXX.) 12°. A-Z^{12}. pp. 2-541. ¶*From sig. E to the end, except for the page number on* Z7^{r}, *apparently identical with the preceding.* [344

FOLLERIO, PIETRO. Dom. Petri Follerii ... canonica Criminalis Praxis ... Marcellina nuncupata. ... Ex Officina Marci de Maria Salernitani, Bibliopolæ Neapolitani. Venetiis, M D LXI. 4°. a-e^{4} A-Z^{4} a-t^{4}. pp. 1-334. (Lea.) [345

-- -- *Another copy.* (Lea.) [346

-- -- Venetiis, Apud hæredes Bartholomæi Rubini. M D LXXXIII. 4°. a-d^{4} A-S^{8}. pp. 2-286. (Lea.) [347

-- ... Petri Follerii de S. Seuerino ... praxis censualis super pragma. de censibus, ... cum Summarijs, & Repertorio, factis per ... Franciscum Antonium Monacum de Vasto Aymonis ... Venetiis, Impensis Marci de Maria, Salernitani, Bibliopolæ Neapolitani. M. D. LIX. 4°. a-b^{4} c^{6} A-Ll^{4}. pp. 2-271. (Lea.) [348

FONSECA, JUAN. Oratio habita ad patres ... Concilii Tridentini ... feria VI. in Parasceue Anno Milesimo D LXII. Patauii, Apud Gratiosum Perchacinum. M D LXII. 4°. A-B^{4}. (Lea.) [349

FONTAINE, JACQUES. De bello Rhodio, libri tres, ... Iacobo Fontano Brugensi autore. Haganoæ apud Ioannem Secerium Anno M. D. XXVII. Mense Augusto. (*Colophon.*) 4°. A-O^{4}. [350

FONTANA, BARTOLOMMEO. Itinerario ouero viaggio da Venetia a Roma ... In Vinegia Appresso di Agostino Bindoni. M. D. L. (*Colophon.*) 8°. A-I^{4}. ff. 1-35. [351

FONTANA, PUBLIO. M. Publii Fontanæ formica, Siue de diuina Prouidentia ... (Bergomi, Typis Comini Venturæ. 1594. ...) 4°. a^4 $A-C^4$. pp. 1-23. ¶*Engraved t.p.* [352

FORCADEL, ÉTIENNE. Henrico III. Francorum et Poloniæ regi, relata gratia, Stephano Forcatulo ... autore. ... Parisiis, Apud Guillielmum Chaudiere ... 1579. ... (Acheué d'imprimer pour la premiere impression le 22. Nouembre. 1578.) 8°. $+^4$ $A-N^8$ O^2. ff. 1-101. [353

-- Prometheus siue, de raptu animorum. ... Parisiis, Apud Guillielmum Chaudiere ... 1578. ... (Acheué d'imprimer pour la premiere impression le 24. Iuillet ...) 8°. $A-C^8$ D^2. ff. 1-23. [354

FOREIRO, FRANCISCO. F. Francisci Forerii Olyssiponen. ... sermo; quam habuit ad Patres, Dominica prima Aduen. Anno MDLXIII. Brixiae, Ad instantiam Ioannis Baptistæ Bozolæ, M D LXIIII. (... Apud Ludouicum Sabiensem: ...) 4°. $A-B^4$ (-B4, *presumably blank*). (Lea.) [355

FORESTI, JACOPO FILIPPO. Supplemento delle croniche del ... Frate Iacopo Philippo da Bergamo ... In Venetia. MDXL. (Stāpate ... per Bernardino Bindoni Milanese ... adi .29. di Maggio.) fol. $*^8$ $**^6$ $A-3B^8$ $3C^6$. ff. I-CCCXL. [356

-- Supplementum Supplementi Chronicarum ab ipso Mundi Exordio vsqȝ ad ... Annum. M.ccccc.x. editum. ... a ... Patre Iacobo Phillippo Bergomate ... (Venetiis impressuȝ Opere & īpensa Georgii de Rusconibus ... M.D.XIII. Die. xx. Augusti.) fol. Aa^{10} $a-z^8$ $\&^8$ $ɔ^8$ $ꝶ^8$ $A-Q^8$ (-Q8, *presumably blank*). ff. 2-335. (Lea.) [357

FORLI. Leggi della communita di Forli. In Bologna, Per Alessandro Benacci. M. D. LXXVII. ... fol. $+^2$ $A-Q^2$. pp. 1-63. (Lea.) [358

-- Ordini, leggi, concessioni, e priuilegii del magistrato de i nouanta pacifici di Forli. In Cesena Appresso Bartolomeo Rauerij. MDLXXXIX. fol. $A-R^4$ S^8 (-S8, *presumably blank*). pp. 1-151. (Lea.) [359

FORMULAR. Formular Berichtlichen Process/ vnd Teutscher Rhetoric/ Nach ietzigem Cantzleijschen Gebrauch ... Getruckt zu Franckenfurd/ am Meyn/ Bei Christian Egenolffen. (... im Herbstmonat. D.M.XXXV.) 4°. $A-S^4$ T^6. ff. I-LXXVII. [360

FORMULARIUM. Formularium diuersorum contractuum ... (Impressum Venetiis per ... Lucam Antoniū de Zontis: ciuem Florentinum. M.ccccc.xxiii. kalendas Augusti ...) 4°. π^4 $A-P^8$. ff. i-CXX. [361

-- Formularium instrumentorum et variorum processuum ... Romae, Apud Bibliopolas socios, ... M. D. LXXXIX. (... Apud Iacobum Ruffinellum ...) 4°. a^6 b^8 $A-Dd^8$ Ee^2. pp. 1-433. (Lea.) [362

FORNARI, SIMONE. La spositione ... sopra l'Orlando furioso di M. Ludouico Ariosto. In Fiorenza Appresso Lorenzo Torrentino 1549 ... (... del mese di Giugno l'anno M D L.) 8°. $A-3D^8$. pp. 3-795. [363

FORNER, FRIEDRICH. Vom Ablass vnd Iubeljar Orthodoxischer vnd Summarischer Bericht: ... Getruckt zu Ingolstatt in der Ederischen Truckerey/ durch Andream Angermayer. M. D. XCIX. 4°. $A-Ll^4$ Mm^2 (-M2, *presumably blank*). pp. 1-256. (Lea.) [364

FORTESCUE, SIR JOHN. A learned Commendation of the politique Lawes of England ... Written in Latine by ... master Fortescue Knight ... And translated into English by Robert Mulcaster. London, Printed by Thomas Wight, and Bonham Norton. 1599. ... 8°. $A-R^8$. ff. 3-132. *S.T.C.* 11196. (Biddle.) [365

FORTI, GIOVANNI BERNARDO. Vocabulista Ecclesiastico Latino e Vulgare ... (Venetijs per Alexandrum de Bindonis. 1518.) 8°. B.L. $a-g^8$. [366

FORTUNIO, GIOVANNI FRANCESCO. Recole grammaticali della volgar lingua. ([Milano,] Ex Officina Minutiana .M.D.XVII. Pridie Sancti. Lucæ.) 8°. $A-G^8$. ff. I-L. [367

-- -- Regole grammaticali ... M.D.XXXIII. (Stampata in Vinegia p Francesco Bindoni, & Mapheo Pasini compagni. ...) 8°. A-F^8 G^4. ff. 2-52. [368

-- -- M D LII. (In Vinegia ... nelle case de' figliuoli di Aldo.) 8°. A-F^8 G^4. ff. 2-51. [369

FOSCHERARI, EGIDIO. Donatio Constantini magni imp. erga Ro. sedem, iuris ciuilis auctoritate comprobata, ac sacræ Scripturæ testimonio roborata ... Per Tiresiam Foscararium Bononien. ... (Impressum vero per Bartholomeum Bonardum Parmensem ... M. D. XLIX. Bononiæ.) 4°. A-R^4 (-R4, *presumably blank*). ff. II-LXVII. [370

FOSSANO. Fossani Subalpinorum vrbis, iura muncipalia ... Augustæ Taurinorum, Apud Antonium Blanchum. 1599. fol. π^4 (-π4) A^4 A-Dd^4. pp. 2-215. [371

FOSSO, GASPAR À. Oratio ad ... Concilium Tridentinum, qua de ecclesiae auctoritate, et imitandis apostolis disseritur, ... die XVIII. Ianuarij. Anni. M. D. LXII. ... Brixiae, Ad instantiam Ioan. Baptistæ Bozolæ. Anno M. D. LXIII. (... Apud Damianum Turlinum. ...) 4°. A^4 B^2. (Lea.) [372

FOUQUELIN, ANTOINE. Antonij Foquelini Veromandui, in Auli Persii Flacci satyras commentarius ... Parisiis, Apud Andream Wechelum ... 1555. ... 4°. *^{4} A-AA^4 BB^2. pp. 1-186. [373

FOX MORCILLO, SEBASTIÁN. Sebastiani Foxii Morzilli Hispalensis de naturæ Philosophia, seu de Platonis & Aristotelis consensione, Libri V. ... M. D. LXXXIX. (VVitebergae typis et impensis Simonis Gronenbergij ...) 8°. a^8 A-Z^8 a-r^8. pp. 1-652. [374

-- Ethices philosophiae compendium, ex Platone, Aristotele, alijsq3 ... auctoribus ... Heidelbergae. (... excudebat Ludouicus Lucius ... M.D.LXI. Mense Septembri.) 8°. A-T^8 V^4. pp. 1-296. [375

FOXE, JOHN. Rerum in ecclesia gestarum ... Commentarij. Pars prima. ... Autore Ioanne Foxo Anglo. Basileae, per Nicolaum Brylingerum, et Ioannem Oporinum. (... M.D.LIX. mense Augusto.) fol. A^4 a-z^4 A-Z^4 aa-qq^4 rr^8 ss-zz^4 Aa-Ff^4 Gg^6 Hh-Ii^4 Kk^6 Ll-Yy^4 (-Yy4, *presumably blank*). pp. 1-732. [376

-- [1] The first Volume of the Ecclesiasticall History, contayning the Actes & Monumentes of thinges passed in euery Kinges time, in this Realme, especially in the Churche of England ... Newly recognised and inlarged by the Author. ... 1576. At London Printed by Iohn Daye ... (*Colophon.*) fol. B.L. *^{4} ¶^{4} ✠^{4} χ^1 A-Y^6 Aa-Yy^6 AA-TT^6 VV-XX^4. pp. 1-771. [2] The second Volume of the Ecclesiasticall History ... *Same imprint.* π^1 B^6 BBb-YYy^6 AAA-RRR^6 SSS-TTT^4 AAAa-YYYy^6 AAAA-YYYY^6 AAAAa-TTTTt^6 VVVVv-YYYYy^4 (-YYYYy2-4). *S.T.C.* 11224. ¶*Lacks all the folding plates, but one of these and portions of 4 others are bound in before* *1. [377

-- -- An abridgement of the booke of acts and monumentes of the church: ... abridged by Timothe Bright ... Imprinted at London by I. Windet, at the assignment of Master Tim. Bright ... 1589. ... (*Colophon.*) 8°. B.L. ¶^{8} (-¶1, *blank*) A-Hh^8 Ii^4 AA-SS^8 TT^4 VV-YY^8 ZZ^4. pp. 1-504, 2-288. *S.T.C.* 11229. (Biddle.) [378

FRACASTORO, GIROLAMO. Hieronymi Fracastorii Veronensis Opera omnia ... Accesserunt Andreae Naugerii ... Orationes duae carminaq. nonnulla ... Venetiis, apud Iuntas, M.D.LV. (*Colophon.*) 4°. ✠^{6} A-3Z^4 3&^{6} a-h^4. ff. 1-285, 2-32. [379

FRACCHI, AMBROGIO NOVIDIO. Ambrosii Nouidii Fracci Ferentinatis Sacrorum Fastorum Libri XII. ... (Excussum Romæ, apud M. Antonium Bladum Asulanum ... XV. Caleñ. Iunij. M. D. XLVII.) 4°. *-3*^{4} A-SS^4 TT^6. ff. 1-169. [380

FRACHETTA, GIROLAMO. Breue spositione di tutta l'opera di Lucretio. ... In Venetia M D LXXXIX. Appresso Pietro Paganini. (... M D LXXXVIII.) 4°. a^4 †+-4†^{4} A-Kk^4. pp. 2-261. [381

-- La spositione ... sopra la canzone di Guido Caualcanti. Donna mi prega &c. ... In Venetia appresso i Gioliti. MDLXXXV. 4°. *^{4} A-O^4. pp. 1-96. [382

FRANCE. *Official documents*. Extraict de toutes les ordonnances Royaulx, desquelles on se peult ayder ... reduictes a Tiltres ... On les vend a Poictiers [chez Jean & Enguilbert de Marnef] ... 1547 8°. A-C^8 D^6. ff. II-XXVIII. ¶D1 *misbound after* D5. [383

-- *Louis XI, king*. Littere clare memo. Ludouici .xi. Francoꝝ Regis ... super abrogatione Pragmatice sanctionis in quarta Sessione ... Lateraneñ. Concilii publice lecte ꝛ recitate. [Romae, Marcellus Silber, c. 1512.] 4°. π^4. (Lea.) [384

-- *François I, king*. Les ordõnances Royaulx faictes par le roy ... Francoys premier ... Touchãt le fait ꝫ admĩistratiõ de ces fiñaces ... Nouuellemẽt imprimees a Paris le vingtiesme iour de Iuĩg. lan mil cinq cens .xxiiii. 16°. a^4. ¶*Probably incomplete*. [385

-- Abclag beder Kõnigen von Franckreych vnd Engelandt/ Auch Rõmischer Kay. May. ... antwort zu Burgos. 22. vnd. 27. Ianuarij/ gehandelt/ Im. 1528. Jar. ... 4°. A-C^4 D^6 (-D6, *presumably blank*). [386

-- Exemplaria literarum quibus & ... Galliarum Rex Frãciscus, ab aduersariorum maledictis defenditur: & controuersiarũ causæ, ex quibus bella hodie inter ipsum & Carolum quintũ Imperatorem emerserunt, explicãtur ... Parisiis. Ex officina Rob. Stephani. M.D.XXXVII. ... (... Postridie Non. August.) 4°. a-z^4 A-C^4 D^6 (D4 + *folded leaf*). pp. 3-215. [387

-- -- *Same imprint*. (... Calend. Septemb.) 4°. a-n^8 o^4. pp. 3-213. [388

-- Copyen etlicher schrifften die der Künig zů Franckrych/ an die Curfürsten vnd andere Fürsten vnnd stãnde des hailigen Rychs/ gesant hat. ... In deütsche sprach vff das trewlichst verdolmetscht. ... Getruckt zů Lyon. 1537. (Gedruckt ... by Claudy Robert im September. ...) 4°. a-m^4 n^2. [389

-- Ordonnances du treschrestien Roy de frãce Francoys premier ... reduictes par tiltres & articles ... M. D. XL. (... imprimees en Auignon par Iehan de channey Lan ... Mil cinq cens. xxxvj. au moys Daoust.) fol. A-T^6. ff. ij-cv. [390

-- Ordonnãces Royaulx sur le faict de la Iustice & abbreuiation des proces par tout le Royaulme de France ... publiees en la court de Parlement a Paris, le sixiesme iour du moys de Septembre Lan Mil.D.XXXIX. ... A Lyon ches Thibault Payen ... 4°. A-G^4. [391

-- Ordonnances sur le faict des monnoyes, estat et reigle des officiers d'icelles. Auec le pourtraict de toutes les especes de mõnoye que le Roy ueult ... auoir cours en son royaulme. ... On les vend a Paris en l'hostel de Estienne Roffet ... 16°. A-F^8. ¶*Date of proclamation 28 April 1541*. [392

-- *Henri II, king*. Edict du Roy ... sur le faict des magazins à sel, ... publie a la chambre des Comptes: le vingt deuxiesme iour de Ianuier, mil cinq cens cinquante & vng. Imprime a Paris pour Felix Guibert ... 8°. A-B^4. [393

-- Auff der Keyserischen schmeheschrifft/ Des Christlichen Kõnigs aus Franckreich/ Antwort vnd verteidigung. [c. 1551.] 4°. A-C^4. ¶*Lacks 2 ll. at the end*. [394

-- Libertas Sendschrifften der Kõniglichen Maiestat zu Franckreich/ etc. ... darinn sie sich jrer yetzigen Kriegsrüstung halben vffs kürtzest ercleret. ... Anno 1552. 4°. A-B^4. [395

-- Epistola Regis Christianissimi ad ... sacri Imperii ordines. Parisiis, Apud Carolum Stephanũ ... M. D. LIII. ... 4°. A-B^4. [396

-- Ordonnance, & Reiglement touchant l'art & manufacture des draps d'or, d'argent & de soye qui se feront a la ville de Lyon ... ottroyez par le Roy Henry second ... A Lyon, Par Iean Pullon, dit de Trin. 8°. A-C^4. ¶*Registered 4 December 1554*. [397

-- Edict du Roy sur la creation des changeurs en tiltre d'offices ... A Paris. Par Iean Dallier ... 1556. 8°. A-B^4. [398

-- Edict du roy sur l'exemption des droictz de la traicte foraine ... pour vn an ... A Paris Pour Vincent Sertenas ... Et pour Iean Dallier ... M.D.LIX. ... 8°. A-B^4. [399

-- *François II, king*. Edict du roy, sur la reuocation et reunion de son dommaine ... A Paris Pour Vincent Sertenas ... Et pour Iean Dallier ... M.D.LIX. ... 8°. A-B^4. [400

-- Ordonnance du roy, sur le faict des traictes de Bledz & Vins ... A Paris Par Vincent Sertenas ... Et Iean Bõfons ... M. D. LIX. ... 8°. A-B^4. [401

-- Edict du roy, contre tous Billonneurs de monnoyes Royalles ... A Paris Pour Iehan Dallier ... M. D. LIX. ... 8°. A-B^{4}. [402

-- De F. II. Lettres patentes et mandement du roy sur le reiglement du Bail à ferme du Sel ... A Paris Par Guillaume Nyuerd ... 8°. A-B^{4}. ¶*Proclaimed 19 December 1559.* [403

-- De F. II. Lettres patentes et mandement du roy sur le reiglement du Bail à ferme des Espiceries & drogueries ... A Paris Par Guillaume Nyuerd ... 8°. A-B^{4}. ¶*Privilege dated 22 December 1559.* [404

-- Edict du roy prohibitif a tous ... officiers Royaux, de prendre n'exiger du peuple deniers n'autres presens ... A Paris Pour Iean Dallier ... Et pour Vincent Sertenas ... M.D.LX. ... 8°. A^{4}. [405

-- *Charles IX, king.* Literae Caroli ... regis exhibitae ab ... Carolo Cardinale de Lothoringia in generali congregatione Die xxiii. nouembris. MDLXII. Oratio ... Cardinalis Lothoringia responsum ... Synodi ad orationem Cardinalis Oratio habita a ... D. Raynaldo Ferrerio Oratori Regis Francorum. Ripae. M D LXII. 4°. A-B^{4} C^{2}. (Lea.) [406

-- Petitiones Caroli noni ... nomine factæ, ab ... oratoribus in Concilio Tridentino. Ripae M D LXIII. 4°. A^{4} (-A4, *presumably blank*). (Lea.) [407

-- Exempla literarum Caroli ... Gallorum regis ad ... Synodum Tridentinam, vnà cum oratione habita à D. Raynaldo Ferrerio eiusdem Regis Oratore, Et Concilij responsione. In congregatione generali Die XI. Februarii. M. D. LXIII. Brixiea [*sic*] ad instantiam Io: Baptistæ Bozolæ. M. D. LXIII. (... apud Ludouicum Sabiensem. ...) 4°. A^{4}. (Lea.) [408

-- Ordonnance du roy et Monseigneur de Barague, Lieutenant generale pour sa Magesté, à Lyon, portant commandement expres, a tous vagabons, de vuyder la ville ... A Lyon, Par Benoist Rigaud. 1565. ... 8°. A^{4}. [409

-- Priuileges de messieurs les consulz de la Ville de Marseille, donnez & Confirmés par le Roy ... A Lyon, Par Benoist Rigaud. 1567 ... 8°. A-C^{4}. [410

-- Les Edict, Declaration, lettres patentes de commission et mandement du Roy, Contenans le pouuoir donné ... aux Huissiers, & Sergens ... de pouuoir executer toutes Lettres patentes, Arrests ... A Paris, Pour Anthoine Houic ... [1568.] 8°. A-B^{4}. ff. 2-8. [411

-- [1] Ordonnance du Roy, pour le reiglement general de ses monnoies. ... A Paris, Par Iean Dallier ... 1572. ... 8°. A-I^{4}. ff. 3-16. [2] Ensuiuent les pourtraits Et Figures Des Pieces qui se treuuent en ce Royaume & sont descriées par la presente ordonnance ... *Same imprint.* A-G^{4} H^{2}. [3] Lettres patẽtes & Declaration du Roy sur la prolongation du cours & mise de l'Escu Sol à cinquante quatre solz ... *Same imprint.* A-B^{4}. [412

-- *Henri III, king.* Ordonnance du Roy Henry III. sur le reglement des Orfeures ... A Paris, Par Iean Dallier ... 1575. 8°. A-B^{4}. pp. 4-16. [413

-- Edict Der Koͤniglichen Wuͤrden in Franckreich/ vber den Frieden/ so von wegen der entpoͤrungen/ welche ... entstanden/ gemacht worden. ... 1576. 4°. A-F^{4}. pp. 1-43. [414

-- Oratio Henrici III. ... Ad tres Gallici populi præcipuos ordines, 1576. octauo Idus Decembr. Parisiis, Ex Officina Federici Morelli ... 1577. ... 8°. A-C^{4}. pp. 3-24. [415

-- Declaration du Roy, sur l'edict faict par sa Majesté ... pour le Reglement general des Monnoyes. A Paris, Pour la Veufue Iehan Dalier, & Nicolas Roffet ... 1578. ... 8°. A-B^{4}. [416

-- Lettres patentes du roy a sa Court des Monnoyes, pour verifier ... les Edicts faicts à Chenonceau sur le restablissement des ... Officiers desdictes Monnoyes. ... A Paris, Par Federic Morel ... 1578. ... 8°. A-B^{4}. pp. 3-15. [417

-- Edict du Roy, de la reduction des offices de Iudicature ... A Paris, Par Federic Morel ... 1582. ... 8°. A-C^{4}. pp. 3-21. [418

-- Articles et propositions, lesquelles le roy a voulu estre deliberees ... en l'assemblee pour ce faicte à S. Germain en Laye, au mois de Nouembre, mil cinq cens quatre vingt & trois. ... M. D. LXXXIIII. 8°. A-X^{4}. pp. 3-168. [419

-- Erklaͤrung Koͤniglicher Maiestat in Franckreich/ der jetzt im Koͤnigreich endtstandenen Empoͤrung wegen. M.D.LXXXV. 4°. A-B^{4} C^{2}. [420

-- Koͤnigliche Declaration Erzehlung etlicher vrsachen/ Warumb Heinricus der dritte ... Koͤnig in Franckreich/ Hertzog Heinrichen von Guise/ zu Bloiss den 23. verflossenen Decembris vmbbringen lassen. Beneben einem Kupfferstuͤck/ darinnen der gantze Actus klaͤrlich abgemalet ist. ... Erstlich Getruckt durch Iohan Walldorff. M. D. LXXXIX. 4°. A-B^4 (B4 + *folded engraving*). [421

-- *Henri IV, king.* Declaration oder Erklaͤrung Koͤn. May. zu Franckreich vnd Nauaren. Auss was Vrsachen jhr Koͤn. Mayt. die General Versam̃lung ... auff den 15. May zukuͤnfftig prorogiert vnd verschoben hat. ... Getruckt zu Strassburg/ bei Bernhart Iobin. Anno M. D. LXXXX. 4°. A-B^4. [422

-- Glaubens Bekentnus Heinrich des 4. ... Koͤnigs in Franckreich vnd Nauarr/ etc. ... Erstlich auss der Frantzoͤsischen Sprach in Latein/ Nu mehr aber in Deutsch gebracht ... 1593. ... 4°. A-B^4. [423

-- Edict du Roy sur la reunion de ... le duc de Guyse, de Messeigneurs ses freres, de la Ville de Rheims, & autres villes & Chasteaux en l'obejssance de sa Majesté. A Rouen. Par Pierre Courant ... M. D. LXXXXV. ... 8°. A-C^4. pp. 3-23. [424

-- Articles accordez par le roy, pour la trefue generale du Royaume. A Lyon, par Thibaud Ancelin et Guichard Iullieron ... M. D. XCV. ... 8°. A-B^4. pp. 3-16. [425

-- Edict du roy, contenant le doublement du droict des petits Sceaux de toutes les Iustices Royalles ... A Paris, Chez Federic Morel, Iamet Mettayer, & Pierre l'Huillier ... M. D. XCV. 8°. A-B^4. pp. 3-14. [426

-- Edict du roy portant creation d'aucuns Offices de Thresoriers, Contreroolleurs generaux, Receueurs & Contreroolleurs particuliers ... A Paris. Par Federic Morel ... M.D.XCVII. ... 8°. A^4. pp. 3-8. [427

-- Edict du Roy, & Declaration sur les precedents Edicts de Pacification. Publié à Paris en Parlement, le xxve. de Februrier, M.D.XCIX. A Paris, Par les Imprimeurs & Libraires ordinaires du Roy. M. D. XCIX. ... 8°. A-O^4. ff. 2-52, pp. 53-57. [428

-- *Chancellerie.* Le grand Stille ⁊ prothocolle de la Chancellerie de France. ... On les vend ... par Arnoul langellier. (Imprime a Paris par Estienne caueiller le .xviii. iour de Ianuier Mil cinq cens .xxxix.) 8°. B.L. ã^8 a-y^8 A-I^8. ff. i-ccxlvii. [429

-- Il thresor du nouueau stille et prothocolle de la Chancellerie de France. ... A Paris. Chez Abel l'Angelier ... CIↃ. IↃ. XCIX. ... 8°. *^{4} **^{8} A-D^8 a-3h^8 3i^4. ff. 1-423. [430

-- *Cour des Aides.* Reglement prouisional faict par le Court des Aides pour le fournissement des greniers à sel ... A Paris Pour Iehan Dallier ... M. D. LIX. ... 8°. A^4. [431

-- *Cour des Monnaies.* Ordonnance faicte par la Court des Generaulx des monnoyes, sur le descry des monnoyes rongnees & legieres ... Publié à Paris, le samedy septiesme iour de Septembre, l'an mil cinq cens soixante. ... A Paris, Par Iehan Dallier ... 8°. A^4. [432

-- *Parlement of Paris.* Ordonnance sur les defences de ne porter Chausses chicquetées & bouffantes le taffetas, Dagues, Espées ne autres bastons offensibles ... A Paris Par Guillaume Nyuerd ... 8°. A^4. ¶*Privilege dated 25 October 1559.* [433

-- L'abbreuiation des procez faicte par la Court de Parlement, Concernants l'Ordonnance & Reglement des Procureurs en icelle. A Lyon, par Benoist Rigaud. M. D. LXXVI. ... 8°. A^4. [434

-- Le nouueau stile de la court souueraine de Parlement, & Forme de plaider & proceder en icelle ... A Paris, Pour Galiot Corrozet ... 1577. ... 8°. A-N^8. ff. 2-103. [435

-- Arrest de la cour de Parlement contre toutes prouisions de Benefices decernees par les Cardinaux Cajetan & de Plaisance ... A Paris, Chez Iamet Mettayer, & Pierre L'huillier ... M. D. XCIIII. ... 8°. A-C^4. pp. 3-29. [436

-- *Parlement of Rouen.* Arrests de la court de Parlement de Rouen, contenans inionction à tous Iuges & Officiers ... informer d'office des assassinats ... & autres crimes & delits, qui seront commis en leur distric. ... A Rouen, Chez Martin le Mesgissier ... 1600. 8°. A-B^4. pp. 3-16. [437

-- *Parlement of Toulouse.* Arrest memorable du Parlement de Tolose: Contenant Vne histoire prodigieuse, de nostre temps, auec ... annotations ... Par ... Iean de Coras ... Prononcé és arrests Generaux, le XII. Septembre M.D.LX. Item, les douze reigles du Seigneur

Iean Pic, de la Mirandole, ... traduites de Latin en François par ledit de Coras. A Lyon. Par Antoine Vincent. M. D. LXV. ... 8°. *8 A-M8. pp. 1-192. [438

-- -- Arrestum siue placitum Parlamenti Tholosani, continens historiam (in casu matrimoniali) admodum memorabilem, ... vnà cum ... Annotationibus ... Ioan. Corasij ... Omnia ex Gallica lingua ... in Latinum conuersa. ... Hugone Suræo Gallo interprete. ... Francofurti Apud Andream Wechelum. M. D. LXXVI. 8°. (:)8 A-R8 S4. pp. 1-179. [439

-- *Church.* Warhaffte Kurtze Beschreibung/ Wie der Neuwgemacht Religion Fried zu Pariss angenommen ... bestettigt worden. ... Anno M.D.LXXVI. (Gedruckt zu Nürmberg/ durch Nicolaum Knorrn.) 4°. A4. [440

-- Erklårung der vrsachen/ welche den Herren Cardinal von Bourbon/ die Pares ... vnd Catholischen Gemeinden des Kőnigreichs Franckreich bewegt/ sich gefasst zůmachen/ wider die/ so sich vnderstehn die Religion vnd den Staht vmbzůstossen. Getruckt zů Augspurg/ bey Michael Manger. M. D. LXXXV. 4°. A4 B2. [441

-- Protestation Der Catholischen/ so die Bůndtnuss wider die Kőnigliche Mt: in Franckreich/ nit vnderschriben haben. M. D. LXXXV. 4°. Aa4. [442

-- Kurtze antwort Eines Catholischen Frantzosen/ auff die Schirmschrifft ... der Neůwverbuntnen ... gemeines wolstands/ welche sich selbs ... die vereinigten Catholischen heissend ... auss Frantzosischer/ in die Teutsche sprach gebracht. Anno 1587. 4°. A-D4 E2. pp. 3-35. [443

-- Response au traite intitulé, Ordre & reglemēt sur les prouisions des benefices en l'Eglise Gallicane, pendant l'empeschement d'aller à Rome. ... M. D. XCVI. 8°. A-L4. pp. 3-87. [444

-- *History.* Eroberung/ plůnderung vnd schlayffung des Gschloss vnd stat Sant Paul/ der statt Monterol vnd Sant Rickir/ sampt der belegerung der statt Terruana in Franckreich. Im monat Iunio. Anno 1537. 4°. [A]4. [445

-- Vrkund vnd anzaygung. Des Hertzogen von Orleans der K. W. in Framckreich [*sic*] Herr brůdern/ die Conspiration belangend der Hertzogen von Nemours vnd Guise ... M.D.LXII. 4°. A4. [446

-- Caroli Kőnigs in Franckreich: Warhafftige Beschreibung aller Handelung/ des zum drittenmal erregten Kriegs in Franckreich ... Alles ... auss Frantzősischer Sprache in die Deutsche gebracht. ... Gedruckt zu Franckfurt am Mayn/ ꝛc. im Jar 1572. (... durch Peter Schmidt/ vnd Sigmund Feirabendt. ...) fol. A-Dd4)(6. ff. 1-106. [447

-- Discours sur la liberte ou captiuité du Roy. M. D. LXII. 4°. A8 B4. [448

-- Grundlicher Warhafftiger Bericht vnd zeytung/ von dem Todt Caroli des neundten Kőnigs in Franckreich ... M.D.LXXIIII. 4°. A4. [449

-- Grűndlicher vnd warhafftiger bericht/ oder Newer zeyttung auss Leon inn Franckreich/ ꝛc. Wie Elendt vnnd Erbårmlich das verschinnen 1587. Jar/ das Teutsch Nauarisch Kriegsuolck ... auch die Schweytzeren ... gewesen ... Gedruckt zu Gånff durch Eustachium Vignon/ ... 1588 Jar. 4°. A-B4. [450

-- Frantzősische Zeittung/ Warhafftiger aussfűrlicher Bericht/ was sich nach Kőnig Heinrichs/ des dritten ... tődlichem Abgange/ so wol in des ... Kőnigs Heinrichs/ des Vierdten ... als in des Hertzogen von Mayne vnd seiner Bundsverwannten/ Kriegshåndeln ... hat verlauffen vnd zugetragen. ... Alles erst newlich auss Frantzősischem in Teutsch gebracht. M.D.Lxxxx. 4°. A-H4. pp. 4-64. ¶*Additional t.p.* (H1r): Relation vnd Bericht/ Von der jűngsten gehaltenen Schlacht bey Dreuss ... M. D. Lxxxx. [451

-- Warhafftig vnd Kurtzer Inhalt Eines heimlichen Rahtschlags/ so der Babst ... nach dem der Hertzog von Alanzon von Pariss gezogen/ gehalten hatt ... Darauss die vrsachen von deren wegen der Kőnig in Franckreich den Hertzogen von Guise vmbbringen lassen zuuernehmen seindt. ... Trewlich auss der Frantzősischen zu Teutscher Sprach gebracht. Getruckt zu Franckfurt am Mayn/ durch Iohannem Basseum. M.D.LXXXIX. 4°. A-E4. pp. I-XXXV. [452

-- Warhafftige newe Zeittung auch Kurtze Erzehlung Wie Henricus Kőnig von Nauarra von seiner vorigen Bekandtnuss abgestanden/ sich zu der Catholischen Rőmischen Kirchen vnd Religion begeben ... Gedruckt zu Důsteldorff/ bey Iohann von Munster/ ... M. D. XCiij. 4°. A4. [453

FRANCHI, FILIPPO. Philippus Franchus in sextum decretalium. ... M. D. XXX VII. (Imprimebant Lugduni Melchior ꝛ Gaspar Trechsel fratres. Impensis ... Hugonem de porta.) fol. B.L. a-n^8 A-N^8 O-P^6 Q-R^8 S^{10} A-B^6 C^4 D^6. ff. 2-246. (Biddle.) [454

FRANCHIS, VINCENZO DE. Decisiones sacri regii consilii Neapolitani ... Præludia item in feudorum vsus ... Iacobutii de Franchis ... Venetiis, apud Iuntas. M D LXXX. fol. *^{4} A-Bb^8 a-f^8 g-h^6. ff. 2-200, 1-31. (Lea.) [455

FRANCIS, S., of Assisi. Opus ... Conformitatũ scilicet vite Beati Frã. ad vitã .d. nr̃i Iesu xp̃i. ... (Impressum Mediolani in edibus Zanoti Castilionei ... 1513. Et perfectum ... xviij. Augu.) fol. B.L. a^{12} a-z^8 ꝛ^8 ꝯ^8 ꝝ^8 A-B^8 C^6 (-C6, *presumably blank*). ff. 1-[229]. ¶*T.p. repaired;* a12, C4, C5 *defective.* (Lea.) [456

FRANCISCANS. Que continentur in hoc uolumine sunt infrascripta uidelicet. Regula beati .p. nostri Francisci. Testamentum eiusdem. Declaratio Greg. pape no. super eandem regulam. Declaratio Ntcolai [*sic*] pape tertii super eandem. Declaratio Clementis pape quinti super eandem. Declaratio quat. magistrorum super eandem. Expositio ... Bonauenture super eandem. Epistola eiusdem ad innominatum magistrum. super tribus articulis ipsius regule. Expositio Bartholomei pisani. super eandem. Quidam ... tractatus per qõnes. super eandem. Declaratio quedam sancti Bernardini. super eandem. Constitutiones & ordinationes Benedicti pape duodecimi. Constitutiones Gulielmi farinerii. Constitutiones Martini pape quinti. Constitutiones & ordinationes beati .p. f. Ioan. de Capistrano. Mare magnum Sixti pape quarti. Bulla aurea eiusdem. (Impressum Brixiæ per Iacobum Britãnicum Brixianum. M.D.ii. xv. calẽ. Ianuarii.) 4°. a-t^8 u^{10} A-C^8. ¶A1^r: tractatus minoricarum dñi Bartoli de saxo ferrato. [457

FRANCK, FABIAN. [Ein Cantzley vnd Titel buͤchlin. ... Orthographia deutsch lernt recht buchstãbig schreiben. Durch M. Fabian Frangken.] (Gedruckt zu Wittemberg durch Nickel Schirlentz. MDXXXII.) 8°. A-L^8 (-A1, L6-8). [458

-- Teutscher Sprach Art vnd Eygenschafft. Orthographia/ Berecht Bůchstaͤbig Teutsch zuschreiben. New Cantzlei ... gerechter Practick ... Zů Franckfurt am Meyn, Bei Christian Egenolph. (... Im Weinmonat. Anno. D. M. XXXI.) 4°. A-L^4. ff. II-XLIIII. [459

FRANCK, SEBASTIAN. Chronica, Zeytbůch vnd geschychtbibel von anbegyn biss in diss gegenwertig ... jar. ... M. D. XXXI. (Getruckt zů Strassburg. Durch Balthassar Beck. Vnd vollendet am Fünfften tag des Herbstmonats. ...) fol. ☞^{6} a-z^6 A-Z^6 aa-zz^6 AA-TT^6 VV^4. ff. ij-D.xxvi. ¶*Additional t.p.* (x4^r): Die Ander Chronica ... der Keyser Jarbůch ... M D xxxj. [460

-- -- M. D. XXXVI. (Getruckt zů Vlm/ bey Iohann Varnier ...) fol. a^8 b-z^6 A-CC^6 Aa-Zz^6 aa-zz^6 a-c^6. ff. ii-ccxcviij, ij-cclxxv. ¶*Additional t.p.* (Aa1^r): Die drit Chronica ꝺ Baͤpst vnd Geystlichen haͤndel ... M. D xxxvj. [461

-- Germaniae chronicon. Von des gantzẽ Teutschlands aller Teutschen voͤlcker herkommen/ Namen/ Haͤndeln/ Guten vnd boͤsen Thaten/ ... Von Noe biss auff Carolum V. ... (Gedruckt zů Augspurg/ durch Alexander Weyssenhorn vñ Henrichen Stainer/ in verlegung vnd costung/ des erbarn Hansen Westermairs .../ vollendt den xv. tag Nouembris/ Anno M. D. XXXVIII.) fol. aa^6 bb^4 cc^6 a-z^6 A-Ee^6 Ff-Gg^4. ff. I-CCCXIIII. ¶Aa *bound after* Bb. (Lea.) [462

-- Paradoxa Ducenta octoginta ... auss der H. Schrifft ... 4°. π^4 A-Z^4 a-v^4 Aa-Cc^4 (-Cc4). ff. I-CLXXII. [463

-- Siben weisen in Gretia beruͤmpt ... Francfurt. Chr. Egen. [c. 1531.] 4°. A-N^4. [464

-- Von ankunfft der Mess vnnd der wandlung brots vnnd weins im ... Sacrament des Altars. Ain disputation Sebastiani Francken/ mit antwort Iohannis Coclei ... M. D. XXXIII. 4°. A-I^4. [465

-- Von dem grewlichenn laster der trunckenheit ... [Augsburg, Heinrich Steiner, 1531.] 4°. A-H^4. [466

FRANCKE, CHRISTIAN. Epistola Pauli Albutii ad Iesuitas. ... Lutetiae Parisiorum, per Gotthardum Vilarmum. Anno M. D. LXXIII. 4°. a-c^4. pp. 3-22. [467

FRANCO, DEMETRIO. Gli illustri et gloriosi gesti, et vittoriose imprese, fatte contra Turchi, Dal Sign. D. Giorgio Castriotto, detto Scanderbeg ... In Vinegia, Presso Altobello Salicato. 1584. Alla Libraria della Fortezza. 4°. *^{4} **^{4} A-Y^4. ff. 1-87. (Lea.) [468

FRANCO, NICOLÒ. Dialoghi piaceuolissimi ...; Espurgati da Giorlamo Gioannini da Capugnano Bolognese. In Vinegia, MDXCVI. Presso Altobello Salicato. 8°. +^{8} A-S^8 T^4. ff. 1-148. [469

-- Dialogo ... Doue si ragiona delle Bellezze. ... In Casale di Monferrato, ne le stampe di Gioanantonio Guidone. Del mese d'Aprile. Del M. DXLII.) 4°. A-T^4 V^2. [470

-- Il Petrarchista, dialogo ..., Nel quale si scuoprono nuoui Secreti sopra il Petrarca. E si dãno a leggere molte lettere, che il medemo Petrarca, In lingua Thoscana scrisse a diuerse persone. ... Venetiis,apud Ioannem Giolitum de Ferrariis M. D. XXXIX. (... del Mese di Ottobre ...) 8°. A-G^8. ff. 2-55. [471

-- Le pistole vulgari ... Venetijs apud Antonium Gardane. M D XXXXII. (*Colophon.*) 8°. A-KK^8 LL^4. ff. 2-267. [472

FRANCO, VERONICA. Lettere familiari a diuersi ... 4°. A-M^4. pp. 1-87. [473

-- Terze rime ... 4°. a^4 (-a4, *probably blank*) A-T^4. ff. 1-73. [474

FRANÇOIS, duc de Anjou. La ioyeuse & magnifique entrée de ... Francoys, fils de France, ... en sa ... ville d'Anuers. A Anuers, De l'Imprimerie de Christophle Plantin. M.D. LXXXII. fol. A-B^4 (B3+χ^2) C-D^4 (D2+χ^2, D3+χ^2, D4+χ^4) E^4 (E1+χ^3, E2+χ^2, E3+χ^2) F^4. pp. 1-46. ¶*Lacks plates* II-VI, VIII, IX, XI, XIII, XV, XVIII, XX, XXII. (Lea.) [475

FRANGEPAN, WOLFGANG. Oratio ad ... Carolum V. ... Ac ad ... Principes: Romani Imperij, facta, ex parte Regnicolarum Croaciæ: ... Augustæ xxiiij. Augusti, Anno 1530. habita. Responsio ... Ioachimi Marchionis Brandenburgensis ... M D XXX. (Augustæ Vindelicorum in officina Alexandri Vueyssenhorn. ...) 4°. A^4. [476

-- -- Ain Oration oder Rede ... durch ... der Crabatischen Lanndtschafft Orator ... Antwortt so der ... Marggraff Ioachim zů Brandenburg ... gegebenn hat. ... (Getruckt zů Augspurg durch Alexander Weyssenhorn ...) 4°. A^4. [477

FRANKFURT AM MAIN. Reformacion der Stat Franckenfort am Meine ... a° 1509. (Gedruckt ... durch Iohãnem Schöffer Burger zů Meintz. ... An dem heiligen abent der vffart vnsers herren ...) fol. 52 *unsigned ll., numbered, except for the first and the last,* II-LI. [478

FRATA E MONTALBANO, MARCO DE LA. Discorsi de principii della nobilta: Et del gouerno ... In Venetia, Nella bottega d'Erasmo di Vicenzo Valgrisi. M D LI. 8°. A-S^8. ff. 2-136. [479

FRATTA, GIOVANNI. La Malteide poema ... In Venetia, Appresso Marc'Antonio Zaltieri. M D XCVI. 4°. a^4 A-P^8 Q^6 (-Q6, *blank*). ff. 1-125. [480

FRAUNCE, ABRAHAM. The lawiers logike, exemplifying the præcepts of Logike by the practise of the common Lawe ... At London, Imprinted by William How, for Thomas Gubbin, and T. Newman. 1588. 4°. [A]^2 ¶^{4} ¶-¶¶^{4} B-Y^4 Aa-Rr^4 (Ii2 + *folded leaf*). ff. 2-151. *S.T.C.* 11344. (Biddle.) [481

FRECCIA, MARINO. Marini Frecciae ... De Subfeudis Baronum, & Inuestituris Feudorum, liber primus, et secundus. Quibus accesserunt nonnulli tractatus ... Neapoli ... MCCCCCLIIII. (Excudebantur per Matthiam Cancer In Aedibus eiusdem ... Frecciæ. ...) fol. a-f^6 g^4 A-SS^6 TT^8 VV-XX^6 YY^8. ff. 1-274. [482

FREGOSO, ANTONIO, PHILEREMO. Dialogo de fortuna ... (Stampata nella ... Citta di Venetia p Nicolo Zopino e Vincẽtio compagno. Nel. M.CCCCC.XXIII. A di. I. de Setembrio.) 8°. A-D^8 (-D8, *presumably blank*). ¶*In verse.* [483

-- Opera noua ... laqual tratta de doi Philosophi, cioe Democrito ... & Heraclito ... (In Venetia per Matthio Pagan ... M D LIIII.) 8°. A-F^8. [484

-- Riso de Democrito: et pianto de Heraclito ... (Impresso in Millano p Zanoto da Castione ... M.ccccc.xv. adi. yi. de Aprile.) 4°. a-e^8 f^{12}. [485

FREIBURG IM BREISGAU. Nüwe Stattrechten vnd Statuten der ... Statt Fryburg im Pryszgow gelegen. ... (... angegangen vff den nüwen iars tag/ ... fünffzehenhundert vnd zwentzig iar. ... zů drucken beuolhen ... durch ... Adam Petri ...) fol. aa^6 A-P^6 (O3 + *folded leaf*) Q^8 R^6 (-R6, *blank*). ff. II-XCVII. [486

FREIGE, JOHANN THOMAS. Ciceronianus, Ioan. Thomæ Freigii, in quo: Ex Ciceronis monumentis, Ratio instituendi Locos communes demonstrata: & Eloquentia cum Philosophia coniuncta, descripta est. Libris decem. Adiecimus Des. Iacotti, de Philosophorum doctrinâ libellum ex Cicerone. Basileæ, per Sebastianum Henricpetri. (... CIↃ. IↃ. LXXIX. Mense Augusto.) 8°.):(^{8} *^{4} a-z^8 A-Q^8. pp. 1-622. [487

-- Rectoratus Ioan. Thomæ Freigii ... eidem per Gymnasij Altorfiani Scholarchas ... demandatus. ... Noribergæ In Officina Typographica Katharinæ Gerlachin, & Hæredum Iohannis Montani. cIↄ. Iↄ. LXXVII. 4°. A-E^4 (E3 + *folded leaf*: Delineatio et σκιαγραφια Scholæ Altorfianae.) F^2. [488

-- Trium artium logicarum, grammaticae, dialecticæ & Rhetoricæ, ... Schematismi ... Epitome Derreri de Regalibus & Iurisdictione: & duae Partitiones ... Basileae Per Sixtum Henricpetri. (... M.D.LXVIII, Mense Septembri.) 8°. a^8 A-M^8 (D8 + *folded leaf*) *^{4} a-f^8 g^4. pp. 1-58. [489

FRELL, GEORG. Zwey Geistliche ABC. Füer die Schüler Gottes ... 8°. A-B^8. [490

FRELLON, JEAN. Lexicon Graeco-Latinum ... è Budæi Commentariis ... locupletatum. Lugduni, apud Ioannem Frellonium, M. D. L. ... fol. *^{4} a-z^8 A-Cc^8 Dd^6. cols. 1-1526. [491

-- Copiosissimus index Latinorum dictionum et phraseon, quae lexico nostro antea edito, respondent. Lugduni, Apud Ioannem Frellonium, M. D. LIII. (... Excudebat Michael Syluius ...) fol. a^{10} b-h^8 i^{10}. [492

FREXIUS, BARTHOLOMAEUS. Bartholomæi Frexii, Turriani, binae orationes. Altera pro pace, per Paulum III. Pont. Max. Christianis reddita ... Altera pro humanorum artium Studijs ... Lugduni apud Seb. Gryphium, 1539. 4°. a-f^4. pp. 2-47. [493

FRÍAS, MARTINO DE. [1] Tractatus perutilis ... 4°. ✠^{2} a^{10} b-n^8. ff. I-XCVI. ¶✠2^r: Dada enla villa de Valla-|dolid a veynte ⁊ vno de Agosto de mil ⁊ quiniētos ⁊ veynte ⁊ ocho. a10^v: Incipit tractatus ... de Arte & modo audiendi confessiones ... [2] tratado del modo y estilo que enla visitacion ordinaria se a de tener. B.L. A-D^8 E^4. ff. ij-xxxiiij. (Lea.) [494

FRIDERICH, MATTHEUS. Widder den Saufteuffel ... Item/ Ein Sendbrieff der Hellischen Sathans/ an die Zutrincker ... Item/ Ein Sendbrieff an die Follen Brüder in Deutschem Lande. M. D. LVII. (Gedrückt zu Franckfurt an der Oder/ durch Iohan. Eichorn ...) 4°. A-S^4. [495

FRIDERUS, PETRUS. Petri Frideri Mindani D. de lingua Latina Opus absolutum ... Basileae, typis Leonhardi Ostenij. Anno cIↄ. Iↄ. XCII. 8°. †^{10} A-Hh^8 Ii^4 (-Ii4, *blank*). pp. 2-502. [496

FRIESE, JOHANN. Bibliotheca philosophorum classicorum authorum chronologica. ... Tiguri apud Ioannem VVolphium typis Frosch. anno M.D. XCII. 4°. α-β^4 A-Z^4 a-e^4. ff. 1-110. [497

FRIGILLANUS, MATTHAEUS. In Matthaei Frigillani Villeborridēsis Bellouaci nimis contractum Compendium de prima philosophia ... Accessit eiusdem ... Stephanoma in animi humani immortalitatis confirmationem, simul & Σχῆμα de partibus iuris. ... Parisiis, Ex Typographia Thomæ Richardi ... 1561. 4°. A-C^4. ff. 2-12. [498

FRISCHLIN, NICODEMUS. Nicodemi Frischlini, de astronomicae artis ... libri quinque. ... Francofurti ad Moenum, excudebat Ioannes Spies. M. D. LXXXVI. (*Colophon.*) 8°. (?)^8 A-Ff^8 Gg^4. pp. 1-469. [499

-- D. Nicodemi Frischlini ... Demonstratio, Graecos non carere Ablatiuo. Argentorati Excudebat Antonius Bertramus Anno M. D. LXXXVI. 4°. A^4. [500

-- Nicodemi Frischlini grammaticae Graecae cum Latina verè congruentis. Pars prima. In qua orthographia, Prosodia, & Etymologia ... Helmstadii Excudebat Iacobus Lucius, impensis Ludolphi Brandes. An. 1589. 8°. $)(^8$ A-Mm^8 Nn^4. pp. 1-567. [501

-- Nicodemi Frischlin nomenclator trilinguis, Graecolatinogermanicus, continens omnium rerum, quæ in probatis omnium doctrinarum auctoribus inueniuntur, appellationes ... Francofurti ad Moenum. Excudebat Ioannes Spies. M.D.LXXXVI. (*Colophon.*) 8°. $(:)^8$ $(::)^8$ A-Mm^8 Nn^4. ff. 1-283. [502

-- [1] Operum poeticorum Nicodemi Frischlini ... pars scenica: in qua sunt, comoediae sex. ... Tragoediae duae. ... Excudebat Bernhardus Iobin. Anno M. D. LXXXIX. (Argentorati ...) 8°. $):(^8$ A-Ii^8 Kk^4. pp. 2-519. [2] Heluetio-Germani, comoedia noua ... *Same imprint.* A-G^8 H^4. pp. 4-118. [503

-- -- *Another copy (lacking the additional comedy).* [504

-- Nicodemi Frischlini ... orationes insigniores aliquot ... editæ. Operâ & studio, M. Georgii Pfluegeri, Vlmani. Argentinae Ex officina Typographica hæredum Bernhardi Iobini. Anno M. D. XCVIII. 8°. a^6 A-Ee^8 Ff^4. pp. 1-456. [505

-- Phasma: Hoc est: comoedia posthuma ... Impressum in Iazygibus-Metanastis, [i.e. Strassburg, per heredes Bernhardi Jobin] ... 1592. ... 8°. A-G^8 H^4 (-H4, *presumably blank*). [506

-- -- *Same imprint.* 8°. A-H^8. [507

-- Nicodemi Frischlini poppysmus grammaticus, pro strigili sua Grammatica, aduersus M. Crusij, & Moropolitarum, Tubingæ Bacchantium Coccysmos ... Pragae Excudebat Michael Peterle. Anno M. D. LXXXVII. 8°. A-Q^8. pp. 2-215. [508

-- Priscianus vapulans. ... comedia ... Erphordiae: Apud Esaiam Mechlerum. Anno M. D. LXXXI. (*Colophon.*) 8°. A-K^8 L^4 (-L4, *presumably blank*). [509

-- Nicodemi Frischlini ... strigilis grammatica ... Eiusdem dialogi tres, aduersus Martinum quendam Crusiū ... M.D.LXXXVII. 8°. α^8 β^6 A-M^8 N^4 a-r^8 s^4. pp. 1-199, 2-149. ¶*Additional t.pp.:* (G3r) Nicodemi Frischlini ... dialogus primus ... M. D. LXXXVII. (a1r) ... Dialogus II. ... M. D. LXXXVII. (g6r) ... Dialogus III. ... M. D. LXXXVII. [510

FRITZHANS, JOHANN. 1524. Wie mann das klar hell gots wort predigen soll ... (Gedruckt [zu Zwickau durch Jörg Gastel] im Tausent Funffhundert vnnd Vier vnnd zweyntzigsten Jare.) 4°. A-D^4. [511

FRIULI. Constitutiones patriae Foriiulii Cum additionibus ... Venetiis, M D LXV. Ex officina Dominici Guerrei et Io. Baptistae, fratrum. 4°. A-EE^4. ff. 3-112. (Lea.) [512

FUCHS, JAKOB. Ain schoͤner Sendbrieff ... Darinn auss heyliger geschryfft Priester Ee beschirmbt vnnd gegründt wirdt ... [Augsburg, Heinrich Steiner,] 1523. 4°. A^4. [513

FUCHS VON RÜGHEIM, GEORG. Der ... Herrn Georgen erwelten ... zu Bischoue zu Bamberg ... Sumarischer ... gegenbericht vnd verantwortung/ auff des ... Echters Marggraue Albrechts von Brandenburg ... Schmachbuch. ... M. D. LVI. fol. A-B^6 C^8 D-Ee^6. ff. II-CLXVII. ¶Ee6 *defective.* [514

-- -- *Another copy* (-Ee6, *errata*). [515

FUCHSBERGER, ORTOLF. Ain gründlicher klarer anfang der natürlichen vnd rechten kunst der waren Dialectica/ durch Ortholphen Fuchsperger von Ditmoning ... auss dem Latein ins teutsch transferiert vnd zůsam̄gefast ... M.D.XXXIII. (Getruckt in ... Augspurg/ Durch Alexander Weyssenhorn.) 4°. π^4 A-Z^4 a-s^4. ff. I-CLIII. [516

-- Kurtze schlossrede wider den jrsall der neügerottenn Tauffer ... Getruckt zu Landsshůt [durch Johann Weissenberger, 1528]. 4°. A^4 B^2. [517

FUENTIDUEÑA, PEDRO DE. Altera concio Doctoris Petri Fontidonii Hispani Segobien. ... habita ad ... Synodum Triden. die Beati Hieronymi xxx. Mensis Septembris. M. D. LXII. Brixiæ

Apud Damianum Turlinum, M. D. LXII. (... Ad instantiam Ioannis Baptistæ Bozolæ. ...) 4°. A-C^4. (Lea.) [518

-- Concio Doctoris Petri Fontidonii ... habita ad ... Synodum Trident. Dominica ... Trinitatis. XXIIII. Maij. M. D. LXII. Brixiæ apud Damianum Turlinum. 4°. A-B^4 C^2. (Lea.) [519

-- -- Patauii Ex officina Laurentii Pasquatii & Sociorum. MDLXII. 4°. A-B^4 C^2. ff. 2-11. (Lea.) [520

-- Petri Fontidonii ... oratio habita ad Patres in ... Concilio Tridentino, nomine ... Claudii Fernandez Quignonii Comitis Lunensis Regis Catholici Oratoris. Die 21. Maii. 1563. Patauii Apud Christophorum Gryphium. M D LXIII. 4°. A-B^4. (Lea.) [521

FULGENTIUS, S. Opera B. Fulgentii Aphri ... Item opera Maxentii Iohannis ... [(Hagenoae, impensis Kobergerorum Norinbergensium, in officina Thomae Anshelmi [15]20.)] fol. a-r^6. ff. II-CII. ¶*Lacks* A-F^6 (Opera Maxentii). (Lea.) [522

FULGENTIUS, FABIUS PLANCIADES. FabI Planciadii Fulgentii V.C. liber de expositione Virgilianæ continentiæ. Iunii PhilargurI ... in Bucolica & Georgica Virgilii Commentariolus. FuluI Vrsini notæ ad Seruium in Bucolica, Georgica & Æneida Virgilij. Velius Longus de Orthographia. Magni AurelI Cassiodori de Orthographia liber. [Heidelbergae,] In officina Sanctandreana, cIↃ IↃ LXXXIX. 8°. A^8 B^4 a-k^8 l^4. pp. 3-24, 3-168. [523

FULGOSIO, RAFFAELLO. [Commentarii in codicem.] Lugduni, Apud Hugonem & hæredes Aemonis à Porta. M. D. XLVII. ... (... excudebant Stephanus Rufinus et Ioannes Ausultus.) fol. B.L. [1] Raphaelis Fulgosij Placentini ... commentariorum in D. Iustiniani Codicem Index ... A-G^8. [2] ... Tomus primus. ... *^{4} a-ff^8 gg^{10}. ff. 1-242. [3] ... Tomus secundus ... A-HH^8 II^6. ff. 2-254. (Biddle.) [524

-- [Commentarii in pandectas.] Lugduni, Apud Hugonem, & hæredes Aemonis à Porta. M. D. XLIIII. (... apud Stephanum Rufinum, ⁊ Ioannem Ausultum.) fol. B.L. [1] Raphaelis Fulgosii Placentini ... in primam Pandectarum partem Commentariorum ... Tomus primus ... a-z^8 A-Q^8. ff. 2-312. [2] ... Tomus secundus ... aa-zz^8 AA-II^8 KK^6. ff. 2-261. (Biddle.) [525

-- Repertoria ... Raphaelis Fulgosij nempè atqȝ Cumani ... Lugduni, Apud Hugonem, & hæredes Aemonis à Porta. M. D. XLIIII. ... (... in typographia ... Stephani Rufini, & Ioannis Ausulti. ...) fol. B.L. a-n^8 o-p^6. (Biddle.) [526

FULIGNI, VALERIO. Bragadino tragedia ... Inpesaro, Apresso Girolamo Concordia ... 1589. 8°. A-I^8. ff. 1-64. [527

FULKE, WILLIAM. A comfortable Sermon of Faith, in temptations and afflictions. ... Imprinted at London by Iohn Awdeley ... 1574. 8°. B.L. A-G^4. *S.T.C.* 11422. [528

FULVIO, ANDREA. L'antichità di Roma ... con le aggiuntioni ... di Girolamo Ferrucci Romano ... In Venetia, Per Girolamo Francini Libraro in Roma ... M D LXXXVIII. 8°. *^{4} A-Ii^8 Kk^{12} (-Kk5-8). ff. 1-260. (Fine Arts.) [529

-- Illustrium imagines (Impræssum Romæ apud Iacobum Mazochium ... M.D.XVII. Die .XV. Mensis Nouembris. ...) 8°. A-GG^4. ff. V-CXX. [530

FUMO, BARTOLOMMEO. Bartholomaei Fumi Placentini ... Summa: quæ Aurea Armilla inscribitur. ... omnia continens, quæ in iure Canonico, apud Theologos, & omnes Summas circa animarum curam diffuse disperseq́ue tractantur. Apud Guillelmum de Millis. 1558 (Methymnae Campi. ...) 4°. ã^4 A-Kk^8 Ll^2. ff. 1-266. (Lea.) [531

-- -- Summa aurea armilla nuncupata, casus omnes ad animarum curam attinentes ... Venetiis, MDLXXXII. Apud Io. Antonium Bertanum. 8°. †-3†^{8} A-4E^8 4F^4. pp. 2-1188. [532

FUNCK, JOHANN. Chronologia, hoc est, Omnium temporum & annorum ab initio mundi, usq; ad annum ... M. D. LIII. computatio ... Item Commentariorum Libri decem ... Basileae, 1554. (... excudebat Iacobus Parcus, expensis Ioannis Oporini ...) fol. α-β^4 A-ZZ^4 (-A1) aa-zz^4 aA-iI^4 A-HH^4. pp. 3-615, 3-245 *present.* [533

FUNCKELIN, JAKOB. Ein Geistlich Spyl von der Empfengknuss vñ Geburt Iesu Christi ... Gedicht ... Anno 1553. vnd gespilt durch die Iugend zů Biel ... (Getruckt zů Zürych by Christoffel Froschouer.) 8°. a-d^{8}. [534

FURIO Y CERIOL, FADRIQUE. Speculi aulicarum atque Politicarum observationum Libelli quinq3 nimirum 1. De Conciliis & Consiliariis Principũ Fridericus Furius, &c. 2. Consiliarius Hippolyti à Collibus, auctior. 3. Palatinus sive Aulicus Eiusdem Autoris ... 4. Aulicus Politicus, Duri de Pascolo. 5. Hypomneses Politicæ Francisci Guicciardini. ... Procurante Andrea Hoffmanno Bibliopola VVitebergensi. Anno M. D. XCIX. 12°. A-V^{12} (B1 + *folded leaf*) X^{6}. [535

-- -- Speculi ... Libelli Sex: nimirum. 1 De educatione Principum Ioannis Sturmii, &c. 2. De Conciliis & consiliariis Principum ... Procurante. Lazaro Zetznero Bibliopola Argentinense. M. D. C. 12°. A-Z^{12} (-Z10-12) + *folded leaf*. [536

FURMAN, JAKOB. Προπεμπτικα Ionæ Hempelo Falcobergensi Silesio, ... honoris faustæque Comprecationis ergò scripta ... CIↃ IↃ XCIII. VVitebergæ, Ex Officina Cratoniana. 4°. A^{4}. [537

FURNIER, ROBERT. De Christo puero, circunciso, et Iesu vocato, concio, Tridenti habita, Calendis Ianuarii, in ... synodi ... Brixiæ, Apud Damianum Turlinum. Ad instantiam Io. Baptistæ Bozolæ. Anno M. D. LXIII. 4°. A^{6}. (Lea.) [538

FURTMAR, WOLFGANG. Rudimenta Latinae grammatices ... collecta. M.D.XXXVI. (Augustae in officina Philippi Vlhardi, Anno. M.D.XXXVII.) 8°. A-C^{8}. [539

G

GABIANI, VINCENZO. I gelosi comedia ... In Vinegia appresso Gabriel Giolito de Ferrari e fratelli. M D LI. (*Colophon.*) 8°. A-G^{8}. ff. 2-54. [1

GAGUIN, ROBERT. La Mer des croniques et miroir historial de Frãce iadis compose en latin ... On les vend a Paris par Philippe le noir ... (... Lan mil cinq cens et trente.) fol. B.L. AA-BB^{6} a-z^{6} ꝛ^{6} A-O^{6} P^{8} (-P8) QQ^{6}. ff. i-C.C.xli. ¶*Translator: Pierre Desray.* [2

GAILDORFINUS, JOANNES. Primitiae Musaꝝ Ioãnis Gaildorfini adolescentis Sueuigenae cõtra Venerem atqȝ cupidinem. ... (Lipsigck imp̃ssit Vuolfgang^{9} Monacensis. 1512.) fol. A-B^{6}. [3

GALENUS, CLAUDIUS. [Omnia Opera.] Apud hæredes Lucæantonij Iuntæ Florentini Venetiis M.D.XLI. (*Colophon.*) fol. [1] Galeni omnia opera ... latinitate donata ... ✠^{8} ✠✠^{6} 1-8^{8} 9^{10}. ff. 2-14, 2-73. ¶*Additional t.p.* (11^{r}): Galeni introductorii libri ... *Same imprint.* [2] Galeni extra ordinem Classium libri ... 4a-4i^{8} 4k^{10}. ff. 2-82. [3] Galeno ascripti libri ... π^{2} aα^{4} bβ-nν^{8} oξ^{10}. ff. 1-115. [4] Galeni prima classis ... a-m^{8} n-o^{6} p-ss^{8} tt^{10}. ff. 3-334. [5] Galeni secunda classis ... 3a^{10} 3b-3m^{8} 3n-3o^{6}. ff. 1-107. [6] Galeni tertia classis ... A-Z^{8} &^{6}. ff. 2-189. [7] Galeni quarta classis ... AA-DD^{8} EE^{10} FF-ZZ^{8} Aa-Cc^{8} Dd-Ee^{6}. ff. 2-221. [8] Galeni quinta et sexta classis ... 3A-3K^{8} 3L^{6} 3M-3Z^{8} AAa-CCc^{8} DDd^{10} EEe-MMm^{8} NNn^{6} OOo^{8} PPp^{10}. ff. 2-306. [9] Galeni septima classis ... 3A-4M^{8} 4N^{6}. ff. 2-285. [4

-- -- Venetiis, M D LXV. (... apud haeredes Lucaeantonii Iuntae.) fol. [1] Galeni omnia quae extant opera In latinum sermonem conuersa. Iuntarum quarta editio. 1^{8} 2^{6} ✠✠^{6} Aa-Hh^{8} Ii^{6} Kk^{10}. ff. 2-79. ¶*Additional t.p.* (Aa1^{r}): Galeni Extra ordinem Classium libri ... Venetiis apud Iuntas M D LXV. [2] Galeni isagogici libri ... 1a-9i^{8}. ff. 1-72. [3] Galeno ascripti libri ... Aα-Iι^{8} Kκ^{10} Lλ-Oξ^{8} Po^{6}. ff. 2-117. [4] Galeni librorum prima classis ... a-z^{8} A-T^{8} V^{6}. ff. 2-341. [5] Galeni librorum secunda classis ... aa^{6} bb-oo^{8}. ff. 2-109. [6] Galeni librorum tertia classis ... 3a-3o^{8} 3p-3q^{6} 3r-3z^{8} 3A-3B^{8}. ff. 2-197. [7] Galeni librorum quarta classis ... 4a-4o^{8} 4p^{10} 4Q-4Q2•^{6} 4q^{6} 4r-4z^{8} 4A-4C^{8} 4D-4E^{6}. ff. 2-220. [8] [Galeni librorum quinta classis ...] 5A-5Z^{8} (-5A1) 5a-5l^{8} 5m^{6}. ff. 2-277. [9] Galeni librorum sexta classis ... 6a-6c^{8} 6d^{4}. ff. 3-21. [10] Galeni librorum septima classis ... 7a-7x^{8} 7y-7z^{10} 7A-7B^{6} 7C-7R^{8} 7S^{6}. ff. 2-322. [11] [Index ...] *^{4} (-*^{4}) a-3t^{8} 3u-3x^{6}. ff. 2-532. [5

-- Cl. Gal. de constitutione artis medicae. ... Lugduni, Apud Gulielmum Rouillium ... 1552. (... excudebat Philibertus Rolletius.) 16°. a-t^{8}. pp. 3-302. (School of Dentistry.) [6

-- Galenus de ossibus ad tyrones. De ... Dissectione libri. De motu Musculorum libri duo. Adiecimus præterea Oribasij de Musculorum dissectione libellum ... Lugduni. Apud Gulielmum Rouillium ... 1551. (... excudebat Philibertus Rolletius.) 16°. A-Y^{8}. pp. 2-349. [7

-- Claudii Galeni Pergameni introductio in pulsus ad Teuthram. Martino Gregorio interprete. Eiusdem de pulsuum vsu. Thoma Linacro interprete. Ludguni, Apud Gulielmum Rouillium ... 1550. (... excudebat Philibertus Rolletius.) 16°. A^{8} (-A4-5) B-F^{8}. pp. 3-94. (School of Dentistry.) [8

GALLO, AGOSTINO. Le vinti giornate dell'agricoltura, et de piaceri della villa ... In Turino Appresso gl'heredi del Beuilacqua, MDLXXX. (*Colophon.*) 4°. *^{8} **^{4} A-Cc^{8} Dd^{6} Ee-Ff^{4}. pp. 1-428. [9

GALLO, JUAN. De laudibus ... Diui Thomæ Aquinatis ... oratio ... ad ... Synodum Tridentinam ... die VII. Martij M. D. LXIII. ... Brixiæ ad instantiam Io: Baptistæ Bozole. 1563. (... apud Ludouicum Sabiensem ...) 4°. A-B^{4}. (Lea.) [10

GALLONIO, ANTONIO. Trattato de gli instrumenti di martirio, e delle varie maniere di martoriare vsate da' Gentili contro Christiani, descritte et intagliate in rame. ... In Roma, Presso Ascanio, e Girolamo Donangeli. 1591. ... (*Colophon.*) 4°. †^{2} A-X^{4}. pp. 1-159. (Lea.) [11

GALLUCCI, GIOVANNI PAOLO. Speculum Vranicum In quo vera loca tum octauæ Sphæræ, tum septem Planetarum ... colliguntur ... Venetijs, Apud Damianum Zenarium. M. D. XCIII. fol. †^{4} A-L^4 (L3 + *folded sheet*). ff. 1-43. [12

GALLUS, CAIUS CORNELIUS. Cornelii Galli ... fragmenta ... [Device of Jehan Petit.] Venũdantur Parrhisiis ... (Impressum ... accuratione ascẽsiana. ... M.CCCCCIII. Die .XXI. Iulii.) 4°. a^8 b^4 c^6. ff. III-XVII. [13

GALLUS, NICOLAUS. Antwort M. Nicolai Galli vnd M. Fla. Illyrici/ auff den brieff etlicher prediger in Meissen/ von der frage/ Ob sie lieber weichen/ denn den Chorrock anzihen sollen. (Gedruckt zu Magdeburg bey Christian Rődinger [1549].) 4°. A-B^4. [14

-- Ein sendbrieff ... zum bericht gegen etlicher leichtfertigen Leut schmehung ... (Gedruckt zu Magdeburg/ durch Michael Lotther.) 4°. A^4. ¶*Dated 26 September 1551.* [15

GAMA, ANTONIO DE. [1] Decisiones supremi senatus regni Lusitaniae ... Nunc denuo ... auctæ ... 1599. Expensis Martini de Cordoua ... Vallisoleti. Apud Didacum Fernandez à Corduba ... (... Excudebant Ioannes de Millis, & Andreas Bolan.) fol. ¶^{8} A^6 B-Xx^8 Yy^4 a-b^8 c^{10}. pp. 6-9, ff. 1-354. [2] Antonii Gammae ... tractatus De Sacramentis præstandis vltimo supplicio damnatis, Ac de testamentis, anatomia, & eorum sepultura. ... *Same imprint.* π^2 A-E^8 F^6. ff. 1-46. [3] Blasii Flores Diaz de Mena Carrionensis ... lucubrationes. In decisiones in supremo Lusitaniae Senatu ... *Same imprint.* π^2 A-H^8 I^4 A^8 b-f^8 G^1 H^8 I^4. ff. 1-68, 1-49. (Lea.) [16

GAMBARO, VINCENZO. Comedia ... Intitulata Mãfrino. (Stampata in Pesaro per Baldassare de Frãcesco Cartholaro. ... 1529. Adi. 6. del mese di Decembre.) 8°. A-D^4. [17

GAMBELLIONIBUS, ANGELUS DE. Angelus de Maleficijs. Angelus de Aretio. Repertorium primi voluminis Maleficiorum in quo continẽtur Tractatus ... Angeli de Aretio: domini Alberti de Gãdino: ac do. Bonifacij de vitellinis de Mantua ... Superaddũtur ... additio. do. Hieronymi Chuchalon Hispani. ... (Lugd. in edibus ... Antonij du Ry ... M.cccccxxx. die. xvij. Maij.) fol. B.L. Aa-Cc^8 a-ff^8 gg^6 +^{8} AA-KK^8 LL^4 a-b^8 A-K^8 L^6. ff. iij-ccxxxviij, j-lxxxiiij, j-lxxxv. (Lea.) [18

-- -- Tractatus de maleficiis Angeli Aretini, cum additionibus ... Augustini Bonfrancisci Ariminensis, ac D. Hieronymi Cuchalon Hispani ... vna cum ... apostillis D. Bernardini de Landriano, nec non aliorum Modernorum. ... Coloniae Agrippinae, Apud Viduam Henrici Falckenburg. Anno M. D. LXXXXIX. 4°. (?)^4 (??)^2 *-4*^{4} A-4G^4 4H^2 (-4H2, *presumably blank*). pp. 2-612. (Lea.) [19

-- Angeli ab Aretio, institutionum D. Iustiniani libr. quatuor commentaria ... D. Purpurati ... Additiones ... [Lugduni,] M. D. XLIX. fol. B.L. a^8 b-zz^6 A-L^6 M^4 AA-DD^6. ff. 1-346. (Biddle.) [20

GAMEREN, HANNARDUS VAN. Bucolica Latina ... Authore Hannardo Gamerio ... Ingolstadij Excudebant Alexander & Samuel Vueissenhornij. M. D. LXV. 8°. A-K^8. ff. 2-80. [21

-- Satyrae duae ... M.D.LXVIII. 4°. A-E^4. [22

-- Turris sacra Dilingana ... Othonis Episcopi Cardinalis Albani & Augustani, Heroico carmine descripta ... Carmen de Sanctorum Reliquijs. 1567. (Dilingæ excudebat Sebaldus Mayer.) 4°. A-V^4. ff. 1-71. [23

GANDINI, LODOVICO. Lettione ... sopra vn dubbio, Come il Petrarca non lodasse Laura expressamente dal Naso. Rime del medesimo. ... In Vinegia Al segno della Pace, 1581. (... Appresso Pietro Dusinelli. ...) 8°. a-c^8 d^{10}. ff. 2-29. [24

GANDINO, ALBERTO. [1] Tractatus diuersi super maleficiis, nempe D. Alberti di Gandino. D. Bonifacij de Vitalianis. D. Pauli Grillandi. D. Baldi de Periglis. D. Iacobi de Arena. Venetiis P. Hieronymus Lilius excudebat. M D LX. 8°. AA-3X^8 3Y^4. pp. 3-663. [2] Indices duo ... *Same imprint.* A-G^8 H^6. (Lea.) [25

GARAY, BLASCO DE. Carta ... de Refrances y sentencias: muy prouechosas que embio vn galan a vna señora. ... [Barcelona,] 1535. 4°. B.L. A^4. [26

GARDINER, STEPHEN. Stephani Winton. episcopi Angli, ad Martinum Bucerum Epistola ... Ingolstadii apud Alexandrum Vueissenhorn. M.D.XLVI. 4°. A-F^{4}. [27

GARETH, BENEDETTO. Tutte le opere volgari di Chariteo ... (Impressa. In Napoli p̱ Maestro Sigismũdo Mayr Alamãno cõ somma diligẽtia di .P. Sũmontio nel anno .M.DVIIII. del mese di Nouẽbre ...) 4°. A-L^{8} M^{10} N-V^{8}. [28

GARGHA, GIOVANNI BATTISTA. Oratio in Octaua Sessioñ. Laterañ. Concilii. unacũ Obedientia magni Magistri Rhodi. [Romae, Marcellus Silber, 1514.] 4°. a-c^{4}. (Lea.) [29

GARIBÁY Y ZAMÁLLON, ESTEVAN DE. Illustraciones genealogicas de los catholicos reyes de las Españas, y de los Christianissimos de Francia, y de los Emperadors de Constantinopla ... En Madrid, Por Luis Sanchez: Año 1596. (... en fin de Abril. ...) fol. A^{4} (+ *engraved leaf*) B-Pp^{4}. pp. 2-297. ¶*Several leaves are oversize and folded. A hand-written folded leaf is inserted after* Pp2. (Lea.) [30

GARIMBERTO, GIROLAMO. Concetti di Hieronimo Garimberto. Et de piu autori. ... In Roma. Appresso Vincenzo Valgrisi. M.D.LI. ... 8°. A^{12} B-Ii^{8}. pp. 9-501. [31

-- -- Concetti diuinissimi di Girolamo Garimberto ... In Vinegia, per Giouanmaria Bonello, M D LI. (*Colophon.*) 8°. a-z^{8} A-H^{8} (-H8, *presumably blank*). ff. 1-239. [32

-- Della fortuna libri sei ... (In Venetia per Michel Tramezzino. M D XLVII.) 8°. A^{8} a^{8} B-T^{8}. ff. 1-150. [33

-- La prima parte delle vite, ouero fatti memorabili d'alcuni papi, et di tutti i cardinali passati. ... In Vinegia, appresso Gabriel Giolito de' Ferrari, M D LXVII. 4°. a-e^{4} A-HH^{8} II^{10}. pp. 1-515. (Lea.) [34

-- Problemi naturali, & morali ... In Vinegia, nella bottega d'Erasmo di Vicenzo Valgrisi. M. D. L. (*Colophon.*) 8°. A-Q^{8} (-Q8, *presumably blank*). pp. 3-239. [35

GARLAND, JOHN OF. Cõposita verboruʒ Iohãnis Sinthis (Impressorũ in Lyptzk p̱ Melchiorem Lotter. Anno ... Milsimoquingentesimoquinto.) fol. B.L. A-B^{6} C^{4} D^{6} E^{4} F-H^{6} (-H6, *presumably blank*). [36

GARNIER, ROBERT. [1] Les tragedies ... A Paris, Par Mamert Patisson ... au logis de Robert Estienne. M. D. LXXX. ... 12°. *^{4} A-Q^{12} R^{8} S^{6}. ff. 1-206. [2] Antigone, ou la pieté ... *Same imprint.* a-d^{12} e^{4}. ff. 2-51. [37

-- -- A Paris Chez Mathieu Guillemot ... [1600.] 12°. A-Cc^{12}. ff. 2-279. ¶*Engraved t.p.* [38

GARNIER, SEBASTIEN. [1] Les huict premiers liures de la Henriade, contenans les faits ... de Henry ... quatriesme ... A Bloys, Chez la Vefue Gomet ... M. D. XCIIII. 4°. A^{4} ē^{4} A-E^{4} A^{4}. pp. 1-39. [2] Les huict derniers liures de la Henriade ... A Bloys, Chez La Veufue Gomet ... M. D. XCIII. (acheué d'imprimer le sixiesme d'Auril ...) ā^{4} ē^{2} A-N^{4} O^{2} P-T^{4} V^{2}. pp. 1-148. [39

-- Les premiers liures de la Loyssee, Contenans, le voyage de Sainct Loys Roy de France ... A Bloys, Chez la Veufue Gomet ... M. D. XCIII. 4°. ā^{4} ē^{2} (-ē2, *presumably blank*) A-E^{4} F^{2} G-H^{4}. pp. 1-59. [40

GARSIA, JUAN. Tractatus De Expẽsis & meliorationibus ... Accesserunt ... tractatus alij per Ioannem Garsiam à Saabedra autoris filiũ ... Pintiæ excudebat apud hæredes a Bernardino Sancto Dominico ... 1592. Expẽsis Martini à Cordoua Bliuipole. (*Colophon.*) fol. π^{2} ¶^{4} a-b^{8} A-LL^{8} MM^{6} A-G^{8} H^{2} I^{6}. ff. 1-278, 1-58. [41

GARTNER, ANDREAS. Dicteria prouerbialia, rhythmica, ab antiquitate mutata, ... cum versione Germanica ... Franc. Apud hæred. Christ. Egen. M D XXCV. (*Colophon.*) 8°. A-Z^{8} a^{6} (-a6, *presumably blank*). ff. 2-127. ¶*Half-titles:* (R4^{r}) Sortelegium rhythmaticum ... (V8^{v}) Prognostica ... (Y4^{r}) Marcolphus. Disputationes, quas dicuntur habuisse ... Salomon ... & Marcolphus ... [42

GARTZE, JOHANN. [Meteorologia Iohannis Garcaei. Vuitebergae 1584.] 8°. A^{8} (-A1, A2) B-3M^{8} 3N^{4} (-3N4, *presuambly blank*). ff. 1-483. [43

GARZONI, GIOVANNI. Chronica. Des ... Herrn Friderichen/ Landgraffen in Düringen ... Geschicht vnd thaten. Durch Iohann Gerson von Bononien ... im Latein beschriben/ vnnd volgendt verdeutscht ... Nürnberg. M.D.XLVI. (Gedruckt ... durch Iohann Daubman. M. D. L.) 4°. A-Q⁴. [44

-- Ioannes Garson de miseria hūana Epistole consolatorie. Epigrammata & Epitaphia. a doctis ... Germāie viris ędita ad Thomā Vuolphiū Iuniorē in obitum fratris (Ioannes Grüninger quarta nonas Martij Anno M.D.V. Argentinę imprimebat) 4°. A⁸ B⁴ C⁸ (-C8, *presumably blank*). [45

-- Io. Garzonis ... de rebus Saxoniae, Thuringiae, Libonotriae, Misnae, et Lusatiae, libri duo. ... Apud ... Basileam. (... apud Io. Frobenium mense Martio an. M. D. XVIII.) 4°. A-B⁴ C¹⁰ D-F⁴ G⁶. pp. 2-59. [46

GARZONI, TOMASO. Il teatro de vari, e diuersi ceruelli mondani. ... In Venetia, Appresso Fabio, & Agostin Zoppini, fratelli. 1588. 4°. A-Cc⁴ Dd². ff. 1-96. [47

GASCÓN, JUAN. Ioannis Gasconii Bilbilitani ... in Logicam, siue Dialecticam Aristot. Cōmentaria. ... Oscæ, Excudebat Ioannes Perez à Valdiuielso ... 1576. (*Colophon.*) 4°. ¶⁴ A-D⁴ E⁶ A-Z⁴ a-t⁴ v-z⁸ Aa-Bb⁸ Cc⁶ Dd-Rr⁸. ff. 1-22, 1-334. [48

GAST, JOHANN. Conuiualium sermonum liber ... per Ioannē Peregrinum Petroselanum. Libellum de uarijs moribus Vrbium, Virorum & Mulierum [Hortensii Landi] ... adiecimus. Basileae M. D. XLI. (... apud Bartholomeum VVesthemerum ...) 8°. A⁴ B-Y⁸ Z⁴. [49

GAUTIER DE LILLE, PHILIPPE. Alexandreidos Galteri ... Libri decem. ... M.D.XXXXI. (Ingolstadii excudebat in officina sua Alexander Weissenhorn. ... Pridie Nonas Aprilis.) 8°. π⁸ A-P⁸ (-P8, *presumably blank*). ff. II-CXVI. [50

GAVARDO, DOMITIO. La rosa ... A San Luca alla libraria del diamante. M D LIIII. 8°. A-E⁴. [51

GAZA, THEODORE. Theodori Gazae introductionis grammaticae libri quatuor, Graece, simul cum interpretatione latina ... Basileae apud Nicolaum Bryling. Anno. M. D. XLV. 8°. a-z⁸ A-X⁸. pp. 3-703. [52

GEBET. Christlich Gebett zů zeit der Thewrung vnd Hungersnot. Getruckt zů Tübingen/ 1573. 8°. A⁴. [53

-- Gebett. Die jn de Hörtzogen von Conde Veldleger jn Franckreich gehalten vnd nach gelegenheyt der zeit gerichtet werden. M. D. LXII. Gedruckt [zu Heidelberg] durch Anthony Cortoys der jung 4°. a⁴. [54

-- Gebet/ Psalmen/ vnd Geistliche Lieder/ jetziger Zeit/ do der Erbfeind der Christenheit/ der Türck so grawsam wütet ... Zu Coburg zusammen zudrucken angeordnet. (Gedruckt zu Erffordt/ bey Iacob Singe ... M. D. LXXXXIII.) 8°. A-B⁸. ¶A2ʳ: Gebett wider den Türcken/ von Doctor Martin Luthern gestellt ... *Other authors named: Johann Haberman, Veit Dietrich.* [55

-- Gebet/ Wider die vorstehende Not des Türcken. ... Gedruckt zu Ihena/ Anno 1566. 4°. A⁴. [56

-- Ein Gebet/ Wider die furstehende Not vnd gefahr der Christenheit/ wegen des Türcken. (Gedruckt zu Erffurd/ durch Esaiam Mechlern. ... M. D. XCIII.) 8°. A⁴. [57

-- Zwey Gebet/ Wider die fürstehende Noth vnnd Gefahr der Christenheit wegen des Türcken. Gedruckt zu Erffordt/ bey Iohann Beck. ... M. D. LXXXXIII. 8°. A⁸. [58

GEBWILER, HIERONYMUS. Grauissimae sacrilegii, ac contemptæ theosebiæ ultionis, ethnicorū Hebræorum & Christianorum uerissimis comprobatæ exemplis syngramma ... Ortum et originem Imperialis Oppidi Hagenou ... Liminaris huius libelli Epistola indicat. Anno M. D. XXVIII. (Hagenoæ Anno ·M. D· XXVIII.) 8°. A-D⁸. (Lea.) [59

-- Libertas Germaniae, qua Germanos Gallis, neminem vero Gallum à Christiano natali, Germanis imperasse ... classicorum scriptorum testimonijs probantur. ... (Argentorati apud Ioannem Scotum ... 1519.) 4°. a-b⁴ c⁸ d⁶. [60

-- Panegiris Carolina cōtinēs Hecatostichon elegiacū carmen in ... Cęsareæ atq3 catholicæ Maiestatis præconiū ... (Excusum Argentinæ per Ioannem Prūss Anno M.D.XXI. Mense Augusto.) 4°. π^6 A^4 b-d^4 e^6. ff. I-XXII. [61

GEBWILER, JOHANNES. Magistralis Totius Paruuli artis Logices compilatio ... Natura Vniuersalium preclare in huius operis calce ... (Basileorum urbe nuper 19. Kal'. ... 1511. Impressi in officicina ... Adæ Petri de Langendorff ...) 4°. B.L. a-$f^{8.4}$ g-$v^{4.8}$ x-y^4 $ż^6$ (-z6, *blank*). [62

GECHAUF, THOMAS. Ermanung zum Creuz in der zeyt der verfolgung. Durch Thomam Venatorium. [Nuremberg, Hieronymus Andreae Formschneider,] 1530. 4°. A-B^4. [63

GEDIK, SIMON. Defensio sexus muliebris, opposita ... disputationi recens editæ, qua ... blasphemè contenditur, Mulieres homines non esse. Simon Gediccus ... 1595 Lipsiæ, imprimebat Michael Lantzenberger. 4°. A-H^4. [64

GEDULTIG, PETER. Warnung Fuͤr dem Baͤpstischen Iubel Iar vnnd Ablass. ... Petrus Patiens ... Gedruckt zu Franckfurt am Mayn/ durch Franciscum Bassee. M. D. LXXVII. 4°. A-K^4. pp. II-LXXIII. [65

GEGENBERICHT. Ein kurtzer warer gegenbricht/ Auff das schnoͤd lesterlich gedicht. ... Gestelt Durch ainen Catholischen ... Christen ... 4°. A^4. ¶*In verse.* [66

GEILER, JOHANN, VON KAISERSBERG. Fragmenta passionis domini nostri Iesu christi. ... Per Iacobum Ottherum ... collecta. ... ([Argentinae,] Ex edibus Matthie Schurerij Mense Nouembri. An. M.D.xi.) 4°. B.L. a-b^6 c^4 d-$m^{8.4.4}$ n^8 o^4 p^6. [67

-- Nauicula penitentie. Per ... Ioannem Keyserspergium ... A Iacobo Otthero Collecta. ... (Ordinatione mgr̄i Ioh̄is otmar locatis expensis per ... Georgiū diemar. ... in Augusta vindelicoꝝ ... impressi et finiti in hebdomada post natiuitatem ... virginis Marie. Anni Millesimi Quingentesimi Vndecimi.) fol. B.L. ☞^{6} A^8 B^6 C^8 d^6 e^8 f^6 g^8 h-k^6 L-M^6. ff. i-lxxx. (Lea.) [68

GELDENHAUER, GERARD. Ad Carolum quintum imperatorem ... Epistola Gerardi Nouiomagi, in qua tractatur, Vtrum hæretici iure supplicijs adfici possunt, nec ne. Anno M. D. XXVIII. 8°. A^8 (-A8, *presumably blank*). (Lea.) [69

GELLI, GIOVANNI BATTISTA. I Capricci del Bottaio ... In Firenze MDXLVIII. 8°. $†^8$ A-O^8. pp. 1-224. [70

-- La Circe ... In Firenze ... MDXLIX. (... appresso Lorenzo Torrentino ..., a di Primo d'Aprile ...) 8°. A-R^8. pp. 8-266. [71

-- -- In Vinegia. Appresso di Agostino Bindoni. M. D. L. (*Colophon.*) 8°. A-L^8. ff. 2-88. [72

-- -- ... Nuouamente accresciuta & riformata. In Fiorenza. M D L. (Stampato ... appresso Lorenzo Torrentino ... a di XXII. de Maggio ...) 8°. A-O^8. pp. 3-224. [73

-- -- La Circe ... nouuellement mise en Francoys, par le Seigneur du Parc, Champenois. A Lyon, chez Guill. Rouillé, ... 1550. ... 8°. A-T^8 V^4 (-V4, *presumably blank*). pp. 11-309. [74

-- Lettura ... sopra lo Inferno di Dante. ... In Firenze [per Bartolommeo Sermartelli] MDLIIII. 8°. A-Q^8 R^2. [75

-- Lettura seconda sopra lo Inferno di Dante ... In Fiorenza MDLV. (... appresso M. Lorenzo Torrentino. ...) 8°. A^{10} B-O^8. pp. 1-218. [76

-- Lettura terza ... sopra lo Inferno di Dante. ... In Fiorenza [per Lorenzo Torrentino,] MDLVI. 8°. A-N^8 (-N8, *blank*). pp. 3-202. [77

-- Lettura quarta sopra l'Inferno di Dante, di Gio. Batista Gelli. ... In Fiorenza [per Lorenzo Torrentino,] MDLVIII. 8°. A-P^8. pp. 4-236. [78

-- La quinta lettura ... sopra lo Inferno ... In Fiorenza [per Lorenzo Torrentino,] M D LVIII. 8°. A-N^8. ff. 2-111. [79

-- La sesta Lettura ... Sopra lo Inferno ... In Fiorenza MDLXI. 8°. A-H^8 I^4. [80

-- Lettura settima ... sopra lo Inferno ... In Fiorenza, Appresso Lorenzo Torrentino, MDLXI. 8°. A-I^8. [81

-- Il Gello ... Sopra Que' due Sonetti del Petrarcha che Lodano il ritratto Della Sua M. Laura. In Fiorenza [per Lorenzo Torrentino]. MDXLIX. ... 8°. A-C^8 D^6. pp. 3-57. [82

-- Il Gello accademico Fiorentino sopra vn luogo di Dante, nel XVI. Canto del Purgatorio ... In Firenze [per Lorenzo Torrentino] M. D. XLVIII. 8°. A-G^8 H^4. pp. 3-115. [83

-- Il Gello sopra vn sonetto di M. Franc. Petrarca. In Firenze [per Lorenzo Torrentino]. MDXLIX ... 8°. A-E^8 F^6 (-F6, *presumably blank*). pp. 3-89. [84

-- La sporta commedia ... In Firenze, per Filippo Giunti. MDXCIII. (*Colophon.*) 8°. A-E^8 F^4. pp. 8-87. [85

-- Tutte le lettioni di Giouam Battista Gelli, Fatte da lui nella Accademia Fiorentina. In Firenze [Lorenzo Torrentino?]. M.D.LI. ... 8°. A-Gg^8 Hh^4. pp. 3-486. [86

GELLIUS, AULUS. Auli Gellii noctium Atticarum libri vndeuiginti. ... (Argentinæ, in Aedibus Ioannis Knoblouchi. Mense Martio. Anno M. D. XVII. Ductu Matthiæ Shurerij.) fol. π^{10} a^8 b-n^6 o^8 p-u^6 x^8. ff. 1-105. [87

-- -- A. Gellii ... noctes Atticae ... Eucharius Ceruicornus excudebat Anno M. D. XXVI. (Coloniæ ... sumptu & ære M. Godefridi Hittorpij ... nonis Martijs.) fol. aa-bb^6 A-T^6. pp. 2-202. [88

-- -- Apud Seb. Gryphium Lugduni, 1550. 8°. a-d^8 a-z^8 A-K^8 L^4. pp. 1-533. [89

-- -- ... Praeterea Petri Mosellani in easdem Annotationes. Basileae per Henricum Petri [1565]. 8°. α-γ^8 A-Z^8 a-z^8 Aa-Kk^8 (-Kk8). pp. 3-47, 1-850. [90

-- -- A. Gellii ... noctes Atticæ. Lugduni Apud Bartholom. Vincentium. M. D. LXXI. (... excudebat Mathias Bonhomme.) 8°. a-d^8 a-z^8 A-N^8. pp. 1-575. [91

-- -- ... Henrici Stephani Noctes Aliquot Parisinae ... Eiusdem H. Stephani Annotationes ... cum Notis Lud. Carrionis ... Parisiis [Henricus Stephanus II]. M. D. LXXXV. ... 8°. A-B^8 a-z^8 A-O^8 O-R^8 S^4 A^8 A^2 A-B^8 A^2 C-N^8 (-C1, N8). pp. 1-23, 1-587, 2-205. ¶*The name of Henricus Stephanus has been inked out wherever it appears.* [92

GELMI, GIOVANNI ANTONIO. Stanze ... In Lode dell' ... Signor Pietro Griti ... In Verona. Appresso Sebastiano dalle Donne. 1589. 4°. A-D^4. [93

GENGENBACH, PAMPHILUS. Der bundtschu. Diss biechlein sagtt von dem bösen fürnemen der bundtschuher ... 4°. [A]^4. [94

-- Ein frischer Combisst/ vom Bapst vnd den seinen ettwann vber Teutsch-Landt eingesaltzen. ... [Strassburg, Jakob Cammerlander, c. 1540.] 4°. A-C^4. [95

-- Liber Vagatorum Der Betler orden. 4°. a^8 b^4. [96

-- Der new Deutsch Bileams Esel. Wie die schoͤn Germania ... ist zuͦr Baͤpst Eselin transformiert worden ... 4°. a-e^4. [97

-- Nouella. ... 4°. A-B^4 C^6. [98

-- Von ainem Waldbruͦder wie er vnderricht gibt Bapst Kaiser Künig vnd allen staͤnden. ... 1522. 4°. [A]-F^4. [99

-- Die zehen allter diser wellt ... (Gedruckt von Hannssen Schobsser zuͦ München. Anno ꝛc. jm̄ xvj. jare.) 4°. A-D^4. [100

GENOA. *Republic.* [Statuta & decreta communis Genuae ...] (Venetiis, Apud Dominicum Nicolinum. M D LXVII.) fol. a-b^6 (-a1, b^6) A^6 (-A2-5) B-Cc^6 Dd^4. ff. 1-160. (Lea.) [101

-- Le leggi et riforme della eccelsa republica di Genoua, fatte ... l'anno M.D.XXVIII. In Pauia. Appresso Girolamo Bartoli. M.D.LXXV. 4°. π^2 A-H^4 I^2. ff. 1-32. [102

-- Leges nouae reipublicae Genuen. ... Die XVII. Martii MDLXXVI. publicatae. Genuae, Apud Marcum Antonium Bellonum ... 1576. ... (*Colophon.*) fol. A-M^4. ff. 2-47. ¶A1 *repaired.* (Lea.) [103

GENOA

-- Nuouo decreto et riforma circa lo vestire degl'huomini. In Genoua M.D.LXXXII. 4°. A^4. [104

-- *Rota.* Reformationes rotae Genuae aeditae anno M. D. LVII. Genuae Apud Antonium Bellonum. 4°. A-K^4. (Lea.) [105

-- [1] Reformationes rotae Genuae aeditae anno M. D. LVII. Genuae. 4°. A-B^8. [2] Ad reformationes rotae, et statuta Genuae, appendix aedita, Anno M.D.LXXII. Genuę M.D.LXXXI. X^6. [106

-- Ad reformationes rotae, et statuta Genuae, appendix aedita, anno MDLXXII. Genuæ Apud Antonium Bellonum, MDLXXII. 4°. A^4 B^2. (Lea.) [107

-- Decisiones rotae Genuae de mercatura ... Genuae anno M.D.LXXXII. (... M.D.LXXXI.) fol. π^2 A-Kk^8 LL^6 A-F^8 G^6. ff. 1-270, 1-54. (Lea.) [108

-- *History.* Narratione delle cose occorse nella citta di Genoua, & del soleuamento del popolo contra i gentilhuomini ... In Perugia Appresso Pietroiacomo Petrucci, & Muchel Porto. M. D. LXXV. 4°. π^4. [109

GENTILI, SCIPIO. Annotationi ... sopra La Gierusalemme liberata Di Torquato Tasso. In Leida [i.e. London, by John Wolfe] 1586. 8°. A-Ll^4 (-A2-4). pp. 1-274. [110

GENTILIS, ALBERICUS. Alberici Gentilis ... de armis Romanis Libri duo ... Hanouiæ Apud Guilielmum Antonium, MDXCIX. 8°. π^2 A-R^8 S^6. pp. 1-284. [111

GENTILLET, INNOCENT. Commentariorum de regno aut quouis Principatu rectè & tranquillè administrando, libri tres ... Aduersus Nicolaum Machiauellum Florentinum. [Genevae, Jacobus Stoer?] CIϽ IϽ LXXVII. 8°. †-$††^8$ A-Yy^8. pp. 1-708. [112

-- -- Discours, sur les moyens de bien gouuerner et maintenir en bonne paix vn Royaume, ou autre Principauté. ... Contre Nicolas Machiauel Florentin. ... Troisieme Edition reueuë. M. D. LXXVIII. (Acheue d'imprimer ... ce dernier iour de Septembre.) 16°. $*^8$ A-$3H^8$. ff. 2-16, pp. 17-843. (Biddle.) [113

-- -- Regentenkunst/ oder Fürstenspiegel. ... Geschriben wider ... Nicolaum Machiauellum ... durch G. N. verteutscht. Gedruckt zu Franckfurt am Mayn. M. D. LXXX. (Gedruckt ... bey Georg Raben/ in verlegung Bernhard Iobins/ ... Buchhendlers in Strassburg. ...) 8°. $)(^8$ A-Z^8 a-z^8 Aa-Nn^8. ff. 1-470. ¶*Translator: Georgius Nigrinus, i.e. Schwartz.* [114

-- Examen Concilii Tridentini: In quo demonstratur, in multis articulis hoc Concilium antiquis Conciliis & Canonibus, Regiaq3 authoritati contrarium esse. ... Geneuæ per Dionysium Probum, & Heliam Viollier. M. D. LXXXVI. 8°. A-Cc^8 Dd^4. pp. 1-398. (Lea.) [115

-- -- Le bureau du Concile de Trente: Auquel est monstré qu'en plusieurs poincts iceluy Concile est contraire aux anciens Conciles & Canons, & à l'autorité du Roy. ... Par Denis Preud'homme. M. D. LXXXVI. 8°. $*_*{*}^4$ A-Bb^8 Cc^6. pp. 1-382. (Lea.) [116

GEOFFREY OF MONMOUTH. Britãnie vtriusq3 regũ ⁊ principũ Origo ⁊ gesta insignia ab Galfrido Monemutensi ex antiquissimis ... monumentis in latinũ sermonẽ traducta: & ab Ascensio cura & impẽdio magistri Iuonis Cauellati in lucem edita: ꝓstant in eiusdem ædibus. (... Ad idus Iulias Anni MDVIII.) 4°. AA^8 A-M^8 N^6. ff. I-CI. [117

-- -- Pontici Virunnii ... Britannicae historiae libri. VI. ... M.D. XXXIIII. (Augustæ Vindelicorum in officina Alexandri VVeyssenhorn. ...) 8°. A-E^8 G^4. [118

GEOPONIKA. Γεωπονικα. De re rustica selectorum libri XX. Graeci ... Io. Alexandri Brassicani opera ... editi. ... Item, Aristotelis de plantis libri duo Græci ... Basileae. (... αναλώμασι Ρόβερτου Χειμερινου ... α φ λ θ [1539], μουνυχιῶνος μηνός.) 8°. α-γ^8 a-z^8 A-L^8 M^4. pp. 1-551. [119

GEORGE OF TREBIZOND. Comparationes phylosophorum Aristotelis et Platonis a Georgio Trapezuntio ... (Venetiis per Iacobum pentium de Leuco ... MDXXIII. nonis Ianuarii.) 8°. a^4 A-V^8 X^4. [120

-- Georgii Trapezuntii rhetoricorum libri ... In ... Basilea. (Cudebat ... Valentinus Curio anno M. D. XXII. mense Augusto.) 4°. aa^6 a-z^4 A-X^4 (-X4, *presumably blank*). ff. 1-175. [121

-- -- Continentur hoc volumine Georgii Trapezuntii Rhetoricorum libri V. Consulti Chirii Fortunatiani libri III. Aquilæ Romani de figuris sententiarum, & elocutionis liber. P. Rutilii lupi earundem figurarum è Gorgia liber, Aristotelis Rhetoricorum ad Theodecten Georgio Trapeauntio interprete libri III. Eiusdem Rhetorices ad Alexandrum à Francisco Philelpho ... uersæ liber. Paraphrasis Rhetoricæ Hermogenis ex Hilarionis ... traductione. Priscianus de Rhetoricæ præexercitamentis ex Hermogene. Aphthonii ... rhetorica progymnasmata Io. Maria Catanæo tralatore. (Venetiis in aedibus Aldi, et Andreae Asulani soceri mense Aprili. M.D.XXIII.) fol. $*^4$ a-t^8 u^{10}. ff. 1-161. [122

GEORGIEVICS, BARTHOLOMAEUS. De Turcarum moribus epitome, Bartholomæo Georgieuiz Peregrino Autore. ... Parisiis, Apud Hieronymum de Marnef, & Gulielmum Cauellat ... 1566. 12°. A-L^8. pp. 3-170. [123

GERALDINI, ANTONIO. Antonii Geraldini ... Bucolicon opus ... in quo ... uitā Christi ... cōplexus est. ... (Excusum ... Viēnæ, solertia Hieronymi Philouallis & Ioānis Singrenii sodaliū. Expensis uero Leonardi & Lucæ Alantse fratrū. Pridie Kalendas Iunii ... M.D.XIII. ...) 4°. a^8 b-c^4 d^6. [124

GERARD VAN HARDERWIJK. Questio de Crucib9 oībusq3 Christi armis inuentis determinata studio Coloniensi. (impressum Nürmberg [per Johannem Weissenburger] Anno 1503.) 4°. π^4. [125

GERBEL, NICOLAUS. Defensio Christianorum de Cruce. id est, Lutheranorum. Cum pia admonitione F. Thomæ Murnar ... Matthæi Gnidij Augusteñ. Epistolæ item aliquot. [1520.] 4°. a-c^4. [126

-- Dialogi. Decoctio. Eckius monachus ... 4°. A-B^4 (-B4, *presumably blank*). [127

-- Dialogi septem ... Authore S. Abydeno, Corallo, Germ. ... [Basileae, 1538.] 4°. a-f^8 g^6. [128

-- Eccius dedolatus authore Ioannefrancisco Cotta lembergio ... (Impressum per Agrippum Panoplium Regis Persarum Bibliopolam L. Simone Samaritano et .D. Iuda Schariottide Consulibus In vrbe Lucernarū Apud Confluentes Rhenū et Istrum [= Erfurt, Matthaeus Maler, 1520].) 4°. B.L. [A]-D^4. [129

-- Oratio ad Carolum ... & Germaniȩ Principes, pro Vlricho Hutteno ... & Martino Luthero, Patriæ, & Christianȩ libertatis adsertoribus Authore S. Abydeno, Corallo, Germ. [Argentorati, Johannes Schott, 1521.] 4°. A^4 B^6. [130

-- Nicolai Gerbelij Phorcensis, pro declaratione picturæ siue descriptionis Græciæ Sophiani, Libri septem. ... Basileae, per Ioannem Oporinum [c. 1550]. fol. α^6 a-z^4 A-O^4 P^8. pp. 1-297. [131

GERHARDT, HANS. Schöne Frag vnd Antwort/ Was ain warhafftiger Christen der recht Glaub/ vnd seyn frucht sey. ... [Augsburg, Heinrich Steiner,] M: D: xxv: 4°. A^4 B^2. [132

GERLACHER, THEOBALD. An die Christelich kirch versamlung ainem Ersamen Radt vnd gemain der Stat Weyl. Herr Theopalden von Bellican Sendbrieff. Im Jar M D XXij. [Augsburg, Melchior Ramminger.] 4°. A-B^4 C^2. [133

-- Epitome dialectices, Theobaldo Billicano autore. ... 8°. A-B^8. [134

GERSON, JEAN CHARLIER DE. [Quarta pars operum Iohannis Gerson ...] (pdeunt ... ex officina Martini flacci iunior? Argeñ. ... Mathie schurer Sletstatini ɔsobrini ei9 opa .iij. kal'. Martij. Anno .1502.) fol. B.L. aa-bb^6 (-aa1) a-c^6 d^8 e^6 f^8 g-h^6 i^8 k^6 l^8 m^6 n-o^8 p^6 q-s^8 t-v^6 x-y^8 z^6 A^8 B^6 C-F^8 G-H^6 I^8 K^6 L-M^8 N-O^6 P^8 Q-R^6 S-T^8. (Lea.) [135

-- -- [1] Prima pars operum Ioannis Gerson ... (... apud Tribotes: p Ioānem Knoblouch. Anno. M.d.xiiij. Kalendis Iunijs.) fol. B.L. a-gg^6 A-E^6 F-G^8. ¶*Additional t.p.* ($A1^r$): Inuentoriū eorum que in tribus primis partibus ... continētur ... [2] Secūda pars operū Ioannis de Gerson ... (Argētoraci ... decimoquīto Kl'as Martij.) A^8 B-Z^6 aA-nN^6 oO^8. [3] Tertia pars ... (... Pridie Idus Aprilis.) aa^8 bb-zz^6 Aa-Zz^6 AA-EE^6. [4] Quarta et nuper conquisita pars ... (... pdie idus Augusti ...) aa^{10} a-z^6 A-P^6 (-P6, *blank*). (Yarnall.) [135a

GERSON

-- Summa theologica et canonica Ioannis Gerson ... Venetiis, M D LXXXVII. Apud Dominicum Nicolinum. (*Colophon.*) 4°. $*^4$ A-B^4 a-c^4 d^2 A-5P^4 5Q^6. ff. 1-433. (Lea.) [136

GERTOPHIUS, JOANNES. Recriminatio Ioan. Gertophii, adulescētis Germani, aduersus furiosissimum Sycophantam Edoardum Leum Anglum, qui ausus est primus Erasmum candidissimum luto aspergere. Epigramma ... Hermanni Buschii ... (Basileae, apud Andream Cratandrum, mense Iunio. Anno M. D. XX.) 4°. A-B^4 C^6. pp. 4-25. [137

GERVAIS DE TOURNAI. Diuina quatuor energumenorum liberatio, facta apud Suessiones ... Iam scripsit Geruasius Tornacensis ... Parisiis, Apud Guillelmum Chaudiere ... M.D.LXXXIII. ... 8°. A-O^8. ff. 2-111. [138

GESNER, CONRAD. Bibliotheca Vniuersalis, siue Catalogus omnium scriptorum ..., in tribus linguis, Latina, Græca, & Hebraica ... Tiguri apud Christophorum Froschouerum Mense Septembri, Anno M. D. XLV. fol. $*^8$ A^6 B^4 a-z^6 A-Zz^6 aa-zz^6 AA-MM^6 NN^8. ff. 1-631. [139

-- -- Bibliotheca instituta et collecta, primum a Conrado Gesnero: Deinde in Epitomen redacta, & ... locupletata, tertiò recognita, & ... aucta, per Iosiam Simlerum: Iam verò postremò ... amplificata, per Iohannem Iacobum Frisium Tigurinum. ... Tiguri excudebat Christophorus Froschouerus. anno M.D.LXXXIII. fol. $*^8$ 3a-3b^6 3c^8 a-z^6 A-Zz^6 AA^6. pp. 1-835. [140

-- Chirurgia. De chirurgia scriptores optimi quique veteres et recentiores ... Tiguri per Andream Gessnerum f. et Iacobum Gessnerum fratres, mense Martio ... M. D. LV. (*Colophon.*) fol. $+^6$ $*^4$ (-*4, *blank*) A-Z^6 a-z^6 Aa-Yy^6 α-β^6 γ^8. ff. 1-408. ¶*Authors: Jean Tagault, Jacques Houllier, Mariano Santo, Angelo Bolognini, Michele Angelo Biondo, Bartolommeo Maggi, Alphonso Ferri, Johann Lange, Claudius Galenus, Oribasius, Jacobus de Dondis, Conrad Gesner.* [141

-- Elenchus scriptorum omnium ... publicatorū atqȝ hinc inde in Bibliothecis latitantium, qui ... claruerunt, ac etiamnum hodie uiuunt: ... nūc uerò ... redactus ...: per Conradum Lycosthenem Rubeaquensem. ... Basileae. (... per Ioannem Oporinum ... M.D.LI. Mense Septembri.) 4°. a-b^4 A-4C^4. coll. 1-1096. [142

-- -- Epitome Bibliothecæ Conradi Gesneri, conscripta primum à Conrado Lycosthene Rubeaquensi: nunc denuo recognita ... per Iosiam Simlerum Tigurinum. ... Tiguri apud Christophorum Froschouerum, mense Martio, anno M. D. LV. (*Colophon.*) fol. $*^6$ a-z^6 A-K^6. ff. 1-184. [143

-- Λεξικον siue dictionarium Graecolatinum ... partim per D. Conradum Gesnerum, partim uerò per Ioan. Hartongum auctum ... Basileæ. (Ex officina Hieronymi Curionis, impensis Henrichi Petri, mense Septembri. Anno MD. LX.) fol. $+^4$ a-z^8 A-3Q^8 3R^{10} Aα-Bβ^4 $\Gamma\gamma^6$. [144

-- Libellus de lacte, et operibus lactariis, philologus pariter ac medicus. Cum epistola ... de montium admiratione. ... Tiguri apud Christophorum Froschouerum [c. 1541]. 8°. A-F^8 G^4 (-G4, *presumably blank*). ff. 2-51. [145

-- Mithridates. De differentiis linguarum ... Obseruationes. Anno M.D.LV. Tiguri excudebat Froschouerus. 8°. A-K^8 (K8 + *folded sheet: the Lord's Prayer in 23 languages*). ff. 1-78. [146

-- [1] Pandectarum siue Partitionum uniuersalium ... libri XXI. ... Tiguri excudebat Christophorus Froschouerus, Anno M.D.XLVIII. fol. $*^6$ a-i^6 k^4 l^6 m^8 n-o^4 p^6 q^8 r^4 s^8 t^6 u^4 x-z^6 A-G^6 H^4 I-Q^6 R^8 S-Ee^6 Ff^8 Gg-Rr^6 aa^6 bb^8. ff. 1-374. [2] Partitiones theologicæ, Pandectarum Vniuersalium ... Liber ultimus. ... Christophorus Froschouerus excudit Tiguri, Anno M. D. XLIX. fol. a^8 aa-zz^6 AA-BB^6 CC^8. ff. 1-157. [147

-- [1] Conradi Gesneri Tigurini ... physicarum Meditationum, Annotationum & Scholiorum Lib. V. ... collecti, ... dispositi ... per Casparum VVolphium Tigurinum ... Tiguri in officina Froschouiana, anno M. D. LXXXVI. fol. aa^6 bb^4 A-Z^6 Aa^8. pp. 1-289. [2] Conradi Gesneri ... physicarum meditationum Liber V. ... *Same imprint.* α-ϕ^6. pp. 3-250. [148

-- Thesaurus Euonymi Philiatri, de remediis secretis ... Lugduni, Apud Balthazarem Arnolletum. M. D. LV. (*Colophon.*) 8°. aa^4 a-z^8 A-K^8 L^4. pp. 1-498. (Smith.) [149

-- -- Tesauro di Euonomo Filatro de rimedi secreti. ... Tradotto di Latino in volgar, per M. Pietro Lauro. ... In Venetia, MDLXXXVIII. Presso Gio. Battista Bonfadio. (*Colophon.*) 8°. A-X^8. ff. 2-152. (Smith.) [150

-- -- Quatre liures des secrets de medecine, et de la philosophie chymique. Faicts Francois par M. Iean Liebaut Diionnois ... A Lyon, par Benoist Rigaud M. D. XCIII. (... De l'Imprimerie des Heritiers de Pierre Roussin. ...) 8°. $*^8$ A-PP^8 QQ^4. ff. 1-293. (Smith.) [151

GESPRÄCH. Eyn freüntlichs gesprech/ zwischen eynem Parfusser münch/ ... vnd einem Loͤffelmacher/ mit namen/ Hans Stösser ... [1521.] 4°. A-D^4. [152

-- Ein gesprech auff des kurtzt zwuschē eynem Christen vñ Iuden/ auch eynem Wyrthe samps seynem Haussknecht/ den Eckstein Christum betreffendt ... (1524) 4°. A-D^4 (-D1). [153

GESTA ROMANORUM. Gesta Romanorum cum applicationibus moralisatis ac misticis (Ex pariss. Anno ... Millesimo quingentesimo decimo septimo die vero vndecimo mensis octobris) 8°. B.L. A-Y^8 z^8 $ꝛ^8$ $ɔ^8$ A-B^8 C^4. ff. ij-ci. [154

-- Die alten Roͤmer. Sittliche Historien vnd Zuchtgleichnussen der Alten Roͤmer ... Itzunt ... verteutscht ... Getruckt zů Strassburg beim Iacob Cammerlander von Mentz. Anno M. D. XXXViij. fol. π^4 A-Y^4 (-N2, N3, Y4, *the last presumably blank*). ff. j-lxxxvij. [155

GEUFFROY, ANTOINE. [1] Aulae Turcicae, Othomannicique imperii, descriptio ... primùm ab Antonio Geufræo Gallicè edita: recens autem in Latinam linguam conuersa, Per VVilhelmum Godeleuaeum. ... Basileae. (... per Sebastianum Henricpetri. Anno M.D.LXXIII. Mense Martio.) 8°. a-c^8 d^4 *-4*^{8} A-X^8 Y^4. pp. 1-340. [2] Cyprium bellum, inter Venetos, et Selymum Turcarum imperatorem gestum, Libris tribus ... descriptum ... Authore, Petro Bizaro. ... $()^8$ α-γ^8 δ^4 Aa-Ss^8. pp. 1-283. [3] Pannonicum bellum, sub Maximiliano II. Rom. et Solymano Turcar. imperatoribus gestum ... descriptum, Per Petrum Bizarum. Vnâ, Cum Epitome illarum rerum, quæ in Europa ... gestæ sunt ... ab anno LXIIII. usq3 ad LXXIII. ... Basileae, per Sebastianum Henricpetri. (... M.D.LXXIII. Mense Febr.) $*^8$ a-c^8 d^4 AA-XX^8. pp. 1-322. [156

-- -- Pars I. Aulæ Turcicæ, Othomannicique imperii descriptio ... Pars II. Solymanni XII. & Selymi XIII. Turcar. impp. contra Christianos ... res gestæ ... ab anno CIↃ.IↃ.XX. usq3 in præsentem annum CIↃ.IↃ.LXXVII. peractæ. ... collectæ: per, N. Honigerum Koningshof. Franc. ... Basileæ. (... per Sebastianum Henricpetri ... CIↃ.IↃ.LXXVII. Mense Martio.) 8°. α-ε^8 ξ^4 A-II^8. pp. 1-509. ¶*Part 2 wanting.* [157

GEWALT. Von gaistlich gewalt vnd würdighait/ Warer vnd rechter gehorsam/ vnnd wievil der Prelaten gepott vnnd gesatz die vnderthon verpinden. 4°. A-C^4. [158

GHERARDO, PIETRO. In foedus et uictoriam contra Turcas iuxta Sinum Corinthiacum Non. Octob. ↀDLXXI. Partam Poemata uaria. Petri Gherardii Burgensis studio ... conquisita, ac disposita. ... Venetiis. ↀDLXXII. Ex Typographia Guerræa. 8°. $*^8$ A-H^8 $H*^8$ $H**^4$ I-Dd^8 Ee^4. pp. 3-439. [159

GHERARDO, QUINTO. Le terze rime piaceuoli ... M D XXXVII. 8°. A-C^4. [160

GHIRARDI, BONETO. La Leonida comedia ... In Venetia. Appresso Paolo Meietto. M D LXXXV. 8°. A-S^8. ff. 1-136. [161

GIACOMINI TEBALDUCCI MALESPINI, LORENZO. Oratione in lode di Torquato Tasso ... In Fiorenza Appresso Giorgio Marescotti MDXCV. 4°. a^2 A-D^4 E^2. pp. 1-27. [162

-- Orationi e discorsi ... In Fiorenza Ne le Case de Sermartelli ... 1597. ... (*Colophon.*) 4°. a^2 A-K^4 L^6. pp. 1-91. [162a

GIAMBULLARI, PIERFRANCESCO. Apparato et feste nelle noze dello ... Duca di Firenze, & della Duchessa sua Consorte, con le sue Stanze, Madriali, Comedia, & Intermedij, in quelle recitati. M. D. XXXIX. (Impressa in Fiorenza per Benedetto Giunta, ... di XXIX d'Agosto.) 8°. A-L^8. pp. 3-171. ¶E2r: Il commodo comedia di Antonio Landi. [163

-- Pierfrancesco Giambullari ... De'l Sito, Fórma, & Misúre, dello Inférno di Dánte. In Firénze per Néri Dorteláta M.D.XLIIII. 8°. A-K^8 L^4. pp. 3-153. [164

-- Pierfrancesco Giambullari Fiorentino, de la lingua che si parla & scriue in Firenze. Et vno Dialogo di Giouan Batista Gelli sopra la difficultà dello ordinare detta Lingua. In Firenze [1551]. ... 8°. A-Bb^8 Cc^4 (-Cc4, *blank*). pp. 3-402. [165

-- Lezzioni ... In Firenze [per Lorenzo Torrentino,] MDLI. 8°. A-K^8. pp. 1-157. [166

-- Lezzioni ... In Firenze [per Lorenzo Torrentino,] MDLI. 8°. A-K^8. pp. 1-157. [166

-- Origine della lingua Fiorentina, altrimenti il Gello ... In Fiorenza. Appresso Lorenzo Torrentino. MDXLIX. ... 8°. A-L^8 $*^8$. pp. 3-176. [167

GIANCARLI, GIGIO ARTEMIO. La capraria comedia di Gigio Arthemio Rhodigino Appresso Francesco Marcolini ... in Venetia M D XXXXIIII. (... il Mese di Maggio. ...) 8°. A^4 B-H^8 I^6. [168

-- La zingana [co]media ... In Mantoua [per Venturino Ruffinelli], del mese di Ottobre nel XLV. (... M. D. XLVI.) 8°. A-L^8 M^4. ff. 2-92. ¶*Label pasted on t.p.* [169

GIGAS, GIROLAMO. Tractatus de pensionibus ecclesiasticis. ... M.D.XLII ... (Venetiis impressum, ... expensis dominorum Francisci & Michaelis de Tremezinis, a Nicolao Bascarino, Mense Maio ...) 4°. +-3+^{8} A-T^8. ff. 2-151. [170

-- ... Hieronymi Gigantis Tractatus de residentia Episcoporum. ... M D XLVIII. (Venetiis apud Nicolaum de Bascarinis. ... Mense Ianuario.) 8°. $*^{12}$ A-K^8. ff. 3-80. (Lea.) [171

GIGAS, JOHANNES. De certitudine religionis Christianae concio ... Addita sunt innocua quædam poëmata. M. D. LI. (Francoforti ad Viadrum, in officina Ioannis Eichorn. ...) 8°. A-C^8. [172

GIKITILLA, JOSEPH BEN ABRAHAM. Portae lucis Hoc est porta Tetragrāmaton iusti intrabūt p̲ eam. ... (Excusa in officina Millerana Augustæ Vindelicorū. quinto Idus Iunias. ... M.D.XVI.) 4°. A^8 B-N^4 (-N4, *presumably blank*). ¶*Translator: Paolo Ricci.* (Lea.) •[173

GILHAUSEN, ISAAC. Grammatica, Das ist: Eine ... Comoedia, von dem schlüssel aller Künsten ... Durch M. Isaacum Gilhausium Marpurgensem. Getruckt zu Franckfort am Mayn durch Nicolaum Bassæum. M D XCVII. 8°. A-K^8. pp. 3-159. [174

GILIO, GIOVANNI ANDREA. La persecutioni della chiesa descritte in cinque libri ... In Vinegia appresso Gabriel Giolito de' Ferrari. M D LXXIII 4°. a-d^4 A-EE^8 FF^6. pp. 1-457. (Lea.) [175

GILLES, NICOLE. [1] Les treselegantes & copieuses Annales, des ... moderateurs des belliqueuses Gaules. ... Compilées par ... Nicole Gilles, iusques au temps du roy Loys vnziesme. Et depuis additionnes ... iusques en Lan mil cinq cents quarāte & sept. ... On les vend ā Paris, par Iehan de Roigny ... M.D.XLVII. fol. a^6 A-Y^6. ff. i-cxxxii. [2] Le second volume des Croniques & Annales de France ... *Same imprint.* (acheuées d'imprimer ... par René Auril ... le vingtiesme iour de Mars ...) aa^6 AA-ZZ^6 $3A^4$. ff. i-Cxlii. [176

-- -- [1] Franszösische Chronica ... durch Nicolaus Falckner ... in hohe Teutsche Sprach gebracht. ... Getruckt ... M. D. LXXII. (Getruckt zu Basel/ bey Niclaus Brylingers seligen Ehrben ...) fol. $()^4$ $†^4$ a-z^6 A-I^6. pp. 1-382. [2] Ander vnd leste Theil Frantzösischer Chronica ... *Same imprint.* $()^4$ $*^4$ Aa-Zz^6 AA-SS^6 TT^8. pp. 1-505. [177

GILLES DE NOYERS, JEAN. Prouerbia cōmunia tam gallico q̄ꝫ latino sermone per ordinem Alphabeticum venusto Carmine contexta ... Preterea de tempore quadragesimali libellus elegans Dyalogi tres. ... Et auli Gelii sententiis a. N. B. T. collectis. ... M.CCCCC.xxix. 16°. B.L. A^8 B-C^4 D^8. [178

GIORDANI, LELIO. Tractatus de maioribus, rerumque capitalium Episcoporum causis ad Papam deferendis, Et Romanæ Sedis origine, atqꝫ authoritate. Authore ... Lælio Iordano ... Venetiis, Apud Dominicum Nicolinum, M D LXXII. 4°. a-f^4 A-R^4 S^6. ff. 1-74. (Lea.) [179

GIORGIO, FRANCESCO. Francisci Georgii Veneti ... de harmonia mundi totius cantica tria (Venetiis in ædibus Bernardini de Vitalibus ... An.D. M.D.XXV. mense Septemb.) fol. ✠^{4} π^{10} A-Z^8 A-S^8 T^6 V^4 a-o^8 p^6 q^8 r-s^6 (-s6, *blank*). ff. I-CCCXXXVIII, II-CXXXVI. [180

GIOVANETTI, FRANCESCO. Pontificum Romanorum liber ex veteribus Germanis desumptus Authoribus per Franciscum Ioannetum ... Bononiae, Typis Alexandri Benatii. MDLXX. ... 4°. ✠-✠✠^{4} 3✠^{2} A-TT^4 a-d^4. pp. 1-336. (Lea.) [181

GIOVANNI DA FANO. Iesus Maria opera utilissima uulgare cōtra le p̲nitiosissime heresie Lutherane. p̲ li simplici. M.D.XXXII. (Giouan Battista Phaello bolognese in Bologna Impresse. ... del Mese di Settembre.) 8°. B.L. ✠^{4} A-N^8. ff. 1-104. [182

GIOVANNI, TITO. La dialettica ... In Vinegia appresso Gabriel Giolito de' Ferrari. M D LXIII. 4°. *8 A-G8 H10. pp. 1-131. [183

GIOVANNINI, ANGELO. Lettioni ... Sopra i Versi Latini del Sanazaro nella Passione di nostro Signore ... In Iesi, Appresso Pietro Farri. M D XCVII. ... 4°. A-X4. ff. 5-77. [184

GIOVIO, PAOLO. [1] Pauli Iouii Nouocomensis.Opera quotquot extant omnia. ... P. Perna[e t]yp. Basil. ty[pis.] CIↃ IↃ LX[XVI]II. (... sumptibus vero Henrico Petri et sibi, communibu ... Calendis Martijs.) fol. (:)6 (-(:)2-6) a-z6 A-L6 A-B6 aa-zz6 Aa-Zz6 AA-HH6 pp. 1-408, 1-617. ¶*T.p. blotted.* [2] Pauli Iouii ... Regionum et Insularum atque Locorum: descriptiones ... Basileae ... M. D. LXXVIII. 3a-3n6 3o4 (*wanting*). pp. 3-156. (Lea.) [185

-- Commentario de le cose de' Turchi ... (Stampata in Roma per Maestro Antonio Blado d' Asola [1531.]) 4°. A-K4 L6. [186

-- -- Turcicarum rerum commentarius ...: Ex Italico Latinus factus, Francisco Nigro Bassianato interprete. ... Argentorati excudebat VVendelinus Rihelius Anno M D XXXVII. (... Mense Septembri ...) 8°. A-E8 F4 G8. ¶*T.p. blotted.* [187

-- Pauli Iouii ... de vita Leonis decimi Pont. Max. libri quatuor. His ... accesserunt Hadriani Sexti Pont. Max. Et Pompeii Columnæ Cardinalis vitæ ... Florentiae Ex officina Laurentii Torrentini ... MDLI. ... fol. ✠4 A-S6 T2 (-S6 T2). pp. 1-204. [188

-- -- Le vite di Leon decimo et d'Adriano sesto sommi pontefici, et del Cardinal Pompeo Colonna ... tradotte da M. Ludouico Domenichi. In Vinegia, Appresso Giouanni de' Rossi, M. D. LVII. (*Colophon.*) 8°. A-Z8 (-A8, *presumably blank*). ff. 9-184. (Lea.) [189

-- Descriptio Britanniae, Scotiae, Hyberniae, et Orchadum, ex libro Pauli Iouii ... (Venetiis apud Michaelem Tramezinum. M D XLVIII.) 4°. A4 a-gg4 hh6. ff. 1-125. [190

-- [1] Dialogo dell'imprese militari et amorose ..., Con vn Ragionamento di Messer Lodouico Domenichi, nel medesimo soggetto. ... In Lione, appresso Guglielmo Rouiglio. 1559. ... 4°. a-z4 A-B4 C2. pp. 5-194. [2] Le imprese heroiche et morali ritrouate da M. Gabriello Symeoni Fiorentino. ... *Same imprint.* a-f4 g2. pp. 3-51. [191

-- -- In Lyone, Appresso Guglielmo Rouillio. 1574. 8°. A-S8 T4. pp. 3-280. [192

-- Pauli Iouii ... Elogia virorum bellica virtute illustrium veris imaginibus supposita ... Florentiae In officina Laurentii Torrentini ... MDLI. fol. a-q6 r-s4 t-z6 A-E6 F8. pp. 3-340. [193

-- -- Gli elogi vite breuemente scritte d'huomini illustri di guerra ... Tradotte per M. Lodouico Domenichi. In Venetia, Appresso Francesco Bindoni. 1560. 8°. A-Oo8. pp. 1-574. [194

-- [1] Pauli Iouii ... illustrium virorum vitae. ... Tomus primus. Basileæ MDLXVII. (... per Henricum Petri et Petrum Pernam ...) 8°. a-z8 A-Kk8. pp. 3-891. [2] Pauli Iouii ... vitarum virorum illustrium tomus secundus. Basileæ MDLXVII. (... Sumptibus Henrici Petri, & Petri Pernæ Typographorum.) a-z8 A-I8 L-O8. pp. 4-482. (Lea.) [195

-- -- Le iscrittioni poste sotto le vere imagini de gli huomini famosi; Le quali à Como nel Museo del Giouio si veggiono. Tradotte di Latino in volgare da Hippolito Orio Ferrarese. In Fiorenza. MDLII. (... appresso Lorenzo Torrentino ... del mese di Dicembri l'anno MDLI.) 4°. ✠6 a-z4 Aa-Hh4 (-Hh4, *presumably blank*). pp. 2-344. [196

-- -- Le iscrittioni poste sotto le vere imagini de gli huomini famosi in lettere. ... In Venetia. Appresso Giouanni de' Rossi (... 1558.) 8°. A-S8. pp. 1-271. [197

-- Lettere volgari ... Raccolte per Messer Lodouico Domenichi. ... In Venetia appresso Giouan Battista et Marchion Sessa f. (... M D LX.) 8°. A-P8 Q4. ff. 2-122. [198

-- Libro ... de' pesci Romani. tradotto in Volgare da Carlo Zancaruolo. ... In Venetia, appresso il Gualtieri. 1560. 4°. A-BB4 (-BB4, *blank*). pp. 3-197. [199

-- La vita di Consaluo Ferrando di Cordoua detto il gran capitano. ... tradotta per M. Lodouico Domenichi. In Fiorenza MDLII. (... appresso Lorenzo Torrentino ... del Mese di Nouembre ...) 8°. A-N8 O12. pp. 3-231. [200

GIOVIO

-- Vita Sfortiae ... ducis ... Romae M. D. XXXIX. (Antonius Bladus excudebat ... mense Nouembri) 4°. a^{4} A-N^{4}. ff. I-XLVIII. [201

-- Le vite de i dodeci Visconti, e di Sforza prencipi di Milano. ... Tradotte per M. Lodouico Domenichi. ... In Vinegia appresso Gabriel Giolito de' Ferrari. M D LVIII. 8°. *-**^{8} A-O^{8}. pp. 1-224. ¶*Lacks the life of Sforza.* [202

GIRALDI, LILIO GREGORIO. [1] Lilii Greg. Gyraldi Ferrariensis Operum quæ extant omnium ... tomi duo. ... Basileae Per Thomam Guarinum. M D LXXX. fol.)(^{8} a-z^{6} A-Ii^{6} Kk^{4} α-β^{6}. pp. 1-666. [2] ... Tomus secundus. *Same imprint.* (*Colophon.*) *^{4} aa-zz^{6} AA-3K^{6}. pp. 2-634. [203

-- Cynthii Ioannis Baptistae Gyraldi ... de Ferraria et Atestinis principibus commentariolum ex Lilii Gregorii Gyraldi epitome deductum. Ferrariae per Franciscum Rubeum, MDLVI. mense Feb. 4°. A-T^{4} t^{4} V-X^{4} Y^{8}. ff. 2-78. ¶*Sig.* t *wrongly imposed.* [204

-- De deis gentium uaria & multiplex Historia ... ... Basileae, per Ioannem Oporinum. (... ex officina Iacobi Parci, sumptibus Ioannis Oporini ... M. D. LX. Mense Augusto.) fol. a-c^{6} A-Z^{6} a-x^{6} y^{4} z^{6} Aa^{8}. pp. 5-31, 1-536. [205

-- Huic libello insunt Lilii Gregorii Gyraldi Ferrariensis Herculis vita. Eiusdem de Musis syntagma ... Epithalamia diuersorum in nuptias Ioan. Sinapii Germani, & Franciscae Bucyronię Gallæ. Iudicium vocalium. Σίγμα accusat Ταῦ, Luciano Samosateo autore, Coelio Calcagnino interprete. Ταῦ diluit accusationem Σίγμα, Coelio Calcagnino autore. ... Basileæ, apud Mich. Ising. M. D. XXXIX. 8°. A^{8} B^{4} a-l^{8} m^{4}. pp. 2-177. [206

-- Lilii Gregorii Gyraldi Ferr. Liber aduersus Ingratos ... Florentiae Excudebat Laurentius Torrentinus ... (... XII. Calend. Decemb. MDXLVIII.) 8°. A-I^{8}. pp. 3-143. [207

GIRALDI CINTHIO, GIOVANNI BATTISTA. Altile tragedia ... In Venetia, Appresso Giulio Cesare Cagnacini M D LXXXIII. 8°. A-I^{8}. pp. 4-144. [208

-- Gli antiualomeni tragedia ... In Venetia, Appresso Giulio Cesare Cagnacini. M D LXXXIII. (... Appresso Nicolò Moretti. ...) 8°. A-G^{8} H^{4}. pp. 3-118. [209

-- Arrenopia tragedia ... In Venetia, Appresso Giulio Cesare Cagnacini. M D LXXXIII. 8°. A-I^{8} (-I8, *presumably blank*). pp. 3-142. [210

-- Cleopatra tragedia ... In Venetia, Appresso Giulio Cesare Cagnacini. M D LXXXIII. 8°. A-H^{8}. pp. 3-127. [211

-- [1] De gli hecatommithi ... Parte prima Nel Monte Regale Appresso Lionardo Torrentino M D LXV. 8°. a^{8} *^{8} a-m^{8} n^{4} 1^{2} o-x^{8} 2^{2} y-hh^{8} 3^{2} ii-qq^{8} rr^{4} 4^{2} ss-3b^{8} 5^{2} 3c-3l^{8} 3m^{4} (-3m4, *presumably blank*). pp. 1-902. [2] La seconda parte de gli hecatommithi ... *Same imprint.* **^{8} 3*^{4} A-D^{8} E^{2} E-P^{8} 6^{2} P-V^{8} X^{4} 7^{2} Y-Aa^{8} 8^{2} Bb-Hh^{8} Ii^{4} Kk^{1} 9^{2} Ll-Ss^{8} Tt^{2} 10^{2} Vu-3G^{8} 3H^{12} 3I^{4} a-c^{8} *^{8}. pp. 1-820. [212

-- -- [1] De gli hecommithi ... Nella quale si contengono tre Dialoghi della vita Ciuile. Parte Prima. In Vinegia M· D· LXVI· Appresso Girolamo Scotto. (*Colophon.*) 4°. *^{8} (-*8, *blank?*) A-P^{4} Q-Pp^{8} Qq^{6}. pp. 1-500. ¶*T.p. repaired:* Prima. *drawn with pen.* [2] ... Parte seconda. ... *Same imprint.* (*Colophon.*) **^{6} a-ff^{8}. pp. 1-464. (Furness.) [213

-- -- Hecatommithi, ouero cento nouelle ... in questa Quarta impressione. Parte Prima. In Venetia, Appresso Fabio, & Agostin Zopini Fratelli. M D LXXX. (... Presso gli Heredi di Francesco Rampazetto. M. D. LXXIX.) 4°. *^{8} A-HH^{8} II^{4}. ff. 1-251. [214

-- -- [1] ... Parte prima. In Venetia, MDLXXXIIII. Appresso Fabio, & Agostin Zoppini Fratelli. (*Colophon.*) 4°. *^{8} A-HH^{8} II^{4}. ff. 1-251. [2] ... Parte seconda. *Same imprint.* A-GG^{8}. ff. 5-231. [215

-- Dell'Hercole ... (In Modena nella stamperia de Gadaldini. M. D. LVII.) 4°. A-V^{8} X-Y^{4} *^{4} †^{4}. pp. 4-353. [216

-- Didone tragedia ... In Venetia, Appresso Giulio Cesare Cagnacini. M D LXXXIII. 8°. A-K^{8} (-K8, *blank*). pp. 4-157. [217

-- Discorsi ... intorno al comporre de i Romanzi, delle Comedie, e delle Tragedie, e di altre maniere di Poesie. .. In Vinegia appresso Gabriel Giolito de Ferrari et fratelli. M D LIIII. (*Colophon.*) *^{4} A-S^{8} *-**^{4} 3*^{8}. pp. 2-287. [218

-- Egle satira ... [Firenze, c. 1550.] 8°. A-F^8. ff. 2-48. [219

-- Epitia tragedia ... In Venetia, Appresso Giulio Cesare Cagnacini. M D LXXXIII. (... Appresso Nicolò Moretti. ...) 8°. A-G^8 H^4. pp. 3-118. [220

-- Euphimia tragedia ... In Venetia, Appresso Giulio Cesare Cagnacini. M D LXXXIII. (... Appresso Paulo Zanfretti. ...) 8°. A-H^8 I^4. pp. 3-135. [221

-- Le fiamme ... In Vinegia appresso Gabriel Giolito de Ferrari. MDXLVIII. 8°. A-L^8 M^4. ff. 2-87. [222

-- Orbecche tragedia ... M.D.XLIII. (In casa de figliuoli d'Aldo, in Vinegia ...) 8°. A-H^8. ff. 2-62. [223

-- -- (M. D. XLVII.) 8°. A-H^8. ff. 2-63. [224

-- -- Orbecche tragedia ... Con l'aggionta di VIII. Tragedie dell'istesso Autore ... In Venetia, Appresso Giulio Cesare Cagnacini. M D LXXXIII. (... Appresso Paulo Zanfretti. ...) 8°. A-H^8 I^4. pp. 3-135. ¶*The eight tragedies are entered separately since these copies are not bound together and lack the general t.p. issued with the collection.* [225

-- Selene tragedia ... In Venetia, Appresso Giulio Cesare Cagnacini. M D LXXXIII. (... Appresso Paulo Zanfretti. ...) 8°. A-I^8 K^4. pp. 3-149. [226

GIRARD, BERNARD DE, sieur du Haillan. De l'estat et succez des affaires de France. Oeuure contenant les choses ... aduenuës durant les regnes des Rois de France, depuis Pharamond ... iusques au Roy Luys vnziesme. ... A Paris, A l'Oliuier de l'Huillier ... 1571. ... 8°. a^8 A-X^8 (-X8, *presumably blank*). ff. 1-165. ¶*Additional t.p.* (T1): Histoire sommaire des comtes et ducs Daniou ... *Same imprint.* (Lea.) [227

-- [1] L'histoire de France ... Tome premier. [Genève] Par Pierre de Saint-André. M. D. LXXVII. 8°. ā^8 ē^8 ī^8 ō^8 ū^2 A-Zz^8 AA-3B^8. pp. 1-1073. [2] ... Tome second. *Same imprint.* a-3x^8 3y^4. pp. 3-1038. [228

GIROLAMI, FLAVIO. Nuoua minera doro ... In Venetia, M.D.LXXXX. Appresso Barezzo Barezzi 4°. *^{4} A-K^4 L/M^4 N-Y^4 Z^2 Aa^4. pp. 2-171. (Smith.) [229

GIROLAMO D'ESTE. Questo e el castello de este. elquale anticamente si chiamaua Ateste ... [Venezia, Boneto Locatello? c. 1500.] 4°. B.L. a-c^4. [230

GIUSTI, VINCENZO. Fortunio Comedia ... In Venetia, MDXCVII. Appresso Marc'Antonio Benibelli. 12°. A-F^{12} G^6. ff. 2-78. [231

GIUSTINIANI, ANTONIO. Die werbung vnd rede des Anthoni Iustinian võ Venedig zu ... Maximilian Romischen Kayser. Auch ... seiner maiestat antwort. Anno ꝛc. 1510. 4°. π^4. [232

GIUSTINIANI, LORENZO. Trattato della disciplina et della perfettion monastica ..., tradotto dal R.P. ... Gregorio Marino ...: con l'aggiunta della uita del medesimo Auttore, tradotta dalla Latina nella uolgar lingua da M. Giouanni Giolito de' Ferrari ... In Venetia appres so Gabriel Giolito di Ferrarii MDLXVIIII. 4°. a-f^4 G^4 A-BB^4 CC^6. pp. 1-240. (Lea.)[233

GIUSTINIANO, BENEDETTO. Benedicti Iustiniani ... oratio ... in funere Innocentii IX. Pont. Max. ... Romæ, Apud Ioannem Martinellum. 1592. ... 4°. A^6. [234

GIUSTOLO, PIETRO FRANCESCO. Iustuli Spoletani opera. ... (Impressum Romæ Per Iacobum Mazochium. Die .y. Ianuarii. M.D.X.) 4°. A^8 B-M^4 N^6. [235

GLANDORP, JOHANN. Iohannis Glandorpii Monasteriensis annotationes in M. Tullii epistolas ... ad familiares ... Editæ studio & opera Reineri Reineccii Steinhemii. ... Basileæ, per Sebastianum Henricpetri. (... CIƆ. IƆ. XXC. Mense Septembri.) 8°. †-3†^{8} a-z^8 A-O^8 (-O8). pp. 1-589. ¶†1 *defective.* [236

-- Onomasticon historiae Romanae ... Reineri Reineccii præfatio. Francofurdi Apud Andreæ Wecheli heredes, Claudium Marnium, & Ioann. Aubrium: MDLXXXIX. ... fol. †^{6} A-PP^6 QQ^4 RR-TT^6 VV^4 (-VV4, *presumably blank*). cols. 1-928, pp. 929-970. [237

GLANVILLA, RANULPHUS DE. Tractatus de legibus et consuetudinibus regni Anglie ... (Londini in ædibus Richardi Totteli. ... [c. 1555.]) 8°. A-R^8. ff. 1-113. *S.T.C.* 11905. (Biddle.) [238

GLAREANUS, HENRICUS LORITUS. De ratione syllabarum breuis isagoge ... Elegiæ quædam ... (Basileae, in aedibus Adae Petri. Anno M D XVI. Mense Nouembri.) 4°. A-D^4 E^6. [239

-- In Q. Horatium Flaccum ... annotationes ... Friburgi Brisgoiae, anno M. D. XXXV. (... apud Ioannem Fabrum Emmeum Iuliacensum.) 8°. a-i^8 k^{10} (-k10, *presumably blank*). pp. 1-153. [240

-- Henrichi Loriti Glareani ... liber de asse, & partibus eius ... Basileae, apud Mich. Isingrinium, M. D. L. fol. A-E^6. ff. 2-25. [241

GLAUBE. Vom Glauben: vn̄d wercken. Vnd wie sich ein mensch gegen Gott durch den glauben halten sol. ... [c. 1520.] 4°. [A]^6. [242

GLYCAS, MICHAEL. Annales ..., qui ... Byzantinam historiam exhibent: nunc primum Latinam in linguam transscripti & editi per Io. Levvenclaium. ... Basileae per Episcopios. M. D. LXXII. (... Mense Septembri.) 8°. α^8 a-z^8 A-M^8 N^{10}. pp. 1-512. [243

GNODALIUS, PETRUS. [1] Dẽr Peu̇risch vnd Protestierende Krieg Das ist/ Histoischer ... Bericht der Bewrischen empörungẽ ... im Jar M.D.XXV. ... in das Teutsch gebracht/ vnd ... vermehret/ Durch M. Iacob Schlussern von Suderburg. ... Getruckt zů Basel fol. *^{4} *^{6} A-M^6 N-O^8. pp. i-clxxvj. [2] Lamberti Hortensij ... beschreibung des Protestierenden kriegs ... Getruckt zu Basel. (... durch Sebastian Henricpetri ... M. D. LXXiij.) Aa-Ll^6 Mm^8. pp. iij-cxlv. [244

GNOMOLOGIA. Γνωμολογιαι παλαιοτατων ποιητων ... Parisiis, M. D. LIII. Apud Adrianum Turnebum ... (*Colophon.*) 4°. π^2 A-E^4 F^2 A^4 a^2 a-d^4. pp. 1-3, 2-44, 1-8, 1-31. [245

GOBEUS, JOANNES. Magistri Ioãnis Gobei Tilliani primaria grãmatices prĩcipia ... Pridie februales Kalendas. (On les vent a Caen ... Michel angier ... [c. 1515.]) 16°. B.L. A^8. [246

GOCLENIUS, RODOLPHUS. Problematum Logicorum ... Pars prima. Marpurgi Excudebat Paulus Egenolphus. M D LXXXIX. 8°. A^4 B-O^8 P^4. ff. 1-116. [247

GOD. Hab Gott lieb vnnd diene jm allein [1520.] 4°. A-C^4 (-C4, *presumably blank*). [248

-- Vom alten vnd neu̇wen Got: Galuben vnd Leer. (Getruckt ... M. D. XXij.) 4°. a-i^4. [249

-- Wie vnd wass massen Gott der Herz/ zů allen zeitten/ gestraffet hab/ die ... wider recht/ fůg/ vnd billichkait/ Geistliche gůter/ eingezogen/ Kirchen vnd Klöster beraubt ... haben. Durch einen gůthertzigen/ Christlichen/ vnd Catholischen/ beschriben ... M.D.LX. (Gedruckt zů Ingolstat [durch Alexander und Samuel Weissenhorn?].) 4°. A-I^4 K^2 L^4. [250

GODEFROY, DENIS. Auctores Latinae linguae in vnum redacti corpus. ... M. Terentius Varro De lingua Latina. M. Verrii Flacci fragmenta. Festi fragmenta à Fuluio Vrsino edita. Schedæ Festi à Pomp. Læto relictæ. Sext. Pomp.Festus, Paulo Diacono coniunctus. Nonius Marcellus. Fulgentius Plantiades. Isidori Originum libri XX. Ex Veteribus grammaticis ... excerpta. Vetus Kalendarium Romanum. De Nominibus & Prænominibus Romanorum. Varii Auctores qui de notis scripserunt. Notæ Dionysii Gothofredi I.C. ad Varronem, Festum, & Nonium. ... [Lugduni,] Apud Guillielmum Læmarium. M. D. XCV. 4°. ***^{4} a-zz^8 3A-3B^8 3C^4 3D-3T^8. cols. 1-1924. [251

GODELMANN, JOHANN GEORG. [1] Iohannis Georgij Godelmanni I.V.D. de magis, veneficis et lamiis, recte cognoscendis & Puniendis, libri tres. His accessit ad Magistratum ... Iohannis Althusij Admonitio. Francoforti Ex officina Typographica Nicolai Bassæi. M. D. XCI. (*Colophon.*) 4°. A^6 B-R^4 S^2. pp. 4-117. [2] Liber secundus. De lamiis. Francoforti, D. M. XCI. A-I^4 K^2 (-K2, *presumably blank*). pp. 1-72. [3] Liber tertius. Quomodo contra magos, veneficas, et Lamias procedatur. Francoforti, M. D. XCI. A-Dd^4 Ee^2. pp. 1-152. (Lea.) [252

GODEN, HENNING. Consilia ... optimo ordine per D. Melchiorem Kling ... distributa ... Vitebergae typis excudebat Ioannes Lufft ... M. D. XLIIII. mense Autumno. (... M. D. XLV.) fol. †^{4} A-Z^6 a-z^6 Aa-Nn^6. ff. II-CCCLIIII. (Biddle.) [253

GODFREY OF BOUILLON. Ein hubscher Tractat wie durch Hertzog Gotfrid von Pullen ... das gelopte landt vnd das heylig grab gewunnen ist worden ... (Gedrückt zu Nürnberg durch Iobst Gutknecht [c. 1517.]) 4°. A^6. [254

GODOI, GIOVANNI DE. Comentari della guerra fatta nella Germania da Carlo Quinto Imperadore ... colle morti di Valenti Giouani, e lor proue ... In Vinegia ... M. D. XLVIII. (... per Comin da Trino di Monferrato. ...) 8°. A-G^8 H^4 (-H4, *blank*). ff. 4-59. [255

GÖBLER, JUSTIN. [1] Chronica der Kriegsshändel/ des ... Keysers vnd Fürsten/ weyland Herrn Maximiliani/ ... der Erst ... Franckfort am Meyn/ Bei Christian Egen. Erben. M. D. LXVI. (*Colophon.*) fol. ℭ^6 ℭℭ^4 A-P^4. ff. I-LXXXVI. [2] Chronica vnd Historien der Braunschweigischen Fürsten herkommen/ Stam̄/ vnnd Geschlecht ... *Same imprint.* (*Colophon.*) A-H^6 I^8 (-I8, *presumably blank*). ff. I-LIII. [256

-- Der Gerichtlich Process/ Auss geschribenen Rechten/ vnd nach Gemeynen im Heyligen Reich Teutscher Nation gebrauch vnd übung. ... Zu Francktur t/ Bei Christian Egenolff. (... M. D. XLIX. Im Mertz.) fol. *^{4} A-Z^6 a-m^6 n^4 o^6. ff. I-CCXIX. [257

-- Statuten Bůch/ Gesatz/ Ordnungen vnd Gebräuch/ Kaiserlicher/ Allgemainer/ vnd etlicher Besonderer Land vnd Stett Rechten. ... Zu Franckfort/ Bei Christian Egenolff. (... M. D. LIII. Im Mertzen.) fol. ♣^{4} A-Z^4 a-q^4. ff. I-CLV. [258

GOLDSTEIN, KILIAN. Chiliani Goldstein processus iudiciarii enchiridion, secundum ius commune et Saxonicum. ... Gerichtlicher Process ... 1585. Franckf. Bey Christ. Egenolphs Erben. 8°. A-P^8 (-P6-8, *presumably blank*). pp. 6-222. (Biddle.) [259

GOMEZ, ANTONIO. Commentariorum, variarumq. resolutionum iuris ciuilis communis et regii. Tomi tres. ... Accesserunt ... Adnotationes Emanuelis Soarez à Ribeira ... Venetiis, Ad candentis Salamandræ Insigne [Christoforo Zanetti] MDLXXII. 4°. *^{4} a-e^4 f^6 A-V^8 Aa-Tt^8 Vu^4 3A-3P^8 3Q^4 (-3Q4, *blank*). ff. 1-439. (Biddle.) [260

-- -- *Another copy* (+ 3Q4). (Lea.) [261

GOMEZ, FERNANDO. Centon epistolario ... Fue estampado. Et correto por el protocolo del mesmo Bachiller Fernanperez Por Iuan de Rei esau costa enla cibda de Burgos el Anno MCD XCIX [= 1599?]. 4°. B.L. A-V^4 X^6. pp. 1-166. [262

GOMEZ DE CASTRO, ALVARO. Aluari Gomez de militia principis Burgūdi ... Alexij Vanegas breuis enucleatio. Mēse nouē. 1540 (Toleti. In ædibus Ioānis de Aiala. 20. die Nouēbris ...) 8°. A-I^8. ff. 5-24. [263

-- De rebus gestis a Francisco Ximenio, Cisnerio, Archiepiscopo Toletano, libri octo. Aluaro Gomecio Toletano authore. ... Compluti, apud Andream de Angulo. ... 1569. (*Colophon.*) fol. ¶^{8} *^{8} A-Gg^8. ff. 1-240. (Lea.) [264

GOMEZ DE HUERTA, JERONIMO. Florando de Castilla lauro de caualleros, compuesto en octaua rima, por el Licenciado Hieronymo de Guerra ... Impresso en Alcala de Henares, en casa de Iuan Gracian que sea en gloria. ... M.D.LXXXVIII. A costa de Iuan Garcia Callejas ... (*Colophon.*) 4°. ¶^{8} A-X^8. ff. 1-168. [265

GONZAGA, CURTIO. Il fidamante poema eroico ... aggiuntiui gli Argomenti dell' ... Signora Maddalena Campiglia, & con le Moralità d'incerto Autore. ... In Venetia. All'insegna del Leone 1591. (*Colophon.*) 4°. ✠^{4} A-Ff^8 Gg^4. ff. 1-275. [266

GONZAGA, LUCREZIA. Lettere della ... Donna Lucretia Gonzaga da Gazuolo ... In Vinegia, MDLII. (... Appresso Gualtero Scotto.) 8°. A-X^8. pp. 2-328. ¶*Sometimes attributed to Ortensio Landi.* [267

GONZAGHI, BONAVENTURA. Canzone di Bonauentura da Reggio, Nelle allegrezze della Creatione del ... Papa Pio Quinto. In Padoua, Appresso Lorenzo Pasquato, M D LXVI. 4°. π^4. [268

-- Ragionamenti ... sopra i sette peccati mortali, & sopra i Setti Salmi Penitentiali ... In Vinegia appresso Gabriel Giolito de' Ferrari M D LXVI. 4°. *-3*^{4} A-Q^4 R^6 (-R6). pp. 1-134. [269

GONZÁLEZ DE MONTES, REINALDO. Sanctae Inquisitionis Hispanicae artes aliquot detectæ, ac palam traductæ. ... Reginaldo Gonsaluio Montano authore. ... Heidelbergæ M.D.LXVII. (... excudebat Michael Schirat ...) 8°. π^2 *-**^{8} A-S^8 T^6. pp. 1-297. (Lea.) [270

-- -- A discouery and playne Declaration of sundry subtill practises of the Holy Inquisition of Spayne. ... Set forth in Latine, by Reginaldus Gonsaluius Montanus, and newly Translated. ... Imprinted at London, by Ihon Day ... 1566. (*Colophon.*) 4°. B.L. A^4 ¶B^4 *B^4 B-Y^4 Aa-Dd^4. ff. 1-99. *S.T.C.* 11996. ¶*Translator: Vincent Skinner.* (Lea.) [271

GORI, GIOVANNI BATTISTA. Vita del gloriosissimo Santo Ansano ... In Siena. ... M.DC. 4°. A^{12}. pp. 3-24. [272

GOSELINI, GIULIANO. Rime ... In Milano. Per Paolo Gottardo Pontio. M.D.LXXII. 4°. A^8 (- *presumably* A5) B-V^4. pp. 3-148. [273

-- -- ... ristampate la quinta volta ... In Venetia, Appresso Francesco Franceschi Senese. M D LXXXVIII. (*Colophon.*) 12°. *^{12} A-Q^{12}. pp. 1-362. [274

GOŚLICKI, WAWRZYNIEC. Laurentii Grimalii Goslicii de optimo senatore libri duo. ... Venetiis, Apud Iordanum Zilettum, M D LXVIII. (*Colophon.*) 4°. *^{4} A-Y^4. ff. 1-83. [275

GOSSON, STEPHEN. Playes Confuted in fiue Actions, Prouing that they are not to be suffred in a Christian common weale ... London Imprinted for Thomas Gosson ... 8°. B.L. π^5 A-G^8. *S.T.C.* 12095. (Furness.) [276

GOTTFRIED, JOHANN. Ein schons buchlein. Võ rechtem warem wullust/ menschlichs lebẽs ... Durch Hern Iohan Gotfridi ... [Speyer, Johann Eckhart, c. 1522.] 4°. a-b^4. [277

GOULET, ROBERT. Compendium recenter editum de multiplici parisiẽsis vniuersitatis magnificentia ... Venundãtur parisiis ... per Toussanum denis ... (... 1517) 4°. B.L. aa^4 a^8 b-d^4. ff. i-xx. [278

GOWER, JOHN. Io. Gower de confessione Amantis. Imprinted at London ... by Thomas Berthelette the .XII. daie of Marche. an. M.D.LIIII. ... fol. B.L. *^{6} A-Ii^6 (-Ii6, *blank*). ff. 1-CXCI. *S.T.C.* 12144. [279

GOZZADINI, LODOVICO. Consilia ... [*Device of Jacobus Giunta.*] ... Repertorio ... Celio Amaseo ... Authore. 1541 (Ex ... Lugduñ. Academia ... 1540. Per Martinum Lescuyer ...) fol. B.L. aa-cc^6 A-Z^6 ⁊^{6} ɔ^6. ff. 1-149. (Biddle.) [280

GOZZE, NICOLÒ VITO DE. Dello stato delle republiche Secondo la mente di Aristotele con essempi moderni Giornate otto ... Con CCXXII. auertimenti ciuili dell'istesso ... Et ... vna Apologia dell'Honor Ciuile. ... In Venetia. CIƆ. IƆ. XCI. Presso Aldo. 4°. †^{4} A-F^4 A-3K^4. pp. 2-449. [281

GRACIÁN DE LA MADRE DE DIOS, JERÓNIMO. Trattato del giubileo dell'anno santo del P.M.F. Girolamo Gratiano ... Tradotto di Spagnuolo in Italiano da Iacomo Bosio ... In Roma, Appresso Luigi Zannetti. 1599. ... (... M D C.) 4°. *^{4} A-Xx^4. pp. 1-334. (Lea.) [282

GRAFFIIS, JACOBUS DE. Decisiones aureæ casuum conscientiae, In Quatuor Libros distributæ ...: Pars Prima. ... Venetiis, M. D. XCVI. Ex Officina Damiani Zenari. 4°. a-k^4 A-3R^8 3S^6 (-3S6, *presumably blank*). ff. 2-509. (Lea.) [283

GRAFTON, RICHARD. A Chronicle at large and meere History of the affayres of Englande and Kinges of the same, deduced from the Creation of the vvorlde, vnto the first habitation of thys Islande: and so by contynuance vnto the first yere of the reigne of ... Queene Elizabeth: ... Anno Domini. 1569. ... (Imprinted at London by Henry Denham, ... at the costes and charges of Richard Tottle, and Humffrey Toye. Anno. 1569. the last of March. ...) fol. B.L. π^6 A-Q^6 R^4. pp. 1-192. ¶*The t.p. is a type-facsimile.* [2] This seconde Volume, beginning at William the Conquerour, endeth wyth ... Queene Elizabeth. ... Anno. 1568. A-Y^6 Aa-Yy^6 3A-3Y^6 4A-4Y^6 5A-5Y^6 6A-6D^6 6E^2 a-b^8 c^6 (-c6, *presumably blank*). pp. 1-1369. *S.T.C.* 12147. (Furness.) [284

-- -- *Another copy, with facsimile t.p., lacking* π^6. [285

GRAMINÄUS, DIEDERICH. Mysticus aquilo, siue Declaratio Vaticinij Ieremię Prophetæ ... Auctore Theodoro Graminaeo ... Item Epistola R.D. VVilhelmi Damasi Lindani ... de hoc eodem negotio. Coloniae, apud Ludouicum Alectorium, & hæredes Iacobi Soteris. Anno M.D.LXXVI. 8°. A-L^8. pp. 4-175. [286

GRANA, NICOLO À. Grauis, vtilis, et perspicua explicatio eorum, Quæ tum ad poenitentes, tum ad confessarios magnopere spectare videntur. ... Brixiæ, in ædibus Polycreti Turlini. (... M. D. C. ...) 4°. †-††^{8} A-P^8 Q^6. pp. 1-251. (Lea.) [287

GRAPALDI, FRANCESCO MARIO. Francisci Marii Grapaldi Parmensis, de partibus ædium, Lexicon ... Basileae, apud Ioan. Vualderum, mense Martio, anno, M. D. XXXIII. (... ex officina Curionana ...) 4°. π^{14} a-z^4 A-L^4 (-L4, *blank*). pp. 1-270. [288

GRASS, MICHAEL. Tractatus de successione tam ex testamento, quam ab intestato ... Per Michaelem Crassum ... Venetiis Apud Paulum Vgolinum. M D XCV. 4°. †-3†^{4} A-Kk^8 (-Kk8, *presumably blank*). pp. 1-526. [289

GRASSIS, PARIS DE. Paridis Crassi Bononien. ... de cerimoniis cardinalium, et Episcoporum in eorum dioecesibus libri duo. ... Romae M.D.LXIIII. ... (... Apud Antonium Bladum ...) 4°. π^6 A-RR^4. ff. 1-157. (Lea.) [290

-- -- Venetiis apud Petrum Dusinellum. M. D. LXXXII. 4°. *^{4} A-Dd^4. ff. 1-106. (Yarnall.) [290a

GRASSO, NICOLÒ. Eutichia. Comedia ... MDXXX. (Stampata in Vinegia per Nicolò d'Aristotile detto Zoppino. ...) 8°. A-F^8. ff. 2-46. [291

GRATAROLI, GUGLIELMO. Alchimiae, quam vocant, artisque metallicae, doctrina, certumq́3 modus ... duobus his Voluminibus comprehensus. ... Basileae, per Petrum Pernam. M.D.LXXII. 8°.):(^{8} a-z^8 A-Y^8 (-Y7-8, *the latter blank*) aa-zz^8 AA-3A^8 3B^4 (-3B4). pp. 1-686, 1-733. (Smith.) [292

GRATAROLO, BONGIANNI. Altea tragedia ... In Vinegia per Francesco Marcolini ... MDLVI. 8°. A-F^8. ff. 2-46. [293

GRATIANUS. ... Decretum aureum domini Gratiani: cum suo apparatu. (in alma Parisiensi achademia/ expensis ⁊ opera Iohannis parui ⁊ Thielman keruer ... Et Iohãnis cabillier ... lugduni ... Anno ... Millesimo quingentesimo sexto die .xxj. octobris.) 4°. B.L. a-z^8 ⁊^{8} ɔ^8 ꝝ^8 A-X^8 AA-XX^8 3A-3D^8 3E^6 A^6 A (*red*)-C (*red*)^8 D (*red*)-E (*red*)^6. ff. ii-V^{cc}lxxxii. (Yarnall.) [293a

-- -- Decreti huius amplissimum argumẽtum. ... (in ... vrbe Lugduneñ. Per Franciscum fradin. ... Mdxij. die ꝟo xxx. mensis Octobri.) fol. B.L. a-z^8 A-Z^8 aa-ff^8 gg^{10} 3a-3g^8 3h^6. ff. II-CCCCXXVI, I-XXXVIII. (Lea.) [294

-- -- Decretum Gratiani ... Venetiis, Apud Iuntas. M·D XCV. fol. a-e^8 f^4 †^{4} A-EE^8 FF^6 GG-5C^8 5D^{10} 5E-6E^8 6F^6 A-H^8 I^4 (-I4, *presumably blank*). pp. 1-1904. (Lea.) [295

GRATIUS FALISCUS. Hoc volumine continentur ... Gratij ... de uenatione Lib. I. P. Ouidij Nasonis Halieuticôn liber acephalus. M. Aurelij Olympij Nemesiani Cynegeticôn Lib. I. Eiusdem carmen bucolicum. T. Calphurnij Siculi Bucolias. Adriani Cardinalis uenatio. M. D. XXXIIII. (Venetijs, in ædibus hæredum Aldi Manutij, & Andreæ soceri, ... Mense Februario.) 8°. A-F^8 G^4. ff. 1-47. [296

-- -- Gratii ... De Venatione Liber I. ... Apud Seb. Gryphium Lugduni, 1537. 8°. a-g^8. pp. 3-107. [297

GRAZIANI, GRAZIANO. Scielta de concetti, de Gratiano Gratiani Granarense. ... In Venetia. M D XCII. Appresso Felice Valgrisio. 8°. a-b^8 A-Cc^8. ff. 1-207. [298

GRAZZINI, ANTONFRANCESCO. La gelosia commedia ... In Fiorenza appresso i Giunti M.D. LXVIII. (*Colophon.*) 8°. A-G^{8}. pp. 3-110. [299

-- -- In Venetia, Appresso Bernardo Giunti, e Fratelli. M D LXXXII. 8°. A-H^{8} I^{2}. ff. 2-66. [300

-- I parentadi comedia ... In Venetia. Appresso Bernardo Giunti, e Fratelli. M D LXXXII. 8°. A-F^{8} G^{2}. ff. 2-50. [301

-- La pinzochera comedia ... In Vinegia, Appresso Bernard Giunti, e Fratelli. M D LXXXII. 8°. A-F^{8}. ff. 4-48. [302

-- La Sibilla comedia ... In Vinegia, Appresso Bernardo Giunti, e Fratelli. M D LXXXII. 8°. A-E^{8} F^{4}. ff. 3-44. [303

-- La spiritata comedia ... In Venetia. Appresso Bernardo Giunti, e Fratelli. M D LXXXII. 8°. A-D^{8}. ff. 5-32. [304

-- La strega commedia ... In Venetia, Appresso Bernardo Giunti, e Fratelli. M D LXXXII. 8°. A-C^{8} D^{16} E^{8}. ff. 2-40. ¶*In the* D *gathering pairs of blank pages alternate with pairs of printed pages.* [305

-- Tutti i trionfi, carri, mascheaate [*sic*] ò canti Carnascialeschi andati per Firenze, Dal tẽpo del Magnifico Lorenzo vecchio de Medici ... à questo anno presente 1559. ... In Fiorenza MDLVIIII. 8°. a^{8} b^{2} A-EE^{8}. pp. 1-465. [306

GREAT BRITAIN. Rerum Britannicarum, id est Angliae, Scotiae, vicinarumque insularum ac regionum, scriptores vetustiores ac præcipui: Galfredi Monumetensis ... de origine & gestis Regum Britanniæ libri XII. Pontici Virunni Britannicæ historiæ libri VI. ... Gildas Sapientis, de excidio & conquestu Britanniæ epistola. Bedae Anglosaxonis Historiæ Ecclesiasticæ gentis Anglorum libri V. Continuatio eiusdem Historiæ, incerto auctore, libris III. comprehensa ... Gulielmus Neubricensis de rebus Anglicis libri V. ... Ioannis Frossardi Historiarum Epitome ... Lugduni, Apud Renatum Potelerium. cIↃ. IↃ. LXXXVII. fol. π^{4} A-G^{6} H^{4} I^{6} K^{4} L-Z^{6} a-f^{6} g^{4} h-z^{6} Aa-Cc^{6} *^{6} (-π4, *6, *presumably blank*). pp. 1-580. (Furness.) [307

GREEK ANTHOLOGY. Ανθολογια διαφόρων ἐπιγραμμάτων παλαιων ... Florilegium diuersorum epigrammatum veterum ... Henr. Steph. ... Anno M. D. LXVI. [Genevae,] Excudebat Henricus Stephanus ... 4°. *^{2} a-ii^{8} kk-rr^{4} ss^{2}. pp. 1-539. [308

-- Epigrammata Græca, selecta ex Anthologia. Interpretata ad verbũ, & carmine, ab Henrico Stephano: quædam & ab aliis. ... Anno M.D.LXX. [Genevae,] Excudebat Henricus Stephanus. 8°. ¶^{4} a-t^{8} v^{4}. pp. 1-311. [309

-- Epigrammatum Graecorum annotationibus Ioannis Brodæi Turonensis, nec non Vincentii Obsopoei, & Græcis ... scholiis illustratorum. Libri VII. Accesserunt Henrici Stephani ... Annotationes. ... Francofurti Apud Andreæ Wecheli heredes Claudium Marnium & Iohannem Aubrium. Anno M. DC. ... fol. ¶¶^{2} A-3C^{6} DDd-FFf^{6} GGg^{4} α-β^{6} γ^{4} δ^{8} ¶^{6}. pp. 1-632, 1-30. [310

GREEK ORTHODOX CHURCH. Τὸ παρὸν εὐχολόγιον ἐτυπώθη ... ἐν τῇ οἰκίᾳ ... Χριστοφόρου τοῦ Ζανέτου ... επιδιορθώσει ... Θεοφανους 'Ιερομονάχου ... α, φ π' [1580] ... 4°. ✠^{4} A-Ω^{8} α-η^{8} ϑ^{4} (-ϑ4, *presumably blank*). ff. α'-σμβ'. (Yarnall.) [310a

GRÉGOIRE, PIERRE. [Syntagma.] Lugduni, Apud Ioan. Pillehotte ... M. D. XCVII. (... Excudebant haeredes Petri Roussin. ...) fol. [1] Syntagma iuris vniuersi, atque legum pene omnium gentium ... Auctore Petro Gregorio Tholosano ... *^{8} A-O^{6}. pp. 1-168. [2] Syntagmatis ... pars secunda. ... Aa-Zz^{6} AA-BB^{6}. pp. 3-298. [3] Tertia ac postrema pars ... †-††^{6} AAa-ZZz^{6} AAA-ZZZ^{6} AAAa-ZZZz^{6} AAAA-BBBB^{6} A-Q^{6} R^{4}. pp. 1-851. [311

-- Syntaxes artis mirabilis, in libros XL. digestae, Tomus Primus. ... Coloniae, Impensis Lazari Zetzneri, cIↃ. IↃ c. 8°. *^{8} a-t^{8} u^{2} (u1 + *1 leaf intended to follow* T6 *and 7 folded ll. signed* u, u2, *&c.*) x^{6} y-z^{8} A-Hh^{8}. pp. 2-97, 2-154, 1-540. ¶*Additional t.pp.:* (g2^{r}) Commentaria in prolegomena syntaxeωn mirabilis artis ... *Same imprint.* (r4^{r}) ... alter tomus. *Same imprint.* (Smith.) [312

GREGORAS, NICEPHORUS. Nicephori Gregorae, Romanæ, hoc est Byzantinæ historiæ Libri XI ...

Nunc ... Hieronymi VVolfii labore, Græcè Latinéque editi ... His adiunximus Laonici Chalcocondylae Turcicam historiã, Conrado Clausero Tigurino interprete ... Basileae, per Ioannem Oporinum, ... 1562. (... Mense Augusto.) fol. α^8 a-y^6 z^4 A-N^6 O^8. pp. 2-271, cols. 275-534. (Lea.) [313

GREGORY NAZIANZEN, S. Hi sunt in hoc Codice libelli X. diui Gregorij Nazanzeni ... (Impressus Argẽtine ꝑ Ioannẽ knoblouch. ... M.d.viij. Hilarij.) 4°. a^4 b^6 c-r$^{4.4.8}$ s^4 t^8. [314

-- Diui Gregorii Nazanzeni ... aliquot ... sermones In Pascha In dictum Matthæi, cum consummasset Ihesus sermones hos &c. Cap. xix. Laudes Cypriani martyris. Oecolampadio interprete. Oratio Oecolampadij ... de expostulatione Christi cum Petro ablutionem pedum recusante. ... (In officina Sigismundi Grim̃ ..., & Marci Vuirsung Augustæ Vindelicorum, ... M.D.XIX. Die .XXII. Mensis Maij.) 4°. a-f^4 g^6 (-g6, *presumably blank*). [315

-- Aldus Romanus omnibus ... S. P. D. Gregorii episcopi Nazanzeni carmina ... e græco in latinum ad uerbum ferè tralata ... (Venetiis ex Aldi Academia mense Iunio. M.DIIII) 4°. A/AA-M/MM$^{18.16}$ N/NN^{18} O/OO^{10}. ¶*The Latin text, on A &c., and the Greek, on AA &c., are interleaved. Includes the gospel of St. John in Greek and Latin.* [316

-- De moderandis disputationibus ... sermo. Ioan. OEcolampadio interprete. (Augustæ Vindelicorum In officina Sigismundi Grym̃ Medici, atqꝫ Marci Vuirsung. ... M.D.XXI.) 4°. a-d^4. [317

-- Due orationi di Gregorio Nazanzeno ... Et il primo sermone di S. Cecilio Cipriano sopra l'Elemosina. Fatte in lingua Toscana dal Commendatore Annibal Caro. ... In Venetia. Appresso Aldo Manutio. M D LXIX. 4°. *^{4} B-S^4 T^6. pp. 1-146. [318

-- -- *Another copy* (-T3-4; T6 *bound after* *4). [319

-- Diui Gregorij ... Nazanzeni, Sententiarũ spiritualium libelli tres, Gręcè editi, & Latinè à Ioanne Lango Silesio uersi. ... Basileae, per Ioannem Oporinum [1558]. 8°. a-d^8. pp. 3-63. [320

GREGORY OF TOURS, S. Gregorii Turonici historiae Francorum libri decem ... Basileæ, per Petrum Pernam 1568 ... 8°. a^8 *^{8} ††^{8} a-z^8 A-Y^8. pp. 1-601, 1-89. ¶*Includes Book XI.* Epistola nuncupatoria *by Matthias Flacius Illyricus.* [321

GREIFFENBERGER, JOHANN. Diss biechlin zaigt an die Falschen Propheten/ vor den vnss gewarnet hat Christus/ Paulus vñ Petrus ... durch Hanns Greyffenberger zů Pfortzhaym. 4°. A-C^4. [322

-- Die welt sagt sy sehe kain besserung vonn den/ die sy Luterisch nennet ... M.D.XXiij. 4°. π^4. [323

GRENIER, NICOLE. Le bouclier de la foy, en forme de Dialogue, contenant deux tomes, extraict de la saincte escripture, & des saincts Peres & plus anciẽs docteurs de l'eglise ... On les vend à Paris ... per Viuant Gaultherot ... 1552. (... le quinziesme iour de Februier ...) 16°. ã^8 ẽ^8 ĩ^4 3a-3z^8 3A-3Z^8 AAa-GGg^8 HHh^4. ff. 1-428. [324

-- -- Spada della fede, per diffesa della chiesa Christiana contra i nimici della verità; ... Tradotto per M. Antonio Bonagratia ... In Vinegia appresso Gabriel Giolito de' Ferrari. M D LXIII. 4°. *^{10} A-R^8 S^4. pp. 1-279. (Lea.) [325

GRESEMUND, DIETRICH. Theodorici Gresemundi. Carmen de Historia Violatę crucis, Et eius vita. Cum interpretatione Hieronymi Gebuileri ... (Excusum Argentinę per Renatum Beck ... M.D.XIIII.) 4°. a-b^4 c-f$^{4.8}$ (-f8, *presumably blank*). [326

GRESER, DANIEL. Eine Leichpredigt zum Begrebnis des ... Herrn Moritzen Hertzogen zu Sachsen ... M. D. Liij. (Gedruckt zu Dressden durch Mattheum Stöckel.) 4°. A-C^4. [327

GRETER, GREGOR. Artickel Auss der Augspurgischen Confession/ vnd derselben Apologia/ dessgleichen auss Doctor Luthers/ Melanchtons/ vnd anderer jhrer Anhänger Büchern vnd Schrifften gezogen ... Getruckt zů Dilingen/ durch Sebaldum Mayer. 1573. 4°. A-Q^4. ff. 2-58. [328

GRETSER, JAKOB. Epistola de historia ordinis Iesuitici, scripta ab Helia Hasemüller, edita à Polycarpo Leiser, nuper promissa a sacerdote Societatis Iesu, superioris Germaniæ ... Dilingae, Excudebat Ioannes Mayer. M. D. XCIV. 4°. A-D^4 E^6. pp. 1-41. [329

-- Nomenclator Latinogræco-Germanicus ... Accessit de verbis anomalis, defectiuis & poëticis commentariolus ... Editio Tertia. ... Ingolstadii, Ex Typographia Adami Sartorii. ... M. DC. 8°. a^8 A-Z^8 a-m^8 n^4. pp. 4-274, 1-201. [330

GRÉVIN, JACQUES. [1] Deux liures des venins ... Ensemble, Les oeuures de Nicandre, Medecin et Poëte Grec, traduictes en vers François. ... A Anuers, De l'Imprimerie de Christofle Plantin. M. D. LXVIII. ... (... M. D. LXVII. au mois d'Octobre.) 4°. *^{4} A-X^8 Y^2. pp. 3-333. [2] Les oeuures de Nicandre ... Ensemble, Deux liures des Venins ... A Anuers, De l'Imprimerie de Christophle Plantin. M. D. LXVII. ... A-K^4 L^6. pp. 3-90. [331

GRIESSMAN, JOHANN. Vnderricht vnd ermanung ... an die Christlich gemain zů Cotbus Wittemberg M.D.XXiij 4°. A-B^4. [332

GRIFONI, GIOVANNI ANDREA. Specchio della lingua Latina. ... In Vinegia. Appresso Egidio Regazzola, & Domenico Caualcalupo compagni. 1575. 8°. A-V^8. ff. 2-152. [333

GRILLANDI, PAOLO. Paulus Grillãdus. Tractat⁹ De Hereticis: ⁊ Sortilegijs omnifariam Coitu: eorumq; penis. Itẽ de Questionibus: ⁊ Tortura: ac de Relaxatione Carceratorum ... 1536 Veneũt Lugδ. apud Iacobũ Giũcti. (... mẽsis Septẽbris die. xij. Benedictus Boninus imprimebat.) 8°. B.L. Aa-Bb^8 A-Q^8. ff. j-cxxviij. (Lea.) [334

-- Tractatus duo: Vnus de sortilegiis D. Pauli Grillandi Castellionis ... Alter de lamiis et excellentia Iuris Vtriusque D. Ioannis Francisci Ponzinibij Florentini ... M.D. XCII. Francoforti ad Moenum. (... apud Martinum Lechlerum, Impensis Hæredum Christiani Egenolphi, Barbaræ, D. Ioannis Cnipij, & Mariæ, Pauli Steinmeyers, viduarum. ...) 8°.)(-)()(^{8} A-S^8 T^6. pp. 1-299. (Lea.) [335

GRILLO. Opera noua ... d'vn villano lauoratore, nomato Grillo. Ilqual volse duuentar medico, in rima historiata, Con piu stanze Nouamente aggionte. (In Venetia, Appresso Fabbio, & Agostin Zoppini fratelli. M.D.L.XXXIIII.) 8°. A-C^8. [336

GRISIGNANO, DECIO. Il Vafro comedia ... In Venetia, Appresso Giacomo Vincenci. M.D.LXXXV. 4°. π^4 A-Ff^4. pp. 1-231. [337

GRISONE, FEDERIGO. Gli ordini di caualcare ... M. D. L. (In Napoli. Appresso Giouan Paulo Suganappo. ...) 4°. π^2 A-HH^4 3A-3G^4. ff. I-CXXIIII. [338

GROSS, HENNING. Magica, Seu mirabilium historiarum de spectris et apparitionibus spirituum ... libri II. Ex probatis, et fide dignis historiarum scriptoribus diligenter collecti. 1597 Islebiæ, Cura, Typis & sumptibus Henningi Grosij Bibl. Lips. ... 4°.)(^{8} A-Hh^8 Ii^6. pp. 1-478. (Lea.) [339

-- -- *Another copy*. (Lea.) [340

GROTO, LUIGI. La Alteria comedia noua di Luigi Grotto cieco d'Hadria. ... In Venetia M D LXXXVII. Appresso Fabio, & Agostino Zoppini Fratelli. 12°. A-G^{12} H^6. ff. 2-90. [341

-- La Calisto noua fauola pastorale. ... In Vinegia, Appresso Fabio, & Agostini Zoppini Fratelli. 1586. (*Colophon.*) 12°. A-G^{12}. ff. 2-81. [342

-- La Dalida tragedia noua ... In Venetia, Appresso Fabio, & Agostin Zopini Fratelli. 1586. (*Colophon.*) 12°. A-F^{12} G^6. ff. 2-77. [343

-- Delle Rime ... In Venetia, Appresso Fabio, & Agostino Zoppini fratelli. 1587. 12°. A-I^{12} K^6. pp. 4-224. [344

-- La Emilia comedia noua ... Recitata in Hadria, il di primo di Marzo. M D LXXIX. ... In Venetia, Appresso gli Zoppini. 1600. 12°. A-F^{12} G^6. ff. 7-78. [345

-- La Hadriana tragedia noua ... In Venetia. Appresso Fabio, & Agostin Zopini fratelli. M D LXXXVI. 12°. A-F^{12}. ff. 2-72. [346

-- Le orationi volgari ... In Venetia, M. D. XCIII. Appresso Fabio, & Agostin Zoppini Fratelli. (*Colophon.*) 4°. a^4 A-Pp^4. ff. 2-152. [347

-- Il pentimento amoroso. Nuoua fauola pastorale ... In Venetia per Francesco Rocca ... M D LXXVI. 8°. A-L^8 M^4. ff. 9-92. [348

-- Il thesoro comedia noua. ... In Venetia. Appresso Agostin Zopini, & Nepoti. 1599. (*Colophon.*) 12°. A-G^{12} (-G11-12, *presumably blank*). ff. 2-81. [349

GROUCHY, NICOLAS DE. N. Gruchii responsio ad binas Caroli Sigonii reprehensiones. Vnam de binis magistratuū comitiis, Alteram de lege curiata. Parisiis, Ex officina Iacobi du Puys ... 1565. (*Colophon.*) 8°. a^4 A-I^4 (-I4, *presumably blank*). ff. 1-35. [350

GRUDÉ DE LA CROIX DU MAINE, FRANÇOIS. Premier volume de la bibliotheque du Sieur de la Croix-du-Maine. ... A Paris, Chez Abel l'Angelier ... M. D. LXXXIIII. ... fol. $\bar{a}^8$ $\bar{e}^6$ $\bar{\imath}^4$ $\bar{o}^4$ A-$3A^6$. pp. 1-558. [351

GRUDIUS, NICOLAUS. Piorum poëmatum libri duo ... Antuerpiæ, Ex officina Gulielmi Silvij ... M.D.LXVI. ... 8°. A-H^8 I^{10}. pp. 1-144. [352

GRUMBACH, WILHELM VON. Copia des Schreibens/ so an ... die Churfürsten vnd Fürsten/ auff den 4. Februarij dieses ... 64. Jars/ zu Wormbs bey einander versamlet/ Wilhelm von Grumbach ... ausgehen lassen vnd vbersandt. 4°. A-E^4. (-E4, *presumably blank*). [353

-- Copia Wilhelm von Grumbachs/ vnd seiner Mituerwandten/ an jre Oheim/ Vettern/ Schweger/ vnd Freunde etc. [c. 1563.] 4°. A^4. [354

-- Der Edlen ... Wilhelmen von Grumbachs/ Ernesten von Mandesloe/ vnd Wilhelmen vom Stein zum Altenstein ... Ausschreiben. ... 4°. A-N^4. ¶*Dated 16 September 1563.* [355

-- Des Edlen ... Wilhelmen vonn Grumpachs Offne/ notgetrangte Klagschrifft ... 4°. Aa-Qq^4 Rr^6. pp. 3-139. ¶*Dated 8 January 1556.* [356

GRYPHIUS, OTTO. Virgiliocentones continentes vitam Saluatoris nostri ... (Typis excusi ab Andrea Burgero Ratisponensi: impensis authoris. ... M. D. XCIII.) 4°. $(:)^4$ $(b)^4$ A-O^4 P^6 (-P6, *presumably blank*). [357

GUAGNINO, ALESSANDRO. Sarmatiae Europeæ descriptio ... Spiræ. ... Apud Bernardum Albinum. M. D. LXXXI. fol. A^4 (A4 + *2 folded ll.*) B-V^6 (-V6, *the pagination continuous notwithstanding*) W-X^6. ff. 1-119. [358

GUALTERUZZI, CARLO. Libro di nouelle, et di bel Parlar Gentile. Nel qual si contengono Cento Nouelle ... In Fiorenza. Nella Stamperia de i Giunti. M D LXXII. (*Colophon.*) 4°. *-$**^4$ $3*^6$ A-X^4. pp. 2-153. [359

GUARINI, ALFONSO. Sponsalitio comedia ... [c. 1550.] 4°. A-F^4 G^2. [360

GUARINI, GIAMBATTISTA. Il pastor fido tragicomedia pastorale ... In Venetia, Presso Gio. Battista Bonfadino. M D XC. 4°. A^4 a^2 B-Ll^4. [361

-- -- Londra. Per Giouanni Volfeo, a spese di Giacopo Casteluetri, MDXCI. (... a XIX. di Giugno. ...) 12°. A-N^{12} O^4 (-O4). pp. 1-298. *S.T.C.* 12414. ¶*Additional t.p.* ($L3^r$): Aminta fauola boschereccia del S. Torquato Tasso. ... 1591 [362

-- Rime ... in questa quarta impressione ricorette. ... In Venetia presso Gio.bat. Ciotti 1599. 12°. A-F^{12} G^6. ff. 3-71. [363

-- Il segretario dialogo ... In Venetia, Appresso Ruberto Megietti. 1594. 4°. a-b^4 c^2 A-Z^4 Aa^2 (-Aa2, *blank*). pp. 1-186. [363a

-- Il verato secondo ouuero replica dell'attizzato accademico Ferrarese In difesa del Pastorfido, Contra la seconda scrittura di Messer Giason De Nores intitolata Apologia. ... In Firenze, per Filippo Giunti. MDXCIII. ... (... MDXCII. ...) 4°. $**^6$ A-T^8. pp. 1-302. [364

GUARNA, ANDREAS. Grammaticale bellum. Nominis & Verbi Regū, de principalitate orationis inter se contendentium. ... (Argentorati Ex Aedibus Schurerianis. Anno M.D.XVI. Mense Aprili.) 4°. Aa-Bb^4 Cc^8. [365

GUARNELLO, ALESSANDRO. Canzone nella ... vittoria Christiana contra infideli ... [Venezia, Domenico & Giovanni Battista Guerra, 1572.] 4°. A^{4}. [366

GUARNIERI, FLAMINIO. L'intrico comedia ... In Rimini, Appresso Gio. Simbeni. 1581. ... 8°. A-I^{8}. ff. 2-70. [367

GUASTAVINI, GIULIO. Del Sig. Giulio Guastauini Risposta all' Infarinato Academico della Crusca. Intorno alla Gierusalemme liberata del Sig. Torquato Tasso. ... , In Bergamo, MDLXXXVIII. Per Comino Ventura, e Compagni. 8°. a^{4} A-I^{4} K^{8} L-M^{4}. ff. 1-88. [368

-- Discorsi et annotationi ... Sopra la Gierusalemme liberata di Torquato Tasso. ... In Pauia, Appresso gli Heredi di Gierolamo Bertoli, ... 1592. 4°. A^{4} A-Vu^{4} *^{4} *-3*^{4} 4*^{6}. pp. 1-344, 1-13. [369

GUAZZO, MARCO. Astolfo borioso ... MDXXXI. ... (Stampato in Vinegia per Nicolo d'Aristotile detto Zoppino. ...) 4°. A^{8} B-O^{4}. ff. II-LX. [370

-- Comedia ... intitolata errori damore. ... (In Venetia ... per Francesco Bindoni, & Mapheo Pasyni cōpagni Nel anno .1526. Del mese di Magio.) 8°. A-G^{4}. [371

-- Cronica ... Prima Editione. ... In Venetia appresso Francesco Bindoni. M. D. LIII. (*Colophon.*) fol. *^{8} **^{6} A-4C^{6} 4D^{4}. ff. 1-435. (Lea.) [372

-- Historie ... M. Marco Guazzo di tutti i fatti degni di memoria nel mondo successi dell' anno M. D. XXIIII. sino a questo presente ... In Vinegia Appresso Gabriel Giolito de Ferrari. MDXLVI. (*Colophon.*) 8°. *^{8} A-3A^{8} (-3A8, *blank*). ff. 1-375. [373

-- Historie ... oue se conteneno le guerre di Mahometto imperatore de turchi ... Con le guerre di suo figliuolo Baiasit ... In Venetia. al segno de la Croce. M.D. XLV. (Impresse ... per Bernardino Bindoni Milanese ...) 8°. A-D^{8}. ff. 2-32. [374

-- Tragedia ... intitolata discordia d'amore. ... MDXXVIII. (In Vineggia per Nicolo d' Aristotile detto Zoppino. ...) 8°. A-I^{4}. [375

GUAZZO, STEFANO. La ciuil conuersatione ... In Vinegia, Presso Altobello Salicato, M D LXXIX. 4°. a-b^{8} A-X^{8}. ff. 1-168. [376

-- -- In Venetia, Apresso Domenico Imberti. M. D. XCIX. 8°. a-b^{8} c^{4} A-Qq^{8} Rr^{4}. ff. 1-316. [377

-- The ciuile Conuersation of M. Stephen Guazzo, written first in Italian, diuided into foure bookes, the first three translated out of French by G. pettie. ... In the fourth is set downe the forme of Ciuile Conuersation ... And now translated out of Italian into English by Barth. Young, of the middle Temple, Gent. Imprinted at London by Thomas East. 1586. 4°. B.L. A^{8} A-Y^{8} Aa-Ff^{8} Gg^{6} (-A1, Gg6, *presumably blank*). ff. 1-229. *S.T.C.* 12423. (Furness.) [378

-- Dialoghi piaceuoli ... In Piacenza, 1587. Ad instantia di Pietro Tini, Libraro in Milano. ... (... Appresso Gio. Bazachi ...) 8°. *^{8} A-Qq^{8} Rr^{4}. pp. 1-586. [379

GÜNTHER XLI, count of Schwarzburg. Aussage/ Graff Günthers vō Schwartzburg/ wider Wilhelm von Grumbach ... Desgleichen/ Christoff Zewitzen/ wider obgenanten Grumbach Aussage ... M.D.LXVII. 4°. A-D^{4} E^{2}. [380

GÜNTHER, RUFF. Grammaticæ institutiones ... M.D.XXVIII. Kalendas Maias. (Excudebat Norimbergæ Fridericus Peypus. ...) 8°. A-C^{8} (-C8, *presumably blank*). [381

GUEVARA, ANTONIO DE. Las obras del ... don Antonio de gueuara ... M. D. xlv. ... (Fue impresso enla ... villa de valladoli: por ... iuā de villaquiran. Acabose a xiii. de iunio. ...) fol. B.L. ℭ^{6} a-z^{8} ⁊^{8} ꝯ^{8} ꝝ^{8} aa^{8}. ff. ij-ccxiiij. ¶*Additional t.pp.:* (q4^{v}) Libro llamado menosprecio de corte ... Año. M.D.xlv. ... (v1) Libro llamado auiso de priuados ... M.D.xlv. ... (42) Libro de los inuentores del arte del marear ... M.D.xlv. (Lea.) [382

-- Vna decada de cesares. ... Fue impresso en Anuers ... por Martin Nucio. ... 8°. B.L. a-z^{8} A-P^{8} Q^{4} (-Q4, *presumably blank*). ff. 2-306. ¶*Privilege dated 8 July 1544.* [383

-- Epistolas familiares ... primera y segunda parte. ... Año 1595. ... En Madrid, por la biuda de Pedro Madrigal. A costa de Miguel Martinez. (*Colophon.*) 4°. ¶^{8} A-Xx^8. pp. 1-797. ¶*Additional t.p.* (Z4): Segundo parte de las epistolas Familiares ... En Madrid Por la biuda de P. Madrigal, Año. 1595. (Lea.) [384

-- -- The Familiar Epistles of Sir Antony of Gueuara ... Translated out of the Spanish toung, by Edward Hellows, Groome of the Leash. ... Printed at London for Raufe Newbery ... 4°. ¶^{4} A-Y^4 Aa-Yy^4 3A-3X^4 (-3X4 *with colophon dated 1574*). pp. 1-512. *S.T.C.* 12432. (Furness.) [385

-- -- Imprinted at London for Ralph Newberrie. 1577. 4°. B.L. A^4 A-Cc^8 Dd^4. pp. 2-400. *S.T.C.* 12434. [386

-- -- Les epistres dorees, et discours salutaires ... Traduites d'Espagnol en Francois par le Seigneur de Guterry ... Ensemble la Reuolte que les Espaignolz firent contre leur ieune Prince, l'An M. D. XX. ... Auec vn Traitté des Trauaux & Priuileges des Galeres ... Traduit ... d'Italien en François. A Paris, Par Iacques Keruer ... 1563. (Imprimé ... par Iean Ruelle ...) 8°. ¶^{8} A-X^8 Aa-Tt^8 3A-3Q^8. pp. 1-335, 1-294, 1-256. [387

-- -- [1] Guldene Sendtschreiben. ... Durch ... Egidium Albertinum, aus der Hispanischen in die Teusche Sprach ... verwendt. Erster Theil. Gedruckt zu Mūnchen/ bey Adam Berg. Anno: M. D. XCVIII. ... 4°. (:)^4 A-3K^4 3L^2. ff. 1-225. [2] Ander Theil. ... *Same imprint.* (*Colophon.*) A^4 A-3X^4. ff. 1-264. [3] Dritter/ Schōnster vnnd letzter Theil. ... Gedruckt zu Mūnchen/ bey Adam Berg. Anno: M. D. XCIX. (*Colophon.*) a^4 A-3G^4 (-3G4, *presumably blank*). ff. 1-208. [388

-- -- Libro primo delle lettere ... Tradotte dal Signor Dominico di Catzelu. ... In Vinegia appresso Gabriel Giolito de' Ferrari. M D LVIII. 8°. *-**^{8} A-EE^8 FF^4 (-FF4, *presumably blank*). pp. 1-453. [389

-- -- Il terzo libro delle lettere ... di lingua Spagnola in Italiano tradotto per Alfonso di Vlloa. ... In Venetia. ... appresso Vincenzo Valgrisio. M D LIX. 8°. *^{8} A-Ee^8. pp. 1-441. [390

-- -- [Lettere.] In Venetia, Appresso Aluisse Zio. M. D. LXIIII. [1] Libro primo delle lettere ... Tradotte dal S. Dominico di Catzelu. ... 4°. ✠^{8} A-P^8. ff. 1-119. [2] Libro secondo ... aa^8 A-R^8. ff. 1-137. [3] Libro terzo ... A^6 B-K^8 L^4. ff. 3-84. [391

-- -- In Venetia, M D LXXV. Appresso gli heredi di Vincenzo Valgrisi. [1] Libro primo delle lettere ... Nuouamente tradotto del S. Alfonso Ulloa. ... 4°. †^{6} A-O^8 P^4. pp. 1-230. [2] Libro secondo ... †^{4} a-r^8. pp. 2-270. [3] Libro terzo ... †^{4} Aa-Ll^8 Mm^4. pp. 2-181. [4] Libro quarto ... †^{4} 3A-3M^8 †-3†^{4}. pp. 1-187. [392

-- -- In Venetia, Appresso la Compagnia degli Vniti. 1585. [1] Delle lettere ... libri quattro. ... 4°. †^{4} A-O^8 P^4. pp. 2-230. [2] Delle lettere ... Libro II. ... *^{4} A-R^8. pp. 2-270. [3] ... Libro III. *^{4} A-L^8 M^4. pp. 2-181. [4] ... Libro IIII. *^{4} A-M^8 †-3†^{4}. pp. 2-189. [393

-- *Libro del emperador Marco Aurelio.* The Diall of Princes. Compiled by ... Don Anthony of Gueuara ... Englysshed oute of the Frenche, by Thomas North ... Anno. 1557. Imprinted at London by Iohn Waylande. (... Mens. Decemb.) fol. B.L. A^2 a-z^6 A-Z^6 ꝛ^8 ꝯ^2. ff. 2-268. *S.T.C.* 12427. [394

-- -- Le liure doré de Marc Aurele ... Traduit de vulgaire Castillan en Frāçois, par R. B. de la Grise ... reueu & verifié sus les exemplaires Latins, & Castillan, par Antoine du Moulin Masconnois. A Paris, Pour Estiēne Groulleau ... 1564. 12°. a-z^8 A-L^8 (-L8). pp. 1-520. [395

-- -- L'horloge des princes auec l'histoire de Marc Aurele ... Traduit de Castillen en François par R. B. de Grise: depuis reueu & corrigé par N. de Herberay ... A Rouen, Pour Claude Micard ... 1576. (... De l'Imprimerie de George l'Oiselet ...) 16°. *^{8} †^{8} a-z^8 A-Zz^8 *^{8}. ff. 1-552. [396

-- -- A Paris, Pour Abel l'Angelier ... 1580. (De l'imprimerie de Nicolas Bonfons.) 8°. ā^8 ē^8 ī^8 ō^8 a-z^8 A-Cc^8 Dd^4. ff. 1-395. [397

-- -- Vita, gesti, costumi, discorsi, lettere di Marco Aurelio Imperatore ... In Vinegia, M. D. XXXXVI. (... In casa de' figliuoli di Aldo.) 8°. A-T^8. ff. 2-148. [398

-- -- M. D. LV. (Stampata in Venetia per Alessandro de Viano. ...) 8°. *^{8} A-T^8. pp. 2-303. [399

-- -- In Venetia, Appresso gli Heredi del Bonelli. 1574. (*Colophon.*) 8°. *⁸ A-X⁸. ff. 1-167. [400

-- -- [1] La institutione del prencipe Christiano, di M. Mambrino Roseo da Fabriano. Con l'aggiunta delle apostille, & d'vn trattato intorno all'ufficio del Consiglio & Consigliere, tratto per M. Lodouico Dolce dal libro Spagnuolo di Furio Ceriolo. ... In Vinegia appresso Gabriel Giolito de' Ferrari. M D LX. 8°. *-**⁸ A-BB⁸. pp. 1-397. [2] Il concilio ... *Same imprint.* *⁸ A-G⁸ H⁴. pp. 1-119. [401

-- -- In Venetia, Appresso Francesco Portonaris da Trino. M D LXII. [1] Libro di Marco Aurelio con l'horologio de principi ... 4°. *⁴ A-B⁸ C⁶ A-L⁸. ff. 2-88. [2] Il secondo libro ... *⁴ A-M⁸. ff. 1-95. [3] Il terzo libro ... *⁴ A-N⁸ O¹⁰. ff. 1-114. [4] Il quarto libro ... (... M D LXIII.) *⁴ A-O⁴ P⁶. ff. 2-61. [402

-- Libro llamado menosprecio de corte y alabança de aldea, Compuesto por ... Antonio de Gueuara ... mise en François par L.T.L. ... *Spanish, French, Italian.* M. D. XCI. [Genève,] Par Iean de Tournes. ... (Acheué d'imprimer le 20 May ...) 16°. †⁴ A-Z⁸ a-l⁸ m⁴. pp. 1-551. ¶*Translator: Louis Turquet de Mayerne.* [403

-- -- Von Beschwerligkeit vnd Vberdruss des Hofflebens: vnd Lob dess Feldbaws oder Landsitzes. ... in Hochteutsch ... vbergesetzet. Lübeck (Gedruckt ... Bey Lorentz Albrecht ... 1600.) 8°. A-Bb⁸ Cc⁴. pp. 2-374. [404

-- Oratorio de' religiosi, et essercitio de' virtuosi ... Tradotto dallo Spagnuolo, per M. Pietro Lauro. ... In Vinegia appresso Gabriel Giolito de' Ferrari. M D LXII. 8°. *⁸ **¹⁰ A-BB⁸ CC⁶. pp. 1-410. ¶*Sig.* CC *misbound in the order 1, 3, 2, 5, 4, 6;* **5 *(signed* **ij*) inserted after* CC3, [**6] *after* CC5. (Lea.) [405

GUICCIARDINI, FRANCESCO. Dell'epitome dell'historia d'Italia ... libri XX. ... In Venetia, Per ordine di Iacomo Sansouino. M D LXXX. 8°. a⁸ (-a8) A-Gg⁸ Hh⁴ 1-3⁸ 4⁴. ff. 1-244. [406

-- -- The historie of Guicciardin, conteining the warres of Italie and other partes ... Reduced into English by Geffray Fenton. ... Imprinted at London by Thomas Vautroullier for VVilliam Norton. 1579. fol. *⁶ (-*1, *presumably blank*) A-5F⁶ 5G⁴ 5H⁸. pp. 1-1184. *S.T.C.* 12458. (Furness.) [407

-- -- *Another copy.* [408

-- -- L'histoire d'Italie ... Translatée ... par Hierosme Chomedey ... A Paris. Pour Iean Dallier ... 1568. ... fol. ã⁴ ¶⁸ A-3Z⁶. ff. j-ccccxiiij. [409

GUICCIARDINI, LODOVICO. Descrittione ... di tutti i Paesi Bassi, altrimenti detti Germania Inferiore. .. In Anuersa M.D.LXVII. Appresso Guglielmo Siluio ... fol. ¶⁶ A⁴ (A4 + *double-leaf map*) B-D⁶ E-F⁴ G² H-I⁴ K⁶ L⁴ M² N-P⁶ Q⁴ R² S⁶ T-V⁴ X⁶ Y-Z⁴ Aa⁸ Bb-Cc⁶ Dd² Ee-Ff⁴ Gg-Ii⁶ Kk² Ll⁶ Mm-Nn⁴ Oo⁶ P⁴ P⁶. pp. 1-296. [410

-- Detti, et fatti piaceuoli, et graui, di diuersi principi, filosofi, et cortigiani. Raccolti del Guicciardini, & ridotti à moralità. In Venetia, Appresso Domenico Farri. M D LXXXI. 8°. *-**⁸ 3*⁴ A-P⁸. pp. 2-218. [411

-- L'hore di ricreatione ... Venetiis, M D LXXXIII. (*Colophon.*) 16°. A-Aa⁸ Bb⁶. pp. 3-350. [412

GUIDALOTTI, DIOMEDE. Tyrocinio de le cose vulgari ... Cioe: Sonetti Canzoni Sestine Strammotti Barzelette Capituli Egloghe E prosa. (Impresso ne Lalma ... Citta di Bologna per me Caligula di Bazaleri ... M.D.IIII. A di. xy. de Aprile.) 4°. A-C⁸ D⁴ E-V⁸ X¹⁰. [413

GUIDELLI, PAOLO. ... Ioanni Suarer ... comiti Arganilli ... Paulus Guidellus ... Tridentinus S. P. D. Brixiae Apud Ludouicum Sabiensem. M. D. LXII. 4°. [A]-B⁴. (Lea.) [414

GUIDELLI, TADDEO. R. P. Magistri Thadaei Perusini ... concio ad ... Concilium Tridentinum, habita in festo ... Ascensionis. M. D. LXII. Brixiae ad instantiam Io: Baptistae Bozolae. M. D. LXIII. (... Apud Ludouicum Sabiensem.) 4°. A⁶. (Lea.) [415

GUIDO DE MONTE ROCHERII. [1] Manipulus curatorum ... In quo de Septē ecclesię sacramentis, de articulis fidei, ac de Eucharistiæ sacramento ad plenū tractatur ... M D XXXVIII. (Venetiis in ædibus Francisci Bindoni, & Maphei Pasini, mense Ianuarii ...) 8°. A-S^8. ff. 2-144. [2] Speculum ecclesie ... M D XXXVIII. (*Colophon.*) a-b^8. (Lea.) [416

GUIDON. Le guidon des practiciens ... Par M. M. N. Aduocat. A Paris, Par Nicolas Bonfons ... 1585. 16°. A-Zz^8 AA-ZZ^8 3A-3E^8. pp. 3-1024. (Biddle.) [417

GUILANDINI, MELCHIORE. Melchioris Guilandini papyrus, hoc est commentarius in tria C Plinij maioris de papyro capita. Accessit. Hieronymi Mercurialis Repugnantia, qua pro Galeno strenuè pugnatur. Item Melchioris Guilandini Assertio sententiæ in Galenum ... Venetiis Apud M. Antonium Vlmum. M D LXXII. 4°. *-**^{4} A-Mm^4. pp. 1-280. [418

GUILELMUS PARISIENSIS. Postille maiores in epistolas ꝛ euangelia per totius anni decursum ... M.CCCCC.VII. Basileę. (Exaratum per ... Iacobū de Pfortzheym ... ad quartūdecimū kalē. Septēbres. ...) 4°. B.L. π^4 a-b^6 e-r$^{8.6.6}$ s^8 t^4 v-hh$^{8.8.8.4}$ ii-mm^8 nn^4 oo-qq^8 rr^4 ss-yy^8 zz^4 AA-DD^8 EE^4 FF-LL^8. ff. I-CCCXCI. [419

GUILLEUS, GULIELMUS. Discorso ... sopra i fatti di Annibale. ... Tradotto per il Dolce. ... In Vinegia appresso Gabriel Giolito de Ferrari e fratelli MDLI. (*Colophon.*) 8°. A-I^8 (-I8, *blank*). ff. 2-69. [420

GUILLAUME LE BRETON. Bellum quod Philippus Francorum Rex cum Othone Augusto, Anglis, Flandrisqȝ gessit, Annos abhinc CCC. conscriptum ... Antuerpiæ apud Martinum Cæsarem, Anno. M.D.XXXIIII. 8°. A-F^8 G^4. [421

GUILLON, RENÉ. De generibus carminum Graecorum ... Parisiis, Excudebat Christianus Wechelus ... M. D. XLVIII. 4°. A-E^4. pp. 2-38. [422

-- Gnomon ... volentibus serio studio rimari arcana Poetarum omnium Græcorum ... Parisiis, Excudebat Christianus Wechelus ... M.D.XLVIII. 4°. A^6 B-M^4. pp. 3-12, 9-94. [423

GULIELMUS APPULUS. Guillielmi Apuliensis rerum in Italia ac regno Neapolitano Normanicarum. Libri quinque. Rothomagi, Apud Richardum Petit, & Richardum l'Allemant. M. D. LXXXII. 4°. †^{4} A-N^4. ff. 1 [=2]-4, 1-52. ¶*In verse.* [424

GULIELMUS, archbishop of Tyre. Historia della guerra sacra di Gierusalemme ...: Raccolta in XXIII. libri ... Tradotta in lingua Italiana Da M. Gioseppe Horologgi. ... In Venetia, Appresso Vincenzo Valgrisi. M. D. LXII. (*Colophon.*) 4°. *-**^{4} 3*^{6} A-Zz^4 AA-ZZ^4 aa-tt^4. pp. 1-702. [425

GUNTHERUS. Ligurini de gestis imp. Cæsaris Friderici primi Augusti libri decē carmine Heroico cōscripti ... A Chunrado Celte reperti postliminio restituti ... (imp̄ssi per ... Erhardū Oeglin ciuem augustēsem Añō Sesquimillesimo & septimo mēse Apprilio) fol. π^2 A-k$^{8.6}$ L-M^6 (-M6, *blank*). [426

GUTIERREZ DE LOS RIOS, GASPAR. Noticia general para la estimacion de las artes, y de la manera en que Se conocen las liberales de las que son Mecanicas y seruiles, con vna exortacion a la honra de la virtud y del trabajo contra los ociosos ... En Madrid, Por Pedro Madrigal, Año M.DC. 4°. §^{8} §§^{8} A-X^8 Y^6. pp. 1-340. (Lea.) [427

GUTMAR, GREGOR. Von den gewis/ vnfehlbarn Gemerck vnd Kennzeychen/ Der wahren/ Alleinseligmachenden Religion ... Vier Predigen ... Durch Gregorium Gutmarum ... Getruckt zu Ingolstatt/ durch Dauid Sartorium. Anno M. D. LXXXXII. 4°. A-Z^4. pp. 1-170. [428

GUZMAN, JUAN DE. Primera parte de la Rhetorica ... Impresso en Alcala de Henares, en casa de Ioan Yniguez de Laquerica. Año. 1589. 8°. ¶^{8} A-Oo^8. ff. 1-291. [429

H

H., W. Auss was vrsach diss Vngewitter über vns erfolge. Den letsten Iunij. Anno M. D. XLVIIII. (Getruckt zů Augspurg/ durch Hans Zimmerman.) 4°. A^{4} (-A4, *presumably blank*). ¶*In verse.* [1

HABERSTOCK, JOACHIM. Epicedion, ac musarum threnodia ... in D. Ferdinandi Romanorum Imperatoris obitum. In D. Maximiliani ... Panegyrus. Item Carmen de ... Christi Iesu natiuitate. Quibus accessit Psalmus Dauid XXX. ... Elegiacôs redditus. ... Monaci excudebat Adam Montanus, Anno M.D.LXIIII. 4°. A-E^{4} F^{2}. [2

HAER, FLORIS VAN DER. Florentii vander Haer, de initiis tumultuum Beligicorum ... libri duo ... Duaci, Ex officina Ioannis Bogardi. M. D. LXXXVII. 8°. A-V^{8} X^{6}. pp. 1-330. (Lea.) [3

HÄTZER, LUDWIG. Eyn vrteyl Gottes vnsers ee gemachels/ wie man sich mit allen goͤtzen vnnd bildnüssen halten sol ... 4°. a^{4} b^{6}. [4

HAGUELON, PIERRE. Petri Hagueloni Lexouiensis Calendarium trilingue, seu de mensibus Hebræorum, Græcorum & Romanorum, Dialogus ... Parisiis, Apud Martinum Iuuenem ... 1557. ... 8°. A-E^{8} (B4 + *folded leaf*). ff. 2-40. [5

HAGUENAU. Vom tag zu Hagenaw Zwen verdeutschte Sendbriefe/ eins Thum̄dechants vnd eins weysen bescheidenen Thum̄herrns. [1540?] 4°. A-D^{4}. [6

HAIDLAUFF, SEBASTIAN. Gewisse/ warhafftige newe zeitung Von der Augspurgerischen Confession verwandten Predicanten/ new angerichter ainigkait. ... M. D. LXXII. (Gedruckt zu Můnchen/ bey Adam Berg.) 4°. A-I^{4}. ff. 2-36. [7

-- -- *Another copy.* [8

HAJEK, TADEÁŠ. Astrologica opuscula antiqua. Fragmentum Astrologicum, incerto autoris, in quo ... aliquot exemplis ostenditur, quomodo medicatio ad Astrologicam rationem sit accommodanda. Liber regum de significationibus Planetarum in duodecim domiciliis Coeli, & de natura duodecim signorum Zodiaci. Liber Hermetis centum Aphorismorum, cum commentationibus Thaddæi Hagecij ab Hagek D. ... Pragæ Excudebat Georgius Melantrichus ab Auentino. M D LXIIII. 4°. A-O^{4} P^{6}. (Lea.) [9

HAKLUYT, RICHARD. [1] The principal nauigations, voyages, traffiques and discoueries of the English Nation ... Imprinted at London by George Bishop, Ralph Newberie, and Robert Barker. Anno 1599. fol. B.L. *-$**^{6}$ A-$3E^{6}$ $3F^{4}$ a-d^{2} (-d2, *blank*). pp. 1-620. [2] The second volume of the principal nauigations ... *Same imprint.* $*^{8}$ A-Cc^{6} 3A-$3R^{6}$. pp. 1-312, 1-204. [3] The third and last volume ... Imprinted at London by George Bishop, Ralfe Newberie, and Robert Barker. Anno Dom. 1600. $(A)^{8}$ A-I^{6} K^{8} L-$4C^{6}$. pp. 1-868. *S.T.C.* 12626. [10

HALL, EDWARD. The vnion of the two noble and illustre famelies of Lancastre & Yorke ... 1550. (Imprynted at London by Rychard Grafton ...) fol. B.L. A^{4} A^{8} B-E^{6} ff^{2} a-g^{6} h^{8} I^{2} a-q^{6} r^{8} s^{4} A-I^{6} K^{8} L^{4} AA-DD^{6} aa-ee^{6} ff^{8} 3a-$3i^{6}$ $3k^{8}$ $3l^{4}$ a-z^{6} A-E^{6} ff^{6} G-Z^{6} (-Z6, *blank*). ff. i-xxxij, i-l, j-C.ii, i-Lxi, j-xxiiij, j-xxxv, i-lxj, i-C.C.lxiij. *S.T.C.* 12723. (Furness.) [11

HAMELMANN, HERMANN. Oldenburgisch Chronicon ... Anno 1599. (Gedruckt zu Oldenburg/ Durch Warner Berendts Erben. ...) fol. a-g^{6} A-G^{6} H^{6+2} I-P^{6} Q^{6+2} R-Hh^{6} Ii^{6+2} Kk-Rr^{6} Ss^{6+2} Tt^{4} (-Tt4) Vu^{8}. pp. 1-494. [12

HANDLUNG. Ein wunderbarlich erschrockenlich hanndlung/ So sich auff den Grun Dornstag diss iars in dem Stetlein Schiltach/ mit einer Brunst durch den Boͤsen geist vormittelst einer Mayd gestifft/ begeben hat. 1533. (Gedrugkt zu Dressden durch Wolffgang Stoͤckel. ...) 4°. A^{4}. [13

HANER, JOHANN. Theses Ioannis Haneri Noribergensis de poenitentia. Lipsiae Excudebat Nicolaus Vuolrab, anno M. D. XXXIX. 4°. A-C^4 (-C4, *presumably blank*). (Lea.) [14

HANGEST, JÉRÔME DE. Introductorium Morale ... Impressum parrhisijs Anno ... Mellesimo quingentesimo vigesimoquarto in ædibus ... Ambrosij girault. 4°. A-S^4. ff. I-LXVII. [15

HANSON, PETER. Offenbarung der newen erschrö̈cklichen vnnd Teuflischen Landtlugen/ so diss 1586. Jars wider die Societet Iesu ... aussgesprengt worden. ... Gedruckt zů Ingolstadt/ durch Dauid Sartorium. Anno M. D. LXXXVI. 4°. A-C^4 D^2. pp. 1-26. [16

HARANGUE. Harangue faicte en la defense de l'Inconstance. A Paris, Chez Abel L'Angelier ... 1598. ... 12°. A^6 B-E^{12} F^6. ff. 1-54. [17

HARIOT, THOMAS. Admiranda narratio ... de commodis et incolarum ritibus Virginiæ ... Latio donata à C. C. A. ... Francoforti ad Moenum typis Ioannis Wecheli, sumtibus vero Theodor De Bry anno CIↃ IↃ XC. Venales reperiuntur in officina Sigismundi Feirabendi (*Colophon.*) fol. a^4 b^6 c^4 d^{8+2} A^6 B^8 C-F$^{8.6}$. pp. 3-34. ¶*The engraved t.p. is that of Church 142 ("second edition; first issue"), but all else corresponds to 140 ("first edition; first issue") as described.* [18

HARMENOPULUS, CONSTANTINE. Προχειρον νομων Κονσταντινου του Ἀρμενοπουλου. Promptuarium iuris ... Interprete Ioanne Mercero. Dionysii Gothofredi I.C. paratitla ad singulos Constantini Harmenopuli titulos ... *Greek and Latin.* [Genevae,] Apud Guillelmum Lœmarium. M. D. LXXXVII. 4°. ¶^{4} A-Mm^8 Nn^4. pp. 1-456. (Lea.) [19

HARTLIEB, JAKOB. De generibus ebriosorum, et ebrietate vitanda. Cui adiecimus de meretricum in suos amatores, & concubinarum in sacerdotes fide: quæstiones ... M.D.LVII. 12°. A-H^{12}. ¶*Additional t.pp.:* (D11^r) De fide meretricum ... in fine Quodlibeti Heydelbergen: determinata à Magistro Iacobo Hartlieb Landonensi ... M.D.LVII. (F11^r) De fide concubinarum ... Quæstio ..., in quodlibeto Heydelbergensi, determinata a Magistro Paulo Oleario Heydelbergensi. [20

-- -- Francoforti ad Moenum. 1581. (... apud Ioannem Spies, Impensis Sigismundi Feyerabenij.) 8°. A-I^8 K^4. [21

HARTUNG, JOHANN. Decuria locorum quorundam memorabilium, ex optimis ... authoribus ... excerptorum ... Basileae, ex officina Ioannis Oporini [c. 1560]. 4°. a-h^4. pp. 4-60. [22

-- Prolegomena in tres priores Odysseæ Homeri Rapsodias. Francoforti, Christianus Egen. excudebat. (D.M.XXXIX.) 8°. A^4 B-E^8 F-G^4. ff. 2-39. [23

HASAN IBN HASAN. [1] Opticae thesaurus. Alhazeni Arabis libri septem ... Eiusdem liber de crepusculis & Nubium ascensionibus. ... adiectis ... commentarijs, à Federico Risnero. ... Basileae, per Episcopios. M D LXXII. (Per Eusebium Episcopium, & Nicolai F. hæredes. ... Mense Augusto.) fol. α^4 a-z^6 zz^6. pp. 1-288. [2] Vitellonis Thuringopoloni opticae libri decem. ... Basileae. *^{4} A-Ff^6 Gg^4 Hh-Rr^6. pp. 1-474. [24

HASENBERG, JOHANN. Ioannis Hasenbergij Bohemi, ad Luderanorum, famosum Libellũ, recens Wittenbergae editũ, Responsio. ... [1530.] 4°. A-D^4. [25

HASENMULLER, ELIAS. Historia Iesuitici ordinis ... Anfe̊nglich in Lateinischer Sprach beschrieben/ Durch M. Eliam Hasenmů̈llern/ vnnd Claudio Aquauiuæ ... ins Teudtsche gebracht/ Durch Melchiorem Leporinum ... Gedruckt zu Franckfurt am Mayn. 1594. 4°. a-d^4 e^2 A-4N^4 4O^2. pp. 1-660. [26

-- Iesuiticum Ieiunium; Siue commemoratio historica de Iesuitarum ieiunio et exercitiis ... Edita à Polycarpo Lysero ... Francofurti ad Moenum, excudebat Iohannes Spies. M. D. XCV. (*Colophon.*) 8°.)(-2)(^{8} A-L^8 M^4. pp. 1-182. ¶*Half-title* (K1^r): Oratio ... habita a M. Daniele Cramero ... [27

-- -- Iesuiticum ieiunium ... ins Teutsche gebracht/ Durch Melchiorem Leporinum ... Gedruckt zu Franckfort am Mayn/ durch Iohann Spies. M. D. XCVI. (*Colophon.*) 4°. A-Cc^4. pp. 3-206. [28

HASENTÖDTER, JOHANN. Chronica. ... Anfangs der Erschaffung aller sichtbarlichen dinge/ biss auff diese ... letzte zeit ... Zu Königsperg bey Iohann Daubman. M. D. LXIX. 4°. ?-3?^{4} A-Z^4 a-z^4 Aa-Rr^4. ff. 2-252. [29

HASSALUS, HERMANNUS. De exornatione carminum, octo cohortes. ... Coloniae. Apud Maternum Cholinum. M.D.LXXXVI. 8°. A-G^8. pp. 3-111. [30

HAUER, GEORG. Ander zwue Predig vom Salue regina ... Ein vorantwortung ... wider die gewesen pröbst zu Nürmberg. ... (Gedrugkt zu Dressden durch Wolffgang Stöckel. 1533.) 4°. A-C^4 D^2 E^4. [31

HAUGWITZ, CHRISTOPH VON. Woher Thumherrn Canonici heissen/ Vnd was jr vnd etlicher anderer jrer Thumpfaffen vrsprüngliche Empter/ gewesen sind. Dialogus. ... Mit einer schrifft D. Iohan. Pomerani/ Von guten Kirchen Ordnungen. Wittemberg/ gedruckt Nickel Schirlentz. 1536. (*Colophon.*) 4°. A-I^4. [32

HAUPTSCHALK. Wider den Hauptschalck vnd todtfeünd des menschē gewissen wie man den stillen sol. ... 4°. A^4. [33

HAVRE-DE-GRÂCE. Briefue Description de l'esiouissance de la reduction du Haure de Grace ..., Qui fut le vingt-huictiesme iour de Iuillet, Mil cinq cens soixante-trois. A Paris Par Guillaume de Niuerd ... 8°. A-B^4. ¶*In verse.* [34

HAYMO, bishop of Halberstadt. D. Haymonis episcopi Halberstattensis homiliarum siue concionum popularium ... pars utraque, hoc est, & hyemalis & æstiualis ... Coloniæ ex officina Iohannis Prael, anno M. D. XXXVI. Mense Septembri. fol. A^4 a-pp^6 qq^8. pp. 2-471. [35

-- Haymonis episcopi Halberstatensis in diui Pauli epistolas omneis interpretatio ... Parisiis Venundatur apud Oudinum Petit ... 1541. 8°. a-z^8 A-Y^8 Z^4. ff. 2-364. [36

HAYNECK, MARTIN. Carmina in honorem ... Georgii Samenhammeri ... nuptias cum ... Catharina ... Iohannis Richteri filia celebrantis ... Scripta ab amicis ... CIↃ. IↃ. LXXIII. ... Lipsiæ Iohannes Rhamba excudebat. 8°. A^8. [37

HAYWARD, SIR JOHN. The first part of the life and raigne of King Henrie the IIII. Extending to the end of the first yeare of his raigne. Written by I. H. Imprinted at London by Iohn Wolfe, ... 1599. (*Colophon.*) 4°. A-V^4 (-V4, *presumably blank*). pp. 1-149. *S.T.C.* 12997. (Furness.) [38

HEDERICH, BERNARD. Schwerinische chronica. ... Rostock Gedruckt durch Christoff Reussner. Anno M D XCVIII. (*Colophon.*) 4°. A-Q^4. [39

HEDERICH, JOHANN. Oratio funebris ... Iulio, duci Brunsuicensi et Luneburgensi ... Helmaestadii Excudebat Iacobus Lucius, Anno M. D. LXXXIX. 4°. A-C^4 D^2. [40

HEDIO, KASPAR. Radts Predig. ... Beschehen ... M. D. XXXIIII. Den xiiij. tag Ienners. Durch Casparn Hedion ... 4°. A-D^4. [41

-- Trost geschrifft. ... Impressum Neuburgi Danubij. M.D.XLVI. (... gedruckt/ bey Hansen Kilian ...) 4°. A-L^4. [42

-- Von dem Zehenden Zwů träffliche Predig/ Beschehen in dem Münster zů Strassburg/ auff den xx. tag Nouembris. Sendtbrieff an das Christlich heüflein im Kinckgaw ... M.D.XXV. 4°. A-C^4. [43

HEERBRAND, JAKOB. Ableinung Vnnd Abfertigung der newen Zeittung auss Constantinopel/ so diss 83. jars zu Wien von einem Iesuiter/ wider die Christliche Augspurgische Confession aussgesprengt. ... Getruckt zu Tübingen bey Georg Gruppenbach/ Anno 1583. 4°. A-L^4 M^2. pp. 1-91. [44

HEERLIED. Ein Heer lied/ für die Christlichen kriegsleut/ so Gottes wort wider den Antichrist/ verthedigen ... Im thon Ir frommen Landsknecht alle ... [Erfurt, Merten von Dolgen,] M D. xlvj. 8°. A^8. [45

HEGENDORF, CHRISTOPH. Encomium Sobrietatis authore Christophoro Hegendorffino Lipsico [c. 1520.] 4°. A-B⁴. [46

-- Encomium Somni ... (Lipsiæ ex ædibus Valentini Schumanni Anno ... Millesimo quingentesimo vndeuigesimo.) 4°. A⁶. [47

-- In actiones Verrinas, et in Topica M. Ciceronis, adnotatiunculæ ... Haganoæ per Iohan. Sec. Anno M. D. XXIX. (*Colophon.*) 8°. a-n⁸. [48

-- Quae iuuenibus eloquentiæ cupidis im primis scribenda sint, ex Fabio ... Item oratio in artium liberalium laudem ... (Impressum Haganoæ per Iohannem Secerium, Anno M.D.XXXI.) 8°. A-N⁸. [49

HEIDENREICH, ESAIAS. Ein lobgesang zu Gott in aller noth ... Sonderlich/ des Türcken ... Im Thon. Aus tieffer noth/ etc. ... Durch E. H. D. Breslaw. 1566. 8°. A⁸. [50

HEILAND, SAMUEL. Aristotelis ethicorum ad Nicomachum libri decem ... per Quæstiones expositi ... Tubingæ, Excudebat Georgius Gruppenbachius, M. D. LXXIX. (*Colophon.*) 8°.):(⁸ A-R⁸ S⁴. pp. 1-278. [51

HEINRICH IV, emperor. Henrici quarti Ro. imperatoris bellum contra Saxones Heroico carmine descriptum. Epistolium Beati Rhenani cum versibus Bap. Mantua. contra errorem cuiusdam Fratricelli de Germanis & Gallis. ... (... prodire fecit ... Ioannes Grüninger ciuis Argentinus ... M.D.VIII.) 4°. A⁶ B⁴ C⁶. [52

HEINRICH VON GORKUM. Tractatus cōsultatorij ... Henrici de Gorychum ... De diuinis nominib⁹ De ꝑdestinatōe et reprobatōe diuina De effectib⁹ salutiferis eucharistie. De processionib⁹ ecclesiasticis De obseruatione festorum De symonia et quodā casu matrimoniali. De iusto bello Cōtinens breue cōsiliū de iure decimarū De superstitionib⁹. De practica eijciēdi demones De temerario iudicio Huyssitarum circa potestatem pape (Impressus Colonie in ... Officina ... Henrici Quentel. ꝑdie idus Apriles. Anno supra Iubileum tercio.) 4°. B.L. a-e⁶ f⁴ g-k⁶ l⁴ m-p⁶. ff. i-lxxxv. [53

HEINRICH VON LANGENSTEIN. Secreta sacerdotum magistri Henrici de Hassia. (Impressum Liptzk per Melchiarem Lotterum Anno millesimo quingētesimo decimo quinto.) 4°. B.L. A⁶ B⁴. [54

HEINRICHSTADT. Heinrichstetische priuilegia. (... geben Heinrichstadt bey unserm Hofflager/ im Jar ... Tausent/ Fünffhundert/ Vier vnd Achtzig/ den 21. Augusti.) 4°. A-E⁴. [55

HELDING, MICHAEL SIDONIUS. Catechismus, Das ist/ Christliche Vnderweisung ... nach warer Euangelischer vnd Catholischer lehr ... durch ... Michaeln Bischoff zu Merseburg ... gepredigt. ... Meyntz/ Druckts Frantz Behem ... M. D. LXI. (*Colophon.*) fol. A⁴ A-Yy⁶ Zz⁴ 3A⁶. ff. I-CCLXXIX. [56

-- -- Catechismus catholicus ... in conciones LXXXIIII. ... distributus ... Latinitate donatus per Tilmannum Bredēbachium Embricens. Coloniæ apud Hæredes Iohannis Quentel & Geruuinum Calenium ... 1562. ... 8°. A*⁸ B*⁴ A-3A⁸. pp. 1-748. [57

-- Etliche schöne/ Christenliche Predig/ von dem Glauben vnd gůten Wercken/ auch von anrüeffung der lieben Heyligen ... Gepredigt zů Augspurg ... M. D. xlvij. ... Gedruckt zů Dillingen/ durch Sebaldum Mayer. Anno M.D.LI. 8°. A-O⁴. [58

-- Predig auff den Grienen donnerstag/ von der Heyligsten Eucharistia ⁊c. Durch Michaeln Meintzischen Suffraganeen ... Getruckt zů Ingolstat/ durch Alexander Weissenhorn. M.D.XLVIII. ... 4°. Aa-Cc⁴. ff. II-XI. [59

HÉLIAN, LOUIS. Ludouici Heliani Vercellensis ... de bello suscipiēdo aduersus venetianos & Turcas oratio ... dicta in Augusta uindelica IIII. Idus Aprilis. Anno ... Millesimoquingentesimodecimo. (Impressum Auguste Vindelicoꝝ. per M. Ioannem othmar ... M.D.X. die XII. Maii.) 4°. a⁸ b⁴ c⁶. ¶c1ʳ: Eiusdem Lodouici Heliani uenatio leonū. Pontifex Max. ... (*in verse*). [60

HELIODORUS OF EMESA. Ἡλιοδώρου Αἰθιοπικῆς ἱστορίας ... Heliodori historiae Aethiopicæ libri decem, nusquam antea in lucem editi. Basileae ex officina Heruagiana an. M. D.

XXXIIII. mense Februario. (*Colophon.*) 4°. a-z⁴ A-G⁴ H⁶. pp. 1-242. ¶*Editor: Vincentius Obsopoeus.* [61

-- -- Heliodori Aethiopicæ Historiæ libri decem, nunc primùm è Græco sermone in Latinum translati: Stanislao VVarschevviczki Polono interprete. Adiectus est etiam Philippi Melanthonis de ipso autore, & hac eiusdem conuersione, iudicium. ... Basileæ, per Ioannem Oporinum. (... M. D. LII. Mense Ianuario.) fol. a-z⁴ A⁴ B⁶ (-B6, *presumably blank*). pp. 8-195. (Lea.) [62

-- -- L'histoire Aethiopique de Heliodorus ... Traduite de Grec en François ... A Paris Pour Estienne Groulleau ... M. D. LIX. (Acheuê d'Imprimer le Mardy douziesme iour de Septembre ...) fol. ❧⁴ A-V⁶ X⁴. ff. 1-122. [63

-- -- I primi cinque canti d'Heliodoro, di M. Hieronimo Bossi. ... (In Milano per Giouann' Antonio Borgio, l'anno M.D.LVII.) 4°. A-I⁸ K⁴. ff. 2-76. [64

-- -- La diletteuole historia di Heliodoro. ... In Genoua M.D.LXXXII (*Colophon.*) 8°. ¶⁸ A-Bb⁸. pp. 1-399. ¶*Translator: Leonardo Ghini.* A3 *defective.* [65

-- -- Historia Ethiopica de Heliodoro. Trasladada de Frances en vulgar Castellano, por vn secreto amigo de su patria, y corregida segun el Griego por el mismo ... En Salamanca, En casa de Pedro Lasso. 1581. A costa de Pedro Landri. (*Colophon.*) 8°. A-Oo⁸ (-Oo8, *presumably blank*). ff. 9-295. [66

HELMBOLD, LUDWIG. Der Iesuiter Orden/ ausser welchem niemand kan Selig werden/ Reimweise beschrieben ... Anno M.D.LXXXIII. (Gedruckt zu Mülhausen/ durch Georgium Hantzsch ...) 4°. A-B⁴. [67

HELMSTÄDT. *Academia Julia.* Piae exequiae Quas ad cohonestandum funus ... Iulii, ducis Brunsuicensium ac Lunaeburgensium ... Academia Iulia Orationibus aliquot ... prosecuta est. ... Helmstadii, Typis Iacobi Lucij, Anno 1589. 4°.)(⁴. [68

HELT, KASPAR. Confessio de mediatore generis Humani Iesu Christo ... VVitebergae. Anno. M.D.LV. (... Ex officina typographica Viti Creutzer.) 8°. A-D⁸ (-D8, *presumably blank*). [69

HÉMARD, URBAIN. Recherche de la vraye anathomie des dents ... A Lyon, par Benoist Rigaud. 1582. 8°. A-G⁸ H⁴. pp. 1-90. (School of Dentistry.) [70

HENETUS, THEODORUS. Ein kurtzer bericht vom Interim ... 1548. 4°. A-C⁴. [71

HENRI II, king of France. La intrata del re Christianissimo Henrico. II. nella citta di Rens et la sua incoronatione. In Vinegia per Paolo Gherardo M D. XLVII. 8°. A-D⁴ (-D4, *presumably blank*). ff. 2-14. [72

HENRICHMANN, JACOB. Grāmatice institutiones ... Ars condendorum carminū Henrici Bebelij ... Centimetrū Mauri Seruij ... Henricus Gran impressit in Hagenau. (... impensis ... Ioannis Rinman de oringau ... Anno ... Millesimo quingētesimodecimoquarto. quindecima die Februarij ...) 4°. a⁶ b⁴ c⁸ d-l⁴·⁴·⁴·⁸ m-v⁴·⁴·⁸ x-y⁴ z⁶. [73

-- Prognostica alioquin barbare practica nūcupata: ab Iacobo Henrichman: latinitate donata ... (Argentine Ioannes gruniger imprimebat M.D.viiij. Adelpho castigatore.) 4°. B.L. [A]⁴. [74

HENRICUS DE HERPF. Speculum perfectionis ... Henrici Hierp. ... M.D.xxiiij. (Venetiis per Ioan. Antonium & fratres de Sabio. Sumptu ... Laurentii Lorii. ...) 8°. ✠⁴ A-N⁸ O¹⁰. [75

HENRIQUEZ, ENRIQUE. Summae theologiae moralis, Tomus Primus. ... Venetiis, ... M. DC. Apud Hæredes Melchioris Sessæ. fol. *⁸ A-4E⁶ 4F⁴ a-k⁶ A-D⁶. pp. 1-895, 2-118. (Lea.) [76

HENRY VIII, king of England. Assertio septem sacramentorū aduersus Martin. Lutherum, ædita ab ... Angliæ ... rege ... Henrico eius nominis octauo. [? Moguntiae, Joannes Schoeffer, 1522.] 8°. A-K⁸ (-K8). pp. 3-158. (Yarnall.) [76a

-- Literarū. quibus ... Hēricus octauus, rex Angliæ ..., respondit, ad quandam epistolā Martini Lutheri, ad se missam, & ipsius Lutheranæ quoq3 epistolæ exemplum. Coloniæ, ... M. D. XXVII. (... ex officina ... Petri Quentell ... mense Februario.) 4°. A-B⁴ C⁶. (Yarnall.) [76b

HERACLITUS. Heracliti ad Democritum de pace elegia. Parisiis. Apud Annetum Briere ... 1559. 4°. A⁴. [77

HERBERSTEIN, SIGISMUND, FREIHERR VON. Rerum Moscouiticarum commentarij Sigismundi Liberi Baronis in Herberstain ... Commentarius de bellis Moscorum ... ab Ioanne Leuuenclaio. ... Basileae, ex officina Oporiniana. 1571. (... Mense Martio.) fol. a⁶ (a6 + 3 *engraved sheets*) b-u⁶ x⁴ y⁶. pp. 1-227. [78

HERBORN, NICOLAUS. Assertiones trecentae ac vigintesex ... ueræ Orthodoxæ, aduersus Francisci Lamberti ... paradoxa impia, ac erroris plena ... [Coloniae, Petrus Quentell, 1526.] 8°. A-E⁸. [79

HERESBACH, CONRAD. [Foure bookes of husbandrie, Collected by M. Conradus Heresbachius, ... containing the whole art and trade of Husbandry, Gardening, Graffing, and Planting ... Newly Englished, and increased by Barnabe Googe, Esquire. ... At London, printed by T. Este, for Thomas Wight. 1596.] (*Colophon.*) 4°. B.L. A-C⁴ (-A1) A-Z⁸ &⁸ 2A². ff. 1-193. *S.T.C.* 13199. (Furness.) [80

HERMAN, NICOLAUS. Ein new Mandat Ihesu Christi ... in welchem er auffgebeut/ allen so jm in der Tauff gehuldet vnnd geschworen haben/ Das sie das verlorne Schlos (Den glauben an sein wort) Dem Teuffel widerrumb abgewinnen sollen/ Gegeben inn diesem 56. Jar/ Am Newen Jars Tage. (Gedrůckt zu Schleussingen/ durch Herman Hamsing.) 4°. a-c⁴. [81

HERMANN VON WIED. Reuerendissimi ... Hermanni, sanctae Coloniensis Ecclesiæ Archiepiscopi, ... Appellatio contra certos quosdam homines ex ... Capitulo Coloniensi, Clero item & Vniuersitate ... [Bonnae, Laurentius Mylius,] Anno M. D. XLV. fol. A-B⁶. (Yarnall.) [81a

-- Nostra Hermanni ... archiepiscopi Coloniensis ... simplex ac pia deliberatio, qua ratione, Christiana & in uerbo Dei fundata Reformatio, Doctrinæ ... instituenda sit ... Bonnae ex officina Laurentii Mylii ... M. D. XXXXV. (*Colophon.*) fol. *⁴ A-X⁶ Y⁴ Z⁶. ff. II-CXXXVI. (Yarnall.) [81b

HERMANN, CHRISTOFF. Ein Predig/ Darinn Grūndtliche Vrsachen angezeigt werden/ das der Iungen Kindertauff/ auss Gott vnnd seinem Wort gemäss sey ... Getruckt zu Tūbingen/ durch Alexander Hock ... 1585. (*Colophon.*) 4°. A-F⁴. [82

HERMANN, WOLFGANG. Frūntliche Ermanung wider ietzt schwebende vffrūrische Leeren vnd jrrthungen Im Reūtters thon gedicht. ... (Gedruckt zů Mūnchen durch Andre Schobsser.) 4°. A-B⁴. [83

-- Persequutiones ecclesiae, quas, ... à Tirannis, Hæreticis & Schismaticis ... sustinuit, & de eorundē sectis, erroribus, fructibus & seditionibus, Collatio ... Vuolphangus Kryiander Otingen. ... conferebat. M. D. XXXXI. ... (Alexander Weissenhorn Ingolstadij Typis excudebat. ...) 4°. π⁴ A-M⁴ N². [84

-- -- *Another copy* (-N2). (Lea.) [85

HERMAS. Pastoris nuntii poenitentiae, Visiones quinq3, Mandata duodecim, Similitudines uero decem, in quibus apparuit & locutus est Hermae, discipulo Pauli apostoli. ... (Argentorati, apud Ioannem Schottum. M. D. XXII.) fol. a-d⁶ e⁸. (Lea.) [86

HERMES TRISMEGISTUS. Mercurii Trismegisti pymander, de potestate et sapientia Dei. Eiusdem Asclepius, de uoluntate dei. ... Iamblichus de mysterijs Aegyptiorum, Chaldæorum, & Assyriorū. Proclus in Platonicum Alcibiadem, de anima & dæmone. Idem de sacrificio & magia. ... Basileae, 1532. (... per Mich. Isingrinium, mense Augusto an. M. D. XXXII.) 8°. A-Ff⁸. pp. 4-480. (Smith.) [87

-- -- Le pimandre ... traduit de l'exemplaire Grec ... Par Francois Monsieur de Foix ... A Bourdeaux, Par S. Millanges ... 1579. ... fol. ã⁶ (-ã2) A⁸ B⁶ C-3A⁸ 3B⁶ 3C⁴ 3D⁶ 3E⁸. pp. 2-741. [88

HERMES TRISMEGISTUS

-- -- Il pimandro ... tradotto da Tommaso Benci in lingua Fiorentina. ... In Firenze [per Lorenzo Torrentino,] 1548. 8°. $*^8$ $**^4$ A-H^8 I^4 (-I4, *blank*). pp. 1-119. (Smith.) [89

HERMOGENES. Hermogemis [*sic*] rhetoris, ad artem oratoriam præexercitamēta, ductu & inuersione Prisciani ... Parisiis In officina Simonis Colinei 1535. 8°. a-b^8. ff. 2-15. [90

-- Ερμογενους περι ιδεων τομοι δυο. Hermogenis de formis orationum tomi duo. Parisiis Excudebat Christianus Wechelus ... 1531 4°. 3A-$3V^4$. [91

HERNANDEZ DE CORDOVA Y AGUILAR, GONZALO. Chronica. Del gran capitan Goncalo Hernandez de Cordoua y Aguilar. ... y los hechos Illustres de don Diego de Mendoça, don Hugo de Cardona, el Conde Pedro Nauarro, y otros ... Con la vida del ... Diego Garcia de Paredes. ... Impresso en Alcala de Henares, en case de Hernan Ramirez ... 1584. A costa del Impressor. (... 1586.), fol. π^2 A-V^8 X^{10} (-X10, *presumably blank*). ff. 1-165. [92

HERO OF ALEXANDRIA. Spiritali di Herone Alessandrino Ridotti in lingua Volgare da Alessandro Giorgi da Vrbino. In Vrbino Appresso Bartholomeo, e Simone Ragusij fratelli. ... 1592. 4°. a^4 A-V^4 X^2. ff. 1-82. (Smith.) [93

HERODIANUS. Ηροδιανου ιστοριων βιβλια. η. Herodiani historiarum lib. VIII. græce pariter, & latine. (Venetiis in aedibus Aldi, et Andreae Asulani soceri, mense Septembri. M.D.XXIIII.) 8°. π^4 A-Λ^8 M^4 1-11^8 12^{10}. ff. 1-92, 2-97. [94

-- -- ... Cum Angeli Politiani interpretatione, & huius partim supplemento, partim examine Henrici Stephani ... Historiarum Herodianicas subsequentium libri duo ... Excudebat Henricus Stephanus anno M. D. LXXXI. 4°. $¶^4$ a-z^4 A-K^4. pp. 1-182, 1-79. [95

-- -- Histoire d'Herodian ... traitant des faicts memorables des successeurs de Marc Aurele ...: Translatee du Grec en François par Iacques des Comtes de Vintemille Rhodien ... Plus, vn discours & aduertissement aux Censeurs de la langue Françoise ... A Paris, De l'Imprimerie de Federic Morel ... M. D. LXXX. ... 4°. a-c^4 d^2 A-Gg^4 Hh^2. pp. 1-225. [96

-- -- Der Fürtrefflich Griechisch geschicht schreiber Herodianus/ den ... Angelus Politianus inn das Latein/ vnd Hieronymus Boner in nachuolgend Teütsch pracht ... (Gedruckt in ... Augspurg/ durch Heynrichen Steyner. Vollendet am XIX. tag Augusti/ Im M.D.XXXI. Jar.) fol. π^4 a-l^6 (-l6) m^4. ff. I-LXX. [97

-- -- (Gedruckt in ... Augspurg/ durch Heynrichen Steyner. Vollendet am XIII. tag Iunij/ Im M.D.XXXII.) fol. π^4 a-l^6 m^4. ff. I-LXVII. [98

-- -- Historia d'Herodiano dello imperio dopo Marco tradotta in lingua toscana ... (Impresso in Fiorenza per gli heredi di philippo di Giunta. ... M.D.XXII. adi .x. Ottobre.) 8°. π^4 $+^8$ A-N^8. ff. 1-109. [99

-- -- Herodiano delle vite imperiali tradotte di Greco per M. Lelio Carani. ... In Vinegia appresso Gabriel Giolito de Ferrari e fratelli. M D LI. (*Colophon.*) 8°. A-Q^8 (-Q8, *blank*). ff. 2-123. [100

HERODOTUS. *Greek.* Ηροδοτου λογοι εννεα ... Herodoti libri nouem ... (Venetiis in domo Aldi mense Septembri. M.DII. ...) fol. AAAA-PPRR^8 ΣΣSS^4. [101

-- -- Ηροδοτου λογοι εννεα ... Herodoti libri nouem ... Georgii Gemisti ... de ijs quæ post pugnam ad Mantineam gesta sunt, Libri II. Vnà cum Ioachimi Camerarii Præfatione, Annotationibus, Herodoti uita ... Basileae, ex officina Heruagiana. (... per Ioannem Heruagium et Bernardum Brand, ... M.D.LVII. Mense Martio.) fol. α^6 β^4 a-z^6 Aa-Cc^6 (-Cc6). pp. 2-310. [102

-- -- Ηροδοτου του Αλικαρνασσέως ἱστορία ... Herodoti Halicarnassei historia ... [Genevae,] Anno M. D. LXX. Excudebat Henricus Stephanus. fol. α-γ^4 a-ff^6 gg^8 hh^6 ii^4. pp. 3-24, 1-362, 1-20. [103

-- -- *Greek & Latin.* Ηροδοτου Αλικαρνασσηος ἱστοριῶν λόγοι θ ... Herodoti Halicarnassei historiarum lib. IX ... Eiusdem Narratio de vita Homeri. Cum Vallæ interpret. Latina ..., ab Henr. Stephano recognita. Item cum iconibus ... Editio secunda. [Genevae,] Excudebat Henricus Stephanus anno M.D.XCII. fol. α-ξ^4 a-$3n^6$ 3o-$3t^4$. pp. 2-731. [104

-- -- *Latin.* Herodoti Halicarnassei ... libri nouem, ... interprete Laurentio Valla. ... Item De genere vitaque Homeri libellus, ... ab ... Heresbachio ... conuersus. Vtriusque translationem emendauit Sebastianus Castalio. Coloniæ, Apud Maternum Cholinum. Anno M. D. LXII. (... Excudebat Godefridus Ceruicornus ... impensis Materni Cholini ... mense August.) fol. Aa^6 A-Z^6 (-Z6, *presumably blank*). pp. 2-273. [105

-- -- ... Ex Ctesia excerptæ historiæ. Icones quarundã memorabiliũ structurarũ. Apologia Henr. Stephani pro Herodoto. ... [Genevae,] Anno M. D. LXVI Excudebat Henricus Stephanus ... fol. 3 *folded plates* **^{6} 3*^{4} 4*^{6} A-V^6 X-Y^4 Z-Bb^6. pp. 1-256, 1-12. [106

-- -- ... Accessit in hac editione Spicilegium Frid. Sylburgij ... Francofurti Apud hæredes Andreæ Wecheli. MDLXXXIIII. 8°. α-δ^8 ε^4 a-z^8 A-T^8 V^{4+1}. pp. 2-72, 1-592. [107

-- -- Francofurti Apud Andreæ Wecheli heredes, Claudium Marnium, & Ioan. Aubrium. M D XCV. 8°. α-δ^8 ε^4 a-z^8 A-O^8 .)(.-2.)(.^{8} 3.)(.^{4} P-T^8 V^4. pp. 3-27, 1-630. ¶*T.p. mounted.* [108

-- -- *French.* Les neuf liures des histoires de Herodote ... Plus vn recueil de George Gemiste dict Plethon, des choses auenues depuis la iournée de Mantinée. ... traduict de Grec en François par Pierre Saliat ... A Paris, Pour Estienne Groulleau ... 1556. fol. a^4 a-z^6 A-R^6 S^4. ff. II-CCXLIII. [109

-- -- *German.* Herodotus ... von dem Persier/ vnd vilen andern kriegen vnd geschichten/ ⁊c. Durch Hieronymum Boner ... inn das ... Teütsch gebracht. M.D.XXXV. (Gedruckt jnn ... Augspurg/ durch Hainrich Stainer vollendet am .xxiij. Iunij ...) fol. π^6 A-Z^6 (-D3-4) a^8. ff. I-CXLVI. [110

-- -- *Italian.* Herodoto Alicarnaseo historico delle guerre de Greci et de Persi, Tradotto di Greco in lingua Italiana oer il Conte Mattheo Maria Boiardo ... M D XXXIII ... (Stampato in Veneggia per Giouann' Antonio di Nicolini di Sabbio. A' instantia di M. Marchio sessa. ...) 8°. ✠^{8} a-z^8 A-R^8 S^4. ff. 1-324. [111

HEROLD, JOHANNES. Haereseologia, hoc est, opus veterum tam Græcorum quam Latinorum Theologorum, per quos omnes, quæ per Catholicam Christi Ecclesiam grassatæ sunt, hæreses confutantur ... Basileæ. (... per Henrichum Petri, mense Septembri anno M.D.LVI.) fol. π^2 *-**^{6} ***^{4} A-Z^6 Aa-Bb^6 AA-ZZ^6 3A-3T^6. pp. 1-798. ¶*Authors:* L. Cælius Lactantius Firmianus, Marius Victorinus, Proclus Episcop. Constantinopolitanus, Theophilus Alexandrinus, Cerealis Episcopus Aphricanus, Gelasius Episcopus Roman., Faustus Episcopus [Rheginus], Agnellus Episcopus, Vigilius, Beatus Fulgentius, Idacius Clarus, Timotheus Episcopus, Vincentius Lirinensis, Prosper Aquitanicus, Ioannes Epsicopus Rom., Antoninus Episcopus [Constantinensis], Rusticus Diaconus, Gẽnadius Scholarius Episc. Cõstantinop. (Lea.) [112

-- Orthodoxographa theologiae ... Doctores numero LXXVI ... Basileae. (... per Henrichum Petri, mense Martio, anno M. D. LV.) fol. a^6 b^8 c^6 A-Z^8 aa-zz^8 AA-ZZ^8 Aa^8 Bb-Cc^6 Dd-Zz^8 Aaa-Bbb^8 Ccc^6 Ddd^8. pp. 1-1522. (Lea.) [113

HERRERA, GABRIEL ALONSO DE. Agricoltura tratta da diuersi antichi et moderni scrittori dal Sig. Gabriello Alfonso d'Herrera, et tradotta di lingua Spagnuola in Italiana, da Mambrino Roseo da Fabriano. ... In Venetia, appresso Valerio Bonelli. M D LXXVII. 4°. a^8 A-Mm^8 Nn^4. ff. 1-284. [114

HERRERA, HERNANDO ALONSO DE. Expositio laurentij vallensis de elegantia lingue latine ... edita per ... Alfonsꝫ herrariẽsem. ... (Salmãticę excussum atqꝫ ... castigatũ: industria ... Laurẽtij ꝺ õdedeis) fol. B.L. a-b^8 c^4. [115

HERTEL, JAKOB. Τα εκ των παλαιων και παντων σοφῶν κωμικῶν ν', Γνωμικὰ ... Vetustissimorum et sapientiss. comicorum quinquaginta, quorum opera integra non extant, sententiae ... Græcè & Latinè collectæ ... Platonii fragmentum, de differentijs Comoediarum. ... Basileae. [c. 1560.] 8°. α-δ^8 a-z^8 A-Dd^8. pp. 1-769. [116

HERTZOG, BERNARD. Schiltwacht bin ich genannt/ Das ist Ein kurtzweilige Bůchlein/ mit vilen Historien vnd Dichtungen ... M.D.LXII. 8°. A-E^8. ff. j-[xxxvii]. ¶D8, E1-8 *defective.* [117

HERVET, GENTIAN. Gentiani Herueti Aurelianensis de residentia episcoporum epistolæ duæ Scripta in Concilio Tridentino, an. 1653 [*sic*]. ... [*post* 1584.] 4°. A-B^4. pp. 3-16. (Lea.) [118

HESHUSIUS, TILEMANNUS. Bekandtnuss vom heyligen Nachtmal des Herren ... Nuͤrnberg. M.D.LXII. (Gedruckt ... durch Iohann vom Berg/ vnd Vlrich Newber.) 8°. A-B^{8}. [119

HESIOD. *Works*. Ησιοδος ο Ασκραιος. (Florentie impressa in edibus Philippi iuntæ ... die .xx. ianuarii. M.D.XV. ...) 8°. a-k^{8} l^{4}. ¶*Includes:* Θεογνιδος ... γνωμαι ελεγιακαι, Γνωμαι διαφοροι, Στιχοι σιβυλλας της ερυθραιας, Χρυσα επη του Πυταγορου, Γριγορίου τοϋ θεολόγου γνῶμαι μονόστιχοι. [120

-- -- Hesiodi Ascraei ... opera, quæ quidem extant, omnia Græcè, cum interpretatione Latina è regione ... Adiectis ... Latino carmine ... uersis, & Genealogiæ deorum à Pylade Brixiano ... descriptæ, Libris V. ... Basileae [1542]. 8°. α^{4} a-z^{8} A-B^{8} C^{4} (-C4). pp. 1-373. [121

-- -- [1] Hesiodi Ascraei ... opera ... Basileae [per Hieronymum Frobenium & Nicolaum Episcopium? 1542?]. 8°. a^{4} a-z^{8} A^{4}. pp. 1-173. [2] ... Ioannis Grammatici Tzetzis expositio librorum Hesiodi ... Basileae. α-ρ^{8}. pp. 3-270. ¶*Lacks the index.* [122

-- -- ... Accessit ... Herculis Scutum, ... carmine à Ioanne Ramo conuersum. ... (Lipsiae Imprimebat Iohannes Steinman typis Voegelianis. Anno M. D. LXXII.) 8°. A-Z^{8} a-e^{8}. pp. 1-500. [123

-- *Works and days*. Hesiodi Poete Georgicoꝝ liber ꝑ Nicolaū de Valle conuersus e greco in latinū (Liptzk ꝑ Iacobū Tanner Herbipolenseꝫ impressus Anno 1504 tertio kalendas Augustas) 4°. B.L. A-B^{6} C^{4} D-E^{6}. [124

-- -- Ησιοδου του Ασκραιου εργα και ημεραι. Hesiodi opera et dies. Vna cum duabus praefationibus, ec ... Enarrationibus Phil. Melanchiam recens conscriptis. Hagenoæ ex Officina Seceriana. Anno M. D. XXXIIII. Mense Februario. (*Colophon.*) 8°. A-L^{8}. [125

-- -- Hesiodi Ascraei opuscula inscripta ερτα και ημεραι, sic recens nunc Latinè reddita. ... Vlpio Franekerensi Frisio autore. Addita est antiqua Nicolai Vallae translatio ... Item accessit Angeli Politiani Rusticus ... Basileæ, apud Mich. Ising. M. D. XXXIX. 8°. A-I^{8} K^{4} (-K4, *presumably blank*). pp. 3-149. [126

HESSE. Reformation gesetze vnd statuten/ vnser Philipsen ... Landtgrauen zu Hessen ... M. D. XXXV. (Gedruckt zu Erffurdt durch Melchior Sachssen ... Inn verlegung Colman Engel/ Buchfuͤrer zu Cassel.) fol. A-B^{6} C^{4} D^{6}. [127

-- Hessische halssgerichts Ordnung in peinlichen sachen ... [1535.] fol. C-G^{6} H^{4} (-H4, *possibly blank*). ff. II-XXXI. [128

-- Landgraff Philipsen zu Hessen etc. ... verantwortung/ an Roͤmische Kay. Maie. ... Auff Hertzog Heinrichs von Braunschweig ... Supplication schrifft ... Anno M. D. XLI. 4°. A-B^{4}. [129

-- Copey wie Landgraffe Wilhelm/ zu Hessen sich gegen der Keyserlichen Maiestat verwaret. Anno. 1552. 4°. A-B^{4}. [130

-- -- *Another copy*. [131

-- Vnser Ludwigs ... Landtgrauen zů Hessen ... Wollenkauffs Ordnung ... Getruckt zů Marpurgk durch Augustinum Colbium ... M. D. Lxxiij. fol. A-B^{4}. [132

-- Antwort der Predicāten in Hessen auff die schrifft des Bischoffs von Meintz/ oder Rabsackes brieff/ De abrogatione matrimonij der Prediger/ vnd von der Dispensation mit dem Bapst zu halten vom brauch des Sacraments sub utraqꝫ specie ... (Gedruckt zu Magdeburg bey Christian Roͤdinger. Anno M.D.XLIX.) 4°. A^{4}. (Lea.) [133

HESYCHIUS ALEXANDRINUS. Ησυχιου λεξικον. Hesychii dictionarium ... fol. a-z^{8} A-B^{6}. cols. 1-776. ¶*The collation is the same as that of the edition published at Haguenau by Thomas Anshelm December 1521.* [134

HEYWOOD, JOHN. The spider and the Flie. ... Imprinted at London ... by Tho. Povvell. anno. 1556. (*Colophon.*) 4°. B.L. A-C^{4} A-Z^{4} Aa^{4} (Aa3 +[ornament]Aaiiii^{4} Aav^{4} Aavi^{4}) Bb^{6} Cc^{4} (Cc1 +[ornament]Ccii^{2}; Cc2 +[ornament]Cciii^{2}) Dd^{4} (Dd1 + *[ornament]Ddii^{2}; Dd3 + ‡*‡Ddiiii^{4}) [ornament]^{2} Ee^{4} (Ee1 + Eeii.^{2}; Ee2 + ☾‡Eeiii^{2} ☾‡^{6}; Ee3 +[ornament]Eeiiii^{2}) Ff^{4} (Ff3 + ¶[ornament]Ffiiii^{4} ¶[ornament]^{4})[ornament]^{2} Gg^{4} (Gg1 + Ggii^{4}) Hh-Ss^{4}. *S.T.C.* 13308. [135

HIEREMIAS, JUDEX DE MONTAGNONE. Epytoma Sapientie. [(impressum Venetijs: impensa Petri Liechtensteyn Coloniensis. ... M.d.v. Tertio kal'. Maias.)] 4°. B.L. π^8 $*^4$ $*A-*H^8$ $*HH^6$ $*I-*R^8$ $*S^{10}$ (-*S10). ff. 1-146. [136

HIEREMIAS, PETRUS. Sermones De Penitentia per quadragesimam ... ([Brixiae] cura Iacobi Britãnici calcographati: ⁊ ... castigatione ... Hieronymi de Bergnano digesti die viij. Octobris. M.cccccij.) 4°. B.L. a-d^8 e^6 A-H^8 I^4 3A-$3H^8$ $3I^{10}$ aa-ee^8 ff^4 3a-$3g^8$ $3h^6$ AA-RR^8 SS^4. ff. ij-xxxvii, iii-lxviij, ii-l, ii-xviii, iii-xliiii, ii-lxii, ii-xl [= cxl]. (Lea.) [137

HIEROCLES. Hieroclis ... in aurea Pythagoræ carmina Commentarius. (Argentorat. In Aedibus Mathiæ Schurerij IX. Kal'. Martias. Anno M. D. XI.) 4°. A^4 B-E^8 F^4 G-H^8. ¶*Translator: Giovanni Aurispa.* [138

-- -- Ιεροκλεους ... υπομνημα εις τα των Πυθαγορειων ἔπη τὰ χρυσᾶ. Hieroclis ... commentarius in aurea Pythagoreorum carmina. Ioan. Curterio interprete. ... *Greek & Latin.* Parisiis, Apud Nicolaum Niuellium ... CIↃ IↃ LXXXIII. ... (Excudebat Steph. Preuosteau,) 12°. $\bar{a}^{12}$ A-O^{12} P^6. pp. III-XXIIII, 1-247. [139

HIERONYMUS DE VILLA VITIS. Panis quotidianus. ... quotidie per totum annum singularem orationem vel meditationem de sancto cuiuslibet dici continet. (... expẽsis ... Ioannis Ryman de Oringau/ ꝑ ... Henricũ gran in ... Hagenaw ciuem/ ... impressus: ... M.d.ix. ipso die sanctoꝶ Prothasij ⁊ Geruasij ...) 4°. $[a]^8$ aa-zz^8 AA-PP^8. [140

HILDEGARDE, S. De praesenti clericorum tribulatione, futurorũq; Temporũ euentu, Diuæ Hildegardis Prophetiarũ ... libellus ... (Haganoe in officina Guilhelmi Seltz ... 1529.) 8°. A-B^8 C^4. [141

HILDESHEIM. Christlike Kerckenordeninge der ... Stadt Hildenssem. Mit einer Voͤrrede Antonij Coruini. (Gedru͠ckt tho Hannouer dorch Henningk Rudem. M. D. XLIIII.) 8°. A-K^8. [142

HIPPOCRATES. Hippocratis Coi ... opera, quæ hactenus ad nos extant omnia. Per Ianum Cornarium ... Latina Lingua conscripta. ... Venetiis Apud Hieronymum Scotum. 1546 fol. $*^4$ A-$2H^6$ aa^4 bb^6 (-bb6, *presumably blank*). ff. 1-138, 1-48. (Furness.) [143

-- -- Του μεγαλου Ιπποκρατους ... τα ευρισκομενα Magni Hippocratis ... opera omnia quæ extant ... Latina interpretatione & Annotationibus illustrata, Anutio Foesio Mediomatrico Medico Authore. Adiecta sunt ... Palladij Scholia Græca ... Francofurti, Apud Andreæ Wecheli heredes, Claud. Marnium, & Ioan. Aubrium. M. D. XCV. fol. $\alpha^{4\pm1}$ A-B^6 C-D^4 AA-RR^6 SS^4 a-k^6 l^4 aa-kk^6 ll^2 3a-$4d^6$ aAa-sSs^6 tTt^4 uVu^6 3A-$4G^6$ $4H^4$ $4I^6$ aaaA-$bbbB^6$ cccC-$dddD^4$ $*^4$ eeeE-$fffF^6$ gggG-$hhhH^4$. pp. 1-30, cols. 31-49, pp. 3-27, cols. 28-41, pp. 42-231, 4-94, cols. 95-153, pp. 3-49, cols. 102-144, pp. 3-257, cols. 258-383, pp. 3-212, cols. 213-253, pp. 4-361, cols. 362-393, pp. 4-33, cols. 34-45. [144

-- Aphorismorum Hippocratis sectiones septem. Ex Franc. Rabelæsi recognitione. Quibus ex Ant. Musæ Commentariis adiecimus & Octauam ... Apud Seb. Gryphium Lugduni 1543. 16°. a-u^8 (-u8, *blank*). pp. 2-318. [145

-- Chirurgia è Græco in Latinum conuersa, Vido Vidio Florentino interprete, cum ... commentarijs. Excudebat Petrus Galterius Lucetiæ Parisiorum, pridie Calendas Maij. M. D. XLIIII. fol. aa^8 bb^{10} a-z^8 A-I^8 K-L^6. pp. 1-533. ¶*Authors: Hippocrates, Galen, Oribasius.* [146

-- Hippocratis magni Coacæ prænotiones. ... Interprete & enarratore Ludouico Dureto, Segusiano. ... Parisiis, Apud Iacobum Du-puys ... M. D. LXXXVIII. ... (... excudebat Dionysius Duvallius, mense Iulio ...) fol. $\bar{a}^6$ A-$3G^6$ (-3G6, *presumably blank*). pp. 1-578. [147

HIRSBECK, PAUL. Etlich predig ... Pauli Hirschpeck ... vom Sacrament ainerlay gestalt ... Item. Apologia ... Georgij Wicelij/ dariñ angezaigt wie er von der Lutherischen sect/ widerumb zu͠ dem alten Catholischen Christlichen glauben kommen sey ... M. D. LVI. 4°. A-X^4. [148

-- Drey predig von dem Hochwürdigen Sacrament des Altars. ... Durch Doctor Paulsen Hirspecken ... Anno. M. D. XLV. 4°. A-O^4. [149

HISTORIE. Eine Warhafftige History/ von einem vngerahtnen Son/ in ein Dialogum gestellet. ... Getruckt zů Strassburg bey Iacob Frölich [c. 1540]. 4°. A-B^{4}. [150

HISTORIEN. Drey schöner Hisstorij/ Von dreyen Heidenischen mörderischen Frawen. M.D.XXXX. (Gedruckt zu Nürnberg bey Hañs Wandereisen.) 4°. π^{4}. ¶*Clytemnestra, Tullia, Cleopatra. In verse.* [151

-- Kurtz viler Historien Handt Bůchlin. ... Zů Strasszburg bey Hans Schotten. M.D.xxxvj. 4°. a-c^{4} d^{2}. ¶*In verse.* [152

HOCKER, JODOCUS. Von Beiden Schlüsseln der Kirchen/ Das ist/ Der Excommunication vnd Absolution ... Mit einer schönen Vorrede M. Cyriaci Spangenbergij. (Gedruckt zu Vrsel/ durch Nicolaum Henricum. Anno 1568.) 8°. A-M^{8} N^{4}. ff. 1-84. [153

HOEST, STEPHAN. Modus Predicandi ... Oratio Pallantis Spangel ... ad Cæsarē Maximilianū ... Epitaphiū Ioannis Keiserspergij ... [per Ioannem Botzheim.] (Argentoraci ... Ex ædibus Ioannis Prūs iunioris. Anno .M.CCCCC.XIII.) 4°. A^{4} B^{6}. [154

HOFFMEISTER, JOHANN. Canones, siue claues aliquot, ad interpretandum sacras Bibliorum scripturas ... M. D. XLV. (Moguntiae ... excudebat Franciscus Behemus ...) 4°. A-G^{4}. pp. 1-51. [155

-- Verbum Dei carnem factum ... Assertio ... M.D.XLV. (Excusum Moguntiæ ... in officina typographica Francisci Behemi.) 4°. π^{4} A-Z^{4} a-e^{4}. pp. 2-320. [156

HOFMANN, MELCHIOR. Dialogus vñ gründtliche berichtung/ gehaltner disputation ... vom ... Sacrament/ oder Nachtmal des Herren. ... M. D. xxix. Getruckt zů Strassburg ... durch Balthassar Beck. 8°. A^{8} B^{4}. [157

HOLDER, WILHELM. Bericht/ Von dem vberkunstreichen Buch des wahnwitzigen Propsts zu Pellan ... D. Peter Muchitsch/ so von jhme/ Schulführung der Würtembergischen Theologen/ intituliert. ... Getruckt zu Tübingen/ bey Georgen Gruppenbach/ Anno 1589. 4°. A-L^{4}. pp. 1-86. [158

HOLINSHED, RAPHAEL. [1] 1577. The Firste volume of the Chronicles of England, Scotlande, and Irelande. Conteyning, The description and Chronicles of England, from the first inhabiting vnto the conquest. The description and Chronicles of Scotland, ... till the yeare ... 1571. The description and Chronicles of Yrelande, ... vntill the yeare. 1547. Faithfully gathered and set forth, by Raphaell Holinshed. At London Imprinted for George Bishop. fol. B.L. ¶^{6} (¶6 *bound in after* *2) *^{2} A-P^{8} Q^{6} r^{1} (Faultes escaped) a-s^{8} t^{1}. ff. 1-124, 1-289. [2] The Historie of Scotlande ... by R. H. *Same imprint.* A^{2} (*b*)^{2} *a*-*b*^{6} A-Ii^{8} Kk^{4} Ll-Mm^{6}. pp. 1-22, 1-518. [3] The Historie of Irelande ... vnto the yeare 1509. Collected by Raphaell Holinshed, and continued till the yeare 1547. by Richarde Stanyhurst. *Same imprint.* ✠^{2} A-C^{8} D^{4} A-D^{8} E^{5} F-G^{8} H^{6} I^{2} ()^{4} (*-()4, presumably blank*). ff. 1-28, pp. 2-115. [4] 1577. The Laste volume of the Chronicles of England, Scotlande, and Irelande, with their descriptions. Conteyning, The Chronicles of Englande from William Conquerour vntill this present tyme. ... At London, Imprinted for Lucas Harrison. ¶^{2} t2-t8 v-z^{8} A-4Y^{8} (+ Eeee.v. *inserted between* 4E4 *and* 4E5 *and folding plate between* 4Y6 *and* 4Y7) 4Z^{2} A-M^{4} N^{2}. pp. 291-1876. *S.T.C.* 13568^{a}. ¶*The Lucas Harrison imprint is not recorded in the* S.T.C. (Furness.) [159

-- -- *Another copy of* [1], [2], [3]. ¶*Lacks* ¶^{6}, ^{3}C6-8, *and all after* ^{3}D1. *A number of leaves defective. Imprint on* ^{2}A1^{r} and ✠1^{r}: Imprinted for Iohn Harrison (*S.T.C.* 13568). (Lea.) [160

-- -- [1] The First and second volumes of Chronicles ... First collected and published by Raphaell Holinshed, William Harrison, and others: Now newlie augmented and continued ... by Iohn Hooker aliàs Vowell Gent. and others. ... (Finished in Ianuarie 1587 ... at the expenses of Iohn Harison, George Bishop, Rafe Newberie, Henrie Denham, and Thomas Woodcocke. At London, Printed in Aldersgate street at the signe of the Starre. ...) fol. B.L. A-Y^{6} A-R^{6} (*-R6, presumably blank*). pp. 1-250, 1-202. ¶*Additional t.p.* (Y5^{r}): The Historie of England ... [2] The Second volume of Chronicles ... 1586 A-E^{6} A-Q^{6} R^{2}. pp. 9-61, 1-183. [3] [The description of Scotland] A-V^{6} (-A1) Aa-Nn^{6} Oo^{4} Pp^{6} Qq-Rr^{5} Ss^{4} Tt^{6} A^{6} B^{8} *^{8} ¶^{8} (*-¶8, presumably blank*). pp. 3-464. ¶*Additional t.p.* (^{5}C1^{r}): The Historie of

Scotland (*bound in* ⁵A1 *position*). ¶Qq3, Rr3, Ss2, Ss3 *are cancels*. [4] [The Third volume of Chronicles ...] (*Colophon.*) A-V^6 (-A1-4) Aa-Vv^6 3A-3V^6 4A-4V^6 5A-5V^6 6A-6T^6 6V^1 A,B,C,D,E^1 F,G,H,I^1 χ^1 7K^6 7L^2 7M^1 7N^6 7O^3 C-G^6 (-G6, *presumably blank*). pp. 1-1592. ¶*For the missing t.p.* (A1) *an 18th-century reprint has been substituted. Lacks cancellandum* 6V-7I^6, *for which the cancels* 6V1, A,B,C,D,E, F,G,H,I, *and an unsigned leaf are substituted, but an 18th-century reprint of* 6V-7G, 7H1 *is inserted before the cancel* 6V1. [161

HOLLANDUS, JOANNES ISAACUS. Magistri Ioannis Isaaci Hollandi ... Opera Mineralia, siue de Lapide Philosophico ... in Latinum sermonem translata, à P. M. G. Middleburgi, Excudebat Richardus Schilders ... 1600. 8°. A-Ee^8. pp. 2-432. (Smith.) [162

HOLOGNE, GRÉGOIRE DE. Gregorii Holonii Leodiensis Lambertias. Tragoedia ... Antuerpiæ Apud Ioannem Bellerum, 1556. (Typ. Diesthemii. XI. Kal. Iun. ...) 8°. A-E^8. [163

HOLTHEUSER, JOHANN. Tabula oeconomica, versibus ... comprehensis ... Anno 1556. (Impressum Erphurdiae [per Georgium Baumann] iuxta fanum S. Pauli.) 8°. A-B^8. [164

HOLTORP, BERNARD. Cantica sacra ... Francoforti Ad Viadrum, ex officina Ioan. Eichorn, Anno 1557. Mense Aprili. 8°. A-D^8. [165

HOLTZWART, MATTHIAS. Emblematum Tyrocinia: Sive picta poesis Latinogermanica. ... Zu Strassburg bei Bernhard Iobin. M.D.LXXXI. ... 8°. a^8 b^4 B-M^8 N^4. [166

HOLY ROMAN EMPIRE. *Laws &c.* Das buch des heiligen römischen reichs vnnderhalltung (Gedruckt jn der ... statt münchen von hannsen schobsser. Anno dñi tausent fünff hundert vnnd eyn jar am tag Blasij ꝛc) fol. A^8 A^6 B^4 a-b^8 c^6 d^8 e-k^6 l-m^8. ff. [i]-lxxxj. [167

-- Extract Auss allen Reichs- vnnd Deputations Abschieden/ vom Jahr 1356. ... was wegen gemeines Müntzwesens ... verordnet worden ... Getruckt in ... Meyntz/ durch Henrich Breem ... M.D.XCVII. (*Colophon.*) fol.)(-2)(^{4} A-O^4 P^6. ff. 1-60. [168

-- *Charles IV, emperor.* Aurea bulla Caroli quarti Romanorum imperatoris ... Moguntiae excudebat Iuo Schoeffer ... M. D. XLIX. fol. A-G^4. ff. 1-25. [169

-- *Maximilian I, emperor.* [Form levying assessments for the imperial court of justice.] Geben zů Worms am [*space*] ... Funffzehenhundert vnd im Newndteñ ... s.sh. 27 × 38 cm. [170

-- Romischer Keyserlicher Maiestat vñ gemeiner Stende des Reichs vff satzung vnd ordnung vff dem Reichstag zu Collen. Anno .XV^c. vnd .XII. vffgericht fol. A^6 B^4. ¶*Dated 26 August 1512.* [171

-- *Charles V, emperor.* Declaratio Caroli imp. et Hispaniarum regis et c. contra Martinum Lutherum ... 4°. π^2. ¶*Dated 19 April 1521.* [172

-- Der Römischen Kaiserlichen Maiestat Edict/ wider Martin Luther Bůcher vñ Lere ... Auch gesetz der Truckerey. 4°. A-C^4. ¶*Dated 8 May 1521.* [173

-- Romischer Kayserlicher Maiestat ordnungen ... wie allenthalben im hailigen Reich ... wider die manigfeltigen vergweltiger/ beschediger/ vnd des ... landtfridens verprecher/ darzu desselben declarirt Echter. ... fol. A-B^8 (-B8, *presumably blank*). ¶*Dated 10, 17 February 1522.* [174

-- [Proclamation on the Turkish menace, with countersignature.] Geben in ... Nůrmberg/ am funfften tag des Monats Septembris ... funffzehundert vnd im drey vnd zwentzigisten ... s.sh. 36 × 49 cm. [175

-- [Form of assessment in support of resistance to the Turks (with the name of Friedrich abbot of S. Egidien in Nůrnberg filled in), with countersignatures.] Geben in ... Nůrmberg/ am Achzehenden tag des Monats Apprilis ... Fünffzehenhundert/ vnnd im Vierundzwaintzigisten ... s.sh. 36 × 49.5 cm. [176

-- Wider die disputatz von Bern. Rö. Kay. M. Mandat wider die ketzerische disputatz zů Bern. Der acht Christenlichen ort in Eydtgnossen Sandtbrieff an die von Bern. 4°. π^6. ¶*Dated 28 December 1528.* [177

-- Ain ernstliche red Kayserlicher Maiestat/ Caroli des fünfften/ die er zů den Hispaniern gethon hat/ von seinem Abschid auss Hispania ... [1529.] 4°. A^4. [178

-- Römischer Kayserlicher Maiestat ausschreyben an die Fürsten/ auff den ytzigẽ angesetzten Reichsstag zu Augspurg. ym 1530. Jar. 4°. A^4. [179

-- [Form letter (with the name of Friderichen Bischouen zuo Munster filled in) announcing the election of his brother Ferdinand as king of the Romans, with countersignature.] Geben in ... Aach ... am zwelftẽ tag des monets Ianuarii Anno &c. im XXXI. ... s.sh. 56 × 36 cm. [180

-- Innhalt dieses Buchleins. 1 Ein Auszug des Kaiserlichen Abschieds im nechsten Reichstags zu Augspurg/ vonn sachen des glaubens. 2 Rathschlag Martin Luthers an den Churfuͤrsten von Sachssen. 3 Erklerung desselbigen Rathschlags/ durch Hern Paulum Abbt der alten Czell. 4 Vormanung zu Frid vnd Eynikeit durch D. Iohan Cocleum ... 5 Ein Epistel M. Phillips Melanchthon/ võ Sitten vnd Tuͤgenden des Kaisers. 6 Summariũ Kaiserlicher Antwort auff der Lutherischen bekentnuͤs zu Augspurg. M. D. xxxi. (Gedrugkt zu Dressden dur[c]h Wolffgang Stoͤckel ...) 4°. $A\text{-}H^4$ I^2 $K\text{-}L^4$. [181

-- Roͤmischer Kaiserlichen Maiestat mandat/ den Fridlichen anstand des Glaubens vnd Religion halben ... Aussgangen im Iar M.D.XXXII. 4°. A^4. [182

-- Roͤmischer Kayserlicher Maiestat ... vnd des Bapsts geschickten werbung/ an Hertzog Iohans Fridrichen zu Sachssen ... Von wegen des kunfftigen Concilij. ... 1533. (Gedruckt zu Wittemberg durch Georgen Rhaw.) 4°. $A\text{-}F^4$. [183

-- [Proclamation concerning the relations of the empire and the papacy, with countersignature and seal.] Geben in ... Neapolis am XXViii. tag des monats Ianuarii. ... Funfzehenhũdert vnd im Sechsunddreissigisten ... s.sh. 31.5 × 43 cm. [184

-- Vnsers herren Kaysers Protestation vnd abschyd von Baͤpstlicher H. vnd dem Consistorio der Cardinaͤl zuͦ Rhom/ den xviij. Aprilis: M.D.XXXVI. ... (Interprete Doct. Cristoph. Scheurl.) 4°. A^4. [185

-- Keyser Carln red/ fridbieten/ vnd handlung mit Bapst Paulus vnd den Cardineln/ zu Rom am andern Ostertag. M. D. xxxvj. Nach lenges in Italianischer zungen beschrieben vnd verdolmetscht. Item ein gesprech Pasquilli vnd der Cardinel ... (Interprete Dost. Christ. Scheurl. 10. Maii. 1536.) [Nuremberg, Johann Petreius, 1536.] 4°. A^4 B^2. [186

-- Eyn Veldtgeschrey des ... Keysers der da ist/ on allen anfang vnd endt/ seinem Kriegssuolck kund gethan/ in diser kriegischen Welt/ damit sie bestendig bey jm bleyben. ... 1536. (Gedrückt zuͦ Nuͤrnberg durch Hans Guldenmunde.) 4°. $A\text{-}B^4$. [187

-- [Proclamation commanding obedience to his brother Ferdinand as king of the Romans, with countersignature and seal.] Geben in ... Barcelona den ersten tag des Monats Februarij. Anno. &c. im Achtunddreissigsten ... s.sh. 37 × 51.5 cm. [188

-- Ordnung/ Statuten vnd Edict/ Keiser Carols des fuͤnfften/ publicirt in ... Bruͤssel ... den 4. Octobris ... 1540. In Brabandischer sprach erstlich aussgangen. 4°. $a\text{-}c^4$. [189

-- Assertio iuris imperatoris Caroli ... quinti, in Geldriæ Ducatu, & Zutphaniæ Comitatu, ædita in Comitijs Ratisbonensibus, anno M.D.XLI. & Confutatio oppugnationum Guilielmi Cliuiæ Ducis, Franckfordiæ exhibitarum, Anno M. D. XXXIX. (Nurenbergæ apud Ioh. Petreium impressum.) fol. $a\text{-}k^4$ l^6. (Biddle.) [190

-- Roͤmisch Kaiserlicher Maiestat Caroli des V. Antwort/ auff Bapst Pauli des III. juͤngstes ausschreiben/ ein Gemain Conciliũ/ so zu Trient solt gehalten werden/ belangend. Aus dem Latin verteuͤtscht/ Anno 1543. 4°. $a\text{-}c^4$ d^2. [191

-- Copey der verschreibung so Karolus der Koͤnig zuͦ Hispanien/ gegen den Chur Fürsten vnd anderen Stenden des H. Roͤmischen Reichs sich verschriben ... M. D. xix. Anno M. D. XLVI. 4°. $A\text{-}B^4$ (-B4, *presumably blank*). [192

-- Der Roͤmischer Kaiserlichen Maiestat erclaͤrung/ wie es der Religion halben im hailigen Reich/ biss zuͦ ausstrag des gemainen Concili gehalten worden soll/ auff dem Reichstag zuͦ Augspurg/ den XV. May/ im M.D.XLVIII. Jar publiciert ... Getruckt zuͦ Augspurg/ durch Philipp Vlhart. 4°. $A\text{-}H^4$ I^2. (Lea.) [193

-- -- Gedruckt zu Franckfort an der Oder/ Durch Nicolaum Wolrab. 4°. $A\text{-}K^4$. [194

-- -- Gedruckt inn ... Meyntz/ durch Iuonem Schoͤffer ... M. D. XLVIII. fol. $A\text{-}I^4$. ff. 2-36. [195

-- Formula reformationis per Caesaream maiestatem statibus ecclesiasticis in Comitijs Augustanis ad deliberandum proposita ... Augustæ Vindelicorum Philippus Vlhardus excudebat. 4°. A-G^4 H^2. ¶*Dated 9 July 1548.* (Lea.) [196

-- [1] Abschied Der Röm. Keys. Maiest. vnd gemeyner Stend/ vff dem Reichsstag zů Augspurg vffgericht ... M. D. XLVIII. ... (Gedruckt inn ... Meyntz/ durch Iuonem Schöffer/ ... M. D. XLVIII.) fol. A-L^4. [2] Der Römischen Keyserlichen Maiestat Erklärung/ wie es der Religion halben/ imm heyligen Reich/ biss zů Ausstrag dess gemeinen Concilij gehalten werden soll ... *Same colophon.* A-I^4. ff. 2-36. [3] Formula reformationis per Caesaream maiestatem Statibus Ecclesiasticis in Comitijs Augustanis ad deliberandum proposita ... Moguntiae, Excudebat Iuo Schoeffer. A-F^4. ff. 2-21. [4] Römischer Keyserlicher Maiestat/ vnd dess heyligen Reichs Landtfriden ... Gedruckt inn ... Meyntz/ durch Iuonem Schöffer/ Anno M.D.XLVIII. (*Colophon.*) A-F^4. ff. 1-23. [5] Der Römischen Kay. Mai. vnd gemeyner Stend ... Cammergerichts Ordnung ... *Same imprint.* A-Z^4 a-z^4 aa^6. ff. 1-180. [6] Der Römischen Keyserlichen Maiestat Ordnung und Reformation/ gůter Pollicey ... *Same imprint.* (*Colophon.*) A-I^4 (-I4, *presumably blank*). ff. 1-34. [197

-- Der Römischen Kay. Mai. vnd gemeyner Stend dess heyligen Reichs angenommene vnd bewilligte Cammergerichts Ordnung ... Gedruckt inn ... Meyntz/ durch Iuonem Schöffer. Anno M. D. XLIX. fol. A-Z^4 a-z^4 aa^6. ff. 1-178. [198

-- Ordonnantie ende Edict des Keysers Kaerle die V. vernieuwt inde Keyserlijcke Radt van Augspurgh/ Inde maent vā September/ des Jaers M.CCCCC.L. Om textirperen die secten ... Geprint te Loeuen/ bij Seruaes Sassenus ... 4°. a-c^4. [199

-- Ordenung vnd Mandat Keiser Caroli V. vernewert im April Anno 1550. Zu aussrotten vnd zu vertilgen/ die Secten vnd spaltung/ Welche entstanden sind/ widder vnsern heiligen Christlichen glauben ... Item ein Register der verworffenen vnd verbottenen Büchern/ Auch von guten Büchern/ welche man inn der Schulen lesen mag. Item eine vermanung des Rectors der Vniuersitet zu Löuen. Item ein ander Keisers Mandat/ von dem selbigen handel im 40. jar ausgangen. ... 4°. A-H^4 I^2. ¶A1^v: Vorrede Matthiae Flacij Illyrici. (Lea.) [200

-- -- Transferit aus einem gedruckten Brabendischen Exemplar. 4°. A-G^4 H^2. (Lea.) [201

-- [Proclamation against plunderers of German towns, with countersignatures and seal.] Geben in ... Augspurg/ am viertzehenden tag des Monats Februarij ... Fünffzehenhundert/ vnd im Ainvndfünfftzigsten ... s.sh. 32 × 44.5 cm. [202

-- [Proclamation forbidding enlistment in foreign armies, with countersignatures and seal.] Geben in ... Augspurg/ am zwelfften tag des Monats Septembris/ ... Fünfftzehenhundert/ vnd im Ainvndfünfftzigisten ... s.sh. 32.5 × 45.5 cm. [203

-- [Proclamation against the rebels Rheingraf Philipp Johann, Sebastian Schertlin, Georg von Reckenrode, and Friederich von Reiffenberg, with countersignature and seal.] Geben ... zů Ynsprugk/ am Neünzehenden tag des Monats Decembris ... Fünffzehenhundert vnd im Ainvndfünfftzigisten ... s.sh. 34 × 48 cm. [204

-- Keyser Karl des fünfften Newe Müntzordnung ... M.D.LI. auffgericht ... Getruckt zů Meyntz/ durch Iuonem Schöffer. fol. A-F^4 G^6. ff. 1-31. [205

-- [Proclamation condemning Albrecht Alcibiades, margrave of Brandenburg, with countersignatures and seal.] Geben in ... Brussel ... am Achzehenden tag des Monats May/ ... Funffzehen hundert/ vnd im vierundfunfftzigisten ... s.sh. 65 × 42.5 cm. [206

-- -- *Another copy* (65 × 48 cm., *defective and lacking the seal*). [207

-- [Proclamation against Albrecht Alcibiades, margrave of Brandenburg, with countersignatures and seal.] Geben ... In ... Brussel ... am Achtzehenden tag des monats Decembris. ... ffunffzehenhundert vnd im viervndfunfftzigisten ... s.sh. 32.5 × 42.5 cm. [208

-- *Ferdinand, king of Hungary and Bohemia.* [Disclaimer of alliance addressed to Johann, elector of Saxony, and Philip, landgrave of Hesse, involving inter alia Ulrich, deposed duke of Württemberg, with countersignatures and seal.] Geben ... in ... Prag den Ersten tag des monats Iuny ... Funffzehenhundert vnd im Achtundzweinczigisten ... s.sh. 42 × 59.5 cm. [209

-- -- Entschuldigūg des ... Herrn Ferdinand ... tzu Vngern/ Behem etc. Künigk ... Vff die vormeinten vñ erdicten verbünthnüs/ welcher Copey yn kurtzen tagen aussgangen ist. 4°. A^4. ¶*Dated 1 June 1528.* [210

-- Zůuermercken die Aussschreyben/ ainer angemassten verpündtnus halben/ vnnd wie darauff/ durch Künigliche Maiestat zů Vngern vnd Boͦhem ... der Kayserlichen Maiestat ... auch ander Churfürsten vnd Fürsten ... verantwortung vnnd enntschuldigung/ dargethon vnd beschehen ... Anno M. D. XXVIII. 4°. A-H^4. [211

-- *Ferdinand, king of the Romans*. [Blank form requiring assistance against the Turks.] Geben in ... Wienn den Dreiundzwaintzigisten tag des Monat Decembris Anno ꝛc. Im Sechssunddreissigisten ... s.sh. 37 × 52 cm. [212

-- Acta aller handlungen/ so sich zwischen ... Ferdinanden/ Roͦmischen/ Hungerischen/ vnd Bohamischen ꝛc Kuͤnig ꝛc. vnnd etlichen personen aus dem Herrn/ Ritter/ vnnd Burger Standt/ der Cron Behaim ... Auss Behemischer in Deutsche sprach Transfferiert ... 1548. (Gedruckt ... in ... Prag ... den vierten des Monats Maij ... Durch Bartholomeum Netholitzky ...) 4°. [A]^2 B-4H^4 4I^{12}. [213

-- [Proclamation encouraging sermons, weekly processions on Friday, &c. as a return to a pure Christian life in the face of the Interim of Augsburg and the danger from the Turks, with stamped signature, countersignatures, and seal.] Geben in ... Wienn/ den zwelfften tag des Monats Septembris/ Anno ꝛc. im Ainvndfuͤnfftzigisten ... s.sh. 34 × 48 cm. [214

-- [Proclamation prohibiting unlawful assembly, agitation, revolt, and the provision of sustenance to wandering armed bands, with countersignature and seal.] Geben in ... Augspurg den Fünffvndzwaintzigisten tag Septembris Anno ꝛc. im Fünffvndfünfftzigisten ... s.sh. 64 × 50 cm. [215

-- Abschiedt Der Roͤmischen Koͤniglichen Maiestat/ vnd gemeiner Stendt/ auff dem Reichsstag zu Augspurg ... M. D. LV. auffgericht. Sampt/ Der Keyserlichen Maiestat Cam̄ergerichts Ordnung ... ernewert/ vnd ... geendert. ... Getruckt inn ... Meyntz/ durch Franciscum Behem ... M. D. LV. fol. A-O^4 a^4 b^6 A-Z^4 a-s^4. ff. 1-51, 1-163. ¶*Additional t.p.* (O2^r): ... Cammergerichts Ordnung ... *Same imprint.* [216

-- [Reaffirmation of the rights and privileges bestowed upon Georg von Hohenheim, named Bombast, and his descendants, by virtue of being master of the Order of St. John in Germany. Mentions his deeds against the Turks and other infidels.] ... geben ist in ... Regenspurg den achten tag des Monats Februarij ... im funfftzehenhundert vnd Siben vnd funfftzigisten ... s.sh. 31 × 41 cm. [217

-- *Ferdinand, emperor*. [Renewal of the mandate for public peace issued earlier at the diet of Augsburg in 1555 and Regensburg in 1557, with countersignature and seal.] Geben inn ... Franckfort am Main/ den Neunzehenden Tag des Monats Martij Anno ꝛc. jm Achtvndfünfftzigisten ... s.sh. 61 × 37 cm. ¶*Slightly defective.* [218

-- Proposition der Roͤmischen Koͤnig. Maie. den Churf. des Reichs ... sampt der instruction des Printzen von Vranien ... 1558. 4°. A^4 B^2. [219

-- [Annulment of the prohibition of the importation or transit of pewter and imposition of duty and taxes instead, with countersignatures.] Geben in ... Wienn den Achtundzwaintzigisten tag Augusti. Anno ꝛc. im Neunundfuͤnfftzigisten ... s.sh. 32 × 45 cm. [220

-- Abschiedt Der Roͦmischen Keyserlichen Maiestat/ vnd gemeyner Stende/ Auff dem Reichsstag zu Augspurg ... M. D. LIX. auffgericht. ... Gedruckt in ... Meyntz/ Durch Franciscum Behem ... M.D.LIX. fol. A-K^4. ff. 1-37. [221

-- Keyser Ferdinandi Newe Müntzordnung ... Gedruckt inn ... Meyntz/ durch Franciscum Behem ... M. D. LIX. fol. A-H^4 I^2. ff. 1-32. [222

-- [Proclamation forbidding the use of grain for the brewing of beer, with countersignature.] Geben in ... Wienn/ am Aindlifften tag Augusti/ Anno ꝛc. im ainvndsechtzigisten ... s.sh. 38.5 × 54.5 cm. [223

-- [Restatement of the promulgation of public peace, with special reference to present abuses.] Geben in ... Wien den Achtundzwaintzigisten tag des Monats Martij ... Tausent Fuͦnfhundert vn̄ im Vierundsechtzigisten ... s.sh. 32.5 × 43.5 cm. [224

-- Abschiedt Der Roͦmischen Keyserlichen Maiestat/ vnd der verordneten ... Stende ... zu Wormbs Anno M.D.LXIIII. Auffgericht. ... Getruckt in ... Meintz/ durch Franciscum Behem/ ... M.D.LXIIII. fol. A-F^4. ff. 1-21. (Biddle.) [225

-- Abdruck Der Roͤm. Keyserlichen May. etc. Mandat vnd befehls/ an den Churfuͦrsten zu Sachssen/ etc. der Achts Execution halben wieder die Echtere/ vnd ... Hertzog Iohan Friderichen von Sachssen etc. ... Anno 1566. ... 4°. A-G^4 (-G4, *presumably blank*). [226

-- *Maximilian II, emperor.* Abdruck der Römischen Key. Maye. ... Ankündigunge der Achts Execution/ gegen Hertzog Iohans Friederichen von Sachssen ... 4°. A^4. ¶*Dated 12 December 1566.* [227

-- Auff vnd abforderunge des Schlosses Grimmenstein vnnd Stadt Gotha ... Von wegen der Römischen Kay. May. Vnd des Churfürsten Hertzogen Augusten zu Sachssen. Geschehen den 25. Ianuarij. Sampt Hertzog Hans Wilhelmen zu Sachssen/ etc. Abforderung obbemeltes Schlos vnd stadt. Anno 1567. 4°. A^4 B^2. [228

-- Abschiedt der Römischen Kayserlichen Maiestat/ vnd gemeiner Stände auff dem Reichstag zu Speyr ... M.D.LXX. auffgericht. ... Gedruckt in ... Meintz durch Franciscum Behem ... M. D. LXXI. (*Colophon.*) fol. π^2 A-O^4 P^6 Q-Aa^4 Bb^6 (-Bb6, *presumably blank*). ff. 1-103, ¶*Additional t.p.* ($P4^r$): Der Römischen Keyserlichen Maiestat/ vnnd dess heyligen Reichs reutter bestallung ... M. D. LXXI. [229

-- *Rudolf II, emperor.* [Proclamation on the preservation of forests, limiting the number of ovens, with countersignatures.] Geben in ... Wienn/ den Achten tag Martij/ im AinvndAchtzigisten ... Jarn. s.sh. 33 × 44 cm. [230

-- -- *Another copy.* [231

-- [Regulations, especially those concerning sanitation, to combat the spread of the plague, with countersignatures.] Geben in ... Wienn den Zwaintzigisten tag Decembris, Anno ꝛc. Im ZwayvndAchtzigisten ... s.sh. 44.5 × 56 cm. [232

-- Publication der Röm: Kay: Mayestat ... an ein E: Raht der Statt Augspurg aussgangen schreibens/ anlangend den Neüwen Calender. 1583. 4°. A-B^4. [233

-- Publication. Der Röm: Kay: May: zwischen der Oberkeit vnnd den Kirchendienern Augspurgischer Confession/ in der Statt Augspurg ... M.D.LXXXVI. 4°. A-D^4 (-D4, *presumably blank*). [234

-- [Reprinting of the privilege granted to Philipp Flach von Schwartzenberg, master of the Order of St. John in Germany.] Geben in ... Speyer am Sibenzehenden Tag Monats Augusti ... Funfftzehenhundert und im neuntzigsten ... Jahren. s.sh. 43.5 × 58.5 cm. [235

-- [Proclamation commanding local officials to supply provisions to the troops fighting the Turks.] Geben in ... Wienn den Sechsten tag Maij/ Anno/ ꝛc. im Viervndneüntzigisten ... s.sh. 33 × 42.5 cm. [236

-- [Mandate ordering the storing of food and munitions in the face of possible attacks by the Turks, signed on the verso.] Geben in ... Wienn den Achtvndzwainzigisten tag Iulij/ Anno/ ꝛc. im Vier vnd Neüntzigisten ... s.sh. 32 × 41.5 cm. [237

-- -- *Another copy, with countersignatures.* [238

-- [Proclamation on the danger from the Turks.] Geben in ... Wienn den Ersten tag Septembris/ Anno/ ꝛc. im ViervndNeüntzigisten ... s.sh. 32 × 43 cm. ¶*Proof sheet with corrections.* [239

-- [Renewed mandate requiring provision for the war against the Turks, with countersignatures.] Geben in ... Wienn/ den Neündten tag Iunij/ Anno/ ꝛc. im SibenvndNeüntzigisten ... s.sh. 32 × 42 cm. [240

-- -- *Another copy.* [241

-- *Hofgericht.* Des Heiligen Römischen Reichs Hoffgerichts zu Rotweil/ Ordnung/ Process/ vnd besondere Gesatz ... Zu Franckfurt Bei Christian Engenolffs Erben. Anno M. D. LXIIII. (*Colophon.*) fol. A-$D^{6.4}$ E^6. ff. I-XVIII. [242

-- *Reichstag.* Was auff dē Reichsstag zu Nüremberg/ von wegen Bebstlicher heiligkeit/ an Keyserlicher Maiestat Stathalter vnd Stende/ Lütherischer sachen halben gelangt/ vñ darauff geantwort wordē ist ... (Gedrückt zu Nüremberg/ durch Friderichen Peypus. M.D.xxiij.) 4°. A-K^4. [243

-- In hoc libello pontificii oratoris continentur legatio, in conuentu Norembergensi, Anno .M.D.xxij. inchoato ... exposita ...: nec non responsione Cęsareæ Maiestatis, ac reliquorum Principum & Procerum nomine reddita. ... (Norembergę, apud Friderichū Peypus. Anno M.D.xxiij.) 4°. a-d^4 A-M^4. [244

-- Abschidt des Reichstags zu Speyer Anno M.D.xxix. ... (Getruckt zů Mentz [durch Johann

Schoeffer für Mathys Auerbach]) fol. A-E^4. [245

-- Pro religione Christiana res gestæ in Comitijs Augustæ Vindelicorū habitis. Anno Dñi M. D. XXX. ... 4°. A-C^4 (-C4, *presumably blank*). [246

-- Supplication: an Kaiserliche Maiestat/ Der Mortbrenner halben/ Auff dem Reichstag/ zu Regenspurg/ Kaiserlicher Maiestat vberantwort ꝛc. Wittemberg. Anno. M. D. XLI. (Gedruckt ... durch Veit Creutzer. ...) 4°. A-M^4 N^6. [247

-- -- Wittemberg Anno. M. D. XLI. 4°. A-H^4. [248

-- Prorogation vnnd Erstreckunge dess Reichsstags im̄ Jar M. D. XLV. in̄ Wormbs gehalten ... [Mainz, Ivo Schoeffer, 1546.] fol. A-B^4. [249

-- *Schmalkaldic League.* Warhafftiger Vnterricht etzlicher Handlungen/ die sich Bapst Pauli/ ... des dritten/ Concilij halben/ das er ... gegen Mantua bestimpt hat/ zwischen Römischer Keiserlicher Maiestet Oratorn ... Doctor Mathiasen Held/ vnd den Churfürst/ Fürsten .../ Auch den Stedten/ so der warhafftigen Euangelischen Bekentnus vnd Confession/ vorwandt sein/ ... zu Smalkalden gehaltenem tage/ zugetragen haben. ... Wittemberg/ Anno M.D.XXXVII. (Gedruckt ... durch Georgen Rhaw.) 4°. A-O^4. [250

-- Vrsachen so die Chůr vnd Fursten: ... durch jr schreiben/ zu erkennen gegeben/ Darümb sie Bapst Pauli/ des namens des dritten/ ausgeschrieben Concilium/ Das er ... gegen Mantua angesatzt/ billich vordechtig/ auch zu gemeiner Christlichen einigkeit/ nicht dienstlich achten vnd halten. Wittemberg/ Anno M.D.XXXVII. (Gedruckt ... durch Georgen Rhaw.) 4°. A-C^4 D^2 E^4. (Lea.) [251

-- Rechtmessige vrsache warumb das Concilium von Paulo dem Rom̄. Bapst des namens dem dritten zů Mantua in Welschenlanden zehalten ... vermeintlich indiciert vnnd verkündt/ vntüglich/ vnnd der kirchen keins wegs erspriesslich zůachten sey ... D. M. XXXVII. 4°. A-B^4. (Lea.) [252

-- Copey odder Abdruck/ einer Recusation/ welche von wegen der Churfürst vnd Fürsten/ Sachssen vnd Hessen ... auff vermeinte nichtige Proces/ des vnreformirten/ vnd parteischen besetzten Cammergerichts ... M.D.XLIII. 4°. A-C^4 D^2. [253

-- Der Churfürsten ... vn̄ Stende der Christlichen Einung/ warhaffter ... Bericht/ Röm. Keis. auch Kön. Maiestaten/ ... vnd Stenden des heiligen Reichs/ von wegen der ... Defension/ welche jre Churf. F.G.G. vnd Sie/ wider Heinrichen/ der sich nennet den jungern von Braunschweig/ furzůnemen gedrungen ... Anno M.D.XLIIII. 4°. A-Z^4 AA^6. pp. 2-187. [254

-- -- *Another copy (*A^4 *only).* [255

-- *Schwäbischer Bund.* Hie hebt sich an. die ordnung der zwelffiarigen aynung des lobliche̅ bunds im land zu Schwaben. zu Esslinge̅ ... in dem funffzehe̅hundersten iar beschlossen ... fol. ff. xxiii *(unsigned but numbered).* ¶*Lacks 4 preliminary ll.* (Register *and one blank).* [256

-- Hernach volgend die schlesser die verprent seindt worden. Von dem schwebischen bund. im iar M.D.xxiij. 4°. π^4. [257

-- Dess Heiligen Römischen Reichs/ vnd desselben angehörigen Stennde dess ... Schwäbischen Krais/ ... Verleichung vnnd verfassung/ Welcher massen ... zů vndertheniger Gehorsame/ auf den die vor aufgerichten ... Religion vnd Landtfriden ... zuerhaltten ... Besigelt zu Vlm/ Montags den XXII Nouembris ... M. D. LXIII. fol. a-o^4 aa-bb^4 cc^6. ff. 2-55, 1-13. ¶*Additional t.p.* (o4^r): Hernach volgen die angehencktn̄ kriegs verfassung ... [258

-- *History.* Ad ... sacri Romani Imperii Electores: Reliquosq3 inclitos in concilio Augustensi Germanorū Principes: Carme̅ exhortatiorū: [Augsburg, Johann Otmar, 1510.] 4°. A^8. [259

-- Grauamina Germanicæ nationis cum remedijs & auisamentis ad Caesaream Maiestatem. (Selestadij impressum in officina Schüreriana [c. 1520].) 4°. A-C^4 (-C4, *blank*). [260

-- Hernach volgend die Zehen Krayss/ wie vnd auff welliche art die inn das gantz Reych ausgethaylt/ vnd im 1532. jar Röm. Kay. Maye. hilff wider den Türckeu [*sic*] zů geschickt haben. [Augsburg, Heinrich Steiner, 1532.] 4°. A-B^4 C^2. [261

-- Newe Zeitung Oder beschreibung/ von der Römischen Kaiserlichen Maiestat Protestation/ Vnd den Ceremonien ... In erhöhung vnd Crönung dess/ hieuor Hertzogen Cosmi Medices/ zu

Florentz etc. ... Geschehen zu Rom am 5. Martij diss 1570. Jars. Auss dem Italianischen ins Teutsch transferiert. 4°. A^4 B^2. [262

-- Warhaffte newe Zeitung Welchermassen die Roͤmische Keys. Maiest. ... von den Polnischen Abgesandten in Wien zu einem Koͤnig in Poland declarirt ... worden. Was auch die Tuͤrckische Botschafft ... anbracht. Folgends/ wie der Gross Fuͤrst aus der Moscaw die ... Tuͤrckische Legation/ tractirt ... Letzlich/ was Bepstliche heiligkeit/ vnd der Gross Fuͤrst aus der Moscaw ... Roͤm. Keys. Maiest. fuͤr Stewr vnd huͤlff wider jhre Feinde zugesagt. Gedruckt zu Leipzig/ M. D. LXXVI. 4°. A^4. [263

-- Eigentliche Bildtnis vnd Abconterfeihung Roͤmischer Keyser/ Koͤnige/ Fuͤrsten vnd Herren ... Anno 1587. 4°. AA-KK^4. [264

HOLYWOOD, JOHN. [Sphaera mundi.] (Impressum Venetiis per [Jacobum Pentium pro] Melchiorem Sessa ... M.D.XIII. Die uero .3. Decembris.) 4°. A-F^8 (-A1, F8, *the latter presumably blank*). ff. 2-47. ¶*Includes:* Ioannis de monte regio disputatiões, Georgii purbachii theoricæ. [265

-- Sphera cum commentis ... videlicet. Cichi Esculani cum textu Expositio Ioannis Baptiste Capuani in eandem Iacobi Fabri Stapulensis Theodosij de Speris Michaelis Scoti Qõnes ... Petri de Aliaco &c. Roberti Linchoniensis Compendium Tractatus de Sphera solida Tractatus de Sphera Campani Tractatus de computo maiori eiusdem Disputatio Ioannis de monte regio Textus Theorice cũ expõne Ioãnis Baptiste Capuani Ptolomeus de Speculis (Venetijs impensa heredum ... octauiani Scoti ...: ac sociorum. 19. Ianuarij. 1518) fol. B.L. A^4 B-FF^8 GG^6 (-GG6, *presumably blank*) §^{4}. ff. 5-253. ¶§1: Tebith de imaginatione Sphere. [266

-- -- *Another copy.* §^{4} *bound between* A *and* B. *Some pages defaced.* (Lea.) [267

-- Liber Ioannis de Sacro Busto de sphaera. Addita est præfatio ... Philippi Mel. ... (Venetijs apud Ioan. Ant. de Nicolinis de Sabio, Sumptu ... Melchioris Sessę. ... MDXXXIIII. Mense Iulij.) 8°. A-D^8 E^6 (-E2). [268

-- -- (Impressum Vitebergæ per Iosephum Klug. M. D. XXXVI.) 8°. A-E^8 F^4. [269

-- Ioannis de Sacrobusto libellus de sphæra. Accessit eiusdem autoris computus Ecclesiasticus, Et alia quædam ... Cum Præfatione Philippi Melanthonis. (Impressum Vuitebergæ apud Iohannem Cratonem. Anno M. D. L.) 8°. A-R^8 (-C8; R8 + 2 *folded leaves*). ¶*Additional t.p.* ($I3^r$): Libellus Ioannis de Sacrobusto, de anni ratione ... Anno M.D.XLV. [270

HOLZMAN, DANIEL. Warhafftige vnd schoͤne beschreibung. Der ersten (von Gott gegebnen) Christenlichen Kunst der Schreiberey ... Dessgleichen von erfindung/ der ... Kunst der Buchdruckerey ... Gedruckt zu Wienn in Osterreich/ durch Steffan Kreutzer ... 1581. 4°. A^4 a^2 B-M^4. ¶*In verse.* [271

HOMER. *Works.* Ποιησεις Ομηρου ... Opus vtrumque Homeri Iliados et Odysseae, ... opera Iacobi Micylli & Ioachimi Camerarii recognitum. Adiecta ... est ... Batrachomyomachia. ... Porphyrij ... Homericarum quæstionum liber. Eiusdem, de Nympharum antro in Odyssea, opusculum. ... Basileae, per Ioan. Heruagium, 1552. fol. A^4 β*^{6} a-z^6 A-K^6 L^8 aa-zz^6 A†-B†^{6} C†^{8}. pp. 1-394, 3-314. [272

-- -- [1] ... Homeri, omnia quae quidem extant opera, Graece, adiecta versione Latina ad verbum ... Basileæ per Nicolaum Bryling. & Bartholomæum Calybæum. Anno M.D.LI. fol. A^6 a-z^6 A^8. pp. 1-292. [2] Odyssea Homeri, reliquaque eius opuscula ... *Same imprint.* A^4 a-z^6 A^6 B-C^8 (-C8, *blank*). pp. 1-317. [273

-- -- Homeri opera Graecolatina, quæ quidem nunc extant, omnia. ... In hæc operam suam contulit Sebastianus Castalio ... Editio tertia, ... ad fidem postremæ editionis Henrici Stephani diligenter expressa. Basileae, per haeredes Nicolai Brylingeri. 1567. (... Mense Martio.) fol. α^6 β^4 a-z^6 A^8 a-z^6 A^6 B-C^8 (-C8, *presumably blank*). pp. 1-292, 1-317. ¶C7 *defective.* [274

-- -- [1] Ομηρου Ιλιας ... Homeri Ilias, seu potius omnia eius quæ extant opera. Studio & cura Ob. Giphanii ... edita ... Argentorati Excudebat Theodosius Rihelius [c. 1575]. 8°.):(^{8} a-$3n^8$ $3o^4$. pp. 3-893. [2] Ομηρου Οδυσσεια, Homeri Odyssea. Eiusdem Batrachomyomachia, Hymni, aliaq; eius opuscula ... Omnia Græcè & Latinè edita ... Cum Præfatione, Scholijs, & Indice D. Giphanij. ... *Same imprint.* †^{8} A-$3H^8$. pp. 3-827. [275

-- -- Homeri poetarum principis, cum Iliados, tum Odysseae Libri XLVIII. Laurentio Vallen. & Raphaele Volaterrano interpr. His recens accessere Ausonij Poëtæ in singulos libros argumenta. Item Βατραχομυομαχία, id est, Ranarum & Murium pugna, Aldo Ma. Ro. interprete Item Deorum hymni XXXII. Iodoco Velareo Verbrokano. interpr. ... Item Homeri uita per Dionem Philosophum, eodem interprete. 1528 ([Antverpiae,] Apud Io. Grapheum mense Aprili ...) 8°. A-Kk^{8} Ll^{4}. ff. 2-259. ¶*Contains the* Iliad *only.* [276

-- *Batrachomyomachia.* Homerus de bello ranarum et murium quem Karolus Aretinus Latinitate donauit. ... (Impressum Pisauri per Hieronymum Soncinum. ... M.D.VIIII. Die uero .xx. mensis Martii. ...) 4°. A^{4} B^{6}. [277

-- *Iliad.* Homeri ... Ilias per Laurentiū Vallēsem Romanū e greco in latinū translata ... (Impressum Liptzk per Melchiorem Lotterū. Anno ... Millesimoq̃ngētesimoduodecimo.) fol. A-P^{6} Q^{4} R^{6}. ff. ij-c. [278

-- -- ... Homeri Ilias, ... Latino carmine reddita, Helio Eobano Hesso Interprete. ... Basileae. (... in officina Roberti VVinter, mense Septembri. Anno M. D. XXXX.) 4°. α^{6} A-Pp^{8} Qq^{6} (-Qq6) Rr-Tt^{4}. pp. 2-617. [279

-- -- Parisiis, Apud Iacobum Bogardum ... 1545. 16°. A-ZZ^{8} a-e^{8}. ff. 2-408. [280

-- -- [1] Les dix premiers liures de l'Iliade d'Homere ...: Traduictz en vers François, par M. Hugues Salel ... A Paris. Pour Vincent Sertenas ... 1555. 8°. A-Bb^{8}. ff. I-CLXXXIII. [2] Les vnzieme, & douzieme liures ... auec le commencement du treziesme, l'Vmbre dudict Salel, faicte par Oliuier de Maigny ... A Paris, Pour Vincent Sertenas ... 1554. A-I^{8}. [281

-- -- [1] Les XXIIII. liures de l'Iliade d'Homere ... Traduicts du Grec en vers François. Les XI. premiers par M. Hugues Salel ... Et les XIII. derniers par Amadis Iamin ...: auec Le premier & second, de l'Odissee d'Homere, par Iaques Peletier du Mans. ... A Paris, Pour Lucas Brayer ... 1577. 8°. ā^{8} ē^{8} ā^{8} (-ā1) a-d^{8} e^{10} f-z^{8} A-C^{4} D^{8} E^{4}. ff. 1-219. [2] Les treize derniers liures de l'Iliade ... *Same imprint.* (Acheué d'imprimer au mois de Ianuier ...) π^{1} A-Z^{8} (-E4-5) a-g^{8}. ff. 1-242. [3] Premier et second liure de l'Odissee ... *Same imprint.* A-D^{8} E^{4}. ff. 2-36. [282

-- -- A Paris, Pour Lucas Breyer ... M. D. LXXX. ... (Acheué d'imprimer le seiziéme iour de Ianuier. ... Par Pierre le Voirrier ...) 12°. ā^{12} A-Qq^{12} (-Qq12, *presumably blank*). ff. 1-408, 2-32. ¶*Additional t.pp.* at R4^{r}, Mm5^{r}. [283

-- -- Les XXIIII. liures de l'Iliade ... Auec Les trois premiers Liures de l'Odissee ... A Paris, Chez Abel l'Angelier ... M. D. XCIX. 12°. ā^{12} A-Ll^{12} Mm^{4}. ff. 1-407. [284

-- -- Dell' Iliade d'Homero, tradotta da M. Bernardino Leo da Piperno, libri dodeci. ... In Roma. Appresso Bartholomeo Toso Bresciano. M.D.LXXIII. 12°. π^{4} A-Bb^{12} Cc^{6}. ff. 2-305. [285

-- -- *Book I.* Il primo libro de la Iliade d'Homero, tradotta di Greco in volgare per M. Francesco Gussano. In Venetia per Comin da Trino di Monferrato l'anno M D XLIIII. 8°. A-C^{8} (-C8, *presumably blank*). ff. 3-23. [286

-- -- *Books I-V.* L'Iliade d'Homero tradotta in lingua Italiana per Paolo La Badessa Messinese. In Padoa, appresso Gratioso Perchacino. M. D. LXIIII. 4°. A-Z^{4}. ff. 2-92. [287

-- *Odyssey.* Homeri ... Odyssea de erroribus Vlyxis. (Argentoraci Ex officina Ioannis Schotti: impēsis ... Georgij Maxilli: al's Übelin ... ad nonū Kal'. Iunij. ... M. D. X.) fol. A-G^{6} H^{4} I^{6}. ff. II-LI. [288

-- -- Odissea Homeri per Raphaelem Volaterranum in Latinum conuersa. ... (Impressum Romæ Per Iacobum Mazochium ... M.D.X. Die .xii. Septembris.) fol. A-M^{6} N-O^{8} P^{6} Q^{10} (-Q10, *blank*). [289

-- -- Premier et second liure de l'Odissee d'Homere. Par Iacques Peletier du Mans. A Paris, Pour Claude Gautier ... 1570. 8°. A-D^{8}. ff. 2-29. [290

-- -- L'Vlisse di M. Lodouico Dolce da lui tratto dall'Odissea d'Homero et ridotto in ottaua rima ... In Vinegia appresso Gabriel Giolito de' Ferrari. M D LXXIII. 4°. *^{8} A-L^{8} M^{6}. pp. 1-186. [291

-- -- L'Odissea d'Homero tradotta in volgare Fiorentino da M. Girolamo Baccelli. ... In Firenze Appresso il Sermartelli. 1582. (*Colophon.*) 8°. †^{4} A-Ss^{8} Tt-Vu^{4}. pp. 1-678. [292

-- -- De la Vlyxea de Homero. XIII. libros traduzidos de Griego en Romance Castellana por Gonçalo Perez. Impresso en Salamanca en casa de Andrea de Portonariis. 1550. ... (... a primero del mes de Hebrero. ...) 4°. aa^{4} A-Z^{8} a-h^{8} i^{4}. ff. 1-250. [293

-- -- Impressa en ... Anuers, en casa de Iuan Steelsio. 1556. ... 8°. A-3K^{8}. ff. 1-440. [294

-- -- *Another copy.* [295

-- *Cento.* Homerici Centones ... Virgiliani Centones. Vtrique in quædam historiæ sacræ capita scripti. Nonni paraphrasis euangelii Ioannis, Græcè & Latinè. [Genevae,] Excud. Henr. Steph. anno M. D. LXXVIII. 8°. ¶^{4} a-b^{8} A-P^{8} Q^{4} a-d^{8} e^{1} a-e^{8} (-e7-8, *blank*). pp. 1-28, 2-247, 1-66, 1-73. ¶*Includes* (a-d^{8} e^{1}): Homerici versus prouerbiales. [296

-- -- *Another copy (lacking* Homerici versus prouerbiales, b7-8, e7-8, *all blank).* [297

-- -- *Another copy (lacking* Homerici versus prouerbiales, *blank* ¶4, *and blank* b8; *sigg.* a-b^{8} *follow* *8 *of* Theocriti aliorumque Poetarum Idyllia, *with which this copy is bound).* [298

HOMERUS LATINUS. Pyndarus de bello Troiano Astyanax maphæi Landensis Epigrammata quædam diuersorum autorū (Impressum Fani ab Hieronymo Soncino Sexto Id. octobris M.D.XV.) 8°. [A]^{4} ✠^{4} B-I^{4}. [299

HOOGSTRATEN, JACOBUS VAN. Ad ... Philippū ... Coloniensis archiepm. Tractat⁹ magistralis declarans q̄ꝫ grauiter peccēt q̄rentes auxiliū a maleficis cōpilat⁹ ab ... Iacobo hoechstrassen ... (Consummatum est ... sub anno ... Millesimo Quingentesimodecimo ... Impressum Colonie per Martinum de werdena.) 4°. B.L. A-B^{4}. [300

-- Defensio scholastica prīcipum almanie ... compilata ab ... Iacobo hochstraten ... contra nouissimum opus ... petri rauēnatis ... (impressum ꝑ me Iohannē Landen ciuē ... Colonieñ. ... M.ccccc.viij. octaua ꝯo die May.) 4°. B.L. A-F^{4}. [301

-- Margarita moralis philosophie ... Per ... Iacobum, de Hoechstraten ... (Impressum Coloniæ, per Petrū Quentel. ... M.CCCCC.xxi.) 4°. B.L. π^{4} A-D$^{4.6}$ E^{6} F-Z$^{4.6.6}$ aa-mm$^{4.6.6}$ nn^{4} oo^{6}. [302

HOPPER, MARTIN. Λεξικον Ελληνορωμαικον, hoc est, dictionarium Graecolatinum ... illustratum & emendatum per: G. Budaeum. L. Tusanum. C. Gesnerum. H. Iunium. R. Constantinum. Io. Hartungum. Mar. Hopperum. ... Basileæ, ex officina Henricpetrina. (... M. D. LXVIII. Mense Septembri.) fol. †^{4} A-Zz^{8} AA-YY^{8} zz^{8} AAa-ZZz^{8} 3A-4C^{8}. [303

HORAPOLLO. Ori Apollinis Niliaci, de sacris AEgyptiorum notis, Ægypticè expressis libri duo, iconibus illustrati ... Nunc primùm in Latinum ac Gallicum sermonem conuersi. Parisiis, Apud Galeotum à Prato, & Ioannem Ruellium ... 1574. 8°. *^{8} A-N^{8} O^{4}. ff. 2-107. [304

HORATIUS FLACCUS, QUINTUS. *Works.* Opa Q. Horatij Flacci ... cum quatuor commētarijs. Acronis. Porphyrionis. Anto. Mancinelli. Iodoci Badii Ascensii ... Cūqꝫ adnotationibus Matthæi Bonfinis: & Aldi Manutii Romani ... Vęnundantur Parrhisiis ... ab ipso Ascensio. ... (... Calen. Octob. ... M.D.XIX. ...) fol. aa^{6} a-z^{8} A-N^{8}. ff. I-CCLXXXVIII. [305

-- -- Q. Horatii Flacci poemata omnia. Centimetrum Marij Seruij. Annotationes Aldi Manutij Romani in Horatium. Ratio mensuum, quibus Odæ eiusdem Poëtæ tenentur eodem Aldo authore. Nicolai Peroti libellus eiusdem argumenti. (Venetiis in aedibus Aldi, et Andreae soceri, mense Nouembri. M. D. XIX.) 8°. A^{8} a-z^{8} &^{8} (-&7-8, *the former blank*). ff. 1-189. [306

-- -- [Q. Horatii Flacci carmina.] (Basileae per Nicolaum Brylingerum, anno M. D. XLIII.) 8°. †^{8} (-†1-2) a-z^{8} A^{8}. pp. 4-379 *visible.* [307

-- -- [1] Opera Q. Horatii Flacci Venusini, Grāmaticorum antiquiss. Helenii Acronis, et Porphirionis Commentarijs illustrata, admixtis interdum C. Aemilii, Iulii Modesti, et Terentii Scauri Annotatiunculis: edita ... per Georgium Fabricium Chemnicensem. Ex Diomedis etiam Obseruationibus ... Hoc quoque accedunt Ioan. Hartungi ... obseruationes ... Basileae. (... apud Henrichum Petri, mense Septembri, anno M. D. LV.) fol. a^{4} b-e^{6} f-g^{4} A-Oo^{6} Pp^{4} Qq^{6}. pp. 2-463. [2] Horatiani huius uoluminis Tomus alter ... Christophorus Landinus in omnia Horat. opera. Franciscus Luisinus Vtinensis in Artem poëticam. Iacobus

Grifolius Lucinianensis in Artem poëticam. Iason de Nores Cyprius in Artem poëticam. Eras. Roterod. Aldi Manutij Ludouici Coelij Angeli Politiani M. Anton. Coccij Sabellici Ioan. Baptistæ Pij Bonon. Iacobi à Cruce Bononiensis Petri Criniti Henrici Loriti Glareani Annotaţiones in Horatij opera. Basileae. (*Colophon.*) †^{4} AA-ZZ^{6} AAa-ZZz^{6} 3A-3M^{6} 3N^{4} 3O^{6}. pp. 701-1411. [308

-- -- [Quinti Horatii Flacci Venusini ... poemata omnia. ... Lugduni, Apud Ioannem Frellonium. 1557. (Excudebat Symphor. Barbierus. ...)] 16°. a^{8} (-a1, a8) b^{8} (-b1) c-t^{8} v^{4} (-v2-4). pp. 3-308. [309

-- -- Quinctus Horatius Flaccus ab omni obscoenitate purgatus. Dilingae, Excudebat Ioannes Mayer. M. D. LXXXV. 8°. A-T^{8}. pp. 3-298. [310

-- -- [1] Dionysii Lambini Monstroliensis ... in Q. Horatium Flaccum ... à se emendatum, ... commentariisque ... explicatum ... Francofurti Apud Andreæ Wecheli heredes, Claudium Marnium, & Ioann. Aubrium. M. D. XCVI. 4°. α^{4} β^{4} a-z^{4} A-Mm^{4}. pp. 1-464. [2] Q. Horatii Flacci sermonum ... Pars altera. *Same imprint.* aa-zz^{4} AA-3Z^{4}. pp. 3-550. [311

-- -- Q. Horatius Flaccus: cum commentariis & Enarrationibus commentatoris veteris, et Iacobi Cruquii Messenii ... Accesserunt, Iani Dousæ Nordouicis in eundem Commentariolus ... Lugduni Barauorum, Ex officina Plantiniana, Apud Franciscum Raphelengium. CIↄ. Iↄ. IIIC. 4°. *-**^{4} A-Z^{4} a-3u^{4}. pp. 1-695. [312

-- -- Quincti Horatii Flacci Opera omnia ... Lugduni Batauorum, Ex Officina Plantiniana, Apud Franciscum Raphelengium. cIↄ. Iↄ. XCVII. 16°. A^{8} (-A2-7) B-N^{8} O^{4}. pp. 15-215 *present.* [313

-- -- Q. Horacio Flacco ... Sus obras con la declaracion Magistral en lengua Castellana. Por el Doctor Villen de Biedma. ... En Granada. Por Sebastian de Mena. Año 1599. A costa de Iuan Diez ... (*Colophon.*) fol. ¶^{4} ¶^{6} A^{8} B-4M^{4} 4N^{2} 4T-4V^{4}. ff. 1-330. [314

-- *Ars poetica.* Quinti Horatij Flacci poetarũ institutiones ad pisones. [Lipsiae, Martin Landsberg, c. 1500.] fol. B.L. A^{6} B^{4}. [315

-- -- Francisci Philippi Pedimontii ecphrasis in Horatii Flacci artem poeticam. ... Venetiis, M. D. XLVI. (Apud Aldi filios. ... Mense Augusto.) 4°. A-P^{4} Q^{6} (-Q6, *blank*). ff. 5-65. [316

-- -- In epistolam Q. Horatij Flacci de Arte Poetica Iasonis de Nores Ciprij ex quotidianis Tryphonis Cabrielij sermonibus interpretatio. Eiusdem ... summa præceptorum de arte dicendi ex tribus Ciceronis libris de oratore collecta. ... Venetiis apud Aldi filios M. D. LIII. (*Colophon.*) 8°. A-Y^{8}. ff. 2-165. [317

-- -- De arte poetica. Ioan. Baptistae Pignae poetica Horatiana ... Venetiis, Apud Vincentium Valgrisium. M D LXI. (*Colophon.*) fol. a-c^{4} d^{2} A-L^{4} M^{16} a-b^{4}. pp. 1-90, 17-28. [318

-- -- La poetica d'Horatio tradotta per Messer Lodouico Dolce. In Vinegia per Francesco Bindoni, & Mapheo Pasini compagni. Del mese di Agosto. MDXXXV. 8°. A-C^{8}. [319

-- *Sermones.* Horatij Flacci Satyrici poete Sermonum Liber Primus. (Impressa Francophordio per Nicolaũ Lamperter & Balthasar Murrer. ... M.D.Viij.) 4°. A-L^{6} M^{4}. ¶F5^{v}: Liber Secundus. *Margin of* L2 *cut out.* [320

-- -- I diletteuoli sermoni, altrimenti satire, e le morali epistole di Horatio, ... insieme con la Poetica. Ridotte da M. Lodouico Dolce dal Poema Latino in uersi Sciolti Volgari. ... In Vinegia appresso Gabriel Giolito de' Ferrari. M D LIX. 8°. A-V^{8}. pp. 3-318. [321

HORNKENS, HEINRICH. Recueil de dictionaires Francoys, Espaignolz et Latins. ... A Bruxelles, Par Rutger Velpius ... 1599. ... 4°. ♣^{4} A-3Z^{4} 4A^{2}. pp. 1-551. [322

HOROZCO Y COVARUVIAS, JUAN DE. Paradoxas Christianas contra las falsas opiniones del mundo. ... In Segouia. Por Marcos de Ortega. Año de 1592. 4°. *^{8} A-Ff^{8} Gg-Ii^{4}. ff. 1-231. (Lea.) [323

HORST, JAKOB. Iacobi Horstij D. de aureo dente maxillari pueri Silesii ... Et de noctambulonum natura, differentiis et causis ... 1595 Lipsiæ, Impensis Valentini Voegelini ... (... imprimebat Michael Lantzenberger. ...) 8°. A-X^{8} Y^{4}. pp. 1-318. (School of Dentistry.) [324

-- -- *Another copy.* (School of Dentistry.) [325

-- Iacobi Horstii ... zwey Bücher: Eins Von dem güldenen Zahn/ so einem Knaben in Schlesien gewachsen ... Vorhin im Latein geschrieben/ Ietzt ... verdeutscht Durch Georgium Coberum. Das Ander Von den Nachtwanderern/ welche im schlaff vmbgehen ... verdeutschet/ Durch Iacobum Horstium den Iüngern. Leipzig ... 1596. (Gedruckt ... bey Michael Lantzenberger. In verlegung Valentini Vögelini/ Buchhändler.) 8°. A-V^{8} (-F1). pp. 1-292. (School of Dentistry.) [326

HORTUS SANITATIS. Ortus Sanitatis De Herbis et Plantis. De Animalibus et Reptilibus. De Auibus et Volatilibus. De Piscibus et Natatilibus. De Lapidibus ... De Vrinis et earum speciebus. [Argentorati, Reinhard Beck,] M.D.XVII. ... fol. B.L. a^{8} b-k^{6} l^{8} m-r^{6} s^{8} t-z^{6} A^{6} B^{8} C-E^{6} F^{8} G-I^{6} K^{8} (-K8) L-M^{6} N^{8} O-R^{6} S^{8} T-Bb^{6} Cc^{8} Dd-Ee^{6} Ff-Gg^{8} Ii-Kk^{8} (-Kk8). [326a

HOST, MATTHAEUS. De numeratione emendata, veteribus Latinis et Græcis vsitata ... Antuerpiæ, Ex officina Christophori Plantini. M. D. LXXXII. 8°. A-D^{8} (D8 + *folded leaf*). pp. 3-62. [327

HOST VON ROMBERCH, JOHANN. Congestorium Artificiose Memorie. V.P.F. Ioānis Romberch de Kyrspe. ... (Venetijs per Melchiorem Sessam ... 1531. Mensis Iulij.) 8°. B.L. A-N^{8}. ff. 2-104. [328

HOTMAN, FRANÇOIS. Der Vnuernünfftige vnd Vnsinnige Bañstrahl des Römischen Antichristischen Bapsts Sixten des V. ... auss Lateinischer Spraach in die Teutsche gebracht/ Durch Alonicum Meliphrona Theutofrancum ... (Getruckt zu Passfurth am Rhein/ Durch Die Gemeinen Liebhaber vnd Furderer der Christlichen Wahrheit vnd Freyheit ... M.D.LXXXVI. Auff den XXI. Tag Herbst Monats ...) 4°. †-3†^{4} A-V^{4} W-Cc^{4}. pp. 2-205. [329

HOVE, ANTONIUS VAN. D. Antonii Houaei Haecmundani ... de arte amandi Christum. Libri tres ... Coloniae. Apud Maternum Cholinum. M.D.LXVI. 8°. a^{8} A-E^{8}. pp. 3-95. [330

-- D. Antonii Houaei ... Odarum, precum, Hymnorum ... liber. Coloniae, Apud Maternum Cholinum. M.D.LXVI. 8°. a-e^{8} *^{4}. pp. 2-78. [331

HOZJUSZ, STANISLAW. D. Stanislai Hosii ... opera omnia ... diligentia D. Doctoris Henrici Dunghæi ... edita. ... Antuerpiæ, In Ædibus Viduæ & Hæredum Ioannis Stelsij. M. D. LXXI. ... (... Excudebat Theodorus Lyndanus ...) fol. *^{6} A-Ll^{6} Mm^{4} Nn-3V^{6}. ff. 1-383. ¶*Additional t.p.* (Nn1^{r}): Confutatio prolegomenon Brentii ... *Same imprint.* [332

-- Dialogus de eo, num calicem laicis, et vxores sacerdotibus permitti, ac diuina officia vulgari lingua peragi fas sit. Authore Stanislao Hosio ... M. D. LVIII. (Dilinge, excudebat Sebaldus Mayer.) 8°. a-q^{8} r^{6}. (Lea.) [333

HRABANUS MAURUS. Rabanus De institutiōe clericorum ... libri tres. Eiusdem epistola ... quota generatione licitum sit matrimoniū. De septem signis matiuitatis domini. De ortu, vita & moribus Antichristi. ... (Phorçe impressit Thomas Anshelmi Badensis ... Mense Augusto. v. Cl'. Septembris. Anno .M.D.V. ...) 8°. a^{6} b^{4} c-d^{6} e-f^{4} g-m$^{6.6.4}$ o^{4} p-s^{6} t^{4} v^{6} x^{4}. [334

HUARTE NAVARRO, JUAN DE DIOS. Examen de Ingenios. The examination of mens Wits. In which, by discouering the varietie of natures, is shewed for what profession each one is apt, and how far he shall profit therein. By Iohn Huarte. Translated out of the Spanish tongue by M. Camillo Camilli. Englished out of his Italian, by R. C. Esquire. London, Printed by Adam Islip. 1598. 4°. A-Y^{8}. pp. 1-133. *S.T.C.* 13893. ¶*Translator: Richard Carew.* (Furness.) [335

-- -- L'examen et parfait iugement des esprits propres & naiz aux sciences. ... Escrit premierement en Espagnol, & mis en François par Gabriel Chapuis, Tourangeau. Se vende a Paris, Chez Claude Micard ... 1588. ... (A Rouen, De l'Imprimerie de George l'Oyselet.) 16°. a-z^{8} A-L^{8}. ff. 1-258. [336

-- -- Essame de gl'ingegni de gli huomini, Per apprender le Scienze: ... di Gio. Huarte: Nuouamente tradotto della lingua Spagnuola da M. Camillo Camilli. ... In Venetia, [Aldine press,] M D XXCII. 8°. *^{8} A-Z^{8}. pp. 2-367. [337

HUBERINUS, KASPAR. Ein Getrewe warnung vor der künfftigen Straff Gottes. ... M.D.XLII. (Getruckt zů Augspurg/ durch Philipp Vlhart.) 8°. A-D⁸. [338

-- Vom Christlichen Ritter. Ain wunderbarlicher kampff der Hellischen Bestien/ wider ainen Euangelischen Christen ... Neuburgæ Danubij. 1545. (... Gedrugkt/ bey Hannsen Kilian ...) 4°. A-T⁴. [339

-- Von Bösen falschen Zungen. ... M.D.XLII. (Getruckt zů Augspurg/ durch Philipp Vlhart.) 8°. A-E⁸ F⁴. [340

-- Warzu das haylige Creůtz nutz vnd gůt sey. Item von den Christlichen waffen. ... M.D.XLII. (Getruckt zů Augspurg/ durch Philipp Vlhart.) 8°. A-E⁸. [341

HUBMAIER, BALTHASAR. Axiomata quae Baldazar Pacimontanus, Musca, Huldrychi Zuinglij in Christo frater, Ioanni Eckio Ingolstadiensi Elephanto, magistraliter examinanda proposuit. ... (Tiguri in ædib. Christophori Froschouer, Anno M.D.XXIIII. Mense Nouembr. die .IIII.) 4°. A⁴. [342

HUG, ALEXANDER. Rethorica vnnd Formularium Teůtsch ... Getruckt zů Tübingen. (... durch Vlrich Morhart/ im Tausent/ Fünffhundert/ vnd Achtvndzweintzigsten Jare.) fol. π⁴ A-QQ⁶. ff. I-CCXXXIIII. [343

HUG, JOHANN. Der heiligen Kirchē vnd des Römischen Reichs Wagen für. (Getruckt in ... Strassbůrg durch Iohannem Grůininger ... vff Montag nach vnser liebē frowē geburt. ... M.d.iiii.) fol. A-D⁶ E⁴ F-L⁶ M². ff. II-LXVI. [344

-- Quadruuium Ecclesie Quattuor prelatorum officium ... ([Paris] ... acheue de imprimer le premier iour daoust lan mil v.c. & neuf pour Guillaume eustace ...) 4°. a-k⁸ l⁶. ff. ii-lxxxiiii. [345

HUGO ARGENTINENSIS. Compendium Theologice Veritatis. (Impressuȝ Venetijs ꝑ ... Petrū de parēghis [*sic*] Pergomēseȝ. ... M.ccccc.x. Die .xxiij. Octob.) 4°. B.L. A-C⁸ D¹² E-K⁸ L¹² (-L12, *presumably blank*). (Lea.) [346

HUGO OF TRIMBERG. Der Renner. ... Darinnen angezeygt wirdt/ eynem Iegklichen Welcher wirden/ wesens/ oder Standts er sey ... allererst im Truck aussgangen. ... 1549. Gedruckt zu Franckfurt am Meyn/ durch Cyriacum Iacobum zum Bock. fol. A-V⁶ X⁴ (-X4, *presumably blank*). ff. 3-123. ¶*In verse*. [347

HUGOBALD, HULDREICH. Ad sanctam Tigurinam ecclesiam Vdalrici Hugualdi epistola. ... [Basileae, Adamus Petri, 1521.] 4°. A-B⁴ C². [348

-- Vdalrichi Hugualdi Durgei adulescentis dialogus ... (Excudebatur [Basileae per Adamum Petri] Anno M. D. XX. Mense Septembri.) 4°. A-K⁴ (-K4, *presumably blank*). pp. 3-78.[349

HULOET, RICHARD. Huloets dictionarie, newelye corrected ... Also the Frenche therevnto annexed, by vvhich you may finde the Latin or Frenche, of anye Englishe woorde you will. By Iohn Higgins ... Londini, In ædibus Thomæ Marshij. Anno. 1572. fol. ¶⁴ A-3A⁶. *S.T.C.* 13941. (Furness.) [350

HULSIUS, LEVINUS. Chronologia. Das ist/ Ein kurtze beschreibung Was sich ... biss auff dieses 1597 Jahr ... verlauffen. ... [Nürnberg,] Typis Christophori Lochneri, M.D.XCVII. Sumptibus Authoris. 4°. π⁴ A-H⁴ I². [351

HUMPHREY, LAWRENCE. Ioannis Iuelli Angli, Episcopi Sarisburiensis vita & mors ... Laurentio Humfredo ... Autore. ... Londini Apud Iohannem Dayum ... 1573. ... 4°. †⁴ *⁴ ¶⁴ ††⁴ *² (-*2, *blank*) A-Y⁴ Aa-Pp⁴ Qq². pp. 1-269. *S.T.C.* 13963. (Yarnall.) [351a

HUNDT, MAGNUS. Compēdiū totius logices: qδ a nōnullis Paruulus Antiquoꝝ appellatur ... Impressum Lyptzk. (... opa ꝑ impēsis Melchiaris Lotter. Anno ... Millesimo quingētesimoseptimo.) 4°. A-Kk⁶. ff. ij-clxxiiij. [352

HUNGARY. Berckhordnung der Freyen ... Perckhstett in der Cron Hungern ... Beschehen ... im Tausent fůnfhundert Fůnffundsechtzigsten Jar. ... Gedruckt zu Wienn in Osterreich/ durch Michael Zimmerman ... fol. A-Q⁴ R⁶. [353

-- Newe Zeittung auss Vngern. Kurtzer Bericht/ der bey dem Marckt Sixo ... den 8. Octobris, Anno 1588. gehaltenen Schlacht. 1588. Erstlich: Gedruckt zu Prag ... durch Hans Schuman. 4°. A^4. [354

HUNGER, WOLFGANG. Volphgangi Hungeri ... in Caroli Bouilli Samarobrini ... vocum Gallicanarum Tabulas, Notæ. ... Argentorati Excudebat B. Iobin. Anno M.D.XXCIII. 8°.):(^{8} A-T^8 V^4. [355

-- Linguae Germanicae vindicatio ... Argentorati Excudebat Bernhardus Iobin. Anno M.D.XXCVI. 8°.):(^{8} A-T^8 V^4. [356

HUNNAEUS, AUGUSTINUS. Breuissimus catechismus catholicus ... nuper vnico schemate comprehensus ... Augustae Taurinorum. Apud hæredes Nicolai Beuilaquæ. 1582. ... fol. A^8. pp. 3-14. (Lea.) [357

-- Aug. Hunnaei de sacramentis ecclesiae Christi axiomata ... Augustae Taurinorum. Apud hæredes Nicolai Beuilaquæ. 1582. fol. A^{10}. pp. 3-18. (Lea.) [358

HUNNIUS, ÆGIDIUS. Die Klaglieder Des heiligen Propheten Ieremie/ aussgelegt vnd erklåret ... in siebentzehen vnterschiedliche Predigten ... Durch Egidium Hunnen ... Gedruckt zu Franckfurt am Mayn/ durch Iohan Spiess. M. D. LXXXVI. 4°.)(^{4} A-Z^4 a-d^4. ff. 1-108. [359

HUS, JAN. Christi Ab incarnationis vsq3 ascensionis Gesta ... (1514. Impressa Landeshutenss octauo Kalendas Maii. per Ioannem Weyssenburger presbiterum.) 4°. A-B^4 (-B4, *presumably blank*). (Lea.) [360

-- [1] Ioannes Huss De Anatomia Antichristi, Liber unus. De mysterijs iniquitatis Antichristi, Fragmentum I De reuelatione Christi, & Antichristi, Fragmentū 2 De abolendis Sectis, & traditionib. hominū. Lib. I De unitate Ecclesiæ, & sçismate uitando Liber I De Euangelica perfectione. Liber I De pernicie traditionum humanarum. Fragment. 3 De regno, populo, uita, & morib. Antichristi. Lib. I Item Fragmentorum collectanea quædam. ... Appendix Othonis Brunnfelsii ... [c. 1525.] 4°. π^8 a-z^4 Aa-Dd^4. ff. i-xcviij. [2] Ioannis Huss Locorum aliquot ex Osee, & Ezechiele prophetis, cap. v. & viij. De abhorrenda Sacerdotum & Monachorum Papisticorum, in Ecclesia Christi abominatione ... Vita item, & regno Antichristi. Tomus secundus. Commendatitia breuis M. Lutheri ... π^4 a-r^4 s^6. ff. ij-lxxiiij. [3] Sermonum Ioannis Huss Ad Populum, tomus tertius. ... π^4 A-H^4 i-k^4 L-N^4. ff. i-li. [361

-- Epistolæ quaedam ... Addita est D. Martini Lutheri Præfatio. Vitembergae ex officina Ioannis Lufft. Anno M.DXXXVII. (*Colophon.*) 8°. A-V^8 X^4 Y^8. [362

-- [1] Ioannis Hus, et Hieronymi Pragensis ... historia et monumenta ... Impressa Noribergæ, in Officina Ioannis Montani, & Vlrici Neuberi. ... M. D. LVIII. (*Colophon.*) fol. a^8 A-$3O^6$ $3P^4$. ff. I-CCCCLXXI. [2] Monumentorum Ioannis Hus, altera pars. ... Norībergæ, anno M.D.LVIII. (... apud Ioannem Montanum, & Vlricum Neuberum.) A^8 B-Nn^6 Oo-Pp^8 Qq-$3O^6$ $3P^8$ (-3P8, *presumably blank*). ff. III-CCCLXVI. (Lea.) [363

-- Liber egregius de vnitate ecclesiae, Cuius autor periit in concilio Constantiensi. (Excubatur ... Mense Augsuto, An. M. D. XX.) 4°. A-Gg^4. pp. 1-231. (Lea.) [364

-- Historia Ioannis Hussi Et Hieronymi Pragensis ... Condemnatio eorundem, per Sacrum Constanciense Concilium. Poggii Florentini de eadem re Epsitola. [c. 1525.] 8°. A-C^8 D^4. [365

-- Processus consistorialis Martyrij Io. Huss, cum correspondentia Legis Gratiæ, ad ius Papisticum, in Simoniacos & fornicatores Papistas. ... Ad uetustatis typum excusus. ... 4°. $[a]^4$ b-d^4 e^6 (-e3-4). [366

-- Le vraye histoire de la vie de M. Iean Hus ... M. D. LXV. 8°. A-K^8. [367

-- Warhafftige Historia von Magister Iohan Hussen ... M. D. XXXViij. (Gedruckt zu Dreszden durch Wolffgang Stöckel.) 4°. a-h^4. [368

HUSAĪN IBN 'ABD ALLĀH, ABŪ 'ALĪ. Auicēne ... opera in lucē redacta ... (Venetijs mandato ... heredū ... Octauiani Scoti ... anno octauo. supra Millesimū qnqesq3 centesimū. Per Bonetū Locatellū ... Sextodecimo kalendas Maias.) fol. B.L. a^8 b^4 c-e^8 f^6 A-O^8 P^6. ff. 2-42, 1-117. (Lea.) [369

HUSAĪN IBN 'ABD ALLĀH

-- [1] Auicennae Liber Canonis De medicinis cordialibus Cantica De remouendis nocumentis in regimine sanitatis De syrupo acetoso. Quorum priores tres ... Andreas Alpagus Bellunensis ... emendationibus, ac Indice ... ornauerat. Postea vero Benedictus Rinius Venetus ... lucubrationibus decorauerat ... Venetiis, apud Iuntas. MDLXII. (*Colophon.*) fol. $*^6$ A-K^8 1-M^4 N-Y^8 Z^6 &^{6} AA-ZZ^8 &&^{8} 3A-$3C^8$ $3D^{10}$ $3E^4$ 3F-$4D^8$ $4E^4$ 1^8 2-3^6. ff. 3-590, 1-20. [2] Index ... *Same imprint.* A-M^6 N^4. ff. 2-76. ¶^{2}N4 *defective.* [370

-- [1] Auicennae ... Libri in re medica omnes ... à Ioanne Paulo Mongio Hydruntino, & Ioanne Costæo Laudensi recognita. ... Venetiis, Apud Vincentium Valgrisium. M D L XIIII. fol. $*^4$ A-S^6 T^4 V-Kk^6 Ll^4 Mm^8 Nn-$4L^6$ $4M^8$. pp. 1-966. [2] Auicennae operum in re medica Tomus secundus ... *Same imprint.* (*Colophon.*) fol. $*^6$ A-Ii^6 Kk^4 Ll-Mm^6 Nn^8 (-Nn8). pp. 1-429. [3] Indices ... *Same imprint.* A-V^6 X^8 (-X8, *blank*). [371

HUTTEN, ULRICH VON. Ad diuum Maximilianum Caesa. Aug. F.P. bello in Venetos euntem, ... Exhortatio. ... (Viennæ Pannoniæ apud Hieronymū Vietorem, & Ioannem Singrenium. Mense Ianuario, anno. M.D.XII.) 4°. A^6 B-C^4. ¶*In verse.* [372

-- In incendium Lutherianum exclamatio ... Anno Domini M.D.XXI. 4°. π^2. ¶*Benzing 150.* (Lea.) [373

-- Ioannis Reuchlin ... Encomion: Triumphanti illi ex Deuictis Obscuris viris: id est Theologistis Colonień. et Fratribus de ordine Predicatorum: ab Eleutherio Bizeno decantatum. [Tubingae? Thomas Anshelm? c. 1515.] 4°. A-D^4 E^6. (Lea.) [374

-- Vlrichi Hutteni equitis Germani opera poetica ... (Anno. M. D. XXXVIII.) 8°. A-S^8 T^4. [375

HUTTICH, JOHANN. Consulum Romanorum Elenchus. ... [Argentinae, Wolfgangus Köpfel.] (... M.D.XXXIIII.) 4°. aa-dd^4 (-bb4). [376

-- Imperatorum Romanorum libellus. Vnà cum imaginibus ... (VVolgangus Caephalius Argentinae ... excussit. ... M. D. XXV.) 8°. A-M^8 N^4. ff. 1-81. [377

-- -- (VVolfgangus Cephalaeus Argentinae ... excussit. ... M.D.XXVI.) 8°. A-M^8 N^4. ff. 1-89. [378

HYGINUS, CAIUS JULIUS. C. Iulii Hygini Augusti Liberti fabularum liber ... Eiusdem poeticon astronomicon, libri quatuor. ... Palaephati de fabulosis narrationibus, liber I. F. Fulgentii Placiadis ... Mythologiarum, libri III. Eiusdem de uocum antiquorum interpretatione, liber. I. Arati Φainomenωn fragmentum, Germanico Cæsare interprete. Eiusdem Phænomena Græce, cum interpretatione latina. Procli de sphæra libellus, Græce & Latine. Basileae apud Ioan. Heruagium Anno, M. D. XXXV mense Martio. (*Colophon.*) fol. α-γ^6 b-d^6 (d3^v, d4^r *blank*) e^8 f-p^6 q^4 r-x^6. pp. 8-246. [379

HYPERIUS, ANDREAS. [1] De honorandis magistratibus Commentarius, in quo Psalmus XX. ... enarratur. ... Eiusdem in psalmum XII. ... paraphrasis. Marpurgi. 8°. π^8 A-S^8. ff. 1-143. [2] In psalmum XII. ... paraphrasis. ... Marpurgi excusum in Officina Christiani Egenolphi. Mense Ianuario. Anno. M. D. XLII. a-d^8 e^4 f^8. ff. 3-44. [380

I

IAMBLICHUS. Index eorum, quae hoc in libro habentur. Iamblichus de mysteriis Ægyptiorum, Chaldæorum, Assyriorum. Proclus in Platonicum Alcibiadem de anima, atq3 dęmone. Proclus de sacrificio, & magia. Porphyrius de diuinis, atq3 dæmonibus. Synesius ... de somniis. Psellus de dæmonibus. Expositio Prisciani & Marsilii in Theophrastum de sensis, phantasia, & intellectu. Alcinoi ... liber de doctrina Platonis. Speusippi ... liber de Platonis definitionibus. Pythagoræ ... aurea verba. Symbola Pythagoræ ... Xenocratis ... liber de morte. Mercurii Trismegisti Pimander. Eiusdem Asclepius. Marsilii Ficini de triplici uita Lib. II. Eiusdem liber de uoluptate. Eiusdem de Sole & lumine libri. II. Apologia eiusdem in librum suum de lumine. Eiusdem libellus de magia. Quod necessaria sit securitas, & tranquillitas animi. ... (Venetiis in aedibus Aldi, et Andreae soceri mense Nouembri M.D.XVI.) fol. A-Y^8 (-Y8). ff. 2-177. (Smith.) [1

-- -- Iamblichus de mysteriis Aegyptiorum Chaldæorum, Assyriorum. Proclus in Platonicum Alcibiadem de Anima, atque Dæmone. Idem de sacrificio & magia. Porphyrius de Diuinis atq; dæmonib. Psellus de Dæmonibus. Mercurii Trismegisti Pimander. Eiusdem Asclepius. Lugduni Apud Ioan. Tornæsium. M. D. LII. 16°. a-z^8 A-L^8. pp. 3-543. (Lea.) [2

IBN ABI AL-RIJAL. Preclarissimus in Iudiciis Astrorum Albohazen Haly filius Abenragel ... (emēdat⁹ ꝑ dn̄m Bartolomeū ꝺ Alten de Nusia germanum ... Impressus [Venetiis] arte ⁊ īpēsis ꝑ. Io. bapti. Sessa. ... Mccccciij. die .iiij. Aprilis.) fol. B.L. A-Z^4 Et^6. ff. 2-98. [3

-- -- Albohazen Haly filii Abenragel libri de iudiciis astrorum, ... de extrema barbarie uindicati, ac latinitati donati, per Antonium Stupam Rhoetum Prægalliensem. ... Basileae ex officina Henrichi Petri. (... mense Martio. Anno M. D. LI.) fol. a^4 b^6 A-Kk^6 Ll^8. pp. 1-410. (Lea.) [4

-- -- Albohazen Haly filii Abenragel ... de iudiciis astrorum libri octo ... Accessit ... Compendium duodecim domorum coelestium, ex ... uetustissimis authoribus ... collectum ... Authore Petro Liechtenstein. ... Basileae, ex officina Henricpetrina. (... M. D. LXXI. mense Martio.) fol. a^6 a^2 A-Zz^6 AA-CC^6. pp. 1-586. [5

IBN SARAFYUN. Iani Damasceni Decapolitani summae inter Arabes autoritatis Medici, therapeuticę methodi ... Libri VII, partim Albano Torino Vitodurano Paraphraste, partim Gerardo Iatro Cremonensi metaphraste. ... Apud ... Basileam per Henrichum Petrum. (... mense Martio, Anno M. D. XLIII.) fol. a-b^6 A-Ss^6. pp. 1-451. [6

IESI. Statuta siue sanctiones, et ordinamenta Aesinae ciuitatis. Alphonsus Lallus Montegallus ... Cancellarius. (Impressum Maceratæ per Lucam Binum Mantuanum, Mense Ianuarii. ... M. D. LXI.) fol. ✠^{6} A-Q^6. ff. 1-96. ¶*Two leaves, the first signed ✠, perhaps belonging to the first gathering, are bound in at the end.* (Lea.) [7

IMOLA, JOANNES DE. [1] Repertorium super Commentariis Ioannis de Imola. ... Lugduni 1548 (Excudebat ... Ioannes Pullonus, alias de Tridino.) fol. B.L. a-h^8 i^{10}. [2] Ioannes de Imola Super Primo Decretalium. ... Accesserunt ... Ioannis de Gradibus ... Additiones ... 1549 (*Same colophon.*) A-MM^8. ff. 2-280. [3] ... Super Secundo Decre[talium]. ... 1547 (Excudebat Lugduni Georgius Regnault.) a-ee^8 ff-gg^6. ff. 2-235. ¶a1-4 *defective.* [4] ... Super Tertio Decretalium. Lugduni, 1547 Aa-Zz^8 3A-3K^8 3L-3M^6. ff. 2-275. ¶3M5 *defective.* (Biddle.) [8

-- [Commentarii super digestis.] Lugduni, 1547. (... excudebat Gaspar Trechsel.) fol. B.L. [1] Index operum Ioannis de Imola. ... A-E^8. [2] Ioannes de Imola, super Prima Infortiati. ... a-v^8 x-y^6. ff. 2-172. [3] ... super Secunda Infortiati. ... A-R^8. ff. 2-136. [4] ... super Prima Digesti noui. ... aa-oo^8 pp-qq^6. ff. 2-241. [5] ... super Secunda Digesti noui. ... AA-YY^8 ZZ-3A^6. ff. 2-187. (Biddle.) [9

-- Consilia Ioannis de Imola. [*Device of Jacobus Giunta.*] 1539 ([Lugduni,] Ioannes Moylin al's de Cambray excudebat.) fol. B.L. A^4 a-f^8 g^{10}. ff. 1-58. (Biddle.) [10

-- Ioannis de Imola ... In Quinto Decretalium Lectura ... edita per ... Hieronymum Gigantem ... Summarijs ... a ... Ioanne Baptista Zilletto decorata. fol. B.L. A-G^4 H^6. ff. 2-33. ¶*Dedication dated* vii. Calen. Decembris ... MDXLI. (Biddle.) [11

INDAGATIO. Indagatio succincta de vera religione: et qui nam specialiter religiosi sint nūcupandi. [c. 1510.] 12°. B.L. π^{6}. [12

INFIAMMATO. Gratiana fauola boscareccia del Infiamato. ... In Vicenza, Appresso Paulo Meieti. 1592. ... 8°. π^{2} A-E^{8} F^{10}. ff. 1-50. [13

INGOLSTADT. *University.* Consilium super iuribus et praeeminentia cancellariatus studii alicuius generalis. ... (Actū Ingolstadij, xvi. Maij, ... M. D. XXiX.) fol. A-D$^{4.6}$ E^{6}. [14

-- Disputatio De Maiestate hominis Christi, in ... Academia Ingolstadiana ... aduersus impias Iacobi Andreæ Schmidelini Theses ... Excudebant VVeissenhornij fratres Ingolstadij 1564. 4°. A-H^{4}. [15

-- Disputatio philosophica de plantis, ex Aristotele ... collecta ... publicè ꝓposita. Præside Iacobo Gretschero ... Respondente ... Casparo Bulling Nerisheimensi. Ingolstadii, Ex officina Typographica Wolfgangi Ederi, Anno M. D. LXXXXI. 4°. A-D^{4} E^{2}. pp. 1-28. [16

-- Expurgatio Rectoris et consilij ... gymnasij Ingolstadiensis ꝑ dn̄o Georgio zingel ... vicecancellario ... contra inuectiuā sub velamine apologie a Iacobo locher philomuso ... confictā. [Augsburg, Johannes Schönsperger, 1505.] 4°. B.L. a^{6} [b^{4}]. [17

-- Sibentzehen Artickel so die Doctorn/ der ... Vniuersitet Ingolstatt/ für Ketzerisch verdammet/ vnd Mayster Arsacij Seehofer vō München offentlich ... widerrufft hatt/ in dem 1523 Jar. [Augsburg, Philipp Ulhart, 1523.] 4°. A^{4}. [18

-- Succincta explicatio difficilimi pulcherrimique prooemii, primi libri physicorum, thesibus nonnullis compraehensa, quas ... in Catholico Ingolstadiensi Gymnasio, sub Præsidio ... Friderici Martini ... publicè tuebitur. F. Georgius Frey Rothensis. ... Ingolstadii Excudebat Dauid Sartorius. M.D.LXXV. 4°. A-C^{4}. [19

INNOCENT III, pope. D. Innocentii papae ... tertij in septem Psalmos poenitentiales Dauidis Commentaria ... Coloniæ, ex officina Melchioris Nouesiani M.D.Li. 8°. a^{8} A-V^{8}. ff. 1-141. [20

-- Liber de contemptu mundi, siue de miseria conditionis humanae, a Domino Innocentio papa tertio compositus. Lipsiae. M. D. XXXIIII. ... (... excudebat Michael Blum. ...) 4°. A-L^{4}. [21

INSTRUCTION. Cy commence vne petite instruction et maniere de viure pour vne femme seculiere. ... On les vend a Paris, en la rue Sainct Iacques, a lenseigne de la Limace, pres Sainct yues [Louis Royer or a predecessor, 1528 or earlier]. 8°. B.L. A-B^{8} C^{4} (-C4, *presumably blank*). [22

INSULANUS MENAPIUS, GULIELMUS. Oratio suasoria ad Carolum Caes. imp. aug. & Franciscum Galliarum regem, de pace & concordia inter ipsos constituenda. ... Basileae, anno M. D. XXXVII. (... in officina Roberti VVinter ... Mense Septembri.) 8°. a-c^{8}. pp. 4-44. [23

INTERROGATIONES. Interrogationes doctrine ... (Imprime a Rouen par Iehan moulin: pour Iehan Mace demourant a rennes: Michel angier demourant a Caen: et richard Mace demourant a rouen ...) 16°. B.L. π^{8}. [24

INTRATIONES. Intrationū excellentissimus liber (Impressum ... London̄ ... in officina ere ac impensis ... Ricardi Pynson ... M.CCCCC.x. Die vero vltima Mensis Februarij.) fol. B.L. Aa^{6} Bb^{4} a-z^{6} ⁊^{6} ꝯ^{6} A-E^{6} F^{4} (-F4, *presumably blank*). ff. j°-c.lxxxv. *S.T.C.* 14116. (Biddle.) [25

-- Intrationum liber ... Excudebat Henricus Smythe ... M.D.XLVI. (... London̄ ... M.CCCCC.XLV die vero primo mensis Nouembris.) fol. B.L. A-D^{6} A-Z^{6} a-s^{6}. ff. i-cc.xliiii. *S.T.C.* 14117. (Biddle.) [26

INTRODUCTIO. Introductio q̄dam vtilissima/ siue Vocabularius quattuor linguarū latine Italice/ Gallice et Alamanice ... (Getruckt in der ... stat Augspurg durch Erhart öglin im jar ... tausend fünff hundert vnd sechtzehen iar am zwölfften tag des Mörtzen.) 4°. A-M^{4}. [27

INTRODUCTORIUM. Elementale introductorium in Nominum, & Verborum declinationes Græcas. ... Item Hieronymi Aleandri Mottensis tabulæ ... (Argentorati, Ex Aedibus Schurerianis, Mense Martio, ann. M. D. XIIII.) 4°. A-D^4 (-D4, *presumably blank*). [28

IRENAEUS, S. Opus eruditissimum Diui Irenaei episcopi Lugdunensis in quinque libros digestum ... emendatum opera Des. Erasmi Roterodami ... Apud ... Basileam anno M. D. XXVI. ... (... apud Ioan. Frob. mense Augusto ...) fol. a-z^6 A-E^6 F^8 G^6. pp. 2-338. [29

IRENAEUS, JOHANNES. Lob vnd vnschuldt der Ehefrauwen. ... Jetzt auss Pommerischer Sprach in Meissnische gebracht ... Durch Andream Hondorff ... Gedruckt zu Franckfurt am Mayn/ M. D. LXIX. (... durch Peter Schmid/ in verlegniss Hieronymi Feyerabends.) fol. A-I^6 K^8. ff. I-LIIII. [30

IRENICUS, FRANCISCUS. Germaniae exegeseos volumina duodecim a Francisco Irenico Ettelingiacensi exarata ... Vrbis Norinbergæ descriptio, Conrado Celte ennarratore. ... (Elaboratum ... typis ac formulis Thomæ Anshelmi, Hagenoæ ... Sumptibus ... Ioannis Kobergii Norinbergeñ. ... M. D. XVIII. Mense Augusto.) fol. π^6 a-z^6 A-T^6 V^8. ff. I-CCXXI. [31

ISABELLA, queen of Hungary. Vier warhafftige Missiuen/ eine der frawen Isabella Kᵒnigin ... in Vngern/ wie vntrewlich der Türck vnd die iren mit ir vmbgangen. Die ander/ eines so in der belegerung bey der Kᵒnigin im Schloss gewest ... Die dritte/ eines Vngern von Gran/ wie es yetz zu Ofen zugehe. Die vierdte/ des Türckischen Tyrannen an die Sibenbürger. Auss dem Latein ins Teutsch gebracht. 4°. a-c^4. ¶*Third letter dated 1541.* [32

ISIDORE, S. Praeclarissimum opus diui Isidori Hyspalensis ...: quod ęthimologiarum intitulat̄ ... (Impressum Parrhisii Opa Iohānis barbier sūptibus Iohannis petit. Anno ... Millesimo quingentesimonono vltim[o] die Mensis Augusti.) fol. a^8 b-r^6 (-r6, *presumably blank*). ff. II-CIII. ¶a1 *defective*. [33

ISOCRATES. *Collections*. Isocratis orationes omnes, ... vna et viginti numero, vnà cum nouem eiusdem Epistolis, è Græco in Latinum conuersæ, per Hieronymum VVolfium Oetingensem. ... Basileae, per Ioannem Oporinum. (... M.D.XLVIII. Mense Augusto.) fol. α^6 A-Gg^4 Hh-Ii^6 aa-yy^4 zz^6 (-zz6, *presumably blank*). pp. 2-251, cols. 1-226, pp. 227-281. [34

-- [1] Ισοκρατους απαντα. Isocratis scripta, quae quidem nunc extant, omnia, Græcolatina ... Hieronymo VVolfio Oetingensi interprete & auctore. ... Basileae, ex officina Oporiniana. 1570. fol. α^6 a-z^6 A-H^6 I^8. cols. 1-738. [2] Hieronymi VVolfii ... Annotationes ... *Same imprint*. (... per Polycarpum et Hieronymum Gemusaeos, & Balthasarum Han, ... Mense Martio.) *^{4} a-z^6 A-P^6. cols. 1-846. [35

-- -- Basileae, ex officina Oporiniana. 1571. (... Mense Martio.) 8°. a-z^8 A-Zz^8 (-Q3-5) AA-FF^8. pp. 1-1121. ¶Q2, FF8 *defective*. [36

-- -- 1587. (... Mense Augusto.) 8°. *Same collation and pagination*. [37

-- -- Basileae, per Hieronymum Gemusæum. 1594. (... ex officina Oporiniana, ... Mense Martio.) 8°. *Same collation and pagination*. [38

-- -- Ισοκρατους λογοι και επιστολαι. Isocratis orationes et epistolae cum Latina interpretatione Hier. VVolfij ... Henr. Steph. in Isocratem Diatribæ VII ... Gorgiae et Aristidis quædam ... Guil. Cantero interprete. [Genevae,] Excudebat Henricus Stephanus anno M. D. XCIII. fol. [symbol]^4 *^{6} **^{4} a-mm^6 nn^4 Aa-Ll^6 A-C^6 D^4 α-δ^4 a^4 b^6. pp. 1-427, 1-131, II-XXXIIII, 1-31. [39

-- *Two or more works*. Ισοκρατους λογι τρεις ... Isocratis orationes tres Euagoras I. In Philippum II. De pace III. Vænundantur ab Iodoco Badio & Ioanne Vatello. 4°. a-l^4. [40

-- Ισοκρατους λογοι απαντες. Isocratis ... orationes ... Haganoæ ex Officina Seceriana, Mense Septembri. Anno M.D.XXXIII. 8°. A-XX^8. ff. 4-354. [41

-- Enseignements d'Isocrates et Xenophon ... Pour bien regner en paix & en guerre. Traduictz de Grec en François, par Loys le Roy dict Regius de Costentin. ... A Paris, Par Vascosan ... M. D. LXVIII. ... 4°. A-M^4. pp. 4-95. [42

-- -- [1] Enseignmens d'Isocrates ... pour induire les ieunes gens, & tous autres, à viure honnestement, & aymer la vertu. Ensemble autres Enseignmens dudict Autheur & de Xenophon, pour bien regner en paix & en guerre. Par Loys Le Roy. A Paris, Chez Federic Morel ... 1579. ... 8°. a-c^8. pp. 3-48. [2] Enseignments d'Isocrate et Xenophon ... *Same imprint.* A-L^8 (-L8). pp. 1-171. [43

-- *Ad Demonicum.* Isocratis ad Demonicū Paranesis: ... per Philippū Beroaldum Iuniorem latinitate donata. Cōplures itē Esopi et Auiani fabelle ... ab Hadriano Barlando ... mutate et aucte. ... (Excusa Augustę Vindelicorū in officina Ioannis Miller IX. Kal'. Iañ ... M. D. XV.) 4°. B.L. A-B^4 C^6. [44

-- -- Oratione d'Isocrate à Demonico ... di Latino in volgare, tradotta da Madonna Chiara Matraini ... In Fiorenza MDLVI. (Stampata ... per Messer Lorenzo Torrentino. ...) 8°. A-B^8. [45

-- *Ad Nicoclem.* In hoc libello ... continentur. Isocratis, de regno gubernando ad Nicolem liber, a Martino Philetico interprete ... Quintii Hæmiliani Cimbriaci ... Comitis Palatini, Epicoedion Tetracolon in diuum Fride. III. Imp. ..., cū Epistola liminari Iacobi Spiegel ... Aloisii Marliani Mediolanen. ... Epistola ... qua Calamitosa Philippi Hispaniæ regis, in Hispaniam nauigatio graphice describitur. Ioachimi Vadiani Heluetii Carmē, ... Friderici .III. patris & Filii Maximiliani, laudes continēs. ... Iacobi Vuimphelingii Selestēsis ... expurgatio contra detractores. (Leonhardus & frater eius Lucas Alantsee ... prodire uoluerūt in lucē, ... Imprimētibus ... Hieronymo Vietore & Ioanne Singrenio ... Viennæ Austriæ Idibus Februarii. Anno M. D. XIIII.) 4°. A-D^4 E-F^6 G-M^4. [46

-- -- La royale et antique oraison composee par Isocrates ... traduict de Grec en Latin par maistre Iean-Loys Viues ..., & de Latin en Françoys par Guy de la Garde ... A Lyon, par Tibauld Payan, M. D. LIX. ... 8°. A-D^8 E^4. pp. 3-72. [47

-- -- Isocrates dela gouernacion del reyno. Al Rey Nicocles. Agapeto Del officio y cargo de Rey ... Dion Dela institucion del Principe ... Traduzidos de lengua Griega en Castellana ... Por ... Diego Gracian. En Salamanca Por Mathias Gast Año M. D. LXX. (*Colophon.*) 8°. A-O^8 (-O8, *presumably blank*). pp. 1-204. [48

-- *De pace.* Isocratis oratio de pace Honofrio Bartholino ... interprete *Greek & Latin.* 8°. [A]^4 B-E^4 A-E^4 F^6 (-F6, *presumably blank*). [49

-- *Evagoras.* Praxis rhetorica generis demonstratiui, in Euagoram Isocratis, exposita a Nicolao Roscio Vicetino ... Cum eiusdem orationis explicatione. Veronæ, Ex typographia Hieronymi Discipuli, M D LXXXVII. 4°. A-M^4 N^2. pp. 1-91. [50

J

JĀBIR AL HAYAN. Alchemiae Gebri ... Ioañ. Petreius Nurembergeñ. denuo Bernæ excudi faciebat. Anno M. D. XLV. (Excusum Bernae ... per Mathiam Apiarium ... Mense Augusti.) 4°. aa-bb^4 a-z^4 A-P^4. pp. 6-302. (Smith.) [1

-- -- *Another copy.* (Smith.) [2

-- In hoc volumine de alchemia continentur hæc. Gebri ... De inuestigatiõe ꝑfectionis metalloꝝ. Liber I. Summæ perfectionis metallorum, siue perfecti magisterij. Libri II. ... Eiusdem De inuentione ueritatis seu perfectionis metallorum. Liber I. De Fornacibus construendis. Liber I. Item. Speculũ Alchimiæ ... Rogerij Bachonis. Correctoriũ Alchemiæ ... Richardi Anglici. Rosarius minor ... Liber Secretorũ Alchemiæ Calidis filij Iazichi Iudæi. Tabula Smaragdina de Alchemia, Hermetis Trismeg. Hortulani ... super Tabulam Smaragdinam ... Commentarius. ... Norimbergæ apud Ioh. Petreium, Anno M. D. XLI. (... Mense Augusto.) 4°. aa-bb^4 cc^2 a-z^4 A-Z^4 &^{4}. pp. 1-373. ¶*Editor: Polydorus Chrysogonus.* (Smith.) [3

JACOBAEUS, VITUS. Academia Ingolstadiensis Carmine illustrata ... Ingolstadii excudebant Alexander, & Samuel Vueissenhornij, fratres Germani. Anno M.D.LXII. 4°. A-F^4. [4

JACOBAZZI, DOMENICO. Reuerendiss. ... patris D. Dominici card. Iacobatii. de consilio tractatus (Romae Excudebat Antonius Bladus Mense Octobri ... M. D. XXXVIII) fol. ✠^{4} ✠^{6} ✠✠^{6} ✠✠✠^{4} A-Zz^6 AA-SS^6 TT^8. pp. 1-783. ¶*Engraved t.p.* (Lea.) [4a

JACOBUS MAGDALIUS, GAUDENSIS. Orariũ aureum poetaꝝ oĩib^9 ... (exaratũ Colonie In officina salubris memorię Henrici Quentell Anno .cccccij. xvij. calendas Ianuarias) 4°. A-B^6 C^4 D^8 E-H$^{4.6}$. [5

-- Stichologia gaudensis. Enchiridion Poetarum. Homeomata Eorundem. Naumachia ecclesiastica cũ carminibus diuersis. (in officina bonę memorię Henrici Quentel ... ĩpressi ... M.ccccciij tercio nonas februarias.) 4°. A^6 B^4 C-H$^{6.6.4}$ I^6 K^4. [6

JACOBUS, PETRUS. Aurea practica libellorum ... (Impressum lugduni per magistrum Iacobum Sacon ... Anno dñi Millesimo quingentesimoꝑmo die sexta mensis nouembris.) 4°. B.L. a-z^8 ꝛ^8 ɔ^8 ꝶ^8 A^6. ff. ij-ccxiij. [7

JACQUIER, NICOLAS. Flagellum hæreticorum fascinariorum ... His recens accesserunt D. Lamberti Danaei de Veneficis, quos vulgo Sortiarios vocant, dialogi. D. Ioachim Camerarii Pabebergensis, in Plutarchi de Oraculorum defectu, epistola. D. Martini de Arles ... de Superstitionibus tractatus. Ioannis Trithemii de Reprobis atq; Maleficis quaestiones III. ... Item D. Thomae Erasti de Strigibus liber. Summa studio & industria F. Ioan. Myntzenbergij ... edita. ... Francofurti ad Moenum, M. D. LXXXI. (Impressum ... apud Nicolaum Bassæum ...) 8°. *-**^{8} 3*^{2} A-Z^8 a-p^8. pp. 1-604. (Lea.) [8

JAHRZAHL. Warhafftige vnnd gewise jarzal aller Zeiten vnd Jaren von Adam ... M D XXXVII. ... (Gedruckt zu Nůrenberg durch Ieronimum Formschneyder.) 4°. [a]^4. [9

JAMOT, FEDERIC. Federici Iamotii medici Bethuniensis varia poemata Græca & Latina. ... Antuerpiæ, Ex officina Plantiniana, Apud Viduam, & Ioannem Moretum. M. D. XCIII. 4°. A-S^4. pp. 2-141. [10

JAMYN, AMADIS. Les oeuures poetiques ... A Paris, Par Mamert Patisson ... au logis de Robert Estienne. M. D. LXXIX. ... 12°. *^{4} A-Z^{12} a-c^{12} (-c12). ff. 1-309. ¶*Wormholes in the last 24 leaves.* [11

JANSEN, CORNELIUS. Cornelii Ianseni ... commentariorum in suam Concordiam, ac totam Historiam Euangelicam partes quatuor. ... Venetiis, Apud Hæredes Melchioris Sessæ. M. D. LXXIX. fol. †^{8} ††^{10} A-Y^8 Z^6 AA-MM^8 NN^4 OO-3H^8. pp. 1-854. ¶*Additional t.pp.:* (M1^r) ... Pars secunda ... *Same imprint.* (AA1^r) ... Pars tertia ... *Same imprint.* (OO1^r) ... Pars IIII. et vltima ... *Same imprint.* [12

JANUS PANNONIUS. Iani Pannonii ... Ad Guarinum Veronensem panegyricus. Eiusdem Elegiarum liber. Et Epigrammatum Syluula. Item Lazari Bonamici Carmina nonnulla. Venetiis, Apud Gualterum Scottum. M D LIII. (*Colophon.*) 8°. A-S8. pp. 3-286. [13

-- Iani Pannonii ... Elegiarũ aureum opusculum. ... (Hieronymus Vietor, & Io. Singrenius Viennæ imprimebãt.) 4°. A-D4. ¶*Letter on* D4v *dated* Pridie Idus Martias. 1514. [14

JAQUEMOT, JEAN. Agrippa ecclesiomastix. Tragoedia ... Genevae, Excudebat Matthæus Berjon. cIↃ. IↃ. XCVII. 8°. A-F8. pp. 3-95. [15

-- Ioannis Iacomoti Barrensis musae Neocomenses. [Genevae,] Excudebat Matthæus Berjon. cIↃ. IↃ. XCVII. 8°. Aa-Pp8. pp. 3-237. [16

JAUDIN, GUILLAUME. Practique pour faire enquestes et examiner tesmoings ... A Lyon, par Ben[o]ist Rigaud. [1]581. 16°. A-R8. pp. 3-258. ¶*T.p. defective.* [17

JAVELLO, CRISOSTOMO. Chrysostomi Iauelli Canapicii in omnibus metaphysicae libris Quæsita testualia Metaphysicali modo determinata. ... Venetijs, Apud Ioannem Mariam Bonellum. M. D. LXVIII. (*Colophon.*) 8°. *-**8 a-z8 A-DD8. ff. 1-399. [18

-- Chrisostomi Iauelli ... Super Octo libros Aristo. de Physico Auditu quaestiones ... Venetiis Apud Hieronymum Scotum 1552 8°. *8 **4 A-EE8 FF4. ff. 1-236. [19

-- Chrisostomi Iauelli ... super Tres libros Arist. de Anima quaestiones ... Venetiis Apud Hieronymum Scotum 1552 8°. *8 **4 aa-zz8 &&8 ↄↄ8 ꝝꝝ4. ff. 1-207. [20

JERIN, ANDREAS, bishop of Breslau. Etliche Sendbrieffe/ Zum zeugnis/ das der Gůldene Zahn noch heutiges tages gůlden/ vnd kein betrug sey. ... Leipzig. ... (Gedruckt ... bey Michael Lantzenberger. ... M. D. XCvj. In verlegung Valentini Vögelini/ Buchhändlers.) 8°. a-b8. pp. 1-30. (School of Dentistry.) [21

JEROME, S. [1] Omnium operum diui Eusebii Hieronymi Stridonensis tomus primus ... cum argumentis et scholiis Des. Erasmi Roterodami ... Apud ... Basileam ex acuratissima officina Frobeniana. fol. α6 β8 (-α5-β8) γ6 δ8 a8 b-s6 t8 u-z6. ff. 1-141. ¶u-z6 *misbound at the end of tomus secundus.* [2] ... tomus secundus ... Basileae. M. D. XVI. [A]6 (-[A]2-3) B-Gg6 Hh8 Ii-Pp6 (-Hh8v-Ii3r) Qq8. ff. 5-238. ¶[A]1 *defective.* [3] Tertius tomus epistolarum diui Eusebii Hieronymi ... AA-XX6 YY8 ZZ6 3a-3e6. ff. 2-169. [4] Tomus quartus epistolarum ... (In ... officina Iohannis Frobenij, apud ... Basileam. Anno .M.D.XVI.) 3A-3Z6 3&6 3ꝝ6. ff. 2-149. [5] Quintus tomus operum ... A-L8 M-Vu6 Xx8 (-Xx8, *blank*). ff. 2-287. [6] Tomus nonus operum ... (Basileae in aedibus Io. Frobennii. Impendio Brunonis, Basilii et Bonifacii Amorbachiorum, ac Ioannis Frobennii ... et Iacobi Rechburgii ... mense Maio. an. M.D.XVI.) a-x6 y4 z6 A-H6 I10 K6 L8. ff. 2-203. ¶*Many pages of this set have been defaced by a former owner.* [22

-- Epistole di S. Girolamo ... Con vna Regola del ... viuere per le Monache ne Monasteri. ... tradotte ... per Giouanfrancesco Zeffi Fiorentino. ... In Venetia nella Stamperia de Giunti. M D LXII. (... M D LXI.) 4°. *-**8 a-3a8 3b6 (-3b6, *presumably blank*). ff. 2-381. [23

-- Epistolas del ... sant Hieronymo. Traduzidas de latin en romance ... por ... Iuan de Molina ... En Burgos por Luys Ortiz y cõpañia, 1554 (... impresso ... en casa de Pedro de Santillana ...) fol. B.L. ✠8 A-Z8 a-g8 h-i6. ff. j-cclij. [24

-- Septẽ diui Hieronymi epistole ... cũ Iohãnis Aesticampiani ... et Epistola ꝛ Sapphico carmine. aliorumq3 ... virorum Epigrãmatibus. ... (Impressum Lypczk ꝑ Melchiorem Lotter ... M.ccccc.viij.) 4°. B.L. A-H6. [25

-- Diui Hieronymi in vitas patrum percelebre opus ... Venundantur Lugduni ab Iacobo huguetan ... ([Impressis Per ... Iacobum Sachon ... M.ccccc.xij. die ꝟo. xx. mẽsis Octobris.]) 4°. A6 a-y8 z4 (-x8, y8, z4). ff. i-clxvij *present.* [26

JESUITS. Iesuiter Spiegel. Das ist: Kurtze Anzeig/ darauss zusehen/ erstlich/ warzu der Iesuiter Orden gestifft ... wie sie sich bisshero in Franckreich gehalten ... Anno M. D. XCVI. 8°. A-Q8 R4. pp. 1-259. [27

-- Newe Zeitung/ Wie ein Iesuwider in Teuffels gestalt/ ein Euangelisch Mensch/ von jhrem

Glauden wollen abschrecken/ vnd darüber erstochen worden/ geschehen in Augspurg. Andere Zeitung. Auch von einem Iesuwider ... Anno 1569. 4°. A^6. ¶*In verse.* [28

JESUS, SOCIETY OF. Auuisi del Giapone de gli anni M.D.LXXXII. LXXXIII. et LXXXIV. Con alcuni altri della Cina dell' LXXXIII. et LXXXIV. Cauati dalle lettere della Compagnia di Giesù. ... In Roma, Per Francesco Zanetti. M. D. LXXXVI. ... 8°. A-M^8. pp. 3-188. [29

-- [1] Epistolæ Iapanicæ, de multorum gentilium in varijs Insulis ad Christi fidem per Societatis nominis Iesu Theologos conuersione. ... Louanii, Apud Rutgerum Velpium, ... 1569. 8°. 1-3^8 A-R^8 S^4. pp. 2-263. [2] Epistolæ Iapanicae ... Pars altera. *Same imprint.* A^8 b-t^8 v^4. pp. 3-310. (Lea.) [30

-- Literae apostolicae, quibus institutio, confirmatio, Et varia priuilegia continentur Societatis Iesu. Romae, In Collegio eiusdem Societatis M. D. LXXVIII. ... 8°. π^2 A-L^8 M^{8+1}. pp. 1-192. [31

-- Nuoui auisi dell'Indie di Portogallo, riceuuti dalli ... Padri della compagnia di Giesu, tradotti dalla lingua Spagnuola nell'Italiana. M D LXVIII. (In Venetia per Michele Tramezzino ...) 8°. A^4 A-G^8 H^4 (-H4, *presumably blank*). ff. 1-59. (Lea.) [32

JEWEL, JOHN. A replie vnto M. Hardinges ansvveare ... Imprinted at London ... by Henry VVykes. Vicesimo Ianuarij. Anno. 1566. ... fol. B.L. $¶^6$ $*^6$ $¶^6$ $¶¶^8$ A^4 B-$3H^6$ $3I^4$ (-3I4, *blank*). pp. 1-641. *S.T.C.* 14607. (Yarnall.) [32a

JOACHIM OF FIORE. Expositio magni prophete Abbatis Ioachim in Apocalipsim. ... Cui adiecta sunt. ⊄ Eiusdē psalteriū dece3 cordaꝝ ... ⊄ Lectura ... in Apocalipsi3 ... Philippi de Mantua ... ([EE8r:] Venetijs in Edibus Francisci Bindoni: ac Maphei Pasini socij. ... 1527. Die vero septimo Februarij.) 4°. B.L. A^4 aa-cc^8 dd^4 A-NN^8 OO^4 (-OO4, *presumably blank*). ff. 2-280. ¶*Additional t.p.* (FF1r): Psalterium decem cordarum Abbatis Ioachim. ... (... Die. XVIII. mensis Martii.) NN1-OO3: ... Tabula ... (... Die vero .xvij. mensis Aprilis.) *The* Lectura *of Philip of Mantua is not present.* (Lea.) [33

-- Abbas Ioachim magnus propheta. ⊄ Hec subiecta in hoc continentur libello. Expositio ... Ioachim: in libru3 beati Cirilli de magnis tribulationib9 ꝛ statu ... ecclesie: ... vna cu3 cōpilatione ex diuersis ꝓphetꝭ ... Theolosphori de Cusentia ... ⊄ Item explanatio ... in Apochalypsi3 de residuo statu ecclesie: ꝛ de trib9 veh vēturis debitis ... ⊄ Item tractatus de antichristo ... Ioānis parisiensis ... ⊄ Item tractatus de septem statib9 ecclesie ... Vbertini de Casali ... (Impressum Venetijs per Laçaꝝ de Soardis. 1516. Die .5. Aprilis.) 4°. B.L. A-T^4. ff. 2-76. (Lea.) [34

-- -- *Another copy.* (Lea.) [35

-- ... Abbatis Ioachim liber cōcordie noui ac veteris Testamenti ... (Venetijs completus fuit ... per Simonem de Luere .13. Aprilis. .1519.) 4°. B.L. a-y^4 $ç^4$ aa-mm^4. ff. 1-135. (Lea.) [36

-- -- *Another copy.* (Lea.) [37

-- ... Abbatis Ioachim florensis scriptu3 super Esaiam prophetam ... (Impressum Venetijs per Laçarum de Soardis. 1517. Die .27. Iunij.) 4°. B.L. aa^8 bb-qq^4. ff. 1-59. (Lea.) [38

-- -- *Another copy.* (Lea.) [39

-- Magnus Abbas Ioachim. ... scriptu3 super Hieremiam prophetam ... (Impressus Venetijs per Laçaru3 de Soardis. 1516. Die .12. Iunij.) 4°. B.L. a^2 b-c^4 d^8 e-f^4 g^8 h^4 i^8 k-l^4 m^6 n^4. ff. 1-61. (Lea.) [40

-- -- *Another copy.* (Lea.) [41

-- [1] Vaticinia, Siue Prophetiæ Abbatis Ioachimi, & Anselmi Episcopi Marsicani ... Vaticinii ouero Profetie ... con le Prefatione, et Annotationi di Pasqualino Regiselmo. *Latin & Italian.* Venetijs M.DC. ... Apud Ioannem Baptistam Bertonum. ... 4°. a-d^4 A-O^4. ¶*Engraved t.p.* [2] Vaticinia seu praedictiones illustrium virorum sex rotis ære incisis comprænsa De successione Summ. Pontificis Rom. Cum ... annotationibus, Hieronymi Ioannini. Vaticini ... d'huomini illustri ... In Venetia Appresso Gio. Battista Bertoni ... M.DC. A^6 B-I^4. ff. 4-36. [42

JOANNES CANONICUS. Ioãnis Canonici qõnes super .VIII. lib. phy. Aristo. ... (Venetijs mãdato heredu3 ... Octauiani Scoti ... ꝛ sociorum. ... 1520. die .8. Maij.) fol. B.L. A^8 $a\text{-}g^8$ h^{10} (-h10, *blank*). ff. 2-8, 1-65. [43

JOANNES OF HILDESHEIM. Historia gloriosissimoꝝ triũ regum integra. ... Sequit̃ sup̱ Matthei Euãgeliũ de festo Egyphanie ... Alberti magni elucidatio. Adijciunt̃ ... Augustini ... sermones tres. ... (Impressa ... Colonie in officina ... liberoꝝ Quẽtell. Anno. M.CCCCC.xiiij. ad Aprilem.) 4°. B.L. $a\text{-}i^{6.6.4}$. [44

JOANNES DE JANDUNO. Habes ... Librorũ meteororũ Aristotelis ... expositionem ... Iohãnis Dullaert de Gãdauo ... (Impresse vero Parrisius a Thoma Kees wesaliense ... 1512. 22. Aprilis.) fol. B.L. $[A]^2$ B^6 c^6 $d\text{-}f^4$ g^6. [45

-- Questiones Ioãnis Iandoni de celo ꝛ mũdo. ... (Venetijs mandato ... Heredum ... Octauiani Scoti ... ac socioꝝ: ... 1519. die .24. Septẽb.) fol. B.L. $aa\text{-}ee^6$. ff. 2-30. [46

-- -- Ioannis de Ianduno In Libros Aristotelis De Coelo & Mundo quaestiones ... adiecimus Auerrois sermonem de substantia orbis, Cum eiusdem Ioannis Commentario ... Venetiis apud Hieronymum Scotum. 1552 (*Colophon.*) fol. $*^4$ $AA\text{-}HH^8$ (-HH8, *blank*). ff. 2-63. [47

-- ... Iohãnis de ianduno qõnes in duodecim libros metaphysice ad intentionẽ Aristotelis. ꝛ ... Auerrois ... disputate. ... Marciantonij zimara annotationes ... (Impresse venetijs mandato ... heredum ... Octauiani Scoti ... Per Bonetum Iocatelum ... octauo idus Martias. i505.) fol. B.L. $A\text{-}M^6$ N^{10} $O\text{-}R^8$ $S\text{-}AA^6$. ff. 2-180. [48

-- Questiones super octo libros phisicorum aristotelis necnon super libros de celo et mundo Magistri Ioannis dullaert de gandauo. Venales reperiuntur ... apud Oliuerium senant ... (... parisius ... impensis ... Oliuerij senant solertia ... Nicolai depratis ... anno dñi millesimo quingentesimo sexto vigesima tertia martij.) fol. B.L. a^8 $b\text{-}t^6$. [49

-- -- Questiones Ioannis de Ianduno de physico auditu ... Helie hebrei Cretensis questiones De primo motore De efficientia mundi De esse essentia ꝛ vno ... (Impressum Venetijs [per Bonetum Locatellum?] ... M.cccccvj. die viij. mensis Maij ...) fol. B.L. π^4 $A\text{-}T^8$. ff. 1-151. [50

-- -- Iandon super physica Questiones ... Ioãnis de Gãdauo ... in octo Libros Aristotelis de physico Auditu p̱ recognitionem .V.P. Ioãnis Romberch Kyrspẽsis ... Qõnes Helie hebrei Cretẽsis. ... (Venetijs arte ꝛ Impensis domini Luceantonij de Giunta Florentini. ... 1520. die primo Martij.) fol. B.L. $♣^8$ $A\text{-}T^8$. ff. 1-151. [51

-- Ioannis de Ianduno ... Super Libros Aristotelis de Anima ... quaestiones ... Venetiis apud Hieronymum Scotum. M D LII (*Colophon.*) fol. $*^8$ $A\text{-}M^8$ $N\text{-}O^6$. ff. 1-107. [52

-- Io. Gandauensis ... Quęstiones, Super Paruis Naturalibus, cum Marci Antonii Zimaræ de mouente Et Moto ... quæstione ... per Albratium Apulum ... emendatæ ... Venetiis, apud Hieronymum Scotum. M D LXX. fol. $*^2$ $A\text{-}V^4$. pp. 1-159. [53

JOANNES PHILOPONUS. Ιωαννου γραμματικου του Φιλοπονου ... υπομνημα. Μαγεντινου σχολια ... Ioan. Gram. Philoponi comentaria in priora analytica Aristotelis. Magentini comentaria in eadem Libellus de syllogismis. ... M D XXXVI. (Venetiis in ædibus Bartholomæi Zanetti Casterzagensis, ære vero, & diligentia Ioannis Francisci Trincaueli ... Mense Aprili.) fol. A^6 $B\text{-}E^8$ $f\text{-}o^8$ p^{10} $aa\text{-}ee^8$ ff^6. ff. II-CXIX, I-XXXXV. [54

-- Ιωαννου γραμματικου ... κατα Προκλου ... Ioannis grammatici Philoponi Alexandrini contra Proclum de mundi aeternitate. ... (Venetiis in ædibus Bartholomæi Casterzagensi, ære ... Ioannis Francisci Trincaueli. ... M.D.XXXV. Mense Maio.) fol. A^4 $B\text{-}L^8$. [55

-- -- *Another copy.* [56

-- Ιωαννης ο γραμματικος εις το περι γενεσεως, και φθορας. Αλεξανδρος ο Αφροδισιευς εις τα μετεωρολογικα. Ο αυτος περι μιξεως. Ioannes Grammaticus in libros de generatione, et interitu. Alexander Aphrodisiensis in meteorologica. Idem de mixtione. ... (Venetiis in aedibus Aldi, et Andreae Asulani soceri anno M. D. XXVII. mense Septembri.) fol. $*^2$ $A\text{-}H^8$ I^6 $K\text{-}S^8$ T^6. ff. 1-147. [57

-- Ioannis grammatici in Posteriora resolutoria Aristotelis Comentaria. ... *Greek*. (Venetiis apud Aldum mense Martio. M. DIIII.) fol. $a\text{-}r^8$ $s\text{-}t^6$ u^8 x^4. pp. 3-295. [58

-- -- Ἰωάννου του γραμματικου, εἰς τὰ ὕστερα ἀναλυτικὰ Ἀριστοτέλους, ὑπόμνημα.

Ἀνωνύμου εἰς τὰ αὐτά. Εὐστρατίου εἰς τὰ αὐτά. Ioannis Grammatici in posteriora resolutoria Aristotelis, commentarium. Incerti authoris in eadem. Eustratii in eadem. ... M D XXXIIII. (Venetiis, in Aedibus hæredum Aldi Manutii Romani, & Andreæ Asulani Soceri, Mense Decembri. ...) fol. a-p^8 q^4 aa-hh^8 ii^4. ff. 3-123, 1-67. [59

-- -- Commentaria Ioannis Grammatici Alexandrei cognomento Philoponi in libros posteriorum Aristotelis. Recens cum Græco exemplari per ... Theodosium collata. ... Venetiis apud Hieronymum Scotum. 1548 (*Colophon.*) fol. A-Q^4. ff. 2-64. [60

JOANNES STOBAEUS. ... Ιωαννου του Στοβαιου εκλογαι αποφθεγματων. Ioannis Stobei Sententiæ ... à Conrado Gesnero ... traductæ ... *Greek & Latin.* Tiguri excudebat Christoph. Froschouerus, anno M. D. XLIII. fol. α-β^6 A-Z^6 a-z^6 Aa-Yy^6. pp. 1-300, ff. 301-536. [61

-- -- Κέρας Ἀμαλθαίας. Ιωαννου του Στοβαιου εκλογαι αποφθεγματων και υποθεκων. Ioannis Stobæi Sententię ex thesauris Græcorum delectæ ... in Sermones siue Locos communes digestę, à Conrado Gesnero ... *Greek and Latin.* Basileae. (... ex officina Ioannis Oporini, sumptibus Christophori Froschoueri, ... M.D.XLIX, Mense Augusto.) fol. α^6 β^4 A-Z^6 Aa-Zz^6 AA-FF^6 GG^4 HH-II^6 KK^4. pp. 2-630. (Lea.) [62

-- -- Ioannis Stobaei sententiae, ex thesauris Graecorum collecta ... per Conradum Gesnerum, ... Latinitati donata. Parisiis, Apud Martinum Iuuenem ... 1552. (... Calend. Maii. ...) 16°. aa-ff^8 gg^{12} a-z^8 A-Nn^8. pp. 1-1041. ¶*Includes also:* Theoctisti sententiae; Cyri Theodori Prodromi dialogus, de exilio amicitiae; Dialogus incerti authoris ... in quo agitur, An virtus doceri possit; Alter dialogus ... in quo docetur, iustitiam esse scientiam; Solonis elegia, citata à Demosthene, ... conuersa à Philippo Melanthone. [63

-- -- Ioannis Stobæi eclogarum libri duo: Quorum prior Physicas, posterior Ethicas complectitur; nunc primùm Græcè editi; Interprete Gulielmo Cantero. Vnà & G. Gemisti Plethonis de rebus Peloponnes, orationes duæ ... Accessit ... eiusdem Plethonis libellus Græcus De virtutibus. ... Antuerpiæ, Ex officina Christophori Plantini ... M. D. LXXV. (... sexto Kalend. Iunii. ...) fol. *^{6} A-Q^6 R^8 S-T^6 V^4. pp. 2-236. ¶*Additional t.p.* (S1^r): Πληθωνος ... πηρι των εν Πελοποννησω πραγματων. ... Plethonis ... orationes duæ. ... *Same imprint.* [64

-- -- Ioannis Stobei Scharpffsinniger Sprüche/ auss den schrifften der ... Griechen ... Durch Georgen Frölich/ genant Letus/ von der Lömnitz ... inn Teütsche sprache gebracht ... M. D. L. ... (Gedruckt zů Basel/ by Iohann Herbst/ genant Oporino/ ... Tusend/ fünffhundert/ fünfftzig vnd ein Jar.) fol. A^6 b-z^6 A-Z^6 aa^6 bb^8. pp. ij-ccccclxvj. [65

JOANNES DE STYNNA. Speculator abbreuiatus, al's Speculum abbreuiatum Ioannis de Stynnia: cũ varijs libellorũ & instrumentorũ tam in iudicijs/ q̄ȝ in contractibus occurrentiũ ... formis ... M.D. Xi. ... fol. B.L. a-z^6 A-I^6 K^8. ff. 2-199. ¶B1, B6 *misbound after* B3. (Lea.) [66

JOBST, WOLFGANG. Omnium academiarum, et quarundam illustrium Scholarum totius Europæ, Erectiones, Fundationes & Confirmationes ... Authore M. Guolphgango Iusto Francophordiano. M. D. LIIII. (Francophorti ad Viadrum excudebat Ioannes Eichorn.) 8°. A-I^8 K^4. [67

-- -- Academiarum et praestantium quarundam scholarum fundatarum Catalogus ... Per Guolphgangum Iustum. Lipsiæ in officina Georgij Hantzsch. 1557. 8°. A-B^8 C^4. [68

JODELLE, ÉTIENNE. Les oeuures et meslanges poetiques ... A Paris, Chez Nicolas Chesneau ... Et Chez Mamert Patisson, ... chez Robert Estienne. M. D. LXXXIII. ... 12°. ā^{12} a-z^{12} A^{12} B^{10}. ff. 1-294. (Furness.) [69

JOHANN JUSTUS, LANDSBERGER. Eyn schöne vnderrichtũg was die recht Euangelisch geystlicheit sy/ vnnd was man vonn den Clösteren halten soll. ... Iohan von Lansspurg. Anno .M.D.xxjx. 8°. A-C^8 D^4. (Lea.) [70

JOHN XXI, pope. [Ioan. Eckii ... in summulas Petri Hispani contemporaria et succincta.] (Augustæ Vindelicorum ex officina Millerana mense Maio M. D. XVI.) fol. B.L. A-S^6 (-A1) T^4. ff. II-CXI. [71

-- -- Petri Hispani summulae logicales, cum Versorii Parisiensis ... expositione. Paruorum item logicalium eidem Petro Hispano ascriptum opus ... Venetiis apud Iuntas, anno M D L. (... Mense Iunio.) fol. ✠-✠✠^{6} a-s^8 t^4. ff. 1-148. ¶*T.p. repaired.* [72

-- -- Venetiis, Apud Dominicum de Farris, M.D.XCIII. 4°. a^8 b^2 A-Nn^8. pp. 1-575. [73

JONAS, JUSTUS. Contra tres pagellas, agri. phagi Georgii VVitzel ... Responsio. (Vuitebergæ apud Georgium Rhaw. 1532.) 8°. A-F^8 G^4. [74

-- Wilch die rechte Kirche/ Vnd dagegen wilch die falsche Kirch ist/ ... Widder das Pharisaisch gewesch Georgij Witzels. ... (Gedruckt ... durch Georgen Rhaw. M.D.XXXIIII.) 4°. A-O^4 P^2 Q^4. [75

JONGIUS, JACOBUS. Argumenta triumphi eloquentiae Guil. Gnaphei, et Troadis Senecae a Iacobo Iongio, Henr. Iunij discipulo, anno ætatis 16. elegiaco carmine Delphi conscripta. Leidæ Excudebat Theodoricus Gerardi Horst ... 1566. 8°. A^8. [76

JORDAN, RAYMOND. Contemplationes Idiotae De amore diuino. De Virgine Maria. De vera patientia. De continuo conflictu carnis & animæ. De innocentia perdita. De morte. Parisijs, in ædibus Henrici Stephani, mense Augusto, M.D.XIX. 4°. a-m^8. ff. 2-95. [77

JORIS, DAVID. Dauid Georgen auss Holand dess Ertzkätzers warhafftige histori/ seines lebens/ vnnd verfürischen leer/ ... vnd wass sich nach seinen absterben mitt jm̃/ vnd seinen verwandten alda verloffen hat. Durch ein Eerwirdige vniuersitet der ... statt Basel/ zů ehren eines Fürsichtigen/ Ersam̃en/ wysen Rathes daselbss beschriben. Getruckt zů Basel jm jor M D LIX. (Getruckt durch Hieronymum Curionem jm jar M D LIX. im Herbstmonat.) 4°. A-H^4. (Lea.) [78

JOSEPHUS, FLAVIUS. Flauii Iosephi opera, in sermonem Latinum iam olim conuersa ... Basileae, ex officina Frobeniana. M. D. LXVII. (... per Ambrosium et Aurelium Frobenios, fratres.) fol. †^{6} *^{4} a-z^6 A-Zz^6 AA-II^6. pp. 2-910. ¶*Translator: Sigmund Gelen.* [79

-- [1] Iosephi ... Zweyntzig bůcher von dem alten geschichten ... Siben bůcher von dem Iüdischen krieg vnd der zerstörũg Hierusalem ... Zwey bůcher wider Appionem Grammaticum ... Von meisterschafft der vernunfft/ oder von den Machabeern ein bůch/ durch ... D. Erasmum von Roterdam im Latein wider besichtigt. ... Item das leben F. Iosephi von Eusebio/ Hieronimo/ Suida/ vnnd Volaterano verzeychnet ... Strassburg. M.D.XLIIII. (Getruckt ... by Balthassar Beck.) fol. a^6 b^8 c-z^6 A-Z^6 aa-mm^6 nn^8 oo-pp^6 qq^8. ff. j-cccxliiij. [2] Flauij Iosephi vom krieg der Iuden ... Anno M. D. XLIIII. rr-zz^6 AA-ZZ^6 aA-dD^6. ff. j-clxxxiij. ¶*Translator: Caspar Hedio.* [80

-- Les cinq liures de l'histoire d'Egesippe ... Mis en François par I. Millet, de Sainct Amour. A Paris, Pour Vincent Sertenas ... 1556. ... (Imprimé ... par Benoist Preuost ...: le dixseptiesme iour de Ianuier ...) 4°. ā^4 ē^4 ī^4 a-z^4 A-Yy^4 Zz^6. ff. 1-278. [81

-- -- Histoire de Fl. Iosephe ... de La guerre, destruction & captiuité des Iuifs: Vn Traitê du martyre des Machabées: La vie de l'Autuer, escrite par luy mesme. Le tout traduit ... en François par Francois Bourgoing. ... À Lion, par Iean Temporal. 1558. (... acheuée ... le septieme de May ... Imprimé ... par N. Edoard, Champenois ...) fol. *^{4} AA-3K^6. pp. 3-271 [=371]. [82

-- -- Les sept liures de Flauius Iosephus de la guerre et captiuité des Iuifz, traduitz de Grec, et mis en Francoys par N. de Herberay ... Á Paris. Par Estienne Groulleau ... 1557. (imprimez ... par Estienne Groulleau ... pour luy, Iean Longis, Vincent Sertenas, & Iean Bonfons ...) fol. ã^6 A-Z^6 Aa^4 Bb-Rr^6. ff. I-CCXXXVII. [83

-- -- De bello Judaico. Egesippus Teũtsch Im Jar M D XXXII Durch Doctor Caspar Hedion vertolmetscht. Strassburg. ... (Getruckt ... durch Balthassar Beck. Vnd volendt am dreissigsten tag Ianuarij ...) fol. π^6 A^8 B-Z^6 a^6 (-a6, *presumably blank*). ff. j-cxxxvj. [84

-- -- Fünff historische bücher Egesippi ... Von dem Iüdischen krieg Von der zerstörung Hierusalem Von grausam̃er straff der Iudē die sich an Christo vñ Apostlen versündigt. ... Durch Doctor Caspar Hedion verteũtscht/ Vnd Getruckt zů Strassburg bey Balthassar Beck Im jar M D XXXVij (... volendt am dreissigsten tag Ianuarij des Tausent Fünffhundertzwey vnnd dreissigsten Iars.) fol. π^6 A^8 B-Z^6 a^6. ff. j-cxxxvj. [85

-- Giosefo nelqual si tratto delle guerre de Giudei ... nella uolgar lingua tradotto ...

(In Veneggia per Vettor .q. Piero Rauano, della Serena & Compagni ... M. D. XXXV.) 8°. a-z8 A-R8 S4. ff. 2-314. [86

-- -- Iosepho de belo Iudaico. Fue impresso enla villa de Anuers, en casa de Martin Nucio. 1551. ... 8°. A-Z8 (-R1, R8, S1-2, S8, Y1) Aa-Ss8 (-Qq1) Tt 6 (-Tt1-2). ff. 2-328. ¶*Translator: Alfons Fernández de Palencia.* [87

JOUBERT, LAURENT. La Prima Parte de gli errori popolari de ... Lorenzo Gioberti ... Tradotta di Franzese in lingua Toscana dal Mag. M. Alberto Luchi da Colle. ... In Fiorenza per Filippo Giunti, MDXCII. ... (*Colophon.*) 4°. *10 A-Q8 R4. pp. 1-240. [88

JOUENNEAUX, GUY. Guidonis Iuuenalis patria cenomani in latine lingue elegantias tam a laurentio valla q̄ȝ a Gellio memorie proditas interptatio ... (... impressū Parisius per Petrum preuost ... Anno dñi Millesimo quingentesimo octauo. die vero decima mensis nouembris.) 8°. B.L. A6 b6 C-Q8.4 R6. ff. ii-cii. ¶R6 *defective.* [89

JUAN MANUEL. El conde Lucanor. Compuesto por el ... principe don Iuan Manuel ... Impresso en Seuilla, en casa de Hernando Diaz. Año de 1575. ... (*Colophon.*) 4°. a-g8 h2 A-M8 N6. ff. 1-97. ¶*Editor: Gonzalo de Argote y de Molina.* [90

JUBELJAHR. Von dem Iubel Iar. ... [Strassburg, Johannes Schwan, 1525.] 4°. A4. ¶*In verse.* [91

JUDICIUM. Iuditium/ eines Predigers inn der Schlesien: Vber Mathie Flacij Illyrici bůchlin/ so er wider Chaspar Schwenckfelden im Truck hat lassen aussgehen. M D LIII. 4°. a-e4. [92

JÜLICH. *Wilhelm V, duke.* Des Durchleuchtigen ... Herrn Wilhelms Hertogen tho Cleue/ Gulich vnd Berge ... Mandat vnd beuelch/ wie es ... mit ... Sectarien/ Busch vnd Winckel Predigern/ oick Vprurischen ... tho halden. Getruckt zu Dusseldorff durch Alberten Buyss. 4°. A-B4. ¶*Dated 23 January 1565.* [93

-- ... Wilhelms Hertzogen Zu Gülich/ Cleue vnd Berg ... Ordnung vnd Reformation des Gerichtlichen Process ... In Cöln durch die Erben Arnoldi Birckmans ... Vnd Iacob Sotern. Anno M.D.LXII. fol. a6 A-Q6 R4 (-R4, *presumably blank*). pp. j-cxcvj. [94

JULIANUS, FLAVIUS CLAUDIAS, emperor. Ιουλιανου αυτοκρατορος τὰ σωζόμενα. Iuliani imperatoris opera quæ extant omnia. A Petro Martinio Morentino Navarro, & Carolo Cantoclaro ... latina facta ... Additus praeterea est a Carolo Cantoclaro eiusdem Iuliani περὶ βασιλείας, & à Theodoro Marcilio ὕμνος εἰς βασιλία Ηλιον ... Parisiis, Apud Dionysium Duvallium ... 1583. ... 8°. A-T8 V12+4 X4. pp. 11-342. ¶*Ends with the letters.* [95

-- Discours de l'empereur Iulian sur les faicts et deportemens des Cæsars. Traduict de Grec en François. ... A Paris, Pour Iean de Bordeaux ... 1580. ... 4°. A-O4. ff. 2-56. [96

JULIUS II, pope. Iulius. Dialogus uiri cuiuspiam eruditissimi ... [Argentorati, Joannes Prüss, c. 1519.] 8°. A-C8 D4. [97

JUNIUS, ADRIANUS. Hadriani Iunii Hornani, medici, Batauia. ... [Lugduni Batavórum,] Ex officina Plantiniana, Apud Franciscum Raphelengium. cIɔ. Iɔ. LXXXVIII. 4°. *-**4 3*2 A-3E4 3F2. pp. 1-411. [98

-- Hadriani Iunii medici emblemata ... Eiusdem ænigmatum libellus ... Antuerpiæ, Ex officina Christophori Plantini. M. D. LXVI. ... 8°. A-H8 I4. pp. 7-134. [99

-- -- Antuerpiae, Apud Christophorum Plantinum. M. D. LXXXV. 16°. A-K8. pp. 3-157. [100

-- -- Lugduni Batauorum, Ex officina Plantiniana, Apud Franciscum Raphelengium. cIɔ. Iɔ. XCVI. 16°. A-K8 L4. pp. 3-167. [101

-- Nomenclator, omnium rerum propria nomina variis linguis explicata indicans ... Antuerpiæ, Ex officina Christophori Plantini ... M. D. LXXVII. (... decimo Kalend. Septembris, anno M.D.LXXVI.) 8°. †4 A-Z8 a-h8 i4. pp. 1-432. [102

-- -- Francofurti Apud Ioannem Wechelum & Petrum Fischerum consortes, MDLXXXXI. 8°. α4 A-Pp8 Qq4. pp. 1-545. [103

-- -- Nomenclator, Hadriani Iunij ... ad scholarum vsum ... accommodatus. Augustæ. Ex officina Michaëlis Mangeri. M D LXXXVIII. 8°. A-T^{8}. pp. 1-288. ¶*Lower margins defective, sometimes impairing the text in the first four gatherings.* [104

-- -- The nomenclator, or Remembrancer ... conteining proper names and apt termes for all thinges ... VVritten ... in Latine, Greeke, French and other forrein tongues: and now in English, by Iohn Higins. VVith ... a dictional Index ... By Abraham Fleming. ... Imprinted at London for Ralph Newberie, and Henrie Denham. 1585 8°. A-Tt^{8}. pp. 1-539. *S.T.C.* 14860. (Furness.) [105

-- Poëmatum ... liber rrimus [*sic*] ... Lugduni, Ex officina Ludovici Elzevirij. Anno cIↄ. Iↄ. XCVIII. 8°. †^{8} A-M^{8} N^{4}. pp. 1-196. [106

JUNIUS, MELCHIOR. Artis dicendi praecepta ... ex Platone, Aristotele, Hermogene, Cicerone, Herenniano magistro, & Quintiliano ... Argentorati Excudebat Antonius Bertamus. M. D. LXXXIX. (*Colophon.*) 12°. A^{8} A-V^{12}. pp. 1-451. [107

-- Scholæ Rhetoricæ, de contexendarum Epistolarum ratione ... Basileæ per Conradum Vualdkirch cIↄ Iↄ XXCVII. 8°.)(^{8} a-u^{8}. pp. 1-319. [108

JUSTICES OF THE PEACE. The contentes of this boke. Fyrst the booke for a Iustice of peace. The boke that teacheth to kepe a courte Baron, or a lete. The boke teachinge to kepe a courte hundred. The boke called returna Breuium. The boke called Carta feodi ... And the boke of the ordinaunce to be observed by the offycers of the Kynges Escheker for fees takynge. (Imprinted at London ... by Richard Tottil, the .xiii. day of Maye ... 1559. ...) 8°. B.L. A-Dd^{8} (-Dd 7-8, *presumably blank*). ff. 2-195. *S.T.C.* 14883. (Biddle.) [109

JUSTIN MARTYR, S. Les oeuures de S. Iustin ... martyr, mises de Grec en Francois, par Ian de Maumont. ... A Paris, De l'imprimerie de Michel de Vascosan ... M. D. LIIII. ... fol. A-Zz^{6} AA-DD^{6} EE^{4} (-EE4, *presumably blank*). ff. 1-297. ¶A1 *repaired.* [110

-- Του αγιου Ιουστινου ... μαρτυρος ... Lutetiae, Ex officina Roberti Stephani ... M. D. LI. fol. (*)^{4} a-t^{8} v^{6}. pp. 2-311. [111

-- Euersio falsorum Aristotelis dogmatum ... Guilielmo Postello interprete. Parisiis, Apud Sebastianum Niuellium ... 1552. 16°. A-K^{8} L^{4}. ff. 2-76. [112

JUSTINIAN I, emperor. *Corpus juris civilis*. Authentica. Imperatoris ... Iustiniani Nouellæ ... Lugduni, Apud Hugonem à Porta. M. D. XLVIII. ... (Excudebat Balthazar Arnoullet.) fol. aa^{8} a-s^{8} A-K^{8} L^{10} AA-FF^{8} GG^{4} *^{6}. pp. 1-288, 1-179, 1-101. ¶*2^{r}: Sequitur noua Arbor Feudorum ... compilata per ... Petrum Rebuffum de Monte Pessulano ... *Part of an edition of the* Corpus juris civilis *in 6 vols*. (Biddle.) [113

-- -- Institutionum D. Iustiniani ... libri quatuor ... Lugduni, Apud Hugonem à Porta. M. D. L. ... (Excudebat Ioannes Ausultus.) fol. A-B^{6} a-p^{8} q^{10}. pp. 1-260. ¶*Part of an edition of the* Corpus juris civilis *in 6 vols*. (Biddle.) [114

-- -- [Corpus juris civilis.] Lugduni, Apud Hugonem à Porta. ... (... Excudebat Ioannes Ausultus.) fol. [1] Digestum vetus. Digestorum, seu Pandectarum Iuris ... in libros quinquaginta collecti ... Tomus Primus ... M. D. LII. ... *^{4} α-ε^{8} ς^{10} a-zz^{8} A-P^{8} Q^{10}. pp. 1-993. [2] Infortiatum, Pandectarum Iuris Ciuilis Tomus Secundus ... M. D. LII. ... AA-CC^{6} a-z^{8} A-Z^{8} aa-ll^{8} mm^{6}. pp. 1-923. [3] Digestum nouum Pandectarum Iuris Ciuilis Tomus Tertius ... M. D. LI. ... aa-bb^{8} cc-dd^{6} a-z^{8} A-Gg^{8} Hh^{10}. pp. 1-866. [4] Codicis ... ex repetita praelectione libri nouem priores ... M. D. LIII. α^{8} β^{10} a-z^{8} A-Z^{8} aa-tt^{8}. pp. 1-1016. ¶*Parts of an edition of the* Corpus juris civilis *in 6 vols*. (Biddle.) [115

-- -- Digestorum seu pandectarum Pars Sexta, à Libro. XXXVII. vsq3 ad XLV. Parisiis ... [Gulielmus Merlin, Gulielmus Desboys, Sebastianus Nivellius,] M.D.LXII. 8°. 6A-6OO^{8} 6PP^{10}. pp. 7-612. ¶*Part of an edition of the* Corpus juris civilis *in 7 vols*. (Biddle.) [116

-- -- [Corpus juris civilis.] *Greek & Latin*. Antuerpiæ, Ex officina Christophori Plantini ... M. D. LXXV. (... XVI. Kal. Apr.) fol. [1] Dn. ... Iustiniani ... digestorum seu pandectarum libri quinquaginta ... Opera ... L. Charondæ ... *^{8} **^{10} A-B^{6} C-Z^{8} a-z^{8} Aa-Ee^{8}. pp. 2-805. [2] Codicis Dn. Iustiniani ... lib. XII. ... AA-ZZ^{8} aa-hh^{8}. pp. 3-494. [3] Authenticæ seu nouellæ constitutiones ... Cum veteri tralatione, Græcis nunc primum Ant. Contij ... opera apposita. Accessit etiam Georgij Haloandri versio ... A^{6} B-P^{8} Q^{6}

Aaa-Hhh^{8} Iii^{6}. pp. 3-246, 1-138. [4] Iustiniani ... edicta. Item Iustini, Tiberii, ac Leonis, aliorumque imperatorum constitutiones. Henrico Agylæo, & Enimundo Bonefidio ... Interpretibus. AAa-BBb^{6} CCc-DDd^{8} EEe^{6} FFf-GGg^{8} HHh-IIi^{6}. pp. 2-126. [5] ... institutionum [iuris] [*sic*] libri IIII. Compositi per Tribonianum ... & Theophilum, & Dorotheum ... aA-cC^{8} dD^{6} A-D^{8} E-F^{6} G^{8}. pp. 5-59. (Biddle.) [117

-- -- [Corpus iuris ciuilis in IIII partes distinctum ... Authore Dionysio Gothofredo ... Lugduni, Ex officina Bartholomaei Honorati ... M.D.LXXXVI.] fol. ¶-¶¶^{6} (-¶1) a^{6} aa-cc^{6} dd^{8} A-Z^{6} aa-zz^{6} 3A-4R^{6} (-4R2-6). cols. j-xxiiij, 1-100, 1-2044 *present*. (Biddle.) [118

-- -- [1] Corpus [i]uris ciuilis Dionysio Gothofredo I.C. recognitum, ... Tomus I. Pandectarum seu Digestorum libri quinquaginta. ... Lugduni, M.D.LXXXIX. 4°. *-**^{8} a-z^{8} Aa-3I^{8} **^{2} A-C^{8} D^{4}. cols. 1-1750, 1-110. ¶*T.p. defective.* [2] Tomus II. Codices Dn. Iustiniani libri XII. ... Leonis Imperatoria Nouellæ CXIII. ... Consuetudines Friderici II. ... Institutionum libri IIII. ... M.D.LXXXIX. (Excudebat Guilielmus Laemarius ... Kal. Ian.) 4°. ¶^{8} ¶¶^{6} **^{2} AA-3D^{8} A-V^{8}. cols. 1-862, 1-588. [119

-- (Codex legalis Iustiniani imp̄atoris ... in Parrhisiēsi academia ... diligentia Andree boucard impressus: ... impensis ... Iohānis petit Thilmāni Keruer ipsiusq3 Andree boucard ... ad .xv. kalendas Nouembris ... M.CCCCC.xij.) 4°. B.L. a-z^{8} ⁊^{8} ꝯ^{8} A-P^{8} Q^{6} aa-ll^{8} mm^{6} nn-zz^{8} AA-II^{8} 3a-3b^{8} 3c^{10}. ff. i-ccccclxxx. ¶*Lacks 4 preliminary ll.* (Biddle.) [120

-- -- Codicis Dn. Iustiniani ... principis, ex repetita prælectione libri nouem priores ... Lugduni, Apud Hugonem à Porta, Antonium Vincentium. M. D. LVIII. ... 4°. α^{8} (-α2-3) β-γ^{8} δ^{2} a-g^{8} h^{4} i-z^{8} A-Zz^{8} AA-3A^{8} 3B^{4} 3C^{8} 3D^{4+1} (EE2 + *folded leaf*, II4 + *folded leaf*). pp. 1-1486. [121

-- Digestum nouum Quod quinquaginta librorū pādectarum calcem appellare possumus ... Andreas Boucard sic renouauit opus. (Impressum ... in ... Parrhisiorum academia: ad idus nouemb. M.d.xxv. Opera ... mea: impensis autem et meis/ ⁊ Ioannis Petit.) 4°. B.L. x^{6} a-ff^{8} A-LL^{8} MM^{10}. ff. i-CCCCxcviii. (Biddle.) [122

-- [Institutiones imperiales.] (Excudebat ... Lugduni ... Ioānes Crespin alias du Quarre. ... M.ccccc.xxxviij. mense Ianuario.) 8°. B.L. aa-ff^{8} (-aa-bb^{8}) gg^{4} a-z^{8} ⁊^{8} ꝯ^{8} ꝶ^{8} A-Z^{8}. ff. j-cccxcij. (Biddle.) [123

-- -- Institutionum, siue elementorum, D. Iustiniani ... Principis, Libri quatuor, A Gregorio Haloandro recēns castigati. ... Parisiis, In ædibus viduæ Claudij Cheuallonij ... 1538. 16°. a-z^{8} A-G^{8}. ff. 2-240. [124

-- -- Institutiones Iustiniani ... Accursii cæterorumq3 Iurisperitorum, præcipue vero Egidii Perrini ... interpretatiōibus, additionibusq3 ... adaucti ... Ex officina Iacobi Giuntæ ... Lugduni ... M. D. XLVIII. (Excudebat ... relicta Ioannis Corispini alias du Quarre. ... mense Aprili.) 8°. B.L. aa-ff^{8} gg^{4} a-z^{8} ⁊^{8} ꝯ^{8} ꝶ^{9} A-Z^{8}. ff. j-cccxcij. (Biddle.) [125

-- -- Institutionum iuris ciuilis libri IIII. Olim a Theophilo Antecessore in eum e Latino vberius diffusiusq̄; translati, & nunc nuper e Græco in Latinum per D. Iac. Curtium Brugensem ... conuersi. ... Venetiis Apud Hieronymum Scotum M D LVI. 16°. A^{8} b-z^{8} A-V^{8}. pp. 1-671. (Biddle.) [126

-- *Novellae*. [1] Authenticae seu nouellæ constitutiones Dn. Iustiniani ... Lugduni, Apud Gulielmum Rouillium, 1571. ... 16°. *-**^{8} A-3G^{8}. pp. 1-843. [2] Authenticorum, seu nouellarum constitutionum ... Pars altera ... *Same imprint*. 16°. A-4R^{8}. pp. 2-1376. (Biddle.) [127

JUSTINUS, MARCUS JUNIANUS. Iustinus hystoricus. (Impressum Venetiis per Bartholomeum de Zanis de Portesio. M.ccccc.iii. die tertio febrarii.) fol. a-i^{6}. ff. ii-54. [128

-- -- Les oeuures de Iustin ... sur les faictz & gestes de Troge Pompée, Contenant. xliiii. liures traduictz de Latin en Frācoys, Nouuellement imprimez A Paris. ... Mil cinq cens. xxxviij. On les vend ... en la boutique de Arnoul et Charles Langelier. (... imprime ... par Denys Ianot ...) fol. B.L. a-b^{4} A-X^{6} Y^{4}. ff. j-cxxvj. ¶*Translator: Guillaume Michel dit de Tours.* [129

-- -- Les histoires vniuerselles de Trogue Pompee, abbregees par Iustin Historien, Translatees ... par Messire Claude de Seyssel ... Premiere edition. A Paris, De l'imprimerie de Michel de Vascosan. M. D. LVIIII. ... (Acheué d'imprimer en Septembre. ...) fol. aa^{6}

A-R^{6} S^{4} (-S4, *presumably blank*). ff. 1-104. [130

-- -- Des Hochberümptesten Geschicht schreybers Iustini/ warhafftige Hystorien/ die er auss Trogo Pompeio gezogē ... Die Hieronymus Boner ... auss dem Latein inn diss volgend Teütsch vertolmetscht hat ... [Augsburg, Heinrich Steyner, 1531.] fol. π^{4} A-V^{6}. ff. I-CXIX. [131

-- -- Iustino ... nelle Historie di Trogo Pompeo. Nuouamente in lingua Toscana Tradotto ... In Vinegia M D XLII. (Stampato ... per Bernardino Bindoni Milanese. ...) 8°. A-V^{8}. ff. 2-160. ¶*Translator: Girolamo Squarciafico.* [132

-- -- Iustino ... abbreuiador de la historia general del ... historiador Trogo Pompeyo ... traduzido en Castellano ... Fue impressa ... enla ... villa de Enuers ... M.D.XLII. y vendese en la casa de Iuan Steelsio ... 8°. a^{8} A-Nn^{8}. ff. 2-258. [133

JUTLAND. Quedam breues expositiões et legum et iuriū concordantie ⁊ allegationes circa leges iucie per ... Kanutuꝫ Ep̄m vibergeñ ... (Impressus haffnie ꝑ Gotfridū de ghemen ... M ccccc viij In profesto scti mathie apostoli.) 4°. B.L. [a]^{4} b-y^{6} A-E^{6} F-G^{4} (-G4, *presumably blank*). ¶C6^{v}: Constitutio Voldemari regis ꝑ Thordonē legiferū articuli ⁊ correctōes leg: quas lille thorddeghñ Dacie legifer cōposuit ... (Lea.) [134

JUVENALIS, DECIMUS JUNIUS. Cōmentarii Ioannis Britannici In Iuuenalem ... (Impressum ... Brixiæ ab Angelo & Iacobo Britānicis fratribus ... Anno ... quingentesimoprimo.) fol. A^{6} a-g^{6} h^{10} i^{6} k-m^{8} n^{6} o-q^{8} r-s^{6}. ff. ii-CXXXVIII. [135

-- -- Liber Satyrarū Iunij Iuuenalis ... (diligentia ... Martini Herbipolensis: Liptzensis ciuis ... pressum. Annoqꝫ ... Millesimoquingētesimo secundo. Quinto Kalendas mensis Augusti ...) fol. B.L. A-N^{6} O^{8}. [136

-- -- Iunii Iuuenalis satyrae ... Vnā cum huiusce dictionis (Satyra) ... elucidatione ... Coloniae apud Ioan. Gymnicum Anno M. D. XLI. 8°. A-K^{8}. pp. 2-157. [137

-- -- Iuuenal tradotto di Latino in volgar lingua per Georgio Summa Ripa Veronese ... ([Venetiis,] P. Alex. Pag. Benacenses. .f. ... [c. 1516]) 8°. a-q^{8}. [138

-- Iuuenalis. Persius. (Venetiis in ædibus Aldi. Mense Augusto. M.DI.) 8°. A-G^{8} H^{10} a^{8} b^{4}. [139

-- -- Iun. Iuuenalis, et Auli Persii Flacci satyrea ... Apud Seb. Gryphium Lugduni, 1538. 8°. a-k^{8}. pp. 2-159. [140

-- -- Iu. Iuuenalis vnà cum Au. Persio ... (Florentiæ per Hæredes Philippi Iuntæ Florentini, mense Maij. M.D.XIX. ...) 8°. A-K^{8}. ff. 2-80. [141

-- -- Iun. Iuuenalis, et Auli Persii Flacci satyrae. Basileae M. D. XLVI. (... per Nicolaum Brylingerum. ...) 16°. a-k^{8}. pp. 1-155. [142

-- -- Apud Seb. Gryphium Lugduni. 1546. 16°. a-k^{8}. pp. 2-159. [143

K

KALENDER. Ein Schöner Geistlicher Kalender/ in welchem das leben vnd sterben ... Gottes ... in lustige Reimen verfasset sindt. ... [Nürnberg, Hans Guldenmund, c. 1540.] 8°. A-B⁸ (-B8, *presumably blank*). [1

KANZLEIBUCH. Neuw Cantzley/ vnd Titelbuch/ in Reden vnd Schreiben ... Franck. Bei Christ. Egen. Erben. M. D. LXXVI. (... In verlegung Doct: Adami Loniceri/ Doct: Iohannis Cnipij/ vnnd Pauli Steinmeyers ...) 8°. A-F⁸. ff. 2-44. [2

KATTELSBURGER, NICOLAUS. Ain Missiue (oder Sendtbrieff) Nicolai Cattelspurger/ darinn ... angezaygt wirt von den falschē leeren/ auch Abgötterey/ byssher gehalten ... [Augsburg, Philipp Ulhart,] 1.5.24. 4°. A-B⁴. [3

KELLER, ANDREAS. Ain Sermon ... Vō gsatz vn̄ Euangelio/ auch wie Christus die kauffer vnd verkauffer auss dem tempel hat tribn̄ ... 1524 ... 4°. a-c⁴. [4

KELLER, MICHAEL. Antwort dem ... Doctor Iohann Bugenhage auss Pomern ... auff die Missiue/ so er an ... Doctor Hesso ... geschickt/ das Sacrament betreffend. Durch Conradt Reyssen zu Ofen gemacht. ... [Augsburg, Philipp Ulhart, 1525.] 4°. A-C⁴. [5

KEMPIS, THOMAS À. De imitatione Christi, et rerum mundanarum contemptu, libri quatuor ... authore, D. Thoma de Kempis. ... Vita Christi ... authore ... Cornelio Iansenio ... Coloniae, In officina Birckmannica, sumptibus Arnoldi Mylij. Anno cIↄ. Iↄ. XCIX. ... 16°. A-Y⁸ R-S⁸. ff. 3-144. [6

-- -- I quattro libri di Gio. Gerson, della imitatione di Christo ... In Vinegia appresso Gabriel Giolito de' Ferrari, M D LVIII. 4°. *⁶ A-M⁸. pp. 1-191. [7

KERTZENMACHER, PETER. Alchimia, Das ist/ Alle Farben/ Wasser/ olea, salia, vnnd alumina, damit man alle corpora, spiritus vnnd calces Prepariert ... [Franckfort am Mayn bey Christian Egenolffs Erben, 1574. (*Colophon.*)] 8°. A-K⁸. ff. 2-79. ¶A1, K8 *defective.* (Smith.) [8

KETTENBACH, HEINRICH VON. Ein Practica practiciert auss der haylgen Bibel/ vff vil zůkünfftig iar ... Anno ... tausent D xxiii. [Nürnberg, Johann Stuchs, 1523.] 4°. A-B⁴. [9

-- Ein Sermon ... wider die falschen Aposteln/ die da haben geprediget/ die Prelaten mögen das haylig Ewangelium verwandeln ... 4°. A-B⁴ (-B4, *presumably blank*). [10

-- Eyn Sermon widder des Bapsts Küchen predyger zu Vlm ... vn̄ sonderlich widd' Peter Nestler ... [Erfurt, Johann Loersfelt,] M. D. XXIII. 4°. [A]-C⁴. [11

KHUNRATH, HEINRICH. Magnesia catholica philosophorum: Das ist/ Höheste Nothwendigkeit/ in alchymia ... (Gedruckt zu Magdeburg/ bey Iohan. Bötcher/ ... M. D. XCIX. Bey Iohan Francken zu bekommen.) 8°. A-M⁸ (-M8, *presumably blank*). pp. 3-187. (Smith.) [12

KIEL, CORNELIS. Etymologicum Teutonicæ linguæ ... Opera Cornelii Kiliani Dufflæi. ... Editio tertia ... Antuerpiæ Ex Officina Plantiniana, Apud Ioannem Moretum. M. D. XCIX. 8°. *⁸ A-Z⁸ a-z⁸ Aa-Bb⁸ (-Bb8, *presumably blank*). pp. 1-764. [13

KIMCHI, DAVID. Hebraicarum institutionum Libri IIII, Sancto Pagnino Lucensi authore, Ex R. Dauid Kimhi priore parte ... transcripti. Ex officina Roberti Stephani ... (... Lutetiae Parisiorum, anno M.D.XLIX. XIII. Cal. Maii.) 4°. a-z⁴ A-Z⁴ aa-ss⁴ tt⁶. pp. 1-515. (Lea.) [14

-- ספר מכלול שחבר... דוד קמחי... נדפס בבית דניאל בומבירגי בשנת ש"ה לפ"ק בויניציאה [Venice, Daniel Bomberg, 1545.] fol. 1-8⁸ 9⁶. ff. ב-סט. [15

-- אוצר לשון הקדש Thesaurus Linguæ sanctæ Ex R. Dauid Kimchi ספר השרשים Sancte Pagnino Lucensi authore. ... [Parisiis,] Ex officina Roberti Stephani ... (Ann. M.D.XLVIII. XII. Cal. Feb.) 4°. *a-*i⁴ a-z⁴ A-Z⁴ aa-zz⁴ AA-ZZ⁴ 3a-3z⁴ 3A-3Z⁴ Aa-Zz⁴ AAa-ZZz⁴ 4A-4K⁴. pp. 2-1495. [16

KINTHISIUS, JODOCUS. In D. Pauli apostoli ad Philippenses, Collecteanea ... Franc. Apud Chr. Egen. (... M.D.XLIIII.) 8°. A-P⁸. [17

KIRCHOFF, LORENZ. Responsum iuris de excommunicatione, duarum quæstionum ... Authore Laurentio Kirchoff ... Rostochii excudebat Iacobus Transyluanus. Anno M. D. LXVI. 4°. A-E⁴ (-E4, *presumably blank*). (Lea.) [18

KIS, ISTVÁN. Speculum Romanorum pontificum, in quo Decreta cum verbo Dei pugnantia, Vitæ cursus, Prodigia horrenda, ... depinguntur Per Stephanum Szegedinum Pannonium. Eiusdem de Traditionibus Pontificiis Quæstiones iucundæ. Anno CIↃ IↃ XXCIV. 8°.)(⁸ a-n⁸. pp. 1-204. (Lea.) [19

KITCHEN, JOHN. Le Court leete & Court Baron collect per Iohn Kitchin de Graies Inne ... In ædibus Richardi Totelli ... 1592. Primo Iulij. 8°. B.L. A⁸ ¶⁴ A-Nn⁸ Oo⁴. ff. 1-289. *S.T.C.* 15021. ¶*Additional t.p.* (Ii7ʳ): Retorna Breuium ... In Ædibus Richardi Tottelli. 1592. [20

KNAUST, HEINRICH. Gegen vnd wider die Spitzbuben/ So hin vnd wider/ in den Landen/ wie eine streuffende Rott/ vmbher ziehen ... Gedruckt zu Erffurdt/ durch Georgium Bawman. M.D.LXXV. 8°. A-F⁸. [21

KNIPSTRO, JOHANN. Antwort der Theologen vnd Pastorn in Pommern/ auff die Confession Andreae Osiandri ... Durch D. Ioannem Knipstrouium ... Gedruckt zu Wittemberg/ Durch Veit Creutzer. 1552. 4°. A-H⁴. [22

KNOBELSDORF, EUSTATHIUS VON. Lutetiæ Parisiorum descriptio ... Parisiis. Apud Christianum Wechelum ... M.D.XLIII. 8°. A-D⁸. pp. 3-61. ¶*In verse.* [23

KOEBEL, JAKOB. Dialogus libertatis ecclesiastice defensorius cum Imperatorum sanctionibus ... (Impressum Oppenheim [per Jacobum Koebel]. ... 15.16.) 4°. π⁴ A⁶ B-C⁴. (Lea.) [24

-- -- *Another copy.* [25

-- Glaubliche Offenbarung wie viell fürtreffener Reich/ vnd Keyserthumb vff Ertrich gewesen/ wo dz Rœmisch Reich herkōme/ auss was vrsach es zů den Edeln Teütschen verandert worden sey. ... (Getruckt zů Meyntz bey Peter Iordan ... für ... Iacob Kœbeln Statschreyber zů Oppenheym/ Im Augstmon. M.D.XXXII.) 4°. [A]-F⁴. [26

-- Eyn Process der gerichts ordenung aus Bepstlichen vnd Keyserlichen rechten ... 1529. (Gedruckt zu Leypzick Melchior Lotther. ...) 8°. A-S⁸. ff. xvij-cxxxiiij. [27

KOERBER, OTTO. Ein Trostpredig beyde für die Schwangern vnd Vnfrůchtbaren Frawen ... gethan ihm 1534 iar. ... (Gedruckt zů Nůrnberg durch Hector Schœffler.) 4°. π⁸. [28

KOLLIUS, JOACHIM. Ein Rechtbuch/ Darinne die Artikele/ so man Lübisch Recht nennet ... Gedruckt zu Hamburg/ durch Hans Binder/ Anno M. D. LXXXVI. 4°. A-Z⁴. [29

KORN, GALLUS. Eyn handlung wie es eynem Prediger Munch czu Nurinberg mit seynen Ordens brudern võ wegen der Euãngelischẽ warheyt gãgen ist. [Wittenberg, Johann Rhau,] Anno M.D.xxij. 4°. A⁴. [30

-- Warumb die Kirch vier Euangelisten hat angenom̃en ... [Augsburg, Melchior Ramminger, c. 1524.] 4°. a⁴ b⁶. [31

KRAGE, TILOMANN. Von dem Bilde Gottes in den ersten Menschen. ... Mit einer Vorrede Philippi Melanthons. 1550. Wittemberg. (Gedruckt ... durch Georgen Rhawen Erben. ...) 4°. A⁶ B-R⁴ S². [32

KRÜGER, PANKRAZ. In Petri Botticheri cancellarii Halberstatensis, ... honorem, de Coniugij dignitate, & ipsius nuptijs Ecloga scripta à Pancratio Crugero, Finsterwaldio. Anno M. D. LXVIII. 4°. A-B⁴ (-B4, *presumably blank*). [33

KÜNIG, NICOLAUS. Kurtzer einfeltiger ... bericht/ von dem Heyligen Ehestandt ... Gedruckt zu Nůrnberg/ bey Vlrich Newber. M.D. LXIX. 8°. A-G⁸ H⁴. [34

KUNHOFER, ENGELHARD. Confessionale cõtinẽs tractatum decem preceptorũ. Et septem viciorũ capitaliũ. ... (Impressus. Nurnberge. an dem Ponerperg [per Johannem Meurl]. sub Anno ... Millesimo quingentesimosecundo) 4°. a^4 b^6 c^4. [35

KYMEUS, JOHANNES. Des Bapsts Hercules/ wider die Deudschen. ... (Gedruckt zu Wittemberg durch Georgen Rhaw. M D XXXVIII.) 4°. A-L^4. [36

L

LABACCO, ANTONIO. Libro d' Antonio Labacco ... nel qual si figurano alcune notabili antiquita di Roma Bolognini Zalterii formis. M. D. LXX. fol. *engraved t.p.* + 28 *plates.* (Fine Arts.) [1

LA CAVALLERIA, PEDRO DE. [1] Tractatus zelus Christi contra Iudaeos, Sarracenes, & infideles. Ab ... Petro de la Caualleria, Hispano ex ciuitate Cæsaraugusta, anno 1450. Compositus ... quem Martinus Alfonsus Viualdus ... edit. ... Venetiis, Apud Baretium de Baretijs. M. D. XCII. ... 4°. *-**^{4} a-k^4 L-M^4 n-p^4 A-Qq^4. ff. 2-156. [2] Aureus Rabbi Samuelis tractatus, ad Isaach Rabbi Sinagogæ ... *Same imprint.* a-b^4 A-E^4. ff. 2-19. (Lea.) [2

LACINIUS, JANUS THERAPUS. Praeciosa ... artis chymiae collectanea de ... Philosophorum lapide. ... Norimbergæ apud Gabrielem Hayn, Ioann. Petrei generum. M.D.LIIII. 4°. a-b^4 A-Hh^4. ff. 1-124 (Smith.) [3

LACTANTIUS FIRMIANUS, LUCIUS COELIUS. L. Celij Lactãtij Firmiani ... de opificio dei vel formatione hominis liber ... (... exitu Colonie in Officina Quẽtell Anno supra sesquimillesimũ sexto. ad festũ Gregorij pape ... diẽ.) 4°. A-B^6 C^4 D^6. [4

-- L. Coelii Lactantii Firmiani diuinarum institutionum libri septem ... Eiusdem De ira Dei De opificio Dei Epitome in libros suos, liber encephalos. Phoenix. Carmen do dominica resurrectione. ... Tertulliani liber apologeticus ... M. D. XXXV. (Venetiis, in aedibus haeredum Aldi, et Andreae soceri, mense Martio ...) 8°. aa^8 bb^4 a-z^8 A-T^8 V^4 X-CC^8 DD^{12} EE-HH^8 *^{4}. ff. 1-328, 1-47. [5

-- -- ... Omnia ex castigatione Honorati Fasitelij Veneti ... restituta. Lugduni, Apud Ioan. Tornæsium, & Gulielmum Gazeium. 1548. 16°. a-z^8 A-Z^8 aa-ff^8. pp. 3-787. [6

-- -- Lugduni. Apud Thomam Soubron. M. D. XCIIII. 16°. a-z^8 A-Mm^8. pp. 3-679. [7

LA FOREST, BERNARD DE. La prenostication nouuelle ... Pour cette presente annee quon dira lan de grace Mil cinq cens ꝛ quatre. 4°. B.L. a^2. ¶*Incomplete.* [8

LAGNIER, PIERRE. M. Tul. Ciceronis insigniores sententiae, ... concinnatæ, inq́; Locos communes digestæ. ... Coloniae, Excudebatur Gualthero Fabritio I.L. Anno 1562. 8°. A-Gg^8. pp. 5-461. ¶*Includes sentences selected from Terence, Demosthenes, and other authors.* [9

-- -- Sententiæ Ciceronis, Demosthenis, ac Terentii. Dogmata Philosophica. Item, Apophthegmata quædam pia. ... Antuerpiae, Ex officina Christoph. Plantini, M.D.LXXXII. (... mense Maio.) 16°. A-B^8 A-Gg^8. pp. 1-478. [10

LAGUS, CONRADUS. Methodica iuris vtriusque traditio ... Ex ore ... Conradi Lagi ... annotata ... Lugduni apud Seb. Gryphium, 1544. 8°. a-z^8 A-Z^8 aa-ff^8. pp. 3-829. (Biddle.) [11

LAING, JAMES. Summarische Historia Vnd Warhafftig Geschicht Von dem Leben/ Lehr/ Bekantnuss vnd Ableyben Martin Luthers vnd Ioann Caluini/ auch etlich anderer ihrer Mitgegehůlffen ... trewlich verteutscht. ... Gedruckt zu Ingolstatt in der Weissenhornischen Truckerey/ bey Wolffgang Eder. Anno M.D.LXXXII. (*Colophon.*) 4°. *-5*^{4} A-Kk^4 (-Kk4, *presumably blank*). pp. 1-363. [12

LA MARCHE, OLIVIER DE. El cauallero determinado, Traduzido de lengua Francesa en Castellana. Por Don Hernando de Acuña. En Anueres, en l'oficina Plantiniana, Cerca la Biuda, y Iuan Moreto. M. D. XCI. ... (*Colophon.*) 4°. *-**^{8} A-N^8 O^4. pp. 2-208. [13

-- Les memoires de Messire Oliuier de la Marche. Auec les Annotations, & corrections de I. L, D. G. ... en ceste seconde edition ... A Gand, Chez Gerard De Salenson ... 1567. ... (Typis Manilii.) 4°. ✠^{8} *^{8} A-Ss^8. pp. 1-655. ¶*Editor: Jean Lautens.* [14

LAMBARDE, WILLIAM. Αρχαιονομια, siue de priscis anglorum legibus libri ... Londini, ex officina Ioannis Daij. An. 1568. ... 4°. A-D^4 E^2 C-Y^4 Aa-Qq^4. ff. 1-140. *S.T.C.* 15141. (Biddle.) [15

-- -- *Another copy (lacking all before ²C1).* (Lea.) [16

-- Eirenarcha: or of The office of the Iustices of Peace ... At London: Imprinted by Ra. Newbery, and H. Bynneman, by the ass. of R. Tot. and Chr. Bar. ... 1582. 8°. B.L. A^4 B-Ll^8 (-Ll8, *presumably blank*). pp. 1-511. *S.T.C.* 15163. (Biddle.) [17

-- -- At London, Printed by Ralph Newbery. ... 1588. (*Colophon.*) 8°. B.L. $[A]^4$ (-A1, *presumably blank*) B-Zz^8 (-Zz8, *presumably blank*). pp. 1-627. *S.T.C.* 15168. (Biddle.) [18

-- -- At London, Printed by Thomas Wight, and Bonham Norton, 1599. ... 8°. B.L. A-N^8 O^4 P-Xx^8 Yy^4. pp. 2-606. *S.T.C.* 15169. (Biddle.) [19

LAMBIN, DENIS. Annotationes, seu emendationum rationes Dionysii Lambini Monstroliensis in librum I. de orat. ad Q. fratrem. Ex bibliotheca Aldina. Venetiis, M. D. LXIX. 8°. A-F^8. ff. 2-49. ¶A8 *misbound before* A2. [20

-- In Adr. Turnebi ... obitum, Nænia, D. Lambino Monstrol. ... auctore. Parisiis. Apud Federicum Morellum ... M. D. LXV. 4°. A^4. [21

LA MOTTE-MESSEMÉ, FRANÇOIS LE PULCHRE DE. Les sept liures des honnestes loisirs de Monsieur de la Motte Messemé ... Plus, vn meslange de diuers Poëmes ... A Paris, Chez Marc Orry ... 1587. 12°. $\dagger^{12}$ A-Z^{12} (-A1) Aa^{12} (-Aa1-5, 8-12). ff. 2-283 *present.* ¶†1 *defective.* [22

LAMPADIUS, HENRICUS. Epitaphiorum, Epicediorum, & Epigrammatum ... Liber vnus. In memoriam & honorem ... Henrici Lampadii ... 8°. A-D^8. [23

LANCI, CORNELIO. Pimpinella comedia ... In Vrbino ... Per Bartholomeo Ragusij. 1588. 8°. A-G^8 H^4. pp. 1-105. [24

-- Scrocca comedia ... In Firenze, Appresso Bartholommeo Sermartelli. ... MDLXXXV. 12°. A-B^{12} C^6. pp. 4-59. [25

-- Il vespa commedia ... In Firenze, Nella Stamperia del Sermartelli. MDLXXXVI. 12°. A-D^{12}. pp. 3-96. [26

LANDAVUS, GERSONITES. Causa tam diuturnae calamitatis ecclesiastici status in Germania. ... Coloniæ ex officina Quenteliana ... M.D.XLVI. mense Martio. 8°. a-c^8 (-c8, *presumably blank*). [27

LANDI, BASSIANO. De incremento ... Venetiis, Apud Balthassarem Constantinum ... M D LVI. (... Apud Ioan. Gryphium. ...) 8°. a-b^8 c^4. ff. 2-20. (Smith.) [28

LANDI, GIULIO. [1] Le attioni morali dell' ... introduttione all'ethica d'Aristotele ... In Vinegia appresso Gabriel Giolito de' Ferrari. M D LXIIII. 4°. $*^4$ $**^8$ $3*^4$ A-X^8 Y^6 Z^1 *(a folded leaf)* AA-II^8. pp. 1-512. [2] Il secondo volume de l'azzioni morali ... In Piacenza appresso Francesco Conti, et Giouan Antonio de' Ferrari compagni. M D LXXV. (MDLXXVI.) $*^4$ $**^6$ A-C^4 (C4 + *folded leaf signed* D*) D-Ii^4. pp. 2-253. [29

LANDI, ORTENSIO. Foricanae quaestiones, in quibus uaria Italorum ingenia explicantur ... Autore Philalethe Polytopiensi Ciue. ... Neapoli excudebat Martinus de Ragusia. Anno. M.D.XXXVI. (*Colophon.*) 8°. A-C^8. ff. 3-24. [30

-- Lettere di molte valorose donne ... In Vinegia appresso Gabriel Giolito de Ferrari. MDXLVIII. (... M D XLIX.) 8°. A-V^8 X^4 (-X4, *presumably blank*). ff. 2-161. ¶*Edited by Landi.* [31

-- Paradossi cioe, sententie fuori Del comun parere ... In Vinegia. MDXLIIII. 8°. A-N^8 (-B1, K8) O^4. ff. 3-106. [32

-- Quattro libri de dubbi con le solutioni ... In Vinegia appresso Gabriel Giolito de Ferrari, et fratelli. MDLII. (*Colophon.*) 8°. A-V^8. pp. 3-318. [33

-- Sette libri de cathaloghi à varie cose appartenenti ... In Vinegia appresso Gabriel Giolito de' Ferrari, e fratelli. M D LII. (... M D LIII.) 8°. A-MM^8 NN^4. pp. 3-567. [34

-- La sferza de scrittori antichi et moderni di M. Anonimo di Vtopia alla quale ... aggiunta una essortatione allo studio delle lettere. ... In Vinegia [per Andrea Arrivabene] M. D. L. 8°. A-I^4. ff. 2-36. [35

-- Varii componimenti di M. Hort. Lando. ... In Vinegia appresso Gabriel Giolito de Ferari, e fratelli. MDLII. 8°. A-D^8 E^{10} F-S^8. pp. 3-288. [36

LANDINO, CRISTOFORO. Christophori Landini Florentini Camaldulensium disputationum opus ... Venundantur Parisiis. a Ioanne paruo ... (... 1511.) 4°. π^8 a^4 b-n$^{4.8}$ o-p^4. ff. II-LXXXIIII. [37

LANDRÉ, CHRISTOPHE. Hauss artzney. ... in Frantzösischer sprach durch den Herrn Christophorum Landrinum ... aussgangen/ nun aber ... zu gutten Teutsch gemacht/ durch Hieremiam Martium. ... M. D. LXXI. (Gedruckt zů Augspurg/ bey Michaël Manger/ in verlegung Georgen Willers.) 8°. a-b^8 c^6. (School of Dentistry.) [38

LANDSBERG, JOHANN. Ain Christliche vnderrichtūg/ wie die Gőtlich geschrifft verleycht vnd geurtayl soll werdē ... 4°. A-B^4. ¶*Preface dated 20 January 1527.* [39

LANGE, JOHANN, of Lemberg. Oratio Ioannis Langij Lembergij, Encomium theologicæ disputationis ... (Lipsiæ, apud Melchiorem Lottherum. ... M.CCCCC.XIX. VI. Calen. Augusti.) 4°. A-B^4. [40

LANGE, JOHANN, Silesian. Ioannis Langi Silesii ... pro Christianis contra Turcas. Elegia. ... Viennæ Pannoniæ in ædibus Ioannis Singrenij. Anno M. D. XXXIX. 4°. A-F^4 G^2 H^4. [41

LANGLAND, WILLIAM. The vision of Pierce Plowman, newlye imprynted after the authours olde copy ... Wherevnto is also annexed the Crede of Pierce Plowman ... Imprinted at London, by Owen Rogers ... The yere ... a thousand, fyue hundred, thre score and one. The .xxi. daye of ... Februarye. 4°. B.L. ✠^{2} A-Hh^4 I^2. *S.T.C.* 19908. ¶*Lacks the* Creed of Piers Plowman. [42

LANGUET, HUBERT. Historica descriptio susceptae à caesarea maiestate executionis contra S. Rom. Imperij rebelles, eorumq̃ue Receptatorem: & captæ vrbis Gothæ, soloq̃ue æquati castri Grimmenstein, ... M.D.LXVII. XIII. Aprilis. M.D.LXVIII. 8°. A-C^8. [43

-- -- Historische beschreibung der ergangenen execution/ wider des Heil. Rőm. Reichs auffrhůrische Echter/ vnd derselben Receptatorn ... Im Jar 1568. 4°. A-H^4 (-H4, *presumably blank*). [44

-- -- Discours De l'execution par la Maiesté Imperiale, contre les rebelles du S. Empire Romain & leur receleur ... Imprimé ... M. D. LXX. 8°. A-C^8 D^4. pp. 4-56. ¶*Translator: Gabriel Chardon.* [45

LA NOUE, FRANÇOIS DE. Del modo di vincere i Turchi, & scacciarli d'Europa ... Discorso del Sig. della Noue. Tradotto da Girolamo Naselli Ferrarese dalla lingua Francesco nell' Italiana. In Ferrara, Appresso Vittorio Baldini ... M.D.C. 8°. a^4 A-H^8. pp. 2-128. (Lea.) [46

-- Discours politiques et militaires ... A Basle, De l'Imprimerie de François Forest. M. D. LXXXVII. 8°. *^{8} a-z^8 A-Bb^8 Cc^4. pp. 2-776. (Lea.) [47

LANQUET, THOMAS. An epitome of chronicles ... gathered ... fyrst, by Thomas Lanquet ..., and now ... continued to the reigne of ... kynge Edwarde the sixt by Thomas Cooper. Anno. M. D. LXIX. ([Imprinted at London ... in the house of Thomas·Berthelet ... M. D. XLIX.]) 4°. B.L. A^4 A-F^4 A-4D^4 (-4D4, *colophon*). ff. 1-292. *S.T.C.* 15217. [48

-- -- Coopers chronicle Conteyning the Whole discourse of the histories as well of this Realme, as of al other countreis ... Nowe latelye ... agmented, vnto the seuenth yere of the raigne of ... Quene Elizabeth ẏ^t nowe is. ℂ Anno 1565. 4°. B.L. a^6 b^2 c-d^8 g^4 h^2 A-Zz^8 A^2 A^8 (-A8, *presumably blank*). ff. 1-377. ¶*Not* S.T.C. 15220; *ends with the accession of Elizabeth.* (Furness.) [49

LANTERI, GIACOMO. Iacobi Lanteri Brixiensis libri duo, de modo substruendi terrena munimenta ad urbes ... quibus aditus hosti præcludatur ... Venetiis, apud Vincentium Volgrisium. M D LXIII. 4°. a^4 A^4 (A4 + *folded leaf*) C-M^4 (M4 + *folded leaf*) O^2 P^2. ff. 1-56. ¶*Additional t.p.* (I1^r): De modo substruendi ... Venetiis, M D LXIII. (Fine Arts.) [50

-- Due dialoghi ... del modo di disegnare le piante delle fortezze secondo Euclide; et del modo di comporre i modelli ... In Venetia appresso Vincenzo Valgrisi, & Baldessar Costantini. M D LVII. 4°. *^{4} A-M^4. p. 1-95. (Fine Arts.) [51

LAPINI, FROSINO. Lettere Toscane ... In Bologna appresso Anselmo Giaccarelli. M. D L VI. 8°. π^4 A-T^8 V^4. pp. 1-311. [52

LA POPELINIÈRE, HENRI LANCELOT VOISIN DE. L'histoire des histoires, Auec l'Idée de l'Histoire accomplie. Plus Le Dessein de l'Histoire nouuelle des François: Et pour Auant-jeu, La Refutation de la Descente des fugitifs de Troye ... A Paris, Chez Marc Orry ... 1599. ... 8°. a-z^8 Aa-Hh^8. pp. 2-495. [53

LA PRIMAUDAYE, PIERRE DE. Suite de l'academie Francoise. ... A Básle. Par Philemon de Hus. M. D. LXXXVII. 8°. *^{8} A-Xx^8 Yy^2. ff. 1-339. [54

LA RAMÉE, PIERRE. Petri Rami ... et Audomari Talæi collectaneæ Præfationes, Epistolæ, Orationes. ... Parisiis. Apud Dionysium Vallensem ... 1577. ... 8°. ã^4 A-Pp^8 Qq^4. pp. 1-612. [55

-- P. Rami actiones duæ, habitæ in Senatu, pro Regia Mathematicæ professionis cathedra. Editio secunda. Parisiis, Apud Andream Wechelum. 1566. ... 8°. A-E^4. pp. 3-40. [56

-- Petri Rami Veromandui Aristotelicae animaduersiones. Lugduni, apud Godefridum & Marcellum Beringos, fratres, 1545. (*Colophon.*) 8°. a-h^8. pp. 2-128. [57

-- -- ... Animaduersionum Aristotelicarum Libri XX. ... Lutetiae. E typographia Matthęi Dauidis ... 1548. (... mense Maij. ...) 8°. *^{8} a-z^8 A-G^8 (-G8, *blank*). pp. 2-473. [58

-- Petri Rami Veromandui Brutinæ Quæstiones ... Secunda editio. ... Parisiis, Ex typographia Matthæi Dauidis ... 1549. 8°. a-h^8 i^4. pp. 3-136. [59

-- Petri Rami ... Liber de militia C. Julii Cæsaris. Cum præfatione Joannis Thomæ Freigii ... Francofurti Apud hæredes Andreæ Wecheli, MDLXXXIIII. 8°. a-o^8. pp. 3-222. [60

-- P. Rami ... liber de moribus veterum Gallorum ... Francofurti, Apud hæredes Andreæ Wecheli. M. D. LXXXIIII. 8°. a-i^8. pp. 3-142. [61

-- Petri Rami praelectiones in Ciceronis orationes octo consulares. Vna cum Ipsius Vita, per Ioann. Thomam Freigium collecta. ... Basileae, per Petrum Pernam. Anno CIↃ IↃ LXXX. 4°. α-ζ^4 θ-ι^4 a-z^4 A-M^4. pp. 5-60, 1-279. ¶*Lacks* In I. de legibus Cic., In librum de fato, In Somnium Scipionis, De optimo genero Oratorum, Distinctiones Rhet. in Quintilianum, In Epistolas Platonis (Aa-Zz^4 AA-TT^4 VV^2). [62

-- Petri Rami Veromandui Pro philosophica Parisiensis Academiæ disciplina Oratio ... Parisiis, Ex typographia Matthæi Dauidis ... 1551. (... Calend. Martii. ...) 8°. a-h^8. pp. 3-125. [63

-- P. Rami ... scholarum Metaphysicarum libri quatuordecim, in totidem Metaphysicos libros Aristotelis. Parisiis, Apud Andream Wechelum. M. D. LXVI. ... 8°. a^8 A-T^8. ff. 1-137. [64

-- P. Rami ... scholarum Physicarũ libri octo, in totidem acroamaticos libros Aristotelis. Parisiis, Apud Andream Wechelum ... 1565. ... 8°. a^8 A-Z^8. ff. 1-171. [65

LASCARIS, CONSTANTINE. In hoc libro haec habentur. Constantini Lascaris Byzantini de octo partibus orõnis Lib. I. Eiusdem de Constructione Liber Secundus. Eiusdem de nomine & uerbo Liber Tertius. Eiusdem de pronomine ... opusculum. ... Cebetis tabula & græca & latina ... De literis græcis ac diphthongis ... Abbreuiationes, quibus frequentissime græci utuntur. Oratio Dominica & duplex salutatio ad Beatiss. Virginem. Symbolum Apostolorum. Euangelium diui Ioannis Euangelistæ. Carmina Aurea Pythagoræ. Phocylidis Poema ad bene, beatéq3 uiuendum. De Idiomatib. linguarum tres tractatus Ioannis grammatici. Eustathii Corinthi cum interpretatione latina. Introductio perbreuis ad hebraicam linguam. (Venetiis apud Aldum mense octobri M.D.XII.) 4°. α-μ^8 ν^4 ξ-π^8 ρ^4 a-f$^{8.10}$ g-m$^{10.8}$ n^6 x^{10} y^8 z^{10} &^{4} aa-bb^8 χ^4. ¶*The Greek and the Latin leaves alternate.* [66

LASCOVIUS, PETRUS MONEDULATUS. De Homine magno illo in rerum natura miraculo et partibus eius essentialibus, Lib. II. ... VVitebergae Per Heredes Iohannis Cratonis Anno M. D. LXXXV. 8°. a^8 b^4 A-Dd^8 Ee^6. pp. 1-439. [67

LASSO DE LA VEGA, GARCIA. Obras de Garcilasso de la Vega con anotaciones de Fernando de Herrera. ... En Seuilla por Alonso de la Barrera, Año de 1580. 4°. ¶^{4} A-N^8 O^4 P-Aa^8 Bb^4 Cc-Xx^8 Yy^4. pp. 1-691. [68

-- -- Obras del ... poeta Garcilasso de la Vega. Em Coimbra. Na Officina de Antonio de Mariz. Per seu Genro, & Heredeyro Diogo Gomez Loureyro ... M.DC. ... 12°. A-G^{12} H^4. ff. 2-76. [69

LASSUS, ORLANDO DE. [Moduli quatuor quinque sex septem octo & nouem vocum Orlando Lassusio auctore. Parisiis, Adrian le Roy & Robertus Ballard, 1577.] obl. 4°. A-M^4 (-A^4) N^2. ff. 5-50 *present.* ¶*Tenor part only.* (Music.) [70

-- [Orlandi Lassi ... fasciculi aliquot sacrarum cantionum ... Noribergae, in officina Gerlachiana, 1582.] obl. 4°. Aa-Rr^4 (-Aa1-3) Ss^2. ¶*Quinta vox only.* (Music.) [71

LATERAN COUNCIL. Edictum contra transgressores constitutionum et ordinationum sacri concilii Lateranensis. 4°. π^2. (Lea.) [72

LATIMER, HUGH. The fyrste Sermon of Mayster Hughe Latimer, whiche he preached before the Kynges Maiest. ... M.D.XLIX. the viii. of Marche. ... (Imprinted at London by Ihon Daye ... and William Seres ... [1549].) 8°. B.L. A-D^8. *S.T.C.* 15272. [73

-- [1] [Frutefull sermons preached by ... M. Hugh Latymer newly Imprinted with others, not heretofore set forth in print ...] (At London Printed by Iohn Daye ... 1571. ...) 4°. B.L. π^2 *(wanting)* a-p^8 q^4. ff. 1-124. ¶*Bound after* [3]. [2] Seuen sermons, made vpon the Lordes Prayer ... At London, Printed by Iohn Daye, ... 1572. A^4 ₵^{2} B-T^8 (-B3-6, C-O, P3-6, Q, S-T) V^4 *(wanting)*. ff. 2-148. ¶*For the missing parts the leaves of the 1562 printing of* Certayn godly sermons *(part of* S.T.C. *15276) with the same signatures and foliation (but not precisely the same text) have been substituted.* [3] Sermons preached by ... M. Hugh Latimer, the xxviij. of Octob. An. 1552. ... At London, Printed by Iohn Daye ... Aa^4 Bb-Ii^8 Kk^4 (- *all after* Ii1). ff. 151-209 *present.* *S.T.C.* 15277. (Furness.)[74

-- -- *Another copy (intact) of* [1] *and* [3] *(bound with part 2 of* S.T.C. *15276).* [75

-- -- Fruitfull Sermons Preached by ... M. Hugh Latimer, newly Imprinted ... At London Printed by Iohn Daye ... 1584. ... *(Colophon.)* 4°. B.L. *^{8} A-Tt^8 Vv^2. ff. 2-331. *S.T.C.* 15280. [76

-- -- Fruitfull sermons preached by ... Hugh Latimer ... At London, Reprinted by Valentine Sims. ... 1596. 4°. B.L. a^6 A-Y^8 Aa-Tt^8 Vv^2 *(wanting)*. ff. 1-329 *present.* *S.T.C.* 15281. [77

-- The seconde Sermon of Master Hughe Latemer whych he preached before the Kynges maiestie ... ẏ .xv. day of Marche. M.ccccc.xlix. ... ([Imprinted at London by Ihon Daye ... and William Seres ...]) 8°. B.L. A-Y^8 Aa-Ee^8 (-Cc^8, Ee6-8). *S.T.C.* 15274. ¶E4^v: The thyrde Sermon ... I7^r: The fourth Sermon ... O2^v: The fifte Sermon ... S7^v: The syxte Sermon ... Aa1^v: The seuenth Sermon ... [78

-- [1] 27 sermons preached by ... Maister Hugh Latimer, as well such as in tymes past haue bene printed, as certayne other commyng to our handes of late, whych were neuer set forth in print ... Imprinted at London by Iohn Day. ... 1562. 4°. A-B^8 C^6 D-Q^8 (-Q1, Q7, Q8). ff. 1-149. ¶*Additional t.p.* (D1): The seuen sermons of ... M. Hughe Latimer, whiche he preached before ... king Edward the .vi. *Same imprint.* C6 *defective, lacking the last five words.* [2] [Certayn godly Sermons, made vppon the lords Prayer ... Whereunto are annexed certaine other sermons ... collected by Augustin Bernher ... *Same imprint.*] A^4 (-A1) ₵^{2} B-T^8 V^4. ff. 1-148. *S.T.C.* 15276. (Furness.) [79

-- -- *Another copy of* [2] *(intact).* [80

LATINI, BRUNETTO. Il tesoro ... MDXXVIII. (Stampato in Vineggia per Gioan Antonio & Fratelli da Sabbio, ad instanza di Nicolo Garanta & Francesco da Salo ... Adi vinti Mazo [*sic*]. ...) 8°. a^8 A-LL^8. ff. 1-271. [81

LATOMUS, BARTHOLOMAEUS. Epistola Austriae ad Carolum Imp. fictitia. ... (Argentinae apud Ioannem Knoblochum mense Nouembri. Anno, M.D.XXI.) 8°. A^8 B^4. ¶*In verse.* [82

-- Refutatio calumniosarum insectationum Martini Bucceri, quibus nouissimis libellis æditisin Bartholomæum Latomum extra ordinem inuectus est. ... Coloniæ ex officina Melchioris Nouesiani, Anno M.D.XLVI. 4°. A-F^4 G^2. [83

LATOMUS, JACOBUS. Articulorum doctrinae Fratris Martini Lutheri per theologos Louanienses damnato℞ Ratio ... (Impressum Antuerpiæ per Michaelem Hilleniũ ... M.D.XXI. vij. die Maij.) 4°. [a]^4 b-y^4 aa-bb^4 cc^6 (-cc6, *blank*). [84

-- Iacobi Latomi ... de confessione secreta. Eiusdẽ de quæstionũ generibus quibus Ecclesia certat intus & foris. Eiusdem de Ecclesia & humanæ legis obligatione. Antuerpiae per M[ichaelem]. H[illenium]. Anno. M.D.XXV. 8°. A-E^8. (Lea.) [85

-- -- Iacobi Latomi ... de confessione secreta. Ioannis Oecolampadii elleboron, pro eodem Iacobo Latomo. (Basileae, per Andr. Cratandrum.) 8°. A-I^8. ¶Epistola *dated 6 May 1525.* [86

-- Iacobi Latomi ... opera, quæ præcipue aduersus horum temporum hæreses ... conscripsit ... Quibus accesserunt eiusdem authoris alia quædam opuscula ... Louanii, Excudebat Bartholomæus Grauius suis impensis, Petri Phalesij, ac Martini Rotarij. Anno, M.D.L. Iulij XXIX. ... fol. a^6 A-Mm^6 Nn^4. ff. 1-214. (Lea.) [87

LA TOUR-LANDRY, GEOFFROY DE. Der Ritter vom Thurn/ Zuchtmaister der Weiber vnd Junckfrawen. Anweisung der Junckfrawen vnd Frawen/ wess sich eyn jede ... halten sol ... Von neuwem verteutscht/ vnd getruckt zů Strassburg beim M. Jacob Cammerlander von Mentz. Anno M. D. XXXviij. fol. π^4 A-O^4. ff. i-lv. ¶*Translator: Marquart vom Steyn.* [88

LAUDIVIO, ZACCHIA, DE VEZZANO. Lettere del gran Mahumeto imperadore de' Turchi; ... ridotte nella volgar lingua da M. Lodouico Dolce. Insieme con le lettere di Falaride Tiranno de gli Agrigentini. ... In Vinegia appresso Gabriel Giolito de' Ferrari. M D LXIII. 8°. A-M^8. pp. 3-192. [89

LAURENTIUS PISANUS. Laurentii presbyteri Pisani paradoxorum theologicorum enchiridion. ... Viennæ Austriæ primus excudebat Ioannes Carbo. 8°. A-E^8. pp. 3-81. [90

LAURET, BERNARD. Casus I quibus iudex secularis potest manus ĩ persõas clericorũ sine metu excõmunicationis ĩponere De priuilegiis clericorum [Bonincontri] De exemptionibus [Baldi de Ubaldis] De carceribus De alimentis [Bartoli] (impressus Parrhisiis pro Ioanne paruo ... Anno ... millesimo quingentesimo decimooctauo Die vero vicesimasexta Mensis Augusti.) 8°. B.L. a-d^8 e^4. (Lea.) [91

LAUTERBECK, GEORG. Regentenbuch Aus vielen trefflichen alten vñ newen Historien ... 1556. (Gedruckt zu Leipzigk durch Iacobum Berwald. ...) fol. *^{6} [illegible]^6 A-Z^6 a-e^6 f^4 (-f4, *presumably blank*). ff. I-CLXXI. [92

LAUTERWALD, MATTHIAS. Was vnser Gerechtigkeit heisse ... angezeiget/ wider des wesentichters Andree Osiandri/ schwermerische entzuckung ... Gedruckt zu Wittemberg/ Durch Veit Creutzer. M. D. LII. 4°. A-C^4 D^2 E^4. [93

LAVATER, LOUIS. De Spectris, lemuribus et magnis atque insolitis fragoribus, variisque præsagitionibus quæ plerumque obitum hominum, magnas clades, mutationésque Imperiorum præcedunt, liber vnus. ... Geneuae. Anchora Crispiniana. M. D. LXX. 8°. ¶^{8} a-r^8. pp. 1-272. (Lea.) [94

-- -- Geneuae apud Eustathium Vignon. M. D. LXXV. 8°. ¶^{8} a-r^8. pp. 1-272. [95

LAVEZIOLA, ALBERTO. Rime ... In Verona, Per Gieronimo Strengari, e fratelli. M D LXXXIII. 8°. a^4 (-a1, *blank*) b^8 A-F^8. [96

LAX, GASPAR. Tractatus paruorum logicaliũ ... (... impressi in ... Cesaraugusta sumptibus ꝛ opera Georgij Coci theutonici ... M.D.xxj. Sexto calendas Decembris.) fol. B.L. a^{6+1} b-m^6 n^4. [97

LAZARILLO DE TORMES. [1] La vida de Lazarillo de Tormes ... En Anuers ... en casa de Guillermo Simon. M. D. LV. 12°. A-D^{12}. pp. 3-94. [2] La segunda parte ... *Same imprint.* A-F^{12} G^6. ff. 2-83. [98

LAZIUS, WOLFGANGUS. De gentium aliquot migrationibus, sedibus fixis, reliquiis, linguarumque initiis & immutationibus ac dialectis, Libri XII. ... Francofurti, Apud Andreæ Wecheli heredes, Claudium Marnium, & Ioannem Aubrium. M D C. fol. A-3M^{6} 3N^{8}. pp. 3-675. (Lea.) [99

LE BRON, NICOLAS. Nic. B. car. ad ... Car. quin. imp. ... (Antuerpiæ typis Antonii Goini an. M. D. XLI.) 8°. A^{8} B^{4} C^{8}. [100

LE BRUN DE SILLY. Brunonis Pomerani Syllae Christiani exercitus disciplina ... Le Brun de Silly. 8°. A-G^{8}. pp. 3-111. ¶*Prologue dated* M.D.XLI. Kal. Maij. [101

L'ÉCLUSE, CHARLES DE. Caroli Clusii Atrebat. Rariorum aliquot stirpium per Hispanias obseruatarum Historia ... Antuerpiæ, Ex officina Christophori Plantini ... M. D. LXXVI. (... quarto Kalend. Martii.) 8°. A-Z^{8} a-l^{8} (-l8, *blank*). pp. 3-529. [101a

LE FÈVRE, JACQUES, d'ÉTAPLES. Artificialis introductio per modum Epitomatis/ in decem libros Ethicorum Aristotelis: adiectis elucidata commentarijs [Jodoci Clichtovei] ... hac in secunda recognitione ... (... absoluta est in Alma Parhisiorum academia per Henricum Stephanum ... 1506 vicesimotertia februarij.) fol. a-f^{8} g-h^{6}. ff. 2-60. [102

-- -- (In orbe veneto ... absolutu3. Per Iacobum Pentium Leucensem ... 1506. Die .14. Octob.) 4°. B.L. a^{2} b-m^{8} (-m8, *presumably blank*). ff. 1-87. [103

-- -- Iacobi Fabri Stapulensis Introductio moralis in Ethicen Aristotelis ... (... In alma Parisiorum academia. 1510) fol. B.L. a^{10}. a1^{r}: Virtutis querimonia ex Baptista Mantuano. a1^{v}: *author's introduction.* a2^{r}: *head-title as above.* [104

-- -- Artificialis introductio Iacobi Fabri Stapulẽsis: In Decẽ Ethicorũ Libros Aristotelis: Adiuncto ... Commẽtario Iudoci Clichtouei Declarata. Leonardi Aretini dialogus de Moribus ... Iacobi Fabri Stapulensis introductio in politicam. Xenophontis dialogus de economia. (Ioannes Groninger: Argentorati ... publicauit. ... M.D.XI. Mense Martio) 4°. B.L. A^{6} B-C^{8} D-G$^{8.6}$ H-I^{8} K-N$^{8.6}$ O^{4} P^{8} Q^{6} R^{4} S-T^{8} V^{4} X^{8}. ff. II-CXXXIX. [105

-- -- Moralis Iacobi Fabri Stapulensis in Ethicen introductio, Iudoci Clichtouei Neoportuensis ... commentario elucidata. Parisiis [In aedibus Simonis Colinæi.] 1528 (... mense Augusto.) fol. A-E^{8} F-H^{6}. ff. 3-56. ¶*Imprint partly erased.* [106

-- Contemplationes idiotae per Iacobũ fabrũ ... M D XXXVIII. (Venetiis in ædibus Bartholomæi de Zanettis Casterzagensis: Sumptibus vero Ioãnis ab ecclesiæ Papiẽsis ... Mense Augusti.) 16°. a-q^{8} r^{4}. ff. 2-131. (Lea.) [107

-- Iacobi Fabri Stapulensis, de Maria Magdalena, & Triduo Christi, disceptatio ... Hagenoæ, ex Neocademia Anshelmiana. (... Mense Decembri. Anno. M. D. XVIII.) 4°. aa-ff^{4} gg^{6}. [108

-- In hoc libro contenta. Epitome compendiosaq3 introductio in libros Arithmeticos diui Seuerini Boetij: adiecta familiare commentario ... [Jodoci Clichtovei.] praxis numerandi ... [Clichtovei.] Introductio in Geometriam ... [Caroli Bovillii.] Liber de quadratura circuli [Bovillii]. Liber de cubiculatione sphere [Bovillii]. Perspectiua introductio [Bovillii]. Insuper Astronomicon. (... impresserũt Volphgangus hopilius et Henricus stephanus ... socii in Almo parisiorum studio ... 1503. Die vicesimaseptima Iunij.) fol. a-o^{8}. ff. ij-cxij. [109

-- [A1^{v}] Iacobi Fabri Stapulensis in politica Aristotelis introductio. (Parisiis. Pridie Nonas Septembris. M.D.XII. ex officina Henrici Stephani ...) fol. A^{10}. ff. 2-10. A3^{r}: [Economica Xenophontis.] [110

-- -- In hoc opere cõtenta. In politica Aristotelis/ introductio: adiecto commẽtario declarata. Oeconomicon Xenophontis: a Raphaele Volaterano traductum. (Parisijs: vicesima secunda die nouembris/ anno ... decimosexto/ supra millesimum & quingentesimum. ex officina Henrici Stephani ...) fol. a-c^{8} d-e^{6}. ff. 2-36. [111

-- -- *Another copy.* [112

LEGACCI, PIERANTONIO. Ecloga a la Martorella ... Intitolata Sauina. (Stampata in Vinegia per Girolamo Pencio da Lecco, Ad instantia di Christoforo da Millano ditto Stampone e suoi compagni. Ne l'anno. M.D.XXVIII. Adi .VI. di Feb.) 8°. A-B^{4}. [113

-- Egloga rusticale ... Intitolata Tognin del Cresta. ... 8°. A-B^8 (-B8, *presumably blank*). [114

LEGH, GERARD. The Accedence of Armorie. (London Printed by Henrie Ballard ... 1597.) 4°. A-S^8 (R8 + *folded leaf*). ff. 1-135. *S.T.C.* 15392. [115

LEGNAGO. Ius ciuile Leniacensium. (Venetiis, MDLV. Apud Nicolaum Tridentinum.) fol. π^2 aa-ff^2 a-z^2 A-R^2 χ^1 *(errata, colophon)*. pp. 1-156. (Lea.) [116

LEGRAND, JEAN MATTHIEU. Io. Mathæi Magni De præsenti Parisiensis Academiæ rerum statu Oratio ... [Parisiis,] Ex Typographia, Dionysij à Prato ... 1588. 8°. A-F^4. pp. 4-46. [117

LEHRE. Wie mā die recht Ewangelisch ler pflantzē mᵒͤcht in der Christenheit/ vnnd was bysshar mengen Doctor die selbig zů bekummen verhindert hat. [Basel, Adam Petri, 1521.] 4°. a^4. [119

LEIGH, VALENTINE. The moste profitable and commendable Science, of Surueiyng ... Imprinted at London, for Andrewe Maunsell ... 1578. 4°. B.L. A-Q^4 (-A1, *presumably blank*). *S.T.C.* 15417. ¶*Sig.* H *consists of 2 folded leaves.* [120

LEIPZIG. Weinordnung der Stadt Leipzig/ Verneůert/ ... M. D. LXV. 4°. A-B^4. [121

-- Dess Raths Zu Leipzig vornewerte Ordnung vnnd Reformation wegen der Tracht vnnd Kleidung/ Auch wie es mit Anstellung der Hochzeiten/ Vorlöbnussen/ Kindtauffen vnd Begräbnussen ... werden sol. ... Anno M. D. XCV. Gedruckt zu Leipzig/ bey Iohan: Beyer. 4°. A-E^4. [122

-- *University.* Endlicher Bericht vnd Erklerung der Theologen beider Vniuersiteten/ Leipzig vnd Wittemberg ... belangend die Lere/ so gemelte Vniuersiteten vnd Kirchen von anfang der Augspurgischen Confession bis auff diese zeit ... gefůret haben ... Mit ... Warnung ... von den streittigen Artikeln/ so Flacius Illyricus ... erregt ... Wittemberg Gedruckt durch Hans Lufft. 1570. 4°. A-3G^4. ff. 2-208. [123

-- Warhafftiger bericht vnd kurtze Warnung der Theologen/ beider Vniuersitet Leipzig vnd Wittemberg/ Von Den newlich zu Ihena im Druck ausgangenen/ Acten des Colloquij/ so zu Aldenburg in Meissen gehalten. 1570. (Gedruckt zu Wittemberg/ duch [*sic*] Peter Seitz. ...) 4°. A-F^4. [124

-- -- Warhafftiger bericht vnd kurtze warnung der Theologen/ beider Vniuersitet Leiptzig vnd Wittemberg ... 1570. [Wittenberg, Peter Seitz.] 4°. A-F^4. [125

-- Ein New lied von der belegerung der ... Stad Leipzig/ von dem Churfůrsten zu Sachssen ... auff den v. tag des Ienners/ im M.D.XLVII. jar/ Ist aber nicht geschehen *rc*. Im thon/ Es geht ein frischer Sommer daher *rc*. 4°. A^6. [126

-- Warhafftiger vnd erschrecklicher Auffruhr zu Leiptzig/ etc. Darinnen Verzeichnet wird/ was sich aussgangs des Leiptzischen Ostermarckts dieses 1593. Jahrs/ mit Stůrmung der Caluinisten Heuser zugetragen ... Durch einen liebhaber der Warheit in Druck gegeben. Gedruckt zu Ihena/ Im Jahr 1593. 4°. A-B^4 (-B4, *presumably blank*). [127

LEISENTRITT, JOHANN. Constitutio. Veteris, apostolicæ et orthodoxæ ecclesiae, breuissime complectens gradus & ... tempora, in quibus liceat, quibusq̃3 prohibeatur, Desponsatos copulare, & nuptias celebrare ... Budissinae. Anno. M.D.LXXII. (... Excudebat Ioannes Wolrab. ...) 4°. A-C^4 D^8. ¶*Folded leaf* D8 *inserted after* D4. (Lea.) [128

LEMNIUS, LEVINUS. Leuini Lemnii medici Zirizæi, de habitu et constitutione corporis, quam Græci χρᾶσιν, Triuiales complexionem, vocant, Libri II ... Francofurti Ex Officina Paltheniana, sumtibus viduæ Petri Fischeri. M. D. XCVI. 16°. ✠^{8} A-M^8. pp. 1-185. (Lea.) [129

-- De miraculis occulti naturæ, libri IIII: Item de vita cum animi et corporis incolumitate recte instituenda, liber vnus. ... 1590. Francofurdi Ex officina typographica Ioannis Wecheli. 8°. †^{8} A-RR^8 (-RR8, *blank*). pp. 1-582. (Smith.) [130

LEMNIUS, SIMON. M. Simonis Lemnii epigrammaton libri III. ... Querela ad Principem. ... M. D. XXXVIII. 8°. A-I^8 K^4. [131

LE MOYNE, JACQUES. Breuis narratio eorum quæ in Florida Americæ prouīcia Gallis acciderunt ... quae est secunda pars Americae. ... Francoforti ad Moenum, Typis Ioānis Wecheli, Sumtibus vero Theodori de Bry Anno M D XCI. Venales reperiuntur in officina Sigismundi Feirabēdii (*Colophon.*) fol.)(^{4} ()(4 + *folded sheet*) a-d^4 A-H^6 (-H2) I^4 K^6 (-K6, *blank*). ¶*Engraved t.p. Additional engraved t.p.* (A1^r): Indorum Floridam prouinciam inhabitantium eicones ... *Same imprint.* [132

LENGENBRUNNER, JOHANN. Erinnerung/ was von Martin Luther/ seiner Lehr/ vnd dañ andern Lutherischen Theologen vnd Predicanten aigentlich zu halten sey. ... 1576. (Gedruckt zu Ingolstatt durch Alexander Weyssenhorn vnd andere seine Miterben. Anno M. D. LXXVII.) 4°. A-H^4. ff. 1-28. [133

LENICAERUS, ALBERTUS. Quarta M. T. Ciceronis contra Catilinam oratio ... explicata. ... VVittebergæ Excudebat Clemens Schleich. M.D.LXXXVIII. 8°. A-K^8 L^4. [134

LENS, JEAN DE. De fidelium animarum purgatorio, libri duo. De limbo patrum, liber tertius. Authore Ioanne Lensæo Belliolano ... Louanii, Excudebat Ioannes Masius, suis & Petri Fabri Bibliopolæ sumptibus. Anno cIↄ. Iↄ. LXXXIIII. ... 8°. *^{8} A-Z^8 a-c^8. pp. 1-397. (Lea.) [135

LENTOLO, SCIPIONE. Italicae grammatices præcepta ac ratio ... Scipione Lentulo Neapolitano non tam authore quam collectore. Secunda Editio. [Genevae,] Apud Eustathium Vignon. cIↄ. Iↄ. LXXX. 8°. A-G^8 H^4. pp. 3-119. [136

LENZONI, CARLO. Carlo Lenzoni in difesa della lingua Fiorentina, et di Dante. Con le regole da far bella et numerosa la prosa. ... In Fiorenza MDLVI (Stampata ... appresso Lorenzo Torrentino ... MDLVII) 4°. A-DD^4 EE^2. pp. 3-204. [137

LEO OF SPERLONGA. Artis notarie Tēpestatis huius Speculum ... editum ... ꝑ ... Leonem spelūcanū ... in ordinem exidere collectuȝ ... a ... Alexandro de Aquila Pomericeo ... MDXXXVIII. (Venetiis per Ioannem Andream dictum Guadagninum ⁊ fratres de Vauassoribus. ... Mense Septmebris.) 8°. B.L. A-Z^8 &^{8} ℴ^8 ℞^{8} a-f^8. ff. 2-252. (Lea.) [138

LEO, JOHANNES, AFRICANUS. Ioannis Leonis Africani, de totius Africæ descriptione, libri .IX. ... Ioan. Floriano interprete. Antuerpiæ Apud Ioan. Latium, M.D.LVI. ... *^{8} *^{8} A-Pp^8. ff. 2-302. [139

LEON, JOHANN. Tragoedia. Die Histori von der Gͤotlichen Offenbarung des waren Messie vnseres Heylandts ... Spielsweise in kͤunstliche Rheimen verfasst ... 1566. (Gedruckt zu Franckfurt am Meyn ...) 8°. A-G^8. ff. 1-45. [140

LEON, LUIS PONCE DE. La perfecta casada, por ... F. Luys de Leon. Tercera impression ... En Salamanca, En casa de Guillelmo Foquel. M.D.LXXXVII. (*Colophon.*) 4°. π^2 A-K^8 L^{10}. ff. 1-89. [141

LEONARDINI, FEDERICO. Alcune rime di diuersi moderni scrittori in morte dell'onorata giouane M. Innocenza Giannotti ... Raccolte per M. Federico Leonardini da Longiano ... In Rimini per Bernardino Pasini ... 1577. 4°. +^{4} A-K^4. ff. 1-40. [142

LEONI, GIOVANNI BATTISTA. Antiloco tragicomedia ... In Ferrara, Appresso Benedetto Mammarelli, Ad istantia di Gio: Battista Ciotti ... 1594. 4°. *^{4} a^4 A-P^4 Q^6. ff. 1-64. [143

-- Considerationi ... sopra l'historia d'Italia di Messer Francesco Guicciardini. ... In Venetia appresso i Gioliti. M D LXXXIII. (*Colophon.*) 4°. *^{4} A-M^8. pp. 1-177. [144

-- Madrigali ... In Venetia presso Gio.bat. Ciotti 1598. 12°. A-B^{12} C^6. ff. 2-30. [145

LEONICO TOMEO, NICCOLO. Nicolai Leonici Thomaei dialogi ... (Venetiis in ædibus Gregorii de Gregoriis. Mense septembri. M. D. XXIIII.) 4°. a-z^4. ff. II-XC. [146

-- Nicolai Leonici Thomaei opuscula ... (... ex impressione repræsentauit Bernardinus

Vitalis Venetus ... MCCCCCXXV. Die .xxiii. Februarii. Ex Venetiis.) 4°. a-b^4 c^6 d-z^4 &^{4} ɔ^4 ℞^{4} A-G^4 H^6 I^4. ff. II-CXXXIX. [147

-- Li tre libri ... de varie historie, nuouamente tradotti in buona lingua volgare. In Venetia. M. D. XLIIII. ... (... per Michele Tramezzino ...) 8°. *^{8} *^{8} A-T^8. ff. 1-150. ¶*Translator: Giouan Battista Castrodardo Bellonese.* [148

-- -- *Another copy.* (Lea.) [149

LEOWITZ, CYPRIAN VON. De coniunctionibus magnis insignoribus superiorum planetarum, Solis defectionibus, & Cometis, in quarta Monarchia, cum eorundem effectuum historica expositione. His ... accessit Prognosticon ab ... 1564 in Viginti sequentes annos. ... Laugingae ad Danubium excudebat Emanuel Salczer ... M.D.LXIIII. 4°. A-N^4. ¶*Additional t.p.* (L1): Prognosticon ab anno Domini 1564. ... L-N^4 *bound in before* A1. (Lea.) [150

LE PETIT, JEAN FRANÇOIS. Dialogisme auquel sont entreparliers l'empire, la France, l'Espagne, l'Vnion des Estats du Pays bas. Rome, Bonne Raison, Le Herault, & le Philosophe Iuge. ... 1600. 4°. A-E^8 F^4. pp. 1-83. [151

LEPIDA, VOLUCRINIA *(pseudonym)*. Theses de cochleatione eiusque venenosa contagione, & multiplicibus speciebus, quas, sub præside Hasione Leflero Narragonensi, ... defendet Volucrinia Lepida Stutzerensis: In Collegij huius facultatis penetralibus, in frequentia vtriusq3 sexus. ... M. D. XCII. 4°. A^6. [152

LE ROY, LOUIS. Considerations sur l'histoire Francoise, et l'vniuerselle de ce Temps ... A Paris, De l'imprimerie de Federic Morel ... M.D.LXX. ... 8°. A-D^4. ff. 2-15. [153

-- Della vicissitudine o mutabile varietà delle cose nell'vniuerso Libri XII. di Luigi Regio Francese Tradotti dal K.^{r} Hercole Cato. ... In Venetia. CIƆ. IƆ. XCII. Presso Aldo. 4°. a^4 a^8 b^4 A-V^8 X^4. pp. 2-327. [154

-- Exhortation aux Francois pour viure en concorde, et iouir du bien de la Paix. Par Louys le Roy. A Paris. Chez Iaques du Puis ... 1570. ... (De l'Imprimerie de Federic Morel ... Au Mois de Septembre.) 8°. A-Q^8. ff. 2-128. [155

-- Ludouici Regii Constantini oratio ad ... Henricum II. Franc. & Philippum Hisp. Reges, de Pace & concordia nuper inter eos inita, & bello religionis Christianæ hostibus inferendo. Parisiis, Apud Federicum Morellum ... 1559. ... 4°. A-E^4. ff. 3-18. [156

LESINA. Capitoli da osseruarsi inuiolabilmente, da tutti i confrati Della ... Compagnia della Lesina. ... Stampata. Per ordine de gli otto Operai di detta Compagnia. [c. 1585.] 4°. A-F^4 (-F4, *blank*). pp. 6-40. [157

LESNAUDERIE, PIERRE DE. Opusculū de doctoribus: ꝛ priuilegijs eorū ... Habetꝛ venale Parhisius apud Frācíscū Regnault ... (Impressum ... expensis ... Francisci regnault ... Et Michaelis angier Cadomensis. ... 1516. die vltima Ianuarij.) 8°. B.L. A-B^8 a-k^8 l^6. ff. ij-lxxxvj. [158

LE SUEUR, PIERRE. De differentia ætatis patrum nostrorum qui sub Romana et Apostolica Ecclesia vixerunt, Et nostræ ... Parisiis. Apud Iacobum Keruer ... 1563. 8°. A-C^8. [159

LETTERE. [1][Lettere volgari di diuersi nobilissimi huomini ... Libro primo. ... M. D. XLIX.] (In Vinegia, nell'anno M D XXXXVIII. In casa de' figliuoli di Aldo.) 8°. A-R^8 (-A1). ff. 2-129. [2] Lettere volgari ... Libro secondo. ... M. D. XLIX. (In Vinegia, nell'anno M. D. XLIX. In casa de' figliuoli di Aldo.) A-P^8. ff. 2-117. ¶*The second book is bound before and the first book after the t.p. of the second book.* [160

-- -- [1] Lettere volgari ... Con la giunta del Terzo libro ... Libro primo. In Vinegia, [Aldine press,] M. D. LXIIII. (*Colophon.*) 8°. A-S^8. ff. 3-141. [2] ... Libro secondo. ... M. D. LXIIII. (In Venetia ...) a-q^8. ff. 2-128. [3] ... Libro terzo ... M. D. LXIIII. Aa^4 Bb-Ee^8 F-I^8 Kk-3E^8 3F^4 (*lacking all after* Ss7). ff. 9-142 *present.* [161

LEVANTO. (Explicit Iurium Municipalium Antiquorum & Recentiorum ... Communis Leuanti Volumen cura & impensa Francisci Payte Notarij ... per ... Antonium Bellonum Thaurini Pedemontarum impressum, ... M.D.XLVIII. die xxviij. Iunij ...) 4°. AA^6 ✠^{6} A-R^4. ff. 1-67. (Lea.) [162

LEVI BEN GERSHON

LEVI BEN GERSHON. ספר מלחמות השם להכלוכוף... לוי בן גרשון נדפס פה ר"יווא דטרי"נט שנת שך לפ"ק [Riva di Trento, Jacopo Mascaria, 1560.] fol. 1-9^8 10^4. ff. ב–עה. [163

LEYDEN. *University. Faculty of Law.* Statuta Collegii Publici Iuridici in Academia Lugdunensi Batavorum ... Lugduni Batavorum, Ex officina Thomæ Basson. cIo. Io. XCVII. 4°. A-B^4. (Lea.) [164

-- Disputatio prima de iustitia et iure, tam scripto quam non scripto ... Præside Iulio à Beyma. ... Exhibet Iohannes Bögelius Gedanensis Pruthenus. ... Lugduni Batavorum, Ex officina Thomæ Basson. cIɔ. Iɔ. XCVI. 4°. A-B^4. (Lea.) [165

-- Disputatio secunda de iurisdictione ... Præside ... Eberardo à Bronckhorst. ... Examinandum proponet Iacobus Douza Amsterodamensis. ... *Same imprint.* 4°. A^6. (Lea.) [166

-- Disputatio tertia de praeparatoriis processus iudicarii, Hoc est, de in ius vocando, et edendo. ... Præside ... Cornelio de Groot ... Discutiendam proponet Hero ab Hottingha Frisius. ... *Same imprint.* 4°. A^6. (Lea.) [167

-- Disputatio quarta de pactis. ... Præside ... Iulio à Beyma Frisio instituit Gisbertus Bouricius Frisius. ... *Same imprint.* 4°. A^6. (Lea.) [168

-- Disputatio quinta de transactionibus ... Præside ... Eberardo à Bronckhorst. Exercitij gratia instituit Eggerdus à Kempen Dantiscanus. ... *Same imprint.* 4°. A^6. (Lea.) [169

-- Disputatio sexta de postulando et his qui notantur infamia. ... Sub Præsidio ... Cornelii de Groot ... Proponit Philippus Lacken Dantiscanus. ... *Same imprint.* 4°. A-B^4. (Lea.) [170

-- Disputatio septima de procuratoribus et defensoribus ... Sub Præsidio ... Everhardi Bronchorst ... Discutiendam proponit Volcuerus Cornelii Medenbliccensis ... *Same imprint.* 4°. A^6. (Lea.) [171

-- Disputatio octava de negotiis gestis ... Sub Præsidio ... Cornelii de Groot ... Propono Arnoldus Limburg Westphalus ... *Same imprint.* 4°. A^6. (Lea.) [172

-- Disputatio nona de dolo malo, et metu ... Præside ... Everardo Bronchorst. ... Examinandam proponit Philibertus à Borsalia. ... *Same imprint.* 4°. A^4 B^2. (Lea.) [173

-- Disputatio decima de restitutione minorum ... Præside ... Cornelio de Groot ... Respondente Cornelio Pynacker Delphico Batavo ... *Same imprint.* 4°. A^6. (Lea.) [174

-- Disputatio undecima de iudiciis et ubi quisque agere vel conveniri debeat ... Præside ... Everardo Bronchorst. ... Excutiendam proponit Petrus Poppo Amstelodamensis. ... Lugduni Batavorum, Ex officina Thomæ Basson. cIɔ. Iɔ. XCVI. 4°. A-B^4. (Lea.) [175

-- Disputatio duodecima de hereditatis petitione ... Præside ... Cornelio de Groot ... Examinandam proponit Dominicus ab Hottingha Frisius. ... *Same imprint.* 4°. A^6. (Lea.) [176

-- Disputatio decima tertia de rei vindicatione et publiciana in rem actione ... Sub Præsidio ... Gerarti Tuningi ... instituit Isbrandus Rietwyck Alcmarianus ... *Same imprint.* 4°. A^6. (Lea.) [177

-- Disputatio decima quarta de iure emphyteutico ... Præside ... Eberhardo Bronchorst. ... instituit Ioannes à Rivieren Hagocomitanus. ... *Same imprint.* 4°. A-B^4. (Lea.) [178

-- Disputatio decima quinta de usufructu. ... Sub Præsidio ... Cornelii de Groot ... Proponit Iacobus VVarnerius Geldrus. ... *Same imprint.* 4°. A^6. (Lea.) [179

-- Disputatio decima sexta de servitutibus urbanorum et rusticorum prædiorum. ... Præside ... Gerardo Tunningo ... Proponit. Samuel Vekemannus Amsterodamensis. ... Lugduni Batavorum, Ex officina Thomæ Basson. cIo. Iɔ. IVC. 4°. A^6. (Lea.) [180

-- Disputatio decima septima de iudiciis mixtis finium regundor. famil. ercisc. communi dividundo. ... Præside ... Everardo Bronchorst. ... Disputandam proponit Petrus Poppo Amstel. ... *Same imprint.* 4°. A^6. (Lea.) [181

-- Disputatio decima octava de rebus creditis, si cer. pet. et de cond. ... Præside ... Cornelio de Groot ... Defendet Iacobus Teylingius Alcmarianus ... *Same imprint.* 4°. A^6. (Lea.) [182

-- Disputatio decima nona de iureiurando ... Præside ... Gerarto Tuningo ... proponit. Reinerus à Persijn Amsterodamensis. ... Lugduni Batavorum, Ex officina Thomæ Basson. cIↄ. Iↄ. XCVI. 4°. A^6 (-A6, *blank*). (Lea.) [183

-- Disputatio vigesima de condictione indebiti ... Præside ... Everardo à Bronchorst. ... Discutiendam proponet. Clemens Fabius Alcmarianus. ... *Same imprint*. 4°. A^6. (Lea.) [184

-- Disputatio vigesima prima de S.C. Macedoniano, et Velleiano. ... Præside ... Cornelio de Groot ... Defendet Timannus à Kuyck Ultraiectinus. ... *Same imprint*. 4°. A^6. (Lea.) [185

-- Disputatio vigesima secunda de deposito sequestratione et compensationib. ... Sub Moderamine ... Gerardi Tuningii ... Proponit. Philippus Lacken Dantiscô Borussus ... *Same imprint*. 4°. A^6. (Lea.) [186

-- Disputatio vigesima tertia de mandato ac societate ... Præside ... Everardo à Bronchorst. ... Discutiendam proponit. Volcuerus Cornelii Medenbl. ... Lugduni Batavorum, Ex officina Thomæ Basson. cIↄ. Iↄ. IVC. 4°. A^8. (Lea.) [187

-- Disputatio vigesima quarta de contrahenda emptione et pactis inter emptorem et venditorem compositis. ... Moderatore ... Cornelio de Groot ... Discutiendam propono. Arnoldus à Limburg Westphalus ... *Same imprint*. 4°. A-B^4. (Lea.) [188

-- Disputatio vigesima quinta de locatione et conductione ... Sub Præsidio ... Gerarti Tuningii ... Ventilandam proponit Philibertus Borsalus Mattiacus ... *Same imprint*. 4°. A-B^4 C^6. (Lea.) [189

-- Disputatio vigesima sexta de pignoribus et hypothecis ... Præside ... Everardo Bronchorstio. Respondente Cornelio Pynacker Delph. Batt. ... *Same imprint*. 4°. A-B^4. (Lea.) [190

-- Disputatio vigesima septima de usuris ... Præside ... Cornelio de Groot ... Tueri conabor Isbrandus Rietwyck Alcmarianus. ... Lugduni Batavorum, Ex officina Thomæ Basson. cIↄ. Iↄ. XCVII. 4°. A^6. (Lea.) [191

-- Disputatio vigesima octava de probationibus et præsumptionibus. ... Præside ... Gerarto Tuningio ... Tueri conabor Cornelius Nicolai Vlissinganus ... *Same imprint*. 4°. A^6. (Lea.) [192

-- Disputatio vigesima nona de fide instrumentorum et testibus ... Præside ... Cornelio de Groot. ... Discutiendam proponit. Timannus à Weede Vltraiectinus. ... *Same imprint*. 4°. A^6. (Lea.) [193

-- Disputatio trigesima de sponsalibus et ritu nuptiarum ... Præside ... Gerardo Tuningio, Respondente Carolo de Varick ... *Same imprint*. 4°. A-B^4. (Lea.) [194

-- Disputatio trigesima prima de iure dotium ... Sub præsidio ... Cornelii de Groot ... Examinandum proponet: Iacobus Warnerius Geldrus ... *Same imprint*. 4°. A^6. (Lea.) [195

-- Disputatio trigesima secunda de tutela et cura ... Sub præsidio ... Gerarti Tuningii ... Defendere conabor Iacobus Brouchoven Leydanus ... *Same imprint*. 4°. A^6. (Lea.) [196

-- Disputatio trigesima tertia de testamentis, qui facere possint et quemadmodum fiant. Præside ... Cornelio de Groot, Respondente Iusto à Dedel Delph. Bat. Examinabitur ... Lugd. Batavor. Ex officina Thomæ Basson. cIↄ. Iↄ. XCVII. 4°. A^6. (Lea.) [197

-- Disputatio trigesima quarta de hæredibus instituendis ... Præside ... Everardo à Bronchorst. ... Examinandam proponit Florentius Teylingius Amsterodamēsis. ... Lugd. Bat. Ex officinâ Thomæ Basson. cIↄ. Iↄ. XCVII. 4°. A^6 (-A6, *blank*). (Lea.) [198

-- Disputatio trigesima quinta de vulgari et pupillari substitutione: ... Præside ... Cornelio de Groot, Examinandum proponit Ioannes Valentinus Saltzman Argentinensis. ... *Same imprint*. 4°. A^8. (Lea.) [199

-- Disputatio trigesima sexta de acquirenda, vel omittenda hereditate, ... Sub præsidio ... Gerardi Tuningii, tueri conabor Iacobus Lettingius Leidensis. ... Lugduni in Batavia, Ex Typographeo Ioannis Patij. Anno cIↄ. Io. XCVII. 4°. A^6. (Lea.) [200

-- Disputatio trigesima septima de legatis ... Sub Præsidio ... Everhardi Bronchorst. Publicè examinandam poponit [*sic*]. Gerhardus â Foegelsanck Frisius. ... Lugduni Batavorum. Ex officinâ Thomæ Basson. cIↄ. Iↄ. XCVII. 4°. A^6. (Lea.) [201

-- Disputatio trigesima octava de conditionibus et demonstrationibus quæ legatis adiiciuntur ... Sub Præsidio ... Cornelii de Groot ... Asserere conabitur Michael Barlandus Goesanus. ... Lugd. Batavor. Ex officina Thomæ Basson. cIↄ. Iↄ. XCVII. 4°. A6. (Lea.) [202

-- Disputatio trigesima nona de lege falcidia et senatus consulto Trebelliano ... Præside ... Gerarto Tuningio ... Examinandam proponit. Iobus Porrenarius Flessinganus. ... *Same imprint.* 4°. A-B4. (Lea.) [203

-- Disputatio quadragesima, de suis et legitimis hæredibus: Et successione ab intestato. ... Præside ... Everhardo Bronchorst, Publicè examinandam proponit, Ioannes Biel Geldrus ... Lugduni Batavorum. Ex officina Thomæ Basson. cIↄ. Iↄ. XCVII. 4°. A-B4. (Lea.) [204

-- Disputatio quadragesima prima de donationibus. ... Præside ... Cornelio de Groot. Exercitij gratia proponit, Reinerus à Rensen Geldr. ... Lugd. Batavor. Ex officinâ Thomæ Basson. cIo. Iↄ. XCVII. 4°. A-B4. (Lea.) [205

-- Disputatio quadragesima secunda de acquirendo rerum dominio ... Moderatore ... Gerarto Tuningio ... Examinandam proponit Petrus Vroesen Roterod. ... Lugduni Batavorum, Ex officina Thomæ Basson. cIↄ. Iↄ. IIIC. 4°. A6. (Lea.) [206

-- Disputatio quadragesima tertia de acquirendo vel amittenda possessione. ... Præside ... Everhardo Bronchorst Disputandam proponit Guilielmus Sypesteyn Vltraiectinus. ... Lugd. Batavor. Ex officinâ Thomæ Basson. cIↄ. Iↄ. XCVII. 4°. A-B4. (Lea.) [207

-- Disputatio quadragesima quarta de usucapionibus et præscriptionibus. ... Sub Præsidio ... Cornelii de Groot. Exercitij gratia disputandam proponit. VValtherus Spaen. ... *Same imprint.* 4°. A6. (Lea.) [208

-- Disputatio quadragesima quinta De re iudicata effectu sententiarum, et interlocutionibus ... sub præsidio ... Gerarti Tuningii ... Discutiendam exhibeo publicè Franciscus Dehnius Lubecensis Saxo ... Lugduni Batavorum Ex officinâ Thomæ Basson. cIↄ. Iↄ. IIIC. 4°. A6. (Lea.) [209

-- Disputatio quadragesima sexta De interdictis sive possessionum extraordinariis actionibus ... Præside ... Everardo à Bronchorst ... Proponit Edoardus Cↄius Gedanô-Borussus. Lugduni Batavorum. Ex officinâ Thomæ Basson. cIↄ. Iↄ. XCVII. 4°. [A]-B4. (Lea.) [210

-- Disputatio quadragesima septima de exceptionibus ... Præside ... Cornelio de Groot ... Discutiendam exhibet Gerardus Geresheim Moguntinus. ... *Same imprint.* 4°. A-B4. (Lea.) [211

-- Disputatio quadragesima octava de verborum obligationibus ... Præside ... Everardo à Bronchorst ... Examinandam proponit Samuel Vekemannus. ... Lugduni Batavorum Ex officinâ Thomæ Basson. cIↄ. Iↄ. IIIC. 4°. [A]-B4. (Lea.) [212

-- Disputatio quadragesima nona de fideiussoribus ... Præside ... Eberharto à Bronchorst ... Exercitij gratia Publicè examinandam propono Nicolaus Heynsius Yperius, Michaelis F. ... *Same imprint.* 4°. A-B4. (Lea.) [213

-- Disputatio quinquagesima de solutionibus, liberationibus, acceptilationibus, ac novationibus. ... Moderatore ... Cornelio de Groot ... Publicè exhibeo Theodorus Rumswinkell. Gochensis Clivius. Lugduni Batavorum, Ex Officinâ Thomæ Basson. cIↄ. Iↄ. IIIC. 4°. A6. (Lea.) [214

-- Disputatio quinquagesima prima de privatis delictis, furto, rapina bonorum et iniuria, re, verbis, ac scripto illata. ... Moderatore ... Gerarto Tuningio ... Publicè discutiendam exhibeo Iacobus à Wynshem Daventr. TransIsulanus. ... *Same imprint.* 4°. A-B4. (Lea.) [215

-- Disputatio quinquagesima secunda et ultima de publicis iudiciis ... Præside ... Everardo à Bronchorst ... Examinandam proponit Iustus Dedel Delph. Batt. ... *Same imprint.* 4°. A-B4. [216

-- Disputationum iuris feudalis prima. De nomine origine & definitione feudi. ... Disquirendam propono Arnoldus à Limburgh. ... Lugduni Batauorum, Ex officinâ Ioannis Patij. Anno 1597. 4°. A6. (Lea.) [217

-- Disputationum iuris feudalis secunda. De diuisione feudi. ... Disquirendam propono Ioannes Valentinus Saltzman Argentinensis. ... *Same imprint.* 4°. B6. (Lea.) [218

-- Disputationum iuris feudalis tertia. De iis qui feuda dare et accipere possunt. ... Disquirendam propono Guilielmus à Sypesteyn, Vltraiectinus. ... *Same imprint.* 4°. C-D^4. (Lea.) [219

-- Disputationum iuris feudalis quarta. De rebus quæ in feudum dari possunt: vbi et de regalibus. ... Disquirendam propono Ioannes Biel Noviomagus. ... *Same imprint.* 4°. E-F^4. (Lea.) [220

-- Disputationum iuris feudalis quinta. De feudi constitutione et adquisitione. ... Ventilandam propono Iacobus Warnerius Geldrus. ... *Same imprint.* 4°. G^6. (Lea.) [221

-- Disputationum iuris feudalis sexta. De obligatione et iure vasalli ex constitutione et acquisitione feudi promanante. ... Disquirendam Exhibeo Eduardus Coius Dantiscanus. ... *Same imprint.* 4°. H-I^4. (Lea.) [222

-- Disputationum iuris feudalis septima. De feudi successione. ... Disquirendam propono Arnoldus à Limburch. ... *Same imprint.* 4°. K-L^4. (Lea.) [223

-- Disputationum iuris feudalis octaua. De feudi alienatione. ... Disquirendam propono Ioannes Valentinus Saltzman Argentinensis. ... *Same imprint.* 4°. M^6. (Lea.) [224

-- Disputationum iuris feudalis nona. De feudi amissione et ad quem amissum devolvatus. ... Disquirendam propono Guilielmus à Sypesteyn Vltraiectinus. ... *Same imprint.* 4°. N^4 O^6. (Lea.) [225

-- Disputationum iuris feudalis decima. De feudis impropriis aut degenerantibus ... Disquirendam propono Ioannes Biel Geldrus. *Same imprint.* 4°. P^6. (Lea.) [226

-- Disputationum iuris feudalis vndecima. De actionibus et probationibus feudorum. ... Disquirendam exhibeo Iacobus Warnerius Geldr. ... *Same imprint.* 4°. Q^6. (Lea.) [227

-- Disputationum iuris feudalis duodecima. De feudalium controuersiarum iudice ac processu iudicario. ... Ventilandam propono Edoardus Coius Dantiscanus Pruthenus. ... *Same imprint.* 4°. R-S^4. (Lea.) [228

LEYSER, POLYCARP. Ein Christliche Leichpredig Bey dem Begrebnus ... Hans Lösern ... Wittenberg. Gedruckt bey Simon Gronenberg. M. D. LXXXI. 4°. A-F^4 G^2. [229

-- Vom Exorcismo. Ein Christlicher ... Bericht. ... Zu widerlegung der ... Schrifft/ welche die Prediger des Fürstenthumbs Anhalt/ in diesem Artickel wider jhn publiciert haben. 1592. Gedruckt zu Ihena/ durch Thobiam Steinman. 4°. A-V^4 X^2. (Lea.) [230

LEZEAU, JEAN. Ioannis Laezii Rupellani amicitia exulans, ex Cyro Theodoro Prodromo Poëta Græco. Eiusdem de Pace carmen. Parisiis, Apud Andream Wechelum ... 1559. 4°. A-G^4. ff. 2-32. [231

L'HÔPITAL, MICHEL DE. Amplissimi cuiusdam viri epistola ad ... Francisc. Lotaringum ducem Guisianum: Cui addita est Elegia Ioach. Bellaii, cum aliquot eiusdem epigrammatis. Parisiis, Apud Federicum Morellum ... 1558. ... 4°. A-B^4. [232

-- De sacra Francisci II. Galliarum regis initiatione, regnique ipsius administrandi prouidentia, Mich. Hosp. sermo. Parisiis, Apud Federicum Morellum ... M. D. LX. 4°. A^4 B^6. [233

-- In Francisci ... Franciæ delphini, et Mariae ... Scotorum reginae nuptias, ... carmen. Parisiis, Apud Federicum Morellum ... 1558. ... 4°. A^4. [234

LIBAVIUS, ANDREAS. D.O.M.A. Alchemia ... Francofurti Excudebat Iohannes Saurius, impensis Petri Kopffij, M. D. XCVII. (*Colophon.*) 4°. a-$3m^4$. pp. 2-424. (Smith.) [235

-- Andreæ LibauI. Halensis ... Neoparacelsica. In quibus vetus medicina defenditur aduersus τερετίσματα, Tum Georgii Anvvald ... Tum Iohannis Gramani ... Francofurti, Excudebat Ioannes Saur, impensis Petri Kopfij. M. D. XCIIII. 8°.)$(^8$)()$(^4$ A-$3C^8$. pp. 1-783. ¶*Additional t.p.* ($Zz7^r$): Anatome Tractatus Neoparacelsici, de pharmaco cathartico ... M.D.XCIIII. (Smith.) [236

-- [1] Rerum chymicarum epistolica forma ... Liber primus ... 1595. Francofurti, Excudebat Ioannes Saurius, impensis Petri Kopfij. 8°. *-$**^8$ A-T^8. pp. 1-300. [2] ... Liber secundus ... *Same imprint.* †-$††^8$ a-z^8 Aa-Pp^8 Qq^4. pp. 1-615. (Smith.) [237

LIBER VAGATORUM. Die Rotwelsch Grammatic/ vnnd barlen der Wanderschafft. ... 4°. A-B^4 C^2 D^4. [238

LIBERTUS. Collectio ... Liberti Episcopi Gericeñ. De crucibus. ... [Basileae, Michael Furter, 1501?] 4°. B.L. A^8. [239

LIBURNIO, NICOLÒ. Elegantissime sentenze et aurei detti de diuersi ... saui cosi Greci, come Latini, Raccolti da M. Nicolo Liburnio; ... in uolgar tradotti da M. Marco Cadamosto da Lodi. In Venetia Appresso Gabriel Gioli di Ferrarij. M. D. XLIII. (... Dil mese d'Agosto.) 8°. A-G^8 H^4. ff. 2-63. [240

-- Le molte et diuerse virtu delli saui antichi da Greci, & Latini auttori in volgar sermone per Messer Nicolo Liburnio tradotte. ... In Vineggia nella Botega di Santo Bernardino. M D XXXVII. (... per Messer Bernardino Stagnino da Trino di Monteferrato. ...) 8°. A-E^8 F^4. [241

-- Le occorrenze humane ... M. D. XXXXVI. (... in casa de' figliuoli di Aldo.) 8°. A-T^8 V^4. ff. 5-147. [242

-- Le Seluette ... (... in Vinegia stampate per Iacopo de Penci da Lecco ... M.D.XIII. del Mese di Maggio ...) 4°. AA^6 A-M^8 N^6 (-N6, *presumably blank*). ff. 1-100. [243

-- Le tre fontane ... in tre libbri diuise, sopra la grammatica, et eloquenza di Dante, Petrarcha, et Boccaccio. ... S'aggiunge ... un Dialogo sopra certe lettere, ouer charatteri trouati per Messer Giouan Giorgio Trissino. (Stampata in Vinegia per Gregorio de Gregorii Del MDXXVI. Nel mese di Febraio.) 4°. ✠^{4} A-H^8 I^6 K^4. ff. 1-73. [244

LICHTENBERGER, JOHANN. Practica ... vonn der grossen Coniunction Saturni vnd Iouis/ im̄ vergangnen M.cccc. lxxxiiij. ... 4°. B.L. A-Q^4 (-Q4). [245

LICINO, GIOVANNI BATTISTA. Rime di diuersi celebri poeti Dell'età nostra ... In Bergamo, MDLXXXVII. Per Comino Ventura, e Compagni. 8°. a-b^8 c^4 A-X^8 Y^4 (-Y4, *blank*). pp. 1-342. [246

-- -- *Variant* (+ Y4; Y3^v *numbered* 42). [247

LIED. Ain Lied für die landsknecht gemacht. ... Im Dennmarcker/ oder im Schweitzer Thon. M.D.XLVI. 4°. A^4. [248

LIEGE. *George of Austria, prince-bishop.* Georgius Dei gratia Episcopus Leodiēsis, Dux Bullonensis, & Comes Lossensis ... [Proclamation summoning a synod.] Datum in ciuitate nostra Leodiensi Decimo quinta Mensis Octobris. Anno Domini Millesimo, quingentesimo, quadragesimo octauo. s. sh. 37.5 × 28.5 cm. [249

LIGNAMINE, CHRISTOPHORUS À. Expositio prolongi magni Auerrois in librum de physico auditu. Impressum Venetijs apud Nicolaum de Bascarinis M. D. L. ... fol. A-C^4 D^6. ff. 3-18. [250

LILIO, ZACCARIA. Breue descrittione del mondo ... tradotta per M. Francesco Baldelli. ... In Vinegia appresso Gabriel Giolito de Ferrari e fratelli. M D LI. (... M D LII.) 8°. A-T^8. ff. 6-146. [251

LINACRE, THOMAS. Thomæ Linacri Britanni, de emendata structura Latini sermonis Libri sex. ... Parisiis Apud Christianum Wechelum ... M. D. XLI. 8°. a-d^8 A-CC^8 DD^6. pp. 1-427. [252

-- -- ... Cum epistola commendatitia Philippi Melanchthonis. ... Basileæ per Nicolaum Bryling. Anno M. D. LIII. 8°. a-z^8 (-a2-4) A-G^8 H^4. pp. 1-459. ¶*T.p. defaced.* [253

-- -- ... Recogniti a Ioachimo Camerario Pabepergensi. ... Accessit libellus eiusdem Camerarij de arte Grammatica, & figuris dictionum ... Lipsiae in officina Valentini Papae. Anno M. D. LVI. 8°. Aa^8 Bb^4 b-z^8 A-Y^8. pp. 1-553. ¶N8^v: Annotationes Casparis Landsidelii Lipsici. X1^r: Annotationes in Linacrum Phil. Bechii. [254

-- Rudimenta grammatices Thomae Linacri, ex Anglico sermone in Latinum uersa, interprete Georgio Buchanano Scoto. Parisiis Excudebat Christianus Wechelus ... M. D. XLII. 8°. A-H^8. pp. 3-127. ¶*Includes Juan Luis Vives,* De ratione studii puerilis. [255

LINCK, SEBASTIAN. Declamatio. De primorum studiorum ordine & ratione, in publica Ingolstadianæ Acdemiæ Schola habita per Sebastianum Linckium ... Anno 37. ... 8°. A-C^8 (-C8, *presumably blank*). [256

-- In nuptias. Osualdi ab Eck & Annæ á Pentzenau, Epithalamium. ... In easdem nuptias Dialogus E. Vuolphij. (Ingolstadii in officina Alexandri Vueissenhorn.) 4°. A-C^4. [257

LINCK, WENCESLAS. Am Vierdtē Sontag der Fasten Letare Euange: mit der Ausslegung. D. Wentzeslaj Linckē ... 4°. A-B^4. [258

-- Bapsts gepreng/ auss dem Cerimonien Bůch. ... An. M. D. XXXIX. (Getruckt zů Strassburg ...) 4°. A^6 A-S^4. [259

-- Matth: 15: Das Euangelion am andern Sontag der Fasten/ mit der Ausslegnng [*sic*] ... (Gedruckt yn ... Zwickaw durch Iörg Gastel. Im XXIIII. Jar.) 4°. A^6. [260

-- Eyn Sermon ... Von anrüffunge der heyligen. ... Aldenburg in Meyssen [Gabriel Kantz]. M.D.xxiij. 4°. A^6 B^4. [261

-- Eyn Sermon von Geistlichem vñ Weltlichem Regiment/ auss dem Euangelio/ Luce .xxij. ... 1536. (Gedrückt zů Nůrnberg durch Hans Guldenmundt.) 4°. A-C^4 D^2. (Lea.) [262

-- Ain Sermon wie der grob mensch vnsers hern esel sein sol in tragen ... Doct. Martinus Luther lobt den Sermō ... M.D.XXi. 4°. A^4. [263

-- Von dreyen Brüdern/ die jnen ainen Vatter erwöleten. ... Durch Nicodemum Noricum. 4°. A^4. [264

-- Das zwölfft Capitel der Epistel an die Ebreer/ mit kurtzer ... ausslegung ... Anno M.D.XLIIII. 4°. A-K^4. [265

LINDEBERG, PETER. Petri Lindebergii ... chronicon Rostochiense Posthumum ... Rostochii, Imprimebatur typis Stephani Myliandri anno cIↄ Iↄ XCVI. 4°. A-Aa^4. pp. 9-174. [266

-- Petri Lindebergii epigrammata in vrbes, et viros aliquot clarissimos ... Rostochii Typis Myliandrinis. Anno CIↃ IↃ XXCVII. 4°. A-C^4. [267

LING, NICHOLAS. Politeuphuia. Wits common wealth. ... Printed by I. R. for Nicholas Ling, ... 1598. 8°. A^4 B-Mm^8. ff. 1-258. *S.T.C.* 15686+. ¶A4 *bound between* A1 *and* A2, Bb4 *after* Bb1, Bb5 *after* Bb7. *Third edition.* (Furness.) [268

LINSCHOTEN, JAN HUYGHEN VAN. Ander Theil der Orientalischen Indien/ Von allen Völckern/ Insulen ... vnd anderen Orten/ so von Portugal ... biss in Ost Indien vnd zu dem Land China ... zu sehen seind. ... in Holländischer Sprach beschrieben/ durch Ioan Hugo von Lindschotten ... in Hochteutsch bracht ... durch Hans Dieterich vnd Hans Israel von Bry Gebrüder. Gedruckt in Franckfurt am Meyn/ durch Iohan Saur. M.D.XCVIII. fol. (?)^6 a-k^4 A-Q^4 R^6 (-R6). ff. I-XXXVIII, pp. 1-138. ¶*Additional t.p.* (a1^r): Folgen hernacher ... Fürblidungen aller frembden Völcker in Orient ... *Same imprint.* [269

-- -- Navigatio ac itinerarium Iohannis Hugonis Linscotani in orientalem siue Lusitanorum Indiam. ... Collecta ... per eundem Belgicè: Nunc vero Latinè reddita ... Hagæ-Comitis Ex officinâ Alberti Henrici. Impensis Authoris & Cornelii Nicolai, prostantq̃ue apud Ægidium Elsevirum. Anno 1599. fol. *^{4} (-*1, *blank*) A^6 B^{6+2} C^{6+6} D^{6+8} E^{6+6} *(one plate repeated)* F^{6+4} G-I^6 K^{8+2} (K4 + 2 *folded leaves*). pp. 1-124. [270

LIONARDO, ALESSANDRO. Dialogi ... della inuentione poetica. ... In Venetia, per Plinio Pietrasanta, M D LIIII. (*Colophon.*) 4°. A-M^4. pp. 3-84. [271

LIPPOMANNO, LUIGI. [1] Historiae Aloysii Lipomani ... De Vitis Sanctorum, pars prima. ... Louanii, Apud Petrum Zangrium Tiletanum, ... 1565. ... fol. *-3*^{6} (-3*2, -3*6, *presumably blank*) A-SS^6. pp. 1-491. [2] Historiae ... pars secunda. ... Louanii, Apud Petrum Sangrium ... (Typ. Reyneri Velpii Dist.) Æ^2 aa-zz^6 3A-3R^6. pp. 1-478. (Lea.) [272

-- Sanctorum priscorum patrum vitæ numero centum sexagintatres, per ... probatissimos auctores conscriptae. Et nuper per R.P.D. Aloysium Lipomanum ... in unum uolumen redactæ ... Venetiis, ad signum spei. M. D. LI. 4°. a^8 a^6 A-3P^8 3Q^6. ff. 2-494. (Lea.) [273

LIPSE, JUSTE. Iusti LipsI ad C. Cornelium Tacitum, curæ secundæ. [Lugduni Batavorum,] Ex officina Plantiniana, Apud Franciscum Raphelengium. cIↄ. Iↄ. LXXXVIII. 8°. *[8] A-K[8]. pp. 1-160. [274

-- Iusti LipsI ad Iac. Monauium epistola, ... cum duabus Ad Abr. Ortelium. Antuerpiæ, Ex officina Plantiniana, Apud Viduam, & Ioannem Moretum. M. D. XCII. 4°. A-B[4]. [275

-- Iusti LipsI admiranda, siue, de magnitudine Romana libri quattuor. ... Secunda editio ... Antuerpiæ, ex officina Plantiana, Apud Ioannem Moretum. M. D. XCIX. ... (*Colophon.*) 4°. A-Z[4] a-d[4]. pp. 4-209. [276

-- Iusti LipsI de amphitheatro liber. ... Cum æneis figuris. Lugduni Batauorum, Ex officina Christophori Plantini. cIↄ. Iↄ. LXXXIV. 4°. A-N[4] a-d[4] e[2] (*folded engraved plates inserted after* B4, H4, b4). pp. 3-98, 3-32. ¶*Additional t.p.* (a1r): Iusti LipsI de amphitheatris quæ extra Romam libellus. ... *Same imprint.* [277

-- [1] Iusti LipsI de militia Romana libri quinque, commentarius ad Polybium. ... Antuerpiæ, ex officina Plantiniana, Apud Viduam, & Ioannem Moretum. M. D. XCVI. ... 4°. *-**[4] A-Z[4] a-r[4] (r4 + *folded plate*) s[6]. pp. 2-330. ¶*T.p. defective.* [2] Iusti LipsI de militia Romana liber quintus. Qui est de ddsciplina. ... M. D. XCV. Aa-Zz[4] AA-NN[4] OO[6]. pp. 3-272. [278

-- Iusti LipsI poliorceticωn siue de machinis. Tormentis. Telis. Libri quinque. ... Antuerpiæ, ex officina Plantiniana, Apud Viduam, & Ioannem Moretum. M. D. XCVI. ... (*Colophon.*) 4°. *-**[4] A-Z[4] a-k[4] l[6]. pp. 1-267. [279

-- I. LipsI Saturnalium sermonum libri duo, Qui de Gladiatoribus. Antuerpiæ, Ex officina Christophori,Plantini. M. D. LXXXII. 4°. *[4] A-V[4]. pp. 1-151. [280

-- -- Lugduni Batauorum, Ex officina Plantiniana, Apud Franciscum Raphelengium. cIo. Io XC. 4°. *[4] A-Y[4], *with 3 (out of 4) large and 8 (out of 12) smaller engraved plates inserted after* *4, B2, C2, D2, G2, I2, K2, L2, M2, R1, R4. pp. 1-175. [281

LISTENIUS, NICOLAUS. Rudimenta musicae ... Augustae Vindelicorum per Henricum Steyner excusum, Mense Octobri, Anno M. D. XXXVI. (*Colophon.*) 8°. A-C[8] (-C1). [282

LITTELTON, SIR THOMAS. *French.* Littletons Tenures. ... Apud Richardum Tottel. ... 1557. (Imprinted at Lōdō ... the .xxviij. daie of October. ...) 8°. B.L. A-Y[8] (-Y8, *presumably blank*). ff. 1-173. *S.T.C.* 15738. (Biddle.) [283

-- -- Les Tenures du Monsieur Littelton ... 1572. (Imprinted at London ... by Rychard Tottill. ...) 8°. B.L. A-X[8] Y[4]. ff. 1-170. *S.T.C.* 15741. (Biddle.) [284

-- -- 1585. (Imprinted at London ... by Rychard Tottill ...) 8°. B.L. A-X[8] Y[4] A-C[8]. ff. 2-171. *S.T.C.* 15747. [285

-- -- Londini In ædibus Ianae Yetsvveirt relictæ Caroli Yetsvveirt ... [c. 1595.] 12°. B.L. A-Q[12] (-A10-12, B[12]). ff. 1-170. *S.T.C.* 15752. (Biddle.) [286

-- -- *English.* Littleton tenures in Englishe. ... (Imprinted at London ... by Richard Tottell the .xvi. daye of Aprill. ... 1556.) 8°. B.L. A-S[8]. ff. 2-142. *S.T.C.* 15767. (Biddle.) [287

-- -- (Imprinted at London ... by Rychard Tottyl. 1574.) 8°. B.L. A-S[8]. ff. 2-142. *S.T.C.* 15770. (Biddle.) [288

-- -- (Imprnted at London ... by Rychard Tottill. 1583. ...) 8°. B.L. A-S[8]. ff. 2-142. *S.T.C.* 15772. (Biddle.) [289

-- -- Imprinted at London by Iane Yetsweirt. 1597. ... 8°. B.L. A-S[8]. ff. 2-142. *S.T.C.* 15776. ¶A1 *mounted.* (Biddle.) [290

LIVIERA, GIOVANNI BATTISTA. Cresfonte, tragedia ... In Padoua, Appresso Paulo Meietto. M.D.LXXXVIII. 8°. §[8] A-F[8]. ff. 1-48. [291

LIVIUS, TITUS. [1] Ex XIIII. T. Liuii decadibus. Prima, tertia, quarta ... Epitome singulorum librorum XIIII Decadum. Historia omnium XIIII Decadum in compendium redacta ab L. Floro. Polybij lib. V ... latinitate donati â Nicolao Perotto. ... (Venetiis in aedibus Aldi, et Andreae soceri, mense Decembri, M. D. XVIII.) 8°. *[8] *[4] 2*-8*[8] *[8] a-zz[8] &&[4]. ff. 1-365. ¶*Additional t.p.* (3*1r): Titi Liuii Patauini decas prima. [2] Index decadis tertiae. (Venetiis in aedibus Aldi, et Andreae soceri, mense Februario. M. D. XIX.) 1-6⁸ *⁸ aa-zz⁸ AA-XX⁸ YY⁴. ff. 1-350. ¶*Additional t.p.* (*1ʳ): ... decas tertia. *Two more volumes were published.* [292

-- T. Liuii Patauini historiarum ab vrbe condita, Decas tertia. ... Basileae, apud Nicolaum Episcopium Iuniorem. M. D. LIIII. (*Colophon.*) 8°. a-z⁸ A-T⁸ (-T8, *presumably blank*). pp. 3-668. [293

-- [1] T. Liuii Patauini, Historiarum ab verbe condita, libri, qui extant, XXXV. ... Secunda editio. ... Venetiis, Apud Paulum Manutium, Aldi F. M D LXVI. fol. a⁶ a-e⁸ f⁶ A-3D⁸. ff. 1-399. [2] Caroli Sigonii scholia ... *Same imprint.* A-N⁸ O⁴ (-O4, *blank*). ff. 3-107. [294

-- [*caption:*] T. Liuii Patauini historiarum ab verbe condita decadis quartae liber primus. (Impressum Francofurti ad Moenum, apud Georgium Coruinum Sigismundum Feierabend. & hæredes VVigandi Galli. M. D. LXVIII.) 8°. 3A-4E⁸ 4F⁴. pp. 1-436. ¶*Presumably part of an edition of the* Libri omnes. (School of Dentistry.) [295

-- Titi Liuii Patauini ... libri omnes ... Francoforti ad Moenum, apud Iohannem & Sigismundum Feyerabendt. M. D. LXXVIII. fol.)(⁴ B⁶ C-D⁴ A-Z⁶ a-z⁶ Aa-3D⁶ 3E-3F⁸ 3G-3H⁶. pp. 1-805. [2] Chronologia in Titi Liuii historiam ... Francofurti ad Moenum, M. D. LXXVIII. (Impressum ... apud Georgium Coruinum ...) A-D⁶. pp. 3-47. [3] In Titi Liuii ... libros ... annotationes, Castigationes & Scholia ... *Same imprint.* *⁶ A-K⁶. pp. 1-119. [4] Caroli Sigonii scholia ... *Same imprint.* A-N⁶ O⁴ A-H⁶ I⁴. ff. 3-82, pp. 1-104. [5] In Titi Liuii ... libros ... obseruationes, ex varijs autorum scriptis collectæ, per Vilhelmum Godeleuæum. ... *Same imprint.* (*Colophon.*) fol. A-H⁶. pp. 3-93. [296

-- The Romane historie written by T. Liuius of Padua. Also, the Breviaries of L. Florus: with a Chronologie to the whole Historie: and the Topographie of Rome in old time. Translated out of Latine into English, by Philemon Holland, Doctor in Physicke. London, Printed by Adam Islip. 1600. fol. A-6F⁶ (-A1, 6F6, *presumably blank*). pp. 1-1403. *S.T.C.* 16613. ¶*The 5 ll. of sig.* A *are mounted and repaired, apparently without loss of text.* (Furness.) [297

-- Les cinq premiers liures de l'histoire Romaine de Tite Liue ... De la traduction de Blaise de Vigenere. A Paris. Chez Nicolas Chesneau ... M.D.LXXIX. ... (Acheué d'imprimer par Henry Thierry ... le 4. iour de Nouembre ...) 8°. †⁴ a-3A⁸ 3F⁴ 3G². pp. 1-734. [298

-- [1] Les decades, qui se trouuent, de Tite Liue, mises en langue Francoise: La premiere, par Blaise de Vigenere Bourbonnois ... La tierce, tournee autrefois par Iean Hamelin de Sarlac ... Le reste, de la traduction d'Anthoine de la Faye. A Paris, Chez Iacques du Puys ... M. D. LXXXIII. ... fol. ā⁸ a-h⁶ i⁴ k-z⁶ A-3K⁶ 3L⁶±² 3M-4R⁶ 4S⁸ a-g⁶ h⁴. pp. 1-462, coll. 463-1752, ff. 1753-1786. [2] La troisiesme decade de Tite-Liue contenant la seconde guerre Punique ... Mise cy deuant en François par Iehan Hamelin de Sarlac: & depuis resuyuie ... par B.D.V. A Paris, chez Iaques du Puis ... M. D. LXXX. ... a⁶ B-KK⁶ LL⁴ 3A-4O⁶ 4P⁸ a-d⁶. ff. 2-201, 2-230. [299

-- [1] Titi Liuij ... Rŏmische Historien ... Getruckt in̄ ... Meyntz/ durch Iuonem Schŏffer/ ... M. D. XLVI. fol. ☞⁶ ☞⁶ A-P⁶ Q⁴ Q-Z⁶ a-h⁶ i⁸ k-z⁶ Aa-Zz⁶ AA-DD⁶ EE⁸. ff. I-CCCCL. ¶*Additional t.pp.:* (²Q1ʳ): Das ander theyl ... (k1ʳ) Das dritt theyl ... [2] Das vierdt theil ... a-n⁶ o-p⁸ (-O8, p1, p8, *the last presumably blank*). ff. II-XCIII. ¶*Translators: Bernhard Schöfferlin, Ivo Wittig, Nicolaus Carbach, Jacob Moltzer.* [300

-- Le deche di .T. Liuio Padouano ... Tradotte nella lingua Toscana, da Iacopo Nardi ... In Venetia M D XLVII. (... nella stamperia degli heredi di Luc'Antonio Giunti Fiorentino ... Nel mese di Marzo.) fol. ✠⁴ 1-3⁶ A-OO⁸ PP¹⁰ QQ-3G⁸ 3H⁶ 3I-3O⁸ 3P⁶ (-3P6, *presumably blank*). ff. 1-485. [301

-- Le deche di T. Liuio Padouano dell'istorie Romane. ... Tradotte in lingua Toscana da M. Iacopo Nardi ... In Vinegia, al segno del seminante. 1574. 4°. †⁸ A-3S⁸ (-A2) 3T¹⁰ a-pp⁸ qq⁴ a-g⁸ h⁴. ff. 1-819. ¶*Additional t.p.* (a1ʳ): Seconda parte delle deche ... *Same imprint.* (Appresso Bartholomeo Rubini. ...) [302

-- Deche di Tito Liuio Padouano delle historie Romane, Già tradotte da M. Iacopo Nardi ...: & hora ... accresciute ... del supplemento della seconda deca, da M. Fra[nc]esco Turchi, Treuigiano. ... In Venetia appresso i Giunti. M D LXXV. (*Colophon.*) fol. *⁴ a-c⁶ A-V⁸

X-Aa^4 Bb-3X^8 3Y^4 (-3Y4, *presumably blank*). ff. 1-18, 1-158, pp. 161-193, ff. 194-537. ¶T.p. *defective.* [303

-- Todas las decadas de Tito Liuio Paduano ... traduçidas en Romançe Castellano ... Anno M. D. LIII. ... (Acabose de imprimer ... en la çiudad ... de Colonia Agrippina, à costas de Arnoldo Byrckmanno ...) fol. a^4 A-Zz ^{6} AA-ZZ^6 aa-3i^6 3k^4 o-r^6 s^2. ff. I-DCVII, LXXXV-CIII. [304

-- Ioachimi Perionii Cormoeriaceni in omnes T. Liuij Conciones ... Annotationes. Vnà cum ipsius T. Liuij Concionibus ... Basileae. 1545. (Ex officina Roberti Winter ...) 8°. α-β^8 a-z^8 A-P^8. pp. 1-590. ¶P8 *defeced.* [305

-- -- Les concions et harengues de Tite Liue ... traduictes en François. A Paris De l'imprimerie de Michel de Vascosan ... M. D. LIIII. ... 8°. A^6 B-Zz^8 AA-CC^8 DD^{10}. ff. 1-393. ¶*Translator: Jean de Amelin.* [306

LLOYD, LODOWICK. The pilgrimage of princes, Newly published by Lodowicke Lloid ... Imprinted at London, by Iohn Wolfe. 1586. 4°. B.L. ¶^{4} (-¶4) ¶¶^{4} A-3I^4. ff. 2-214. *S.T.C.* 16625. [307

LOACES, FERNANDO DE. Perutilis ⁊ singularis q̄stio: seu tractatus super noua paganorū regni Valentie cōuersione: Editus p̱ ... Ferdinādum de Loazes Oriolēss ... (impressus Valentie per Ioannē Iāfredū: expensis Ferdinādi δ loazes. die .xxix. mēsis Aṗlis. ... 1525.) fol. B.L. A-E^6. ff. II-XXX. (Lea.) [308

LOAYSA, GARCIA DE. Collectio conciliorum Hispaniæ, diligentia Garsiæ Loaisa elaborata ... Madriti. Excudebat Petrus Madrigal. M. D. XCIII. fol. a^4 b-c^6 d^8 A-4B^6. pp. I-xxxix, 1-778. (Lea.) [309

L'OBEL, MATTHIAS DE. Kruydtboeck oft Beschrÿuinghe Van allerleye Ghewassen, Kruyderen, Hesteren, ende Gheboomten: deur Matthias De Lobel ... T'Antwerpen By Christoffel Plantyn M. D. LXXXI. (*Colophon.*) fol. π^2 A-Z^6 a-z^6 AA-ZZ^6 aa-oo^6 (-oo6, *blank*) Aa-Zz^6 aA^6 bB^4 (-bB4, *presumably blank*) cC^4 dD^6 (-dD6, *blank*) ††^{8} a-e^4 ¶-¶¶^{4} 3¶^{6}. pp. 1-994, 1-312, 1-15. ¶*Engraved t.p.* [309a

LOCATI, UMBERTO. Cronica dell'origine di Piacenza, ... ridotta ... nella volgare nostra fauella. In Cremona per Vincenzo Conti M D LXIIII. (... M. D. LXV.) 4°. A-ZZ^4 (-B1) 3a-3e^4. pp. 3-393. [310

-- Opus quod iudiciale inquisitionum dicitur ex diuersis theologis et I.V.D. ... extractum ... Romae Apud Hæredes Antonii Bladii ... M. D. LXX. 4°. ✠^{4} a^2 b-d^4 E^4 A-3S^4. pp. 1-511. (Lea.) [311

-- Praxis iudiciaria inquisitorum ... His accesserunt quædam Sancti Officij decreta ... Editio secunda ... Venetijs, Apud Damianum Zenarium. 1583. 4°. a-c^8 A-Kk^8. pp. 1-527. (Lea.) [312

LOCCATELLI, EUDOSIO. Vita del glorioso padre San Giouangualberto fondatore dell'Ordine di Vallombrosa. Insieme con le Vite di tutta i Generali, Beati, e Beate, che ha ... hauuto la sua Religione ... In Fiorenza MDLXXXIII. Appresso Giorgio Marescotti. (*Colophon.*) 4°. *^{4} A-Z^4 AA-Vv^4 Xx-Yy^4 (-Yy4, *presumably blank*). pp. 1-330. (Lea.) [313

LOCHER, JAKOB. Apologia Iacobi Locher Philomusi: contra poetarum acerrimum Hostem Georgium Zingel ... [Argentorati, Johannes Grüninger, c. 1505.] 4°. A-B^4. [314

-- Exhortatio heroica ... ad Principes Germanię & status pro ... Hispaniarū Rege Carolo ... [1521.] 4°. A^6. [315

-- Hęc in libello continentur. Poemation ... de Lazaro mendico ... carmen augurale de ... cęsare Maximiliano ... Epigrāma cōtra oblocutores maiestatis cęsareę Carmen ... de festo Conceptionis beatę Marię uirginis. ... [1510.] 4°. A-B^6. [316

-- Rosarium celestis curie. et patrie triūphantis. ... (Impressum Nurnberge p̱ Fridericū Peypus. ... M.V^c.xiiii.) 4°. a-b^4. [317

-- Spectaculum ... more tragico effigiatum. In quo christianissimi Reges. aduersum truculentissimos Thurcos consilium ineunt ... Eiusdem iudiciū Paridis de pomo aureo. de triplici hominum vita. ... [Augustae, Johannes Froschauer, 1502.] 4°. a^6 b^4 c^6 d-e^4. [318

-- Threnodia siue funebris lamentatio. in laudem ... Heduigis ... Georgij Comitis palatini rheni ... cõiugis ... ... [Augustae, Johannes Froschauer, 1502.] 4°. a-b^4. [319

LODI. Decreta, edita et promulgata in synodo diocesana Laudensi ... anno M. D. LXXXXI. .. Mediolani, Apud Pacificum Pontium. 1591. ... 4°. ✠^{4} A-I^4 ✠^{2} A-N^4. pp. 1-70, 1-100. (Lea.) [320

LODOVICI, FRANCESCO DE. Triomphi di Carlo ... (Stampato in Vinegia per Mapheo Pasini & Francesco Bindoni cõpagni ... MDXXXV. del mese di Settembre ...) 4°. ✠^{4} A-CC^8 DD^6. ff. 1-214. [321

LÖWENKLAU, JOHANN. Historiae Musulmanae Turcorum, de Monumentis ipsorum exscriptæ, libri XVIII. Opus Io. Leunclauii Amelburni ... Francofurti Apud heredes Andreæ Wecheli, Claudium Marnium & Ioann. Aubrium. M D XCI. ... fol.)(^{6}):(^{4} A^6 B^4 C-Ss^6 Tt^4 Vu^6. pp. 2-17, 1-02 [= 20], cols. 21-898. [322

-- Neuwer Musulmanischer Histori ... Gestellt durch Hansen Lewenklaw von Amelbeurn. 1590. ... Gedruckt zu Franckfurt am Meyn/ bey Andres Wechels seligen Erben/ nemlich/ Claudi de Marne vnd Iohan Aubri. fol.)?(^{6} a-h^6 i^{6+2}. pp. 1-104. [323

LOLLIO, ALBERTO. Delle orationi ... volume primo. Aggiuntaui vna lettera del medesimo in laude della villa. ... In Ferrara Appresso Valenti Panizza Mantouano, M DLXIII. 4°. A-$3V^4$ $3X^2$. ff. 1-244. [324

-- Oratione consolatoria ... in morte dello ... Signor Marco Pio ... In Vinetia appresso Gabriel Giolito di Ferrarii MDXLV. (*Colophon.*) 4°. A-E^4. ff. 2-19. [325

LOMAZZO, GIOVANNI PAOLO. Rime di Gio. Paolo Lomazzi Milanese pittore, diuise In sette Libri. ... In Milano, Per Paolo Gottardo Pontio, l'anno 1587. ... (*Colophon.*) 4°. A-Oo^8. pp. 3-560. ¶*Additional t.pp. with the same imprint:* ($C1^r$) Libro primo de grotteschi, di Gio. Paolo Lomazzi ... ($E8^v$) Libro secondo de grotteschi ... ($K1^r$) Libro terzo ... ($N8^r$) Libro quarto ... ($T5^r$) Libro quinto ... ($CC3^r$) Libro setto ... ($II1^r$) Libro settimo, et vltimo ... ($Kk4^r$) Breue trattato della vita dell'auttore descritta da lui stesso in rime sciolte. ... [326

LOMBARDELLI, ORAZIO. L'arte del puntar gli scritti ... In Siena, appresso Luca Bonetti. 1585. ... 8°. A-Q^8. pp. 3-256. [327

-- Della eccellenza libri due ... In Fiorenza Appresso Giorgio Marescotti. 1578. ... 8°. A^4 B-H^8. pp. 1-112. [328

-- Discorso intorno ai contrasti, che si fanno sopra la Gierusalemme liberata di Torquato Tasso ... In Ferrara, Ad instanza di Giulio Vassalini. ... 1586. (... Appresso Vittorio Baldini ...) 8°. A-K^8. pp. 3-156. [329

-- -- In Mantoua, per Francesco Osanna. M D LXXXVI. (*Colophon.*) 12°. A-D^{12} E^4. pp. 3-100. [330

-- I fonti Toscani ... In Firenze Appresso Giorgio Marescotti. MDXCVIII. 8°. †^{8} A-L^8. pp. 1-133. [331

LOMBARDI, BERNARDINO. L'Alchimista comedia di M. Bernardino Lombardi Comico Confidente. ... In Vinetia, M D LXXXVI. Appresso gli Heredi di Marchiò Sessa. (*Colophon.*) 12°. A-H^{12}. ff. 2-91. (Smith.) [332

LOMBARDO, GIOVANNI DONATO. Nouello prato de' Prologhi di Gio. Donato Lombardo da Bitonto, detto il Bitontino. ... In Messina, Presso Fausto Bufalini. 1589. (*Colophon.*) 8°. *^{8} A-O^8. pp. 1-223. [333

LOMBARDO, GIOVANNI FRANCESCO. Ioan. Francisci Lombardi Neapolitani ... oratio. Habita ad Patres Concilij Tridentini, die Sancti Stephani Protomartyris. Anno M. D. LXI. Brixiae Ad instantiam Io: Baptistæ Bozolæ. M. D. LXIII. 4°. A^6. (Lea.) [334

LOMBARDY. Leges longobardorum seu capitulare ... Carolimagni impatoris ... p ... Nicolaum boherii ... editis ... [*Privilege to Simon Vincent of Lyon dated 3 June 1512.*] 4°. B.L. aa-vv^8 xx^6. ff. iij-clx. (Biddle.) [335

LOMME, JEAN. Secunda appellatio quorūdā religiosoruȝ sācti germani de pratis cū quadam eplā. 8°. B.L. π^8 (-π8). ¶*Appellants: Jean Lomme, Guillaume Guerry, Pierre Gringet.* [336

LONGUEIL, CHRISTOPHE. Christophori Longolii epistolarum libri IIII. Bartolomæi item Riccij de imitatione libri tres. A Io. Michaële Bruto emendati. Lugduni, apud haered. Seb. Gryphii, 1563. 16°. a-z^8 A-T^8 ā^2. pp. 3-672. [337

-- -- ... Doctorum item aliquot Epistolarum ad eundem Longolium, Liber I. Quibus eiusdem uita ... est præmissa. Basileae, per Eusebium Episcop. & Nicolai fratris hæredes. Anno M.D.LXX. (... Mense Septemb.) 8°. α-β^8 a-z^8 A^6. pp. 1-374. [338

-- Christophori Longolii orationes duæ pro defensione sua in crimen lesæ maiestatis ... Oratio una ad Luterianos Eiusdem epistolarum libri quatuor. Epistolarum Bembi & Sadoleti liber unus. Longolij uita ... (Florentiæ per Hæredes Philippi Iuntæ. ... M.D.XXIIII. Mense Decembris. ...) 4°. a-u^8 x^4. ff. 2-163. [339

LONICER, JOHANNES. Catechesis De bona Dei uoluntate ... Deqȝ sanctorum cultu & inuocatione. ... [Argentorati, Johannes Schott, 1523.] 4°. a-i^4. [340

-- Figurarum, promissionum, historiarum, caeremoniarum, Victimarum, & Sacrificiorum: Ex Testamento uetere ... συναθροισις. ... Franc. Apud Hæred. Chr. Egen. Anno M.D.LX. 8°. A-N^8. pp. 3-187. [341

LONICER, PHILIPP. [1] Chronicorum Turcicorum, ... Accessere, narratio de Baiazethis filiorum seditionibus; ... Et Iohannes Auentini Liber, in quo causa miseriarum, quibus Christiana Respub. premitur, indicantur, ... tomus primus. ... Collecta, sermoneque latino exposita, à ... D. Philippo Lonicero ... Impressum Francoforti ad Moenum M.D.LXXVIII. (Impressum ..., apud Iohannem Feyerabendt. Impensis Sigismundi Feyerabendt. ...) fol.)(^{4} A-Z^4 a-h^4 i^6 k^4. ff. 1-130. ¶i4 *bound between* i2 *and* i3; *margins of* i2 *and* i4 *repaired.* [2] Chronicorum Turcicorum ... tomus secundus. ... Francoforti ad Moenum, ex officina Georgij Coruini, impensis Sigismundi Feyrabendij, M.D.LXXVIII. (*Colophon.*) a^4 (*bound between* S4 *and* T1 *of tomus primus*) A-D^6 E-Z^4 a-g^4. pp. 1-255. [3] Chronicorum Turcicorum, in quibus vita, indoles, et aduersus Turcas res gestae Georgii Castrioti ... Libris XIII. describuntur à Marino Barletio, Scodrensi sacerdote: tomus tertius. Accesserunt autoris eiusdem libri III. de Scodra ... *Same imprint and colophon as* [1]. *^{4} A-Z^4 a-zz^4. ff 1-271. (Lea.) [342

-- -- [1] Chronicorum Turcicorum, In quibus Turcorum origo, principes, ... bella, ... reique militaris ratio ... exponuntur ... Tomus primus. ... Collecta ... à ... Philippo Lonicero ... 1584. Francofurti Excudebat Ioan. Wechelus, impensis Sigismundi Feyerabendij. (... M.D.LXXXIIII.) 8°. *^{8} A-Z^8 a-c^8. pp. 1-435. [2] Chronicorum Turcicorum ... tomus secundus. ... 1584. ... Francofurti. (*Same colophon.*) *^{8} Aa-Oo^8. pp. 1-208. [343

LOOS, CORNELIUS. Duellum fidei et rationis: si in Eucharistiæ sacramento, verè sit corpus Christi ... Moguntiæ, Typi inuentricis: Apud Casparum Behem, Anno M. D. LXXXI. 8°. A-P^8. [344

LÓPEZ MADERA, GREGORIO. Excelencias de la monarchia y reyno de España. ... Por Diego Fernandez de Cordoua ... 1597. A costa de Martin de Cordoua ... fol. ¶^{4} A^4 (-A4) a^8 A-K^8 L^4. ff. 1-84. (Lea.) [345

LÓPEZ MALDONADO, JUAN. Cancionero de Lopez Maldonado. ... Impresso en Madrid, en casa de Guillermo Droy ... Acabose a cinco de Febrero. Año de .1586. 4°. π^4 *^{8} A-Y^8 Z^4 (-Z4). ff. 1-189. [346

LÓPEZ PINCIANO, ALONSO. Philosophia antigua poetica ... En Madrid, Por Thomas Iunti. M.D.XCVI. 4°. †^{4} A-3X^4. pp. 1-535. [347

LÓPEZ DE UBEDA, JUAN. Vergel de flores Diuinas. Compuesto por el Licenciado Iuan Lopez de

Vueda natural de Toledo ... Impreso en Alcala de Henares por los herederos de Iuan Gracian ..., A costa de Luys Mendez ... Año .1588. (*Colophon.*) 4°. [¶]^4 ¶¶^{8} A-Cc^8 Dd^{12}. ff. 2-204. [348

LORD'S SUPPER. Vonn des Herren Nachtmal/ der papisten Messen vnnd etlichenn Newen yrrthumen. ... M.D.XXVI. 8°. A-D^8. [349

LORENZINI, NICOLÒ. Il peccator contrito ... In Fiorenza, per Filippo Giuntà, M D XCI. ... (*Colophon.*) 4°. *^{8} A^4 B-O^8. pp. 1-206. ¶*In verse.* [350

-- Vita del glorioso S. Giouan Gualberto Azzini ... In Firenze Appresso Giorgio Marescotti. 1599. 4°. †^{4} ††^{2} A-L^4 M-Ee^8 Ff^2. pp. 1-358. [351

L'ORME, PHILIBERT DE. Nouuelles inuentions pour bien bastir et a petits fraiz ... A Paris, De l'Imprimerie de Federic Morel ... M.D.LXI. ... fol. A-K^6 L-M^4. ff. 1-57. (Fine Arts.) [352

LOS, WOLFF. Vonn Erbschafften der Erb vnd Lehengůter ... Zu Franckfurt durch Dauidem Zephelium. ... M.D.LVI. (*Colophon.*) fol. A-E^6 F^4. ff. ij-xxxiij. ¶*T.p. mounted.* [353

LOSCOS, AUGUSTINUS. Oratio habita ad patres Concilii Tridentini die. S. Gregorii. M. D. LXII. ... Brixiæ apud Damianum Turlinum. 4°. A^6. (Lea.) [354

LOSS, LUCAS. [1] Exemplorum in grammaticis Philippi Melanthonis Latinis ... completio, & breuis interpretatio. Liber prior. ... Franc. Apud Hæredes Chr. Egen. M. D. LX. 8°. A-X^8. ff. 2-165. [2] Liber II. exemplorum in syntaxi et prosodia ... interpretatio. ... *Same imprint.* (*Colophon.*) A-T^8. ff. 3-153. [355

LOTICH, PETER, SECUNDUS. Carmen, in nuptias ... Iohannis Guilielmi, Ducis Saxoniæ, ac ... Susannae Dorotheae, ... Principis Friderici Palatini Elect. f. ... Heidelbergae, Per Ludouicum Lucium. M. D. LX. 8°. a-b^8 c^2 d^4. [356

-- Poemata ... Lipsiæ, in officina Voegeliana. ... 8°.)(^{6} (-)(6) A-O^8 P^{10}. pp. 1-242. ¶*Preface dated* 1563. [357

LOTTINI, GIOVANNI AGNOLO. Sacra rappresentazione di San Lorenzo. ... In Firneze, Presso Michaelagnolo di Bart. Sermartelli. MDXCII. 8°. a^4 A-F^8. pp. 1-95. [358

LOTTO DEL MAZZA. I Fabii comedia di Lotto del Mazza calzaiuolo Fiorentino. In Fiorenza Per Valente Panizzij & Marco Peri. MDLXVII. (... Ad istantia di Giouanni Baldi. ...) 8°. A-F^8 G^4. ff. 4-51. [359

LOUIS XI, king of France. La cronique du ... Roy Loys vnziesme ... On les vend à Paris ... en la boutique de Galliot du Pré ... 1558. (... 1557.) 8°. π^2 A-X^8. ff. 1-167. [360

LOUVAIN. *University.* Condemnatio Doctrinalis Librorum Martini Lutheri: per quosdam magistros nostros Louanieñ. ⁊ Colonieñ. facta. [c. 1520.] 4°. A^6. [361

-- Die handlung der Vniuersithet Leuen wider Doctor Martinus Luther. [Strassburg, Johann Knoblouch, 1520.] 4°. A^6. [362

-- Zwen vnd dreissig Artickel/ die allgemeinen Religion vnd Glauben belangend/ von den Theologen der hohē Schůl zu Lōuen ... aussgangen. Anno M.D.Xlv. ... 4°. A-B^4. [363

LUBBERTUS, SIBRANDUS. Sibrandi Lubberti de papa Romano libri decem, Scholasticè & Theologicè collati cum disputationibus Roberti Bellarmini ... Apud Aegidium Radaeum ... in Academia Franekerana. CIↃ.IↃ.XCIIII. 8°. ☛^{6} A-3N^8 3O^2. pp. 1-903. (Lea.) [364

LUBIN, EILHARD. Eilhardi Lubini in Q. Horatii Flacci poemata quæ exstant omnia paraphrasis scholastica noua ... Rostochii Ex Typographia Christophori Reusneri, anno M. D. XCIX. 4°. A-H^4 I^2 A^2 B-F^4 G^2 A^2 B-I^4 K^2 A^2 B-E^4 F^2 A^2 B-E^4 F^2 A-I^4 A^2 B-I^4 K^2 A^2 A-M^4 [N]^2 (N1 *signed* M, N2 *signed* K2) A^2 B-E^4 F^2 A^2 B-F^4 G^2. ¶*Additional t.pp.* at ^{2}A1^r (M. D. IIC), ^{3}A1^r, ^{4}A1^r, ^{5}A1^r (*all three* M. D. XCVIII), ^{6}A1^r, ^{7}A1^r, ^{9}A1^r, ^{10}A1^r (*all four* cIↃ IↃ Ic) ^{11}A1^r (M. D. XCIX). [365

LUCANGELI, NICOLÒ. Successi del viaggio d'Henrico III. ... re di Francia, e di Polonia, dalla sua partita di Craccouia fino all'arriuo in Turino. ... In Vinegia appresso Gabriel Giolito de' Ferrari. M D LXXIIII. 4°. A-H^{4}. pp. 3-64. ¶*Lacks portrait opposite t.p.* [366

LUCANUS, MARCUS ANNAEUS. M. Annæi Lucani de bello ciuile, vel Pharsaliae Libri decem, Gregorii Bersmani Annaebergensis studio ... emendati, scholijsq̃; illustrati. ... 1589. Lipsiæ. ... (... imprimebant haeredes Ioannis Steinmanni, Impensis Henningi Grossij ...) 8°.)?(^{8})*(^{4} A-Kk^{8} Ll^{4}. pp. 1-533. ¶*Includes:* Commendationes Ioach. Camerarii in librum primum Pharsaliæ, Nota Iosephi Scaligeri in eclogam ad Pisonem, Annotationes Iacobi Micylli, Theodori Pulmanni Craneburgii variarum lectionum libellus. [367

-- -- Lucano delle guerre ciuili di Giulio Morigi ... Con aggiunta sino alla morte di Cesare. ... In Rauenna, Appresso Francesco Tebaldini da Osimo. M D LXXXVII. 4°. +^{6} A-Nn^{8}. pp. 1-574. [368

-- -- Lucano ... En que se tratan las guerras Pharsalicas ... Traduzido de Latin en Romance Castellano, por Martin Lasso de Oropesa. En Anuers, En casa de Iuan Cordier. 1585. ... 8°. ¶^{8} A-Bb^{8}. pp. 1-397. [369

-- -- Lucano traduzido ... en prosa Castellana ... En Burgos. En casa de Phelippe de Iunta. M.D.LXXXVIII. (... 1578.) fol. ¶^{8} A-Bb^{8} Cc^{6}. pp. 1-411. [370

LUCCA. Lucensis ciuitatis statuta ... (Ioannes Baptista Phaellus Bononiensis Lucensi Aere publico Lucæ impressit ... MDXXXIX. Cal. Martiis.) fol. A^{6} (-A6, *blank*) B-ZZ^{6} 3A^{8} 3B-3F^{6} 3G^{8} 3H-3I^{6} 3K^{6+1} 3L^{6}. ff. i-cccxxxix. [371

-- [1] Leggi, et decreti del Magnifico Consiglio generale della citta di Lucca sopra li malefiti et il portare dell'armi ... [Lucca, Vincenzo Busdrago.] fol. a^{4} B^{4} C^{2}. [2] Statutum de poena portantis arma. Lucæ. 1561. A^{4} B^{2} (-B2, *presumably blank*). (Lea.) [372

-- *Rota.* Capitula magnifici domini praetoris DD. iudicum rotae, et iudicis ordinarii Lucensis ciuitatis. Lucae apud Vincentium Busdracum. fol. A-F^{4}. pp. 4-45. ¶F3^{r}: Finis capitularum rotae die prima Settembris MDLXI. (Lea.) [373

-- Nouissimae decisiones rotae Lucensis, Barnaba Cornazzano ... Auctore & Collectore ... Venetijs, Apud Damianum Zenarum MDXCVIII. fol. a-d^{6} e^{4} A-Bb^{6}. ff. 1-149. (Lea.) [374

-- *Confraternità della Santissima Trinità.* Statuti della vernerabile Confraternità della santissima Trinita De' Pellegrini, & Conualescenti Della Citta di Lucca. 4°. π^{6} A-O^{4}. ff. 2-56. (Lea.) [375

-- *Corte de' mercadanti.* Li statuti de la corte de mercadanti de la magnifica citta di Lucca. In Lucca per Vincenti Busdraghi MDLVII. fol. A-Cc^{4} Dd^{6}. pp. 1-205. [376

LUCIAN OF SAMOSATA. *Works.* Λουκιανοῦ ἅπαντα. Luciani Samosatensis opera ... omnia ... Basileae, anno M.D.XLV. [per Michaelem Isengrin.] 8°. α^{8} A-Z^{8} a-z^{8} &^{8} *^{8}. pp. 2-765. [377

-- -- Les oeuures de Lucian de Samosate ...: traduites du Grec, par Filbert Bretin Aussonois ... Repurgees de parolles impudiques & profanes. A Paris, Pour Abel l'Angelier ... M. D. LXXXII. ... fol. ā^{4} (-ā4) ē^{6} (-ē6) A-Ii^{6} Ll-4C^{6} 4D-4E^{4}. pp. 1-856. [378

-- *Two or more works.* Luciani Samosatensis dialogi aliquot, D. Brasmo [*sic*] Rot. et Thoma Moro interpretib. Eiusdem Oratio, Calumniæ non esse temerè credendum: &, Encomium Demosthenis: ex Philippi Melanchthonis uersione. Apud Seb. Gryphium Lugduni, 1541. 8°. a-z^{8} A-K^{8} L^{4}. pp. 2-534. [379

-- I diletteuoli dislogi: le vere narrationi: le facete epistole di Luciano philosopho: di greco in volgare nouamente tradotte ⁊ historiate. (Stampato in Vinegia per Nicolo di Aristotile detto Zoppino ... MDXXV. del mese di Settembre.) 8°. +^{8} A-FF^{8}. ff. I-CCXXX. [380

-- -- I dialogi piaceuoli ... tradotte per M. Nicolo da Lonigo ... In Venetia. M D XXXXI. (... per Giouanni de Farri & fratelli, da Riuoltella. ...) 8°. A-EE^{8}. ff. 2-223. [381

-- -- In Venetia. MDLI. (... per Giouanni Padoano. ...) 8°. A-EE^{8} (-EE8, *presumably blank*). ff. 2-223. [382

-- *De mercede conductio.* La vita de cortigiani di Luciano ... Interprete Giulio Roselli

Fiorentino. M.D.XLII. ... (In Vinegia, per Venturino di Roffinelli. ...) 8°. A-C4 (-C4, *presumably blank*). ff. 2-11. [383

-- *Dialogi deorum*. Λουκιανοῦ Σαμοσατέως θεῶν διάλογοι. Luciani Samosatensis deorum dialogi numero .70. una cum interpretatione e regione latina ... Ioannes Schottus. Argentinę ... elaborauit ... 1515. 4°. a-x4. [384

-- *Selected dialogues*. Luciani Samosatensis dialogi aliquot Græci ... Basileæ apud Valentinum Curionem, Mense Febr. an. M. D. XXII. (*Colophon.*) 4°. A-O4. [385

-- L. Luciani Samosateni Dialogi ... (Pressi sunt ... Lipsi in edibus Lotterianis Anno ... decimotertio, Mense Decembri,) 4°. A-B6 (-A3) C4 D-F6. [386

-- Luciani Samosatensis dialogi selectiores, ... Græce Latineq; ... Augustæ Vindelicorum, in officina Typographica Michaelis Mangeri. M.D.LXXXVII. 8°. A-Y8 Z6. ff. 2-8, pp. 9-340. [387

-- Spiegel der Menschlichen blödigkeit. Drei schöner Gesprech Luciani/ Sampt vil andern lustigen vnd nützlichen Historien. ... verteütscht. Durch I. Vielfelt M. D. LXIIII. (Getruckt zu Strassburg bei Iosia Rihel/ Anno M.D.lxiiij ...) 4°. π4 A-I4. ff. ij-xxxij. [388

LUCIENBERG, JOHANN. Inclyta Æneis: P. Virgilii Maronis ... in regiam tragicocomoediam, seruatis vbique heroicis versibus ... redacta. ... Francofordiæ Moeni, anno CIↃ. IↃ. LXXVI. (... apud Paulum Reffelerum.) 4°. ✠8 *.*.4 A-R8. [389

-- Ioannis Lucienbergij Thesaurus Poeticus ... 4°. *8 a-t8 **4 A-N8 3*4 Aa-Zz8 Aaa-Ppp8 AAa-ZZz8 3a-3c8 3d10 3A-3C8. [390

LUCILIUS, GAIUS. C. Lucili, Suessani Auruncani, ... satyrarum quæ supersunt reliquiæ. Franciscus Iani f. Dousa collegit, disposuit, & Notas addidit. Lugduni Batauorum, Ex officina Plantiniana Francisci Raphelengij. cIↄ. Iↄ. IIIC. 4°. *4 ¶4 †4 A-R4 S2. pp. 2-139. [391

LUCIUS, CYRIACUS. De neosophistica. Kurtze Erinnerung/ Dass man die New Sophistische Lehr/ welche ... der heiligen Christlichen Religion/ vnd Policey/ sehr einreisset/ Fleissig erwegen/ vermeyden vnd abstellen ... soll. ... Getruckt zu Ingolstatt/ durch Wolffgang Eder. Anno M.D.Lxxxvi. (VI. Id. Sextil. ... typis absoluebatur ...) 4°. A-E4 F2. pp. 1-36. [392

LUCRETIUS CARUS, TITUS. [In Carū Lucretiū poetā Cōmētarij a Ioāne Baptista Pio editi. (Bononiæ typis ... Hieronymi Baptistæ de Benedictis ... Kal. Maii 1511.)] fol. π4 (-π4) A-NN6 OO8 (-OO8). ff. II-CCXVI *present*. [393

-- -- .T. Lucretii Cari de rerum natura libri .VI. (Impressum Florentiae sumptibus Philippi Giuntæ ... M.D.XII. Mense Martio) 8°. A8 a-q8 r10. ff. II-CXXV. [394

-- -- Lucretius. (Venetiis in aedibus Aldi, et Andreae soceri mense Ianuario M. D. XV.) 8°. *8 a-q8. ff. 1-125. [395

-- -- [T. Lucretii Cari de rerum natura libri sex ... Antuerpiae, ex officina Christophori Plantini. CIↃ.IↃ.LXVI.] (Excudebat Antuerpiæ Christophorus Plantinus anno M. D. LXVI.) 8°. *-**8 (-*1) A-Hh8 (-Hh8, *blank*). pp. 1-477. [396

-- -- ... A Dion. Lambino Monstroliensi ... emendati, ac ... illustrati ... Lutetiae, anno CIↃ. IↃ. LXXX. Apud Ioannem Bene‿natum. ... 4°. a-e4 f2 A-Zz4 AA-3C4 3D2. pp. 1-627. ¶*T.p. repaired.* [397

LUDOLPHUS DE SAXONIA. Ludolfi Carthusiensis ... in Psalterium expositio. ... Psalmi penitentiales et cōfessionales ... Francisci Petrarche ... Additur in margīe ... Augustini accuratissima de hebreo in latinū trāslatio. ... Venundatur Parrhisijs ... a magr̄o Bertholdo Rembolt ⁊ Iohāne paruo. (Anno ... Millesimo quingentesimo. xiiij. die vero decima Marcij.) 4°. B.L. aa-dd8 a-z8 A-F8 G4. ff. j-ccxxxij. [398

-- -- Ludolphi Chartus. in Psal. Dauid ... Enarratio ... [Lugduni,] A. Vincent. (... M.cccccxlij.) 8°. B.L. aa-ee8 a-z8 A-AA8. ff. 1-372. [399

LÜBECK. Der Kayserlichen Freyen ... Reichs-Stadt Lübeck Statuta vnd Stadt Recht. ... aus alter Sechsischer Sprach on Hochteudsch gebracht. Gedruckt zu Lübeck/ durch Iohan Balhorn ... 1586. (*Colophon.*) 4°.)(^{4} (:)^4 (?)^2 A-Ee^4. [400

LÜDTKE, MATTHÄUS. Historia Von der erfindung/ Wunderwercken vnd zerstörung des vermeinten heiligen Bluts zur Wilssnagk. ... Durch Matthæum Ludecum ... Gedruckt zu Wittenberg/ durch Clemens Schleich/ Anno 1586. 4°. A-Cc^4 Dd^2. [401

LUIGINI, FEDERICO. Il libro della bella donna ... In Venetia, per Plinio Pietrasanta, MDLIIII. (*Colophon.*) 8°. A-H^8 I^4. pp. 3-130. [402

LUIGINI, MARCO ANTONIO. Espositione dell'XI. et XII. cap. del IIII. lib. d'Esdra ... Nuouamente composta per ... Marco Antonio Louisino Vdinese ... In Venetia, appresso Mattheo Boselli, M. D. LXXI. 4°. +^{4} A-Z^4 a-c^4. ff. 1-92. [403

LUIS DE GRANADA. [1] Tutte l'opere del R. Padre Fra Luigi di Granata ... Nuouamente tradotte di Spagnuolo in Italiano da diuersi auttori ... E questo è il primo fiore della nostra Ghirlanda Spirituale. ... In Vinegia appresso Gabriel Giolito di Ferrarii M D LXVIII. 4°. *^{8} A-L^8. pp. 3-174. [2] Memoriale della vita del Christiano ...: nuouamente tradotto di Spagnuolo in Italiano da M. Giouanni Miranda. ... E questo è il secondo fiore della nostra Ghirlanda Spirituale. ... *Same imprint.* *^{8} A-N^8. pp. 1-208. [3] Deuotissime meditationi ... Nuouamente tradotte di Spagnuolo in Italiano da M. Pietro Lauro Modonese. ... E questo è il terzo fiore della nostra Ghirlanda Spirituale. ... *Same imprint.* *^{10} A-N^8 O^4 (-O4). pp. 1-214. [404

-- -- *Another copy.* [1] *lacks* L8; *8 *misbound before* *2. [405

-- Specchio della vita humana ... tradotto di di [*sic*] Spaguolo [*sic*] in Italiano dal Signor Giouanni Miranda. ... In Vinegia appresso Gabriel Giolito de' Ferrari. MDLXVIII. 12°. *^{12} A-R^{12}. pp. 1-408. [406

-- Trattato dell'oratione, et della meditatione, nel quale si tratta de' principali misteri della fede nostra ... tradotto dallo Spagnuolo, per ... Vincenzo Buondi Mantouano. ... In Vinegia appresso Gabriel Giolito de' Ferrari. M D LXI. 8°. *^{8} [**]^4 (-**1-3) A-CC^8 (-CC7-8). pp. 1-414. (Lea.) [407

-- -- In Venetia, appresso Giorgio Angelieri, M. D. LXXXII. 4°. [1] La prima parte ... a^8 A-R^8. ff. 1-135. [2] La seconda parte ... a^4 A-K^8. ff. 1-80. [3] La terza parte ... a^4 A-G^8. ff. 1-56. [4] La quarta parte ... π^4 a-g^8 (-g8, *presumably blank*). ff. 1-55. ¶*Additional t.p.* (f1): Breue confessionario del R.P.F. Francesco D'Euia ... Nuouamente Tradotto dalla lingua Spagnuola ... per Camillo Camilli. ... *Same imprint.* [408

LULL, RAMON. Arbor sciētie ... Venales habentur Lugdun̄. ... in domo Francisci fradin impressoris. (Anno ... Millesimo quingentesimo decimoquinto .iiij. Nonas Maij.) 4°. B.L. a-z^8 A-E^8. ff. ij-ccxxiiij. [409

-- Ars Iuris ... (Impressum Rome [per Ioannem Beplin] apud Iacobū Mazochium Die .II. men̄. Apri. M.D.XVI.) 4°. A-G^4. ff. V-XXVII. ¶*Editor: Salvator Gavellus.* [410

-- ... Raymundi Lull. ars magna/ generalis et vltima ... per magistrum Bernardum la Vinheta ... elimata. ... Symon vincent. ... (Lugduni per Iacobum Marechal ... sumptibus vero Simonis Vincent ... M.cccccxvij. quinto idus mayas.) 4°. B.L. A^4 B-Q^8 R^4. ff. j-cxxiiij. [411

-- Codicillus seu vade mecum ... Secunda editio ... Coloniae Apud Hæredes Arnoldi Birckmanni, Anno M. D. LXXII. ... 8°. A-P^8 Q^4. pp. 3-248. (Smith.) [412

-- Raimundi Lullii Maioricani de alchimia Opuscula quæ sequuntur. Apertorium. Item. Magica naturalis. Item. De secretis naturæ, Seu de Quinta essentia liber unus. ... Norimbergæ, apud Iohan. Petreium. M.D.XLVI. (*Colophon.*) 4°. a-z^4 A-D^4 E^6 (-E6, *blank*). ff. 2-113. (Smith.) [413

-- -- *Another copy.* [414

-- Raimundi Lullii ... De secretis naturæ siue Quinta essentia libri duo. His accesserunt, Alberti Magni ... De mineralibus & rebus metallicis Libri quinq3. ... repurgata ... per M. Gualtherum H. Ryff ... M.D.XLI. Mense Martio. ... (Argentorati apud Balthassarum Beck. ...) 8°. A-Z^8 a^8. ff. 1-183. (Smith.) [415

-- -- Venetijs apud Petrum Schoeffer Germanum Maguntinum. Anno M. D. XLII. (Venundantur ... apud Io. Baptistam [Pederzanum] ...) 8°. A-X^8. pp. 3-324. [416

-- -- ... Adiecta est eiusdem epistola ad Regem Robertum de Accurtatione lapidis Philosophorum: cui adiunctus est tractatus de aquis ex scriptis Raymundi super Accurtationis epistolam ... collectus. Coloniae Apud Ioannem Birckmannum Anno D. M. LXVII. ... 8°. [A]^4 B-Aa^8 Bb^4. pp. 1-376. (Lea.) [417

-- -- *Another copy*. (Smith.) [418

-- -- Raymundi Lulii ... libelli aliquot Chemici ... opera Doctoris Toxitæ editi. ... Basileae. Apud Petrum Pernam. M.D.LXXII. 8°.):(^{8} a-z^8 A-G^8 a-b^8. pp. 1-480. [419

-- -- Basileae. Typis Conradi Waldkirchii. Anno cIo DC. 8°. a-z^8 A-D^8. pp. 1-397. (Smith.) [420

-- Rẹmundi Lulli ... Metaphysica noua: & Philosophiæ in Auerroistas expostulatio. Vẹnundantur Parrhisiis in officina Ascensiana. (... ad Decimum Kalendas Martias ... MD.XVI.) 4°. A-B^8 C^4. [421

-- Raymundi Lullii opera ea quae ad adinuentam ab ipso artem Vniuersalem ... pertinent. ... Argentinæ. Sumptibus Lazari Zetzneri. cIↃ Io XCIIX. 8°. (?)^4):(^{8} ():(8 + *folded leaf*) a-z^8 A-Ss^8. pp. 3-992. [422

-- Quaestiones dubitabiles super quattuor libris sententiarū cum quaestionibus solutiuis Magistri Thomae attrabatēsis. (Opera: & Impensa Ioānis Tacuini Tridinēsis ... cusum est ... M.CCCCC.VII. die .XV. Iulii.) 4°. AA-KK^8 LL^6. ff. II-LXXXIIII. [423

-- Raymundi Lulli ... testamentum, duobus libris vniuersam artem Chymicam complectens ... Item eiusdem compendium animae transmutationis srtis metallorum ... Coloniae Agrippinae Apud Ioannem Byrckmannum Anno M. D. LXVI. ... 8°. A^4 B-Ii^8 (Bb1 + *folded leaf*, Ee2 + *folded leaf*). ff. 2-240. (Smith.) [424

-- -- *Another copy* (- *folded ll.*). (Smith.) [425

-- -- Coloniae Agrippina. Apud Ioannem Birckmannum. Anno. M. D. LXXIII. 8°. A^4 B-Hh^8 (Aa1 + *folded leaf*, Bb1 + *folded leaf*). ff. 1-231. (Smith.) [426

-- -- *Another copy* (- *folded leaf with* Aa1; *folded leaf with* Bb1 *defective*). (Smith.) [427

LUNA, FABRICIO. Vocabulario, di cinq; mila Vocabuli Toschi ... M.D.XXXVI. (Stampato in Napoli per Giouanni Sultzbach Alemano ... adi 27. di Ottobre ...) 4°. A-Gg^4. [428

LUPICINI, ANTONIO. Architettura militare ... In Fiorenza M.D.LXXXII. Appresso Giorgio Marescotti. (*Colophon*.) 4°. A-L^4. pp. 3-88. (Fine Arts.) [429

LUPULUS, SIGISMUND. Rudimenta grammatices ad puerorū utilitatem cōscripta ... M. D. XXXI. (Augustæ ex aedibus Heynrici Steyner ...) 8°. A-D^8. [430

LURBE, GABRIEL DE. Budigalensium rerum chronicon. Auctore Gabr. Lurbeo ... Editio secunda aucta ... Burdigalæ. Excudebat S. Millangius ... cIo. Io. xc. 4°. A-C^8 D^6. ff. 3-28. [431

-- -- Chronique Bourdeloise Composée cy-deuant en Latin par Gabriel de Lurbe ... Et par luy ... traduitte en François. Auec deux siens discours ..., l'vn de la conuersion du Roi, & l'autre des Antiquitez n'aguieres trouuées hors ladicte ville. A Bourdeaus, Par S. Millanges ... 1594. 4°. A-Q^4 R^6 (-R1, R4). ff. 2-60, pp. 58-69. ¶*Additional t.p.* (Q1^r): Discours sur les antiquitez trouuees pres le Prieure S. Martin les Bourdeaus en Iuillet 1594. ... A Bourdeaus, Par S. Millanges ... 1595. [432

LURCHER, ERHART. Ein hüpsche historiē von einem Ritter genant herr Thorelle ... (Getruckt zů Strassburg [durch Johann Knoblouch].) 4°. A^8 B-C^6. ¶*In verse*. [433

LUSIGNANO, STEFFANO DI. Description de toute l'isle de Cypre ... Par R. Pere F. Estienne de Lusignan ... traduite en François. A Paris, Chez Guillaume Chaudiere ... 1580. ... 4°. ā^4 ē^4 ī^2 a-z^4 A-Zz^4 AA-HH^4 II^2. ff. 1-292. [434

-- Les genealogies de soixante et sept ... maisons ... yssuēs de Meroūée, fils de Theodoric

2. Roy d'Austrasie ... Par R.P. Estienne de-Cypre, de la Royale Maison de Lusignan ... A Paris, Chez Guillaume le Noir ... M. D. LXXXVI. ... 4°. $\bar{a}^{4}$ $\bar{e}^{2}$ A-Ii^{4}. ff. 1-128. [435

-- Histoire contenant vne sommaire description des Genealogies, Alliances, & gestes de tous les Princes ... qui ont iadis commãdé és Royaumes de Hierusalem, Cypre, Armenie, & lieux circonuoisins. ... A Paris, Chez Guillaume Chaudiere ... 1579. ... 4°. *^{4} a-s^{4}. ff. 1-72. [436

LUTHER, MARTIN. [1] Tomus primus omnium operum ... D. M. L. ... Ienae excudebat Christianus Rhodius. 1556. (*Colophon.*) fol. *^{6})(^{6} A-Z^{6} a-z^{6} AA-ZZ^{6} aa-zz^{6} Aa-Dd^{6} Ee^{8} (-Ee8, *presumably blank*). ff. I-CCCCCLXXIX. [2] Tomus secundus ... [Ihen]ae. [Excud]ebat [Christianus] Rhodius. [155]7. (*Colophon.*) *^{6} A-Z^{6} a-z^{6} AA-ZZ^{6} aa-zz^{6} 3A-3H^{6}. ff. 1-603. [3] Tomus tertius ... Ihenae. Excudebat Hæredes Christiani Rhodij. 1557. *^{4} A-Z^{6} a-z^{6} AA-ZZ^{6} aa-3b^{6} (-3b6). ff. 1-564. [4] Tomus quartus ... Ihenae, excudebat, [Hae]redes Christiani Rhodij. Anno M.D.LVIII. (*Colophon.*) *^{4} A-6Y^{6}. ff. 1-822. ¶*Tomes 2 and 4 very fragile, with many defective leaves.* [437

-- -- [1] Tomus primus omnium operum ... D. M. L. ... Ienae. Impressum in Officina Typographica Donati Richtzenhaini, & Thomæ Rebarti. Anno M.D.LXIIII. (... M. D. LXV.) fol. *^{6})(^{6} A-4X^{6} 4Y^{4}. ff. 1-540. [2] Tomus secundus omnium operum ... D. Mart. Luth. ... Ienae. Ex Officina Hæredum Thomæ Rebarthi. Anno M.D.LXXXI. [illegible]^{6} A-5B^{6} 5C^{8}. ff. 1-571. [3] Tomus tertius omnium operum ... D. M. L. ... Ienæ Ex Officina Hæredum Thomæ Rebarthi. Anno M.D.LXXXII. *^{4} A-4V^{6} 4X^{8} (-4X8, *presumably blank*). ff. 1-540. [4] Tomus quartus et idem vltimus omnium operum ... Doct. Mart. Luth. ... Ienae Excudebat Christianus Rhodius. M. D. LXX. (*Colophon.*))(^{4} A-6T^{6} 6V^{2}. ff. 1-806. (Lea.) [438

-- Die ander Epistel Sanct Petri/ Vnd eine S. Iudas gepredigt vñ ausgelegt ... Vuittemberg (Gedruckt ... durch Nickel Schyrlentz.) 4°. A-I^{4}. ¶*Benzing 1841.* [439

-- Auff das Vermeint Keiserlich Edict/ Ausgangen jm 1531 jare/ nach dem Reichstage des 1530 jars. Glosa. ... Wittemberg. DMXXXI. (Gedrückt ... durch Nickel Schirlentz.) 4°. A-G^{4}. [440

-- Ein Brieff ... Wider die Sabbather ... Wittemberg 1538 (Gedruckt ... durch Nickel Schirlentz ...) 4°. A-H^{4} (-H4, *blank*). [441

-- [1] Colloquia, meditationes, consolationes, consilia, iudicia, sententiæ, Narrationes, Responsa, Facetiæ ... Tomus primus. ... Francofurti ad Moenum. (... per Nicolaum Bassum & Hieronymum Feyerabent.) 8°.)(^{8})()^{8} A-Z^{8} a-h^{8} i^{4}. ff. 1-238. [2] Colloquia ... Tomus secundus. Francofurti ad Moenum M. D. LXXI. (*Same colophon.*) Aa-3K^{8} 3L^{4}. ff. 2-153 [= 253]. (Lea.) [442

-- Colloquia Oder Christliche Nützliche Tischreden ... durch Herrn M. Iohannem Aurifabrum ... zusammen getragen ... Leipzig/ M. D. LXXVII. 1.2.3.6. (Gedruckt ... durch Iacob Berwalds Erben. ...) fol. a-g^{6} h^{4} A-4V^{6}. ff. 1-505. [443

-- Das Elltern die kinder zur Ehe nicht zwingen noch hyndern ... [Wittenberg, Lukas Cranach & Christian Döring, 1524.] 4°. A^{4} B^{2}. [444

-- Das Ihesus Christus eyn geborner Iude sey ... Wittemberg [durch Nickel Schirlentz]. M.D.xxiij. 4°. A-C^{4} D^{2} E^{4}. [445

-- De votis monasticis ... iudicium. VVittembergae [Melchior Lotter, 1522]. 4°. Aa-Pp^{4}. (Lea.) [446

-- Deutsch Auslegung des sieben vnd sechzigsten Psalmen/ von dem Ostertag/ Hymelfart vnd Pfingsten. ... Wittemberg M. D. XXIIII. (Gedruckt ... Melchior Lotter der Iünger. ...) 4°. A-E^{4} F^{6}. [447

-- Enarrationes Seu Postillæ ... maiores ... Quibus ... adiectas aliquot Homilias, accessit etiam Apologia Græcorum de igne Purgatorio ... per Ioannem Hartungum latinitate donata ... Basileae. (... per Ioannem Heruagium ... M.D.XLVI. Mense Martio.) fol. α^{6} β^{4} A-Zz^{6} AA-3O^{6}. ff. 1-493. [448

-- Epistel Sanct Petri gepredigt vnd aisgelegt ... Vuittemberg. M.D.XXiij. (Gedruckt ... durch Nickel Schyrlentz ...) 4°. A-Z^{4} aa-cc^{4}. [449

-- Epistolarum ... Tomus primus, continens scripta ... ab anno millesimo quingentesimo septimo, vsque ad annum vicesimum secundum a Iohanne Aurifabro ... collectus. Anno M. D.

LVI. Ihenae. Excudebat Christianus Rhodius. (*Colophon.*) 4°. A⁴ *⁴ *² B-Z⁴ a-z⁴ AA-ZZ⁴ aa-zz⁴ 3A⁴ (-3A4, *presumably blank*). ff. 1-367. (Lea.) [450

-- Secundus tomus epistolarum ... continens scriptas ab anno Millesimo quingentesimo vigesimosecundo, vsq; in annum vigesimum octauum. A Ioanne Aurifabro collectus. Eislebii excudebat [Andreas Petri anno M.D.LXV.] 4°. A⁶ (-A6, *probably blank*) B-Z⁴ a-z⁴ Aa-4H⁴. ff. 1-396. ¶*T.p. and a few other leaves defective and repaired.* (Lea.) [451

-- Ein frage des gantzen heiligen Ordens der Kartenspieler vom Karnoffel/ an das Concilium zu Mantua. gebessert. 1537 [Wittenberg, Nickel Schirlentz, 1537?] 4°. A⁴. ¶*Doubtfully Luther's.* [452

-- Ein herpredig wider den Türckē. ... Wittemberg. M.D.XXX. (Gedruckt zu Nurnberg durch Friderich Peipus. 1530.) 8°. A-E⁸ F⁴ (-F4, *presumably blank*). [453

-- Kurtz Bekentnis vnd Artickel vom heiligen Abendmal ... was hievon ... zu Sachssen/ bisher ȯffentlich geleret/ ... worden ... Gedruckt zu Wittenberg/ durch Hans Lufft. 1574. (*Colophon.*) 4°. A-K⁴ L². [454

-- M.D.XX. Ain kurtze vnderweysung wie man beichten sol: auss Doctor Martinus Luthers Augustiner wolmainung gezogen. [Augsburg, Silvan Otmar.] 4°. A⁶. [455

-- Ordenung vnd bericht wie es furterhin (mit ihenen so das ... Sacrament empfahen wollen) gehalten sol werden. Item zwo predig/ die Vffersteung Christi ... Wittemberg [durch Michael Lotter]. MDXXV. 4°. A-H⁴. [456

-- Ein sendbrieff ... Von Dolmetzschen̄ vnd Fürbit der heiligenn. [Nürnberg, Georg Rottmaier,] M.D.XXX. 4°. a-b⁴ c². ¶"M Iohanni Weibringero | suo hospiti M Luther dd". [457

-- Eyn Sermon von dem gutten hyrten. Iohannis x. ... Wittemberg [Johann Grunenberg]. 1523. 8°. A-B⁸ (-B1-3, B6-8, B7-8 *being blank*). [458

-- Ein Sermon Von dem Heubtman zu Capernaum/ Matth. viij. ... M. D. XXXV. (Gedruckt zu Wiitemberg durch Georgen Rhaw.) 4°. A-E⁴. [459

-- Ain sermon von der wirdigen empfahung des ... leychnams Christi/ gethon am grůndonerstag Wittenberg ... [Augsburg, Silvan Otmar,] M.D.XXj. 4°. A⁶. [460

-- Vnterricht der Visitatorn an die Pfarherrn im Kurfürstenthumb zů Sachssen. Wittemberg. [Nürnberg, Friedrich Peypus,] MDXXVIII. 4°. A-H⁴. [461

-- Vermanung zum Sacrament des leibs vnd bluts vnsers Herrn. ... Wittenberg. M. D. XXX. (Gedruckt durch Melcher Sachssen.) 8°. A⁶ B⁸ C⁴ D⁸. [462

-- Vieler schȯnen Sprůche aus Gȯttlicher Schrifft Auslegung. ... Heinrichstadt Gedruckt durch Conrad Horn. 1595. (*Colophon.*) 8°. A-Qq⁸. ff. 1-325. [463

-- Vom Eelichen Leben. ... Wittemberg [durch Johann Grunenberg]. M.D.xxij. 4°. A-D⁴. [464

-- -- Vom Ehelichen Leben. ... Vuittemberg [durch Melchior Lotter]. M. D. xxiij. 4°. A-E⁴. [465

-- Vom Kriege/ Wider den Turcken. ... Wittemberg. M D XLII. (Gedruckt ... durch Nickel Schirlentz ...) 4°. A-I⁴ K⁶. [466

-- Vom Missbrauch der Messen. ... Wittemberg. 1523. (Gedruckt ... Melchior vnd Michael Lotther gebrůder ...) 4°. A-P⁴ Q⁶. [467

-- Von Anbeten des Sacraments des heyligen leychnams Christi. ... Wittemberg [durch Melchior Lotter den J.]. Anno M. D. xxv. 4°. A-D⁴ E² F⁴. [468

-- Von dem aller nȯttigisten/ Wie man diener der kirchen welen vnd eynsetzen sol. ... Wittemberg. Im. xxiiij. iar. (Gedruckt ... Melchior Lotter der Junger. ...) 4°. A-I⁴. ¶*Translator: Paul Speratus.* [469

-- Von den gutten wercken. ... Wittemberg. M.D.XXV. (Getruckt ... bey Melchior Lother dem iunger ...) 4°. Aa-Nn⁴ Oo⁶. [470

-- Von den Schlüsseln ... Wittemberg. M.D.XXX. (Gedruckt ... durch Hans Lufft. ...) 4°. A-K⁴. [471

-- Von der Beicht ob die der Bapst macht habe zu gepieten. ... Wittenbergk [durch Johann

Grunenberg, 1521]. 4°. A-G⁴. ¶*Lacks* Der hundert vñ achtzehnt Psalm ..., *included in some other copies.* [472

-- -- Vuittemberg [durch Melchior Lotter den J.]. 1523. 4°. A-M⁴. ¶*With the psalm.* [473

-- Von der Freyheit eynes Christen menschen. ... Vuittemberg [durch Melchior Lotter den J.]. M.D.Xxiij. 4°. a-b⁴ c⁶. [474

-- Von der heiligen Tauffe: predigten. ... Wittemberg. M.D. XXXV. (Gedruckt ... durch Georgen Rhaw.) 4°. a⁴ A-M⁴ N² O⁴. [475

-- Von der Kirchen/ Was/ wer/ vnd wo sie sey/ vñ wo bey man sie erkennen sol. ... 1540. 4°. a-d⁴. [476

-- Von menschen leren zů meyden. ... Wittenberg. [Augsburg, Heinrich Steiner,] M.D.XXij. 4°. A⁴ B⁶. [477

-- Ein Widderuff vom Fegefeur. ... Wittemberg. 1530. (Gedrůckt ... durch Georgen Rhaw.) 4°. A-F⁴. ¶*Presentation copy to Johann Weibringer, signed* M L dd. [478

-- [Zwo Predigt vber der Leiche des Kurfürsten Hertzog Iohann zu Sachsen/ D. Martinij Luthers.] (Gedruckt zu Wittemberg/ durch Nickel Schirlentz/ im jar MDXXXIII.) 8°. A-C⁸ (-A1). [479

LUTRIA, JOANNES DE. Questiones per vtiles librorum de anima Cum adiectione textus noue trãslationis Ioãnis Argiropoli bisanti circa questiones. ... (Impressum Venetijs per Iacobum de leuco Impensis vero Leonardi Alantsee ciuis Viẽnensis Anno .1508. die .21. Ianuarij.) 4°. B.L. A-G⁸ H⁶. [480

LUTZENBURG, BERNARD. Catalogus haereticorum ... in cuius calce & de Luthero nonnihil deprehendes. Aeditio tertia ... Cui tractatus eiusdem de purgatorio adiectus est. M. D. XXVII. 8°. a-x⁸. (Lea.) [481

-- -- *Another copy.* (Yarnall.) [481a

-- Concilium generale malignantium cum Digressionibus pro concilio generali orthodoxoꝶ militantium. ... Anno. D. M. XXVIII. 8°. A-D⁸ E⁴. (Lea.) [482

LUXEMBOURG, JEAN DE. Repudio della Reina Maria d'Inghilterra, Sorella del Duca di Cleues, & difesa sua con molta eloquentia in uerso il Re, tradotto di Franzese in Toscano dal Cap. Gio: Battista del Grillandari, Fiorentino. In Bologna per Antonio Giaccarello & Pelegrino Bonardo Compagni. 1558. 4°. A-F⁴ G². [483

LYCOPHRON. [1] Λυκοφρονος Αλεξανδρα, το σκοτεινον ποιημα. ... Lycophronis Chalcidensis Alexandra, siue Cassandra: ... Isacii Tzetzis Grammatici Commentarijs ... illustratum atqȝ explicatum ... Ioannis Tzetzæ Variarum historiarum liber, ... Pauli Lacusii Veronensis opera ad uerbum Latinè conuersus ... Basileae. (... ex officina Ioannis Oporini, ... M.D.XLVI. Mense Martio.) fol. α-β⁴ A-X⁴ Y⁶. pp. 1-180. [2] Ιωαννου του Τζετζου βιβλιον ιστορικον ... Accessit quoque, Nicolai Gerbelii praefatio ... Basileae. *⁴ Aa-3L⁴. pp. 1-268. [484

-- -- ... Cum versione Latina Gulielmi Canteri. Eiusdem Canteri ... Annotationes ... [Heidelbergae,] Apud Hieronymum Commelianum. Anno cIↄ Iↄ XCVI. 8°. †⁸ a-m⁸. pp. 1-192. [485

-- -- Lycophronis Chalcidensis Alexandra. Poẽma obscurum. Ioannes Meursius. Recensuit, & Libro Commentario illustravit. Altera Editio ... Accessit Iosephi Scaligeri Iull Cæs. F. versio centum locis emendatior. *Greek and Latin.* Lugduni Batavorum, Ex officinâ Ludovici Elzevirii. Anno cIↄ. Iↄ. IC. (... Excudebat Ioannes Balduini. VIII. Kal. Maias. ...) 8°. A-Z⁸ (-A6, A7) a⁸. pp. 4-350. [486

-- -- ... è Græco in Latinum sermonem ... uersa ... per Bernardum Bertrandum Rheginũ ...: unà cũ ... Isacij Tzetzis ... commentarijs ... Basileae, per Ioannem Oporinum. (... M.D.LVIII. Mense Iunio.) 8°. a-z⁸ A-D⁸ E¹⁰. pp. 4-387. [487

LYCOSTHENES, CONRADUS. Prodigiorum ac ostentorum chronicon, Quæ præter naturæ ordinem, motum, et operationem ... ab exordio mundi usque ad hæc nostra tempora, acciderunt. ... Basileæ, per Henricum Petri. (... mense Augusto anno M. D. LVII.) fol. a⁴ b² A⁶ B-C⁴ D-Zz⁶ AA-II⁶ KK⁴ LL⁶. pp. 1-670. (Lea.) [488

LYCURGUS. Oratio Lycurgi contra Leocraten ... Cum Præfatione Phi. Melanth. Vitebergae edita in officina Iohannis Lufft M.D.XLV. (*Colophon.*) 8°. $+^8$ A-E^8. [489

LYNDEWODE, WILLIAM. Prouinciale seu Constitutiones Anglie ... (... diligentia ... Andree Bocard ... In ... parisiana academia. Anno ... Millesimo quingentesimoprimo. Maij vero die .xxviij.) fol. B.L. a^8 b^6 c-g^8 h^6 i-q^8 r^6 s-z^8 $ꝛ^8$ $ɔ^6$ A-B^6 C^8 (-C8, *presumably blank*). ff. ii-Cxcii. *S.T.C.* 17107. (Biddle.) [490

LYON. Triomphes, pompes et magnificences faicts a Lyon, pour la paix. A Paris, De l'imprimerie de Federic Morel ... M. D. LIX. 4°. A^4. [491

LYSIAS. Lysiae Atheniensis ... orationes duæ Latinitati datæ. (Romae apud Iacobum Mazochium. M.D.XV. nonis Aprilis.) 4°. [a]-c^4 d^6. ¶*Translator: Janus Vitalis Panormitanus.* [492

M

M., I. D. S. Sentences selectes de Periander, Publian, Seneque, & Isocrate: tournées en Poësies Françoises. A Paris, Pour Vincent Sertenas ... M.D.LXI. ... 8°. A-H^4 (-H4, *presumably blank*). ff. 2-30. [1

MACCHIAVELLI, LUCA. Oratio de laudibus Ferrariensium ... Bononiæ Peregrinus Bonardus Excudebat. M. D. LX. (*Colophon.*) 4°. A-D^4 E^2. pp. 3-35. [2

-- Fratris Lucae Macchiauellij Bononiensis ... Oratio de liberali educatione ... Bononiæ, Peregrinus Bonardus Excudebat. 1561. 4°. A^8. [3

MACER, KASPAR. Ein Bittpredig/ Wider den grausamen erschröcklichen erbfeind/ vnd durchächter des hailigen Christlichen glaubens ... den Türcken ... Getruckt zů Ingolstatt/ durch Alexander vnd Samuel Weissenhorn. Anno M.D.LXVII. 4°. A-F^4. ff. II-XXIIII. [4

-- De optimo genere oratorum M. T. Ciceronis, in duas Aeschinis & Demosthenis Orationes, Præfatio, cum facili Enarratione ... Ingolstadij excudebant Alexander & Samuel Vueissenhornij. 8°. A-D^8. ff. 1-24. [5

-- Drey kurtze bittpredig. ... Gedruckt zu Můnchen/ bey Adam Berg. Anno M.D.LXXII. ... 4°. A-E^4. [6

-- Euangelische Fragstuck/ Auss D. Martin Luthers Bůchern ... gezogen ... Getruckt zů Ingolstat/ durch Alexander Weissenhorn. Anno M.D.LXX. 4°. A-K^4. ff. II-XXXX. [7

-- Hymnorum liber, cui de laudibus sacrarum scripturarum, et B. Ioannis Euangelistæ accessit oratio ... Anno M. D. LXII. (Impressum Ingolstadij, per Alexandrum & Samuelem Vueissenhornios.) 8°. A-D^8. [8

MACHIAVELLI, NICOLÒ. Discorsi di Nicolo Machiauelli, Fiorentino, sopra la prima deca di Tito Liuio ... (In Vinegia per Giouan'Antonio de Nicolini da Sabio, ad instantia de M. Merchiore Sessa. ... MDXXXVII. Del Mese d'Agosto.) 8°. *^{8} A-BB^8. ff. 1-200. [9

-- -- Discorsi. Nicolai Machiavelli Florentini disputationum De republica ... Libri III. ... Ex Italico Latini facti. Ursellis Ex Officina Typographica Cornelij Sutorij M. D. XCIX. (*Colophon.*) 12°. A-Aa^{12} (-Aa10-12, *blank*). pp. 1-546. [10

-- Il principe ... La vita di Castruccio Castracani da Lucca ... Il modo che tenne il Duca Valentino per ammazare Vitellozo, Oliuerotto da Fermo, il .S. Pagolo, & il Duca di Grauina ... I ritratti delle cose della Francia, & della Alamagna ... M D XXXV. 8°. ✠^{4} A-K^8 L^4 (-L4). ff. 1-83. [11

-- -- Nicolai Machiauelli ... de Principe libellus: ... ex Italico in Latinum sermonem uersus per Syluestrum Telium Fulginatem. Basileae apud Petrum Pernam. M. D. LX. 8°. *^{8} a-m^8. pp. 1-176. [12

MACIEJ Z MIECHOWA. Tractatus de duabus Sarmatiis Asiana et Europiana et de contentis in eis. (Excusa Auguste Vindelicoꝝ [per Sigismundum Grimm & Marcum Wirzung]. ... M.D.xviij. die vero .iiij. mensis Augusti.) 4°. B.L. a^6 b-g^4. [13

MACROBIUS, AMBROSIUS AURELIUS THEODOSIUS. Aur. Theodosii Macrobl ... opera. Ioh. Isacius Pontanus recensuit ... Lugduni Batauorum, Ex officina Plantiniana, Apud Franciscum Raphelengium. cIo. Io. XCVII. 8°. *^{8} A-Xx^8 *-**^{8} ✠^{8}. pp. 1-697. [14

-- Hoc volumine continentur. Macrobii interpretatio in somnium Scipionis a Cicerone confictum. Eiusdem Saturnaliorum libri septem. ... Nicolaus Angelius ... correxit. imprimiq3 curauit. (Venætiis In Ædibus Ioannis Tacuini de Tridino ... M.D.XXI. Die XVIII Iulii. ...) fol. aa^4 A-M^8 N^{10} (-N10, *presumably blank*). ff. I-CV. [15

-- -- Eucharius Ceruicor. excudebat Anno M. D. XXVI. (Coloniæ ... impensa M. Godefridi Hittorpij ... pridie Nonas Ianuarias.) fol. Aa^6 Bb^4 a-n^8 o-p^6 q-s^8. ff. 2-140. [16

-- -- ... Censorinus De die natali ... (Venetiis in aedibus Aldi, et Andreae Asulani soceri. M.D.XXVIII. mense Aprili.) 8°. *^{8} ✠^{8} a-z^8 &^{8} A-Q^8 R^4. ff. 1-322. [17

-- -- Lugduni, apud Seb. Gryphium, 1556. 8°. a-z^8 A-R^8. pp. 3-567. [18

MACROPEDIUS, GEORGIUS. Lazarus. Comoedia sacra ... Coloniae Excudebat Petrus Horst. Anno 1557. 8°. A-D^8. [19

-- -- *Another copy.* [20

-- Petriscus Georgii Macropedii, fabula ... (Busciducis apud Gerardū Hatardū. ... M.D.XXXVI. Mense Octobri.) 8°. A-D^8. [21

MAFFEI, GIOVANNI CAMILLO. Scala naturale, ouero fantasia dolcissima ... Intorno alle cose occulte, e disiderate nella Filosofia. ... In Venetia, Per Gio. Varisco, e compagni. M D LXXXI. 8°. A-R^8 S^4. ff. 2-140. [22

MAFFEI, GIOVANNI PIETRO. De vita et morib. Ignatii Loiolae, qui Societatem Iesu fundauit, libri III. ... Romae, Apud Franciscum Zannettum. M.D.LXXXV. (*Colophon.*) 4°. +^{2} A-Cc^4 Dd^2. pp. 1-200. (Lea.) [23

-- -- Coloniae, Apud Maternum Cholinum. Anno M.D.LXXXV. ... 8°. (?)^8 (?)^4 A-Z^8 (-Z7-8, *blank*). pp. 1-363. [24

MAFFEI, RAFFAELE, of Volterra. Commentariorum vrbanorum Raphaelis Volaterrani octo et triginta libri. ... Oeconomicus Xenophontis, ab eodem Latio donatus. Lugduni apud Sebastianum Gryphium, M. D. LII. (*Colophon.*) fol. a-c^6 a-z^6 A-Z^6 aa-ee^6. cols. 1-1218. [25

MAGANZA, GIOVANBATTISTA. Frotola de Magagno Per la Vittuoria de i nuostri Segnore contra i Turchi. 4°. A^4. ¶*Dedication dated:* Da Vicenza ai xxv. d'Ottore, del 1571. (Lea.) [26

MAGDEBURG. *Rat.* Der Von Magdeburgk Ausschreiben an alle Christen. Anno M. D. L. den XXIIII. Marcij. Gedruckt zu Magdeburgk durch Michel Lotther. 4°. A-C^4. [27

-- Der von Magdeburgk verantwortung alles vnglimpffs/ so ihnen in ihrer Belagerung von den Magdeburgischen Baals Pfaffen ... begegenet. Gedrůckt zu Magdeburgk durch Michel Lotther. 1550. 4°. A-I^4 K^2. [28

-- -- Der von Magdeburgk widerlegung vnnd verantwortung ... Gedrůckt zu Magdeburgk bey Michel Lotther. 1551. (*Colophon.*) 4°. A-K^4 L^2. [29

-- Ein warhafftiger Bericht deren von Magdeburg/ des ihenen was Montags nach Matthei nechst verschinen/ ... Am xxij. tag Herbstmonats/ im jor M. D. L. 4°. A^4. [30

-- -- Ein warhafftiger Bericht dero von Magdeburgk/ des ihennen was Mantags nach Matthei nechst verschienen ... 1550. (Gedruckt zu Magdeburgk durch Michel Lotther. ...) 4°. A-B^4. [31

-- Deren zu Magdeburgk/ so widder die Adiaphora geschrieben haben/ jhres vorigen schreibens beschlus ... Anno 1551. am tag Simonis vnd Iude. 28. Octobris. 4°. A-C^4. [32

-- Des Rades der Oldenstadt Magdeborch Ordenunge/ aner Gelöffte vnd Werdtschop. M.D.LX. (Gedrůcket tho Magdeborch/ dorch Ambrosij Kerckeners seligen Eruen. ...) 4°. A-C^4 D^2. [33

-- Nothwehre Des Raths vnd Syndici/ auch etzlicher Pastorn ... der Altenstadt Magdeburgk/ Wieder das ... Buch/ so vnlangst vnter dem Namen ... D. Tilemanni Heshusij Nothwendiger entschůldigung vnd verantwortung/ etc. ... 4°. a-o^4 A-H^4. ¶*Dated 18 February 1563.* [34

-- *Church.* Der Prediger zu Magdeburgk ware/ gegrůndte Antwort/ auff das rhůmen ihrer Feinde ... (Gedruckt zu Magdeburgk durch Michael Lotther. 1551.) 4°. A-C^4 D^2. [35

-- Etliche Artickel zu Notwendiger Kirchen ordnung gehörig/ welcher sich die Pfarherr vnd Diener der Kirchen zu Magdeburg ... entschlossen haben ... 4°. A^4 B^2. ¶*Dated 3 April 1554.* [36

-- Fides scholasticorum Magdeburgensium, de nonnullis doctrinae Christianæ Articulis ... Magdeburgi Per Ioachimum VValden ... M. D. LXIIII. 4°. A-E^4. ¶*In verse.* [37

MAGDEBURG CENTURIATORS. [1] Ecclesiastica historia ... Per aliquot studiosos & pios uiros in urbe Magdeburgica. ... Basileae, per Ioannem Oporinum. 1560. (... opera et expensis partim Ioannis Oporini, partim Nicolai Brilingeri ... Mense Februario.) fol. α-γ^6 a-t^6

^{4} A-Kk^{6} aa^{4} bb-mm^{6} nn^{4} 3*^{4} 3a-3m^{6} 3n^{8} 3o-3t^{6}. cols. 1-382, 3-672, 1-248, 1-374. ¶*Half-titles:* (1^{r}) Primae centuriae liber Secundus. (aa1^{r}) Secunda centuria historiae ecclesiasticæ. (3*1^{r}) Tertia centuria ... [2] Quarta centuria ecclesiasticae historiae ... *Same imprint.* (... Mense Martio.) a-z^{6} A-Zz^{6} AA-EE^{6}. pp. 4-11, cols. 13-1574. [3] Quinta Centuria ecclesiasticae historiae ... Basileae, per Ioannem Oporinum. (... M. D. LXII. Mense Martio.) α^{6} a-z^{6} A-Rr^{6} Ss^{4} Tt-Yy^{6} Zz^{4}. cols. 1-1526. [4] Sexta Centuria ecclesiasticae historiae ... Basileae, per Ioannem Oporinum: 1562. (... mense Augusto.) a-z^{6} A-T^{6}. pp. 4-13, cols. 15-872. [5] Septima Centuria ecclesiasticae historiae ... Basileae, per Ioannem Oporinum. 1564. (... mense Martio.) a-z^{6} A-D^{6} E^{8} F-H^{6} I^{4} K^{6}. pp. 4-20, cols. 21-668. [6] Octaua Centuria ecclesiasticae historiae ... Basileae, per Ioannes Oporinum & Heruagium. (... ex officina Ioannis Oporini, ... M. D. LXIIII. Mense Septembri.) α^{6} a-z^{6} A-P^{6} Q^{8} R-S^{6} T^{8}. cols. 1-942. [7] Nona Centuria ecclesiasticae historiae ... Basileae, per Ioan. Oporinum, & hæredes Ioan. Heruagij. (... ex officina Ioannis Oporini, ... M. D. LXV. Mense Septembri.) a-z^{6} A-C^{6} D^{4} E-F^{8}. cols. 1-640. [8] Decima Centuria ecclesiasticae historiae ... Basileae, per Ioannem Oporinum. 1567. (... Mense Septembri.) a-z^{6} A-F^{6} G^{8} H-I^{6} K^{8}. pp. 4-6, cols. 7-722. [9] Vndecima Centuria ecclesiasticae historiae ... *Same imprint and colophon.* a-z^{6} A-M^{6} N^{8}. pp. 4-14, cols. 15-766. [10] Duodecima Centuria ecclesiasticae historiae ... Basileae, ex officina Oporiniana. 1569. a-z^{6} A-Zz^{6} AA-OO^{6} PP^{4} QQ^{6}. pp. 4-8, cols. 9-1930. [38

-- -- *Another copy of* [3] *and* [4]. (Yarnall.) [38a

-- -- *Another set, with the following differences:* [1] Basileae, per Ioannem Oporinum. (... expensis Ioannis Oporini ... M. D. LXIIII. Mense Augusto.) α-γ^{6} a-t^{6} **^{4} A-Ii^{6} Kk^{8} αα^{4} aa-cc^{4} dd-nn^{6} oo^{4} pp^{6} 3*^{4} 3a-3m^{6} 3n^{8} 3o-3q^{6}. cols. 1-382, 1-684, 1-284, 1-320. [2] (Basileae, per Ioannem Oporinum ... M. D. LX.) a-z^{6} A-Zz^{6} AA-EE^{6} FF^{4}. [4] Basileae, per Ioannem Oporinum. M. D. LXII. (... ex officina Ioannis Oporini ... M. D. LXIII. mense Martio.) a-z^{6} A-R^{6} S^{4} T^{6}. pp. 4-13, cols. 15-870. [5] *With a different setting of the indexes* (F-K) *and without errata on* K6^{r}. [8] *Last column erroneously numbered* 723. [11] Decimatertia Centuria ... Basileae, ex officina Oporiniana. 1574. (... Mense Ianuario.) a-z^{6} A-Ll^{6} Mm^{4} Nn-Pp^{6} Qq^{8}. pp. 4-7, cols. 9-1378. (Yarnall.) [38b

-- -- *Another copy of* [5] *and* [6]. (Yarnall.) [39

MAGENTINUS, LEO. Magentini Mitilanensis ... expositio, In librum Perihermeneias hoc est de interpretatione Aristotelis, ex Amonio ... congesta ... Hieronymo Leursio Veronensi interprete ... Venetiis. M. D. XXXIX. (... apud Octauianum Scotum.) fol. A-E^{4}. ff. 3-19. [40

MAGNI, PIETRO PAOLO. Discorsi ... Intorno al sanguinar i corpi humani ... Roma ... MDLXXXIIII. (... Appresso Bartholomeo Bonfadino, & Tito Diani. ...) 4°. +^{6} A-M^{4} N^{6}. pp. 1-106. ¶*Engraved t.p.* [41

-- -- Discorsi ... sopra il modo di Sanguinare ... In Roma anno .D.M.LXXXVI. (... Per Bartholomeo Bonfadino ...) 4°. *^{6} A-P^{4} (-P4, *presumably blank*). pp. 2-117. ¶*Engraved t.p.* [42

MAGNUS, OLAUS. Historia Olai Magni ... de gentium Septentrionalium ... Basileæ, ex officina Henricpetrina. (... M. D. LXVII. Mense Martio.) fol. ⊛^{6} ✦-✦✦^{6} (+ *folded leaf*) α-ε^{6} a-z^{6} A-Zz^{6} AA^{6} BB^{8}. pp. 2 [= 1]-854. (Lea.) [43

MAHEUSTRE. Dialogus d'entre le maheustre et le manant. Contenant les raisons de leurs debats & questions en ces presens troubles au Royaume de France. M. D. XCIIII. 8°. A-P^{8} Q^{4} (-Q4, *presumably blank*). ff. 2-123. [44

-- -- M. D. XCIIII. 8°. A-T^{8} V^{6}. ff. 2-158. [45

MAILLARD, OLIVIER. Passio domini nostri Iesu christi ... declamata. [*Device of Jehan Petit.*] 8°. A-B^{8}. (Lea.) [46

-- ... Oliuerii Maillardi ... Sermones de aduẽtu ... Prostant in edibus Ioãnis petit. ([Excudebat Michael Lesclencher] ... .M.ccccc.xv penultima Nouembris.) 8°. B.L. a-o^{8} p^{4} q^{6} (-q6, *presumably blank*). ff. ii-cxvj. (Lea.) [47

MAINARDI, ARLOTTO. Scelta di facezie, tratti Buffonerie, motti, e burle. Cauate da

Diuersi Autori. ... In Firenze, Appresso i Giunti. 1579. ... (... 1580.) 8°. $*^2$ A-K^8 L^4 M^2. pp. 2-171. [48

-- -- Scelta di facetie, motti, burle, et buffonerie, Del Piouano Arlotto, & altri Auttori. ... In Venetia [appresso Domenico Farri], M D XCV. 8°. A-L^8. ff. 2-87. [49

-- -- In Venetia. M. D. XCIX. 8°. A-F^8 (-F8). ff. 2-47. [50

MAINZ. *Archdiocese*. Ein mandat des ... Cardinals [Albrecht von Brandenburg] zů Meintz/ widder die Luttherische lere. ... Item ein ander mandat der gemeynen Leyen ... [c. 1524.] 4°. a-f^4. [51

-- Vndergerichts ordnung des Ertzstiffts Meyntz ... M. D. XXXV. (Gedrůckt zů Meyntz durch Iuonem Schöffer ... volendet an dem zehenden tag des Meyen.) fol. A-G^4. ff. II-XXVII. [52

-- -- Vndergerichts Ordnung des Ertzstiffts Meyntz ... Meyntz Drucks Franciscus Behem ... M. D. LIX. fol. A-G^4. ff. II-XXVII. (Biddle.) [53

-- *Provincial council*. I Statuta prouincialia Moguntina [vetera et noua] ... Tractat⁹ scī Thomę δ articul' fidei ꝛ sacris ... II Constitutiones D. Ioannis Epī Tusculani per alemãniam. III Casus excommunicatōnū ex vetere ꝛ nouo iure collecti IIII Copia bulle dñi Eugenij ... Calixti ... Sixti ... V Ser. d. Ioãnis gerson de iure pariochiali VI Decretū Ducis Mediolaneñ de q̄rta funeralium ꝛ legatorū parochianis soluēda Ordinate mēorie in missa exemplū VII Septē p̄paramenta celebraturorū Nouē licita motiua celebrandi (expēsis ... Cōradi hyst ciuꝫ Spireñ. ꝑ ... Henricū Gran in ... opido Hagenau ciuem ... imp̄ssa: ipso die sancti Kiliani ... M.D.xij.) 4°. B.L. A^8 B^4 a-$m^{8.4.4}$ n^6 o^8. ff. I-LXXVIII. [54

-- Constitutiones concilii prouincialis Moguntini ... His accessit institutio ad pietatem Christianam ... Moguntiæ, M.D.XLIX. (... apud D. Victorem, ... excudebat Franciscus Behem ... Mense Septembri ...) fol. a^8 A-D^6 E^8 F-Vu^6 Xx^8. ff. I-CCLXVII. [55

-- -- *Variant without the imprint*. [56

-- *History*. Fragestücke vnde Artikel/ Auff welche die Priesterschafft im Stifft Meintz/ zuforderung des Teufflischen Pabsthumbs/ jtzo Examiniert werden. ... 4°. A^4. [57

-- Veraynigung der fůnff Chur vnnd Fürsten/ Meintz Trier Pfaltz Wirtzburg vnd Hessen. M.D.xxxiij. 4°. π^4. [58

MAIRHOFER, MATTHIAS. Predicanten Spiegel/ Darinn zusehen/ wie jetziger Zeit der Predicanten Lehr ... nicht Apostolisch ... sey. Insonderheit Wider Philips Heylbrunners/ Lauingischen Predicanten Censur ... Getruckt zu Ingolstatt/ durch Adam Sartorium. Anno M. DC. 4°. $(:)^4$ A-Z^4 a-z^4 Aa-Gg^4 Hh^2. pp. 1-416. [59

MAJOR, JOHN, of Haddington. Historia Maioris Brittaniæ, tam Anglię q̄ Scotię, ... e veterum monumentis concinnata. Vęnundatur Iodoco Badio Ascensio. (Ex officina Ascensiana ad Idus Aprilis. MDXXI.) 4°. A^{10} b-p^8 q-s^6 t^8. ff. IX-CXLVI. (Furness.) [60

MAJOR, JOHANNES, of Joachimsthal. Iohan. Maioris Ioachimi operum pars prima. VVitebergæ ex officina typographica Hæredum Georgij Rhauu. Anno M. D. LXIII. 8°. A-X^8 Y^4. [61

-- Exequiæ ... Augusto, Duci Saxoniæ ... habitæ in Academia VVittebergensi ... VVittebergae. Ex officina Cratoniana 1586. 4°. A-C^4. ¶*In verse*. [62

-- Iohan. Maioris ex Valle S. Ioachimi, D. liber poematum ... VVitebergæ Iohannes Schvvertel excudebat. Anno M. D. LXXVI. 8°. A^4 B-M^8 N^4. [63

-- Parentalia anniuersaria ... D. Philippo Melanthoni, &c. ... Anno 1569. 4°. A-C^4 D^2. [64

MALACIOLA, T. CURTIUS. Dialogus, bulla ... Excusum, Impensis & opera Iohannis Coticulæ, (Callyrius Trulla, apud Burlassiam Cataduppæ regis Stratiotarum Metropolim, Excudebat [Eberburgi, c. 1520].) 4°. A^4. (Lea.) [65

MALATESTA, GIUSEPPE. Della nuoua poesia ouero della difese Del Furioso, dialogo ... In Verona. Per Sebastiano dalle Donne. 1589. (*Colophon*.) 8°. $*^8$ A-S^8. pp. 1-285. [66

MALAVOLTI, ORLANDO. [1] [Historia de' fatti e guerre de' Sanesi ...] 4°. a^4 *(wanting)* *^{2} a^6 A-H^8 I^4. ff. 1-68. ¶*Additional t.p.* (*1^r): Dell'historia di Siena ... La Prima Parte. ... In Venetia, M.D.XCIX. Per Saluestro Marchetti Libraro in Siena ... [2] ... la seconda parte. ... *Same imprint.* 4°. a^2 a-c^4 A-3B^4 3C^6. ff. 1-198. [3] [... la terza parte ...] 4°. +^{2} (-+1) a-c^4 A-Rr^4 Ss^6. ff. 1-166. [67

MALAVOLTI, UBALDINO. Rime dello Sbattuto Filomato ... raccolte dal Bidello della Accademia Filomata. ... Venetia, M.D.XCVII. Appresso Mattio Valentini, Ad Instanza di Saluestro Marchetti Libraro in Siena. 8°. A-I^8 (-I8, *blank*). [68

MALDONADO, JUAN. Ioannis Maldonati Hispaniola ... 1535. (Burgis in officina Ioannis Iuntae mense Octobri anno M.D.XXXV.) 8°. A-K^8 L^4. pp. 1-149. [69

MALEGUZZI, FLAMINIO. La Theodora comedia ... In Venetia, Appresso Domenico Farri. M.D.LXXII. 8°. A-G^8. ff. 3-56. [70

MALESPINI, RICORDANO. Historia antica ... Dall'edificazione di Fiorenza per insino all'anno M.CCLXXXI. Con l'aggiunta di Giachetto Suo Nipote Dal detto anno per insino al 1286. ... In Fiorenza Nella stamperia de i Giunti M.D.LXVIII. (*Colophon.*) 4°. *-**^{4} A-Aa^4. pp. 1-173. [71

-- -- In Fiorenza. Per Filippo Giunti M. D. IIC. ... (*Colophon.*) 4°. *-**^{4} A-Gg^4. pp. 1-225. [72

MALIPIERO, GIROLAMO. Seraphicae Hieronymi Maripetri ... in diui Francisci vitam Christiano carmine ... (Venetiis in ædibus Ioannis Tacuini de Tridino. M.D.XXXII. pridie Calendas Iulii.) 4°. ✠^{4} A-CC^4 (-CC4, *presumably blank*). ff. I-CIII. ¶P3-4 *misbound after* O4. [73

-- Il Petrarcha spirituale ... (Stampato per Francesco Marcolini da Forlì, in Venetia ... M D XXXVI. Del mese di Nouembre) 4°. A-RR^4 (-RR4, *presumably blank*). ff. 2-161. [74

-- -- (Stampato per Francesco [Marcolini] da Furlì, in Venetia ... M D XXXVIII. Del mese di Settembre.) 8°. A-V^8 X^4 (-X4, *presumably blank*). ff. 2-153. ¶X3 *defective*. [75

-- -- (In Venetia ... M.D.XLV. nel mese di Genagio.) 8°. A-Y^8 Z^4 (-Z4, *presumably blank*). ff. 2-169. [76

-- -- In Venetia, appresso Domenico Farri. 1567. (*Colophon.*) 8°. a^8 b^4 A-X^8 Y^4. ff. 1-161. [77

MALOMBRA, BARTOLOMMEO. Nuoua canzone nella ... vittoria contra infideli ... In Venetia, M.D.LXXI. ... 4°. A^4. [78

MAMERANUS, NICOLAUS. Iter caesaris ex Inferiore Germania ab Anno 1545 Vsq3 Augustam Rheticã in superiore Germania. Anni 1547. ... Authore Mamerano Lucemburgeñ. Augustæ excudebat Philippus Vlhardus. M.D.XLVII. 8°. A-B^8. [79

-- Von anrichtung des newen Euangelij/ vnd der alten Libertet oder Freyheit Teutscher Nation ... (Gedruckt zu Cölln/ durch Henricũ Mammeranum ... 1552.) 4°. A-G^4. [80

MAMORIS, PETRUS. Nature verborum ... cum Interrogationib^9 Item Nature verborum a Peroto Sulpicio/ et compluribus alijs grammatice auctoribus ... excerpte. (Impresse Cadomi per Laurẽtium hostingue Impensis ... Michaelis angier ... [c. 1511].) 16°. B.L. A-B^8 C^2. [81

MANCINELLI, ANTONIO. Ant. Mancinelli. Carmen de Floribus. Carmen de Figuris. De Poetica Virtute. Vitæ Carmen. (Impressum Venetiis. Per Ioannem de Cereto alias Tacuinum de Tridino. Mccccc.ii. die .xx. Iunii.) 4°. A-H^8 I^4. [82

-- Antonii Mancinelli De parentum cura in liberos. ... De Filiorum erga parentes Obedientia Honore, & Pietate. (Argentorat. in aedibus Schurerianis. Mense Iulio. Anno. M. D. XII.) 4°. Aa-Ee$^{4.8}$. ff. II-XXVIII. [83

-- Ant. Mancinelli. Sermonum Decas ... (Impressum Romæ ... per ... Eucharium Silber Alias

Franck MDIII. Die Maii Vltimo.) 4°. A^8 a-p^8 q^4. ¶A1^v, A2^r *and* A7^v, A8^r *reversed in imposition.* (Lea.) [84

-- -- Venundantur Parrhisijs in ædibus Ioannis parui & Iodoci Badij Ascensij. (ad exemplar impręssionis eorundem Romę ... MDXI.) 4°. A^6 a-i^8 k^6 (-k6, *presumably blank*). ff. I-LXXVII. [85

MANCINI, CELSO. Celsi Mancinii Rauennatis ... de somniis, ac synesi per somnia. Risu, ac ridiculis. Synaugia Platonica. ... Ferrariæ, Apud Victorium Baldinum ... CIO.IↃ.XCI. (*Colophon.*) 4°. a^4 A-Ee^4. pp. 1-211. [86

MANCINI, DOMENICO. Tractatus dominici Mācini de passione domini. ... (Impressum Liptzk per Iacobum Thanner Anno 1.5.0.8.) 4°. B.L. A-B^6 C^4 D^6. [87

MANFREDI, MUZIO. Lettione ... Nella quale, con la interpretatione d'vn Sonetto del Sig. Caualier Gio. Galeazzo Rossi, ... si discorre dell'honore reciproco fra gli Huomini, e le Donne. In Bologna, Appresso Alessandro Benacci. M D LXXV. 4°. A-H^8. pp. 3-64. [88

-- La Semiramis Tragedia ... Ristampata in Pauia, Per gli Heredi di Girolamo Bartoli. 1598. ... 12°. A-F^{12}. pp. 3-140. [89

MANIÈRE. Par quantes manieres doit on cōmencer sō latin a faire ... (Imprime per Laurens hostingue et Iamet loys demourant a rouen. pour Raulin gaultier ... [c. 1515.]) 16°. B.L. A^8. [90

MANNARINO, CATALDO ANTONIO. Glorie di guerrieri e d'amanti in nuoua impresa nella Citta di Taranto succedute. Poema Heroico ... Con gli Argomenti et Annotationi di Lodouico Chiari ... Appresso Gio: Giac: carlino et Ant. Pace. Napoli 1596. (*Colophon.*) 4°. a-b^8 A-X^8 Y^4. pp. 1-344. ¶*Engraved t.p. Additional t.p.* (A5^r): Obligantea delle lodi di Alberto I. Acquauiua d'Aragona, X. duca d'Atri, &c. ... In Napoli, Nella Stamperia di Gio. Iacomo Carlino, & Antonio Pace. M. D. XCVI. [91

MANSFELD. Grauen Albrechts vorantwortung. ... 4°. A-D^4 E^2. ¶*Dated 18 December 1548.*[92

-- Kurtze Antwort vnd Gegenbericht/ Der Prediger/ in der Graffschaft Mansfeldt. Vff Der Herrn Theologen/ beider Vniuersiteten/ Leiptzig/ Vnd Wittemberg ... Auch M. Cyriaci Spangenbergs sůnderliche Antwort ... Gedruckt zu Eissleben/ durch Andream Petri. M.D.LXX. 4°. A-K^4. [93

-- Kurtzer Bericht/ Wes sich die Prediger/ In ... Mansfelt/ in jrem Synodo zu Eisleben dieses 1562 Jares/ den 24. Februarij ... der/ fur zweien jaren in Deutscher vnd Lateinischer sprach/ ausgegangenen Confession halben ... vergliechen haben. Gedruckt zu Eisleben bey Vrban Gaubisch. (*Colophon.*) 4°. A-F^4 G^6. [94

MANTOVA, DOMENICO. Rime ... In Venetia, per Plinio Pietrasanta, M D LIII. 8°. a-c^8. pp. 3-45. [95

-- -- *Another copy.* [96

MANTOVA BENAVIDES, MARCO. Annotationi breuissime, soura le rime Di M. F. P. ... In Padoua. Appresso Lorenzo Pasquale. M D LXVI. 4°. $+^4$ A-X^8 Y^4. ff. 1-171. [97

-- [Collectanea.] Mense Maio. MDXLV. Venetiis (... Apud Aurelium pincium Venetum ... elaborata.) fol. B.L. [1] Marci Mantuæ Bonauiti, Patauini ... collectanea ad primam, et secundam .ff. vete. partem ... A-N^4. ff. 3-76. [2] ... collectanea ad primam, et secundam .C. partem ... AA-QQ^6 RR^8. ff. 3-103. (Biddle.) [98

-- Collectaneorum iuris, Tomus secundus: in primam et secundam .ff. noui partem, inq̄ue primam & secundam partem Infor. Venetiis, Ioan. Gryphius excudebat, M.D. LVIII. fol. $*^4$ A-C^6 D^4 A-D^6 E^4 A-E^6 F-G^4 A-K^6. ff. 1-22, 2-27, 2-38, 2-60. (Biddle.) [99

-- Marci Mantua Bonauitis, Patauini, ... dialogus de concilio. (Venetiis, [Aurelius Pincius,] MDXLI. Mense Mai.) 4°. A-O^4 P^6. [100

-- M. Mantuae Bonauiti ... enchiridion rerum singularium. ... Venetiis ad signum Putei. MDLI. (... apud Bartholomæum Cæsanum. ...) 8°. aa-bb^8 cc^4 a-z^8 A-HH^8. ff. 1-428. (Biddle.) [101

-- Epitoma virorum illustrium qui vel scripserunt, vel iurisprudentiam docuerunt in Scholis ... Authore Mantua, Patauino ... Patauij, Gratiosus Perchacinus Excudebat. 1555. 8°. A-K⁸ (-K8, *blank*). ff. 2-72. [102

-- Opereta ... de Lheremita di messer Marco Mantouano ... (Impresso in Milano per Ioanne Angelo Scinzenzeler ... .M.D.XXIII. adi .xix. de Octobre.) 8°. A-E⁸ (-E8, *presumably blank*). [103

MANUALE. Manuale piarum orationum ex antiquis, et Catholicis patribus ... per patres Societatis Iesu reuistum ... Venetiis, apud Iuntas. M D LXXII. (*Colophon.*) 8°. ✠⁸ ✠✠⁸ A-Gg⁸. ff. 1-240. (Yarnall.) [103a

MANUEL COMNENUS, emperor. Legatio Imp. Cæsaris Manuelis Comneni aug. ad Armenios, siue Theoriani cum Catholico disputatio ... Adiunximus Leonis Magni Græcolatinam epistolam, rectæ fidei columnam, Io. Damasceni contra Manichæos dialogum, Leontii Byzantini sectarum historiam, Const. Harmenopuli de ijsdem. Fidei confessiones Harmenopuli, Augustini, Hilarij. ... Latina faciente Leunclauio. ... Basileæ. Ex Officina Petri Pernæ. M.D.LXXVIII. 8°.):(⁸ a-z⁸ A-R⁸. pp. 2-605. (Yarnall.) [103b

MANUZIO, ALDO, the elder. Aldi manutij Romani ... lucubrationes Grãmatice. iam secũdo ... expresse. ... Liptzk Impressit Melchior Lotter Anno Millesimo quingentesimo tredecimo. (*Colophon.*) 4°. B.L. A⁶ B-K⁶·⁶·⁴ L⁶ M⁴ N⁶ (-N6, *presumably blank*). [104

MANUZIO, ALDO, the younger. De quaesitis per . epistolam libri . III ... Venetiis, [Aldine press,] ꝏ .D.LXXVI 8°. π⁴ A-H⁸ A-G⁸ A-F⁸ O⁴. pp. 2-125, 2-106, 2-103. [105

-- Eleganze, insieme con la copia della lingua Toscana, e Latina. ... [*Device of Aldus.*] In Venetia, MDLXV. 8°. A-AA⁸. ff. 3-192. [106

-- Epitome orthographiae ... Venetiis. ꝏ .D.LXXV. Apud Aldum 8°. †⁸ A-Q⁸ R⁶. pp. 1-268. [107

-- In Q. Horatii . Flacci Venusini Librum de . arte . poetica ... Commentarius. ... Venetiis. ꝏ .D. LXXVI Apud Aldum 4°. *-**⁴ A-Q⁴ (-Q4, *presumably blank*). pp. 2-99. [108

MANUZIO, PAOLO. Adagia quaecumque ad hanc diem exierunt, ... ab omnibus mendis vindicata ... emendata à F. Angelo Rocch. ... Venetijs, Apud Hieronymum Polum. 1578. 4°. *⁴ A-O⁴ P² A-3S⁸. cols. 1-2042. [109

-- Apophthegmatum ex optimis vtriusque linguae scriptoribus Libri VIII. ... Editio tertia. Coloniæ, Impensis Lazari Zetzneri. cIↄ cI XCVI. 16°.):(⁸ **⁸ 3*⁶ a-z⁸ A-Mm⁸. pp. 1-926. (Lea.) [110

-- Commentarius Pauli Manutii in epistolas M. Tullii Ciceronis ad M. Iunium Brutum, & ad Q. Ciceronem fratrem. Venetiis, [Aldine press,] M.D.LVII. ... 8°. A⁸ B² C-V⁸. ff. 2-144. [111

-- Epistolarum Paul Manutii libri IIII. Eiusdem quæ præfationes appellantur. Venetiis, [Aldine press,] M.D.LX. (*Colophon.*) 8°. A-Y⁸ yy⁴ Z-GG⁸. ff. 1-229. [112

-- -- [1] Epistolarum Pauli . Manutii libri . X duobus . nuper . additis Eiusdem quae Praefationes appellantur. Venetiis. ꝏ DLXXI In Aedib. Manutianis 8°. A-GG⁸ HH⁴. pp. 2-469. [2] Pauli . Manutii epistolarum lib. IX et . X ... *Same imprint.* (*Colophon.*) a-d⁸ e⁴ A-I⁸ K⁴. pp. 4-67, 4-139. [113

-- -- Paulli Manutii epistolarum libri XII vno nuper addito. Eiusdem quae, praefationes appellantur. Venetiis, M D XCV. Apud Dominicum de Farris. 8°. a⁸ A-Tt⁸. pp. 1-536, 1-127. [114

-- In epistolas Ciceronis ad Atticum, ... commentarius. ... Venetiis, M. D. LIII. (... apud Paulum Manutium, Aldi filium ...) 8°. *⁴ A-3F⁸. ff. 1-414. [115

-- Tre libri di lettere volgari ... In Venetia, [Aldine press,] M. D. LVI. ... 8°. A-R⁸. ff. 2-135. [116

-- -- In Pesero per Bartolomeo Cesano. MDLVI. 8°. A-R⁸. ff. 2-135. [117

MANWOOD, JOHN. A treatise and discourse of the Lawes of the Forrest ... At London

Printed by Thomas Wight and Bonham Norton. 1598. ... 4°. B.L. *-**^{4} A-D^4 E-Z^8 Aa^4 Bb^2. ff. 1-167. *S.T.C.* 17291. (Biddle.) [118

-- -- *Another copy* (-Z8, *blank*, Aa^4 Bb^2). (Furness.) [119

MANZOLLI, PIETRO ANGELO. Marcelli Palingenii Stellati ... Zodiaci vitæ: hoc est, De hominis vita ... Libri XII. ... Lugduni, Apud Ioannem Tornæsium ... 1566. 16°. a-cc^8. pp. 3-366. [120

-- -- Basileæ, Typis Brylingerianis. Anno M. DC. (... M. DCI. Mense Ianuario.) 16°. a-y^8. pp. 2-331. [121

MARABOTTO, CATTANEO, & ETTORE VERNAZZA. Libro de la vita mirabile & dottrina santa, de la beata Caterinetta da Genoa, Nel quale si contiene vna ... dimostratione & dechiaratione del purgatorio. ... (Stampata in Genoua, per Antonio Bellono. ... M. D. L. I.) 8°. ✠^{8} A-LL^8. ff. 1-271. (Lea.) [122

MARBURG. *University.* ... Praeside ... Hermanno Vulteio ... in ... Marpurgensium Academia LL. Professore ordinario, hæc De Injuriis & Famosis libellis enunciata, publicè disputanda proponit Hector Mithobius Junior Saxo. Marpurgi, Excudebat Augustinus Colbius, Anno, 1584. 4°. A^6. [123

MARCELLINI, VALERIO. Il diamerone ... Oue ... si mostra, La Morte non esser quel male, che'l senso si persuade. Con vna ... discorso intorno alla lingua uolgare. ... In Vinegia appresso Gabriel Giolito de' Ferrari. M D LXV. 4°. a-c^8 A-H^8 I^4 (-I3-4, *presumably blank*). pp. 2-128. [124

MARCELLINO, EVANGELISTA. Della vanita del mondo dialoghi dodici ... In Camerino, Appresso Girolamo Strengari, & gli Heredi d'Antonio Gioioso. M D LXXX. 4°. *^{4} A-DD^4 EE^6. pp. 1-198. ¶*Additional t.p.* (Xi^r): Dialogo della pouerta ... *Same imprint.* [125

MARCELLO, CRISTOFORO. Christophori Marcelli ... de authoritate summi pontificis et his quae ad illam pertinent. Aduersus impia Martini Lutherii dogmata. (Florentiae per Haeredes Philippi Iuntae. ... M.D.XXI. Mense Iunij ...) 4°. B^6 a-r^8 s^{10}. ff. 1-145. [126

-- Christophori Marcelli ... In quarta Lateranẽ. Concilii Sessione Habita Oratio .iiii. Idus Decembris .M.D.XII. (Impressum Rome per [Joannem Beplin, venales apud] Iacobum Mazochium .xiii. Ianuarii. M.D.XIII.) 4°. A^4 B^6. (Lea.) [127

-- Christophori Marcelli ... Oratio ad Iulium .ii. Põt. Max. ... [Romae, Marcellus Silber, c. 1511.] 4°. A^6. [128

MARCELLO, PIETRO. De vita, moribus, et rebus gestis omnium ducum Venetorum ... Historia: Auctoribus Petro Marcello, patricio Veneto, Syluestro Girello Vrbinate, & Heinrico Kellnero ... Francofurtensi ... M. D. LXXIIII. (Impressum Francofurti ad Moenum, apud Paulum Reffeler, impensis Sigismundi Feyerabent.) 8°.)(^{8} A-Z^8 a-d^8. ff. 2-218. (Lea.) [129

-- -- Vite de' prencipi di Vinegia di Pietro Marcello. Tradotte in volgare da Lodouico Domenichi. ... In Venetia per Plinio Pietrasanta. M D LVII. (*Colophon.*) 4°. ✠^{4} A-DD^4. pp. 1-191. [130

MARCH, MOSEN AUSIAS. Les obres del ... poeta Ausias March. ... M.D.XXXXV. (Foren impeses ... en la ... Ciutat de Barcelona per Carles amoros Prouencal en lany M.D.xxxxv. a .xxij. del mes de Desembre.) 8°. ✠^{4} A-V^8 X^{12}. ff. ij-CLxxij. [131

-- -- [Las obras del poeta Mosen Ausias March ... Impresso en Valladolid, Año de. 1555.] (... En casa de Sebastiã Martinez ... a veynte dias đ Febrero ...) 8°. A-LL^8 (-A1, A8) MM^4. ff. 7-276. [132

MARCHANT, JACQUES. De rebus Flandriae memorabilibus liber singularis. ... Ab eodem Flandriæ Principes carmine descripti. ... Antuerpiæ, Ex officina Christophori Plantini. M. D. LXVII. (... mense Martio.) 8°. A-E^8 F^4. pp. 3-86. (Lea.) [133

MARCHESINI, EGIDIO. Oratio in funere Hieronymi Seripandi cardinalis ..., habita Bononiae ... IIII. Nonas Aprilis. Pataui, Apud Christophorum Gryphium, M D LXIII. 4°. A^4. (Lea.) [134

MARCOBRUNI, PAOLOEMILIO. Raccolta di lettere di diuersi Principi, & altri Signori ... Fatta dal Signor Paoloemilio Marcobruni. ... In Venetia, Appresso Pietro Dusinelli, 1595. 4°. a^8 b^2 $A\text{-}Bb^8$. pp. 2-399. [135

MARCOLINI, FRANCESCO. Dell'origine de' barbari, che distrussero per tutto'l mondo l'imperio di Roma, ... Libri Vndici. ... In Venetia per Plinio Pietrasanta. M D LVII. 4°. a^4 $A\text{-}II^4$. pp. 1-210. [136

MARENZIO, LUCA. Canto Il secondo libro de madrigali a sei voci. ... In Venetia Appresso Angelo Gardano. M D LXXXIIII. 4°. $A\text{-}C^4$ (-B4, C4, *the latter presumably blank*). (Music.) [137

MARGARIT Y PAU, JUAN DE. Episcopi Gerundensis paralipomenon Hispaniae libri decem ... Apud ... Granatam. Anno. M. D. XLV. Mense Octobri. fol. π^2 $aa\text{-}nn^6$ (-nn6, *blank*). ff. I-LXXVII. [138

MARGARITA. Margarita Facetiarum Alfonsi Aragonum Regis Vafredicta Prouerbia Sigismundi & Friderici tertij Ro. Imp̃atoꝝ Tropi siue sales Ioannis Keisersberg ... Marsilij Ficini Florentini de Sole opusculum. Hermolai Barbari Orationes. Facetię Adelphinę. (Impressum per ... Iohannem gruniger. Anno ... Nono. supra Millequingentos. Argentine.) 4°. A^8 B^4 $C\text{-}D^6$ $E\text{-}G^8$ $H\text{-}K^6$ L^8 M^6 $N\text{-}O^4$ $P\text{-}Q^6$. [139

MARGUERITE, queen of Navarre. L'heptameron des nouuelles ... Remis en son vrsy ordre ... par Claude Gruget Parisien. A Paris, Par Iean Caueiller ... 1560. ... (Imprimé ... par Benoist Preuost ...) 4°. $\bar{a}^4$ $a\text{-}z^4$ $A\text{-}Gg^4$. ff. 1-212. [140

MARGUES, NICOLAS. Description du monde desguisé. ... A Paris, De l'Imprimerie de Thomas Richard ... 1563. 4°. $A\text{-}B^4$. ¶*In verse.* [141

MARIANI, GIOVANNI. Rasonato de mercantia ... M D XXXV. (In Vinegia per Gjouan'Antonio da Sabbio. ... Del mese di Zugno.) 8°. $A\text{-}Y^8$. [142

-- -- Tariffa ristampata da nuouo ... (In Vinegia per Giouan'Antonio e Pietro Fratelli de Nicolini da Sabio, ad instantia de l'auttore Zuane Mariani. 1543 Del Mese di Gienaro.) 12°. $A\text{-}K^{12}$ $*^6$. [143

MARICONDA, ANTONIO. Tre giorna[te] delle fauole d[e] l'Aganippe ... In Napoli. Appresso Gio. Paulo Suganappo. M. D. L. (*Colophon.*) 4°. $✠^8$ $✠✠^4$ $A\text{-}Z^4$ $aa\text{-}ii^4$. ff. I-CXXIIII. ¶✠1 *defective.* [144

MARIETA, JUAN DE. [1] Historia ecclesiastica de todos los santos, de España. ... En Cuenca, en casa de Pedro [de]l Valle ... M.D.XCVI. A costa de Christiano Bernabe. ... (En Cuenca. En casa de Iuan Masselin ... M.D.XCIIII.) fol. π^6 $A\text{-}X^8$ X^4. ff. 1-159. ¶*T.p. repaired.* [2] Secunda parte, de la historia eclesiastica de España ... En Cuenca, en casa de Pedro del Valle ... M.D.XCVI. A costa de Christiano Bernabe ... (... M.D.CXV.) π^2 $A\text{-}Dd^8$ Ee^6. ff. 1-212. [3] Tercera parte ... En Cuenca, en casa de Pedro del Valle ... M.D.XCVI. A costa de Christiano Bernabe ... $A\text{-}P^8$ Q^4. ff. 4-117. [4] Tratado, de las fundaciones de las Ciudades y Villas principales de España ... En Cuenca, en casa de Pedro del Valle ... M.D.XCIII. A costa de Christiano Bernabe. $A\text{-}G^8$ (-G8, *perhaps blank*). ff. 2-53. ¶A5, G7 *defective.* (Lea.) [145

MARINELLI, GIOVANNI. [1] La prima parte della copia delle parole ... In Venetia, Appresso Vincenzo Valgrisi. M. D. LXII. 4°. $*^4$ $A\text{-}Z^8$ a^4. ff. 1-187. [2] La seconda parte ... *Same imprint.* A^6 $B\text{-}Qq^8$ Rr^{10}. ff. 2-321. [146

MARINEO, LUCIO. L. Marinei Siculi ... opus de rebus Hispaniae Memorabilibus ... (Impressum Compluti per Michaelem de Eguia, Absolutũqꝫ est mense Maij. ... M.D.XXXIII.) fol. $✠^8$ $A\text{-}Q^8$. ff. ij-cxxviij. [147

-- Sumario dela vida/ y heroycos hechos de ... don Fernando y doña ysabel ... (Fue impresso ... enla ... Ciudad de Seuilla: por Dominico de Robertis a catorze dias del mes de nouiembre. Año de Mil/ y quinientos/ y quarenta/ y cinco.) 4°. B.L. $A\text{-}K^8$. ff. ij-lxxix. [148

MARINO, MARCO. תבה נח arca Noe thesaurus linguae sanctae nouus. ... Venetiis, Apud Iohannem Degaram. ꝏ. D. XCIII. fol. †-††^{6} A-4N^{6}. ff. 1-492. ¶*The second part is wanting.* [149

MARLIANI, GIOVANNI BARTOLOMMEO. Topographia antiquae Romae. ... Apud Seb. Gryphium Lugduni. 1534. 8°. *^{4} a-u^{8} x^{4} (-x4). pp. 1-313. [150

-- Bartholomaei Marliani vrbis Romae topographia ... Cui accessere Hieronymi Ferrutij Romani ... additiones ... Venetiis, Apud Hieronymum Franciscum, Bibliopolam in Vrbe ... M D LXXXVIII. (*Colophon.*) 8°. *^{8} A-Z^{8}. ff. 1-176. (Fine Arts.) [151

MARMITTA, GIACOMO. Rime ... In Parma, Appresso di Seth Viotto. M. D. LXIIII. 4°. A^{4} A-Z^{4} a-c^{4}. pp. 1-198. [152

MARMOL-CARAVAJAL, LUIS DEL. Primera parte de la descripcion general de Affrica ... En Granada en casa de Rene Rabut. Año de 1573. Vendense en casa de Iuan Diaz ... (*Colophon.*) fol. *^{6} A-Nn^{8} Oo^{6+1} ✠^{8} ††^{8}. ff. 1-294. [153

MAROTTA, GIACOMO. Iacobi Marottæ Marilianensis ... In Porphyrij Isagogen, siue quinque prædicabilia, ... expositio ... Neapoli, Apud Horatium Saluianum. M D XC. fol. §^{2} A-V^{6} X^{10}. pp. 1-258. [154

MARSCHALCK, HAUG. Der Blinden fůrer bin ich genennt/ Dem der sich selbs blind erkennt. ... Von Iohann Schnewyl ... [Augsburg, Philipp Ulhart,] M.D.XXVI. 4°. A-H^{4}. [155

-- Eyn Edles schönes lieblichs Tractetleyn/ von dem reynen hymlischen: ewigen wort ... [Nürnberg? 1524.] 4°. A-B^{4}. [156

-- Eyn Ermanung/ Reymensweys/ an vnsern ... hern Carolum/ ... das wort Gottes tzu erhalten ... M D XXX. 4°. A^{4}. [157

-- Das Hailig ewyg wort gots/ was dz ... in aym rechten Christen zů erweckñ vermag ... Im Jar. M. D. XXiij. (Gedruckt in ... Augspurg. Durch Melcher Ram̃inger.) 4°. A-C^{4}. [158

-- Wer gern wölt wissen wie ich hiess/ Zů leesen mich hett nit verdriess. ... Iohann Schnewyl von Strassburg. 4°. A-B^{4} C^{2} D-E^{4}. [159

MARSIGLI, IPPOLITO DE. [1] Consilia et singularia omnia D. Hippolyti de Marsiliis. ... M. D. XXXVII. (Lugduni Impressa nomine ... Hugonis de porta: et do. Lucemburgi de Gabiano sociorum ...) fol. B.L. A-M^{8} N-P^{6} AA-GG^{8} HH-II^{6}. ff. 2-114, 1-68. [2] Mariana ... (... per ... Iacobum myt. ... Mense Martio.) 3A-3I^{6} 3K^{4} A-B^{6}. ff. 2-58. (Biddle.) [160

-- Mariana. ... singularia septingenta ... Venetiis. M D L V. (... apud Cominum de Tridino ...) 8°. a-d^{8} A-Q^{8}. ff. 2-127. [161

-- -- *Another copy* (-Q8, *blank*). (Lea.) [162

MARSILIUS AB INGHEN. Questiões ... Marsilii in libros Aristotelis de generatione et corruptione ... (Impsse Argẽtine ĩ officina Martini flach iunioris, ix. kal'. octobres. ... 1501.) fol. B.L. a-f$^{8.6}$ g^{6} h^{8} i-n^{6} o^{8} p^{6}q^{8}. [163

MARSILIUS OF PADUA. Opus insigne cui titulum fecit autor defensorem pacis, quod quęstionem illam ... De potestate papae et imperatoris ... tractet ... (Absolutum est [Basileae, Valentin Curio?] ... sesquimillesimo xxij. ...) fol. A^{6} ꝁ-ꝁꝁ^{6} b-z^{6} A-G^{6} H^{8}. (Lea.) [164

-- -- Ain Kurtzer Auszug des ... Fridschirmbůchs/ Marsilij von Padua. Dariñ der Kayser vnd Babste gewalt ... gehandelt wirdt. ... Durch M. Marxen Müller von Westendorff ... verteutscht ... Neuburgi Danubii. M. D. XLV. ... (Gedruckt ... bey Hannsen Kilian ...) fol. A-N^{6} O^{4}. ff. I-LXX. [165

MARTELLI, LODOVICO. Stanze e canzoni ... M.D.XXXVII. (Stampata in Vinegia per Pietro de Nicolini da Sabio. Ad instantia di Messer Nicolo de Aristotile detto Zoppino. Del mese di Settembrio. ...) 8°. A-D^{8}. [166

MARTELLI, NICOLÒ. Il primo libro delle lettere ... MDXLVI. (In Fiorenza [per Anton

Francesco Doni] a instanza dell'Auttore, ... adi xviij del Mese di Giugno.) 4°. A-Z^4. ff. 5-91. [167

MARTIAL D'AUVERGNE. Aresta amorum. Cum erudita Benedicti Curtij Symphoriani explanatione. Lugduni apud Seb. Gryphium M. D. XXXIII. 4°. a^4 a-z^4 A-S^4. pp. 1-321. [168

MARTIALIS, MARCUS VALERIUS. Martialis. (Venetiis in aedibus Aldi, mense Decembri. M.DI.) 8°. A-Z^8 &^{8}. [169

-- -- Martialis. (Venetiis in aedibus Aldi et Andreae soceri mense Decembri M. D. XVII.) 8°. A-Z^8 &^{8}. ff. 2-190. [170

-- -- M. Val. Martialis epigrammaton libri XIIII. ... Apud Seb. Gryphium Lugduni, 1553. 8°. a-z^8 A^4 (-A4, *presumably blank*). pp. 2-368. [171

-- -- Lugduni, apud haered. Seb. Gryphii, 1559. 16°. a-z^8 A-B^8 (-B8, *presumably blank*). pp. 3-398. [172

-- -- Basileae per Nicolaum Bryling. Anno 1563. (*Colophon.*) 16°. a-z^8 A-B^8. pp. 2-394. [173

MARTINELLI, BONIFAZIO. Annotationi sopra la Gierusalemme liberata. Del Sig. Torquato Tasso. ... In Bologna, Per Alessandro Benacci. M D LXXXVII. ... 4°. A-S^4. pp. 3-142.[174

MARTINENGHI, LUCILLO. Canzoni sonetti et sestine. In lode della sacra Sindone conseruata in Turino. ... In Brescia, Appresso Policreto Turlini. Ad instanza di Gio. Battista Borelli. (.. 1590.) 8°. A-B^8. pp. 3-32. [175

-- Quattro canzoni, con la espositione ... In Brescia, Appresso Pietro Maria Marchetti. M.D.XCII. ... 8°. †^{8} B-I^8. pp. 1-129. [176

-- Sestina con la espositione ... In Brescia, Appresso Policreto Turlini. 1591. Ad instanza di Gio. Battista Borelli. 8°. A-D^8. pp. 2-50. [177

-- Vita di Santa Margherita detta Pelagia. Ridotta nell'ottaua Rima ... In Brescia, Appresso Policreto Turlini. Ad instanza di Gio. Battista Borelli. (... 1590.) 8°. A-O^8 P^4. ff. 2-110. [178

MARTINENGHI, TITO PROSPERO. Theotocodia siue parthenodia opus eximium In laudem Deiparae Virginis. ... Romae Excudebat Franciscus Zanettus. M.D.LXXXIII. (*Colophon.*) 4°. A-Bb^4 (-A4). pp. 9-198. [179

MARTINEZ DE CASTRILLO, FRANCISCO. Coloquio breue cōpēdioso, Sobre la materia đ la [dē]tadura, y marauillosa obra đ la boca. ... Estāte en Valladolid. 1557. ... (Fue impreso en la ... villa de Valladolid. En casa de Sebastian Martinez ... Acabose a veynte dias del mes de Marzo. ...) 8°. A^{12} B-S^8 T^4. ff. [10]-152. ¶A1, B1-2 *defective*. (School of Dentistry.) [180

MARTINIUS, PETRUS. מפתח לשון הקדש that is the key of the holy tongue: Wherein is conteined, first The Hebrue Grammar ... of P. Martinius. Secondly, A practize upon the first, the twentie fift, and the syxtie eyght Psalmes ... Thirdly, A short Dictionary ... All Englished ... By Iohn Udall. Imprinted at Leyden, By Francis Raphelengus, cIↃ. IↃ. XCIII. 8°. A-N^8 (-N8) a-l^8 (-l8, *blank*) Aa-Ff^8 Gg^4 (-Gg4). pp. 4-204, 3-174, 3-98. *S.T.C.* 17523. [181

MARTIRANO, CORIOLANO. Coriolani Martirani Cosentini ... Tragoediae. VIII. ... Comoediae II. ... Odysseae lib. XII. Batrachomyomachia. Argonautica. Neap. M D LVI. ... (Ianus Marius Simonetta Cremonensis ... excudebat. Mense Maio ...) 8°. †^{4} A-KK^8 LL^4 MM-ZZ^8 &&^{8} (-&&7, *blank*). ff. 1-370. [182

MARUCINI, LORENZO. Rime de diuersi autori Bassanesi, raccolte dall' ... M. Lorenzo Marucini. ... In Venetia, Appresso Pietro de' Franceschi, & Nepoti. M D LXXVI. (*Colophon.*) 4°. *^{6} A-V^4. pp. 2-157. [183

MARULIĆ, MARKO. Mar. Maruli Spalatensis de institutione bene beateq; uiuendi libri sex ...

Coloniæ, ex officina Eucharij Ceruicorni, anno M. D. XXX. mense Aug. (Impensis ... Godefridi Hydorpij, ciuis Coloniensis.) 8°. Aa-Cc^8 Dd^4 a-zz^8 A-H^8. pp. 2-863. [184

MARY, the Virgin. Salue Regis mater misericordie ... 4°. π^2. ¶π1^r, π2^v *blank*. [185

MARZI, GIOVANNI BATTISTA. Ottauia Furiosa commedia ... In Fiorenza. Per Filippo Giunti. M D LXXXIX. (*Colophon.*) 8°. A-K^8 L^4. pp. 3-167. [186

MASCHER, GIROLAMO. Il fiore della retorica ... In Vinegia per Giouanni Bariletto, M D LX. (*Colophon.*) 8°. A-HH^8 II-KK^4. ff. 2-252. [187

MASI, TEODORO. Oratio Fratris Theodori Masii Mantuani ..., quam habuit ad patres in Concilio Tridentino, die octaua Martij ... Brixiae Apud Ludouicum Sabiensem. M. D. LXII. 4°. A-B^4. (Lea.) [188

MASSOLO, PIETRO. Sonetti morali di M. Pietro Massolo ..., hora Don Lorenzo monaco Casinese. ... In Bologna per Antonio Manutio ... M. D. LVII. 8°. *^{4} A-O^8. [189

MASSON, JEAN PAPIRE. Papirii Massoni annalium libri quatuor: Quibus res gestæ Francorum explicantur. ... Lutetiæ, Apud Nicolaum Chesneau ... M.D.LXXVII. ... (Excudebat Henricus Thiery, prime Cal. Decemb. ...) 4°. ā^4 A-Zz^4 AA-3E^4. pp. 1-538. [190

MASSONIO, SALVATORE. Dialogo dell'origine della citta dell'Aquila ... con l'aggiunta ... di alcuni huomini della stessa Città, che per hauere scritto, & date in luce libri di diuerse professioni, sono degni di memoria. ... Nell'Aquila, Appresso Isidoro, & Lepido Facij Fratelli. M. D. XCIIII. (... 1593.) 4°. A-V^4. pp. 17-158. (Lea.) [191

MASSUCCI, NICOLÒ. Il velettaio Commedia ... In Firenze Per li Giunti. M D LXXXV ... (*Colophon.*) 8°. A-F^8. pp. 91-183. [192

MATASILANI, MARIO. La felicità del serenissimo Cosimo Medici granduca di Toscana. ... In Fiorenza. ... Appresso Giorgio Marescotti. MDLXXII. 4°. ☧-2☧^{4} A-G^4. pp. 1-47. [193

MATHESIUS, JOHANN. Bergpostilla/ Oder Sarepta Darinn von allerley Bergkwerck vnd Metallen ... Sampt der Iochimsthalischen kurtzen Chroniken/ biss auff das 1578. jar. ... Nürmberg. M D LXXXVII. (Gedruckt ... bey Katharina Gerlachin.) fol.)(^{6} x^6 A-Ss^6. ff. 1-215. (Smith.) [194

MATRAINI, CHIARA. Lettere della Signora Chiara Matraini, gentildonna Luchese, con la prima, e seconda parte delle sue Rime. Stampata in Lucca, Per Vincenti Busdraghi 1595. ... Ad instanzia di Ottauiano Guidoboni. 8°. *^{4} A-F^8 G^{12}. pp. 1-120. [195

-- Rime et prose ... In Lucca per il Busdrago, del M D LV. 8°. A-F^8 G^4. pp. 3-103. [196

MATTHIEU, PIERRE. [1] Histoire des derniers troubles de France. Soubs les regnes des Rois ... Henry III. ... & Henry IIII. ... Imprimé l'An de Grace, M. D. XCIX. 8°. ā^4 A-Y^8 Z^4 Aa-Ii^8 Kk^6. ff. 1-111, 1-74. ¶*Additional t.p.:* (Z4) Le cinquiesme liure ... Imprimé ... M. D. XCIX. [2] Recueil des edicts et articles accordez par le Roy Henry IIII. pour la rèvnion de ses subiets. Imprimé ... M. D. XCIX. ā^2 a-p^8 q^4. ff. 1-123. (Lea.) [197

-- Summa constitutionum summorum pontificum, et rerum in Ecclesia Romana gestarum à Gregorio IX. vsque ad Sixtum V. ... Per Petrum Matthæum ... Lugduni, sumptibus Petri Landry. M. D. LXXXVIII. ... 4°. α-υ^4 a-z^4 A-4Y^4 †-5†^{4}. pp. 1-914. ¶†1^r: Index ... Per Petrum du Boys ... (Lea.) [198

MATTIOLI, PIETRO ANDREA. [1] Petri Andreæ Matthioli ... opera quæ extant omnia ... Nunc à Casparo Bauhino ... notis illustrati ... M. D. XCVIII. fol. π^1 *^{4} **^{6} b-i^6 A-4Q^6 4R^8 4S-4T^4. pp. 1-1027. [2] Petri Andreæ Matthioli Senensis ... apologia aduersus Amathum Lusitanum ... Francofurti, Ex officina Typographica Nicolai Bassæi. M. D. XCVIII. AA-TT^6 VV-XX^4 (-XX4, *blank*). pp. 3-236. [198a

-- Discorsi ... nelli sei libri Di Pedacio Dioscoride Anazarbeo della materia Medicinale. ... In Venetia, [Ap]presso Vincenzo Valgrisi. MDLXVI[II.] fol. *-**^{6} 3*^{4} a-l^6 m^{6+1}

A-6M 6. pp. 1-1511 *present.* ¶*T.p. repaired;* 614 *ff. remargined with occasional loss of text. Lacks 2 or more leaves at the end.* [198b

-- [Kreutterbuch ... zum dritten mal ... gemehret ... durch Ioachimum Camerarium ... Franckfurt am Mayn, 1600.] fol. *4 A-4M6 4N2. ff. 1-460. ¶*Lacks 6 preliminary ll.* N1-2 *defective. Translator: Georg Handsch.* (School of Dentistry.) [199

MAURUS, HARTMANN. De necessario bello aduersus Turcas ... Anno. M. D. XXX. 4°. B.L. A-D4 (-D4). [200

MAXIMUS, S. Του αγιου Μαξιμου εκατοντάδεσ ...centuriae quatuor de Charitate, opera Vincentij Obsopoei uersæ ... Praeterea aliquot Psalmi παραφραστικῶς tractati carmine elegiaco, per eundem ... Haganoæ, per Iohannem Secerium, Anno M. D. XXXI. (*Colophon.*) 8°. A-HH8 II4. [201

MAXIMUS TYRIUS. Maximi Tyrii ... sermones e Graeca in Latinam linguam versi Cosmo Paccio interprete. ... (Impręssum Romę apud Iacobum Mazochium ... M.D.XVII. Die .XV. Mensis Octobris. ...) fol. a-s6 t8. ff. II-CXV. [202

MAYER, SEBASTIAN. Des Bapsts vnd seiner Gaistlichen Jarmarckt. ... 1535. ... [Augsburg, Philipp Ulhart.] 4°. A-X4. ff. 2-84. [203

-- Summarium der schődlichen tődtlichen gyfften/ so in disem Mandat vergriffen/ vff das du frummer Christ dich dar vor wissest zů hůten das du nitt gyfft für brott essest. (Gedruckt zů Hohensteyn/ durch Hanns Fürwitzig [i.e. Augsburg durch Philipp Ulhart, 1523].) 4°. A-B4. [204

MAYRONIS, FRANCISCUS DE. [1] Illuminati doctoris Fratris francisci de Mayronis In primuȝ sentētiaꝝ foecūdissimuȝ scriptū sum cōflatus nominatuȝ. ... (Exactum Venetijs ... expēsis heredū ... Octauiani scoti ... ꝑ Bonetū Locatellum ... 3° kal'. Augustas. i504.) fol. B.L. Aa10 Bb-Ss8 Tt6. ff. 1-149. ¶Tt4r: correctū atque ꝺcoratū sūma cura ... Mauritij de hibernia ... [2] Scriptum luculentissimū in secundū sententiaꝝ ... Francisci Maronis ... (Venetijs ... expensis heredum ... Octauiani Scoti ... Per Bonetuȝ Locatellum ... i505. i4. kal'as maias.) A-C8 D6. ff. 2-29. [3] Scriptum luculentissmum in Tertiū sentētiaꝝ ... (Venetijs ... expensis hereduȝ ... Octauiani Scoti ... Per Bonetum Locatellum ... i506. Sexto kal'as Iunias.) AA-BB8 CC6. ff. 2-22. [4] Scriptū luculentissimū in quartuȝ sentētiaꝝ ... (Venetijs ... expensis heredum ... Octauiani Scoti ... Per Bonetum Locatellum ... i507. die. 24. nouembris.) a-f8 g10. ff. 2-57. (Lea.) [205

-- Quodlibettales questiones ... (Venetijs ... expensis heredum ... Octauiani Scoti ... Per Bonetū Locatellum ... i507. die. iij. feb.) fol. B.L. A-D8 E-F6 (-F6, *presumably blank*). ff. 2-42. ¶F5r: Correcte ... cura ... Mauritij ꝺ hibernia ... E6, F1-5 *damaged.* (Lea.) [206

MAZZIO, GIOVANNI MARIA. [1] Opinionum Ioannis Marii Mattii Brixiani ... Libri tres. In quibus plurima loca auctorum Latinorum & Graecorum ... explicantur; aut corrupta emendantur: adcesserunt aliquot carmina ... Alexandriae Statiellae, ex Officina Herculis Quinctiani Kalen. Mai. CIↃ.IↃ.IIC 4°. †-††4 A-Bb4. pp. 1-200. [2] Eiusdem ... libellus de orthographia. ... *Same imprint.* (*Colophon.*) ✦4 A-F4. pp. 1-32. [207

MAZZOLINI, SILVESTRO, da Prierio. Reuerendi patris F. Siluestri Prieriatis ... de strigimagarum, Dæmonumque Mirandis, Libri Tres, vna cum praxi ..., Et ratione formandi Processus contra ipsas ... Romae, In Aedibus Po. Ro. M . D . LXXV. ... (*Colophon.*) 4°. a-c4 A-Kk4. pp. 1-262. (Lea.) [208

-- Epithoma responsionis ad Martinum Lutherum per Fratrem Syluestrum de Prierio. Martini Lutheri epistola ad lectorem. [Wittenbergae, Melchior Lotter junior, c. 1520.] 4°. A-B4 C6. [209

-- R.P. Fratris Siluestri Prieratis ... in ꝑsumptuosas Martini Luther cōclusiōes de ptāte pape dialog9. 4°. B.L. A-C4. [210

-- Sūmario ꝑ cōfessarsi breuissimo e doctrinale di maistro Siluestro ... 12°. B.L. a12. [211

-- [1] Syluestrinae Summæ ..., Pars Prima, Ab ... Syluestro Prierate ... Lugduni, Apud Symphorianum Beraud. M. D. LXXII. 4°. a-z^8 A-I^8 K^6 (-K6, *presumably blank*). pp. 1-515. [2] Syluestrinae Summæ, ... Pars Secunda ... *Same imprint.* aa-zz^8 AA-LL^8. pp. 3-542. (Lea.) [212

MAZZONE, MARCANTONIO. [1] I fiori della poesia Dichiarati, & raccolti da Don Marcantonio Mazzone di Miglionico da tutte l'opere Di Virgilio, Ouidio, & Horatio ... In Venetia, Appresso Francesco de'Franceschi Senese. M.D.XCIII. 4°. †^{6} a-g^8 h^4 A-X^8 Y^4. pp. 1-344. [2] De fiori della poesia Parte Seconda. ... *Same imprint.* a-h^8 i^4. pp. 3-136. [213

MAZZONI, JACOPO. Della difesa della Comedia di Dante. Distinta in sette libri. Nella quale si risponde alle oppositioni fatte al Discorso di M. Iacopo Mazzoni ... Parte prima. Che contiene li primi tre libri. ... In Cesena. ... Appresso Bartolomeo Rauerij. L'Anno MDLXXXVII. 4°. *^{6} A-H^4 I^2 a-c^8 d^2 A-Zz^8 (N2 + *folded leaf*) 3A^2. pp. 1-739. [214

-- Discorso de dittongi ... In Cesena Appresso Bartolomeo Rauerio. 1572. ... (*Colophon.*) 8°. A-D^8. ff. 2-30. [215

MECHLIN. Coustumen vsancien ende stijl van procederen der stadt ... van Mechelen ... (Gheprint Tantwerpen by Michielen van Hoochstraeten ... M.D.XXXV. In October.) 4°. A-R^4. ff. I-lxiiij. (Biddle.) [216

-- Costumen vsanciē ende stijl van procederen der Stadt vrijheyt/ ende Iurisdictie van Mechelen ... In den Jare ... M.CCCCC. ende. Vūftich. (Gheprint Thantwerpen ... by my Ian van Ghelen. ... M.CCCCC. eñ. LXI.) 8°. A-H^8. ff. I-xlvi. [217

-- Ein warhaffte grawsam̄e Geschicht/ So geschehen ist zů Mechel in Brabandt/ Allda hat man ain Můter mit vier Kindern/ vmb des Euangeliums wegen/ gefangen ... M. D. Lvj. 4°. A-B^4. [218

MECKLENBURG. Kirchenordnung: Wie es ... Im Hertzogthumb zu Meckelnburg etc. gehalten wird. Witteberg. 1552. (... durch Hans Lufft. ...) 4°. A-Z^4 a-l^4. ff. 3-136. [219

-- -- Witteberg. Gedruckt durch Hans Lufft. 1554. 4°. A-Z^4 a-n^4. ff. 2-144. (Yarnall.) [219a

MEDICI. Medici antiqui omnes, qui ... diuersorum morborum genere & remedia persecuti sunt ... Venetiis, M. D. XLVII. (Apud Aldi filios. ...) fol. *-**^{6} a^8 *^{2} b-h^8 i^6 k^{10} l-z^8 A-Q^8 R^6. ff. 1-[317]. ¶*Authors:* Aurelius Cornelius Celsus, Q. Serenus, Trotula, Marcellus, Scribonius Largus, Soranus Ephesius, C. Plinius Secundus, L. Apuleius Madaurensis, Antonius Musa, Aemilius Macer, Strabus Gallus, Cælius Aurelianus, Theodorus Priscianus. (School of Dentistry.) [220

MEDICI, LORENZINO DE'. Aridosio comedia ... In Vinegia appresso Matio Pagan. (*Colophon.*) 8°. A-M^4 (-M4, *presumably blank*). ff. 2-47. [221

MEDICI, LORENZO DE'. Poesie uolgari ... In Vinegia, M. D. LIIII. (... in casa de' figliuoli di Aldo ...) 8°. A-CC^8. ff. 2-205. [222

MEDICI, SEBASTIANO. Summa omnium haeresum et catalogus schismaticorum, haereticorum, Et Idolatrarum. ... Florentiae In Officina Sermartelliana. 1581. (Apud Bartholomæum Sermartellium. ...) 8°. †^{4} A-3C^8 3D-3E^4. pp. 1-784. (Lea.) [223

-- Tractatus de promouendis episcopis. Auctore Sebastiano Medice ... Maceratæ, Apud Sebastianum Martellinum. M. D. XCI. (*Colophon.*) 12°. ✠^{4} A-L^{12} M^8. pp. 25-301. (Lea.) [224

MEDICI, VITALE. Omelie fatte alli Ebrei di Firenze Nella Chiesa di Santa Croce, et sermoni fatti in piu compagnie della ditta città. ... In Firenze Nella Stamperia de'Giunti. 1585. ... (*Colophon.*) 4°. ¶^{4} A-P^4. pp. 1-112. [225

MEDINA, MIGUEL. [1] Disputationum de indulgentiis, aduersus nostrae tempestatis haereticos, ... liber vnus. ... Venetiis, Ex officina Stellæ, Iordani Zileti. M. D. LXIIII. 4°. a^4 b^2 A-Hh^4 Ii^2. ff. 2-126. [2] Explicationes in quartum symboli apostolici articulum. ...

Same imprint. A-D^4 (-D4, *presumably blank*). ff. 2-15. (Lea.) [226

MEDUNA, BARTOLOMMEO. Dialogo sopra la miracolosa vittoria ottenuta dall'Armata della Santissima Lega Christiana, contra la Turchesca. ... In Venetia. M. D. LXXII. 4°. A^4. [227

-- Lo scolare ... Nelquale si forma a pieno vn perfetto Scolare ... In Venetia, Presso Pietro Fachinetti. 1588. 4°. a^4 A-Hh^4 Ii^2. ff. 2-126. [228

MEETKERCKE, ADOLPHE VAN. Adolphi Mekerchi Brugensis de veteri et recta pronuntiatione linguæ Græcæ commentarius ... Accessit appendix de Græcorum accentibus ... Antuerpiæ, Ex officina Christophori Plantini ... M. D. LXXVI. 8°. A-K^8. pp. 3-155. [229

MEIER, GEORG. De origine et autoritate Verbi Dei ... Additus est catalogus Doctorum Ecclesiæ Dei ... Autore Georgio Maiore. Francoforti ad Viadrum excudebat Iohannes Eichorn. Anno M. D. LIIII. 8°. A-G^8 H^4. [230

-- Enarratio epistolae Pauli, scriptae ad Philippenses. Autore Georgio Maiore. [Wittenberg, Johann Lufft,] M. D. LIX. 8°. A-X^8. ff. 1-159. [231

-- Homeliæ in epistolas dierum dominicorum et Festorum. Doct: Georg: Maior. ... VVitte-bergæ. Excudebat Iohannes Lufft. Anno. 1563. fol.)(^{8} a-e^6 f^4 B-Y^6 Z^4 a-z^6 Aa-Rr^6 Ss^8 Tt-Zz^6 AA-ZZ^6 aa^8 (-aa8, *presumably blank*). ff. 1-551. [232

-- Oratio de ... Georgio Principe in Anhalt & Ascania &c. à Georgio Maiore ... recitata in renunciatione publici testimonij de ... Henrico Sthenio Mundero ... Vitebergae. anno. 1554. 8°. A-B^8. [233

-- Quaestiones rhetoricae, ex libris M. Ciceronis, Quintiliani, & Philippi Melanth. Collectæ ... per Georgium Maiorem. Magdburgae. Excussit Michael Lotther. (... M. D. XLIIII.) 8°. A-M^8 (-M8, *presumably blank*). [234

-- Refutatio horrendae prophanationis coena domini. ... A Georgio Maiore. Iterum recognita. Cum præfatione Philippi Melanthonis. VVitebergae. Ex officina Typographica Viti Creutzer. Anno M. D. LV. 8°. A^{12} B-S^8. [235

-- Sententiae veterum poetarum, per Georgium Maiorem in locos communes digestæ ... Antonii Mancinelli de Poetica uirtute Libellus. ... Lutetiae Ex officina Roberti Stephani ... M. D. LI. 8°. a-p^8 q^4. pp. 3-240. (Lea.) [236

-- -- ... Aurelii Prudentii ἐνχειρίδιον noui & veteris instrumenti. ... Parisiis, Apud Benedictum Preuost ... 1552. (... nono Calend. Mart.) 16°. ā^8 ē^8 a-v^8. ff. 1-160. [237

-- Testamentum Doctoris Georgii Maioris. ... Wittemberg. Gedruckt durch Hans Lufft. Anno M. D. LXX. 4°. A-B^4. [238

-- Vitae patrum, in vsum ministrorum verbi ... Per D. Georgium Maiorem. Cum præfatione D. Doctoris Marti. Luth. VVitebergæ. 1562. (Impressum ... per Vitum Creutzer. ...) 8°. A-Ss^8 Tt^4. ff. 2-257. [239

-- Zwo Predig vber das Euangelium/ Iohann. j. ... Durch D. Georg. Maior. ... Gedruckt zu Wittemberg/ Durch Veit Creutzer. 1552. (*Colophon.*) 8°. A-H^8. [240

MEIGRET, AMÉDÉE. Questiones Fra. Amadei Meygreti Lugdunensis ... in libros de celo ⁊ mũdo Aristotelis. [*Device of the brothers de Marnef.*] Venundantur Parrhisii ... (... .18. kal'. Decēbris. 1514.) fol. B.L. π^4 a-l^6. ff. I-LXVI. [241

MEISSEN. *Heinrich V, burgrave.* Abtruck Der Verwarung ... Marggraff Albrechten dem Jüngern zů Brandenburg ⁊c. zugeschickt. Darinnen ... die vrsachen angezaiget werden/ welcher halb jre Kün. Maie. vnd Churf. Gn. nicht haben vmbgehen kœnnen/ zů beschützung derer aignen Land ... Anno M.D.LIII. 4°. A-B^4. [242

-- -- Abtruckt der abklag vnd verwarung schrifft/ des ... Herrn Heinrichen ... Burggraffen zu Meissen ... Aussgangen zu Osterrode/ den 1. Iulij/ Anno 1553. 4°. [A]-C^4. [243

-- -- Przelozieniá Wohrada z Němčiny na Czesko ... Létha Pánie M.D.Liij. (Wytisscěno w Starém Městě Prazském/ w Pondělij po Hwatém Iakubu/ v Gifijka Melantricha Rozdalowského.) 4°. A-C^4. [244

-- Warhafftige Beschreibung/ des wunder seltzamen vnbekandten Vogels/ deren etliche in

Meissen vnd Düringen/ dieses LXI. Jars/ gesehen vnd geschossen worden sind/ Sampt ... andern schrecklichen Wunderzeichen ... 4°. A^4. ¶*In verse.* [245

MELANCHTHON, PHILIPP. Aduersus furiosum Parisiensium theologastrorum decretum, Philippi Melanchthonis pro Luthero apologia. 4°. A-B^4 C^6. [246

-- Annotationes ... in Euangeliũ Matthei ... (Excusum [Basileae per Valentinum Curionem] anno M. D. XXIII. mense Maio.) 8°. A-F^8 G^{10}. ff. 2-57. [247

-- -- Philippi Melancthonis in euangelium Matthei annotationes ... (Excudebatur anno. M. D. XXIII. mense Decembri.) 8°. a-f^8 g^4. ff. 2-51. [248

-- -- ... Item in eundem Euangelistam, & in Lucam ... Scholia ... (Haganoæ, per Iohannem Secerium Anno M. D. XXVI.) 8°. A-V^8 X^4. ff. 4-159. [249

-- Philippi Melanchthonis, annotationes in Iohannem ... una cum Epistola commendatitia M. Lutheri ... Ex ... Hagenoa. (... per Iohannem Secerium [1524].) 8°. A-R^8 S^4 T^8. ff. 2-152. [250

-- Bedencken auffs interim ... 1548. 4°. A-C^4 D^2. [251

-- Didymi Fauentini aduersus Thomam Placentinum, pro Martino Luthero theologo, oratio. ... Anno M. D. XXI. 4°. A-I^4 K^6. [252

-- Philippi Melanthonis elementorum Rhetorices Libri duo: Martini Crusii quæstionibus et Scholijs explicati ... Adiectis aliquot epistolis et carminibus ... Basileae, ex officina Oporiniana. (... M. D. LXX. Mense Augusto.) 8°. a-z^8 A-Y^8 Z^4. pp. 4-663. [253

-- Enarratio symboli Niceni ... Cum præfatione Philippi Melanthonis ... VVitebergæ. ... Ex officina Iohannis Lufft. 1550. 8°. A-V^8. ff. 1-151. [254

-- Epistolæ Pauli scriptae ad Romanos, Enarratio edita â Philippo Melanthone Anno 1556. ... VVitebergae [per haeredes Petri Seitz]. 8°. A-M^8 a-u^8. ff. 1-89, 1-160. (Yarnall.) [254a

-- Epistolæ selectiores aliquot ... Editæ a Casparo Peucero. ... VVitebergæ excudebat Iohannes Crato. Anno M. D. LXV. 8°. A-Pp^8 (-Pp6, *errata*, Pp7-8, *blank*). pp. 1-575. [255

-- Epistolarum D. Philippi Melanchthonis Farrago, in Partes tres distributa ... a Ioanne Manlio passim collecta ... Basileae, per Paulum Queckum: M.D.LXV. (... Mense Martio ...) 8°. α^8 a-z^8 A-O^8. pp. 2-550. (Lea.) [256

-- -- *Another copy.* [257

-- Die Erste Epistel Sant Paulus an die Corinther/ Ausgelegt ... 1527. (Gedrückt durch Ioseph Klug. zu Wittemberg. ...) 8°. A-Y^8 (-Y8, *presumably blank*) Aa-Qq^8 q-c^8 d^4. ff. 2-302. ¶A2^v: Philippo Melanch: *(signed on* A3^v*)* Martinus Luther. A4^r-Y7^v: *commentary on Romans.* Aa2^v-Kk5^r: *commentary on 1 Corinthians.* Kk6^r-Qq8^r: *commentary on 2 Corinthians.* a1^r-b3^v: Vorrede auff die Epistel S. Paulus zu den Römern. Martin Luther. [258

-- Ein gewisser vnd klarer vnterricht/ von der Gerechtigkeit/ die fur Gott gilt/ Gezogen aus den Schrifften der heiligen Propheten vnd Aposteln/ newlich durch Herrn Philippum Melantho. Latinisch gestellt. Gedruckt zu Wittemberg durch Hans Lufft. M. D. XLI. 4°. A-S^4 (-S4, *presumably blank*). [259

-- Grammatica Latina ... Syntaxis, seu de constructione libellus eiusdem. De periodis. De quantitate syllabarum. Quarta editio. Parisiis. Ex officina Roberti Stephani. M.D.XXXIII. (... XIII. Cal. Decemb.) 8°. A-K^8. pp. 5-157. [260

-- -- Philippi Melanchthonis grammatica Latina. ... Basileae, per I[o]annem Oporinum. (... M.D.LX. Mense Iunio.) 8°. a^8 a-z^8 A-E^8. pp. 4-447. ¶*T.p. defective.* [261

-- Historia de vita et act[is] ... Martini Lutheri ... Adiecta est præterea de Obitu eius breuis Narratio, Cum Oratione D. Io. Pomerani, in funere habita, quæ nunc primum in Latinum Sermonem conuersa sunt, per Matthiam Ritterum Francofor. 1557. 8°. A-L^8. ¶*T.p. repaired.* (Lea.) [262

-- Initia doctrinae physicæ ... VVitebergæ, Per Iohannem Lufft. 1550. 8°. A-Z^8 a-c^8. ff. 9-206. [263

-- -- Vitebergae excudebat Iohannes Crato, anno M.D.LXX. 8°. A-Cc^8. pp. 2-363. [264

-- Integrae Græcæ grammatices institutiones ... [1520.] 4°. A-L^8 M^4 (-M4). [265

-- -- Grammatica Graeca ... recognita ... M. D. XXXVIII 8°. A-S^8 T^4. [266

-- Heubtartikel Christlicher Lere/ im latin genandt/ Loci Theologici/ Etwa von Doctore Iusto Iona in Deutsche sprach gebracht/ jetzund aber im M.D.LIII. jar/ von Philippo Melanthon widerumb durchsehen. Wittemberg. 1554. (Gedruckt ... Durch Veit Creutzer.) 4°. A-Z^4 a-ii^4 Aa-3P^4. ff. I-CCXI, I-CXLIII. [267

-- -- Loci præcipui theologici. ... His accesserunt definitiones Theologicæ ... eodem autore. ... Lipsiae omnia in officina Valentini Papae elaborata atque edita. Anno M. D. LVII. 8°. A-Z^8 a-z^8 Aa^8 Bb^4. pp. 2-664. [268

-- Philippi Melanchthonis moralis Philosophiæ Epitome. Item in quintum librum Ethicorum Arist: Commentarius ... (Argentorati apud Cratonem Mylium mense Martio, anno M. D. XXXIX.) 8°. π^8 A-R^8. pp. 1-267. [269

-- Ob auch die Christē mit guttem gewissen/ fur gericht handeln vnd gerichtliche ordenungen brauchen mů̊gen/ ein kurtzer vnterricht. ... 1529. (Gedruck zu Zwickaw durch Gabriel Kantz ...) 8°. A^8. [270

-- Oratio dicta in funere Friderichi Saxoniæ Ducis. Oratio de Legibus. Oratio de Gradibus. Praefatio in Aeschinis & Demosthenis orationes. Oratio Critiæ contra Theramenem ex Xenophonte. ... Haganoæ, excudebat Iohan. Secer. Anno M. D. XXV. (*Colophon.*) 8°. Aa-Dd^8 Ee^4. [271

-- Responsiones ... ad impios articulos Bauaricæ Inquisitionis. VVitebergæ excudebant haeredes Georgij Rhaw. Anno M. D. LIX. (... Mense Augusto.) 8°. A-K^8. (Lea.) [272

-- -- VViterbergæ excudebant hæredes Georgij Rhaw. Anno M. D. LIX. (... Mense Septembri.) 8°. A-K^8 (-K8, *presumably blank*). (Lea.) [273

-- Philippi Melanchthonis sermo habitus apud iuuentutē Academiæ Vuittenberg. de corrigendis adulescentiæ studijs. Rodolphus Agricola Phrisius de studiorum omnium colluuie ... (Basileae apud Io. Frobenium mense Ianuario, anno M. D. XIX.) 4°. A-B^8 C^6. pp. 2-26. [274

-- Vrsach Warumb die Stende/ so der Augspurgischen Confession anhangen/ Christliche leer erstlich angenommen/ vnnd endtlich dabey zůuerharren gedencken. Auch Warumb das vermaindte Trientische Concilium weder zůbesůchen/ noch darein zů willigen sey ... M.D.XLVI. (Getruckt zů Augspurg durch Valentin Othmar.) 4°. A-F^4 G^2. [275

-- Ain warhafftigs vrtayl/ ... vō .D. Martin luthers leer/ dem Cardinal vñ Bäbstlichen legaten gen Stůgarten zůgeschickt. M.D.XXIIII. Ain schöne offenbarung des Endchrists/ durch Iohan. bugeñ. Pomeranū. [Augsburg, Simprecht Ruff, 1524.] 4°. a-b^4 c^2. [276

MELANDER, OTHO. Resolutio præcipuarum Quæstionum criminalis adversus Sagas Processus, cum refutatione nova ... Purgationis Sagarum per aquam frigidam, adversus Guilielmum Adolphum Scribonium ... Lichae, apud Nicolaum Erbenium, Anno M. D. XCVII. 8°.)(^{8} A-I^8. pp. 1-131. [277

MELCHIORI, OTTAVIO. In ... Cardinalem Cynthium Aldobrandinum ... Carmina. Venetiis, M.D.XCVII. Apud Georgium Angelerium. ... 4°. π^4. [278

MELDEMANN, NICOLAUS. Ein kurtzer bericht vber die recht warhafftig Contrafactur/ Türckischer belegerung der Stat Wien ... welche ... durch Niclaus Meldeman yetzt verfertigt/ getrückt vñ aussgangen ist. [1530.] 4°. A^4. [279

MELEGHINI, TOMMASO. De Contractibus summatiȝ versibus elegis editus libellus ... interprete .d. Polydamante Tiberto ... (Impressum Cęsenę per Amadeum ⁊ eius socios ... M.D.XXV. Quarto kalē. Decembris ...) 4°. B.L. ✠-✠✠^{4} A-N^4 O^6. ff. I-LVI. [280

MELHOFER, PHILIPP. Offenbarung der allerheimlichisten heymlicheit/ der ytzigen Baals priester ... genannt Canon oder die Styllmess. ... [Augsburg, Philipp Ulhart,] M. D. XXV. 4°. A-O^4 P^2 Q^4. [281

-- -- [Augsburg, Philipp Ulhart, c. 1530.] 8°. A-K^8. [282

MELLINI, DOMENICO. Descrizione dell'entrata Della ... Reina Giouanna d'Austria ... fatto in Firenze ... In Fiorenza appresso i Giunti MDLXVI. ... (*Colophon.*) 8°. A-K^8. pp. 1-128. [283

-- Dominici Mellinii Guidonis f. in veteres quosdam scriptores, Maleuolos Christiani Nominis Obtrectatores. Libri Quatuor. Florentiæ, In Officina Typographica Georgii Marescoti. M D LXXVII. (*Colophon.*) fol. a^8 b^2 A-L^6 M^4. pp. 1-140. ¶B1 *misbound after* B6. [284

-- Vita di Filippo Scolari, volgarmente chiamato Pippo Spano ... In Fiorenza, Appresso Giorgio Marescotti. (... Per Bartholomeo Sermartelli, Adistanza di Giorgio Marescotti. MDLXX.) 8°. A-D^8 E^4. pp. 7-71. [285

MEMMINGEN. *Order of S. Anthony.* Indulgẽtie ⁊ certa priuilegia ordinis sancti Anthonii. [Memmingen, Albrecht Kunne, c. 1500.] s.sh. 30 × 38 cm. *(folded, with an impression on each recto).* B.L. [286

MEMMO, GIOVANNI MARIA. Dialogo ... nel quale ... si forma un perfetto Prencipe, & una perfetta Republica, ę parimente un Senatore, un Cittadino, un Soldato, & un Mercatante ... In Vinegia appresso Gabriel Giolito de' Ferrari. M D LXIII. (*Colophon.*) 4°. $*^4$ A-I^8 K^2 L-N^8 (-N8, *presumably blank*). pp. 1-198. [287

-- Tre libri della sostanza et forma del Mondo ... (In Venetia per Giouanni de Farri & fratelli. ... M D XLV.) 4°. A^4 a-s^4 t^2. ff. 1-76. [288

MENA, JUAN DE. [1] Las .ccc. del ... poeta Iuã de mena: cõ otras .xxiiij. coplas y su glosa y la coronacion del mesmo poeta: ⁊ otras cartas: ⁊ coplas ⁊ cãciões. ... (Fueron empremidas ... ẽla ... cobdad ỏ Seuilla: por Iacobo crõberger alemã año de mil ⁊ q̃niẽtos ⁊ dezisiete a veynte ⁊ quatro de setiembre.) fol. B.L. a-n^8 (-m^8). ff. ij-ciiij. [2] [La Coronacion ...] (Fue empremida ... enla ... cibdad de Seuilla por Iacobo cronberger Aleman año ... de mill ꝫ quinientos ꝫ veynte años. A ocho dias del mes de Março.) a-b^8 (+a1) c^6. [289

-- [1] Copilacion ỏ todas las obras del ... poeta Iuã de mena ... Año. M.D.y.xlviij. Años. (Fue impressa ... enla ... cibdad de Toledo en casa de Fernando de sancta catalina defunto ... Acabose a quinze dias del mes de Diziembre. Año ... Del mil ⁊ quinientos ⁊ quarenta y siete Años.) fol. B.L. a-n^8. ff. ij-ciiii. [2] La coronacion ... Impresso. Año. M.D.xlviij. A-B^8 C^{10}. ff. ij-xxvj. [290

-- -- Todas las obras ... con la glosa del Comendador Fernan Nuñez ... En Anuers. En casa de Martin Nucio ... M.D.LII. 8°. A-Vv^8 (-Vv8). ff. 2-343. [291

-- -- *Another copy.* [292

-- -- Las obras ... corregidas ... por ... Francisco Sanchez ... En Salamanca. En casa de Lucas de Iunta. 1582. (*Colophon.*) 12°. $*^8$ (-*8) A-M^{12} N^4. ff. 2-148. [293

MENDOZA, BERNARDIN DE. Commentaires memorables ... des guerres de Flandres & pays bas depuis l'an 1567. ... A Paris. Chez Guillaume Chaudiere ... M.D.LXXXXI. ... 8°. $ā^8$ $ē^8$ $ī^8$ $ō^4$ A-$3C^8$ (-3C8, *presumably blank*). ff. 1-342. ¶*Translator: Pierre Crespet.* (Lea.) [294

MENGHI, GIROLAMO. Compendio dell'arte essorcistica, et possibilita delle mirabili, & stupende operationi delli demoni, & de' Malefici. ... In Bologna, Per Giouanni Rossi. MDLXXX. ... 8°. †-$3†^8$ $4†^4$ A-T^8 V^4. pp. 1-312. (Lea.) [295

MENGIN, NICOLAUS. Venediger Chronica. Mit angezoͤigtẽ vrsachẽ des schaͤdlichẽ Kryegs/ do mit sye bitz haͤr võ Roͤmischer Key. Maiestaͤt so schwaͤrlich gestrafft seind. 4°. a^8 b-c^4 d^8. [296

MENINI, OTTAVIO. Etlicher Franckreichischen Stenden/ erbaͤrmliche Klage vber ihren langwirigen Kriegswesen/ an den ... Bapst zu Rom/ Clementen den Achten ... Vertiert auss dem Lateinischen/ so Gedruckt war zu Venedig/ durch Dominico Nicolini Im Jahr 1593. 4°. A^4. [297

MENIUS, JUSTUS. An die Hochgeborne Furstin/ Fraw Sibilla Hertzogin zu Sachssen/ Oeconomia Christiana/ das ist/ von Christlicher Haushaltung ... Mit einer schoͤnen Vorrede/ D. Martini Luther. Wittemberg. M.D.XXXV. (Gedruckt zu Wittemberg/ durch Hans Lufft. M.D.XXXVI.) 8°. A-H^8. [298

-- Censurae: Das ist/ Erkendtnis aus Gottes Wort vnd heiliger Schrifft/ Vber die Bekendtnis Andreæ Osiandri ... [Erfurt, Gervasius Stürmer,] Anno 1552. 4°. A-F^4. ¶*Signed by 10 theologians besides Menius.* [299

-- Censurae Der Fürstlichen Sechsischen Theologen zu Weymar vnd Koburg. Auff die Bekendtnis des Andreæ Osiandri. ... Zu Erffurd/ bey Geruasius Sthürmer/ Gedrückt. Anno M. D. LII. 4°. AA-DD⁴. [300

-- Von der Berechtigkeit die für Gott gilt. Wider die newe Alcumistische Theologiam Andreæ Osiandri. ... 1552. (Zu Erffurdt trückts Geruasius Sthürmer ...) 4°. A⁶ B-T⁴. ¶A3-4 *misbound after* B2. [301

-- Von der Notwehr vnterricht. ... MDXLIX. 4°. A-G⁴. [302

MENNEL, JAKOB. De inclito atq3 apud Germanos rarissimo actu ecclesiastico Kaleñ. Augusti Auguste Celebrato ... 1518. [Augustae, Sigismund Grimm & Marcus Wirzung, 1518.] 4°. B.L. A-B⁴. [303

MENNI, VINCENZO. Regole della Thoscana lingua ... Con vn Breue modo di Comporre varie sorti di Rime. (In Perugia. Per Andrea Bresciano ... 1568.) 8°. A-K⁴. ff. 3-38. [304

MENOT, MICHEL. Fratris Michaelis menoti ... sermones quadragesimales vna cũ nonnullis alijs tractatibus ... [Parisiis, Enguilbert de Marnef, 1519 *or later*.] 8°. B.L. a⁸ a-p⁸ aa-hh⁸ A-BB⁸ (-BB6-8). ff. j-cxcvi. [305

MENSING, JOHANN. Grundtliche vnterrichte: Was eyn frommer Christen ... halten sol ... M. D. XXVIII. (... Am .xviij. tage Februarij.) 4°. A-I⁴ K² L⁴. ff. 2-42. [306

-- Replica Auff das wutige vnd vnchristliche schandbuchlyn Eberhardts Wydensehe ... (Gedruckt Im Tausent. Funfftzehen hundert/ vnd Sechs vnd zwentzigsten Jare Am .iij. tage Nouembris.) 4°. A-M⁴ N² O⁴. [307

-- Von der Concomitantien: vnnd ob Hiesus Christus ... ym Sacramẽt seyns ... leibs vñ bluts volkõmen sey: Widder Merten Luthers ... schmehungen ... [Franckfurt an der Oder, Johann Jamer, 1529.] 4°. A-N⁴. ff. j-xlviij. [308

MERCATI, FRANCESCO. Il sensale comedia ... In Fiorenza appresso i Giunti MDLXI. (*Colophon.*) 8°. A-F⁸. pp. 7-96. [309

-- -- *Another copy.* [310

MERCENARI, ARCANGELO. Dilucidationes Arcangeli Mercenarii a Monte Sancto ... In plurima Aristotelis perobscura, & nonnulla Auerrois loca. ... Venetiis, Apud Paulum & Antoniũ Meietos fr. biblio. Patau. M.D.LXXIV. (*Colophon.*) 4°. a-b⁴ A-Nn⁴ Oo². pp. 1-295. [311

-- -- Archangeli Mercenarii ... dilucidationes ... Additae sunt disputationes de Putredine contra Thomam Erastum ... Tertia editio. ... Venetiis, Apud Paulum Meietum Bibliopolam Patauinum. M D LXXXVIII. 4°. a-f⁴ A-4R⁴. pp. 1-687. [312

-- -- Lipsiæ, Anno M. D. XC. (... imprimebant haeredes Iohannis Steinmanni, Impensis Hæredum Ernesti Võgelini. ...) 4°.)?(⁸ A-Mm⁸ Nn⁴ a-aa⁸. pp. 1-548, 3-380. ¶*Additional t.pp.:* (a1ʳ) Disputatio de putredine ... a Thoma Erasto ... *Same imprint and colophon.* (h6ʳ) Archangeli Mercenarii ... de putredine disputatio ... [313

MERCIER, JOSIAS. Iosiæ Merceri ad nouam Taciti editionem aliquot Notæ. Parisiis, Apud Ambrosium Drouart ... M. D. XC. 8°. A-C⁸. ff. 2-24. [314

MERCURIALIS, HIERONYMUS. Hieronymi Mercurialis, de arte gymnastica, libri sex ... Secunda editione aucti ... Parisiis, Apud Iacobum du Puys ... 1577. 4°. *⁴ A-3F⁴ 3G⁶ (-3G6, *blank*). ff. 2-201. (Hutchinson Gymnasium.) [315

MERGENTHAL, HANS VON. Gründliche vnd warhafftige beschreibung der ... Reise vnd Meerfart in das heilige Land nach Hierusalem/ des ... Herrn Albrechten/ Hertzogen zu Sachssen ... Dabey ein kurtzer Ausszug der Pilgramschafft ins gelobte Land/ Hertzog Wilhelmen zu Sachssen ... Leipzig ... (Gedruckt ... durch Zachariam Berwaldt/ In verlegung Henningi Grossen ... M. D. LXXXVI.) 4°. A-P⁴. [316

MESMES, JEAN PIERRE DE. La grammaire Italienne, composée en Françoys. ... A Paris, Par

Estienne Groulleau ... 1548. 16°. ã^4 A-Q^8. pp. 1-251. [317

MESSAHALAH. De elementis et orbibus coelestibus, liber antiquus ... Cui adiectum est scriptum cuiusdam Hebræi de Eris seu interuallis regnorum, & de diuersis Gentium annis ac mensibus. Item ... scriptum cuiusdam Saraceni, continens prȩterea prȩcepta ad usum tabularum Astronomicarum utilissima. Quæ omnia ad ueteris Archetypi lectionem ... collata ... dicauit Ioachimus Hellerus ... Noribergæ excudebant Ioannes Montanus, & Vlricus Neuberus. ... M. D. XLIX. 4°. A^4 a^4 α^4 *^{2} B-Y^4 Z^2. [318

MESSINA. Consuetudines nobilis ciuitatis Messane suique districtus ... Panhormi per Iouannem Mattheum de Maida ad instantia Ioannis Francisci Carara ... M D L VIIII. (*Colophon.*) 4°. A-B^4. (Lea.) [319

MESSKRAM. Der Wůcherer Messkram oder Jarmarckt. Ein Newer Pasquillus/ Ob der Wůcher Sünde ... M D XLIIII. 4°. A-L^4. [320

METEREN, EMANUEL VAN. Historia Belgica nostri potissimum temporis ... [Antverpiae? 1598.] fol. (?)^4 (+ *folded sheet*) A-3E^6 3F^4 3G-3H^6. pp. 1-623. (Lea.) [321

MEURER, NOE. Handtbůchlein/ Oder Compendium. Darinnen Sũmarie ... alle vnd jede des Heiligen Rômischen Reichs Abschied/ Ordnungen vnd Constitutiones ... Gedruckt in ... Meyntz/ durch Casparum Behem. M.D.LXXXVI. (*Colophon.*) 4°.):(^{4} (:)^4 a-Aa^4 Bb^6 A-R^4. ff. 1-101, 2-97. [322

-- Loci communes: Aller des Hayligen Rômischen Reiches Ordnungen/ gehaltener Reichstâge vnd Abschied/ gemeyne Titul: ... Gedruckt zu Franckfurt am Meyn ... M. D. LXVIII. (... bey Georg Raben/ Sigmund Feyerabend/ vnd Weygand Hanen Erben. ...) fol.)(^{4} A-Z^6 a-z^6 Aa-3H^6. ff. I-CCCCLXII. (Lea.) [323

MEXÍA, PEDRO. Dialoghi di Pietro Messia tradotti ... di Spagnuolo in volgare da Alfonso d'Vlloa. ... In Venetia, per Plinio Pietrasanta. MDLVII. (*Colophon.*) 4°. a-b^4 A-R^4. pp. 1-125. [324

-- Silua de varia lecion ... 1550. Impresso en Anuers por Martin Nucio. ... 8°. a-b^8 A-PP^8. ff. 2-303. [325

-- -- [1] Les diuerses lecons de Pierre Messie ... auec trois dialogues, ... mises en François par Claude Gruget Parisien ... Augmentees ... de la suite d'icelles, faite par Antoine du Verdier ... A Lyon, par Barthelemy Honorat. 1580. 8°. a-z^8 A-T^8. pp. 3-661. [2] Les diuerses lecons d'Antoine du Verdier ... *Same imprint.* *^{8} **^{2} a-z^8 A-D^8 E^6. pp. 1-422. ¶E5-6 *misbound, in reverse order, after* **1. [326

MEYER, ANTOINE. Antonii Meieri vrsus siue de rebus diui Vedasti ... Libri iij. ... Lutetiae. Apud Carolum Roger ... 1580. 8°. A-G^8. pp. 3-111. ¶*In verse.* [327

MEYER, JAKOB. [1] Annales, siue historiæ rerum Belgicarum, a diuersis auctoribus ... ad haec nostra vsque tempora ... & in duos Tomos distinctæ. ... Francofurti ad Moenum, expensis Sigismundi Feyerabendij ... M. D. LXXX. (... apud Georgium Coruinum ...) fol. a^4 A-C^6 D-Z^4 a-z^4 Aa-Gg^4 Hh^6. pp. 1-427. [2] Rerum maxime memorabilium in Brabantia, Flandria, Hollandia, Selandia ... tomus II. ... *Same imprint and colophon.* a-y^4 z^6. pp. 3-187. ¶*Authors:* Jacobus Meyerus Baliolanus, Hadrianus Barlandus, Gerhardus Geldenhaurius, Jacobus Marchantius, Ludovicus Guicciardinus, Philippus Gallaeus, Gerhardus Candidus. (Lea.) [328

-- Commentarii Siue Annales rerum Flandricarum libri septendecim ... Antuerpiæ In ædibus Ioannis Steelsii. M. D. LXI. (Excudebat Ioan. Grapheus ...) fol. a^8 b^{10} A-ZZ^8 3A^6. ff. 2-374. (Lea.) [329

MEZZABARBA, ANTONIO. Le rime ... (In Vinegia per Francesco Marcolini da Forlì ... M D XXXVI. del mese di Maggio.) 4°. A-N^4. ff. 2-52. [330

MICHAEL DE HUNGARIA. Sermones Michaelis de vngaria predicabiles ... (Impressum parisius pro Iohanne Petit ... Anno dñi millesimo quingẽtesimo ꝑmo die ꝟo .xxij. mẽsis Decẽbris.) 8°. B.L. A^{10} a-o^8 (-o8, *presumably blank*). [331

MICHAELIS, SEBASTIEN. Pneumalogie, ou discours des esprits en tant qu'il est de besoing, pour entendre & resouldre la matiere difficile des Sorciers, comprinse en la sentence contre eux dõnee en Auignon ... 1582. ... A Paris, Chez Guillaume Bichon ... 1587. ... 8°. $\bar{a}^8$ A-P^8 Q^6. ff. 1-122. (Lea.) [332

MICHELE, AGOSTINO. Cianippo tragedia ... Et è la prima ... sino ad hora publicate dalle Stampe, che sia scritta in prosa. ... In Bergamo, Per Comin Ventura. cIↄ Iↄ xcvI. 4°. a^4 A-K^4. ff. 1-40. [333

MICHELIUS, JOSEPHUS. Apologia Chymica, aduersus inuectiuas Andreæ Libaui calumnias ... Middelburgi, Excudebat Richardus Schilders ... 1597. 8°. $*^4$ B-Aa^8 Bb^6. pp. 1-364. (Smith.) [334

MIDDENDORP, JAKOB. Academiarum vniuersi terrarum orbis. libri tres ... Coloniae, Apud Maternum Cholinum. M. D. LXXXIII. ... 8°. $(?)^8$ $2(?)^4$ A-Ss^8. pp. 1-634. [335

MILAN. *Laws &c.* Constitutiones · dominii· Mediolanensis. (Im̄pssum Mediolani, p̲ Vincētiū Medā, Calusci Impēsa, ... prima M.D.xlj. Decembris.) fol. π^4 (-π1 *or* π4) A-O^8 P^4. [335a

-- -- Venduntur Mediolani per Bernardum Caluschum ... Apud Valerium, & Heironymum Metios fratres ... MDLII. (... die. xx. Decembris.) fol. A^{10} B-N^8 O^6 P^4. ff. 1-114. [336

-- -- Nouariæ [apud] Franc. Sesallum. M D LXVII. 4°. a^4 A-L^8 M^6 N-P^4 Q^6. pp. 1-185. ¶*T.p. repaired.* (Lea.) [337

-- -- Mediolani Apud Valerium & Hieronymum fratres Metios. M D LXXIIII. (*Colophon.*) fol. $♦^4$ A-B^6 C^{10} A-N^8 O^6 P^4. ff. 1-114. [338

-- -- [1] Quarta editio ... Nouariæ, Apud hæredes Fr. Sesalli. Ad instantiam Melchioris Peroti, M.D.XCVII. 4°. a^4 $\dagger\dagger^2$ A-K^8 A^8 B^{10}. pp. 1-156. [2] Ordines excell. Senatus. ... *Same imprint.* χ^4 $\dagger^8$ $**^6$ A-G^8 H^{10}. pp. 1-124. (Lea.) [339

-- Statuta Mediol.ⁱ cum appostillis ... Catelliani Cottae ... Quibus ... adiectus est Elenchus, vnâ cum Annotationibus ... ab ... Antonio Rubeo ... Mediolani, Apud Io. Antonium Castellionæum impensis .D. Io. Baptistæ, et Fratrum de Serono. Anno. M.D.LII. (... M.D.L.) fol. π^2 A-I^8 A-T^8 V^{10} χ^2 A-T^8 V^{12}. ff. 1-161, 1-164. (Lea.) [340

-- Statuta criminalia Mediolani E tenebris in lucem edita ... Bergomi, Typis Comini Venturæ, cIↄ Iↄ XCIII. Sumptibus Antonij de Antonijs Bibliopolæ Mediolanensis. 4°. a-b^4 A-H^4. ff. 1-32. (Lea.) [341

-- *Senate.* Ordines ab ... Senatu Mediol. nuper editi. Mediolani Apud Antonium de Antoniis. M. D. LXII. fol. A^6. [342

-- Ordines ac decreta, constitutionumq'. declarationes aliquae, ab excell. Senatu aeditae ... Cum Indulto Leonis Decimi Pont. Max. Ordinibus Vermatiæ, & alijs. ... Nouariae apud Franciscum Sesallum, M D LXXIIII. 4°. †-$\dagger\dagger^4$ A-D^8 E^6 F-G^4 (-G4, *presumably blank*). pp. 7-96. (Lea.) [343

-- -- Nouariæ in ædibus Fr. Sesalli. M D LXXXIII. ... 4°. A^4 a^4 B-H^8 I^4 i^2 k^4. pp. 1-124. (Lea.) [344

-- -- Bergomi CIↃ IↃ XCVI. Typis Comini Venturæ. Sumptibus Antonij de Antonijs Bibliopolæ Mediolanen. 4°. A^4 A-N^4. pp. 1-104. (Lea.) [345

-- *Accademia dei Trasformati.* Sonetti de gli academici Trasformati di Milano. (In Milano per M. Antonio Borgi nel .1548. del mese di Decembre.) 8°. A-G^8 H^{10}. [346

MILAN. *Diocese.* Acta ecclesiæ Mediolanensis, a Carolo cardinali ... archiepiscopo condita ... Mediolani, Ex Officina Typographica quon. Pacifici Pontij. ... M. D. XCIX. ... fol. $\dagger^6$ A-$5N^6$ $5O^8$ (+ 3 *folded ll. signed* A, B, C) a-r^6 s^4. pp. 1-1273. (Lea.) [347

-- *Province.* Constitutiones et decreta condita in prouinciali synodo Mediolanensi. Sub ... Carolo Borrhomaeo ... archiepiscopo Mediolani. ... Venetiis, [Aldine press,] M. D. LXVI. 8°. $*^8$ A-S^8 T^4. pp. 2-216. (Lea.) [348

-- Constitutiones et decreta Condita In prouinciali Synodo Mediolanensi Quarta. ... Anno M. D. LXXVI. ... Mediolani, in Typographia Seminarij. M.D.LXXX. (*Colophon.*) 8°. $\dagger^8$ (-†2-3) A-Z^8 $\&^{12}$. pp. 1-343. (Lea.) [349

-- Constitutiones et decreta Condita In prouinciali Synodo Mediolanensi Quinta. ... Anno M. D. LXXIX. ... Mediolani, in Typographia Seminarij. M.D.LXXX. (... Apud Michaelem Tinum, Typographum Seminarij ...) 8°. $+^{8}$ (-+2,3) A-Bb^{8}. pp. 1-349. (Lea.) [350

MILICH, LUDWIG. Schrap Teufel. Was man den Herrschafften schuldig sey/ Womit das Volcke beschwert werde ... M.D.LXVIII. (*Colophon.*) 8°. A-X^{8}. [351

MINADOI, TOMMASO. Historia della guerra fra Turchi, et Persiani, descritta ... In Roma Nella Stamperia di Iacomo Tornerio, & Bernardino Donangeli. M D LXXXVII. (... Appresso Alessandro Gardano, & Francesco Coattini Compagni. ...) 4°. $+^{6}$ A-Z^{8} Aa^{4}. pp. 1-360. [352

MINCUCCI, ANTONIO. Repertorium domini Antonij de Prato Veteri. (Venetiis impressuȝ per Simonem de Luere: Impēsis ... Andree de Torresanis de Asula. 18. nouembris .1502.) fol. B.L. 1-13^{10} 14^{8} (-148, *presumably blank*). ff. 2-137. (Biddle.) [353

MINGO REVULGO. Coplas de Mingo Reuulgo glosadas por Hernando de Pulgar. Año M.D.XCIIII. 12°. I^{8} (*t.p.*, I6, I7, 5 *unsigned ll.*) K-L^{12} M^{6}. [354

MINI, PAOLO. Difesa della citta di Firenze, et de i Fiorentini. Contra le calunnie & maledicentie de maligni. ... In Lione, appresso Filippo Tinghi. M.D.LXXVII. 8°. a-x^{8} (-x8, *presumably blank*). pp. 3-329. [355

MINSHEU, JOHN. [A dictionarie in Spanish and English, first published by Richard Perciuale Gent. Now enlarged ... by Iohn Minsheu ... Imprinted at London, by Edm. Bollifant. 1599.] fol. A^{6+2} (-A1) B-Kk^{6} i^{4} b-g^{6} h^{8} k-o^{6} p^{4}. pp. 1-391, 3-84, 1-68. *S.T.C.* 19620. ¶*Additional t.pp.:* (i1r, *misbound before* A2) A Spanish grammar ... *Same imprint.* (h6r) Pleasant and delightfull dialogues in Spanish and English ... By Iohn Minsheu ... *Same imprint.* [356

MINTURNO, ANTONIO. Antonii Sebastiani Minturni de poeta, ... libri sex. ... Venetiis, ann. M D LIX. (... Apud Franciscum Rampazetum. ...) 4°. a^{4} A-$4B^{4}$. pp. 1-567. [357

-- Lettere ... In Vineggia appresso Girolamo Scoto. 1549 8°. $*^{8}$ A-Aa^{8} (-Aa8, *blank*). ff. 1-190. [358

MIRANDOLA, OTTAVIANO. Viridarium Illustrium Poetaꝝ ... (Venetiis ... impressum ꝑ Bernardinū de Vital' Venetū ... M.D.VII. Die .20. Nouēbris.) 4°. π^{4} a-f^{8} g^{10} a-z^{8} A-E^{8} F^{4}. ff. 1-227. [359

-- -- Illustrium poetarum flores, Per Octauianum Mirandulam collecti, et in locos communes digesti. Venetiis, Apud Gio. Baptistam Bonfadium, M D LXXXVI. 12°. A-Cc^{12} (-Cc12, *presumably blank*). ff. 2-[309]. [360

MIRROR FOR MAGISTRATES. The Seconde part of the Mirrour for Magistrates ... From the Conquest of Cæsar, vnto the commyng of Duke William the Conquerour. Imprinted by Richard Webster, ... 1578. 8°. B.L. $*^{4}$ $**^{2}$ A-Q^{4} R^{2}. ff. 1-66. *S.T.C.* 3131. ¶*Author: Thomas Blennerhasset.* [361

-- The Mirour for Magistrates ... Newly imprinted, and with the addition of diuers Tragedies enlarged. At London ... by Henry Marsh, being the assigne of Thomas Marsh. 1587. ... (*Colophon.*) 4°. $[A]^{4}$ (-[A]4, *presumably blank*) B-C^{4} A-Mm^{8}. ff. 1-272. *S.T.C.* 13445. [362

MIZAULD, ANTOINE. Antonii Mizaldi Monluciani De Arcanis Naturæ, Libelli quatuor. Editio tertia ... Lutetiae. Apud Iacobum Keruer ... 1558. 16°. A-V^{8}. ff. 2-158. (Smith.) [363

MOCCIA, PIETRO. Petri Mochii Senensis de cruciatu, exilioque Cupidinis ... dialogus. (Venetijs ꝑ Bernardinū Vitalē Veñ.) 8°. A-D^{4} E^{2}. [364

MOCENIGO, ANDREA. Andreas Mocenigus ad lectorem. ... [π1v] ... Epithalamion ... Petri Mantuani & Corneliæ Patauinæ. 4°. π^{4}. [365

-- Andreæ Mocenici P.V.D. bellum Cameracense. (Impressum Venetiis per Bernardinum Venetum de Vitalibus anno .M.D.XXV. quinto idus Augusti ...) 8°. a-z^{8} $\&^{4}$. [366

-- -- La guerra di Cambrai ... Scritta dal ... Andrea Mocenico Gentilhuomo Vinitiano. Tradotta di Latino in lingua Thoscana. In Vinegia M D XLIIII. (... per Giouanni Padoano. ...) 8°. $*^8$ A-R^8 S^4. ff. 1-140. ¶*Translator: Andrea Arrivabene.* [367

MODENA. *Laws &c.* Libri quinque statutorum inclytae ciuitatis Mutinae. Ioannes de Nicolis Mutinensis excudebat ... M.D.XLVII. fol. ♣^{6} A-YY^6 ZZ^8 3A^2 (-3A2, *presumably blank*). ff. I-CXXXX. (Lea.) [368

-- Reformationes nonnullorum statutorum ... ciuitatis Mutinae. Mutinae, Apud Paulum Gadaldinum, & Fratres. M. D. LXX. fol. A-B^4 C^6. ff. 2-14. [369

-- [1] Gride ducali prouisioni, gratie, et ragioni della citta di Modona. ... In Modona. ... (Mutinae apud Paulum Gadaldinum. M.D.DLXXV. [*sic*].) fol. ♣^{6} A-I^6 K^8. pp. 1-128. [2] Statuta salinae, et gabellarum ciuitatis Mutinae ... Mutinae. ... ♣^{6} ♣♣^{4} A-N^6 O^4 P^2. pp. 1-165. [3] Stima della gabella di Modena sopra le mercantie. In Modona. ... A-B^6 C^4. (Lea.) [370

-- Statuta et ordinationes ad publicum totius ciuitatis beneficium ... Mutinae. Apud Paulum Gadaldinum. ... fol. A-D^4 E^6. pp. 3-44. ¶*Dated 5 November 1577.* (Lea.) [371

-- Libro delle prouisioni, decreti, instromenti, gratie, ordini, ragioni, et altre cose degne di memoria per beneficio della ... citta di Modono. Ristampata di nuouo com molte additioni ... In Modona. Per Paolo Gadaldino. M. D. LXXVIII. (*Colophon.*) fol. ♣^{4} (-♣4, *presumably blank*) a-b^6 c^4 A-D^4 E-H^6 h^6 I-DD^6 dd^4 EE-KK^6 LL-MM^4. ff. 1-46, 1-30, 1-36, 1-51, 1-42. (Lea.) [372

-- Libri quinque statutorum ... ciuitatis Mutinae ... Mutinae. Apud Paulum Gadaldinum. ... M. D. XC. (*Colophon.*) fol. ♣^{6} ₵^{6} ♣♣^{2} A-T^8 V^{10}. pp. 1-324. ¶*Many margins repaired.* [373

-- Gratie concesse dal ... Don Cesare da Este, duca sesto di Ferrara, ... Alla Communità di Modona ... In Modona. Appresso Francesco Gadaldino. M.D.XCVII. ... fol. A^6. ¶*All margins repaired.* [374

-- *Collegio de' notari.* Statuta almi Collegii dominorum Notariorum ciuitatis Mutinae ... Ioannes Nicolus Mutinensis Excudebat ... M.D.XLVIIII. fol. A-C^8. ff. I-XXIII. (Lea.) [375

-- Responsa diuersorum super statutis Mutinae exclusius foeminarum ... MDXCV. fol. A-D^6 E-F^4 (-E4, *the pagination continuous notwithstanding*) A-B^6 C^4. pp. 3-59, 3-31. ¶*The t.p. is repeated on* ^{2}A1^r. [376

MODUS. Modus.vacandi.et.acceptandi.beneficiorum. [Romae, Jacobus Mazochius, c. 1510.] 4°. π^4. [377

MÖRLIN, JOACHIM. Epistolæ quædam ... ad D. Andream Osiandrum, Et Responsiones. M D LI. 8°. A-C^8. [378

MOLINO, ANTONIO. Dialogo, ouer contrasto d'amore di Messer Antonio Molino cognominato Burchiella. ... In Vinegia per Comin da Trino. M. D. XLVIII. 8°. [A]^4 B-G^4. ff. 3-28. [379

MOLINO, GIROLAMO. Rime ... In Venetia, MDLXXIII. 8°. ♣^{8} ♣♣^{8} A-D^8 E^{8+2} F-Q^8. ff. 2-121. [380

MOLITOR, ULRICH. Tractatus de lamiis et pythonicis ... anno 1489. Parisiis, Apud Ægidium Corrozet ... 1561. 8°. A-E^8. ff. 2-40. [381

MOLZA, FRANCESCO MARIA. Commento di Ser Agresto da Ficaruoloi sopra la prima ficata del Padre Siceo. (Stampata In Baldacco, per Barbagrigia da Bengodi ... Vscita fuora co'Fichi, alla prima acqua d'Agosto. l'Anno. M. D. XXXIX.) 4°. A-N^4 (-N4, *presumably blank*). ff. 2-4, pp. 5-77. [382

-- La nimpha Tiberina del Molza ... con altre sue rime. Et de altri diuersi autori ... 8° ♣^{8} A-D^8. ff. 2-40. [383

MOMBRIZIO, BONINO. [A2^r] Bonini Mōbritii ... Trenodiæ in funere ... Gal'. Marie: Sfor. &c.

(Mediolani Apud Alexandrũ Minutianũ die secundo mẽsis Martii. M.ccccciiii.) 4°. a-e^4 f^2. [384

MONDELLO, FRANCESCO. Isifile tragedia ... In Verona. Appresso Sebastiano, & Giouanni dalle Donne. M. D. LXXXII. 4°. A-E^8 F^4. pp. 8-83. [385

MONHEIM, JOHANN. Breuis et succincta Græcæ Grãmatices institutio autore Ioanne Monhemio. [Coloniae,] Excudebat Hero Alopecius. Anno M. D. XLI. 8°. A-D^8. ¶B1-4 *misbound after* B8. [386

MONNER, BASILIUS. Bedencken vonn dem kriege/ der Anno/ ꝛc. sechs/ siben/ vnd viertzig im land zů Meissen vnd Sachsen gefůrt ist ... Durch Cchristian [*sic*] Aleman/ mit einer kurtzen vorrede Christoff Cůnrads. ... Gedruckt zů Basel/ M. D. LVII. (... durch Bartholome Ståhele ...) 4°. A-H^4. [387

MONSERRAT, GUILIELMUS DE. Guillelmi de monserrat ... cõmentum sup̃ pragmatica sanctione ... (Impressꝰ Parisius in Bellouisu [per Iaonnem Marchand] Pro Iohanne Petit ... .1509. die .24. Mensis Septembris.) 8°. B.L. a-n^8 (-n8, *presumably blank*). (Yarnall.) [387a

MONSTRELET, ENGUERRAND DE. [1] Volume premier des chroniques d'Enguerran de Monstrelet ... A Paris, Chez Pierre l'Huillier ... M. D. LXXII. fol. ā^4 ē^4 ī^4 A-3H^6 A^4 B^2. ff. 1-324. [2] Volume second ... A Paris, A l'Oliuier de Pierre l'Huillier ... 1572. ... †^{8} A-Kk^6 Ll^4 A^4. ff. 1-201. ¶†2-8 *misbound before* †1. †1-2 *defective*. [3] Volume troisiesme ... *Same imprint as* [1]. ā^4 ē^6 A-TT^6 VV^4 a^6 b^4 (b4 *signed* c). ff. 1-255. [388

MONTAMAGNO, BUONACCORSO DE. Rime del Montemagno da Pistoia coetaneo del Petrarca ... In Roma per Antonio Blado ... [1559.] 8°. A-E^4. ff. 2-16. [389

MONTANO, MARCO. Rime ... In Vrbino, Appresso Domenico Frisolini ... MDLXXV. (*Colophon.*) 4°. A-I^4 k^4 L^4. ff. 2-44. [390

MONTANUS, DOMINICUS. Ein new Jar/ So Bapst Paulus der vierde ... den Lutherischen gedenckt mit zu teilen. ... M. D. LVI. 4°. A-B^4. [391

MONTANUS, PETRUS. Satyrae ... Argentorati, apud Christianum Egenolphum. An. M.D.xxix. 8°. A-B^8. [392

MONTEMAYOR, JORGE DE. Las obras de George de Monte mayor ... En Anuers. En casa de Iuan Steelsio, Año de M. D. LIIII. ... (Fue impresso ... en casa de Iuan Lacio. ...) 12°. A-Z^{12} Aa^4. ff. 1-257. [393

-- Cancionero del excellentissimo poeta George de Monte mayor ... En Salamanca, En casa de Domingo de Portonrijs ... 1571. ... (*Colophon.*) 8°. A-Y^8 Z^4. ff. 4-179. (Furness.) [394

-- Los siete libros de la Diana ... En Anuers En casa de Iuan Stelsio. Año .M.D.LXI. ... 12°. A-T^{12} V^2. ff. 1-230. [395

-- -- [1] Los siete libros de la Diana ... En Anuers. En casa de Pedro Bellero. Año 1580. 12°. A-T^{12}. ff. 2-228. ¶*T.p. defective.* [2] Segunda parte de la Diana ... En Anuers. En casa de Pedro Bellero. Año 1581. A-T^{12} V^6 (-V6, *presumably blank*). ff. 7-224. ¶*Includes the 8th book.* [396

-- -- [1] ... In Venetia, Appresso Giacomo Vincenci. 1585. 12°. A-T^{12}. ff. 2-228. [2] ... *Same imprint.* A-T^{12} V^6 (-V6, *blank*). ff. 2-228. ¶*Includes the 8th book.* [397

-- -- Diana of George of Montemayor: Translated out of Spanish into English by Bartholomew Yong of the Middle Temple Gentleman. At London, Printed by Edm. Bollifant, Impensis G. B. 1598 fol. a^4 A-Rr^6 Ss^8. pp. 1-496. *S.T.C.* 18044. (Furness.) [398

-- -- [1] La Diane de Georges de Montemaior. ... traduites d'Espagnol en François. ... A Tours, Chez Georges Drobet ... M.D.XCII. 12°. ā^6 A-P^{12}. ff. 1-170. [2] La seconde partie de la Diane ... A Tours, M. D. XCII. A-T^{12}. ff. 2-202. [3] La troisiesme partie ... *Same imprint.* A-H^{12} I^4. ff. 2-96. ¶*Translators: Nicole Colin and Gabriel Chappuys.* [399

MONTERENZI, ANNIBALE. Scholia D. Annibalis Monterentii ... ad nonnullas pactorum formulas instrumentis inserendas. Bononiae, Peregrinus Bonardus Excudebat. 1561. fol. A^8 B^6 C^4. pp. 2-33. (Lea.) [400

-- -- *Another copy.* (Lea.) [401

MONTE SANCTI SAVINI, FABIANUS. Tractatus de emptione et venditione ... Auctoribus ... Fabiano De Monte S. Sabini, & Francisco Zoannetto ... Venetiis, ad signum iurisconsulti. M D LXXV. (... Apud Bartholomæum Rubinum. ...) 8°. †-††^{8} A-Hh^8 Ii^4. pp. 1-502. [402

MONTFORT, SIMON DE. Preclara Frācorū facinora variaqȝ ipsorum certamina ... [Parisiis, 1530?] 8°. A-G^8. (Lea.) [403

MONTHOLON, JEAN DE. [1] Promptuarium Diuini iuris & vtriusqȝ humani ... a Ioanne Montholonio Eduensi ... elaboratum ... Parisiis In ædibus Henrici Stephani, 1520 fol. ℭ^6 a^{10} b-z^8 A-Z^8 aa-dd^8 ee-ff^6. ff. I-CCCCX. [2] Tomus secundus Promptuarij ... Parisiis Ex officina Henrici Stephani. 1520 (... die ante Nouēbris Calēdas septima ...) AA-ZZ^8 3a-$3s^8$ $3t^{10}$ (-3t10, *presumably blank*). ff. II-CCCXXXI. (Lea.) [403a

MONTI, SCIPIONE DE. Rime et versi in lode della ... D^{na}. Giouanna Castriota Carr. duchessa di Nocera ... Scritti in lingua Toscana, Latina, et Spagnuola Da diuersi huomini ... Et raccolti da Don Scipione de Monti. ... In Vico Equense Appresso Gioseppe Cacchi, M.D.LXXXV. (*Colophon.*) 4°. *-**^{4} A-Hh^4. pp. 2-222. [404

MONTIFALCHIUS, PETRUS JACOBUS. Petri Iacobi Montifalchii de cognominibus deorum opusculum. (Perusie in aedibus Hieronymi Francisci Chartularii Augusto mense M.IIIIIXXV. ...) 4°. A-Z^4. ff. 2-91. ¶01^r: Petri Iacobi Montifalchii de sacris celebritatibus. Y3^r: De hostiis seu victimis antiquorum. [405

MONTIGIANI, COSIMO. Trattato de l'anno del santissimo giubileo, E dell'Indulgentie della nuoua legge. ... In Fiorenza, Appresso Giorgio Marescotti. 1575. (*Colophon.*) 8°. A-D^8 E^4. pp. 3-66. (Lea.) [406

MORA, DOMENICO. Il soldato ... In Venetia appresso Gabriel Giolito di Ferrarii MDLXX. (... Per Giouan Griffio. M D LXIX.) 4°. a^8 A-Ii^4 (-Ii4, *blank*). pp. 2-254. [407

MORAES, SEBASTIÁN DE. Libro de la breue relacion de la vida y muerte ... dela princesa de Parma ... Con las annotaciones del padre ... Diego Perez ... Impresso ... MDLXXXVII. En Barcelona en casa de Hieronymo Genoues. (Impresso ... en casa de Iayme Cendrad ...) 8°. *^{8} A-X^8. ff. 1-162. ¶*Translated from the Italian by Francisco de Alvarado.* [408

MORATA, OLYMPIA FULVIA. Olympiæ Fuluiae Moratæ ... orationes, Dialogi, Epistolæ, Carmina, tam Latina quàm Græca ... Hippolytæ Taurellæ elegia ... Basileæ apud Petrum Pernam. M. D. LXII. 8°. *^{8} A-R^8 S^4. pp. 2-278. [409

-- -- Olympiæ Fuluiae Moratae ... Opera omnia ... Quibus, præter C. S. C. Epistolas selectas & orationes: ... M. Antonij Paganutij fabulæ ex Aesopo Latinè factæ, & Ioannis Boccacij quædam ex Italico. Basileae. Ex officina Petri Pernae. M. D. LXXX. 8°. *^{8} **^{4} A-Ll^8 Mm^4. pp. 1-551. [410

MORATO, FULVIO PELLEGRINO. Del significato de colori e de mazzolli. ... In Vinegia. (... per Gioanne Padoano. ... M. D. LI.) 8°. A-C^8 D^4. [411

-- Rimario de tutte le cadentie di Dante, e Petrarca ... M. D. XXXIII. (Stampato in Vinegia per Francesco di Alessandro Bindoni, & Mapheo Pasini, Compagni ... Del mese di Ottobrio.) 8°. A-C^8 D^4. [412

MORAVIA. Epistola LIIII. nobilium Morauiæ, pro defensione Iohannis Hussi, ad concilium Constantiense ... 4°. a^4 b^6. ¶a4^v: Constantiæ XVI. Calend. Ianuarias, Anno M. D. XXIIII. (Lea.) [413

MORCATI, PIETRO. Sermo habitus Tridentini Dominica quarta post Pentecostem ... Ripae, ad instantiam Baptistæ Bozolæ. M. D. LXII. 4°. A^8. (Lea.) [414

MORDECAI BEN HILLEL. ספר רב מרדכי ... [Kraków, 1589.] fol. 1-2^4 3-8^8 9^4 10^2 11-18^8 19-20^6 21-24^8 25^6 26^8 27^6. ff. ב-קפה. [415

MORE, JOHN. A table from the beginning of the world to this day. ... Printed by Iohn Legate Printer to the Vniuersitie of Cambridge. And are to be sold [by Anthony Kitson] at the signe of the Sunne in Pauls Churchyard in London. 1593. 8°. ¶^{8} (-¶1, *blank*) A-Q^8 R^4. pp. 1-237. *S.T.C.* 18074. [416

-- -- *Another copy* (-¶1, ¶8, *both blank*). [417

MORE, SIR THOMAS. Epigrammata ... Thomae Mori Britanni ... Apud ... Basileam. (... apud Ioannem Frobenium mense Decembri. Anno. M. D. XX.) 4°. a-n^4 o^6. pp. 2-115. [418

-- Doctissima D. Thomæ Mori ... Epistola, in qua respondet Literis Ioannis Pomerani ... Louanii, Ex officina Ioannis Fouleri. M.D.LXVIII. 8°. *^{4} A-G^8. ff. 2-55. (Yarnall.) [418a

MOREL, GUILLAUME. De verbis anomalis commentarius ... Parisiis, Apud viduam Guil. Morelij. 1566. 8°. A-L^8 M^{10}. pp. 3-196. [419

-- Locorum In M. T. Ciceronis partitionibus oratorijs difficiliorum explicatio ... Parisiis, Apud eundem Guilielmum Morelium ... (... Calend. Iunijs, 1549.) 4°. A-H^4 I^6. pp. 3-74. [420

-- Obseruationum Gulielmi Morelii Tilliani in M. T. Ciceronis libros quinque de finibus bonorum et malorum, commentarius. ... Parisiis, Apud Ioannem Lodoicum Tiletanum ... 1546. (... M. D. XLV.) 4°. A^4 A-Y^4 Z^6. pp. 2-171. [421

MORELLO, TEODORICO. Enchiridion ad verborum Copiam ... Ioannes Gymnicus excudebat Coloniæ, anno M. D. XXXII. 8°. *^{8} A-L^8. pp. 2-175. [422

-- -- Coloniae excudebat Martinus Gymnicus, Anno M. D. XLVI. 8°. †^{8} A-L^8. pp. 2-175. [423

MORELOT, JEAN. Discours de M. Iean Morelot ... Aux ... Gouuerneurs de la Citê Imperiale de Besanson. A Besanson, Par Iaques Foillet. cIↄ Iↄ XXCIIX. 4°. A-B^4. pp. 3-15. [424

MORETO. Moreto. 4°. A^6. ¶*Dedication dated 15 May 1543. In verse.* A2-5 *defective.* [425

MORGENSTERN, GEORG. Eine Predigt vber den Text Luce am zehenden Capitel ... M. D. LVII. (Gedruckt zu Eisleben/ durch Vrbann Kaubisch.) 4°. A-H^4. [426

MORI, ASCANIO DE. Prima parte delle nouuelle ... In Mantoua, Per Francesco Osanna M D LXXXV. ... 4°. *^{4} A-R^4 S^2. pp. 1-139. [427

MORICE, JAMES. A briefe treatise of Oathes exacted by Ordinaries and Ecclesiasticall Iudges ... [London? before 1600.] 4°. A-G^4 H^2 (-H2, *presumably blank*). pp. 3-58. *S.T.C.* 18106. (Biddle.) [428

MORIENUS. Alchimyspiegel: oder Kurtz entworffene Practick/ der gantzen Chimischen Kunst ... Alles in zweyen lustigen Gesprěchen verfasset: vnnd das erste ... auss dem Arabischen von Roberto Castrensi in latein ... in vnser Teutsche Sprach vbergesetzt/ durch Theophilum Cæsarem August. Gedruckt zu Franckfort am Meyn/ bey Christ. Egen. Seel. Erben. M. D. XCVII. 8°.):(^{8} (-):(8) A-G^8. ff. 1-56. ¶*Additional t.p.* (E8^r): Das ander Gesprěch von der kunst Alchimisterey ... M. D. XCVII. (Smith.) [429

-- Artis auriferae, quam chemiam vocant volumen secundum quod continet Morieni Romani scripta de Re Metallica, atque de Occulta ... antiquorum Medicina, cum aliȷs Authoribus ... Basileæ, Typis Conradi Vualdkirchii. cIↄ Iↄ XCIII. 8°. Aa-Zz^8 AA-KK^8 (-KK8) LL^{10} *(wanting)*. pp. 3-525. ¶*T.p. blotted. Additional authors: Bernardus Trevisensis, Arnaldus de Villanova, Roger Bacon.* (Smith.) [430

MORIGI, PAOLO. Historia dell'origine di tutte le religioni ... Raccolta dal ... Fra Paolo Moriggia Milanese ... In Venetia, appresso Pietro da Fino, M D LXIX. 8°. a^8 A-Dd^8 (-Dd8, *presumably blank*). ff. 1-216. (Lea.) [431

MORIN, NICOLAS. Tractatus Catholice eruditionis ad testimoniū & legem recurrens, confutansq3 libellum perniciosum velamine elemosine pauperibus Lugduni impense propalatū, Editione exaratus Fratris Nicolai Morini Blesensis ... Veneunt Lugduni in officina Guillermi Boulle ... (... impressus apud Ioannē Crespin al's du carre. ... Mcccccxxxij. mensis Septembris die quarto.) 8°. a-k^{8}. ff. III-LXXX. (Lea.) [432

MORING, GERARD. Vita Hadriani sexti Pontificis Maximi ... Louanij ex officina Rutgeri Rescij, Mense Nouemb. .1536. (*Colophon.*) 4°. A-M^{4} N^{6}. (Lea.) [433

MORINUS, JOHANNES. Principia grammaticalia magistri Iohānis morini (Imprimees a Rouen per Richard Goupil pour Raulin gaultier ... [c. 1512.]) 16°. B.L. π^{8}. [434

MORITZ, elector of Saxony. Hertzog Moritzen Churfürsten zu Sachssen/ *c. Lieder ... (M. D. LIII.) 8°. A^{8}. [435

MORITZ, landgrave of Hesse. Poetices methodice conformatæ Libri Duo ab ... Mauritio Hassiae Langravio &c. concinnati. ... Cassellis, Excudebat VVilhelmus VVesselius Anno 1598. 8°.)(^{8} A-F^{8}. [436

MORIZI, MARCANTONIO. Oratione di Marcantonio Moritio da Fermo ... nella morte dell' ... M. Francesco Frizimeliga Paduano ... In Venetia, [per Vincenzo Valgrisi,] MDLVIII. 4°. A^{4} B^{2}. [437

MORNAY, PHILIPPE DE. Excellent discours de la vie et de la mort. ... A Paris, Chez Thomas Perier ... M. D. LXXXIII. ... 16°. ā^{8} A-M^{8}. ff. 1-96. [438

MORONE, BERNARDINO. Liber Creationis: Distinctionis: Ornat^{9}: Quietis: *r* recreationis: Cū allegoria totius opis ... (Impressum Mediolani per Gotardum Ponticum ... Ad instantiā Ioānis Antonii de Varedeo. Die .xx. Iunii. M.CCCCCX.) fol. a^{4} A^{4} B-C^{6} D^{4} E-H^{6}. ff. I-XLIIII. [439

MORONE, GIOVANNI. Verba prolata ab ... Ioanne cardinale Morono Primo Præsidente ... concilii Tridentini, in eius prima comparitione in Generali Congragatione Die Martis XIII. Aprilis M D LXIII. Ripae Ad instantiam Ioannis Baptistæ Bozolæ. M D LXIII. 4°. A^{2}. (Lea.) [440

MORONE, GIROLAMO. Inprestanda obedientia Leoni .X. Pon. Max. pro Maximiliano Sfortia Mediolani duce ... oratio. (Impressum Mediolani per Zanottum de Castiliono.) 4°. A^{4}. [441

-- -- [Romae, Joannes Beplin, c. 1513.] 4°. A^{4}. [442

MOSCHOPULOS, MANUEL. Του σοφωτατου και λογιωτάτου Μανουήλου τοῦ Μοσχοπούλου ... Manuelis Moschopuli de ratione examinandæ orationis libellus. ... Lutetiae, Ex officina Roberti Stephani ... M. D. XLV. ... (... pridie Cal. Ian.) 4°. a-z^{4} A-I^{4} K^{6}. pp. 3-216. [443

MOSHAIM, JACOBUS DE. Orationes duæ ... ab ... Gymnasio Viennensi in susceptiōe R. Principū ac Eporum Laibacensis. Seccouiensisq3, & Tergestini. Anno .M.D.XVII. habitæ ... (Ioannes Singrenius impressit Viennæ. M.D.XIX.) 4°. A-B^{4}. ¶*Additional author: Andreas Endlich.* [444

MOTTANUS, JOANNES. Paean de Christi Resurrectione opera ... Parisiis, Ex officina Simōnis Caluarini ... 1557. 4°. A^{4}. [445

MOUCHY, ANTOINE DE. Antonii Monchiaceni Democharis ... ad patres ... Concilii Tridentini Sermo, feria sexta, die parasceues Anno 1563. nona Aprilis. Brixiae ad instantiam Io: Baptistæ Bozolæ. M. D. LXIII. 4°. A-B^{4} C^{6}. (Lea.) [446

MÜLLER, GEORG. Augspurgische handel so sich daselbsten wegen der Religion ... zugetragen. ... [Wittenberg,] Gedruckt bey Matthes Welack/ anno M. D. LXXXVI. 4°. A-T^{4} V^{2}. [447

-- Ein Christlich Psalter Gebett. ... auss den CL. Psalmen Dauids zusamen gezogen. G. M. D. Gedruckt zu Vlm/ durch Iohañ Antonij Vlhart. M.D.LXXXV. 4°. A^{4} B^{2}. [448

-- Christlicher Sendtbrieff An einen Ersamen ... Raht/ der ... Reichsstadt Cölln/ welcher hiemit ... gebeten wirdt/ der Vnderthanen daselbs/ so der Augspurgischen Confession ... zugethan ... das öffentliche exercitium Religionis ... zu zulassen ... Geschrieben von Georgio Mylio ... Gedruckt in ... Heydelberg/ durch Iohann Spies. M. D. LXXXIII. (*Colophon.*) 4°. A-D^4. pp. 3-29. [449

-- Declamatiuncula cum carmine Elegiaco & Sapphico de salutifera natiuitate seruatoris ... Autore Georgio Mylio. Adiectis ... quorundam Poëmatibus. Lipsiae excudebat Georgius Hantzsch [c. 1555]. 8°. A-D^8 E^4. [450

-- Oratio funebris de Augusto ... Saxonum Duce ... 11. Februar. 86. Dresdæ defuncto. Habita ... a Georgio Mylio Augustano ... Vitebergae Excusa typis hæredum Iohannis Cratonis, Anno M, D, LXXXVI. 4°. A-G^4. [451

-- S. Vrbans Predigt ... Wittemberg/ Gedruckt bey Matthes Welack [1586]. 4°. A-C^4. [452

-- Send vnd Trostbrieff ... an ... die Euangelische Burgerschafft in Augspurg/ vber jrem betrübten Zustande/ da jhnen jhre liebe Seelsorger vnd Prediger abgeschafft ... Wittemberg/ Gedruckt bey Matthes Welack/ M.D.LXXXVI. 4°. A-B^4 (-B4, *presumably blank*). [453

MÜLLER, TOBIAS. Kurtzer bericht/ Von der eigenschafft dieser Jare vnd vnserer gegenuertigen zeit/ auch was von dem newen Bepstischen Calender ... zu halten sey. Gestellet Durch M. Thobiam Mollerum Crimuicensem, Astronomum. Gedrucket Anno 1585 ... 4°. A-B^4. [454

MÜNSTER. Historia der belegerung vnd eroberung der Statt Münster Anno 1535. Getruckt .17. Iulij. 4°. $[A]^4$. [455

-- Newe zeyttung/ Wie die Statt Münster eroberet vnnd gewunnen worden ist/ ... den Fünff vnd zwayntzigsten Iunij/ des tausent fünff hundert vnd fünff vnd dreissigsten jar. [1535.] 4°. A^4. [456

MÜNTZER, THOMAS. Bekentnus Thomas Muntzers .../ Gescheen in der guthe dinstage nach Cantate Anno 1525 Ein Sendbrieff Thomas Müntzers an die zu Mülhausen. 4°. a^4. [457

MÜNTZER, VALENTIN. Chronographia oder Beschreybung der Jaren/ vonn anfang der Welt biss auff ... M.D.XLIX. ... (Getruckt inn ... Bernn in Vchtlandt/ Durch Mathiam Apiarium. Inn Costen ... Cyriaci Iacobi ... zů Franckfort am Meyn/ vnd volendet vff den ersten tag Martij. Im M.D.L. Jar.) 4°. A-Z^4 a-z^4 Aa-Ff^4. ff. II-CLXXXVI. [458

MUHAMMAD. I. Acta Mechmeti I Saracenorum principis natales, vitam, victorias, imperium et mortem eius ominosam complectentia. ... II. Vaticinia Seueri et Leonis ... Impp. ... Iconibus ... exornata ... per Io. Theodorum & Io. Israelem de Bry fratres. 1597 4°. $*^4$ A-G^4 H^2 I-N^4 O^2. pp. 1-96. [459

-- Machumetis Saracenorum principis, eius que successorum vitae, doctrina, ac ipse Alcoran, ... quæ ... D. Petrus Abbas Cluniacensis ... ex Arabica lingua in Latinam transferri curauit. His adiunctæ sunt confutationes multorū ... authorum ..., unà cum ... Philippi Melanchthonis præmonitione. ... Hæc omnia in unum uolumen redacta sunt, opera & studio Theodori Bibliandri ... [Basileae,] M.D.L. Mense Martio. fol. α-β^6 a-t^6 $*^4$ A-P^6 aa-nn^6 oo^4 pp-uu^6. pp. 1-227, cols. 1-358, pp. 4-235. ¶*Half-titles:* ($*1^r$) Confutationes legis Mahumeticae ... Adiecta quoq; est Lodouici Viuis Valentini ... Censura ... Item Ioannis Cantacuzeni Constantinopolitani regis ... orthodoxa assertio, ... per Rodolphum Gualtherum Tigurinum ... in latinum sermonem conuersa. ... ($aa1^r$) Historiae de Saracenorum siue Turcarum origine, ... rebus gestis ... [460

-- Mahometis Abdallæ filii theologia dialogo explicata, Hermanno Nellingaunense interprete. Alcorani epitome, Roberto Ketenense Anglo interprete. Iohannis Alberti Vuidmestadij ... Notationes falsarum impiarumq; opinionum Mahumetis ... M. D XLIII. 4°. a-p^4 q^2. [461

MUHAMMAD IBN HASANJÁN. Annales Sultanorum Othmanidarum, a Turcis sua lingua sripti [*sic*]: ... a Ioanne Gaudier dicto Spiegel, interprete Turcico Germanice translati. Ioannes Leunclauius ... Latine redditos illustrauit ... editio altera. Francofurdi, Apud Andreæ Wecheli heredes, Claudium Marnium, & Ioan. Aubrium. M D XCVI. fol. A-X^6 Y^4 A^6 B^8. pp. 3-260. [462

MUHAMMAD OF BAGHDAD. De superficierum diuisionibus liber Machometo Bagdedino ascriptus nunc primum Ioannis Dee Londinensis, & Federici Commandini Vrbinatis opera in lucem editus. Federici Commandini de eadem re libellus. Pisauri M D LXX. Apud Hieronymum Concordiam ... 4°. ♣^{4} A-H^4 I^6. pp. 2-76. [463

MUNICH. *Collegium Societatis Jesu.* Assertiones in vniuersam logicam Aristotelis, ... in Ducali Societatis Iesu Monachiensi Gymnasio ad disputandum propositæ. Præside M. Antonio Balduino ... Respondente ... Balthasaro Schellio ... Monachij excudebat Adamus Berg. Anno M. D. LXXV. 4°. A^6. [464

-- Naturalis Philosophiæ quatuor priores partes, conclusionibus explicatæ ... Præside M. Ferdinando Alber ... Respondente ... Osuualdo Stadler Monachiensi. Monachij excudebat Adamus Berg. M.D.LXXV. 4°. A^6. [465

MUNSTER, SEBASTIAN. ערוך Dictionarium Chaldaicum ... Basileae apud Io. Fro. anno M.D.XXVII. (... mense aprili.) 4°. a-z^4 A-Hh^4 Ii^6. pp. 1-434. [466

-- שילוש לשונות Dictionarium trilingue, in quo scilicet Latinis vocabulis ... respondent Græca & Hebraica ... Basileae apud Henricum Petrum mense Augusto anno M. D. XXX. (*Colophon.*) fol. A-V^6 (-V6, *presumably blank*). pp. 5-238. [467

-- עיקר הדקדוק Hebraicae grammaticæ præcipua illa pars quæ est de uerborum coniugationibus & eorum affixis ... Basileae excudebat Henricus Petrus. (... mense Augusto An. M. D. XXXVI.) 8°. a-f^8 (-a6). pp. 3-95. [468

-- משיח Messias Christianorum et Iudæorum Hebraicè & Latinè. ... Basileae apud Henricum Petrum. (... Augusto anno M. D. XXXIX.) 8°. A-K^8 א-ט^8. pp. 3-153. ¶*Half-title* (א1): הויכוח Christiani hominis cum Iudæo ... colloquiū ... (*Colophon.*) [469

MUNTANER, RAMON. Chronica, o descripcio dela fets, e hazanyes del inclyt rey Don Iaume primer Rey Darago ... En Valencia, en casa de la viuda de Ioan Mey Flandro. 1558. fol. *^{6} **^{10} A-Ii^8 (-Z-Aa^8, Gg^8, Hh-Ii^8). ff. j-CLxxvj, CxCiij-CCxxxix *present.* [470

MURET, MARC-ANTOINE. M. A. Mureti iuuenilia. ... Bardi Pomeraniæ, ex officina principis. Anno cIↃ. IↃ. XC. 8°. A-H^8 (-H8, *presumably blank*). pp. 2-126. ¶*Contents:* Tragoedia Iulius Caesar. Elegiae. Satyrae duae. Epigrammata. Epistolae tres. Odae sex. (Furness.) [471

-- M. Antonii Mureti ... oratio: habita Romæ in Funere Caroli IX. Gallorum Regis. Parisiis, Ex Officina Federici Morelli ... M. D. LXXIIII. ... 4°. A^4 B^2. [472

-- [1] M. Antonii Mureti ... orationes XXIII ... Eiusdem interpretatio quincti Ethicorum Aristotelis ad Nicomachum. Eiusdem hymni sacri, & alia quaedam poemata. Venetiis. ⅭⅠↃ D. LXXV Apud Aldum. 8°. (^{8} A-V^8 a-c^8. pp. 2-320, 2-37. [2] M. Antonii Mureti ... hymnorum sacrorum liber ... *Same imprint.* A-D^8. pp. 6-57. [473

-- -- Venetiis, Apud Ioan. Alberti. 1586. 8°. ♣^{4} A-T^8 v^8 A-C^8 D^4 a-b^8 c^6. pp. 1-320, 6-56, 1-37. [474

-- M. Antonii Mureti ... Orationum Ciceronis in Catilinā explicatio. Parisiis, Apud Robertum Coulombel ... M.D.LXXXI. ... 8°. A-N^8 O^4. ff. 2-107. [475

-- [1] M. Antonii Mureti ... orationum volumina duo ... Coloniae Agrippinae, Apud Ioannem Gymnicum ... M.D.XCII. ... 8°. †^{4} A-Q^8 R-S^4. pp. 1-272. [2] ... Orationum volumen secundum ... *Same imprint.* †^{4} Aa-Ll^8 Mm-Nn^4. pp. 1-189. [3] Caroli Sigonii ... orationes septem, quarum priores quatuor sunt pro Eloquentia. V. De Latinæ linguæ vsu Retinendo. VI. De Laudibus Historiæ. VII. De Laudibus Studiorum humanitatis. *Same imprint.* a-f^8. pp. 3-93. [476

-- M. Antonii Mureti variarum lectionum libri VIII ... Venetiis, ex officina Iordani Zilleti, M D LIX. 4°. A-Gg^4. ff. 2-99. [477

-- -- M. Antonii Mureti variarum lectionum libri XV. ... Antuerpiæ, Ex officina Christophori Plantini ... M. D. LXXX. 8°. *^{8} **^{4} A-Z^8 a-c^8 d^4. pp. 1-422. [478

-- -- Antuerpiae, Apud Christophorum Plantinum, M. D. LXXXVI. 8°. A-Z^8 a-e^8. pp. 3-325. [479

MURMELLIUS, JOANNES. Ioannis murmellij Ruremūdēsis elegiaꝝ moraliū libri quattuor ...

(Impressum ... M.d.octauo) 4°. B.L. A-B⁶ C⁴ D-G⁶ (-G3-4) H⁴. [480

-- Isagoge Ioannis Murmelii ... In decem prædicamenta Aristotelis. Parisiis, Apud Simonem Colinæum. 1538. 8°. a-c⁸. ff. 2-24. [481

-- Pappa noua ... Supaddita est etiā forma declinādi p̱ primā cōiugationē ... Ex opere grammatico Iacobi Montani Spirensis (Excusum ad iustū auctoris exēplar Colonie, in ędib⁹ Quētelianis ... M.ccccc.xxi.) 4°. B.L. A-F⁶·⁴ G⁴. [482

-- Scoparius Ioannis Murmellij. in barbariei propugnatores: & osores humanitatis, ex diuersis illustrium virorū scriptis ... (Impressum ... Colonie in edib⁹ Quentelianis. Anno .M.CCCCC.xviij.) 4°. B.L. A⁶ B-E⁶·⁴. [483

-- Tabulae Ioannis Murmellii ... in artis componendorum versuum Rudimenta. ... Coloniae Excudebat Petrus Horst. Anno 1558. 8°. A-C⁸. [484

MURNER, THOMAS. Thomas Murner de augustiniana hieronymianaqꝫ reformatione poetarum. (Impressum Argentine [per Martinum Flach] ... M.D.IX.) 4°. a⁸ b-c⁴ d⁸ e-g⁴ h-i⁸. ff. II-XLV. [485

-- Von Doctor Martin⁹ luters lerē vnd predigen. Das sie argwenig seint/ vn̄ nit gentzlich glaubwirdig zů halten. ([Strassburg, Johann Grüninger,] Tausent CCCCC. vn̄ .xx. Vff sant Katherinē abent getruckt ...) 4°. A-D⁴ E⁶. [486

MUSCULUS, ANDREAS. Vnderrichtung/ Vom Wucher/ Geitz vnnd Reichthumb. Item/ von Christlichem vnd Gottseligem gebrauch/ der zeitlichen Gütter ... M. D. LXXXVIII. (Getruckt zu Tübingen/ bey Alexander Hock ...) 8°. A-E⁸. pp. 7-70. [487

-- Vom Hosen Teuffel. Gedruckt zu Franckfurt an der Oder/ durch Iohan. Eichorn/ anno. M.D.LVI. 4°. A-E⁴. [488

MUSLER, JOHANN. Von schůlzuchte. ... (Gedruckt zů Nůrmberg bey Georg Wachter. M.D.XXIX.) 8°. A-F⁸ G⁴ H⁸. [489

MUTIUS, HULDREICH. De Germanorum prima origine, moribus, institutis ... libri Chronici XXXI ex probatioribus Germanicis scriptoribus in Latinam linguam tralati. ... Basileae apud Henricum Petrum. (... mense Augusto. Anno M.D.XXXIX.) fol. A-D⁴ a-z⁴ A-X⁴ Y⁶. pp. 1-363. [490

MUZI, GIOVANNI BATTISTA. Della cognitione di se stesso dialogi ... In Fiorenza Nelle Case di Filippo Giunti. Nel'An. MDXCV. (*Colophon.*) 4°. +⁴ A-Aa⁴ (-Aa1) Bb⁶. pp. 1-190. [491

MUZIO, GIROLAMO. Battaglie di Hieronimo Mutio Giustinopolitano, Per diffesa dell' Italica lingua ... In Vinegia, Appresso Pietro Dusinelli. 1582. 8°. *¹² A-Dd⁸. ff. 1-216. [492

-- Difesa del Mutio Iustinopolitano. Della messa. De' santi. Del papato. Contra le bestemmie di Pietro Vireto. ... In Pesaro, Appresso gli Heredi del Cesano del M.D.LXVIII. ... 8°. ✤⁸ A-DD⁸ (-DD8, *presumably blank*). p. 1-402. [493

-- Il duello. ... In Vinegia appresso Gabriel Giolito de Ferrari e fratelli. MDLI. (*Colophon.*) 8°. A-P⁸ (-P8, *presumably blank*). ff. 2-119. [494

-- Egloghe ... In Vinegia appresso Gabriel Giolito de Ferrari e fratelli. MDL. (*Colophon.*) 8°. A-Q⁸. ff. 2-128. [495

-- Il gentilhuomo ... In Venetia, Appresso gli Heredi di Luigi Valuassori, & Gio. Domenico Micheli. M. D. LXXV. 4°. (⁴ ((⁴ A-Nn⁴. pp. 2-286. [496

-- Lettere ... In Firenze, Nella Stamperia di Bartholommeo Sermartelli. MDLXXXX. 4°. *⁴ A-P⁸ Q⁶. pp. 1-252. ¶A4 *misbound after* A2, A6 *after* A3. [497

-- Le mentite Ochiniane ... In Vinegia appresso Gabriel Giolito de Ferrari e fratelli. MDLI. (*Colophon.*) 8°. A-Z⁸ AA⁴. ff. 4-185. [498

-- -- *Variant with colophon dated* MDLII. [499

-- La poluere del Mutio. (In Milano Imprimeuano i fratelli da Meda. 1564.) 8°. A-F⁸ G⁴. ff. 2-52. [500

-- Le Vergeriane ... Discorso se si conuenga ragunar concilio. ... In Vinegia appresso

Gabriel Giolito de Ferrari e fratelli. M D L. (*Colophon.*) 8°. A-DD^8 EE^4. ff. 2-218. [501

MYLIUS, JOANNES. Poēmata Ioannis Mylii. L[ib]enrodensis ... M. D. LXVIII. 8°. A-Z^8 a-s^8 (-s8, *presumably blank*). ¶A1 *defective.* [502

N

NABOTH, ALEXIUS. Für die deudsche Kirche. Von vnterscheid des Gesetzes vnd Euangelij/ beider Testamenten vnd Pfingsten/ Vnd von der Rechtfertigung für Gott/ vnd heiligung des Menschen. ... Gedruckt zu Wittemberg/ Durch Veit Creutzer. 1549. 4°. A-N⁴. [1

NACHTIGALL, OTMAR. Allegoriae Psalmorum Dauidis ... ab Ottomaro Luscinio, Argentino ... tractatæ. ... Plectra in singulos Psalmos ... Apud ... Augustam. M. D. XXIIII. (Excusum ... per Sympertū Rŭf, impendijs ... Sigismundi Grimm ...) 8°. a-e⁸ f⁶ A² B-K⁸ A-I⁸. ¶*Additional t.p.* (²A1ʳ): Psalterium Dauidis ... è Græco & Hebraicis dialectis, ab Ottomaro Luscinio Argentino latinitati redditum. [2

-- Collectanea sacrosancta, grȩce discere cupientibus non aspernanda. ... *Greek and Latin.* Ioannes Schottus Argentineñ. prȩlo literario excussit. 1515. 4°. a-d⁴. [3

-- Grunnius sophista siue pelagus humanæ miseriæ, Ottomari Luscinij Argentini ... M. Grunnij Corocottæ Testamentum. (Argentinae apud Ioannem Knoblouchum, mense Decembri. Anno, M.D.XXII.) 8°. A-G⁸ H⁴. ff. 2-59. [4

-- Ioci ac sales mire festiui, ab Ottomaro Luscinio Argentino partim selecti ..., partim ... uisi & auditi ... (Excusi sunt ... typis Symperti Ruff, ... Impensa uero D. Sigismundi Grimmij Medici, Augustæ Vindelicorū. Idibus Februarij. ... D.M.XXIIII.) 8°. A-O⁸. [5

-- Graece et Latine. Moralia quaedam instituta, ex uarijs authoribus. Cato noster, Maximo planude græco interprete. Aurea carmina Pythagoræ. Phocylidis poema exhortatorium. Senarij morales ... Cebetis Tabula. ... (Augustae Vindelicorum, per Simpertum ruff, Expensis D. Sigismundi Grim, mense Decembri ... 1523.) 8°. A-T⁸ V⁴ X⁸. [6

-- Senarii Graecanici Quingenti ... Singuli moralē quandā sententiā ... ferētes, Othmaro Nactgall Argentino, Metaphraste. ... *Greek and Latin.* Ioannes Knoblouch notis æreis excepit Argentoraci [1515]. 4°. a-b⁶ c-d⁴ e⁶. pp. 5-49. [7

NANCEL, NICOLAS DE. Nic. Nancelii Trachyeni Nouiodunensis αὐτοσχέδια, in Ioannis Despauterii Niniuitæ Quantitatem syllabarum ... Parisiis, Apud Dionysium Du-Val ... 1579. ... 4°. ã⁴ ẽ² A-K⁴ L². pp. 1-84. [8

NANI MIRABELLI, DOMENICO. Polyanthea Opus ... floribus exornatum compositum ... Anno 1507 Venetijs (... arte ⁊ impensis Petri Liechtenstein Coloniensis Germani. ... die .17. Februarij.) fol. a-z⁸ A-C⁸ D-E⁶ F⁸ (-F8, *presumably blank*). ff. I-CCXIX. [9

-- -- Anno M.D.XII. Basileae. (... in officina libraria Adæ Petri de langendorff ... Mense Augusto: ... Sumptu Leonhardi Alantsæi & Lucæ fratrū: ciuitatis Viennensis ciuium.) fol. *Same collation and foliation.* ¶F2-7, a8 *misbound after* a1. [10

NANNI, GIOVANNI. Antiquitatū variarū volumina .XVII. A ... Io. Annio ... Vȩnundātur ab Ioanne Paruo ⁊ Iodoco Badio. (Impressæ rersus opera Ascensiana ad .X. Kalendas Octob. ... M.D.XV.) fol. a⁶ a-t⁸ v-x⁶ y⁸ (-y8, *presumably blank*). ff. I-CLXXI. [11

NANNINCK, PIETER. Petri Nannii Alcmariani in P. Virgilii Maronis bucolica commentaria ... Basileae, per Ioannem Oporinum. (... M. D. LIX. Mense Februario.) 8°. a-t⁸. pp. 4-288. [12

NANNINI, REMIGIO. Orationi in materia ciuile, e criminale, tratte da gli historici Greci, e Latini, ... raccolte, e tradotte per M. Remigio Fiorentino. ... In Vinegia appresso Gabriel Giolito de' Ferrari. M D LXI. 4°. *⁸ A-FF⁸ GG¹⁰. pp. 1-483. [13

-- Orationi militari, raccolte per M. Remigio Fiorentino, da tutti gli historici Greci, e Latini ... In Vinegia, alla Insegna della Concordia. M D LXXXV. (... Appresso Gio. Antonio Bertano. ...) 4°. a-b⁸ c⁴ A-3Q⁸ 3R⁶. pp. 2-1004. [14

-- Rime di M. Remigio Fiorentino ... M D XLVII. (Stampate in Vinegia per Francesco Bindoni & Mapheo Pasini compagni, il mese di Giugno. ...) 8°. A-E⁸. ff. 2-38. [15

NAOGEORGUS, THOMAS. [1] De dissidiis componendis ... Libri II. ... Adiuncta est etiam Satyra ... in Ioannem Del'la Casa ... Basileae. 1559. 8°. a-h⁸. pp. 4-123. [2] In catalogum Hæreticorum nuper Romæ editum, Thomae Naogeorgi Satyra. ... Anno 1559. a-b^8 c^4. pp. 2-39. [16

-- Hamanus tragoedia noua ... Anno M. D. XLIII. mense Aprili. (Lipsiae. Ex officina typograpgica ... Michaēlis Blum. ...) 8°. A-H^8. [17

-- Hieremias. Tragoedia noua ... Basileæ [1551]. 8°. *^{8} A^2 B-N^8 O^2. [18

-- Incendia seu Pyrgopolinices tragoedia ... VVitebergae [Georgius Rhau]. M. D. XLI. 8°. A-G^8. ff. 2-53. [19

-- Regnum Papisticum. ... [Basileae, Joannes Oporinus,] 1553. Mense Iunio. 8°. a-l^8. pp. 4-171. ¶*In verse.* [20

-- Satyrarum libri quinque priores: ... His sunt adiuncti, de Animi tranquillitate duo libelli: unus Plutarchi, latinus ab eodē factus: alter Senecę ... Basileae, per Ioannem Oporinum. (... M.D.LV. Mense Iulio.) 8°. a-t^8 (-t8, *presumably blank*). pp. 4-300. [21

-- Tragoedia alia noua Mercator, seu iudicium ... Anno LX. 8°. A-H^8 I^4. [22

-- Tragoedia noua Pammachius ... Excusum Vitebergæ, Typis Ioannis Luft Anno .M.D.XXXVIII. Tertio Idus Maij 8°. A-L^8. [23

-- Ein Christlich/ vnd gantz lustig Spiel/ Darinn des Antichristischen Bapstthumbs/ Theufflische lehr ... dargeben wird ... aus dem Latein ... inn deudsche Reim versetzt durch Ioan Tyrolff zu Cala an der Saal. ... (Gedruckt zu Zwickaw/ durch Wolffgang Meyerpeck.) 8°. A-N^8 O^4. [24

NAPIER, JOHN. A plaine discouery of the whole Reuelation of Saint Iohn ... Set foorth by Iohn Napier L. of Marchistoun younger. Whereunto are annexed certaine Oracles of Sibylla, agreeing with the Reuelation ... Edinburgh printed by Robert Walde-graue ... 1593. ... 4°. A-S^8 (-A1, *presumably blank*) T^4. pp. 1-269. *S.T.C.* 18354. [25

NAPLES. *Laws &c.* Pragmatice regni noue et antique ... Neapoli. Apud Ioannem Paulum Suganappum. ... (... excudebat Ioannes Sultzbachius. Anno. M. D. XXXXIIII.) fol. B.L. 3A-3E^6 3F^4. ff. 1-33. (Lea.) [26

-- Consuetudines Neapolitanae, vna cum nouis additionibus Felicis de Rubeis, Vincentij de Franchis, Iacobi Anelli de Bottis, ... Atque Thomæ Nauclerij ... Venetiis, Apud Petrum Dusinellum, sumptibus Nicolai de Bottis. M D LXXXVIII. fol. †^{6} a-b^8 ♣^{6} A-OO^6. pp. 1*-12[*], 1-396, ff. 2-24. (Lea.) [27

-- Priuilegii, et capitoli, con altre gratie Concesse alla ... Città di Napoli, & Regno per li ... Rî di Casa de Aragona ... In Venetia, Per Pietro Dusinelli, Ad instantia di Nicolò de Bottis, M D LXXXVIII. fol. †^{6} ††^{4} A-Z^8 (-Z8, *presumably blank*). ff. 2-183. (Lea.) [28

-- -- *Another copy.* (Lea.) [29

-- *Juan de Zúñiga, conde de Miranda, viceroy.* Banno et comandamento ... [Order fixing taxes for those who leave the city during the summer, dated 24 December 1587.] Impress. Neap. Apud Hęredes Matthiæ Cancer. 1588. s.sh. 31 × 21 cm. (Lea.) [30

-- Philippus Dei gratia rex etc. ... [Proclamation setting forth a petition to the king, dated 13 January 1588.] Neapoli Apud Hęredes Matthię Cancer. M.D.LXXXVIII. fol. π^2. (Lea.) [31

-- Banno et comandamento ... [Order forbidding the hoarding of foodstuffs, dated 17 June 1588.] Impress. Neap. Apud Hæredes Matthiæ Cancer. 1588. s.sh. 31 × 21 cm. (Lea.) [32

-- Banno et comandamento ... [Order requiring any one storing grain to report it, dated 20 July 1588.] Impress. Neap. Apud Hæredes Matthię Cancer. 1588. s.sh. 31 × 21 cm. (Lea.) [33

-- *Consiglio di stato.* Decisiones sacri regii consilii Neapolitani, Ab ... I.C. Clarissimis ... collecta, Matthæo de Afflictis, Antonio Capycio, Thoma Grammatico. ... Venetiis, apud Hieronymum Scotum M D LXXII. (*Colophon.*) 4°. a-m^8 A-4R^8. pp. 1-1375. (Lea.) [34

-- -- Decisiones sacri regii consilii Neapolitani, per ... Matthaeum de Afflictis ... collectae. Iis Cęsaris Vrsilli ... Adnotationibus ... illustratę ... Venetiis, Ad Signum Concordiæ, M D LXXXIIII. (... Apud Ioan. Antonium Bertanum.) fol. a-c^6 D-G^6 A-3M^6 3N^4

(-3N4, *presumably blank*). ff. 2-351. (Lea.) [35

-- *Diocese.* Constitutiones, et declarationes quaedam apostolicae super reformatione, et ... Tridentini Concilij decretis editę ... Neapoli. Apud Io. de Boy. 1567. 4°. A-N^4 (-N4, *presuamably blank*). (Lea.) [36

-- Decreta synodi dioeces. Neapolitanae celebratae ... quarta Kal. Ian. M.D.LXVII. Neapoli Apud Io. de Boy. 1568. 4°. A-B^4. pp. 3-16. (Lea.) [37

-- Acta et decreta synodi Neapolitanae Neapoli MDLXVIII. Impensis Anelli Sanuiti. Vænundantur Apud Antonium Baccolum. ... 4°. †-††^{4} 3†^{2} A-Y^4 Z^6 Aa-Dd^4. pp. 1-214. ¶*Sig.* 3† *misbound before* ††. (Lea.) [38

NARDI, JACOPO. Comedia di amicitia [Firenze, Gian Stephano di Carlo da Pavia, c. 1510.] 4°. a-b^8 c^4. [39

-- Le storie della citta di Firenze ... In Firenze MDLXXXIIII. Nella Stamperia di Bartolommeo Sermartelli. ... 4°. a^8 A-Bb^8 Cc^4. pp. 1-390. (Lea.) [40

-- Vita d'Antonio Giacomini Tebalducci Malespini. In Fiorenza Ne le Case de Sermartelli ... 1597. ... 4°. a^4 A-I^4 K^6. pp. 1-77. [41

NARR. Der gůt frum Lutherisch Pfaffen narr hayss ich Der mich kaufft der lesse mich. 4°. A^4. [42

NARRATIONES. Herein is conteined the booke called Nouæ Narrationes, the booke called Articuli ad Nouas Narrationes, and the booke of diuersitees of courtes. ... 1561. In aedibus Richardi Tottell. ... (... the firste daye of Aprill. ...) 8°. B.L. A-P^8. ff. 2-120. *S.T.C.* 18363. (Biddle.) [43

NAS, JOHANN. Angelus Paræneticus contra solam fidem delegatus: Das ist/ Der Warnungs Engel/ wider den Solen Glauben aussgesandt ... Getruckt zu Engelstatt/ Anno M. D. LXXXVIII. (Getruckt zu Ingolstatt/ durch Wolffgang Eder. ...) 4°. A-Ee^4 (-Dd2-3, Ee4, *the last presumably blank*). pp. 1-201. [44

-- ἀντιπράξεις τῶν ἀστρολόγων, Das ist/ Die vnfelig gewisest Practica practicarum, auff das yetzig vnd nachfolgende jar ... Ionas Philosognysius practicierts. (Getruckt zů Ingolstatt.) 4°. A-G^4. [45

-- Concordia Alter vnnd newer/ guter/ auch bőser Glaubens ... Anno M. D. LXXXIII. (Getruckt zu Műnchen/ bey Adam Berg. ...) 4°. *^{4} (:)^4 ✠^{2} A-3S^4 3T^2. ff. 1-257. [46

-- -- *Another issue.* Ananeosis. Vieler Wunderbarlichen Religions Hǎndel beschreibung ... [Műnchen, Adam Berg,] M.D.LXXXVIII. 4°. (:)^4 A-3S^4 3T^2. ff. 1-257. [47

-- Examen Chartaceæ Lutheranorum Concordiæ, Das ist/ die Aussmusterung vnnd Widerlegung dess Nagelnewgeschmidten Concordi Buchs ... Doctor Iacob Andre ... Ingolstatt. Anno cIↃ. IↃ. LXXXI. (... In der WeyssenHorrnischen Truckerey/ bey Wolffgang Eder ...) 4°. A-3G^4. pp. 1-421. [48

-- -- *Another copy.* [49

-- Noua nouorum: ... Das ist/ Allenthalbische Newezeittung/ von der Bergischen Vǎtter newangestellten concordien ... Anno M. D. LXXXI. 4°. A-G^4. [50

-- -- Noua, supra noua nouorum ... Anno [1581]. 4°. A-X^4. [51

-- Præludium In Centurias hominum, sola fide perditorum: Das ist/ Newer Zeittung Vorgang/ vnd lengerwarter Enderung/ von der grossen Gloggen zu Erfurdt ... Anno. M.D.LXXXVIII. (Getruckt zu Ingolstatt/ durch Wolfgang Eder. ...) 4°. A-H^4. pp. 1-52. [52

-- Schaw Leser diese Bilder an/ Vnd dich darbey selbsten gemahn/ Wass massn Ecclesia militans, Heu clamet parturiens ... [c. 1588.] s.sh. 64.5 × 38.5 cm. ¶*Defective.* [53

-- Widereinwarnung/ An alle frōme Teutschē Ein Vermanung/ Auff dass sie sich/ vor denen vnlǎngst widerauffgerichten Abgőttereyen vnnd Missbrǎuchen/ hůten ... Ingolstatt/ 1577. (Gedruckt ... durch Alexander Weyssenhorn vnd andere seine Miterben. ...) 8°. A-T^8 V^4. pp. 1-297. [54

-- -- *Another copy.* [55

-- Zwölff Wolgegründter Predig/ von der ... Sacrament des Altars ... Getruckt zů Ingolstatt durch Alexander Weissenhorn. M.D.LXVIII. (*Colophon.*) 8°. A-Z^8 a-s^8. ff. 2-327. [56

-- Von Bruder Iohan Nasen Esel vnd seinem rechten Tittel F.I.N.S.A.C. oder/ F.I.N.S.C.E. ... G. N B. 4°. A-H^4. ¶*In verse.* [57

NATTA, GIORGIO. Trac. dñi Geor. nate Astēsis ð statu. exclu. femĩas a succes. (impressum Ast per me Franciscū Syluaȝ Anno M.cccccxviij. die .xxvj. Aprilis. Impensa ... Alberti Bruni ⁊ Balthasaris de Gabiano ciuiū Ast.) fol. B.L. 3a-3e^6 3f-3g^4. ff. I-XXXVII. (Biddle.) [58

NATTA, MARCANTONIO. Marci Antonii Nattae Astensis orationes. ... Papiæ. Apud Franciscum Moschenium. Cal. Decembris. M.D.LII. (*Colophon.*) 4°. a^4 b-l^8. ff. 1-80. [59

NATURA BREVIUM. *French.* Natura breuium. The olde tenures. Lyttylton tenures. The new talys. The articles vppon the new talys. Diuersyte of courtes. Iustyce of peace. The chartuary. Court baron. Court of hundrede. Returna breuium. The ordynaunce for takynge of fees in the escheker. ... ([London,] Prentyd by w. Rastell ... 1534) 8°. B.L. [✦]^4 ✦✦^{4} 3✦^{6} A-V^4 a-z^4 Aa-Kk^4. pp. 2-423. *S.T.C.* 18394. (Biddle.) [60

-- Natura breuium, newly ⁊ moost trewly corrected ... (Imprinted at London ... by Wyllyam Myddylton [c. 1545] ...) 8°. B.L. A-Y^8 Z^4. ff. i-C.lxxiiii. *S.T.C.* 18396. ¶*In this copy* Z1-3 *are in duplicate.* (Biddle.) [61

-- Natura breuium in French. [Londini,] In ædibus Richardi Tottell. 1566. ... (... 1567 Ianuarij vicesimo primo. ...) 8°. B.L. A-Z^8. ff. 2-180. *S.T.C.* 18399. (Biddle.) [62

-- -- La vieux Natura breuium dernierment corr[igee] et amend' ... Londini. In ædibus Richardi Tottelli. 1580. ... 8°. B.L. A-Z^8 (-Z8). ff. 2-180. *S.T.C.* 18401. ¶A1 *defective.* (Biddle.) [63

-- *English.* Natura breuiū newly corrected in Englisshe ... (Imprynted at London ... by Wyllyam Myddylton. An. 1544.) 8°. B.L. A-X^8 AA^8 BB^4. ff. ii-C.lxxxviii. *S.T.C.* 18407. (Biddle.) [64

-- -- Natura breuium in Englishe ... (Imprinted at London ... by Richard Tottill. ... [c. 1570]) 8°. A-X^8 (-X8, *presumably blank*). ff. 2-164. *S.T.C.* 18410. (Biddle.) [65

NAUCLER, JOHANN. [1] Memorabilium omnis aetatis et omnium gentium chronici commentarii ... Adiecta Germanorum rebus Historia de Sueuorum ortu, institutis ac Imperio. Compleuit opus Nicolaus Basellius Hirsaugiensis ... Ex Tubinga Sueuiae vrbe ... fol. π^8 a-ii^6. ff. I-CLXXXXI. [2] D. Ioannis Naucleri ... chronicarum historiarum secundum volumen ... (... impensis ... Cunradi Breuning, Kiliani Veszler, & Ioannis Zuysel ciuium Tubingensis. Impressum ... opera Thomæ Anshelmi Badensis, Mense Martio, Anno M.D.XVI.) π^{14} A-N^6 O^8 P-ZZ^6 Aa-Ee^6 Ff^4 Gg^6. ff. I-CCCXVII. [66

-- -- D. Iohannis Naucleri ... chronica ... ab initio mundi vsqȝ ad ... M. CCCCC. Cum Auctario Nicolai Baselij ab ... M.D.I. in annum M.D.XIIII. Et Appendice noua ... ab anno videlicet M.D.XV. vsqȝ in annū pręsentem ... Rhapsodis partim D. Cunrado Tigemanno, partim Bartholomæo Laurente. Coloniæ ex officina Petri Quentel, ... M.D.XLIIII. mense Martio. (... pridie Idus Martias ...) fol. A*-C*^{6} a-4r^6 4s^4 (-4s4, *presumably blank*). pp. 1-1042. (Lea.) [67

NAUM, JODOCUS. Assertio sacrosancti testamenti Christi contra μυστηριομάχους ... Sigenæ Nassoviorum Ex officina Christophori Corvini. cIↄ Iↄ xcVI. 8°. A-G^8. pp. 3-109. [68

-- Testamenti Christi falsati in integrum restitutio; cuidam Vdalrico Christmanno ... opposita a Iodoco Naum Süntzheimense ... Hanouiæ Apud Guilielmum Antonium, MDXCVII. 8°. A-P^8 (-P8, *blank*). pp. 3-235. [69

NAUSEA, FRIDERICUS. Ad sacratissimum caesarem Ferdinandum ... super huius anni ... M.D.XXXI, & quolibet alio Cometa exploratio. 4°. a-c^4 d^6. pp. 6-35. [70

-- Anonymi Philalethi Eusebiani in vitas, miracula, passionesq̄ȝ Apostolorum Rhapsodiæ. ... M. D. XXXI. (Coloniæ, in ædibus Quentelianis ...) 4°. a-b^4 A-T^4 (-T4, *blank*). ff. III-LXXV. [71

-- Friderici Nauseae Biancicampiani ... Catholicarum in totius anni tam de Tempore quàm de Sanctis euangelia Postillarum & Homiliarum epitome, siue Compendium. Coloniæ ex officina Petri Quentel ... M.D.XLIII. mense Augusto. (.. Mense Septembri.) 4°. a^4 A-$3Y^4$ (-3Y4, *presumably blank*). pp. 2-540. [72

-- F. Nauseae Blancicampiano in artem poeticen, carminumque condendorum. primordia. Eiusdem syntagma de conficiendis epistolis ... (Impressum Venetiis per Gregorium de Gregoriis, Anno .M.D.XXII. die .xvi. Maii.) 8°. A-O^8 P^4. ff. 2-115. ¶P4 *mounted.* [73

-- Friderici Nauseae ... in ... Erasmum Roterodamum ... monodia. Eiusdem uita ex Beati Rhenani Epistola ad Archiepiscopum Coloniensem. Parisiis Ex officina Christiani Wecheli ... M. D. XXXVII. 8°. A-C^8. [74

-- Frederici Nauseae ... Libri Mirabilium Septem. ... Coloniae apud Petrum Quentell. Anno M. D. XXXII. 4°. $*^6$ A-T^4. ff. II-LXVI. (Lea.) [75

-- Sermones quadragesimales. ... Aeditio prima. Coloniæ, Anno M. D. XXXV. ... (... apud Petrum Quentell ... Mense Augusto.) fol. A^6 A-M^6 N-O^4 (-O4, *presumably blank*). ff. II-LXXIX. [76

NAVAGERO, ANDREA. Andreae Naugerii ... orationes duae, carminaque nonnulla. ... (Impraessum Venetiis ... Prælo Ioan. Tacuini. M. D. XXX. IIII. Id. Mart.) fol. π^2 a-b^4 c^2 d-f^4 g^2 i-k^4 l^6. ff. I-XLI. [77

-- Il viaggio fatto in Spagna, et in Francia, ... alla Cesarea Maesta di Carlo V. ... In Vinegia appresso Domenico Farri. 1563. 8°. A^4 A-H^8 I^4. ff. 1-68. [78

NAVARRE. *Henri III, king.* Erjnnerung Des Königs von Nauarren an die Königliche Mt: inn Franckreich. M.D.LXXXV. 4°. A^4. [79

-- Weytere Declaration/ oder Ercläerung: So Henricus der Khönig von Nauarra: auf der Catholischen vorgeendes Declarirn/ vnd sonst in Franckreich beschehen Protestieren ... gethon hat. ... Gedruckt ... M. D. LXXXV. 4°. A-C^4. [80

NEANDER, MICHAEL. [1] Ethice vetus et sapiens veterum Latinorum sapientum. ... Pars prima. ... Anno M. D. LXXXI. (Islebii. Imprimebat Vrbanus Gubisius) 8°. A-G^8 (-G8, *presumably blank*). ff. 1-55. [2] Ethice vetus et sapiens ... Pars altera. Islebii Vrbanus Gubisius excudebat. Anno CIↃ. IↃ. XIXC. a-c^8 D-L^8. ff. 2-88. [81

-- Græcæ linguæ erotemata ... Basileae, ex officina Oporiniana. (... M. D. LXXVI. Mense Martio.) 8°. a-z^8 A-D^8 E^{10} (E10 + *folded leaf*). pp. 4-451. [82

-- Sanctae linguæ Hebrææ Erotemata ... Basileae, per Ioannem Oporinum. 8°. a-n^8. pp. 3-208. [83

NEGRI, FRANCESCO. Erschreckliche Newe Zeitung/ so der itzige Babst Iulius 3. an zweien Christen geübt/ die er ... ermordet hat. Verdeudscht durch M. Bartholomeum Wagner ... 1551. 4°. A-C^4. [84

NEGRI, GIROLAMO. Hieronymi Nigri Veneti ... in Lazari Bonamici funere. Oratio. ... Eiusdem ad ... Franciscum Capilistium Patauinum in morte Hannibalis filij Consolatio. Veneetiis [*sic*]. M. D. LIII. 8°. A-B^4. ff. 2-8. [85

NEGRI, STEFANO. [1] Stephani Nigri ... è grȩco Authoꝝ subditoꝝ Trãslationes. uidelicet. Philostrati Icones. Pythagorȩ Carmẽ aureũ Athenȩi collectanea Musonij ... de prĩcipe optimo Isocratis ꝺ regis muneribus oꝛo. alia multa ... (Mediolani impressum ꝑ Io. de Castelliono impẽsis Andreæ Calui. ... M.ccccc.xxi. Mensis Iulij.) 4°. AA^4 A-P^4 Q^2. ff. i-lx. ¶*Additional t.p.* ($M1^r$): Cõmẽtarioli Stephani Nigri in Aurea Carmina Pythagorȩ ... [2] Opus de nimia obsoniorum appetentia ... de Musonio græco excerptum. ... (Impressum Mediolani per Io. de Castelliono ... M.D.XXI. Mensis Augusti.) 4°. A-Y^4 Z^6. ff. ij-xciij. ¶*Additional t.p.* ($R1^r$): Stephani Nigri chriȩ quinqȝ: prȩfationes tres in Homerum: ĩ pindarũ: in. T. Liuiũ ... [86

-- -- Stephani Nigri quae quidem praestare ... monimenta, nempe translationes ... Basileae excudebat Henricus Petrus. (... mense Augusto, anno M.D.XXXII.) 4°. a-c^4 A-Zz^4 AA-EE^4. pp. 1-405. ¶*Contents (the t.p. notwithstanding):* Philostrati icones, Commentarioli Stephani Nigri in aurea carmina Pythagorae, Stephani Nigri chriae quinque, Praefatio in

Homerum, Praefatio in Pindarum, Praefatio in Titum Livium, Opus de nimia obsoniorum appetentia ex Musonio, Epistola ad Marlianum. [87

NEGRO, FRANCESCO, Veneto. Frācisci nigri ... Compēdiosa Ars de Epistolis artifitiose exarandis. ... (Impressum Liptzk per Baccalariū wolffgangum Monacensem. ... M.ccccc.ij.) 4°. B.L. A-B[6] C[4] D-E[6] F[8]. [88

-- Quæ in hoc perutili opusculo continentur. Francisci Nigri ... de Grammatica libri decem ... Georgii Valle de Orthographia opusculum ... Libanii Sophistæ de componendis epistolis præceptiones ... per philelphum traductæ. (Impressum Mediolani per ... Petrum Martirem & Fratres de Mantegatiis ad impensas ... Nicolai Gorgonzolis ... M.ccccc.yii. die .xix. iulii.) 4°. a-x[8] &[8] y[8] (y1-3 *signed* a1-3) z[4]. ff. 9-i68. [89

NEGRO, MARINO. La pace comedia ... In Venetia, per Francesco Rocca ... MDLXI. (*Colophon.*) 8°. A-I[8]. ff. 3-71. [90

NELLENBURG, CHRISTOFF LADISLAUS, count of. Warhaffte verantwortung vnd grůndtlicher bericht Dess ... Herrn/ Christoff Ladisslai/ Grauen von Nellenburg ... Auff Graue Herman Adolff von Solms ... Mandat ... M. D. XC. 4°. Aa-Ee[4]. pp. 1-36. (Lea.) [91

NELLI, PIETRO. Le satire alla carlona di Messer Andrea da Bergamo. ... In Vinegia Per Pauolo Gherardo. M. D. XLVI. 8°. A-M[8] N[4]. ff. 2-100. [92

NENNA, GIOVANNI BATTISTA. Il Nennio. Nel quale si ragiona di nobilta. ... M. D. XXXXII. (Impresso in Vinegia per Andrea Vauassore detto Guadagnino & Fratelli. ...) 8°. A-M[8] (-M8, *presumably blank*). [93

NEOBAR, CONRAD. Compendiosa facilisque artis Dialecticæ ratio, in puerorum gratiam nunc primum conscripta ... Argentorati in ædibus Vuendelini Rihelij. Anno M. D. XXXVI. Mense Augusto. 8°. A-E[8]. [94

NEPOS, CORNELIUS. Aemilii Probi vitae excellentium imperatorum ... Ti. Pomponii Attici vita per Cornelium Nepotem descripta. Plutarchi liber de illustrium mulierum virtutibus. Eiusdem paralelia. (Argentorat. In Aedibus Schurerianis. Ann. M. D. VI. XII. Kal'. April'.) 4°. A[4] B-E[8] F[4] G[8] H[4] I-O[8]. [95

-- Les vies des plus grands ... capitaines, et personnages Grecs et barbares faictes par Aemylius Probus ... Et mises en Francois par B. de Girard seigneur du Haillan ... A Paris, A l'Oliuier de Pierre l'Huillier ... 1568. ... 4°. †[4] A-V[4]. pp. 1-159. ¶*Imprint defaced.* [96

-- Emillio Probo de gli huomini illustri di Grecia. Tradotto per Remigio Fiorentino. ... In Vinegia appresso Gabriel Giolito de Ferrari e fratelli. MDL. (*Colophon.*) 8°. *[4] A-H[8] I-K[4]. ff. 1-72. ¶*1 *defective.* [97

NERI, TOMMASO. Apologia ... in difesa Della Dottrina del R.P.F. Girolamo Sauonarola ... In Fiorenza appresso i Giunti. MDLXIIII. (*Colophon.*) 8°. A-P[8]. pp. 2-212. [98

NESEN, GULIELMUS. Epistola de magistris nostris Louaniensibus, quot, & quales sint, quibus debemus magistralem illam damnationem Lutherianam. [c. 1520.] 4°. A-D[4]. [99

NESER, AUGUSTIN. Ein newe Catholische Predig. Auff des Tūrcken Niderlag/ mit hůlff Gottes ... Gedruckt zu Můnchen/ bey Adam Berg. Anno M.D.LXXII. 4°. A-Q[4]. ff. II-LXIII. [100

NETHERLANDS. Ordinancie, edict, ende gebot, ... des Conincx, op tstuck vande criminele Iusticie in dese zyne Nederlanden. Tantwerpen, Ghedruct by Christoffel Plantijn ... M. D. LXX. ... 4°. A-F[4] A-B[4] C[2]. pp. 3-47, 3-19. [101

-- [1] Summari Verclærung Der billichen Vrsachen/ vvelche die Stend von disen Niderlanden bezwungen haben/ vmb sich zur gegenwehr wider den Herrn Don Iohann von Oesterreich zuuersehen ... Zu Antorff/ Durch Wilhelm Silvium ... M. D. LXXVIII ... 4°. ‡[4] (-‡3) B-I[4] I-N[4]. pp. 5-107 *present.* [2] Hernach volgen die abgeworffene oder auffgehaltene Brieff ... A-H[4]. pp. 2-63. ¶*Sigg.* C-I *of* [1] *and* C-H *of* [2] *transposed in binding.* [102

-- Kriegs Zeittung. Auss dem Niderland/ was sich ... zwischen dem ... Prinzen von

Oranigen/ ... vnd seim widersächer dem Duc de Alba mit Scharmützlen vnd einnemung der Statt Sauttroy ... verlauffen hat. M.D.LXVIII. 4°. A⁴. [103

NETTER, THOMAS. [1] Thomae VValdensis ... doctrinale antiquitatum fidei ecclesiæ catholicæ: ... in tres tomos digestum; ... Tomus Primus. Venetiis, Apud Iordanum Zilettum, M D LXXI. fol. §⁸ (+ *² *bound after* §2) §§-4§⁶ A-3B⁶ 3C⁴ (-3C4, *presumably blank*). pp. 1-581. [2] Thomae VValdensis ... doctrinalis ... Tomus Secundus. ... *Same imprint.* *⁴ **⁶ 3*⁸ A-Xx⁶ Yy⁸ (-Yy8, *presumably blank*). ff. 1-271. [3] ... Tomus Tertius. ... *Same imprint.* †⁴ ††-4†⁶ a-3d⁶ *⁶ **⁸ (-**8, *presumably blank*). ff. 1-299. ¶*1-**7: Fratris Ioannis Baptistae Rubei ... breues elucidationes pro Thoma VValdense ... (Lea.) [104

NEUFVILLE, FRANÇOIS DE. De l'origine et institution des festes et solemnitez ecclesiastiques. ... A Paris. Chez Iean Hulpeau ... M.D.LXXXII. ... 8°. ā⁸ ē⁸ ī⁶ A-O⁸ P⁶. ff. 1-116. [105

NEUMEISTER, HEINRICH. Der Päbstische Betlermantel. ... Anno 1590. 4°. A-C⁴. [106

NEVIZZANO, GIOVANNI. ... Io. de Neuizanis ... Silua nuptialis ... (... impssit in ... Ciuitate Astēsi Frāciscus de silua. Mcccccviij. in octaua parasceue.) fol. B.L. aa-dd⁶·⁴ ee⁶. ff. II-XXVI. (Biddle.) [107

-- -- Syluae nuptialis libri sex. In quibus ... materia Matrimonij, Dotium, Filiationis, Adulterij, Originis, Successionis, & Monitorialium ... discutitur ... ... Lugduni, apud Bartholomaeum Vincentium. M. D. LXXII. (Excudebat Ioannes Marcorellius ...) 8°. a-b⁸ A-Pp⁸. pp. 1-601. [108

NICANDER OF COLOPHON. Nicandri ... Theriaca & Alexipharmaca in Latinos uersus redacta, per Euricium Cordum, Medicum. ... Francofordiae Apud Christianum Egenolphum. (... M. D. XXXII.) 8°. A-E⁸. [109

NICEPHORUS CALLISTUS. [1] Nicephori Callisti Xanthopuli ... ecclesiasticæ historiæ libri decem et octo. ... opera ... Ioannis Langi ... è Græco in Latinum sermonem translati ... Adiecimus quoque ... Magni Aurelij Cassiodori Tripartitam, quam vocant, Historiam ... Parisiis, Apud Gulielmum Cauellat ... 1562. fol. ††⁶ a-z⁶ A-CC⁶. cols. 1-1174. [2] Historiae ecclesiasticae quam tripartitam vocant libri XII. ... Parisiis, Apud Ægidium Gorbinum ... 1573. A-N⁶ O⁴ P⁶ *-3*⁶. pp. 3-165. (Lea.) [110

-- -- L'histoire ecclesiastique de Nicefore fils de Calliste Xanthouplois ... traduicte ... du Latin en Francois ... A Paris, chez Michelle Guillard, veufue de Guillaume Desbois ... 1567. ... fol. †-3†⁴ *-3*⁴ a-b⁶ c-z⁴ A-Z⁴ Aa-Zz⁴ AA-ZZ⁴ AAa-ZZz⁴ AAA-GGG⁴. ff. 2-492. (Lea.) [111

NICETAS CHONIATA. [1] Historia de gl'imperatori Greci, descritta da Niceta Coniate ... Alla quale s'e' aggiunta l'historia di Niceforo Gregora ... Amendue tradotte da M. Lodouico Dolce, Et ricontrate co' testi Greci, & migliorate da M. Agostino Ferentilli. ... In Venetia appresso Gabriel Giolito di Ferrarii MDLXVIIII. 4°. *-**⁴ 3*² A-H⁸. pp. 1-127. [2] Secondo et terzo libro dell'historie ... *Same imprint.* A-B⁴ C² a-q⁸. pp. 1-254. [3] Historie di Constantinopoli, descritte da Niceforo Gregora ... *Same imprint.* *-3⁴ A-T⁸. pp. 1-302. [112

NICOLAI, JOANNES BAPTISTA. [1] Regularum iuris, tam ciuilis, quam pontificii, ex celeberrimis ... doctoribus, vtputa, Azone, Andrea Tiraquello, Antonio Corseto, Bartholomæo Socino, Benedicto Vadio, Bernardo Diazio, Claudio Batandro, Donato Fina, Damaso, Francisco Turzano, Georgio Viuienno, Henrico Rysvvichio, Iacobo Nouello Veneto, Ioanne Nicolai, Matthæo Chæriano, Petro Duenna, Pandulpho Prateio, Scipione Ianuario, & Sebastiano Medices; praeterea Bartolo, Baldo, Iasone, aliisque ... Tomi Duo. ... Opera ... Ioan. Baptistæ Nicolai ... Tomus Primus. Francofurti ad Moenum, Impensis Sigis. Feyrabendt. M. D. LXXXVI. fol.)(⁴ A-3K⁶. pp. 2-669. [2] Tomus secundus ... repurgatus, a Matthia Sasbouto ... Francofurti ad Moenum. M. D. LXXXVI. (... apud Iohannem Spies ...) A-Z⁶ a-q⁶ r-s⁴ t-z⁶ Aa-Ee⁶ Ff-Gg⁴ (-Gg4, *blank*). pp. 4-482. (Lea.) [113

NICOLAS D'ARLES. De haereticis aureus tractatus, primū nunc Ioan. Nicolai Arelatani I.V.D. opera ... in lucem missus ... Primus. D. Gondissalui Villadiegi Hispani quinq; & uiginti quæstiones amplectitur. Secundus Ioan. Nico. Arelatani quinquaginta pronunciatæ ... in corpus unum congestæ. M. D. XXXVI. [Lugduni,] Væneunt apud Vincentium Portonariū. ... 8° a-k^{8} l^{4} m-n^{8} (-n7-8, *blank*). ff. 2-83. (Lea.) [114

NICOLAUS VON DINCKELSPÜHL. Nycholai Dünckelspühel Tractatus [octo] ... 1516 (... finē ... posuit Ioannes Schottus Argeñ. 3. Kal'. Septēbris ...) fol. B.L. a^{6} (-a6) a-z^{6} A^{4} B-D^{6}. ff. 1-163. [115

NICOLAUS DE PLOVE. Tractatus sacerdotalis de sacramētis deq3 diuis officiis: et eoꝝ administrationibus. (Imp̄ssus Argētine ꝑ Marti. iu. flach. ... M.ccccc.iij.) 4°. B.L. a-q^{8}. (Lea.) [116

NICOLAUS, PETRUS. Ad S.D.D.N. Clementem VII. Opus de immortalitate animorum secundū Platonem ⁊ Aristotelem ... (Ioannes Maria ex Simonettis Cremonensis imprimebat Fauentiæ ... M. D. XXV. XIII. Cal'. Nouembris.) fol. A-N^{4} (-N4, *blank*). ff. II-LI. [117

NICOLETTI, GIULIO. Stanze spirituali ... In Vicenza, Appresso Perin Libraro, & Giorgio Greco compagni. 1585. 4°. A^{4}. [118

NICONITIUS, FRANCISCUS. [1] Francisci Niconitii ... Allegationum Prima pars. (Venetiis.) fol. B.L. A-F^{6}. ff. 2-36. ¶*Dedication dated* III. Idus Februa. M.D.XXXVI. [2] ... secunda pars. Venetiis [Aurelius Pincius,] 1548 A-B^{6} C-H^{4} H^{4}. ff. 2-40. (Biddle.) [119

NICOT, JEAN. Le grand dictionaire François-Latin ... Recueilli des obseruations de plusieurs hommes doctes, entre autres de M. Nicod ... [Genevae,] De l'imprimerie de Iacob Stoer M.D.XCIX. 4°. †^{4} a-zz^{8} Aa-Pp^{8} Qq-Rr^{4} (-Rr4, *blank*). pp. 1-990. [120

NIDER, JOHANNES. De lepra morali. ... (impressos Parisij Impensa ... Iohannis petit. Gaufridi de marnef. et Francisci regnault ... Anno dñi millesimo quingentesimo vndecimo sexto. Kal'. Iunij.) 8°. B.L. a-l^{8} (-l8, *presumably blank*). (Lea.) [121

-- Formicarius Ioannis Nyder ... Dialogus ad vitam christianam exemplo conditionum ... 1517 (sumptibus ... Io. Knoblouchi/ ⁊ Pauli Götz/ Ioānes Schott⁹ prelo suo Argentina restituit.) 4°. B.L. π^{4} a-p^{8}. ff. I-XCI. (Lea.) [122

NIFO, AGOSTINO. Augustini Niphi Medices ... de Auguriis Lib. II. ... adiecimus Ori Apollinis Niliaci de hieroglyphicis notis Lib. II. à Bernardino Vicentino latinitate donatos. Basileae apud Iohannem Heruagium, anno M. D. XXXIIII. (*Colophon.*) 8°. a-m^{8}. pp. 3-190. [123

-- Augustini Niphi ... Suessani de falsa diluuij prognosticatione ... (... .M.D.XX. mense Februarii, impressum ...) 4°. A-B^{4} C^{6}. [124

-- Augustini Niphi Suessani de Immortalitate anime. Libellus. (Venetijs impensa heredum ... Octauiani Scoti ... ac sociorum 27. Octobris. 1518) fol. B.L. [A]^{2} a-d^{6}. ff. 1-24. [125

-- Euthici Augustini Niphi Philotei Suessani de nostrarum calamitatu3 causis liber ... (Venetijs exactum ... expensis heredū ... Octauiani Scoti ... Per Bonetum Locatellum ... i505. tertio nonas Aprilis.) fol. B.L. a-e^{6} f^{4} (-f4, *presumably blank*). ff. 2-33. [126

-- Augustini Niphi Medicis ... de pulchro liber. (Romæ apud Antonium Bladum Anno .D. M.D.xxxi.) 4°. A-Z^{4} &^{4} AA-PP^{4}. ff. IIII-CLVIII. [127

-- De re aulica ad Phausinam libri duo ... (Neapoli Ioannes Antonius de caneto papiensis excudebat Anno . M . D . XXXIIII. Die . XXIIII . Iulii.) 4°. a^{4} A-H^{8} I^{4}. [128

-- Dilucidarium Augustini Niphi Suessani ... metaphysicarum disputationum, in Aristotelis Decem & quatuor libros Metaphysicorum ... Venetiis, Apud Hieronymum Scotum. MDLIX. (... MDLX.) fol. A-Z^{8}. pp. 1-363. [129

-- Augustini Eutychi Niphi ... Epitomata rethorica ludicra ... (Venetiis a Philippo pincio Mantuano. impressum. ... M.CCCCCXXI. Die xxiii. Octobris.) 8°. π^{8} a-y^{8}. ff. I-CLXXV. [130

-- Euthici Augustini Niphi philothei Suessani in Auerroys de animae beatitudine ... (Venetijs imp̄ssa mandato ⁊ expēsis heredu3 ... Octauiani Scoti ... Modoetiensis. Per p̄sbyterum

Bonetum Locatellum Bergomense3. ... 1508. Die. 23°. mēsis Decēbris.) fol. B.L. a-b^8 c^6 d^4 (-d4, *presumably blank*). ff. 2-25. [131

-- ... Augustini Niphi Suessani In duodecimu3 Metaphysices Aristotelis ⁊ Auerrois volumen ... (Venetijs impensa heredum quondam ... Octauiani Scoti ... ac sociorum. 12. Februarij. 1518) fol. B.L. A-F^6 (-F6, *presumably blank*). ff. 2-35. [132

-- Eutyci Augustini Niphi ... in librū destructio destructionum Auerrois Cōmentarij ... Eiusdem Augustini Codicillus de Sensu agente. Lugd. apud Iacobum Giunctam. M D. XLII. (... impressum per Theobaldum Paganum. ...) 8°. Aa-3V^8 3X^4. ff. 2-346. [133

-- Augustini Niphi ... Suessani in priora analytica Aristotelis commentaria ... Venetiis Apud Hieronymum Scotum. 1549. (*Colophon.*) fol. *^{6} A-Y^6 Z^8. ff. 1-140. [134

-- ... Augustini Niphi Suessani in quattuor libros de celo et mundo et Aristote. et Auero. expositio (Impressum Neapoli per Sigismundum Mayr Alemanum Anno ... Millesimoquingentesimo decimoseptimo Die uero uigesimotertio mensis Martii.) fol. π^2 A-N^8 O^{10} aa-hh^8 ii^6 Aa-Ii^8 Kk^6. ff. i-cxiii, ii-lxvi, ii-lxxviii. (Lea.) [135

-- Augustini Niphi de Medicis ... Suessani Libellus. De rege et tyranno. (Impressum Neapoli per .M. Euangelistā Papieñ: ... M.D.XXVI. Die .xxiii. Mensis Ianuarii ...) 4°. A-O^4 (-O4, *presumably blank*). [136

-- Augustini Niphi super tres libros de anima (Impressum Venetijs per Petru3 de Quarengijs Bergomensem. ... impēsis dñi Alexādri Calcidonij Pisaurieñ. M.ccccc.iij. Die .x. Maij.) fol. B.L. a^6 b^{12} c-s^6 t^4 (-t4, *presumably blank*). [137

NIGER, ANTONIUS. Primae grammatices Græcæ partis rudimenta, olim quidem per Iohannem Mecelerum edita: iam vero per Antonium Nigrum medicum locupletata ... Lipsiæ, Excudebat hæredes Georgij Defneri, M. D. LXXXVII. 8°. A-P^8. pp. 1-228. [138

NILUS AMYRANUS, S. Beatissi. patris Nili ... Sententiæ morales e græco in latinum versæ. Bilibaldo Pircheimero Norimbergensi Interprete. ... (Argentorati Ex ædibus Schurerianis, Mense Septembri Anno M. D. XVI.) 4°. A-B^4. [139

-- -- Vil schõner spruch des heyligen ... S. Nili ... Durch hern Willibaldum Pirckheymer/ aus Krichischer sprach ins Deudsch gepracht. 1536. (Gedruckt zu Nűrenberg durch Hieronimum formschneyder.) 8°. A-B^8 C^4. [140

NIZZOLIO, MARIO. Marii Nizolii Brixellensis de veris principiis et veneratione philosophandi contra pseudophilosophos, libri IIII. ... Parmae Apud Septimum Viottum. 1553. (... Mense Maij ...) 4°. *^{6} A-Yy^4 a^4 b^6. pp. 1-360. [141

-- Marii Nizolii Brixellensis obseruationes, omnia M. T. Ciceronis verba, vniuersamque Dictionem complectentes ... Nunc tandem Cælij Secundi Curionis labore ... auctus ... Basileæ. ... (... per Ioannem Heruagium, Anno M.D.LI. mense Augusto.) fol. α^6 β^4 a-z^6 A-3I^6 3K^8 3L^6. cols. 1-1904. [142

-- -- Nizolius, siue Thesaurus Ciceronianus, ... Cælij Secundi Curionis Herculeo labore ... quarta parte auctior ... Basileae, apud Ioannem Heruagium. (... M. D. LIX. Mense Martio.) fol. α^8 a-z^6 A-Zz^6 AA-YY^6 ZZ^8. cols. 1-3096. [143

-- -- Nizolius siue thesaurus Ciceronianus, Post Mar. Nizolii, Basilii Zanchi, & Caelii Secundi Curionis, ... operas, Per Marcellum Squarcialupum Plumbinensem ... digestus, & illustratus. ... [Basileae, ex officina Heruagiana, per Eusebium Episcopium 1576.] (Basileae, per Eusebium Episcopium, ... M.D.LXXVI. Mense Septembri.) fol. α^8 a-z^6 A-Rr^6. cols. 1-1498. ¶*T.p. defective.* [144

-- -- Nizolius siue thesaurus Ciceronianus Caelii Secundi Curionis labore ... auctus, Marcelli subindè Squarcialupi studio mactus digestúsque: Nunc demum à Iacobo Cellario Augustano ... locupletatus. ... Basileae ex officina Heruagiana per Eusebium Episcopium. CIↃ IↃ XXCIII. (... Mense Septembri.) fol. α^6 β^4 a-z^6 A-Qq^6 Rr^4 Tt^6. cols. 1-1538. [145

NOBILI, FLAMINIO. Flaminii Nobilii Lucensis ... De Hominis Felicitate, libri tres. De vere & falsa voluptate, libri duo. De Honore, liber unus. Marpugi, Ex officina typographica Pauli Egenolphi. cIↄ Iↄ xcvI. 8°. A-Bb^8 Cc^4. pp. 3-395. ¶*Editor: Conrad Ritterhausen.* [146

NODÉ, PIERRE. Declamation contre l'erreur execrable des maleficiers, sorciers, Enchanteurs, Magiciens, Deuins, & semblables obseruateurs des superstitions ... Plus les Articles ... condemnez à Paris par la faculté de Theologie: auec vne ... Preface faicte ... par M. Iehan Gerson ... A Paris, Chez Iean du Carroy ... 1578. ... 8°. ā^{8} ā^{2} A-E^{8} F^{4}. pp. 1-78. ¶F1, F4 *misbound between* F2 *and* F3. (Lea.) [147

NOGAROLA, ISOTTA. Isotae Nogarolae Veronensis, dialogus, quo, vtrum Adam vel Eua magis peccauerit ... Venetiis [Aldine Press], M.D.LXIII. 4°. A-E^{4}. pp. 1-34. [148

NOGAROLA, LUIGI. Ludouici Nogarolæ Comitis dialogus. Qui inscribitur Timotheus, siue de Nilo. Venetiis, Apud Vincentium Valgrysium. M D LII. (... Ioan. Gryphius excudebat. ...) 4°. a-k^{4}. ff. 2-39. [149

NONIUS MARCELLUS. Nonius Marcellus de proprietate sermonum. ... restitutus ... industria Hadriani Iunii ... Fulgentij Placiadæ libellus De prisco sermone ... Antuerpiæ, Ex officina Christophori Plantini, cIↄ. Iↄ. LXV. 8°. A-Z^{8} a-p^{8} a-b^{8} c^{4}. pp. 1-592. [150

NONNUS PANOPOLITA. Νουνου ... Διονυσιακα. Nonni Panopolitae Dionysiaca ... Cum lectionibus ... Gerarti Flakenburgij Nouiomagi ... Antuerpiæ, Ex officina Christophori Plantini. cIↄ Iↄ LXIX. 8°. ‡^{8} ‡‡^{4} A-Ω^{8} α-ω^{8} Αα-Ιι^{8} Κκ^{4}. pp. 1-899. [151

NORES, GIASONE DE. Apologia contra l'auttor del Verato di Iason de Nores ... In Padoua, M. D. XC. appresso Paolo Meietti. 4°. ¶^{4} A-N^{4}. ff. 1-52. [152

-- [1] Breue institutione dell'ottima republica: Di Iason de Nores, raccolta ... da tutta la Philosophia humana di Aristotile ... Introdutione del medesimo ridotta poi in alcune Tauole sopra i tre libri della Rhetorica d'Aristotile. ... In Venetia, appresso Paolo Megietti, M D LXXVIII. 4°. A-O^{4}. ff. 2-56. [2] Introduttione ... *Same imprint.* a-h^{4}. [153

-- Discorso di Iason Denores intorno à que' principii, cause, et accrescimenti, che la comedia, la tragedia, et il poema heroico riceuono dalla philosophia ... In Padoua, Appresso Paulo Meieto 1587. 4°. ¶^{4} A-L^{4}. ff. 1-43. [154

-- Oratione di Iason Denores al ... Principe di Venetia Sebastian Veniero, per nome di quei Gentil'huomini del Regno di Cipro, che ... si trouarono presēti nel tēpo della sua ... creatione ... In Padoua Per Lorenzo Pasquati 1578. 4°. a-c^{4} d^{2} A^{6}. ¶A1^{r}: Oratione di Giouanni Battista Bell'hauere Nella creatione del ... Prencipe di Venetia ... [155

-- Panegirico di Iason de Nores in laude della ... rep. di Venetia ... In Padoua, M.D.XC. appresso Paolo Meietti. (*Colophon.*) 4°. ¶^{4} A-K^{4}. ff. 1-40. [156

-- Poetica di Iason Denores Nella qual ... si tratta secondo l'opinion d'Arist. della Tragedia, del Poema Heroico, & della Comedia. ... In Padoua, Appresso Paulo Meietto. M.D.LXXXVIII. (*Colophon.*) 4°. ✱^{4} ††^{2} A-Qq^{4}. ff. 1-156. [157

-- Tauole di Iason Denores del mondo, et della sphera, ... introduttione a' libri di Aristotile Del Cielo, Delle Meteore, & De gli Animali. Con la spheretta del ... M. Triphon Gabriele ... In Padoua appresso Paulo Meietto MDLXXXII. 4°. π^{2} A-F^{4}. ff. 1-24. [158

NORI, GIULIO. Bellum Geminianense, eiusdem loci Iulio Norio auctore ... (Senis Apud Lucam Bonettum. 1584.) 4°. A^{4}. ¶*In verse.* [159

NORMANDY. Le grand coustumier du pays ⁊ duche de Normandie ... Aussi y est le texte en latin ... Nouuellemēt imprime a Rouen par Nicolas le roux: pour Francoys regnault ... de Paris. pour Iehan Mallard demourant a Rouen ... ⁊ pour Girard anger/ demourant a Caen ... 1539. fol. B.L. ✱^{6} a-s^{8} t^{6} v^{4} ✱^{4} A-H^{8} I^{4} K^{8} L^{6}. ff. j-clx, i-lxxxij. [160

-- Coustumes du pais de Normandie ... A Paris. Pour Martin le Mesgissier ... à Roüen ... 1586. (... Par Iean le Blanc ...) 4°. ā^{4} ē^{4} ī^{2} A-GG^{4} A-L^{4}. ff. 1-128, 1-43. [161

NOSTREDAME, JEAN DE. Le vite delli piu celebri et antichi primi poeti Prouenzali ... in lingua Franzese da Gio: di Nostra Dama poste: & hora da Gio: Giudici in Italiana tradotte ... In Lione, Appresso d'Alesandro Marsilij. L'anno M. D. LXXV. 8°. A-R^{8}. pp. 3-254. [162

NOTARIATBUCH. Notariatbůch ... Kantzleibůch ... Getruckt zu Franckenfort am Meyn/ Bei Christian Egenolffen. (M. D. XXXIIII. Im Augstmonat.) fol. $*^4$ A-R^6 S^4 (-S4, *presumably blank*). ff. I-CV. [163

NOTTURNO NAPOLITANO. Comedia noua ... intitolata gaudio d'amore. ... (Stampata in Vinegia ad instantia di Christoforo ditto Stampone. Nel M.D.XXVI. A di. yii. Genaro.) 8°. A-K^4. ff. III-XXXVIII. ¶A2 *misbound after* A3. [164

-- Opera noua ... ne la quale si contiene Epistole Capitoli Sextine Sonetti Stambotti [*sic*] [*Device of Benedetto Hectoris of Bologna.* 1520?] 12°. A^{12}. [165

NOVELLUS, JACOBUS. Practica et theorica causarum criminalium, ... per Dominum Iacobum de Nouello ... Venetiis, Petrum Bosellum excudere faciebat. M D LV. 8°. A-K^8 L^4. ff. 4-75. [166

-- Tractatus singularis Defensionem omnium reorum, quascunque accusationes & inquisitiones pro quibuscunque Criminibus instruens. ... Venetijs, ex officina Dominici Guerrei, & Io. Baptistæ fratrum. M D LXVIII. 8°. $*^4$ A-M^8 N^4. pp. 2-176. [167

-- Volumen statutorum, legum, ac iurium D. Venetorum ... Venetiis, M D LXIIII. (... Apud Cominum de Tridino Montisferrati, Anno M D LXIII.) 4°. a-d^8 (-a1, *presumably blank*) A-Cc^8 Dd^4. ff. 2-212. ¶*Additional t.p., engraved* ($A1^r$): Statuta Veneta. M D LXIIII. *Sig.* S *wrongly imposed.* (Lea.) [168

NOZZOLINI, ANNIBALE. Rime ... In Lucca [Vincenzo Busdragho] M. DLX. 4°. ✠^{4} A-Ff^4. pp. 1-232. ¶*Engraved t.p.* [169

NUCIARELLIS, HIERONYMUS DE. Contenta in Volumine per ... Hieronymum de Nuciarellis Romanū correcta ⁊ emendata. ... Passus super Vniuersalia ⁊ Predicamenta Aristotelis ... Francisci Maironis. Formalitates eiusdem ... De principio complexo eiusdem ... De terminis Theologicis eiusdem. Formalitates Petri Thome ... De secundis intentionibus Opusculum eiusdem Magistri Hieronymi. De ente ꝛ essentia Diue Thome ... Tria principia rerum naturalium Antonij Andree ... Expositio Francisci Maironis super octo libros Physicorum ... De cuiuscunqꝫ scientie subiecto magistri Cometij hispani. Questiones super libros de anima ... Ioānis Scoti. Necnō de vniuocatione entis eiusdem Francisci Maironis. (Venetijs Impensa Heredum ... Octauiani Scoti ... ac Sociorum. 3. Augusti. .1517.) fol. B.L. a-o^6. ff. 2-84. [170

NÚÑEZ, PEDRO JUAN. Apposita M. T. Ciceronis, collecta a Petro Ioanne Nunnesio Valentino ... Valentiae, Excudebat vidua Ioannis Mey. 1556. 8°. A^8 a-z^8 aA-oO^8 A-F^8 (-F8, *presumably blank*). ff. 1-296, 1-44. [171

-- Pet. Iohan. Nunnesii Valentini institutionum rhetoricarum libri quinque. Editio altera ... Barcinone ... Ex Typographia Iacobi Cendrat. An. 1585. (*Colophon.*) 8°. $*^8$ A-Hh^8. pp. 1-464. [172

NÚÑEZ DE AVENDAÑO, PEDRO. De exequendis mandatis regum Hispaniæ, quæ rectoribus ciuitatum dantur, & hodie continentur in titulo. 6. lib. 3. Recopilationis; vulgò nuncupatis Capitulos de Corregidores, prima et secunda pars. ... Item de Venatione tractatus eiusdem authoris ... Madriti, Apud Petrum Madrigal. 1593. Venundantur in ædibus Francisci Lopez. (*Colophon.*) fol. ¶^{4} A-Ll^8 Mm^6 ¶^{8} ¶¶-3¶^{6}. pp. 1-555. (Lea.) [173

NUNES DE LEÃO, DUARTE. Orthographia da lingoa Portuguesa. ... Pelo Licenciado Duarte Nunez de Lião. Em Lisboa, Per Ioão de Barreira ... M.D.LXXVI. 4°. A^4 A-I^8 K^6. ff. 1-78. [174

NÚÑEZ DE ORIA, FRANCISCO. Doctoris Francisci Nunnii ab Oria de Casaruuiis Montanis Lyræ Heroycæ libri quatuordecim. ... Salmanticæ Apud hæredes Mathię Gastij M. D. LXXXI. (*Colophon.*) 4°. ¶^{4} A-Ee^8 Ff^{8+1}. pp. 1-463. [175

NÜRNBERG. *Rat.* Ains Erbern Rats der Stat Nüremberg ... verantworttung ... gegen dem vnbewerlichen des ... Marggraf Cazimirus zu Brandenburg ausschreiben ... [c. 1520.] fol. π^{16}. [176

-- Handlunng Eynes Ersamenn weysen Rats zu Nürnberg mit jren Predicantten Newlich geschehen ꝛc. M D xxv. 4°. A-D^4. [177

-- Was eynn Erbar Rathe/ der Stadt Nürmberg/ yre Burgerschafft zu gut/ in mancherley Artickeln/ So sie sich habē beschweren mügē/ nachgelassen ... hat. Item auch von den vylfeltigen Feyertag ... [Erfurt, Melchior Sachse,] M.D.XXV. 4°. A^4 B^2. [178

-- Eynes erbarn Raths der stadt Nüremberg ordnung von hochzeyten vñ derselben wirtschafften ... [Nürnberg, Friedrich Peypus, 1526.] 8°. A^8. [179

-- Mandata oder Gesetze/ Ierlich am Ersten oder Andern Suntag inn der Vasten/ auff dem Lande zuuerkünden. Anno 1548. 4°. A-E^4 F^2 G-I^4 K^2 L-Q$^{4 \cdot 2}$. [180

-- -- Vernewte Policeyordnung/ Mandata vnd Gesetz ... Anno M. D. LXXII. (Gedruckt zu Nürmberg durch Dieterich Gerlatz.) 4°. A-M^4 N^2. [181

-- Ains Erbarn Raths der Stat Nürmberg ... Bericht/ der landfridbrüchigen Empörung/ vheindlicher thaten vnd handlungen/ so Marggraf Albrecht zu Brandenburg ꝛc. der Jüngern ... Im 1552 vnd 1553 Jaren geübt hat. ... 4°. A-O^4. ¶*Dated 5 June 1553.* [182

-- Andere ains Erbarn Raths der Stat Nürmberg warhaffte verantwortung ... vff des ... Echters vnd Landfridprechers/ Marggraf Albrechts des jüngern von Brandenburg ... lasterschriften ... M. D. LIIII. 4°. A-N^4. [183

-- [Proclamation of the council against swearing.] Decretum in Senatu 9 Aprilis. 1558. s.sh. 33 × 42 cm. [184

-- [1] Exceptiones cum insertis probationibus defensionum. Herren Burgermaister vnd Raths der Statt Nürmberg/ Contra Die Herren Marggrauen zu Brandenburg ꝛc. ... Product. Spirae 26. Novemb. Anno 1563. ... 1. fol. A-G^6 H^8. ff. 2-49. [2] Exceptiones Eines Erbarn. Raths der Statt Nürmberg/ Contra Die Herrn Marggrauen zu Brandenburg ꝛc. ... Product. Spiræ 26. Novemb. 1563. ... 2. a-e^6. ff. 2-30. [3] Exceptiones wider die intitulirte Additionales respective Elisivos prioribus additos den 20. Martij Anno 1538. producirt. Eines Erbarn Raths der Statt Nürmberg/ Contra Die Herrn Marggrauen zu Brandenburg ꝛc. ... Product. Spiræ 26. Novemb. Anno 1563. 3.)(^{8} χ^4 (-χ4, *presumably blank*). ff. 2-7. [185

-- [1] Exceptiones et respective replicæ et duplicæ: Herren Burgermaister vnd Raths der Statt Nürmberg/ Contra Herrn Marggrauen Georg Friderichen zu Brandenburg ... Product. Spiræ 3. Octob. Anno 1569. ... 1. fol. Aa-Hh^6. ff. 2-47. [2] In puncto possessorii, replicæ et respective duplicæ, Herren Burgermaister vnd Raths der Statt Nürmberg/ Contra Herrn Marggrauen Georg Friderichen zu Brandenburg ... Product. Spiræ 3. Octob. Anno 1569. ... 2. AA-PP^6 QQ^8. ff. 2-96. [3] Probationes, cum annexis Replicis & confutationibus, Herren Burgermaister vnd Raths der Statt Nürmberg/ Contra Herrn Marggrauen Georg Friderichen zu Brandenburg ... Product. Spiræ 3. Octob. Anno. 1569. 3. ... aa-cc^6 dd^4. ff. 2-21. [186

-- Conclusiones Herren Burgermaister vnd Raths der Statt Nürmberg/ Contra Marggrauen Georg Friderichen zu Brandenburg ... Product. Spiræ 9. Aprilis, Anno 1573. fol. 3a-3c^6 3d^8. ff. 2-25. [187

-- Conclusiones Herren Burgermaister vnd Raths der Statt Nürmberg/ Contra Herrn Marggrauen Georg Friderichen zu Brandenburg ... Product. Spiræ 6. Maii, Anno 1578. fol. 3A-3E^6 3F^{10}. ff. 2-38. [188

-- Eins Erbern Raths der Statt Nürmberg/ verneute Policeyordnung vnd verpot der Hoffart ... M D LXXXIII. 4°. A-D^4. [189

-- [1] Gravamina in angestellter Revision sachen/ Burgermeister vnd Raths der Statt Nürmberg/ als gewesnen Beklagten/ Contra Den ... Herrn Georg Friderichen Marggrafen zu Brandenburg ꝛc. als gewesnen Cläger. ... Product. Spiræ 8. Iunii Anno 1585. fol. A-RR^6 SS^4 TT^6. ff. 2-247. [2] Copia Etlicher Brieflicher Vrkunden vnd Beylagen/ auf welche sich in den übergebnen Grauaminibus inn angestelter Reuision sachen/ Burgermeister vnd Raths der Stat Nürmberg ... Contra Den ... Herrn Georg Friderichen Marggrauen zu Brandenburg ꝛc. ... Produ. Spiræ 8. Iunij, Anno 1585. a-r^6 s^8. ff. 2-109. [190

-- Leges ac statuta ampliss. Senatus Norimbergensis, ad Medicos, Pharmacopoeos, & alios pertinentia. ... Typis Christophori Lochneri. ... M D XCIII. fol. A^6. [191

-- *Theologians.* Epistola theologorum Norimbergensium, ad Doctorem Rupertum à Mosham, Decanum Patauiensem, ... in qua uenenata eius conuicia, mendacia, & noxia dogmata percelluntur, & ... confutantur. 4°. A-B^4. ¶*Dated 21 November 1539. Signed:* Vuenceslaus Lincus,

Andreas Osiander, Vitus Theodorus, Thomas Venatorius. [192

NUTI, GIULIO. Pie rime sopra la felice vittoria de Christiani contra il Turco. ... In Perugia. Per Valente Panizza ... M. D. LXXI. 4°. A-H^4. [193

O

OCAMPO, FLORIAN DE. [1] Los cinco libros primeros dela Cronica general de España ... Impresso en Medina del Campo por Guillermo de Millis. Año. 1553. ... fol. A-Tt^{8} Vv^{10}. ff. ij-cccxxxvj. [2] La coronica general de España. Que continuaua Ambrosio de Morales ... En Alcala de Henares, En casa de Iuan Iñiguez de Lequerica, en Setiembre, del año M. D. LXXIIII. (*Colophon.*) ✠^{6} ✠^{8} A-B^{6} C-O^{8} P^{10} Q-3F^{8} 3G^{6} 3F^{8} 3I-3K^{6}. ff. 1-418. [3] Los. autros. dos. libros. vndecimo. y. duodicimo. de. la coronica. general. de España. ... en Abril, del año M. D. LXXVII. (*Colophon.*) ()^{8} ✠^{10} 2✠^{8} A-Ee^{8} Ff^{6}. ff. ¶2-¶17, 1-225. [4] Las antiguedades de las ciudades de España. ... Que escreuia Ambrosio de Morales . ... M. D. LXXV. (... M. D. LXXVII.) π^{2} ¶^{4} A-P^{8} Q-R^{6}. ff. 1-131. [5] Los cinco libros postreros de la coronica general de España. ... Impresso en Cordoua por Gabriel Ramos Bejarano ... 1586. A costa de Francisco Roberte ... (*Colophon.*) §^{6} 2§^{8} A-Vv^{8} Xx^{6}. ff. 1-350. [1

OCHINO, BERNARDINO. Ain Gesprech/ der flaischlichen vernunfft ... verteütscht. ... (Getruckt zů Augspurg/ durch Philipp Vlhart.) 4°. A-B^{4} C^{2} D^{4} (-D4, *presumably blank*). [2

-- [1] Prediche di Bernardino Ochino da Siena. ... [Basel, c. 1545.] 8°. a-z^{8} A-D^{8}. [2] La seconda parte delle prediche ... aa-zz^{8} AA-KK^{8}. [3] La terza parte ... Aaa-Zzz^{8} AAa-LLl^{8}. [4] La quarta parte ... 4A-4Y^{8}. (Yarnall.) [2a

OCHOA DE LA SALDE, JUAN. Primera parte de la Carolea inchiridion, que trata dela Vida y Hechos del ... Don Carlos Quinto ... M.D.LXXXV. ... (Fue impressa ... a costa de su mismo Author, en su propria posada, en Lisboa, por Marcos Borges, Antonio Ribero, e Anton Aluarez ... Acabose a los xx. del mes de Deziembre ...) fol. a^{6} A-3H^{8} 3I^{12} 3K^{8} (-3K8, *presumably blank*). ff. 1-444. [3

OCKHAM, WILLIAM. Venerabilis inceptoris fratris Gulielmi de villa Hocchã Anglie: ... Summule in lib. Physicorum adsunt. (Impresseq3 Venetijs per Lazarum de Soardis, Anno. 1506. Die. 17. Augusti.) 4°. B.L. π^{2} A-D^{8}. ff. 1-32. [4

OCLAND, CHRISTOPHER. Anglorum prælia ab anno Domini .1327. ... vsque ad annũ Domini .1558. Carmine summatim perstricta. Item De pacatissimo Angliæ statu, imperante Elizabetha, ... Narratio. ... Londini: Apud Radulphum Nuberie, ex assignatione Henrici Bynneman ... 1582. ... 8°. A^{4} B-T^{8} V^{4}. pp. 2-63. ¶*Additional t.pp.:* (I5^{v}) Ειρηναρχια Siue Elizabetha. De pacatissimo Angliæ statu ... *Same imprint.* (N1^{r}) Alexandri Neuilli Kettus ... Liber vnus. Londini, Ex officina Henrici Binnemani ... 1582. ... *S.T.C.* 18773. [5

ODDI, SFORZA DEGLI. I morti viui comedia ... In Venetia, Appresso Gio. Battista Sessa, e fratelli. M D LXXXII. (*Colophon.*) 12°. A-H^{12} (-H12, *presumably blank*). ff. 7-93. [6

-- Prigione d'Amore commedia ... In Fiorenza, per Filippo Giunti. MDXCII. ... (*Colophon.*) 8°. A-K^{8}. pp. 1-143. [7

ODO MAGDUNENSIS. Aemilius Macer de herbarum virtutibus, cum Ioannis Atrociani cõmentarijs ... Strabi Galli ... Hortulus uernantissimus. Apud Friburgum Brisgoicum. (... apud Ioannem Fabrum Emmeum Iuliacensem. M.D.XXX.) 8°. a^{4} A-N^{8} O^{4}. ff. 1-108. [8

-- Macri de materia medica lib. V. versibus conscripti. Per Ianum Cornarium ... emendati ac annotati ... Franc. Chr. Ege. (... M. D. XL.) 8°. a^{8} b^{4} A-Q^{8} R^{4}. ff. 1-232. [9

ODOFREDO DA BOLOGNA. [Commentaria in digestum.] (Iacobus Saccon ... absoluebat ... Lugduni sumptibus ... Vincẽtij de portonarijs ... 1519. ...) fol. B.L. [1] Egregia ... commentaria ... in primam .ff. veteris partem ... domini Odoffredi ... (... die vltima Ianuarij.) a-z^{8} A-M^{8} N-P^{6} A-C^{6}. ff. 2-297. [2] Aurea ... lectura ... super secunda parte digesti veteris ... (... die .ix. decẽbris ...) aa-zz^{8} ꝛꝛ^{8}. ff. 2-192. (Biddle.) [10

ODONI, RINALDO. Discorso di Rinaldo Odoni, per uia Peripatetica, oue si dimostra, se l'anima, secondo Aristotele, e mortale, o immortale. In Venetia, [Aldine Press,] M. D. LVII. 4°. A-K^{4}. ff. II-XXXVI. [11

OECOLAMPADIUS, JOANNES. De non habendo pauperum delectu, ... Epistola utilissima. Basileae, [per Andream Cratandrum,] Anno M. D. XXIII. 4°. a-c4. [12

-- Ioh. Oecolampadii dialogus, quo Patrum sententiam de Coena Domini bona fide explanat. Huldrichi Zuinglii Confessio Fidei ad Carolum V. Imp. Philippi Melanchthonis iudicium de controuersia Coenę Domini ... Ioh. Iacobi Grynaei Exomologesis ad Deum Opt. Max. Basileæ Typis Conradi Vualdkirchii. M. D. XC. 8°.):(8 a-s8. pp. 3-288. [13

-- In epistolam Ioannis apostoli Catholicam primam, ... demegoriæ, hoc est homiliæ una & XX. Basileae apud Andream Cratandrum, an. M. D. XXIIII. mense Iunio.) 8°. a-m8 n4. ff. 2-99. [14

-- Oecolāpadij iudiciū de doctore Martino Luthero. [Leipzig, Valentin Schumann, 1520.] 4°. A4 (-A4, *presumably blank*). [15

-- Ain schȯ̈ne Epistel ... an Caspar Hedion/ das es zymlich/ nutz/ vn̄ gůt sey/ das die Epistel vn̄ das Euangelium in dem ampt der Mess/ in teūtscher sprach ... gelesen vnd verkündet werd durch Iohañem diepolt zů Vlm verteūtscht. [Augsburg, Sigmund Grim, 1522.] 4°. A-D4. [16

-- Ain Sermon ... von dem verss im Magnificat. Exultauit spiritus meus ... [Augsburg, Sigmund Grim & Marcus Wirsung, 1520.] 4°. A4. [17

OGIER, SIMON. Simonis Ogerii Audomaropolitae Lutetia. ... Duaci, Ex officina Ioannis Bogardi ... M.D.XC. 8°. A-C8 (-C8, *presumably blank*). pp. 2-47. [18

OLDENDORP, JOHANN. Actionum iuris ciuilis loci communes ... Item, de formula libelli per quem editur actio ... Coloniae apud Ioannem Gymnicum. Anno M. D. XXXIX. 8°. α-β8 A-P8. pp. 1-238. (Biddle.) [19

-- De iure singulari breuis ennarratio ... Coloniae excudebat Ioannes Gymnicus. Anno M. D. XXXIX. 8°. a-b8 A-G8. pp. 2-86. (Biddle.) [20

-- Formula inuestigandae actionis ... De probationibus ... Coloniae, Excudebat Ioannes Gymnicus. Anno M. D. XXXVIII. 8°. A-F8. (Biddle.) [21

-- Iuris naturalis, gentium, et ciuilis ἐισαγωγή. Leges XII. tabularum, interpretationibus ... illustratæ. Epitome successionis ab intestato ... Coloniae excudebat Ioannes Gymnicus. Anno M. D. XXXIX. 8°. a-d8 A-Q8. pp. 1-224. (Biddle.) [22

-- Vsucapionum et praescriptionum tempora ex iure Ciuili ... Coloniae Ioannes Gymnicus excudebat. Anno 1558. 8°. A-K8. (Biddle.) [23

OLDOINO, ERCOLE. Orlando ... In Venetia, M. D. XCVIII. Appresso Francesco de'Franceschi Senese. ... 4°. a4 A-O8 (-O1, O8, *the latter blank*). ff. 1-111. [24

OLDRADI, ANGELO DELLI. Il poeta comedia nuoua ... In Venetia (... per Comin da Trino di Monferrato M. D. XLIX.) 8°. A-D8 (-D8, *blank*). ff. 2-31. [25

OLIMPO DEGLI ALESSANDRI, CAIO BALDASSARE. Ardelia opera nuoua. Nellaquale si cōtiene Mattinate, Sonetti, Stanze, Capitoli, Dialoghe, e diuersi Strambotti ... In Siena [c. 1550]. 8°. A-E8. [26

-- Gloria damore ... (Stampata in Vinegia per Giouann Padouanno. Nel .M.D.XXXXIIII. Del Mese de maggio.) 8°. A-D8 E4. [27

-- Linguaccio. Libro nouo chimato linguaccio .... 8°. A-C8 D4. ¶B2 *(signed* B*) misbound before* B1, B3 *after* B4. [28

-- Opera noua Damore chiamata Camilla. ... (In Vinegia per Giouāne Padoano ... M D XXXXIIII.) 8°. A-H8. [29

-- Pegasea ... (Stampata in Venetia per Bernardino di Bindoni Milanese ... M.D.XXXVIIII. Nel Mese de Febraro.) 8°. A-I8. [30

OLIVETANS. Constitutiones et reformationes congregationis Oliuetanae. Determinatae in capitulo generali anno M. D. LXIIII. ... Neapoli Apud Io. de Boy. 1568. (*Colophon.*) 4°. *-**4 A-R4. ff. 1-67. ¶*1: *engraving*. *2: *t.p.* (Lea.) [31

OLIVIERO, ANTONIO FRANCESCO. [1] La Alamanna ... (In Venetia, Appresso Vicenzo Valgrisi.

MDLXVII.) 4°. A^{8} A-V^{8}. pp. 2-316. [2] *Same title.* (*Colophon.*) a-x^{8}. pp. 5-330. [3] Carlo quinto in Olma ... (*Colophon.*) aa-bb^{8} cc^{6}. ff. 3-43. [4] L'origine d'amore ... (*Colophon.*) 3a^{8}. pp. 1-15. [32

ONOSANDER. Onosandro Platonico dell'ottimo capitano generale, et del suo vfficio. Tradotto di Greco in lingua volgare Italiana per M. Fabio Cotta ... In Vinegia appresso Gabriel Giolito de Ferrari MDXLVI (*Colophon.*) 8°. A-F^{8} G^{4}. ff. 1-46. [33

ONGARO, ANTONIO. Alceo fauola pescatoria ... In Venetia, Appresso Francesco Ziletti. 1582. 8°. a^{8} A-G^{8}. ff. 2-54. [34

OPERETTA. Operetta, nella quale si contengono Prouerbij, Sententie, Detti, & modi di ragionare ... [Venezia, Alessandro Bindoni, 1520?] 8°. A-C^{8} (-C8, *presumably blank*). ff. 2-23. [35

OPORINUS, JOANNES. Christianae poeseos opuscula aliquot ... Adiecta ... disticha, totius Noui Testamenti Epitomen ... Basileae [per Joannem Oporinum, c. 1542]. 8°. a^{4} a-z^{8} A-G^{8} H^{4} B-S^{8}. pp. 1-494, ff. 2-135. ¶*Authors:* Petrus Rossetus, Scipio Capycius, Janus Vitalis Panormitanus, Io. Franc. Quintianus Stoa, Eobanus Hessus. [36

-- Librorum per Ioannem Oporinum partim excusorum hactenus, partim in eiusdem Officina uenalium ... Basileae, 1552. (... Ex officina Ioannis Oporini ... Mense Maio.) 8°. A-E^{8}. pp. 3-76. [37

OPPIANUS. Οππιανου αλιευτικων βιβλια πεντε. Του αυτου κυνηγετικων βιβλια τεσσαρα. Oppiani de piscibus libri V. Eiusdem de uenatione libri IIII. Oppiani de piscibus Laurentio Lippio interprete ... (Venetiis in aedibus Aldi et Andreae soceri mense Decembri M. D. XVII.) 8°. a-x^{8}. ff. 3-166. [38

-- -- Oppiani Poëtæ Cilicis de venatione Lib. IIII. De piscatu Lib. V. Cum Interpretatione Latina, Commentariis ... opera Conradi Rittershusii Brunswicensis ... Lugduni Batauorum, Ex officina Plantiniana, Apud Franciscum Raphaelengium. cIↄ. Iↄ. XCVII. 8°. †-††^{8} α-γ^{8} δ^{4} A-Z^{8} a-b^{8} c^{4} *^{4} AA-XX^{8} YY^{4} αα-κκ^{8} λλ^{4}. pp. 1-376, 1-344, 2-164. [39

OPSOPOEUS, VINCENTIUS. De arte bibendi libri tres, autore Vincentio Obsopoeo. ... (Norimbergæ apud Ioh. Petreium, Anno M.D.XXXVII.) 4°. a^{6} b-n^{4}. ¶*In verse.* [40

-- -- De arte bibendi libri tres ... Quibus adiunximus de arte iocandi libros quatuor, Matthiæ Delij Hamburgensis ... Francoforti ad Moenum. 1578. (... ex officina hæredum Christiani Egenolphi, impensis Adami Loniceri, Ioannis Cnipij Andronici secundi, Doctorum, & Pauli Steinmeyers. ...) 8°. A-F^{8} G-H^{4} I-O^{8}. ¶O4^{v}: In ebrietatem, Nicodemi Frischlini Elegia. [41

-- In Graecorum epigrammatum libros quatuor Annotationes ... Vincentio Obsopoeo autore. ... Basileae. (... in officina Nicolai Brylingeri, anno M. D. XXXX. Mense Septembri.) 8°. α^{8} a-z^{8} A-O^{8} P^{4}. pp. 1-570. [42

ORADINI, LUCIO. Due lezzioni ... lette publicamente nell'Accademia Fiorentina. In Fiorenza. Appresso Lorenzo Torrentino. M. D. L. ... 8°. A-F^{8}. pp. 3-96. ¶*On two sonnets of Petrarch.* [43

ORANTES, FRANCISCO. Oratio F. Francisci Orantii Hispani, Habita in ... Synodo Tridentina, die ... Sanctorum omnium, anno 1562. Venetiis, M D LXIII. Ex officina Iordani Zileti. (*Colophon.*) 4°. A-D^{4}. ff. 2-16. (Lea.) [44

ORATIONES. Orationes clarorum hominum ... ad principes ... habitae. In Academia Veneta, M. D. LIX. 4°. *-**^{4} A-Vu^{4} (-Vu3-4, *blank*). ff. 1-176. [45

-- -- *Another copy* (-Rr-Vu^{4}). [46

ORDNUNG. Ein ordnung eines vernūnfftigen hausshalters. [Nūrnberg, Johann Stuchs?] 1530. 8°. [a]^{6}. [47

ORESME, NICOLAS. Isthec epistola fuit a paucis diebus casu reperta in libro quodā tabularum alphonsi regis ... Clemens sextus episcopus Romanus circa annū christi .Mil.

Trecentesi. Quadragesimũ q̃ntũ regnauit. 4°. B.L. π^4. ¶*Authorship uncertain.* [48

-- Epistola Luciferi ad spirituales circiter ante Annos Centum ... descripta. Autore Nicolao Oren. ... (Magdeburgæ excudebat Michael Lotther. Anno 1549.) 8°. A-B^8 C^4. ¶A2: Christiano lectori ... Matthias Flacius Illiricus. [49

ORIBASIUS. Oribasii Sardiani collectorum medicinalium libri XVII. ... Ioanne Baptista Rasario, medico, Nouariensi, interprete. Venetiis, apud Paulum Manutium, Aldi f. ... [1555.] 8°. *^{4} A-Z^8 a-z^8 &^{8}. pp. 1-252 [= 752]. [50

-- Oribasii Sardiani synopseos ... libri nouem: quibus tota medicina in compendium redacta continentur: Ioanne Baptista Rasario Nouariensi medico interprete. Venetiis ... (... apud Paulum Manutium, Aldi filium, M. D. LIIII.) 8°. A-DD^8. ff. 5-216. [51

ORIGENES ADAMANTIUS. [1] Origenis Adamantii Operum Tomi Duo Priores ... Venundantur [Parisiis] cum reliquis Ioanni Paruo: Iodoco Badio: et Conrado Resch. fol. a-d^8 a-z^8 &^{6} Aa^6 Bb-Mm^8 Nn^6 Oo-Qq^8 Rr-Ss^6 Tt^8 Vv^6 Xx^8 (-Xx8, *blank*). ff. I-CXC, I-CLVII. [2] Tertius et quartus Tomi Operum Origenis Adamantii ... *Same imprint.* 3A^6 3a^6 3B-3z^8 3&^{8} 3ɔ^8 3ꝶ^8 3A^8 3B^{10}. ff. 1-CCXXIIII. ¶3A1 *defective.* [3] Quartus tomus ... *Same imprint.* 4a-4x^8 4y^{10}. ff. I-CLXXV. [52

ORLÉANS. Coustumes generales, des bailliage, et preuosté d'Orleans, & ressorts d'iceux. Reueuës ... par Leon Trippault ... A Orleans. Par Eloy Gibier ... 1570. ... 8°. *^{8} a-i^8 k^4 A-D^8 E^4. pp. 1-152, 1-69. [53

D'ORLÉANS, LOUIS. Aduertissement, des Catholiques Anglois aux François Catholiques, du danger où ils sont de perdre leur Religion ... 1586. 8°. A^4 B-I^8. pp. 4-133. [54

-- -- ... En ceste derniere Edition augmenté. ... 1586. 8°. A^4 B-I^8. pp. 4-133. (Lea.) [55

OROLOGI, GIUSEPPE. Vita dell'illustrissimo Signor Camillo Orsino, discritta da Gioseppe Horologgi, nella quale si vengono ... a narrare tutte le guerre successe dalla uenuta di Carlo VIII. Re di Francia in Italia, sin'all'anno MDLIX. ... In Vinegia appresso Gabriel Giolito de' Ferrari. M D·LXV. 4°. *^{12} A-S^4. pp. 1-141. [56

ORONSUSPE, MICHAEL. De misterio sanctissimae Trinitatis concio, Doctoris Oronsuspe Nauarri Olitensis ... Habita in ... Synodo Tridentina Dominica Sanctæ Trinitatis VI. Iunij. M D LXIII. Pataulii, Apud Christophorum Gryphium, M D LXIII. 4°. A^4. (Lea.) [57

OROSIUS, PAULUS. Paulo Orosio tradotto di Latino in volgare per Giouanni Guerini da Lanciza nouamente stampato. ([Toscolano,] P. Alex. Pag. Benacenses. F. Bena. .V. .V. [1520?]) 8°. a-x^8 y^4. [58

ORPHEUS. Orphei poetarum vetustissimi Argonauticōn opus Græcũ, cũ interpretatione Latina incerti autoris ... Apud ... Basileam, ... M. D. XXIII. (... in aedibus Andreae Cratandri, mense Iunio. ...) 4°. a-o^4. [59

ORSI, AURELIO. Aurelius Vrsus ... De Bello Belgico. ... Perusiæ 1586. (... ex Typographia Andreæ Brixiani ...) 4°. π^2 A-D^4 E^2 (-E2, *presumably blank*). ¶*In verse.* [60

-- Aurelii Vrsi Perettina siue Syxti V. pont. max. horti Exquilini. Romae, Apud Ioannem Martinellum. 1588. ... 4°. A-C^4 D^6. pp. 4-35. [61

ORSINI, FULVIO. Imagines et elogia virorum illustrium et eruditor ... Ex bibliotheca Fului Vrsini M.D.LXX Romæ Ant. Lafrerij Formeis [(Venetiis in aedibus Petri Dehuchino.)] fol. A-O^4 (-O4). pp. 3-109 *present.* ¶*Engraved t.p.* [62

-- Virgilius collatione scriptorum Græcorum illustratus, opera et industria Fuluii Vrsini. Antuerpiae, Ex officina Christophori Plantini. Anno cIↄ. Iↄ. LXVII. ... (... mense Nouembri.) 8°. ❧^{8} A-Z^8 a-g^8. pp. 1-473. [63

ORTA, GARCIA DE. Aromatum, et simplicium aliquot medicamentorum apud Indos nascentium historia: ... D. Garcia ab Horto ... auctore: ... Latina facta, & in Epitomen contracta à Carolo Clusio Atrebate. Antuerpiæ, Ex officina Christophori Plantini, cIↄ. Iↄ. LXVII. ...

(... Mense Aprili.) 8°. A-Q8 R4. pp. 3-250. [64

ORTELIUS, ABRAHAMUS. Abrahami Ortelii Antuerpiani synonymia geographica ... Antuerpiæ, Ex officina Christophori Plantini ... M.D.LXXVIII. (... Prid. Kal. Augusti.) 4°. †4 A-Z4 a-z4 AA-EE4 FF6. pp. 49-417. [65

-- Il theatro del mondo ... In Brescia, Appresso la Compagnia Bresciana. M D XCVIII. ... (*Colophon.*) 4°. †4 A-N8 O-P6. pp. 1-215. ¶*Translator: Pietro Maria Marchetti.* [66

ORTIZ, FRANCISCO. ... Francisci Ortiz ... de Ornatu animæ liber vnicus. M. D. XLIX. ... (Compluti excudebat Ioannes Brocarius anno ... millesimo quingentesimo quadragesimooctauo. Mense Nouembri.) 4°. ♦10 a-i8 (-i8, *presumably blank*). ff. II-LXX. (Lea.) [67

ORZECHEOWSKI, STANISLAW. Stanislai Orichouii Roxolani chimæra: siue de Stancari funesta Regno Poloniæ Secta. ... Coloniæ, Apud Maternum Cholinum. Anno 1563. (Typis Godefridi Ceruicorni.) 8°. §8 a4 A-Y8 (-Y8, *blank*). ff. 2-170. ¶*Folded leaf attached to binding.* [68

-- Stanislai Orichouii Poloni Turcicae duae ... Romae. CIↃ IↃ XCIV Apud Heredes Ioannis Lilioti. 4°. a4 A-F4. pp. 1-48. [69

OSIANDER, ANDREAS. Bedencken auff das Interim ... 1548. 4°. A-E4 F2. [70

-- Coniecturæ de vltimis temporibus, ac de fine mundi ... Norimbergæ apud Iohan. Petreium ... M.D.XLIIII. 4°. a-i4. [71

-- -- Vermuͤtung von den letzten zeiten ... 1545. Zu Nuͤrnberg Truckts I. Petreius. 4°. a-o4. [72

-- Ain guͦt vnderricht vnd getrewer Ratschlag ... wess mā sich ... vnnsern hailigen glauben vnnd Christliche leer betreffend/ halten soll ... Geschriben an ain Erbern/ Weysen Rhat der ... Stat Nürnberg durch jre prediger. M:D:xxv. 4°. A-I4 (-G3-4, H4). ¶*Signed by Dominicus Sleupner and Thomas Venatorius as well as Osiander.* [73

-- Ordnung wie man Tauffet bisher ym Lateyn gehalten/ verteütscht. ... Andreas Osiander. Nürnberg. 4°. a-b4. [74

-- Vnterricht an ein sterbenden menschen. ... Nürmberg. M.D.XXXVIII. (Gedruckt ... bey Leonhart Milchtaler.) 4°. A-B4. [75

-- Von den Spoͤttern des worts Gottis. ... 1545. Zu Nuͤrnberg Truckts I. Petreius. 4°. a-k4. [76

-- Wie vnnd wohin/ ain Christ die grausamen plag der Pestilentz fliehen soll. ... [Nürnberg, 1533.] 4°. A-D4. [77

-- -- Wie/ vnd wo hin ... Ein predig ... Vormals im 1533. jar aussgangen/ vnd yetzo ... gepessert. ... Zu Nuͤrmberg truckts Iohan Petreius am 27 Octobris/ Anno 1543. 4°. a-e4. [78

OSIANDER, LUCAS. Abfertigung Der vermeindtē Replic/ Christophori Rosenbusches/ Iesuiters ... wider Lucam Osiandrum ... Getruckt zu Tuͤbingen/ bey Georgen Gruppenbach/ Anno 1587. 4°. A-I4 K2. pp. 1-74. [79

-- Ableinung Der Lugen/ Verkerungen vnnd Loͤsterungen/ mit denen Bruͦder Iohann Nass in seinen Centurijs der Euangelischen Warheiten ... die Christlich Lehr der Augspurgischen Confession ... antastet. ... Getruckt zuͦ Tübingen/ Anno 1569. 4°. A-P4 Q2. pp. 1-120. [80

-- Bedencken Ob der newe Paͤpstische Kalender ein Notturfft bey der Christenheit seie ... Tuͤbingen/ bey Georgen Gruppenbach. M. D. LXXXIII. (*Colophon.*) 4°. A-G4. pp. 2-49. [81

-- Ein Christliche Predig Vber der Leich der ... Fraͤwlin Eua Christiana/ Graͤuin zu Wuͤrtemberg ... Getruckt zuͦ Tübingen/ bey Georg Gruppenbach 1575. 4°. A-C4. pp. 1-22. [82

-- [1] Epitomes historiae ecclesiasticæ centuria I. II. III. ... Tubingæ apud Georgium Gruppenbachium, anno M. D. XCII. 4°.)(4 2)(2 A-X4 A-O4 A-P4. pp. 1-159, 1-102, 1-114. [2] Epitomes historiæ ecclesiasticae centuria quinta. ... Tubingæ, Apud Georgium Gruppenbachium anno M. D. XCVII.):(4 A-3R4 3S2. pp. 1-494. [3] ... centuria Sexta. ... Tubingæ, Apud Georgium Gruppenbachium, Anno M. D. XCVIII.):(4 a-rr4. pp. 1-309. [4] ... centuria Septima. ... Tubingæ, Typis Georgij Gruppenbachij, anno M. D. XCIX.):(4 a-uu4.

pp. 1-339. ¶*This set includes the 8th century and two parts of the 16th, dated 1602, 1602, and 1603 respectively.* [83

-- Ein Predig. Aus dem Lobgesang der Prophetin Hanna ... Getruckt zu Tübingen/ durch Georg Gruppenbach. 1577. 4°. A-C^4 D^2. pp. 1-25. [84

-- Ein Predig/ Bey der Leych ... Iacobi Andreæ ... Getruckt zu Tübingen/ bey Alexander Hock ... M. D. LXXXX. 4°. A-E^4. [85

-- Ein Predig vber der Leich Dess ... Herren Frantzen Kurtzen ... Gehalten zu Stutgarten ... den 30. Augusti/ Anno 1575. ... Getruckt zů Tübingen/ bey Georg Gruppenbach/ 1575. 4°. A-B^4 C^2. pp. 1-16. [86

-- Warnung Vor der Iesuiter blutdurstigen Anschlägen vnnd bösen Practicken. ... Getruckt zu Tübingen/ bey Georgen Gruppenbach. Anno/ 1585. 4°. A-F^4. pp. 1-43. [87

-- Zwo kurtze Hochzeit Predigen ... Getruckt zu Tübingen/ bey Alexander Hock ... M. D. LXXXX. 4°. A-E^4. [88

-- Zwo Predigen/ Die eine/ von dem Ampt Christlicher Obrigkeit/ vnnd gottseliger Vnderthanen. Die ander/ von vnserm Herrn Ihesu Christo ... Getruckt zu Tübingen bey Georg Gruppenbach/ Anno 1580. 4°. A-E^4. pp. 1-36. [89

OSIUS, HIERONYMUS. Elegia de laudibus ... Christiani Regis Daniæ, &c. ... VVitebergæ excudit Vitus Creutzer. Anno 1559. 8°. A^8 B^4. [90

-- Theognidis versio, item Pythagorae, Phocylidis, Tyrtæi, & Solonis paraphrasis, necnon alia uaria poemata ac Epigrammata ... VVittebergae impressum in officina haeredum Georgii Rhau. Anno 1558. 8°. A^8 A-R^8. [91

OSORIO DA FONSECA, JERONYMO. Hieronymi Osorii Lusitani ... de Gloria, libri V. ... Eiusdem de nobilitate Ciuili & Christiana, Libri V. ... Coloniae, Apud Gosuinum Cholinum. cIↄ. Iↄ. XXCIII. 12°. +^{12} A-X^{12}. pp. 2-504. [92

-- Hieronymi Osorii Lusitani ... de rebus, Emmanuelis regis Lusitaniae ... annis sex, ac viginti, domi forisq́; gestis; libri duodecim. ... Coloniae Agrippinae, Apud Hæredes Arnoldi Birckmanni. cIↄ. Iↄ. LXXIV. 8°. +-++^{8} A-3F^8 *-**^{8} (-**8, *presumably blank*). ff. 4-412. (Lea.) [93

-- Hieronymi Osorii ... in Gualterum Haddonum Anglum, de Religione libri tres. Eiusdem epistola ad Elisabetham Angliae reginam. Editio tertia ... Accessit recens Christophori Longolii ... oratio. Dilingae, Excudebat Sebaldus Mayer. M. D. LXXVI. 16°. A-Z^8 a-b^8. pp. 2-397. (Lea.) [94

OSUNA, FRANCISCO DE. Pars occidentalis in accommodas hisce temporibus euangeliorum Quadragesimalium expositiones ... Per F. Franciscum ab Ossuna Bethicum in lucem prodita. ... Venetiis, Apud Iacobum Simbenum. M. D. LXXII. (*Colophon.*) 8°. *^{8} A-3C^8. pp. 1-781. (Lea.) [95

-- Primera parte del libro llamado Abecedario spiritual ... (Fue ĩpresso ẽla ... villa ꝺ medina ꝺl cãpo por Pedro ꝺ Castro. A costa de Iuã de espinosa ... Acabose a veynte dias del mes de Setiembre: Año de mil ⁊ quinientos ⁊ quarenta ⁊ quatro Años.) 4°. B.L. a-y^8 z^4. ff. iij-clxxx. [96

-- Segunda parte del libro llamado Abecedario spiritual: ... (Impresso enla ... ciudad de Seuilla: en casa de Iuan Varela ... a .xx. de Agosto de .M.d.xxx. Años.) 4°. B.L. a-z^8 ⁊^{8} ꝯ^8. ff. II-CXCVIII. [97

-- Tercera parte del libro llamado Abecedario spiritual ... 1544. (impresso enla ... ciudad de Burgos en casa de Iuã de junta. Acabose a cinco dias ꝺl mes de Enero. ...) 4°. a-z^8 A-D^8 E^6. ff. j-ccxxij. (Lea.) [98

-- -- *Another copy.* [99

-- Ley de amor y quarta parte del Abecedario espiritual ... Año. 1536. (Fue impresso ... Enla ... ciudad de Burgos. En casa del señor Iuan de Iunta Florentino. Acabose a. xxxj.

dias del mes de Março ... a costa del señor Iuan de Espinosa ... de medina del Campo.) 4°. B.L. a-z^8 A-B^8 C^6. ff. ij-ccvi. [100

-- Quinta parte: del abecedario spiritual ... 1542. (Fue Impresso en la ... ciudad de Burgos. En casa de Iuan de Iunta. A quinze dias del mes de Abril ... a costa del señor Iuan de Espinosa ... de Medina del Campo.) 4°. B.L. ✠^{10} A-Dd^8 Ee^6. ff. j-ccxxj. [101

OTTHACIUS, NICOLAUS. Nicolai Otthacii nobilis Iustinopolitani poemata varia. Venetijs. M. D. XLV. ... (... per Bartholomæum cognomento Imperatorem, & Franciscum eius generum. ...) 16°. A-C^4. [102

OTTO VON FREISING. Ottonis episcopi Frisingensis Leopoldi Pii marchionis Austriae F. chronicon, siue rerum ab orbe condito ad sua vsq3 tempora gestarum, Libri octo. Eiusdem de gestis Friderici I. Cæs. Aug. Libri duo. Radeuici Frising. Canonici de eiusdem Frid. gestis Libri II. priorib. additi. Guntheri poetæ Ligurinus, siue de gestis Friderici, Libri X. Addita sunt & alia ... Basileae, apud Petrum Pernam, M. D. LXIX. ... fol. *^{8} a-ff^6 †^{8} (-†8, *presumably blank*) a^6 B-S^6. pp. 1-346, 1-196. ¶*Includes:* M. Alberti Argentinensis chronici fragmentum (O1^r-R3^r). (Lea.) [103

OTTONAJO, GIOVANNI BATTISTA. La ingratitudine, comedia ... In Fiorenza M D LIX. (... appresso i Giunti. ...) 8°. A-C^8. [104

OTTONELLI, GIULIO. Discorso del Sor Giulio Ottonelli sopra l'abuso del dire sua santità, sua maestà sua altezza, Senza nominare il Papa, l'Imperatore, il Principe. Con le difese della Gierusalemme Liberata del Signor Torq. Tasso dall'oppositioni degli Academici della Crusca. ... In Ferrara, Ad instanza di Giulio Vassalini. ... 1586. (... Per Vittorio Baldini ...) 8°. †^{4} A-L^8 a-b^4. pp. 1-175. [105

-- -- *Another copy, lacking the tavola* (a-b^4). [106

OVIDIUS NASO, PUBLIUS. *Works.* [1] Quae hoc volumine continentur. Annotationes in omnia Ouidij opera. ... Ouidii metamorphoseon libri XV. (Venetiis in aedibus Aldi, et Andreae soceri mense Februario M.D.XVI.) 8°. π-^{6}π^8 (*the first ll. of these gatherings are numbered* 2-4, 5-8, 9-12, 13-16, 17-20, 21-24) a-z^8 A-B^8 C^4. ff. 2-204. [2] P. Ouidij Nasonis uita per Aldum ... Heroidum epistolæ Amorum libri III. De arte amandi libri III. De remedio amoris libri II. De medicamine faciei Nux Somnium Pulex & Philomela ... (Venetiis in aedibus Aldi, et Andreae soceri mense Maio. M. D. XV.) Aa-Bb^4 aa-hh^8 ii^4 kk-oo^8 pp^4 qq-yy^8 zz^4 AA^{10}. ff. 1-172. [3] Cla. Ptolemaei inerrantium stellarum significationes per Nicolaum Leonicum ê græco translatæ. ... P. Ouidii Nasonis fastorum lib. VI. Tristium lib. V. De Ponto lib. IIII. In Ibin Ad Liuiam. (Venetiis in aedibus Aldi, et Andreae soceri mense Ianuario M. D. XVI.) 22 *ll. numbered* 2-21 3a-3k^8 3l^6 3m-3s^8 3t^6 3u-3z^8 3A-3E^8 3F^4. ff. 2-227. [107

-- -- *Another copy of* [3]. [108

-- -- P. Ouidij Nasonis uita per Aldum ex ipsius libris excerpta. Heroidum epistolae. Amorum lib. III. De arte amandi lib. III. De remedio amoris lib. II. De medicamine faciei. Nux. Somnium. Pulex & Philomela ... (Venetiis in aedibus haeredum Aldi, et Andreae soceri, mense Ianuario. M. D. XXXIII.) 8°. Aa^8 Bb^4 aa-hh^8 ii^4 kk-oo^8 pp^4 (-pp4, *blank*) qq-zz^8 AA^4. ff. 1-172. ¶*The 2nd vol. of a 3-vol. edition.* [109

-- *Two or more works.* Publij Ouidij Nasonis opuscula: ... de Nuce de Philomena et de pulice. [*Device of Gilles de Gourmont.* c. 1510.] 4°. a^6. [110

-- Compendiosa ⁊ vberrima elucidatio in Ouidiū de arte amandi et remedio amoris. Per Bartholomeum merula mantuanum ... a Guillermo Ramesio sagiensis ... emendata cū annotationib^9 ... (impressit Lugduni ... Iacobus myt ... M.ccccc. ⁊ xiiij. viij. Idus augusti.) 4°. B.L. a^4 b-c^8 d-g$^{4.8}$ h^4 i-k^8. ff. ij-lxj. [111

-- P. Ouidii Nasonis libri de arte amandi et de remedio amoris. Vna cum ... commētariis R.D. Bartholomei Merulae ... (Impressum Venetiis in Aedibus Ioannis Tacuini de Tridino ... MDXVIII. Die .XX. Februariii [*sic*] ...) fol. A-H^6. ff. 2-46. [112

-- -- ... Annotationes ... Io. Baptiste Pii. Io. Baptiste Egnatii. Philippi Beroaldi Iunioris: & Pontici Virunni ... Venundantur apud Lignanos ... (Impressit Mediolani ... Augustinus de Vicomercato. Ad instantiam D. Ioan. Iacobi & fratres de Legnano. ... M.D.XXI.

die .xiii. Iunii.) fol. AA4 A-G6 H8. ff. i-l. [113

-- P. Ouidii Nasonis fastorum lib. VI. Tristium libri V. De Ponto lib. IIII. Item, Claudii Ptolemaei in errantium Stellarum significationes ... Scholia Philippi Melanchthonis. Basileae. (... per Henrichum Petri, Anno M. D. LVI. Mense Martio.) 8°. A-Kk8. pp. 3-465. [114

-- *Separate works*. P. Ouidij Nasonis Sulmonēsis ... tres de arte amādi libelli ... (Impressum Liptzk per ... Martinum Herbipolensem Anno ... Millesimo quingentesimoseptimo.) 4°. A-E6 F-L4.6. [115

-- Pub. Ouidii Nasonis De Ponto Libri Quatuor. ([Argentorati,] Ex ædibus Schurerianis, Mense Martio. ... M. D. XX.) 4°. A-H8.4 I8 K6. [116

-- -- ... Cum argumentis ... Viti Amerbachij. M. D. XLI. ... (Argentorati ex officina Cratonis Mylii ...) 8°. A-Q8. pp. 1-245. [117

-- P. Ouidii Nasonis ... heroides epistolae ... Adiunximus ... adnotata ab Ioanne Baptista Egnatio, obseruationes Constantii Fanensis ... Adiecta est ... versuum dispositio, ac interpretatio, per Aaronem Battaleum Triuiliensem ... excogitata. Ad haec Ioannis Scoppae expositiones ... Venetiis, apud Ioannem Mariam Bonellum. M. D. LVIII. (*Colophon.*) fol. A-K8 L-M6 (-M6, *presumably blank*). ff. 5-91. [118

-- -- Epistole del famosissimo Ouidio vulgare In octaua rima ... (Impresso in Milano per Rocho ꝛ Fratelli da Valle ad Instantia de Meser Nicolo da Gorgonzola a di .xxviii. de Zenaro. M.ccccc.xviii.) 4°. B.L. a-e8 f6. ff. 2-46. [119

-- -- Epistole d'Ouidio di Remigio Fiorentino diuise in due libri. ... In Vinegia appresso Gabriel Giolito de' Ferrari. M D LX. 12°. A-O12 (-O11-12, *blank*). pp. 3-330. [120

-- -- L'epistole d'Ouidio, tradotte in terza rima da Camillo Camilli ... In Venetia, Appresso Gio. Battista Ciotti. MDLXXXVII. 12°. A-K12. ff. 1-119. [121

-- -- Epistole d'Ouidio di Remigio Fiorentino. ... In Venetia, Appresso Lucio Spineda. M D XCIX. 12°. A-N12. pp. 3-311. [122

-- I fasti di Ouidio tratti alla lingua volgare per Vincenzo Cartari Regiano. In Venetia M D LI. ... (... per Francesco Marcolini il mese di Aprile ...) 8°. A-KK8 LL2. ff. 2-264. [123

-- Metamorphosis Ouidiana Moraliter a Magistro Thoma vvaleys Anglico ... explanata. Venundantur in edibus Francisci Regnault ... (Anno dñi Milesimo quingetesimo decimo quinto. die vero .xxiii. mensis Martij.) 8°. B.L. A8 B6 a-m8 n6. ff. i-cii. [124

-- -- P. Ouidij Nasonis metamorphoseos libri moralizati ... cum ... Lactātij Firmiani Cocli in singulas fabulas argumentis ... & tropologica ... enarratione per ... Petrum Lauinium ... Adnotationes præterea ... Philippi Beroaldi: Ioānis baptistæ pii: Iani Parrhasii: Lodouici Coelii Rhodigini: & Iacobi Bononiēsis: huc curauit adiiciēdas Ioānes Theodericus Bellouacus. ... Venundantur Lugduni ab Iacobo huguetan ... (Impressum ... in edibus Simonis biuilaque Anno domini Millesimo quingentesimo decimo octauo pridie nonas Maias.) 4°. B.L. a-z8 (-y2) ꝛ8 ɔ8 (-ɔ5) ꝶ8 A6 A6 (-A6). ff. i-CCVI. [125

-- -- P. O. Nasonis metamorphoseos libri. XV. nunc primum in lucem dati catsigatissimi [*sic*]. ... (Florentiæ per hæredes Philippi Iuntæ. ... M.D.XXII. Kal. Septēb.) 8°. A-E8 a-z8 &8 ɔ8 ꝶ8. ff. 1-208. [126

-- -- Metamorphoseon Pub. Ouidii Nasonis Sulmonensis Libri XV. Raphaelis Regii Volterrani ... explanatio, cum nouis Iacobi Micylli ... additionibus. Lactantii Placidi in singulas fabulas argumenta. ... Iacobi Phanensis, Coelij Rhodigini, Ioan. Baptistæ Egnatij, Henrici Glareani, & Gilberti Longolii ... annotationes ... Venetiis apud Hieronymum Scotū. MDLIII (*Colophon.*) fol. *4 A-T8 V10. ff. 1-162. [127

-- -- Ouidii Metamorphoseon libri XV. ... Venetiis, apud Ioan. Gryphium, M D LXX. (*Colophon.*) 8°. *8 A-Dd8. pp. 1-432. [128

-- -- Pub. Ouidii Nasonis metamorphoseon libri XV. ... Ex postrema Iacobi Micylli Recognitione. Francofurti ad Moenum. M. D. LXXIX. (Impressum apud Georgium Coruinum, impensis Iohannis Feyerabendij.) 8°. *8 a-oo8. pp. 1-573. [129

-- -- The .xv. Bookes of P. Ouidius Naso, entytuled Metamorphosis, translated oute of Latin into English meeter, by Arthur Golding Gentleman ... 1567 Imprynted at London, by Willyam

Seres. (*Colophon.*) 4°. B.L. a-b⁴ A⁴ B-Y⁸ Aa-Dd⁸. ff. 2-200. *S.T.C.* 18956. ¶*T.p. mounted and defective, lacking the last letter in* Bookes. (Furness.) [130

-- -- [1] [Le Grand Olympe des histoires poetiques du prince de poètes Ouide Naso.] 8°. A-I⁸ (-A1) K⁴. ff. 2-76. [2] La seconde partie du grand Olympe des histoires poetiques contenans cinq liures ensuyuans de la Metamorphose d'Ouide ... 1543 Aa-Kk⁸ Ll⁴. ff. 2-84. [3] La tierce partie du grand Olympe des histoires poetiques ... 1543 3A-3M⁸ 3N⁴. ff. 3-97. [131

-- -- Six liures de la Metamorphose d'Ouide, traduictz ... en Rime Françoise ... par Françoys Habert d'Yssouldun ... A Paris, De l'imprimerie de Michel Fezandat ... 1549. 8°. a-o⁸ A-H⁸ (-H8, *presumably blank*). [132

-- -- Le trasformationi di M. Lodouico Dolce ... In Venetia appresso Gabriel Giolito de Ferrari e fratel. MDLIII. 4°. *⁸ A-T⁸ V-X⁴. pp. 2-309. [133

-- -- Le metamorphosi d'Ouidio in ottaua rima col testo Latino ... tradotte da M. Fabio Marretti ... Apud Bologninum Zalterium, et Guerreos fratres, unanimes socios. Venetiis. M. D. LXX. 4°. *⁴ A-GG⁸. pp. 4-479. ¶*Engraved t.p.* [134

-- -- Le metamorfosi di Ovidio Ridotte da Gio Andrea dell'Anguillara in ottaua rima. Con le Annotationi di M. Gioseppe Horologgi, & gli Argomenti, & Postille di M. Francesco Turchi. ... M.D.LXXXIV. In Vin. Presso Bern. Giunti. 4°. †⁸ A-Kk⁸ Ll¹⁰. pp. 2-539. ¶*Engraved t.p.* [135

-- -- Libro del metamorphoseos ⁊ fabulas del ... Ouidio ... traduzido de latin en romance. ... M. D. L. (Fue impressa ... ēla ... cibdad ꝺ seuiblla en casa ꝺ Sebastiā Trugillo ... Acabose a quinze dias ꝺl mes ꝺabril Año de M.D.L.) 8°. B.L. a-z⁸ ⁊⁸ A-O⁸ P⁴ (-P4, *presumably blank*). ff. xv-ccciij. ¶*Translator: Jorge de Bustamante.* [136

-- -- Los quinze libros de los Metamorphoseos de ... Ouidio. Traduzidos en verso suelto y octaua rima por Antonio Perez ... En Salamanca. En casa de Iuan Perier ... 1580 (*Colophon.*) 12°. ¶¹² ℭℭ⁶ A-Kk¹². ff. 1-396. [137

-- -- [1] Las transformaciones de Ouidio: Traduzidas ... en tercetos, y octauas rimas, Por el Licēciado Viana. ... Con el comento ... Impresso en Valladolid, por Diego Fernandez de Cordoua ... M.D.LXXXIX. ... 4°. ¶-¶¶⁸ 3¶⁴ A-Y⁸ Z⁴. ff. 1-179. [2] Anotaciones sobre los quinze libros de las Trāsformaciones ... Por el Licenciado Pedro Sanchez de Viana. ... *Same imprint.* A-Nn⁸. ff. 5-314. [138

-- -- *Another copy* (-¶4-5). [139

-- -- Las transformaciones de Ouidio en lengua Española ... En Anuers, En casa de Pedro Bellero. M. D. XCV. ... 8°. a⁸ b¹⁰ A-Ff⁸ Gg¹⁰ (-Gg10, *presumably blank*). ff. 1-241. ¶b5-6 *misbound after* Gg5. *Translator: Jorge de Bustamente.* [140

-- Publij Ouidij Nasonis Sulmonensis quinqȝ libri Tristium ... (Impressum Liptzck per Iacobū Thanner Herbipolitanū. Anno dn̄i Millesimo quingentesimodecimoquarto) 4°. A-F⁶ G⁴ H-N⁶. [141

OXFORD. Vera relazione del martirio Di due Reuerendi Sacerdoti, & due Laici. Seguito l' Anno 1589. in Oxonio Città di Studio in Inghilterra. Stampata in Roma, ... & ristampata in Firenze l'Anno 1590. 8°. A⁴. [142

P

P., J. L. Discours sur le diuorce qui se fait par l'adultere, & s'il est permis à l'homme de se remarier. Par I. L. P. ... A Paris, Chez Iean Richer ... 1586. ... 8°. A-F^4 (-F4, *presumably blank*). ff. 2-33. [1

PACHYMERES, GEORGIUS. Georgii Pachymerii in vniuersam Aristotelis disserendi artem epitome Ioanne Baptista Rasario Interprete. Venetijs apud Hieronymym Scotum. 1545. (*Colophon.*) 8°. A-H^8. ff. 2-61. [2

PACIFICO DA NOVARA. Somma pacifica, Composta già piu di cent'anni, ... ridotta in miglior lingua, riformata, & illustrata ... Per il R. P. Francesco de Treuigi ... In Venetia, appresso Domenico, & Gio. Battista Guerra, fratelli. M D LXXIIII. 8°. a-b^8 c^4 A-Cc^8. pp. 1-420. (Lea.) [3

PADILLA, PEDRO DE. Eglogas pastoriles de Pedro de Padilla y Iuntamente con ellas algunos Sonetos del mismo Auctor. ... In Seuilla En casa de Andrea Pescioni, ... 1582. A costa de Antonio Viuas ... 4°. π^4 A^4 B-Gg^8 Hh^{10}. ff. 1-246. [4

PADUA. Statuta Patauina ... correcta per ... Bartholomeum Abborario ... (Venetiis per Guilielmum de Fontaneto Montisferrati: sumptibus ... Hieronymi Giberti ciuis Patauini. ... M.D.XXVIII. octauo Calendas Februarii.) fol. AA-CC^8 A-R^8 S^6. ff. 1-cxlij. (Lea.) [5

-- Gli statuti de Padoua tradotti de Latino in Vulgare ... Stampati In Padoua appresso Giacobo Fabriano. Del M. D. XLIX. 4°. A-$3F^4$. ff. 2-206. (Lea.) [6

-- *Academici Eterei.* Rime degli academici eterei ... [Padova, Gratioso Perchacino, 1567?] 4°. § ^{4} A-X^4. ff. 1-76. ¶*Engraved t.p.* [7

PĀMINGER, SOPHONIAS. Sophoniæ Pamingeri Patauini poematum libri duo ... His accessit liber poematum Balthaseris Pamingeri ... Norimbergæ, In Officina Typographica Valentini Neuberi. M. D. LVII. 8°. A-M^8 N^2. [8

PAGANI, MARCO. [1] Il primo libro delle rime ... In Vinegia, appresso Domenico Farri. M D LVII. 8°. A-I^8. ff. 5-72. [2] Il secondo libro ... *Same imprint.* A-I^8. ff. 3-71. [9

PAGNI, SERAFINO. Trattato, e dichiarazione dell'indulgenze. Con vn discorso della Concezzione della ... Vergine Maria. ... In Firenze Nella Stamperia di Bartholomeo Sermartelli. MDLXXXVIII. (*Colophon.*) 8°. A-G^8. pp. 3-112. (Lea.) [10

PAGNINI, SANTE. קצר הדקדוק Institutionum Hebraicarum abbreuiatio ... Parisiis. Ex officina Caroli Stephani ... M. D. LVI. (... Idib. Februar.) 4°. A-Q^4. pp. 8-126. [11

PAIVA DE ANDRADA, DIEGO DE. Concio habita ad patres in Concilio Tridentino congregatos, ab ... Didaco de Payua, d'Andrade, Lusitano ... Dominica secunda post Pascha Anno M D LXII. Brixiae, apud Ioannem Baptistam Bozolæ Anno M D LXII. (*Colophon.*) 4°. A-B^4. ff. 2-7. (Lea.) [12

-- Orthodoxarum explicationum libri decem ... Præsertim contra Martini Kemnicij ... audaciam ... Auctore Iacobo Payua Andradio Lusitano ... Coloniae Apud Maternum Cholinum, M. D. LXIIII. 8°. a-b^8 A-$3F^8$ $3G^{8+2}$. pp. 1-826. [13

PALACIOS, MIGUEL DE. Magistri Michaelis de Palacio Granatẽsis ... in tres libros Aristotelis de anima Commentarij ... Salmanticæ. Excudebat Ioannes à Canoua. M V. LVII. (... 14. calendas Iunij.) fol. π^2 $*^6$ A-Oo^8 Pp^{10}. ff. 1-315. [14

PALAEPHATUS. Palaephati ... Opusculum De non Credendi Fabulosis narrationibus/ Interprete Philippo Phasianino Bononiensi. (Impressum Bononiæ Per Benedictum hectoris ... Idibus Aprilis ... M.D.X.V. ...) 4°. A-C^8 D^4. [15

-- -- (Argentorati ex Aedibus Matthiæ Schurerii Mense Ianuario. Anno M. D. XVII.) 4°. A^4

B^8 C-D^4 E^8 F^4. ff. [III]-XXXI. [16

PALATINATE. Kirchenordnung Wie es mit der Christlichen Lehre/ Administrierung der heiligen Sacramenten vnd Ceremonien/ in ... Ludwigen Pfaltzgrauen bey Rhein ... Füurstenthumb gehalten werden soll. Gedruckt in ... Heydelberg/ Durch Iacob Müller. M. D. LXXVII. 4°. A-Rr^4 Ss^2. ff. 2-160. (Yarnall.) [17

-- Pfaltzgraff Ludwigs Churfürstens/ etc. neuw ... Policey: Allmusen: vnnd Ehe Ordnunge/ Auch Widertäuffer Edict. Gedruckt in ... Heydelberg/ durch Iohan Spies. M.D.LXXXIII. 4°.)(^{4} A-Y^4. ff. 1-88. ¶*Additional t.p.* (V2^r): Churfürstlichen Pfaltz Widertäufferischen Irthumbs halb gegebene Instruction. *Same imprint.* [18

PALATINO, GIOVANNI BATTISTA. Libro nuouo d'imparare a scriuere tutte sorte lettere antiche et moderne ... (Stampata in Roma ... nelle Case di M. Benedetto Gionta, per Baldassarre di Francesco Cartolari Perugino, Il di XII d'Agosto M. D. XXXX.) 4°. [A]^4 B-N^4. [19

PALEARIO, AONIO. Aonii Paleari Verulani epistolarum lib. IIII. orationes XII. de animorum immortalitate lib. III. ... Basileae, apud Ioannem Oporinum [c. 1567]. 8°. A-Qq^8 Rr^4. pp. 4-617. [20

-- -- Basileae apud Thomam Guarinum [c. 1570]. 8°. A-Qq^8. pp. 4-609. [21

PALEOTI, GABRIEL. De bono senectutis ... Romae Ex Typographia Aloysij Zannetti. 4°. a-c^4 d^6 A-V^4 X^6 Y-Gg^4 Hh^2 Kk-Pp^4. pp. 1-258. [22

PALEOTTI, ALFONSO. Esplicatione del lenzuolo, oue fu inuolto il Signore & delle Piaghe in esso impresso ... In Bologna per gli heredi di Gio. Rossi ... 1598 4°. †-††^{8} 3†^{1} A-L^8 M^6 (-M6, *presumably blank*). pp. 1-146. ¶*Engraved t.p.* A3, A4 *defective.* (Lea.) [23

PALLADIO, ANDREA. [1] I quattro libri dell'architettura Di Andrea Palladio. ... In Venetia, Appresso Bartolomeo Carampello. 1581. (*Colophon.*) fol. A^2 B-I^4. pp. 1-67. [2] Il secondo libro ... In Venetia, Appresso Dominico de' Franceschi. 1570. AA-KK^4. pp. 3-66. [3] [Il terzo libro ... In Venetia, appresso Bartolomeo Carampello. 1581.] 3A-3E^4 (-3A1) 3F^{2+1}. pp. 3-46. [4] Il quarto libro ... *Same imprint.* 4A-4R^4. pp. 3-133. (Fine Arts.) [24

-- -- [1] Il terzo libro dell'architettura ... In Venetia, Appresso Dominico de' Franceschi. 1570. fol. 3A-3F^4. pp. 3-46. [2] Il quarto libro ... *Same imprint.* (*Colophon.*) 4A-4R^4. pp. 3-128. (Fine Arts.) [25

PALLAVICINO, GIUSEPPE. Delle lettere ... Libri tre ... In Venetia. Appresso Francesco Rampazetto. (... M D LXVI.) 8°. *^{8} A-Ii^8 Kk^4. pp. 1-259. [26

PALLAVICINO, ROLANDO. Statuta Pallauicinia. Cum additionibus ... eorum in terris subiectis Ill. D. Rolando de Curtemaiori obseruandis. Et cum annotationibus ... Petri Pectoreli, & Hieronymi Vitalis. His accessere Statuta, & Ordines Collegij DD. Notariorum Buxeti ... Parmae, Ex Officina Erasmi Viotti, M. D. LXXXII. fol. *^{6} (-*6, *presumably blank*) A-S^6 T^4 (-T4, *presumably blank*). pp. 1-222. (Lea.) [27

PALMERÍN DE OLIVA. Histoire de Palmerin d'Oliue ... A Paris. Pour Galiot du Pré ... 1573. 8°. ā^8 ē^8 A-Zz^8 Aa-Ii^8 KK-OO^8 PP^4. ff. 1-496. [28

PALMIERI, MATTEO. Libro della vita ciuile ... [Firenze, heirs of Filippo Giunti, c. 1528.] 8°. A-M^8 N^4 (-N4, *blank*). ff. 2-99. ¶K4, M4 *ff. repaired.* [29

-- -- (In Firenze per li heredi di Philippo di Giunta ... M.D.XXIX. alli 5. di Settembre.) 8°. A^4 B-Q^8. ff. 2-125. [30

PALMIRENO, JUAN LORENZO. Laurentij Palmyreni de copia rerum et artificio oratorio libellus ... Valentiæ, Ex typographia Ioannis Mey. 1564. (Vendense en casa del autor ...) 8°. A-K^8 L^2. ff. 2-76. ¶*Additional t.p.* (F7^r): Laurentij Palmyreni de inuentione liber secundus ... *Same imprint.* [31

-- Laurentij Palmyreni de vera & facili imitatione Ciceronis ... Cæsaraugustæ. 1560. (Fue impresso ... en casa de Pedro Bernuz. Acabose a nueue dias del mes de Março ...) 8°. A-P8 Q12. [32

-- [1] Prima pars rhetoricæ Laurentii Palmyreni ... Valentiae. Ex typographia Ioannis Mey. 1567. 8°. A-G8 H4. pp. 2-118. [2] Tertia & vltima pars rhetoricae ... Valentiæ, Ex typographia Ioannis Mey. 1566. (Eas habet venales Palmyrenus in suis ædibus Valentiæ ...) A-I8 K2. pp. 2-148. [33

-- Rhetoricę prolegomena Laurentino Palmyreno praelegente excepta. Excipiebat autem ... Iosephus Medina ... Valentiae Ex typographia Ioannis Mey. 1564. (*Colophon.*) 8°. A-B8. ff. 2-16. [34

-- -- Valentiae. Ex typographia Ioannis Mey. 1567. 8°. A-C8. pp. 5-31. [35

PANFILO, GANIMEDE. Gli centonici et historici capitoli et alcuni pieni di sdruccioli, e Bisticci, & altri versi ... In Camerino, Appresso gli Heredi d'Antonio Gioioso, & Girolamo Stringari, M D LXXIX. 4°. A-HH4 II2. ff. 2-125. ¶II1-2 *in duplicate.* [36

-- Rime, e versi sciolti, con sdruscioli bistici. E Centoni ... 4°. A-L4. [37

PANTALEON, HEINRICH. Militaris ordinis Iohannitarum, Rhodiorum, aut Melitensium equitum, rerum memorabilium ... gestarum ... Historia Noua ... Basileæ, [Thomas Guarinus,] Anno M. D. LXXXI. fol.):(6 a-z6 A-I6 K8. pp. 135 [= 1]-387. [38

-- [1] Prosopographiae heroum atque illustrium virorum totius Germaniæ, pars prima. ... Basileae in officina Nicolai Brylingeri, Anno 1565. (*Colophon.*) fol. ()6 a-z6 A8 +6. pp. 2-291. [2] ... Pars secunda. ... Basileae, in officina Nicolai Brylingeri, 1565. a4 A-Nn6 Oo8 *6. pp. 1-480. [3] ... Pars tertia, eaque primaria. ... Basileae, in officina haeredum Nicolai Brylingeri, Anno 1566. A6 AA-ZZz6 Aaa6 a6. pp. 1-565. [39

PANTHEO, GIOVANNI AGOSTINO. [1] Ars et theoria transmutationis metallicæ cum Voarchadúmia ... Vęneunt apud Viuantium Gautherotium ... 1550. 8°. A-D8 E2. ff. 2-34. [2] Voarchadumia contra alchimiã ... Parisiis, Apud Viuentium Gualtherot ... 1550. A-H8. ff. 2-55. [40

-- Voarchadumia contra Alchi´miam: Ars distincta ab Archimi´a, & Sophia ... Ioannis Augustini Panthei ... Venetiis [per Joannem Tacuinum]. Diebus. Aprilis. M. D. XXX. 4°. A-P4 Q6 (-Q6). ff. 2-69. (Smith.) [41

PANVINIO, ONOFRIO. Epitome pontificum Romanorum ... Gestorum ... Venetiis, Impensis Iacobi Stradæ Mantuani. M. D. LVII. fol. *4 A-Mm6 Nn8 Oo-Pp6. pp. 1-428. ¶*1 *defective.* [42

-- [1] Onuphrii Panuinii Veronensis ... fastorum libri V a Romulo rege vsque ad ... Carolum V ... Venetiis, Ex Officina Erasmiana Vincentij Valgrisij. M D LVIII fol. a4 b6 A-Rr6 Ss4. pp. 3-480. [2] ... commentariorum appendix. ... *Same imprint.* *4 A6 B-D4 E-G6. pp. 1-72. [3] ... de ludis saecularibus liber ... *Same imprint.* A-G6. pp. 3-82. [43

-- Onuphrii Panuinii ... reipublicae . Romanae commentariorum libri . tres Et alia quaedam ... Venetiis Ex Officina Erasmiana apud Vincentium Valgrisium, M D LVIII. 8°. a8 A-Z8 a-z8 Aa-Oo8. pp. 1-947. (Lea.) [44

-- Di F. Onofrio Panuinio Veronese ... Le sette chiese principali di Roma. Tradotte da M. Marco Antonio Lanfranchi. In Roma per gli heredi di Antonio Blado 1570 ... (*Colophon.*) 8°. π4 A-X8 Y6. pp. 1-346. (Lea.) [45

PAPADOPULO, NICOLÒ. [1] Epistola ... à Sultan Selin Imperator de Turchi. ... [c. 1572.] 8°. A-B4. [2] Risposta de Sultan Selin ... a tutti i sonetti a lui fatti da diuersi Auttori, & in uarie lingue. ... Opera di M. Nicolo Papadopulo ... A4 B8 C4. [46

PAPE, GUY. Dn. Guidonis Papae ... Decisiones Grationopolitanæ. ... Venetiis, Apud Andræam Muschio. 1569. 8°. A-Ff8 GG-3T8. pp. 8-967. [47

-- -- ... Rote decisiões capelleqȝ tholosane: ⁊ nouissime scripta per eũdẽ Guidonem Pape ... cũ ... addi. Hẽri. Ferrãdat Niuer. ... 1528 (... die. ij. mensis Septembris. Sumptu ... Guilielmi Boulle hoc ... opus excusum est Lugduni in edibus ... Antonij Blanchardi.) 8°. B.L. A-B8 C4 a-kk8 ll4. ff. I-CCLXVII. (Lea.) [48

PAPON, JEAN. Recueil d'arrestz notables des courts souueraines de France. ... A Lyon par

Iehan de Tournes, M. D. LVI. ... (Acheué d'imprimer le quatriesme de Nouembre ...) fol. a-zz^{4} A-V^{4} X^{4+1}. pp. 3-504. [49

PARABOSCO, GIROLAMO. Comedie ... cioè, La Notte, Il Viluppo, I Contenti, L'Hermofrodito, Il Pellegrino, Il Marinaio. ... In Vinegia appresso Gabriel Giolito de' Ferrari. M D L X. 12°. A-E^{12} A-D^{12} A-C^{12} A-C^{12} D^{6} (-D6, *presumably blank*) A-E^{12} A-D^{12}. ff. 2-59, 2-48, 2-36, 2-41, 2-59, 2-47. [50

-- I contenti comedia ... In Vinegia appresso Gabriel Giolito de' Ferrari. MDLX. 12°. A-D^{12}. ff. 2-47. [51

-- I diporti ... In Vinegia. MDLVIII. 8°. A-O^{8} P^{4}. ff. 2-115. [52

-- La fantesca comedia noua ... In Vinegia, Appresso Stephano di Alessi ... 1557. 8°. A-F^{8} (-F8, *presumably blank*). pp. 3-94. ¶B8 *defective*. [53

-- Il ladro comedia noua ... In Venetia, per Francesco e Pietro Rocca Fratelli, l'anno MDLV. (*Colophon.*) 8°. A-I^{4} K^{6}. ff. 5-41. [54

-- [1] Lettere amorose ... Libro primo. ... In Vinegia, appresso Domenico Farri. M.D.LXIIII. 8°. A-I^{8}. ff. 3-71. [2] ... Libro secondo. ... *Same imprint*. A-F^{8}. ff. 3-4 [= 47]. [3] ... Libro terzo. ... *Same imprint*. A-G^{8}. ff. 3-55. [55

-- -- Lettres amoureuses de Messer Girolam Parabosque ... reduites de l'Italien en volgaire François, par Hubert Philippe de Villiers. ... A Lyon par Benoist Rigaud [c. 1575]. 16°. A-Y^{8}. pp. 3-350. ¶*T.p. blotted*. [56

-- La Progne tragedia noua ... In Venetia a San Luca al segno della Cognitione. M.D.XLVIII. (... per Comin da Trino. ...) 8°. A-D^{8}. ff. 2-32. [57

-- Il Viluppo comedia noua ... In Vinegia appresso Gabriel Giolito de' Ferrari. M D LXVII. 12°. A-E^{12}. ff. 2-59. [58

PARADIN, GUILLAUME. Anglicae descriptionis compendium ... Parisiis, Apud Viuantium Gualtherot ... 1545. ... 8°. A-I^{4}. pp. 3-70. [59

-- Chronique de Sauoye ... A Lyon par Ian de Tournes ... M. D. LXI. ... (*Colophon.*) fol. A-C^{4} D^{6} a-zz^{4} A-G^{4} H^{6}. pp. 1-435. [60

-- De antiquo statu Burgundiae liber. ... Lugduni, Apud Stephanum Doletum. 1542 ... 4°. A-X^{4}. pp. 2-158. [61

-- Gulielmi Paradini Anchemani epigrammata. Accessit Francorum regum series ... Lugduni, apud Ant. Gryphium. M. D. LXXXI. 4°. A-I^{4}. pp. 3-72. [62

-- Histoire de notre tems. Faite en Latin par M. Guillaume Paradin, & par lui reuuē & mise en François. ... A Lyon, Par Pierre Michel. 1558. 16°. A-C^{8} a-z^{8} A-Ii^{8} (-Ii8, *presumably blank*). pp. 1-835. (Lea.) [63

PARAMO, LUIS DE. De origine et progressu Officii Sanctae Inquisitionis, ... libri tres. Autore Ludouico à Paramo Boroxensi ... Matriti, Ex Typographia Regia. cIↄ. Iↄ. XCIIX. (... Apud Ioannem Flandrum. ...) fol. *^{8} a-f^{8} g^{4} A-3I^{8} 3K^{4}. pp. 1-887. (Lea.) [64

PARÉ, AMBROISE. Deux liures de chirurgie. ... 1. De la generatiō de l'homme ... 2. Des monstres ... A Paris, Chez André Wechel. ... 1573. 8°. ā^{8} ē^{4} a-z^{8} A-P^{8} Q^{6}. pp. 1-619. [65

PARIS. *Collège de Rheims*. Elegia et epigrammata super defensione priuilegiorum Academiæ. Praisiis, Ex Typographia Dionysij à Prato ... 1570. 4°. A-B^{4}. [66

PARISIO, PIETRO PAOLO. Commentaria ꝛ rescripta ... in titulum de exceptionibus in secūdo libro Decretalium. ... (Venetijs per Baptistam de Tortis Mccccxxij. die .xx. Octobris.) fol. B.L. AA-HH^{6} II-KK^{4}. ff. 2-55. (Biddle.) [67

-- Commentaria ... in titulum De prescriptionibus. (Venetijs per Baptistam de Tortis die .xxviij. Nouembris. Mccccxxij.) fol. B.L. 3A-3H^{6} 3I-3K^{4}. ff. 2-55. (Biddle.) [68

-- [Consilia.] Venetiis MDXLIII (... apud Aurelium Pincium Venetum ... impressum.) fol. B.L. [1] Primum volumen consiliorum, ac responsorum Petri Pauli Parisij ... (... MDXLII

...) A-Hh^{8} Ii^{6}. ff. 2-253. [2] Secundum volumen ... (... MDXLII ...) aa-zz^{8} ꝛꝛ^{8} ꝯꝯ^{8} ꝝꝝ^{8} AA^{8} BB^{10}. ff. 2-225. [3] Tertium volumen ... (... M D XLIII.) 3a-3z^{8} 3ꝛ^{8} 3ꝯ^{4}. ff. 2-195. [4] Quartum volumen ... (... M D XLIII.) 4a-4z^{8} 4ꝛ^{8} 4ꝯ^{8} 4ꝝ^{4}. ff. 3-202. [5] Repertorium siue index ... A-R^{8} S^{6} T^{4}. ff. 3-8. (Biddle.) [69

PARMA. Decreto gratioso. In Parma. Nella Stamperia di Erasmo Viotti. fol. π^{2}. ¶*Dated 13 July 1585.* [70

-- Ordini, et constitutioni ducali, Nell'errettione del ... Ducale Consiglio. In Parma. Appresso Erasmo Viotto. M. D. LXXXIX. fol. A^{4}. (Lea.) [71

-- Statuta magnificæ ciuitatis Parmae. Cum annotationibus ... D. Bartholomei a Prato, D. Vincentij Blondi, D. Iacobi Carpesani, D. Ludouici Zandermariæ, D. Antonij Cantelli, D. Innocentij Blondi, Et aliorum Doctorum ... Hac secunda editione ... emendata. ... Parmae. Ex Officina Erasmi Viothi, M. D. LXXXX. (*Colophon.*) fol. *^{10} A-Ee^{8} Ff^{4} [♦]^{2} A-Cc^{8}. ff. 1-228, 1-207. ¶*Additional t.p.* (♦1): Annotationes ad statuta mag. ciuitatis Parmae ... *Same imprint.* (Lea.) [72

-- Constitutiones ducalis cameræ Parmæ, et Placent. Parmae, Apud Erasmum Viothum. M. D. XCIV. fol. A^{14} B^{10}. (Lea.) [73

PARRHASIUS, AULUS JANUS. Iani Parrhasii liber De rebus per epistolam quæsitis. ... Francisci Campani Quæstio Virgiliana. Anno M. D. LXVII [Genevae,] Excudebat Henricus Stephanus ... 8°. ¶^{4} a-r^{8} s^{4}. pp. 1-272. [74

PARSONS, ROBERT. Elizabethae Angliae reginae haeresim Caluinianam propugnantis saeuissimum in Catholicos sui regni edictum ... cum responsione ad singula capita Per D. Andream Philopatrum ... Romæ, Ex Typographia Aloysij Zannetti. 1593. 4°. ❦^{2} A-3Q^{4} 3R^{2}. pp. 1-485. (Lea.) [75

-- The first booke of the Christian exercise, appertayning to resolution. ... [Rouen,] Anno. 1[5]82. ... 12°. A^{6} B-T^{12}. pp. 1-431. *S.T.C.* 19353. ¶*T.p. defective.* [76

PARTENIO, BERNARDINO. Della imitatione poetica. ... In Vinegia appresso Gabriel Giolito de' Ferrari, MDLX. 4°. *^{8} A-P^{8} Q^{6}. pp. 1-248. [77

-- -- De poetica imitatione libri quinque. ... Venetiis, Apud Ludouicum Auancium. MDLXV. (... M D LXVI.) 4°. A-SS^{4}. ff. 3-160. [78

PARUTA, PAOLO. Della perfettione della vita politica ... Libri tre. ... In Venetia, M D LXXIX. Appresso Domenico Nicolini. fol. a-c^{4} A-L^{4} M^{6} N-Qq^{4}. pp. 1-315. [79

PARVULUS. Habes hic amande lector textũ Paruuli/ qꝺ aiũt/ pĥie natural' cũ cõmentarijs ... Matthie Qualle Carniolani ... (Impẽsis ... Ioãnis rynman in officina ... Hẽrici Gran ... in ... Hagenaw imp̃ssus. ... 1513. vigesimaoctaua die Septembris ...) 4°. B.L. a-i^{8} k^{6} l^{4} m^{8}. [80

-- Paruulus philosophie naturalis cum expositiõe textuali ac dubiorum ... dissolutione ad intentionem Scoti cõgesta ... a Ioanne Stobnicensi ... (Impressum Cracouie impensis domini Joannis Haller ... M.d.vij. et finitum vltima die Aprilis) 4°. B.L. a^{6} b^{8} c^{4} d^{8} e^{4} f^{6} g^{8} h-l$^{4.8}$. [81

-- -- Paruulus philosophiae naturalis ... (Impressu [Viennae] Anno M. D. XXI.) 4°. A-C^{4}. [82

PASI, BARTOLOMMEO DI. Tarifa de i pesi, e misure corrispondenti dal Leuante al Ponente ... In Vinegia per Paolo Gherardo. M. D. LVII. (... per Comin da Trino. ...) 8°. †^{8} ††^{4} A-BB^{8}. ff. 1-200. [83

PASI, CURIO LANCELLOTTO. Emendatũ Quadringentis in locis: vbi multa diminuta pleraqꝫ apocripha. manibꝰ Cur. Lancilotti Pasij Ferrariẽsis laureati: qui est operis autor. ... Titulus de litteratura non vulgari. (Antonius Ranotus & Eustachius Hebertus in Augusta Taurinorum imprimebãt ... M.D.XX.VI. Id. Octobris.) 4°. AA^{8} a-z^{8} A-D^{8} E^{6} ♦^{8} ♦♦^{6}. ff. I-CCXXI. [84

PASQUALIGO, LUIGI. Il fedele comedia ... In Venetia, Appresso Bolognino Zaltieri,

M D LXXVI. (*Colophon.*) 8°. a8 A-L8 M4. pp. 1-184. [85

-- Gl'intricati Pastorale del ... Sig. Aluise Pasqualigo. ... In Venetia, Appresso Francesco Ziletti. M D LXXXI. 8°. A-I8. ff. 10-71. [86

PASQUIL. Carmina quæ ad pasquillum fuerunt posita in anno .M.CCCCC.IX. (Finis Rome [per Jacobum Mazochium].) 4°. A-C4 D6. [87

-- Carmina, ad Pasquillum Herculem obtruncantem Hydram referentem posita Anno M. D. X. (Impressum Rome per magistrum Iacobū Mazochiū. ...) 4°. a-e4 f6. [88

-- Carmina Apposita Pasquillo anno. M.D.xiij. 4°. [A]-B4 C6. [89

-- Pascuillus Ain warhafftiges buchlin Erklerēd was list die Rômer brauchen/ mit Creiren viler Cardināl/ auff das sy alle Bistumb Deūtscher land vnder sich bringen. [Nürnberg, Jobst Gutknecht, c. 1520.] 4°. A6. [90

-- Pasquillorum Tomi duo. ... Eleutheropoli [*i.e.* Basileae, Joannes Oporinus?] MDXLIIII. 8°. *8 a-z8 A-R8 (-R8). pp. 1-537. [91

-- Pasquillus Nouus dolos fraudesqȝ Concubinarum mire complectens ... 16°. aa-bb8. [92

-- Pasquillus Romanus ad rectores ciuesque Galliae. M D XXXVI. 4°. A4. [93

-- Pasquillus semipoeta. De bello religionis causa à Carolo v. Cæsare & Romano Pontifice nuper Germaniæ illato. Anno M. D. XLVI. 4°. a-b4. [94

-- Ein sinreicher Pasquillus/ der aller erst von Rom kommet/ vnd vnser aller Herrn ... kriegsshandlungen vnd andere leuff meldet. Mense Iunio. 1537. 4°. [A]4. [95

-- Ein vnterredung zwisschen dem Pasquillen vnd Deudschen/ von dem zukünfftigen Concilio zu Mantua. ... MDXXXVII 4°. A-B4. [96

-- -- Ein vnderredung zwischē dem Pasquillen vnd Deutschen/ vonn dem zůkünfftigen Concilio zů Mantua. ... MDXXXVII. 4°. A4 B2. [97

-- Pasquillus. Ein Colloquium oder Gesprech wider die ... lere/ Andree Osiandri ... Anno M.D.LII. 4°. A-I4. ¶*In verse.* [98

PASQUINO. Compositioni Nuoue del faceto homo Maestro Pasquino di Parione: tradotte di Latino in Volgare da Marforio suo carissimo cōpagno antico. ... (Stampata [Roma?] a instātia di Paris Mantoano ... 1547.) 8°. A4. [99

PASSAU. Articuli reformationis, omnibus ... Sacerdotibus Episcopatui ac Dioecesi Patauiensi supra Anasum subiectis prescripti ... Patauiæ Apud Matthaeum Nenninger. M. D. XC. 8°. A-E8. [100

PASSERAT, JEAN. In Adriani Turnebi obitum ... elegia ... Parisiis, Apud Federicum Morellum ... M. D. LXV. 4°. A4. [101

-- Ioannis Passeratii ... Kalendæ Ianuariæ. Lutetiæ, Apud Mamertum Patissonium ... Ex officina Rob. Stephani. CIↃ IↃ XCVII. ... 4°. ã2 A-R4. ff. 1-67. [102

-- Io. Passeratij præfatiuncula in disputationem de Ridiculis, quæ est apud Ciceronem in libro secondo de Oratore. Lutetiæ, Apud Mamertum Patissonium ... In officina Roberti Stephani. M. D. XCV. 8°. A-C4 D2 (-D2, *blank*). ff. 2-13. [103

PASSI, CARLO. La selua di varia istoria ... Laquale auanti andaua attorno stampata sotto nome fittitio di Annotationi dell'Infortunio nella prima, e seconda parte delle Istorie di Monsig. Giouio. ... In Venetia appresso Giorgio de'Caualli. 1564. 4°. A4 b-dd4 3a-3f4 3g2. ff. 1-103. ¶*Presumably part of an edition of the* Istorie *of Giovio.* [104

-- -- [1] La selua di varia istoria ... In Vinegia, Presso Altobello Salicato, M D LXXII. 4°. A-DD4. ff. 1-105. [2] Tauola nella quale si contengono i nomi antichi, et moderni, Delle Prouincie, Città, Castella, Popoli, Monti, Mari, Fiumi, & Laghi, de'quali Mons. Paolo Giouio ha fatta nelle sue Istorie mentione. ... *Same imprint.* A-F4 G2. ff. 2-25. ¶*Presumably parts of an edition of the* Istorie *of Giovio.* [105

PASTORIS, HEINRICH. Practica deutsch von vergangen/ vñ zůkunfftigen dingen (wider die zů

Speyer gedruckt) auss der Heiligen schrifft ... getzogen. Auff das. 1524. ɾc jar. ... Gedruckt zů Errfordt durch Michel Buchfurer. 4°. A^4. [106

PASTRENGO, GUGLIELMO DE. De originibus rerum libellus authore Gulielmo Pastregico Veronese. ... Expurgatus ... à Michaeleangelo Blondo ... (Impressum Venetijs per Nicolaum de Bascarinis. ... M. D. XLVII.) 8°. A-Q^8 R^4. ff. 2-131. [107

PATELLIUS, DEIPHOBUS. ... Deiphobi Patellii de virtutis laudibus oratio ... Senis, apud Lucam Bonettum. ... MDXCV. 4°. A-G^4. pp. 3-56. [108

PATERNO, LODOVICO. Le nuoue fiamme ... In Lyone, appresso Guglielmo Rouillio. 1568. 16°. a-z^8 A-M^8 (-M8, *presumably blank*). pp. 4-541. [109

-- Nuouo Petrarca' ... In Venetia, Appresso Gioan'Andrea Valuassori, detto Guadagnino. MDLX. 8°. a^8 A-Ss^8. pp. 1-624. [110

PATRIZI, FRANCESCO. Di M. Francesco Patritio la citta felice. Del medesimo, Dialogo dell' honore, il barignano. Del medesimo, Discorso della diuersita de' furori poetici. Lettura sopra il sonetto del Petrarca. La gola, e'l sonno, e l'ociose piume. In Venetia per Gio-uan. Griffio MDLIII. (... Alli. 30. di Gennaio.) 8°. A-S^4. ff. 4-69. [111

-- Della retorica dieci dialoghi di M. Francesco Patritio ... In Venetia, appresso Francesco Senese, M D LXII. 4°. $*^6$ A-P^4 Q^2 (-Q2, *blank*). ff. 1-61. [112

-- Francisci Patricii discussionum Peripateticarum Tomi IV. ... Basileae ad Perneam lecythum ... CIↃ IↃ XXCI. fol. $()^6$ a^4 b-z^6 A-Q^6 R^4 S^6 T^8. pp. 3-479. ¶*Additional t.pp.:* (()3^r) ... tomus Primus ... *Same imprint.* ($q1^r$) ... tomus Secundus. ... *Same imprint.* ($B1^r$) ... tomus Tertius. ... *Same imprint.* ($H1^r$) ... tomus Quartus. ... *Same imprint.* [113

-- [1] Le liure de police humaine ... extraict des ... volumes de François Patrice ... par maistre Gilles d'Aurigny, ... & nouellement traduict de Latin en Frãçois, par maistre Iehan le Blond ... 1546. On les vend à Paris par Charles l'Angelié ... (*Colophon.*) 8°. $*^8$ A-O^8. ff. 2-101. [2] La seconde partie du liure de police humaine ... *Same imprint.* $**^4$ Aa-Nn^8 Oo^4. ff. 1-108. [114

-- [1] Francisci Patricii noua de vniuersis philosophia. ... Ferrariae, Apud Benedictum Mammarellum. Anno MDXCI. ... fol. a^4. [2] Francisci Patricii Zoroaster. et eius CCCXX oracula Chaldaica ... latine reddita. ... *Same imprint.* $*^2$ a^2 D3-8 E^4. ff. 3-11. [3] Hermetis Trismegisti Libelli integri xx. Et Fragmenta. Asclepii ... libelli III. ... *Same imprint.* π^2 $\dagger^4$ $\dagger\dagger^2$ $*^6$ B-O^4. ff. 1-51. [4] Mystica Aegyptiorum et Caldæorum, à Platone voce tradita. ... *Same imprint.* $[A]^2$ B-O^4. ff. 1-51. [5] Francisci Patricii panaugia. Vniuersae lucis tractatio ... *Same imprint.* π^2 A-C^8. ff. 1-23. [6] Francisci Patricii Panarchiae. De rerum principiis primis. Libri octo. ... *Same imprint.* $*^2$ F-G^8 H^2 $*^2$ K-M^4 N1 $*^2$ N2-4 O-R^4 χ^2 S-V^4 χ^2 X-Bb^4 Cc^6 Dd-Mm^4 $*^2$ Nn-Vu^4 Xx^2 †-$\dagger\dagger^4$ (†1-3 *bound after* 3†2) $3\dagger^2$. ff. 1-153. ¶*Additional t.pp.:* ($^2*^r$) Francisci Patricii panarchias. De summa trinitate, ac diuinitate. Lib. VI. ... *Same imprint.* ($\chi 1^r$) Francisci Patricii Pampsichia nouae philosophiae, Tomus III. ... *Same imprint.* ($^2\chi^r$) Francisci Patricii pancosmiae. Mundi corporei principia et constitutio. Lib. VIII. ... *Same imprint.* ($Cc4^r$) Francisci Patricii pancosmiæ. De aethere, ac rebus coelestibus. Lib. XIIII. *Same imprint.* ($^3*^r$) Francisci Patricii pancosmiae. De aere, aquis, terra. Libri Decem. ... *Same imprint. According to the register,* [2]-[4] *should follow* Xx2. [115

-- Franc. Patricii philosophiae, de rerum natura. Libri II. priores. Alter de Spacio Physico, Alter de Spacio Mathematico. Ferrariae, Excudebat Victor. Baldinus ... MDLXXXVII. 4°. A-F^4 G^2. ff. 2-26. [116

-- Il sacro regno de'l gran' Patritio de'l uero reggimento, e de le uera felicità de'l Principe, e beatitudine humana. ... (In Vinegia per comin de Trino di Monferrato, L'anno M.D.XLVII.) 4°. A^6 *-$**^4$ A-BB^8 CC^4 DD^2. ff. 2-206. ¶*Translator: Giovanni Fabrini.* [117

-- -- In Vinegia, M. D. LIII. (... in casa de' figliuoli di Aldo. ...) 8°. *-$**^8$ $3*^8$ A-ZZ^8 (-ZZ7). ff. 1-368. [118

PAUL III, pope. Ein kostlich Triumph/ Gepreng/ vnd Fassnacht spil/ so man diss jar dem Babst zu Ehren/ zu Rhom gehalten/ ... zu Rhom gedruckt hat/ gantz fleyssig verteutscht.

... Adi. 15. Maij/ Anno 1545. in Deutsch yetzt erstlich getruckt. 4°. a-c^4. [119

PAULIANUS, JOANNES BAPTISTA. De iobeleo et indulgentiis libri tres, recollecti ex repetitione ... (Romæ apud Valorium, & Aloisium Doricos fratres. Anno M.D.L.) 8°. *^{4} A-Q^8. pp. 1-255. [120

PAULINUS, FABIUS. In eundem M. Tullii Ciceronis, dialogi de oratore Librum Primum. ... scholia. ... Venetiis, Apud Franciscum Francisciumn Senensem. M D LXXXVII. 4°. A-F^4. ff. 2-24. [121

PAULUCCIO, SIGISMONDO. Continuatione di Orlando furioso, Con la morte di Ruggiero ... M D XLIII. (In Vinegia per Gioann'Antonio, e Pietro fratelli, di Nicolini da Sabio: Ad instantia di M. Nicolo d'Aristotile detto il Zoppino. ...) 4°. A-GG^8 HH^4. ff. 3-243. [122

PAULUS DE SANCTA MARIA. Scrutinium Scripturarum. ... Recognitum ... per ... Christophorum Sanctotisium ... Burgensem. Cui addita est ipsius D. D. Pauli vita ... Burgis. Apud Philippum Iuntam. 1591. (*Colophon.*) fol. π^2 A-E^8 F^{10} G-Nn^8. pp. 1-572. ¶L13^v-Nn^v: Epistola Rabbi Samuel ad Rabbi Isaac. Oo^{10} *wanting*. (Lea.) [123

PAULUS VENETUS. Tractatus summularum logice .... (Impresse Venetijs p̱ Lucaȝ antonium de Giuntis Florentinuȝ. ... 1517. Die .xxix. Decemb.) 4°. B.L. a-f^8. [124

PAUSANIAS. Παυσανίας Pausanias (Venetiis in aedibus Aldi, et Andreae soceri mense Iulio. M. D. XVI.) fol. π^2 αα-ρρ^8 σσ^6. pp. 2-282. [125

PAVESI, CESARE. Il targa, doue si contengono le Cento, & cinquanta Fauole. Tratte da diuersi Autori antichi, Et ridotte in versi, & Rime Italiane ... Impressione Quarta. In Venetia, Presso gli Heredi di Francesco Ziletti. M. D. LXXXVII. 12°. A-I^{12}. pp. 3-215. [126

PAVIA. Statuta ciuitatis et Principatus Papiæ ... Ticini, Ex Typographia Hieronymi Bartoli. MDXC. fol. A^4 A^4 A-X^6 Y^8. pp. 1-247. (Lea.) [127

-- *Accademia degli Affidati*. Rime de gli academici Affidati di Pauia. ... Nella ... citta di Pauia. Appresso Girolamo Bartoli. MDLXV. (*Colophon.*) 4°. *^{6} A-Ii^4. pp. 1-255. [128

PAWŁOWSKI, STANISŁAW. Rudolphi secundi, ... Romanorum Imperatoris ... D. Stanislai Pawlowski, Episcopi Olomuceñ: ... Venceslai Senioris Bercæ, Baronis de Daub ... Oratorum ad ... Sigismundum Tertium, Poloniæ & Sueciæ Regem ... Oratio, in Comitiis Generalibus Cracouiæ habita, Die 27. Mensis Februarij, ... 1595. (Cracouiæ, In Officina Lazari, ... 1595.) 4°. A-D^4. (Lea.) [129

PECHAM, JOHN. Perspectiua communis. ... emendata ... Per Georgium Hartmannum Norimbergensem. Norimbergæ apud Iohan. Petreium. Anno M. D. XLII. 4°. a-o^4. [130

PEDIONEUS, JOANNES. Ioannis Pedionei Constantini ... de Bello Germanico liber. ... M. D. XLVII. 4°. A-F^4. ff. 1-20. [131

-- Ioannis Pedionei ... de Claris Oratoribus Libri duo. Eiusdem elegiae II. ... Ingolstadii ex officina Typographica Alexandri Vueissenhorn. M. D. XLVI. 4°. A-F^4. ff. 1-56. [132

-- Ioannis Pedionei ... Hymnorum Liber. Eiusdem odae VII. Oratio de Ciceronis, & eloquentiæ laudibus. ... Ingolstadii excudebat Alexander Vueissenhorn. Anno XLIX. 8°. A-H^8 I^4. [133

-- -- *Variant*. Ingolstadii excudebat Alexander Vueissenhorn. Anno L. 8°. A-H^8 I^4. [134

PEELE, JAMES. 1569. The Pathe waye to perfectnes, in th'accomptes of Debitour, and Creditour ... Imprinted at London ... by Thomas Purfoote ... 16. August. fol. B.L. *^{4} A-K^6 L^4 M-Mm^6. *S.T.C.* 19548. [135

PEGIE, MARTIN. De iure protomiseos congrui, vel retractus. Vom Vorkauff, Eynstād, Kauffzugrechten. ... durch ... Martinum Pegium ... Strassburg/ In verlegung Lazari Zetzners. M .D XCVI. fol. A-O[4]. ff. 1-53. [136

-- Einstandtrecht/ In Latein Ius protomiseos, congrui, vel retractus genannt ... Accesserunt præterea eiusdem autoris Consiliorum seu Responsorum Tyrocinia ... Getruckt zů Ingolstatt/ durch Alexander vnd Samuel Weissenhorn gebrůder. Anno M.D.LXIIII. fol. *[6] A-O[4]. ff. I-LV. (Biddle.) [137

PEIFER, DAVID. Imperatores Turcici, Libellus de ... rebus gestis principum gentis Mahumeticæ, Elegiaco carmine conscriptus ... Basileae, per Ioannem Oporinum. 8°. A-D[8] E[4]. pp. 4-71. [138

-- Tyranni Turcici. De de [*sic*] vita et rebus gestis principum gentis Othomannicæ, Libelli duo, Scripti Carmine Elegiaco; aliaque poemata ... VVittebergæ. Typis Zachariæ Cratonis. Anno M. D. LXXXVII. 4°. A-S[4]. [139

PELAGIUS, ALVARUS. Aluari Pelagij de plāctu eccl'ie ... libri duo ... (Impressum est ... in ... Lugdunensi emporio apud ... Ioannem Cleyn ... Anno ... sesquimillesimo supra decimū septimo ad Calendas Augustas.) fol. B.L. A-C[6] ✣[6] a-z[8] A-K[8] L[6]. ff. I-CCLXX. ¶✣1 *defective*. (Yarnall.) [140

-- -- *Another copy*. (Lea.) [141

PELBART, OSWALD, de Themeswar. [1] Aureum sacrae theologiae rosarium; Iuxta Quatuor Sententiarum Libros quadripartitum. ... A R.P. Pelbarto de Themesvvar ... Venetiis, Ex Officina Francisci Ziletti. MDLXXXVI. (... MDLXXXV.) 4°. a[4] a[8] b[4] A-Gg[8]. ff. 2-239. [2] ... Thomus Secundus. ... *Same imprint and colophon*. a-b[8] A-Yy[8] (-Yy8, *presumably blank*). ff. 2-359. [3] ... Tomus Tertius. ... Venetiis, Ex Officina Damiani Zenarij. MDLXXXVI. a[8] A-Hh[8]. ff. 1-248. [4] ... Tomus Quartus. ... *Same imprint*. a[8] A-Ii[8] Kk[4]. ff. 2-260. (Lea.) [142

-- Pomerium sermonum. De sanctis Pars estiualis (Impssuꝫ Rothomagi ꝑ ... Petrū Oliuier pro ... Francisco regnault. Anno dn̄i vicesimoprimo supra millesimū ⁊ quingētesimū die vero quīta mensis Aprilis.) 8°. B.L. A[8] B[4] A-X[8] Aa-Xx[8] 3A-3E[8] 3F-3G[6]. [143

PELETIER, JACQUES, du Mans. Iacobi Peletarii Cenomani, In Euclidis Elementa Geometrica Demonstrationum Libri sex. ... Lugduni, apud Ioan. Tornæsium et Gul. Gazeium. M. D. LVII. ... fol. A[4] a-p[6]. pp. 1-166. [144

PELLEGRINO, CAMILLO. Replica ... alla riposta de gli accademici della Crusca Fatta contra il Dialogo dell'Epica Poesia in difesa ... dell'Orlando Furioso dell'Ariosto. ... In Vico Equense. Appresso Gioseppe Cacchij. M. D. LXXXV. 8°. A[8] B[4] C-Y[8] Z[6]. pp. 1-327. [145

PELLISSON, JEAN. Contextus vniuersae grammatices Despauterianae. ... Venetiis, Apud Francis. Bindonum. M. D. LVIII. (*Colophon*.) 8°. A-M[8]. pp. 3-191. [146

-- Rudimenta prima Latinæ grammatices. ... Modus examinandæ Constructionis in oratione ... MDXXXVII. (Impressum Venetijs per D. Melchiorem Sessam. ...) 8°. A-I[8] K[4]. ff. 2-75. [147

-- -- Venetiis, apud Francis. Bindonum. M. D. LVI. 8°. A-G[8]. pp. 2-112. [148

PELUSIO, GIANO. Iani Pelusii Crotoniatae ad proceres Christianos cohortatio. Neapoli. Apud Io. de Boy. 1567. 8°. A-F[8]. ff. 2-47. [149

PENA, PETRUS. Noua stirpium aduersaria. ... Auctoribus Petro Pena et Matthia de Lobel ... Additis Guillielmi Rondellettii aliquot Remediorum formulis ... Antuerpiæ, Apud Christophorum Plantinum ... M.D. LXXVI. ([Pp7[v]] Londini. 1571. Calendis Ianuarijs, excudebat prelum Thomæ Purfoetij ... [5*4[r]] ... VII. Calend. Augusti.) fol. π^2 *[6] A-Oo[6] (N3 + *slip*) Pp[6+1] Qq-Rr[4] *-5*[4] †-††[4]. pp. 1-471, 1-15. *Incorporates S.T.C.* 19595. [150

-- -- *Another copy*. [150a

PENSA, GIROLAMO. Epigrammi Toscani ... Nel Monte Regale [per Lionardo Torrentino] MDLXX. ... 4°. A[4] B-Y[8] Z[4] aa-cc[4]. pp. 3-344. [151

PÉRAULT, GUILLAUME. [1] Summae virtutum ac vitiorum. Tomus primus. ... Guilielmo Peraldo ... auctore. Antuerpiae. Apud Martinum Nutium. 1588. 8°. A-Kk^8. ff. 9-250. [2] ... Tomus secundus. ... *Same imprint.* A^8 Bb^2 A-Cc^8. ff. 1-196. [3] Summae virtutum ac vitiorum per figuras. Summarium. *Same imprint.* A-D^8. [152

PERAULT, RAYMOND, cardinal. [*Blank indulgence dated* M.ccccc.ij.] s.sh. 22 × 17 cm. B.L. [153

PEREIRA, BENITO. Benedicti Pererii ... De Communibus omnium rerum naturalium Principiis & Affectionibus, libri quindecim. ... Parisiis, Apud Thomam Brumennium ... M. D. LXXXV. ... 4°. ā^4 ē^6 a-z^8 A-Ii^8. pp. 1-839. [154

-- Benedicti Pererii Valentini ... Aduersus fallaces & superstitiosas artes. Id est, De Magia, De obseruatione Somniorum, & de Diuinatione Astrologica. Libri tres. Lugduni, ex officina Iuntarum. M. D. XCII. 8°. A-Q^8 R^4. pp. 3-258. (Lea.) [155

PERETTI, BATTISTA. Historia di S. Zeno vescouo di Verona et martire Raccolta ... In Verona, Nella Stamperia di Girolamo Discepolo. M D XCVII. 4°. [A]^4 B-K^4 L^6. pp. 5-86.[156

PEREZ, ANTONIO. Relaciones ... Impresso en Paris. ... M. D. XCVIII. 8°. †^{4} ā^8 ē^6 A-X^8 Y-Cc^4 Dd-Ll^8 Mm^4. ff. 1-218, pp. 219-222, ff. 1-19. [157

PEREZ DE MOYS, JUAN. Philosofia secreta. Donde debaxo de historias fabulosas ... En Madrid en casa de Francisco Sanchez ... M.D.LXXXV. 4°. π^6 ¶^{8} A-Mm^8 Nn^4. ff. 1-284. [158

PERGOLA. Statuta terrae Pergulae. Impressa Pisauri Apud Hieronymum Concordiam ... M D LXVII. fol. A^4 B-T^6 V^8 X^6 Y^8. ff. 3-134. (Lea.) [159

PERIANDER, GILLES. Hortus Amorum floribus illustrium Germanorum poetarum ... illustratus, ab Ægidio Periandro Brabantino, Bruxellensi ... Francofurti ad Moenum, per Martinum Lechlerum, impensis Sigismundi Feyrabend & Simonis Huteri. 1567. (... Mense Augusto.) 8°. A-Z^8 a-o^8 (-o8, *presumably blank*). ff. 2-293. [160

PERINGER, DIEPOLT. Ain schōne auslegūg über das gōtlich gebet. ... [Augsburg, Silvan Otmar,] Im .XXij. jar. 4°. A^4. [161

-- -- Eyn schöne Ausslegung ... M.D.XXiiij. 4°. A^4. [162

PÉRION, JOACHIM. Ioachimi Perionii ... de optimo genere interpretandi Commentarij. Parisiis Apud Ioannem Lodoicum Tiletanum ... M. D. XL. ... (*Colophon.*) 4°. A^4 A-FF^4. pp. 1-229. [163

-- De Romanorum et Græcorum magistratibus libri tres. ... Parisiis, In officina Caroli Perier ... 1560. ... 4°. A-O^4 P^2. ff. 1-51. [164

-- Ioachimi Perionii ... Dialogorum de linguæ Gallicæ origine, eiúsque cum Græca cognatione, libri quatuor. ... Parisiis, Apud Sebastianum Niuellium ... 1555. ... 8°. a-d^8 e^4 A-T^8. ff. 1-149. [165

-- Ioachimi Perionii Benedictini Cormoeriaceni oratio, qua Nicolai Groscij calumnias atque iniurias ostendit & refellit. Parisiis, Apud Thomam Richardum ... 1554. 8°. A-L^8 M^4. ff. 2-91. [166

-- Ioachimi Perionii ... pro Ciceronis oratore contra Petrum Ramum, oratio. ... Lutetiæ Parisiorum per Nicolaum Diuitem ... 1547. 8°. A-F^8 G^4. ff. 3-53. [167

PERKINS, JOHN. A profitable Booke ... treating of the lawes of England. Apud Richardum Tottell. ... (Imprinted at London ... 1567.) 8°. B.L. A-B^8 C^4 B-Y^8. ff. 1-168. *S.T.C.* 19635. (Biddle.) [168

-- -- Apud Richardum Tottell. ... (Imprinted at London ... the 14. daye of December. 1576.) 8°. B.L. *Same collation and foliation.* *S.T.C.* 19636. (Biddle.) [169

-- -- Apud Richardum Tottell. ... (Imprinted at London ... 1586.) 8°. B.L. *Same collation and foliation. S.T.C.* 19638. (Biddle.) [170

-- -- London, Apud Richardum Tottell. ... (... 1593.) 8°. B.L. *Same collation and foliation. S.T.C.* 19639. *Printed on large paper.* (Biddle.) [171

PERKINS, WILLIAM. An exposition of the symbole or creede of the apostles ... corrected by William Perkins. ... Printed by Iohn Legat printer to the Vniuersitie of Cambridge. 1596. 4°. π^4 A-Dd^8 Ee^2. pp. 1-441. *S.T.C.* 19704. [172

-- The foundation of Christian religion: gathered into sixe Principles. ... London, Printed by the Widoe Orwin, for Iohn Porter. 1597. 4°. Aa-Qq^8 Rr^4. pp. 1-258. *S.T.C.* 19712. ¶*Additional t.pp.:* ($Mm3^r$) An exposition of the Lords Prayer ... London, Printed by Felix Kingston, for Iohn Porter, and Ralph Iackson. 1597. (Qq^r) A graine of mustard-seed, or the least measure of grace that is or can bee effectual to Saluation. ... London, Printed by Felix Kingston, for Ralph Iackson, and Hugh Burwell. 1597. [173

-- A golden chaine, or the description of theologie, containing the order of the causes of Saluation and Damnation ... Written in Latine, and translated by R. H. Hereunto is adioined the order which M. Theodore Beza vsed in comforting afflicted consciences. The second edition, much enlarged ... Printed by Iohn Legate; Printer to the Vniuersitie of Cambridge. 1597. 4°. A-O^8 P^4 (-P4, *presumably blank*). pp. 4-218. *S.T.C.* 19663. ¶*Translator: Robert Hill. Lacks 2 folded leaves.* [174

-- A salve for a sicke man: or, a treatise concerning the nature, differences, and kindes of death; as also the right manner of dying well. Printed by Iohn Legat, printer to the Vniuersitie of Cambridge. 1597. 4°. A-I^8. *S.T.C.* 19743. ¶I7, I8 *defective. Additional t.pp.:* ($D2^r$) A declaration of the true manner of knovving Christ crucified. ... *Same imprint.* ($E3^r$) A discourse of Conscience ... The second Edition. *Same imprint.* [175

PERNEDER, ANDREAS. [1] Institutiones. Auszug vñ anzaigung etlicher geschriben Kayserlichen vnnd des heyligen Reichs rechte ... Mit ainer Vorrede des ... herrn Wolffgang Hunger ... Gedruckt/ zů Ingolstat durch Alexander Weyssenhorn. ... M. D. XLVI. (*Colophon.*) fol. A-E^4 F^6 A-Z^4 a-k^4. ff. I-CXXXII. [2] Gerichtlicher Process ... *Same imprint.* (*Colophon.*) a-c^4 A-Z^4 a^6. ff. I-XCVII. [3] Der Lehenrecht ... Gedruckt/ zů Ingolstat durch Alexander Weyssenhorn. ... M. D. LXV. (*Colophon.*) A^6 A-I^4 K^6. ff. I-XLI. [4] Von straff vnnd Peen aller vnnd yeder Malefitzhandlungen ain kurtzer breicht ... *Same imprint.* (*Colophon.*) A^4 a-f^4. ff. I-XXIII. [5] Sũma Rolandina. ... Gedruckt/ zů Ingolstat durch Alexander Weissenhorn. ... M. D. XLVI. a^4 a^6 Aa-Ee^4 Ff^6 Gg-Nn^4 Oo^6. ff. I-LIX. [176

PERONDINI, PIETRO. Magni Tamerlanis Scytharum Imperatoris vita ... [Ambergae,] Ex typograheio [*sic*] Forster. M. D. XCVII. 12°. A-C^{12}. pp. 3-66. [177

PEROTTI, NICOLÒ. In hoc volumine habentur haec. Cornucopiae, Siue linguę latinę cõmentarii ... Sypontini libellus, quo Plynij epistola ad Titum Vespasianum corrigitur. Cornelli Vitellii in eum ipsum libellum Sypontini Annotationes. M. Te. Varronis de lingua latina libri .iii. Quartus. Quintus. Sextus. Eiusdem de Analogia libri tres. Sexti Pompeii Festi vndeuiginti librorum fragmenta. Nonii Marcelli Compendia ... (Thusculani, apud Benacum in ædibus Alexandri Paganini. Mense Aprili. M.CCCCC.XXII.) 4°. 50 *ll. signed* [1]-50 A-Z^{12} &^{12} ɔ^{12} ꝶ^{12} AA^6. cols. 1-1268. [178

PERRACHE, JACQUES. La vanite du ieu, la miserable condition et fin damnable de ceux qui le suyuent, Et les moyens de s'en retirer. Poeme ... Par le Cap. Perrache Gentil-hom. Prouençal. A Paris, Pour Mathieu Guillemot. M.D.LXXXVII. 8°. A-D^8 (-A8). ff. 1-23. [179

PERSIUS FLACCUS, AULUS. Persij Flacci ... satyraꝝ liber. [Lipsiae, Martin Landsberg, c. 1500.] fol. B.L. A^6 B^4 C^6. [180

-- -- A. Persii satyrarum liber I. D. Iunii Iuuenalis satyrarum lib. V. Sulpiciæ satyra I. ... Cum veteribus commentariis ... P. Pithoei ... Notæ ... adiectæ sunt. [Heidelbergae,] In officina Sanctandreana cIↄ. Iↄ. xc. 8°. $\bar{a}^6$ A-I^8 K^2. pp. 1-146. ¶*Lacks the commentaries* (Aa^8 B-P^8). [181

PERSONA, GOBELINUS. Doctoris Gobelini Personae ... cosmodromium, Hoc est, chronicon vniuersale, ... ab orbe condito vsq3 ad annum ... 1418. ... nunc in lucem editum, studio et opera Henrici Meibomii Lemgouiensis ... 1599. Francofurti, Apud Andreæ Wecheli heredes, Claudium Marnium, & Ioannem Aubrium. fol. *^{6} A-Cc^{6} Dd-Ee^{4}. pp. 1-304. (Lea.) [182

PERSONALI, FRANCESCO. Quaestiones non minus vtiles, quam vniuersis forum practantibus necessariæ, cum tractatibus de Inditijs & Tortura, & de Gabellis, D. Francisci Personalis ... Venetiis Apud Hæredem Hieronymi Scoti. M D LXXXV. (*Colophon.*) 4°. †-5†^{4} A-Kk^{4} Ll^{2}. pp. 2-267. (Lea.) [183

PERUGIA. Sommario de capi principali Che secondo lo Statuto del Cardinal di Cortona deueno osseruare i Vicarij del contado di Perugia ... Cauato in questa volgar lingua ... In Perugia. M.D.LXXVI. 4°. A-E^{4} F^{6}. (Lea.) [184

PESARO. Statuti del Collegio mercantile de la Citta di Pesaro. M.D.XXXII. (Impresso in ... Pesaro ad instantia del ... Collegio mercantile per Baldasserre de Francesco Cartulario da Perusa ... adi VI. de Giuno.) 4°. π^{4} A-D^{4} E^{6} F^{2}. [185

PESCATORE, GIOVANBATTISTA. Morte di Ruggiero continuata alla materia de l'Ariosto ... A San Luca al segno del diamante M D LVII. (In Vinegia per Comin da Trino di Monferrato.) 8°. A-AA^{8}. ff. 2-190. [186

-- -- La suite de Roland furieux ... Mise d'Italien en François par Gabriel Chappuys Tourangeau. A Lyon, par Barthelemy Honorati. ... 1583. (Acheué d'Imprimer le dernier Ianuier. ...) 8°. *^{4} a-z^{8} A-B^{8} C^{4}. pp. 1-408. [187

PASCETTI, ORLANDO. La regia pastorella, Fauola Boschereccia ... In Vinegia, Appresso Girolamo Polo. MDXCVII. 12°. A-E^{12}. ff. 2-59. [188

PETER OF BLOIS. Wie iemmerlich vnd schendtlich der Babst sampt seinẽ Bischouen vnd geistlichen/ die arme Scheflein Christi ... schindet. Durch ... Petrum Blesensem/ welcher fuͤr CCCC. jaren geleht hat. Mit einer Vorrede Matthiæ Flacij Illyrici. ([Magdeburg,] Gedruckt bey Christian Roͤdinger.) 4°. A^{4}. [189

PETRARCA, FRANCESCO. *Latin works.* [1] Librorum Francisci Petrarche Impressorum Annotatio Vita Petrarche edita per Hieronymum Squarzaficum Alexandrinum. (Impressum Venetiis per Simonem Papiensem dictum Biuilaquam. ... 1503. die uero .15. Iulii.) fol. ✠^{4} A-K^{8} L^{6} M-AA^{8} BB-CC^{6} aa-dd^{8} ℭ^{10} a-z^{8} &^{8} ɔ^{4} 1-7^{6} 8^{8}. [2] Bucolicum Carmen ... cum comento Beneuenuti Imolensis ... A-E^{6}. [190

-- -- *Another copy (lacks the* Bucolicum Carmen; *t.p. defective).* (Lea.) [191

-- -- Francisci Petrarchae Florentini ... Opera quę extant omnia. ... Adiecimus ... quæ Hetrusco sermone scripsit carmina ... Basileæ excudebat Henrichus Petri. (... Mense Martio, anno M. D. LIIII.) fol. †^{4} (-†2-3) ††^{6} 3†^{4} A-Z^{8} aa-pp^{8} qq^{10} (-qq10, *blank*) Aa-Zz^{8} AA-OO^{8} PP^{6} QQ^{8} AAa-HHh^{8} AAA-DDD^{8} EEE^{10}. pp. 1-1375. ¶*Additional t.pp.:* (Aa1^{r}) Operum Francisci Petrarchæ ... Tomus Secundus ... (AAa1^{r}) Operum ... Tomus Tertius ... (AAA1^{r}) Operum ... Tomus quartus ... [192

-- -- [1] Francisci Petrarchae ... Opera quæ extant omnia ... Basileæ, per Sebastianum Henricpetri. fol. †^{4} ††^{6} 3†^{4} A-Ll^{8} Mm^{10} AA-3L^{8} 3M-3N^{6}. pp. 1-1131. ¶*Additional t.p.* (AA1^{r}): Tomus II. ... [2] Tomus III. ... (... CIƆ. IƆ. XXCI. mense Martio.) aa-ff^{8} gg-hh^{6} ii-mm^{8} nn-oo^{6}. pp. 3-205. ¶*Additional t.p.* (ii1^{r}): Tomus IIII. ... [193

-- -- Librorum Francisci Petrarche ... (Impressum Venetijs per Simonẽ de Luere: impensa domini Andree Torresani de Asula .17. Iunij. 1501.) fol. B.L. a^{10} b-e^{8} f^{10} ff^{8} g-o^{8} p-r^{10} s-y^{8} ç^{8} A-F^{8} G-I^{6} K^{10} L-M^{6} N-O^{8} ✠^{4} 1-7^{8} 8-11^{6} 12-13^{8} 14-15^{10} 16-17^{6} 16-18^{6} 19-23^{8} 24^{6}. ¶*Additional t.p.* (✠1^{r}): Annotatio nonnullorum librorum seu epistolarum Francisci Petrarche. ... [194

-- *Chronica (suppositious).* Chronica delle vite de pontefici et imperatori Romani composta per .M. Francesco Petrarcha allaquale sono state aggiunte quelle che ... insino alla eta nostra mancauano. (Stampata in Venetia per Maestro Iacomo de pinci da Lecco ... MDVII. Adi .iii. di di [*sic*] Decembre.) 4°. A-L^{8} M^{4}. ff. II-XC. [195

-- *De rebus memorandis.* De rebus memorandis. Franciscus Petrarcha ... von ... fuͤrtreflichen handlungen ... inns Teutsch gebracht durch M. Stephanum Vigilium Pacimontanum ...

Hierzů seindt kommen der sieben Weisen in Grecia Sprichwörter/ ... in Rheimen/ durch ... Casparum Bruschium/ gestellt. ... Franckfurt am Meyn/ Bey Christian Egenolffs seligen Erben. M. D. LXVI. (*Colophon.*) fol. A-E^{6} G-T^{6} (-T6, *presumably blank*). ff. I-CII. [196

-- *De remediis utriusque fortunae*. Francisci Petrarchae ... de Remediis utriusque Fortunæ ... libri duo ... Lutetiae, Apud Nicolaum Boucher ... 1547. 16°. a^{8} A-3F^{8}. ff. 1-415. [197

-- -- Lugduni, apud Clementem Baudin. M.D.LXXVII. 16°. a-z^{8} A-Z^{8} aa-kk^{8}. pp. 3-884. [198

-- -- Opera di M. Francesco Petrarca, de rimedi da l'una et l'altra fortuna, ... tradotta per Remigi Fiorentino. ... In Vinetia. Appresso Gabriel Giolito di Ferrarii MDXLIX. (*Colophon.*) 8°. A-3F^{8} 3G^{4}. ff. 2-416. ¶*T.p. repaired.* [199

-- -- Frãcisco petrarcha de los remedios cõtra prospera y aduersa fortunia. M.D.XXX.iii. (... impresso enla ... cibdad de Seuilla. En casa de Iuan varela de Salamanca. Acabose a veynte ⁊ seys dias đl mes se Abril. Año ... de mill ⁊ quiniẽtos ⁊ treynta ⁊ quatro años.) fol. B.L. A^{4} a-t^{8} v-x^{6} (-x6, *presumably blank*). ff. j-[c]lxiij. [200

-- *Rime*. Opere volgari di Messer Francesco Petrarcha. (Impresso in Fano Caesaris per Hieronimo Soncino nel .M.D.III. adi VII de Luglio) 8°. a-z^{8} &^{8} A^{8}. [201

-- -- [1] Sonetti et Canzõe de Miser Francescho Petrarcha. (Stãpadi in Milano per Ioãne Angelo scinzenzeler) fol. A-N^{8} O-P^{6}. ff. II-CXVI. [2] Opera del ... Miser Francesco Petrarcha con li cõmenti sopra li Triumphi: Soneti: ⁊ Canzone historiate ... per Miser Nicolo Perãzone ... Miser Bernardo Lycinio sopra li Triũphi. Miser Francesco Philelpho. Miser Antonio de Tempo. Hieronymo Alexandrino. Sopra Soneti ⁊ Canzone [*Device of Iacomo e frat. de Legnano.*] ([Stampado ... per Ioanne Angelo scinzenzeler. ... M.CCCCCXII. adi .VIII. del mese di Mago.]) a^{10} b-r^{8} (-r8). ff. II-CXXVIII. [202

-- -- Il Petrarcha. (Impresso in Vinegia nele case d'Aldo Romano, nel'anno MDXIIII del mese di Agosto.) 8°. a-z^{8} A-C^{8}. ff. 2-184. [203

-- -- [1] Opera del ... misser Francescho Petrarcha con el cõmento de misser Bernardo Lycinio sopra li triũphi. Con misser Frãcescho Philelpho: Misser Antonio de tempo: Misser Hieronymo Alexãdrino sopra li Soneti ⁊ Canzone ... historiate ... per misser Nicolo Peranzone. ... (Stampadi in Venetia per Augustino de Zanni da Portese nel .M.D.XV. adi .xx. Mazo.) fol. a^{10} (-a3) b-r^{8}. ff. I-CXXVIII. [2] Sonetti ⁊ Canzone ... (*Same colophon.*) A-N^{8} O-P^{6}. ff. II-CXIII. [204

-- -- Canzoniere et triomphi ... (Impresso in Florentia per Philippo di Giunta nel .M.D.XV. di Aprile. ...) 8°. a-z^{8} &^{8} ɔ^{8}. ff. 2-193. [205

-- -- [1] Li sonetti canzone triumphi del Petrarcha con li soi commenti ... (... stampadi per Gregorio de Grigorij in Venesia del mese de Maggio. M.D.XIX. ...) 4°. A-T^{8} V^{6}. ff. 2-158. [2] Triomphi ... con la ... spositione (... In Venegia impressi nel anno .M.D.XIX. del mese di Zugno per Meser Bernardino stagnino ...) ✠^{6} AA-ZZ^{8}. ff. 1-184. [206

-- -- *Another copy of* [1]. [207

-- -- Petrarca. (Impresso in Vinegia nelle case de Gregorio de Gregoriis nel'anno M.D.XXIII. del mese de Marzo.) 12°. A^{2} B-R^{12} S^{6}. ff. L-CxCII. [208

-- -- Le volgari opere del Petrarcha con la espositione di Alessandro Vellutello da Lucca. ... MDXXV. (Stampate in Vinegia per Giouanniantonio & Fratelli da Sabbio del mese d'Agosto ...) 4°. AA^{8} BB^{4} A-Bb^{8} Cc^{4} a-f^{8} g^{10}. ff. 1-201. [209

-- -- Li sonetti, canzoni et triomphi ... historiati. (Stampato in Vinegia per Melchiore Sessa ... MDXXVI.) 8°. a-z^{8} A^{8} B^{4} C^{8}. ff. 2-196. [210

-- -- Il Petrarcha con l'espositione d'Alessandro Vellutello ... M D XXVIII (Stampate in Vinegia per Maestro Bernardino de Vidali Venetiano del mese di Febraro L'anno ... Mille cinquecento uentiotto.) 8°. AA^{6} BB^{4} A^{8} B-Yy^{4} a-n^{4} (-n4, *blank*). ff. 1-185. ¶AA6 *misbound after* BB4. *T.p. mounted.* [211

-- -- Li sonetti, canzoni et triomphi ... historiati. MDXXX. (Stampato in Vinegia per Nicolo d'Aristotile detto Zoppino. ...) 8°. A-AA^{8} B^{4} CC^{8}. ff. 2-196. [212

-- -- Il Petrarcha con l'espositione d'Alessandro Vellutello ... MDXXXVIII (Stampate in Vinegia per Bartolomeo Zanetti Casterzagense, Ad instantia di Messer Alessandro Vellutello, e di Messer Giouanni Giolitto da Trino ...) 4°. A-BB^{8} CC^{12}. ff. III-160. [213

-- -- [1] Il Petrarca con le osseruationi di Messer Francesco Alunno. M. D. XXXIX. (Stampato ... per Francesco Marcolini da Forlì ... Del mese di Dicembre.) 8°. A-Z^8 AA^4. pp. 1-354. [2] Le osseruationi ... (Impressa in Venetia per Francesco Marcolini da Forlì il mese di Ottobre nel M D XXXIX.) A-XX^4. ¶*Engraved t.p.* [214

-- -- Il Petrarcha colla spositione di Misser Giouanni Andrea Gesualdo. ... MDXXXXI. (Stampato in Vinegia per Giouann' Antonio di Nicolini & fratelli da Sabbio ...) 4°. a-c^8 A-3B^8 ♦^{4} aa-ii^8 kk^4. ff. I-CCCLXXXIIII. [215

-- -- Il Petrarcha con l'espositione d'Alessandro Vellutello ... In Venetia appresso Gabriel Gioli di Ferrarii M D XXXXIIII. (... M D XLIII.) 4°. A-CC^8 D^4. ff. 3-197. [216

-- -- In Vinegia appresso Gabriel Giolito de Ferrari MDXXXXVII. (*Colophon.*) 4°. *^{8} A-DD^8. ff. 1-215. [217

-- -- I sonetti le canzoni et i capitoli ... M. D. XLIX. (In Vinetia per Pietro de Sabio, ad instantia di Francesco Rocca, e Fratelli. ...) 12°. A-Q^{12} R^6 (-R6, *presumably blank*). ff. 3-190. [218

-- -- Sonetti canzoni e triomphi ... con la spositione di Bernardino Daniello da Lucca. ... In Vinegia M.D.XLIX. (... per Pietro & Gioanmaria Fratelli de Nicolini da Sabio, Ad instanza di M. Gioambattista Pederzano ... & compagni.) 4°. *^{8} **^{4} A-GG^8. ff. 2-237. [219

-- -- Il Petraraca [*sic*] con le osseruationi di M. Frrncesco [*sic*] Alunno da Ferrara ... In Vinegia per Paulo Gherardo. M. D. L. (... per Comin da Trino di Monferrato ...) 8°. A-Z^8 AA^4. pp. 1-354. [220

-- -- Il Petrarcha con l'espositione d'Alessandro Vellutello ... In Vinegia appresso Gabriel Giolito de Ferrari e fratelli. M D L. (*Colophon.*) 4°. *^{8} A-DD^8. ff. 1-213. [221

-- Il Petrarca. In Lione, per Gioanni di Tournes. M. D. XXXXX. 16°. a-z^8 A-D^8. pp. 2-416. [222

-- -- [1] Il Petrarca ... In Lyone, appresso Guglielmo Rouillio. 1551 ... 16°. a-z^8 A-N^8 †^{8} *^{8}. pp. 2-576. [2] Tauola di tutte le rime ... *Same imprint.* a-t^8. pp. 3-294. [223

-- -- Il Petrarca ... corretto da Girolamo Ruscelli. Con alcune annotationi, & un pieno Vocabolario del medesimo ..., et con uno .. rimario di M. Lanfranco Parmegiano ... In Venetia, per Plinio Pietrasanta. M. D. LIIII. (*Colophon.*) 8°. ❧-2 ❧^{8} A-BB^8 *,*,^{8} *,*,-2*,*,^{8} ✠-5✠^{8} a-o^8 (-o8, *presumably blank*). pp. 2-388. ¶C3 *defective.* [224

-- -- [1] Il Petrarca ... Insieme ... Annotazioni, tratte delle ... Prose di Monsignor Bembo ... In Lyone, appresso Gulielmo Rouillio. 1558. ... 16°. a-z^8 A-N^8 *-3*^{8}. pp. 5-577. [2] Tauola di tutte le rime ... *Same imprint.* a-t^8. pp. 3-294. [225

-- -- [1] Il Petrarca. Nuouamente reuisto ... da M. Lodouico Dolce. Con alcuni ... Auertimenti di M. Giulio Camillo ... In Vinegia appresso Gabriel Giolito de' Ferrari. M D LX. 12°. A-Q^{12} R^6. pp. 4-396. [2] Annotationi di M. Giulio Camillo ... In Vinegia appresso Gabriel Giolito de' Ferrari M D LVII. a-l^{12}. ff. 3-132. [226

-- -- [1] Il Petrarcha ... Insieme con alcune ... Annotationi, tratte dalle ... Prose di Monsignor Bembo ... In Venetia, appresso Nicolò Beuilacqua. 1562. (*Colophon.*) 12°. A-V^{12} X^6. pp. 2-490. [2] Tauola di tutte le rime ... *Same imprint.* a-l^{12}. pp. 3-259. [227

-- -- Il Petrarca con l'espositione d'Alessandro Vellutello ... In Vinegia, per Giouan. Griffio. M D LIIII. (*Colophon.*) 4°. *^{8} A-DD^8. ff. 1-214. [228

-- -- In Vinegia appresso Gabriel Giolito de Ferrari. MDLVIII. (*Colophon.*) 4°. *^{8} **^{4} A-DD^8. ff. 1-216. [229

-- -- In Venetia, Appresso Nicolo Beuilacqua. M D LXIII. (*Colophon.*) 4°. *^{8} **^{4} A-DD^8. ff. 2-212. [230

-- -- [1] Il Petrarca ... Insieme con alcune ... Annotationi, tratte dalle ... Prose di Monsignor Bembo ... In Venetia, Appresso Nicolò Beuilacqua. 1564. (*Colophon.*) 12°. A-V^{12} X^6. pp. 3-490. [2] Tauola di tutte le rime ... *Same imprint.* a-l^{12} (-l12, *presumably blank*). pp. 3-259. [231

-- -- Il Petrarca. ... In Lyone, appresso Gulielmo Rouillio. 1564. 16°. *^{8} a-z^8 A-B^8. pp. 1-387. [232

-- -- Il Petrarca ... In Lyone, Appresso Gulielmo Rouillio. 1574. ... 16°. *-**8 A-Rr8. pp. 19-558. [233

-- -- [Il Petrarca; con l'espositione di M. Gio. Andrea Gesualdo. ... In Venetia, Appresso Alessandro Griffio. MDLXXXI.] (... M D LXXXII.) 4°. *-**8 (-*1-3) 3*2 A-3F8 (-3F8, *presumably blank*). ff. 1-418. ¶*With a pen facsimile of the t.p., on the verso of which *3 is pasted down.* [234

-- -- Le rime del Petrarca breuemente sposte per Lodouico Casteluetro. ... In Basilea ad istanza di Pietro de Sedabonis. M D LXXXII. (Si finì di stampare il di 4. di Maggio ...) 4°.)(-2)(4 A-Zz4 AA-KK4 aa-zzz4 Aaa-Ccc4 Ddd2. pp. 1-447, 1-378. [235

-- -- Il Petrarca con l'espositione di M. Alessandro Velutello. ... In Venetia, Appresso Gio. Antonio Bertano. MDLXXXIIII. 4°. †8 ††4 A-DD8. ff. 2-213. [236

-- -- Le Petrarque en rime Francoise auecq ses commentaires, traduict par Philippe de Maldeghem ... A Bruxelles. Chez Rutger Velpius ... M. D. C. ... 8°. *8 †4 A-Mm8. pp. 1-547. [237

-- -- Los sonetos y canciones del poeta Francisco Petrarcha, que traduzia Henrique Garces de lengua Thoscana en Castellana. ... En Madrid Impresso en casa de Guillermo Droy ... 1591. (*Colophon.*) 4°. ¶6 †8 A-Y8 Z2. ff. 1-178. [238

-- *Trionfi*. Triomphos de Petrarca. Translacíon ... de toscano en castellão: fecho por antonio de obregõ ... (Fue impresso ... enla ... cibdad de Seuilla en casa del jurado Juã varela ... Acabo se a cinco dias del mes de Setiembre: del año ... de mill ⁊ quinientos ⁊ treynta ⁊ dos años.) fol. B.L. a-s8 t-v6 (-v6). ff. ij-clv *present*. [239

PETRONIUS ARBITER. Petronii Arbitri satyricon ... Lugd. Batauorum, Ex officia Plantiniana, Apud Franciscum Raphelengium. cIↄ. Iↄ. XCVI. 16°. *8 **4 A-Z8 a8 b6 (-b6, *presumably blank*). pp. 1-393. [240

PETRUS DE ABANO. [1] Comincia la geomantia di Pietro d'Abano, tradotta di Lattina lingua nel volgare idioma. In Venetia, per Curtio Troiano de i Nauò. M. D. LVI. 8°. A-G8 H4. ff. 2-60. [2] La seconda parte della geomantia ... In Vinegia, Per Curtio Troiano. M. D. LII. A-H8. ff. 2-24. [241

PETRUS CHRYSOLOGUS. Diui Petri Chrysologi archiepiscopi Rauennatis sermones ... M. D. XXXIIII. ... (Io. Baptista Phaellus Bononien. Bononiae impressit, III. Kal. Iunii. ...) 4°. *8 A-Rr8. ff. 1-318. [242

PETRUS LOMBARDUS. Petri Lombardi Parrhysiensis ... Sententiarum Textus ... Cuilibetqȝ distinctioni Henrici Gorichemij propositiones. Egidij de Roma elucubrationes. Henrici de Vurimaria additiões. ... Anno M.D.XIII. ... ([N5v] Lodouicus hornken nup Basileæ ... mensis ꝓo Iulias die .28. ... p ... Adã Petri de langẽdorff ... ĩprimi fecit ...) fol. B.L. π4 a-z6 A-K6 L4 M-Q6 R8. ff. 1-213. [243

-- -- Petri Lombardi ... sententiarum libri IIII. ... Per Ioannem Aleaume ... pristino suo nitori ... restituti ... Parisiis, Apud Iacobum Keruer ... 1564. (Excudebat Mauricius Menier ... mense Aprili.) 8°. *8 a-z8 A-Ll8 Mm4. ff. 1-456. [244

-- -- Magistri sententiarum libri quatuor. ... Venetiis, Apud Camillum & Franciscum Franceschinis Fr. 1566 8°. *8 a-z8 A-Ll8 Mm2. ff. 1-456. [245

PETRUS DE VICENTIA. De beate uirginis conceptione Ducentorum: & sexdecim ... Doctorum ... sententia. [Venetiis, Simon de Luere.] 8°. B.L. a-f4 (-f4). ff. 2-23. (Lea.) [246

PETRUS, SUFFRIDUS. De Frisiorum antiquitate et origine libri tres ... Coloniae Agrippinae, In Officina Birckmannica, sumptibus Arnoldi Mylii Anno M. D. XC. ... 8°. †-††8 A-X8. pp. 1-335. [247

-- De illustribus ecclesiae scriptoribus Authores præcipui veteres: I. D. Hieronymus Stridonensis ... II. Gennadius Massiliensis ... III. Isidorus Hispalensis ... IIII. Honorius Augustodunensis ... V. Sigebertus Gemblacensis ... VI. Henricus de Gandauo ... opera Suffridi Petri Leouardiensis Frisij ... Coloniae Apud Maternum Cholinum. cIↄ. Iↄ. LXXX. ... 8°. a-c8 A-Dd8. pp. 1-431. [248

PEUCER, CASPAR. Commentarius de præcipuis generibus diuinationum, in quo ... discernuntur artes & imposturæ Diabolicæ ... VVitebergæ excudebat Iohannes Lufft. Anno M. D. LXXII. 8°. A-3O^{8}. ff. 1-440. (Lea.) [249

-- -- [VVitebergae, excudebat Iohan. Schvvertel.] (... M. D. LXXVI.) 8°. A-3R^{8} (-A1, *t.p.*; -3R8, *presumably blank*). ff. 1-451. ¶[A8] *misbound before* A2. *Lacks folding table.* (Lea.) [250

-- -- Les deuins ou commentaire des principales sortes de deuinations ... Nouuellement tourné en François par S. G. S. ... En Anuers, par Heudrik Connix. M. D. LXXXIIII. 4°. *^{4} **^{2} a-z^{4} A-3Q^{4} (-3Q4, *presumably blank*). pp. 1-653. ¶*Translator: Simon Goulart.* [251

PEUTINGER, CONRAD. De mirandis Germaniae antiquitatibus, sermones conuiuales ... Argentorati apud Christianum Egenolphum. (... 1530.) 4°. A-C^{4} D^{6}. [252

-- ... Chonradi Peutingeri, Augustani, ... Oratio pro ... Ciuitate Augusta Vindelicorum, Imp, Cæs, Charolo ... Brugis in Comitatu Flandrēsi pronūciata, Eiusdem Epistola olim scripta ad ... Bernhardinū Caruasalum ... (Simon Cocus et Gerhardus Nicolaus Ciues Anduerpienses ... excudebant, Kalendis Mai, Anno supra Millesimum Quingentesimum, XXI) 4°. A-B^{4}. [253

PEZEL, CHRISTOPH. Etliche gewisse grūnde fūr die einfeltigen/ wie vnnd wobey man eigentlich die rechten Sacramentirer vnd Schwermer erkennen soll. ... M. D. LXXXVIII. 8°. A-B^{8}. [254

PEZZI, LORENZO. Vinea domini Cum breui descriptione sacramentorum, et Paradisi, Limbi, Purgatorij, atq3 Inferni ... per D. Laurentium Petium de Colonia ... Venetiis Apud Hier. Porrum MDLXXVIII. ... 8°. A^{8} *^{4} B-N^{8} (-E8, *blank*; -N8, *presumably blank*). pp. 1-186. ¶*Engraved t.p.* [255

PFEFFINGER, JAKOB. Abusus ecclesiae Romanae. MDXXXIII. 8°. [a]^{8} b^{4}. [256

-- Eine Predigt/ vber die Leich des ... Herren Moritzen Hertzogen vnd Churfursten zu Sachssen ... Gethan zu Leipzig/ den 19. Iulij ... M. D. LIII. ... (Gedruckt zu Leipzig/ durch Iacobum Berwald.) 4°. A-B^{4}. [257

-- Warhafftige Copey einer Schrifft/ so die ... Predicanten zu Leiptzig/ an Hertzog Moritzen zu Sachsen gethan/ etc. Desgleichē eine andere Copeyschrift/ des ... Herrn Nicolai Amssdorff ... an den Bischoff zu Merssburg etc. ... M. D. xlvij. 4°. A-B^{4}. ¶*Signed also by Georgius Mohr, Nicolaus Faucke, Steffanus Schonbach, Vincencius Stang, Caspar Lindener.* [258

PFLUG, JULIUS VON. Grūndtlicher vnd Christlicher Bericht/ Ob einer mit gutem gewissen die alte Catholische Religion verlassen ... mōge. ... Zu Cōlln/ Durch Maternum Cholinum. M. D. LXXI. ... 4°. A-I^{4} K^{2}. [259

PHALARIS. Φαλαριδος καὶ Βρουτου επιστολαι. Phalaridis & Bruti epistolae. His præfixa Epistolarum conscribendarum methodus, Græcè & Latinè. [Heidelbergae,] Apud Hieronymum Commelinum. cIↃ IↃ XCVII. 8°. A-C^{8} A-P^{8}. pp. 2-45, 2-240. [260

-- -- Epistole Phalaridis p Franciscū Aretinum traducte (Impressum Liptzk p Iacobū Thanner ... 1502. ...) 4°. B.L. A-G^{6}. [261

-- -- Les epistres de Phalaris, et d'Isocrates: auec le manuel d'Epictete. La tout traduit de grec en françoys. ... A Anuers, De l'Imprimerie de Christophle Plantin 1558. 12°. A^{6} B-P^{12} Q^{6}. ff. 2-186. ¶*Additional t.p.* (K10^{r}): Les epistres d'Isocrate traduites par Loys de Matha. *Same imprint. Other translators: Claude Gruget, Antoine Dumoulin.* [262

-- -- L'epistole di Phalaride ... Tradotte dalla lingua Greca nella volgare Italiana ... In Vinegia Appresso Gabriel Giolito de Ferrari. MDXLV. (*Colophon.*) 8°. A-H^{8}. ff. 2-59. [263

PHANUCIIS, PHANUCCIUS DE. Tractatus De Inuentario Hæredis, ac eius beneficio. ... Cui accedit, eiusdem Authoris, ... Responsum, super Statuto Lucensi. ... Venetiis, M. D. LXXIIII. Apud Hæredes Vincentij Valgrisij. (... MDLXXIII. ...) 8°. a-d^{8} A-Rr^{8}. ff. 2-314. (Lea.) [264

PHAYER, THOMAS. [A boke of Presidentes. ... 1550.] (Londini Ex officina Richardi Graftoni ...) 8°. ♣^{6} (-♣1, ♣6) *^{4} (-*4, *blank*) a-v^8 x^4. *S.T.C.* 3331. ¶x4 *defective*. (Biddle.) [265

-- -- A Booke of Presidents exactly written in manner of a Register ... 1583. Imprinted at London, by Iohn Charlewood, the assigne of Richard Tottle. 8°. B.L. [A]^8 B-Y^8 (-Y8, *presumably blank*). ff. ii-C.lix. *S.T.C.* 3342. (Biddle.) [266

PHILANDRIER, GUILLAUME. Gulielmi Philandri Castilionii Galli ... in decem Libros M. Vitruuii Pollionis de Architectura Annotationes. ... (Impressum Romæ [typis Antonii Bladi] apud Io. Andream Dossena Thaurineñ. ... M. D. XLIIII.) 8°. a^8 A-Z^8 &^{8} AA^8 BB^4. pp. 2-369. (Fine Arts.) [267

PHILO JUDAEUS. Φιλονος Ιουδαιου εις τα του Μωσεως ... Philonis Iudaei in libros Mosis de mundi opificio, historicos, de legibus. Eiusdem libri singulares. ... Parisiis, Ex officina Adriani Turnebi ... M. D. LII. ... (... Cal. Septemb.) fol. α^6 A-Z^8 a-y^8 z^4 AA-CC^6 DD^2. pp. 2-716. [268

-- Les oeuures de Philon Iuif ... Mises de Grec en François, par Pierre Bellier ... A Paris, Chez Michel Sonnius ... M. D. LXXV. ... fol. ✝^{4} A-Qq^6 ā^4 ē^6 ī^6 ō^6 ū^6. pp. 1-468. [269

PHILOSTRATUS. Φιλοστράτου ... βιβλία ὀκτώ. Εὐσεβίου ... ἀντιῤῥητικὸς... Philostrati de uita Apollonii Tyanei libri octo. Iidem libri latini interprete Alemano Rinuccino florentino. Eusebius contra Hieroclem q3 Tyaneum Christo conferre conatus fuerit. Idem latinus interprete Zenobio Acciolo florentino ... (Venetiis apud Aldum Mense Martio. M.DI. ... mense februario. M. D II.) fol. a-g^8 h^{10} Apoll.^{8} a-h^8 i^{10}. ff. 1-73. [270

-- -- La vita del gran philosopho Apollonio Tianeo, ... tradotta nella lingua volgare da M. Lodouico Dolce. ... In Vinegia appresso Gabriel Giolito de Ferrari. M D XLIX. (... M D L.) 8°. A-HH^8 (-HH8, *blank*). ff. 3-247. [271

-- Flauii Philostrati de Vitis Sophistarum Libri duo, Antonio Bomfino interprete. ... ([Argentorati,] Ex aedibus Schurerianis Mense Martio. ... M D. XVI.) 4°. π^4 A^4 B-G$^{8.4.4}$ H^8 I^4 K^8. ff. I-LVI. [272

PHRYGIO, PAULUS CONSTANTIUS. Chronicum regum regnorumque omnium catalogum ... Basileae apud Iohan. Heruag. anno, M. D. XXXIIII. fol. a^4 a-z^6 A-T^6 V^8 α-γ^6 δ^8. pp. 1-516. [273

-- Oratio Constantii Eubuli Mouentini, de uirtute Clauiū, & Bulla condemnationis Leonis Decimi, Contra Martinum Lutherum ... [Selestadii, Lazarus Schūrerius, c. 1521.] 4°. A-B^4 C^6. [274

PIACENZA. Statuta et decreta antiqua ciuitatis Placentiae. Apud Andream Gallum ... (Brixiae apud Ludouicum Sabiensm. ... M. D. LX. Ad instantiam ... Andreae Galli bibliopolae Placentini.) fol. a-d^6 e^2 A-N^6 O^8 AA-GG^6. ff. 1-128. (Lea.) [275

-- -- *Another copy*. (Lea.) [276

-- Facultates magistratuum, iudicum, et officiorum vrbis Placentiae, et status. ... Parmae Apud Seth viottum 1561. (... Ad instantiam D. Ioseph Scurzani, Bibliopolæ Placentini ...) fol. A-C^4. (Lea.) [277

-- Additiones ad nouas constitutioones [*sic*] Magistratuum Vrbis nostrę Placentię. Placentiae Apud Ioseph Scurzanum. fol. A-C^2. (Lea.) [278

-- Nouae constitutiones de forma, et ordine procedendi in causis ciuilibus Placentiae. Parmae, Apud Seth Viottum. M D LXVII. fol. A-C^4. (Lea.) [279

-- Ordini et bandi Ducali Generali da osseruarsi ... nella ... Città di Piacenza ... In Piacenza Appresso Vincenzo Conti 1569. ... fol. A-F^2. (Lea.) [280

PIATTI, PIATTINO. Huic libello haec insunt. Platini Plati Mediolanēsis ... Libellus de carcere Item Marcellini Verardi Cæsenatis Fernandus seruatus. (Argentorati Ex officina Matthię Schurerij Selestensis Mense Aprili Anno M. D. XIII.) 8°. A^8 B^4 C^8. ¶*In verse*. [281

PIBRAC, GUY DU FAUR DE. Ornatissimi Cuiusdam Viri, De Rebus Gallicis, Ad Stanislaum Eluidium, Epistola. Et Ad Hanc De Iisdem Rebus Gallicis Responsio. 1573. 4°. A-N^4. pp. 3-102. (Lea.) [282

-- Oratio habita a Guidone Fabro oratore Caroli Galliarum regis ... in generali Congragatione, & subsequenter. Responsum synodi in admissione oratorum eiusdem Regis ... datum ... IIII. Iunij. M. D. LXII. Ripae: ad instantiam Petri Antonii Alciatis. M. D. LXII. 4°. A^6. (Lea.) [282a

-- ... Vidi Fabri Pibracii ... tetrasticha Græcis & Latinis versibus expressa, Authore Florente Christiano. Lutetiæ, Apud Federicum Morellum ... M.D.LXXXIIII. 4°. A-H^4 I^6. ff. 2-34. [283

PICARD, JEAN. Ioannis Picardi Toutreriani De Prisca Celtopædia, libri quinque. ... Parisiis. Ex typographia Matthæi Dauîdis ... 1556. ... 4°. $\bar{a}^6$ a-z^4 A-K^4. pp. 1-250. [284

PICCHA, GREGORIO. Rime in lode dela santita di ... Papa Paolo IIII. ... & d'altri ... Signori ... [c. 1555.] 8°. A-D^4. [285

PICCOLOMINI, ALESSANDRO. L'amor costante. Comedia del Signor Stordito Intronato, Composta ... L'anno del XXXVI. ... In Vineggia per Agustino Bindoni. L'Anno M.D.L. 8°. A-K^8. ff. 4-78. [286

-- Cento sonetti. ... In Roma Appresso Vincentio Valgrisi M.D.XLVIIII. 8°. $*^8$ A-H^8 I^4. [287

-- Comedia intitolata Alessandro ... [Venezia, per Andrea Arrivabene? c. 1540.] 8°. A^8 $*^4$ B-G^8 H^4. ff. 3-60. [288

-- De la institutione di tutta la vita de l'homo nato nobile e in citta libera. libri X. ... Venetijs apud Hieronymum Scotum. M.D.XLIII. ... (*Colophon.*) 8°. A-MM^8 (-MM7-8). ff. 3-274. [289

-- -- Della institution morale ... Libri XII. ... In Venetia, MDLXXV. Appresso Giordano Ziletti. (... appresso Gio. Antonio Bertano ...) 4°. $*^4$ a-d^4 A-MM^8. pp. 1-559. [290

-- -- *Another copy.* [291

-- -- La philosophie et institution morale ... Mise en Francois, par Pierre de Lariuey Champenois. ... A Paris, Chez Abel l'Angelier ... M. D. LXXXV. ... 8°. $\bar{a}^8$ A-$3K^8$ $3L^2$. pp. 1-902. [292

-- Dialogo de la bella creanza de le donne. De lo Stordito Intronato. M.D.XXXX. (Stampata in Brouazzo per dispetto d'un asnazzo ... [= Venezia, per Comin da Trino.]) 8°. A-E^8. ff. 2-39. [293

-- -- Dialogo, nel quale si ragiona della bella creanza delle donne. ... In Venetia, Appresso Domenico Farri [1562]. 8°. π^8 A^4 B-E^8 F^4. ff. 1-40. [294

-- Instrumento della filosofia naturale ... In Venetia, Appresso Daniel Zaneti. M D LXXVI. 4°. a^4 A-H^8 I^{10}. ff. 1-72. [295

-- Lettura del S. Alessandro Piccolomini Infiammato fatta nell'Accademia degli Infiammati. M. D. XXXXI. (Stampata in Bologna per Bartholomeo Bonardo & Marc'antonio da Carpi ... Del Mese di Luglio.) 4°. A-E^4. [296

-- [1] Parte prima della filosofia naturale ... In Venetia, Appresso Daniel Zaneti, & compagni. M D LXXVI. 4°. a^8 A-K^8 L^6. ff. 1-83. [2] Parte seconda ... *Same imprint.* $+^4$ A-O^8. ff. 1-111. [297

-- Rime, et versi Nella Morte del ... Mons. Alessandro Piccolomini ... In Siena Appresso Luca Bonetti. M.D.LX[X]IX. ... 4°. A-F^4. pp. 4-46. [298

PICCOLOMINI, FRANCESCO. [1] Francisci Piccolominei Senensis ... Librorum ad Scientiam de Natura attinentium pars prima. ... Venetiis, Apud Franciscum de Franciscis Senensem MDXCVI. fol. $*^4$ $*^6$ $**^8$ A-Hh^6. ff. 1-186. [2] ... pars secunda. ... *Same imprint.* a-b^6 a-t^6 u^4. ff. 1-118. [299

-- Vniuersa philosophia de moribus ... Venetiis, MDLXXXIII, Apud Franciscum de Franciscis Senensem. fol. $†^{10}$ A-Nn^8 Oo^{10} a-b^8 c^6. pp. 2-596. [300

PICCOLOMINI, GIACOMO. Epistolae Iacobi Picolomini ... una cũ ... Cōmētarijs res gestas sui tp̄ris cōtinētibus ... (In Aedibus Minutiani Inp̄ssum Mediolani. M.D.XXI. Mensis Martij. Die. iiij.) fol. a^4 a-z^8 &^{8} ɔ^8 ℞^{8} aa^4 A-Z^8 &^{8} ɔ^8 ℞^{6}. ff. 1-414. (Lea.) [301

-- Testamentum Iacobi Picolomini Cardinalis Papiensis, ad memoriam humanæ imbecillitatis & funebrium impensarũ contemptum ... [c. 1524.] 4°. A^4. [301a

PICEDI, PAPIRIO. Oratione ... In morte della ... Donna Maria di Portugallo Prencipessa di Parma ... In Parma, M D LXXVIII. Appresso Seth Viotto. 4°. A-E^4. [302

PICO DELLA MIRANDULA, GIOVANNI. Opera Ioannis Pici, Mirandule Comitis Concordie ... (... imp̄ssit ... Ioannes Prũs Ciuis Argentinus. ... M.CCCCCIIII. Die vero .XV. Marcij.) fol. π^6 aa^6 A-Z^6 a-n^6. ff. I-CCXVI. [303

-- -- Ioannis Pici Mirandulae omnia opera. ... (Impressum Venetiis per Gulielmum de Fontaneto de Monteferrato. ... M.D.XIX. Die .XXII. Martii.) fol. A^{10} a-q^8 r^4 s-z^8 &^{8} ɔ^8 ℞^{8} A-C^8 D-E^{10}. [304

-- -- [1] Opera omnia, Ioannis Pici, Mirandulae Concordiaeque comitis ... Basileæ, ex officina Henricpetrina. (... M. D. LXXII. mense Martio.) fol. $*^8$ a-f^6 g^4 a^6 A-Zz^6 AA-QQ^6 RR^8. pp. 1-759. [2] Opera omnia Ioannis Francisci Pici ... Tomus Secundus. ... Basileae. Ex officina Henricpetrina, (... CIↃ IↃ LXIII. mense Martio.) $*^6$ aA-zZ^6 aAA-zZZ^6 $aaAA$-$zzZZ^6$ AAA-ZZZ^6 $AAAa$-$MMMm^6$ $NNNn^8$ $OOOo$-$YYYy^6$ $ZZZz^4$ A-K^6 L^8. pp. 2-1378. ¶*Sig.* * *repaired.* [305

-- -- *Another copy of tomus I.* (Lea.) [306

-- Conclusiones nongentae, in omni genere scientarum: quas olim Io. Picus Mirandula Romæ disputandas proposuit ... Adiectum est Panepistemon Angeli Politiani, hoc est omnium scientiarum ... descriptio. [Nurembergae, Johannes Petreius,] 1532. 8°. A-M^8 N^2. pp. 4-195. [307

-- Le sette sposizioni ... intitolate heptaplo, sopra i sei giorni del Genesi. Tradotte in lingua Toscana da M. Antonio Buonagra ... e da M. Pompeo de la Barba ... In Pescia MDLV. (Stampato ... appresso Lorenzo Torrentino ...) 4°. A-K^8. pp. 11-158. [308

PICO DELLA MIRANDOLA, GIOVANNI FRANCESCO. Io. Francisci Pici Mirandulæ Dñi ... De Animæ immortalitate digressio. (Impressum Bononiæ a Hieronymo de Benedictis ... M.D.XXIII. Mense Iulio. ...) 4°. a-e^4. ff. 2-20. [309

-- Ioannis Francisci Pici Mirandulae domini ... de rerum praenotione libri nouem. Pro veritate religionis/ contra superstitiosas vanitates editi. ... ([u8] formis excusa die. xxij. Decemb. Ann. M.D.vi. ... [o7] Argentoraci Pridiæ Kaleñ. Februarias ann. M.D.VII. ... Ioannes Knoblochus Imprimebat: Recognouit Mathias Schürerius.) fol. π^4 A-V^6 p-s^6 t-u^8 a-c^6 d^8 e^6 f^{10} g^4 h-k^6 l^8 m-n^6 o^8 A-D^6 E^4 F^8. (Lea.) [310

-- -- *Another copy.* ¶*Bound in the order* π^4 A-V^6 a-c^6 d^8 e^6 f^{10} g^4 h-k^6 l^8 p-s^6 t-u^8 A-D^6 E^4 F^8 m-n^6 o^8 *(-o8, blank).* [311

-- Ioannis Francisci Pici Mirandulae domini ... examen vanitatis doctrinae gentium, et veritatis Christianae disciplinae ... (Impressit Mirandulae Ioannes Maciochius bundenius ... Anno ... millesimo quingentesimo uigesimo. ...) fol. π^6 A-LL^6 MM^4. ff. I-CCVIII. [312

-- Ioannis Francisci Pici Mirandulae ... liber de prouidentia Dei contra philosophastros. (... M.D.VIII. No. nouembr. In suburbio Noui ... Benedictus Dulcibellus Mãgius Carpēsis exscripsit ...) fol. A-D^6 (-A6) E-G^4. [313

-- Staurostichon hoc est carmen de mysteriis dominicæ crucis nuper in germaniam delapsis ... Cum Iacobi Spiegel Selestani enarratione ... (Tubingæ in ædibus Thomæ Anshelmi Badensis. M.D.XII. mense Iulio.) 4°. a-$p^{4.4.8}$. ff. II-LXXX. [314

PICTORIUS, MARIUS. Oratio in funere ... Salomes ducis Munsterbergi ... Huic accessit Næniæ tàm Latinæ quàm Italicæ insignium Poetarum. Venetiis, apud Vincentium Valgrisium. M D LXVIII. (*Colophon.*) 4°. $[A]^4$ B-N^4. pp. 4-103. [315

PIENTINI, ANGELO. Delle demostrationi degli errori della setta Macomettana Libri cinque. ... In Firenze Appresso Giorgio Marescotti. 1588. ... 4°. A^4 A-$3A^4$ $*^4$. pp. 1-371. (Lea.) [316

PIERIUS, CHRISTIANUS. Christus crucifixus: carmen cothurnatum catastrophicumq3 ... Concinnatore ... Christiano Pierio Coloniensi. ... Francoforti ad Moenum, M. D. LXXVI. (... ex officina haeredum Christiani Egenolphi, impensis Adami Loniceri, Ioannis Cnipij, Doctorum, & Pauli Steinmeyers. ...) 8°. A-G^8 (-G7-8, *presumably blank*). [317

-- Paupertas Poetarum, praestigiis pertinacique Plutonis pugna parata, primitusque per pauperem Pierium Poetam publicata. ... Tubingæ, Apud viduam Vlrici Morhardi. M.D.LXVI. 4°. A-B^4 C^2. [318

PIERRE DE CLUNY. D. Petri venerabilis ... contra Heinricianorum & Petrobrusianorum hæreses, Epistolæ duæ ... Ingolstadii in officina Alexandri Vueissenhorn. M. D. XLV. 4°. Aa^4 A-Z^4 a-i^4 k^2. ff. 1-129. ¶*Includes:* 1) Sancti Bernardi ... Sermones Tres ..., 2) quædam S. Bernardi epistolæ. (Lea.) [319

PIERRE DES VAUX-DE-CERNAY. Histoire des Albigeois, et gestes de noble Simon de Mont-fort. Descrite par F. Pierre des Vallées Sernay ... Et rendue de Latin en François, par M. Arnaud Sorbin ... A Paris, Chez Guillaume Chaudiere ... 1569. ... 8°. ā^8 ē^2 A-AA^8 B^6. ff. 1-190. (Lea.) [320

PIETRO DA LUCCA. Fundamento della vita Christiana ... (Et e in Bologna ... imp̄ssa per mi Hieronimo d̄ Benedicti ... M.D.XV. A di. primo d̄ Aprile.) 4°. A-I^4 K^6. [321

-- Opusculo de trenta documenti. ... (In Bologna per hieronymo di Beneditti. Adi .xx. de luio M.D.XVIII.) 4°. a-f^4 g^6. [322

PIGHIUS, ALBERTUS. Hierarchiæ ecclesiasticae assertio ... Coloniæ, Melchior Nouesianus excudebat, ... M. D. XXXVIII. fol. β^8 γ^6 A-VV^6 XX^4 YY^6 a^6 b-c^4. ff. II-CCLXVII. (Lea.) [323

PIGNA, GIOVANNI BATTISTA. Io. Baptistae Pignae carminum lib. quatuor ... Caelii Calcagnini carm. lib. III. Ludouici Areosti carm. lib. II. ... Venetiis, ex officina Erasmiana, Vincentii Valgrisi. M.D.LIII. 8°. A-T^8 V^4 X^8. pp. 3-312. [324

-- Il duello ... In Vinegia, nella bottega d'Erasmo, appresso Vincenzo Valgrisi. 1554. 4°. a^2 A-Qq^4. pp. 1-270. [325

-- Gli heroici ... In Vinegia appresso Gabriel Giolito de' Ferrari, M D LXI. 4°. A-M^4 N^6 *-**^{4}. pp. 3-105. [326

-- Historia de principi di Este ... In Vinegia, Appresso Vincenzo Valgrisi. M D LXXII. (*Colophon.*) 4°. a^4 A-3D^8 3E^4. pp. 2-798. [327

-- Il principe ... In Venetia. (... appresso Francesco Sansouino. M. D. LXI.) 4°. *^{4} A-V^4. ff. 1-71. [328

-- I romanzi ... Ne quali della Poesia, & della vita dell' Ariosto ... si tratta. ... In Vinegia, nella bottega d'Erasmo, appresso Vincenzo Valgrisi. 1554. 4°. α^2 A-Bb^4. pp. 1-174. [329

PIGNONE. La presa del Pignone, et l'ordine che ha tenuto la maesta del re Filippo a prenderla, & la quantita delle galere, & il numero delli soldati ... Che si ritrouorono alla ditta impresa ... Con vna littera Mandata dal gran Turcho ... Stampata in Milano [per Francesco Moscheni] ... 1564. 4°. A^4. [330

PILADE, GIOVANNI FRANCESCO BOCCARDO. Carmen Egregi Pylade Scolasticū Guilhelmi Ramesei Sagiensis Cōmentario ... Venundatur. Lugduni in officina Ludouici Lanchart ... (Impressi ... in calcographia Stepha. baland. ... M.cccccviij. pridie nonas Ianua.) 8°. B.L. a-q^8 r^{10}. [331

PIMPINELLI, VINCENZO. Vincentii Pimpinelli ... Oratio Augustæ habita xij. Kal. Iulij. M D XXX. [Augustae, per Alexandrum Weissenhorn.] 4°. A-B^4. [332

-- -- (Excusum Augustæ Vindelicorum per Alexandrum Vueyssenhorn. XV. Iulij. M. D. XXX:) 4°. π^4 A-C^4. [333

-- -- Ain Oration/ oder rede/ vor Rō. Kaiserlicher Mai. ... Im eingāg des yetzt schwebenden Reichsstag ... auff das fleyssigst verteutscht. Augspurg. 1530. (Getruckt ... durch Alexander Weyssenhorn ...) 4°. A-C^4. [334

PINADELLO, GIOVANNI. Inuicti quinarii numeri series quæ summatim a superioribus pontificibus et maxime a Sixto quinto res præclare quadriennio gestas adnumerat ... auctore Ioanne Pindello Taruisino Romæ M.D.LXXXIX (... Apud Franciscum Zannettum. ...) 4°. A-K⁴ (-A2-3, K4, *the latter presumably blank*). ff. 4-38 *present*. ¶*Engraved t.p.* [335

PINDAR. *Greek*. Πινδαρου, Ολυμπια. Νεμεα. Πυθια. Ισθμια. ... Impressi Romæ per Zachariam Calergi Cretensem ... (... χιλιοςω φιέ [1515] ...) 4°. α⁴ β-θ⁸ ι⁶ κ-μ⁸ ν-ξ⁶ A-H⁸ Θ¹⁰ I-P⁸. ¶β4ʳ *next to last line ends* τῆς; A1-2 *unsigned*; A3ʳ *caption and initial letter printed in red.* [336

-- -- *Greek & Latin*. [1] Pindari Olympia, Pythia, Nemea, Isthmia. Cæterorum Octo Lyricorum carmina, Alcaei, Sapphus, Stesichori, Ibyci, Anacreontis, Bacchilidis, Simonidis, Alcmanis, Nonnulla etiam aliorum. Omnia Græcè & Latina. Anno M. D. LX [Genevae,] Excudebat Henr. Stephanus ... 16°. a-nn⁸. pp. 3-576. ¶*Lacks part 2 (the eight other poets).* [337

-- -- [2] Carminum poetarum nouem, lyricæ poeseωs principū fragmenta. ... Editio II. ... Anno M. D. LXVI [Genevae,] Excudebat Henr. Stephanus ... 16°. A-FF⁸ GG⁴. pp. 3-568. ¶*Lacks part 1 (Pindar).* [338

-- -- [1] Πινδαρος. Pindari Olympia, Nemea, Pythia, Isthmia. ... Latinam interpretationem M. Æmilius P. Fr. Porti c. f. ... recognouit ... [Heidelbergae,] Apud Hieronymum Commelinum ... cIↄ Iↄ XCIIX. 8°.):(⁸ A-L⁸. pp. 3-16, 1-176. [2] Λυρικοι. Carminum poetarum nouem ... *Same imprint*. A-M⁸. pp. 3-191. [339

-- -- [1] Pindari Olympia, Pythia, Nemea, Isthmia. ... Editio IIII. Graecolatina, H. Steph. recognitione ... locupletata. [Genevae,] Excudebat Paulus Stephanus. Anno M. DC. 16°. a-nn⁸. pp. 3-576. [2] Carminum poetarum nouem ... *Same imprint*. A-FF⁸ GG⁴. pp. 3-472. [340

-- -- [1] Pindari Olympia, Pythia, Nemea, Isthmia. Cæterorum octo Lyricorum carmina ... Omnia Græcè & Latinè. ... Antuerpiae, Ex officina Christophori Plantini, anno CIↃ. IↃ. LXVII. 16°. a-r⁸. pp. 3-270. [2] Carminum poetarum nouem ... fragmenta. Alcaei, Sapphus, Stesichori, Ibyci, Anacreontis, Bacchylidis, Simonidis, Alcmanis. Pindari. Nonnulla etiam aliorum. *Same imprint*. A-M⁸ N⁴. pp. 4-196. [341

-- -- *Latin*. Pindari Thebani ... Olympia. Pythia. Nemea. Isthmia. Per Philippum Melanchthonem Latinitate donata ... Basileae, per Ioannem Oporinum. (... M.D.LVIII. Mense Iunio.) 8°. a-h⁸. pp. 4-126. [342

-- -- ... Per Ioan. Lonicerum latinitate donata: adhibitis enarrationibus ... Tiguri [per Andream Gesner]. M.D.L.X. 8°. α⁸ a-z⁸ A-Ee⁸. pp. 3-779. [343

-- Αριστολογια Πινδαρικη ... Aristologia Pindarica Graecolatina. ... opera ac studio Michaelis Neandri Sorauiensis. Basileae, per Ludouicum Lucium. (... M. D. LVI. Mense Augusto.) 8°. α-β⁸ a-z⁸ A-D⁸ E⁴. pp. 1-434. [344

PINELLI, LUCA. Libretto d'imagini, et meditationi sopra alcuni misterii della passione di Christo ... Composto da vn religioso ... In Napoli [per Giovanni Giacomo Carlino & Antonio Pace, c. 1595]. 8°. π² + 22 *engraved ll.* [345

PINGONE, FILIBERTO. Inclytorum Saxoniae Sabaudiaeq. principum arbor gentilitia ... Augustae Taurinorum Apud hæredes Nicolai Beuilaquæ, M.D.LXXXI. ... fol. a⁶ A-P⁴. pp. 1-120. [346

PINICIANUS, JOANNES. Contenta hoc libello Carmen ad libellū vt sibi patronum querat Virtus et voluptas Carmen de origine ducum Austrie. et alia. Carmen de armis Venetorum ... [Augustae, Silvanus Otmar, 1511.] 4°. a⁸ b⁶. [347

-- Ioānis piniciani Promptuarium uocabulorum ... MDXVI (Siluanus Otmar ... Auguste Vindelicorum impressit. ... XXVI. Ianuarii) 4°. B.L. A⁶ A-E⁴ A-P⁸·⁴·⁴ Q⁸ R⁶. [348

PINO DA CAGLI, BERNARDINO. [1] Della nuoua scielta di lettere di diuersi nobilissimi huomini ... libro primo. Con un Discorso Della commodità dello scriuere, di M. Bernardino Pino. In Venetia, MDLXXXII. 8°. †-3†⁸ A-Gg⁸ Hh⁴. pp. 1-478. [2] ... libro secondo. *Same imprint*. a-pp⁸ (-pp8) qq⁴. pp. 3-605. [349

-- L'euagria. Ragionamenti famigliari ... In Vinegia, Presso Gio. Battista Sessa, & fratelli. M.D.LXXXIIII. 12°. A-G¹² H⁶. ff. 2-90. [350

-- Gli affetti regionamenti famigliari ... In Vinegia, Appresso Iacomo Simbeni, ad instanza di Marco Amadoro. 1569. 8°. A-I^{8} (-I8, *blank*). ff. 2-71. [351

-- Gli ingiusti sdegni, comedia ... In Venetia, Appresso Giuseppe Guglielmo. MDLXXVI. 12°. A-E^{12}. ff. 2-59. ¶*T.p. repaired.* [352

PINU, JOSEPH A. Carmen continens narrationem non quidem historicam sed confictam ... 8°. A^{8}. ¶*Head-title:* Carmen continens narrationem de diuina institutione magistratus & subditorum. [353

-- Carmen elegiacum in natalem diem Iesu Christi ... scriptum ... VVitebergae. 1556. 4°. A^{6}. [354

-- Iosephi a Pinu Auerbachii eteostichorum liber. Eiusdem ænigmatum de annis natalibus illustrium ... uirorum libellus. VVitebergæ excudebat Iohannes Lufft anno M. D. LXI. 8°. A-G^{8} (-G8, *presumably blank*). [355

PIO, GIOVANNI BATTISTA. Annotamenta Ioānis Baptiste Pii Bononiēsis. (Excussum ... apud Ioānem Antoniū Platonicū de Benedictis ciuem bononiensem ... .M.DIIII. die .x. Ianuarii.) fol. A^{2} B-R^{6} S^{4} T-V^{6}. [356

-- Elegidia ... (Impressum Bononiæ per Io. Antoniū de Benedictis ... Die .xx. Decembris. M.D.ix. ...) 4°. A^{8} B-Z^{4}. [357

PIOBESI, AYMON DE. Commentarii in consuetudines Aruerniae, editi per D. Aymonem Publitium Pedemontanum ... Parisiis, Apud Arnoldum Angelier ... 1548. (*Colophon.*) fol. a^{6} b^{4} A-Ff^{6} (-Q6, R1-3, Ff6, *the last presumably blank*). ff. I-CLXXIII. [358

PIPERARIO, ANDREA. Andreæ Piperarii Cremonensis oratio ... ad Leonem .X. Pont. Max. (Romę [per Stephanum Guileretum & Herculem Nani] ... M.D.xiii. Die viii. Nouembris ...) 4°. A^{8}. [359

PIRCKHEIMER, WILIBALD. Germaniae ex variis scriptoribus ... explicatio. Authore Bilibaldo Pirckeymero ... Norembergæ apud Io. Petreium, Anno M. D. XXX. 8°. A-D^{8} E^{4}. [360

PIRSTINGER, BERTHOLD. Tewtsche Theologey (Gedruckht ... in ... München durch Hansen Schobser ... am lessten tag des augstmonets ... M.CCCCC.XXviij. jar.) fol. A^{4} B-Z^{6} a-s^{6} t^{8}. [361

-- Theologia Germanica in qua continentur articuli de fide, euangelio, virtutibus et sacramentis: quorum materia iam nostra tempestate controuerti solet. M. D. XXXI. (Excusum Augustæ Vindelicorum, per Alexandrum Vueyssenhorn, Expensis ... Martini Silbereysen, An. M.D.xxxi.) fol. A-Z^{6} a-o^{6}. (Lea.) [362

-- -- *Another copy.* [363

PISA, COUNCIL OF. Cōuocatio Generalis Concilij parte Principum. (Impressum Norinbrege p̱ ... Ioannē Weyssenburger Presbyterū. 1512.) 4°. B.L. Aa^{4}. [364

PISCINA, FRANCESCO. Disputatio Francisci Piscinae ... An statuta Feminarum exclusiua porrigantur ad bona forensia. In Monteregali, MDLXX. Sumptibus Bartholomæi Galli, & Francisci Dulcij. ... 8°. ✤-✤✤^{8} A-N^{8}. pp. 1-208. (Biddle.) [365

PISTORIUS, JOANNES. [1] Anatomiae Lutheri pars prima. ... Gedruckt zu Cöln/ durch Arnoldum Quentel ... M. D. XCV. 4°. *^{6} *a-*i^{4} A-Z^{4} Aa^{6} a-gg^{4} A-N^{4} O^{6}. pp. 1-72, 1-194, 1-240, 1-115. [2] Anatomiae Lutheri pars secunda. ... Gedruckt zu Cöln/ durch Arnoldum Quentel ... M. D. XCVIII. a*-d*^{4} e*^{2} A-4M^{4}. pp. 1-20, 1-646. [366

-- Artis cabalisticae: hoc est, reconditae theologiae et philosophiæ, scriptorum: Tomus I. ... Ex D. Ioannis Pistorii, Nidani ... Bibliotheca. ... Basileæ, per Sebastianum Henricpetri. (... M. D. XXCVII. Mense Aprili.) fol.):(^{4} α-γ^{6} δ^{4} a-z^{6} A-Ff^{6} Gg-Hh^{4} Ii-Pp^{6} Qq^{4} Rr-Zz^{6} AA-OO^{6}. pp. 1-979. [367

-- Ein hundert Vnwarheyt/ Beneben Achtzehen vnd mehrern verfälschungen der Schrifft/ vnd Viertzigen vngeschickten Consequentzen So in den ersten siben kleinen Blettern ... in D.

Aegidij Hunnij ... Buchlen/ dass er wider D. Pistorij Theses von der iustification ... geschriben ... Getruckt zu Costantz am Bodensee/ bei Leonhart Straub/ In verlegung Arnoldi Quentels, Buchtruckerherrn zu Cölln. Anno M.D.XCV. 4°. (:)^4 A-R^4. pp. 9-135. [368

PITHOU, PIERRE. Annalium et historiae Francorum Ab anno ... DCCVIII. ad ann. DCCCCXC. scriptores coætanei XII. ... Ex Bibliotheca P. Pithoei ... Francofurti Apud Andreæ Wecheli heredes, Claudium Marnium, & Ioann. Aubrium. M D XCIIII. 8°.)(^{8} A-Qq^8. pp. 1-572. ¶*Authors:* Flodoardus Remensis, Guillaume de Nangis, Odorannus, Conradus Urspergensis, S. Arnulphus, Paulus Warnefridus, Constantinus Manasses, Theganus, Nithardus, Abbo Cernuus. [369

-- -- *Another copy.* (Lea.) [370

-- Historiae Francorum ab anno ... DCCCC. ad ann. M.CC.LXXXV. scriptores veteres XI; in quibus Glaber Helgaudus Sugerius Abbas M. Rigordus Guillermus Brito Guillermus de Nangis & anonymi alij. ... Ex bibliotheca P. Pithoei ... Francofurti Apud Andreæ Wecheli heredes Claudium Marnium & Ioannem Aubrium. M. D. XCVI. fol. π^2 A-Tt^6 Vu-Yy^4 Zz^6. pp. 1-504. (Lea.) [371

PIUS II, pope. Aneae Syluii Piccolominei Senensis, qui ... Pius ... secundus appellatus est, opera quæ extant omnia ... His quoque accessit gnomologia ex omnibus Syluii operibus collecta ... Basileae, ex officina Henricpetrina. ... (... M.D. LXXI. mense Augusto.) fol. a-b^6 c^4 d^6 *-3*^{6} *†-*†††^{6} *††††^{4} A-Zz^6 Aaa-Zzz^6 AAa-PPp^6 QQq-RRr^4 SSs-XXx^6 YYy^8 α^6 β^4 γ^6. pp. 1-1086. ¶*Additional t.p.* (α1): Gnomologia ... collecta, Per Conradum Lycosthenes Rubeaquensem. ... Basileæ. (Lea.) [372

-- Pii Pont. Max. decadum Blondi epitome ... Basileae apud Ioannem Bebelium M. D. XXXIII. (... octauo Calend. Septemb.) fol. α-β^6 A-M^6 N^4. ff. 2-75. [373

-- [Equitis Franci et adolescentulæ mulieris Italæ practica artis amandi ... Cui præterea ... alia quædam ... Authore Hilario Drudone.] (Ursellis ex officina typographica Cornelij Sutorij. Anno M D C.) 12°. A-V^{12} (-A1) X^{10}. pp. 3-495. [374

-- Germania Enee Siluij ... (Excusum ĩ ... vrbe Argentineñ. per Renatũ Beck ... Anno ... Sesquimillesimo. XV. XVI. Kal'. Iulij.) 4°. π^4 A-M$^{4.4.8}$ N-O^4 P^6. ¶A3, A4 *defective.* [375

PLACENTIUS, JOANNES LEO. Pugna porcorum per P. Porcium Poëtam ... M.D.XXX. 8°. A^8. [376

PLANTSCH, MARTIN. Opusculum de sagis maleficis ... (Phorce in ædibus Thome Anshelmi impẽsisq3 Sigismundi Stir ciuis Heilprunnensis Anno septimo supra .M. & .D. ... mense Ianuario.) 4°. a-e^8 f^4 g^6. [377

PLATINA, BARTOLOMMEO. ... Platynae hystoria de Vitis pontificum ... (Venetiis a Philippo pincio Mantuano. ... M.CCCCCIIII. die .XXII. Augusti.) fol. a-r^8 s^{10} A-F^8 G^6. ff. ii-cxlyi. ¶A1^r: ... Platynæ dialogus de falso & uero bono. B6^r: Platynae dialogus contra amores ... C6^r: Dialogus ... de uera nobilitate ... D4^r: Platinæ de optimo ciue liber primus ... F1^v: Platynae Panegyricus in laudem ... Bessarionis ... F5^v: ... Platynæ oratio de pace Italiæ confirmanda & bello Thurcis indicendo. F6^r: Diuersorũ academicorum panegyrici in parentalia .B. Platynæ [378

-- -- Historia B. Platinæ de vitis pontificum Romanorum. ... Annotationum Onuphrii Panuinij accessione nunc illustrior reddita. ... Coloniae, apud Maternum Cholinum. M. D. LXXIIII. ... fol. †-††^{6} A-NN^6 3A-3D^6 3E^4 3F-3I^6 a-h^6.i^4. pp. 1-429, 57-104, 1-72. (Lea.) [379

-- -- Bap. Platinae historia, Von der Bäpst vnd Keiser leben. ... Strassburg. M. D. XLVI. (Gedruckt ... bey Wendel Rihel ...) fol. AA^6 BB-CC^4 A-Z^6 a-z^6 Aa^6 Bb^8 (-Bb8, *presumably blank*). ff. j-cclxxxj. ¶*Translator: Caspar Hedio.* [380

-- -- Platina delle vite de' pontefici ... Tradotto di Latino in lingua volgare ... In Venetia, Per Francesco Lorenzini da Turino, M D LX. (... Per Comin da Trino di Monferrato. M D LXV.) 8°. a^4 B-Zz^8 AA-GG^8 HH^4 *^{8}. ff. 7-426. [381

PLATO. *Works. Greek.* Απαντα Πλατωνος ... Platonis omnia opera ... Basileae, apud Henrichum Petri. (... M. D. LVI. Mense Martio.) fol. α^6 α-ω^6 Αα-Ωω^6 ΑαΑ-ΗηΗ^6 ΘθΘ-ΙιΙ^8 ΚκΚ-ΜμΜ^6 ΝνΝ^4. pp. 1-690. [382

-- -- *Greek & Latin.* [1] Πλατωνος απαντσ τα σωζομεναι. Platonis opera quæ extant omnia. Ex noua Ioannis Serrani interpretatione ... Henr. Stephani ... iudicium, & ... emendatio. 1578 [Genevae,] Excudebat Henr. Stephanus ... fol. $*^4$ $**^6$ $3*^8$ A-Xx^6 Yy^8 (-Yy8, *blank*). pp. 1-542. [2] Platonis ... operum tomus secundus ... ¶^{4} AA-5P^6 5O^4. pp. 3-992. [3] ... tomus tertius ... ¶^{4} 4A-4B^6 4C-4D^4 4E-5L^6 5M^8 5N^4 5O^6 5P-5Z^4 a-f^4. pp. 1-416, 1-139. [383

-- -- *Latin.* Omnia diuini Platonis opera tralatione Marsilii Ficini ... [Basileae in officina Frobeniana an. MDLI.] (Basileae apud Hier. Frobenium et Nic. Episcopium, an. M D LI. Mense Martio.) fol. α^6 a-z^6 A-Zz^6 AA-II^6 KK^8 LL-OO^6. pp. 1-952. ¶α1 *defective.* [384

-- -- ... tralatione Marsilii Ficini, emendatione ... Simonis Grynaei ... Venetiis, apud Ioannem Mariam Bonellum. M. D. LVI. (*Colophon.*) fol. α-γ^6 δ^8 a-z^6 A-Hh^6. pp. 1-646. ¶α1 *defective.* [385

-- *Two or more dialogs.* [Platonis ... Dialogi IIII ... Iano Cornario ... interprete. His accesserunt Fabularum aliquot poeticarum allegoriae ex Psello ... et ipsius Cornarii Venator Actaeon ... MDXLIX.] (Basileae apud Frobenium et Episcopium mense Augusto M. D. XLIX.) 8°. a-l^8 (-a1) m^4. pp. 4-180. ¶*Contents:* Alcibiades I, II, Hipparchus, Amatores. [386

-- Il Liside di Platone de l'amicitia, Tradotto da Francesco Colombi: et il furore poetico, Tradotto da Nicolo Triuisani in lingua Toscana. ... In Vinegia. M. D. XLVIII. 8°. $*^4$ A-H^4. ff. 1-32. [387

-- I Dialoghi di Platone intitolati L'Eutifrone, ... L'Apologia di Socrate, Il Critone, ... Il Fedone, ... Il Timeo ... Tradotti di lingua Greca in Italiana da M. Sebastiano Erizzo ... In Vinegia, Presso Giouanni Varisco, e Compagni. (... M. D. LXXIIII.) 8°. a^8 b^4 A-Ss^8 (-Ss7-8, *presumably blank*). ff. 1-327. ¶b4 *defective.* [388

-- *Phaedo.* Le Phedon de Plato traittant de l'immortalite de l'ame ... Le dixiesme liure de la Republique, en ce qu'il parle de l'immortalité ... Deux passages du mesme autheur à ce propos, l'vn du Phedre, l'autre du Gorgias. La remonstrance que fait Cyrus Roy des Perses à ses enfans & amys ... escritte par Xenophon. Le tout traduit de Grec en François ... par Loys le Roy, dit Regius. A Paris, Chez Sebastien Nyuelle ... 1553. 4°. A-YY^4. pp. 1-350. [389

-- *Phaedrus.* Il Fedro ... di Platone, Tradotto in lingua Toscana per Felice Figliucci Senese. In Roma. Nel M D XLIIII. ... (... Per Francesco Priscianese Nel M D LXIIII.) 8°. A-I^8 L^8. ff. 4-79. [390

-- *Republica.* Sebastiani Foxii Morzilli Hispalensis commẽtatio in decem Platonis libros de Republica. ... Basileae, apud Ioannem Oporinum. (... M. D. LVI. Mense Septembri.) fol. a^6 A-Cc^4 Dd^6. cols. 1-416. ¶*Translator: Marsiglio Ficino.* [391

-- -- La republica di Platone, tradotta dalla lingua Greca nella Thoscana dall'eccellente ... Pamphilo Fiorimbene da Fossembrone. ... In Vinegia appresso Gabriel Giolito de Ferrari, et fratelli MDLIIII. (*Colophon.*) 8°. $*$-$**^8$ A-FF^8 GG^4. ff. 2-8, pp. 17-451. [392

-- *Timaeus.* M. T. Cic. Timęus, siue de Vniuersitate liber ... Adiectæ sunt ... Annotationes ... Parisiis, Apud Thomam Richardum ... 1549. 4°. a-c^4. ff. 2-12. [393

-- -- Timaeus Platonis, siue de vniuersitate, interpretibus, M. Tullio Cicerone, & Chalcidio, vna cum eius docta explanatione. Parisiis, M.D.LXIII. Apud Guil. Morelium ... (Absoluebat Ioannes Benenatus pridie Kalendas Maias 1569.) 4°. A-Cc^4 Dd^2. pp. 3-212. [394

-- -- [1] Le Timee de Platon ... translaté de grec en françois ... par Loys le Roy ... Trois oraisons de Demosthene ... dittes Olynthiaques ... A Paris, De l'imprimerie de Michel de Vascosan. M. D. LI. ... (... le XXII iour de Ianuier. M. D. LII.) 4°. A-B^4 ãã^2 C-Ee^4 Ff^6. ff. 9-115. [2] Trois oraisons de Demosthene ... *Same imprint.* A-E^4 F^6. ff. 9-25. [395

-- -- Le Timee de Platon ... Plutarque de la creation de l'ame ... A Paris, Par Abel l'Angelier ... M.D.LXXXI. 4°. A-Rr^4 $*^4$ (-*4, *presumably blank*). ff. 9-159. [396

-- -- Il dialogo di Platone, intitolato il Timeo ... Tradotto di lingua Greca in Italiana da M. Sebastiano Erizzo ... mandato in luce da Girolamo Ruscelli. ... In Venetia per Comin da Trino M D LVIII 4°. $*^4$ A-K^4 L^2 (-L2, *presumably blank*). ff. 1-41. [397

-- *Selections*. Dicta notabilia, et in thesaurum memorie reponēda, Platonis. Aristotelis. Cōmentatoris. Porphirij. Gilberti poretani. Boetij. Senece. Apuleij ... Quibus addita sunt ... Aristotelis problemata ... M. D. XXXII. (Impensis Venetiis per magistrum Sebastianū Vincentinum impresse. ... die .XXVII. Iunij ...) 8°. a-l^8 m^6. ff. II-XCIIII. [398

-- -- [1] Dicta notabilia ... Addita sunt Marcantonii Zimaræ Problemata ... Ad signum Putei. M D XXXVII. (Venetiis per Ioannem Patauinum & Venturinum Roffinellis. ...) 16°. A-Z^8 $\&^8$ $ɔ^8$. ff. 2-198. [2] Marci Tulii Ciceronis ac Publi. Terentii facundissime authoritates. *Same imprint and colophon.* A-H^8. ff. 2-63. [399

-- -- Dicta notabilia ... Venetiis ad Signum Spei. 1548. 16°. A-Z^8 Aa^6. ff. 2-189.[400

-- Diuini Platonis gemmae, siue illustriores sententiæ, ... à Nicolao Liburnio Veneto collectæ. ... Parisiis, Apud Benedictum Preuost ... 1552. (*Colophon.*) 16°. A-Q^8 (-Q8, *presumably blank*). ff. 2-127. [401

PLATZ, CONRAD WOLFGANG. Kurtzer/ Nottwendiger/ vnnd Wollgegrundter bericht/ Auch Christentliche vermanung/ von der Grewlichen ... Zauberey ... ([Tübingen, widow of Ulrich Morhart,] Anno. M.D.LXvj.) 8°. A-H^8. [402

-- Oberkeits Ampt Schenckung. Von den drey ... Tugenten/ aller vnd jeder Oberkeit ... Getruckt zu Tübingen/ bey Alexander Hock ... 1577. 4°. A-C^4. [403

PLAUTUS, TITUS MACCIUS. Ex Plauti comoediis. XX. ... (Venetiis in aedibus Aldi, et Andreae Asulani soceri, mense Iulio. M. D. XXII.) 4°. *-$**^8$ a-z^8 A-M^8 N^4. ff. 1-284. [404

-- -- M. Actii Plauti comoediae viginti. Apud Seb. Gryphium Lugduni, 1549. 16°. a-z^8 A-Q^8 aa-zz^8 AA-EE^8 FF^4. pp. 3-1078. [405

-- -- M. Accii Plauti comoediae XX. ... studio Ioachimi Camerarii Pabeperg. ... editæ ... Basileae, per Ioannem Heruagium [1552]. 4°. a-z^8 A-Ii^8. pp. 3-910. ¶*The name of Camerarius has been inked out.* [406

-- -- M. Accii Plauti comoediae viginti, olim a Ioachimo Camerario emendatæ: nunc ... restitutæ, opera ... Ioannis Sambuci Tirnauiensis Pannonij. Aliquot ... C. Langij, Adr. Turnebi, Hadr. Iunij, & aliorum ... obseruationes. Antuerpiae, Ex officina Christophori Plantini. cIɔ.Iɔ.LXVI. 16°. A-Z^8 a-Gg^8. pp. 10-847. [407

-- -- M. Accius Plautus ... opera Dionys. Lambini Monstroliensis emendatus: ab eodémque commentariis explicatus. ... [Genevae,] Apud hæredes Eustathij Vignon. M. D. XCV. 4°. $¶^4$ A-Zz^8 AA-KK^8 LL^4 MM-PP^8 QQ^2. pp. 1-920. [408

-- M. Actii Plauti Asinii ... Comoediæ quinqȝ. 1 Amphitryo. 2 Asinaria. 3 Aulularia. 4 Captiui duo. 5 Curculio. Cum lucubratiunculis ex commentarijs Pyladę Brixiani, ornati. ... (Argentorati. Ex Aedibus Matthiæ Schürerij Mense Augusto. ... M.D.XIIII.) 4°. a-b^8 c-d^4 e^8 f-h^4 i^6 k^4 l^8 m-n^4 o^6 p-$s^{4\cdot8}$ t-v^4 x-$Ee^{4\cdot8}$ Ff^8. ff. I-CLVI. [409

-- M. Plauti ... Comoedia prima: cui Amphitryo nomē ab auctore ip̄o inditū est. ... Lipsiae apŏ Melchiorē Lotthel̶ Anno ... Millesimo q̄ngētesimo vigesimoprimo. 4°. A-E^6. [410

-- -- Comedia di Plauto intitolata l'Amphitriona, tradotta dal latino al uolgare, per Pandolfo Colonnutio, ... & nuouamente stampata. MDXXX (Stampata in Vinegia per Nicolo d'Aristotile detto Zoppino. ...) 8°. A-H^8. ff. 2-64. [411

-- Comedia Ridiculosa di Plauto intitolata Asinaria tradotta de latino in uolgare in terza rima ... M D XXX (Stampata in Vinegia per Nicolo d'Aristotile detto Zoppino. ...) 8°. A-F^8. ff. 2-47. [412

-- Aulularia Plautina ... quæ &si alias incompleta/ a Codro Vrceo tamen est perfecta. ... (Impressum Albiburgii per Ioannē Viridimontanū Anno. M.D.IX.) 4°. A^6 B-F^4. [413

-- -- Plauti ... Aulularia ab Antonio Codro Vrceo ... restituta ... (Lipsiæ in ædibus Valentini Schumañ Anno ... Millesimo quingentesimo decimoseptimo.) 4°. A-B^6 C^4 D^6. [414

-- Comedia di Plauto intitolata Menechini, dal latino in lingua uolgar tradotta, ... & nuouamente ristampata. MDXXX (Stampata in Vinegia per Nicolo di Aristotile detto Zoppino. ...) 8°. A-E^8. ff. 2-39. [415

-- Il Penolo. Comedia antica di Plauto ... tradotta ... M.D.XXVI. (Stampato nella ... citta di Vinegia ... per Francesco di Alessandro Bindoni, & Mapheo Pasini, compagni. ... Del mese di Zugno.) 8°. A-F^4 (-F3-4, *blank*). [416

-- Stichus Plautinus ... (Impressa ... Lipsi in edibus Melchiaris Lotteri anno millesimo quingentesimo duodecimo.) fol. A-B^6. [417

PLENIGEN, DIETRICH VON. Hienach volgt ain kurtzer ausszuge den ich Dieterich von Plenigen zu Eysenhofen ... vom Seneca gethon hab ... gethutscht Anno ꝛc. CCCCC.xv. den xviij tag des monatz Augusti. ... (... gedruckt zu Landsshůt von herr Iohann Weyssenburger ... M.CCCCC. vnnd xv. am den x. tag des September.) 4°. A-D^4. [418

-- In disem buchlein ist begriffen ein anntwort auff zwo fragen: ... wie es zu kom̄: das sich wenig mēschen jrs stands benuegen lassent: ... wie es zů gang das wenig leuͤt ... das ware guͤt erkennen/ vnnd das poͤss dauon zů vnderschaiden wissent ... (... gedruckt zu Landsshůt Anno ... Tausent funff hundert vnnd sechtzehen. Am Pfintztag nach Ambrosy: Durch herr Iohañ Weyssenburger.) fol. A-D^6. [419

PLETHO, GEORGIUS GEMISTUS. Georgij Gemisti Plethonis ... Quatuor Virtutum explicatio, græcè & latinè, ... Adolpho Occone Physico Augustano interprete. De moribus philosophorum locus ex Platonis Theæteto, item græcè & latinè, eodem interprete. Adiunximus, Aristotelis de virtutibus & vitiis libellum ..., quatuor eius interpretibus ... Basileae, per Ioannem Oporinum. 8°. a-i^8. pp. 1-127. ¶*Preface dated* M.D.LII. Calendis Ianuarij. [420

PLINIUS CAECILIUS SECUNDUS, GAIUS. Quæ in isto continentur opusculo. C. Plinii iunioris epistolæ per Philippum beroaldū emendatæ ... Etiā eiusdem auctoris panegærycus in laudem Trayani imperatoris: & de iuris illustribus libellus. (Impressum Venetiis per Albertinū Vercellensem. ... M.CCCCCI. Die .XX. Aprilis.) 4°. a-k^8 l^{10} m^8 n^4. [421

-- -- C. Plinii Secundi Nouocomensis Epistolarum libri X. Eiusdem Panegyricus Traiano Principi dictus. Eiusdem de Viris illustrib. in re militari, & in administranda rep. Suetonij Tranquilli de Claris Grammaticis, & Rhetoribus. Iulij Obsequentis Prodigiorum liber. ... (Venetiis in aedib. Aldi, et Andreae Asulani soceri mense Iunio. M.D.XVIII.) 8°. *-3*^{8} 4*^{4} a-kk^8. pp. 1-525. [422

-- -- Basileae, apud And. Cratand. an. M. D. XXX. ... 8°. α^8 a^4 b-z^8 A-P^8 Q^4. pp. 2-562. [423

-- -- Epistole di G. Plinio, di M. Franc. Petrarca, del S. Pico della Mirandola et d'altri ... huomini. Tradotte per M. Lodouico Dolce. ... In Vinegia appresso Gabriel Giolito de Ferrari. MDXLVIII. (*Colophon.*) 8°. *^{4} A-V^8 X^4. ff. 1-164. [424

-- Cay Plinij des Andern Lobsagung ... Durch herrn Dietrichen vō Pleningē ... geteütscht. ([Strassburg,] Getruckt [durch Martin Flach] vnd vollendet in dem Jare ... Fünfftzehundert vnnd zwentzig Jare. ... an dem Achtzehenden tag des Newmonadts.) fol. π^4 A^4 B-G^6 H^8 (-H8, *blank*). [425

PLINIUS SECUNDUS, GAIUS. [1] C. Plinii Secundi naturalis historiae prima pars. M. D. XL. (Venetiis, in aedibus haeredum Aldi, et Andreae Asulani soceri, M. D. XXXVI.) 8°. A-F^8 a-z^8 A-P^8 Q^4. ff. 1-314. [2] C. Plinii Secundi naturalis historiae secunda pars. M. D. XXXV. (Venetiis, in aedibus haeredum Aldi, et Andreae Asulani soceri ...) aa-zz^8 AA-PP^8. ff. 2-303. [3] ... tertia pars. M. D. XXXV. (*Same colophon as* [1].) 3a-3z^8 3A-3O^8. ff. 2-295. [4] Index in C. Plinii nat. Hist. Libros ... Venetiis M D XXXVIII. (*Colophon.*) A-GG^8 HH^{12} (-HH12, *blank*). [426

-- -- C. Plinii Secundi historiae mundi libri triginta septem. ... Annexæ sunt ... Castigationes Sigismundi Gelenij. ... Lugduni, ex officina Godefridi et Marcelli Beringorum fratrum, M.D.XLVIII. fol. a-b^8 a-z^6 A-R^6 S^4 3a-3c^6 a-k^6 l^4. cols. 1-976. ¶*Additional t.p.* (^{3}a1^r): Index ... Lugduni excudebant ... Beringi ... M. D. XLVIII. [427

-- -- *Another copy* (-a2-4). [428

-- -- Basileae M. D. LIIII. (... per Hier. Frobenium, et Nic. Episcopium, M D LV.) fol. A-C^6 a-z^6 A-Hh^6 Ii^8 3a-3e^6 a-n^6 (-n6, *presumably blank*). pp. 1-663. [429

-- -- [1] L'histoire du monde de C. Pline Second ... mis en François par Antoine du Pinet ... Premier Tome. A Lyon, ... Par Claude Senneton. M.D.LXII. ... fol. a^6 *-**^{6} 3*^{4} a-z^6 A-Kk^6 Ll^4 A-N^6 (-N6). pp. j-xxxj, 1-678. ¶*Additional t.p.* (^{2}A1^r): Table des noms et matieres ... *Same imprint.* [2] ... Tome second. ... *Same imprint.* a-b^8 C-Zz^6 AA-RR^6 SS^8 a-h^6 i^4. pp. 1-745. ¶*Additional t.p.* (^{2}a1^r): Table ... *Same imprint.* [430

-- -- Caij Plinij Secundi von Veron/ Natürlicher History Fünff Buͤcher. ... durch Heinrich von Eppendorff verteütscht. ... Zů Strassburg/ bey Hans Schotten ... M. D. xliij. fol. a-v^6. pp. iiij-ccxxxv. [431

-- -- Historia naturale di C. Plinio Secondo di Latino in volgare tradotta per Christophoro Landino ... In Venetia appresso Gabriel Iolito di Ferrarii M. D. XXXXIII. (*Colophon.*) 4°. *-3*^{8} A-3M^8 3N^4. pp. II-DCCCCXXXIIII. [432

-- -- Historia naturale di G. Plinio Secondo, Tradotta per M. Lodouicho Domenichi. ... In Venetia, Appresso Gio. Battista Vscio. 1589. 4°. a-c^8 A-4E^8 4F^4 (-4F4, *presumably blank*). pp. 4 [=3]-1184. [433

-- C. Plinij Praefatio. ... (Impress. Vuittenburgii in officina Ioannis Grunenbergii. Anno .M.D.XVIII.) 4°. A^6. [434

PLOTINUS. Plotini ... operum philosophicorum omnium libri LIV. in sex enneades distributi ... Græcè editi, cum Latina Marsilii Ficini interpretatione & commentatione. Basileae ad Perneam Lecythum M D XXC. (... Ex Officina Petri Pernæ. ... Kalend. Iunii.) fol. α-γ^6 a-z^6 A-Rr^6 Ss^8 Tt^6 Vu-Xx^8. pp. 1-771. [435

-- -- Plotini ... De rebus Philosophicis libri LIIII. ... Basileae, per Thomam Guerinum. Anno M. D. LIX. fol. †^{6} *^{8} a-z^6 A-Pp^6 α-δ^6. ff. 1-365. [436

PLOWDEN, EDMUND. 1571. Les Comentaries, ou les Reportes ... de dyuers cases ... en les temps des Raygnes le Roye Edwarde le size, le Roigne Mary, le Roy & Roigne Phillipp & Mary, & le Roigne Elizabeth. In Ædibus Richardi Tottelli. Octobris. 24. (*Colophon.*) fol. B.L. ¶^{4} A-5H^4 5I^2 (-5G4, 5H^4, 5I^2). ff. 1-395 *present*. *S.T.C.* 20040. [437

-- -- [1] 1578. Les Commentaries, or Reportes ... In Ædibus Richardi Tottelli. Octobris 20. ... (*Colophon.*) fol. B.L. ¶^{6} A-C^4 A-5G^4 5H^6 A-SS^4 TT^6. ff. 1-565, 1-15. ¶*Additional t.p.* (^{3}A1): Cy ensuont certeyne Cases Reportes per Edmunde Plowden. Anno. 1579. (... 15. die Iunij. ...) [2] Vn Report fait per vn vncerteine authour del part de vn argument del Edmund Plowden ... (... 1579.) A-D^4. ff. 1-15. *S.T.C.* 20041/20042. (Furness.)[438

PLUTARCH. [1] Πλουταρχου Χαιρωνεως τα σωζομενα παντα. Plutarchi Chæronensis quæ exstant omnia. Cum Latina interpretatione Hermanni Cruserij: Gulielmi Xylandri, et doctorum virorum notis ... Francofurti, Apud Andreæ Wecheli heredes, Claudium Marnium, & Ioannem Aubrium. M.D.XCIX. fol. †-††^{6} A-4S^6 4T^4 4V-4X^6 α-η^6 θ^4 ι^6 κ^4 A-B^6 C^4. pp. 2-1076, 3-114. [2] Plutarchi ... omnium ... operum tomus secundus ...)(^{4} a-5c^6 5d^4 5e-5h^6 5i^4 *-6*^{6} 7*^{4} a^6 aa^6 aaa^6 (-aaa6, *blank*). pp. 1-1147, 1-56, 1-80. [439

-- *Moralia*. Plutarchi opuscula. LXXXXII. ... *Greek*. (Venetiis In ædibus Aldi & Andreæ Asulani Soceri. mense Martio. M.D. IX.) fol. ✠^{8} a-z^8 &^{8} aa-3s^8 3t^6. pp. 1-1050. [440

-- -- Πλουταρχου ... ηθικα συγγραμματα ... Plutarchi Chaeronei moralia opuscula ... Basileae per Hier. Frobenium et Nic. Episcopium. M. D. XLII. (*Colophon.*) fol. *^{6} α-ω^6 Αα-Ωω^6 ΑΑ-ΩΩ^6 ΑαΑ^8. pp. 1-877. [441

-- -- Plutarchi Chaeronei ... Opuscula ... omnia ... (Venetiis per Io. Ant. & fratres de sabio, sumptu ... Melchioris Sessa. ... M D XXXII. Mēse Martio.) 8°. a-d^8 a-z^8 &^{8} ɔ^8 ℞^{8} A-SS^8. ff. 1-536. [442

-- -- Basileae, in officina And. Cratandri, Mense Septembri, an. M. D. XXX. (*Colophon.*) fol. a-c^6 A-Ss^6 Tt^4. ff. 2-249. [443

-- -- Les oeuures morales & meslees de Plutarque, Translatees du Grec en François par Messire Iacques Amyot ... A Paris, De l'Imprimerie de Michel de Vascosan. M. D. LXXII. ... (Imprime ... par Vascosan Et Federic Morel ...) fol. a^6 (-a6) A-3N^6 3O^4 3P-5T^6 5V^4 5X^2 a-g^6. ff. I-668. [444

-- -- [1] Tugentspiegel der hoch vnd Weltweisen. ... XXj. Buͤcher. ... Auss Plutarcho/ durch Heinrich Eppendorff verteutscht. M.D.LI. (Zů Strassburg bey Hans Schotten M.D.XXXV.) fol. π^4 a-cc^6. pp. j-ccxcvj. [2] Plutarchi ... kurtz/ weise/ vnd hoͤffliche Sprüch ... a-z^6 A-Dd^6 E^6 (-E6, *presumably blank*). pp. j-dxcij. [445

-- -- Morales de Plutarco Traduzidos de lengua Griega en Castellana. ... Impresso en Alcala de Henares por Iuan de Brocar. M.D.xlviij. ... fol. B.L. aa^6 bb^4 A-Z^8 a-b^8 c^4. ff. j-ccj. ¶*Translator: Diego Graciano de Alderete.* [446

-- *Moralia. Selections.* Plutarchi Cheronei Opuscula ... Vęnundantur ab Ioanne Paruo & Iodoco Badio. (In ędibus Ascensianis ad .VI. Kalen. Martias ... MDXIIII.) fol. A^8 a-s^8 t^6. ff. I-CXLIX. [447

-- De natura et effectionibus Dæmonum libelli duo Plutarchi Cheronensis, cum explicationibus, & Prooemio Ioachimi Camer. ... Editi Lipsiae in officina Voegeliana ... [1576]. (*Colophon.*) 8°. A-N^8. pp. 1-151. ¶*T.e.*, De oraculorum defectu liber, De figura E I consecrata Delphis. *Translator: Adrien Turnèbe.* (Lea.) [448

-- Opuscules de Plutarche Cheronee. Traduictz par maistre Estienne Pasquier ... A Lyon, Par Iean de Tournes. 1546. 8°. a-n^8 o^4. pp. 6-216. [449

-- Le tresor des morales de Plutarque de Chæronæe ... redigez en bon ordre & disposition en langue Françoise. Par François Le Tort, Angeuin. A Paris, Chez Iean Poupy ... M. D. LXXVII. ... 8°. $\bar{a}^8$ a-z^8 A-M^8 N^2 O-Gg^8 Hh^6 Ii-Kk^8 Ll^2. pp. 1-888. ¶*Additional t.p.* ($O1^r$): Le tresor ... Tome second. *Same imprint.* [450

-- [1] Alcuni opusculetti de le cose morali del diuino Plutarco in questa nostra lingua nuouamente tradotti. In Venetia, nel M D XLIX. ... (... per Michele Tramezino ...) 8°. A-Y^8. ff. 7-176. [2] Seconda parte de le cose morali di Plutarcho, recate ... in questa nostra lingua, da M. Giouanni Tarchagnota. ... In Venetia, Nel M D XXXXVIII. (*Same colophon.*) $*^4$ a-ll^8. ff. 1-272. [451

-- -- In Venetia, Per Comin da Trino di Monferrato. M D LXVII. (*Colophon.*) 8°. a-x^8 a-nn^8 oo^4 (-oo4, *presumably blank*). ff. 3-163, 2-289. [452

-- Opere morali di Plutarcho, nuouamente tradotte, per M. Lodouico Domenichi, Cioè Il conuito de'sette saui. Come altri possa lodarsi da se stesso senza biasimo. Della Garrulità ... In Lucca per Vincenzo Busdragho MDLX. 8°. A-H^8. pp. 3-128. [453

-- *Conjugalia praecepta.* Ein schon herlich Buchlin/ einer ... vnderweisung/ wie sich zwey Eeleut gegen einander halten sollen ... jetzt erstlich auss dem Latein in Teutsch transsferiert ... Anno M. D. XXXXV. (Getruckt zu Augspurg/ durch Hainrich Stayner/ am v. tag Iunij ...) 4°. A-E^4. [454

-- Plutarchi Chaeronei de Exilio Angelo Barbato Interprete. (Impressum Nurenbergæ per Fridericum Peypus. M.D.XVII. Die. XV. Iulii) 4°. A^4 B^6. [455

-- Plutarchi de loquacitate liber. Latinè redditus ab Ioanne Caselio. ... Rostochii Ex officina typographica Myliandrj. Anno CIↃ IↃ XIC. 4°. A-G^4 $*G^4$ H-M^4. [456

-- *De latenter vivendo.* Plutarchi Chaeronei disceptatio num recte dictum sit λάθε βιώσας, id est, sic viue, vt nemo te sentiat vixisse. [Romae, Franciscus Minitius Calvo, c. 1523.] 4°. A^4. [457

-- Plutarchi Cheronei de Philosophorum Placitis libellus ..., interprete Guilielmo Budeo. (Argentorati, Ex ædibus Schurerianis Mense Iulio. M D XVI.) 4°. π^4 A-B^4 C-D^8 E-G^4. ff. I-XXXV. [458

-- [1] Πλουταρχου ... περι πρωτου ψυχρου. Plutarchi Chaeronei de primo frigido. Parisiis, Ex officina Adriani Turnebi ... M. D. LII. ... 4°. A-C^4. pp. 3-21. [2] Plutarchi Chaeronei commentarius de primo frigido, Adriano Turnebo interprete. *Same imprint.* χ^2 D-F^4. pp. 1-24. [459

-- *De sera numinis vindicta.* Plutarchi Chaeronei ... De his qui tarde a Numine corripiuntur Libellus. (Argentorati, ex Aedibus Schurerianis, Mense Martio, Anno M. D. XIIII.) 4°. A^4 B^8 C-D^4 E^6. [460

-- *De recta ratione audiendi.* Plutarchi Chaeronei commentarius, περὶ τοῦ ἀκούειν, Id est, de officio auditoris quid legendo ... ab Ottomaro Luscinio latinitate donat[9]. Item de docenda uirtute. ... 8°. a-c^8. ¶*Dedication dated* Augustæ. pridie Iduū Octobrium. ... M. D. XXV. [461

-- Plutarchi Chaeronei de vitanda vsura libellus ..., interprete Bilibaldo Pirchimerio ... [Romae, Franciscus Minitius Calvo, c. 1525.] 4°. A^6. [462

-- *De vitiosa verecundia.* De la honte vicieuse, traicté composé par Plutarque de Cheronee, & traduict en nostre langue, par François le Grand. A Paris, Chez Charles Estienne ... M. D. LIIII. 8°. A-B^8 C^4. pp. 3-40. [463

-- *Vitae parallelae.* Les vies des hommes Illustres Grecs & Romains, Comparees ... per Plutarque de Chæronçe, Translatees de Grec en François. A Paris, De l'imprimerie de Michel de Vascosan. M. D. LVIII[I]. ... (Acheué d'imprimer en May. M. D. LVIIII.) fol. A^8 $b-z^6$ $A-Zz^6$ $AA-ZZ^6$ $AAa-ZZz^6$ $AAA-GGG^6$ $HHH-III^4$ $A-C^6$ $D-E^4$. ff. 1-734. ¶A1 *defective. Translator: Jacques Amyot.* [464

-- -- ... Ausquelles sont adioustees ... les vies de Annibal & de Scipion l'Africain, traduites de Latin en Francois par Charles de l'Escluse. ... A Lausanne. Par Francois le Preux. ... M. D. LXXV. (*Colophon.*) fol. A^8 $B-Zz^6$ $Aaa-Zzz^6$ $AAa-ZZz^6$ $AAA-TTT^6$ VVV^8 $XXX-ZZZ^6$ $\&^4$. pp. 1-1336. [465

-- -- Plutarchus Teutsch. Von dem leben vnd Ritterlichen geschichten/ der ... Griechen vnd Rômern ... newlich verteutscht ... Getruckt zů Augspurg durch Heinrich Steiner. M. D. XXXIIII. (... Am sibenden tag Martij ...) fol. π^4 $A-Cc^6$ Dd^8. ff. I-CLXIIII. ¶*Translator: Jeronymus Boner.* [466

-- -- Ankunfft/ Leben vnd wesen ... der Griechen vnnd Römer ... ins Teutsch bracht/ Durch ... Hieronymum Boner ... M. D. XLVII. (Gedruckt inn ... Colmar durch Barptolomeum Grieninger/ vnd vollendet den neün und zweintzigsten tag Martij ... M. D. XLI.) fol. π^4 $A-X^6$ Y^8 $Z-4M^6$ $A-Dd^6$. ff. I-CCCCLXXXIIII, I-CLXI. [467

-- -- Plutarchus ... von den herrlichsten ... Männern ... vnder den Rômern vnd Griechen ... Durch ... Guilielmum Xylandrum/ von Augspurg/ angefangen/ vnd ... durch ... Ionas Lôchinger vollendet. ... Getruckt in ... Franckfort am Mayn ... M. D. LXXX. (... durch Peter Schmid/ in verlegung Sigmund Feyrabends. ...) fol. $(?)^4$ $A-4P^6$ $4Q^4$ (-4Q4, *presumably blank*). ff. 2-495. [468

-- -- [1] La prima parte delle vite di Plutarcho di greco in latino: ⁊ di latino in volgare tradotte ... MDXXV (Stampate in Vinegia per Nicolao di Aristotile detto Zoppino ... del mese di Luglio.) 4°. $A-PP^8$ (-PP8, *presumably blank*). ff. II-CCCIII. [2] La seconda ⁊ vltima parte delle vite di Plutarcho ... M.D.XXV. (Stampate in Vinegia per Nicolao di Aristotile detto Zoppino ... dil mese di Martio.) $a-dd^8$ $Aa-Bb^8$. ff. III-CCXV. [469

-- -- Le vite de gli huomini illustri Greci et Romani, di Plutarco Cheroneo ..., tradotte nuouamente da M. Francesco Sansouino. ... In Venetia, Appresso Vincenzo Valgrisi. 1564. 4°. $*^4$ $A-YY^8$ ZZ^4 $3A-3B^4$. pp. 2-726. ¶*Part I only. Lacks one or more gatherings at the end.* [470

-- -- [1] Vite di Plutarco Cheroneo de gli huomini illustri Greci et Romani, nuouamente tradotte per M. Lodouico Domenichi et altri, et ... confrontate co'testi Greci per M. Lionardo Ghini: con la vita dell'auttore, descritta da Thomaso Porcacchi ... In Vinegia, appresso Gabriel Giolito de' Ferrari, MDLXVII. 4°. a^4 $A-K^4$ $A-3G^8$ $3H^6$. pp. 1-860. [2] Seconda parte delle vite di Plutarco ... *Same imprint.* a^4 $a-e^4$ $a-ff^8$ gg^4. pp. 1-470. [471

-- *Vitae parallelae. Selections.* Les Vies de huit ... personnages Grecz & Romains, mises au paragon lune de lautre: escrites en Grec par Plutarque de Cherronee: & depuis translatees par ... George de Selue ... A Lyon, per Iean de Tournes. M. D. XLVIII. 16°. $a-z^8$ $A-Z^8$ $aa-cc^8$ dd^4. pp. 4-791. [472

-- Las vidas de dos illustres varones, Cimon Griego, y Lucio Lucullo Romano, ... escritas ... por ... Plutarcho de Cheronea, y al presente traduzidas en estilo Castellano. [Basel, Johann Oporinus,] M. D. XLVII. 4°. $A-Tt^4$. pp. 3-332. [473

-- El primero volumen de las vidas de illustres ... varones Griegos y Romanos pareadas, escritas ... por ... Plutarcho de Cheronea, & ... traduzidas en estilo Castellano. En Argentina, en casa de Augustin Frisio ... M D. LI. (... â çostas d' señor Pedro de Porres, en el mes de Mayo ...) fol. π^1 $A-Zz^6$ $AA-FF^6$ GG^8 $3A-3L^6$ $3M^8$. ff. 1-320, 1-71. [474

-- *Selections.* Apoftemmi di Plutarco ... Tradotti in lingua Toscana per M. Gio. Bernardo Gualandi Fiorentino. ... In Vinegia appresso Gabriel Giolito de' Ferrari. M D LXV. 4°. $*-**^4$ $3*^6$ $A-QQ^8$ RR^4. pp. 1-632. [475

-- -- In Vinegia appresso Gabriel Giolito de' Ferrari. M D LXVI. *Same collation and pagination.* ¶*Variant with a different setting of the dedication.* [476

-- Apopthegmas del ... Philosopho/ y Orador Plutarcho Cheroneo ... traduzidos de lẽgua Griega en Castellana: ... por Diego Gracian ... (Fue ímpressa ... en la ... vniuersidad de Alcala de Henares en casa de Miguel de Eguia acabose a treinta de Iunio de Mil y Quinientos y Treinta y tres Años.) 4°. B.L. $a-i^8$ k^6. [477

POCATERRA, ANNIBALE. Due dialogi della vergogna ... In Ferrara Appresso Benedetto Mammarelli. MDXCII. ... (*Colophon.*) 8°. A-P^8. pp. 7-209. [478

POCCIANTI, MICHELE. Catalogus scriptorum Florentinorum omnis generis ... Cum additionibus ferè 200. scriptorum ... Lucæ Ferrinij ... Florentiae, apud Philippum Iunctam, M. D. LXXXIX. ... (*Colophon.*) 4°. *^{2} A-L^8 M^4. pp. 1-171. [479

POEMATIA. Poematia aliquot insignia illustrium Poetarum recentiorum ... Basileae, anno M D XLIIII. Per Robertum VVinter. (*Colophon.*) 16°. a-p^8. ¶*Authors:* Laurentius Mondanarius, Petrus Bembus, Augustinus Beatianus, Camillus Palaeotus, Julius Camillus, Aaron Batalaeus, Eucharius Synesius, Baptista Persius, Joannes Arnolletus, Bucius Aenicola, Franciscus Philelphus, Janus Vitalis, Petrus Cursius, Claudius Budinus, Paulus Cerratus, Paulus Belmisserus, Quintianus Stoa. [480

POEONIUS, MARTIN. Ein Schön Lied Vom ... Sacrament des Leibs vnd Bluts Ihesu Christi ... 8°. A^4. ¶A2 *misbound after* A3. [481

POGGI, BELTRAMO. La Cangenia tragicomedia ... In Fiorenza Appresso i Giunti. MDLXI. (*Colophon.*) 8°. A-D^8 E^4. pp. 7-70. [482

POGGIO BRACCIOLINI, GIAN FRANCESCO. Poggii Florentini ... historiae conuiuiales disceptatiuae orationes inuectiuae epistolae descriptiones quaedam: et faceciarum liber (Impressum Argentine per ... Ioānem Knoblouchū. III. Idus Februarij. ... M. D. X.) fol. a-m^6 AA-EE^6. ff. II-LXXII, I-XXIX. [483

-- Facecie di Poggio Fiorentino, Historiate ... MDXXXI. (In Venetia ... per Frācesco Bindoni, & Mapheo Pasini, Nell'anno M.D.XXXI.) 8°. A-F^8. ff. 2-48. [484

-- Istoria di M. Poggio Fiorentino. Tradotta di Latino in Volgare da Iacopo suo figliuolo. Riueduta ... per M. Francesco Serdonati ... In Fiorenza. Per Filippo Giunti. M. D. IIC. (*Colophon.*) 4°. ¶^{2} A-R^8 S^2. pp. 1-258. [485

-- Wie Hieronymus von Prag ain anhānger Iohannis Huss durch das conciliū zů Costentz für ain ketzer verurtailt vn̄ verprānt worden ist ... 4°. A^6. [Augsburg, 1521.] *Translator: Nicolaus von Wyle.* [486

POITOU. Le coustumier de poictou ... Imprime a Paris. Lan Mil cinq cens et six. Et sont a vendre en lostel de Iehan de marnef ... fol. B.L. a-n^6 (-n6, *presumably blank*). ff. ii-lxix. (Biddle.) [487

-- -- Coustumier du pais de Poictou. ... On les vend a Poictiers [chez Jean & Enguilbert de Marnef] ... 1547 8°. *^{8} a-l^8 m^2. ff. I-CX. ¶*1 *defective.* [488

POLAND. [*caption*] Confoederatio generalis Ich ... Rad Koronnych/ Duchownych y Swietskich/ y Rycerstwá z Woiewodztw Wielgopolskich ... fol. B.L. A^8 (-A8). [488a

-- Statuta Regni Poloniæ in ordinem alphabeti digesta. A Ioanne Herburto de Fulstin ... Samoscii Martinus Lenscius ... excudebat. M. D. XC. VII. ... fol.)(^{6} A-3Y^4 3Z^6 (-3Z6, *presumably blank*). pp. 1-546. (Lea.) [489

POLANUS, AMANDUS. Amandi Polani à Polansdorff logicæ libri duo; juxta naturalis methodi leges conformati ... Herbornae Nassaviorum Excudebat Christophorus Corvinus. MDXC. 8°. (:)^8 2(::)^4 A-O^8 P^4. pp. 1-232. [490

POLE, REGINALD. De concilio liber Reginaldi Poli cardinalis. Romae, M. D. LXII. Apud Paulum Manutium Aldi F. 4°. A-S^4. ff. 1-64. ¶R3^r: ... de baptismo Constantini magni imperatoris. [490a

-- -- *Another copy.* (Yarnall.) [491

-- De summo pontifice Christi i[n] terris vicario, ei[us]que officio & potestate, Liber ... Louanii, apud Ioannem Foulerum Anglum. M.D.LXIX. ... 8°. *^{8} A-T^8 V^4. ff. 2-151. ¶*T.p. defective.* (Yarnall.) [491a

-- Reformatio Angliae ex decretis Reginaldi Poli cardinalis ... anno M. D. LVI. Romae, M. D. LXII. Apud Paulum Manutium Aldi F. 4°. A-G^4. ff. 2-27. (Yarnall.) [491b

POLIFILA. Polifila, comedia piaceuole e nuoua ... In Fiorenza. MDLVI. (... appresso i Giunti. ...) 8°. A-F8 (-F8, *blank*). [492

POLITI, AMBROGIO CATARINO. ... Fratris Ambrosij Cath. ... Apologia pro veritate Catholice ... Doctrine. Aduersus ... Martini Lutheri Dogmata. ... (Florentiæ p hæredes Philippi Iuntæ. ... M.D.XX. Vigesimo. Mēsis Decēbr.) fol. a6 b-c8 d6 e-m8. ff. 3-96. [493

-- Compendio d'errori, & inganni Luterani, contenuti in vn libretto ... intitolato, Trattato vtilissimo del benefitio di Christo crucifisso. ... In Brescia ... M.D.XLIIII. (... per Damiano Turlino. Nel mese de Zugno. ...) 8°. A-G8. ff. 2-56. [494

-- Discorso ... contra la dottrina, et le profetie di fra Girolamo Sauonarola. ... In Vinegia appresso Gabriel Giolito di Ferrarij M D XLVIII. 8°. *8 A-M8 N4. ff. 1-100.[494a

POLLEN, JOHANN. Ioannis Pollii Wesphali poetae ... opuscula ... Tiguri excudebat Froschouerus [c. 1550]. 8°. A-I8. ff. 2-72. [495

POLLICARIUS, JOHANNES. Antwort auff das buch Osiandri/ von der Rechtfertigung des Menschen. ... Gedruckt zu Wittemberg/ Durch Veit Creutzer. M.D.LII. 4°. A-G4. [496

-- Antwort Auff das vergiffte bůch des Bischoffs zů Naumburg ... wider vnsere Lehr vnd Kirchen. ... Getruckt zů Strassburg durch Samuel Emmel. M.D. LVII. 4°. A-I4 K6. ff. ij-xxxviij. [497

-- Historia Von der himelfart vnsers Herrn ... Gedruckt zu Leiptzigk durch Georgen Hantzsch. M.D.LIIII. 4°. A-S4. [498

-- Ein Sendbrieff ... von der Schlacht/ vnd abschied aus diesem leben/ des ... Hertzog Moritzen/ Churfürsten zu Sachsen ... M. D. LIII. (Gedruckt zu Leiptzig durch George Hantzsch.) 4°. A-C4. [499

POLLICH, MARTIN. Martini Mellerstat polichii Theoremata aurea ... 4°. A4 B6. [500

POLLINI, GIROLAMO. L'historia ecclesiastica della riuoluzion d'Inghilterra ... In Roma, Presso Guglielmo Facciotti. M. D. XCIV. ... Ad Istanza di Gio. Angelo Ruffinelli. (*Colophon.*) 4°. a8 b4 A-3C8 3D-3G4 (-3G4, *blank*). pp. 1-766. (Lea.) [501

POLLUX, JULIUS. Ιουλιου Πολυδευκους, πιναξ. Iulii Pollucis index. (Venetiis apud Aldum mense Aprili. M.DII.) fol. π4 AA4 αα-νν8. [502

POLYAENUS. Πολυαινου στρατηγηματων βιβλοι οκτω. Polyaeni stratagematum libri octo. Is. Casaubonus Græcè nunc primum edidit ... CIƆ. IƆ. XXCIX. Apud Ioan. Tornaesium ... Lugdunensem. 16°. ¶8 a-z8 A-CC8. pp. 2-754. [503

-- -- *Another copy, with* Coloniæ Allobrogum *added to the imprint.* [504

-- -- Gli stratagemi di Polieno ... tradotti fedelmente dalla lingua Greca nella Thoscana per M. Lelio Carrani. ... In Vinegia appresso Gabriel Giolito de Ferrari, e fratelli MDLII. (*Colophon.*) 8°. A-Z8 AA-BB4. ff. 2-188. (Lea.) [505

POLYBIUS. Polybii historiarum libri quinque in Latiam conuersi linguam, Nicolao Perotto interprete. (Venetiis in aedibus Aldi et Andreae soceri, mense Februario, M. D. XXI.) fol. A-I8. ff. 2-71. ¶*Part of* Ex XIIII. T. Liuii Decadibus prima tertia quarta ... Polybii libri V de rebus Romanis ... quos in locum secundae Decadis substituimus ... (1520-1521). [506

-- -- Polybii ... historiarum libri quinque. Nicolao Perotto, interprete. Apud Seb. Gryphium Lugduni, 1548. 16°. a-z8 A-O8. pp. 3-592. [507

-- -- Les cinq premiers liures des histoires de Polybe Megalopolitein, auec trois Parcelles du VI. un du VII. un du VIII. & un du XVI. Autrefois traduits ... par Louis Maigret ... Ausquelz de nouueau sont ajoutees les subsequentes Parcelles des liures IX. X. XI. XII. XIII. XIIII. XV. XVII. ... A Lion par Ian de Tournes, M. D. LVIII. ... fol. A6 a-z6 (a6 + *folded leaf*) A-E6 F-G4. pp. 1-335. [508

-- *Selections.* Εκ των Πολυβιου ... εκλογαι περι πρεσβειων. Ex libris Polybii Megalopolitani selecta de legationibus; Et alia ... Ex bibliotheca FuluI Vrsini. Antuerpiae, Ex officina Christophori Plantini M. D. LXXXII. 4°. π4 A-Z4 a-z4 Aa-Kk4 A-Z4 (-Z4, *blank*). pp. 2-447, 1-182. [509

-- Liber ex Polybii historiis excerptus de militia Romanorum, et castrorum metatione inuentu ... a, lano Lascare in Latinam linguam translatus. ... (Ioannes Antonius de Sabio excudebat. Venetiis MDXXVIIII. Kalendis Martiis.) 4°. a-f^4. ff. 2-24. [510

POMERANIA. Bekentnus vnd Lehr der Kirchen in Pommern. ... Anno 1593. ... (Gedruckt zu Alten Stettin ... durch Ioachim Rheten. ...) 4°. 1-5^4 A-Hh^4. ff. 2-20, 2-123. [511

POMPONAZZI, PIETRO. Petri Pomponatii ... Opera. De naturalium effectuum admirandorum causis, Seu de Incantationibus Liber. Item de Fato: Libero arbitrio: Prædestinatione: Prouidentia Dei, Libri V. ... Basileae, ex officina Henricpetrina. (... M. D. LXVII. mense Martio.) 8°. a^8 a-c^8 A-V^8 X^4 Aa-Zz^8 AA-VV^8. pp. 1-1015. [512

-- Petri Pomponatii Mantuani ... de naturalium effectuum causis, siue de Incantationibus ... Adiectis breuibus scholijs à Gulielmo Gratarolo Physico Bergomate. ... Basileæ. (... per Henrichum Petri, mense Augusto, an. M.D.LVI.) 8°. †^{8} A-Y^8. pp. 1-349. (Lea.) [513

-- Petri Pomponatii ... Dubitationes in quartum Meteorologicorum Aristotelis librum. ... Venetiis, Apud Franciscum Francisci. 1563. fol. *^{6} A-G^6 H^8. ff. 1-50. [514

-- Tractatus de immortalite animae. ... (Impressum Bononiæ per Magistrū Iustinianum Leonardi Ruberiensem ... M.ccccc.xyi. Die sexta Nouembris.) fol. A-C^6. [515

-- -- Petri Pomponatii ..., tractatus de immortalitate animæ. M.D.XXXIV. 12°. A-E^{12} F^{14}. pp. 3-147. (Furness.) [516

-- -- *Another copy.* (Lea.) [517

-- -- *Another edition.* 12°. A-F^{12}. pp. 3-144. [518

POMPONIO LETO, GIULIO. Opera Pomponii Laeti. Romanæ historiæ compendium ... Pomponius De Romanorum Magistratibus. De Sacerdotijs. De Iurisperitis. De Legibus ... Item. De Antiquitatibus vrbis Romæ libellus, qui Pomponio adscribitur. Pomponii Epistolæ aliquot familiares. Pomponij vita, per .M. Antonium Sabellicum. (Argentorati in libraria officina Matthiæ Schürerij ... Mense Ianuario. ... M.D.X.) 4°. A^2 B-E$^{8.4}$ F^4 G-K$^{8.4}$ L^4 M^8. ff. I-LXVII. [519

-- Compendio del'historia Romana di Pomponio Leto ... tradotto per Messer Francesco Baldelli. I magistrati sacerdotii. Dottori di leggi, & le leggi de Romani scritte del medesimo ... In Vinetia appresso Gabriel Giolito di Ferrarii MDXLIX. (*Colophon.*) 8°. A-Q^8. ff. 2-126. ¶A2 *and* A7 *transposed in binding.* [520

POMPONIUS MELA. [Pomponius Mela. Iulius Solinus. Itinerarium Antonini Aug. Vibius Sequester. P. Victor de regionibus vrbis Romæ. Dionysius Afer de situ orbis Prisciano interprete.] (Venetiis in aedibus Aldi, et Andreae soceri mense Octobri M. D. XVIII.) 8°. a-z^8 (-a1) A-F^8 G^4 (-G4). ff. 2-233. [521

PONCE DE LEON, GONZALO. Responsio ad librum Leonharti Vvaramundi, Hæretici Caluiniani, in causa Coloniensi. ... Romae, Apud Franciscum Zanettum. M.D.LXXXV. (*Colophon.*) 4°. †-††^{4} 3†^{2} A-Z^4 Aa^2. pp. 1-184. (Lea.) [522

PONTANI, GUGLIELMO. ... Guilielmi Pontani Perusini Quotidianarum Lectionum Vespertinarum Enarrationes. Venetiis [Alviso de Tortis,] MD XLI. fol. B.L. A-B^4 C-K^6 L^8 M-BB^6 Aa-Bb^6. ff. 2-147. (Biddle.) [523

PONTANO, GIOVANNI GIOVIANO. Ioannis Iouiani Pontani Opera. ... (Impressum Venetiis per Bernardinum Vercellensem ... M.CCCCC.I. Die primo Kalendas Martii.) fol. a^8 b-z^6 &^{8} (-&8, *blank*). [524

-- -- Pontani opera. ... (Venetijs in ædibus hæredum Aldi Manutij, & Andreæ soceri, mense Augusto, M.D.XXXIII.) 8°. *^{8} a-hh^8. ff. 1-247. [525

-- [1] Ioannis Iouiani Pontani ... opera quæ soluta oratione composuit, omnia: in Tomos tres digesta. Primus ... Basileae, M. D. XXXVIII. (... per Andream Cratandrum, mense Martio ...) 4°. α-γ^4 a-z^4 A-Zz^4 AA-HH^4. pp. 1-615. [2] ... Tomus secundus ... *Same imprint and colophon.* α^4 a-z^4 A-Zz^4 AA-FF^4. pp. 1-596. [3] ... Tomus tertius. ... *Same imprint.* (mense Septembri. ... M. D. XXXI.) a-x⁴ y⁶. pp. 1-169. [4] Ioannis Iouiani Pontani de rebus coelestibus Libri XIIII. Eiusdem de Luna fragmentum. Basileæ, Anno M. D. XXX. a⁶ b-z⁴ A-Cc⁴. pp. 2-382. [526

-- Pontani de immanitate (Neapoli per Sigismundum Mayr Germanum ... MDXII Kal. Quin. ...) fol. a-b⁶ c⁴. [527

-- Pontani de sermone et de bello Neapolitano. (Excusum opus Neapoli p̱ Sigismundum Mayr Alemanũ ... mense Augusto: MDVIIII. assistente ... P. Summontio ...) fol. a-g⁸ A-G⁸. ¶*Additional t.p.* (A1r): Pontani de bello Neapolitano et de sermone (... mense Maio ...) [528

-- Le guerre di Napoli ... nuouamente di Latino in lingua Italiana tradotte. In Venetia, Nel M. D. XXXXIIII. (... per Michel Tramezino ...) 8°. *⁴ A-M⁸ N⁴. ff. 2-98. [529

PONTANO, LODOVICO. [Lectura in corpus juris civilis.] Lugduni, Apud Hugonem & haeredes Aemonis à Porta. M. D. XLVII. ... (... excudebant Stephanus Rufinus, et Ioannes Ausultus.) fol. B.L. [1] D. Ludouici Pontani Romani ... Lectura ... in primam digesti veteris partem ... a-i⁸ k¹⁰. ff. 2-81. [2] ... Lectura ... super secunda parte digesti veteris ... A-I⁸. ff. 2-72. [3] ... Lectura ... super Prima parte infortiati ... (... Excudebat Ioannes Ausultus.) a-aa⁸. ff. 2-191. [4] Fragmenta ... in Secundam Infortiati partem ... (... Excudebat Ioannes Ausultus.) A-E⁸. ff. 2-39. [5] ... Lectura super prima parte digesti noui ... a-q⁸ r⁶. ff. 2-133. [6] ... lectura ... super secunda parte digesti noui ... A-L⁸. ff. 2-88. [7] ... Lectura ... in primam codicis partem ... a-m⁸. ff. 2-96. [8] ... Lectura ... super secunda parte codicis ... A-K⁸. ff. 2-79. [9] Index, seu Repertorium D. Ludo. Romani. ... M. D. XLVIII. ... (... idus Febr. 4. ... Ioannes Ausultus ... emisit ...) fol. B.L. A-M⁸ N¹⁰. (Biddle.) [530

-- [1] Excellentissimi Iurisconsulti quorum singularia in hoc uolumine ɔtinẽtur hi sunt. Ludouicus Romanus cum additionibus Ioannis Baptiste castellionei. Franciscus cremensis ... Matthesillanus ... Domin⁹ Antonius Corsectus siculus. fol. B.L. a-c⁸ d¹⁰. ff. 2-33. [2] Singularia siue notabilia dicta collecta per Francischum cremensem ... aa¹⁰. ff. 3-10. [3] Singularia siue notabilia dicta Mathesilani ... A-B⁸. ff. 2-16. [4] Singularia domini Anto. corsicti siculi. (Apud Alexãdrum Minutianum Mediolani iterum Impressa M.ccccc.vi. Die vltimo Februarii.) a-c⁸ d⁶. ff. 2-30. (Lea.) [531

POPE. Des Bapsts vnd der Pfaffen Badstub. [Augsburg, Valentin Otmar,] M. D. XLVI. 4°. A-B⁴ C². ¶*In verse.* [532

POPPIUS, MENSO. Septem cyclopeidon libri ... Heroico carmine elaborati ... per Mensonem Poppium Eurothalassium, aliâs Osterzeensem, Frisium ... Anno. 1555. (Impressum in Campis Elysijs, a ciue Vtopiensi, calendis græcis, Mensis, Ianuarij. ...) 8°. A-X⁸. ff. 2-168. [533

PORCACCHI, TOMMASO. Lettere di XIII. huomini illustri. ... Allequali ... ne sono state aggiunte molte. ... In Venetia. Appresso Fabio & Augustin Zoppini Fratelli 1584. 8°. ♣⁸ A-3K⁸. ff. 1-448. [534

PORCIA, JACOPO, conte di. Iacobus Purlillarum comes de liberorum educatione. (Argentoraci Ex officina Ioannis Schotti: Impensis ... Georgii Maxilli (al's übelin) ... IIII. idus Augusti. ... D. M. X.) 4°. a⁴ b⁶. [535

PORPHYRIUS. Porphyrii in Aristotelis prædicamenta per interrogationem & responsionem ... explanatio, nunc primum in Latinam linguam conuersa ... Ioanne Bernardo Feliciano authore. Parisiis, Ex officina typographica Michaëlis Vascosani ... M. D. XLVIII. ... 8°. A-L⁸. ff. 2-88. [536

-- Porphyrii Institutiones ... Ioachimo Perionio ... interprete. ... Tertia editio. Parisiis, Apud Ioannem Lodouicum Tiletanum ... M.D.XLVI. 8°. A-C⁴ D⁶. ff. 2-12. [537

PORRI, ALESSIO. Vaso di verità nel quale si contengono dodeci Resolutioni uere, à dodeci ... Dubbi, fatti intorno all' ... Antichristo. ... In Venetia Apresso Pietro Dusinelli e Girolamo Porri. MDXCVII. 4°. a-c⁴ A-O⁴. ¶*Engraved t.p.* [538

PORRINO, GANDOLFO. Rime ... (In Venetia per Michele Tramezzino. M D L I.) 8°. *^{8} a-m^{8} n^{4}. ff. 1-100. [539

PORSIUS, HENRICUS. Iter Byzantinum ... 8°. A-L^{8}. pp. 1-175. ¶*With other poems. Part 2 of* Historia belli Persici ... (Francofurti, excudebat Ioannes Wechelus, impensis Sigismundi Feyerabendt, 1583). [540

PORTA, GIOVANBATTISTA DELLA. De humana physiognomonia ... libri IIII. ... M D XCIII. Hanouiæ Apud Guilielmum Antonium, impensis Petri Fischeri Fr. 8°.)(^{8} A-Oo^{8}. pp. 1-534. [541

-- De occultis literarum notis ... Libri IIII. ... Montisbeligardi Apud Iacobum Foillet, Expensis Lazari Zetzneri M. D. XCIII. 8°. ()^{8} a-r^{8} A-B^{8} C^{4} (-C3, C4). pp. 1-275, 2-24. [542

-- Magiae naturalis, siue de miraculis rerum naturalium libri IIII. ... Neapoli apud Matthiam Cancer. M. D. LVIII. ... fol. a-b^{4} A-T^{4} V^{6}. pp. 1-163. [543

-- -- De miraculis rerum naturalium libri IIII. ... Antuerpiae, ex officina Christophori Plantini: M. D. LX. ... (... Kalendis Februarii ...) 8°. ¶^{8} A-R^{8}. ff. 1-135. (Lea.) [544

-- -- Magiae naturalis ... Antuerpiae, Ex officina Christophori Plantini, M. D. LXVII. 16°. A-T^{8} V^{10}. pp. 3-324. [545

-- -- Io. Bapt. Portae Neapolitani magiae naturalis libri XX. ... Neapoli, Apud Horatium Saluianum. D. D. LXXXVIIII. (*Colophon.*) fol. a-b^{4} A-Pp^{4}. pp. 1-303. [546

-- -- Francofurti Apud Andreæ Wecheli heredes, Claudium Marnium, & Ioann. Aubrium. M D XCI. 8°.)(^{8}):(^{8})::(^{2} A-Tt^{8}. pp. 1-669. [547

-- -- De i miracoli et marauigliosi effetti della natura prodotti. Libri IIII, ... nouamente tradotti di Latino in lingua uolgare ... In Venetia appresso Lodouico Auanzi. MDLX. 8°. *-**^{8} A-V^{8} X^{4} (-X4, *presumably blank*). ff. 1-163. [548

PORTA, MALATESTA. Il rossi o vero del parere sopra alcune obiettioni, Fatte dall' Infarinato Academico della Crusca. Intorno alla Gierusalemme liberata del Sig. Torquato Tasso. Dialogo ... In Rimino, Appresso Giouanni [Si]mbeni. 1589. ... (*Colophon.*) 8°. +^{8} A-Q^{8} R^{2}. pp. 1-258. ¶*T.p. wormholed.* [549

PORTA, PETRUS À. ... Petri â Porta Carmen De Amore. Cremona apud Vincentium Comitem Ann. 1566. 4°. A-B^{4} (-B4, *presumably blank*). [550

PORTOLANO. Il portolano del mare, nelqual si dichiara minutamente del sito di tutti i porti ... In Venetia, Appresso Daniel Zanetti, & compagni. M. D. LXXVI. 4°. A-D^{8} E^{10}. ff. 1-39. (Lea.) [551

PORZIO, SIMONE. De conflagratione Agri Puteolani, Simonis Portii Neapolitani epistola. Florentiae [per Laurentium Torrentinum] M D LI. 8°. a^{4}. pp. 3-8. [552

-- Simonis Portii Neapolitani de humana mente disputatio. Florentiae Apud Laurentium Torrentinum. MDLI. 4°. A-L^{4} M^{6} (-M6, *blank*). pp. 3-98. [553

-- Se l'huomo diuenta buono o cattiuo volontariamente. Disputa dello ... Filosofo M. Simone Portio Napoletano. Tradotta in volgare par Giouam Batista Gelli. In Fiorenza, Appresso Lorenzo Torrentino. M D LI. 8°. A-H^{8} I^{6}. pp. 3-139. (Lea.) [554

POSIO, ANTONIO. Thesaurus ... in omnes Aristotelis, et Auerrois libros ... Venetiis M D LXII. (... Apud Cominum de Tridino Montisferrati. ...) 8°. *^{8} A-3S^{8}. [555

POSSEVINO, ANTONIO. [1] Antonii Posseuini ... bibliotheca selecta Qua agitur de ratione studiorum ... Romæ Ex Typographia Apostolica Vaticana. M. D. XCIII. fol. *^{4} A-3H^{6} 3I^{8}. pp. 1-663. [2] ... Pars Secunda. ... *Same imprint.* *^{4} a-i^{6} k^{4} l-cc^{6} dd^{8}. pp. 1-321. [3] ... Cicero collatus cum Ethnicis, & sacris Scriptoribus. ... *Same imprint.* (Excudebat ... Dominicus Basa ...) A-B^{6} C^{2} a-b^{6}. pp. 3-28. [556

POSSEVINO, GIOVANNI BATTISTA. Dialogo dell' honore ... In Vinegia appresso Gabriel Giolito de Ferrari e fratelli. M DLIII. 4°. $*^4$ A-T^8 V^{10}. pp. 2-322. [557

POSTEL, GUILLAUME. [1] De la republique des Turcs: & là ou l'occasion s'offrera, des meurs & loy de tous Muhamedistes Par Guillaume Postel Cosmopolite. A Poitiers Par Enguibert de Marnef. ... M. D. LX. 4°. $()^4$ a-h^8. pp. 1-127. [2] Histoire et consideration de l'origine, loy, et coustume des Tartares, Persiens, Arabes, Turcs, & tous autres Ismaelites ou Muhamediques ... *Same imprint.* A-C^8 D^6. pp. 3-57. [3] La tierce partie des orientales histoires ... *Same imprint.* $()^4$ aa-ee^8 ff^6 (-ff6, *presumably blank*). pp. 1-90. [558

POU, ONOFRIO. Thesaurus puerilis ... Editio secunda ... Barcinone Apud Ioannem Paulum Marescal. 1580. ... 8°. $†^8$ (-†8) A-Ee^8 (-Ee1, Ee8, *the latter presumably blank*). ff. 1-214. ¶†1, Ee7 *repaired;* Q4 *defective.* [559

-- -- Barcinone. Ex Typographia Iacobi à Cendrat ... M. DC. 8°. A-Dd^8 (-Q8) Ee^4. ff. 3-216. [560

POZZO, MODESTA. Il merito delle donne, Scritto da Moderata Fonte ... In Venetia, M. DC. Presso Domenico Imberti. 4°. a^4 A-V^4 (-V4, *presumably blank*). pp. 1-158. [561

-- Tredici canti del Floridoro, Di Mad. Moderata Fonte. ... In Venetia. M.D.LXXXI. (... Nella Stamparia de' Rampazetti.) 4°. $*^4$ A-O^4 P^6. ff. 2-62. [562

POZZO, PARIS DE. Duello: libro de Re, Imperatori, Principi, Signori, Gentil'huomini; & de tutti Armigeri ... (Stampato in ... Venetia per [Gregorio de Gregoriis pro] Marchio Sessa, & Piero dela Serena Compagni. Adi .X. Marzo. M.D.XXV.) 8°. A-Y^8 Z^6 a^8. [563

-- Trac. de re mili. ꝛ duel. ... Tractatus de re militari ꝑ ... Do. Paridem de puteo compilatus totā materiā duelli singularisq3 certaminis egregie continens ... 1543 (Impressum Lugduni ꝑ Benedictū Bonñyn ... die .vij. mensis Septembris. 8°. B.L. Aa-Bb^8 Cc^4 A-S^8 T^4. ff. j-cxlvij. [564

PRAETORIUS, ABDIAS. Propositiones de sacramento disputandæ in Ludo Magdeburgensi, ultimo Augusti, Anno 1554. Godescalcus Prætorius. [Magdeburgi] Ex officina Michaelis Lottheri Anno 1554. Mense August. 8°. A^8. [565

PRAETORIUS, HIERONYMUS. [Cantiones sacrae.] Hamburgi Excudebat Philippus de Ohr Anno cIↄ Iↄ IC. 4°. [1] Cantus. Cantiones sacræ de præcipuis festis totius Anni 5. 6. 7. & 8. Vocum. ... A-I^4. [2] Tenor. ... A-I^4. [3] 5ta. Vox. ... A-I^4. [4] Sexta Vox. ... A-G^4. [5] 7tima Vox. ... A-E^4 F^2. [6] Octaua Vox. ... $[A]^4$ B-E^4. ¶*Altus and bassus wanting.* [566

PREDIGT. Ein gemeyne Predig zů den Kriegssleüten/ so wider die vnglaubigen kriegen wőllen. ... M. D. XXXXII. (Getruckt zů Augspurg/ durch Haynrich Stainer.) 4°. A-B^4. [567

-- Ain predig vom Wolff zů den Genssen. [Augsburg, Melchior Ramminger, 1523.] 4°. a^4. [568

PRINCIPIA. Prīcipia grāmaticalia ... (Imprime a rouen ... pour Raulin gaultier ... [c. 1510.]) 16°. B.L. π^8. [569

-- Principia siue maxima legū Anglie ꝛ Gallico illo ... sermone collecta, et sic in Latinum translata ... [Londini,] Richardus Lant excudebat. (Anno xxxviii. regni Regis Henrici octaui [= 1546] xxiiii. die Mensis Decembri.) 8°. B.L. A-B^8. *S.T.C.* 20394. (Biddle.) [570

PRIOLI, MICHELE. Michaelis Prioli epicedion ... M D XCIIII. 4°. A^4. [571

PRISCIANESE, FRANCESCO. Francisci Priscianensis argumentorum obseruationes in omneis Ciceronis epistolas. ... Venetiis, M D XLIX. (Apud Aldi filios. ... Mense Septembri.) 8°. A-H^8 (-H8, *presumably blank*). ff. 9-63. ¶*Bound in at the end is* Pauli Manutii in Asconium Pedianum scholia, *ff.* M2-M8 *of* Asconii Pedianii expositio in quasdam Ciceronis orationes (Apud Paulum Manutium, Aldi filium, M. D. LIII.) [572

-- Francesco Priscianese Fiorentino, della lingua Romana. (Stampato in Vinegia per Bartolomeo Zanetti da Brescia nel mese d'Agosto. M. D. XL.) 4°. π^8 Aa-Zz^8 AA-II^8 Kk-Oo^8 Pp^4. ff. I-cclxxxxi. [573

PRISCIANUS CAESARIENSIS. Prisciani grammatici Caesariensis libri omnes. ... (Venetiis in aedibus Aldi, et Andreae Asulani soceri. Mense Maio M. D. XXVII.) 4°. 14 *ll. signed* 1-[14] a-z^8 A-O^8 P^6. ff. 1-299. [574

-- Naturæ præpositionū ex Prisciano. Parisiis. Apud Franciscum Stephanum. M.D.XXXVIII. 8°. A-B^8. pp. 3-32. [575

PRIULI, ALVISE. Le rime ... (... stampata In Venetia del MDXXXIII del mese de Settembrio.) 4°. ✠^{8} A-V^8 X^{10} (-X10, *presumably blank*). [576

PROBUS, MARCUS VALERIUS. Vlaerii [*sic*] Probi grammatic de interpretandis romanorū litteris opusculum ... (Impressum Romæ per iacobum mazochium ... M.CCCCC.VIIII. Die .XXV. Aprilis.) 4°. a-e^4. [577

PROCLUS. Astronomica veterum scripta isagogica Græca & Latina. ... [Heidelbergae,] In officina Sanctandreana, clↃ IↃ LXXXIX. 8°. π^2 (-π2, *blank*) A-K^8 L^6 A-T^8. pp. 2-170, 1-302. ¶*Authors: Proclus (translated by Thomas Linacre), Leontius Mechanicus, Aratus Solensis (translated by Cicero, Festus Rufus, Germanicus Caesar), C. Julius Hyginus.* [578

-- La sfera di Proclo Liceo tradotta da Maestro Egnatio Danti ... con l'vso della Sfera del medesimo. In Fiorenza Nella Stamperia de'Giunti. M D LXXIII. 4°. *^{4} A-G^4 χ^4 A-B^4 C^6. pp. 1-53, 6-33. [579

PROCOPIUS CAESARIENSIS. Procopius de bello Persico. (Noxamque Iacobo Mazochio bibliopolae pendat. Impressum Romæ per ... Eucharium Silber al's Franck. Castigatum per Andream Nucium ... M D IX. Nonis Martiis.) fol. A-P^6. [580

-- Iustiniani augusti historia ... Opera ... Procopii Caesariensis, Agathiae Myrrinaei, Iornandis Alani ... Noua editio ... Geneuae. Apud Franciscum le Preux. M. D. XCIIII. 8°. *^{8} A-Zz^8 ā^8 AA-3D^8. pp. 1-1136. [581

-- Procopio Caesariense de gli edifici di Giustiniano imperatore di Greco in volgare tradotti per Benedetto Egio da Spoleti. ... (In Vinegia per Michel Tramezino MD XLVII.) 8°. a^8 A-G^8 H^4. ff. 1-59. [582

-- Procopio Cesariense de la guerra di Giustiniano imperatore contra i Persiani, lib. II. De la guerra del medesimo contra i Vandali, lib. II. Di Latino in volgare tradotti per Benedetto Egio da Spoleti. ... (In Vinegia per Michele Tramezino. M D XLVII.) 8°. A^8 a-bb^8. ff. 1-200. [583

-- Procopio Cesariense de la longa & aspra guerra de Gothi libri tre, di Latino in volgare tradotte per Benedetoo Egio da Spoleti. In Venetia. M. D. XLIIII. ... (... per Michele Tramezino. ...) 8°. A^8 A-II^8. ff. 2-253. [584

PROLAGHI, ZANOBI. Lettere e trattati familiari ... In Fiorenza Appresso Bartolomeo Sermartelli. MDLXXI. (*Colophon.*) 4°. *-5*^{4} A-4E^4. pp. 1-591. [585

PROPHEZEIUNG. Ain Prophecey vnd Weissagung von den Vier erben Hertzog Iohansen von Burgundi/ der vonn dem Tūrcken gefangen des Jars 1395. wie es in ꝺ zeit jrs regimēts ergeen solte biss auf Künig Karol in Hyspanien ... durch ein heydnischē mayster/ Astolgan genañt ... [c. 1530.] 4°. A^4. [586

PROSE. Prose antiche di Dante, Petrarcha, et Boccaccio, et di molti altri ... ingegni ... M D XLVII. (Stampate in Fiorenza appresso il Doni a di primo d'Agosto ...) 4°. A-K^4. pp. 9-78. ¶A1^r: *engraved frontispiece;* A2^r: *t.p.* [587

PROSPER OF AQUITAINE. Diui Prosperi Aquitanici ... opera ... Lugduni apud Seb. Gryphium, 1539. fol. *^{6} a-i^6 k^8 A-N^6 O^4 P-Tt^6. pp. 1-124, 1-499. ¶Qq5-6, Rr-Tt^6 *defective.* [588

-- Opuscula de gratia et libero arbitrio ... Venetiis, M. D. XXXV. (... Apud Octauianum Scotum.) 8°. A-H^8. pp. 3-127. [589

PROTESTANT PRINCES. Le raggioni, perche. i. principi Protestanti inuulgano la confederatione fatta fra Pappa Paulo III, Antichristo Romano, & Carlo .v. Contra di Germania, & la bolla insieme. M.D.XLVI. 4°. A-B^4. [590

PROU DES CARNEAUX, NICOLAS. Homeri epitheta omnia ex Iliade et Odyssea, Vnà cum interpretatione textus Eustathij in eadem difficiliora. Lugduni, apud Thomam Soubron. M. D. XCIIII. (Excudebat Guichardus Iullieron. ...) 16°. A-K8 L4. pp. 3-161. [591

PROVENCE. Les statutz, et coustumes de Prouence ... Auec commentaires ... par maistre Lois Masse ... Imprimé en Auignon par Pierre Roux. 4°. a4 aa4 3a4 A-V4. pp. 1-160. ¶*Privilege dated 13 September 1557. Wormholes in* a4. [592

PRUDENTIUS CLEMENS, AURELIUS. Aurelij Prudentij Clementis ... Libelli Cum cōmento Antonij Nebrissensis. ... (Fuit impressum ... Lucronij per Arnaldum guillermū de Brocaria, et finitur die seconda mēsis Septēbris Anno ... Millesimo quingentesimo duodecimo.) 4°. a4 A-M8 (-A1) N4 a-l8 m4. [593

-- -- Aurelii Prudentii Clementis ... Psychomachia. Cathemerinon. Peristephanon. Apotheosis. Hamartigenia. Contra Symmachum ... Enchiridion Noui & Veteris testamēti. ... scholia, per Ioannem Sichardum. Item Commentarius Erasmi Roterodami in duos hymnos. Basileae per Henrichum Petrum. (... mense Augusto anno M.D.XL.) 8°. a8 A-Z8 aa-ll8 mm4. pp. 1-552. [594

-- -- [1] Aurelius Prudentius Clemens Theodori Pulmanni Cranenburgii, et Victoris Giselini opera ... emendatus, et ... eiusdem ... Giselini commentarius. Antuerpiæ, Ex officina Christophori Plantini, CIƆ. IƆ. LXIV. ... (... III. Non. Augusti.) 8°. A-Y8. pp. 3-350. [2] Victoris Giselini ... commentarius. *Same imprint.* (... VI. Kal. Nouemb.) A-K8 L4. [595

-- Prudentij carmen de martyrio diui Cassiani Francisci Petrarcę carmen de diua Magdalena Rodolphi Agricolę carmen de diuo Iudoco In Petrum Rauennatē sylua Ioānis Murmellij Eiusdem epigrāmatum liber. [Coloniae, haeredes Henrici Quentel, 1508.] 4°. B.L. a4 *only.* [596

-- Psichomachia religiosi Prudentii. ... (Castigata per Ioan. Foenisecam Augn̄. ... impressæ Augustæ per Erhardum öglin. ... M.D.VI.) 4°. a8 b-c6. [597

PRUSSIA. Des Durchleüchtigsten ... Herrn Albrechten des Eltern Margraffen zu Brandenburg ... Mandat An ihr ... Vnderthanen aussgangen den 11 Augusti/ anno. M.D.LV. Gedruckt zu Königsperg inn Preussen/ durch Iohann Daubman. 4°. A-B4. [598

PSELLUS, MICHAEL CONSTANTINE. Ψελλου των περὶ ἀριθμητικῆς σύνοψις. Pselli Arithmetices compendium. Parisiis. In officina Christiani Wecheli. M.D.XXXVIII. 4°. A-B4. pp. 3-14. [599

-- Libelli aliquot in Quinque Porphyrii Voces, & decē Philosophiæ Prædicamenta introductorii, è Greco in Latinum conuersi. ... Parrisiis apud Ioannem Lodoicum Tiletanum ... M. D. XXXVIII. 8°. A-B8. pp. 2-32. ¶*Additional authors: Nicephorus Blemmydes, Georgios Pachymeres. Translator: Jacopo Foscarini.* [600

PTOLEMAEUS, CLAUDIUS. Claudii Ptolemaei Pelusiensis Alexandrini omnia, quae extant, opera, geographia excepta ... Basileae apud Henricum Petrum, mense Martio, anno M. D. XLI. (*Colophon.*) fol. a-b6 c2 A-D6.4 E-H6 I4 K-N6 O-Q4 R6 S-T4 V6 X-Bb4 Cc-Gg6 Hh4 Ii-Kk6 Ll-Mm4 Nn6 Oo4 Pp-Rr6 Ss8 Tt-Zz6 Aa-Bb6. pp. 1-511. [601

-- Claudii Ptolemaei liber de analemmate, a Federico Commandino Vrbinate instauratus, & commentariis illustratus ... Eiusdem Federici Commandini liber de Horologiorum descriptione. Romae, M. D. LXII. Apud Paulum Manutium Aldi F. 4°. *4 (-*2-4) A-Z4 &4. ff. 2-93. [602

-- [1] La geografia di Claudio Tolomeo Alessandrino, Nuouamente tradotta di Greco in Italiano da Ieronimo Ruscelli ... In Venetia, Appresso Giordano Ziletti ... M. D. LXIIII. 4°. *4 A-YY4. pp. 2-358. [2] Espositioni et introduttioni vniuersali, di Ieronimo Ruscelli sopra tutta la Geografia di Tolomeo. Con XXXVI. nuoue Tauole ... *Same imprint.* α-η4 *28 double-page maps of the "old" series and 34 (wanting XI, XII) of the "new", bound in a highly irregular order* A-F4. [3] Discorso vniuersale di M. Gioseppe Moleto ... *Same imprint.* A-F4. pp. 3-47. [603

-- [1] Κλ. Πτολεμαιου μεγάλης συντάξεως βιβλ. ιγ̃. Θεωνος Αλεξλνδρέως ἐις τὰ ἀυτὰ ὑπομνημάτων βιβλ. ιᾱ. Claudii Ptolemaei Magnæ Constructionis ... lib. XIII. ... Basileae apud Ioannem Vualderum, an. M. D. XXXVIII. ... (... Μαιμακτηριῶνος πρώτη.)

fol. a^6 α-ω^6 $\alpha\alpha$-$\beta\beta^6$ $\gamma\gamma^8$. pp. 1-327. [2] ... Theonis Alexandrini ... commentariorum lib. XI. Basileae Apud Ioannem Vualderum. A^4 a-mm^6 nn^8. pp. 2-425. [604

-- Ptolemaei mathematicæ constructionis Liber primus græce & latine editus. Additæ explicationes aliquot locorum ab Erasmo Rheinholt Salueldensi. VVitebergae Ex Officina Iohannis Lufft. Anno 1549. 8°. A-O^8 Π^8 P^4. ff. 1-123. [605

-- Quadriparti. Ptolo. Que in hoc volumine continentur hec sunt. Liber quadripartiti Ptolomei. Centiloquium eiusdem. Centiloquium Hermetis. Eiusdem de stellis beibenijs. Centiloquium Bethem. ⁊ de horis planetaꝝ. Eiusdem de significatione triplicitatū ortus. Centum quinquaginta ꝓpōnes Almansoris. Zahel de interrogationibus. Eiusdem de electionibus. Eiusdem de tēpoꝝ significationibus in iudicijs. Messahallach de receptionibus planetarum. Eiusdem de interrogationibus. Epistola eiusdem cū duodecim capitulis. Eiusdem de reuolutionibus annorum mundi. (Venetijs ... sumptibus hereduȝ ... Octauiani Scoti ... ⁊ socioꝝ ... 1519. sexto februarij.) fol. B.L. aa^6 A-Q^8 R-S^6. ff. 1-140. [606

-- -- Cl. Ptolemæi Pelusiensis Mathematici operis quadripartiti, in Latinum sermonem traductio: Adiectis libris posterioribus, Antonio Gogaua Grauiens. interprete ... Item, de sectione conica ... Deq̄ȝ Speculo Vstorio, Libelli duo ...: restituti ... Cum præfatione D. Gemmae Frisii ... Louanii Apud Petrum Phalesium, ac Martinum Rotarium, Anno M. D. XLVIII. Mense Octobri. (... excudebat Iacobus Batius ...) 4°. A-R^4 S^2 T^4. [607

-- -- Εις την τετραβιβλον του Πτολεμαιου εξηγητης ἀνώνυμος. In Claudii Ptolemæi quadripartitum enarrator ignoti nominis, quem tamen Proclum fuisse quidam existimant. Item Πορφυριου ... εισαγωγη ... Porphyrii ... introductio in Ptolemæi opus de affectibus astrorum. Praeterea Hermetis ... de reuolutionibus natiuitatum libri duo ... Basileæ. ... (... ex officina Petriana. Anno M. D. LIX. mense Septembri.) fol. a-b^6 A-R^6 Aa-Ee^6 Ff^8. pp. 1-279. ¶*T.p. repaired.* [608

PULCI, LUCA. Ciriffo Caluaneo. Libro intitolato Ciriffo Caluaneo, et il pouere Aueduto ... Composto il primo Libro per Luca Pulci: il resto ꝑ Bernardo Giambulari Fiorentini. ... 1535 (In Vinegia Nelle case de Pietro de Nicolini da Sabbio ... del mese di Ottobre.) 4°. A-R^8 S^4. [609

-- -- Ciriffo Caluaneo di Luca Pulci ... Con la Giostra dal Magnifico Lorenzo De Medici. Insieme con le Epistole Composte Dal Medesimo Pulci. ... In Fiorenza Nella Stamperia de' Giunti M D LXXII. (*Colophon.*) 4°. $*^2$ A-F^4 G^8 H^4 I^2. pp. 2-121. [610

-- Epistole di Luca de Pulci ... al magnifico Lorenzo de Medici. (Impresso in Firenze adpetitione di Frācesco di Iacopo Cartolaio uocato il Conte. .B. .Z.) 8°. A-L^4. [611

PULCI, LUIGI. Il Morgante ... In Fiorenza, Nella Stamperia di Bartolomeo Sermartelli. MDLXXIIII. (*Colophon.*) 4°. $\dagger^8$ A-Aa^8 Bb^4. pp. 2-390. [612

PULGAR, HERNANDO DE. Chronica. De los ... reyes Catholicos don Fernando y doña Ysabel ... Compuesta por el Maestro Antonio de Nebrixa ... Impressa en Valladolid, en casa de Sebastian Martinez. Año de M. D. LXV. fol. π^2 A-Qq^8 Rr^6. ff. 1-313. (Lea.) [613

PURBACH, GEORG. Theoricae nouae planetarum ... ab Erasmo Reinholdo Salueldensi pluribus figuris auctæ ... M. D. XLII. (Vitembergæ per Ioannem Lufft. ...) 8°. A-Z^8 (H8 + *folded leaf*, I1 + *folded leaf*, O2 + *folded leaf*) a-g^8. [614

PURGATORIUM. Purgatorium detractorum saluberrimū ... (Impressum ... Colonie ... M.ccccc.ix. in domo Quentell .x. kal'. Nouēbris) 4°. B.L. a-d^6 c^4. [615

PURPURATUS, JOANNES FRANCISCUS. Purpurate interpretationes ... (... imprimebat ... in eadem Taurinoꝝ vrbe: Anthonius Ranotus. Anno ... millesimo quingentesimo vigesimo quarto octauo calendas Maij.) fol. B.L. a-d^6 e-g^4 Aa-Dd^6 Ee-Ff^4. ff. II-LXXVI. (Biddle.) [616

-- [1] Ioannis Frācisci Purpurati ... in .ij. ff. vete. partem commentaria ... Addita repetitione .L. manifeste turpitudinis .ff. de iureiurando. Et repetitione .L. admonendi. eodem titulo. (... imprimebat ... ī ea taurinorū vrbe Antoniꝰ ranotꝰ Anno ... vigesimosexto supra millesimū qgētesimū kleñ. februarij.) fol. B.L. A-P^6. ff. II-LXXXIX. [2] Repertorij Tabula super cōmento tituli .ff. si certuȝ petatur: ⁊ de iureiurādo ... A-C^6. (Biddle.) [617

-- [1] Tabula seu repertoriū sup̱ sequenti cōmento ... fol. B.L. A^6. [2] Ioannis Francisci Purpurati de Pinerolio ... in primā C. partem. cōmētaria. ... (Imprimebat ... Antonijus Ranotus in eadem Taurinoꝝ vrbe. ... 1523. die .xv. Ianuarij.) a-g^6. ff. II-XL. (Biddle.) [618

PYTHAGORAS. [1] Opus aureum et scholasticum, in quo continentur Pythagoræ carmina aurea, Phocylidis, Theognidis & aliorum poëmata ... Edita ... cura Michaëlis Neandri Sorauiensis. Lipsiae. ... 4°. A^8 B-Z^4 Aa-$5F^4$. pp. 3-789. ¶*Additional t.p.* ($P1^r$): ... Theognidis ... gnomologia Graecolatina ... Lipsiae ... [2] Aurei operis Pars altera. Νειλου ... κεφαλαια, η παραινεσεις. Nili episcopi et martyris capita, seu praeceptiones de Vita pie, Christianè ac honestè exigenda, Graecolatinè: a Michaële Neandro Sorauiense conuersa & exposita. ... (Lipsiae, imprimebat Iohannes Steinman, anno M. D. LXXVII.) A-$3M^4$ $3N^6$. pp. 3-268, 2-191. ¶*Additional t.p.* ($Nn3^r$): ... Cointi Smyrnaei ... Ilij Excidij libri duo. Reditus Græcorum, capta Troia, liber vnus. ... editi labore, Laurentij Rhodomanni Cherusci. Lipsiae. *Includes also* Coluthi Helenae raptus, Tryphiodori de Troiae excidio, Luciani Samosatensis somnium. [619

-- -- Poemata Pythagorae et Phocylidis Graeca. Cum duplici interpretatione Viti Amerbachij. ... M.D.XXXIX. (Argentorati apud Cratonem Mylium mense Sept. ...) 8°. A-K^8 L^{10}. pp. 3-176. [620

-- -- Argentorati apud Christianum Mylium. 1565. 8°. A-K^8 L^4. pp. 3-163. [621

Q

QUADRAMIO, EVANGELISTA. La vera dichiaratione di tutte le metafore, similitudini, & Enimmi de gl'antichi Filosofi Alchimisti ... Oue ... si mostra l'errore, & ignoranza (per non dir l'inganno) di tutti gl'Alchimisti Moderni. Per Frate Euagnelista Quattrami ... In Roma, Appresso Vincentio Accolti ... 1587. 4°. $\dagger$-3$\dagger^4$ A-Ii^4 (-Z^4, Ii1, Ii4, *the last presumably blank*). pp. 1-230. (Smith.) [1

QUEMADA, GABRIEL DE. Breue Compendium quæstionū quæ æueniunt in praxi in materia Fiscali coram iudicibus Fisci sanctæ Inquisicionis. ... (Toleti Apud Michaëlem Ferrer. M.D.LXIIII.) 8°. A-M^8. ff. 3-86. (Lea.) [2

QUERELA. Querela Martini Luteri, seu Somnium. ... Basileae. (... ex officina Ioannis Oporini, ... M. D. LIIII. Mense Martio.) 8°. a-d^8. pp. 3-62. [3

QUERHAMER, KASPAR. Labyrinthus Lutheri. Sechs vnd dreissig Stell vnd Ort/ da ... Luther ... jhm selbs zuwider lehret. ... durch Caspar Querhamer von Hall/ vnd D. Iohannem Cochleum ... zusamen gezogen ... Getruckt zu Ingolstatt. Anno M.D.LXXXIII. 8°. A-C^8. pp. 1-43. [4

QUINTIANUS STOA, JOANNES FRANCISCUS. In preciosissimam Galliarum Reginę Britonumq3 Ducis Annę mortem Threnos ... Vęnundantur ab Ioanne paruo & Ascensio [1515]. 4°. a-c^4. [5

-- Quę hoc in libello continentur ... disticha in omneis fabulas. P. Ouidij Nasonis Methamorphoseon Eiusdem Elegia qua deflet philippum Beroaldū ... Eiusdem in immaturam Reginę annę fatū Threnos ... carmina ... Regis Scotie epitaphia ... 4°. a^4 B-K^4 L^6. [6

QUINTILIANUS, MARCUS FABIUS. M. Fabii Quintiliani ... institutionum Oratoriarum Libri XII. ... Eiusdem Declamationum Liber. Basileae, ex aedibus Ioannis Bebelii, mense Augusto, anno M. D. XXIX. fol. A-B^4 a-z^4 A-Bb^4 Cc^6 A-O^4. ff. 2-198, 2-54. [7

-- -- [1] M. Fabii Quintiliani institutionum oratoriarum libri duodecim. ... Apud Seb. Gryphium Lugduni, 1549. 8°. a-z^8 A-Z^8 aa-bb^8. pp. 3-646. [2] ... declamationes vndeuiginti. ... *Same imprint.* a-r^8 (-r8, *presumably blank*). pp. 2-269. [8

-- M. F. Quintilianus. (Venetiis in aedibus Aldi, et Andreae soceri mense Augusto. M.D.XIIII.) 4°. *^{4} a-z^8 A-E^8 F^6. ff. 1-230. [9

-- -- *Another copy.* [10

-- -- M. Fabii Quintiliani Institutionum Oratoriarum libri XII diligentius recogniti M D XXII. ... (Venetiis in aedibus Aldi, et Andreae soceri mense Ianuario. M.D.XXI.) 4°. *^{4} a-z^8 A-E^8 F^6. ff. 1-230. [11

-- -- Eucharius Ceruicornus excudebat, anno M. D. XXVII. mense Aug. (Coloniæ ... impensa M. Godefridi Hydorpij, quarto nonas Augusti.) fol. AA^4 a-h$^{8.6}$ i-bb^6 cc^8. ff. 2-330. [12

-- -- Ioannes Soter excudebat Coloniæ, anno M D XXVIII. Mense Aug. 8°. aa^8 a-z^8 A-M^8 N^4. pp. 2-567. [13

-- Mar. Fabii Quintiliani ... Declamationum liber. Lugduni apud Seb. Gryphium, anno 1536. 8°. aa-pp^8 qq^4. pp. 2-247. [14

-- -- Basileæ per Nicolaum Bryling. Anno M.D.XLIX. 8°. a-s^8 t^6. pp. 1-297. [15

-- -- M. Fab. Quintiliani declamationes, quæ ex CCCLXXXVIII. supersunt, CXLV. ... Calpurnii Flacci excerptæ X. rhetorum minorum LI. ... Dialogus de oratoribus ... Ex bibliotheca P. Pithoei I.C. Lutetiæ, Apud Mamertum Patissonium ... in officina Roberti Stephani. M. D. LXXX. ... 8°. ā^8 ē^6 A-Gg^8. pp. 1-458. [16

R

RABENHAUPT, NICOLAUS. Oration in teütsch welchermassē die Römisch Kayserlich Mayestat/ jnnamen Stathalters Regenten/ vnd Camer Rethe/ der Niderösterreichischen Lannde/ durch der Küniglichenn Mayestat Canntzler in Niderösterreich/ Herrnn Niclasen Rabenhaupt vonn Suchee/ ꝛc. empfangē worden ist ... 1532. 4°. A^4. [1

RACCOLTA. Raccolta di varii poemi Latini, e volgari: Fatti ... nella felice Vittoria reportata da Christiani contra Turchi. In Venetia, Appresso Giorgio Angelieri. 1571. (... A instantia di M. Lorenzo Parma.) 4°. A-G^8 H^4. ff. 1-56. [2

RAEMOND, FLORIMOND DE. L'Anti-christ et l'Anti-papesse. ... Edition seconde ... A Paris, Chez Abel l'Angelier ... M. D. XCIX. ... (De l'Imprimerie de Denis Binet, ce cinquiesme Iuin. ...) 4°. ā^4 ē^4 ī^4 ō^2 A-6K^4 6L^2. pp. 1-485. ¶*Half-titles:* (4V2) L'Anti-papesse. ... (5Y3) De la couronne du soldat. Traduict du Latin de Q. Septim. Tertullian. Par Florimond de Remond ... (6F2) Aux martyrs traduict du Latin de Q. Septim. Tertullian. Par Florimond de Remond ... (Lea.) [3

RÄTSELBÜCHLEIN. Eyn newe Spinstůb/ oder Räterschbůchlin. ... Getruckt zů Strassburg bey M. Iacob Cammerlandern von Mentz [c. 1535]. 4°. A-F^4. [4

RAGAZZONI, GIROLAMO. Oratio habita in sessione nona, et vltima, ... Concilii Tridentini: ... Prid. & Non. Decembris. M. D. LXIII. ... Brixiae: Ad instantiam Io: Baptistæ Bozole. M. D. LXIII. (... apud Ludouicum Sabiensem.) 4°. A^4. (Lea.) [5

RAGGUAGLIO. Vero et minuto ragguaglio di quanto è successo nella felicissima Armata della santa lega ... a questo presente giorno terzo di Settembre. M. D. LXXII. In Roma per gli Heredi di Antonio Blado ... 4°. A-B^2. [6

RAGIONAMENTI. Ragionamenti familiari de diuersi Autori ... In Vinegia al segno del Pozzo. M. D. L. (... per Pietro, & Zuanmaria fratelli di Nicolini da Sabbio ...) 8°. A-Q^4. ff. 2-65. [7

RAIDA, BALTHASAR. Widder das lester vnd lügen büchlin Agricole Phagi/ genant Georg Witzel. Antwort/ ... Vorrede D. Martini Lutherij. Wittemberg. MDXXXIII. (Gedruckt ... durch Nickel Schirlentz.) 4°. A-F^4. [8

RAIMONDI, RAFAELLO. [Commentationes in pandectas.] Lugduni, Apud Hugonem, & hæredes Aemonis à Porta. M. D. XLIIII. (... in Typographia ... Stephani Rufini, et Ioannis Ausulti.) fol. B.L. [1] Raphaellis Cumani ... Cōmentationes ... in eius Pandectar. partis Primam (quam Infortiatum vulgus ... vocitat) ... A-V^8 X^6. ff. 2-165. [2] ... Cōmentationes ... in eius Pandectar. partis Secūdam ... AA-SS^8 TT^6. ff. 2-150. [3] ... in eius pandectarum partis Priman, quæ vulgi censura Digesti Noui appellatione differtur, Prælectiones ... 3a-3y^8. ff. 2-176. (Biddle.) [9

-- Consilia vtriusque Raphaelis ... Rapha. Cumani, necnō Raphaelis Fulgosij Consilia ... Lugduni. Apud hæredes Iacobi Giunctæ. 1548 (... Excudebat Hector penet ...) fol. B.L. a-z^8 ꝛ^8 ꝯ^{10} A-B^6. ff. 2-201. (Biddle.) [10

RAINERIO, ANTONIO FRANCESCO. L'altilia comedia ... M.D.L. (Stampata nella ... Cità di Mantoua per Venturino Roffinelli il xx. di Settember. ...) 8°. A-N^4. ff. 2-52. [11

-- ... Cento sonetti. ... M.D LIII. (Impressi in Milano per Gio. Antonio Borgia.) 4°. A-L^8. ¶*Half-title* (D6^r): Seguono alchuni altri sonetti del medesmo authore, con le risposte di diuersi. Et del medesmo authore canzoni sestine stanze madrigali et pompe. ... *Additional t.pp.:* (F5^r) ... Pompe di. M. Antonfrancesco Rainerio. ... (I1^r) ... Breuissime Espositione di M. Hieronimo Rainerio ... soura li cento sonetti & l'altre Rime ... M D LIIII. [12

RAINOLDS, WILLIAM. Caluino-Turcismus id est, Caluinisticæ perfidiae, cum Mahumetana collatio, et dilucida vtriusque sectae confutatio: Quatuor Libris explicata. ... Authore Gulilemo Reginaldo Anglo ... Antuerpiae, In ædibus Petri Belleri ... M. D. XCVII. ... 8°. a-b^8 A-3T^8 (-3T8, *presumably blank*). pp. 4-1038. (Lea.) [13

RAMPINI, ANDREA DE', de Isernia. Andreas de Isernia super vsibus feudorum. ... [*Device of Jacobus Giunta.*] 1541 (Excussum Lugduni typis ... Ioannis Dominici Guarnerij.) fol. B.L. a-p^{8}. ff. 2-111. (Biddle.) [14

RAMUS, JOANNES. Oikonomia, seu dispositio regularum vtriusque iuris in locos communes ... Coloniae Agrippinae, Ad Intersignium Monocerotis. Anno M.D.LXX. 8°. †^{8} A-N^{8}. pp. 2-204. (Lea.) [15

RAMUSIO, GIOVANNI BATTISTA. Primo volume, & Terza editione delle nauigationi et viaggi raccolto gia da M. Gio. Battista Ramusio ... In Venetia nella stamperia de Giunti. L'anno M D LXIII. (... nel mese di Gennaio ...) fol. a^{4} b-d^{8} e^{10} a-u^{8} x^{10} y-3b^{8} 3c^{10} (-3c10, *blank*). ff. 2-34, 1-394. [16

-- -- *Another copy.* [17

-- Secondo volume delle nauigationi et viaggi ... In Venetia nella stamperia de Giunti. L'anno M D LIX. (... M D LVIII.) fol. 1^{8} ✠^{2} 2-5$^{6.4}$ A-S^{8} T-V^{6}. ff. 3-28, 1-155. [18

-- -- [1] In Venetia, Appresso i Giunti. MDLXXXIII. (*Colophon.*) fol. 1-2^{6} 3^{4} 4^{6} 5^{4} A-II^{8}. ff. 2-18, 1-256. [2] La descrittione della Sarmatia Europea, del ... Caualiere Alessandro Guagnino Veronese, Tradotta dalla lingua Latina nel volgare Italiano dal ... M. Bartholomeo Dionigi da Fano. (*Colophon.*) A-X^{4} Y^{6}. ff. 1-90. [19

-- Terzo volume delle nauigationi et viaggi ... In Venetia nella stamperia de Giunti. L' anno M D LVI. (*Colophon.*) fol. 1^{6+6} 2-6^{6} 7^{4} a-yy^{8} zz^{10} 3a-3d^{8} 3e^{8+2} 3f^{4} 3g^{8+2} 3h^{8+4} 3i^{6} 3k^{6+2} (-3k6, *presumably blank*). ff. 1-453. [20

-- -- In Venetia nella stamperia de' Giunti. L'anno M D LXV. (*Colophon.*) fol. A^{6} B-D^{8} E^{10} a-yy^{8} zz^{10} 3a-3c^{8} 3d^{8+2} 3e^{8} 3f^{4} 3g^{8+4} 3h^{8+4} 3i^{6} 3k^{6+2} (-3k6). ff. 1-34, 1-456. [21

RANCHIN, GUILLAUME. Reuision du Concile de Trente, contenant les nullitez d'iceluy: les griefs des Rois & Princes Chrestiens: de l'Eglise Gallicane & autres Catholiques. [Genève,] L'An de Grace, M. DC. 8°. *^{8} a-cc^{8} dd^{4} ee^{2} A-CC^{8} ¶^{8}. pp. 1-428, 1-409. (Lea.) [22

RANTZAU, HEINRICH. Belli Dithmarsici, ab ... Daniae rege Friderico II. et ... Holsasatiæ Ducibus, Iohanne & Adolpho fratribus, gesti, Anno ... M.D.LIX. vera descriptio, Duobus libris comprehensa. ... Argentorati Per Bernhardum Iobinum. Anno 1574. 8°. A-P^{8}. pp. 3-14, 1-209. [24

-- Catalogus imperatorum, regum ac principum qui astrologicam artem amarunt, ornarunt & exercuerunt: quibus additæ sunt Astrologica quadam prædictiones ... tractatus de annis Climactericis ... edita à Theophilo Siluio ... Antuerpiæ, Ex officina Christophori Plantini ... M. D. LXXX. 8°. A-G^{8}. pp. 3-109. [25

RAO, CESARE. L'argute, et facete lettere ... In Trento, Ad instantia di Marc'Antonio Pallazzolo 1585. (... Per Gio. Battista, & Giacomo Fratelli Gelmini. ...) 8°. †^{8} A-P^{8}. ff. 1-120. [26

-- -- In Venetia, MDXCVIII. Appresso la Compagnia Minima. 8°. A-O^{8} (-O8, *presumably blank*). ff. 2-105. [27

RAPHAEL PLACENTINUS. Armeniados Libri. X. Scenæ IIII Polystichorum Liber I Epigrammatum Libri III ... (Cremonæ Impressum per Franciscum Ricardum de Luere. ... M.D.XVIII. Die uero .XVI. Mensis Martii.) 8°. A^{4} B-Y^{8} Aa-Oo^{8}. [28

RAPICIO, GIOVITA. Iouitae Rapicii Brixiani de numero oratorio libri quinque ... Eiusdem paraphrasis in psalmos Dauidis, & quædam carmina. ... Venetiis, M. D. LIIII. (... in ædibus Pauli Manutij, Aldi filij ...) fol. A-EE^{2} A-I^{2} 1:^{2}. ff. 2-56, 1-20. [29

RAPPO DE SANTERENTIO, FRANCESCO. Lima Spirituale. ... (Impressa ... Bologna per Hieronymo di Benedicti ... M.D.xiiii. adi. ulitmo de Martio.) 4°. A-K^{4} L^{6}. ff. 2-46. [30

RASARIO, GIOVANNI BATTISTA. Ioannis Baptistæ Rasarii, de victoria Christianorum ad Echinadas Oratio ... (Rostochii excudebant Iohannes Stockelman & Andreas Guttervvitz M. D. LXXII.) 8°. A-B^{8}. [31

RASTELL, WILLIAM. A colleccion of entrees ... & diuers other matters. ... [Londini,] In ædibus Richardi Tottell. ... M.D.LXVI. decimo quarto die Maij. (*Colophon.*) fol. B.L. π^4 A-4H^8 4I-4K^6. ff. 1-627. *S.T.C.* 20730. (Biddle.) [32

-- -- *Another copy.* (Biddle.) [33

-- -- In ædibus Richardi Tottel. ... 1574. vicesimo secundo Ianuarij. (*Colophon.*) fol. B.L. π^4 A-4H^8 4I-4K^6. ff. 1-627. *S.T.C.* 20731. (Biddle.) [34

-- An exposition of certaine difficult and obscure wordes, and termes of the lawes of this Realme ... In ædibus Richardi Tottelli. ... (Imprinted at London ... 1579.) 8°. A^4 A-Cc^8 Dd^4 (-Dd4, *presumably blank*). ff. 1-196. *S.T.C.* 20707. (Biddle.) [35

-- A table Collected of the yeares of oure Lorde God, and of the yeares of the Kynges of Englande ... Lõndini. M.D.LXI. (... Ex officina Ioannis Waley ... 3. die Mens. Nouemb.) 8°. B.L. A-L^8. *S.T.C.* 20733. (Biddle.) [36

RATSCHLAG. Eyn Christenlicher Ratschlag vnnd vnterrichtung/ Welcher gestalt sich alle Christenliche personen/ von Obern vnnd vnterthanen halten sollen/ das jne das in vermoͤg vnnd nach anzaygung eins sundern Artickels im abschied des iüngst gehalten Reichstag zu Speyer/ diss .1526. Jars. verleibt ... 4°. [A]-B^4 C^2 D^4. [37

-- Eyn Ratschlag/ Den etliche Christenliche Pfarherrn ... 1525 (Gedruckt zů Nuͤrnberg durch Iobst Gůtknecht.) 4°. π^6 A-Bb^4 Cc^6. ff. 1-105. [38

RAUSCHER, HIERONYMUS. Der Hundert vnd Fuͤnff vnd zweintzigste Psalm ... gepredigt vnd ausgelegt ... (Gedruckt zu Koͤnigsperg in Preussen/ durch Iohann Daubman. M.D.LV.) 4°. A-V^4 X^6. [39

-- Ein nůtzliches gesprech eines Christlichen Fursten mit seynen Reten/ Predigern/ vnd einem Barfusser Moͤnich/ Von vrsach des gegenwertigen vnglucks in Teutschen Landen ... [Jena, Christian Roͤdinger, 1555.] 4°. A-D^4. [40

RAVENNA. Statutorum seu iuris ciuilis ciuitatis Rauennae. Cum reformationibus Hieronymi Ruginii Rauen. ... libri V. ... Rauennae; Petrus, & Camillus Ioannellij Fratres, industria Sigismundi Bordognę, excudebant. M.D. LXXXX. ... (... M.D.XCI.) fol. π^2 +^{2} A-C^6 D^1 E-M^6 N^4 O-T^6 V^2. ff. 2-108. (Lea.) [41

RAVERINUS, PANTHALEON BERTHELONAEUS. Epitome in prosodiam ex varijs scriptoribus ... collecta ... Accessit ex Despauterio ... quæ de Prosodia carmine scripsit ... Venetiis, Apud Hæredes Melchioris Sessæ. M D LXXV. 16°. a-t^8. pp. 3-293. [42

RAVESTEYN, JODOCUS. Confessionis Siue doctrinæ, quæ nuper edita est à Ministris, qui in Ecclesiam Antwerpiensem irrepserunt ... Confutatio. ... Editio secunda ... Louanii, Apud Petrum Zangrium ... 1567. 8°. A-X^8 Y^4. ff. 1-168. [43

RAVISIUS, JOANNES, TEXTOR. Ioannis Rauisii Textoris Niuernensis epithetorum opus ... Accesserunt de Carminibus ad veterum imitationem artificiosè componendis præcepta bona ... à Georgio Sabino. Parisiis, Apud Michaëlem Sonnium ... M.D.LXXV. 8°. ã^4 a-z^8 A-Vv^8 Xx^4 (-Xx4, *presumably blank*). ff. 1-531. (Lea.) [44

RAZZI, GIROLAMO. La balia comedia ... In Fiorenza appresso i Giunti, 1560. 8°. A-G^8. ff. 3-55. [45

-- Vite di quattro Huomini Illustri; M. Farinata Vberti, Gualtieri Duca D'Atene, M. Saluestro De'Medici, e Cosimo Il Vecchio. Scritte da D. Siluano Razzi ... In Firenze, Nella Stamperia de'Giunti. 1580. ... (*Colophon.*) 8°. +^{8} A-Q^8 R^4. pp. 1-260. [46

RAZZI, SERAFINO. Cento casi di coscienza. ... Ristampati con aggiunta d'alcuni casi de' Cambij, & vn Trattato de'Censi. ... In Venetia, Appresso Iacomo Vicenzi. MDLXXXV. (... Appresso Ventura de Saluador, Ad instanza di Iacomo Vicenzi.) 12°. +^{12} A-S^{12}. pp. 2-423. ¶R1, R2 *misbound between* R4 *and* R5. (Lea.) [47

REALINO, BERNARDINO. Bernardini Realini Carpensis in nuptias Pelei et Thetidis Catullianas commentarius. Eiusdem aliquot in varia scriptorum loca annotationes. ... Bononiæ apud Anselmum Giaccarellum M D. LI. 4°. A-R^4. ff. 1-64. ¶*The* A *gathering may be incomplete.* [48

REBHUN, PAUL. Hausfried Was füer vrsachen den Christlichen Eheleuten zubedencken/ den lieben Hausfriede in der Ehe zuerhalten. ... Witteberg. 1563. (Gedruckt ... durch Lorentz Schwenck.) 8°. A-S^8. [49

REBUFFI, PIERRE. [1] Concordata inter ... Papam Leonem decimum, & ... regem Franciscum ... primũ ... ædita. Cum interpretationibus ... D. Petri Rebuffi ... IIII. Aeditio. Parisiis. Apud Galeotum Pratensem ... 1545 ... 4°. ✠-7✠^{4} A-ZZ^4 a-h^4. pp. 1-429. [2] Tractatus nominationum ... Aa^2 Bb-Xx^4 Yy^2. pp. 1-166. [3] Tractatus de pacificis possessoribus ... (... decima quinta die mensis Septembris ...) aa-kk^4. pp. 1-74. (Lea.) [50

-- Feudorum declaratio ... Coloniae Apud Ioannem Birckmannum. M. D. LXI. 8°. A-H^8. pp. 3-127. (Biddle.) [51

RECUEIL. Brief recueil de toutes les sortes de ieux, qu'auoient les anciens Græcz & Romains ... 1542 ... On les vend à Paris ... par Andry roffet. 16°. A-B^8. [52

REDALDO, GIOVANNI. Kalendarium per annos centum. Ad vsum ... Fratrum Minorum ... Venetiis, Apud Iuntas, M D LXXXII. (... 1573.) 8°. ✠^{8} A-EE^8 FF^4 ✠✠^{4} (-✠✠1, ✠✠4). [53

REGENSBURG. Bericht vnd Vermanung/ Eines Er. Cammerer vnd Raths der Stadt Regenspurg ... deren ... geurlaubten füenff Kirchendienern halben. ... (1588. Gedruckt zu Regenspurg/ bey Iohann Burger.) 4°. A-B^4. [54

-- Eyn wegsprech gen Regenspurg zů/ ynss Concilium/ zwischen eynem Byschoff Hůren wirt/ vnd· Kůntzen seinem Knecht. ... MDXXV (Gedruckt zů Arnaw an der Elb jn Böhem durch Hans Hoss von Brawn [i.e., zu Hagenau durch Armand Farckall]. ...) 4°. a-e^4. [55

REGGIO EMILIA. Statuta magnificae communitatis Regii. Regii, Apud Herculianum Bartholum. MDLXXXII. ... (*Colophon.*) fol. *^{8} A-3L^6 3M^8 3N^6 3O^4 3P^6. ff. 3-349. [56

REGIOMONTANUS, JOHANNES. In Ptolemæi ... almagestum ... libri tredecim ... Noribergæ apud Ioannem Montanum, & Vlricum Neuberum, Anno M. D. L. fol. [A]^6 B-S^6 T^8 (-T8, *blank*). [57

REGISTRUM. 1595 Registrum omnium breuium ... Londini In ædibus Ianæ Yetsweirt relictæ Caroli Yetsweirt ... fol. ¶^{4} ¶¶^{6} A-3F^6 3G^4 3H-3Y^6. ff. 1-321, 1-85. *S.T.C.* 20838. (Biddle.) [58

REGOLI, SEBASTIANO. Sebastiani Reguli Brasichellensis in primum Aeneidos Virgilii librum Ex Aristotelis de arte poetica, & Rhetorica præceptis explicationes. Bononiae, Ex Typographia Ioannis Rubei ... M D LXIII. 4°. A-FF^4 GG^2. pp. 3-220. [59

REGULAE. Regule grammaticales regimina et constructiones. (Impressum Liptzk per Melchior Lotter ... M.cccccciij.) 4°. B.L. A^6 B^4 C^6. [60

REICHERSDORFF, GEORG VON. Chorographia Transyluaniæ, quæ Dacia olim appellata ... Viennæ Austriæ excudebat Egidius Aquila ... M. D. L. 4°. A-K^4 (K3 + *folded leaf*). ff. 1-31. [61

REINECK, REINER. Oratio de historia, eiusque dignitate ... a Reinero Reineccio Steinhemio. Francofurti apud And. Wechelum, M. D. LXXX. fol. a-c^6. pp. 1-31. [62

-- Oratio funebris de ... Iulio, duce Brunouic. et Luneburg. ... Helmaestadii Excudebat Iacobus Lucius, Anno M.D.LXXXIX. 4°. A-G^4. ¶*Additional t.pp.:* (D4^r) Exequiae. ... Auctore M. Henrico Meibomio ... Helmestadii Anno CIƆ. IƆ. LXXXIX. (G1^r) Ecloga Daphnis, in qua sub nomine Daphnidis lugetur obitus ... Iulii ... Ducis ... Auctore M. Henrico Papaeburgero ... Helmaestadii Excudebat Iacobus Lucius, Anno M. D. LXXXIX. [63

REINHARD, MARTIN. Vnderrichte wie sich ain frũmer Christ bey den Papistischen Messen ... halten soll ... Martinus Reynhart ... M. D. xxiiij. 4°. A^4. [64

-- Wess sich Doctor Anndreas Bodenstein von Karlstadt mit Doctor Martino Luther beredt zů Ihenn ... Item Die handlung Doctor Martini Luther mit dem Rath vnnd Gemeyne/ der Stat Orlamünd/ am tag Bartolomei ... A. ꝯc̄. xxiiij ... [Bamberg, Georg Erlinger, 1524.] 4°. A-C^4. [65

REINHOLD, ERASMUS. Oratio de Casparo Crucigero, ab Erasmo Rheinholt Salueldensi recitata, die uicesimo Augusti. Anno, 1549. VVitebergæ. In officina Typographica Viti Creutzer. 8°. A-B^8. [66

REINIER, JEAN. Mopsi, et Nisæ Lugdunensium μεταμορφώσεις, Ioanne Rænerio autore. Lugduni Apud Ioannem Franciscum de Gabiano. 1541. 4°. A-C^4. pp. 3-23. [67

REISCH, GREGOR. Margarita philosophica (... Friburgi ꝑ Ioannē Schottū Argeñ. citra festū Margarethę ... M.CCCCC.III.) 4°. π^8 1-4^8 a-h^8 (h6 + *folded leaf*) i^8 (i7 + *folded leaf*) k-q^8 r^6 A-B^8 C^4 D-K^8 L-M^6 aa-dd^8 ee^4 ff^6. ¶*Engraved t.p.* [68

REISNER, ADAM. [Ierusalem ... descripta. Francofurti, 1563.] (Francofurti ad Moenum, per Georgium Coruinum, Sigismundum Fierabent, & Hæredes Vuigandi Galli.) fol. A^6 (*wanting*) A-Z^6 (B6 + 2 *leaves*) a-z^6 Aa-Hh^6 Ii^4 Kk^6. pp. 3-635. ¶*Translator: Johann Heyden.* [69

REM, BERNHARD. Ain Sendtbrieff an ettlich Closterfrawen zu sant katherina vnd zu sant niclas in Augspurg [Augsburg, Philipp Ulhart, 1523.] 4°. A^4 B^2. [70

REMY, NICOLAS. Nicolai Remigii ... daemonolatreiae libri tres. ... Coloniæ Agrippinæ. Apud Henricum Falckenburg. Anno Iↄ. cIↄ. XCVI. (... Typis Lamberti Andreæ. ...) 8°. †-††^{8} A-Cc^8. pp. 1-414. (Lea.) [71

REPETITIONES. Primum volumen Repetitionum diuersorum doctorū in iure canonico ... vna cum Reportorio ... Hieronymi de Marliano Mediolanensis ... i5i9 ... (Impressum Mediolani per Ioannem Angelum scinzenzeler ... die .xx. Aprilis.) fol. B.L. a^6 b^4 c-z^6 ⁊^{6} ↄ^6 ꝝ^6 A-G^6 A-E^6. ff. II-CXCVI. (Biddle.) [72

-- Repetitionum seu commentariorum in varia iurisconsultorum responsa Volumen Secundum. Repetitiones ... pertinent ad posteriorem partem primi Tomi Pandectarum. Lugduni, Apud Hugonem à Porta, & Antonium Vincentium. M. D. LIII. fol. B.L. a-pp^8 qq^6. ff. 2-310. (Biddle.) [73

REPGOW, EYKE VON. Die Lehenrecht verdeũtscht ... Mit erklerung vnnd ausslegung etlicher Lateinischer vnnd Wälscher wort ... Zu Wormbs truckts Sebastianus Wagner. (... M. D. XX[X]VII.) fol. ✠^{4} A-G^4. ff. I-XXVIII. ¶G3-4 *defective.* [74

-- Sachsenspiegel Auffs newe vbersehen/ mit Summarijs vnd newen Addicionen ... Durch ... Christoff Zobel ... zugericht ... Leiptzig. Anno M. D. LXIX. (... Bey M. Ernesto Vögelin ...) fol.)(^{6} A^6 B^4 C-Z^6 a-z^6 Aa-4E^6 4F^4. ff. I-DXXVIII. [75

-- -- Leipzig. Anno M. D. LXXXII. (... Bey Iohann Steinman ...) fol. *Same collation and foliation.* (Biddle.) [76

RESCHEL, THOMAS. Dictionarium Bohemicolatinum ... Impressum Olomucij, apud Ioannem Guntherum. M. D. LXII. (*Colophon.*) 4°. A^2 A-V^4 W-Vv^4 Ww-3E^4. [77

-- Dictionarium Latinobohemicum ... Impressum Olomucij, apud Ioannem Guntherum. M.D.LX. 4°. a^4 A-5A^4 5B^2. [78

RESENDE, GARCIA DE. Choronica que tracta da vida e ... virtudes ... do ... Dom Ioão ho Segundo ... Em Lisbo[a] Im[pressa em] casa de Simão Lopez ... M.DXC.V.I. (*Colophon.*) fol. ✚^{6} A-R^8. ff. i-cxxxiiij. ¶✚1 *defective.* [79

RESPONCE. Responce faicte par vn Religieux des Feullars, à la lettre que son pere luy auoit escrit, pour le retirer de Religion. M.D.LXXXVIII. 8°. A-I^4. pp. 3-72. [80

RESPONSA. [1] Responsorum, iuris, siue consiliorum, partim a ... aliquot academiis, partim à ... Germaniæ Iurisconsultis conscriptorum, ... Tomi duo. ... Francofordiae apud haeredes Christiani Egenolphi Hadamarij. M. D. LXVIII. (*Colophon.*) fol. *,*^{4} AA-ZZ^6 aa-uu^6 A-Z^6 a-r^6. pp. 1-490, 1-454. [2] Responsorum ... tomus III. ... Francofordiae apud haeredes Christiani Egenolphi Hadamarij. M. D. LXXI. (*Colophon.*) a-b^6 c^4 A-Z^6 a-t^6. pp. 1-511. [81

REUCHLIN, JOHANNES. Ioannis Reuchlin Phorcensis ... liber de verbo mirifico. Lugduni apud Ioan. Tornaesium. M. D. LII. 16°. a-y^8 (-y8, *blank*). pp. 2-324. (Lea.) [82

-- -- *Another copy.* [83

-- Ioannis Reuchlin Phorcensis Sergius uel Capitis caput cum commentario Georgij Symler. (Phorce in ædibus Thomæ Anshelmi Anno .M.D.VII. mense Septembri.) 4°. a-f$^{6.4}$ g-k$^{4.6}$. pp. I-LXXXVII. [84

REUDEN, AMBROSIUS. Compendium grammaticæ Hebrææ ... VVitebergae Typis excusum Cratonis. Anno M. D. LXXXVI. 8°. A-C^{8}. [85

REUSNER, HIERONYMUS. Pandora, Das ist/ Die Edleste Gab Gottes/ oder der ... Stein der Weisen ... Getruckt zu Basel. Anno M.D.LXXXII. (... bey Samuel Apiario.) 8°. (:)^{8} A-N^{8} O^{8+1} P-T^{8} V^{2}. pp. 1-309. ¶(:)8, C8, R3-4 *defective.* R4, R3 *misbound after* R1. (Smith.) [86

REUSNER, NICOLAUS. Ænigmatographia Siue sylloge ænigmatum et griphorum conuiualium ... Ex recensione Nicolai Reusneri Leorini ... Francofurti Impensis M. Georgij Draudij & Philippi Angeli. M. D. IC. 12°.)(^{12} A-E^{12} a-p^{12} (-p12, *presumably blank*). pp. 1-120, 1-358. [87

-- Icones sive imagines virorum literis illustrium. ... Additis eorundem elogiis diversorum auctorum. Ex Secunda recognitione ... Curante Bernhardo Iobino. ... Argentorati. CIↃ IↃ XC. 8°.)(^{8} A-Z^{8} a-e^{8} (-e7-8, *the latter blank*). pp. 1-428. [88

-- -- *Another copy* (-c7-8, e7-8). (Smith.) [89

-- Nicolai Reusneri Leorini Lauinga ... Lauingae Rhetorum Typis Emanuelis Salzeri, excusum, Anno 1567. 8°. A-B^{8}. [90

-- Parentalia siue Charistia ... Ioan. Friderico I. ... eiusq; Filio ... Ioan. Vuilhelmo, Saxoniæ Ducibus, ... habita, Ienæ ad V. Non. Martij, Anni M. D. XCI. ... Accessit Iusti Lipsii oratio de Ioanne VVilhelmo Saxoniæ Duce &c. Ienæ Typis Tobiæ Steinmanni Anno M. D. XCII. 4°. A-F^{4} G^{2}. [91

REUTER, QUIRIN. Oratio de vita et morte ... Iohannis Casimiri Palatini Rheni ... cIo. Io. XCII. Heidelbergae Typis Abrahami Smesmanni, Impensis Henrici Auenæ. 4°. A-D^{4}. [92

REYGER, ARNOLD DE. Arnoldi de Reyger Iurisc. disputationum siue diatribarum iuris ciuilis Ex Institut. D. Iustiniani Imp. ... libri quatuor. ... Ienae Typis Tobiæ Steinmanni. Anno cIo. Io. XCIII. 4°. A-B^{4} A^{6} A^{6} A^{4} A-B^{4} A^{6} A-B^{4} A^{6} A^{6} X^{2} A-B^{4} C^{2} A^{6} A^{6} A-B^{6} A-B^{6} A^{4} A-B^{4} A-B^{4} A^{6} A-B^{4} X^{2} A-B^{4} A^{6} A^{6} A-C^{4} A-B^{4} C^{2} A^{4} A-B^{4} A^{6} A^{4} A^{6} X^{2} A^{6} A^{6} A-C^{4} A-B^{4} A-B^{4} A-B^{4} A-B^{4} A-B^{4} A^{4} A-B^{4} C^{2}. ¶*With 41 additional t.pp. and many inserted blank leaves.* (Lea.) [93

REYMUNDUS. Reymundus Offenbarung. Ist gefunden worden/ jn einem alten Bůch. Vor vil Jaren geschryben. 4°. A^{4}. ¶A3 *repaired.* [94

RHEGIUS, URBANUS. Anzaygung dass die Romisch Bull mercklichen schaden in gewiss in manicher menschen gebracht hab/ vnd nit Doctor Luthers leer/ durch Henricū Phoeniceum von Roschach. ... 4°. A-E^{4}. [95

-- Argument disses biechleins. Symon Hessus zeygt an Doctori Martino Luther vrsach/ warumb die Lutthерische bücher von den Coloniensern vnd Louaniensern verbrent wordē sein ... 4°. A-C^{4} D^{6}. ¶D5^{v}: Datum zu Zeringen im̄ Bryssgaw/ am .vj. tag des Ianuarij. im̄ XXj. jar. [96

-- -- Argument dises büechleins. ... [Augsburg, Sigmund Grim, 1521.] 4°. A-D^{4} E^{6}. [97

-- Dialogus. Ein lůstig vnd nützlich Gesprech/ vom zukünfftigen Concilio zu Mantua ... (Gedruckt zu Wittemberg durch Ioseph Klug. 1537.) 4°. A-H^{4}. [98

-- Dialogus von der schoͤnen predigt/ die Christus Luc. 24. von Ierusalem bis gen Emaus ... gethan hat ... 1537. (Gedruckt zu Wittemberg durch Ioseph Klug.) 4°. *^{4} A-Zz^{4} a-x^{4} (-x4, *presumably blank*). [99

-- Doctrina ... contra desperationem propter peccata, è quarto Capite ad Roman. Item, Dialogus inter Satanam & poenitentem peccatorem. ... 1545. (Francofurti ex officina Petri Brub. ...) 8°. A-F^{8} G^{6}. [100

-- Erklerung der zwölff artickel Christlichs galubens ... Wittemberg. 1524. 8°. A8 B4 C8 D4 E-F8 G2. [101

-- -- Eyne vorklarynge der twelff Artikel der Christiliken louen ... 1525. (Gedrückt to Erfford dorch Iohannem Loersfelt. ...) 8°. A-E8 F4 G-I8. ¶D8r: Eine korte vorklaringe etliker ... pūcte/ ... to einem rechten vorstande der hilligen schrifft ... [102

-- Ernstliche erbietung der Euangelischē Prediger an den gaystlichen Stand/ die yetzigen leer betreffend. ... [Nürnberg, Friedrich Peypus, 1524.] 4°. A-B4. [103

-- Fulmen in votariam monasticen ... Magdeburgi apud Michaelem Lottherum. M. D. XXXVII. (*Colophon.*) 8°. A8 B4 C8. [104

-- Ain gesprech büchlin/ von ainem Weber vnd ainem Kramer uber das Büchlin Doctoris Mathie Kretz von dem haimlichen Beycht/ so er ... geprediget hat: im M:D:XXiiij. Vtz Rychssner Weber: 4°. A4 B2 C-D4. [105

-- Noua doctrina. ... M. D. XXVI. ... 8°. A-E8. pp. 1-75. [106

-- Opusculum de dignitate sacerdotum ... (In officina excusoria Ioannis Miller Augustæ Vindelicorum .XI. Kalen. Martij. ... 1519.) 4°. a-i4 k6. [107

-- Ain schöner dialogus Cüntz vnnd der Fritz Die brauchent wenig witz ... Vñ sind güt Luthrisch bauren [1522.] 4°. A4. [108

-- Ain Sermon von dem hochwirdigen sacrament des Altars/ gepredigt ... am tag Corporis Christi. M.D.XXi. [Augsburg, Silvan Otmar.] 4°. A6. [109

-- Ain Sermō. Von der kyrchweyche ... M.D.XXII. Jar. 4°. A-B4. [110

-- Vnderricht Wie ain Christenmensch got seinem herren teglich beichten soll ... M.D.XXI (Gedruckt zu Augspurg durch Siluanū Ottmar ...) 4°. a4. [111

-- Vom hochwürdigen Sacrament des Altars: ... [Augsburg, Philipp Ulhart,] M.D.xxiij. ... 4°. a-d4. [112

-- Von leibaygēschaft oder knechthait/ wie sich Herren vnnd eygen leüt Christlich halten sollend/ Bericht ... zü Augspurg gepredigt. M D XXV. 4°. A-E4. [113

-- ... Von Reuw Beicht. Büss. kurtzer beschluss ... Im Jar. M D XXiij. [Augsburg, Melchior Ramminger.] 4°. A-B4. [114

-- Von volkomenhait vnd frucht des leidens Christi/ Sampt erklärung der wort Pauli Colos. 1. ... [Augsburg, Simprecht Ruff, c. 1524.] 4°. A-B4 C2 D4. [115

-- Wider den newē irrsal Doctor Andres von Carlstadt/ des Sacraments halb/ warnung. ... [Augsburg, Simprecht Ruff, 1524.] 4°. A-E4. ¶*T.p. border defective.* [116

RHENANUS, BEATUS. Ioannis Geileri Caesaremontani ... vita. ... [1510.] 4°. a6. [117

-- Beati Rhenani Selestadiensis rerum Germanicarum libri tres ... Vita Beati Rhenani, à Ioanne Sturmio ... conscripta. Basileae, M D LI ... (... per Hieronymum Frobenium, et Nicolaum Episcopium, mense Martio ...) fol. A-D6 a-q6 r8. pp. 2-206. [118

RHODES. Warhafftige Newe zeytung/ der ... belegerung vnd Bestreyttung/ der ... Stat Rhodiss/ So der herr der Turcken ... zweyvnndtzweintzigsten jars furgenomen vnd gethan hat. [1523.] fol. A4. [119

RHODIUS, W. Das die Magdeburger nicht vmb Weltliche sachen/ oder Pfaffengüter ... verfolget werden. ... Magdeburg/ Anno M. D. LI. (Gedruckt ... bey Christian Rödinger. ...) 4°. A-C4 D2. [120

RHYS, JOHN DAVID. Cambrobrytannicæ Cymræcæue linguae institutiones et rudimenta ... conscripta à Ioanne Dauide Rhaeso Monensi Lanuaethlæo ... Londini Excudebat Thomas Orwinus. 1592. fol. *-3*4 (-3*4, *errata, but with the following folded leaf*) A-Z4 (I3 + *folded leaf*) Aa-Pp4 (-Pp4, *presumably blank*). pp. 1-304. *S.T.C.* 20966. [121

RIBADENEYRA, PEDRO DE. La vie du R. Pere Ignace de Loyola ... Nouuellement traduicte du Latin du ... Pere Pierre Ribadanera ...: & enrichie de plusieurs choses tirees du ... P. Pierre Maffee ... En Auignon, De l'Imprimerie de Iaques Bramereau. 1599. 8°. ā8 A-Oo8 Pp2. pp. 1-594. [122

-- La vie du ... Pere Iaques Laynez Second General De La Compagnie de Iesus. Auec vn sommaire de la vie du R.P. Salmeron. ... Et nouuellement mise en François. A Lyon, pour Abraham Cloquemin. 1599. 8°. $*^8$ A-P^8 Q^4. pp. 1-248. [123

RIBSCH, HEINRICH. Disceptatio. an vxor sit ducēda in publica disputatione Lipsensi enarrata a magistro Henrico Ribsch philocalo Budingio. (Impressum Nürmberge p̲ venerabile Dñm Io. W[eissenberger].) 4°. B.L. A-B^6 C^4. ¶*Dedicatee's letter dated:* Septimo Idus Octobris Anno. 1509. [124

RICARDUS ANGLUS. I. Correctorium alchymiae Richardi Anglici. Das ist. Reformirte Alchimy. II. Rainmundi Lulli Apertorium, & Accuratio Vegetabilium. ... III. Das Kōnigs Gebers auss Hispanien Secretum ... Zu Strassburg bey B. Iobins seligen Erben. Anno M. D. XCVI. 8°.)(^{8} A-T^8. ff. 2-151. ¶D6^v: Ex latino in Germanicum versum & conscriptum per L. Pomisium, ... 1559. (Smith.) [125

RICCARDI, GREGORIO DI. Varii pensier amorosi ... Intitolato Pretiosa Margarita ... M. D. XXXIX. (In Perugia. A instanza d'Hippolito detto Il Ferrarese. ... Dil mese di Zugno.) 8°. A-M^4. ¶*Many lower margins cropped.* [126

RICCHI, AGOSTINO. Comedia ... intittolata i tre tiranni ... M. D. XXXIII. (Stampata in Vinegia per Bernardino de Vitali, Adi xiiij di Settēbre ...) 4°. A-B^4 a-q^4. [127

RICCHIERI, LODOVICO, of Rovigo. Lodouici Caelii Rhodigini lectionum antiquarum libri XXX. ... Basileae M D XLII (... per Hier. Frobenium et Nicol. Episcopium ...) fol. α-ο^6 π^4 A-F^6 a-z^6 A-Z^6 aa-zz^6 AA-ZZ^6 aA-eE^6 fF^4 gG^6. pp. 1-1182. [128

-- -- Basileae, per Ambrosium et Aurelium Frobenios fratres. (... M. D. LXVI. mense Martio.) fol. α-ν^6 ξ^8 ρ-υ^6 φ^4 a-z^6 A-Z^6 aa-zz^6 AA-ZZ^6 Aa-Ee^6 Ff^4 Gg^6. pp. 2-1182. [129

RICCHO, ANTONIO. Opera ... Intitulata Fior de Delia. ... (Impressum Venetiis per Maestro Manfredo Bono da Monteferrato da Sustreuo del. M.D.VII. Adi XV del mese de Marzo.) 8°. A-P^4. ¶N1^r: Farsa. O2^r: Farza. [130

-- -- (Impressum Venetiis per Georgio de Rusconi ... M.D.XIIII. Adi .XII. Luglio.) 8°. A-P^4. [131

RICCI, BARTOLOMMEO. Apparatus Latinae locutionis. ... Argentorati apud Mathiam Apiarium M. D. XXXV. (... die quarto Martij.) 4°. π^4 π^{14} a-z^4 A-Zz^4 AA-LL^4 MM^2. pp. 2-605. [132

-- Bartholomaei Riccii de imitatione libri tres ... Venetiis, M. D. XXXXIX. (... per Petrum & Ioānem Mariam Fratres & eius Nepotem de Nicolinis de Sabio. ...) 8°. A-L^8. ff. 3-86. [133

-- Bartholomaei Riccii in Bartholomaei Ferrini funere oratio. ... 4°. A-B^4. [134

RICCOBONI, ANTONIO. Antonii Riccoboni commentarius in vniuersam doctrinam oratoriam Ciceronis ... M. D. XCVI. ... Francofurti, Apud Andreæ Wecheli hæredes Claudium Marnium, & Ioannem Aubrium. 8°. A-Y^8. pp. 3-309. [135

-- De gymnasio Patauino ... Commentariorum Libri Sex ... Patauij, Apud Franciscum Bolzetam. M. D. IIC. ... 4°. $*^4$ ✠^{4} A-Oo^4. ff. 1-148. ¶*Adams* R496. [136

-- Antonii Riccoboni Rhodigini de historia commentarius. Cum fragmentis ... M. Porcii Catonis censorii, Q. Claudii Quadrigarii, L. Sisennae, C. Crispi Salustii, M. Terentii Varronis ... Venetiis, Apud Ioannem Barilettum M D LXVIII. (*Colophon.*) 8°. A-MM^8 $*^4$. ff. 2-278. [137

-- -- ... De Historia Liber. Cum fragmentis historicorum veterum Latinorum ... Basileae Ex Officina Petri Pernæ Anno M. D. LXXIX. 8°.):(^{8} a-z^8 Aa-Kk^8 Ll^4. pp. 1-513. [138

RICHARD OF ST. VICTOR. Richardii Sancti Victoris ... omnia opera ... Prostant Lugduni apud Iacobum Giunti. 1534 (... excudebāt ... Nicolaus Petit/ ꝛ Hector Penet ...) fol. B.L. aa^6 a-c^8 d-z^6 A-K^6. ff. j-cciij. [139

RICHARD, JEAN. Cagasanga reistro Suyssolansqnettorum. Per Magistrum Ioannem Baptistam Lichiardum Recatholicatum Spalipercinum Poëtam. Parisiis, Apud Ioannem Richerium ... 1588. 12°. F^{12}. ff. 2-9. [140

RICHARDOT, FRANÇOIS. Oratio habita in sessione octaua, ... Concilii ... Tridentini ... M. D. LXIII. Brixiae. Ad instantiam Io: Baptistae Bozolæ. M. D. LXIII. (... apud Ludouicum Sabiensem.) 4°. A^{4}. (Lea.) [141

RICHEOME, LOUIS. Apologia Societatis Iesu in Gallia ... Scripta à religiosis eiusdem societatis ...: et hoc anno 1599. Burdegalæ excusa. Nunc primùm Latinè reddita. ... Ingolstadii. Ex Typographia Adami Sartorii. ... M. D. XCIX. 8°. A-H^{8}. pp. 1-120. ¶*Translator: Jakob Gretser.* [142

RICHIER, CHRISTOPHE. De rebus Turcarũ ... libri quinque: Christophoro Richerio Thorigneo Senone ... authore. ... Parisiis. Ex officina Rob. Stephani ... M. D. XL. (... III. Non. Martii.) 4°. a^{4} b-h^{8} i^{4}. pp. 3-115. [143

RICHIUS, JOANNES. Epithalamium de nuptiis ... Iohannis Ernesti, Ducis Saxoniæ, ... Et ... Ducissæ Brunsuicensis & Luneburgensis. ... VVitembergæ. Anno M. D. XLII. 4°. A^{4} B^{2}. [144

RICHLICHIUS, ANDREAS. Diuus Paulus apostolus, et Iudas Iscariotes, proditor ... adducti. ... Wirceburgi, Ex Officina Typographica Henrici Aquensis. 1591. 4°. †^{4} A-M^{4}. [145

RICHTER, MATTHIAS. De vera pace ecclesiae, et de seditione duplici ecclesiastica, et, politica, libelli duo ... per Matthaeum Iudicem. ... Anno M. D. LXVI. 8°. A-F^{8}. pp. 3-93. [146

RICIUS, PAULUS. In apostolorum simbolum (iuxta peripateticorum dogma dialogus ... (Augustæ vindelicæ officina [Johannis Miller] ... exaratũ ... Anno ... sesquimillesimo .XIIII. Pridie Nonas Apriles.) 4°. a^{8} b-k^{4} l^{6} (-l6, *presumably blank*). [147

RICOLDUS DE MONTECRUCIS. Contenta Ricoldi ... contra sectam Mahumeticam ... Libellus. Cuiusdam diu captiui Turcorũ ... de vita & moribus eorundem ... libellus ... Adiũct^{9} est ĩsup libell^{9} de vita & morib^{9} Iudæorũ. (... impressorũ Parisijs ĩ officina Henrici Stephani ... M D XI. 16. Aprilis.) 4°. a-h$^{4.8}$ i^{4} k^{6} l^{4}. ff. 2-62. ¶*Lacks the* Libellus de vita & moribus Judaeorum. [148

RIDOLFI, LUCA ANTONIO. Ragionamento hauuto in Lione, da Claudio de Herberè gentil'huomo Franzese, & da Alessandro degli Vberti, gentil'huomo Fiorentino, sopra alcuni luoghi del Cento Nouelle del Boccaccio. ... In Lione, Appresso Guglielmo Rouillio. 1557. 4°. A-N^{4} (-N4, *presumably blank*). pp. 3-100. [149

-- -- In Lione, appresso Guglielmo Rouillio. M. D. LX. *Same collation and pagination* (-N4). [150

-- Tauola di tutte le rime de i sonetti e canzoni del Petrarca. ... In Venetia, Appresso Nicolò Beuilacqua. M D LXIIII. (*Colophon.*) 12°. a-l^{12}. pp. 3-259. [151

RIDOLFI, PIETRO. Historiarum Seraphicæ religionis libri tres ... A F. Petro Rodulphio Tossinianensi ... Venetijs apud Franciscum de Franciscis Senensem MDLXXXVI. (*Colophon.*) fol. A^{4} b^{8} c^{6} A-K^{6} L^{4} M-BB^{6} CC^{4} DD-3F^{6} *3G^{6} 3G-3M^{6} (-3M6, *presumably blank*). ff. 4-336. ¶*Engraved t.p.* (Lea.) [152

RIEGER, MARTIN. Christliche Hochzeit Predig Vom vngehorsam der Kinder/ so wider den willen der Eltern sich in heiligen Ehestand eintringen. Gehalten zu Augspurg ... den 12. Iunij Anno 1581. ... Getruckt zů Laugingen/ durch Leonhart Reinmichel. 4°. A-B^{4}. [153

-- Ein Christliche Predig Von dem verborgnen Schatz vnd kostlichen Perlein ... Getruckt zu Tũbingen/ bey Alexander Hock/ 1586. 4°. A-B^{4} C^{2}. [154

RIMBERTINUS, BARTHOLOMAEUS. Insignis atq3 preclar^{9} de deliciis sensibilibus paradisi liber: cum singulari tractatu de quattuor inflictibus. Venundatur ab Ioanne paruo ⁊ Iodoco Badio. (... ad sextum idus Martij .mdxiiij. ...) 8°. B.L. π^{4} a-h^{8} i^{4}. ff. i-lxviii. [155

RIME. Delle rime di diuersi nobili huomini ... nella lingua Thoscana. ... Libro secondo. ... In Vinegia appresso Gabriel Giolito de Ferrari MDXLVIII. (*Colophon.*) 8°. A-Aa^{8} (-Aa8, *presumably blank*). ff. 1-177. [156

-- Rime di diuersi antichi autori Toscani ... Di Dante Alaghieri Lib. IIII Di M. Cino da Pistoia Libro I Di Guido Caualcanti Libro I Di Dante da Maiano Libro I Di Fra Guittone d'Arezzo Lib. I Di diuerse Canzoni e Sonetti senza nome d'autore Libro I. (Stampata in Vinegia per Io. Antonio, e Fratelli da Sabio. ... MDXXXII.) 8°. A-S^8 T^4. ff. 2-148. [157

-- Rime di vari autori ... In Oruieto, Per Baldo Saluiani. 1586. 4°. *^{4} A-R^4. pp. 3-152. [158

-- [Libro quarto] delle rime di diuersi eccellentiss. autori nella lingua volgare. ... In Bologna presso Anselmo Giaccarello. M. D. LI. (*Colophon.*) 8°. A-Z^8. pp. 3-328. ¶*Editor: Ercole Bottrigaro. The first two words of the title have been erased.* [159

-- [Rime di diuersi illustri signori Napolitani ... Libro Quinto. ... In Vinegia appresso Gabriel Giolito de Ferrari et fratelli. MDLII.] (*Colophon.*) 8°. *A^8 (-*A1-3) A-EE^8. pp. *1-*10, 1-448. [160

-- Rime diuerse di molti eccell. auttori. In Venetia Ad instantia di Alberto di Gratia detto il Thoscano. 8°. A-C^4. [161

RIMINO, SERAFINO DI. Ethica, et politica sotto breuissime regole ritratte ... da due Orationi D'Isocrate in versi sciolti. In Venetia, Appresso Gio: Antonio Rampazetto. M D LXXXIIII. (*Colophon.*) 4°. A-F^4 G^2. ff. 3-25. [162

RINALDI, GIOVANNI DE'. Il mostruosissimo mostro ... Diuiso in due Trattati. Nel primo de' quali si ragiona del significato de' Colori. Nel secondo si tratta dell'herbe, & Fiori. ... In Ferrara, Ad instanza di Alfonso Caraffa. ... 1588. (... Per Vincenzo Galdura. ...) 8°. A^4 A-I^8 K^4. pp. 1-157. [163

RINGELBERG, JOACHIM FORTIUS. Ioachimi Fortii Ringelbergii Andouerpiani lucubrationes ... nempe liber de Ratione studij ... Basileae. Anno M. D. XLI. (... apud Bartholomeum VVesthemerum ...) 8°. a-z^8 A-Dd^8. pp. 3-796. [164

RINGHIERI, INNOCENTIO. Cento giuochi ... ritrouati ... In Bologna per Anselmo Giaccarelli M. D. LI. (... alle spese dell'authore ... alli. XXV d'Agosto ...) 4°. †^{4} A-SS^4. ff. 1-162. [165

RIVIUS, JOANNES. De Consolandis aegrotantibus, ijsdemq3 ad mortem animandis, Liber ... Basileae [1547]. 8°. A-H^8. pp. 4-113. [166

-- De erroribus pontificiorum, seu de abusibus Ecclesiasticis. ... Basileae [1547]. 8°. Aa-Ee^8. pp. 3-69. [167

-- De seculi nostri felicitate, et hominum erga Dei beneficia ingratitudine, liber. ... [Basileae,] 1548 8°. A-R^8 S^4. pp. 3-259. [168

-- Ioannis Riuii Atthendoriensis, de spectris et apparitionibus vmbrarum, seu de vetere superstitione liber. Anno M.D.XLI. 8°. a-k^8. [169

-- [1] Ioannis Riuij ... de titulo et inscriptione ... Crucis, libellus. Eiusdem, De perpetuo conflicta piorum cum carne, mundo, diabolo ... Basileae. 8°. a-m^8. pp. 4-160. [2] ... de officio pastorali ministrorum Ecclesiae in Pagis. Eiusdem, De uero erga Deum amore, Sermo. 1549. A-L^8 M^4. pp. 3-162. ¶[2] *misbound before* [1]. [170

RIZZONI, MARCO. Marci Veronēsis ... opusculum de oratorio pronunciandi modo. 4°. *8 ll. signed* .I.-.VIII. [171

ROBERT LE MOINE. Historia di Roberto monaco della guerra fatta da principi Christiani, Contra Saracini per l'acquisto di terra Santa, Tradotto per M. Francesco Baldelli. In Fiorenza [per i Giunti] MDLII. ... 8°. A-R^8. pp. 3-272. (Lea.) [172

ROBORTELLO, FRANCESCO. Hilarii Cantiunculae hendacasyllaborum liber. Venetiis. M D LV. (... apud Plinium Petramsanctam ...) 8°. A-H^8. pp. 2-121. [173

ROCCA, ANGELO. Bibliotheca ex praecipuis ... theologis, quos scripturales vocant: ... A ... Angelo Rocchensi ... compilata ... Romae. Ex Typographia Vincentij Accolti. M. D. LXXXIII. 4°. A-H^4. [174

-- Osseruationi intorno alle bellezze della lingua Latina ... In Venetia, CIƆ.IƆ.XC. Presso Aldo. 8°. A-Cc^8. pp. 3-375. [175

ROCCHETTA, AGOSTINO. Rime ... In Fiorenza appresso Lorenzo Torrentino MDLVIII. (*Colophon.*) 8°. A-E^8. pp. 3-74. [176

ROCHUS, PERUSINUS. Rochi Perusini de epistola componenda Liber. Editio Tertia. ... Dilingae Excudebat Ioannes Mayer. cIɔ. Iɔ. XXCVIII. 8°. A-P^8. pp. 1-237. [177

RODOANO, GUGLIELMO. Tractatus ... de rebus ecclesiae non alienandis ... Gulielmi Redoani ... Placentiae Apud Franciscum Comitem. 1572. fol. *^{4} A-4F^4 (-A2, A3). pp. 1-600. (Lea.) [178

-- Tractatus de simonia ... Auctore ... Gulielmo Redoano. ... Ex officina Dominici Guerrei, & Io. Baptistæ fratrum. Venetiis, M.D.LXV. 4°. a^4 b-e^8 A-Xx^8 Yy^4. ff. 1-356. (Lea.) [179

-- Tractatus de spoliis ecclesiasticis in quo ... omnes species bonorum per prælates occasione ecclesiæ comparatorum, per mortem relictorum, Spolia nuncupatorum tractantur ... Romæ, Ex Officina Bartholomæi Grassi, M. D. LXXXV. (... Ex Typographia Vincentij Accolti ...) 4°. +^{4} A^8 B-E^4 F-KK^8. pp. 2-457. (Lea.) [180

RODELLA, GIUSEPPE. Sermoni diuersi da nozze, da conuiuio, da communione, et anco da morti. ... In Venetia, Appresso Domenico Nicolino. M D LXV. 8°. A-E^8 F^4. ff. 2-40. [181

RODRIGUEZ DE ALMELA, DIEGO. Valerio δlas hystorias escolasticas δla sagrada escritura ⁊ δlos hechos despaña cōlas batallas cāpales. Copiladas por Fernan perez de guzman. ... (Fue impresso enla ... ciudad de Toledo en casa de Iuan de ayala. Acabose a diez dias del mes de Enero. Año de mil ⁊ quinientos ⁊ quarenta ⁊ vn años.) fol. B.L. a^{10} b-l^8. ff. j-lxxxvij. (Lea.) [182

-- Impresso ... en Medina del cāpo. Por Francisco del Canto. Año de M. D. LXXIIII. 8°. A-Oo^8 (-Oo8, *presumably blank*). ff. 9-295. [183

ROEDINGER, JOHANN. Schmeichel oder Fuchsschwentze Teufel/ Das ist/ Klarer Bericht von Schmeichlern ... durch Iohannem Rhodium secundum, Rockhusanum ... (Gedruckt zu Erffurdt/ Durch Esaiam Mechler ... [1581?]) 8°. A^8 A-G^8 H^4. [184

ROESSLIN, EUCHARIUS. De partu hominis, et quae circa ipsum accidunt. Libellus D. Eucharij Rhodionis, Medici. Franc. Chri. Egen. [1532.] 8°. A-K^8. ¶K8 *repaired.* [185

-- -- The birth of mankynde, otherwyse named the womans booke. ... By Thomas Raynalde Phisition. [London, Richard Jugge.] (1565.) 4°. B.L. A^4 B-G^8 H^{8+2} I^8 K^{8+2} L-S^8 T^6. ff. i-Cxxxi. *S.T.C.* 21157. [186

ROFFIGNAC, CHRISTOPHE DE. Commentarii omnium a creato orbe historiarum. Christophoro Roffin. ... auctore. ... Lutetiae, M. D. LXXI. Apud Ioannem Bene natum. ... 4°. ā^4 ē^4 a-z^4 A-Z^4 aa-zz^4 AA-DD^4 EE^2. pp. 1-500. [187

ROJAS, JUAN. De hæreticis, vnà cum quinquaginta Analyticis assertionibus, & priuilegijs inquisitorum. ... (Valentiae, ... Ex typographia Petri à Huete, ... 1572.) 8°. ℭ^{10} A-Gg^8. pp. 1-480. (Lea.) [188

ROJAS, MARTIN. Oratio D. F. Martini Roias Portalrubei ... Tridenti in generali congregatione, Die VII. Mensis Septembris. M. D. LXIII. habita. Brixiae ad instantiam Io: Baptistae Bozolae. M. D. LXIII. 4°. A^4. (Lea.) [189

ROLLENHAGEN, GEORG. Froschmeuseler Der Frosch vnd Meuse wunderbare Hoffhaltunge. ... Gedruckt zu Magdeburgk/ durch Andream Duncker/ ... 1600. 8°. A-3C^8 3D^6. [190

-- Der post Reutter bin ich genandt/ Dem Hinckenden Bothen wol bekandt. ... 1590. 4°. A-F^4. [191

ROMANUS, ADRIANUS. Parvum theatrum urbium sive urbium praecipuarum ... Descriptio. ... Francoforti Ex officina Typographica Nicolai Bassæi. Anno M. D. XCV. 4°.):(^{4} A-3C^4 3D^2. pp. 2-365. [192

-- -- *Another copy.* (Fine Arts.) [193

ROME. [1] S: P: Q: R: Statuta et nouæ reformationes vrbis Romæ ... in sex libros diuisa ... (Impressum per ... Stephanū Guillereti ... M.D.XXIII. Quarto Kal'. Iulias ...) fol. A-G^6 H^8 AA-PP^6 QQ^{10} RR^8 a-c^6 d^4. ff. 1-44, 1-31, 1-67, 1-21. ¶*Lacks book 6* (a-g^6). [2] Noua vrbis Romæ statuta super causis ciuilibus ... (Impressum Rome apud Stephanum Guillireti ... M.D.XXI. die xxviii. Mensis Septembris ...) a-c^6 (-b3, b4). ff. 2-16. (Lea.) [194

-- [1] Statuta almae vrbis Romae ... Romae, In Aedibus Populi Romani. M D LXXX. fol. [a]^4 b^6 A-P^4 Q^2 R-Dd^4 χ^2. pp. 2-210. [2] Gratiae immunitates, & facultates per summos Romanos Pontifices ... concessæ. A-L^4. pp. 1-88. (Lea.) [195

-- Statuta almae vrbis Romae ... Romæ, in ædibus Populi Romani. Apud Georgium Ferrarium. M. D. XC. (*Colophon.*) fol. a-b^4 A-Tt^4. pp. 1-301. (Lea.) [196

-- Iacobus ... Cardinalis Sabellus ... Vicarius Generalis ... [Publishes a decree of the Council of Trent concerning marriages.] Romae. Apud Antonium Bladum ... 1564. fol. π^2. (Yarnall.) [196a

-- Reformatione ⁊ Tassa delli pagamenti de farsi alli Guardiani delle Carcare, & Esecutori. Romae. Apud Antonium Bladum ... 1564. fol. π^2. ¶*Issued by Cardinal Guido Ascanio Sforza, papal chamberlain.* (Yarnall.) [196b

-- *Archiconfraternità della Pieta de Carcerati.* Statuti della venerabile Archicompagnia della Pieta de Carcerati di Roma. ... (In Rome, Appresso Giouanni Osmarino Gigliotto. M.D.LXXXIII.) fol. A-K^4 L^6. pp. 1-79. (Lea.) [197

-- *Compagnia del Santissimo Sacramento.* Statuti o ver constitutioni della Compagnia del Santissimo Sacramento, Eretta nella Chiesa di san Pietro di Roma sotto Papa Paolo III. ad eccitare la deuotione del Popolo. In Roma per Antonio Blado ... 4°. A-B^4. (Lea.) [198

-- *History.* Warhafftige vnnd kurtze bericht Inn der Summa/ wie es ietzo/ im Tausent Funff hundert vñ Siben vnd zwayntzigsten Jar Den vj. tag May/ durch Rômischer Kayserlicher/ vnd Hispanischer Küniglicher Mayestet kriegs volck/ In eroberunng der Stat Rom ergangen ist/ biss auff den xxj. tage Iunij. [Augsburg, Heinrich Steiner, 1527.] 4°. A-C^4. [199

-- Warhafftige Newe Zeitung/ Was sich fůr Empôrung nach des Bapsts Pauli des iiij. Todt ... zu Rom zugetragen hat ... Vom Rom geschriben an einen guten Freundt in Deudtschlande. 4°. π^4. ¶*Dated 19 August 1559.* [200

ROME, CHURCH OF. Calendarium ad vsum Romanum. Antuerpiae, Ex officina Christophori Plantini. 1566. 8°. A^8. [201

-- Hoc in libello omnes continentur Patriarchatus, Archiepātus. Metropoles. ac Episcopatus: totius Catholice ecclesie ... (Vindelice Auguste jmpressit mḡr joħes Otmar Anno Millesimo quingentesimo quinto ⁊c̄.) 4°. B.L. A^6. (Lea.) [202

-- *Cancellaria Apostolica.* Regule Cācellarie cum Commento ⁊ cum Priuilegio. (Impressum Rome ... per ... Eucharium Zilber alias Frāck. Anno. Mccccciiii. die. v. mensis Iunii. ...) 4°. B.L. a-l^6 m^8. [203

-- Regulae: ordinationes ⁊ Constitutiones Cancellariæ ... Pauli ... Pape. III. in Cancellaria Apost. Lactaę & publicatę Anno M.D..XXXIIII. ([H4^v] Romae apud Valerium Doricum.) 4°. A-N^4. ¶*Additional t.p.* (I1): Regulae Quinque Cācellariæ Apostolicæ ... (Lea.) [204

-- [1] Regulæ omnes, ordinationes, et constitutiones Cancellariæ ... Pauli ... Papæ IIII. ... Parisiis, Apud Viduam Francisci Renauld ... 1555. 4°. A-H^4. ff. 2-32. [2] Duae regulae cancellariae, prior moderatio & ampliatio indultorum ... Romanæ Ecclesiæ Cardinalium. Altera, reseruatio mensium Apostolicorum ... per ... Paulum ... Papam IIII. 1555. A-B^4. ff. 2-8. (Lea.) [205

-- Prouinciale omnium ecclesiarum cathedralium vniuersi orbis. Cum cuiusque regionis monetæ nomenclatura ac ualore, nuper ex libro Cancellariæ Apostolicæ excerptum. Brixiae ad instantiam Io: Baptistae Bozolæ. M. D. LXIII. (... apud Ludouicum Sabiensem.) 4°. A-C^4. (Lea.) [206

-- *Camera apostolica.* Capitulatione per il nuouo appalto de le dogane di Roma. A gli xiii. d'Ottobrio. M D LXIIII. [Roma, per Antonio Blado ... MDLXIIII.] fol. π^2. ¶*Printed form with blanks to be filled in.* (Yarnall.) [206a

-- Capitoli del nouo Appalto delle Lumiere. [1565.] fol. A^4. *¶Printed form with blank spaces to be filled in.* (Yarnall.) [206b

-- *Cardinals.* Nomina tituli et appellationes S.R.E. car. nunc viuentium. ... [c. 1515.] 4°. π^2. (Lea.) [207

-- *Collegium Fabricae Basilicae Principis.* In Tertio et Quarto de contrahendo. Collegium Fabrice Basilice Principis Apłoŭ de vrbe ... [A form granting dispensation for marriage in order to raise money for the building of St. Peter's.] [Romae, c. 1510.] s.sh. 21.5 × 35 cm. *¶Engraved on vellum.* [208

-- *Councils.* [1] Conciliorum quatuor generaliũ Niceni, Constātinopolitani, Ephesini, ⁊ Calcedonēsis. ... Tomus primus. Quadraginta quoqȝ septem Cōciliorum prouincialium authenticorum. Decretorum etiam sexaginta nouem pontificum, ... Isidoro authore. Item Bulla Aurea Caroli. iiij. Imperatoris, de electione regis Romanorum. Parisijs. Apud Franciscum Regnault. 1535. 8°. B.L. $A\text{-}C^8$ $a\text{-}z^8$ $A\text{-}R^8$ S^6. ff. i-cccxix. [2] Tomus secundus Cōciliorum generalium. ... *Same imprint.* (... mēse Mayo.) $♣^8$ $aa\text{-}zz^8$ $Aa\text{-}Dd^8$ Ee^6. ff. 1-ccxxij. *¶Editor: Jacques Merlin.* (Lea.) [209

-- *Index librorum prohibitorum.* Index librorum prohibitorum, Cum regulis confectis per Patres a Tridentina Synodo delectos ... Venetiis, Apud Andream Muschium. 1565. (*Colophon.*) 12°. $A\text{-}B^{12}$ C^{10}. ff. 2-34. (Lea.) [210

-- Index auctorum et librorum, qui ab officio sanctae Rom. & vniuersalis Inquisitionis caueri ab omnibus ... mandātur ... 8°. *¶Collation uncertain because of shaved margins; perhaps* A^8 B^6. *A copy of the so-called index of Paul IV, probably printed at Rome by Antonio Blado or his heirs some time after 1559.* (Lea.) [211

-- Index librorum prohibitorum, cum regulis confectis per patres a Tridentina synodo delectos ... Cum Appendice in Belgio, ex mandato Regiæ Cathol. Maiestatis confecta. Antuerpiæ. Ex officina Christophori Plantini. M. D. LXX. 8°. $A\text{-}G^8$. pp. 3-108. (Lea.) [212

-- -- *Another copy.* (Yarnall.) [212a

-- Index et catalogus Librorum prohibitorum, mandato ... Gasparis a Quiroga, ... in regnis Hispaniarum Generalis Inquisitoris, denuò editus. ... Madriti Apud Alphonsum Gomezium ... M.D.LXXXIII. ... (*Colophon.*) 4°. A^4 $*^2$ $A\text{-}M^8$. ff. 1-96. (Lea.) [213

-- -- *Another copy.* (Lea.) [214

-- Index expurgatorius librorum qui hoc seculo prodierunt ... concinnatus, anno MDLXXI. Apud Ioannem Mareschallum Lugdunensem MDLXXXVI. 16°. $A\text{-}Y^8$. pp. 1-292. (Lea.) [215

-- Index librorum prohibitorum cum regulis confectis Per Patres à Tridentina Synodo delectos ... Romæ, apud Impressores Cam. ... 1596. 12°. $A\text{-}D^{12}$ E^2 (-E2, *presumably blank*). pp. 3-98. (Lea.) [216

-- -- *Another copy.* (Lea.) [217

-- -- Romae, Apud Impressores Camerales. ... 1596. 8°. $A\text{-}D^8$. pp. 3-64. (Lea.) [218

-- -- Vrbini Apud Bartholomæum, & Simonem Ragusios fratres. 1596. ... (*Colophon.*) 8°. $A\text{-}H^8$ I^4. ff. 1-50. (Lea.) [219

-- -- Romae, Et Ferrariȩ, Apud Victoriũ Baldinum. ... M.D.XCIX. 8°. $A\text{-}H^8$. pp. 1-125. (Lea.) [220

-- Index expurgatorius librorum qui hoc sæculo prodierunt ... concinnatus: anno MDLXXI. ... Præfatio Doct. Ioannis Pappi ... [Argentorati,] Impensis Lazari Zetzneri. Anno 1599. 12°. $)($ ^{12} $A\text{-}R^{12}$ S^4. pp. 1-363. (Lea.) [221

-- *Inquisition.* Repertorium inquisitorum prauitatis haereticae. ... Correctionibus, & Annotationibus ... Quintilliani Mandosij, ac Petri Vendrameni ... auctum. ... Venetiis, M. D. LXXXVIII. Apud Damianum Zenarum. (*Colophon.*) 4°. $+^8$ $A\text{-}3D^8$. pp. 1-797. (Lea.) [222

-- -- *Another copy.* (Lea.) [223

-- Die Artickelen ende besluyten der Inquisitie van Spaegnien/ om die vande Nederlanden te overvallen ende verhunderen. (Aldus gheoordelt inder Stadt van Madril den 16. dach Februarij Anno 1568.) 4°. A^2. (Lea.) [224

-- -- *Another copy.* (Lea.) [225

-- *Liturgies.* Missale scd'm vsum Carmelitaꝝ cum annotationibus ... Venalia reperiuntur ... ad intersignum diui Claudij [Parisiis, Franciscus Regnault, 1512]. 8°. 1-5^{8} a-n^{8} o^{12} p-z^{8} ꝛ^{8} ꝯ^{8} ꝝ^{8} A-F^{8} G^{10} ✠^{4}. pp. cxj-cclxvj. [226

-- Missale Romanum ... Venetiis, Apud Iohannem Variscum, & Pagninum de Paganinis. (... M. D. LXXXV.) 4°. B.L. a-c^{8} A-Kk^{8} Ll^{4}. pp. 1-534. (Yarnall.) [226a

-- [1] Sequẽtiarum lucul ẽta interpretatio ... ꝑ Ioan. adelphū physicū Argẽtiñ. collecta. Anno dñi. M.D.XIII. 4°. B.L. a^{8} b-y$^{8.4.4}$ z^{8}. ff. III-CXXXVI. [2] De ... diue virginis Marie Psalterio: triplex Hecatosticō Hermanni Buschij monasteriensis. cum quibus alijs carminibus. Ma. Diui Cipriani ... de ligno salutifere crucis carmen heroicū Claudiani ... inuocatio ad Christum pro Theodosio cesare Augusto. A-B^{6}. [3] Hymni de tempore ꝛ de sanctis ... Anno dñi. M.D.XIII. (Impressi per Ioannem knoblouch ... Argentinoꝝ impressorem: Vltima die Martij ...) C^{4} D-P$^{8.4.4}$ Q-R^{8}. ff. I-LXXX. [227

-- Sequentie de tempore & sanctis per totum annum. Anno dñi. M.D.XVI. (Impressum Argentinæ per Iohannem Knoblouch. ... XVII. die Iulij.) 4°. a^{4} b^{8} c^{4} d^{8} e^{6}. ff. I-XXV. [228

-- Rituum ecclesiasticorum siue sacrarum cerimoniarum .S.S. Romanæ ecclesiæ libri tres ... (Gregorii de Gregoriis Excussere ... Venetiis .M.D.XVI. Die .XXI. Mensis Nouembris.) fol. ✠^{6} A-G^{8} H-I^{6} K-R^{8} S-T^{6} (-T6, *presumably blank*). ff. I-CXLIII. ¶*By Agostino Patrizio Piccolomini.* (Yarnall.) [228a

-- Martyrologium Romanum ... Gregorii XIII. Pont. Max. issu editum. Accesserunt notationes ... Auctore Caesare Baronio Sorano ... Romae Ex Typographia Dominici Basæ. M D LXXXVI. fol. a-b^{6} c^{4} A-3I^{6} 3K^{4} (-3K4, *presumably blank*). pp. II-XXIV, 2-588. ¶3C4 *ff. defective.* (Yarnall.) [229

-- Martyrologio Romano. ... Publicado por mandado de Gregorio. XIII. ... Traduzido ... de lẽgua Latina en la Españ ola: por ... Dionysio Vazquez ... Impresso, en Valladolid por Diego Fernandez de Cordoua ... M. D. LXXXVI. 4°. ¶¶^{4} ¶¶-3¶^{4} A^{4} B-Mm^{8} Nn^{4}. ff. 1-212. [229a

-- *Constitutions.* Die verteütschtẽ Text aus den Bebstlichen Rechten: vnd vil andren glaubwirdigen geschrifftẽ ... [Strassburg, Johann Knoblauch, 1521.] 4°. A-E^{4} F^{6}. [230

-- Collectio diuersarum constitutionum et litterarum Rom. pont. A Gregorio VII. usque ad ... Gregorium XIII. ... Romae Apud heredes Antonij Bladij ... M.D.LXXIX. ... fol. a^{4} A-4V^{4} A-F^{4} A-DD^{4} EE^{2} a-b^{4} A-I^{4} K^{4}. pp. 1-711, 1-220, 1-76. (Lea.) [231

-- *Rota.* Decisiones reuerendorum Patrum Dominorum Rotæ ... annotationibus ad ipsas studio Camilli Melle ... exornatæ. ... (Venetiis, apud Michaelem Tramezinum M D L. ... M D LI.) fol. *-3*^{4} A-D^{4} A-Q^{6} (-Q6, *presumably blank*) A-T^{6} V^{4} A-C^{4} D^{6} (-D6, *presumably blank*). ff. 1-15, 1-95, 1-118, 1-17. (Lea.) [232

-- Decisiones sacrae rotae ... Per R.P.D. Cæsarem de Grassis ... Bononiensem ... lucubratæ. Quas ab Auctoris ei proposito exemplari, Paulus Granuccius ... descripsit ... Romae, Apud Paulum Bladum ... M. D. LXXXX. (*Colophon.*) fol. ✠-✠✠^{4} A-Ff^{4} a-c^{4} d^{6}. pp. 2-231. (Lea.) [233

-- Decisiones sacrae rotae compendiariae ... Per R.P.D. Achillem de Grassis ... Bononiensem ... lucubratæ. Quas ab Auctoris exemplari ei proposito Paulus Granuccius ... descripsit ... Romae, Apud Paulum Bladum ... M. D. LXXXX. (*Colophon.*) fol. †-††^{4} a-x^{4} A-D^{4} E^{6}. pp. 2-167. (Lea.) [234

-- *Nicholas I, pope.* Nicolai primi pont. maximi epistolae. Romae apud Franciscum Priscianensem. M.D.XLII. fol. π^{6} A-O^{6}. pp. II-CLXVII. [235

-- -- Antiqua et insignis Epistola Nicolai Pape. i. Ad Michaelem Imperatorẽ ... Eiusdem Nicolai PP. Decreta ... Breuis historiarū illius tẽporis cōmemoratio, ex Reginone ... Defensio Ioannis Episcopi Roffeñ & Thome Mori, aduersus Richardum samsonem Anglū. per Ioannem Cochleum. Fragmenta quarundã Tho. Mori Epistolarum ad Erasmum Rot. & ad Ioannem Coc, Lipsiae MDXXXVI Ex Officina Melchioris Lottheri. (*Colophon.*) 4°. A-Cc^{4} Dd^{6}. [236

-- *Gregory IX, pope.* Decretales Gregorii noni pontificis ... Lugduni, Apud Hugonem à Porta, & Antonium Vincentium. M. D. LVIII. ... (... Excudebat Petrus Fradin.) 4°. aa-dd^{8} ee^{2} a-z^{8} A-Z^{8} Aa-Zz^{8} AA-CC^{8}. pp. 1-1151. (Lea.) [237

-- -- Decretales ... Venetiis, Apud Iuntas. M D XCV. fol. a-c^{8} d^{4} ++^{4} A-4Q^{8} 4R^{10}. pp. 1-1388. (Lea.) [238

-- *Boniface VIII, pope.* [Decretalia.] (per Ioannes: Amorbachium/ Petri ⁊ Froben impressus: ... M.D.xi. ...) fol. B.L. [1] Sextus decretalium liber a Bonifacio .VIII. in concilio Lugdunensi editus Cum Glossematū diuisionibus: que ex nouella Iohānis andree ... sunt ... apposite. Interpretamētis dñi Helie et Dominici de sancto Geminiano. ... (... ad tertiū decimū Kal'. decēbres.) π^{6} a-y^{8} z^{6} (-z6). ff. 1-177. [2] Clementis Quinti constitutiones in concilio viennensi edite. Cum ... Additionibus Ioānis de Imola et Francisci Zabarelle. ... (... ad .xvii. kl's. nouēbris. ...) A-I^{8} K^{4}. ff. 2-72. [3] Extrauagātes viginti Iohānis vigesimisecundi. Cum Interpretamentis Domini Zenzelini et Iohānis Francisci de Pauinis. ... AA-EE^{8}. ff. 2-39. [4] Extrauagantes cōmunes ... cū glossis ⁊ interpretatione dñi Guillermi de monte ... cū glossa ... Ioannis monachi ... ⁊ petri presbyteri ... cū cōmentario dñi Ioānis francisci de pauinis ... Additio insup ... Petri bertrandi ... Aa-Dd^{8} Ee^{10} (-Ee10, *presumably blank*). ff. 2-39. (Lea.) [239

-- -- (Venetiis nup īpressus per heredes ... Octauiani Scoti ...) 4°. B.L. [1] (... M.CCCCCXXV. Decīo cal. decēbris.) A-II^{8} KK-LL^{10}. ff. 2-276. [2] MM-3B^{8}. ff. 1-112. [3] (... M.ccccc.xxiij. die .xviij. Augusti.) 3C-3K^{8}. ff. 2-64. [4] (... M.CCCCCXXV. decimo calendas Decembres.) 3L-3S^{8}. ff. 1-64. [5] Constitutiones domini Eugenij .iiij. ... Bulla Iulij .ii. de electiōe romani pōtificis ... Item bulla eiusdem de concessione testandi edificantibus in vrbe ... 3T^{12} (-3T12, *presumably blank*). ff. 2-11. (Biddle.) [240

-- -- Venetiis, MDLXVII. 4°. [1] aa-bb^{8} cc^{2} a-x^{8} (+ 2 *inserted tables*) y-z^{8} A-F^{8}. pp. 1-463. [2] AA^{8} aa-mm^{8}. pp. 1-191. [3, 4] ... Venetiis, MDLXVI. (... MDLXVII.) π^{2} 3a^{8} AA-QQ^{8} RR^{4}. pp. 1-262. (Lea.) [241

-- -- [1] Liber sextus decretalium ... Venetiis, Apud Iuntas. M D XCV. fol. †^{4} A-Oo^{8}. pp. 1-592. [2] Clementis papae V. constitutiones ... *Same imprint.* A-D^{8} P^{10}. pp. 5-243. [3] Extrauagantes tum viginti D. Ioannis papae XXII. tum communes ... *Same imprint.* P11-12 a-q^{8} r^{4} s-t^{8}. pp. 1-262. (Lea.) [242

-- *Clement V, pope.* [1] Tabula Clementinarum. fol. B.L. ₡₡^{4}. ff. 1-4. [2] Clementinarum constitutiones ... Clementis pape quinti constitutiones vna cum profundo apparatu dñi Ioannis Andree. ... A-I^{8}. ff. 2-71. [3] Tabula Extrauagantium .xx. Ioannis .xxij. 3₡^{2}. [4] Extrauagantes .xx. Ioannis .xxii. AA-EE^{8}. ff. 2-40. [5] Tabula extrauagantium cōmunium. 4₡^{2}. ff. 1-2. [6] Extrauagantes communes. 3A-3C^{8} 3D^{4} (-3D4). ff. 2-27. ¶*Perhaps part of an edition of the decretals of Boniface VIII.* (Lea.) [243

-- *Pius II, pope.* Pii papae II bulla retractationum omnium, dudum, per eum in Minoribus adhuc agentem ... Brixiae: Ad instantiam Io: Baptistæ Bozole. M. D. LXIII. (... apud Ludouicum Sabiensem.) 4°. A-B^{4}. (Lea.) [244

-- *Innocent VIII, pope.* Bulla Innocenti octaui. 4°. π^{4}. ¶*Dated Sexto Idus Maij 1488.* [245

-- -- *Another copy.* (Lea.) [246

-- *Julius II, pope.* Bulla Prima Annatarum. (Impresse Rome in Campo flore [per Eucharium Silber].) 4°. B.L. π^{4}. ¶*Dated 5 Kal. Augusti 1505.* π3^{r}: Bulla Secunda Annatarum. [247

-- Sanctissimi D. Iulij Papæ II. Litteræ quibus olim confirmauit erectionem Monte Pietatis Ciuit. Bononiæ. (Dat. Bonon. Anno ... Millesimo Quingentesimo sexto, decimo Calendas Martij ...) 4°. A^{4}. (Lea.) [248

-- Monitorium contra Venetos (Impssum Rome per ... Iacobū Mazochiū ... Anno Sexto [1509].) 4°. A^{10} (-A10, *presumably blank*). [249

-- -- Bulla intimatiōis generalis Concilii apud Lateranum per ... Iuliū Papā .ii. edita. (Impressum Rome per Iacobum Mazochium ... Vltima Iulii [1511].) 4°. a^{4} b^{6}. ¶a1^{v} *blank.* [250

-- -- Bulla intimatiōis ... per ... Iuliuȝ Papam .ii. edita. *Same colophon.* 4°. A^{4} b^{6}. ¶A1^{v}: *certificate of Hieronymus de Ghinucciis, papal auditor.* (Lea.) [251

-- Bulla monitorii apostilici contra tres ... cardinales vt redeant ad obedintiam S.D.N. pape ne scisma in ecclesia sanacta [*sic*] Dei oriatur. 4°. A-B^{4}. ¶B3^{v}: Datū Romæ ... M.CCCCC.XI Quinto Kal' Augusti. (Lea.) [252

-- Bulla super sententia priuationis in publico consistorio facte ꝑ S.D.N. Contra .D. Ber. Caruaialē Guillermū Brizonettū et Frāciscū de Borgia olim S.R.E. Cardinales ad furam rei memoriam. [Romae, Marcellus Silber? 1511.] 4°. A⁴ b-c⁴. (Lea.) [253

-- Bulla Monitorii ⁊ declarationis in cursus priuatiōis ⁊ aliaꝝ penaꝝ: cōtra prelatos Gallice natiōis hic expressos: qui interuenerūt in Pisano cōciliabulo cū Scismaticis. [Romae, Joannes Beplin, 1511.] 4°. A⁶. (Lea.) [254

-- Iulii Secundi Pontificis Max. decretū ...: ī Quinta Sessione Sacri Cōcilii Lateraneñ. de Creatione sūmi Pont. approbatū. [Romae, Marcellus Silber, 1512.] 4°. A⁶. (Lea.) [255

-- Bulla vltima conuocationis et inuitationis cardinalium absentium et prelatorum Gallice nationis ad celebrationem concilii Lateranen. cum declaratione nullitatis gestorum per conciliabulum Pisanum per ... Iulium .II. Pont. Max. edita. [Romae, Joannes Beplin, 1512.] 4°. π⁴. ¶*Isaac 12072A.* (Lea.) [256

-- Bulla Secunde sessionis ... Concilii Lateraneñ. approbans ⁊ renouans damnationeȝ ⁊ reprobationem Pisani Conciliabuli: ⁊ annullans omnia ⁊ singula in illo gesta ⁊ gerenda: celebrate die .xvii. Maii. M.d.xii. [Romae, Marcellus Silber, 1512.] 4°. π⁴. (Lea.) [257

-- Publicatio Sanctissimi federis inter S.d.n. Iulium Secundum Pont. Max. ac ... Maximilianū Electum Imp. ... [Romae, Marcellus Silber, 1512.] 4°. π⁴. (Lea.) [258

-- Bulla tertie sessionis habite in ... Concilio lateraneñ. tertio noñ. Decēbris. M.D.xii. ... [Romae, Joannes Beplin, 1512.] 4°. π⁴. (Lea.) [259

-- Bulla Quarte Sessionis habite in ... Cōcilio Lateraneñ. Quarto Idus Decemb. M.d.xii ... [Romae, Marcellus Silber, 1512.] 4°. π⁴. (Lea.) [260

-- Cedula Quinte Sessionis prorogationis in causis Reformationis ⁊ Pragmatice Sanctionis: habite in ... Concilio Lateraneñ. Quartodecimo Kal' Martii. M.d.xii. ... [Romae, Marcellus Silber, 1513.] 4°. π². (Lea.) [261

-- Intimatione Della Bolla di Papa Iulio II. Che nissuno debba vsare, e conuertire Denari, e Robbe del Monte di Pietà in altri maneggi, se non per seruitio, & vso si esso Monte. (In Bologna, per Alessandro Benacci. 1586. ...) 4°. s. sh. 20.5 × 14.5 cm. [262

-- *Leo X, pope.* Bulla Leonis PP. X. super erectioñ. ac vnioñ. quarumdā ecclesiarū & Iuris concessionis patronatus, ac presentādi ad illas in fauorem ... Comitum Pallauicinorum de Curte Maiori placentiñ. Diocesis. fol. A². ¶*Dated 15 Kal. Maii 1513.* [262a

-- Bulla Sexte Sessionis: habite in ... Concilio Lateraneñ. Quinto Kal'. Maii .M.D.xiii. ... [Romae, Marcellus Silber, 1513.] 4°. π⁴. (Lea.) [263

-- Edictum ... Leonis Pape .X. super prorogatione Lateraneñ. Concilii. [Romae, Marcellus Silber, 1513.] 4°. π². (Lea.) [264

-- Tres Deputationes facte per S. dñm nostrum ... Cardinalium/ & Prelatoꝝ per Concilium electoꝝ ... super diuersis materiis & negociis tractādis & expediendis in Concilio Lateraneñ. ... [Romae, Marcellus Silber, 1513.] 4°. π⁴. (Lea.) [265

-- Bulla Continens materiam Pragmatice/ Reformationis Curie Romañ. Officialium ... lecta Die. XVII. Iunii. M.d.xiii. in Septima Sessioñ sacri Laterañ. Cōcilii ... [Romae, Marcellus Silber, 1513.] 4°. π⁴. (Lea.) [266

-- Bulla seu cedula reformationis officialium Romane Curie Lecta in .viii. Sessione Sa. Lateraneñ. Concilii ... per ... Leonem .X. Pont. Max. ... edita. [Romae, Marcellus Silber, 1513.] 4°. A⁴. (Lea.) [267

-- Bulla siue Cedula materiā uniuersalis Pacis: ⁊ destinationis Legatoꝝ de latere: per ... Leonem .X. Pont. Max. sacro approbante Concilio [Lateranensi] edita. ... [Romae, Marcellus Silber, 1513.] 4°. π⁴. (Lea.) [268

-- Bulla seu Cedula in materia fidei: edita per ... Leonem .X. Pont. Max. Sacro approbante Concilio. ... in Octaua Sessione: in Laterañ. Basilica celebrata. [Romae, Marcellus Silber, 1513.] 4°. π⁴. (Lea.) [269

-- Bulla super Societatibus Officialorum Romañ. Curie. 4°. A⁶. ¶a6ᵛ: Datꝫ Rome ... Anno ... Millesimoquingentesimoquartodecimo: Pridie Idus Ianuarii ... (Lea.) [270

-- Bulla Concilii in Decima Sessione super materia Montis pietatis ... [Romae, Marcellus Silber, 1514.] 4°. A⁴. (Lea.) [271

-- -- *Another copy.* (Lea.) [272

-- Bulla Reformationis ... Leonis .X. Pont. Max. Sacro approbante Concilio [Lateranensi] edita. ... [Romae, Marcellus Silber, 1514.] 4°. a-c[4] d[2]. (Lea.) [273

-- Bulla in materia Prelatorum circa exemptos ⁊ alia plura: lecta ... in Decima Sessione ... Lateraneñ. Concilii. [Romae, Marcellus Silber, 1515.] 4°. A[6]. (Lea.) [274

-- Bulla super materia Pragmatice Sanctionis: ⁊ Indictionis future Sessionis sc3 Vndecime: Lecta in Decima Sessione ... Lateraneñ. Concilii ... [Romae, Marcellus Silber, 1515.] 4°. π[2]. (Lea.) [275

-- -- *Another copy.* (Lea.) [276

-- Bulla ... Leonis Pape .X. super moderatione priuilegioꝝ per Sedē Apostolicā Fratribus Mendicātibus: ⁊ aliis Religiosis cōcessorum: ... in Vndecima Sessione in ... Lateraneñ. Basilica solenniter celebrata. [Romae, Marcellus Silber, 1516.] 4°. π[4]. (Lea.) [277

-- Cōcordata inter ... Papam Leonem decimum, et Christianissimum ... Regem Franciscum ... primū, in supremo Parlamenti curia Parisius vigesimasecūda mēsis Martii. Anno ... Millesimo Quingētesimo decimoseptimo ... Vna cum Ioānis Dayma Baionēsis ... commentariolis ... 1535 (Lugduniq3 ... typis excusa in edibus ... Iacobi Myt ... Expensis vero Guilelmi de Guelques.) 8°. B.L. aa[8] a-z[8] A-G[8]. ff. j-ccxi. (Lea.) [278

-- Bulla noua in Cena Dñi. Cum nonnullis additionibus nunq̄ Impressa. ... (Impressum Rome per Stephanum Guillireti M:D.XVII. Die. xi. Aprilis.) 4°. A[6]. (Lea.) [279

-- Bulla Canonizationis Sancti Francisci de Paula/ ordinis fratrum Minimorum institutoris. .... 4°. a-d[4]. ¶*At end: privilege of Nicolas de la Barre dated 12 May 1520.* (Lea.)[280

-- Wie die Bebstlich geschickte Botschafft yre werbung gethan/ haben An den ... hertzog Friderich tzu Sachssen ... vnnd seyner ... Antwort ... [Leipzig, Valentin Schumann.] (1520) 4°. A[4]. [281

-- *Adrian VI, pope.* Wie der Hailig Vatter Bapst Adrianus eingeritten ist zů Rom Auff den .XXVIII. Tag des Monats Augusti. Im jar M.D.XXII. Darbey ain gesprech von dreyen personen. 4°. A[4]. [282

-- *Clement VII, pope.* Bulla Clementis papae septimi [20 August 1524]. (Impressum Romę, apud Ludouicum Vicentium Et Lautitium Perusinum.) 4°. A-D[4]. (Lea.) [283

-- [1] Bulla Clementis PP. VII. confirmationis institutionis collegii militum .S. Petri et aliorum priuilegiorum concessionis. 4°. A-B[4]. ¶*Dated 16 October 1526.* [2] Bulla erectionis [Leonis X] officii dominorum militum .S. Petri ... A-C[4] D[6]. [284

-- [Inspeximus issued by Thomas de Prato, bishop of Clermont, of a bull of Clement VII 17 Kalend. Decembris 1526 addressed to King Francis I for the collection of subsudies for defense against the Turks.] Datum Apud sanctū germanū [*illegible*] Die vij[a] Mensis Ianuarij anno Domini millesimo, quigentesimo, vigesimo Sexto. s.sh. 52 × 49.5 cm. ¶*Place, day, and month filled in by hand.* [285

-- *Paul III, pope.* Pauli tertii Pont. Max. ad Carolum V. Imp. Epistola hortatoria ad pacem. Ipsius Caroli tum ad eam, tum ad alias eiusdem, Concilij conuocatorias responsio. Francisci ... Francorum Regis aduersus ipsius Caroli calumnias, Epistola apologetica ... [Parisiis, Robertus Stephanus, 1543.] 8°. a-e[8] f[4]. pp. 3-87. [286

-- Indulgentie, stationi, & Gratie, Concesse dal ... Paulo, ... Papa Terzo: Ad Instantia della ... Signora Eleonora Osorio, sopra li Rosarii, & Aue Marie, che da sua Santità sone state Benedette. 4°. π[2]. ¶π2[v]: Dat. Ro. ... die tertia Februarii. ... M.D.XLIIII ... (Lea.) [287

-- Christianum de fide, et sacramentis, edictum. Romae, Antonius Bladus imprimebat. M. D. XXXXV. 4°. aa[4] A-M[4]. pp. 1-94. (Lea.) [288

-- S. D. N. D. Pauli ... papae III. Bulla ... oecumenici et generalis Concilij, ... celebrandi, seu prosequendi. Cum reuocatione suspensionis ... [Ingolstadii, Alexander Weissenhorn,] M. D. XLV. 4°. A[6]. [289

-- Bapst Pauli des dritten Bulla/ vnd beruffung zů einem gemaynen Consilium ... zů Trient/ zů halten. Anno M. D. XLV. 4°. A-B[4]. (Lea.) [290

-- Bulla des Antichrists/ dadurch er das volck Gottes widderumb inn den eisern ofen der Egiptischen gefengknis denckt zuziehen ... (Gedruckt zu Magdeburg durch Christian Rö-dinger. M.D.L.) 4°. A-D^4. ¶*Preface by Matthias Flacius Illyricus.* [291

-- Scripta quędam papae et monarcharum, de concilio Tridentino ... Cum praefatione Mathiæ Flacij Illyrici. ... Basileae [1560?]. 8°. a-i^8 k^4. pp. 4-152. [292

-- *Paul IV, pope.* [Writ (printed form with blank spaces to be filled in) issued by Franciscus Albericus de Racaneto, apostolic prothonotary, summoning members of the conclave convened by the pope at Rome and setting forth two bulls on the subject. 1555.] fol. A-B^4 C^2. (Yarnall.) [292a

-- Priuilegia auctoritates, facultates, indulgentiæq3 Fabricæ Basilicæ Principis Apostolorū Sancti Petri de Vrbe, à quàmpluribus Ro. Pontificibus concessæ ... Romae M.D.LVIIII. 4°. A-KK^4. ff. 1-131. (Lea.) [293

-- *Pius IV, pope.* Facultates, ac Priuilegia Archiconfraternitatis Monasterii Beatæ Mariæ Virginis Annuntiatæ, & Hospitalis Catechumenorum de Vrbe. fol. π^2. ¶*Dated 23 January 1560.* (Yarnall.) [293a

-- Reuocatio omnium Indulgentiarum, quæstarum, & aliarum facultatum, quæ deseruntur per Commissarios, cum reductione ad uisitantes personaliter Ecclesias originales. [Romae, Antonius Bladus, 1561.] fol. A^2. (Lea.) [294

-- ... Pii ... Papæ IIII. bulla Reformationis Officii Sacræ Poenitentiariæ. Ripae: ad istantiam Petri Antonii Alciatis. 1562. 4°. A^4. (Lea.) [295

-- Bulla ... Pii ... papae IIII. super reformatione tribunalium ordinariorum Vrbis et Romanæ Curiæ, Conseruatorū, Fisci procuratorum, & aliorum officialium, ac ab eis dependentium. Brixiea [*sic*] ad instantiam Io: Baptistæ Bozolæ. M. D. LXIII. (... apud Ludouicum Sabiensem. ...) 4°. A-C^4 D^2. (Lea.) [296

-- Motus proprius ... Pii ... quarti, super parrochialium, ac aliarum ecclesiarum curatarum collationibus, necnon iuramento, & fideiussione præstañ. de residendo. Brixiae Ad instantiam Io: Baptistæ Bozolæ. M. D. LXIII. (... Apud Ludouicum Sabiensem. ...) 4°. A^4. (Lea.) [297

-- Bulla ... Pii quarti Super facultate concesssa Presidentibus ... Montis Pietatis Ciuitatis Bononiæ ... Bononiæ, Apud Victorium Benatium. M.D.XCVI. 4°. A^8. pp. 3-15. (Lea.) [298

-- -- *Another copy.* [299

-- -- Bononiae, Apud Victorium Benatium. M.D.XCVI. 4°. A-B^4. [300

-- Motus proprius Contra Mercatores ... exercētes Cambia sicca, vsuraria, & illicita. Romae Apud Antonium Bladum ... 1564. fol. π^2. [301

-- S.D.N.D. Pii ... PP. IIII. Constitutiones, seu ordinationes, seu decreta, seu statuta sex ... Romæ apud Antonium Bladum ... fol. A^4. ¶*Dated 8 August 1565.* (Yarnall.) [301a

-- Confirmatio literarum fe. re. Pii iiii. super reuocatione Licentiarum extrahēdi granum, bladas, & legumina ... Romae, apud Antonium Bladum ... M.D.LXVI. fol. π^2. (Yarnall.) [301b

-- *Pius V, pope.* Decreto di N.S. Pio Papa Quinto contra Homicidi, & altri delinquenti, o Banditi del Regno di Napoli. Romae, apud Antonium Bladum ... 1566. fol. π^2. (Yarnall.) [301c

-- Bolla del ... signor nostro Pio ... Papa Quinto, contra gli accettanti homicidi, banditi, & huomini di mal affare ... Publicata in Bologna li iii. Settemb. M D LXVI. In Bologna, per Alessandro Benacci. ... 4°. π^2. [302

-- Edictum super reformatione Cleri Vrbis. (Romae, apud Antonium Bladum ... M. D. LXVI.) fol. A^2. (Lea.) [303

-- Breue S.D.N.D. Pij ... Papa V. quo D. Bartholomæus Bussottus Thesaurarius deputatur Collector generalis omnium spoliorum ecclesiasticorum in vniuersa Italia. Romæ apud Antonium Bladum ... 1566. fol. A^2. (Yarnall.) [303a

-- Motus proprius ... Pii ... Papæ V. Super modo relaxandi carceratos. Romae. Apud Hæredes Antonij Bladij ... M.D.LXVIII. fol. π^2. (Lea.) [304

-- Sanctiss. D.N.D. Pii PP. V. constitutio De extinctione officiorum Ministri, Vicarii, & Visitatoris generalis in ordine Fratrum Tertij ordinis Sancti Francisci, Et De submissione huius ordinis Ministro generali, & Prouincialibus Fratrum Minorum de obseruantia ... (Romae. Apud Hæredes Antonii Bladi ... 1568.) fol. π^2. (Yarnall.) [304a

-- S.D.N.D. Pii papae V. constitutio super forma creandi census. Bononiæ Typis Alexandri Benacij. M D LXIX. ... 4°. A^4. [305

-- -- ... constitutio. Super forma ... Bononiae Typis Alexandri Benacci. M D LXIX. 4°. A^4. (Lea.) [306

-- Moderatione delle constitutioni, et delle Gride che concedono faculta dinominar Banditi. Publicata dal ... Signor Nostro Pio Papa Quinto. In Bologna per Alessandro Benacci. alli 5. Luglio MDLXX. ... 4°. π^2. (Lea.) [307

-- Bulla S.D.N. Pii papae V. reuisionis et recuperationis bonorum Ecclesiasticorum male Alienatorum. Romae Apud Hæredes Antonij Bladij ... M. D. LXX. 4°. π^4. (Lea.) [308

-- Bulla S.D.N. Pii papae. V. quod duae sententiae in ea parte in qua erunt conformes faciant rem iudicatam. Romae Apud Hæredes Antonij Bladij ... M. D. LXX. 4°. π^2. (Lea.) [309

-- Bulla S.D.N. Pii papae V. applicationis fabricae medietatis relictorum piorum non exactorum per triennium. Romae Apud Hæredes Antonij Bladij ... M. D. LXX. 4°. π^2. (Lea.) [310

-- Breue ... di N.S. Papa Pio V. con li capitoli del Cambio Reale di Bologna. In Bologna, Per Giouanni Rossi ... MDLXX. ... fol. A^6. [311

-- Bulla S.D.N.D. Pii papae V. Assignationis, & applicationis Fabricæ Basilicæ Principis Apostolorum de Vrbe, omnium fructuū ... ex bonis ecclesiarum alienatis perceptorum ... Romae, Apud Hæredes Antonij Bladij ... M. D. LXXI. 4°. A^6 (-A6, *presumably blank*). (Lea.) [312

-- Declaratio S.D.N. Pii papæ V. super derogatione Concilij Tridentini. Romae Apud Hæredes Antonij Bladij ... 1571. 8°. π^4. (Lea.) [313

-- *Gregory XIII, pope.* Processus fulminatorius et executiuus bullae a ... Gregorio XIII. pontifice max. emanatae. Ad fauorem fori mecatorum Bononiae. Bononiae, Apud Ioannem Rossium 1578. ... fol. A^6. [314

-- *Sixtus V, pope.* Constitutione ... di N.S. Sisto Papa Quinto. Contra coloro, ch'essercitano l'arte dell'Astrologia giudiciaria, & qualunque altra sorti di diuinationi ... Et contra coloro, che leggono, & tengono libri intorno à tal materia &c. Tradotto in volgare ... Stampata in Roma da gli Heredi di Antonio Blado ... 1586. Ristampata in Bologna, per Alessandro Benaci. M D LXXXVI. 4°. $A\text{-}B^4$. (Lea.) [315

-- Sanctissimi D.N.D. Sixti ... papae V. constitutio super Temeraria Tori separatione, ac publicis adulterijs, stupris, & lenocinijs in quibusdam casibus seuerius coercendis. Romae, Apud Hæredes Antonij Bladij ... M D LXXXVI. fol. π^2. (Lea.) [316

-- La bulle et constitution de ... Sixte cinquiéme, sur les cōfidences des Benefices. A Paris, Chez Guillaume Bichon ... 1589. 8°. $A\text{-}C^4$. pp. 1-21. [317

-- Schreiben Sixti. V. PP. An Graff Iohan/ von Manserscheid ꝛc. Bischoffen zu Strassburg/ ꝛc. Belangendt die Reformation dess Bistumbs vnd hohen Stiffts daselbst ... [30 April 1588]. M. D. XCII. 4°. $A\text{-}C^4$. (Lea.) [318

-- *Gregory XIV, pope.* Constitutio S.D.N.D. Gregorii ... papae XIIII. Super Immunitate Ecclesiarum. Romae, Apud Paulum Bladum ... M. D. XCI. fol. π^2. (Yarnall.) [318a

-- *Clement VIII, pope.* Constitutione di N.S. Papa Clemente VIII. Sopra il buon Gouerno, & retta administratione delle Intrate delle Communità, & Vniuersità dello Stato Ecclesiastico. Tradotta di Latino in Volgare ... Stampata in Roma per Paolo Blado ... Et Ristampata in Bologna per Vittorio Benacci. ... 4°. A^6. ¶*Dated 15 August 1592.* [319

-- Sanctissimi D.N.D. Clementis ... papa VIII. Pręceptum de depositio pecuniarum facien. super Montem Pietatis Ciuitatis Bononiæ. (Bononiæ, Apud Victorium Benaccium.) s. sh. 39 × 25.5 cm. ¶*Dated 5 October 1592.* [320

ROME, the empire. Notitia vtraque dignitatum cum Orientis, tum Occidentis vltra Arcadij, Honorijque Tempora. Et in eam Guidi Panciroli ... commentarium. ... Item de Magistratibus Municipalibus eiusdem Auctoris Liber ... Venetiis, M. D. XCIII. Apud Franciscum de Franciscis Senensem. fol. a^8 b^6 A-Bb^8. ff. 1-298. ¶*Additional t.p.* ($Aa1^r$): De magistratibus municipalibus ... Venetiis, Apud Franciscum de Franciscis Senensem. 1593. [321

RONCHEGALLUS, JOANNES. Io. Ronchegalli Gioldi Ferrariensis ... in titulum institutionum de bonorum possessionib. Interpretatio ... Florentiæ Ex officina Laurentii Torrentini. MDXLVIII. fol. A-M^6. pp. 1-136. (Biddle.) [322

RONDINELLI, DIONISIO. Galitia fauola pastorale ... In Verona, Per Girolamo Strengari, e fratelli. M D LXXXIII. 8°. A-E^8. [323

RONDINELLI, GIOVANNI. Orazione ... Delle lodi della Reina di Francia Caterina de' Medici ... In Firenze Appresso Antonio Padouani. 1588. 4°. $[A]^2$ B-D^4. pp. 1-24. [324

RONSARD, PIERRE DE. P. Ronsardi ad pacem exhortatio Latinis versibus de Gallicis expressa a Francisco Thorio Bellione. Parisiis, Apud Andream Wechelum ... 1558. ... 4°. A-B^4. [325

ROSCIO, LUCIO VITRUVIO. L. Vitruuii, Roscii, Parmensis, ... de conficiendis epistolis isagogicon. ... M D XXXVIII. (Venetijs, ex ædibus Francisci Bindoni, et Maphei Pasini ...) 8°. A-G^8 H^4. ff. 2-60. [326

-- L. Vitruuii, Roscii, Parmensis, de modo docendi, atque studendi, ac de claris puerorum moribus Libellus ... (Venetiis, ex ædibus Francisci Bindoni, et Maphei Pasini ... M D XXXVIIII.) 8°. A-E^8 F^4. [327

-- Grammaticarum quaestionum, et elegantiarum. Libri tres ... Venetiis per Gabrielem Iolitum de Ferrariis M.D.XXXXIII. (... M. D. XXXXII.) 8°. A-Q^8. pp. 1-235. [328

ROSELLI, ALESSANDRO. Salus Italica. [Florentiae, Philippus Giunta, c. 1515.] 4°. a-c^4. [329

ROSELLO, LUCIO PAOLO. Considerationi deuote intorno alla uita e Passione di Christo ... In Vinegia M. D. LI. (... per Comin da Trino di Monferrato ...) 8°. A-O^8 (-O8, *presumably blank*). ff. 2-111. [330

-- Discorso di penitenza raccolto ... da un ragionamento del ... Cardinal Contareno. In Vinegia del M. D. XLIX. 8°. A-F^4. ff. 2-24. [331

-- Il ritratto del vero gouerno del prencipe dal l'essempio viuo del gran Cosimo de' Medici. ... con due orationi d'Isocrate ... tradotte dal medesimo di Greco in uolgare Italiano. ... In Vinegia, al segno del pozzo [Andrea Arrivabene]. M D LII. (... per Giouanmaria Bonelli. ...) 8°. A-N^8 O^4. ff. 2-107. [332

ROSEMONDT, GODSCHALCK. Confessionale siue libellus modum Confitendi pulcherrime cōplectes. ... Anno Mil. CCCCC.XIX. Men. Iunij. Die .xxvij. (Impressum Anduerpie Per me Michaelem Hillenū Hoochstratanū. ... MCCCCCXIX. Die vero viii. Iulij.) 8°. B.L. $[A]^8$ B-Y^8 AA-KK^8. ff. ij-CCli. (Lea.) [333

ROSENBUSCH, CHRISTOFF. Christophori Rosenbuschs Replica. Auff dess Calumnianten Lucæ Osiandri Verantwortung wider die Iesuiter. ... 1586. Gedruckt zu Ingolstadt/ durch Dauid Sartorium. 4°. A-Ii^4 Kk^6. pp. 1-258. [334

ROSENTHAL, HEINRICH VON. Synopsis totius iuris feudalis conclusionibus, seu sententiis in certa ac familiaria capita digesta ... Excudebat Eustathius Vignon, Atrebat. M D LXXXIIX. 4°. $*^4$ $**^4$ $***^2$ A-Zz^4 AA-II^4. pp. 1-422. ¶*Additional t.p.* (**1): Iuris feudalis conclusiones aliquot miscellaneæ, quas ... in ... Basiliensi Academia ... defendet. Henricus Rosenthal Montensis. Anno ... M. D. LXXXVIII. (Lea.) [335

ROSIERES, FRANÇOIS DE. Stemmatum Lotharingiæ ac Barri ducum tomi septem. ... Parisiis, Apud Guilielmum Chaudiere ... 1580. ... fol. $*^8$ (*8 + 2 *folded ll.*) $ā^6$ $ē^6$ $ī^6$ $ō^6$ $ū^8$ a-z^6 A-D^6 E^8 F-$3O^6$. ff. ii-xxxii, 1-460. ¶*Additional t.p.* ($F1^r$): ... tomus quartus. ... *Same imprint.* [336

ROSSETTO, PIETRO. P. Rosseti Poetæ Laureati, Paulus. Vænundatur Badio ... ([Parisiis,] Sub prelo Ascensiano ad .XV. Calē. Aprilis M.D.XXII. Et rursum cū his scholiis, Calen. Aug. M.D.xxvii. ...) 8°. a-l^8 m^4. ff. II-XCII. [337

ROSSI, BARTOLOMMEO DE'. Ornamenti di fabriche antichi et moderni ... di Roma Con le sue dichiaratione fatti da Bartolommeo Rossi fiorentino Ad Instanza di Andrea della Vaccaria ... Parte Seconda ... Ioannes maius Romanus delineauit ... MDC. obl. fol. ff. 50, *including the t.p., each with 2 engravings.* [338

ROSSI, GIROLAMO. Hieronymi Rubei historiarum Rauennatum libri decem hac altera editione libro vndecimo aucti ... Venetiis, MDLXXXIX. Ex Typographia Guerræa. (*Colophon.*) fol. †^{4} A-4G^6 a-d^6 e^4. pp. 2-900. (Lea.) [339

ROSSI, PAOLO. Il commíssario comedia rurale ... A Fermo, Presso gl'Heredi di Sertorio de' Monti, & Gio: Bonibello. 1596. (*Colophon.*) 8°. A-H^8 I^4. pp. 3-135. [340

ROSSO, PAOLO DEL. La fisica di F. Paulo del Rosso, Caualiere di S. Giouanbatista. ... In Parigi. Par Pierre le Voirrier. 1578. 8°. A^4 B-G^8 H^6 (-H6, *presumably blank*). pp. 1-103. ¶*In verse.* B2 *misbound after* B3. [341

ROTA, BERARDINO. Berardini Rotae, equitis Neapolitani, poemata. ... Venetiis, apud Gabrielem Giulitum de Ferrariis. Anno MDLXVII. 8°. *^{8} **^{6} A-L^8. pp. 3-25, 1-176. [342

-- Berardini Rotae ... carmina. ... Neapoli. Apud Iosephum Cacchium MD LXXII. (*Colophon.*) 4°. *^{4} †^{4} A-S^4. ff. 1-72. [343

-- Sonetti ... in morte della S. Portia Capece sua moglie. (In Napoli appresso Mattia Cancer Del mese di Marzo MDLX.) 4°. A-GG^4. pp. 1-191. [344

-- [1] Sonetti, et canzoni ..., con l'egloghe pescatorie ... In Vinegia, appresso Gabriel Giolito de' Ferrari. M D LXVII. 8°. *^{12} A-N^8 (-N8) a^8 b^2. pp. 1-204. [2] Egloghe pescatorie ... In Vinegia, appresso Gabriel Giolito de' Ferrari. MDLXVI. A-F^8 G^4. pp. 3-97. [345

ROTH, FRIEDRICH. Leichpredigt ... Bey der Begrebnis ... Hans Hoiers/ Grafen vnd Herrn zu Manssfeld ... Gehalten ... den vierden Aprilis, Anno 1585. ... (Gedruckt zu Eissleben/ bey Vrban Gaubisch ...) 4°. A-K^4. [346

ROTING, MICHAEL. Etlicher Iungen Prediger zu Nůrnberg verantwortung gegen der anklag Andreæ Osiandri ... (Gedruckt zu Magdeburg bey Christian Rődinger [1552].) 4°. A-C^4 D^2. [347

ROTMAR, VALENTIN. Annales Ingolstadiensis academiæ ... Ingolstadii Ex Typographia VVeissenhorniana, apud VVolfgangum Ederum, Anno M. D. XXC. ... 4°. *-**^{4} A-Rr^4 Ss^6. ff. 1-164. [348

-- Orationes funebres quatuor. In obitum ... Martini Eisengreinii ... His accesserunt quorundam carmina funebria. ... Ingolstadii Excudebat Dauid Sartorius. M. D. LXXVIII. 8°. A^8 a^4 B-H^8 I^4. ¶*Additional authors: Johann Holonius, Kaspar Franck, Albert Hunger, Cyriacus Lutz, Philipp Menzel, Johann Engerd, Sixtus Volhard Wenger.* A8^v-a4^v: Catalogus librorum Domini Eisengreinij. [349

ROVERE, GIROLAMO DELLA. Hieronymi Ruuere, pueruli annum agentis decimum, carmina. ... P. P. Venturi ... epistola gratulatoria. ... (Papię apud Io. Mariā Simoneti Cremoneñ. 1540.) 4°. a-d^4 e^6. ff. 2-22. [350

RUBERTI, BATTISTA DE. Osseruazioni de astrologia et altre appartenenze, Circa della Medicina, & mutazione de tempi. ... In Firenze. 1567. (... per i figliuoli di Lorenzo Torrentino, & Carlo Pettinari Compagno. ...) 4°. A-O^4 (-O4, *presumably blank*). pp. 3-108. [351

RUBYS, CLAUDE DE. Sommaire explication des articles de la coustume du pays et duche de Bourgongne. ... A Lion, par Benoist Rigaud. M. D. LXXXVIII. ... 8°. A-S^8. pp. 3-288. [352

RUCELLAI, GIOVANNI. Rosmunda tragedia ... In Fiorenza Appresso i Giunti. 1568. (*Colophon.*) 8°. A-C^{8}. pp. 4-47. [353

RUDOLPHINUS DE PASSAGERIIS, ROLANDINUS. Flos Vltimarum voluntatum. D. Rolandini passagerij ... cū additionibus. D. Petri de Vnzola Bononiensis: Necnon Domini Baptiste guarini Brixiensis: Ac. D. Bartholo. abhor. Patauini ... (Ioānes Baptista Sessa ... Venetijs impressit. ... M.ccccli. Die vero primo Augusti.) 4°. B.L. a-s^{4}. [354

-- [1] Summa totius artis notariae, Rolandini Rodulphi Bononiensis ... Hac nouissima vero editione à M. D. Leonardo à Lege ... recognita ... Cui ... accessit ... Tractatus Angeli à Gambilionibus de testamentis. ... Venetiis, Apud Franciscum Rampazetum. M. D. LXXIIII. (*Colophon.*) fol. *^{6} a-z^{8} A-R^{8} S^{4} T-3L^{8} 3M^{10}. ff. 1-632. ¶*Additional t.p.* (T1^{r}): Rolandini Rodulphi ... Tomus Secundus, siue Apparatus Petri de Vnzola in nonum Capitulum de iudiciis summæ Rolandinæ. ... *Same imprint.* [2] Ziliola M. D. Leonardi a Lege ... *Same imprint.* A-E^{8}. (Lea.) [355

RUINI, CARLO. [Consilia.] Lugduni, Apud Hugonem, & haeredes Aemonis à Porta. ... M.D.XLVI. (... excudebant Stephanus Rufinus, et Ioannes Ausultus.) fol. B.L. [1] Primum volumen consiliorum, seu responsorum, ... a-z^{8} A-S^{8} T^{6}. ff. 3-333. [2] Secundum volumen ... a-z^{8} A-O^{8} P^{6}. ff. 2-302. [3] Tertium volumen ... a-z^{8} A-M^{8} (-M8, *presumably blank*). ff. 2-279. [4] Quartum volumen ... a-z^{8} A-B^{8} C-D^{6}. ff. 2-211. [5] Quintum volumen ... a-z^{8} A-D^{8}. ff. 2-215. [6] Index ... in quinque volumina responsorum ... a-m^{8} n^{6}. (Biddle.) [356

-- Caroli Ruini ... in tit. digestorum de no. ope. nuncia. ... (Impressum Bonoñ. apud Vincentium Bonardum Parmēsem ... & Marcū Antoniū Carpensem ... M.D.XXXV. Die .XXIIII. Decembris.) fol. A-E^{6} F^{4}. ff. II-XXXIIII. (Biddle.) [357

-- Lectura ... in secūdam Infortiati partem ... (Impressum Bononie per Hieronymum de Benedictis ... 1526. ...) fol. B.L. A-Q^{6} R-S^{4}. ff. II-CIIII. (Biddle.) [358

-- Lectura ... Super secunda .ff. Noui ... [*Device of Baptista de Tortis.*] ([F6] Venetijs per Thomam de Pectenatis Vercellensem. Impensis vero Bernardini de Benalijs. Die viij. Martij. 1530. [G2] ... .1530. Die .21. Martij.) fol. B.L. A^{6} B-E^{4} F^{6} GG^{6} G^{2}. ff. II-XXVIII. (Biddle.) [359

-- ... Caroli Ruyni Lectura vltima super prima Infortiati ... MDXXXVIII (Venetijs: ex impressione Baptiste de Tortis.) fol. B.L. A-D^{4} E^{6} F-O^{4}. ff. 2-58. (Biddle.) [360

RUPERTUS, abbot of Deutz. Ruperti abbatis ... Tuitiensis ... Commentariorum, in Apocalypsim Iohannis libri .XII. Frans Birckman. Apud ... Coloniam ... M. D. XXVI. Aeditio prima. (*Colophon.*) fol. aa^{6} a-t^{6} u^{4}. pp. II-CCXXXV. [361

-- Ruperti abbatis ... Tuitiensis ... Commentariorum, in Euangelium Iohannis libri .XIIII. Frans Birckman. Apud ... Coloniam ... M. D. XXVI. Aeditio prima. (*Colophon.*) fol. π^{8} a-gg^{6} hh^{4}. pp. II-CCCLXVII. [362

-- Ruperti abbatis ... Tuitiensis ... De diuinis Officijs libri .XII. Frans Birckman. Apud ... Coloniam ... M. D. XXVI. Aeditio prima. (*Colophon.*) fol. π^{6} a-p^{6} q^{4}. pp. III-CLXXXVII. [363

-- Ruperti abbatis ... Tuitiensis ... Opera duo ... In Matthaeum ... Libri XIII. De glorificatione Trinitatis ꝛ precessione spiritus sancti libri IX. Apud ... Coloniam ... M.D.XXVI. Aeditio prima. (... Impēsis ... Francisci Birkman ... Pridie Idus Iunias.) fol. aa^{4} a-q^{6} r^{4} χ^{8} A-K^{6} L^{4}. pp. II-CXCIX, III-CXXV. ¶L2 *misbound before* L1, L4 *before* L3. [364

-- -- *Another copy (-L4, blank).* [365

RUPECISSA, JOANNES DE. Ioannis de Rupescissa ... de consideratione Quintæ essentię rerum omnium ... Arnaldi de Villanoua Epistola de Sanguine humano distillato. Raymundi Lullij Ars operatiua & alia quædam. ... Accessit Michaelis Sauonarolae Libellus ... de aqua Vitæ ... Item Hieronymi Cardani Libellus de Aethere, seu Quinta essentia Vini. Basileae. 8°. a-y^{8} (-i^{8}, 12-7, y6-8, y7-8 *being blank*). pp. 10-341. ¶Epistola nuncupatoria *dated May 1561.* (Smith.) [366

RUSCELLI, GIROLAMO. De' commentarii della lingua Italiana ... libri VII. ... In Venetia, appresso Damian Zenaro ... M D LXXXI. 4°. *^{8} A-Nn^{8}. pp. 1-574. [367

-- Del modo di comporre in versi nella lingua Italiana, trattato ... In Venetia appresso Gio. Battista et Melchior Sessa fratelli. (... M D LXIII.) 8°. A-3H^8 (-3H8, *presumably blank*). pp. 1-866. [368

-- -- In Venetia Appresso gli Heredi di Marchiò Sessa. M D LXXII. (*Colophon.*) *Same collation and pagination.* [369

-- Del tempio alla diuina signora Donna Giouanna d'Aragona ... prima parte ... In Venetia, per Plinio Pietrasanta, M. D. LV. 8°. ✝-3✝^{8} A-Z^8 Z-AA^8 BB^2 a-h^8 i^2 1-n^8 o^2. pp. 2-388, 2-159. [370

-- I fiori delle rime de poeti illustri, nuouamente raccolti ... da Girolamo Ruscelli ... In Venetia, Per Giouanbattista et Melchior Sessa fratelli. 1558. (*Colophon.*) 8°. *-**^{8} 3*^{4} A-L^8 2L^8 M-PP^8 QQ^4 ✠-✠✠^{8}. pp. 17-608. [371

-- -- In Venetia, Appresso gli heredi di Marchiò Sessa. M D LXIX. (*Colophon.*) 12°. a-b^{12} A-Dd^{12} Ee^6. ff. 2-294. [372

-- In Venetia, Appresso gli heredi di Marchiò Sessa. M D LXXIX. (... Appresso Pietro Dehuchino. ...) 12°. a-b^{12} A-Cc^{12}. ff. 2-290. [373

-- [1] Lettere di principi ..., libro primo, Nuouamente mandato in luce da Girolamo Ruscelli ... In Venetia, Appresso Giordano Ziletti ... M. D. LXII. (*Colophon.*) 4°. A-B^4 A-3I^4. ff. 1-219. [2] ... Libro Secondo. ... In Venetia, Appresso Giordano Ziletti. M D LXXV. 4°. a^4 b^2 A-3R^4 3S^6. ff. 2-257. [3] ... Libro terzo. ... In Venetia, Appresso Giordano Ziletti. M D LXXVII. 4°. *^{4} b^4 A-4C^4. ff. 2-278. [374

-- -- *Additional copies of* [1] *and* [2]. (Lea.) [375

-- -- *Another edition of* [1]. In Venetia, presso Francesco Toldi. M D LXXIII. 4°. a-h^4 A-Hh^8. ff. 2-247. [376

-- -- [1] Delle lettere di principi ... Libro Primo. ... In Venetia, Appresso Francesco Ziletti. M D LXXXI. 4°. A^6 A-Ff^8 Gg^4. ff. 1-286. [2] ... Libro Secondo. ... *Same imprint.* 4°. A^6 A-Bb^8 Cc^4 (-Cc4, *blank*). ff. 1-203. [3] ... Libro Terzo. ... *Same imprint.* (*Colophon.*) 4°. *^{8} A-Mm^8 Nn^4. ff. 1-284. [377

-- -- *Another copy of* [3]. (Lea.) [378

-- Lettura ... sopra vn sonetto dell' ... Marchese della Terza ... In Venetia per Giouan Griffio, l'anno M D LII. 4°. a^6 A-T^4 V^6. ff. 1-77. [379

-- Rime di diuersi eccellenti autori Bresciani, ... raccolte ... da Girolamo Ruscelli; tra le quali sono le rime della Signora Veronica Gambara, & di M. Pietro Barignano ... In Venetia, per Plinio Pietrasanta, M D LIIII. 8°. *^{8} A-O^8 P-Q^4 χ^8. pp. 1-234. [380

-- -- *Another copy* (-χ8, *blank*). [381

-- Tre discorsi ... L'uno intorno al Decamerone del Boccaccio, L'altro all' Osseruationi della lingua volgare, Et il terzo alla tradottione dell'Ouidio. ... In Venetia M D LIII. (... per Plinio Pietrasanta. ...) 4°. A-II^4 LL-OO^4. pp. 3-287. [382

-- Vocabolario delle voci Latine dichiarate con l'Italiane ... In Venetia, Appresso gli Heredi di Valerio Bonello. M D LXXXVIII. (*Colophon.*) 4°. *^{8} A-M^8. ff. 1-95. [383

RUSCONI, GIOVANNI ANTONIO. Della architettura ... libri dieci. ... In Venetia, appresso i Gioliti. M.D. XC. fol. [a]^2 b-c^2 A-NN^2. pp. 1-143. (Fine Arts.) [384

RUTILIO, BERNARDINO. Iurisconsultorum vitae, veterum quidem, ... unà cum eiusdem Decuria. Recentiorum vero ... per Ioannem Fichardum Francofurtensem. Ad haec Indices duo ...: Per Io. Neuizanum, Lud. Gomessium, & Io. Fichardum collecti. Basileae. (*Device of Thomas Platter.*) 4°. α-γ^4 A-Qq^4. pp. 1-263. [385

RUTILIUS LUPUS, PUBLIUS. De figuris sententiarum ac verborum ... libri duo ... Aquilæ Romani liber vnus. Iulii Rufiniani de iis quæ ab Aquila prætermissa erant, libellus, & præterea eiusdem libri duo. Parisiis. Ex officina Roberti Stephani ... M. D. XLI. (... XVI. Cal. Octobr.) 8°. a-e^8 (-e8, *presumably blank*). pp. 3-57. [386

RUTILIUS NAMATIANUS, CLAUDIUS. Claudius Rutilius ... de laudibus vrbis, Etruriae, et Italiae. (Bononiæ in ædibus Hieronymi de Benedictis ... M.D.XX.) 4°. A-E^4. [387

RYD, VALERIUS ANSELMUS. Catalogus annorum et principum geminus ab homine condito, vsque in praesentum ... Ex ... vrbe Berna. ... M. D. XL. (... per Matthiam Apiarium. ...) fol. $*^6$ a-k^6 1^8. ff. I-LXVIII. [388

RYFF, WALTHER HERMANN. [Die gross chirurgei oder volkommene Wundtartznei ... Durch Gwaltherus H. Ryff ... In Franckfurt bei Chr. Ege. (... M.D.XLV. Im Merzen.)] fol. ^{6} (- 1) a-z^6 A-H^6 (-F6, G-H) I^4 (*wanting*). ff. I-CLXXIII *present*. ¶h6 *defective*. (School of Dentistry.) [389

S

SABELLICO, MARCO ANTONIO COCCIO. Opera Mar. Ant. Sabellici ... (Impressi Venetiis p̄ Albertinū de Lisona Vercellensem. M.ccccc.ii. Die .xxiiii. Decembris.) fol. a-i^{6} k-l^{8} m-x^{6} y^{8} A-M^{6}. ff. 2-136. [1

-- M. Antonii Sabellici De rerū et artiuꝫ inuentoribus poema ... [Parisiis,] Venale reperitur in domo Iohannis Lamberti ... 4°. A-B^{4}. [2

-- Marci Anthonij Sabellici ... duodecim oratiōes ... [Parisiis.] 4°. a^{4} b^{8} c-d^{4} e^{8} f-h^{4}. ¶*Dedication dated 1509.* [3

-- ... Marci Antonii Cocci Sabellici exemplorum libri decem. ... (Ioannes Bartholomeus fecit. Venetiis. M.D.VII. Septembris. mensis: die. XIX. ...) 4°. π^{4} A-MM^{4} NN^{6}. ff. I-CXLVI. [4

-- -- (... Matthias Schurerius Selestatensis ... Argentorati ... exscripsit. iij. Nonas Nouēbris. Anno. M. D. XVIII.) fol. π^{4} a-c^{6} d^{4} e^{6} f^{4} g^{6} h^{8} i^{4} k-n^{6} o^{4} p-q^{6} r^{4} s^{6}. ff. I-XCIX. [5

-- -- Exempelbůch Marci Anthonij Sabellici von wunderbarlichen Geschichten ... Durch M. Leonard Brunner ... verteutscht. Zů Strassburg durch Iacob Cammerlandern von Mentz getruckt. Anno M.D.XXXV. fol. π^{4} A-Z^{4} a-b^{4} c^{6}. ff. ij-cvj. [6

-- Le historie Vinitiane ... In Vinegia per Comin da Trino, l'anno M. D. LIIII. (*Colophon.*) 4°. *-3*^{4} A-GG^{8} HH^{4}. ff. 3-244. [7

SABEO, FAUSTO. Epigrammatum ... Libri quinque. ... Romæ apud Valerium, & Aloisium Doricos fratres Brixien. M D. LVI. (*Colophon.*) 8°. A-3H^{8}. pp. 3-872. [8

SABINUS, GEORG. Cæsares Germanici descripti ... 4°. A-B^{4}. ¶*Dedication dated 1532. In verse.* [9

-- Fabularum Ouidii interpretatio, ethica, physica, et Historica, ... in vnum collecta & edita studio ... T.T. ... Accessit etiam ex Natalis Comitis Mythologijs de fabularum vtilitate ... tractatio. Cantabrigiæ, Ex officina Thomæ Thomæ ... 1584. 8°. ¶^{8} A-Qq^{8} R^{8}. pp. 1-638. *S.T.C.* 18951. [10

-- Poēmata ... [Leipzig,] In officina Voegeliana [1563] ... 8°. A-Z^{8} a-m^{8} (-m8, *blank*). pp. 2-532. [10

SABINUS, TROILUS. Troili Sabini oratio de laudibus scientiarum, habita ... Romae ... 4°. A^{4} B^{6}. [12

SABUNDE, RAYMOND DE. Theologia naturalis ... Venetiis, Apud Franciscum Ziletum. M D LXXXI. (*Colophon.*) 8°. a-b^{8} c^{4} A-3D^{8}. ff. 1-400. [13

-- -- Viola anime per modū dyalogi inter Raymundum Sebūdium ... ꝑ dominū Dominicū seminiuerbium. De hominis natura ... tractans ... (Colonie Impēsis ... Hērici Quētell denuo Impressus ... M.CCCCC.j. Die. decimosexto mensis Iulij.) 4°. B.L. aa^{4} A-B^{6} C^{4} D^{8} E-F^{4} G^{8} H-P$^{4 \cdot 6}$. [14

SACCHETTI, CESARE. Rappresentatione di Santo Christoforo martire, ridotta a vso di comedia ... In Fiorenza MDLXXV. 4°. A-D^{4} E^{2}. pp. 4-36. [15

SACCO, BERNARDO. De Italicarum rerum varietate et elegantia, libri X. ... Eiusdem de Papiensis Ecclesiæ dignitate ... Ad hæc, de dignitate Gymnasij Ticinensis Henrici Farnesii Eburonis encomium ... Cum autoris Sacci vita ... Ticini, Apud Hieronymum Bartolum. MDLXXXVII. 4°. a^{6} a-b^{8} c^{4} A-S^{8}. pp. 1-287. [16

SACHS, HANS. [1] Sehr Herzliche Schoͤne vnd warhaffte Gedicht. ... Durch ... Hans Sachsen ... Getruckt zu Nuͤrnberg bey Christoff Heussler. ... M. D. LVIII. (... XVI. Tag Februarij.) fol. π^{4} ✿^{4} A-ZZ^{6} a-yy^{6} (-yy6, *presumably blank*). ff. I-CCCCCXLV. [2] Das ander Buch ... Gedruckt zu Nuͤrnberg durch Christoff Heussler ... M.D.LX. Jar. (*Colophon.*) ✿^{4}

✠^{4} (-✠4) A-P^{6} AA-TT^{6} a-z^{6} Aa-Ii^{6} aa-xx^{6} yy^{4}. ff. I-XC, I-CXIIII, I-CXCII, I-CXXX. ¶T.p. *mounted.* [3] [Das dritt vnd letzt Buch ... Gedruckt zu Nürmberg bey Christoff Huessler. M.D.LXI.] ✠^{4} (-✠1) A-XX^{6} (-XX6) a-zz^{6} 3A-3D^{6} A☙-O☙^{6} (-O☙6, *presumably blank*). ff. I-CCLXIIII, I-CCC, I-LXXXIIII. [4] Das vierdt Poetisch Buch. ... M. D. LXXVIII. (Gedruckt zu Nürnberg/ durch Leonhardt Heussler/ In verlegung Ioachim Lochners.))(^{6} A-VV^{6} (-X6) a-t^{6} v^{4}. ff. I-CXXV *present*, I-CXX, I-CXIX. [5] Das fünfft vnd letzt Buch. ... M. D. LXXIX. Gedruckt zu Nürnberg/ durch Leonhard Huessler. (... In verlegung Ioachim Lochners.) (:)^{4})(^{4} A-Z^{6} a-z^{6} Aa-Zz^{6} (-Zz6, *presumably blank*). ff. II-CCCCXIIII. [17

-- All Römisch Keiser nach ordnung/ vnd wie lang yeder geregiert hat ... (Getruckt zu Nürmberg [durch Johann Petreius] Anno M.D.XXX.) 4°. A-C^{4}. [18

-- Anzeygung/ wieder das Schnöd Laster der Hurerey. Mehr der Sabat brecher. ... (Gedruckt zu Nüremberg/ durch Georg Merckel. ... 1553.) 4°. A^{4} B^{2}. [19

-- Der Büler Artzney. Mehr die Neun Geschmeck in dem Eelichen stand. ... (Gedruckt zu Nüremberg/ durch Georg Merckel. ...) 4°. A-B^{4} B^{2}. [20

-- Disputation/ zwischen einem Chorherren vnnd Schumacher ... [Augsburg, Melchior Ramminger, 1524.] 4°. A^{2} B^{4} C^{2}. ¶A1 *defective.* [21

-- Die drey Klaffer. Mer des klaffers zung Mehr der Hederlein bin jch genandt/ zenckischen Leüten wol bekant. ... (Gedrflck zu Nüremberg/ durch Georg Merckel. 1553.) 4°. A-B^{4}. [22

-- Die Gemarthert Theologia. Mer das Klagent Ewangelium. ... (Gedrückt zu Nürmberg/ durch Georg Merckel. 1553.) 4°. A-C^{4}. [23

-- Eyn gesprech eynes Euangelischen Christen/ mit einem Lutherischen ... 1524. ... [Nürnberg, Hieronymus Hoeltzel.] 4°. A-C^{4}. [24

-- Ein gesprech von dē Scheinwercken der Gaystlichē/ vnd jren gelübdten ... (Anno. 1524.) 4°. A-B^{4}. [25

-- Ein gesprech zwischen Sanct Peter vnd dem Herren/ von der jetzigen Weldt lauff. Mehr ein gesprech zwischen eim Waldtbrůder vñ eim Engel/ von dē heimlichen gericht Gottes. ... (Zu Nüremberg truckts/ Georg Merckel ...) 4°. A-B^{4}. ¶A1 *defective.* [26

-- Der klagent waldbrůder vber alle Stendt/ auff erden. Mehr der waldtbruder mit dem Esel/ der argen weldt thut nimandt recht. ... (Gedruckt zu Nüremberg/ durch Georg Merckel. ...) 4°. A-B^{4}. [27

-- Klagredt der waren Freundtschafft/ vber das volck Christlicher landt/ welches sie flüchtig verlassen můss Mer die brüderlich lieb hat keyn Fuss mehr. ... (Gedruckt zu Nüremberg/ durch Georg Merckel. ...) 4°. A-B^{4}. [28

-- Klagredt der weldt/ ob jrem verderben/ dargegen ein straffredt jrer grundtlosen bossheyt. Mehr ein klagred der wilden Holtzleut vber die vntrewen Welt. ... (Gedruckt zu Nürnberg durch Georg Merckel.) 4°. A-B^{4}. [29

-- Nachred das greulich laster/ sampt seinen zwölff Eygenschafften. ... (Gedruckt zu Nüremberg/ durch Georg Merckel. ... 1553.) 4°. A-B^{4}. [30

-- Der Narren fresser. Mehr das Narren Bad. ... (Gedruckt zu Nüremberg/ durch Georg Merckel. ... 1553.) 4°. A-B^{4}. [31

-- Der Thurnier spruch. Alle Thurnier/ wo/ wie vnd wenn sie im Teutschlandt gehalten sind worden. ... (Gedruckt zů Nürnberg durch Hans Guldenmundt. 1541.) 4°. A-B^{4}. [32

-- Der Todt ein Endt/ aller yrdischen ding. ... (Gedruckt zu Nüremberg/ durch Georg Merckel [c. 1550].) 4°. A-C^{4}. [33

-- Des veriagten Frids Klagredt/ vber alle stendt der Weldt. Mehr ein Klagredt der Neün Muse oder künst vber Teudtschlandt. ... (Gedruckt zů Nüremberg/ durch Georg Merckel. ...) 4°. A-B^{4} C^{2}. [34

-- Vonn dem verlornen redenten gülden. ... (Gedruckt zu Nüremberg/ durch Georg Merckel. ... 1553.) 4°. A-B^{4} C^{2}. [35

SACK, SIEGFRIED. Zwo Predigten ... wie ein Christen Mensch/ beides das Reich Gottes/ vnd auch zeitliche narung in der Haushaltung erlangen könne. ... Durch Siegfridum Saccum Northusanum D. Bey Iohan Francken. M. D. LXXX. (Gedruckt zu Magdeburgk/ Durch Wilhelm Ross. ...) 4°. A-I^{4}. [36

SACRANUS, JOANNES. Errores Atrocissimorum Ruthenorum. [c. 1507.] 4°. B.L. π^4. [37

SACRATUS, SEBASTIANUS. Oratio de studiis liberalium artium ... Epigrammata diuersorum auctorum ... Iacobi Sadoleti cardinalis oratio de Pace ad Imperatorem Carolum Quintum ... Lucae apud Vincentium Busdragum. MDXLIX. 8°. A-R^4 S^2. ff. 1-66. [38

SADOLETO, JACOPO. Iacobi Sadoleti ... de bello Turcis inferendo, Oratio. Eiusdem argumenti, Othonis Brunfelsii ad Christianos Principes Oratio. Iacobi Fontani de Rhodi expugnatione Epistola. Petri Nannii Alcmariani Declamatio. Ludouici Viuis de uita Christianorum sub Turca opusculum. Basileae M. D. XXXVIII. (... per Thomam Platterum ... Mense Martio.) 8°. A-O^8 P^4 Q^8. pp. 3-247. [39

-- Iacobi Sadoleti de laudibus Philosophiæ Libri duo. Lugduni apud Seb. Gryphium, 1538. 4°. a-z^4 A-E^4. pp. 3-222. [40

-- Ia. Sadoleti de liberis recte instituendis, liber. Apud Seb. Gryphium Lugduni, 1533. 8°. A-I^8 K^4. pp. 3-149. [41

-- Duo ... poemata heroica. ... Iacobi Sadoletii, & Francisci Sfondrati. Quorum alterum inscribitur Curtius, alterum vero De raptu Helenæ. In Academia Veneta, M. D. LIX. 4°. $*^4$ A-F^4. ff. 1-24. [42

-- Iacobi Sadoleti ... epistolarum libri sexdecim. ... Vita eiusdem autoris per Antonium Florebellum. Lugduni, apud haered. Seb. Gryphii. 1560. 8°. a-z^8 A-Y^8 (-Y8, *blank*). pp. 2-716. [43

SAGREDO, DIEGO DE. Raison d'architecture antique ... nouuellement traduicte d'Espaignol en François ... A Paris, Pour Gilles Gourbin ... 1555. (Imprimé par Benoist Preuost ...) 4°. a-g^8. ff. 2-56. (Fine Arts.) [44

SAINT-DENIS, ANTOINE DE. Les comptes du monde auantereux contenant liiij. discours. Par A.D.S.D. De nouueau augmentees de cinq discours modernes ... A Paris, Chez Claude Michard ... 1582. 16°. a-z^8 A-P^8. pp. 1-588. [45

ST. GERMAN, CHRISTOPHER. The dyaloges in Englishe, betwene a Doctour of diuinitie and a studēt in the lawes of Englād ... (Londini in aedibus Richardi Toteli. An. 1554. ... 8°. B.L. A-Y^8 Z^4. ff. 3-182. *S.T.C.* 21571. (Biddle.) [46

-- -- (Londini in ædibus Richardi Tottelli, Anno. 1575.) 8°. B.L. A-Y^8 Z^4. ff. 2-177. *S.T.C.* 21573. (Biddle.) [47

-- -- (Londini in Ædibus Richardi Tottelli Anno 1580.) 8°. B.L. A-Y^8 Z^4. ff. 3-177. *S.T.C.* 21574. (Biddle.) [48

-- -- *Another copy.* (Furness.) [49

-- -- The Dialogue ... Imprinted at London ... by Richard Tottill. 1593. ... 8°. B.L. A-Y^8 Z^4 (-Z3-4). ff. 3-176. *S.T.C.* 21575. (Biddle.) [50

-- -- At London, Printed by Thomas Wight, and Bonham Norton. 1598. ... 8°. B.L. A-Y^8 Z^4. ff. 3-176. *S.T.C.* 21576. (Biddle.) [51

SALAMANCA. *University.* Estatutos hechos por la ... vniuersidad de Salamanca. En Salamanca Impresso Por Diego Cusio. Año. MDXCV. (... a tres dias del mes de Hebrero.) fol. A-G^8 H^6. ff. 2-55. [52

SALAMONI, MARIO. Marii Salamonii patritii Romani de principatu libri VI. Parisiis, Excudebat Dionysius du Val ... 1578. ... 8°. $\bar{a}^8$ A-H^8 I^4. pp. 1-115. [53

SALBACH, MARTIN. Carminum ... libri Septem ... Vitebergae excudebat Iohannes Crato. Anno M. D. LXXIII. (*Colophon.*) 8°. A-Nn^8. ¶A1 *defective.* [54

SALCEDO DE AGUIRRE, GASPAR. Pliego de cartas. ... En Baeça. por Iuan Baptista de Montoya. ... 1594. (*Colophon.*) 4°. π^4 (-π3) $+^{10}$ A-Bb^8 (-K8) Cc^6 (-Cc6, *presumably blank*). ff. 1-204. ¶*Engraved t.p.* [55

SALERNO. De conseruanda bona valetudine Opusculum Scholæ Salernitanæ ... Cum Arnoldi Nouicomensis Enarrationibus. ... repurgata ... Opera & studio Ioannis Curionis, & Iacobi Crellij. ... De electione meliorum Simplicium, ... Rhytmi M. Othonis Cremonensis. Item, S. Augustini Concio, de uitanda ebrietate, Carmine reddita. ... Franc. Apud Chr. Egen. (... M D LI.) 8°. *^{8} A-T^{8}. ff. 1-147. (Smith.) [56

-- -- ... Item: ... Epigramma Anastasij ad Armatum. Victus & cultus ratio, ... per Ioachimum Camerarium. ... De moderatione cibi & potus, ... Philippi Melanth. De uictus salubris ratione priuatorum, Polybii tractatus, Andernaco interprete. ... Franc. apud hæred. Chr. Egen. (... M. D. LVII.) 8°. α^{8} β^{4} A-Z^{8} a-m^{8} n^{4}. ff. 1-281. [57

-- -- ... Cum ... Arnoldi Villanouani ... Exegesi. Per Ioannem Curionem Berckensem ... recognita ... Franc. Apud Hæredes Chr. Egen. Anno M. D. LIX. (*Colophon.*) 8°. α^{8} β^{4} A-Z^{8} a-m^{8} (-m8, *presumably blank*). ff. 1-279. ¶α1 *repaired.* [58

SALICETUS, JOANNES, ECKIUS. Elegia Ioannis Saliceti Eckij, contra Petri Lempergij Gorlicensis calumniam. M. D. XLIIII. (Ingolstadii ex officina Alexandri Vueissenhorn.) 4°. a-b^{4}. [59

-- Threni in obitum Ioannis Eckii ... Obijt ann. M.D.XLIII. IIII. Idus Februarij. ... [Ingolstadii, Alexander Weissenhorn, 1543.] 4°. A^{4} B^{2}. [60

SALIGNAC, BARTHÉLEMY. [1] Itinerarium sacræ Scripturæ. Hoc est, Sanctæ Terræ ... descriptio ... Magdeburgi, Excudebat Paulus Donatus, Impensis Ambrosij Kirchneri, Anno M.D.XCIII. ... 4°. A-P^{4}. [2] Itinerarium Hierosol: ... Anno M. D. LXXXVII. Aa-Mm^{4} Nn^{2}. [61

SALĪM II, sultan. Goleta. Warhafftige eigentliche Beschreibung/ Wie der Türck ... die ... Vestung Goleta ... zugetragen hat. ... (M.D.LXXiiij. Gedruckt erstlich zu Nürmberg/ Nachmals zu Erffurdt/ durch Conradum Dreher.) 4°. A-B^{4}. [62

SALINAS, MIGUEL. Rhetorica en lengua Castellana ... M. D. XLI. (Fue impressa ... en la ... vniuersidad ὁ Alcala de Henares en casa de Ioã de Brocar/ a ocho dias del mes de Febrero ...) 4°. B.L. ✠^{4} a-o^{8} p^{6}. ff. j-cxvij. [63

SALLUSTIUS CRISPUS, GAIUS. C. Crispi Salustii, de coniuratione Catilinæ, & bello Iugurthino, historiæ ... (Viennæ Pãnoniæ in ædibus Hieronymi Vietoris, & Ioannis Singrenii, sociorum, Expensis uero Leonhardi, & Lucæ Alantseæ fratrũ. XII. Calendas Nouembres. Anno. M. D. XI.) 4°. a-h$^{8.8.4.4}$ i-k^{8} l^{4} m^{6}. [64

-- -- C. Crispi Sallustii de coniuratione Catilinae historia. Eiusdem de bello Iugurthino. Portij Latronis declamatio contra L. Catilinam. M. T. Ciceronis orationes quatuor in L. Catilinam. C. Crispi Sallustij in M. T. Ciceronem inuectiua. M. T. Ciceronis responsio. Fragmenta quædam ex libris historiarum C. Crispi Sallustij. ... Basileae, ex officina typographica And. Cratandri, An. M. D. XXIX. 8°. a-z^{8}. pp. 1-308. [65

-- -- C. Crispi Sallustii De L. Sergij Catilinæ coniuratione, ac Bello Iugurthino historiæ. ... Lugduni, apud Seb. Gryphium, 1549. 8°. a-s^{8}. pp. 3-261. ¶*Includes:* 1) M. T. Ciceronis ... recriminatio, 2) Eiusdem orationes quatuor contra L. Catilinam, 3) Fragmenta ... Sallustij. [66

-- -- C. Sallustii . Crispi coniuratio . Catilinae et . bellum . Iugurthinum fragmenta eiusdem historiarum ... Scholia . Aldi . Manutii ... Romae. M.D.LXIII. (... M.D.LXIV. Apud Paulum Manutium.) 8°. A^{8} A-BB^{8} (-BB8, *presumably blank*). ff. 2-178. [67

-- -- [1] C. SallustI Crispi operum, quæ exstant, Noua editio. Edente et recensente Ludouico Carrione. Antuerpiæ, Ex officina Christophori Plantini, ... cIↄ. Iↄ. LXXIX. 8°. A-P^{8}. pp. 4-236. [2] In C. Salustii Crispi Catilinam, et Iugurthinam, Ioannis Riuii Castigationum lib. II. Aldi Manutii Paulli f. Scholia. Cypriani a Popma Emendationes. In historiarum lib. VI. A Ludouico Carrione collectos, auctos, & restitutos. Eiusdem Lud. Carrionis Scholia. *Same imprint.* a-q^{8} r^{4}. pp. 3-249. [68

-- -- L'histoire de C. Crispe Saluste touchant la coniuration de L. Serge Catelin, auec la premiere harangue de M. Tulle Ciceron contre luy: ensemble la guerre Iugurthine, & la harangue de Portius Latro contre Catelin: traduittes de Latin en François, par Loys Meigret Lyonnois. ... Imprimée à Paris chés Chrestien Wechel ... le 25. de Mars, ... 1547. 8°. A-S^{8} T^{4}. pp. 2-295. [69

-- -- Salustio con alcune altre belle cose: volgareggiato per Agostino Ortica della Porta Genouese. (Empresso in Vinegia p̲ Bernardin Vinitiano di Vitali nel anno ... M.D.XVIII. adi .xxiii. di Aprile.) 4°. A-S^8 T^{12} (-T12, *presumably blank*). [70

-- -- *Another copy.* [71

-- -- (Impresso in Vinegia per Zorzi di Rusconi Milanese. ... M.D.XVIII. Adi .XXIII. d'Aprile.) 8°. A-T^8 V^4. [72

-- -- (Impresso in Vinegia per Marchio Sessa e Piero de Rauani Compagni del M.D.xxiii. Adi .18. Magio) 8°. A-R^8. ff. 2-136. [73

-- -- Salustio tradotto ... MDXXXI. (Stampato in Vinegia ... per Francesco di Alessandro Bindoni, & Mapheo Pasini compagni. .... Del mese di Nouembrio.) 8°. A-Q^8. ff. 2-127.[74

-- -- L'historia di C. Crispo Sallustio ... per Lelio Carani tradotta. In Fiorenza. M D L. (Stampato ... appresso Lorenzo Torrentino ... del mese d'Aprile ...) 8°. ❦^{10} A-R^8 S^6. pp. 1-181. [75

-- -- La historia di Gaio Sallustio Crispo, ... tradotta dal Signor Paulo Spinola. ... In Venetia, per Gio. Andrea Valuassori. M. D. LXIIII. (... MDLXIII.) 8°. A^8 A-O^8. pp. 1-224. [76

-- C. Crispi Salustij Liber de Bello Iugurtino. (Impressum Liptzk per Iacobū Thanner. Anno dñi Millesimo quingentesimodecimoquinto.) fol. B.L. A-F$^{6.6.4}$ G^6. [77

-- C. Crispi Sallustii lib. de cōiuratione L. Ser. catilinae. (Impressus Constautie [*sic*] per Ioannem Schaͤffeler ... M.ccccc v. Duodecimo die Iunij.) 4°. B.L. a-f$^{6.6.4}$. [78

-- -- ([Lipsiae] ... ab Herbipolēsi Martino [Landsberg] ... impressum ... Anno ... Decimo supra millesimū quingentesimūqȝ.) fol. B.L. A-B^6 C^4 D^6. [79

SALMON, JEAN. Salmonii Macrini Iuliodunensis carminum libellus. Parisiis Apud Simonem Colinæum 1528. 8°. A-B^8. [80

-- Salmonii Macrini ... hymnorum libri sex ... Parisiis. Ex officina Roberti Stephani. M. D. XXXVII. (... VII. Idus Febr.) 8°. a-p^8. pp. 4-238. [81

-- Salmonii Macrini ... Hymnorum selectorum libri tres. ... Parisiis. Ex officina Roberti Stephani ... M. D. XL. (... XVI. Cal. Iulii.) 8°. a-g^8 h^4. pp. 3-118. [82

-- Salmonii Macrini ... lyricorum libri duo ... Epithalamiorum liber vnus ... Parisiis ex officina Gerardi Morrhii Campensis. M. D. XXXI. ... 8°. A-F^8 G^4. [83

-- Salmonii Macrini ... Næniarum libri tres, De Gelonide Borsala uxore ... Lutetiae Apud Vascosanum ... M. D. L. 8°. A-I^8. pp. 2-144. [84

-- Salmonii Macrini ... Odarum libri Sex ... Seb. Gryphius excudebat Lugduni, anno M. D. XXXVII. 8°. a-n^8 o^4 p-q^8. [85

-- Salmonii Macrini ... Odarum libri tres ... Io. Bellaii ... Poemata aliquot ... Parisiis Ex officina Rob. Stephani ... M. D. XLVI. ... 8°. A-K^8. pp. 3-159. [86

SALUSTE, GUILLAUME, sieur du Bartas. Ioannis Edoardi du Monin, Burgundionis Gyani[,] Beresithias, siue mundi creatio, Ex Gallico G. Salustij du Bartas Heptamero expressa. .. Eiusdem Edoardi manipulus poëticus ... Parisiis, Apud Ioannem Parant. M. D. LXXIX. ... 8°. ä^8 A-Q^8 R^3 + a^5 b-h^8. ff. 1-131, pp. 1-104. [87

SALVIANUS MASSILIENSIS. Saluiani Massiliensis presbiteri de gubernatione Dei et de iusto præsentíque eius iudicio libri VIII. ... Eiusdem epistolarum Lib. I. Ex Bibliotheca P. Pithoei I.C. [Genevae,] Apud Iacobum Chouët. 1600. 16°. (:)^8 a-t^8. pp. 1-297. [88

SALVIATI, JOSEPHE. Regola di far perfettamente col compasso la voluta Et del capitello Ionico ... In Vinetia Per Francesco Marcolini. M D LII. ... (... di Giugno.) fol. A^4. (Fine Arts.) [89

SALVIATI, LIONARDO. Cinque lezzioni ..., Cioè due della Speranza, vna della Felicita, e l'altre due sopra varie materie: ... con l'occasione del Sonetto del Petrarca. Poi che vol, & io piu volte habbiam prouato. In Firenze. Appresso i Giunti. 1575. ... 4°. A-H^4 I^2. ff. 2-34. [90

-- Considerazioni di Carlo Fioretti da Vernio, intorno a vn discorso di M. Giulio Ottonelli da Fanano sopra ad alcune dispute dietro alle Gierusalem di Torq. Tasso. ... In Firenze Per Antonio Padouani M. D. LXXXVI. 8°. A-K^8 (-K8, *presumably blank*). pp. 5-157. [91

-- De dialogi d'Amicizia ... libro primo ... In Firenze Appresso i Giunti 1564. (*Colophon.*) 8°. A-F^8 G^4. pp. 2-86. [92

-- [1] Degli auuertimenti della lingua sopra'l Decamerone Volume Primo ... In Venezia. M D LXXXIIII. ... (... Presso Domenico, & Gio. Battista Guerra, fratelli. ...) 4°. a-d^4 A-Xx^4 YY^4 ZZ^6. pp. 6-335. [2] Del secondo volume degli auuertimenti ... Libri due ... In Firenze. Nella Stamperia de' Giunti. 1586. ... (*Colophon.*) *^{4} a-b^4 c^6 A-Z^4. pp. 1-154. [93

-- Lo'nfarinato secondo ouuero dello'nfarinato Accademico della Crusca, risposta al libro intitolato Replica di Camillo Pellegrino ec. ... In Firenze Per Anton Padouani. MDLXXXVIII. ... 8°. *^{8} A-Cc^8 A^8 *^{8} (-*8, *presumably blank*). pp. 1-398. [94

-- Orazione ... Nella Morte dello ... S. Don Garzia, De Medici. ... In Firenze appresso i Giunti. 1562. 4°. A-B^4. [95

-- Orazione ... Nella quale si dimostra la Fiorentina fauella, & i Fiorentini Autori essere a tutte l'altre lingue, ... e a tutti gli altri Scrittori ... lunga superiori Da lui ... recitata nella Fiorentina Accademia il di vltimo d'Aprile. 1564 ... In Firenze Appresso i Giunti 1564 ... 4°. A-C^4 D^2. [96

-- Il Primo Libro delle orazioni ... In Firenze. Nella Stamperia de' Giunti. M D LXXV. (... M D LXXIIII.) 4°. a^4 A-X^4. pp. 9-161. [97

-- Dello Infarinato Accademico della Crusca Risposta all' apologia di Torquato Tasso Intorno all'Orlando Furioso, e alla Gierusalem liberata. ... In Firenze Per Carlo Meccoli, e Saluestro Magliani. 1585. 8°. ¶^{8} A-I^8 K^4. pp. 1-149. [98

-- Seconda orazione ... Nella Morte dello ... S. Don Garzia, De Medici. ... In Firenze appresso i Giunti. M.D.LXII. 4°. A-B^4. [99

-- Terza orazione ... Nella Morte dello ... S. Don Garzia De Medici. ... In Firenze appresso i Giunti. MDLXIII. 4°. A-C^4. [100

SALWECHTER, JAKOB. Dboeck van Exceptien inden Rechte ... Gheprint Tantwerpen ... by Hans de Laet/ Anno. M. D. Liiij. ... 8°. a-g^8. (Biddle.) [101

-- De maniere om een Proces te voeren ... Gheprint Tantwerpen ... by Hans de Laet/ Anno. M.D. eñ Liiij. ... 8°. A-H^8. (Biddle.) [102

SAMBUCUS, JOANNES. Emblemata, et aliquot nummi antiqui ... Tertia editio. ... Antuerpiæ. Ex officina Christophori Plantini. Iɔ. cIɔ. LXIX. 16°. A-Y^8 (-Y8). pp. 4-350 *present.* [103

SÁNCHEZ, FRANCISCO. De autoribus interpretandis, siue De Exercitatione, Francisci Sanctii Brocensis ... Antuerpiæ, Ex officina Christophori Plantini ... M. D. LXXXII. (... cIɔ. Iɔ. LXXXI. Mense Septemb.) 8°. A-B^8. pp. 3-28. [104

-- Francisci Sanctij Brocensis, ... Grammatices Latinae institutiones, caeterae fallaces & prolixae. ... Salmanticae Excudebat Ioannes Ferdinandus. Anno. M. D. XCV. 8°. A-F^8 A^4. ff. 2-48. [105

-- Francisci Sanctii Brocensis ... Minerua: seu de causis linguæ Latinæ. ... Salmanticae, Apud Ioannem, & Andręam Renaut, fratres. 1587 (*Colophon.*) 8°. A-Ll^8 *-**^{8} +^{8} (-+1, +8, *the latter presumably blank*). ff. 5-271, 1-16. (Lea.) [106

SÁNCHEZ, PEDRO. Historia moral y philosophica, En que se tratan las vidas de doze Philosophos, y Principes antiguos ... Impresso en Toledo, en casa de la biuda de Iuan de la Plaça. Año. 1590 ... fol. ♦^{10} A-Zz^8 3A^4 ¶^{8} (-¶6-8). ff. 2-372. [107

SÁNCHEZ DE ARÉVALO, RODRIGO. Liber incipit de origine ac differentia principatus imperialis et regalis ... (Impressum Rome apud Stephanū Guillireti ... M.D.XXI. die .iiii. Mensis Octobris ...) fol. A-P^6 Q^4 (-Q4, *presumably blank*). ff. 3-93. [108

-- Speculum vite humane ... Author ... fuit ... Rodericus Episcopus zamorẽsis Castellanus ... (Simon autẽ beuelaqua ... in ... Lugdunensium vrbe imprimebat. Anno ... Millesimoquingentesimodecimosexto. sexto nonas Maij.) 8°. B.L. A-B⁸ a-p⁸. ff. 1-119. [109

SÁNCHEZ DE LA BALLESTA, ALONSO. Dictionario de vocablos Castellanos, aplicados a la propriedad Latina. ... En Salamanca, En casa de Iuan y Andres Renaut ... M.D.LXXXVII. 4°. ¶⁴ ¶¶²⁺¹ A-Vv⁸ a-e⁴. pp. 1-688. [110

SANDEUS, FELINUS MARIA. Consilia seu responsa ... Lugduni, Apud hæredes Iacobi Iuntæ, M.D.LII. ... (... Thomas Bertellus ... excudebat.) fol. a-m⁶ A⁶ B⁸. ff. 4-68. (Biddle.) [111

SANDFURT, WILHELM. De perpetua ecclesiae Dei in mundo conseruatione ... sectiones viginti. ... Autore Guilielmo Santphurdio. 1553. (Francofurti in officina Petri Brubachii ...) 8°. A-H⁸ I⁴. pp. 3-125. [112

SANDOVAL, PRUDENCIO DE. Chronica del inclito emperador de España, Don Alonso VII. ... Año 1600. En Madrid, Por Luis Sanchez. (*Colophon.*) fol. [¶]-3¶⁴ A-Ss⁶. pp. 1-491. [113

SAN GIORGIO, BENVENUTO DE. De origine Guelphorum, et Gibellinorum ... In quo ostenditur, quantum hac in re Clariss. scriptores ... à ueritate aberrauerint. (Basileae, apud Andream Cratandrum. Mense Ianuario, anno M.D.XIX.) 4°. a⁶. ff. 2-6. [114

-- -- *Another copy.* [115

-- Montisferrati Marchionum ⁊ Principũ Regie propaginis: successionũq3 series ... (Impressa in oppido Tridini ... Impẽsis dñi Ioannis de ferrariis al's de Iolitis ... M.cccccxxj. die .xij. Mensis Martij.) 8°. B.L. A-F⁴. [116

SAN GIORGIO, GIOVANNI ANTONIO DA. Praepositus super quarto decre. ... cũ additiõibus ... Benedicti de Vadis ... autẽ cum ... summarijs Henrici Ferrãdat Niuernensis ... [*Device of Jacobus Giunta of Lyons.*] 1541 fol. B.L. a-v⁸ x⁶. ff. 2-155. (Biddle.) [117

-- Domi. Praepo. super feudis. ... Lugduni, Apud Hæredes Iacobi giuntæ. M. D. XLVIII. fol. A¹⁰ a-s⁶ t-v⁸. ff. 1-124. (Biddle.) [118

SANLEOLINO, SEBASTIANO. Serenissimi Cosmi Medycis primi Hetruriae Magniducis Actiones ... Florentiæ, Typis Georgij Marescoti 1578. (*Colophon.*) 4°. a-b⁴ A-Kk⁴ LL-MM⁴. ff. 1-132. [119

SAN MARTINO, MATTEO, Conte da. Le osseruationi grammaticale e poetiche della lingua Italiana. ... In Roma per Valerio Dorico, e Luigi fratelli del M.D.LV. (*Colophon.*) 8°. A-P⁸ Q⁴. pp. 3-245. [120

-- Piscatoria et ecloghe del San Martino. [Venezia, Gabriel Giolito, c. 1544.] 8°. A-L⁸ M⁴. [121

SANNAZARO, JACOPO. Iacobi Sannazarii opera omnia Latine scripta ... M. D. XXXV. ... (Venetiis, in aedibus haeredum Aldi Manutii, et Andreae Asulani soceri, mense Septembri ...) 8°. a-e⁸ A-H⁸. ff. 3-40, 1-63. [122

-- -- Apud Seb. Gryphium Lugduni, 1536. 8°. a-m⁸ n⁴. pp. 2-198. [123

-- -- Lugduni, Apud Antonium Gryphium. 1569. 16°. a-m⁸ n⁴ (-n4, *presumably blank*). pp. 2-198. (Lea.) [124

-- Arcadia del Sannazaro ... (Impressa in Napoli per Maestro Sigismundo Mayr: con ... diligenza di Petro Summontio: ... MDIIII. del mese di Marzo. ...) 4°. A-L⁸ M⁶ N⁴. [125

-- -- Libro pastorale nominato Archadio de Iacobo sanazaro neapolitano. (Impresso in Milano per Ioanne Angelo Scinzenzeler. ... M.ccccc.iiii. a di .viiii. di Zenaro.) 4°. a-e⁸ f⁴ (-f4, *presumably blank*). [126

-- -- Arcadia del Sannazaro ... [Napoli, c. 1508.] 4°. A-N⁸. [127

-- -- (Impresso in Vinegia nelle case D'Aldo Romano nel'anno MDXIIII nel mese di Settembre.) 8°. A-K⁸ L¹⁰. ff. 2-89. [128

-- -- M.D.XXXIIII. (Impresso in Vinegia nelle case delli heredi d'Aldo Romano, et Andrea socero ...) 8°. A-L^8 M^4. ff. 2-91. [129

-- -- Arcadia di Messer Giacopo Sannazaro ... M.D.XXXIX. (Per Giouanni Andrea di Vauassori detto Guadagnino. ... Del mese d'Aprile.) 8°. A-K^8 L^4. [130

-- -- Arcadia del Sannazaro. ... ritornata alla sua vera lettione. Da M. Lodouico Dolce. In Vinegia appresso Gabriel Giolito de' Ferrari, e fratelli. M D LVI. 12°. A-F^{12} G^6. ff. 3-78. [131

-- -- Arcadia di M. Iacopo Sannazaro. Nouamente corretta ... da Thomaso Porcacchi. ... In Venetia, Appresso Antonio Ferrari. M D,LXXXI. (... Appresso Oratio de' Gobbi. ...) 12°. $*^{12}$ A-L^{12} (-L12, *presumably blank*). pp. 1-25[3]. [132

-- Synceri. De partu Virginis. (In ædibus ... Andreæ Matthæi Aquiuiui Hadrianorum Interamnatumq3 Ducis per Antonium Fretiam Corinaldinum ciuemq3 Neap. ... MDXXVI Maio Mense Neapoli.) fol. A-G^6 g^4 H-K^6 L-M^4. ¶H1r: ... Piscatoria. *Printed on vellum.* [133

-- -- Actii Synceri Sannazarii de partu Virginis libri tres. Lamentatio de morte Christi. Piscatoria. Parisiis ex officina Roberti Stephani ... M.D.XXVII. (... V. Idus Maii.) 8°. a-f^8. [134

-- -- Del parto della Vergine del Sanazaro libri tre, Tradotti in versi Toscani da Giouanni Giolito de' Ferrari. ... In Venetia, appresso i Gioliti. MDLXXXVIIII. 4°. π^4 A-R^4 S^2. [135

-- Rime di M. Giacopo Sannazaro. ... reuiste, per M. Lodouico Dolci. In Venetia. Appresso Oratio de' Gobbi. M. D. LXXXI. 12°. A-D^{12}. pp. 3-94. [136

-- -- *Variant.* In Venetia. Appresso Antonio Ferrari. M. D. LXXXI. [137

-- -- Rime ... ripuragte ... per M. Borgarurutio [*sic*] Borgarucci. In Venetia, M D LXXXIX. Appresso Pietro Marinelli. 12°. A-D^{12}. pp. 3-96. [138

-- Sonetti, è canzoni del Sannazaro. M.D.XXXIIII. (In Vinegia, nelle case delli heredi d'Aldo Romano, & Andrea socero, ... nel mese di Luglio.) 8°. A-F^8 G^4. ff. 2-48. [139

-- -- In Venetia appresso Gabriel Gioli di Ferrarii M D XXXXIII. (*Colophon.*) 8°. A-F^8 G^4. ff. 2-48. [140

SAN PEDRO, DIEGO HERNANDO DE. Carcer damore del ... Meser Lelio di Manfredi Ferrarese [Vinegia, Zorzi di Rusconi, 1514.] 8°. A-O^4 P^6. ¶*6-line colophon erased. Printed on vellum.* [141

SANSOVINO, FRANCESCO. Cento nouelle scelte da piu nobili scrittori della lingua volgare ... In Venetia, M D LXVI. 4°. $*^4$ A-$3O^4$. ff. 2-238. [142

-- Le ciento nouelle antike 4°. A-I^4. ff. I-XXXI. ¶*Probably part of a copy of the 1571 ed. of the* Cento nouelle scelte (Venetia, Appresso gli Heredi di Marchiò Sessa). [143

-- Concetti politici ... Raccolti da gli Scritti di diuersi Auttori Greci, Latini, & Volgari ... In Venetia, MDLXXVIII. Appresso Giouanni Antonio Bertano. 4°. *-$**^4$ A-Mm^4. ff. 1-140. [144

-- Cronologia del mondo ... In Vinegia, Presso Altobello Salicato, M D LXXXII. 4°. $*^8$ $**^6$ A-Z^8 Aa^6 (-Aa6, *blank*). ff. 1-189. [145

-- De gli huomini illustri della casa Orsina ... libri quattro. ... In Venetia. Appresso Bernardino, & Filippo Stagnini, fratelli. MDLXV. (Stampata ... per Domenico Nicolini ...) fol. A-O^4 P^6 Q-X^4 Y^6. ff. 2-92. [146

-- Del secretario ouero formulario di lettere missiue et responsiue ... Libri Quattro. ... In Venetia. MDLXXIII. (*Colophon.*) 8°. $\dagger^8$ A-Q^8. ff. 1-126. [147

-- Delle lettere amorose di diuersi huomini illustri. Libri noue. ... In Venetia, Appresso gli Eredi del Bonelli. 1574. (*Colophon.*) 8°. $*^8$ A-R^8. ff. 1-135. [148

-- Dell'historia vniuersale dell'origine et imperio de Turchi ... libri tre. ... In Venetia, appresso Francesco Rampazetto. M D LXIIII. (*Colophon.*) 4°. $*^4$ A-LL^8 MM^4 NN-$3L^8$. ff. 1-457. [149

-- [1] Diuerse orationi volgarmente scritte da molti huomini illustri de tempi nostri. ... Raccolte ... per Francesco Sansouino. ... In Venetia. (... appresso Fran. Sansouino.

M D LXI.) 4°. *^{8} a-z^4 &^{4} ꝯ^4 ꝝ^4 A-Y^4. ff. 1-104, 1-88. [2] Delle orationi ... Parte Seconda ... In Venetia (*Same colophon.*) *^{4} A-NN^4. ff. 1-150. [3] Di Francesco Sansouino in materia dell'arte libri tre ... In Venetia, M D LXI. (*Same colophon.*) A-M^4. ff. 2-48. [150

-- -- Delle orationi ... parte prima. ... In Venetia M D LXXV al segno della luna. 4°. *^{4} ◆◆^{4} A-4A^4 *^{4} A-T^4. ff. 1-345. ¶*Additional t.p.* (^{2}*1^r): Delle orationi ... parte seconda. ... *Same imprint.* [151

-- Gl'annali Turcheschi ouero vite de principi della casa Othomana ... In Venetia MDLXXIII. (... Appresso Enea de Alaris. ...) 4°. a-c^4 A-Ee^4. pp. 1-224. [152

-- L'historia di casa Orsina ... In Venetia, Appresso Bernardino, & Filippo Stagnini, fratelli. M D LXV. (... Appresso Nicolo Beuilacqua ...) fol. *^{4} A^{10} A-Ll^4 (C4 + *folded leaf*). ff. 2-135. [153

-- Informatione ... a soldati Christiani et a tutti coloro che sono su la potentissima armata della ... Signoria di Venezia. Fatta contra Selim secondo re de' Turchi l'anno MDLXX. [Venezia, 1570.] fol. A^{10} (+ *engraved plate*). (Lea.) [154

-- Le osseruationi della lingua volgare de diuersi huomini illustri, cioè Del Bembo, Del Gabriello, Del Fortunio, Dell'Acarisio. Et di altri Scrittori. ... In Venetia. M D LXV. (... appresso Fr. Rampazetto. ...) 8°. *^{8} A-RR^8 SS^4. ff. 1-324. ¶*Lacks an extra leaf between* Q1 *and* Q2. [155

-- Sette libri di sattire di Lodouico Ariosto. Hercole Bentiuogli. Luigi Alemanni. Pietro Nelli. Antonino Vinciguerra. Francesco Sansouino. E d'altri scrittori. ... raccolti per Francesco Sansouino. In Venetia, Appresso Nicolò Beuilacqua. 1563. (*Colophon.*) 8°. *^{8} A-Cc^8 (-Cc8, *presumably blank*). ff. 1-206. [156

-- -- *Another copy.* [157

-- Il simulacro di Carlo quinto imperadore ... In Venetia, Appresso Francesco Franceschini, M. D. LXVII. (... appresso Francesco Franceschini, & Iseppo Mantelli. ...) 8°. a^8 A-Q^8 R^4. ff. 2-139. [158

-- Venetia citta nobilissima et singolare, Descritta in XIIII. Libri ... In Venetia, appresso Iacomo Sansouino. M D LXXXI. (Stampata ... Appresso Domenico Farri. ...) 4°. A^4 A^6 B-3Z^4 a-g^4 h^6 aa-hh^4 ii^6. ff. 1-286, 1-38. [159

SANTAREM, PEDRO DE. Petri Santernae Lusitani ... tractatus de assecurationibus & sponsionibus Mercatorum ... Venetiis apud Baltassarem Constantinum ... M D LII. 8°. A-G^8 H^4. ff. 3-52. [160

SANTIAGO. *Archbishopric.* Constituciones synodales, del arçobispado de Sanctiago, hechas por ... Francisco Blanco Arçobispo ... Año de 1576. Impressas en Madrid ... En casa de Pierres Cosin. Año de 1579. 4°. π^2 A-L^8 M^4. ff. 1-91. (Lea.) [161

SANTOTIS, CRISTOBAL. Concio R. P. Mag. Christophori Sanctotisii, Hispani, Burgensis ... Habita ad ... Synodum Tridentinam. De signis ueræ Ecclesiæ agnoscendæ. Dominica tertia Quadragesimæ M D LXIII. Venetiis, ex officina Iordani Ziletti. M D LXIII. 4°. a-e^4. (Lea.) [162

SANUDO, PIETRO AURELIO. ... Recens Lutheranarum assertionum oppugnatio, per Magistrum Petrum Aurelium Sanutum Venetum ... Venetiis ... M D XLIII. (Apud Aldi filios ... Mense Iulio.) 4°. A-CC^4. ff. 2-95. ¶A2, A3 *misbound after* B4. (Lea.) [163

SANUTO, LIVIO. Al ... cardinal di Trento la rapina di Proserpina ... M. D. LIII. 8°. A-F^8. ff. 2-48. [164

SAPIDUS, JOANNES. Epigrammata ... [Selestadii, Lazarus Schürer, 1520.] 4°. a-f^4 g^6. [165

SARACENUS, JOANNES ANTONIUS. Summo Pont. Leoni X. ... pro re. pub. Senen. [Romae, Marcellus Silber, 1513.] 4°. π^4. [166

SARCERIUS, ERASMUS. Ein ander Leichpredigte/ vber die Leiche/ vnsers ... Churfuͤrstens zu

Sachssen/ auff den 20. tag Iulij ... M. D. LIII. (Gedruckt zu Leiptzig Durch Iacobum Berwaldt.) 4°. A-E^{4}. ¶*Sig.* C *misbound before sig.* B. [167

-- -- *Another copy.* [168

-- Einer Christlichen Ordination/ form vnd weise ... ... M. D. LIIII. (Gedruckt zu Eisleben/ durch Vrbanum Kaubisch ...) 4°. A-G^{4}. [169

-- Corpus iuris matrimonialis. ... Getruckt zu Franckfurt am Mayn/ im jar M. D. LXIX. fol.)(^{4})(^{6} A-3F^{6} 3G^{4}. ff. I-CCXCXVI. [170

-- Leichpredigte/ des ... Herrn Moritzen Hertzogen/ vnd Churf. zu Sachssen ... Geprediget zu Leiptzig den 15. Iulij ... M. D. LIII. ... (Gedruckt zu Leiptzig Durch Iacobum Berwaldt.) 4°. A-E^{4}. [171

-- Eine Predigte/ auff dem grossen Landtage zu Leipzig/ gethan/ ... M.D.LIII. Den xxj. Augusti. ... (Gedruckt zu Leipzig/ durch Iacobum Berwaldt.) 4°. A-E^{4}. [172

-- Rhetorica ... Francoforti, Apud Chr. Egenolphum. (... 1546. Mense Iunio.) 8°. A-O^{8}. ff. 2-110. [173

SARDI, ALESSANDRO. Alexandri Sardi Ferrariensis, de moribus ac ritibus gentium libri III. ... Venetiis, Ex officina Stellæ Iordani Zilleti. 1557. (*Colophon.*) 8°. *^{8} A-R^{8}. pp. 1-265. [174

-- Discorsi del S. Alessandro Sardo Della Bellezza. Della Nobiltà. Della Poesia di Dante. De i Precetti Historici. Delle qualità del Generale. Del Terremoto. ... In Venetia appresso i Gioliti. M D LXXXVI. 8°. *-3*^{8} 4*^{4} A-N^{8}. pp. 1-207. [175

SARDI, GASPARO. Historie Ferraresi ... In Ferrara appresso Francesco Rossi da Valenza. MDLVI. 4°. [A]^{4} (-A2) B-Ss^{4} Tt^{2} (-Tt2). pp. 5-330. ¶*At the end a copy of a later printing of the 11th book* (Dd3-4, Ee-Gg^{4}) *has been bound in.* [176

SARTORIUS, JOANNES. Selectissimarum Orationum Germanice redditarum ... aduersus barbariem exercitus ... Quibus accesserunt & aliæ quædam Sartorij, ab Henrico Iunio Selectæ orationes ... Antuerpiae, Ex officina Ioannis Loëi, Anno 1565. 8°. A-K^{8} L^{4} M-N^{8} O^{4} (-O4, *presumably blank*). ff. 4-10[3]. [177

-- -- Linguæ Latinæ phrases: vel ... orationum ... exercitus ... Antuerpiæ, Apud Henricum Henricium ... 1573. ... (... Typis AEgidii Radaei.) 8°. A-M^{8} N^{4}. ff. 2-100. [178

SASSO, PAMPHILO. Opera del preclarissimo poeta Miser Pamphilo Sasso Modenese ... (Venetiis per Guilielmum de Fontaneto de Monferrato. M.ccccc.xix. Adi primo Febraro.) 4°. a-k^{8} (-a4-5, k8, *the last presumably blank*). [179

SATAN. Expostulation vnd straffschrifft Satane des Fürsten diser welt mit hertzog Heintzen von Braunschweig/ seinem geschworen diener ... Getruckt in Vtopia [1541]. 4°. a-c^{4}. [180

SATTLER, BASILIUS. Eine Christliche Leichpredigt ... gethan Bey der Begrebnus ... Elisabeth von Veltheim ... Gedruckt zu Helmstedt durch Iacobum Lucium Anno 1580. 4°. A-C^{4} D^{2}. [181

SAVILE, SIR HENRY. Rerum Anglicarum scriptores post Bedam praecipui ... Londini, Excudebant G. Bishop, R. Nuberie, & R. Barker ... cIo Io XCVI. fol. ¶^{2} A-R^{6} S^{8} T-Dd^{6} Ee^{4} Ff-4R^{6} 4S^{4} *-**^{4} 3*^{6} A-H^{2}. pp. 4-520. *S.T.C.* 21783. ¶*Additional t.pp.:* (A1^{r}) Willielmi monachi Malmesburiensis, De gestis Regum Anglorum, Libri quinque. Eiusdem Historiæ Nouellæ, libri duo. Eiusdem de Pontificibus Anglorum, lib. quinque. *Same imprint.* (Ff1^{r}) Henrici archidiaconi Huntindoniensis historiarum libri octo. *Same imprint.* (Qq1^{r}) Rogeri de Houeden annalium Pars prior, & posterior. *Same imprint.* (4K4^{r}) Chronicorum Ethelwerdi libri IIII. Ingulphi ... Historiarum, Lib. vnus. *Same imprint.* [182

SAVIOLO, VINCENTIO. Vincentio Sauiolo his Practise. In two Bookes. The first intreating of the vse of the Rapier and Dagger. The second, of Honor and honorable Quarrels. London Printed by Iohn Wolfe. 1595. 4°. A-H^{4} &-3&^{4} I^{4} (-I1 *cancelled*) K-2G^{4} ¶^{2} 2H-2M^{4} (-A1, 2M4, *presumably blank*). *S.T.C.* 21788. ¶*Additional t.p.* (O1^{r}): Of honor and honorable Quarrels. The second Booke. London, Printed by Iohn Wolfe. 1594. (Furness.) [183

SAVONAROLA, GIROLAMO. Confessionale R.F. Hieronymi Sauonarolae ... Additis nonnullis ex Concilio Tridentino, præcipuè excommunicationū sententijs, ac alijs ad matrimonij negotium pertinentibus ... Per ... Alexandrum Saulium ... collectis, & reuisis. Taurini. MDLXXVIII. (... Apud hæredes Nicolai Beuilaquæ. ...) 8°. A-L^8. ff. 2-88. (Lea.) [184

-- Habes hic Lector, Dialogū de Fratre Hieronymo Nicolai Sauonorola Ferrariensi ... laqueo suspenso, igne atq3 aqua consumpto. Epistolam Ioachimi Turrani, Veneti ... & Frācisci Ramalicii ... Hispani, ad Alex: VI. de Hiero: & Syluestro Floren: & Dominico de Pisia cōplicib^9 damnatis. Epistolam Alexādri Papę approbantis conciones in Hiero: factas, lepore refertam. M. D. XXI. 4°. A^4. (Lea.) [185

-- Fratris Hieronymi. Sauonarolæ Ferrariēsis expositiōes in psalmos. Qui regis israel. Miserere mei deus. In te domine speraui. Item Regulæ quedam ... ad omnes religiosos attinentes. Oratio: uel psalmus. Diligam te domine. (Impressęq3 Venetiis ... per Cęsarem Arriuabenū Venetum ... M.D.XVII.) 8°. A-N^4. ff. II-LIII. (Lea.) [186

-- Libri fratris Hieronymi de ferraria ... de simplicitate Christiane vite. Venundantur ab Ioanne paruo Henrico iacobi ⁊ ipsorū impressore Ascensio (impressum ... Parrhisiis ... Ad Sextū Calēdas Iunias ... M.D.XI. ...) 8°. B.L. A-G^8 H^4. (Yarnall.) [186a

-- -- Opera di Frate Hieronymo Sauonarola da Ferrara, della semplicita della uita Christiana ... In Venetia al segno della speranza. MDXLVII. 8°. A-H^8. ff. 2-64. [187

-- Opera singolare del ... F. Hieronimo Sauonarola cōtra L'astrologia diuinatrice in corroboratione delle refutatione astrologica del. S. conte Ioan. Pico de la Mirandola ... In Vinegia MDXXXVI. (... per M. Bernardino Stagnino ...) 8°. B.L. A-E^8. ff. 2-38. (Lea.) [188

-- Oratione di Hieremia propheta laquale Fra Girolamo da Ferrara ha cōfortato sidebba dire ogni di da qualunche fedele christiano. [Firenze, Lorenzo Morgiani & Johannes Petri.] 4°. π^2. (Lea.) [189

-- Prediche del Rev. P.F. Hieronymo Sauonaruola ... sopra alquanti salmi & sopra Aggeo Profeta ... raccolta dalla sua uiua uoce Da frate Stefano da Codiponte ... M D XLIIII. (In Vineggia per Bernardino de Bindoni Milanese. ...) 8°. a^8 A-Z^8 AA^4. ff. 2-185. [190

-- Prediche ... sopra il Salmo quam bonus Israel Deus ... da Fra Girolamo Giannoti da Pistoia in lingua volgare tradotte. ... MDXXXIX. (Stampata in Vinegia per Brandino & Ottauiano Scoto a di sedese di Mazo. ...) 8°. ✠^{8} A-PP^8. ff. 1-302. (Yarnall.) [190a

-- [a2^r] Regole a tutti li Religiosi molto utile/ cōposte da Frate Hieronymo da Ferrara ... 4°. a^4 (-a1). [191

-- *Suppositious work.* Il nouo cortegiano de vita cauta et morale. ... 4°. A^8 B-Q^4. [192

SAVOY. *Charles III, duke.* Philippi chenrem Oratoris ... Caroli Sabaudie ducis ad Iulium .II. ... Oratio. M.cccccvi. xx. Aprilis. 4°. π^4. [193

SAXO GRAMMATICUS. Danorum Regū heroūq3 Historię ... Saxone Grammatico ... cōscriptę ... (... impressit in ... Parrhisiorum academia Iodocus Badius Ascensius Idibus Martiis. MDXIIII. ...) fol. Aa^8 a-z^8 A-B^8 (-B8, *blank*). ff. I-CXCVIII. [194

-- -- Danica historia libris XVI ... conscripta. ... Francofurti ad Moenum Ex officina Typographica And. Wecheli. M.D.LXXVI. (*Colophon.*) fol. ã^4 A-Gg^6 Hh^4. pp. 1-342. (Lea.) [195

SAXONY. *Laws &c.* Sechsische oberhofgerichts Ordenung. (Hatt gedruckt tzu Leyptzigk/ Melchior Lotter. Im .M.D.xxix.) 4°. A-B^4 (-B1) C^6. [196

-- Ordnungen/ Hertzog Ernsten/ Hertzog Albrechten/ Hertzog Moritzen/ vn̄ Hertzog Augusten/ Chur vnd Fürsten zu Sachssen ... 1573 Dressden. (... Auffs naw vmbgedrucket/ durch Matthes Stöckel/ vnd Gimel Bergen. ...) 4°.)(^{4} A-3T^4. ff. 2-239. [197

-- Das Gantze Sechsisch Landrecht ... Durch Doctor Melchior Klingen von Steinaw ... Leipzig. M. D. Lxxvij. (Gedruckt ... bey Hanss Steinman ...) fol.)(^{6} A-Z^6 a-u^6 x^8. ff. I-CCLXII. [198

-- Sachsisch Lehenrecht vnnd Weichbilt ... Durch ... Christoff Zobel ... zugerichtet. ... Leipzig. Anno M. D. Lxxxix. (... Bey Hans Steinmans Erben. ...) fol.)?(^{6}):(^{2} a-l1^6

)(^{2} A-3B^6 3C^8 (-3C8, *presumably blank*). ff. I-CXCII, I-CLXII. ¶*Additional t.pp.:* ()(1) Magdeburgisch Weichbildt ... Leipzig. M. D. Lxxxix. (Ee1) Remissorium Oder Register vber den Sachsenspiegel/ Lehenrecht vnnd Weichbild ... Leipzig. M. D. Lxxxviij. [199

-- *Johann I, elector.* Ausschreiben durchs Chur vnd Furstenthumb zu Sachssen ... zuerhaltung Christlicher zucht/ belangend. M. D. XXXj. 4°. A-B^4. [200

-- *Georg, duke.* Des Churfursten vnd Hertzog Georgen zu Sachssen voreynigung der Blackerey vnd Mutwilligen Befehder halben. M. D. XXXIII. 4°. A-C^4. [201

-- *Johann Friedrich I, elector.* Warhafftige Copey/ Einer schrifft/ des Churfürsten zu Sachssen/ an die Landsstende ... (Gedruckt zu Wittemberg durch Georgen Rhaw.) 4°. A-E^4. ¶*Dated 1538.* [202

-- De iniustis processibus iudicii camerae imperialis, protestatio & petitio Principum, & coeterorum confoederatorum in causa veræ religionis ... 1538 (Impressum Vitebergæ per Georgium Rhau. Anno M. D. xxxviij. Mense Decembri.) 4°. A-E^4 F^2 G^4. [203

-- Anderer Abdruck/ des ... Herrn Iohans Fridrichen/ Hertzogen zu Sachssen ... verantwortungen auff Hertzog Heinrichs von Braunschweig ... (Gedruckt zu Wittemberg/ durch Georgen Rhaw. M.D.XL.) 4°. a-cc^4 dd^6. [204

-- Auffgebot vnnd warnungssschrifft/ So die Chur/ vnd Fürsten zů Sachssen etc. ... des grawsamen Erbfeyndes der Christenheit/ des Türcken/ persönlichen anzugs halben ... verkündigen lassen. M.D.XLI. 4°. A^4. [205

-- Des ... Herrn Johans Fridrichen/ Hertzogen zu Sachssen ... Verantwortung/ Wider des ... Barrabas/ auch hurnsüchtigen Holofernes von Braunschweig. ... Anno 1541 ... (Gedruckt zu Wittemberg durch Georgen Rhaw. ...) 4°. A-Y^4 (-Y4, *presumably blank*). [206

-- Meiner genedigsten ... Herren Hertzog Johans Friderichen Churfürsten zu Sachssen/ etc. Vnnd Herren Philipsen Landgraffen zu Hessen/ etc. warhafftige aussfürung/ das Marggraue Hansen von Brandenburg nit gebürt/ sich in der Key. Maiestat dienst wider jr Chur vñ Fürstliche gnad ... einzulassen ... Sambt Bapst Pauli des dritten Gottlos gifftig schreiben/ an gemeine Aydgnossen ... Anno M.D.XLVI. 4°. A-C^4. [207

-- Von Gottes gnadẽ Iohañes Friderich/ Hertzog zu Sachssen/ Philips Lantgraue zu Hessen/ vnd gemeiner Christlicher einung verordnete Krieges Räthe. An Hertzogen Wilhelmen zu Bayern. M. D. xlvi. Den III. Augusti. 4°. A^4. [208

-- Historia vnnd erzelung des Handlung/ so in dem ... Köningreich Behem ... den Churfürsten zu Sachssen, Herzog Iohans Fridrichen etc. Vnd seine Land vnd Leut zu vberzihen ... sich zugetragen vnd ergangen ... M. D. XLVII. 4°. A-F^4. [209

-- *Moritz, elector.* Des Durchlauchtigen ... Herrn Moritzen Hertzogen zu Sachssen ... Newe Landsordnunge. 1543. (Gedruckt zu Leipzig durch Nickel Wolraben. ...) 4°. A-C^4 D^6. [210

-- *Heinrich, duke.* Agenda. Das ist/ Kirchenordnung ... Für die Diener der Kirchen in Hertzog Heinrichen zu Sachsen V.G.D. Fürstenthumb gestellet. ... Gedruckt zu Leipzig/ durch Georg Hantzsch. M. D. LV. 4°. A-T^4 V^2. ff. II-LXXII. (Yarnall.) [210a

-- *Johann Friedrich II, duke.* Des Durchleuchtigen ... Herrn Iohans Friderichen des Mittlern/ Hertzogen zu Sachssen ... in Gottes wort/ Prophetischer vnd Apostolischer schrifft/ gegründete Confutationes ... etlicher ... Irrthumen ... M. D. LIX. Ihena. Gedruckt durch Thomam Rebart. 4°. A^6 B-T^4 V^6. ff. 1-78. [211

-- Copey Der antwort/ so Hertzog Iohansfridrich zu Sachssen der Mittler/ etc. des Reichs abgesandten Botschafften/ auff jr anbringen vnd werbung/ Wilhelmen von Grumbachs/ Ernst von Mandelslo/ vnd Wilhelmen vom Steins halben gegeben. Anno M.D.LXVI. 4°. A-P^4 (-P4, *presumably blank*). [212

-- *August I, elector.* Copeien/ Derer Schrifften/ so zwischen dem Churfürsten vnd Hertzog Iohansfriedrichen dem Mittlern/ zu Sachssen/ etc. Graff Günthers von Schwartzburgs/ vnd Wilhelmen von Grumbachs ... ergangen. Anno 1566. 4°. A-Bb^4 Cc^2. ¶A1 *repaired.* [213

-- Vorwarnungs Schrifft/ so Churfürst Augustus zu Sachssen/ etc. ... zu volge der Römischen Key. May. etc. vnd des heiligen Reichs zu Augspurg vornewerten Acht vnd einmütiglich beschlossenẽ Execution/ wider ... Hertzog Iohan Friderichen von Sachssen/ ausgehen lassen. ... 1567. ... 4°. A^4. [214

-- Notwendige warhaffte verantwortung/ bestendige ablehnunge vnd wiederlegung der ... auflagen/ damit ... Augustus Hertzog zu Sachsen ... von Hertzog Iohans Friedrichen von Sachssen/ als ... Wilhelmen von Grumbachs/ vnd seiner anhenger ... in der Antwort/ welche er den 12. tag Iulij nechstuor schienen/ des Reichs Gesandten ... gegeben ... M. D. XLVII. 4°. A^6 B-L^4 M^2 (-M2) a-p^4 (-p4, *presumably blank*). ¶*Half-title* (a1r): Hiernach volgen die Copien/ welche in des Churfürsten zu Sachssen Antwort ... angezogen. [215

-- -- *Another copy of* a-p^4 (-p4). [216

-- Kurtze vorantwortung des Churfürsten zu Sachsen/ Hertzogen Augusti/ ꝛc. etlicher erdichteten vnwarhafftigen Bezichtigung halben/ So ... wider seine Churf. G. ausgebreitet worden. ... M.D.LXVII. 4°. A-B^4. [217

-- Des Durchlauchtigsten ... Herrn Augusten Hertzogen zu Sachsen ... Verordenungen vnd Constitutionen des Rechtlichen Proces ... Dressden/ 1572. (... Gedruckt durch Matthes Stöckel vñ Gimel Bergen. ...) 4°. π^4 (-π4) A-D^4 E^2 F-Ll^4. ff. 1-113. [218

-- *Friedrich Wilhelm, duke.* Der Durchlauchtigen ... Herren Friederich Wilhelms/ vnd Herren Iohansen Gebrüdern/ Hertzogen zu Sachsen ... Policey vnd Landesordnunge ... 1589. Gedruckt zu Ihena/ durch Thobiam Steinman. ... (*Colophon.*) 4°. A-V^4. [219

-- *Johann Casimir, duke.* Der Durchlauchtigen ... Herrn Iohann Casimirn/ vnd Herrn Iohan Ernsten/ Gebrüdere/ Hertzogen zu Sachsen ... Hofgerichts Ordnung ... Anno M. D. XCVIII. auffgerichtet. ... 4°. A-I^4. [220

-- *Landtag.* Aussschreiben vnnd erklerunge/ welcher gestalt/ vnnd zu was Terminen, die ... 1594. Jars/ zu Coburgk gehaltenem Landtage/ bewilligte Sechssjärige Landstewer ... eingebracht werden soll. Coburgk. Anno M. D. XCV. 4°. A-C^4 D^2. [221

-- *Ministers.* Der Prediger/ der Iungen Herren/ Iohans Friderichen Hertzogen zů Sachssen/ ꝛc. Sönen Christenlich bedencken auff das Interim. ... M. D. XXXXVIIII. 4°. A-B^4 C^2. [222

-- -- 1549. 4°. A-C^4. [223

-- *History.* Warhafftige Abcontrafactur vnd Bildnůs aller GrosHertzogen/ Chur vnd Fürsten/ welche vom Jahr ... 842. bis auff das jetzige 1587. Jahr ... regiert haben. ... Gedruckt in ... Dressden/ durch Gimel Bergen von Lübeck. Anno M. D. LXXXVII. 4°. $*^4$ A-I^4. [224

SBROLIUS, RICHARDUS. Richardi Sbrulii Equitis Foroiuliani ... Moduli aliquot. ... (Impressa sunt Hec/ Auguste/ apud Iohannē Erphordianū. ... M.D.xviiii. iii. Id. Nouembris:) 4°. A^6. [225

-- Richardi Sbrulij ... Principalis Marchiæ Brādeburgensis Triumphus. ... (... M.D.Xiiij. Idibus Octob. Ioannes Hanaw Impressit. In Academia Frāckfordiana. ...) 4°. A-$D^{4.6}$ E^6. [226

SCALIGER, JOSEPH JUSTUS. Epicedium ... Iani Dousae f. ... Lugduni Batavorum, Ex officinâ Ioannis Patij. cIↄ. Iↄ. IIC. 4°. A-B^4 C^2. [227

SCALIGER, JULIUS CAESAR. Iulii Caesaris Scaligeri animaduersiones in historias Theophrasti. Lugduni, Apud Ioannam Iacobi Iuntæ F. M. D. LXXXIIII. ... 8°. A-Cc^8 Dd^4. pp. 7-424. ¶Dd^4 *misbound between sigg.* A *and* B *of* A598, *with which this is bound.* [228

-- Iulii Caesaris Scaligeri ... De Causis linguæ Latinæ libri tredecim. [Genevae,] Apud Petrum Santandreanum. M. D. LXXX. 8°. $¶^8$ $††^8$ A-Ee^8 Ff^4. pp. 1-451. ¶*T.p. defective.* [229

-- -- Apud Petrum Santandreanum. M. D. LXXXIIII. 8°. *Same collation and pagination.* [230

-- -- Apud Petrum Santandreanum. M. D. XCVII. 8°. $¶^8$ $¶¶^4$ A-Ee^8 Ff^4. *Same pagination.* ¶*T.p. defective.* [231

-- Iulii Caesaris Scaligeri ... de sapientia et beatitudine libri octo, quos Epidorpides inscripsit. Geneuae, excudebat Eustathius Vignon, M. D. LXXIII. 8°. A-Q^8 R^2. pp. 3-260. [232

-- Iulii Caesaris Scaligeri exotericarum exercitationum lib. XV. De Subtilitate ... Francofurti Apud Andream Wechelum. M. D. LXXVI. 8°. $\bar{a}^8$ a-z^8 A-$3H^8$ (-3H8, *presumably blank*). pp. 1-1129. [223

-- -- Francofurti Apud Andreæ Wecheli heredes Claudium Marnium, & Ioann. Aubrium, M D XCII. 8°. ā^{8} a-z^{8} A-3H^{8}. pp. 1-1129. [234

-- Iulii Caesaris Scaligerii ... in libros de plantis Aristoteli inscriptos, commentarii ... [Genevae,] Apud Ioannem Crispinum. M. D. LXVI. (*Colophon.*) fol. a-m^{6} n^{4}. pp. 3-143. [235

-- Iulii Caesaris Scaligeri in luctu filij Oratio ... Apud Seb. Gryphium Lugduni, 1538. 8°. a-c^{8} d^{4} (-d4, *presumably blank*). pp. 3-54. [236

-- [1] Iulii Caesaris Scaligeri ... Poetices libri septem ... [Lugduni,] Apud Antonium Vincentium. M. D. LXI. fol. a^{4} a^{4} b-z^{6} A-H^{6}. pp. 1-364. [2] Iulii Caesaris Scaligeri ... in librum de Insomnijs Hippocratis commentarius ... a-c^{6} D^{4}. pp. 3-54. [237

-- -- [Genevae,] Apud Petrum Sanctandreanum. M. D. XCIV. 8°. ¶^{8} **^{4} a-z^{8} A-Rr^{8} Ss^{4}. pp. 2-945. [238

SCALIGER, PAUL. Encyclopaediæ, seu Orbis disciplinarum ... Epistemon: Pauli Scalichii de Lika ... Basileae, per Ioannem Oporinum. (... M. D. LIX. Mense Februario.) 4°. a-z^{4} A-4K^{4} (4K4 + 2 *folded half-sheets*). pp. 4-755. [239

SCAMOZZI, VINCENZO. Discorsi sopra l'antichità di Roma ... Con XL. Tauole in Rame In Venetia Appresso Francesco Ziletti MDLXXXIII fol. †^{2} A-B^{8} + 40 *double-page plates (with letterpress on the first recto of each sheet and on the second verso of plates 2, 8, 24)* + *leaf of errata*. (Fine Arts.) [240

SCAPULA, JOANNES. Lexicon Graecolatinum nouum ... Basileae Ex officina Heruagiana, per Eusebium Episcopium. ... M D XXC. fol. a^{6} a-z^{6} A-Zz^{6} AA-II^{6} KK^{6+2} LL-SS^{6} TT^{10} α-θ^{6}. cols. 1-1878, 7-190. [241

SCELTA. [1] Scelta di rime di diuersi moderni autori. ... Parte Prima. ... In Genoua, Appresso gli Heredi di Gieronimo Bartoli. ... 1591. 8°. A-K^{8}. pp. 3-153. [2] ... Parte seconda. ... In Pauia MDXCI. Per gli Heredi di Girolamo Bartolo. ... 8°. A-I^{8}. pp. 3-131. [242

SCHADE, PETER. Annotationes Petri Mosellani Protogensis in ... Auli Gellij Noctes Atticas. ... [c. 1540.] 8°. A-M^{8}. [243

-- -- *Another copy.* [244

-- -- Petri Mosellani ... in Auli Gellii noctes Atticas, annotationes. Lugduni, apud Seb. Gryphium, 1542. 8°. a-n^{8} o^{4}. pp. 3-213. [245

-- De ratiōe disputandi, præsertim in re Theologica, Petri Mosellani ... oratio ... Epistola quædam Erasmi, ad Petrum Mosellanum ... Epistola item Erasmica, ad D. doctorem Martinum Lutherium. [Leipzig, Melchior Lotter, c. 1520.] 4°. A-D^{4}. [246

-- Petri Mosellani ... in M. Fab. Quintiliani rhetoricas institutiones annotationes. ... Basileae apud Adamum Petrum mense Aug. an. M.D.XXVII. (*Colophon.*) 8°. a-x^{8} (-a1, *presumably blank*). pp. 3-324. [247

-- Paedologia Petri Mosellani ... Dialogi XXXVII. Christophori Hegendorphini Dialogi pueriles XII. ... M.D.XXXIII. (Augustæ Vindelicorum, per Alexandrum Veyssenhorn.) 8°. A-C^{8} D^{10}. [248

-- Tabulae in schemata et tropos Petri Mosellani. In rhetorica Philippi Melanchthonis. Item in copiam duplicem Erasmi Roterodami. Argentorati, anno, M. D. XLIX. (... excudebat Iacobus Iucundus ...) 8°. A-D^{8} E^{4}. [249

SCHATZGEYER, KASPAR. Omnia opera ... Gasparis Schatzgeri ... Epistola eliminaris Eckii. ... Ingolstadii in officina Alexandri Vueissenhorn. M.D.XLIII. fol. aa^{6} A-Z^{6} a-z^{6} Aa-Mm^{6}. ff. 1-333. [250

-- De vita Christiana. Et monastici instituti ... Authore Gasparo Sasgero Mino. [Tübingen, Ulrich Morhart, c. 1525.] 8°. a-n^{8}. [251

-- Examen nouarum doctrinarum pro elucidatione ueritatis Euangelicæ & catholicæ ... Autore Caspare Sasgero Minorita. (Vlmae apud ... Ioannem Grüner. Anno. M.D.XXIII.) 4°. A-Q^{4}. [252

-- Fürhalltung xxx artigkl ... (Gedruckt ... durch Hannssen Schobsser jnn der ... Statt München/ Am̄ tag des heyligen Iohannsen ... Im̄ M D vnd XXV. jar.) 4°. A-P⁴. [253

-- Ein gietliche vn̄ freüntliche anntwort vn̄ vntterricht/ auf eines Eersamen/ der warheyt begerenden/ Christlichen Burgers von Nürmberg ... sandt brieff ... (Gedruckt jn der ... Statt Münchn̄. durch Hannssen Schobsser jm̄ M.D.XXvj.) 4°. A-H⁴ I² K-L⁴. [254

-- Tractatus de missa ... Authore Gaspare Sasgero Minorita. (Excusum Tubingae per Hulderichum Morhardum. An. M. D. XXV. mense Ianuario.) 8°. a-l⁸. [255

-- Traductio Sathanae, hoc est, diabolicæ fraudis detectio, qua ... falsos & impios errores ... disseminat. ... Autore patre Chaspare Sasgero Minorita. ... Tubingae, anno M.D.XXX. (... apud Hulderichum Morhardū ...) 8°. π⁸ A⁴ B-O⁸ P⁴. ff. 1-116. [256

-- Vnius articuli, dissolubilitatem matrimonij contingentis, uera declaratio ... contra Lutheranū dogma ... Authore Gaspare Sasgero minorita. (Excusum Tubingae per Hulderichum Morhardum. ... M.D.XXV.) 8°. A⁸ B⁴ (-B4, *presumably blank*). [257

-- Vom fegfeür oder volkōmner Raynigung der ausserwölten/ Das ... das Fegfeüer nit aussgelescht ist. ... M D XXV Jar (Gedruckt ... jn ... München. am̄ abend der bekerung des heyligen hymelfürsten Pauli/ durch Hannssen Schobsser. ...) 4°. A-K⁴. [258

-- Vonn Christlichē satzungen vn̄ leeren/ am Christförmigs leben (der werck halben) betreffend ... Im̄ jar M D XXiiij. (Gedruckht jnn ... Münchn̄ durch Hannssen Schobser. ... Am̄ Sambsstag nach Aller heyligen tag.) 4°. A-G⁴ (-G4, *presumably blank*). [259

-- Ainn warhafftige Erklerūg wie sich Sathanas Inn disen hernach geschriben vieren materyenn vergwentet vnnd erzeugt vnnder der gestalt eynes Enngels des Liechts. ... [Augsburg, Heinrich Steiner,] M. D. XXVI 4°. A-M⁴. [260

SCHEGK, JAKOB. Iacobi Schegkii Schorndorffensis Commentaria in ... Organi Aristotelis libros ... Tubingæ apud viduam Vlrici Morhardi, M.D.LXX. (... mense Augusto.) fol.)(⁶ A-4K⁶ 4L⁴. pp. 1-624. [261

-- Iacobi Schegkii ... in octo Physicorum ... libros Aristotelis, Commentaria ... Commentarius in Aristotelis de Anima libros tres ... Basileae. (... per Ioannem Heruagium ... M.D.XLVI. Mense Augusto.) fol. α⁶ A-Rr⁶ Ss⁴. pp. 1-485. [262

-- [In reliquos naturalium Aristotelis libros commentaria ... Item, eiusdem in x libros ethicorum annotationes ... Basileae, per Ioannem Heruagium, Mar. 1550.] fol. α⁸ (*wanting*) a-z⁶ A-Z⁶ Aa⁸ (*wanting*). pp. 1-539. [263

-- Philosophia naturalis (quae acroamata solitus fuit appellare Aristoteles) omnes disputationes ... Tubingae ex officina Vlrici Morhardi. Anno M. D. XLIII. 8°. π² A-N⁸ O⁴ (-O4). ff. 1-107. [264

SCHENCK, JAKOB. Auslegung des spruchs S. Pauls zu den Colossern aus dritten Capitel/ Ir Weiber seid vnterthan Ewren Mennern ꝛc. ... D. Iacobum Schenck. Wittemberg. 1540. (... durch Ioseph Klug. ...) 4°. A-H⁴. [265

-- Eine Predigt von Iudas Geitz ... Wittemberg. 1541. (Gedruckt ... durch Georgen Rhaw.) 4°. A-G⁴. [266

SCHERER, GEORG. Erster Theil/ Aller Schrifften/ Bücher vnnd Tractätlein/ welche Georg Scherer ... aussgehen lassen. ... Gedruckt im Closter Bruck Præmonstratenser Ordens/ in Mähren/ Anno 1599. fol.)(⁶⁺¹ A-V⁶ W⁶ X-Z⁶ a-v⁶ w⁶ x-z⁶ Aa-Vv⁶ Ww⁶ Xx-3V⁶ 3W⁶ 3X-4O⁶ 4P-4S⁴. ff. 1-663. [267

-- Bericht/ Ob der Bapst zů Rom der Antichrist sey ... Gedruckt zů Ingolstadt durch Dauid Sartorium. ... M. D. LXXXV. 4°. A-X⁴. pp. 1-153. [268

-- Ein bewerte Kunst vnd Wundsegen Für Schiessen/ Stechen/ Hawen/ Rauben/ Brennen/ ꝛc. ... Gedruckt zu Wienn in Osterreich/ bey Leonhardt Formica. M. D. XCV. 4°. A-M⁴. [269

-- Ein Christliche Heer-Predig ... Gedruckt zu Wienn in Osterreich/ bey Leonhard Formica. M. D. XCV. (*Colophon.*) 4°. A-D⁴. [270

-- Eigentliche Abcontrafehung einer newen vnerhörten Monstrantzen: Darinnen Magister Maximilianus Biber/ Lutherischer Predicant/ die Partickel vn̄ Oblaten für seine Communicanten ... herumb getragen ... Ingolstadt bey Dauid Sartorio. ... M. D. LXXXVIII. 4°. A-O⁴. pp. 1-103. [271

SCHERER

-- Fortsetzung Dess Triumphs der Warheit/ wider Lucam Osiandrum. ... Gedruckt zů Ingolstadt/ durch Dauid Sartorium. M.D.LXXXVIII. 4°.)(^{4} A-Aa^4. pp. 1-191. [272

-- Der Lutherische BettlerMantel. ... (Getruckt zu Ingolstat/ durch Wolffgang Eder/ Anno M. D. LXXXVIII.) 4°. A-B^4. ff. 1-7. [273

-- -- (Gedruckt zu Wienn in Osterreich/ durch Leonhard Nassinger.) 4°. A-B^4 (-B4, *presumably blank*). ff. 1-6. [274

-- -- *Another copy.* [275

-- Ein Predig Vom Gotsleichnams Fest vnnd Vmbgang. ... Gedruckt zu Grätz in Steyr/ bey Georg Widmanstetter. ... M. D. LXXXVIII. 4°. A-E^4. ff. 2-20. [276

-- Rettung der Iesuiter Vnschuld wider die Grifftspinnen Lucam Osiander. ... Gedruckt zů Ingolstadt/ durch Dauid Sartorium. Anno M. D. LXXXVI. 4°. A-K^4. pp. 1-72. [277

-- Scala Iacob. Die Him̃els Layter. ... Gedruckt zu Bruch an der Teya [Druckerei der Prämonstratenserstiftes]. 1595. 4°. A-E^4 F^6. [278

-- Trattato del R. Padre Giorgio Scherer ... Nel quale ... proua non esser vero, che già sia stato in Roma vna Donna Pontefice. Tradotto dalla Lingua Tedesca nell' Italiana da Nicolò Pierio. In Venetia, appresso i Gioliti. MDLXXXVI. (*Colophon.*) 8°. A-C^8 D^4 (-D4, *presumably blank*). pp. 1-48. [279

-- Ein trewhertzige Vermahnung/ Dass die Christen dem Türcken nicht Huldigen ... sollen. ... Gedruckt zu Bruck an der Teya [Druckerei des Prämonstratenserstiftes]. 1595. 4°. A-G^4. [280

-- Triumph Der Warheit/ wider Lucam Osiandrum. ... Gedruckt zů Ingolstadt/ durch Dauid Sartorium. M.D.LXXXVII. 4°. A-X^4. pp. 1-159. [281

SCHEURL, CHRISTOPH. Epl'a D. Schewrli ad Charitatem Pirchameram. Carmen Conradi Celtis ad eandem. Epistola Pilati ad Tyberium Cesarem. Epistola Lentuli ad Tyberium Cesarem. Epistola Abgari ad Iesum Saluatorem. Epistola responsiua ad Abgarum. Vtilitates Misse. Exemplum Enee Siluij de vendente missam. Vtilitates orationis pro defunctis. Exemplum pulchrum quod contigit Bononie. Sequentia Dies ire. Carmen ad diuum Christophorum. (Ioannes Weyssenburgius ... imprimebat Nurenberge quinto Nonas Mayas. Anno Tertiodecimo.) 4°. B.L. A-B^4. [282

SCHIAFENATO, GIOVANBATTISTA. Rime ... (Stampate in Vinegia per Giouann'Antonio de Nicolini da Sabio. Nel MDXXXIIII.) 8°. a-l^8. [283

SCHILLE, HANS VAN. Form vnd weis zu bauwen ... Maniere, de bien bastir ... Chasteaux, forteresses, Villes ... Antuerpiæ Apud Theodorum Gallæum. Mr Hans van Schille Ingenieur et geographe inuentor. fol. *engraved t.p.* + 14 *plates*. (Fine Arts.) [284

SCHILTER, ZACHARIAS. Illustrissimo ... Augusto, duci Saxoniæ ... defuncto ... parentatio Facta ab ... Academia Lipsiensi ... & quidem orationibus duabus, quarum altera habita fuit à Zacharia Schiltero ... Alter verò à M. Iohanne Albino ... Anno ... supra sesquimillesimum LXXXVI. (Lipsiæ, imprimebat Iohannes Steinman. ...) 4°. A-L^4. [285

-- Oratio de obitu ... Annæ, natæ reginæ Daniæ, ... Augusti, Ducis Saxoniæ Electoris &c. coniugis ... Vna cum ... versibus Epicedijs M. Iohannis Albini ... Die mensis Octobr. VII. ... M. D. LXXXV. Lipsiæ, imprimebat Iohannes Steinman. 4°. A-F^4. [286

SCHINDLER, ANDREAS. Carmen Sapphicum in natalem Domini Iesu Christi ... VVitebergæ Excudebant hæredes Iohannis Cratonis, Anno M. D. LXXX. 4°. A^4. [287

SCHLESWIG. Christlyke Kercken Ordeninge/ De yn̄ den Fürstendömen/ Schlesswig/ Holsten etc. schal geholden werdenn. (Gedrücket thó Magdeborch/ dorch Hans Walther. Anno. M. D. XLII.) 4°. A-Z^4. ¶*Margins repaired.* [288

SCHNABEL, JOHANN. Warhafftige vnd erschröckliche Geschicht/ welche sich ... zugetragen hat/ mit einem ... Schmidtsgesellen ... der ... vmb das Fest S. Matthiæ Apostoli, dieses 1589. Jars ... von einer gantzen Legion Teüffeln/ hefftig besessen ... worden ist. ... Durch M. Ioannem Schnabeln Ingolstadiensem ... Vnd M. Simonem Marium, Bauarum ... Gedruckt zu Wirtzburg/ durch Heinrich von Ach. ... 4°. A-D^4. [289

SCHNAUSS, CYRIACUS. Ein Lobspruch/ oder gantz hertzliche Dancksagunge/ zů der ... dryfeltigkeit Gottes ... 1552. ... 4°. A⁴. [290

-- Pasquillus. Newe Zeyttung vom Teüffel. ... 1546. 4°. A-E⁴. [291

-- -- Pasquillus. New Zeyttung Vom Teuffel. ... 4°. A-C⁴. [292

SCHOENER, JOANNES, CAROLOSTADIUS. Ioannis Schoneri Carolstadii opusculum astrologicum ... Tractatus integer electionum M. Laurentij Bonicontrij Miniarensis. Assertio contra calumniatores Astrologiæ D. Eberhardi Schleusingeri ... Norimbergæ apud Iohan. Petreium ... M.D.XXXIX. (*Colophon.*) 4°. A-O⁴. [293

-- -- *Another copy* (-O4, *blank*). (Lea.) [294

SCHOENER, JOHANN, of Waltershof. Feudalium disputationum libri duo ... Francofurti, Apud Andreæ Wecheli heredes, Claudium Marnium, & Ioan. Aubrium. MDXCVII. 8°.):(-2):(⁴ 3):(² (+ *folding leaf*) A-Zz⁴)(⁴ 3A-3T⁴. pp. 2-454. (Lea.) [295

SCHOENITZ, ANTON. Anthonij Schenitz Notwehre/ auff das ertichte Buch/ vnter Graff Philipsen von Mansfelt ... namen/ ausgegangen. Wittemberg. M. D. XXXIX. (Gedrückt ... durch Hans Lufft ...) 4°. A-R⁴ (-R4, *presumably blank*). [296

-- Warhafftiger bericht Anthonij Schenitz/ wie sich die sachen zwisschen dem Cardinal von Meintz ꝛc. vnd seinem Bruder Hansen Schenitz zugetragen ... Wittemberg. M. D. XXXVIII. (Gedruckt ... durch Hans Lufft. ...) 4°. A-H⁴. [297

SCHONHEINTZ, JAKOB. Apologia astrologie. (Exaratum per ... Georgiū Schenck in ... ciuitate Nurmberga Anno ... Millesimo q̄ngentesimo scđo. Mensis vero Septembris die xxi. finit.) 4°. B.L. A-C⁸. (Lea.) [298

SCHOORL, ADRIAAN. Adriani Scorelii Bataui poemata. ... opera Guilielmi Mennentij Antuerpiani correcta ... Cornelij Valerij Vltraiectini Triumphi. Antuerpiae, Ex officina Christoph. Plantini. cIↄ. Iↄ. LXVI. 16°. A-F⁸ (-F6-8, *presumably blank*). pp. 2-88. [299

SCHOPPE, GASPAR. Narratio historica eorum, quae in nuptiis Philippi III. Hispaniarum regis cum Margarita Austriaca: item Alberti Austriæ Archiducis cum Isabella Clara Eugenia Hispaniarum Infante Ferrariæ celebratis memorabilia acciderunt. ... Ingolstadii, Ex Typographia Ederiana, apud Andream Angermarium. M. D. XCIX. 4°. A-B⁴. pp. 1-10. [300

SCHOPPER, HARTMANN. In ἐπισκοπομίμεσιν ... adolescentis Vdalrici à Riethaim ... qua in ipso SS. Innocentium festo de more Academiæ Dilinganæ ... functus est, Elegiæ tres. Vna, Hartmanni Schopperi Nouoforensis Norici. Altera, F. Ioannis Ruostalleri Coenobitæ S. Galli. Tertia, M. Melchioris Zuntzeri Schrattenbachij ... Quibus accessit in aduentum ... Othonis, Cardinalis Albani & Augustani Episcopi, Elegia gratulatoria eiusdem M. Melchioris Zuntzeri ... Dilingæ Excudebat Sebaldus Mayer. M.D.LXV. 4°. A-D⁴. [301

SCHORE, ANTONIUS VAN. De ratione discendae docendaeque linguæ Latinæ & Græcæ, libri duo. ... Argentorati excudebat Iosias Rihelius, Anno M. D. LXIII. 8°. A-Y⁸ Z⁴. ff. 1-146. [302

-- Phrases linguae Latinae: ratióque obseruandorum eorum in authoribus legendis ... Antonio Schoro authore. ... Coloniae Agrippinae, Excudebat Petrus Horst. M.D.LXXIII. 8°.)(⁸ A-Rr⁸ Ss⁴ *present.* ¶*Lacks 10 ll. or more at end.* [303

SCHOSSER, JOHANN. Aliquot insignia clarorum hominum, elegiaco carmine celebrata ... Addita est elegia L. Iohannis Codicij, scripta in honorem eiusdem Schosseri ... Francofurti ad Viadrum anno M.D.LVII. (Ex officina Iohannis Eichorn.) 8°. A-B⁸. [304

-- Poëmatum ... libri XI. Accesserunt epistolarum ... libri III. Francofordiae ad Viadrum excudebat Andreas Eichorn, impensis auctoris. ... M.D.LXXXV. ... 8°. A-Mm⁸. [305

SCHOTTENIUS, HERMANNUS. Vita honesta, siue virtutis: Quomodo quisque viuere debeat ... adiecimus Institutionem Christiani hominis, per Adrianum Barlandum Aphorismis digestum. ... Formula honestæ vitæ, siue de quatuor Virtutibus, consarcinatio. Martino Episcopo Dumiensi, authore. ... hactenus Senecæ falsò adscriptus. ... Lugduni, aub scuto Coloniensi. 1545 (... excudebant Ioannes et Franciscus Frellonii, fratres. ...) 8°. A-F⁸ G⁴. pp. 1-92. [306

SCHRADER, LUDOLF. [1] Dn. Ludolphi Schraderi ... Tractatus Feudalis, ... tomus primus. ... in lucem editus, ... opera, Ioannis Brandis Hildeschemensis ... Francofurti, Ex Officina Paltheniana. 1594. fol. A^6 A-3Q^6 3R^4. pp. 1-751. [2] ... tomus secundus ... *Same imprint.* (... Prostat in Taberna Feierabendiana.))(^{4} Aa-4Z^6 5A^8. pp. 1-637. (Biddle.) [307

SCHRADIN, JOHANN. Expostulation/ das ist Klag vnd Verweiss Germanie/ ... gegen Carolo Quinto dem Kayser ... (M. D. XLVI. Den XX. Augusti.) 4°. A-C^4. ¶*In verse.* [308

SCHRAMM, JOHANN, VON SCHWEIDNITZ. Fasciculus Historiarum, Das ist: Historien vnd Exempel/ der alten Keyser/ Koͤnige ... Auch anderer Personen/ so in jrem Stande vnd Beruff den Regimenten/ ihnen selbst/ vnd andern nuͤtzlich oder schedlich gewesen. ... Leipzig ... M. D. LXXXIX. (Gedruckt ... durch Zachariam Berwaldt/ Inn vorlegung Henningi Grossen ...) fol.):(^{8} A-Ii^6 Kk-Mm^4 Nn^6. ff. 1-200. [309

SCHROEGEL, GEORG. Elegia εγκωμιαστικη in ... vrbem Handouerpiam ... Antuerpiae, Ex officina Christophori Plantini, anno M. D. LXV. 4°. A-D^4. [310

SCHROT, MARTIN. Apocalipsis. Ain frewden geschray über das gefallen Bapstumb ... 4°. A^4. [311

-- Dialogus. Ain wunnderbarlichs/ seltzams Gespraͤch: ... Vom Gellt/ vnd der Armuͦt. ... [1550?] 4°. A-D^4. [312

-- Vrsprung vnnd Vrsach diser Auffrur/ Teutscher Nation. ... [Nürnberg, Christoph Gutknecht, 1546?] 4°. A^4 B^2. ¶*In verse.* [313

SCHRYVER, CORNELIS. Querela proditi Christi, per nouos quosdam suos ... Ischariotas Turcochristianos. Item in ... Martini à Roshem Gelrogalli, latrocinium, psalmi CXXIII. Paraphrasis. Vate Cornelio Grapheo. Antuerpiae, Ex officina Ioannis Graphei M. D. XLIII. 4°. A-B^4. [314

-- De Triumphe vā Antwerpen. (Geprint Tantwerpen/ doer Peeter Coecke van Helst/ gesworen Printere/ by Bielis van Diest. 1550.) 4°. A-O^4. (Fine Arts.) [315

SCHURERIUS, AMBROSIUS. Ambrosij Schurerij I.C. de haereditatibus quae ab intestato deferuntur ... doctrina ... Vrteyl vnd vrtelmessige Spruͤche ... Eiusdem authoris methodica de gradibus consanguinitatis & affinitatis explicatio. ... (Leipzig/ Bey M. Ernesto Voͤgelin. M. D. Lxvij.) 4°. Aa^8 Bb^4 A-Z^8 a-q^8 (m1 + 4 *folded ll.*) r^{8+6} (r8 + 2 *folded ll.*). pp. 1-554. (Lea.) [316

SCHWARZ, GEORG. Anticaluinismus, Das ist: Gründtliche Entdeckung dess gantzen Caluinischen Glaubens vnd Wesens ... Durch Georgium Nigrinum ... Gedruckt zu Franckfurt am Mayn/ durch Iohann Spies. M. D. XCV. (*Colophon.*) 4°. a-d^4 e^2 A-4A^4 4B^2. pp. 1-544. [317

-- Bapistische Inquisition vnd guͤldē Flüs der Roͤmischen Kirchen. Das ist. Historia vnd ankunft der Roͤmischen Kirchen/ vnd sonderlich vom Antichristischen wesen/ inn Siben Bücher verfast ... zusammen getragen von Georgio Nigrino. ... sonderlich wider Doctor Georgen Eders Euangelische Inquisition vnd gulden Flüss zugericht ... Anno M.D.LXXXII. fol. A-I^6 K^8 a-z^6 A-Oo^6 Pp^4 QQ^6 RR^4. pp. 1-728. (Lea.) [318

-- Gewisser/ Notturfftiger Beschlag/ sampt Guͤrt/ Sattel vnd Zaum/ der Frenckischen/ Iesuwidrischen/ Nerrischen/ Cacolischen Esels/ Iohan Nasen zu Ingelstat. Zubereit von Georgio Nigrino Battimontano. ... (Gedruckt zu Vrsel/ durch Nicolaum Henricum.) 4°. A-S^4 T^2 (-T2, *presumably blank*). [319

-- [*caption*] Hypodromus Oder Nachtrab ... wie man Priester vnd Prediger der Kirchen ordenlich wehlen/ beruͦffen/ vnd einsetzen soll/ auff Georg Nigrini anhalten vnnd schreiben inn Truck verfertigt. (Gedruckt zu Ingolstadt/ durch Dauid Sartorium.) 4°. A-Z^4 a-g^4. ff. 1-155. (Lea.) [320

-- Wilkom vnd Abdanck der Antigratulation Iohan Nasen/ des Muͤnchs zu Ingelstat. Georgius Nigrinus Battimontanus. ... 4°. A-Q^4. [321

SCHWARTZENBACH, LEONHARD. Synonyma. Formular Wie man ainerley rede vnd mainung/ mit andern mehr worten ... schreiben/ vnd ausssprechen sol. ... Gedruckt zu Franckfurt am

Mayn/ M. D. LXIIII. (... Getruckt ... durch Georg Raben/ in verlegung Sigmund Feyerabents vnd Simon Hüters. ...) fol. A-R⁶. ff. II-C. [322

SCHWARZENBERG, FRIEDRICH VON. Widerbericht vnd verantwortung mit einuerleibten protestationen herren Friderichen Freyherren zů Schwartzenberg vnd zů Hohenlandtsperg ... Contra Ludwigen der sich von Hutten vnd einen Ritter nennt. Am Keyserlichen Cammergericht einbracht M. D. xxxv. fol. a⁶ B⁶. [323

SCHWARZENBERG, JOHANN VON. Beschwerung der alten Teüfelischen Schlangen mit dem Gőtlichen wort. ... (Gedruckt [zu Augsburg durch Heinrich Steiner] jm̄ M.D. vnd xxv. Jar.) 4°. A-Z⁴ a-n⁴ o² p⁴. ff. I-CXLII. [324

-- Eynn Schőner Sendtbrieff ... An Bischoff zu Bamberg aussgangen/ Darinn er ... vrsachen anzeygt/ wye vnd warůmb ehr seyn Tochter auss dem Closter daselbst ... hin weg gefűrt ... Ein vorred ... Andreas Osiander. Nurenberg [Friedrich Peypus]. Anno. M.D.XXiiij. 4°. A⁴ B² C⁴. [325

SCHWARTZENBERG, PAUL VON. Epigrammata D. Pauli a Svvartzenberg, ... Landspergij dominij ... M. D. XXXVIII. (Augustae Vindelicorum, excudebat Henricus Steyner ... Mense Aprili.) 4°. A-I⁴. [326

SCHWEBEL, JOHANN. Hauptstűck vnd summa des gantzen Euangeliums ... Durch Iohan. Schweblin ... M. D. XXV. 4°. A-D⁴. [327

SCHWENDI, LAZAR, Freiherr von. Parere del Signor Lazaro Suendi Alemanno, come si possa resistere à Turchi. In Ferrara, Appresso Vittorio Baldini, ... M.D.C. 8°. A-B⁸ C⁶. pp. 3-44. (Lea.) [328

SCHWENKFELD, CASPAR. Bericht/ von Chaspar Schwenckfelds leere. M. D. XLVII. 4°. a⁶.[329

-- Ain Christlicher Sendbrieff an Gaistliche personen geschriben. ... [Ulm? Hans Varnier?] M. D. XLVII. 4°. A-O⁴. [330

-- Ein Christlicher Sendbrieff an gűte freünde auff M. Speckers Strassburgischen predicanten bűch das er ... newlich im truck hat lassen aussgeen. Durch ainen liebhaber der Glorien Christi geschriben. ... 1556. 4°. A-E⁴. [331

-- Vom Euangelio Christi Vnd Vom Missbrauch des Euangelij. ... [1552.] 4°. A-QQ⁴. ff. 1-CXLI. [332

-- Vom worte Gottes. ... Damit auch auff Matthie Flacij Illyrici schmachbůchlen/ mit auffdeckung seiner vilfaltigen Irrthumb wirt geanthwurt. Item/ Iudicium vber Osianders leere von der Iustification. ... 4°. π⁴ A-Oo⁴ (-Oo4, *presumably blank*). ff. I-CXLVII. [333

SCLEZA, GIORGIO. Ad Adrianum sextum Pont. Max. mittitur musa Georgii Scleza Cretensis. (Impressum Romæ per magistrum Marcellum [Silber]. 5. Nōn. Iulii [1522].) 4°. π⁴. [334

SCOPPA, LUCIO GIOVANNI. L. Io. Scopae grammatice. ... (Venetiis apud hæredes Petri Rauani, & socios ... M. D. XLVI. Mense Ianuarii.) 8°. A-D⁸ A-QQ⁸ RR⁴. pp. 1-631. [335

SCRIBONIUS, WILHELM ADOLF. De Sagarum natura et potestate ... Physiologia ... Vbi de purgatione earum per aquam frigidam. Contra Joannem Evvichium ... & Her. Neuvvaldum ... Marpurgi, typis Pauli Egenolphi. 1588. 8°. ¶⁸ A-Q⁸ R⁴. ff. 1-132. [336

-- Responsio ad examen ignoti patroni veritatis de purgatione Sagarum per aquam frigidam ... Francofurdi Apud Joannem Wechelum. M D XC. 8°. A-D⁸ (-D8, *presumably blank*). pp. 1-56. (Lea.) [337

SCROFA, CAMILLO. I cantici di Fidentio Glotto Crysio Ludimagistro ... In Fiorenza. Appresso Antonio Padouani MDLXXII. 8°. A-C⁸. pp. 3-44. [338

SCYLITZA, JOANNES. Historiarum compendium, Quod incipiens à Nicephori Imperatoris, à Genicis obitu, ad Imperium Isaaci Comneni pertinet. A Ioanne Curopalate Scillizzæ ... conscriptum: Et ... à Ioanne Baptisto Gabio, è Græco, in Latinum conuersum. ... Venetiis, M D LXX. Apud Dominicum Nicolinum. (*Colophon.*) fol. a⁴ b⁶ A-PP⁴. ff. 1-151. [339

SEBASTUS, ALPHONSUS AEMILIUS. Pasquillus. Der vertriben von Rhom/ so yetzund diser zeyt in Teütschland im ellend vmb zeücht. Durch Alphonsum Aemilium Sebastum erstlich inn Latein gemacht/ hernach in Teütsch transsferiert worden. 4°. A-C^4. [340

SECCHI, NICOLÒ. Gl'inganni comedia del Signor N. S. Recitata in Milano l'anno 1547. ... In Fiorenza appresso i Giunti MDLXII. (*Colophon.*) 8°. A-F^8 G^4. pp. 4-101. [341

-- -- In Venetia, Appresso Bernardo Giunti, e Fratelli. M D.LXXXII. 8°. A-G^8. ff. 2-56. (Furness.) [342

SECKERWITZ, JOHANN. Valedictio Austriae. Scripta a Iohanne Secceruitio discidente in patriam. Viennæ Austriæ ex Officina Caspari Stainhoferi, Anno M. D. LXIX. 4°. A-B^4. [343

SECOND, JAN. Ioannis Secundi Hagiensis opera. Nunc primum in lucem edita. ... Traiecti Batauorum Harmannus Borculous excudebat. Anno XLI. 8°. A-T^8 V^4 X^8. [344

-- -- ... nunc secundùm in lucem edita ... Parisiis, Apud Iacobum Dupuis ... 1561. 16°. A-X^8 Y^4. ff. 2-172. [345

SEEHOFER, ARSACIUS. Die Artickel so Mayster Arsacius Sehofer von München durch die Hohenschůl zů Ingelstat beredt am abent vnser Frawen geburt nechstuerschinen widerrůffet vñ verworffen hat. Actum. Ingelstat M.D.XXiij. Wie eyn Christliche fraw des adels in Bayern ... die Hohenschůl zů Ingelstat ... straffet. 4°. A^4 B^2 C^4. [346

-- Die Artickel warumb der rector vnd Rethe der Hohenschůl zů Ingolstatt zwungen vnd genötigt haben/ zům widerspruch Mayster Arsacium Seehofer von München ... (M. D. XXiiij.) 4°. A-F^4. [347

SEGAR, SIR WILLIAM. The Booke of honor and Armes. At London, Printed by Richard Ihones ... 1590. 4°. π^2 ($-\pi 2$) A-N^4 Nn^4 O-Y^4 Z^2. pp. 1-104, 1-75. *S.T.C.* 22163. ¶*Additional t.p.* ($A1^r$): The booke of honor and Armes. VVherein is discoursed the causes of Quarrell, and the nature of Iniuries, with their repulses. ... (Furness.) [348

SEGNI, AGNOLO. Ragionamento ... Sopra le cose pertinenti alla poetica ... In Fiorenza, Nella Stamperia di Giorgio Marescotti. ... MDLXXXI. 8°. a^4 A-D^8 E^4. pp. 1-70. [349

SEGNI, BERNARDO. Il trattato sopra i libri dell'anima d'Aristotile ... In Fiorenza MDLXXXIII. Appresso Giorgio Marescotti. Ad instanza di Giouanni di Michele da Passignano ... 4°. ☙-2☙^{4} 3☙^{2} A-Cc^4 DD-EE^4. pp. 1-201. [350

SEGNI, GIULIO. Tempio all' ... Signor Cinthio Aldobrandini Cardinale ... (In Bologna, Presso gli Heredi di Giouanni Rossi. MDC. ...) 4°. $+^6$ A-Xx^4 Yy^2 A-Bb^4 Kk^4 a-c^4 d^2. pp. 2-354, 1-207. [351

SEIDEL, BRUNO. Loci communes prouerbiales de Moribus, Carminibus antiquis conscripti: Cum interpretatione Germanica ... Basileae, ex officina Oporiniana. 1572. 8°. a^4 b-o^8 p^4. pp. 1-216. [352

SEINSHEIM, GEORG LUDWIG VON. Georg Ludwigen von Seinssheim/ ꝛc. Kurtze Ablainung vnd Verantwortung/ etlicher ... Zulagen/ Die Wilhelm von Grumbach/ vnd seine Zugewandte ... zugemessen worden. Getruckt ... M D XC. fol. A-C^4. pp. 3-22. [353

SELLARIUS, HEINRICH. [Epitome Chronicorum, ac Magis insignium Historiarum Mundi velut Index ...] (Francofurti, Christianus Aegenolphus Hadamarius excudebat. Mense Augusto. 1533.) 8°. A-H^8 (-A1) I^6. ff. 3-70. (Lea.) [354

SELNECCER, NICOLAUS. Ein Christliche/ kurtze vnd nötige Predigt aus dem Euangelio Luc. 2. ... Aus dem munde ... nachgeschrieben ... Leiptzig/ M.D LXXX. (Gedruckt ... durch Iohan: Beyer ...) 4°. A-D^4. [355

-- Drey Predigten ... Vom Reichen man vnd armen Lazaro ... Ein Büchlein von den Bettlern/ genant expertus in truphis ... Sampt einer vorrede D. D. Martini Lutheri. Leiptzig ... M D.LXXX. (... bey Iohann Beyer ...) 4°. A-M^4. [356

-- Propositiones, et Quæstiones, in octo libros Physicorum Aristotelis ... Basileae, ex officina Oporiniana. (... M.D.LXIX. Mense Ianuario.) 8°. a-k^8. pp. 3-158. [357

-- Theophania. Comoedia ... de primorum parentum conditione ... VVitebergae excudebat Lau. Schuenck. 1560. 8°. A-E⁸. [358

SENECA, LUCIUS ANNAEUS. *Works*. Opera L. Annaei Senecae ... per Des. Erasmum Roterod. & Matthæum Fortunatum ... emendata ... Adiecta sunt Scholia D. Erasmi Roterodami ... Beati Rhenani in Ludum de morte Claudij Caesaris. Rodolphi Agricolæ in Declamationes aliquot Commentraioli [*sic*]. Fernandi Pinciani castigationes in uniuersum opus. ... Basileae [per Joannem Hervagium, c. 1541]. fol. a^8 a-z^6 A-Mm^6 Nn^4 AA-GG^6 HH^8 II-KK^6 LL^4 (-LL4). pp. 2-701. [359

-- -- L. Annaei Senecae ... opera quæ extant omnia, Coelii Secundi Curionis ... cura castigata ... Basileae, M. D. LVII. (... per Ioannem Heruagium, et Bernardum Brandum ... Mense Augusto.) fol. α^8,a-z^6 A-Ss^6 Tt^4 (-Tt4, *blank*). pp. 2-761. ¶α4-6, a1 *defective*. [360

-- -- L. Annaei Senecae ... opera, Quæ extant, omnia ... Nouæ huic editioni accesserunt ... Authore Dionysio Gothofredo I.C. Basileae, per Eusebium Episcopium. Anno, M. D. XC. 8°.):(^{8} a-h^8 A-V^8 aa-oo^8 pp^4 Aa-Gg^8 Hh^4 AA-SS^8. pp. 1-121, 1-319, 1-232, 1-120, 1-287. [361

-- -- L. Annæus Seneca a M. Antonio Mureto correctus et notis illustratus. Accedunt seorsim Animaduersiones ... Iani Gruteri opera. [Heidelbergae,] Ex Typographeio Hieronymi Commelini, CIↃ IↃ XCII. fol. π^1 A-Pp^6 Qq^8 Rr-Tt^4 Vv^6 Xx^4. pp. 1-516. ¶*Lacks the* Animadversiones. π1 *defective*. [362

-- -- *Variant*. Ex Typographeio Hieronymi Commelini, CIↃ IↃ XCIII. fol. π^1 A-Pp^6 Qq^8 Rr-Tt^4 Vv^6 Xx^4 $(.\cdot.)^4$ Yy-$5P^4$ $5Q^6$ $+^4$ $++^6$. pp. 1-1031. ¶*Additional t.p.* ((.˙.)1ʳ): Iani Gruteri animaduersiones ... Ex Typographeio Hieronymi Commelini, anno M.D.XCIIII. *Includes* M. Annaei Senecae rhetoris, controuersiarum libri X, Suasoriarum liber vnus. [363

-- -- *Variant*. Ex Typographeio Hieronymi Commelini, anno M.D.XCIIII. [364

-- -- [1] L. Annæi Senecae opera. Cum Emendationibus & Notis M. Antonij Mureti. Accedunt vita Senecæ. Animaduersiones Iani Gruteri studio concinnata ... [Genevae,] Apud Ioannem Le Preux. M. D. XCV. 16°. †-3†^{8} ¶^{8} a-z^8 A-Dd^8 Ee^4 Ff-Hh^8. pp. 2-806. ¶*Additional t.p.* (¶1ʳ): L. Annæi Senecae epistolæ CXXIII. ... Sumptibus Ioannis le Preux. M. D. XCIIII. [2] L. Annæi Senecae operum, tomus secundus. ... *Same imprint*. a-z^8 A-Xx^8. pp. 3-1038. [365

-- *Two or more works*. Seneque de la prouidence diuine. De la clemence. De la consolation de la mort. A Lyon, Par Michel Beublin. M.D.XCVI. 12°. a-i^{12}. pp. 3-216. ¶*Translator: Ange Cappel*. [366

-- Les oeuures morales et meslees de Seneque. Traduites de Latin en François, par Simon Goulart Senlisien. ... Deuxiesme Edition ... A Paris, Chez Iean Houzé ... M. D. XCVIII. ... fol. $+^4$ $\bar{a}^6$ $\bar{e}^6$ $\bar{\imath}^6$ $\bar{o}^4$ A-B^6 C^4 D-$4D^6$ A-M^6. pp. 1-42, 1-889, 3-138. [367

-- Cinco libros de Seneca. ... (Imprimidas enla ... ciudad de Toledo. Enel año ... de Mill ꝛ quinientos ꝛ diez Años. A quinze dias del mes de Mayo.) fol. B.L. a^8 b^7 c-p^6 (-p6, *presumably blank*). ff. XIII-LXXXIX. ¶*A made-up copy, the first 15 ll. coming from a copy of the Seville 1491 ed. of* Las obras. *Translator: Alonso de Cartagena*. [368

-- -- Los cinco libros de Seneca en Romance. ... M.D.XXX. (Fue impresso ... enla ... vniuersidad de Alcala de Henares: en casa de Miguel de Eguia. ... Acabose a veynte y ocho dias del mes de Enero.) fol. B.L. a-k^8 l^4. ff. ij-lxxvj. [369

-- *Separate works*. Entiere traduction des Epistres de Seneque ... Par le Seigneur de Pressac ... Et le Cleandre, ou de l'Honneur, & de la Vaillance, discours fait par ledit Seigneur de Pressac. ... A Lyon, Par Michel Beublin. M.D.XCVI. 12°. A-X^{12}. pp. 1-462. [370

-- -- L'epistole di Seneca ridotte nella lingua toscana, per il Doni. ... In Vinegia MDXLIX. (... MDXLVIII. Per Aurelio Pincio.) 8°. $*^8$ A-Z^8 (-A1) AA-XX^8. pp. 3-680 *present*. [371

-- -- Epistolas de Seneca en Romance ... (Fueron impressas ... En la vniuersidad ꝺ Alcala ꝺ Henares en casa de Miguel de Eguia a .xv. ꝺ Enero M.D.xxix. años.) fol. B.L. a-k^6 l-m^8. ff. ij-lxxiij. [372

-- *De beneficiis*. Lucius Anneus Seneca vanden Weldaden. ... vertaelt duer Dierick Coornhert. Tot Haerlem by Ian van Zuren. 1562. ... 8°. $*^8$ A-Ee^8 Ff^{10}. [373

-- -- Seneca de benifizii tradotto in volgar Fiorentino da Messer Benedetto Varchi. In Firenze MDLIIII. (Stampati ... per Lorenzo Torrentino ... del mese di Settembre ...) 4°. A-DD^4. pp. 1-204. [374

-- -- In Fiorenza Nella Stamperia dei Giunti M D LXXIIII. 8°. a-b^8 A-T^8. pp. 2-304. [375

-- *De consolatione.* Seneque de la consolation de la mort. A Paris. Pour Felix le Magnier ... MVLXXXIIII [*sic*]. ... (Acheué d'Imprimer le 29. Iuing. 1584.) 8°. ā^4 ē^4 A-Q^4. ff. 1-63. ¶*Translator: Ange Cappel.* [376

-- Seneca De quattuor virtutibus Cardinalibus [*spurious*]. (Impressum Viennę pannonię per Ioannem Singreniū Expensis Bartholomei Werlen ... 1519) 4°. A-B^6 C^4 D^6. ¶*With translation in German verse.* [377

-- L. Annei Senecae naturalium quaestionum libri VII. Matthæi Fortunati in eosdem libros ... annotationes. ... (Venetiis in aedibus Aldi et Andreae Asulani soceri, mense Februario. M.D.XXII.) 4°. *^{6} a-g^8 h^{10} i-q^8 r^6. ff. 1-180. [378

-- *Proverbia.* Prouerbios de Seneca. (Impressos en seuilla por Iuan crōberger. A .v. dias de nouiēbre. Año ... δ mil y ꝗniētos. y. xxxv) fol. B.L. a^4 b-h^8 i^6. ff. j-lxij. [379

-- -- Introduction a los Prouerbios de Seneca: Por el doctor Pero Diaz ... *Latin & Spanish.* En Medina del Campo Vendense en casa de Adrian Ghemart. M.D.LII. (Fue impressa ... en casa de Guillermo de Millis. ...) fol. B.L. a^8 A-I^8 K^6. ff. j-lxxiij. [380

-- Senecae tragoediae. (Venetiis in aedibus Aldi et Andreae soceri mense Octobri M. D. XVII.) 8°. a^4 b-z^8 A-D^8 E^4. ff. 1-207. [381

-- -- *Another copy.* (Lea.) [382

-- -- [1] L. Annaei Senecae Cordubensis tragoediae. ... Heidelbergæ, cIↄ Iↄ LXXXIX. 8°. *^{4} A-Aa^8. pp. 1-384. [2] Iusti LipsI animaduersiones ... cIↄ. Iↄ. LXXXVIII. A-G^8 a-c^8 d^4. pp. 3-112, 3-56. [383

-- -- Seneca his tenne tragedies, translated into Englysh. ... Imprinted at London ... by Thomas Marsh. 1581. (*Colophon.*) 4°. B.L. A^4 B-Ee^8 Ff^4 (-A1, Ff4, *presumably blank*). ff. 1-217. *S.T.C.* 22221. (Furness.) [384

-- -- Le tragedie de Seneca, tradotte da M. Lodouico Dolce. ... In Venetia, appresso Gio. Battista et Marchion Sessae. (... M.D.LX.) 12°. *^{12} A^6 B-FF^{12}. ff. 1-347. [385

-- *Selections.* Les authoritez, sentences et singuliers enseignemens du grant censeur ... Seneque ... [Paris,] On les vend ... en la boutique de Denis Ianot. Et en ... la boutique de Iehan Longis. ... ([A1^v] acheue dimprimer ... le dieuxiesme iour de May. Mil cinq cens. XXXIIII. [P8^v] Imprimees par Denys Ianot, pour Pierre sergent, & Iehan Longis ...) 8°. A-P^8. ¶P4 *misbound after* P6. [386

SENIGALLIA. Statutorum et reformationum magnificae ciuitatis Senogaliæ. Volumen. ... Pisauri. Apud Hieronymum Concordiam. M. D. LXXXIIII. (*Colophon.*) fol. π^2 A-Z^4 Aa-Zz^4 AA-FF^4 (-FF4, *possibly blank*) ✠^{4} ✠✠^{4} ✠✠^{4}. ff. 1-202. (Lea.) [387

SENS. Coustumes du Bailliage de Sens & anciēs ressorts d'iceluy ... A Sens, De l'Imprimerie de Gilles Richeboys, M. D. LVI. ... 4°. A^6 a-m^4 A-Y^4 Aa-Ii^4. pp. 1-95, 1-174, 1-70. [388

-- Ordinationes Synodales ciuitatis & diocesis Senonensis ... Venale reperitur Señ: in edibus Ioannis de la Mare ... 1554. (... Excudebat Franciscus Girault ...) 8°. ✠$^{8+1}$ A-F^8 G^2. ff. 1-49. [389

SENTENCIAS. Primera parte de las sentencias que hasta nuestros tiempos, ... por diuersos Autores escritas ... Y traduzidas en el nuestro comun. ... M. D. LIIII. (Fue impressa ... en la ... ciudad de Coimbra, por Ioan Aluarez ... Acabose a veinte dias de Março. De mil y quinientos y cincuenta y cinco años.) 4°. A-X^8 Y^4 (-Y4, *presumably blank*). pp. 8-340. [390

SEPINUS, GERVASIUS. Geruasii Sepini Salmurei erotopaegniωn libri tres ad Apollinem. Parisiis. Ex officina Christiani Wecheli ... 1553. 8°. A-P^8 Q^4. pp. 3-246. [391

SERARIUS, NICOLAUS. Contra nouos noui Pelagiani et chiliastae, Francisci Puccii Filidini errores ... libri duo ... Wirceburgu Ex officina typographica Georgij Fleischmanni. Anno

M. D. XCIII. 4°. A^4 A-K^4. pp. 1-78. (Lea.) [391a

SERDONATI, FRANCESCO. De' fatti d'arme de' Romani, libri tre. ... In Venetia. Appresso Giordan Ziletti, e compagni. M. D. LXXII. (Stampata ... per Christoforo Zanetti ...) 4°. *-$**^4$ A-Y^4. pp. 1-170. [392

SERENI, AURELIO. Aurelij sereni Monopolitani. Opuscula (Romae Impressum [per Stephanum Guileretum & Herculem Nani] anno .M.ccccc.xii. Die uero viii. Mensis Martii.) 4°. A-F^4. [393

SERLIO, SEBASTIANO. [1] Il primo libro d'architettura, di M. Sebastiano Serlio Bolognese. (In Vinetia per Cornelio de Nicolini da Sabbio a instantia de Marchio Sessa.) fol. A-D^4 A-H^4. ff. 2-16, 1-31. [2] Il terzo libro ... In Venetia ... (... per Pietro de Nicolini da Sabbio, Ad instantia di Marchione Sessa. M. D. LI. fol. $[A]^2$ B-V^4. pp. IIII-CLV. [3] Regole generali di architettura ... In Venetia ... (*Same colophon.*) fol. A-T^4. ff. II-LXXVI. [4] Quinto libro ... In Venetia. (*Same colophon.*) fol. 3A-$3C^4$ $3D^6$. ff. 2-18. (Fine Arts.) [394

-- -- Tutte l'Opere d'Architettura di Sebastiano Serlio Bolognese; Doue si ... aggiunto ... da M. Gio. Domenico Scamozzi. In Venetia, M D LXXXIIII. Presso Francesco de'Franceschi Senese. 4°. a^4 a^4 c-f^4 A^4 B-F^8 G^4 G-I^8 K-P^4 Q-S^8 T^4 II-QQ^4 RR-ZZ^8 $3A^8$ $*^4$ A-O^8 P^{10} a-c^8 d^4 (-d4, *presumably blank*). ff. 2-219, pp. 1-243, ff. 4-27. ¶*Additional t.pp.:* ($A1^r$) Libro primo d'architettura ... *Same imprint.* ($C5^r$) Il second libro di prospettiua ... ($G1^r$) Il terzo libro ... ($II1^r$) Regoli generali di architettura ... ($YY5^r$) Quinto libro ... ($*1^r$) Il settimo libro ... *Same imprint.* (*Colophon.*) ($^2a1^r$) Libro estraordinario ... *Same imprint.* (Fine Arts.) [395

-- Des Antiquites, Le troisiesme liure translaté d'italien en franchois. ([Anuers, Imprimé pour P. Coeck d'Alost par G. van Diest, 1550.]) fol. A-R^4 S^6 (-S1, S4-6). ff. 3-71 *present.* [396

-- Tercero y quarto libro de architectura ... Traduzido de Toscano en lẽgua Castellana, por Francisco de Villalpando ... Impresso ... en Toledo en casa de Iuan de Ayala. Año de 1573. A costa de Miguel Rodriguez ... (*Colophon.*) fol. A-V^4 A-T^4. ff. II-LXXX, pp. II-V, ff. VI-LXXVIII. (Fine Arts.) [397

-- Extraordinario libro di architettura ... In Lione, per Giouan di Tournes. M. D. LI. ... fol. A^6 A^6 + 50 *plates.* ¶*Additional t.p.* ($^2A1^r$): Liure extraordinaire de architecture ... A Lyon, par Iean de Tournes. M. D. LI. (Fine Arts.) [398

-- -- In Lione, appresso Guglielmo Rouillio. M. D. LX. ... fol. A^6 + 28 *plates (out of 50), all mounted.* [399

SERREIUS, JOANNES. Grammatica Gallica ... Argentorati, Excudebat Antonius Bertramus. 8°.)(^{8} A-K^8. pp. 1-156. [400

SERVILIO, GIOVANNI. La congiuratione de Gheldresi contra la citta Danuersa ... volgarizzata per Francesco Strozzi. ... M D XLIII. (In Vinegia per Giouanni Britto Intagliatore. ... Nel mese d'Ottrobre [*sic*].) 8°. A-E^8. [401

SEVEN SAGES. I compassioneuoli auuenimenti di Erasto. ... di Greco ridotta in Volgare. ... In Venetia. Appresso Francesco Bindoni. 1558. 8°. A-Q^8. pp. 3-250. [402

-- -- In Venetia, Appresso Gerolamo Caualcalouo. M D LXV. 8°. A-S^8. ff. 2-134. [403

-- Ludus septem sapientum, de Astrei regii adolescentis educatione ... (Impressum Francoforti ad Moenum, apud Paulum Reffeler, Impensis Sigismundi Feyrabent.) 8°. A-N^8. [404

SEVERUS, PONTANUS. Encomium Eccii. Authore Pontano Seuero Traiectensi. M. D. XXX. 8°. a^8 b^2. [405

SEVILLE. Ordenanças de Seuilla. ... (Impressas ... enla ... cibdad de Seuilla por Iuan varela de slamanca ... Acabaronse de imprimir a catorze dias del mes de febrero ... M.d.xxvij.) fol. B.L. a^{8+1} b-r^8 s^{10} t-z^8 A-G^8 H^{10} (-H10, *presumably blank*). ff. I-CCII. [406

SEVILLE

-- Synodo diocessano quel ... Don Christoual de Rojas y Sandoual Arçobispo de Seuilla ... Celebro ... Año de .M.D.lxxij. Impresso en Seuilla ... En casa de Iuan Gutierrez. 4°. a-c^8 (-c8, *presumably blank*). ¶c2, c7 *interchanged in binding*. (Lea.) [407

SEXTUS EMPIRICUS. Sexti philosophi Pyrrhoniarum hypotypωsεων libri III ... Interprete Henrico Stephano. [Genevae,] Anno M. D. LXII. Excudebat idem Henricus Stephanus ... 8°. A-S^8. pp. 2-188. [408

SEYSSEL, CLAUDE DE. [1] D. Claudij de Seyssello ... In. vj. ffoꝝ. partes. ꝛ primam .C. vnicuiqꝫ legi ... fol. B.L. A-H^6 I^4. [2] Lectura ... super prim: parte .ff. veteris ... aa-ff^8 gg^6 hh^4. ff. I-LVIII. [3] Lectura ... in primam Infortiati ... AA-II^8 KK^6 LL^4. ff. I-LXXXII. [4] Lectura ... In primam .ff. noui ... 3A-3F^8 3G^6. ff. I-LIIII. [5] ... Commentaria In .ij. ff. noui par. ... (Venetijs per Thomaꝫ Ballarinū Vercellensem. ... M.ccccc.xxxv. Die .12. Mensis Aprilis.) 3a-3e^8 3f^6. ff. I-XLVI. [6] Lectura ... In primā Codicis ... A-C^8 D^6. ff. I-XXX. (Biddle.) [409

SIBER, ADAM. Adami Siberi gemma gemmarum, seu Nomenclatoris Had. Iunii Epitome. Adiunctis neaniscis I. S. Idea formandorum studiorum Rhodol. Agricolae. ... Lipsiæ Iohannes Rhamba imprimebat. M. D. LXXIX. 8°. A-V^8. pp. 3-317. [410

SIBUTUS, GEORG. De diui Maximiliani Cesaris aduentu in Coloniam ... (... Disseminatū ē h' opus Colonie in edibus Quentel. ... M.D. quinto post principium Sextilis. al's. Augusti Et iteꝝ impressum in eodē mēse in ... Hantwerpia Per me Godofridum. Bac.) 4°. B.L. a^6 b^4 c^6. [411

SIBYLLA, Herzogin von Sachsen. Vom Christlichen abschied aus diesem tödlichen leben Der ... Fraw Sibyllen ... Des ... Churfürsten Iohans Fridrichs Hertzogen zu Sachssen ꝛc. Ehegemahl. Daneben auch/ Des ... Hertzogen zu Sachssen Churfursten ꝛc. abschiedt. 1554. 4°. A^4 B^2. [412

SIBYLLINE ORACLES. Sibyllina Oracula de Graeco in Latinum conuersa, et in eadem annotationes. Sebastiano Castalione interprete. ... Basileae. (... ex officina Ioannis Oporini ... 1546. Mense Augusto.) 8°. a^8 b^4 A-H^8 I^4. pp. 1-135. [413

SICHARDT, JOHANNES. Antidotum contra diuersas omnium fere seculorum haereses. ... Basileæ excudebat Henricus Petrus, mense Augusto, anno M. D. XXVIII. (*Colophon.*) fol. α-γ^6 a-z^6 A-X^6 Y^4 Z^6. ff. 1-275. ¶*Authors: Justin Martyr, S. Athanasius, Marius Victorinus Afer, S. Hilary, S. Ambrose, Theophilus, Idacius, Cyril of Alexandria, Proclus, Timotheus, Vincent of Lerins, Prosper of Aquitaine, Victor, Cerealis, Gelasius, John bishop of Rome, Faustus, Antoninus, Agnellus, Rusticus.* (Lea.) [414

SICILY. [1] Constitutiones regni Sicilie Per ... Andream de Ysernia, Et alios doctores cōmentate ... M.CCCCC.XXXXV. Neapoli. Apud Ioannem Paulum Sugganappum. ... (*Colophon.*) fol. B.L. ✠^{6} ✠✠^{4} ℭ^4 a-n^6 o^4 p-z^6 ꝛ^6 ꝯ^6 ꝝ^6 aa-cc^6 dd^4. ff. 1-175. [2] Capitula Regni Siciliae: (Excussum ... sumptibus Ioannis Pauli de suganappis ... Neapoli excudebat Ioannes Sultzbachius. Anno M.D.XXXXIIII.) A-E^6 F^8 G-K^6 L-M^4 AA-BB^6. ff. 1-69. 1-12. ¶G1^r: ... Repertorium ... AA1^r: ... Ritus magne Curie ... redacti per dominum Cesarē de Perinijs. [3] Pragmatice regni noue et antique ... *Same imprint.* (*Colophon.*) 3A-3E^6 3F^4 ff. 1-33. (Lea.) [415

-- [1] Regni Siciliae capitula ... recognita ... Per ... Rainmundum Raimundettam ... Venetiis, Ex Officina Dominici Guerræi, & Io. Baptistæ fratrum. MDLXXIII. fol. *^{4} A-LL^8 MM^6. pp. 2-559. [2] Index alphabeticus ... *Same imprint.* a-d^6. [3] Pandectae reformatae, et de nouo factae ... *Same imprint.* A-D^8 E^4. pp. 4-70. (Lea.) [416

SIENA. *Laws &c.* Bandi, ordini, e prouisioni, appartenenti al gouerno Della Città, e Stato di Siena. Publicati dal giorno 19. di Luglio 1557. ... fino à quest'Anno 1584 ... In Siena, Appresso Luca Bonetti. 1584. 4°. +^{4} A^4 aa^4 B-Bb^4. ff. 1-8, pp. 9-198. (Lea.) [417

-- Bando di promessione di Gratia, o di permutatione alli Condennati, ò Contumaci, che vorranno ritornare ad habitare à Siena ... (Bandito ... il di 19. di Dicembre [1585?] ...) 4°. π^2. [418

-- Bando sopra i premii da darsi a chi ammazzerà, ò darà in potere della Giustitia Banditi, Assassini, & altri delinquenti. (Bandito ... il di 28. di Nouembre 1587.) 4°. π^2. [419

-- Dichiarazione, Et moderatione del Bando Pubblicatosi in materia delli premii da darsi a chi dà nelle mani della Giustizia li notorii omicidarii, & altri delinquenti infrascritti. (Bandito ... il di 22. d'Ottobre 1588.) 4°. π^2. [420

-- Bando generale della proibitione dell'Arme per la Città, e Stato di Siena. Pubblicato il 14. di Dicembre 1588. 4°. A^4. [421

-- Bando contro li giocatori, Dannatori, Discoli, Oziosi, & Insolenti. (Bandito ... il di 4. di Nouembre 1589.) 4°. π^2. ¶*Includes:* Bando che non si giuochi à Carte, ò Dadi; nè si stia à vedere. (Bandito ... il di 12. d'Aprile 1597.) [422

-- Bando Sopra l'Estrazzione Del Bestiame Vaccino, & altro, à fauore de'Vergari. (Bandito il dì 4. di Luglio 1590.) In Siena. 1590. 4°. A^4. ¶90. *pasted over* 89. [423

-- Bando, ò Moderazione sopra li sfoggi, e vestire nella citta di Siena, e suo stato. In Siena. (Bandito ... il dì 17. di Maggio 1594.) 4°. A^6 (-A6, *presumably blank*). [424

-- *Accademia degli Intronati.* Dieci paradosse degli academici Intronati da Siena. ... In Milano Appresso Gio. Antonio degli Antonij. 1564. (... Imprimeuano i fratelli da Meda. ...) 8°. $A\text{-}F^8\ G^4$. ff. 4-52. [425

-- Il sacrificio. Comedia de gli Intronati celebrato ne i giuochi d'un Carnouale in Siena. ... In Venetia. Appresso Altobello Salicato, M D LXIX. 12°. $A\text{-}F^{12}$. ff. 3-72. ¶$B2^r$: Prologo de gli Ingannati de gli Intronati. [426

-- -- *Another copy.* ¶*First two ll. badly wormed and repaired; imprint partly illegible.* (Furness.) [427

-- -- In Vinegia. Presso Domenico Caualcalupo. M D LXXXV. 8°. $A\text{-}I^8$. ff. 2-69. (Furness.) [428

-- -- *Another copy.* [429

SIGMARIUS, SEBASTIAN. Cicadae encomium. ... [Viennae, Johannes Singriener,] M. D. XL. 4°. $A\text{-}B^4$. [430

SIGONIO, CARLO. Caroli Sigonii de antiquo iure ciuium Romanorum libri duo. Eiusdem de antiquo iure Italiae libri tres. ... Venetiis, ex officina Iordani Zileti, M D LXIII. (*Colophon.*) 4°. $\alpha^4\ \beta^2\ A\text{-}P^4\ P*^4\ Q^4\ R*^4\ R\text{-}Z^4\ a\text{-}o^4\ p^2$. pp. 1-281. ¶*Lacks part 2.* (Biddle.) [431

-- Caroli Sigonii de antiquo iure Italiae libri tres ... Venetiis, apud Iordanum Ziletum M D LX. (*Colophon.*) 4°. $*\text{-}**^4\ A\text{-}NN^4$. ff. 2-128. (Biddle.) [432

-- Caroli Sigonii de antiquo iure prouinciarum libri duo. ... Venetijs, ex officina Iordani Ziletti, M D LXVII. 4°. $A^6\ B\text{-}EE^4$. pp. 2-198. [433

-- Caroli Sigonii de Atheniensium, Lacedaemoniorumq. temporibus liber. ... Venetiis, M D LXIIII. Ex Officina Dominici Guerrei, & Io. Baptistæ fratrum. (*Colophon.*) 4°. $A\text{-}N^4$. ff. 1-48. (Biddle.) [434

-- Caroli Sigonii de dialogo liber. ... Venetiis, apud Iordanum Ziletum, M. D. LXII. 4°. $A\text{-}Q^4$. ff. 1-57. [435

-- Caroli Sigonii de episcopis Bononiensibus libri quinque. Bononiae MDLXXXVI Per Alexandrum Benatium (*Colophon.*) 4°. $A^2\ A\text{-}Ss^4$. pp. 1-259. [436

-- Caroli Sigonii de rep. Atheniensium libri IIII. Eiusdem de Athenien. Lacedaemoniorumq. temporibus liber ... Bononiae Apud Ioannem Rubrium. M D LXIIII. 4°. $a^4\ A\text{-}FF^4\ GG^2$. pp. 1-235. ¶*Part 2 wanting.* (Biddle.) [437

-- -- Venetiis, Apud Vincentium Valgrisium. M D LXV. 8°. $A\text{-}T^8$. ff. 2-15[1]. (Biddle.) [438

-- Caroli Sigonii de republica Hebræorum libri VII ... Francofurti Apud hæredes Andreæ Wecheli, M. D. LXXXIII. 8°. $A\text{-}Cc^8$. pp. 3-392. [439

-- Caroli Sigonii de vita Laurentii Campegii cardinalis liber. ... Bononiae, Apud Societatem Typographiæ Bononiensis. MDLXXXI. ... 4°. $\dagger^4\ A\text{-}O^4$. pp. 1-108. [440

-- Caroli Sigonii emendationum libri duo. ... Venetiis, [Aldine press,] M. D. LVII. 4°. A^4 a^4 B-Ss^4. ff. 2-159. (Biddle.) [441

-- Caroli Sigonii historiarum de occidentali imperio, libri XX. ... Basileae, ex officina Thomae Guarini, M.D.LXXIX. (... M. April.) 4°. A-Zz^4 AA-ZZ^4 3A-$3O^4$. pp. 4-524, cols. 525-664. (Lea.) [442

-- Caroli Sigonii historiarum de regno Italiae Libri Quindecim. ... Bononiæ, Apud Societatem Typographiæ Bonon. MDLXXX. ... (*Colophon.*) fol. A-Oo^6 Pp^8 Qq-$3I^6$ $3K^4$ $+^6$ a-i^6 k^4. pp. 3-666. [443

-- Regum, consulum, dictatorum, ac censorum Romanorum fasti ... Eiusdem de Nominibus Romanorum liber. Kalendarium uetus Romanum ... & Pauli Manutij de ueterum dierum ordine opinio ... Venetiis, M. D. LV. Apud Paulum Manutium, Aldi F. ... (*Colophon.*) fol. A^4 B-Q^2. [444

SILIUS ITALICUS, GAIUS. Silius Italicus ... de secundo bello punico. ... (... M.cccccciiij. ... impressum cura et impensis ... Martini Herbipolensis cũ Argumentis Hermanni Buschij.) fol. B.L. A-Pp^6 (-Pp6, *presumably blank*). [445

SILVAGIUS, MATTHAEUS. Lectura seu expositio ... super octo libros phisicorum Aristo. cũ aliquibus annotationibus ... Frãcisci Mayronis. ... Venetiis. M D XLII. ... (... in ædibus Francisci Bindonei, & Maphei Pasinei. Mense Ianuarij. ... M D XLIII.) 8°. A-M^8 N^4. ff. 2-96. [446

SILVANUS, C., GERMANICUS. C. Siluani Germanici in pontificatum Clementis septimi Pont. Opt. Max. panegyris prima. Eiusdem in statuam Leonis decimi Pont. Max. sylua. (Rome in ædibus Ludouici Vicentini et Lautitij Perusini ... M.D.XXIIII. XII. Kl. Ian.) 4°. A-L^4. [447

SILVESTRI, JACOPO. Opus nouum ... pro cipharis ... (Impressum Romæ [per Marcellum Silber]. Anno M.D.XXVI.) 4°. A-L^4. ff. 2-44. [448

SIMANCAS, DIEGO. Iacobi Simancae Pacensis episcopi enchiridion iudicum violatae Religionis, ad extirpandas hereses theoricen & praxim ... complectens. ... Cui accesserunt ... opuscula duo ... vnum, annotationum in Zanchinum. Alterum, de patre hæretico. ... Venetiis, Ex officina Iordani Zileti. M D LXIX. 8°. *-$3*^8$ A-Q^8 R^4. ff. 1-125. (Lea.) [449

-- -- Iacobi Simancae ... theorice et praxis haereseos, siue enchiridion iudicum violatae religionis. ... Venetiis, Ex Officina Iordani Ziletti, M. D. LXXIII. 8°. *-$3*^8$ A-T^8 V^4. ff. 1-154. (Lea.) [450

-- Institutiones catholicae quibus ... diseritur quicquid ad præcauendas & extirpandas hæreses necessarium est, authore Iacobo Septimancensi ... Vallisoleti, Ex officina Ægidij de Colomies ... 1552 (*Colophon.*) fol. π^6 a-z^8 A-F^8 (-F8, *presumably blank*). ff. I-CCXXX. (Lea.) [451

-- -- Iacobi Simancae ... de catholicis institutionibus liber, Ad præcauendas & extirpandas hæreses admodum necessarius, tertio nunc editus. ... Romae, In Aedibus Populi Romani ... M. D. LXXV. (*Colophon.*) 4°. a-d^4 A-$3S^4$ $3T^6$. pp. 2-522. (Lea.) [452

SIMEONI, GABRIELE. Comentarii di Gabriello Symeoni Fiorentino sopra alla tetrarchia di Vinegia, di Milano, di Mantoua, et di Ferrara ... M. D. XLVIII. (In Vinegia per Comin da Trino di Monferrato ...) 8°. A-Q^8. ff. 5-113. [453

-- Le satire alla Berniesca ... con vna Elegia sopra alla morte del Re Francesco Primo, & altre Rime a diuerse persone. ... Nel. M. D. XLIX. (In Turino pro Martino Crauotto. ...) 4°. a-b^4 c^6 d-h^4 i^6 k^4 l^6. [454

SIMLER, JOSIAS. De republica Heluetiorum Libri duo. ... Tiguri excudebat Christophorus Froschouerus. 1577. 8°. $*^8$ A-Cc^8 Dd^4 (-Dd4, *blank*). ff. 1-207. [455

-- Vita clarissimi philosophi et medici ... Conradi Gesneri Tigurini ... Item, Epistola Gesneri de libris à se editis. ... His accessit Caspari VVolphii Tigurini ... hyposchesis ... Tiguri excudebat Froschouerus, 1566. 4°. A-N^4. ff. 2-52. [456

SIMONETA, GIOVANNI. Historie di Giouanni Simonetta delle ... imprese fatte dallo inuittissimo Francesco Sforza Duca di Milano nella Italia, Tradotta in lingua Thoscana da

Cristoforo Landino Fiorentino ... In Vinegia al segno dil pozzo [Andrea Arrivabene] M D XLIIII. (... per Bartolomeo detto l'Imperador, & Francesco suo genero. ...) 8°. *-3*^{8} A-3D^{8} 3E^{4}. ff. 1-403. [457

-- Sfortiade fatta Italiana de li gesti del generosi ... Francesco Sforza, ... Duca di Milano ... In Venetia per Curtio Troiani di Nauo ... M D XLIII. (... per Venturino Roffinello. M.D. XLIIII.) 8°. A-3I^{8} 3K^{4}. ff. 2-440. ¶*Translator: Sebastiano Fausto.* [458

SIMONETTI, CESARE. Madrigali ... In Verona, Appresso Girolamo Discepoli. M D XC. 8°. A-M^{8}. pp. 3-186. [459

SIMONIS, NICOLAUS. ... Exercitium signorũ sacerdotaliũ seu Ars memoratiua sacerdotũ siue rationale Pro cõdigna oꝑatione. orõne. celebratione et ꝯtẽplatione. ... (M.cccccxiiij. circiter gymnasium: vel vt vulgo placet bursam Kuck impressus ... Colonia [per Henricum de Nussia] ...) 8°. B.L. A^{8} B-S^{4}. ff. ij-lxxiiij. [460

SIMPLICIUS. Σιμπλικιου υπομνήματα ... Simplicii Commentaria in tres libros Aristotelis de anima. Alexandri Aphrodisici cõmentaria in librum de sensu, & sensibili. Michaelis Ephesii annotationes ... M. D. XXVII. (Venetiis in aedibus Aldi, et Andreae Asulani soceri ... mense Iunio.) fol. **^{4} aa-ll^{8} mm^{4} nn-pp^{8} qq^{10} rr-zz^{8} &&^{6}. ff. 1-187. [461

-- Simplicii ... commentarius in enchiridion Epicteti ... Angelo Caninio Anglariensi interprete. ... Venetiis Apud Hieronymum Scotum. M. D XLVI. (*Colophon.*) fol. π^{2} A-G^{6} H-I^{4}. pp. 1-100. [462

-- Σιμπλικίου ... σχόλια ... εἰς τὰς Ἀριστοτέλους Κατηγορίας. Simplicii ... in ... Categorias siue Prædicamenta ... commentaria ... Iusti Velsij ... industria, elaborata. Basileae apud Michaëlem Isingrinium, anno M.D.LI. fol. α^{6} a-s^{6} t^{4}. ff. 2-211. [463

SINAPIUS, JOANNES. Declamatio aduersus ignauiam, & sordes eorum, qui literas Humaniores negligunt ... Parisiis Venit in ædibus Aegidij Gormontij. M.D.XXXI. (Imprimebat [Petrus] Vidouæus suis typis.) 8°. A-B^{8} C^{4} (-C4, *presumably blank*). [464

SINAPIUS, SIMON. Der XIII. Psalm/ Gesangweiss gestellet/ vnd kurtz ausgelegt. Item/ Ein ander ... Lied/ zur zeit der Pestilentz ... Durch D. Simonem Sinapium/ zu Franckfurt an der Oder. Anno, M. D. LIX. 4°. A^{2} B^{4}. [465

SKALICH, PAUL. Pauli principis de la Scala et Hun ... primi tomi miscellaneorum, ... effigies ac exemplar ... vaticinorum & imaginum Ioachimi Abbatis Florensis Calabriæ, & Anselmi Episcopi Marsichani, super statu ... Pontificum Rhomanæ Ecclesiæ, contra ... Theophrasti Paracelsi ... pseudomagicam expositionem, vera ... explanatio. Coloniae Agrippinae, Ex Officina Typographica Theodori Graminæi. Anno M. D. LXX. 4°. *^{4} **^{2} A-T^{4}. pp. 1-152. [466

SLEIDAN, JOHANN. Ioannis Sleidani commentariorum de statu religionis & Reipublicæ, Carolo Quinto Cæsare, Libri XXVI. Vnã cum apologia ab ipso Authore conscripta ... Argentorati Excudebat Theodosius Rihelius. [1565?] 8°. a^{8} A-3I^{8} 3K^{6}. pp. 1-872. ¶F4^{r}, *l.* 6 *ends:* bel-. (Lea.) [467

-- Les oeuures de I. Sleidan qui concernent les histoires qu'il a escrites. ... A Geneue, chez Eustache Vignon. M. D. LXXIIII. fol. ¶$^{4+2}$ A-Z^{6} Aa-Zz^{6} AA-ZZ^{6} AAa-DDd^{6}. ff. 1-457. [468

-- Ioannis Sleidani orationes duae, vna ad Carolum quintum caesarem: altera ad Germaniae Principes omnes ac ordines imperii. ... Anno M.D.XLIIII. Argentinæ excusæ apud Cratonem Mylium. Et nunc ... edita ... Studio & opera Conradi Rittershusii Brunsuuic. ... Helmæstadii Excudebant hæredes Iacobi Lucij, Anno M.D.XCVIII. 8°. A-Q^{8}. pp. 1-229. ¶*Includes:* Henrici Meibomii ... Anagrammatum adoptiuorum libellus. (Lea.) [469

SLOTANUS, JOANNES. D. Ioannis Slotani Geffensis ... disputationum aduersus hæreticos Liber unus: In quo sub propugnatione articulorum Iusto Velsio Coloniæ propositorum omnes fermè huius seculi controuersiæ discutiuntur. ... Coloniae, Apud Ioannem Bathenium. Anno M. D. LVIII. 8°. *^{8} ¶^{8} A-3K^{8} 3L^{4}. ff. 1-441. (Lea.) [470

-- -- *Another copy* (-3L4). (Lea.) [471

SMIDENSTEDT, HARTWIG. Oratio funebris de ... Iulio, Brunouicensium ac Lunæburgensium Duce: Habita à M. Hartuico Smidesteto. Helmaestadii Excudebat Iacobus Lucius, Anno M. D. LXXXIX. 4°. A-E^4. [472

SNELLIUS, RODOLPHUS. Snellio-Ramæum philosophiæ syntagma ... Quibus Præfatio D. Rhodolphi Goclenii ... præfixa est. ... Francofurti, Ex Officina Typographica Ioannis Saurij, impensis hæredum Petri Fischeri. M D XCVI. 8°. A-R^8 S^6. pp. 3-282. [473

SNEPFFIUS, THEODORICUS. Oratio de vita et morte ... Christophori Ducis VVirtenebrgici & Teccij ... qui Anno LXVIII. ... Stutgardiæ piè defunctus ... est. ... Accesserunt etiam Epicedia & Carmina doctissimorum virorum. Tubingæ, [vidua Ulrici Morhard,] 1570. 4°. A-M^4. pp. 3-96. ¶*Possibly incomplete: catchword on* M4^v. [474

SOAREZ, CYPRIANO. De arte rhetorica libri tres. ... Auctore, Cypriano Soario ... Veronae, Apud Sebastianum, a Donno. 1582. 8°. A-O^8. ff. 3-90. [475

-- -- De arte rhetorica libri tres. ... Federici Ceruti Veronensis commentarijs illustrati. Coloniae Agrippinae, [A]pud Ioannem Gymnicum ... M. D. XCI. 8°. $+^8$ A-Q^8 R^2 a-i^8 k^2. pp. 1-243, 1-148. [476

SOBIUS, JAKOB. Philalethis ciuis Vtopiensis dialogus, de facultatibus Rhomanensium nuper publicatis. Henno rusticus. [Basileae, Andreas Cratander, 1520.] 8°. A-C^8 D^4. [477

SOCCINO, BARTOLOMMEO. Bartholo. Soci. commentaria in primam partem infortiati. ... M. D. XXXII. (sumptu ... Lucembergi de Gabiano Lugduni fuerũt excusa in officina Ioannis Crespin al's du carre ... die decimooctauo mensis Septembris.) fol. B.L. a-z^8 (-a2-8, b-d^8) aa-cc^8 dd-ee^4 ff-ii^8 kk-ll^6 mm-ss^8 tt^{10}. ff. 23-330 *present.* ¶*Additional t.pp.:* (o1^r) ... commentaria in secundam partem Infortiati. M. D. XXXII. (ff1^r) ... in primam digesti noui partem commentaria. ... M. D. XXXII. (mm1^r) ... commentaria in secundam digesti noui partem. ... M. D. XXXII. (ss1^r) ... commentaria in titu. cod. de edendo ... M. D. XXXII. (Biddle.) [478

SOCCINO, MARIANO. [1] Prima pars consiliorum Mariani & Bartholomei de Socinis Senensium. ... [Lugduni, Jacobus Giunta,] 1537 fol. B.L. a-z^8 $ꝛ^8$ $ꝯ^8$. ff. 2-187. [2] Secunda pars ... 1537 aa-yy^8. ff. 2-168. (Biddle.) [479

-- [1] Consilia Mariani Socini iunioris ... pars prima. ... Venetiis 1544 fol. B.L. A-LL^8 A-E^6 F^8. ff. 3-271. [2] ... Secunda pars ... Venetiis. 1545 aa-zz^8 $ꝛꝛ^8$ $ꝯꝯ^8$ $ꝶꝶ^8$ AA-CC^8 DD-EE^6. ff. 2-243. (Biddle.) [480

SOCIO, NOBILE. Le miserie de li amanti ... (Stampata in Vinegia per Maestro Bernardino de Vitali Veneciano MDXXXIII) 4°. a-y^4 z^2. [481

SOLINUS, GAIUS JULIUS. Solinus de memorabilibus Mundi ... Venundatur Parrhisiis ... [per Joannem Petit]. 4°. π^4 a-c^8 d^4 e-f^8. ff. I-XLIIII. ¶π1^v: Ex officina nostra [Ascensii] litteraria ad idus iulias Anni .M.D.III. [482

-- -- Solino delle cose marauigliose del mondo, tradotto dall' ... S. Gio. Vincenzo Belprato conte di Anuersa. ... In Vinegia appresso Gabriel Giolito de' Ferrari. M D LVII. (*Colophon.*) 8°. A-P^8. pp. 4-237. [483

SOLIS, GIULIO CESARE DE. L'origine di molte citta del mondo ... In Venetia, Appresso Gio. Antonio Rampazetto; 1593. 4°. A-C^8 D-E^6 F-I^8 K^4. ff. 2-72. ¶F1^r: Di Milano, et altre citta principali di tutta Italia [*in verse*]. [484

SOLOMON, king of Israel. Somnia Salomonis Regis Filii Dauid. (Impressus Venetiis Arte & impensis ... Iohã. Baptiste Sessa. ... 1501. die .xvi. octobris.) 4°. A-O^4. ff. 2-56. (Lea.) [485

SONETTI. Sonetti è canzoni di diuersi antichi autori Toscani ... (Impresso in Firenze per li heredi di Philippo di Giunta ... M.D.XXVII. Adi VI. del mese di Luglio.) 8°. AA^4 a-s^8 t^4. ff. 2-148. ¶*Authors named:* Dante Alaghieri, Cino da Pistoia, Guido Cavalcanti, Dante da Maiano, Guittone d'Arezzo. [486

-- -- Rime di diuersi antichi autori Toscani ... (Stampata in Vinegia per Io. Antonio, e Fratelli da Sabio. ... MDXXXII.) 8°. A-S^8 T^4. ff. 2-148. [487

SOPHOCLES. Σοφοκλεους τραγωδιαι επτα μετεξηγησεων. Sophoclis tragaediae septem cum commentariis. ... (Venetiis in Aldi Romani Academia mense Augusto. M. DII.) 8°. α-γ^8 δ^4 ε-η^8 ϑ^4 ι-λ^8 μ^4 ν-σ^8 τ^{10} υ-φ^8 χ^{10} ψ-ω^8 αα^8 ββ^4. [488

-- -- Σοφοκλεους τραγωδιαι επτσ ... (Florentiæ per hæredes Philippi Iuntæ: ... M.D.XXII. sexto kal'. Nouembris.) 4°. ※^{4} a-z^8 &^{10}. ff. 2-193. [489

-- -- ... Vnà cum omnibus Græcis scholiis, & cum Latinis Ioach. Camerarij. Annotationes Henrici Stephani in Sophoclem & Euripidem ... [Genevae, Henricus Stephanus,] Anno M.D.LXVIII. ... 4°. *^{4} a-3k^4 31^2 A-Gg^4 Hh^2. pp. 1-461, 3-142. ¶*Half-title* (A1^r): Commentatio explicationum omnium tragoediarum Sophoclis, Autore Ioachimo Camerario Pabepergensi. [490

-- -- *Another copy of the* Commentatio. [491

-- -- Tragoediae Sophoclis quotquot extant carmine Latino redditæ Georgio Ratallero ... interprete. Antuerpiae M.D.LXX Ex officina Gulielmi Siluij ... 8°. *^{8} A-Ii^8 (-Ii8, *presumably blank*). pp. 2-486. [491a

-- Sophoclis tragici Aiax flagellifer. Callimachi Cyrenaei hymni in Iouem & Apollinem. Ioanne Lonicero interprete. Genetliacon diuo Vilhelmo iuniori Cattorum principi factum, Ioanne Lonicero autore. *Greek and Latin.* Basileae ex officina Heruagiana anno M.D.XXXIII mense Augusto. 4°. a-p^4 q^6. pp. 2-129. [492

-- Elettra tragedia di Sofocle, Fatta volgare dall' ... Signor Erasmo delli signori di Valuasone ... In Venetia, Appresso i Guerra fratelli. ... 1588. 8°. A^8 B-C^{16} D^{20}. ff. 9-60. [493

-- Edipo tiranno di Sofocle tragedia. In lingua volgare ridotta dal ... Signor Orsatto Giustiniano ... In Venetia, Appresso Francesco Ziletti. 1585. 4°. *^{4} **^{2} a-k^4 l^6. ff. 2-46. [494

-- -- Edipo tiranno tragedia di Sofocle. Ridotta dalla Greca nella Toscana lingua da M. Pietro Angelij Bargeo. In Firenze, Appresso Bartolomeo Sermartelli. M D LXXXVIIII. 8°. A-D^8 E^4. pp. 3-72. [495

SORANZO, LAZARO. L'Ottomanno ... Quarta editione. In Napoli, ... Per Costantino Vitale. M. D. C. 4°. †-††^{4} 3†^{2} A-Dd^4 Ee^2. pp. 1-202. ¶†1 *defective.* [496

SORBIN, ARNAULD. Arnaldi Sorbini ... Tractatus de Monstris ... Parisiis, Apud Hieronymum de Marnef, & Gulielmum Cauellat ... 1570. ... 16°. a-b^8 A-R^8. ff. 1-134. [497

SOTO, DOMINGO DE. [1] Commentariorum F. Dominici Soto Segobiensis ... in quartum sententiarum, Tomus Primus. ... Venetiis, MDXCVIII Ex Officina Ioannis Zenarij. 4°. a-c^8 A-4A^8. pp. 1-1120. ¶*Lacks* 4B^4. [2] ... Tomus Secundus. ... *Same imprint.* *-**^{8} 3*^{6} A-3B^8 3C^2. pp. 1-772. (Lea.) [498

-- R. P. F. Dominici Soto ... De Iustitia, & iure, libri decem. ... Venetiis, M D XCIV. Apud Minimam Societatem. 4°. a-d^8 A-3R^8 (-3R8, *presumably blank*). pp. 4-1006. (Lea.) [499

SOTO, PEDRO DE. Assertio catholicae fidei circa articulos confessionis nomine ... Ducis Wirtenbergensis oblatæ ... Concilio Tridentino, XXIIII. Ianuarij Anni M. D. LII. ... Coloniae, Ioannes Nouesianus excudebat, Anno M.D.LV. 4°. A-Z^4 a-x^4 y^8 (*with 8 blank pp.*) z-ee^4. [500

-- -- ... Accessit his defensio aduersus Prolegomena Brentij. ... Antuerpiae. Apud Martinum Nutium ... M. D. LVII. ... 4°. A^4 B-T^8 (-T8, *presumably blank*). ff. 1-143. ¶*Lacks the* Defensio. (Lea.) [501

SPACH, ISRAEL. Gynæciorum siue de mulierum ... Affectibus & Morbis, libri Græcorum, Arabum, Latinorum veterum et recentium ... M. D. XCVII. ... Argentinae, Sumptibus Lazari Zetzneri. fol. *^{8} **^{6} 3*^{4} α^6 β^8 a-q^6 r^8 s-z^6 A-Vv^6 Xx^4 Yy-Zz^6 AA-3A^6. pp. 1-28, 2-1080. ¶*Authors: Felix Plater, Moschion, Cleopatra, Theodorus Priscianus, Trotula, Nicolas de la Roche, Lodovico Bonacciuoli, Jacques Du Bois, Jakob Rueff, Hieronimo Mercuriali, Giovanni Baptista*

Monti, Vettore Trincavello, Albertino Bottoni, Jean Le Bon, Ambroise Paré, Jean Ailleboust, Gaspard Bauhin, Khalef ibn 'Abbās, Abū Al-Kāsim, Maurice de la Corde, Martin Akakia, Luis de Mercado. [502

SPAGNUOLI, BAPTISTA, MANTUANO. Omnia opera Baptistae Mantuani ... (Impressum Bononiæ per Benedictum Hectoris ... M.DII. Die uero xi. Iunii. ...) fol. π^{4} a-t^{6} u^{4} x-z^{6} &^{6} ɔ^{6} ꝶ^{6} A-H^{6} I-K^{8} L-BB^{6} CC^{8} DD-OO^{6} PP^{8}. ff. i-ccclxxxix. [503

-- Aeglogae Fratris baptistae Mātuani Carmelitae de honesto amore et foelici eius exitu cum quadam alia aegloga cōtra amorē nouiter addita. (Brixiæ Impressæ per Bernardinum Misintā de Papia. ... M.D.II. Idibus Sextilibus.) 4°. a^{6} b^{8} c-f^{6} g^{4}. (Furness.) [504

-- Baptiste Mantuani Bucolica seu adolescentia: in decem æglogas diuisa, Ab Iodoco Badio Ascensio ... exposita ... Carmen eiusdē de sancto Ioanne Baptista. Dialogus eiusdem de uita beata. Hermanni Buschij de contēnendo mūdo ... (Excussit Ioannes Prūs iunior Ciuis Argentinensis. Anno ... Sesquimillesimo Decimoquarto.) 4°. [A]^{6} B^{4} C-O$^{8.4.4}$ P^{8} Q^{4} R^{8} S^{6}. ff. I-LXXVIII. [505

-- Baptistæ Mantuani ... duarum Parthenicum libri: cum cōmentario Sebastiani Murrhonis Germanni Colmariensis ... (Impressum Argentinæ [per Joannem Schott] quinto Kalēdas Septembres. ... M.CCCCCI.) 4°. a-b^{6} A^{8} B^{4} C-O$^{8.8.4}$ P-R^{8} S^{6} X^{8} Aa-Ee^{8} Ff^{4} Gg-Hh^{8} Ii^{4} Kk-Ll^{6} a^{6}. ff. I-CXXII, I-LXXII. [506

-- Baptiste Mantuani ... epigrāmatū liber ... (... Melchiar Lotter ... Lypsensis excusoria incude formauit. Anno ... .M. quingnetesimoseptimo Idibus vero Iulijs.) 4°. B.L. A-D^{6}. [507

-- Nouem F. Baptiste Mātuani ... opa præter cætera moralia: ... quidē Iodoci Badii Ascensii explanatione elucidata omnia/ ... Sebastiani Murrhonis & Sebastiani Brantii Germanoꝝ ... elucidatiōe decorata ... Venundantur ab Ioāne Paruo et ipso Ascensio Parrhisiis: Et ab Iacobo Forestario Rothomagi ... (... MDVII. Ad Calendas Decemb.) fol. B.L. ✠^{10} a^{6} b-z^{8} A-R^{8} S^{4} T^{8}. ff. I-CCCXXIX. [508

SPAIN. *Ferdinand V & Isabella, king & queen.* Quaderno delas alcaualas. Leyes del quaderno nueuo delas rentas delas alcaualas y franquezas. Fechas enla vega de granada. ... (Fue impressa ... enla ... cibdad de Toledo. Acabase a treynta dias del mes de Agosto: año ... de mill ⁊ quiniētos ⁊ diez años.) fol. B.L. a-d^{8}. (Lea.) [509

-- -- Impresso en Alcala de Henares, en casa de Salzedo librero. Año M.D.LVIII. (... A .xviij. dias del mes de Agosto. ...) fol. A-E^{8}. ff. ij-xxix. (Lea.) [510

-- *Charles I, king.* Reportorio de todas las prematicas, y capitulos de cortes, hechos por su magestad, desde el año de mil y quinientos y veynte y tres, hasta el año de mil y quinientos y cincuenta y vno: hecho por ... Andres de Burgos ... de Astorga. ... Venden se en Medina del campo, en casa de Guillermo de Millis ... 1551. (... Acabo se a veynte dias del mes de Iulio. ...) fol. ✠^{4} A-H^{6} I^{8}. ff. i-xlv. ¶A^{6} *misbound after* B6. (Lea.) [511

-- Quaderno de algunas leyes, que no estan enel libro delas pragmaticas, que por mandato de sus Magestades se mandan imprimir este año de M.D.XLIIII. (Fueron impressas ... enla ciudad de Salamanca en casa de Ioan de Canoua/ acabaron se a diez y seys dias del mes de Nouiembre de .M. D. Lvj.) fol. B.L. A^{12}. (Lea.) [512

-- Capitulos y leyes discedidos en las cortes que su Mag. del Emperador nr̄o señor Mādo tener, y se tuuierō en esta villa đ Madrid el año q̄ passo de .1552. Cō los capitulos q̄ se determinarō y pueyeron en las cortes q̄ por su mādado se tuuierō en esta villa de Vall'id el año q̄ passo de .1555. ... [y] este pñte año de .1558. ... Impressas en Valladolid en casa de Sebastian martinez. Año .1558. (*Colophon.*) fol. B.L. A-H^{6} I^{8} K^{6} A-B^{6} C^{8}. ff. ij-lxij, ij-xx. ¶G1, G2, G5, G6 *misbound after* D6; G3, G4 *after* H5; H1, H6 *after* G4. (Lea.) [513

-- *Philip II, king.* Philippi II. ... edictum De Librorum prohibitorum Catalogo obseruando. Antuerpiae, Ex officina Christophori Plantini. M. D. LXX. ... 8°. A^{8}. (Lea.) [514

-- -- *Another copy.* (Yarnall.) [514a

-- Cortes de Cordoua del año de setenta, y de Madrid del año de setenta y tres. Quaderno de las leyes y Pragmaticas que su Magestad mando hazer ... Impressas en Alcala, en casa de Andres de Angulo. Año de. 1575. ... A costa de Francisco Lopez ... fol. π^{2} A-E^{8} F-G^{6}. ff. 1-52. (Lea.) [515

-- *Consejo*. Ordenanças del cõsejo Real de su Magestad. ¶ y los Arãzeles q̃ han ẟ guardar los Relatores. ... Impresso en Valladolid. Año de. M. D. LVI. ... (... encasa ẟ Sebastiã Martinez ... Acabose a veynte dias del mes ẟ Nouiembre. ...) fol. B.L. A-E⁴ F⁶. ff. iij-xxvj. (Lea.) [516

-- *History*. Erzelung der Künigreych in Hispanien auch der selben jårlich nutzung vnd einkom̃ens mit sampt dẽ herschafften dem selben Künigreych zůgehörig. Mer ein alte Prophecey Kay. Carl betreffend. M. D. XXXII. 4°. A-B⁴. [517

-- Werbung der potschaftẽ der ... Kůnig Karolus võ Hispanien/ vñ kůnig Franciscus von Frãckreich an die Curfursten zu Frãckfurt im Monat Iunij/ Im xix. ⁊c geschehen. 4°. A⁶. [518

SPANDUGINO, TEODORO. I commentari di Theodoro Spandugino Cantacuscino Gentilhuomo Constantinopolitano, dell'origine de principi Turchi, & de'costumi di quella natione. In Fiorenza appresso Lorenzo Torrentino ... MDLI. ... (*Colophon*.) 8°. a⁸ A-N⁸ (-N7-8, *blank*). pp. 1-202. [519

SPANGENBERG, CYRIACUS. Catechismus, Die Funff Hauptstůcke der Christlichen Lere ... Gedruckt zu Vrsel/ Durch Nicolaum Henricum. ... 1592. (*Colophon*.) 4°.)(⁴ ?¿⁴ .·.⁴ A-Z⁴ a-z⁴ Aa-3N⁴ 3O⁶ A-O⁴. [520

-- Ehespiegel Das ist/ Alles was von dem heyligẽ Ehestande/ nutzliches/ nötiges/ vnnd tröstliches mag gesagt werden/ In LXX. Brautpredigten ... Getruckt zu Strassburg/ durch Theodosium Rihel. Im Jar/ M. D. LXXVIII. 8°.)(⁸ ✠⁸ A-3P⁸. ff. I-CCCCLXVIII. [521

-- Elegantiarum Veteris Adami. Decades sex. Formular Bůchlin/ der alten Adamssprache. ... Anno M. D. LXIIII. (Gedruckt zu Eisleben durch Vrban Gaubisch. ...). 8°. A-O⁸ (-O8, *presumably blank*). [522

-- Historia Vom Anfang/ vnd Irsprung/ Fortgang vnd Zunemen/ der Vnsinnigen/ Gifftigen vnd Schedlichen Secten/ der Manicheer. ... 1579. 4°. A-Z⁴ a-h⁴ *². [523

-- Der Iagteüfel. Bestendiger vnnd Wolgegründter bericht/ wie fern die Jagten rechtmessig/ vnd zugelassen. ... Anno M.D.LXI. (Getruckt zu Wormbs/ bey Philips Köpffel/ in verlegung Weygand Han ...) 8°. ₵⁴ A-P⁸ Q⁴ (-Q4, *presumably blank*). [524

-- Mansfeldische Chronica Der Erste Theil. ... M. D. LXXII. (Gedruckt zu Eisleben ... Durch Andream Petri. ...) fol. π⁶ A-4Y⁶ 4Z⁸. ff. 1-503. [525

-- -- Såchssische Chronica ... Hievor vnter dem Tittel Mansfeldischer Chronica erster Theil ... in Truck gegeben. .. Gedruckt zu Franckfort am Mayn/ in Verlegung Sigmundt Feyerabends ... M. D. LXXXV. (Gedruckt ... Bey Christoff Raben ...) fol.)(⁶ A-M⁶ N-4S⁴. pp. 1-728. [526

-- [Wider die bösen Sieben, ins Teufel Karnöffelspiel.] ... (Gedruckt zu Ihena/ durch Thomam Rhebart/ vnd Donat Richtzenhayn.) 4°. [a]⁴ b⁴ (*wanting*) c² A-Z⁴ a-z⁴ Aa-Mm⁴ (-Kk⁴). ¶a1 *defective*. [527

-- Wider die Vnchristliche Ermanung/ so Iulius Pflug ... hat ausgehen lassen. Gegenbericht vnd Warnung. ... Gedruckt zu Eisleben/ durch Vrban Gaubisch. 1562. 4°. A-I⁴. [528

SPANGENBERG, JOHANN. Eine Christliche vnterrichtung wie man gůther vnnd reichtumb Christlich gebrauchen möge ... Aus den bůchern Doct. Martini vnd anderer getzogen ... Durch Ioannẽ Spangenberg ... M. D. XL. (Gedruckt zu Erffurdt durch Melcher Sachssen ...) 8°. A-D⁸. [529

-- Computus ecclesiasticus ... VVitebergæ Ex officina Hæredum Georgij Rhau. M.D.LIII. 8°. A-F⁸ G⁴. [530

-- Des Ehelichen Ordens/ Spiegel vnd Regel ... Wittemberg. 1563. (Gedruckt ... durch Peter Seitz.) 8°. A-Y⁸. [531

-- Ein Geistlich Bad der Seelen ... 1540. (Gedruckt zu Erffurd durch Melcher Sachssen ...) 8°. A⁸. [532

-- Margarita theologica, continens praecipuos locos doctrinæ Christianæ ... Cum Præfatione D. Gasparis Crucigeri. Anno M.D.XLVII. 8°. A-K⁸ L⁴. pp. 2-154. [533

SPECULUM. ... Speculũ et alphabetum sacerdotũ ⁊ quare quotidie tenentur celebrare Item diui Raimũdi lulli ɔtẽplatiões abbreuiate ... 8°. B.L. A⁸. [534

SPENGLER, LAZARUS. Antwort auff das vnwarhafft gedicht: so Iohan Cocleus ... Widder den gedrückten auszug Bepstlicher rechten: newlich hat ausgehen lassen. D. Hieronymus von Berchnishausen etc. ... [c. 1530.] 4°. A-I^4. [535

-- M.D.XX. Schutzred vn̄ christenliche antwurt ... auf etlicher vermaint widersprechen/ mit anzaigunge/ warumb Doctor Martini Luthers leer ... verworffen ... werden soll ... [Augsburg, Silvan Otmar, 1520.] 4°. A^4 B^6. [536

SPERBER, JULIUS. Kabalisticæ precationes, siue selectiores sacrosancti Nominis Divini Glorificationes E Sacrorum Bibliorum fontibus ... Magdeburgi apud Iohannem Francum 1600. 8°. *^{8} A-S^8 T^4. pp. 1-296. (Lea.) [537

SPERONI DEGLI ALVAROTTI, SPERONE. Canace tragedia di Messer Sperone Speroni nobile Padouano. Stampata l'anno M. D. XLVI. (In Fiorenza per Francesco doni ...) 8°. A-E^8. ff. 2-40. [538

-- -- Canace tragedia ... Alcune altre sui compositioni, & vna apologia, & alcune lettioni in difesa della Tragedia. ... In Venetia, M.D.XCVII. Presso Giouanni Alberti. 4°. A^4 A^4 B-Q^8 R^4 (-R4, *blank*). pp. 1-253. [539

-- Dialoghi ... In Venetia. Per Francesco Lorenzini da Turino. M D LX. 8°. A-V^8. ff. 2-160. [540

-- Orationi ... In Venetia, MDXCVI. Presso Ruberto Meietti. (... Per Giouani Alberti. Ad instantia di Paulo Meieti.) 4°. A^4 A-Dd^4. pp. 1-215. [541

SPEYSER, JOHANN. Ain. Sermon. Sontag Reminiscere in halten sonders freuels endtscheidung des glauben ... M D XXIII. 4°. A-B^4. [542

SPI., M. Epigrammata quinque, addita per eundem authorem hexastichon de Pace acta inter .S. Iulium III. P.M. & Henricum .ij. Regem Gallorum. [c. 1552.] 4°. π^2. [543

SPINA, BARTOLOMMEO DE. Opuscula ... (Impressuȝ Venetijs per Gregoriū de gregorijs. ... 1519. die .x. mensis Septembris.) fol. B.L. A^4 B-K^6 L^4 (-L4, *presumably blank*). [544

-- ... Bartholomaei Spinei Pisani ... quaestio de strigibus, vna cum tractatu de praeeminentia Sacræ Theologiæ, & quadruplici Apologia de Lamiis contra Ponzinibium. ... Romae, In Aedibus Populi Romani, M D LXXVI. (*Colophon.*) 4°. +^{4} A-Y^4 Z^2. pp. 1-180. (Lea.) [545

SPINELLO, ALESSANDRO. Cleopatra tragedia ... In Vinegia. M.D.L. ... (... per Pietro de Nicolini da Sabbio ...) 8°. A-F^8 G^4. ff. 2-51. [546

SPINOLA, FRANCESCO. Concetti della lingua Latina di un ualente huomo letteratissimo ... In Venetia, appresso Bolognino Zaltieri, 1562. 8°. A-H^8 I^6. pp. 3-139. [547

SPOLETO. Statutorum magnificae ciuitatis Spoleti. Liber primus. M.D.XXXXII. ... (Impressa & absoluta Spoleti per ... Lucam Bini Mantuanum, In ædibus hæredum Zucharelli Marcelli Spoletini, ac ... recognita per ... Constantinum Ferrantinū ... M.D.XLIII. quinto idus Martii.) fol. A-K^6 L-M^4. ff. 2-LXVIII. ¶*Another copy of* L2-L3, *printed on conjugate leaves, the first correctly signed, whereas in the book it is missigned* Kii, *is laid in.* (Lea.) [548

SPONTONE, CIRO. Hercole difensore d'Homero. Dialogo ... In Verona, Nella Stamparia di Girolamo Discepolo. M D XCV. 8°. a-b^8 c^4 (-c4) A-N^8 O^4 (-O4, *presumably blank*). pp. 1-213. ¶a1 *defective.* [549

SPRENGER, JAKOB. Malleus maleficarum ... His ... adiecimus, Bernhardi Basin opusculum de artibus magicis ... Item. D. Vlrici Molitoris Constantiensis, de Lamijs & Pythonicis mulieribus Dialogus. Item. D. Ioannis de Gerson ... de probatione Spirituum, libellum. Item. D. Thomæ [Murner] ... libellum, de Pythonico contractu. ... Francofurti ad Moenum, apud Nicolaum Bassæum. M. D. LXXX. 8°. A^8 B^4 A-Z^8 a-z^8 Aa-Dd^8 (-Dd8, *presumably blank*). pp. 1-737. ¶*All the leaves of* ^{1}A *are damaged.* (Lea.) [550

SPRETER, JOHANN. Von Renndten/ Gülten/ Zinsen/ Zehenden/ Neüwbrüchē vn̄ W°ucher des neüwen vn̄ alten Testaments ꝛc. ... (Getruckt z°u Basel/ durch Bartholomeum Westheymer. Anno 1543.) 4°. A-D^4 E^6. [551

STAMLER, JOHANN. Dyalogus Iohannis Stamler Augustñ. de diuersarum gencium sectis et mundi religionibus (Impressum Auguste: per Erhardum oglin. & Ieorgiū Nadler Cura ... Wolfgangi Aittinger ... 1.50. & .8. die. 22. mensis May. 7c.) fol. a-f^{6} (-f6, *presumably blank*). ff. II-XXXII. ¶*Engraved t.p.* (Lea.) [552

STANFORD, SIR WILLIAM. An exposicion of the kinges prerogatiue ... by ... sir William Staunford Knight ... 1568. (Imprynted at London ... by Rychard Tottel ...) 4°. B.L. A-K^{8} L^{6}. ff. 6-85. *S.T.C.* 23214. (Biddle.) [553

-- -- 1577. Imprinted at London ... by Richard Tottel ... (*Colophon.*) 4°. B.L. A-K^{8} L^{6}. ff. 1-85. *S.T.C.* 23216. (Biddle.) [554

-- -- Imprinted at London ... by Richard Totthil. 1590. 4°. B.L. A^{4} B-K^{8} L^{6}. ff. 6-84. *S.T.C.* 23217. [555

-- -- *Another copy.* (Biddle.) [556

-- Les plees del coron ... Composees per ... Guilliaulme Staunforde Chiuauler ... 1560. In ædibus Richardi Tottelli. ... (Imprinted at London ...) 4°. ℭ^{8} a^{6} A-Z^{8} &^{8} ɔ^{6}. ff. 1-198. *S.T.C.* 23220. (Biddle.) [557

-- -- 1574. In ædibus Richardi Tottelli. ... (Imprinted at London ...) 4°. ¶^{8} a^{6} A-Z^{8} &^{6} ɔ^{6}. ff. 1-193. *S.T.C.* 23222. (Biddle.) [558

-- -- 1583. In Ædibus Richardi Tottellj. ... (Imprinted at London ...) 4°. ℭ^{8} ℭℭ^{4} A-Z^{8} &^{8} ɔ^{6}. ff. 1-196. *S.T.C.* 23223. (Biddle.) [559

-- -- *Another copy.* [560

STAPHYLEUS, JOHANNES. Vrsach der Statt Rom eroberung vnd zerstörung/ durch Keyserliche Maiestat Kriegs volck. Anno im .M. D. xxvij. am .vj. Maij beschehen. Ein Oration ... [Strassburg, Johann Prüss, 1521.] 4°. A-B^{4}. [561

STAPHYLUS, FRIDERICUS. Apologia D. Friderici Staphyli, cuius præcipua argumenta sunt, De Vero germanoq; scripturæ sacræ intellectu, De Sacrorum Bibliorum in idioma vulgare tralatione, De Luteranorum concionatorum consensione. ... Latinitate donata, opera F. Laurentij Surij ... Coloniæ apud Hæredes Iohannis Quentel & Geruinum Calenium, 1561. 8°. a-c^{8} d^{4} A-CC^{8}. ff. 1-206. [562

-- Defensio Friderici Staphylii aduersus Philippum Melanthonem, Shvvenckfeldianum Longinum, Andream Musculum, Mat. Flacc. Illyricum, Iacobum Andream Shmidelinum, Aedificatores Babylonicæ turris Martini Lutheri. ... Parisiis Apud Gulielmum Guillard & Amelium Varencorium ... 1559. 8°. A-I^{8}. ff. 2-72. [563

-- Historia de vita, morte, et iustis Caroli V. ... Augustæ Vindelicorum Philippus Vlhardus excudebat. ... 1559. Calend. Iunij. 4°. A-Z^{4} a-f^{4} g^{6}. [564

-- Nachdruck zůuerfechtung des Bůchs Vom rechten waren verstandt des Göttlichen worts/ vnd Von der Teütschen Bibel verdolmetschung. Wider Iacob Schmidlen ... M. D. LXII. (Gedruckt zů Ingolstat durch Alexander vnd Samuel Weyssenhorn gebrůder. ...) 4°. aa-bb^{4} A-Z^{4} a-z^{4} Aa-Nn^{4}. ff. 1-235. [565

-- Vom letsten vnd grossen Abfall/ so vor der zůkunfft des Antichristi geschehen soll. ... Getruckt zů Ingolstatt/ durch Alexander vnd Samuel Weissenhorn. M.D.LXV. (*Colophon.*) 4°. α-β^{4} A-Z^{4} a-x^{4}. ff. 1-175. ¶*Preface dated at* Ingolstat. [566

-- -- *Another edition. Same imprint, collation, and foliation.* ¶*Preface dated at* Ingolstatt. [567

-- Vortrab zů rettung des Bůchs. ... Wider Iacob Schmidle ... Durch Fridericum Staphylaw. Gedruckt im 1561. Jar. (Gedruckt zů Ingolstat. ...) 4°. A-I^{4}. [568

STAPLETON, THOMAS. [1] Promptuarium morale super euangelia dominicalia totius anni ... Pars Æstiualis. ... Anuterpiae, in officina Plantiniana, Apud Viduam, & Ioannem Moretum. M. D. XCIII. ... 8°. †^{8} A-Ss^{8}. pp. 1-640. [2] ... Pars Hiemalis. ... *Same imprint.* *-**^{8} 3*^{4} A-3B^{8} 3C^{4}. pp. 2-750. (Yarnall.) [568a

STARTZLER, CONRAD. Ain Sermon Conradi Startzler ... 1524. 4°. A^{4} B^{2}. [569

STATIUS, PUBLIUS PAPINIUS. La Thebaide di Statio ridotta dal Sig. Erasmo di Valuasone in ottaua rima ... In Venetia Appresso Francesco de' Franceschi Senese. M. D. LXX. 4°. *^{4} A-V^8. ff. 4-159. [570

STAUFF, ARGULA VON. An ain Ersamen Weysen Radt der stat Ingolstat/ ain sandtbrieff/ von Fraw Argula vō grunbach geborne von Stauffen. [Augsburg, Philipp Ulhart, 1523.] 4°. A^4. [571

-- Ain Christenliche schrifft ainer Erbarn frawen/ vom Adel dariñ sy alle Christenliche stendt ... ermant/ Bey der warhait/ vñ dem wort Gottes zů bleyben ... Argula Staufferin. [Augsburg, Philipp Ulhart,] M. D. xxiii. ... 4°. A^6. [572

-- Dem Durchleuchtigistē ... Friderichen/ Hertzogen tzů Sachssen ... Anno .M.D.xxiiij. Argula Staufferin. [Augsburg, Philipp Ulhart.] 4°. π^2. [573

-- Dem Durchleüchtigen ... Iohansen/ Pfaltzgrauen bey Reyn ... Argula Staufferin. [Augsburg, Philipp Ulhart, 1523.] 4°. A^4. [574

STAYGMAYER, HANS. Ain kurtze vnderrichtung von der waren Christlichē brůderschaft ... [Augsburg, Philipp Ulhart,] M.D.xxiiij. 4°. A^4. [575

STECHAU, BALTHASAR VON. Warhafftige bestendige verantwortung vnd bericht/ der Erbarn ... Balthasers von Stechaw/ grossen Vogts zu Wulffenbüttel/ Balthasars von Hünaw/ Iohan Hamsters vñ Steffan Schmids ... wider Hertzogen Heinrichen zu Braunschweig vnd Lüneburg etc. ... Abdruck ... (Gedruckt zu Wulffenbüttel durch Henningk Rüdem. M. D. XLI.) 4°. A-F^4. [576

STECHMANN, JOHANN. Διαλογισμος in honorem ... Iohannis Clotzii ... Marpurgi, Excudebat Augustinus Colbius ... 1573. 4°. A^4 B^6. [577

STEENE, WILHELM VAN DEN. Methodus dialectices, Aristotelicam doctrinam capessentibus apprimè utilis. Guilhelmo Lapidano Veruiacense autore. Apud Seb. Gryphium Lugduni, 1540. (*Colophon.*) 8°. a-i^8 k^4. pp. 2-149. [578

STEEWECH, GODESCALC. Godescalci StewechI Heusdani in L. Apuleii opera omnia quæstiones et coniecturæ. ... Antuerpiae, Ex officina Christophori Plantini. M. D. LXXXVI. (*Colophon.*) 8°. A-O^8. pp. 3-212. [578a

STEINACH, HANS LANDSCHAD VON. Ain Missiue vō ... Hans Landtschadt zů Steynach Ritter/ an ... Ludwygen ... Pfaltzgrauff bey Reyn ... Von wegen der götliche leer/ zů beschirmen. ... Im jar. 1522. 4°. a-b^4 c^2. [579

STELLA. Stella clericorum ... (Impressum Liptzk per Melchiarem Lotterum. ... M.ccccc.xv.) 4°. B.L. A^6 B^4. [580

STELLA, CHERUBINO DI. Poste per diuerse parti del mondo. Con tutto le Fiere notabili ... Aggiontoui ... il viaggio di Gierusalem ... In Venetia, Presso Daniel Zanetti 1598. ... 12°. A-L^{12}. ff. 4-124. [581

STELLA, ERASMUS. Erasmi Stellae Libonothani de Borussiae antiquitatibus libri duo. Apud ... Basileam. (... apud Ioannem Frobenium mense Martio an. M. D. XVIII.) 4°. a-e^4. pp. 2-38. [582

STELLA, TILEMANN. Kurtzer vnd klarer Bericht vom Gebrauch vnd nutz der newen Landtaffeln ... Wittemberg. Gedruckt durch Hans Krafft. Anno. 1560. 8°. A-C^8. [583

STEPHAN VON LANDSKRONA. Himelstrass. im latin genant Scala celi. (In ... Augspurg. Von Maister hanssen Othmar/ durch verlegung des ... herñ Iohann Rynmañ von Oringen. Vnnd geendt auff freitag nach dem achten corporis christi. ... Tausent funff hundert vnd zehen jar.) fol. a-y$^{8.6}$ z^{8} $^{.10}$ (-.10, *presumably blank*). ff. ij-Clxvii. [584

STEUCO, AGOSTINO. Augustini Steuchi Eugubini ... De Aqua Virgine in Vrbem reuocanda. Lugduni apud Seb. Gryphium, M. D. XLVII. 4°. a^4 b^6. pp. 3-19. [585

-- Augustini Steuchi ... contra Laurentium Vallam, De false Donatione Constantini. Libri duo. Eiusdem De restituenda nauigatione Tiberis. Lugduni apud Seb. Gryphium, M. D. XLVII. 4°. a-b^4 a-z^4 A-E^4 F^6. pp. 1-234. [586

STEVART, PETER. Apologia Oder Rettungschrifft Fuͤr die ... Societet Iesu: Wider Polycarpi Leysers falscherdichte Histori ... durch Herrn Cleophas Distlmeyer ... in die Teutsche Sprach gebracht. Getruckt zu Ingolstatt/ durch Wolffgang Eder. Anno M. D. XCIIII. 4°. A-Z^4 a-l^4. pp. 1-265. [587

STIGEL, JOHANN. Ad inuictissimum ... Carolum Quintum, ... Germaniæ Epistola gratulatoria. ... Anno M. D. XLI. (Impressum Norimbergæ per Ioh. Petreium ... Pridie Nonarum Iulij.) 4°. a-d^4. ¶*In verse.* [588

-- In reditum ... Ioannis Friderici Ducis Saxoniæ ... hymnus ad Spiritum Sanctum ... Eclogae duae Daphnis et Aristaeus ... (Excudebantur in ... Noriberga Typis Ioachimi Helleri Leucopetræi ... M. D. LIII. Mense Februario.) 4°. A-K^4 L^6. [589

-- [1] Poematum Ioannis Stigelii liber I. continens sacra. Ienæ Excudebat Donatus Ritzenhayn, & Thomas Rebart. 1566. ... 8°. A-P^8. [2] ... Liber II. Continens sacra. *Same imprint.* A-P^8. [3] ... Liber tertius continens elegiarum libros tres. Ienæ Excudebat Donatus Ritzenhayn, & Thomas Rebart. 1567. ... A-R^8. [4] ... Liber quartus, continens elegiarum libros tres. Ienæ Excudebat Donatus Ritzenhayn, Anno 1568. ... A-M^8. [590

-- Warhafftiger Bericht/ wie der ... Hertzog Iohans Friderich/ der Elter/ Hertzog zu Sachsen ... von dieser Welt abgeschieden. Aus einem Sendbrieff/ Iohannis Stigelij. Gedruckt zu Ihena/ durch Christian Roͤdinger. Anno. 1554. 4°. A^4 B^2. [591

STÖFFLER, JOHANNES. Ioannis Stoefleri Iustingensis ... in Procli Diadochi ... Sphæram mundi ... commentarius. ... Ex ædibus Morhardinis nostris Tubingæ ... M. D. XXXIIII. ... (*Colophon.*) fol. π^8 (-π8) A-O^6 P^4 Q-Z^6 (-Z6, *presumably blank*). ff. 1-133. [592

-- [1] Der Newe gross Römisch Calender ... von ... Iohann Stoͤffler ... aussz Latin/ in Teütsche Sprach verwandelt. ... 1522. Getrůckt zů Oppenheym. fol. π^6 A-$F^{6.4}$ G^4 A^6. [2] Der Römisch Kalender ... Gedruckt zů Oppenheym. 1518 (... von Iacob Koͤbeln ... getruckt Am 24. tag des Mertzen. ...) fol. B^8 C^4 D^6 E^8 18 *unsigned ll.* [593

STÖR, STEFAN. Von der Priester Ee disputation/ durch Stephanum Stoͤr Diessenhoffen ... am xvj. tag Februarij jm̃ xxiiij. jar gehalten. 4°. A-G^4 H^6. [594

STOLZ, JOHANN. Vier Trostpredigten vber den Leichen des Churfuͤrsten zu Sachsen/ Hertzogen Iohans Fridrichen etc. vnd seiner Gemahel Hertzogin Sibilla ... Gethan zu Weimar durch Niclas von Amsdorff etc. vnd Iohan Stoltzen. 1554. ... 4°. A-N^4 (-N3-4). ¶*The fourth sermon, by Amsdorf, was omitted.* [595

STRABO. Στράβωνος γεωγραφικῶν βίβλοι ἑπτὰ καὶ δέκα. Strabonis rerum geographicarum libri septemdecim. À Guilielmo Xylandro Augustano ... recogniti ... Basileae, ex officina Henricpetrina. (... CIↃ IↃ LXXI. Mense Augusto.) fol. ✠^{6} (+ *folded map*). α-θ^6 ι^4 a-k^6 l^8 m-r^6 s^8 t-z^6 A-B^4 C-D^6 E^2 F^6 G-I^2 K^4 L^2 M^6 N^8 O-Dd^6 Ee^2 Ff-Gg^6 Hh^2 Ii^8 Kk-zZ^6 AA^6 BB^2 CC-DD^6 EE^8 FF^2 GG^4 HH^6 II^4 KK^2 LL^6 MM^4 NN-OO^2 PP-SS^6 TT^4 VV^2 XX^8 YY^4 (-YY4, *presumably blank*). pp. 1-977. [596

-- -- Strabonis ... Geographia decem et septem libros cõtinens E greco In latinã a Gregorio Typhernale et Guarino Veronẽse cõuersa ... Veneunt [Parisiis] Ab Egidio gourmont ... (M.D.Xij. decĩo Calendas Februarij.) fol. B.L. A^6 b^8 a-z^6 ꝛ^6 ꝯ^8. ff. i-clii. [597

-- Valentinus Curio lectori. En tibi ... Strabonis geographicorum cõmẽtarios, ... à Conrado Heresbachio ... recognitos. ... Basileae an. M. D. XXIII. (... in aedibus Valentini Curionis ... mense Martio.) fol. π^4 Aa^6 Bb^8 a-z^6 A-Z^6 &^{8}. pp. 2-566. [598

-- -- ... Item, epitomae ..., nunc primum de Græco sermone in Latinum conuersæ, Hieronymo Gemusæo ... interprete. Basileae apud Ioan. Vualder. M. D. XXXIX. ... fol. a^4 b-g^6 h^4 a-z^6 A-Bb^6 (-Bb6). pp. 2-549. [599

-- -- [1] La prima parte della geografia di Strabone, di Greco tradotta in volgare Italiano da M. Alfonso Buonacciuoli ... In Venetia, appresso Francesco Senese. M D LXII. 4°. a-d^8 e^4 A-BB^8. ff. 1-220. [2] La seconda parte ... In Ferrara. Appresso Francesco Senese. M D LXV. a^6 b-f^4 A-Rr^4. pp. 1-320. ¶b^4 *misbound after* c4. [600

STRACCHA, BENVENUTO. ... Benuenuti Stracchae patritii Anconitani de mercatura, seu mercatore tractatus. Venetiis. M. D. LIII. ... 8°. *8 ††-5†8 A-Nn8. ff. 1-287. [601

STRADA, JACOBUS DE. [Epitome thesauri antiquitatum, hoc est, impp. Rom. Orientalium & Occidentalium Iconum ... Ex museo Iacobi de Strada Mantuani ... Lugduni, apud Iacobum de Strada, et Thomam Guerinum, M.D.LIII.] (Lugduni, Excudebat Ioannes Tornæsius. ... acheué d'imprimer le premier de Septembre 1553.) 4°. A-L4 (-A1) a-z4 A-V4. pp. 1-339. [602

-- -- Epitome du thresor des antiquitez, C'est à dire, Pourtraits des vrayes Medailles des empp. ... Traduit par Iean Louueau d'Orleans. A Lyon par Iaques de Strada, et Thomas Guerin, M. D. LIII. 4°. aa-cc4 a-z4 A-Gg4. pp. 1-394. [603

STRAPAROLA, GIOVANNI FRANCESCO. Le XIII. piaceuoli notti ... In Venetia, M D LXXX. 8°. A-Ss8. ff. 2-3[22]. [604

STRASSBURG. *Rat.* Ordnung ainer Ersamen Oberkait zů Strassburg/ wie offentliche ergerliche laster daselbst/ ... gestrafft werden. 4°. A-B4. ¶*Dated 25 August 1529.* A2-3 *misbound after* B3. [605

-- Nach dem wir Meyster vnnd Rath der statt Strassburg ... [Orders regulating the baking of bread.] decretum Mitwoch nach Lamperti. Anno rc. xxxj. s. sh. 46.5 × 29.5 cm. [606

-- Wir Iacob Zorn zum Riedt der Meyster/ vnd der Rathe zů Strassburg ... [Orders restricting military service abroad.] decretum/ donderstag den zwölfften Octobris/ Anno/ M. D. xxxj. s.sh. 23 × 29 cm. [607

-- Als nun eyn zeit her/ ettlich burger vnd auch frembde ... [Proclamation forbidding citizens away from home to marry by Catholic rites.] Decret. Montag den zwölfften Februarij. Anno rc. xxxvij. s.sh. 21 × 31.5 cm. [608

-- Wir Peter Sturm der Maister/ vnd der Rhat zů Strassburg ... [Order prohibiting the sale or purchase of wine, fruit, grain, vegetables, etc.] decretum Samstag den dreitzehenden Septembris/ ... fünffzehenhundert dreissig vnd neün jar. s.sh. 43 × 44 cm. [609

-- Wir Hildtbrandt von Mülnheim Maister vnd der Rath zů Strassburg ... [Order proscribing the Anabaptists.] Actum freytag den neundten Aprilis ... fünfftzehen hundert vnnd viertzigjar. s.sh. 46 × 30.5 cm. [610

-- *Commissarien.* Acta vnd Handlungen Der Kais: naher Strassburg verordneter Cōmissarien/ belangend der Euangel: Capitularn auss vnd abschaffung ... M.D.LXXXVI. ... 4°. a4 A-Z4 (-R1) a-c4. pp. 1-201. ¶*Additional t.p.* (L3r): Acta vnd Handlungen Der Key: May: Commissarien/ vnd eines Ersamen Rhats der Statt Strassburg ... M. D. LXXXVI. (Lea.) [611

-- *Academia.* Disputatio de patrimonio mulierum ...: in inclyta Argentoratensium Academia publicè proposita à Georgio Obrechto IC. Respondente Adamo Huenerero Argentoratensi. Argentorati excudebat Antonius Bertramus [1586]. 4°. A-D4. [612

-- *Cathedral chapter.* [*caption*] Eines Hoch vnd Ehrwirdigen Thumcapituls hoher Stifft Strassburg ec. grůndtliche warhafftige verātwortung vnd widerlegung/ deren von Graff Christoff Ladislaen von Thengen ... Calumnien vnd Schmächschrifft ... 4°. A-M4. pp. 1-93. (Lea.) [613

-- *Diocese.* Statuta et decreta synodi dioecesanae Argentoratensis. Moguntiae Excudebat Franciscus Behem, M. D. LXVI. fol. :)(:4 A-B4 a-c4 D-Ee4):(4 3A-3E4. ff. I-CXI, I-XIX. ¶*Additional t.pp.:* (A1r) ... Erasmo ... Episcopo Argentinensi ... *Same imprint.* ():(1r) Formula examinis Ecclesiastici ... *Same imprint.* [614

-- *Ministers.* Ordnūg des herren Nachtmal: so man die Messz nennet sampt der Tauff vñ Insegung der Ee/ Wie yetzt die diener des wort gottes zů Strasszburg/ Erneüwert vnnd ... gebessert haben ... M. D xxv. 4°. A-C4. [615

STRATIUS, JOANNES. Ad ... Leonoram, Galliae reginam, ... de eius felicitate & matrimonio, cum ... Francesco Gallorum Rege, Gratulatio. ... Parisiis apud Sorbonam, ex officina Gerardi Morrhij Campensis. impensis Ioannis Petri ... M.D.XXX. pridie Iduum Iulij. 4°. A-B4 (-B4, *presumably blank*). pp. III-XIIII. [616

STRAUSS, JAKOB. Auffrůr/ Zwytracht vñ vnainigkait/ zwischen waren Euangelischen Christen fürzůkomē ... [Augsburg, Heinrich Steiner,] M.D.XXVI. 4°. A-B4 C2 D4. [617

-- Das der war leyb Christi vnd seyn heiliges blůt/ im Sacramēt gegenwertig sey/ richtige erklerūg auff das new bůchleyn. D. Iohannes Haussscheyn ... [Augsburg, Heinrich Steiner,] M.D.XXVII. 4°. A-K^{4}. [618

-- Ein Sermon In der deutlich angezaiget/ vñ gelert ist dye pfaffen Ee/ yn Euangelischer leer nit zu der freyhayt des fleyschs/ vnd zu bekrefftigē dē alten Adā ... XXiij. ... [Augsburg, Georg Nadler, 1523.] 4°. A-B^{4}. [619

-- Ain trostliche verstendige leer über das wort sancti Pauli. ... Geprediget ... M.D.XXII. ... [Augsburg, Silvan Otmar.] 4°. A-B^{4} C^{6}. [620

STREUBER, PETER. Christliches Gutachten/ Wie etwan der schwere Streit/ so in der Reformierten Kirchen Gottes ein lange zeit hero (leider) gewesen vnd noch ist ... köndte auffgehaben ... werden ... Anno M. D. XCI. 4°. A-D^{4}. [621

STRIGEL, VICTORINUS. In Erotemata dialecticae Philippi Melanchthonis. υπομνηματα Victorini Strigelij. Excepta de ore ipsius ... [*Device of Matthaeus Harnisch of Neustadt.*] Anno cIↄ. Iↄ. XCI. 8°.):(^{8} A-3X^{8}. pp. 1-1075. [622

STROZZI, GIOVAMBATTISTA. Madrigali ... In Firenze. Nella Stamperia del Sermartelli. MDXCIII. (*Colophon.*) 4°. a-b^{4} A-T^{4}. pp. 2-152. [623

STROZZI, GIOVANNI. Oratio habita a ... Ioanne Strozio oratore ... Cosimi ducis Florentiæ & Senarum in eius comparitione, die XVIII. Martij. M. D. LXII. Vna cum responsione ... Synodi. Ripae. Ad instantiam Baptistæ Bozzolæ. 1562. 4°. A^{4}. (Lea.) [624

-- Oratio habita ... Portugaliae Algarbiorumque Regis Sebastiani Nomine, in Concilio Tridentino. Die IX. februarij. M. D. LXII. Vna cum responsione ... Synodi. Ripae. Ad instantiam Petri Antonii Alciatis, 1562. 4°. A^{4}. (Lea.) [625

STROZZI, TITO VESPASIANO & ERCOLE. Strozzi poetae pater et filius. (Venetiis in aedibus Aldi et Andreae Asulani soceri. M.DXIII.) 8°. A^{8} A-M^{8} N^{4} a-t^{8}. ff. 2-99, 1-152. [626

STUCK, JOHANN WILHELM. Carolus magnus rediuiuus, hoc est, Caroli magni ... cum Henrico M. Gallorum & Nauarrorum Rege ... comparatio ... M. D. XCII. [Tiguri, apud Ioannem Vuolphium typis Frosch.] 4°. A-V^{4} (-V4, *colophon*). ff. 2-79. [627

-- Vita ... Iosiae Simleri Tigurini ... in eiusdem obitum Carmina. Tiguri excudebat Frosch. anno M.D.LXXVII 4°. A-E^{4}. ff. 2-20. [628

STÜMMEL, CHRISTOPH. Studentes, comoedia de vita studiosorum, Nunc primum in lucem ædita, authore M. Christophoro Stummelio, f. Eiusdem Carmen de iudicio Paridis. Addita est Præfatio Iodoci VVillichij, & epilogus à M. Christophoro Cornero. Coloniae. Excudebat Petrus Horst. Anno 1565. 16°. A-F^{8}. [629

-- -- Magdeburgi. Apud Iohannem Francum. 16°. A-E^{8} (-E8, *presumably blank*). [630

STUMPF, JOHANN. Des grossen gemeinen Conciliums zů Costentz gehalten ... beschreybung ... Durch Iohann Stumpffen. Item von Iohann Hussen vnnd Hieronymo von Prag ... [Zürich, Christopher Froschauer, 1541.] fol. aa-bb^{6} a-z^{6} A-F^{6}. ff. I-CLXXIIII. [631

STURM, JOHANN. Ioannis Sturmii ad VVerteros fratres, Nobilitas literata. Liber vnus. Argentorati per VVendelinum Rihelium, Anno M. D. XLIX. (*Colophon.*) 8°. A-G^{8}. ff. 2-55. [632

-- Ioan. Sturmii Classicę epistolæ. ... Argentorati excudebat Iosias Rihelius. M.D.LXV. 8°. A^{6} A^{6} B-I^{8} K^{4}. ¶K4 *defective.* [633

-- De literarum ludis recte aperiendis Liber. ... Argentorati, Anno M. D. LVII. (... Apud Rihelios Fr. ...) 8°. A-F^{8}. ff. 3-46. [634

-- Libri duo Ioannis Sturmii de periodis vnus. Dionysii Halicarnassaei de collocatione Verborum Alter. Argentorati Vuendelinus Rihelius. M. D. L. 8°. A-D^{8} E^{4} B-G^{8} H^{4}. ff. 1-52. [635

-- Ioannis Sturmii, partitionum dialecticarum Libri quatuor. ... Argentorati per VVendelinum Rihelium. Anno M. D. XLIX. 8°. A-Y^{8} Z^{4} b-q^{8} r^{4}. ff. 1-170, 1-124. [635a

STURM, KASPAR. Exequiæ, Sive Honores funebres, quibus ... Vilelmum Hassiæ Landgravium ... filius ac hęres Dominus Mauritius ... mandavit ... Marpurgi, Excudebat Paulus Egenolphus M. D. XCII. 4°. A-F^4. pp. 3-47. [636

-- Warhafftig anzaygung wie Kaiser Carl der fünft ettlichen Fürsten auff dem Reychstag zů Augspurg im M.CCCCC.XXX. jar gehalten/ Regalia vnd Lehen vnder dem fan gelihen/ was such ... für Räthe vnd Adels personen auff solchem Reichstaf gehept haben. (Getruckt zů Augspurg durch Philipp Vlhart ...) 4°. A-B^4 C^6 D-F^4 G^2 H^4. ¶C5-6 *misbound after* C2. [637

STURTZ, CHRISTOFF. Oratio memoriæ ... Dn. Dauidis Chytræi ... à ... Christophoro Sturcio ... Rostochii Excusa Typis Myliandrinis, Impensis Laurentij Alberti bibliopolæ ... Lubecensis. Anno M.D.C. 4°. A-F^4. [638

STYRIA. *Ferdinand, king of the Romans.* [Mandate concerning fiefs, with stamped signature.] Geben in ... Wienn am Sechsvndzwajntzigisten tag Nouembris/ Anno ꝛc. jm Vierundfünfftzigisten ... s.sh. 32 × 43 cm. [639

-- *Ferdinand, Roman emperor.* [Mandate prohibiting the sale and export of horses, which adversely affects the mining of iron, with countersignatures.] Geben in ... Wienn/ am zwölfften tag Augusti/ Anno/ ꝛc. im Sechtzigisten ... s.sh. 32.5 × 44 cm. [640

-- *Karl, archduke of Austria.* Des ... Fürstenthumbs Steyer/ Landt vnd Peindlich Gerichts Ordnung ... M. D. LXXXIII. (Getruckt zů Augspurg/ durch Michael Manger. ...) fol. a^6 A-I^6 K^4. ff. 1-56. [641

-- *Siegmund Friedrich, freiherr zu Herberstein.* [Proclamation requiring provisions to lift the siege of Canisa by the Turks, with seals.] Datum Grätz den Sechzehenden Septembris/ des Ain tausent Sechshundertisten Jahr. s.sh. 33 × 49 cm. [642

-- *Landschaft.* [Notice of assessment of taxes addressed to Hanns Rindsmaull, with seals.] Datum Grätz den [*filled in by hand:*] xiiij tags Apprilljs Anno jm xliiij. s.sh. 32 × 41.5 cm. [643

-- [Notice of assessment of taxes addressed to Michell Rindsmaull, with subscription and seals.] Datum Grätz am Fünffundzwaintzigisten tag des Monats September. Anno ... jm Achtunduiertzigisten. s.sh. 31 × 45 cm. [644

-- [Notice of assessment of taxes addressed to Hanns Rindsmaull and heirs, with seals.] Datum Grätz den Sechsten tag May Anno ꝛc. jm Neünunduiertzigisten. s.sh. 32 × 43.5 cm. [645

-- [Notice of assessment of taxes addressed to Niclas Pernner, Herr zu Pernegkh, with seals.] Datum Grätz den Vierundtzwaintzigisten tag des Monats Iunij Anno Dñi ꝛc. im Ainundfunfftzigistn [*sic*]. s.sh. 33 × 42.5 cm. [646

-- -- *Another copy addressed to Michell Rindsmaull, with subscription.* [647

-- [Notice of assessment of taxes addressed to Niclas Pernner, with seals.] Datum Grätz den Letzten tag Ianuarij. Anno ꝛc. im Zwayvndfünfftzigisten. s.sh. 32 × 43 cm. ¶*Defective.* [648

-- -- *Another copy (defective) addressed to Michell Rindsmaull, with subscription.* [649

-- [Notice of assessment of taxes addressed to Hanns Rindsmauls Erben, with seals.] Datum Grätz den Sibenzehenden tag Marcij Anno ꝛc. im Dreyundfünfftzigisten. s.sh. 33 × 44 cm. [650

-- -- *Another copy addressed to Niclas Pernner.* [651

-- [Notice of assessment of taxes addressed to Niclas Pernner, with seals.] Datum Grätz den Sibenzehenden tag Martz/ Anno ꝛc. im Viervndfünfftzigisten. s.sh. 34 × 43.5 cm. [652

-- -- *Another copy addressed to Michl Rindsmaul.* [653

-- [Notice of assessment of taxes addressed to Michl Rindsmaul, with subscription and seals.] Datum Grätz am montag nach Iubilate [1555.] s.sh. 33 × 43.5 cm. ¶*Defective.* [654

-- [Notice of assessment of taxes addressed to Niclas Pernner, with seals.] Geben zů Grätz den Ersten tag May/ Anno ꝛc. im Sechsundfünfftzigisten. s.sh. 31 × 43 cm. [655

-- [Notice of assessment of taxes addressed to Michael Rindsmaul, with subscription.] Geben zů Grätz den letsten tag Ianuarij. Anno ꝛc. jm Sibenundfünfftzigisten. s.sh. 31.5 × 44 cm. [656

-- [Notice of assessment of taxes addressed to Michl Rindtsmaul, with seals.] Geben zů Grätz/ den fünfftzehenden tag Octobris/ Anno ꝛc. jm Sibenundfünfftzigisten. s.sh. 32 × 45.5 cm. [657

-- [Notice of assessment of taxes addressed to Niclas Pernner, with seals.] Actum Grätz den Ersten tag Decembris/ Anno ꝛc. jm Sibenundfünffzigisten Jar. s.sh. 31 × 43 cm. [658

-- Newe Ordnung hilff vnnd anlag so von ainer gemainen ... Landtschafft des Hertzogthumbs Steyer ... wieder den Erbfeindt ... den Türckhen ... Gedruckt zů Wienn in Osterreich/ durch Hanns Singriener. 1557. fol. A^6. [659

-- [Notice of assessment of taxes addressed to Michaell Rindszmaull, with subscription and seals.] Actum Grätz den letzten tag Ianuarij/ Anno ꝛc. im Sechtzigisten. s.sh. 32 × 43.5 cm. ¶*Worn at the folds.* [660

-- [Notice of assessment of taxes addressed to Michell Rindszmaull, with subscription and seals.] Actum Grätz den letzten tag Ianuarij/ Anno ꝛc. im Ainundsechzigisten. s.sh. 32.5 × 44 cm. [661

-- [Notice of assessment of taxes addressed to Niclas Perner, with seals.] Actum Grätz den letzten tag Martij Anno ꝛc. im Dreyvndsechzigisten. s.sh. 32 × 43 cm. [662

-- [Notice of assessment of taxes addressed to Michell Rindsmaull, with subscription and seals.] Actum Grätz den letzten tag Aprillis Anno ꝛc. im Viervndsechzigisten. s.sh. 32 × 44 cm. [663

-- [Notice of assessment of taxes addressed to Michel Rindsmaull, with subscription and seals.] Actum Grätz den letzten tag Martij Anno ꝛc. Fünffvndsechzigisten. s.sh. 32.5 × 44.5 cm. ¶*Worn at the folds.* [664

-- [Notice of assessment of taxes addressed to Michell Rindsmaull, with subscription and seals.] Actum Grätz den letzten tag Ianuarij/ Anno ꝛc. Im Sechs vnd sechtzigisten. s.sh. 34 × 44 cm. ¶*Worn at the folds.* [665

-- [Notice of assessment of taxes addressed to Michell Rindsmaull, with subscription and seals.] Actum Grätz den xx. Martij. Anno M. D. LXVII. s.sh. 32 × 43.5 cm. [666

-- [Notice of assessment of taxes addressed to Niclasen Perner Herr zů Perneck in der Vesenaw ꝛ Wittib vnd Erben, with seals.] Datum Grätz den Ersten Februarij Anno ꝛc. im Achtvndsechzigisten. s.sh. 33.5 × 42 cm. [667

-- [Notice of assessment of taxes addressed to Niclasen Perner, with seals.] Actum Grätz den Erstn [*sic*] tag Ianuarij anno ꝛc Im Neunvndsechtzigsten. s.sh. 31 × 41.5 cm. [668

-- [Notice of assessment of taxes addressed to Niclasen Perrner, with seals.] Actum Grätz den Ersten Ianuarij/ Anno ꝛc. Im Sibentzigisten Jhar. s.sh. 31.5 × 43 cm. [669

-- [Notice of assessment of taxes addressed to Niclasen Perner, with seals.] Actum Grätz den Funfftzehenden tag Martij Anno im zway vnd sibenzigisten. s.sh. 43.5 × 59 cm. [670

SUCHTEN, ALEXANDER VON. De secretis antimonii Liber vnus ... translatus ... per M. Georgium Forbergium Mysium. ... Geor. Phaedronis ... Aquila coelestis, siue correcta Hydrargyri præcipitatio. Basileae per Petrum Pernam. Anno 1575. 8°. a-g^8. pp. 3-112. ¶f2^r: Theophrasti Paracelsi de Narcoticis ægritudinibus ... (Smith.) [671

-- -- *Another copy.* (Smith.) [672

SUETONIUS TRANQUILLUS, GAIUS. Cōmentationes condite a Philippo Beroaldo adiecta paraphrastica. M. Ant. Sabellici interpretatione in Suetonium Tranquillum ... Eiusdem Philippi Beroaldi uita per Barptolomæum Blanchinum composita. ... Venundantur Parrhisiis ... (Impressum ... opera ... Ioannis Philippi: ære ... Lodouici Hornken & Godofredi Hittorpii. M.D.XII.) fol. a-z^6 &^{6} ꝯ^6 ℞^{6} aa-zz^6 &&^{6} ꝯꝯ^6 ℞℞^{6} 3a-3c^6 A-B^6 C^8 (-C8, *blank*). ff. I-CCCXXXIIII. [673

-- -- C. Suetonii Tranquilli XII. caesares. Item, Io. Baptistæ Egnatij Veneti, de Romanis principibus, libri III. Eiusdem Annotationes in Suetonium. Annotata in eundem ... per D. Erasmum Roter. His Accesserunt, Ausonius poëta de XII. Cæsaribus ... Eiusdem tetrasticha de Cæsaribus ... Parisiis, Apud Hieronymum de Marnef ... 1564. 16°. A-QQ^8. ff. 2-293. [674

-- -- C. Suetonius Tranquillus von Gebůrt/ Leben ... der XII. ersten Roͤmischen Keyser ... Gedruckt zů Strassburg bei M. Iacob Cammerlander von Mentz. Anno M.D.XXXVI. fol. π^4 A-X^4 Y^6 (-Y6, *presumably blank*). ff. ij-lxxxix. [675

-- -- Le vite de dodici cesari ... Tradotte in lingua Toscana per M. Paolo del Rosso cittadino Fiorentino. In Roma nel M. D. XLIIII. (Stampato in Roma per Antonio Blado Asulano, ad instanza, & à spese di M. Francesco Priscianese Fiorentino. ...) 8°. aa^4 A-Z^8 (-A1) AA-KK^8 (-KK7-8, *presumably blank*). ff. 9-262. [676

SULAIMAN II, sultan. Newe Zeitung. Des Tuͤrckischen Keisers Absagbrieff/ so er newlich dem Roͤmischen Koͤnige Ferdinando/ bey seinem Legatus zugesandt. ... M.D.LVI. 4°. A^4. [677

-- Oration. Tuͤrckischer Botschafft/ an die Key. May. zu Franckfort. ... Des Tuͤrckischen Keysers Friedtbrieff ... Franckfurt M. D. LXII. 4°. A^6. [678

-- -- [Literae Sultani Sulemanni Turcarum imp. missae Constantinopolo ad Ferd. Imperatorem Rom. & ab Ebrahimo Strotschio, Polono, apostata, redditæ Francofordiæ ... Anno MDLXII. ... Patauii.] 4°. A^4 (-A1-2) B^2. [679

SUMMENHARD, KONRAD. Conradi Sūmenhart Cōmentaria in Summā physice Alberti magni ... (... excuse a ... Henrico gran ... in Hagenaw. ... Vale ... 1507 septimo kal'. maias.) fol. a-f$^{8.8.6}$ g^8 h-l^6 m-z$^{8.6.6.6}$ ⁊^{6} ꝯ^8. [680

SUMMERHART, HEINRICH. Ain hüpsche frag von ainem iüngling an ainen altten Cartheüser/ wie die Epistel ad Titū .j. Zů versteen sey ... hat solchs auffgeschriben mit namē hainrich Summerhart von Colmar. [Augsburg, Melchior Ramminger] Im Jar. M D XXIIII. 4°. a^4. [681.

SUNCZEL, FRIEDRICH. Collecta ⁊ exercitata ... ī octo libros Phisicorum Arestotelis ... (Impressa sub hemisperio veneto Impensis Leonardi Alātse Bibliopole viennensis Arte ... Petri Liechtenstein Coloniensis āno .M.d.vj. Die .xxviij. Mensis madij ...) 4°. B.L. a^8 b^4 c-s^8 t^4 v^8. [682

SURGANT, JOHANN ULRICH. Manuale curatorum predicandi prebens modū ... (... impressus [Basileae per Michaelem Furter]: Anno ... Millesimo q̄ngentesimotercio: Mensis ꝟo Augusti die decimoquarto.) 4°. B.L. π^8 A^8 B-R$^{8.4}$ S-V^8. ff. I-CXXVII. [683

-- -- (... impressus [Basileae per Michaelem Furter]: Anno ... Millesimo q̄ngentesimosexto: Mēsis ꝟo Ianuarij.) 4°. B.L. π^8 A^8 B-R$^{8.4}$ S-V^8 (-V8, *blank*). ff. I-CXXVII. [684

-- Regimen studiosorum 4°. B.L. a-d^8. [685

SURIUS, LAURENTIUS. Commentarius breuis rerum in orbe gestarum, ab anno ... 1500. vsque in annum 1567. ...congestus ... Coloniae, Apud Geruinum Calenium, & hæredes Iohannis Quentel, Anno M. D. LXVII. ... 8°. a^8 A-3Q^8 3R^4. pp. 1-936. [686

-- -- Commentarius ... ab anno ... M. D. vsque in annum M. D. LXXIIII. ... Nunc verò recēns ... ad annum M. D. LXXXVI. opera & studio Michaelis ab Isselt Amorfortij perductus. ... Coloniae, Apud Geruinum Calenium, & hæredes Ioannis Quentelij, Anno M. D. LXXXVI. ... 8°. a-f^8 A-4F^8. pp. 1-1199. (Lea.) [687

-- -- Kurtze Chronick oder Beschreibung der vornembsten haͤndeln vnd geschichten/ so sich ... zugetragen/ vom jar ... M.D. biss auff das jar M. D. LXVIII. ... verteutscht durch Henricum Fabricium Aquensem, P. Getruckt zu Coͤln/ durch Gerwinum Calenium/ vnd die Erben etwan Iohan Quentels/ ... M.D.LXVIII. fol. A^6 a-5a^4 5b^6 (-5b6, *presumably blank*). ff. 1-377. [688

-- -- Ander teil/ kurtzer Chronick Vnserer zeit ... vom Jar ... M.D.XXXVII. biss auff das Jar M.D.LXII. ... verteutscht durch Henricum Fabritium ... Zu Coͤln/ Durch Geruinum Calenium/ vnd die Erben Iohan Quentels ... M.D.LXXXVI. ... 8°. a-rr^8 ss^{10}. ff. 2-229. [689

-- [1] Tomus primus conciliorum omnium ... Coloniae Agrippinae Apud Geruuinum Calenium, & Hæredes Iohannis Quentelij, ... M.D.LXVII. ... fol. a*^{6} a-3x^6 3y-3z^4. pp. 2-819. ¶3z2-4 *defective*. [2] Tomus secundus ... A*^{4} A-4T^6. pp. 1-1054. [3] Tomus tertius ... A*^{2} A-4H^6 4I^4. pp. 2-930. [4] Tomus quartus ... *a*^{2} *a-4*o^6 4*p^4. pp. 1-1003. [5] In quatuor tomos conciliorum omnium ... index. ... **a-**k^4 **l^6. (Lea.) [690

SUSANNIS, MARQUARD DE. Tractatus de coelibatu sacerdotum non abrogando ... Venetiis. M. D. LXV. (... apud Cominum de Tridino Montisferrati. ...) 4°. *-4*^{4} A-V^4 X^2. ff. 2-81. (Lea.) [691

-- Tractatus ... de Iudaeis et aliis infidelibus, & de inimicis Crucis Christi, tam visibilibus, quam inuisibilibus. ... Venetiis. MDLXVIII. (... Apud Cominium de Tridino Montisferrati. ...) 4°. †-††⁴ 3†⁶ A-3F⁴ 3G². ff. 1-210. (Lea.) [692

SUSENBROTUS, JOANNES. Σὺν δὲ θεοὶ μάκαρες. Epitome troporum ac schematum et grammaticorum & Rhetorum ... Tiguri apud Christophorum Froschouerum [1557]. 8°. A-G⁸ H⁴. pp. 1-110. [693

-- Grammaticae artis institutio ... ex Grãmaticorũ Coriphæis ... concinnata. Etymologia ... Prosodia ... Syntaxis ferè ex Thoma Linacro. De constructæ orationis distinctione & ordine naturali. ... 8°. A-T⁸. ff. 1-150. ¶*Dedication dated 1539. T.p. repaired.* [694

SUSO, HEINRICH. D. Henrici Susonis ... opera. ... à Sueuico idiomate Latinè reddita à ... Laurentio Surio ... Coloniae Agrippinae, In officina Birckmannica sumptib. Arnoldi Mylij. Anno cIↄ. Iↄ. LXXXVIII. 8°. a⁸ a⁴ B-Xx⁸ Yy². pp. 9-656. (Lea.) [695

-- Diss buch da gedicht hat der erleücht vater Amandus/ genañt Seüss. begreift in jm vil gůter gaistlicher leeren ... (... gedruckt ... in ... Augsburg. Durch maister Hannsen Othmar ... Durch verlegung des ... herrn Iohann Rynnman von öringen ... In dem jar ... Tausent fünffhundert vnd zwölff jar auff den xx tag des monats Iunij ...) fol. A⁸ B-Z⁶ (-Z6) aa-ff⁶ gg⁸ (-gg1). ff. ii-ccxxxiii. ¶gg7 *defective.* [696

SWINBURNE, HENRY. A briefe treatise of testaments and last willes ... London Printed by Iohn Windet. 1590. (... 1591.) 4°. A⁴ (-A1, *blank*) B-C⁴ B⁴ C-Pp⁸ Qq² Rr-Tt⁴. ff. 3-293. *S.T.C.* 23547. (Biddle.) [697

SYLBURG, FRIEDRICH. Ετυμολογικον το μεγα. ... Etymologicon magnum ... [Heidelbergae,] E Typographeio Hieronymi Commelini ... MDXCIIII. fol.):(⁴ A-Ll⁶ Mm⁴ A-T⁴ V⁶. cols. 1-828, pp. 1-163. [698

-- Saracencia, siue Moamethica: in quibus ... Moamethicae Sectæ ... dogmatum Elenchus: ex Euthymii Zigabeni Panoplia Dognatica. De ... Moamethe historia; incerti auctoris. Saracenorum ... Catechesis, & Saracenismi anathematizatio. Ex Theophanis & Anastasii Ecclesiastica historia ... narratio. Græce et Latine ... [Heidelbergae,] Ex typographeio H. Commelini, Anno 1595. 8°.):(⁴ A-I⁸ K⁴. pp. 1-152. [699

-- -- *Another copy.* (Lea.) [700

SYLVESTER, FRANCISCUS. Concio de duplici mysterio abominationis vno, desolationis altero. Habita à F. Francisco vicedomino Ferrarien. ... Ad ... Synodum Tridentinam. Dominica XXIIII. post Pentecosten, Quæ fuit XXII. Nouemb. ... M D LXII. Brixiæ Apud Damianum Turlinum, ... Imprimebatur. Ad instantiam Ioannis Baptistæ Bozolæ. Anno M. D. LXII. (*Colophon.*) 4°. A⁴ B⁶. (Lea.) [701

SYLVIUS, PETER. Von den vier Euangelion ... Das ist von den irrigen Artickeln/ der vier vnchristlichen ketzereyen. Nemlich der Pickarden/ der Muscouitern/ des Wigkleffs/ vnd des Husss. Auss welchen allen/ Lutther/ seyn funfft Euangelium/ ... tzusamen gelesen vnd tzuhauffen gesetzt ... Anno. M. D. xxviij. (Gedruckt tzu Leypsick Freytag noch Viti. ...) 4°. A-F⁴. [702

SYMMACHUS, QUINTUS AURELIUS. Symmachi ... Epistolæ familiares. Item Laudini Equitis hierosolymitani in epistolas Turci magni traductio. (Argentoraci Ex officina Ioannis Schotti: Impensis ... Georgii Maxilli (al's übelin) ... III. idus Augusti ... M. D. X.) 4°. a-f⁸·⁴·⁴ g⁸ h⁶ A⁶ B⁴. [703

SYNESIUS CYRENAEUS. Synesij Cyrenæi, Aegyptii, seu de prouidentia, Disputatio: conuersa in Latinum sermonem ... Addita epistola eiusdem Synesij ad Orum ... Elaborata omnia ab Esromo Rudingero Pabepergensi. Basileae, per Ioannem Oporinum. (... M. D. LVII. Mense Martio.) 8°. a-m⁸. pp. 4-191. [704

-- Synesii ... Epistolæ ..., Gręcè ac Latinè editæ: Thoma Naogeorgo Straubingensi interprete. Basileae, per Ioannem Oporinum. (Finis ... 25 Aprilis 1558.) 8°. α-γ⁸ b-z⁸ A-I⁸. pp. 18-515. [705

SYNONYMA. Hie hebent an die synonima die man nēt gezierte geblůmbte/ vñ colores der schonen hoffkunstrethoricken formierē. (1522) 8°. a-c^8. [706

SYRIANUS. Syriani antiquissimi interpretis in II. XII. et XIII. Aristotelis libros metaphysices Commentarius, a Hieronymo Bagolino ... latinitate donatus. In Academia Veneta, M. D. LVIII. (*Colophon.*) 4°. *^{4} A-Hh^4. ff. 2-132. [707

T

TABOUROT, ÉTIENNE. [1] Les bigarrures Du Seigneur des Accords: ... Liure Premier. ... A Paris, Chez Iean Richer ... 1588. 12°. ā^{12} ē^{2} A-T^{12} V^{8}. ff. 1-236. [2] Les bigarrures ... Quatriesme liure. Auec les Apophthegmes du Seigneur Gaulard, augmentees. *Same imprint.* A-K^{12} L^{4}. ff. 1-124. [1

TACITUS, PUBLIUS CORNELIUS. Cornelius Tacitus ... M. D. XXXIIII. (Venetiis, in aedibus haeredum Aldi Manutii Romani, et Andreae Asulani soceri, mense Nouembri ...) 4°. *^{8} **^{4} a-h^{8} i^{4} k^{8} L^{8} m-z^{8} A-K^{8}. ff. 1-260. [2

-- -- C. Cornelii Taciti opera quæ exstant. Ad exemplar quod I. Lipsius quintum recensuit. ... Commentarii eiusdem LipsI ... Guil. Barclayus præmetia quædam ex vitâ Agricolæ libauit. ... Parisiis, Apud Ambrosium Drouart ... cIↃ. IↃ. XCIX. 8°. *^{8} A-3C^{8} 3D^{4} 3E^{8} 3F^{4} (-3D4, *presumably blank*) a-pp^{8} qq^{4} (-qq4, *presumably blank*). pp. 1-790, 2-568. [3

-- -- [1] ... Iustus Lipsius postremùm recensuit. Additi Commentarii ... cum Curis secundis. Accessit seorsim C. Velleius Paterculus cum eiusdem LipsI auctoribus notis. Antuerpiæ, Ex officina Plantiniana, Apud Ioannem Moretum. cIo. IↃc. ... 4°. *^{4} **^{2} A-Zz^{4} AA-BB^{4} CC^{6}. pp. 1-385. [2] Iusti LipsI ... liber commentarius ... *Same imprint.* **^{4} a-hh^{4}. pp. 1-246. [3] Iusti LipsI ... notæ. *Same imprint.* (*Colophon.*) Aa-Oo^{4}. pp. iij-lxxxij. [4

-- -- Les oeuures de C. Cornelius Tacitus ... nouuellement mis en Francois ... A Paris, Pour Abel l'Angelier ... M. D. LXXXII. (Acheue d'imprimer le vingtiesme iour de Iuillet ... Par Pierre le Voirrier ...) fol. ā^{6} ē^{4} A-Yy^{6} Zz-3D^{4} 3E-3F^{6} 3G^{4} 3H^{6}. pp. 2-602. ¶*Translators: Claude Fauchet and Étienne de la Planche.* [5

-- P. Cornelii Taciti ... annalium ab excessu Augusti ... libri sedecim qui supersunt ... recogniti ... per Beatum Rhenanum. ... Basileæ in officina Frobeniana anno M D XLIIII. (... per Hieronymum Frobenium et Nicolaum Episcopium ...) fol. aa-ff^{6} a-z^{6} A-V^{6}. pp. 1-492. [6

-- -- The annales of Cornelius Tacitus. The description of Germanie. M. D. XCVIII. (Printed at London by Arn. Hatfield, for Bonham and Iohn Norton.) fol. π^{4} (-π1, *presumably blank*) A-Y^{6} Z^{4}. pp. 1-271. *S.T.C.* 23644. ¶*Translator: Richard Greneway.* (Furness.) [7

-- -- The ende of Nero and beginning of Galba. Fower bookes of the histories of Cornelius Tacitus. The life of Agricola. The second Edition. M. D. XCVIII. (Printed at London by Edm. Bollifant, for Bonham and Iohn Norton.) fol. ¶^{6} A-S^{6} T^{4} V^{6} (-V6, *presumably blank*). pp. 1-227. *S.T.C.* 23643. ¶*Translator: Sir Henry Savile.* (Furness.) [8

-- -- Les cinq premiers liures des annales ... Traduictz nouuellement de Latin en Francoys. ... A Paris, Pour Vincent Sertenas ... 1548. (... acheué d'imprimer le treiziesme iour de Juing ...) 4°. a^{4} A^{4} B-F^{8} G^{4} H-M^{8} N^{4} O-Dd^{8} Ee^{2}. ff. 1-205. [9

-- -- Gli annali di Cornelio Tacito ... Nuouamente tradotti di Latino in lingua Toscana da Giorgio Dati Fiorentino. ... In Venetia, ad instantia de' Giunti di Firenze. M. D. LXIII. (Stampata ... per Domenico Guerra, & Gio. Battista suo fratello ...) 4°. *-***^{8} A-OO^{8} PP^{6}. ff. 2-301. [10

-- -- Le historie auguste di Cornelio Tacito, Nouellemente fatte Italiane. ... In Vinegia, Appresso Vincenzo Vaugris ... M. D. XLIIII. 8°. A-3G^{8}. ff. 2-422. [11

-- -- L'imperio di Tiberio Cesare Scritto da Cornelio Tacito nelli annali Espresso in lingua Fiorentina propria da Bernardo Dauanzati Bostíchi. In Fiorenza per Filippo Giunti. MDC. ... (*Colophon.*) 4°. *^{6} A-Dd^{4} Ee^{6}. pp. 2-603 [= 203]. [12

-- Cornelij Taciti ... de situ. moribus. et populis Germanie. ... (Impressum ... Lips in edibus Melchior Lotters. ... M.D. Nono. Vltimo die Decembris.) 4°. B.L. A-C^{6} D^{8}. [13

-- -- Andreae Althameri Brenzii scholia in Corneliū Tacitū Rom. historicū, De situ, moribus, populisq3 Germaniæ ... (Typis excudebat Norimbergæ Fridericus Peypus, impensis ... Leonardi de Aich ... Anno ... vicesimo nono, supra sesquimillesimum.) 4°. A-R^{4}. ff. 1-59. [14

-- -- Commentaria Germaniae in P. Cornelij Taciti ... libellum de situ, moribus, & populis Germanorum ... Andreae Althameri diligentia ... elucubrata. Anno M. D. XXXVI. (Norimbergæ apud Ioh. Petreium ...) 4°. aa-ff^{4} a-z^{4} A-V^{4}. pp. 1-341. [15

TAEGIO, BARTOLOMMEO. Le risposte di M. Bartolomeo Taegio giureconsulto ... In Nouara appresso Francesco e Giacopo Sesalli. M. D. LIIII (*Colophon.*) 8°. A^4 A-S^8. ff. 3-142. [16

TAGLIENTE, GIOVANNI ANTONIO. Formulario nuouo che insegna dittare lettre missiue, & responsiue ... M.D.XXXII. (Stampato in Vinegia per maestro Bernardino de Vitali Vinitiano ...) 8°. A-E^8. [17

TAHUREAU, JACQUES. Les dialogues ... A Paris, Chés Gabriel Buon ... 1566. ... 8°. $\bar{a}^8$ $\bar{e}^4$ A-Q^8 R^4. pp. 1-264. [18

TAILLEPIED, NOËL. Recueil des antiquitez et singularitez de la ville de Rouen. ... A Rouen, Chez Raphael du petit Val ... M. D. LXXXVII. 8°. A-S^8 (-S8, *presumably blank*). pp. 1-265. [19

TAISNIER, JEAN. Opus mathematicum octo libros complectens, ... quorum sex priores libri ... Cheiromantiæ Theoricam, Praxim ... continent. Septimus Physiognomiæ dispositionem, hominumq3 omnium qualitates & complexiones. Octauus Periaxiomata de faciebus Signorum ... Coloniae Agrippinae Apud Ioannem Birckmannum & Wernerum Richwinum, ... M. D. LXII. fol. $*^6$ A-Z^4 Aa-Zz^4 AA-ZZ^4 aa-ii^4 KK^4. pp. 2-614. (Lea.) [20

TALENTONE, GIOVANNI. Discorso in forma di lezzione ... fatto ... con l'occasione del principio del quarto Canto del Purgatorio di Dante ... In Milano, Per Francesco Paganello, Ad instanza di Antonio de gli Antonij. ... M.D.XCVII. 4°. *-$**^4$ A-K^4 A^6 (A6 + *folded leaf*) pp. 1-80. [21

TALON, OMER. Audomari Talaei rhetorica ... Quinta ... æditio ... Tremoniae, Excud. Albertus Sartorius, Anno 1557. 8°. A-E^8. [22

TANCRED OF BOLOGNA. Tancreti ... ordinis iudiciarii tractatus. Lugduni excudebat Godefridus & Marcellus Beringi, fratres, M.D.XLVII. (*Colophon.*) 8°. a-o^8 p^{10}. pp. 2-240. [23

TANI, NICOLÒ. La cognata comedia ... In Padoa, Appresso Paulo Meieto M D LXXXIII. 8°. π^4 A-K^8 L^4. ff. 1-83. [24

TANSILLO, LUIGI. Stanze amorose, sopra gli horti delle donne & in lode della menta. La Caccia d'amore del Bernia. In Venetia, 1574. 12°. A-D^{12} (-D12, *blank*). ff. 3-46. [25

-- Stanze in lode della menta. ... Venetiis. M. D. XLIII. 8°. A-D^4. [26

TAPPERT, RUARD. Explicationis articulorum venerandae facultatis sacrae theologiae Generalis Studii Louaniensis circa dogmata Ecclesiastica ab annis triginta quatuor controuersa ... tomus primus. Authore ... Ruardo Tapper ab Enchusia ... Antuerpiae Apud Ioannem Bellerum ... M. D. LV. ... fol. a-d^4 A-$3F^4$ $3G^6$. pp. 1-402. (Lea.) [27

TARAFA, FRANCISCO. Francisci Taraphæ Barcinonen. De origine, ac rebus gestis Regum Hispaniæ liber ... Antuerpiæ, In Ædibus Ioannis Steelsij. M. D. LIII. ... (Typis Ioannis Latij.) 8°. A-O^8. pp. 4-201. [28

TARCHANIOTA MARULLUS, MICHAEL. Michael Tarch. Marullus, Hieron. Angerianus, et Ioan. Secundus, Poetae elegantissimi: Nunc primùm in Germania excusi. Spiræ Nemetum Apud Bernardum Albinum M. D. XCV. 12°. $+^4$ A-X^{12} Y^8 (-Y8, *presumably blank*). pp. 1-517. ¶*Additional t.pp.:* (H6) Hieronymi Angeriani Neapolitani, Ἐωτοπαίγνιον [*sic*]. *Same imprint.* (L4) Ioannis Secundi Hagiensis ... opera ... *Same imprint.* (Lea.) [29

-- Michaelis Tarchaniotae Marulli Constantinopolitani Epigrammata & Hymni. Parisiis, Apud Iacobum Dupuis ... 1561. 16°. a-l^8 m^4. ff. 2-92. [30

TARSIA, GIOVANNI MARIA. Oratione o vero discorso ... Fatto nell'essequie del diuino Michelagnolo Buonarroti. Con alcuni Sonetti, & prose latine e volgari ... In Fiorenza Appresso Bartolomeo Sermartelli. MDLXIIII. 4°. A-C^4 D^6. ¶D3r: Discorso di M. Benuenuto Cennini ... [31

TARTAGNI, ALESSANDRO, DA IMOLA. [Consilia.] M. D. XXXII (Lugduni Iacobus myt imprimebat.) fol. B.L. [1] Consiliorum Alexandri volumen primum. ... a-o^8. ff. 2-111. [2]

Consiliorum ... volumen secundum. ... aa-ss^8 tt-vv^6. ff. 2-156. [3] ... volumen tertium. ... A-L^8 M^6. ff. 2-94. [4] ... volumen quartum. ... AA-LL^8 MM-NN^6. ff. 2-100. [5] ... volumen quintum. ... Aa-Rr^8. ff. 2-139. [6] ... volumen sextum. ... a-x^8. ff. 2-167. [7] ... volumen septimum. ... aa-pp^8 qq^4. ff. 2-124. [8] Repertorium ... a-i^8 k^6. (Biddle.) [32

-- Alexander Imolensis, in primam et secundam digesti veteris partem. Commentariorum ... Tomus primus, vnà cum ... Francisci de Curte, & Bernardini Landriano Additionibus. Quibus accessit ... Hieronymi Loreti Repertorium ... Lugduni, M. D. LII. (... excussa fuere, per Iacobum Faure ⁊ Petrum Taconem.) fol. B.L. A^{10} B-AA^8 (-AA8, *presumably blank*). ff. 1-191. (Lea.) [32a

TARTALEA, NICOLÒ. Quesiti et inuentioni diuerse de Nicolo Tartaglia ... Appresso de l' auttore M D LIIII. (In Venetia per Nicolo de Bascarini ...) 4°. A-II^4 (S2 + *leaf pasted on*). ff. 5-128. [33

TARTARET, PIERRE. [1] Expositio magistri petri Tatareti in summulas Petri Hispani vna cũ passibus Scoti ... in marginib⁹ sparsis ... Additus est tractatus insolubiliũ eiusdem ⁊ obligatoriorũ magistri Martini molenfelt ex Liuonia. fol. B.L. a-n^6 o^8 p^4. ff. 2-87. [2] Magistri Petri tatareti cõmentarij in Isagogas Porphyrij et libros logicorũ Aristotelis ... A-O^6 P-Q^8 R^6. ff. 2-100. [3] Commẽtarij Petri tatareti in libros philosophie naturalis et metaphysice Aristotelis. Eiusdẽ in Aristotelis sex ethicos libros questiones. ... (Basilee [per Joannem Froben] ... Anno ... Millesimo quingentesimo decimoquarto/ decimaquinta Martij.) AA-VV^6 XX^4 3A-3C^6 3D^8. ff. 2-118, 1-26. [34

-- -- Petri Tatareti Parisiensis ... in summulas Petri Hispani exactae explicationes. Per R.P.F. Saluatorem Bartol. ... recognita ... Venetiis, Apud Hæredes Melchioris Sessæ. M D LXXXI. (... Alexander Gryphius Excudebat ... M D LXXX.) 4°. *^{8} **^{4} A-Cc^8. ff. 1-207. (Lea.) [35

-- [1] ... Petri Tatareti ... in quartum librum sententiarum opus. ... purgatum. Per Fratrem Constantium Sarnanũ ... Thomus primus. [Neapoli,] Apud Horatium Saluianum. 1579. ... 8°. ¶-¶¶^{8} ¶¶¶^{4} A-NN^8 OO^2. ff. 1-289. [2] ... Thomus secundus. *Same imprint.* §-§§^{8} PP-4H^8 4I^4. ff. 297-620. (Lea.) [36

-- Petri Tatareti ... In triplicem Aristotelis Philosophiam; Physicam, Metaphysicam, & Ethicam, ... lucubrationes. ... Venetiis, Apud hæredes Melchioris Sessæ. M D LXXI. (*Colophon.*) 8°. *^{8} **^{4} A-3D^8. ff. 1-400. [37

-- -- Petri Tatareti ... in Aristotelis philosophiam, Naturalem, Diuinam, & Moralem, exactissima commentaria ... Addita sunt ... due quæstiones R. P. M. Iacobini Bargij ... Omnia ... expurgata per R. P. F. Saluatorem Bartol. de Assisio ... Venetiis, Apud Hæredes Melchioris Sessæ. M D LXXXI. (... Alexander Gryphius Excudebat ...) 8°. a^8 b^4 A-3D^8. ff. 1-398. [38

-- -- Petri Tatareti ... Commentaria. Per R. P. F. Liuium a Lege Venetum ... repurgata. ... Duæ Quæstiones R. P. M. Iacobini Bargij ... Tertia pars. Venetiis, Apud Hæredes Melchioris Sessæ. M. D. XCII. (... Georgius Angelerius Excudebat ...) 8°. a^8 b^4 A-3D^8. ff. 1-398. [39

-- Questiões Magistri Petri Tatareti super sex libros Æthicoꝝ Aristotelis ... Venundãtur Parisius ... apud Iohannẽ Frellon ... (Impresse ... in intersignio Speculi iuxta collegium Lombardorum Expensis ... Iohannis Frellon et Gaufridi Hamelin ... 1509. Die vero .x. mensis Septembris.) 8°. B.L. A-K^8 L^4. ff. iii-lxxxiiii. [40

-- -- *Another copy.* [41

-- Petri Tatareti ... regulae morales ... Per R. P. F. Liuium a Lege Venetum ... repurgata. ... Venetiis, Apud Hæredes Melchioris Sessæ. M. D. XCII. (*Colophon.*) 8°. +^{8} A-G^8 H^4. ff. 1-60. [42

TASSARA, ANTONIO. In notariorum excessus errores atque pecata Compendium ... Venetiis [per Cominum de Tridino Montisferrati] M.D.XLVI. 8°. A-L^8 (-B1). ff. 3-88. (Lea.) [43

TASSO, BERNARDO. L'Amadigi ... In Vinegia appresso Gabriel Giolito de' Ferrari. MDLX. 4°. *^{4} A-PP^8 QQ^4. pp. 1-612. [44

-- -- In Venetia, Appresso Fabio, & Agostino Zoppini Fratelli. M D LXXXIII. (*Colophon.*) 4°. *^{4} A-Yy^{8} Zz^{6}. pp. 1-731. [45

-- Il Floridante ... Con gli Argomenti à ciascun Canto del Signor Antonio Costantini ... In Bologna, per Gio. Rossi. MDLXXXVII. ... 8°. †^{4} A-I^{8} K-L^{4}. pp. 1-158. [46

-- Li due libri delle lettere ... In Venetia, Appresso Vincenzo Valgrisi, & Baldessar Costantini. M D LVII. 8°. A-Oo^{8}. pp. 3-585. [47

-- -- In Venetia Appresso P. Gironimo Giglio, e compagni. M. D. LIX. (*Colophon.*) 8°. *^{8} a-ij^{8} kk^{2}. ff. 1-255. [48

-- [Rime.] In Vinegia appresso Gabriel Giolito de' Ferrari. M D LX. 12°. [1] Rime di Messer Bernardo Tasso. ... *-**^{12} A-M^{12} N^{8}. pp. 1-304. [2] Delle rime di Messer Bernardo Tasso. Libro quarto. ... A-C^{12}. pp. 3-67. [3] Rime ... Libro quinto. ... A-E^{12}. pp. 3-120. [4] Salmi ... A-C^{12}. ff. 2-48. [5] Ode ... A-F^{12}. pp. 3-142. [49

-- -- *Another copy of* [4] *and* [5]. [50

TASSO, ERCOLE. Dell'ammogliarsi piaceuole contesa Frà i due moderni Tassi, Hercole, cioè, & Torquato ... In Bergamo. cIↃ IↃ XCIII. Per Comin Ventura. 8°. a^{4} A-N^{4}. ff. 1-55. ¶I2^{r}: Che bene sia di prender moglie, Diffesa del Sig. Torquato Tasso, contra la predetta Declamatione. [51

-- -- In Bergamo, Per Comin Ventura. cIↃ IↃ xcv. 4°. a^{4} A-D^{8} I-L^{8}. ff. 1-56. [52

TASSO, FAUSTINO. Le historie de' successi de' nostri tempi ... Diuise in Tredici Libri. ... dal fine dell'anno M D LXVI. fino al principio dell'anno M D LXXX. ... In Venetia, Presso Domenico, & Gio. Battista Guerra, fratelli. M D LXXXIII. (*Colophon.*) 4°. a-c^{8} d^{4} A-3E^{8}. pp. 2-815. (Lea.) [53

TASSO, TORQUATO. [1] Rime, et prose ... Parte Prima. ... In Ferrara. Ad instanza di Giulio Vassallini. M. D. LXXXIII. (Appresso Vittorio Baldini. 1582.) 12°. ❦^{12} A-O^{12} A-E^{12}. pp. 2-335, 3-118. [2] Rime, e prose ... Parte Seconda. ... *Same imprint and colophon.* ❦^{12} A-V^{12} X^{6}. pp. 2-490. [54

-- -- [1] Delle rime, et prose ... parte prima. ... In Vinetia, MDXXCIII. Presso Aldo. 12°. *^{12} A-Y^{12}. pp. 2-144, 18-120, 8-171, 2-66. [2] ... parte seconda. ... *Same imprint.* *^{12} A-Z^{12}. pp. 2-144, 4-276, 8-84. [3] Aggiunta alle rime, et prose ... In Vinegia, MDXXCV. Presso Aldo. a^{12} A-D^{12} (-D10-12, *blank*). pp. 2-90. [55

-- -- *Another copy of* [2]. ¶Il Padre di Famiglia (V-Z^{12}) *bound separately.* [56

-- -- [Delle rime et prose ... Parte prima. ... In Ferrara appresso Simon Vasalini. MDLXXXV.] (... nella Stamperia di Giulio Cesare Cagnacini, & Fratelli. ...) 12°. †^{12} A-Y^{12} (*lacks all before* M2). pp. 7-171 (M4^{r}-T2^{v} Il forno), 1-54 (T10^{r}-X12^{v}, Lettera ... Nella quale paragona l'Italia alla Francia, Il Romeo ...) *present.* [57

-- -- [1] Rime, et prose ... Parte prima. ... In Ferrara. Ad instantia di Giulio Vasalini. MDLXXXIX. (... Presso Vittorio Baldini ...) 12°. ❦^{12} A-F^{12}. pp. 2-144. [2] Aminta ... In Ferrara, MDLXXXIX. A-C^{12}. pp. 3-72. [3] Delle prose ... Parte Prima. In Ferrara. 1589. A-L^{12}. pp. 3-195, 2-54. [4] Rime, et prose ... Parte seconda. *Same imprint and colophon.* ❦^{12} A-C^{12}. pp. 1-72. [5] Il re Torrismondo tragedia ... In Ferrara, Appresso Giulio Cesare Cagnacini, & Fratelli. CIↃ IↃ XXCVII. (... 1588.) A-E^{12}. ff. 1-54. [6] Il Rinaldo ... In Ferrara, MDLXXXIX. (... Appresso Vittorio Baldini ...) A-L^{12}. pp. 3-261. [7] Il padre di famiglia. ... *Same imprint.* A-E^{12}. pp. 3-79, 2-31. [8] ... Parte terza. ... *Same imprint and colophon as* [1]. ❦^{12} A-F^{12}. ff. 2-71. [9] Delle prose ... Parte Terza. In Ferrara, MDLXXXIX. A-R^{12}. ff. 2-200. [10] ... Parte quarta. ... In Venetia, MDLXXXIX. Appresso Giulio Vasalini. †-††^{12} A-H^{12}. pp. 1-192. [11] Delle prose ... Parte Quarta. M. D. XC. A-H^{12} I^{6} †^{6}. pp. 1-201. [12] Gioie di rime, e prose ... Quinta, e sesta parte. ... In Venetia, Ad instanza di Giulio Vasalini Libraro in Ferrara MDLXXXVII. (*Colophon.*) †-††^{12} A-H^{12}. ff. 1-94. [13] Dialoghi e discorsi ... In Venetia, Appresso Giulio Vasalini. 1587. A-R^{12}. ff. 3-203. [58

-- Aminta fauola boscareccia di M. Torquato Tasso. ... In Vinegia [presso Aldo]. M.D.LXXXI. 8°. (^{4} A-D^{8} E^{4}. pp. 2-70. [59

-- -- In Tours, Appresso Iametto Maitaier M.D.XCI. 12°. A-H$^{8.4}$ I^{2}. ff. 2-50. [60

-- -- In Ferrara, MDXCIX. Per Vittorio Baldini ... (*Colophon.*) 12°. A-C^{12} D^6. pp. 3-82. [61

-- Apologia del S. Torquato Tasso. In difesa della sua Gierusalemme liberata. Con alcune altre Opere, parte in accusa, parte in difesa dell'Orlando Furioso dell'Ariosto. Della Gierusalemme istessa, e dell' Amadigi del Tasso Padre. ... In Mantoua, Per Francesco Osana. M D LXXXV. 12°. a^8 A^{12} (-A1) B-I^{12} k^4 (-k4). pp. 5-219. ¶*Lacks the Della Cruscans' defense of Ariosto* (^{1}A-$^1E^{12}$). *Additional t.p.* (A2^r): Apologia del S. Torquato Tasso. ... *Same imprint. Half-titles:* (E4^r) Lettere diuerse scritte dal Signor Torquato Tasso. ... (G10^v) Parere del Signor Francesco Patrici, in difesa dell'Ariosto (H12^r) Difese dell'Orlando furioso ... fatte dal S. Horatio Ariosto. [62

-- -- In Ferrara, Appresso Giulio Cesare Cagnacini, et Fratelli. 1585. (*Colophon.*) 8°. $+^8$ A-G^8 A-O^8 P^2. [63

-- -- In Ferrara Ad instãza di G. Vasalini ... 1586. (... Appresso Vittorio Baldini ...) 8°. ¶^{8} A-V^8 X^4. pp. 2-227. [64

-- Canzone ... nella creatione del ... Papa Gregorio XIIII. ... In Roma, Nella Stamperia di Vincenzo Accolti ... M. D. LXXXXI. 4°. A^8 (-A8, *presumably blank*). [65

-- Dialogo dell'imprese ... Nella Stamperia dello Stigliola In Napoli, Ad instantia di Paolo Venturini. (*Colophon.*) 4°. π^2 A-I^4. [66

-- Discorsi ... Dell'arte poetica; et in particolare del Poema Heroico. Et insieme il primo libro delle lettere [poetiche] ... In Venetia, MDLXXXVII. Ad instanza di Giulio Vassalini Libraro à Ferrara. 4°. $+^4$ A-Dd^4. ff. 1-108. [67

-- Discorsi del poema heroico ... Nella Stamperia dello Stigliola In Napoli, Ad instantia di Paolo Venturini [c. 1594]. (*Colophon.*) 4°. a^4 A-X^4 Y^6. pp. 1-179. [68

-- Discorso della virtu feminile, e donnesca ... In Venetia, Appresso Bernardo Giunti, e fratelli. M D LXXXII. 4°. A-B^4. ff. 2-8. [69

-- Discorso della virtù heroica, et della charità ... In Venetia, Appresso Bernardo Giunti, e fratelli. M D LXXXII. 4°. A-B^4 C^2. ff. 2-10. [70

-- Il forno, ouero della nobiltà dialogo ... In Vicenza, Appresso Perin libraro, & Georgio Greco campagni. M D LXXXI. 4°. a^4 A-L^4 M^6. ff. 1-49. [71

-- -- Il forno della nobilta ... In Ferrara, Appresso Vittorio Baldini. M. D. LXXXII. (*Colophon.*) 12°. A-E^{12}. pp. 3-118. ¶*Identical with sigg.* ^{2}A-^{2}E *of* T54 *except for the substitution of a t.p. for the half-title.* [72

-- -- Il forno, Ouero della nobiltà ... In Vinetia, M D XXCIII. Presso Aldo. 12°. A-H^{12}. pp. 8-171. [73

-- Di Gierusalemme conquistata ... libri XXIIII. ... In Roma, M. D. XCIII. Presso à Guglielmo Facciotti. ... 4°. $*^6$ A-Mm^4 Nn^6. pp. 2-290. [74

-- -- In Pauia M. D. XCIV. Appresso Andrea Viano. ... Ad instanza de Antonio de gli Antonij. (*Colophon.*) 4°. A^4 A^4 B-V^8 X^{10}. pp. 1-303. [75

-- -- In Parigi, Appresso Abel l'Angelieri ... M.D. LCXV. [= 1595.] 12°. $ã^{12}$ A-Qq^{12} (-Qq12, *blank*). ff. 2-361. [76

-- Gerusalemme liberata ... Aggiunti ... gli Argomenti del Sig. Oratio Ariosti. In Casalmaggiore. CIƆ IƆ LXXXI. Appresso Antonio Canacci, & Erasmo Viotti. (*Colophon.*) 4°. $+^8$ A-Q^8. pp. 1-254. [77

-- -- In Lione, Appresso Alessandro Marsilij. M.D.LXXXI. (... Nella stamperia di Petro Roussin. ...) 16°. A-Tt^8. ff. 2-333. [78

-- -- Gierusalemme liberata ... Tratta dal vero Originale ... In Ferrara 1581. (... Per Vittorio Baldinj. ...) 4°. $+^4$ A^8 B-DD^4. pp. 1-208. [79

-- -- Il Goffredo ... In Venetia, Appresso Gratioso Perchacino M.D.LXXXI. 4°. $*^8$ $**^4$ A-P^8 Q^4. ff. 1-118. [80

-- -- La Gierusalemme liberata, ouero il Goffredo ... In Parma. Nella Stamperia d'Erasmo Viotto. ... M. D. LXXXI. 4°. $*^4$ A-R^8 S^6. pp. 1-242. [81

-- -- Gierusalemme liberata ... In Ferrara, Appresso Domenico Mammarelli, e Giulio Cesare Cagnacini, 1582. (*Colophon.*) 12°. $+^{12}$ A-Aa^{12} Bb^6. pp. 1-376. [82

-- -- [1] Il Goffredo ... Con l'aggiunta de' cinque Canti del Sig. Camillo Camilli. In Venetia, presso Francesco de' Franceschi Senese 1583 4°. $*^8$ $**^4$ A-Q^8. ff. 2-115. [2] I cinque canti ... *Same imprint.* $*^4$ A-G^4 H^2 (-H2, *presumably blank*). ff. 1-29. [83

-- -- Gierusalemme liberata ... In Mantoua, Per Francesco Osanna. M.D.LXXXIIII. (*Colophon.*) 4°. $*^8$ A-O^8 P^6. pp. 1-236. [84

-- -- [1] Il Goffredo ... In Vinegia, Presso Altobello Salicato. 1585. ... 4°. $\dagger^{10}$ A-Q^8. ff. 2-127. [2] Cinque canti ... *Same imprint.* A-D^8. ff. 2-32. [85

-- -- [1] In Vinegia, Presso Altobello Salicato, 1588. ... 12°. $\dagger^{12}$ A-Bb^{12}. pp. 1-576. [2] Cinque canti ... *Same imprint.* A-F^{12}. pp. 3-143. [86

-- -- [1] In Vinegia, Presso Altobello Salicato, 1589. ... 4°. $\dagger^{10}$ A-Q^8. ff. 2-127. [2] Cinque canti ... In Vinegia, Presso Altobello Salicato, MDLXXXVIII. ... A-D^8. ff. 2-42. [87

-- -- [1] In Vinegia, Presso Altobello Salicato. M D XC. 12°. $\dagger^{12}$ A-Bb^{12}. pp. 1-576. [2] Cinque canti ... *Same imprint.* A-F^{12}. pp. 3-143. [88

-- -- La Gierusalemme liberata ... Con le Figure di Bernardo Castello, & le Annotationi di Scipio Gentili, e di Giulio Guastauini. In Genoua. M.D.LXXXX. (... Appresso Girolamo Bartoli. ...) 4°.)(^{6} A-Q^8 A-D^8 E^4 A-B^8 C^4 $♣^4$. pp. 2-255, 1-71, 2-40. [89

-- -- [1] Goffredo ... In Vinegia, Presso Altobello Salicato. M D XCIII. ... 4°. $*^{10}$ A-Q^8. ff. 2-127. [2] Cinque canti ... *Same imprint.* A-D^8. ff. 2-42. [90

-- -- [1] In Vinegia, MDC. Presso gli Heredi di Francesco de' Franceschi. 4°. $\dagger^{10}$ A-Q^8. *Engraved ll. inserted after* †10, A6, B3, B8, C5, D3, E1, E8, F5, G3, G8, H5, I3, I8, K6, L2, L6, M4, N2, O2. ff. 2-127. [2] Cinque canti ... *Same imprint.* A-D^8. ff. 2-32. [91

-- -- Godfrey of Bulloigne, or The Recouerie of Ierusalem. Done into English Heroicall verse, by Edward Fairefax Gent. Imprinted at London by Ar. Hatfield, for I. Iaggard and M. Lownes. 1600 (*Colophon.*) fol. A^4 B-Kk^6 Ll^4. pp. 1-392. *S.T.C.* 23698. (Furness.) [92

-- -- *Another copy.* [93

-- -- Quatre chants de la Hierusalem de Torquato Tasso. Par Pierre de-Brach, Sieur de la Motte Montussan. ... A Paris, Chez Abel l'Angelier ... M. D. XCVI. 8°. $\bar{a}^{4+1}$ A-M^8. ff. 2-96. [94

-- -- La Hierusalem du Sieur Torquato Tasso. Renduë Françoise par Blaise de Vignere Bourbonnois. A Paris, Chez Abel l'Angelier ... cIↄ. Iↄ. XCIX. ... 8°. $\bar{a}^8$ $\bar{a}^8$ (-ā1) $\bar{e}^2$ A-Ss^8 Tt^2. pp. 1-658. [95

-- -- Scipii Gentilis Solymeidos libri duo priores de Torquati Tassi Italicis expressi. Venetiis, Apud Altobellum Salicatium, 1585. ... 4°. A-F^4 G^2. ff. 5-26. [96

-- -- Ierusalem libertada, Poema heroyco ... Traduzido ... en Castellana por Iuan Sedeño ... En Madrid por Pedro Madrigal. 1587. A costa de Esteuan y Francisco Bogia. (*Colophon.*) 8°. $\dagger^8$ A-Xx^8 Yy^6. ff. 1-341. ¶†1 *defective.* [97

-- Il Gonzaga secondo, ouero del giuoco, dialogo ... In Venetia, Appresso Bernardo Giunti, e fratelli. M D LXXXII. 4°. A-E^4. ff. 2-20. [98

-- -- *Another copy.* [99

-- [1] Delle lettere familiari del Sig. Torquato Tasso, ... libro primo. ... In Bergamo, MDLXXXVIII. Per Comino Ventura, e Compagni. 4°. a^4 b^2 A-Hh^4. ff. 1-124. [2] ... libro secondo. ... In Bergamo, Per Comino Ventura. M D LXXXVIII. (*Colophon.*) a^4 A-Dd^4 (-Dd4, *presumably blank*). ff. 1-107. [100

-- Il messaggiero dialogo ... In Venetia Appresso Bernardo Giunti, e fratelli. M D LXXXII. 4°. π^2 A-I^4. ff. 1-36. [101

-- Il re Torrismondo tragedia ... In Bergamo, MDLXXXVII. Per Comino Ventura, & Compagni. 4°. A^4 A-T^4 V^6 (-V3, V4). ff. 1-82. [102

-- -- In Vinegia, M D LXXXVII. Per Girolamo Polo. 8°. A-H^8. ff. 2-63. [103

-- -- In Verona, Appresso Girolamo Discepolo, 1587. Ad instantia di Marc'Antonio Palazzolo. 8°. a^8 A-G^8. ff. 1-56. [104

-- Il rimanente delle rime nuoue ... In Ferrara per Vittorio Baldini ... 1587. 12°. A-C^{12} D^{6}. pp. 3-84. [105

-- Delle rime ... parte prima ... In Vinegia, [Presso Aldo,] M D XXCII. 12°. $*^{12}$ A-V^{12} (*lacking all after G5*). pp. 2-153 *present*. [106

-- -- [1] Delle rime ... parte prima. ... In Brescia, Appresso Pietro Maria Marchetti. M.D.XCII. ... (*Colophon.*) 8°. $\dagger^{4}$ (-†8, *blank*) A-X^{8} Y^{4}. pp. 1-341. [2] ... parte seconda. ... In Brescia, Appresso Pietro Maria Marchetti. 1593. (*Colophon.*) $\dagger^{4}$ A-M^{8} N^{4}. pp. 1-194. [107

-- -- *Another copy of the first part* (-Y4, *blank*). [108

-- Il Rinaldo ... In Vinegia M D LXX. Appresso Francesco de'Franceschi Sanese. (*Colophon.*) 4°. A^{4} B-G^{8} H^{2}. pp. 1-100. [109

-- Risposta ... al discorso del Sig. Oratio Lombardelli Intorno à i contrasti, che si fanno sopra la Gierusalemme liberata. In Ferrara Per Vittorio Baldini. ... 1586. 8°. A-B^{8}. pp. 3-31. [110

-- -- Parere ... Sopra il discorso del Signor Horatio Lombardello ... In Mantoua, per Francesco Osanna ... M D LXXXVI. 12°. A^{12} B^{6}. pp. 6-33. [111

-- Risposta ... alla lettera di Bastian Rossi, academico della Crusca, in difesa del suo dialogo del Piacere Honesto, et detta lettera. Et vn discorso del medesimo Tasso, sopra il parere fatto del Sig. Franc. Patricio, in difesa di Lodouico Ariosto. ... In Ferrara, Nella Stamperia di Vittorio Baldini. Ad instanza di Giulio Vassalini. 1585. 8°. $*^{8}$ A-G^{8} H^{4}. pp. 1-117. [112

-- Scielta delle rime ... Prima, e Seconda Parte. ... In Ferrara, Appresso Domenico Mammarelli, e Giulio Cesare Cagnacini Compagni. 1582. (... Nella Stamperia delli Heredi di Francesco di Rossi.) 8°. $*^{8}$ A-F^{8} A-F^{8}. pp. 2-95, 1-93. [113

-- -- In Ferrara, Per Vittorio Baldini. 1582. (*Colophon.*) 4°. $*^{4}$ A-M^{4} N^{2} A-L^{4} M^{4+1}. pp. 1-95, 1-93. [114

-- Il secretario ... In Ferrara, Appresso Giulio Cesare Cagnacini, & Fratelli. M.D.LXXXVII. (*Colophon.*) 8°. A-C^{8} (-C8, *presumably blank*). pp. 1-39. [115

-- -- [1] Il secretario et il primo volume, delle lettere famigliari ... In Venetia, Appresso Giacomo Vincenzi. M D LXXXVIII. (*Colophon.*) 8°. a^{8} A-Q^{8} (-Q8, *blank*). pp. 1-247. [2] Il secondo volume delle lettere familiari ... In Venetia Appresso Giacomo Vincenzi. M. D. LXXXIX. A^{8} A-L^{8}. pp. 2-174. [116

-- -- In Vinegia, M D XCVI. Presso Altobello Salicato. [1] (*Colophon.*) 8°. A^{8} A-P^{8} Q^{4}. pp. 1-247. [2] A^{4} A-L^{8}. pp. 1-174. [117

TATTI, GIOVANNI. Della agricoltura ... libri cinque. ... In Venetia, appresso F. Sansouino, et compagni. MDLX. (*Colophon.*) 4°. $*^{4}$ A-3A^{4}. ff. 1-187. [118

TAULER, JOHANN. Historia et enarratio vitae ... Quæ pariter multas institutiones, doctrinas, cōcionesq; complectitur ... 8°. A-Tt^{8} Vu^{4}. ff. 2-337. (Lea.) [119

TEGLIACCI, STEFANO. Oratio habita in decima Sessione [concilii Lateranensis] Die Quarta Maii. M.D.XV. per ... Stephanum Archiepm Patraceñ. [Romae, Marcellus Silber, 1515.] 4°. A-C^{4}. (Lea.) [120

TEIXEIRA, JOSÉ. Exegesis genealogica, sive explicatio arboris gentilitiæ ... Galliarum Regis Henrici ... IIII. ... Lugduni Batavorum, Ex officina Plantiniana, Apud Franciscum Raphelengium. cIɔ. Iɔ. XCII. 4°. *-$**^{4}$ A-Aa^{4}. pp. 1-192. ¶*Lacks 3 terminal leaves found in some copies.* [121

TEJEDA, GASPAR DE. Estilo de escreuir cartas ... Compuesto por Gaspar de Texeda ... 1549. (Fue impresso, enla ... Villa de Valladolid. A costa y en casa de Sebastiā Martinez ... Acabose a veynte y dos dias del mes Nouiembre ...) 8°. B.L. A-Y^{8}. ff. jx-clxxvj. [122

TELESIO, ANTONIO. Antonii Thylesii Consentini in odas Horatii Flacci auspicia ad iuuentutem Romanam. [Romae, Franciscus Minitius Calvus, c. 1525.] 4°. A^{4} B^{6}. [123

TELESIO

-- Antonii Thylesii Consentini poemata. ... (Romæ in ædibus F. Minitii Calui Anno M.DXXIIII. Mense Maio.) 4°. A-H⁴. [124

TELESIO, BERNARDINO. Bernardini Telesii Consentini de rerum natura iuxta propria principia. Libri IX. ... Neapoli Apud Horatium Saluianum. M. D. LXXXVI. ... fol. π^1 $§^4$ $†^2$ A-Ii^6 Kk-Ll^4. pp. 1-400. [125

TEMPO, ANTONIO DE. Antonius de Tempo de Ritimis vulgaribus. ... (Impressa Venetijs per Simonē de Luere. 20. Iunij. 1509. ...) 8°. B.L. a-l^4. ff. 2-44. [126

TENGLER, ULRICH. Der neũ Layenspiegel Von rechtmässigen ordnungen in Burgerlichen vnd peinlichñ Regimenten. Mit Additõn. (Volbracht ... In der ... Satt [*sic*] Augspurg ... von Maister Hansen Othmar ... Durch ... Costen ... johann Ryñman von ðringen ... vollendet in vigilia Corporis Christi des jars ... Fünfzehenhundert/ vñ im aylften jar.) 4°. ☞^{8} ¢^{4} $§^6$ A-$V^{8.6}$ W-$Z^{8.6}$ a-$d^{8.6}$ e^6 f^4 g-$l^{8.6}$. ff. i-cclviii. (Lea.) [127

-- -- Layenspiegel. .... M. D. XXXVI. (Getruckt zů Strassburg/ durch Iohannem Albrecht/ am .iij. tag des Hornungs ...) fol. ¢^{6} A-Y^6 (-Y6, *presumably blank*). ff. I-CXXVIII.[128

TENURES. The olde. Tenures. (Imprinted at London ... by Wyllyam Myddylton [c. 1540] ...) 8°. B.L. A-B^8. *S.T.C.* 23884. (Biddle.) [129

TEODORO DA SUIGO. Confessionario ... (Impresso in Milano per Iohanne Angelo Scinzenzeler. ... M.cccccx. Adi .xx. de Marzo.) 8°. B.L. A-I^8. (Lea.) [130

-- -- (Impresso in Milano per Zanoto da Castiono adi .viij. de Agosto ... M.ccccc.xiiij.) 8°. B.L. A-G^8 H^6. (Lea.) [131

TERENTIANUS MAURUS. Terentiani Mauri Niliacae ... de literis, syllabis, pedibus et metris, tractatus ... Nicolao Brissæo Montiuillario commentatore & emendatore. ... Parisiis Apud Simonem Colinæum 1531 (... primo, mense Octobri.) 4°. a^8 ✠^{2} b-p^8 q^6. ff. 1-117. [132

TERENTIUS AFER, PUBLIUS. Pub. Terentij Comici ... sex ... fabule ... in officina Melchiaris Lotteri ... impresse. ... (Lipsi ... Mense Iunio, Anno, M,D,XII,) fol. A-S^6. [133

-- -- P. Terēti⁹ ... restitutus Cum elucubratiũculis Petri Marsi & adnotatiõibus ... Pauli Malleoli ... exornatus. ... M.D.XIIII. (Per Ioannē prüs ... Argentineñ. ... stanneis caracteribus mandatæ: In fine Augusti ...) 4°. a-b^8 c-$z^{4.4.8}$ A-B^4 C^8 D^4 E^8. ff. I-CXLVI. [134

-- -- Habes in hoc enchiridio ... P. Terentii comoedias, ex Des. Erasmi & Io. Riuii castigationibus & annotationibus ... Des. Eras. in genera carminum annotationes & ex eiusdem Chiliadibus adagia & sententiæ omnes explicate, quibuscũq; aut vsus est aut manifeste allusit Terentius. ... Argumenta Donati, P. Malleoli & Christ. Hegen. ... Petri Marsi in omnes fabulas ... commentarii ... Coloniae excudebat Io. Prael. M.D.XXXIIII. Mense Martio. 12°. A-$Tt^{8.4}$. pp. 2-392. [135

-- -- P. Terentii comoediæ sex, tum ex Donati cõmentariis, tum ex optimorum ... exēplarium collatione ... emendatæ. Aelii Donati ... commentarii ... Calphurnii in tertiam Comoediam ... interpretatio. ... carminũ genera, ... opera Des. Erasmi Roterodami ... Parisiis. Ex officina Roberti Stephani. M.D.XXXVI. (... Nonis Aprilis.) fol. a-z^8 (-v4-5) A^8 B^6 (-B6, *blank*). pp. 16-378. [136

-- -- Habes hic amice lector P. Terentii comoedias, vna cum scholiis ex Donati, Asperi, et Cornuti commentariis decerptis ... Carminum genera ... studio & opera Des. Erasmi Roterodami ... Basileae, in officina Frobeniana anno M. D. XXXVIII (... per Hieronymum Frobenium, & Nicolaum Episcopium, Mense Martio ...) fol. α^6 β^8 a-z^6 A-I^6 K^8 (-K2-7). pp. 2-386 *present*. [137

-- -- P. Terentii Afri comoediae omnes, Donati, Asperi, Cornuti, Ioan. Calphurnii ... commentariis illustratæ, ... vnà cum argumentis Phil. Melan. D. Erasmi Roter. de metris Comicis ... Antuerpiae, apud Ioan. Steelsium ... M. D. XXXIX. (Typis Ioan. Graphei.) 8°. *^{8} A-$3I^8$. ff. 2-419. [138

-- -- Pub. Terentii Aphri comoediae sex ex Donati commentariis ... restitutæ. ... Venetiis ex officina Erasmiana, apud Vincentium Valgrisium. MDXLVI. 8°. A-V^8. ff. 2-159. [139

-- -- P. Terentii Afri ... comediae ... Elenchum interpretum ... Parisiis, Apud Ioannem de Roigny ... 1552. ... (... excudebat Benedictus Preuotius ... decimoseptimo Calendas Decembris, Anno 1551.) fol. a^{6+1} $b-z^6$ $A-YY^6$. pp. 3-776. [140

-- -- P. Terentii Afri ... comoediae omnes. Cum ... commentariis Aelii Donati, Guidonis Iuuenalis Cenomani, Petri Marsi ... Stephani Doleti ... Ioannis Calphurnii Brixiensis ... D. Erasmi Roterodami annotationes in genera carminum ... Philippi Melanchthonis ... argumenta. Antonii Goueani Epistola ... de castigatione harum comoediarum. ... Barptolomæi Latomi ... Argumenta ... Ioãnis Riuij Attendoriensis Castigationes ... Henrici Loriti Glareani ... iudicium. ... Venetiis Apud Bartholomæum Cæsanum. Anno M. D. LIII. (*Colophon.*) fol. $*^6$ $**^8$ $A-Qq^6$ (-Qq6, *presumably blank*). ff. 1-238. [141

-- -- Il Terentio Latino. Comentato in lingua Toscana ... Da Giouanni Fabrini da Fighine, Fiorentino. ... In Venetia, Appresso Giambattista, & Marchiò Sessa, & fratelli. ... (... M. D. LXV.) 4°. $A-Dd^8$ Ee^6 $Kk-Zz^4$ $AA-FF^4$ GG^2. pp. 1-438. [142

-- -- Terence in English. Fabulae comici ... poetæ Terentii omnes Anglicæ factae ... industria R. B. ... Cantabrigiæ ex officina Iohannis Legat. 1598. 8°. $¶^4$ $A-Q^8$ R^4 $S-Ff^8$ G^2. pp. 1-[455]. *S.T.C.* 23890. ¶*Translator: Richard Bernard.* (Furness.) [143

-- -- Les sis comedies de Terence ... mises en Françoys ... A Anuers. Chez Iean VVaesberghe ... (... M.D.LXVI.) 8°. A^4 $B-Oo^8$ Pp^4 (-Pp4, *presumably blank*). ff. 2-273. ¶*Translator: Jean Bourlier.* [144

-- -- Les six comedies de Terence, corrigees par M. Ant. de Muret. ... *Latin & French.* A Paris, Chez Iaques Nicole ... 1583. 16°. $\bar{a}^8$ $A-Zz^8$. ff. 1-367. [145

-- -- Comedie Di Terentio nuouamente di latino in volgare tradotte. ... M. D. XXXIII. (Stampate in Venetia per ... Bernardino Vidale, ad instantia di M. Iacob da Borgofrancho, del mese di Luglio ...) 8°. $a-x^8$ y^4. ff. 2-171. [146

-- -- M. D. XXXVIII. (Stampate in Venetia per M. Iacob da Borgofrancho, Pauese, del mese di Marzo. ...) 8°. $a-x^8$. ff. 2-168. [147

-- -- Le comedie di Terentio uolgari ... In Vinegia, M. D. XLVI. (... In casa de' figliuoli di Aldo.) 8°. $A-X^8$. ff. 2-168. [148

-- -- Las seys comedias de Terentio ... traduzidas en Castellano por Pedro Simon Abril natural de Alcaraz. ... *Latin and Spanish.* Impresso en Alcala, Por Iuan Gracian. Año de 1583. (*Colophon.*) 8°. $¶^8$ $A-Vv^8$. ff. 3-344. [149

-- Andria Des Terentii Comoedia/ Deutsch gemacht/ Vnd in Reim verfasset Durch M. Henricum Ham ... Wittemberg. Gedruckt bey Simon Gronenberg. M.D.[L]XXXV. 8°. $A-D^8$. [150

-- Eunuchus Des poeten P. Terentij andere Comoedia/ Deutsch gemacht/ vnd in Reim verfasset durch M. Iosuam Ponerum ... Mit einer vorrede M. Stephani Riccii des Eldern. ... 8°. $A-E^8$ F^4 (-F4). ¶A6r: Zeugnis D. Martini Lutheri/ aus der Auslegunge vber den 101 Psalm genomen/ was von dieser Comoedia ... zu halten sey. *Preface dated* 1586. [151

-- -- Eunuco. Comedia di Terentio Intitulata l'Eunuco, dal Latino al Volgare tradotta, ... & Nuouamente stampata del MDXXXII. (Stampata in Vinegia per Nicolo d'Aristotile detto Zoppino del mese di Luio. ...) 8°. $A-D^8$ E^4. ff. 2-36. [152

-- Locutioni di Terentio: Ouero, modi famigliari di dire: ... Scielti da Aldo Mannucci. ... In Vinetia, [Aldine press,] M D LXXXV. 8°. $a-c^8$ d^4 $A-O^8$ $Aa-Ee^8$. pp. 2-220. [153

-- Flovvers or eloquent Phrases of the Latine speech, gathered out of al the sixe Comedies of Terence. VVherof those of the first thre were selected by Nicolas Vdall. And those of the latter three novv to them annexed by I. Higgins ... Imprinted at London ... by Thomas Marshe. 1581 ... 8°. B.L. A^4 $A-Cc^8$ Dd^2. *S.T.C.* 23903. (Furness.) [154

TERRACINA, LAURA. Discorso sopra tutti li primi canti d'Orlando furioso ... In Vinetia appresso Gabriel Giolito di Ferrarii MDL. (*Colophon.*) 8°. $A-K^8$ L^4 (-L4, *presumably blank*). ff. 2-83. ¶*In verse.* [155

-- -- Discorso sopra il principio di tutti i canti d'Orlando furioso ... ricorretto. In Vinegia appresso Gabriel Giolito de Ferrari e fratelli MDLI. (*Colophon.*) 8°. $A-L^8$. ff. 2-88. [156

-- -- In Vinegia, Appresso Domenico Farri. 1567 8°. $A-L^8$. ff. 5-88. [157

-- Quinte rime ... In Vinegia appresso Gio. Andrea Valuassorio detto Guadagnino. MDLII. 8°. $A-I^8$. ff. 2-69. [158

-- Rime ... In V[i]negia appresso Gabriel Giolito de' Ferrari. M D LX. 8°. A-G^8. ff. 3-56. ¶G2^v: Rime d'alcuni ... ingegni in lode della S. Laura Terracina. [159

TERTULLIANUS, QUINTUS SEPTIMIUS FLORENS. Opera Q. Septimii Florentis Tertulliani ... per Beatum Rhenanum Selestadiensem è tenebris eruta ... Basileae, an. M. D. XXVIII. mense Martio. (... in officina Frobeniana ...) fol. AA^6 a-b^6 BB^4 a-z^6 A-Ll^6 Mm^4. pp. 1-692. ¶a-b^6, *index and colophon, intended to follow* Mm4. [160

-- Q. Septimii Florentis Tertulliani ... præscriptiones aduersus Hæreses omnes. Des ... Tertulliani/ ... verlegung aller Ketzereyen. ... Sampt einer Apologi vnnd schutzschrifft ... Alles durch Laurentium Albertum Francum. .. Getruckt zů Dilingen durch Sebaldum Mayer. M. D. LXXII. 4°. A-V^4 X^2. ff. 1-73. [161

TESAURO, ANTONINO. Nouae decisiones sacri Senatus Pedemontani ... Venetiis, M. D. XCI. Apud Hieronymum Polum. 4°. a-c^8 d^4 A-Pp^8 Qq^4 *-$**^8$. ff. 1-308. (Lea.) [162

TESTAMENTUM. Testamentum duodecim patriarcharum, filiorum Iacob, per Robertum Lincolinensem Episcopum, è Græco in Latinum uersum. ... Iuliani Pomerii ... contra Iudæos libri tres. ... Haganoæ, per Iohannem Secerium Anno M. D. XXXII. Mense Februario. 8°. A-Q^8 R^4 (-R4). [163

-- Testament vnnd Abgschrifft der zwölff Patriarchen der Sünen Iacobs ... (Getruckt in ... Bern/ durch Mathiam Apiarium. In kosten vnnd verlegũg Iacobi Ciriaci säligen Erben. Im 1554. Jar.) 12°. A-V^6. [164

TEUTLEBEN, VALENTIN VON. Apologia: et responsio ... Valentini Episcopi Hildesemeñ. aduersus confictas calũnias Erici, & Henrici Ducum Brũsuiceñ. ... Romae M. D. XL. (Antonius Bladus Asulanus Excudebat.) 4°. A-I^4 K^6. [165

TEUTONIC KNIGHTS. Kurtze vnd einfeltige Beschreibung/ aller Hohemeister Deutsches Ordens S. Mariæ/ des Hospitals zu Ierusalem/ ꝛc. ... Gedruckt zu Königsperg in Preussen bey Georgen Osterbergern. (... 1584.) 4°. Aa-Nn^4. [166

THELOALL, SIMON. Le digest des Briefes originals ... Londini. In Ædibus Richardi Tottelli. Octobris decimo quarto. 1579. ... (*Colophon.*) 8°. $¶^8$ A-$3G^8$. ff. 1-424. *S.T.C.* 23934. (Biddle.) [167

-- -- *Another copy* (-¶4). (Lea.) [168

THEMISTIUS. Libri paraphraseos Themistii ... in Aristotelis commentarios De Memoria & Reminiscentia. De Somno & Vigilia. De Insomnijs. De Diuinatione per Somnium. Hermolao Barbaro Patritio Veneto Interprete. Basileae excudebat Henricus Petrus, mense Martio, Anno M D. XXX. (*Colophon.*) 8°. A-F^8. [169

THEOCRITUS. θεοκριτου ειδυλλια. Theocriti Edyllia. Louanii apud Theodoricũ Martinũ Alostẽsem. An. M.D.XXVIII. 4°. A-Q^4. [170

-- -- [1] θεοκριτου ειδυλλια ... Theocriti idyllia, Hoc est, parua Poëmata XXXVI. Eiusdem Epigrammata XIX. Eiusdem Bipennis, & Ala. Praeter haec et Latina versio Carmine ... reddita, per M. Eobanum Hessum, & Ioachimi Camerarij Scholia ... accessere. M. D. XLV. 8°. a-z^8 &^{8} aa^4. ff. 2-194. [2] Theocriti Syracusani eidyllia trigintasex, Latino carmine reddita ... Francofurti ex officina Petri Brubacchij. M.D.XLV. A-N^8 O^4. [171

-- -- *Another copy.* [172

-- -- M. D. LIII. 8°. a-z^8 &^{8} aa^4 A-N^8. ff. 5-194. ¶A1^r: Francofurti ex officina Petri Brubacchij. ... [173

-- -- Theocriti aliorumque Poetarum Idyllia. Eiusdem Epigrammata. Simmiæ Rhodii Ouum, Alæ, Securis, Fistula. Dosiadis ára. Omnia cum interpretatione Latina. In Virgilianas et Nas. imitationes Theocriti, Obseruationes H. Stephani. [Genevae,] Excudebat Henricus Stephanus, anno M. D. LXXIX. 16°. $*^8$ a-z^8 Aa-Ee^8 3a-$3m^8$. pp. 2-447, 1-128. [174

-- -- Theocriti Syracusani opera Latine à Ioanne Trimanino ... expressa ... (Venetiis per Ioan. Ant. de Nicolinis de Sabio. Sumptu uero D. Melchioris Sessæ. Anno D. MD XXXIX.) 8°. A-K^8. ff. 2-77. [175

THEODORETUS. Theodoriti Cyrensis episcopi de Curatione Gręcarum affectionum libri duodecim, Zenobio Acciaolo interprete. Parisiis In officina Henrici Stephani. 1519 ... (... mense Iulio ...) fol. a-o^8. ff. 2-112. [176

-- L'histoire de Theodorite ... Traduicte du Grec en Francoys, par D. M. Mathée. ... On les vend a Poictiers a l'enseigne du Pelican [par Jean & Enguilbert de Marnef] 1544 8°. ā^8 ē^4 a-z^8 A-D^8 E^4. ff. i-ccxx. [177

-- Θεοδωριτου επισκοπου Κυρου, λόγος ὄντως πάγχρυσος περί τῆς Αγάπης. Theodoriti episcopi Cyri, oratio ... de caritate siue dilectione. ... Græce simul & Latine recens edita. Interprete Gerardo Vossio. ... Romæ, in Ædibus Populi Romani, M D LXXX. 4°. a^4 A-G^4. pp. 1-51. [178

THEODOSIUS TRIPOLITA. Θεοδοσιου Τριπολίτου σφαιρικῶν βιβλία. γ. Theodosii Tripolitæ sphæricorum, libri tres ... Iidem latinè redditi per Ioannem Penam ... Parisiis, Apud Andream Wechelum ... 1558. ... 4°. ā^4 a-g^4 A-I^4. pp. 1-54, 2-68. [179

THEOGNIS. [1] Theognidis Megarensis sententiae cum versione Latina, ... VVitebergae excudebat Laurentius Schuenck. 1561. 8°. A-F^8. ff. 1-46. [2] Explicatio sententiarum Theognidis ... auctore ... Philippo Melanthone ... Collecta à Iohanne Maiore ... VVitebergae excudebat Laurentius Schuenck. 1560. (*Colophon.*) A-S^8 T^4. ff. 2-137. [180

THEOLOGIA DEUTSCH. Theologia Teutsch. Diss ist ein ... Bůchlein/ von rechtem verstandt/ Was Adam vnd Christ sey/ Vnd wie Adam in vns sterben/ vnd Christus erstehen soll. ... [Franckfurt a/M., David Schöffel,] 1555 12°. A-V$^{8.4}$ (-A2-3, V2). ¶S4 *misbound before* S3. [181

-- Theologia Germanica. ... Quomodo sit exuendus vetus homo, induendusq̃ue nouus. Ex Germanico translatus, Ioanne Theophilo interprete. Antuerpiae, Ex officina Christophori Plantini. 1558. ... 16°. A-H^8 (-H7-8, *blank*). pp. 3-124. [182

THEOPHRASTUS. Theophrasti de causis plantarum libri VI. Theodoro Gaza interprete. Luteciæ, Ex officina Christiani VVechel. 1529 (... Idibus Nouēbris ...) 8°. **^{8} A-Z^8 Et^6. pp. 2-354. [182a

THEOPHYLACTUS. Theophylacti archiepiscopi Bulgariae, in quatuor Euangelia enarrationes ... Ioanne Oecolampadio interprete. [Basileae, Andreas Cratander,] Anno M. D. XXV. fol. α^8 a-z^6 A-M^6 N^8. ff. 2-217. [183

-- Theophylacti Bulgarorum archiepiscopi, In quatuor Euangelistas, in D. Pauli Epistolas, in minores aliquot Prophetas, ... enarrationes: Philippi Montani studio recognitæ & emendatæ. Eiusdem Theophylacti in Acta Apostolorum ... Explicationes, ... Laurentio Sifano I.C. interprete. ... Basileæ, ex officina Heruagiana, per Eusebium Episcopium, ... M. D. LXX. (... Mense Septembri.) fol. α^4 a-z^6 A-D^6 E^4 F-Z^6 Aa-Rr^6 Ss^4 Tt-Zz^6 AA^6 BB^4 CC^6 DD^4 (*wanting*) EE^6. pp. 1-824. (Lea.) [184

THETI, CARLO. [1] Discorsi delle fortificationi ... In Venetia, M. D. LXXXIX. Appresso Francesco de Franceschi Senese. fol. †^{2} A-L^2 M^6. pp. 1-47. [2] Discorsi delle fortificationi ... In Venetia, appresso Nicolo Moretti. M. D. LXXXVIII. χ^2 A-D^2 D-E^2 G^4 H-Q^8 R^4 S^2 T-V^8 X-Y^4 (-Y4) A-S^2. pp. 1-86, 1-70. ¶V3-8 *misbound after* X4. (Fine Arts.) [185

THEVENEAU, NICOLAS. Paraphrase aux lois municipalles, et coustumes du comté et pays de Poictou ... A Poitiers, Par Enguilbert de Marnef, & les Bouchetz, freres. 1565. 4°. *^{8} A-GG^8 HH^6. pp. 1-386. [186

THEVET, ANDRÉ. Les singularitez de la France Antarctique, autrement nommé Amerique ... A Paris, Chez les heritiers de Maurice de la Porte ... 1558. ... 4°. ā^8 a-z^4 A-T^4. ff. 1-166. ¶*Sig.* ā *bound in the order 1, 2, 7, 8, 5, 6, 3, 4.* [187

-- -- A Anuers, De l'imprimerie de Christophle Plantin ... 1558. ... 8°. A-X^8 Y^4. ff. 1-163. [188

-- -- The new found vvorlde, or Antarctike ... written in the French tong, by ... Andrevve Theuet ... Imprinted at London, by Henrie Bynneman, for Thomas Hacket. ... (... 1568.) 4°. B.L. *^{4} A^4 B-S^8 T^4. ff. 2-138. *S.T.C.* 23950. [189

-- -- Historia dell' India America detta altramente Francia antartica, di M. Andrea Teuet; tradotta di Francese ... da M. Giuseppe Horologgi. ... In Vinegia appresso Gabriel Giolito de' Ferrari. M D LXI. (*Colophon.*) 8°. *-**^{8} A-Z^8 (-Z8, *presumably blank*). pp. 1-363. [190

-- -- In Venetia appresso i Gioliti. M D LXXXIIII. (*Colophon.*) *Same collation* (+ Z8) *and pagination.* [191

THOMA, FRANZ. Sponsa Christi: Das ist Warhaftige/ gründliche erweisung/ wie das wort/ oder nam Catholisch, seinem rechten verstand nach/ eine aigentliche ... nota ... sey/ der ... Römischen ... Kirchen ... Gedruckt zu München/ bey Adam Berg. ... M. D. LXXXVI. 4°. A-G^4. [192

THOMAS AQUINAS, S. [... Thome Aquinatis, Prima Secunde ... Thome a Vio ... commentarionibus illustrata ...] fol. B.L. ✣-3✣^{8} (-✣1) a-x^8 y^6. ff. 1-173. ¶*Extract from* Opera seu summa theologiae *published at Lyons in 1552.* [193

-- Doi aurei opuscoli o vero tractati ... El primo del modo de la ɔfessione ⁊ purita de consciẽtia. El secundo de li diuini costumi. Dechiarati ... del Reuerendo ... Guasparre da Perosia ... (S[t]ampati in ... Perusia: per Girolamo: figliolo del sopradicto Francesco cartholaio: ... Adi xiij. de Febraio. M.ccccc.x.) 4°. B.L. A-F^8. [194

-- Liber quattuor causarum. Beati Thome de Aquino ... (Anno ... Millesimo quingentesimo decimoseptimo Die vero .iiii. mensis Decembris.) 16°. B.L. a-b^8. [195

-- Ordo, ac series quinque nouorum indicum generalium. ... Augustae Taurinorum, Apud hæredes Nicolai Beuilaquæ. 1582. fol. a^8 B^8 c-o^8. (Lea.) [196

-- Diui Thomae Aquinatis ... secundum scriptum appellatum, Super quatuor libros Sententiarum ... Parisiis, Apud Gulielmum Chaudiere ... 1574. 8°. a-i^8 A-Zz^8 AA-3F^8 3G^4. ff. 1-616. (Lea.) [197

-- [Summa.] Antuerpiae, Ex officina Christophori Plantini ... M. D. LXXV. fol. [1] S. Thomae Aquinatis summa totius theologiae ... *^{10} A-V^8 X^6. pp. 1-332. [2] Prima secundae partis summae theologicae ... **^{4} a-x^8 (-x8, *presumably blank*). pp. 2-334. [3] Secunda secundae ... †^{6} Aa-Zz^8 aa-ii^8. pp. 1-524. [4] Tertia pars ... ††^{8} aA-vV^8 AA-PP^8 QQ^6. pp. 2-318, 1-249. [5] Aug. Hunnaei de sacramentis ecclesiae Christi axiomata ... (... tertio Nonas Iunias.) a-o^8. [198

THOMAS DE CELANO. Legenda dela Gloriosa Verzene Sancta Clara: Traducta de latino in ... vulgare. Cōposta per ... Sancto Bonauentura. (In Venetia ... per Simone de Luere. Adi. VII. Luio. M.D.XIII.) 4°. a-h^4 i^6 (-i6, *presumably blank*). ff. 2-37. [199

THOMAS GRAMMATICUS. Thomæ Grammatici Neapoli ... Allegationes ⁊ Consilia ... Eiusdem vota ... Venetiis M D XLII. (... Impressa in officina Comini de Tridino Impensis ... Petri de Dominicis mercatoris librorum Neapoli Mense Ianuario. ...) fol. B.L. π^8 A-I^6 K^4 L-P^6 Q^8. ff. 1-95. (Biddle.) [199a

THOMAS À KEMPIS. Of the Imitation of Christ ... made 170. yeeres since by one Thomas of Kempis ... translated ... by Thomas Rogers. ... At London Printed by Henrie Denham ... 1589. (*Colophon.*) 12°. A-O^{12}. pp. 1-277. *S.T.C.* 23978. [200

THOMAS MAGISTER. Θομᾶ τοῦ μαγίστρου ... ἐκλογαί ... Thome Magistri per alphabetum, hoc est elementorum ordinem attici eloquii, elegentie ... (... impressus per Zachariam Caliergi Cretensem ... ἐν ῥώμη ... Χιλιοστῷ φ ι ξ' [1517]. Μηνὸς μαρτιου ...) 8°. π^2 α-ω^4 Α-Θ^4 Ι^2. [201

THOU, CHRISTOPHE DE. Coustumes de la cité & ville de Rheims ... Redigées ... Par nous Christofle de Thou President, Barthelemy Faye, & Iacques Viole Conseillers du Roy ... A Rheims. Chez Iean de Foigny ... 1571. 4°. A-G^8 H^2. ff. 2-56. [202

-- V. ampliss. Christophori Thuani tumulus. ... Lutetiæ, Apud Mamertum Patissonium ..., in officina Rob. Stephani. M.D.LXXXIII. 4°. A-P^4. pp. 3-117. [203

THUCYDIDES. Θουκυδίδης μετα σχολιων ... Thucydides cum scholiis ... Accessit praeterea diligentia Ioachimi Camerarij ... unà cum annotationibus eius. ... Basileae ex officina Heruagiana anno M. D. XL. (*Colophon.*) fol. α*6 β*6 α6 b-z6 A-D6 E8 F10 (-F10, *presumably blank*). pp. 1-225, 1-177. [204

-- -- Θουκυδίδου τοῦ Ὀλόρου περὶ τοῦ Πελοποννησιακοῦ πολέμου βιβλία ὀκτώ. Thucydidis Olori filii de bello Peloponnesiaco libri octo. Iidem Latinè, ex interpretatione Laurentii Vallae, ab Henrico Stephano recognita. ... [Genevae,] Anno M. D. LXIIII. Excudebat Henricus Stephanus ... fol. *8 a-s8 t6 A-S6 T4. pp. 1-297, 1-216. [205

-- -- Thucydidis de bello Peloponnesiaco libri VIII. ... In hac secunda editione ... habes: Vitam Thucydidis ex Marcellino ...: eiusdem integræ Historiæ Chronologiam ... Adhuc ... Orationum ... Catalogum ... Francofurdi, Apud heredes Andreæ Wecheli, Claudium Marnium & Ioann. Aubrium. MDLXXXIX. 8°. ¶-¶¶8 A-Oo8. pp. 1-558. [206

-- -- Thucydidis Atheniensis de bello Peloponnesiaco libri octo; e Graeco sermone in Latinum noua interpretatione conuersi. Cum annotationibus ... Auctore Georgio Acacio Enenckel, L. Barone Hoheneccio. ... Tubingae, Apud Georgium Gruppenbachium. M. D. XCVI. 8°.):(-2):(8 (2):(8 + *folded leaf*) A-Zz8 (-Yy-Zz8). pp. 1-690. ¶*The missing pages of the index are replaced by four leaves, signed* r, *from the index of another book, probably* Aesopi Phrygis, et aliorum fabulae, *printed, according to the colophon on* r4r, *by Gryphius at Lyon in 1554.* [207

-- -- Lhistoire de Thucydide Athenien ... Translatee en langue Francoyse par feu Messire Claude de Seyssel ... (imprime a Paris en lhostel de maistre Josse Badius ... le dixiesme iour Daoust, Lan Milcinqcens vingtsept.) fol. ā8 ē8 a-z8 A-L8 M10. ff. I-CCLXXXI. [208

-- -- (... imprime a Paris [1530?].) fol. B.L. ā6 ē4 A-LL6. ff. i-C.xci. ¶*T.p. border of Egidius Gormontius.* LL5v: *device of François Regnault.* [209

-- -- A Paris, De l'imprimerie de Michel de Vascosan. M. D. LVIIII. ... (Acheué d'imprimer en Apuril. ...) fol. a6 a6 A-Rr6 Ss4. ff. 1-244. [210

-- -- Histoire de la guerre des Peloponnesiens et Atheniens ... Nouuellement traduicte de Grec en François: par Louys Iausaud, D'Vzez. [Genève,] Pour Iaques Chouet. ... 1600. 4°. ¶4 ¶¶2 3¶-4¶4 A-3Z4 a-c4. pp. I-XIIII, 1-551. [211

-- -- Gli otto libri di Thucydide ... Nuouamente dal Greco idioma, nella lingua Thoscana ... tradotto, per Francesco di Soldo Strozzi Fiorentino. ... In Venetia. Apresso Vincenzo Vaugris ... M. D. XLV. 8°. *8 **4 a-z8 A-Ii8. ff. 1-440. [212

-- -- Historia de Thucydides. ... Traduzida de lengua Griega en Castellana ... por ... Diego Gracian ... En Salamanca En casa de Iuan de Canoua. M. D. LXIII. (*Colophon.*) fol. ✠8 A-Bb8 Cc10 Dd-Ee6 (-Dd1). ff. j-ccx. [213

THURMAIR, JOHANN. ... Imp. Henrici quarti ... vita. Eiusdem epistolæ, inuentæ a Ioanne Auentino. ... Friderici ducis Saxonie. &c̄. epistole ad Ioannem Auentinum. Eiusdem principis capita rerum quas ipsi absoluit Auentinus. Ad eundem principem Auentini carmina. Auctores quidam quos Auentinus inuenit, & qui nondum impressi sunt. Sodalitatis literarie Boiorum carmina. ... (Excussum Augustæ Vindelicorū in sigismundi Grimm Medici & Marci Vuirsung officina, Mense Augusto. ... M.D.XVIII.) 4°. a-g6.4.4. [214

-- [1] ... Rudimenta gramaticae ... Ioannes Auentinus Thurinomarus edidit ... (Impressum Auguste in officina Milleriana. Impensis ... Erhardi Sampachs granatoris Vniuersitatis Angilostadensis. An. M.D.XVII. die 8 Ianuarij.) 4°. A4 B8 C-D4 E8 F4 G8 H-L4 M-T8.4 V-X4 Y6. [2] ... Encyclopedia orbisque doctrinarum ... Aa-Dd4 Ee6 χ2. [215

THURNEISSER ZUM THURN, LEONHARD. Archidoxa. Dorin der recht war Motus, Lauff vnd Gang ... der Planeten/ Gstirns/ vnd gantzen Firmaments Mutierung ... Gedruckt zu Berlin im Grawen Closter Anno 1575. (*Colophon.*) fol. ✤6)(2 A-K6 L2. ff. 1-60. ¶*In verse.* [216

-- Magna alchymia Dass ist ein Lehr vnd vnterweisung von den ... Naturen/ Arten vnd Eigenschafften/ allerhandt wunderlicher Erdtgeweschssen ... Item onomasticum ... Etliche ... Nomina ... Gedruckt in Cölln/ Durch Iohannem Gymnicum ... M.D.LXXXVII. fol. *2)(2 ()2 A-Nn2 χ1)(2 *present.* pp. 1-144. ¶*Lacks the* Onomasticum. *T.p. mounted. A reissue, with a new t.p., of works published in 1583.* (Smith.) [217

THURÓCZI, JÁNOS. Der hungern Chronica ... Im druck yetz new aussgangen. Anno 1534. (... verteutscht/ vnd also zusamen gebracht ... durch herr Hansen Haugen zum Freystein ... in druck verordnet auff kosten ... Hansen Matzkers Bürger in Wien. ...) fol. a-p4 q6. ff. 2-165. [218

-- -- Der Hungern Chronica ... Angefangen von jrem ersten Künig Athila/ vnnd volfüret biss auff Künig Ludwig/ so im M.D.xxvj. jar ... vmbkōmen ist. ... M.D.xxxvj. (Getruckt in ... Augspurg/ durch Philipp Vlhart. ...) 4°. A-X^4 (-X4, *presumably blank*). [219

THYRAEUS, PETRUS. ... Petri Thyraei Nouesiensis ... de Apparitionibus Spirituum tractatus duo ... Coloniae Agrippinae Ex Officina Mater. Cholini, sumptibus Gosuini Cholini. Anno M.D.C. 4°. (:)-2(:)^4 A-3P^4. pp. 1-486. (Lea.) [220

-- ... Petri Thyraei Nouesii ... de daemoniacis liber vnus ... Coloniae Agrippinae, Ex Officina Mater. Cholini, sumptibus Gosuini Cholini. Anno M. D. XCIIII. 4°. †^{4} A-Q^4 R^2. pp. 3-130. (Lea.) [221

-- -- Daemoniaci, Hoc est: de obsessis a spiritibus daemoniorum hominibus, liber vnus. ... Editio secunda ... Coloniae Agrippinae, Ex officina Mater. Cholini, sumptib⁹ Gosuini Cholini. Anno M. D. XCVIII. ... 4°. (:)^4 2(:)^2 A-Bb^4 Cc^2. pp. 3-207. [222

-- -- *Another copy*. (Lea.) [223

-- ... Petri Thyraei Nouesii ... de variis tam spirituum, quam viuorum hominum prodigiosis Apparitionibus, & nocturnis infestationibus libri tres ... Coloniae Agrippinae, Ex Officina Mater. Cholini, sumptibus Gosuini Cholini. Anno M. D. XCIIII. 4°. †-††^{4} A-T^4. pp. 1-159. (Lea.) [224

-- Loca infesta, Hoc est: de infestis, ob molestantes daemoniorum et defunctorum hominum spiritus, locis, liber vnus. ... Accessit eiusdem Libellus de Terriculamentis nocturnis ... Coloniae Agrippinae, Ex officina Mater. Cholini, sumptib⁹ Gosuini Cholini. Anno M.D.XCVIII. 4°. (:)-2(:)^4 A-Xx^4. pp. 1-352. [225

-- -- Lugduni, apud Ioannem Pillehotte ... M. D. XCIX. 8°. ā^8 ē^4 A-Ll^8. pp. 1-543. (Lea.) [226

TIBALDEO, ANTONIO. Opere del thebaldeo da Ferrara. Sonetti cclxxxiij Dialogo j Epistole iij Egloge iiij Desperata j Capitoli xix ... (Impresso nela ... citta di Venetia per Georgio de Rusconi Milanese. ... M.CCCCCI. A di .ii. Septembrio.) 4°. [A]^4 B-L^4. [227

-- Di M. Antonio Tibaldeo Ferrarese l'opere d'amore ... MDXXX. (Stampato in Vinegia per Nicolo di Aristotile detto Zoppino. ...) 8°. A-Q^8 (-Q8, *presumably blank*). [228

-- -- In Vinegia M. D. XLIIII. (... per Bartolomeo detto l'Imperador, e Francesco Vinetiano ...) 8°. A-R^8. ¶I5^v *defective*. [229

TILEMANN, FRIEDRICH. A. A. M. M. Discursus philologicus, de historicorum delectu ... VVitebergae, Imprimebat VVolfgangus Meisnerus, Sumptibus Clementis Bergeri ... 1597. 8°.)(^{8})(^{8} A-Cc^8. pp. 1-407. [230

TILMANN, GODEFROY. Allegoriae simul et tropologiae in locos vtriusque Testamēti selectiores iudicio collecte ... è monimentis vnius & triginta Authorum. ... Parisiis, Apud Sebastianum Niuellium ... 1574. 8°. ā^8 a-z^8 A-Z^8 &^{8} Aa-Zz^8 AA-LL^8. ff. 1-619. [231

TINNOLI, GIOVANNI. Ioannis Tinnoli Perusini præfatio In Priora Analytica Aristotelis ... Eiusdem quæstio, An propositio sit genus affirmationis, & negationis. (Perusiae, apud Andream Brixianum, M. D. LXVII.) 8°. *^{4} A-D^8 E^4. ff. 1-34. [232

TIO, ANGELO. ... Angelus Thyus Hydruntinus. De subiecto logices ... Patauii Bernardinus de Bindonis Mediolanensis & Iacobus Fabrianus socii excudebant ... M. D. XLVII. (Venetijs sumptibus .D. Angeli Titij ... Mense Maio) fol. A-G^6. ff. 1-36. [233

TIRABOSCHI, LUCREZIO. Oratio habita ad patres in Concilio Tridentino. Quarta Dominica Quadragesimae ... M. D. LXIII. ... Brixiae Ad instantiam Io: Baptistæ Bozolæ. M. D. LXIII. 4°. A^6. (Lea.) [234

TIRAQUEAU, ANDRÉ. Andreae Tiraquelli ... commentarii, de nobilitate, et de iure primigeniorum. ... Basileae, M. D. LXI. (... per Hieronymum Frobenium, & Nicolaum Episcopium ...) fol. *^{8} α-γ^6 a-z^6 A-Z^6 Aa^8 Bb-Zz^6 AA-OO^6 PP^8. pp. 1-588, 2-415. [235

-- Andreae Tiraquelli ... commentarii. In .1. Boues. §. hoc sermone. ff. de uerbor. signif. Venetiis Apud Dominicum Lilium. MDLV. (*Colophon.*) 8°. a-c^8 d^4 A-K^8 L^4. ff. 1-84. [236

-- Andreae Tiraquelli Fontenaii ... commentarij, in .1. Si vnquam .C. de reuo. donat. ... Veneunt Parisijs apud Poncetum le Preux ... M.D.XXXV. (... ex officina Ludouici Cyanei sumptibus ... Galeoti a Prato, & Ponceti le Preux ... mense Aprili.) fol. aa-cc^8 a-z^8 &^{8} A^8. pp. 1-397. [237

-- Andreae Tiraquelli ... de priuilegiis piae causae tractatus ... Lugduni, apud Guliel. Rouillium, M. D. LX. fol. A-B^4 C^2 a-z^4 A^4. pp. 1-190. (Biddle.) [238

-- -- Venetiis, Apud Franciscum Laurentium, de Turino. M D LXI. 8°. a-b^8 A-M^8. pp. 1-190. [239

-- Andreae Tiraquelli ... ex commentariis in Pictonum consuetudines, sectio, de legibus connubialibus, et iure maritali, Quinta hac ... editione ... recognita ... Lugduni, apud Guliel. Rouillium ... M. D, LX. fol. α-β^6 a-z^6 A-Z^6 aa-oo^6 a-f^6 g^4. ff. 1-360. (Biddle.) [240

-- -- *Another copy.* [241

-- Andreae Tiraquelli ... Tractatus de Præscriptionibus ... Venetiis, Apud Franciscum Laurentium, de Turino. M D LXI. 8°. a^8 b^4 A-G^8 H^4. pp. 1-118. [242

-- Andreae Tiraquelli ... Tractatus le mort saisit le vif. Parisiis, Apud Iacobum Keruer ... 1550. ... (Excudebat Guil. Morelius ... Id. Octobris.) 8°. a-c^8 d^6 A-T^8 V^2. pp. 1-306. [243

TITELMANN, FRANZ. Compendium dialecticae ... ad libros logicorum Arist. ... utile ... Parisiis. Apud Christianum Wechelum ... M.D.XXXIX. 8°. A-C^8 D^4. pp. 2-52. [244

-- De rerum naturalium consideratione Libri Duodecim ... Coloniae ex officina Melchioris Nouesiani, Anno M. D. XLIIII. 8°. π^8 *^{8} **^{4} A-Z^8 a-n^8. ff. 1-288. [245

-- -- Compendium philosophiæ naturalis ... libri XII. ... Lugduni, apud Barthol. Vincentium, M. D. XCVI. 8°. a-z^8 A-D^8. pp. 3-415. [246

-- In omnes epistolas apostolicas ... Elucidatio ... Antvverpiae. Apud Ioannem Steelsium ... M. D. XL. 8°. A-KK^8 LL^4. ff. 5-267. (Lea.) [247

-- Libri sex de consyderatione Dialectica. ... Excudebat secundo, Symon Cocus [Antuerpiae] ... M.CCCCC.XXXVII. Mense Aprili. (... Mense Iulio.) 8°. A-Z^8 a-g^8. ff. 1-222. [248

-- Tractatus de expositione mysteriorū Missæ. Sacri canonis Missæ duplex expositio. Tractatus sanctarum meditationum pro cordis in deo constabilitione. ... Antuerpiæ, apud Guilielmū Vorstermannū. ... m.ccccc.xxx. 8°. A-C^8 D^4 E-H^8 I^4 K-M^8 N^4 O-R^8. (Yarnall.)[248a

TIXIER, JEAN, DE RAVISY. Ioannis Rauisii Textoris Niuernensis Epithetorum opus ... repurgatum, opera Valentini Cherleri Elsterburgensis. Accesserunt de carminibus ad veterum imitationem artificiosè componendis præcepta ... collecta à Georgio Sabino. Venetiis, Ad Signum seminant[is] M D LXXII. 4°. †^{4} A-3C^8. pp. 1-783. ¶*T.p. defaced.* [249

-- Ioannis Rauisii Textoris Niuernensis officina, ... redacta per Conradum Lycosthenem ... Eiusdem Rauisij Cornucopiæ libellus ... Item eiusdem autoris ... epistolæ ... Basileae, apud haeredes Bryling. Anno M.D.LXVI. 4°. a-b^4 a-z^4 A-Z^4 aa-zz^4 Aa-Zz^4 3a-3i^4. cols. 1-1596. [250

TODI. Constitutiones synodales ecclesiae Tudertinae. Tam antiquæ sub ... vetustioribus Episcopis: quam nouæ sub ... Angelo Cæsio Episcopo Tudertino promulgatæ ... Perusiae. Ex ædibus Io: Bernardini Rastellij. MDLXXVI. 4°. A-Q^4. pp. 2-112. (Lea.) [251

TOLEDO, FRANCISCO DE. D. Francisci Toleti ... commentaria, Vnà cum Quæstionibus, in octo libros Aristotelis de physica auscultatione. Item, in lib. Arist. de generatione et corruptione. ... Coloniæ Agrippinæ, In Officina Birckmannica sumptibus Arn. Mylij, anno M. D. LXXXV. ... (... Typis Godefridi Kempensis.) 4°. *^{4} A-4T^4. ff. 1-359. [252

-- -- Coloniae Agrippinae, In Officina Birckmannica sumptibus Arnold. Mylij. Anno M. D. XCIII. ... *Same colophon, collation, and pagination.* [253

-- D. Francisci Toleti ... commentaria vnà cum Quæstionibus in tres libros Aristotelis De Anima ... Coloniae Agrippinae, Apud hæredes Arnoldi Birckmanni. Anno M.D.LXXVI. ... 4°. *^{4} A-Yy^4. ff. 1-179. [254

-- -- [Parisiis, apud Iacobum du Puys, 1581.] 4°. ✠⁴ (-✠1) A-Ss⁴ Tt². pp. 1-332. ¶*Possibly belongs to the 1582 edition with the same collation and pagination.* [255

-- -- Coloniae Agrippinae, In officina Birckmannica. Anno cIↄ. Iↄ. LXXXIII. ... (... Typis Godefridi Kempensis.) 4°. *⁴ A-Yy⁴. ff. 1-179. [256

-- -- Coloniae Agrippinae, In officina Birckmannica. Anno cIↄ.Iↄ.XCIV. ... *Same colophon, collation, and foliation.* [257

-- Summa casuum conscientiæ, Siue De instructione sacerdotum, libri septem: item De peccatis Liber vnus, cum Bullæ Coenæ Domini dilucidatione ... Coloniae Agrippinae Sumptibus Lamberti Rasfeldt. Anno M.L.XCIX [*sic*]. 8°. †⁸ ††⁴ A-3H⁸ 3I⁴ (-3I4, *presumably blank*). pp. 1-799. (Lea.) [258

-- Tractatus de septem peccatis mortalibus, cum Bullæ Coenæ Domini dilucidatione. ... ... Constantiae, Apud Nicolaum Kalt ... M. DC. 8°.)(⁴ A-P⁸ (-A1, *but with no apparent loss of text*). ff. 1-119. (Lea.) [259

TOLMER, JOHANN. De papatu Romano ... liber, versu heroico tractatus ... Lugduni Batauorum, M. D. LXXXXIII. 8°. A-H⁸. pp. 4-125. [260

TOLOMEI, CLAUDIO. Il cesano, dialogo ... nel quale ... si dee ragionevolmente chiamare la volgar lingua. ... In Vinegia appresso Gabriel Giolito de Ferrari, et fratelli. M D LV. (*Colophon.*) 4°. A-N⁴. pp. 2-97. [261

-- De le lettere ... libri sette. ... In Vinegia, Appresso Domenico Giglio. 1558. (*Colophon.*) 8°. A-PP⁸. ff. 2-296. [262*

-- Due orazioni in lingua Toscana. Accusa Contra Leon Secretario, di secreti riuelati. Difesa. In Parma. Appresso Sette Viotto. M. D. XLVII. il di primo di Gennaio. 4°. A-F⁴. [263

-- Oratione de la pace ... (... stampata poi in Roma da Antonio Blado Asolano nel .M.D.XXXIIII. di Marzo.) 4°. A-L⁴. [264

-- Versi, et regole de la nuoua poesia Toscana. (In Roma per Antonio Blado d'Asola. Nel M. D. XXXIX. Del Mese d'Ottobre.) 4°. a⁴ A-Y⁴. [265

TOMITANO, BERNARDINO. Bernardini Tomitani Patauini ... Animaduersiones aliquot In Primum Librum Posteriorum Resolutoriorum. Contradictionum solutiones in Aristotelis et Auerrois dicta, in Primum Librum Posteriorum Resolutoriorum. In nouem Auerrois Quęsita Demonstratiua, Argumenta. Venetiis apud Iunctas. M. D. LXII. (*Colophon.*) 4°. ✠⁸ A-R⁸. ff. 1-136. [266

-- Quattro libri della lingua Thoscana ... Oue si proua la philosophia esser necessaria al perfetto Oratore, & Poeta ... In Padoua. Appresso Marcantonio Olmo. M D LXX. (... Per Lorenzo Pasquati, Ad instantia di Innocente Olmo. L'Anno M D LXIX.) 8°. *⁶ a-z⁸ Aa-Ee⁸ Ff¹⁰ Gg-Oo⁸ Pp¹² Qq⁸ Rr¹⁰ Ss-3G⁸ 3H⁴. ff. 1-426. [267

-- Ragionamenti della lingua Toscana ... (In Venetia per Giouanni de Farri & fratelli ... M D XLV.) 8°. a-dd⁸ ee⁴. pp. 3-439. [268

TOMMAI, PIETRO. Petri Rauennatis ... Aurea nō nulla opuscula ... (Impressum Erffordie per Wolfgangū Schenck. Anno Millesimoquingentesimo tercio) 4°. B.L. A-G⁶ H-I⁴ (-I4, *presumably blank*). (Lea.) [269

TOMMASI, ZACCHARIA DI. I felici pronostichi, da verificarsi, contro à infedeli a fauor della chiesa Christiana. Contenuti in Cinque Canzoni ... In Venetia, Appresso Nicolò Beuilacqua. M. D. LXXII. 4°. A-G⁴ H². ff. 3-30. [270

TOMMASO ILLIRICO. In Lutherianas hèreses clipeus Catholicæ Ecclesiæ ... (Taurini ... Anthoniu⁹ Ranot⁹ excudit. ... M.D.XXIIII. octauo Idus Iulii.) 4°. AA-BB⁸ a-z⁸ &⁸ ↄ⁴. ff. I-CXCVI. [271

TORELLI, POMPONIO. La Merope tragedia ... In Parma. Appresso Erasmo Viotto. M. D. LXXXIX. 4°. A⁴ B-H⁸. pp. 1-108. [272

-- Trattato del debito ... In Parma, Nella Stamperia di Erasmo Viotti, 1596. ... 4°. ✠⁴ Bb⁸ A-Aa⁸. ff. 1-192. [273

TORQUEMADA, ANTONIO DE. Iardin de flores curiosas, en q̄ se tratā algunas materias de humanidad, philosophia, theologia, y geographia ... En Salamanca. En casa de Iuan Baptista de Terranoua. M.D.LXX. ... (*Colophon.*) 8°. *[8] A-Nn[8]. ff. 1-286. [274

-- -- Giardino di fiori curiosi, in forma di dialogo ... tradotto di Spagnuolo in Italiano, per Celio Malespina. In Vinegia, Presso Altobello Salicato. 1590. ... 4°. *-3*[4] A-Kk[4] (-Kk4, *presumably blank*). pp. 1-262. [275

TORQUEMADA, JUAN DE. [Questiones spiritualis ɔuiuij delicias preferentes, super euangelijs tam de tempore q̄ȝ de sanctis, edita a ... iohanne de turre cremata. ... Venundantur lugduni ab Stephano Gueynard ...] (Impresse lugδ. per iohānem de vingle. ... M.ccccc. nono die ɣo. xviij. mensis Ianuarij.) 8°. B.L. ¶[12] (-¶1) a-z[8] A-H[8] I[12]. ff. j-cclx. ¶5-6 *misbound after* ¶8. (Lea.) [276

TORRES, FRANCISCO DE. Francisci Turriani De Matrimoniis clandestinis explicatio. Venetiis, Ex officina Iordani Ƶileti ... M D LXIII. 4°. A-C[4]. ff. 2-12. [277

-- Epistola Francisci Turriani ... contra Vbiquistas Arianistas. Ingolstadii, Ex Officina Typographica Dauidis Sartorij. ... M. D. LXXXIII. 4°. A-C[4] D[2]. pp. 1-26. [278

TORRES Y AGUILERA, GERONIMO DE. Chronica, y Recopilacion de varios successos de guerra que ha acontescido en Italia y partes de Leuante y Berberia, desde ... año de M.D.LXX. hasta ... el de M.D.LXXIIII. ... En Çaragoça. Impressa en casa de Iuan Soler, ... M. D. LXXIX. ... (... a los veynte dias del mes de Febrero ...) 4°. ¶[8] A-P[8] Q[4] (-Q4, *presumably blank*). ff. 1-123. (Lea.) [279

TORSELLINI, ORAZIO. Horatii Tursellini Romani ... Lauretanæ historiae, libri quinque. ... Moguntiæ Apud Balthasarum Lippium, Sumptibus Arnoldi Mylij. ... cIↄ. Iↄ. c. 8°. (.·.)[8] A-Bb[8] Cc[2]. pp. 1-397. (Lea.) [280

TOSCANELLA, ORAZIO. Dittionario volgare et Latino ... ... In Venetia, M D LXVIII. (... Per Comin da Trino da Monferrato. ...) 4°. *[4] a-i[4] k[6] A-3Q[4] (-Z2-3, Mm4). ff. 2-248. [281

-- Modo di studiare le pistole famigliari di M. Tullio Cicerone ... In Vinegia, appresso Gabriel Giolito de' Ferrari. M D LXVII. 4°. a[4] A-BB[4] (-BB4, *presumably blank*). pp. 1-197. [282

-- Osseruationi ... Sopra l'Opere di Virgilio ... In Vinegia, appresso Gabriel Giolito de' Ferrari. M D LXVI. 8°. *[8] *-3*[8] A-DD[8] EE[4] (-EE4, *presumably blank*). pp. 1-438. [283

-- Prontuario di voci volgari, et Latine ... In Venetia, Appresso Vincenzo Valgrisi. MDLXV. 4°. A-R[8]. [284

TOSCANO, GIOVANNI MATTEO. Peplus Italiæ. ... In quo illustres viri ... recensentur. ... Lutetiæ. Ex officina Federici Morelli ... 1578. ... 8°. ā[8] A-H[8]. pp. 1-128. [285

TOSI, GIOVANNI. De vita Emmanuelis Philiberti ... Subalpinorum principis, libri duo. Ioannis Tonsi ... Augustæ Taurinorum Apud Io. Dominicum Tarinum. cIↄ Iↄ xcvI. (*Colophon.*) fol. †[4] †[4+1] A-Ff[4] Gg[2]. pp. 1-235. [286

TOULOUSE. Conciles de Tholose, Besiers et Narbonne, ensemble les ordonnances de Comte Raimond ... contre les Albigeois: & l'Instrument d'accord entre ledit Raimond & sainct Loys, Roy de France ... Rendu de Latin en François, P. M. Arnauld Sorbin ... A Paris, Chez Guillaume Chaudiere ... 1569. ... 8°. ā[6] A-D[8] E[2]. ff. 1-33. (Lea.) [287

-- Consuetudines Tolosae ... Et quæstionibus ... Ioan. de Casaveteri ... Veneunt Tolosae, in officina Anthonij Vincentij, Apud Ludouicum Yuernaige. Impressum per Anthonium Gorcium 1544. ... 4°. A-T[4] V[6]. ff. 1-73. [288

TOURAINE. [Le coustumier de touraine ...] (Imprime pour Anthoine verard ... a Paris. ... acheue dimprimer ... le .vi. iour de mars mil cīq cēs ⁊ sept) 8°. B.L. a-p[8] (-a1). (Biddle.) [289

-- Les coustumes du pais et duche de Touraine ... A Tours. Par Pierre Regnard ... 1567. 4°. a-b[4] A-N[4] O[2]. pp. 1-108. [290

-- [1] Proces verbal de Messieurs de Thou president, Faïe, & Viole ... Sur la reformation des Coustumes de Touraine, par eulx faicte en l'an 1559. A Tours, Par Oliuier Tafforeau ...: pour Laurent Richard, & Zacharie Griueau, & Pierre Regnard ... 1566. 4°. a^4 b-h^8 i^4. ff. 3-64. [2] Ordonnances du roy Charles neufiesme, ... Faictes en son Conseil, Sur les plainctes ... des trois Estats, tenus en la ville d'Orleans. (Acheué d'imprimer le premier iour de Septembre ...) A-I^4. [291

TOXITES, MICHAEL. Methodus legendi in alphabetariorum gratiam atque vsum ... Tubingæ apud Viduam Vlrici Morhardi. M. D. LVIII. 8°. A-D^8. ¶A1 *defective.* [292

-- Querela anseris vel de ingratitudine hominum elegia ... Argentorati M.D.XL. 8°. a-b^8 (-b8, *blank*). [293

TRACTAET. Een Tractaet van Criminele saken ... Gheprint Thantwerpen ... by Hans de Laet/ Anno M.D. eñ Liiij. 8°. A-H^8 I^4. (Biddle.) [294

TRACTATULUS. De Testamentis Tractatulus de Testamentis. Codicillis. Causa mortis donatiōe. ... (Impressum ... Liptzk arte et expensis ... Vuolfgangi Monacēsis (al's Stőckel) Anno supra Millesimūquingentesimū nono. Die vero .xviij. Mensis Ianuarij ...) fol. B.L. A-E^6 F^4 G-X^6 χ^8. ff. 2-106, 1-10. (Lea.) [295

TRACTATUS. Tractatus De ruine ecclesie planctu ... (Impressum Hagnoe [per Henricum Gran, c. 1505.]) 4°. *A-*B^4. [296

-- [Tractatus.] M. D. XLIIII. (Lugduni, per Georgium Regnault ...) fol. B.L. [1] Primum Volumen Tractatuū, e varijs iuris interpretibus collectorum. ... a-z^8 A-P^8 Q^{10}. ff. 3-314. [2] Secundum Volumen ... aa-zz^8 AA-GG^8 HH^6 II^4. ff. 2-250. [3] Tertium Volumen ... aA-zZ^8 Aa-Gg^8 Hh^6. ff. 2-245. [4] Quartum Volumen ... 3a-$3z^8$ 3A-$3C^8$ $3D^6$. ff. 3-214. [5] Quintum Volumen ... aaA-zzZ^8 AAa-MMm^8. ff. [2]-280. [6] Sextum Volumen ... aAa-zZz^8 AaA-CcC^8 DdD^6. ff. 2-213. [7] Septimum Volumen ... 4a-$4z^8$ 4A-$4G^8$ $4H^6$ $4I^4$. ff. 2-250. [8] Octauum Volumen ... AAAa-$ZZZz^8$ aaaA-$gggG^8$ $hhhI^4$. ff. 2-243. ¶hhhH3 *defective.* [9] Nonum Volumen ... aaAA-$zzZZ^8$ AAaa-$QQqq^8$. ff. 2-312. [10] Decimum Volumen ... †a-$†z^8$ †A-$†S^8$. ff. 2-327. [11] Vndecimum Volumen ... †aa-$†zz^8$ †AA-$†NN^8$ $†OO^6$. ff. 2-294. [12] Duodecimum Volumen ... ‡a-$‡z^8$ ‡A-$‡M^8$ $‡N^6$ $‡O^4$. ff. 2-289. [13] Index ... a-z^8 A-Q^8 R^6. (Biddle.) [297

-- Tractatus criminales ... De Fama, Thomę de Piperata. De Brachio implorando per iudicem ecclesiasticum à iudice seculari ..., Martini de Fano. De inquisitionibus ad interprętationem .l. si uacantia .c. de bonis uacantibus lib. x. Angeli de vbaldis. De Quæstionibus, Antonij de Canario. De Syndicatu officialium, Antonij Rondinelli. ... Venetiis M D LXII (... Apud Aurelium Pincium.) 8°. a-e^8 A-T^8. ff. 1-151. (Lea.) [298

TRAGUS, HIERONYMUS. Hieronymi Tragi, de stirpium ... nomenclaturis ... Commentariorum Libri tres, ... nunc in Latinam conuersi, Interprete Dauide Kybero ... Hi accesserunt ... praefationes duae: ... Conradi Gesneri ... Praeterea ... adiectus est Benedicti Textoris Segusiani de Stirpium differentijs, ... ex Dioscoride ... Libellus ... (Argentorati Excudebat Vuendelinus Rihelius, Anno M. D. LII.) 4°. a-c^8 d^{10} A-Zz^8 AA-ZZ^8 3A-$3K^8$. pp. 1-1200. [298a

TRAUT, VEIT. Türckischer Kayser Ankunfft/ Krieg vnd Sig/ wider die Christen/ biss auff den zwelfften yetzt Regierenden Tyrannen Soleymannum ... Getruckt zů Augspurg durch Hainrich Stainer. M.D.XLIII. (... Am V. Decembris ...) fol. A-C^6 D^8 (-D8, *presumably blank*). ff. I-XXIII. [299

TREGIANI, DOMENICO. Il ladro Cacco fauola pastorale Del Desioso Academico Insipido Senese ... In Venetia, Presso Gio. Battista Ciiotti Senese. MDLXXXIII. 8°. A-F^8. [300

TRELLON, CLAUDE DE. Les oeuures poetiques du Sieur de Trellon. ... A Lyon, Pour Claude Michel Libraire de Tournon. M. D. XCIV. 12°. A-Cc^{12}. pp. 3-600. [301

TREMELLIUS, IMMANUEL. Grammatica Chaldaea et Syra ... [Genevae,] Excudebat Henricus Stephanus, M. D. LXIX. 4°. A-K^8. pp. 3-155. [302

TRENT. Constitutiones ... Ludouici ... Episcopi Tridenti, &c. in dioecesana synodo Promulgatæ Anno 1593. Tridenti, Apud Ioan. Baptistam Gelminum. 1594. 4°. A-C^{12} D^{10} (-D10, *presumably blank*). ff. 2-44. (Lea.) [302a

TRENT, COUNCIL OF. Acta Concilij Tridentini. ... Parisiis, Ex officina Reginaldi Calderij, & Claudij eius filij. 1546. ... 8°. A-H^{8}. (Lea.) [303

-- -- *Another copy.* (Yarnall.) [304

-- Acta et decreta ... Tridentinae synodi. Ann. M. D. XLVI. et XLVII. Vna cum admonitione legatorum sedis Apostolicæ ... in prima Sessione. Ac orationibus tribus per diuersos prelatos ... Mediolani ... M. D. XLVIII. 8°. A-I^{8}. pp. 2-70. ¶*Orators named: Cornelius Placentinus, Ambrosius Catharinus.* (Lea.) [305

-- Bulla indictionis sacri oecumenici concilii. Breue Pii PP. IIII. super ordine sedendi in concilio. Declaratio facta per ... Legatos super Decreto ... Pij Papæ IIII. Decretum primum publicatum in prima Sessione ... Die XVIII. Ianuarij. MDLXII. Primum decretum publicatum in secunda Sessione ... Die XXVI. Februarij. M D LXII. Decretum publicatum in Sessione tertia ... Die XIIII. Maij M D LXII. Vna cum decreto publicato in sessione Quarta ... Die IIII. Iunij. M D LXII. Patauii, apud Christophorum Gryphium, M D LXIII. 4°. A-B^{4}. (Lea.) [306

-- Canones, et decreta ... concilii Tridentini ... Romae, M D LXIV. Apud Paulum Manutium, Aldi F. In ædibus Populi Romani. (*Colophon.*) fol. A-T^{6} V^{8} X^{6}. pp. 5-239. (Yarnall.) [307

-- [1] Canones, et decreta ... Concilii Tridentini ... Mediolani Apud Antonium Antonianum. 1564. (... Apud Valerium, & Hieronymum fratres Metios.) 4°. A-K^{8} L^{10} +^{10}. ff. 4-89. [2] Index librorum prohibitorum, cum regulis confectis per patres a Tridentina Synodo delectos ... *Same imprint and colophon.* A-D^{4}. ff. 2-15. (Lea.) [308

-- -- Canones et decreta ... concilii Tridentini. ... Adiectus est index Librorum prohibitorum ... Anno M. D. LXIIII. (Dilingæ, excudebat Sebaldus Mayer.) 8°. A-Z^{8} a-k^{8} Aa-Ee^{8}. ff. 3-264, 2-40. (Lea.) [309

-- -- [1] Anno M. D. LXV. (Dilingæ, excudebat Sebaldus Mayer.) 8°. A-Z^{8} a-m^{8}. ff. 3-274. ¶*Adds:* Oratio ... Hieronymi Raggazzoni Veneti ... in postrema ... sessione publice recitata (11^{r}-m2^{v}), Index ... (m3^{r}-m8^{v}). [2] Index librorum prohibitorum. ... Aa-Ee^{8}. ff. 2-40. (Lea.) [310

-- Catalogus legatorum patrum oratorum theologorum, qui à principio vsque in hodiernum diem, ad ... Tridentinum Synodum conuenerunt ... Brixiae Ad instantiam Io: Baptistæ Bozolæ. Anno M. D. LXIII. XIIII. Mensis Augusti. (... apud Ludouicum Sabiensem.) 4 . A^{4} B^{6}. (Lea.) [311

-- -- Nomina ... patrum, Qui conuenerunt ad Concilium Tridentinum. ... Pataui Apud Christoforum Gryphium. M D LXIII. 4°. A-B^{4}. (Lea.) [312

-- Catechismus, Ex Decreto Concilii Tridentini, ad parochos ... Romae, In ædibus Populi Romani, apud Paulum Manutium, M D LXVI. fol. A^{2} B-II^{6}. pp. 2-359. (Yarnall.) [312a

-- -- Venetiis, Apud Aldum. 1582. 8°. *^{8} A-RR^{8}. pp. 3-616. [313

-- -- Catechismo ... tradotto ... Dal ... Alesso Figliucci ... In Venetia M.D.LXVII. Appresso Aldo Manutio ... 4°. π^{4} A-ZZ^{4} aa-xx^{4}. pp. 2-519. [314

-- -- In Venetia MDLXIX. Appresso Aldo Manutio ... 8°. A-PP^{8} a^{8} b^{4}. pp. 8-608. [315

-- [1] Decreta, publicata in sessione nona et vltima, ... Concilii Tridentini, ...III. & IIII. Decemb. M. D. LXIII. Brixiae: Ad instantiam Io: Baptistæ Bozolæ. M. D. LXIII. (... Apud Ludouicum Sabiensem.) 4°. B-D^{4}. [2] Catalogus legatorum, patrum, Oratorum, & Theologorum omnium ... (Brixiae apud Ludouicum Sabiensem. M. D. LXIII.) aa^{4} bb^{6}. (Lea.) [316

-- -- *Another copy.* (Lea.) [317

-- Decreta de sacramento matrimonii, et de reformatione, publicata in sessione octaua, ... Concilii Tridentini ... XI. Nouemb. M. D. LXIII. Brixiae: Ad instantiam Io: Baptistæ Bozolæ. M. D. LXIII. (... apud Ludouicum Sabiensem.) 4°. A-C^{4} D^{2}. (Lea.) [318

-- -- *Another copy.* (Lea.) [319

TRENT, COUNCIL OF

-- Doctrina de communione sub vtraque specie et paruulorum publicata in sessione quinta ... Concilij Tridentini ... Die XVI. Iulij. MDLXII. Decretum de reformatione publicatum in eadem Sessione ... Pataui Apud Laurentium Pasquatium & Socios. M D LXII. 4°. A^4. (Lea.) [320

-- Generale, concilium Tridentinum continens omnia quæ ab initio vsquæ ad finem in eo gesta sunt. Venetiis, Ad signum Spei. 1552. 4°. A-E^8 Ee^8 F^8 G^2 A^4. (Lea.) [321

-- -- Alle Handlung vnd Session des ... Concilij/ zu Trent ... Verteutscht vnd getruͦckt ... M.D.Lxiiij. zu Coͤllen bey Iaspar Gennep. 4°. A-Z^4 a^4. ff. v-xcij. [322

-- Des hayligen Tridentinischen Concilij Satzungen/ von den haymlichen oder winckel heyraten. Item Von raichungen der Zehenden/ vnd dass man sich der Kirchen vnnd gaistlichen Guͤter verbotner weiss nit gebrauchen solle. Getruckt zuͦ Dilingen durch Sebaldum Mayer. 4°. A-B^4 (-B4, *presumably blank*). (Lea.) [323

-- Vniuersum sacrosanctum Concilium Tridentinum ... Brixiæ. Cura et impensis Io: Baptistae Bozolae. M. D. LXIII. 4°. $†^4$ A-CC^4. ff. 1-103. (Lea.) [324

-- -- *Another copy.* (Lea.) [325

-- -- Le saint, sacré, vniuersal, et general Concile de Trente ... Traduit de Latin en François, par Gentian Heruet d'Orleans ... A Rheims, Chez Iean de Foigny ... 1577. ... 12°. $ā^8$ A-Mm^{12} Nn^4 Oo^{10}. ff. 1-453. (Lea.) [326

-- -- A Paris, Chez Nicolas Chesneau ... M. D. LXXXIIII. 8°. $ā^8$ A-PP^8 QQ^4. pp. 1-296. [327

-- Vera, et catholica doctrina, quod in missa verum sacrificium, et propitiatorium offeratur; Promulgata in Sessione sexta concilii Tridentini Die XVII. Mensis Septembris. M D LXIII. ... Pataui, apud Christophorum Gryphium, M D LXIII. 4°. A^6. (Lea.) [328

-- Recusationschrifft der Christlichen Augspurgischen Confessions verwandten Stende/ wider das vermeint/ von Bapst Paulo dem dritten/ weiland zu Trient indicirt ... Concilium ... Mit einer Vorrede Math. Fla. Illyr. vnd Nicolai Galli. ... (... nachgedruckt/ durch Michael Lotther/ zu Magdeburg. Anno 1551.) 4°. A-E^4 F^2. [329

-- Was von dem ietzt ausgeschriebenen Tridentischen Concilio zu halten sey/ Drey gesprech. ... 1551. 4°. A-F^4 G^6. [330

TRETER, THOMAS. In Quinti Horatii Flacci Venusini ... poemata omnia, rerum ac verborum ... Index ... Antuerpiæ, Ex officina Christophori Plantini ... cIↄ. Iↄ. LXXV. (... cIↄ. Iↄ. LXXVI. Idibus Martii.) 8°. A-O^8 P^4. pp. 3-230. [331

TREULINGER, JOHANN. Warnung. Erinnerung/ vnd Christliche Ermanung/ sampt gründtlichem bericht/ von yetziger Kriegs yebung in Teűtscher Nation. ... M.D.XLVII. 4°. A-E^4. [332

TREUTLER, HIERONYMUS. Oratio historica de vita et morte ... VVilhelmi Hassiæ Landtgravii ... Marpurgi, Imprimebat Paulus Egenolphus ... M. D. XCII. 4°. A-P^4. pp. 3-119. [333

TREVISO. Statuta prouisionesq. ducales ciuitatis Taruisii. ... Venetiis, M. D. LXXIIII. fol. π^2 a-d^4 A-$3A^6$ $3B^6$ A-B^6 a-b^4 c^6. ff. 1-296, 1-12. ¶*T.p. repaired.* [334

TRINCI, FRANCESCO MARIANO. Comedia di amore cōtro auaritia & pudicitia ... (Impresso in Siena ad instantia di Giouanni di Alexandro Libraro. a di .9. di Marzo .1514.) 8°. a-c^4 d^6. [335

-- Commedia del matrimonio Composta per il peregrino Ingenio di Mariano Maniscalcho da Siena. (Stampata in Siena Per Michelagniolo di Bernardino: Ad instantia di Giouanni di Alexandro Libraio A di .XXVII. di Octobre. .M.D.XXXIII.) 8°. A-B^8 C^4. [336

-- Pieta d'Amore: Comedia composta per Mariano Maniscalco da Siena. ... In Siena [c. 1550]. 8°. A-C^8. [337

TRIPPAULT, LÉON. Celt'-Hellenisme, ou, etymologic des mots francois tirez du Græc. ... Par Leon Trippault, sieur de Bardis ... A Orleans. Par Eloy Gibier ... 1580. ... 8°. $*^4$ A-Qq^4. pp. 2-311. [337a

TRISSINO, GIOVANNI GIORGIO. Dialωgω del Trissinω intitulatω il castellanω, nel quale si tratta de le lingua Italiana. ... [Vicenza, Tolomeo Janiculo da Bressa, 1529.] fol. A-B^8 C^4. [338

-- Epistola del Trissino de la vita, che dee tenere una Dωnna vedova. (Stampata in Roma per Lodovico Vicentino, e lautitio nel MDXXIIII ...) 4°. A-C^4. [339

-- La Italia liberata da Gotthi de Trissinω. Stampata in Rωma per Valeriω e Luigi Dorici A petiziωne di Antoniω Macrω Vincentinω MDXLVII. di Maggiω ... ([Zz6^r] Stampata in Venezia per Tωlomeω Ianiculω da Bressa ... MDXLVIII. di Nωvembre. [3z8^r] ... di Ωttωbre.) 8°. *^{8} A-N^8 O^{8+2} P-Yy^8 Zz^{10} (Zz9 + *folded leaf*) 3a-3y^8 3z^{12}. ff. 1-175, 2-181, 1-184. [340

-- La pωetica di M. Giωuan Giorgiω Trissinω. (Stampata in Vicenza per Tωlωmeω Ianiculω, Nel MDXXIX. Di Aprile.) fol. a-r^4 s^2. ff. II-LXVIII. [341

-- Rime del Trissinω. (Stampata in Vicenza per Tωlωmeω Ianiculω, ... MDXXIX.) 4°. aa-nn^4. [342

-- I ritratti de le bellissime donne dItalia ... (Stampata in Roma per Rutilio Caluo nel M. D. XXXI.) 4°. A-B^4. [343

-- [La Sophonisba tragedia ...] (Stampata in Roma per Lodovico Vicentino Scrittore, & Lautitio Perugino Intagliatore, nel MDXXIIII del mese di Luglio) 4°. a-n^4 (-a1, a4). [344

-- -- La Sωphωnisba del Trissinω. (Stampata in Vicenza per Tωlωmeω Ianiculω, Nel MDXXIX. Di Maggiω) 4°. a-n^4. [345

-- -- la Sophonisba, tragedia del Trissino ... In Vinegia, appresso Francesco Lorenzini da Turino, MDLX. 8°. A-E^8 F^2. ff. 2-41. [346

-- -- In Venetia, Presso Domenico Caualcalupo. M D LXXXVII. 8°. A-E^8. ff. 2-39. [347

TRISTABOCCA, PASQUALE. Altus Missarum cum quinque vocibus. Auctore Paschalis Tristabuchii De Aquila. Liber primus. ... Venetijs Apud Iacobum Vincentium. M D XC. 4°. G-L^4 M^2. pp. 2-25. [2] Quintus ... *Same imprint.* N-T^4 V^2. pp. 2-25. (Music.) [348

TRISTRAM. [1] L'opere magnanime de i due Tristani caualieri della Tauola Ritonda. ... 8°. a^8 a-kk^8 (-kk8, *blank*) b^4 (-b4, *presumably blank*). ff. 1-263. [2] [Di Don Tristano il giouane. Libro secondo.] (In Venetia per Michele Tramezino. M D LV.) A-SS^8 (-A1) a^6. ff. 1-337. [349

TRITHEMIUS, JOHANNES. Chronica. Vom vrsprung herkommen vnd zunemen der Francken/ ... durch ... Iacob Schenck ... verteutscht ... Getruckt zů Franckfurt am Mayn. M. D. LXIII. (Getruckt ... bey Hans Hechler/ in verlagung Sigmund Feyerabends/ vnd Simon Hůters. ...) 8°.)(^{8} A-Y^8. ff. 1-173. [350

-- De origine gentis principumque Bauarorum commentarius ... Francofurti. ... 1549. (... per Cyriacum Iacobum.) 4°. A-I^4 (-I4, *blank*). ¶A1 *mounted*. [351

-- Dn. Iohannis Tritthemii abbatis Spanheimensis, de scriptoribus ecclesiasticis ... liber vnus ... Appendicum ... posterior nunc recens additur, authore Balthazaro Werlino Colmarieñ. ... Coloniæ ex officina Petri Quentel, mense Martio anni M.D.XLVI. ... (*Colophon.*) 4°. A-D^4 a-3q^4. pp. 1-494. [352

-- Ioannis Trithemii ... de septem secundeis, id est, intelligentijs. siue Spiritibus Orbes post Deum mouentibus ... Coloniae Apud Ioannem Birckmannum. Anno M.D.LXVII. 8°. A-L^8. pp. 3-175. [353

-- Ioannis Tritemii ... Epistolarum familiarium libri duo ... Haganoae ex officina Petri Brubachij, 1536. 4°. A^4 a-xx^4. pp. 2-344. [354

-- Liber de triplici regione claustralium ⁊ spirituali exercicio monachorum ... Venundantur ... In parrisiorum lutetia (impressum ... per Anthoniū bōnemer pro Gofrido de marnef ... M.ccccc.vii. die quarta augusti.) 4°. B.L. A-O$^{8.4}$ P^4. ff. i-lxxxviiii. [355

-- Ioannis Tritemii ... Liber Octo questionū ... (Impressum Oppenheym [per Jacobum Kōbel] Impensis Iohānis Hasselbergeñ/ de Augia ... M.D.XV. xx. Mensis Septembris.) 4°. A^6 B-H^4 I^6 (-I6, *presumably blank*). (Lea.) [356

-- -- Antwort Herrn Iohan Abts zů Spanhaim/ auff acht fragstuck/ jme von weylandt Herrn

Maximilian Röm. Kayser ... fürgehalten/ .., in das Teütsch erstlich transsferiert. ... Gedruckt zů Ingolstat durch Alexander vnnd Samuel Weyssenhorn gebrüder. M. D. LV. 4°. A-Q^4 R^2 S^4. [357

-- -- *Another copy.* [358

-- Polygraphiae libri sex ... (Impressum [Oppenhemii per Jacobum Kōbel] ductu Ioannis Haselberg de Aia bibliopolae ... M. D. XVIII. Men. Iulio.) fol. B.L. a-b^6 A^8 B-Z^6 a-m^6 n^8 o-r^6 A^6 B-C^4. [359

-- -- ... Additae sunt etiam aliquot Locorum Explicationes ... Per ... Adolphum à Glauburg, Patricium Francofortensem. Francoforti 1550. (... ex officina Cyriaci Iacobi. ...) 4°. *-4*^{4} a-e^4 A-Zz^4 a-i^4 d-i^4. [360

-- -- Coloniae, Apud Ioannem Birckmannum, & Theodorum Baumium. 1571. 8°. A-Pp^8. pp. 3-554. [361

-- -- *Another copy.* [362

-- -- Polygraphie, et Vniuerselle escriture Cabalistique ..., Traduicte par Gabriel de Collange, natif de Tours en Auuergne. A Paris, Pour Iaques Keruer ... 1561. ... 4°. ā^8 ē^{10} a-z^8 A-P^8. ff. 1-300. ¶*Additional t.pp.:* (B1) Clauicule, et interpretation sur le contenu és cinq liures de Polygraphie ... Traduicte & augmentée par Gabriel de Collange ... *Same imprint.* (I1) Tables et figures planispheriques ... Par Gabriel de Collange ... A Paris, 1561. (Lea.) [363

-- -- *Another copy.* [364

-- Sermones et Exhortationes ad monachos ... (Impressi ... Argentine per Ioannē Knoblouch ... Impēsis Ioānis haselbergers de augia ... M.D.xvi. die vero .xxv. mensis Augusti.) fol. B.L. a^8 b-m^6. ff. ij-LXXIIII. [365

TRITONI, MARCANTONIO. M. Antonii Tritonii Vtinensis mythologia in qua hæc continentur. Disputatio de fabula, & fabulari sermone. Fabulosa exempla ... ex Ouidiana Metamorphosi ... selecta. Epitome in Ouidij Metamorph. libros ... Bononiæ, Ex Officina Alexandri Benacij, & Ioannis Rubei sociorum. MDLX. 4°. a^6 b-e^4 A-Q^4. pp. 1-120. [366

TROMBETA, ANTONIO. [1] Antonij trombette Patauini ... opus in Metaphysicā Arist. ...: Cum qōnibus ... antiquioribus ...: ꝛ formalitates eiusdē cum additionibus ... (Venetijs [Jacobus Pentius de Leuco] ... M.ccccc.iiij.) fol. B.L. A-O^8 (-O8, *presumably blank*). ff. 2-111. [2] Insigne Formalitatū Opus de mēte Doctrois Subtilis ... adiūctisq; resolutissimis ... Tuanensis Archiepi̅ Mauritij: necnō ... Antonij de Fantis Taruisini Annotationibus ... A-B^6. ff. 2-12. [3] Auree scoticarum formalitatum lucubrationes ... edite ab ... Antonio Trombeta ... Aa-Bb^6 Cc^8. ff. 2-20. [367

TROPIANUS, THAMAS. Compendium coniurationis contra daemones vexantes, humana corpora. ... Panormi Ex Typographia Io. Baptistæ Maringhi. MDXCVIII. 4°. A-M^4. pp. 1-88. (Lea.)[368

TROTA, AMBROSIUS. Der Mordtbrenner Zeichen vnd Losunge ... Anno. M. D. XL. 4°. A-B^4.[369

TROTTO, BERNARDO. Dialoghi del matrimonio, e vita Vedouile ... In Turino. M D LXXVIII. (... Appresso Francesco Dolce. ...) 4°. *^{4} A-Gg^4 a-d^4 e^6. pp. 1-238. [370

TROTZENDORFF, VALENTIN. Precationes ... Valentini Trocendorfii, ... ex eius ore exceptæ, & editæ opera Laurentii Ludouici Leobergensis. ... VVitebergae M. D. LXIIII. (... Excudebat Iohannes Crato. ...) 8°. A-V^8. [371

TRUTFETTER, JODOCUS. Sūmule totius logice ... ꝑ Iodocum Truttuetter Isennachcensem ... compilate ... (Expressum ... ab Lupambulo Schenck ... Erphurdie Quindecimo Calēdas Septembres. Anno ... Quingentesimoprimo supra Millesimum. ...) 4°. A^4 B-ZZ^6 3a-3u^6 3x-3y^4.[372

TUBERINUS, JOANNES. Ad Georgiū inclytum Saxoniae ducē ... Musithias de Cælitibus, & sacris Historijs in Musas nouem digesta ... (excussit ... Melchiar Lotherus Auanus ... in ... vrbe Lipsica ... MDXIIII ... Quarto Maij.) fol. a^8 A-Zz^6 a-n^6 o^4 p^6. ff. ij-ccclxi. [373

TÜBINGEN. *University*. Constitutiones atque leges ... in Tubingensi academia nuper instituti Collegij Ducalis VVyrtembergici, &c. Tubingae, Typis Georgij Gruppenbachij, anno M. D. XCVII. fol. A-D^4 (-D4, *presumably blank*). pp. 1-28. [374

TÜRCK, BERNARDIN. Das der Türck/ ein Erbfeind aller Christen ... klare beweysung aus den geschichten bissher in kurtzen jaren von jme begangen. ... 1542. 4 . a^4 b^2. (Lea.) [375

TUNSTALL, CUTHBERT. De arte supputandi libri quatuor, Cuthberti Tonstalli. Parisiis. Ex officina Roberti Stephani. M.D.XXXVIII. (... XVI. Cal. Nouemb.) 4°. a-p^8 q^{10}. pp. 3-259. [376

TURAMINI, ALESSANDRO. Sileno fauola boscareccia ... In Napoli: Nella Stamparia dello Stigliola ... M. D. XCV. (*Colophon.*) 8°. ✠^{8} A-K^8 L^{12}. pp. 1-184. ¶L8-L12 *defective*. [377

TURCO, CARLO. Agnella comedia nuoua ... In Vinetia. [Aldine press,] M D LXXXV. 8°. A-H^8 I^4. [378

TURKEY. Anschlag wider die grausamen vnd blutdürstigen Thiraney des Türcken ... M.D.XXXXI. 4°. π^6. [379

-- Auszug eines Brieffs ... was das Türckisch Regiment vnd wesen sey/ vnd wie er es mit den landē/ so er erobert zühaltē pflegt/ kürzlich in Teutsche sprach gebracht ... [Nuremberg, Jobst Gutknecht,] M. D. XXvj 4°. A^4. [380

-- Chronica vnnd beschreibung der Türckey ... von eim Sibenbürger xxij. jar darinn gefangen gelegen yn Latein beschrieben/ verteütscht Mit eyner schönen Vorrhed [durch Martin Luther]. ... Anno M. D. XXX. (Gedruckt zu Nürmberg durch Fridericum Peypus.) 4°. A-M^4 N^2 O^4. ¶*Translator: Sebastian Franck*. (Lea.) [381

-- Commentario de le cose de Turchi, et del S. Georgio Scanderbeg ... M D XXXX. 8°. A-F^8. ff. 3-48. [382

-- De origine imperii Turcorum, eorumque administratione & disciplina ... Cui libellus de Turcorum moribus, collectus à Bartholomæo Georgieuiz, adiectus est. Cum præfatione ... Philippi Melanthonis. Vitebergæ anno M. D. LXII. 8°. A-M^8. [383

-- De Turcicarum et Barbarossae Triremium naufragio nuper in sinu Hadriatico facto. Epistola. [1538.] 4°. A^4 B^2. [384

-- Die gross erlegung des Türckischen heers vom Sophi in Persien beschehen. ... Sampt der eroberung des Türcken Schatz/ vnd der Frewlin seiner Versperr oder Frawenzimers/ in der ... Stat Tawris in Persien. Aus Italianischer sprach yetz new verteutscht. 15. Maij. 1535. 4°. [A]^4. [385

-- Rerum gestarum Turcarum et Sophi Persarum imp. de anno M.D.XIIII. breuiarium. (Impressum Augustæ [Johann Miller, 1514].) 4°. A^4. ¶*Wormholes in* A3-4. [386

-- Türkische grosse Niderlag. Warhaffte ... Beschreibung/ der zeweyen grossen ... Schlachten/ so der ... König in Persia/ dem Mustapha Bassa/ Türckischen Obristen ... aberhalten. ... [M. D. LXXIX.] (Gedruckt zu Nürnberg/ durch Leonhard Heussler.) 4°. A-B^4. ¶*Lower margin of* A1 *shaved*. [387

TURNÈBE, ADRIEN. Adriani Turnebi aduersariorum tomi III. ... Basileae Per Thomam Guarinum. MDLXXXI. fol.):(^{4} a-q^6 r^4 s-z^6 A-Mm^6. cols. 1-1200. ¶*Additional t.pp.:* (s1^r) ... tomus secundus. ... Basileae, MDLXXX. (Q1^r) ... Tomus tertius ... Basileae, MDLXXXI. Ee1^r: In Adriani Turnebi aduersariorum libros quaedam obseruationes [Io. Spondani] ...[388

-- Adriani Turnebi V.C. lucubrationes variæ. C. Plinii Historiæ naturalis Præfatio emendata & annotationibus illustrata. In M. T. Ciceronis I. Academicas Quæstiones, II. De Fata, III. De Legibus Libros tres, vna cum Apologia, IV. In Orationem pro C. Rabirio per duellionis res, Commentarii ... [Heidelbergae,] Apud Hieronymum Commelinum, Anno cIↄ Iↄ XCVII. 8°. A-B^8 C^4. pp. 3-40. ¶*The first part only (of six)*. [389

-- Poltrotus Meræus Adr. Turnebi. M.D.LXVII. Excudebat Henricus Stephanus, Geneuæ. 4°. A^6. [390

TURNÈBE

-- Adriani Turnebi ... tumulus, A Doctis quibusdam viris, è Græco, Latino, & Gallico carmine excitatus. Parisiis, Apud Federicum Morellum ... M. D. LXV. 4°. A^4. ¶*Authors: Joachim du Bellay, Jean Dorat, Pierre Ronsard.* [391

TURNER, ROBERT. [1] Roberti Turneri Deuonii ... Orationes XIV. ... Commentationes in loca scripturæ ... Ingolstadii, Ex Officina Typographica Dauidis Sartorii. Anno M. D. LXXXIIII. 8°.)(^{8} A-Q^8. pp. 1-253. [2] ... panegyrici sermones duo ... Ingolstadii, Ex Officina Typographica Dauidis Sartorii. Anno M. D. LXXXIII. (*Colophon.*) a-p^8. pp. 1-224. [392

TURNER, WILLIAM. [1] [The first and seconde partes of the Herbal of William Turner ... Imprinted at Collen by Arnold Birckman ... M. D. LXVIII. ...] fol. *^{4} (*wanting*) A^2 (*wanting*) A-B^6 C^8 D-S^6 (-Q6, R1, R6, S1) T^4 (-T4). pp. 1-213. [2] The seconde parte of Vuilliam Turners Herball ... *Same imprint.* π^2 A-Ee^6 (-A3-4, H6, K1, L5-6, O6, S5, X4-5, Cc1-2, Ee2-5) Ff^4 (-Ff4, *blank?*) Gg^2 (*wanting*). ff. 1-171. [3] The thirde parte ... *Same imprint.* *^{4} 3A-$3G^6$ (-3G6, *presumably blank*). pp. 1-81. *S.T.C.* 24367. ¶*Lacks part 4.*[392a

TUSCANY. Istoria delle cose auuenute in Toscana; Dall'anno 1300. al 1348. ... Scritta per Autore, che ne' medesimi tempi visse. ... In Firenze, Nella Stamperia de' Giunti. 1578. 4°. a-c^4 A-Dd^4 Ee^2. pp. 1-217. [393

-- *Cosimo I, grand duke.* Prouisione ... Che li banditi condennati in pena afflittiua, ò confinati, cosi del Dominio di Fiorenza, come di Siena, siano descritti à vn Libro particolare, sotto certo modo & forma. Publicato il di 14. d'Ottobre. 1569. Nuouamente Ristampata. In Fiorenza, nella Stamperia di lor'Altezze. Appresso Giorgio Marescotti. 1572. 4°. A^4. (Lea.) [394

-- Prouisioni dell'Archiuio Publico della Città ... stabilite. ... il di. xiiii. di Dicembre. 1569. ... In Fiorenza. Nella Stampa Ducale. 1569. 4°. A-D^4. pp. 3-32. (Lea.) [395

-- -- *Another copy.* [396

-- Prouisione per la quale prohibisce il giuocare a qual si voglia giuoco Inscritte, in pegni, o a credenza, sotto graui pene pecuniarie, e d'honore. Fatta ... Il di 24. di Dicembre. 1569. ... In Fiorenza Appresso Filippo Giunti, e' fratelli. 4°. A^4. (Lea.) [397

-- -- In Fiorenza. Nella Stamperia di Lor'Altezze. Appresso Giorgio Marescotti. MDLXXIII. 4°. A^4. (Lea.) [398

-- Perdono, et libera assolutione fatta per gratia, & per suo Moto proprio, dal ... Gran Duca di Toscana. A tutti li descritti della sua Militia dell'uno & dell'altro Stato di Fiorenza, e da Siena, Bāditi, cōdennati, & incorsi in qual si voglia pregiuditio, per alcune particulari transgressioni, & errori comessi da loro nell'impresa d'Vngaria. (Bandito ... questo di 24. di Dicembre. 1569.) In Fiorenza. Nella Stampa Ducale. 1569. 4°. π^2. (Lea.) [399

-- Bando che non si possa intromettere nelle quistioni d'altrui, ne fare Cartelli ne portarli ne Lettere, o imbasciate, ne far quadriglie, o dare aiuto ne fauore in dette quistioni. Publicato ... sotto Di 7. di Gennaio. 1569. In Fiorenza 1569. 4°. π^2. (Lea.) [400

-- Deliberatione ... Fatta il Di 26. di Gennaio. MDLXIX. Attenēte alli Notari ... In Fiorenza. MDLXIX. 4°. π^2. (Lea.) [401

-- -- In Fiorenza, Appresso Giorgio Marescotti. 4°. π^2. (Lea.) [402

-- Bando et dichiaratione sopra il capitolo XVIII. et XIX. Della legge dell'Archiuio publico ... Dell'obbligo de gl'heredi legatarij, & fideicommissarij. Publicato il di xiii. di Marzo. MDLXIX. Nuouamente Ristampato. In Fiorenza. Appresso Giorgio Marescotti. MDLXXIII. 4°. π^2. (Lea.) [403

-- Prouisione sopra il cuoiame vaccino da tomaie, et sua conciatura. ... il Di 7. d'Aprile. MDLXX. In Fiorenza Nella stamperia de'Giunti. 4°. π^2. (Lea.) [404

-- Deliberationi circa il modo et osservanza di piu capi delle leggi dell'Archiuio Publico. Publicato addi IX. d'Aprile MDLXX. In Fiorenze Appresso Giorgio Marescotti. 4°. π^2. (Lea.) [405

-- -- In Fiorenza. Appresso Giorgio Marescotti. MDLXXII. 4°. A^2. (Lea.) [406

-- Prouisioni concernanti il negotio et carico dell'Archiuio Publico. Fatte ... Il di xi d'Aprile. MDLXX. In Fiorenza. Nella Stampa Ducale. 1570. 4°. A^4. pp. 3-8. (Lea.) [407

-- -- *Another copy.* (Lea.) [408

-- Bando sopra le leggi et deliberationi nuouamente fatte. Circa, i Negotij dell'Archiuio Publico. Publicato il di 22. d'Aprile M D LXX. In Fiorenza Appresso i Giunti. 4°. π^2. (Lea.) [409

-- -- In Fiorenza. Appresso Giorgio Marescotti. MDLXXIII. 4°. A^2. (Lea.) [410

-- -- *Another copy.* (Lea.) [411

-- Bando Della prohibitione dell'arme di gamba, & de'giubboni, o imbusti rinforzati con agora, or magliente, che seruon per arme, & del prestare arme defensiue. Publicato ... sotto di xi. di Luglio ... 1570. In Fiorenza nella stampa Ducale MDLXX. 4°. A^2. (Lea.) [412

-- Prouisione et decreto ... Fatto il di XXVII. di Luglio MDLXX. Disponente Che tutte le Communitā dello stato di S. Altezza doue sono Archiuii, sieno tenute mandar tutte le scritture publiche che in essi si ritrouano, Al nuouo Archiuio della Cittā di Fiorenza. ... In Fiorēza nella stampa Ducale 1570. 4°. A^2. (Lea.) [413

-- -- In Fiorenza. Appresso Giorgio Marescotti. MDLXXIII. 4°. A^2. (Lea.) [414

-- Prouisione sopra la prohibitione delli abrenuntii Stamignioni: Ferrādine, & Erbagi ... Publicata il di 27. di Luglio. M. D. LXX. Fiorēza nella Stāpa di lor'Altezze. 4°. π^2. (Lea.) [415

-- Bando Et Legge, Contro a quelli Che incettano, Grani, & Biade. Publicata l'Anno. 1570. (Bandito ... questo di. 5. d'Agosto. M. D. LXX.) (In Fiorenza Nella Stamperia di lor'Altezze.) 4°. A^4. (Lea.) [416

-- -- Publicato l'Anno 1578. In Fiorenza, Nella Stamperia di Giorgio Marescotti. 1578. 4°. A^4. (Lea.) [417

-- Bando delle portate da darsi de Grani, Biade, & bocche. Publicato questo di 9. d'Agosto. 1570. In Fiorenza nella Stampa di lor'Altezze. 4°. π^2. (Lea.) [418

-- Legge sopra ogni sorte di scommesse. Fermata il di 3. di Ottobre. MDLXX. In Fiorenza. Nella Stāpa di lor'Altezze. MDLXX. 4°. A^2. (Lea.) [419

-- -- Legge di loro altezze seren. sopra ogni sorte Di scommesse. Fermata il di 3. di Ottobre. MDLXX. In Fiorenza Nella stamperia d'i Giunti MDLXXIIII. 4°. π^2. (Lea.) [420

-- Obligo de i notai di dar le copie duplicate alle parti de i contratti Stati rogati da loro & non rimessi ancora nell'Archiuio. (Stabilita & fermata ... il di primo di Febbraio MDLXXI.) In Fiorenza, Appresso Giorgio Marescotti. 4°. π^2. (Lea.) [421

-- Bando ... Sopra le Scaglie, Pubblicato A di 7. di Febbraio. M DLXXI. In Fiorenza Nella Stamperia de'Giunti. 4°. A^2. (Lea.) [422

-- Prouisione sopra l'ordine deuon tenere gl'esentionati ... per godere le loro immunitā fatta ... il di viii. di Febbraio. 1571. In Fiorenza. Nella Stampa di loro Altezze Serenissime. 1571. 4°. π^2. (Lea.) [423

-- Bando, et prohibitione dell'armi che si chiamano stiletti, quadrelli, sfondagiachi, & altre armi simili, Publicato ... questo di 27. di Febbraio. 1571. In Fiorenza Nella Stampa di loro Altezze, 1571. 4°. A^2. (Lea.) [424

-- Aggiunta fatta al bando delli stiletti quadrelli et sfondagiachi. Publicata Firenze sotto di 13. di Marzo. MDLXXI. s.sh. 49.5 × 20.5 cm. (Lea.) [425

-- Ordini Sopra Il gouerno delli comuni Del Contado, et Montagna di Pistoia. Deliberati il di 4. di Maggio. 1571. ... In Fiorenza, Nella Stamperia de' Giunti. 4°. A-B^4. (Lea.) [426

-- Legge et bando ... Sopra l'Extratione de'Grani, Biade, & altre Grascie, del Suo Ducale Stato. Publicato l'Anno. M. DLXXI. (Bādito ... questo di 27. di Giugno. M.D.LXXI.) In Fiorenza. Nella Stampa di lor'Altezze Serenissime MDLXXI. 4°. A^4. (Lea.) [427

-- Ordine ... Cosi sopra quello, & di quali instrumenti si debbe paghare all'Archiuio, come ancora circa il matricolare li Notai. Addi 20. di Luglio. M.D.LXXI. Nuouamente Ristampato. In Fiorenza. Nella Stamperia di Lor'Altezze. Appresso Giorgio Marescotti. 1572. 4°. A^2. (Lea.) [428

-- Prouisione de' ... conseruadori dell'Archiuio Publico Fiorentino Concernente l'obbligo de'Notari, di notificare à detto Archiuio, & suoi Ministri i proprij Protocolli, che si ritrouauano auanti quello, quali ancora hanno presso di lorò, & degli heredi, in manderueli dopo la morte di ciascheduno de' predetti Notari. Stampata in Fiorenza nell'Anno 1571. Et ristampata per Giorgio Marescotti, nel 1573. 4°. A^2. (Lea.) [429

-- Ordine, et modo sopra libelli diffamatorii, Fatto ... Sotto di 23. di Gennaio. MDLXXII. In Fiorenza. Appresso Giorgio Marescotti. MDLXXIII. 4°. A^2. (Lea.) [430

-- Nuouo Ordine sopra il dare, et rinnouare patente, et bullettini a descritti delle bande. Confirmata ... il di vltimo di Marzo MDLXXII. Nuouamente Ristampato. In Fiorenza, Nella Stamperia Ducale, Appresso Giorgio Marescotti. MDLXXIIII. 4°. π^2. (Lea.) [431

-- Legge, et prouuisione in fauor di quelli che Di nuouo andassino ad habitare familiarmente nel Contado di Pisa per lauorare, & cultiuare la terra, Ottenuta ... Il di XXIX. d'Aprile MDLXXII. In Fiorenza, Nella Stamperia de' Giunti. MDLXXII. 4°. A^4. (Lea.) [432

-- Riforma, et prouisione concernente l'autorità Del Magistrato de' Conseruatori di Legge ... & altri Rettori del suo Dominio. In beneficio delle pouere persone litiganti, Ottenuta ... il dì 29. d'Aprile MDLXXII. In Fiorenza, Nella Stamperia de'Giunti. MDLXXII. 4°. A^4. (Lea.) [433

-- Bando ... Sopra il Cōdurre Pesce, & del modo di venderlo in Fiorenza. Deliberato il dì 23. di Maggio 1572. In Fiorenza. Nella Stamperia di Lor'Altezze. Appresso Giorgio Marescotti. 1572. 4°. A^2. [434

-- Prouisione, et ordine che li contratti fatti, & rogati da Calē di Marzo 1569. in quà, & che si trouano, & si trouerranno nell'Archiuio publico Fiorentino dopo la morte di quei Notari, che ne saranno rogati si deuino deporre & mettere nell'Archiuio del Proconsole, per perpetua conseruatione. Fatto ... Il di 18. di Luglio. 1572. (In Fiorenza. Appresso Giorgio Marescotti Stampator di lor'Altezze. M.D. LXXII.) 4°. A^2. (Lea.) [435

-- Bando sopra il commertio libero tra li Stati di Fiorenza, e Siena, E che di quelli non si possa estrarre ne'paesi alieni qual si voglia sorte di Bestiame Vaccino. Fermato questo di 24. di Settembre MDLXXII. In Fiorenza. Nella Stamperia di lor'Altezze. Appresso Giorgio Marescotti. 1572. 4°. A^4. (Lea.) [436

-- Prouisione nuouamente fatta sopra l'apostille, cancellature, Rasure, Rastiature, & in qual forma si deuino descriuere le somme, quantità, tempi, & numeri dentro al corpo degli Instrumenti, Con la moderatione sopra delle nudità de' Contratti fatti ... (Bandito ... 8. di Marzo. 1573.) In Fiorenza, Alla Stamperia di lor'Altezze, Appresso Giorgio Marescotti, 1574. 4°. A^2. (Lea.) [437

-- Prouisione et ordine. Che le pouere persone habitanti nello stato di Fiorenza possino conuenire li Cittadini Fiorentini dauanti al Magistrato de'Conseruadori di Legge, per le liti, che mouer volessino contra essi. Fatto ... questo di 7. di Luglio 1573. In Fiorenza Nella stamperia de'Giunti. 4°. π^2. (Lea.) [438

-- Legge sopra il modo di procedere nelle Cause Delle Confiscazione. ... Ottenuta ... sotto di xi. di Decembre MDLXXIII. In Fiorenza Nella stamperia de'Giunti. 4°. A^4. (Lea.) [439

-- Proibizione ... Delli Scudi Leggieri, Pubblicata l'Anno MDLXXIII. (Addi di Nouembre. MDLXXIII.) In Fiorenza, Appresso Giorgio Marescotti. MDLXXV. 4°. A^2. (Lea.) [440

-- Bando del modo, et come li hosti et abergatori Possano comperare il Vino, Et come, & quando lo possano riuendere alle loro Hosterie, & Aberghi. (Bandito ... 3. di Gennaio 1574.) In Fiorenza, Nella Stamperia Ducale, Appresso Giorgio Marescotti. MDLXXIIII. 4°. A^2. (Lea.) [441

-- *Francesco I, grand duke*. Bando della proibitione delle scommesse Sopra la vita, & morte de Papi, & altri Signori, cosi Temporali, come Spirituali, Publicato ... sotto li 7. di Giugno, MDLXXIIII. In Fiorenza, Nella Stamperia ducale, Appresso Giorgio Marescotti, MDLXXIIII. 4°. π^2. (Lea.) [442

-- -- In Fiorenza nella Stamperia de'Giunti 1574. 4°. A^2. (Lea.) [443

-- Bando ... Sopra il prestare Caualli a vettura Secondo la nuoua Riforma del Sale. Pubblicato il di 15. d'Agosto MDLXXIIII. In Fiorenza, Nella Stamperia Ducale, Appresso Giorgio Marescotti. MDLXXV. 4°. A^2. (Lea.) [444

-- Bando della nuoua riforma del sale. ... Nuouamente publicato il Dì 4. d'Ottobre 1574. In Fiorenza, Appresso i Giunti. ... 4°. A^4 B^2. (Lea.) [445

-- Bando che' vetturini non possino fare Compagnia con Albergatori, Ne Vetturino con altro Vetturino, & Ordine fra Procacci, & Vetturini. (Bandito ... 9. di Nouembre 1574.) In Fiorenza Nella Stamperia de'Giunti. 4°. π^2. (Lea.) [446

-- Instruzione ... Sopra le cose de Coiami di tutto'l Dominio Fiorentino, Alli Rettori si esso Dominio. A di 7. d'Aprile 1575. In Fiorenza. Appresso i Giunti. 4°. A^4. (Lea.) [447

-- Bando ... Che non si posse estrarre Piantoni, ò altre Piante di Vliui. Publicato questo di 14. d'Aprile. 1575. In Fiorenza, Nella Stamperia Ducale, Appresso Giorgio Marescotti. MDLXXV. 4°. A^2. (Lea.) [448

-- Prouisione fatta ... Sopra l'Ordine da tenersi di non poter cauar senza Gabella fuori del Dominio ... Sete nate, ò da nascere di sorte alcuna per benefitio dell'Arte, & dell' Vniuersale. Publicata il di 10. di Giugno 1575. In Fiorenza, Appresso Giorgio Marescotti. MDLXXV. 4°. A^4. (Lea.) [449

-- Bando che non si possa cauare dello stato ... Salina senza Licentia. (Bandito ... 30. di Luglio 1575.) In Fiorenza, Appresso Giorgio Marescotti. MDLXXV. 4°. π^2. (Lea.) [450

-- Bando delle portate da darsi de' grani, et biade, Publicato questo di d'Agosto 15 In Fiorenza, Nella Stamperia di Giorgio Marescotti [1575?] 4°. A^4. (Lea.) [451

-- Bando che non si possa comperare vino per riuendere, Et à chi è permesso, & quanto sono obbligati li Vinattieri. (Bandito ... 11. d'Ottobre. 1575.) In Fiorenza, Appresso Giorgio Marescotti. MDLXXV. 4°. A^2. (Lea.) [452

-- Bando di proroga di dare le portate Che hauessi compero Vino, & non l'hauessi date. (Bandito ... 29. di Nouembre 1575.) In Fiorenza, Appresso Giorgio Marescotti. MDLXXV. 4°. A^2. (Lea.) [453

-- Prouisione sopra li drappi forestieri, et lor gabelle, Con la prohibitione delli Ori falsi. Fatta ... il dì 16. di Dicembre MDLXXV. In Fiorenza, Appresso Giorgio Marescotti. MDLXXV. 4°. A^4. (Lea.) [454

-- Bando rinnouato circa il mettere insieme e Riscontri delle Polize dei Macinato per farne la Reuisione Generale, Publicato il di noue di Maggio. 1576. In Fiorenza, Appresso Giorgio Marescotti. MDLXXVI. 4°. A^2. (Lea.) [455

-- Prouisione nuouamente fatta sopra l'ordine di poter estrarre del Dominio di S. Altezza Sete, & Doppi nostrali, oltro al modo dell'altra Legge per ciò fatta sin'à di x. di Giugno. 1575. Stabilita ... il dì 15. di Maggio 1576. In Fiorenza, Appresso Giorgio Marescotti. MDLXXVI. 4°. A^6. (Lea.) [456

-- Bando attenente all'arte di Porta Santa Maria, Circa il vendere li Ori, & Arienti filati, & tirati. (Bandito ... 16. di Maggio 1576.) In Fiorenza, Appresso Giorgio Marescotti. MDLXXVI. 4°. A^4. (Lea.) [457

-- Bando attenente all'arte di Porta Santa Maria, Per conto delle Matricole da pagarsi per quelli, che esercitano delli Esercitii, & Membri sotto posti alla dett'Arte. ... (Bandito ... 26. di Maggio 1576.) In Fiorenza, Appresso Giorgio Marescotti. MDLXXVI. 4°. A^4. (Lea.) [458

-- Bando contro a banditi rebelli, assassini, et homicidiarii, Publicato ... sotto dì 29. di Maggio 1576. In Fiorenza, Appresso Giorgio Marescotti. MDLXXVI. 4°. A^4. (Lea.) [459

-- Prouisione, et nuoua riforma attenente all'arte di Porta Santa Maria concernente l'esercitio degli orefici ... publicata ... il dì 9. di Giugno 1576. In Fiorenza, Appresso Giorgio Marescotti. 1576. 4°. A^4 B^2. (Lea.) [460

-- Bando del douer piantare gelsi. Publicato il di 16. di Giugno 1576. In Fiorenza Appresso i Giunti. 4°. π^2. (Lea.) [461

-- Deliberatione che non si possa agucchiare stame, o lana nel contado, et Distretto Di Fiorenza. ... Sotto do 9. d'Agosto 1576. In Fiorenza Appresso i Giunti. 4°. π^2. [462

-- Bando fatto per li ... maestri di zecca ... Che'l non si possa dare aggio alle Monete, Publicato il dì 2. di Nouembre 1576. In Fiorenza, Appresso Giorgio Marescotti. 4°. A^2. (Lea.) [463

-- Bando circa l'ordine da tenersi per quelli che comperano Panno à Taglio. ... Il di 18. di Dicembre 1576. In Fiorenza Appresso i Giunti. 4°. π^2. (Lea.) [464

-- Bando della nuoua riforma de' conseruadori et officiali d'honesta. Publicato il di 3. di Marzo, 1577. In Firenze, Appresso i Giunti, 1577. 4°. A^4. (Lea.) [465

-- Bando ... Sopra le Potentie della città di Firenze. Publicato il di 18. Giugno 1577. In Fiorenza. 1577. 4°. π^2. (Lea.) [466

-- Bando delle proibitioni delle Monete forestiere, e Fiorentine tose, Eccettuato per vn'anno solo tre sorte di Monete Genouese. Publicato a di 24. di Luglio. 1577. In Fiorenza, Appresso Giorgio Marescotti. 1577. 4°. A^4. (Lea.) [467

-- Bando della proibitione delli scudi leggieri et di oro basso Publicato questo dì 12 d' Agosto. 1577. In Fiorenza, Appresso Giorgio Marescotti. 1577. 4°. A^2. (Lea.) [468

-- Deliberatione de Sig. Riformatori dell'Arte di Porta Santa Maria Quanto alle Drapperie, nella quali e lecito metter Sete crude. Et circa le tasse da pagarsi per i Merciai, che voglion tenere a vendere Drappi. (Bandito ... questi di 17. d'Agosto 1577.) In Fiorenza, Appresso Giorgio Marescotti. 1577. 4°. A^2. [469

-- Bando sopra alli archibusi a ruota di maggior misura con la serpentina, Che si comprendino nel Bando della Prohibitione dell'Arme in Hasta. Publicato ... il dì 4. di Settembre 1577. In Fiorenza, Appresso Giorgio Marescotti. 1577. 4°. A^4. (Lea.) [470

-- Editto delle prohibizioni dell'ingresso delle meretrici. In alcuna Chiesa, & altri luoghi pij Della Citta, & Diocesi di Firenze. (Datum ... Nonis Settembris. MDLXXVII.) In Firenze. Appresso i Giunti. 4°. π^2. (Lea.) [471

-- Bando per conto de tiralori, battilori, tessitori d'Oro, & altri Artieri sottoposti all' Arte di Por Santa Maria. Che fussino andati, ò che andassino per l'auuenire à lauorare fuori dello stato, & Dominio Fiorentino, Fatto ... il di xxx. d'Aprile 1578. In Fiorenza, Nella Stamperia di Giorgio Marescotti. 1578. 4°. A^2. (Lea.) [472

-- Proroga d'vn'anno fatta sopra la prohibitione Del non potere estrarre del Dominio Stracci, Bozzoli, ne altre Rigaglie. (Adi 3. di Giugno 1578.) In Fiorenza, Nella Stamperia di Giorgio Marescotti. 1578. 4°. A^2. (Lea.) [473

-- Prouisioni circ' alcuni ordini dell'Archiuio Publico Fiorentino, Di limitationi di pene, & dell'obligo, che li Notai deuino tener vn Protocollo a parte per e testamenti, & altre cose ... A di 13. di Giugno 1578. In Fiorenza, Nella Stamperia di Giorgio Marescotti. 1578. 4°. A^2. (Lea.) [474

-- Bando et ordinatione che le strade publiche si mantenghino sempre in buono essere. Publicato il di 14. Giugno 1578. In Firenze. Appresso i Giunti. 4°. A^4 B^2 (-B2, *presumably blank*). (Lea.) [475

-- Bando de' tre proueditori dell'arte di Por Santa Maria, Per Conto de Drappi forestieri. (Bandito ... 13. d'Ottobre. 1578.) In Fiorenza, Nella Stamperia di Giorgio Marescotti. 1578. 4°. A^2. (Lea.) [476

-- Legge, et bando ... Sopra l'Estrattione de' Grani, Biade, & altre Grasce del suo Ducale stato. Publicato l'Anno M.DLXXVIII. In Fiorenza, Nella Stamperia di Giorgio Marescotti. 4°. A^4. (Lea.) [477

-- Bando et prohibitione de giuochi, et biscazze. (Bandito ... 18. di Maggio 1579.) In Fiorenza, Nella Stamperia di Giorgio Marescotti. M D LXXIX. 4°. A^2. (Lea.) [478

-- Nuoua prouuisione dell'Archiuio Publico Fiorentino. (Bandito ... 20. d'Aprile 1581.) In Fiorenza, Nella Stamperia di Giorgio Marescotti. MDLXXXI. 4°. A^2. (Lea.) [479

-- Bando che per vn'anno prossimo si possino spendere Le tre sorte di Monete di Roma. (Bandito ... 11 d'Agosto 1581.) In Fiorenza, Appresso Giorgio Marescotti. M. D. LXXXI. 4°. A^2. (Lea.) [480

-- Legge, et prouisione penale contra quelli, Che diuerranno all'atto del fallimento, & cessatione, massimo con fraude, ò dolo. ... Sotto dì XX. d'Aprile 1582. In Firenze, Nella Stamperia de i Giunti. ... 4°. A^4. (Lea.) [481

-- Decreto sopra la cognitione et decisione delle nullità de' Contratti, & altri atti gabellabili. (A di 18. di Settembre 1582.) In Fiorenza MDLXXXII. Appresso Giorgio Marescotti. 4°. A^2. (Lea.) [482

-- Bando e prohibitione del non poter tenere ne vsare Palline, Gocciole, Migliaruole, Dadi, Palle ramate, ò altro che la palla grossa sola nel tirare gli archibusi publicato ... el dì primo di Luglio 1583. In Fiorenza, Appresso Giorgio Marescotti, MDLXXXVI. 4°. A^2. (Lea.) [483

-- Prouisione ottenuta nel Senato de' 48. Sotto di 8. di Marzo 1584. In correzzione dello statuto, de incendiis, & vastis, &c. In Fiorenza. Appresso Giorgio Marescotti. 1584. 4°. A^2. [484

-- Bando che non si possa fare Scommesse, à Mastio, ò Femmina. (Bandito ... 6. di Nouembre. 1585.) In Fiorenza, Appresso Giorgio Marescotti. 1585. 4°. π^2. (Lea.) [485

-- *Ferdinand I, grand duke.* Bando e prouisione sopra le scommesse da farsi per causa di promotioni Di Cardinali, & ordini da tenersi per li Sensali di dette Scommesse. (Bandito ... 16. di Febbraio. 1587.) In Firenze Per Iacopo, e Bernardo Giunti. 1587. 4°. π^4. (Lea.) [486

-- Bando contro gl'estrattori delle grasce Del Capitanato di Pietra Santa. (Bandito ... 1. di Febbraio 1589.) In Firenze, appresso Giorgio Marescotti. M D LXXXIX. 4°. A^4 (-A4, *presumably blank*). (Lea.) [487

-- Bando contro a sensali di scommesse di cardinali. (Bandito ... 24. di Marzo 1589.) In Firenze, appresso Giorgio Marescoti. ... 4°. π^2. (Lea.) [488

-- Bando attenente alli aderenti, et aiutanti delli sensali principali Deputati sopra le Scommesse di Sede Vacante, & promotione di Cardinali. (Bandito ... 14. di Nouemb. 1589.) In Fiorenza, Appresso Georgio Marescotti. M D LXXXIX. 4°. A^4. (Lea.) [489

-- Bando e prohibitione di scommesse sopra la promotione de cardinali. (Bandito ... 27. di Dicembre. 1589.) In Firenze, appresso Giorgio Marescotti. M D LXXXIX. 4°. A^4 (-A4, *presumably blank*). (Lea.) [490

-- Bando et prohibitione del giuoco di carte Et dadi per la Città di Firenze Et per lo Stato & dominio Fiorentino. (Bandito ... 7. Gennaio 1590.) In Firenze Appresso Giorgio Marescotti. 4°. A^4 (-A4, *presumably blank*). (Lea.) [491

-- Priuilegii concessi Di nuouo ... Alli Archibusieri à Cauallo. (xj. di Giugno 1590.) 4°. π^2. (Lea.) [492

-- Bando sopra la proibizione del Sale Forestiero. (Bandito ... 14 di Dicembre 1590.) In Firenze, Per Giorgio Marescotti M.D.XC. ... 4°. π^2. (Lea.) [493

-- Deliberatione ... sopra l'esentioni, & priuilegij di nuouo concessi a tutti quelli che andaranno ad habitare, & habitassino nella Terra di Liuorno, & suo Capitaneato. Questo dì 12. di Febbraio 1591. ... In Firenze, Appresso Giorgio Marescotti. 4°. A^4 (-A4, *presumably blank*). (Lea.) [494

-- Per Ordine delli ... Otto di Balia [wagers on the death of the pope and the promotion of cardinals made since 19 March 1590 are nullified. March 1591.] s.sh. 20 × 20.5 cm. (Lea.) [495

-- Bando e prohibitione del giuocare à Scommesse, Sopra l'elettione de' futuri Pontefici. (Bandito ... 4. di Aprile. 1591.) In Fiorenza Appresso Giorgio Marescotti. 1591. 4°. A^2. (Lea.) [496

-- Prouisione sopra le donne maritate, O che si mariteranno a' Forestieri. (Bandito ... 28. di Maggio. 1591.) In Fiorenza, Appresso Giorgio Marescotti. 1591. 4°. A^4 (-A4, *presumably blank*). (Lea.) [497

-- Ordine e instruzione per i capitani delle bande di S.A.S. In Firenze Appresso Giorgio Marescotti [after 1592]. 4°. A^4. (Lea.) [498

TYNDALE, WILLIAM. The whole workes of W. Tyndall, Iohn Frith, and Doct. Barnes ... At London Printed by Iohn Daye ... 1573. (... 1572.) fol. B.L. A-Y^4 Aa-Yy^6 AA-EE^6 FF-GG^4 HH-XX^6 YY^4 3A-$3Q^6$ (3A1 + *3A2-4*) $3R^4$. pp. 1-478, 3-376. *S.T.C.* 24436. ¶*Additional t.pp.:* ($GG3^r$) The workes of ... Iohn Frith ... ($3A1^r$) The workes of Doctour Barnes. [499

-- The exposition of the fyrste Epistle of seynt Ihon with a Prologge before it: by W. T. [Antwerp, Martin de Keyser.] (The yere ... 1531. in September.) 8°. B.L. A-H^8 (-H8, *blank*). *S.T.C.* 24443. [500

TYPOETS, JAKOB. Iac. Typotii. Epistolæ II. Ad ordines imperii. De Salute Patriæ. Halæ Saxonum. Typis Pauli Greberi, anno M.D.XCVIII. 8°. A-Z^8. pp. 1-72. (Lea.) [501

-- Iacobi Typotii, orationes Turcicæ tres. Quarta, Quinta, & Sexta. I. Pro Christianis contra Turcas. Habita Rebus Secundis, II. Pro salute Omnium, contra Paucorum insolentiam. Habita Rebus Dubiis, III. Spes ostentatur, contra Opinionem Pseudochristianorum. Habita rebus adversis. Halæ Saxonum, Typis Pauli Greberi, anno M.D.XCVIII. 8°.)(^{8} ^{2})(^{8} A-N^8. pp. 1-207. (Lea.) [502

TYROL. *Ferdinand, king of the Romans.* [Proclamation against disorderly legal proceedings, especially excessive eating and drinking, with seal.] Geben zů Ynnsprugk am Vierundzwaintzigisten tag des Monats Martij/ Anno dñi im Fünfftzehenhundert vnd Zwayvnduiertzigisten ... s.sh. 25.5 × 37 cm. [503

-- *Ferdinand, archduke of Austria.* [Proclamation setting prices of meals and wine for different classes of consumers, with countersignatures and seal.] Geben in ... Ynnsprugg/ den Aindlifften tag Decembris. Anno ꝛc. im Achtundsechtzigisten ... s.sh. 72.5 × 52 cm. ¶*Defective.* [504

-- [Mandate on legal fees, with countersignatures and seal.] Geben in ... Ynssprugg/ den Neuntzehenden tag Monats Maij/ Anno ꝛc. Sechssvndactzig. s.sh. 79 × 56.5 cm. [505

-- Fürstlicher Durchleuchtigkayt Ertzhertzog Ferdinand zů Osterreich ... Ordnung vnd Reformation gůter Policey/ in ... Graffschafft Tirol. 4°. A-G^4 H^2. ff. I-XXIX. ¶*Dated 14 December 1573.* [506

U

UBALDI, ANGELO DEGLI. [Commentaria in digestum.] Lugduni [Jacobus Giunta]. 1548. (... Exarata per Georgium regnault.) fol. B.L. [1] Angelus de Perusio super Prima Infortiati. ... purgata. per ... Nico. de Lacu de Alice. ... A-H^{8} I^{10}. ff. 2-73. [2] ... super Secunda Infortiati. ... AA-FF^{8} GG^{10}. ff. 2-57. [3] ... super Prima Digesti noui. ... a-f^{8} g-h^{6}. ff. 2-53. [4] ... super Secunda Digesti noui. A-Q^{8}. ff. 2-128. [5] ... super Prima parte Digesti veteris. ... antepositis summariis ... per ... Nico. de Lacu de Alice. ... A-AA^{8} BB^{6}. ff. 2-197. [6] ... super Secunda parte Digesti veteris. ... A-K^{8} L^{6}. ff. 2-85. [7] Repertorium ... a-m^{8} n^{10}. (Biddle.) [1

-- Angelus de Perusio super Codice. ... cum additio ... Francisci Cursii ... Lugduni [Jacobus Giunta]. 1548 (Impressum ... per Thomam Bertheau.) fol. B.L. a-z^{8} A-L^{8} M-N^{6}. ff. 2-284. (Biddle.) [2

UBALDINI, GIOVANNI BATTISTA. Istoria della casa de gli Vbaldini, e de' fatti d'alcuni di quella Famiglia. Libro primo. ... E la vita di Niccola Acciaioli ... de scritta da Matteo Palmieri. ... In Firenze, Nella Stamperia di Bartolommeo Sermartelli. MDLXXXVIII. 4°. a^{10} A-H^{8} (B4 + *folded double leaf*) I^{2} K-M^{8}. pp. 1-181. ¶*Additional t.p.* (K1^{r}): La vita di Niccola Acciaioli ... Descritta in lingua latina da Matteo Palmieri ... E fatta volgare da M. Donato Acciaioli ... *Same imprint. Between sigg.* I *and* K *7 leaves, probably from another book, are inserted:* [A1, *mounted*] All'Illustriss. e Reuerendiss. Sig. Card. Vbladino legato di Bologna. In Bologna, per Theodoro Mascheroni, & Clemente Ferroni. ... 1625. A2^{r}: *dedication signed* Cornelio Ghirardelli. A2^{v}: *commendatory poem.* a3^{r}-a6^{v}: Antichita dell'illustrissima, & Inclitissima Famiglia Vbaldina. [a7] *blank.* [3

UBALDINI, GIOVANNI PAOLO. Carmina poetarum nobilium Io. Pauli Vbaldini studio conquisita. ... Mediolani Apud Antonium Antonianum. 1563. (... Apud Valerium ac fratres Metios. ...) 8°. A-N^{8} O^{4}. ff. 2-107. [4

UBALDIS, BALDUS DE. Practica Baldi. ... Practica iuris vtriusq3 ...: cum additionib9 dñi Antonij de Cremonte ... et cu3 pristinis apostillis ... Celsi Hugonis dissuti. ... 1528 (Impressum Lugduni in calcographia ... Antonij Blanchard ... die vero .vj. Februarij.) 4°. B.L. A^{8} B^{4} a-m^{8}. ff. I-XCVI. ¶m8^{v}: *device of* Sy. vincẽt. (Biddle.) [5

-- -- 1530 ... Venũdant̃ Lugd. a Iacobo Giunti ... (Impressum ... in calcographia ... Ioannis Crespini.) 8°. B.L. A-N^{8}. ff. j-xciij. (Lea.) [6

-- Tractatus exquisitissimi. De questionibus et tormentis secundum Baldum. ... De testibus secundum Bartholum ... De sponsalibus ⁊ matrimonijs ẜm Iohannẽ andree (... impẽsis Iohis Barbier calcographi atq3 bibliopole alma vniuersitatis Parrhisieñ ... impressa. Anno ... Millesimo quĩgẽtesimo octauo: tercio idus octobris.) 8°. B.L. a-q^{8}. ff. i-cxxvij. (Lea.) [7

UBERTI, FAZIO DEGLI. Opera di Faccio Degliuberti Fiorentino Chiamato Ditta Mundi. ... (Impresso ĩ Venetia per Christofaro di Pensa da mãdelo Adi .iiii. setẽbrio M.CCCCC.I.) 4°. a-z^{8} &^{8} ɔ^{8} ꝶ^{8} A-G^{8} H^{4} (-H4, *presumably blank*). [8

UGONI, FLAVIO ALESSIO. Flauii Alexii Vgonii ... De maximis Italiæ atque Græciæ calamitatibus. ... In Academia Veneta, M. D. LIX. (*Colophon.*) 4°. a^{4} A-H^{4} I^{6} K-R^{4} S^{6}. ff. 2-74. [9

-- Dialogo della vigilia, et del sonno del ... Signore Vgoni ... In Venetia, Appresso Pietro da Fine. CIϽ IϽ LXII. 8°. A-F^{8}. pp. 1-80. [10

-- Discorso ... Della dignità & eccellenza della gran città di Venetia. ... In Venetia, Appresso Pietro da Fine. CIϽ IϽ LXII. 8°. aa-bb^{8}. pp. 1-24. [11

-- Ragionamento ... nel quale si ragiona di tutti gli stati dell'humana uita. In Venetia, Appresso Pietro da Fine. CIϽ IϽ LXII. 8°. AA-HH^{8}. pp. 1-116. [12

-- -- *Another copy.* [13

-- Trattato ... della impositione de' nomi. In Venetia, Appresso Pietro da Fine CIϽ IϽ LXII. 8°. Aa-Bb^{8}. pp. 1-22. [14

UGONI, MATTIA. Synodia Vgonia episcopi Phamaugustani. De conciliis [Brixiae, 1534.] fol. B.L. π^1 Aa^4 A-Z^6 ꝛ^8. ff. 1-145. (Lea.) [15

UGONI, POMPEO. Pompeii Vgonii aduersus barbaros Latini candoris hostes oratio ... Romae, Ex Typographia Vincentij Accolti. ... M. D. LXXXVIII. ... 4°. A-B^4. [16

-- Pompei Vgonii Romani ... de lingua Latina Oratio. ... Romae, ... M.D.LXXXVI. Apud Ioannem Martinellum. (*Colophon.*) 4°. A^4 B^6. pp. 3-18. [17

-- Pompeii Vgonii Romani ... oratio de laudibus literarum. ... Romae, Apud Iacobum Ruffinellum. M D LXXXVIII. ... 4°. A^4. [18

ULLOA, ALFONSO DE. Commentari del Sig. Alfonso Vlloa, della guerra, che il ... duca d'Alua ... ha fatto contra Guglielmo di Nansau ... Insieme con le cose occorse tra la reina d' Inghilterra, l'Ambasciatore Catolico appresso quella Maiestà, & il sopra detto Duca d'intorno all'arresto fatto di alcune naui ... Et quel, che piu auuenne fino alla morte del Principe di Condè in Francia ... In Venetia, appresso Bolognino Zaltieri. M D LXX. 4°. *-**^{4} A-M^4 N^2. pp. 2-99. [19

-- La historia dell'impresa di Tripoli di Barberia, della presa del Pegnon di Velez della Gomera in Africa, Et del successo della ... armata Turchesca, uenuta sopra l'isola di Malta l'anno 1565. La descrittione dell'Isola di Malta. Il disegno dell'Isola delle Zerbe ... [Venezia, Alfonso de Ulloa, 1566.] 4°. a-b^4 b^2 (b2 + *folded leaf*) A-Y^4. ff. 2-87. [20

-- Vita dell' ... imperator Carlo V. ... Terza impressione ... In Venetia, Appresso Vincenzo Valgrisio. M D LXVI. 4°. A-VV^8 a-b^4 c^2. ff. 5-344. [21

-- -- In Venetia, Dalla Bottegha d'Aldo. M. D. LXXV. 4°. A-XX^8. ff. 2-344. [22

ULM. Ordnung die ain Ersamer Rath der Statt Vlm/ in abstellung hergeprachter etlicher misspreuch ... (Verkündt ... vff Sontag nach Sant Osswalds tag/ Anno, ꝛc. xxxj.) fol. a-d^6 e^4 f^6. [23

ULNER, HERMANN. Copiosa supellex elegantissimarum, Germanicae et Latinae linguae, phrasium ... aucta ... VVolffgango Gruningio Hirsfeldiano. ... Francoforti ad Moenum per VVendelinum Hom. Anno M. D. LXXXVI. (*Colophon.*) 8°. a-b^8 A-Pp^8 (-Pp8, *blank*). pp. 1-547. [24

ULSTADT, PHILIPP. Coelum philosophorum, seu secreta naturae ... ex authoribus ... Iohanne de Rupescissa, Raymundo, Lullio, Arnoldo de uilla noua, Albertoq; Magno, à Philippo Vlstadio ... collectus. ... Argentorati excudebat Iacobus Cammerlander Moguntinum. Anno M. D. XXXV. fol. π^4 A-L^4. ff. 1-44. (Smith.) [25

-- -- Coelum philosophorum ... Adcessit Ioan. Anto. Campesij Directorium Summæ summarum Medicinæ. ... apposimus Rosarium Philosophorum, Magistri Arnaldi de Villanoua. Lugduni, Apud Gulielmum Rouillium 1572. 16°. A-TT^8. pp. 3-649. (Smith.) [26

-- -- Le Ciel des Philosophes, ou sont contenus les secretz de nature ... On les vend à Paris par Viuant Gaultherot ... 1550. 8°. ¶^{8} A-M^8 N^2. ff. 1-98. (Smith.) [27

UNGER, BASIL. Zwo Predigten Eine Bey der Leich. Des ... Herrn Wilhelmen Grauen ... zu Hennenberg ... durch M. Basilium Vnger ... Die andere. zu Schmalkalden durch ... Christophorum Fischer ... gethan. Sampt etlichen Epitaphijs. M. D. LIX. (Ienae Excudebat Thomas Rebart. ...) 4°. A-G^4 H^6. [28

UNTERREDUNG. Ein vnderred des Bapsts vnd seiner cardinalen wie im zu thun sey/ vnd das wort Gottes vnder zu trucken ... 4°. a-d^4. [29

UNTERRICHT. Vnderricht auss Göttlichen vnd Gaystlichen Rechten ... ob ain Priester ain Eeweyb/ oder Concubin/ das ist/ ain beyschlaff haben möge. Von eynem Ainsidel lange zeyt in Polnischer Hayd gewonet ... M. D. XXVI. ... 4°. A-D^4. [30

-- Vnterricht vnnd Antwurt/ auff die siben todtsünd/ Achtsaligkait/ vñ Zehen gebott/ so der Gott loss hauff/ denen so in Christo glaubē (die sy Lutherisch nennē) zů Schmach aussgeben M.D.xxiiii. 4°. A-B^4. [31

UNTERWEISUNG. M.D.XXIII Ain schöne/ gaistliche/ vnd der hailigen schrifft gegründte vnderweysung von wegen der gelübten. 4°. A-C^4 (-C4, *presumably blank*). [32

URANIUS, HENRICUS. Compendium Hebraeae Grammatices ... Basileae, ex officina Henricpetrina. (... mense Ianuario anno M.D.LXVIII.) 8°. A-F^8 G^4. pp. 3-102. [33

-- De seruilium literarum apud Hebraeos vsu et officijs ... Coloniae Agrippinae, Ad intersignium Monocerotis, Anno M. D. LXX. 8°. A-H^8 I^4. pp. 1-120. [34

URBANUS BOLZANIUS. Vrbani grammaticae institutiones, Græcæ ... Basileae, apud Valentinum Curionem, anno M. D. XXX. (... mense Septembri. ...) 4°. a-z^4 A-Ii^4. ff. 1-215. [35

URCEO, ANTONIO, CODRO. In hoc Codri volumine haec continentur. Orationes. seu sermones ... Epistolæ Siluæ Satyræ Eglogæ Epigrammata (Impressum Bononiæ per Ioannem Antoniū Platonidem ... Mcccccii. die uero .VII. Martii. ...) fol. A^8 B-I^6 L-Q^6 R^4 S^6 T^4 A^8 B-H^6 I^4 α^8. [36

URSIN, JEAN. Elegiae de peste de eaque medicinae parte quae in victus ratione consistit. ... Alexandriae 1549. (Excudebant Franciscus et Simon, Moscheni, fratres Bergomenses. ...) 4°. A-G^4. pp. 3-48. [37

URSINUS, CASPAR. Hoc in libello hæc continentur. Monosticha Regum Italiæ, Albanorum, Romanorū, & virorum illustrium, tum Cæsarum ... Monosticha summorum Pontificum Rom. ... Eiusdem Carmen ad Adrianum Sextum ... Epigrammata quædam selectiora. (Excusum Viennæ Austriæ, per Ioannē Singreniū. ... M.D.XXVIII. ...) 4°. A-E^4. [38

-- Oratio de ... electione ... Ferdinandi Archiducis Austriæ in Regem Romanorum ... Coloniæ, Per me Petrum Quentell. Anno M. D. XXXI. 4°. A-B^4. [39

-- In hoc libello haec habentur. Oratio dominica in uersus adstricta ... Aurea carmina Pythagoræ græce, ac deinde latina eodem Vrsino interprete. Eiusdem epistola ad D. Erasmū Rhoterodamum. Eiusdem varia Epigrammata. (Viennæ Austriæ per Ioannē Singreniū. Anno. XXIIII.) 4°. A-B^6. [40

-- Querela Austriae, siue epistola ad reliquam Germaniam ... M. D. XXXI. (Augustæ Vindelicorum per Alexandrum Vueyssenhorn.) 4°. A-C^4. ¶*In verse.* [41

UVA, BENEDETTO DELL'. Il pensier della morte ... In Firenze. Appresso Bartolomeo Sermartelli. MDLXXXII. 4°. A^4 a-e^4. pp. 1-40. ¶*In verse.* [42

-- [1] Le vergini prudenti ... Cioe Il Martirio di S. Agata. Lucia. Agnesa. Giustina. Caterina. ... In Firenze Nella Stamperia di Bartolommeo Sermartelli. MDLXXXVII. 4°. π^4 A-M^8 N^4. pp. 1-198. [2] Il pensier della morte ... *Same imprint.* a-c^8. pp. 1-40. [3] Il Doroteo ... *Same imprint.* aa^8. pp. 3-16. [43

V

VAIR, LEONARDO. De fascino libri tres ... Venetiis. CIO IO XXCIX. Apud Aldum. 8°. a^8 A-R^8 a-c^8 (a1-2 *signed* S1-2). pp. 1-375. ¶c7^v: Libri di stampa d'Aldo, che si trouano al presente. (Lea.) [1

-- -- *Another copy.* (Lea.) [2

-- -- Trois liures des charmes, sorcelages, ou enchantemens. ... mis en François par Iulian Baudon, Angeuin. ... A Paris, Chez Nicolas Chesneau ... M. D. LXXXIII. ... 8°. $\bar{a}^8$ A-Qq^8. pp. 1-503. (Lea.) [3

VALDES, ALFONSO DE. Due dialoghi l'vno di Mercurio et Caronte. Nelquale ... si raccõta quel che accade nella guerra dopo l'anno. M. D. XXI. L'altro di Latantio et l'archidiacono. Nequale ... si trattano le cose auuenute in Roma nell'ãno M. D. XXVII. Di spagnuolo in Italiano ... tradotti ... 8°. A-Z^8. ff. 14-183. [4

VALDES, JUAN. Le cento & dieci diuine Considerationi del S. Giouãni Valdesso ... In Basilea, M. D. L. 8°. a^8 b^4 A-Gg^8 Hh^4. ¶Z1-Z4 *misbound after* Z8. *Two printings of sheet* Gg *are present.* (Lea.) [5

VALENCIA, PEDRO DE. Academica siue de iudicio erga verum ... opera Petri Valentiæ Zafrensis ... Antuerpiae, Ex officina Plantiniana, Apud Viduam, & Ioannem Moretum. M. D. XCVI. 8°. A-H^8. pp. 3-124. [6

VALENTIN ET ORSON. Historia de i due .... fratelli Valentino et Orsone ... Tradotta nuouamente di lingua Francese in Italiana. ... In Venetia, appresso Vincenzo Valgrisi, & Baltessar Costantini. 1558. 8°. A-Dd^8. pp. 3-421. [7

VALENTINO, GIOSEPPE STEFANO. Breui, bolle, et indulgenze concesse da diuersi pontefici ... alli diuoti Christiani della Compagnia del Santissimo Rosario, Già raccolte da Gioseppe Stefano Valentino ... In Venetia, Appresso Bernardo Giunti. M D LXXXVII. 4°. A-I^4. pp. 3-68. (Lea.) [8

VALERA, DIEGO DE. La coronica de España abreuiado ... Año M:D:xlij. (Fue impressa ... enla ... ciudad de seuilla en casa de Iuã cromberger ... Año ... de mil y quiniẽtos y quarenta y tres. A .ix. ðl mes de Abril.) fol. B.L. $+^6$ a-l^8 m-n^6. ff. j-c. [9

VALERAND DE LA VARANNE. Decertatio fidei et heresis [Parisiis, Robertus Gourmont.] 4°. A^6 b-d^6. ¶A1^v: Valarandus de varanis ... Ex parisiis Anno Millesimo quinquagesimo quinto. [10

VALERIANO, GIOVANNI PIERIO. Pierii Valeriani amorum libri .V. ... Amicitia Romana. Carpionis Fabula. Protesilaus Laodamiæ Respon. Leucippi Fabula. ... In Vinetia appresso Gabriel Giolito di Ferrarii. MDXLIX. (*Colophon.*) 8°. $*^8$ A-O^8. ff. 1-111. [11

-- Pierii Valeriani hexametri odae et Epigrammata. Apud Gabrielem Iolitum de Ferrariis et fratres. M. D. L. (*Colophon.*) 8°. A-R^8. ff. 2-136. ¶*Some leaves repaired, obscuring signatures.* (Lea.) [12

-- Ioannis Pierii Valeriani hieroglyphicorum, ex sacris Aegyptiorum literis, libri octo. Florentiae. MDLVI. fol. $(*)^2$ a-k^6 l^2. pp. 1-120. [13

-- Pierii Valeriani Ioathas rotatus. (Impressum Ro. Per Stephanum [Guileretum] & Herculem [Nani] Socios. III. Cal. Iunias. M.D. XII.) 4°. A-F^4. [14

-- Io. P. Valeriani Bellunensis, oratio in funere Hieronymi Turriani ... ([Venetiis] Ex ædibus Lazari Soardi. ... Habita Patáuii, VIII. Id. Ianu. ...) 4°. A-B^4. [15

-- Pro sacerdotum Barbis. ... Parisiis Excudebat Christianus Wechelus ... M.D.XXXIII. 8°. A-C^8. pp. 3-47. [16

VALERIIS, VALERIUS DE. Aureum sane opus, in quo ea omnia ... explicantur, quæ scientiarum omnium Parens, Raymundus Lullus ... tradit. ... M.D.LXXXIX. Augustæ Vindelicorum imprimebat Michaël Manger. ... 4°. A-Z^4 Aa^2. pp. 1-179. [17

VALERIUS MAXIMUS. Valerij Maximi ... de factis ac dictis memorabilib^9 Exemplorū Libri nouem ... Venduntˉ Lipsi ꝑ Melchiarē Lotterū ... (Anno ... Millesimo ꝙngētesimo duodecimo.) fol. A-X^6 Y^4 Z^6. [18

-- -- Valerii Maximi opus cū Oliuerii cōmentariis ... cum paucis annotationibus: quas sub Theophili nomine Arcadicus ... marginibus inspersit. Addite sunt ... Ascensii familiaria ... interpretamenta ... [Device of Lodovicus Hornken.] (Impressum Mediolani Apud Leonardum Vegiū ... M.CCCCC.XIII. Die Vltimo Februarii.) fol. a^6 A-D^8 (D *signed* C) E-F^6 G-K^8 L^6 M-O^8 P^6 Q^8 R-S^6 T-X^8 Y^6 Z^4 AA-LL^8 MM^{10}. ff. I-CLXV, I-XCVII. [19

-- -- Valerii Maximi factorum dictorumque memorabilium libri nouem. ... Mogunt. anno M. D. XXX. (... apud Ioannem Schoeffer mense Ianuario ...) 8°. π^{12} A-Z^8 a-l^8. pp. 1-543. [20

-- -- Parisiis, Apud Hieronymum de Marnef, & Gulielmum Cauellat ... 1570. 16°. A-II^8. pp. 2-487. ¶*Sigg. C-D misbound after F8.* [21

-- -- Valerius Maximus von Gschichten der Rœmer vnd aussers Volcks ... Durch Petrum Selbet ... verteutscht. Getruckt zů Strassburg bei Iacob kammerlandern. Anno M.D.XXXV. (*Colophon.*) fol. π^4 A-T^4 V^6. ff. j-lxxxij. [22

-- -- Valerio Maximo volgare. ... (impresso in Venetia per Agustino de Taie da Portese del Mille e cinquecēto e noue Adi .2. de Zugnio.) fol. a-o^6 p^4. ff. III-LXXXVII. [23

-- -- Valerio Massimo, de' detti, et fatti notabili de' Romani. ... Tradotto da M. Giorgio Dati Fiorentino. ... In Venetia, Appresso Marc'Antonio Zaltieri. M D LXXXVI. (*Colophon.*) 8°. a-b^8 A-RR^8. ff. 2-320. [24

VALERIUS, CORNELIUS. Ethicae, seu de moribus philosophiæ ... descriptio. ... Lugduni, apud Theob. Paganum. M D. LXVIII. 8°. A-E^8. pp. 3-80. [25

-- Physicae, seu de naturæ philosophia institutio ... Antuerpiæ, Ex officina Christophori Plantini. cIɔ. Iɔ. LXVIII. 8°. A-F^8 G^4. pp. 3-103. (Smith.) [26

-- Tabulae totius dialectices ... Coloniae Agrippinae, Ad Intersignium Monocerotis, M. D. LXX. 8°. A-L^8. [27

VAL MARINO. Volumen statutorum, legum, ac iurium comitatus Vallis Mareni, ac Gastaldiæ Soligheti. Nuperrimè à Francisco Guerra I.V.D. à Latino Sermone ad Vernaculam Linguam ... traductorum. ... Venetiis, Apud Georgium Angelerium. 1600. ... (*Colophon.*) 4°. a-c^4 A-Z^4. pp. 9-183. ¶Z2, Z3 *repaired.* (Lea.) [28

VALLA, GIORGIO. [1] Georgii Vallae Placentini ... de expetendis, et fugiendis rebus opus ... fol. *^{8} ◻^{6} a-nn^8 oo-pp^6. [2] Georgii Vallae Placentini expetendorum, ac fugiendorum. quod struebat volumen vigesimumquartum ... (Venetiis in aedibus Aldi Romani, impensa, ac studio Ioannis Petri Vallae filii ... mense Decembri. M.D.I.) A-TT^8. [29

VALLA, LORENZO. Laurentius Valla de libero arbitrio. Apologia eius aduersus Calumniatores ... Item, Contra Bartoli libellū ... Epistola. ... (Basileae. Apud Andream Cratandrum, mense Nouembri, anno M. D. XVIII.) 4°. a-g^4 h^6. ff. 2-34. (Lea.) [30

-- Dialectice Laurētii Vallę libri tres ... Venales sunt in ędibus Ascensianis & Bibliopolarū de Marnef. (Impressum ... in ædibus Ascensianis Anno nono ... supra Millesimū ac quīgētesimum ad Calendas Septemb.) fol. π^2 A-G^6 H^4. ff. I-XLV. [31

-- De Voluptate ac vero Bono Laurentii Vallę declamationes ac disputatiōes in libros tris contractę. ... ([Parisiis,] in ędibus Ascensianis ad. V. Idus Martias M.D.XII. ...) 4°. A-M^8 N^4. ff. III-C. (Lea.) [32

-- Laurentii Vallae elegantiarum Latinae linguae libri sex. De Reciprocatione Sui, & Suus, libellus eiusdem. ... ab Ioanne Rænerio emendata omnia. Lugduni apud Seb. Gryphium, 1543. (*Colophon.*) 8°. a-z^8 A-K^8. pp. 3-486. ¶D1^v, D2 *defective. Wormholes in* E5 *ff.* [33

-- -- Laurentii Vallae de linguae Latinae elegantia libri sex ... Eiusdem de reciprocatione Sui & Suus libellus: & in errores Antonij Raudensis & Poggij Florent. adnotationes. Vnà cum adnotationibus Ioannis Theodorici ... Coloniae Agrippinae, Apud Ioannem Gymnicum ... M. D. LXXVII. 8°. A-3I^8. pp. 8-833. [34

VALLA

-- Laurentii Vallensis ... in Latinam Noui testamenti interpretationem ex collatione Gręcorum exemplarium Adnotationes ... Venundantur Parrhisiis ... (... in ædibus Ascensianis ad idus aprilis. M.D.V.) fol. A-G^6 H^4. ff. I-[XLV]. ¶*Foliation partly erased.* [35

VALLE, BATTISTA DELLA. Vallo libro continente appertinentie à Capita iiij, retenere, & fortificare una Città ... (Stampato in Venetia per Nicolo d'Aristotile detto Zoppino. MDXXIX.) 8°. a^8 A-I^8. ff. 1-71. (Fine Arts.) [36

VALLE, GIROLAMO DELLE. Tractatus carminibus elegantissimis conscriptus de passione domini. [Lipsiae, Martinus Landsberg, c. 1500.] 4°. B.L. 13 *unsigned ll.* [37

-- -- Iesuida Hieronimi Paduani ... Venundatur Erffordie in Officina Matthei maler ... [c. 1515.] 4°. A-B^6. [38

VALLE BREMBANA SUPERIORE. Statuta, decreta, ordines, et ordinamenta Vallis Brembanae citra Augugiam, Episcopatus Bergomi ... Bergomi, Typis Cominis Venturæ. M D LXXXIX. fol. a^4 A-K^4. ff. 1-39. (Lea.) [39

VALLE SABBIA. Statuti de Val di Sabbio. In Bressa appresso iac.° britannico i573. (*Colophon.*) 4°. π^1 A-F^4 ♣^{6}. pp. 1-120. ¶*Engraved t.p.* (Lea.) [40

VALLENSIS, ROBERTUS. De veritate et antiquitate Artis Chemicæ ... Testimonia & Theoremata ... Parisiis, Apud Federicum Morellum ... M.D.LXI. 16°. A-F^8. (Smith.) [41

VALPOLICELLA. Priuilegia et iura communitatis, et hominum Vallis Pulicellae ... Veronae, M D LXXXVIII. Ex Typographia Hieronymi Discipuli. 4°. *-**^{4} 3*^{2} A-Hh^4 (-Hh4, *presumably blank*). pp. 1-246. (Lea.) [42

VALSERANO, ISIDORO. Trattato d'indulgentie. ... In Venetia, Appresso Domenico Farri. MDLXXXIII. 4°. +^{6} A-Q^4. ff. 1-4, pp. 5-114. (Lea.) [43

VALTELLINA. Li statuti de Valtelina riformati nella Cità di Coira nell'anno ... M.D.XLVIII. ... ꝑ M. Giorgio Trauerso con l'aiuto di M. Giacomo Cataneo ... in questo ordine ridotti ... & dalla Latina nella volgare lingua tradotti ... In Poschiauo per Dolfino Landolfo. M.D.XLIX. fol. A-Gg^4 (-Gg4, *presumably blank*). ff. 2-117. (Lea.) [44

VALTURIO, ROBERTO. En tibi lector Robertum Valturium ... de re militari Libris XII ... quàm cum Veronæ inter initia artis chalcographicæ Anno M.cccclxxxiii. inuulgaretur. Parisiis, Apud Christianum Wechelum ... Ī.D.XXXII. Mense Iulio. (*Colophon.*) fol. a^6 A-Ii^6. pp. 2-383. [45

VAN DIEVE, PIETER. [1] Petri Diuæi Louaniensis de Galliae Belgicæ antiquitatibus liber I. ... Accessit ... H. Nuenari de eadem Gallia Belgica Commentariolus. Antuerpiæ, Ex officina Christophori Plantini. M.D.LXXXIIII. 8°. A-D^8 (A8 + *folded leaf*) E^4. pp. 3-62. [2] H. Nuenari ... commentariolus ... *Same imprint.* A-B^8. pp. 4-29. [46

VANEGAS DE BUSTO, ALEJO. Primera parte delas diferencias de libros q̃ ay enel vniuerso. ... 1540. Febr. 28. (Fue impressa ... enla ... ciudad de Toledo en casa de Iuã de Ayala. Acabose a .xxviij. dias del mes de Hebrero. ...) 4°. B.L. ♣^{8} a-z^8 ꝛ^8 A-F^8. ff. j-ccxl. [47

-- Tractado de Orthographia y accẽtos enlas tres lenguas principales ... M.D.xxxj. Men. Octob. (Fue impressa ... enla ... ciudad de Toledo en casa de Lazaro Saluago Ginoues. Acabose a siete dias de mes de Octubre. ...) 4°. B.L. a-e^8 f^6. [48

VANNUCCI, ROBERTO. Sermocinales artes Roberti Vannuccij Florentini vbi de Dialectica atqȝ Grammatica tractatur. Eiusdem dialogus de arte sermocinali eiusdem carmina. Venetijs M.D.XLV ... (... Apud Cominum de Tridino Montisferrati ...) 8°. A-K^8. ff. 2-79. [49

VARCHI, BENEDETTO. [1] De sonetti Parte prima. ... In Fiorenza apresso M. Lorenzo Torrentino. M D L V. (*Colophon.*) 8°. **^{8} A-S^8 T^4. pp. 3-272. [2] De' sonetti ... parte seconda. In Fiorenza appresso Lorenzo Torrentino MDLVII. Aa-Pp^8. pp. 3-224. [50

-- L'Hercolano dialogo ..., Nel qual si ragiona generalmente delle lingue, & in particolare della Toscana, e della Fiorentina ... In Fiorenza, Nella stamperia di Filippo Giunti, e Fratelli, MDLXX. (*Colophon.*) 4°. *^{4} **^{2} A-YY^4 ZZ^2. pp. 2-339. [51

-- -- In Vinegia, M D LXX. Appresso Filippo Giunti, e Fratelli. (*Colophon.*) 4°. *^{8} A^4 B-V^8 X^2. pp. 1-282. [52

-- Lezzioni ... Lette da lui publicamente nell'Accademia Fiorentina ... In Fiorenza, per Filippo Giunti, M D XC. ... (*Colophon.*) 4°. *^{4} †^{8} A-Xx^8. pp. 1-682. [53

-- -- *Another copy.* [54

-- Orazione funerale ... sopra la morte del S. Giouanbatista Sauello. In Fiorenza 1551 (... per li Eredi di Bernardo Giunta. ...) 4°. A-D^4. [55

-- Sonetti spirituali ... Con alcune Risposte, & Proposte di diuersi Eccellentissimi ingegni. Nuouamente stampati. In Fiorenza Nella Stamperia de' Giunti. 1573. ... 4°. A-R^4. pp. 1-128. [56

VARENNIUS, JOANNES. Ioannis Varennii Mechliniensis περὶ προσῳδιῶν libellus ... Ἐμμανουὴλ Μοσχοπούλου περὶ προσῳδιῶν. De dialectis Græcis ... Parisiis, Apud Andream Wechelum. 1566. 8°. A-C^8. ff. 2-24. [57

VARGAS MEXIA, FRANCISCO DE. Francisci Vargas ... De Episcoporum iurisdictione, Et Pontificis Max. auctoritate, responsum. Romae, M. D. LXIII. Apud Paulum Manutium Aldi F. in aedibus Populi Romani. 4°. A-Y^4. pp. 1-160. (Lea.) [58

VARGAS Y TOLEDO, ALFONSO DE. Alphonsi archiepiscopi Toletani ... In tres Aristotelis Libros de anima ... quaestiones ... Venetiis, Ad Insigne Stellæ Iordani Ziletti. M D LXVI. fol. *^{6} A-I^6 K^4. pp. 1-116. [59

VARRO, MARCUS TERENTIUS. M. Terentii Varronis opera quæ supersunt. In lib. de ling. Lat. Cōiectanea Iosephi Scaligeri. In lib. de re rust. Notæ eiusdem. Alia in eundem scriptorem, trium aliorū, Turn. Vict. August. Editio tertia ... [Genevae, Henricus Stephanus II,] Anno M. D. LXXXI. 8°. a-z^8 A-K^8 aa-ii^8 a^8 Bb-Ee^8. pp. 5-143, 5-255, 2-48, 3-129, 3-77. [60

VASEO, JUAN. Rerum Hispaniae memorabilium annales, a Ioanne Vasaeo Brugensi, et Francisco Tarapha Barcinonensi, ... ad hæc vsq3 tempora deducti. ... Quibus accessit ... rerum à Philippo Secūdo ... gestarum descriptio: omniumq̄; Regum Hispaniæ genealogia, recens ex Italico translata. Coloniae, Apud Ludouicum Alectorium, & hæredes Iacobi Soteris, Anno M. D. LXXVII. 8°. A^8 A-3G^8 3H^4. pp. 1-781. (Lea.) [61

VATTER, HANS. Grůndlicher vnnd warhaffter Bericht/ was sich mit dem Mann/ der sich Hanns Vatter von Mellingen/ ... genennt/ ... zugetragen vnnd verloffen hat. M. D. LXII. Gedruckt zu Nürmberg/ bey Valentin Geyssler. 4°. A-B^4 C^2. [62

VAULX, CLAUDE DE. Regales Gallorum regis triumphi Parrisiis celebrati in gratiam Nuptiarum filiæ illius Elizabet cum Hispaniarum Rege, Et Margaritæ sororis illius cum insubrum Duce ... Parisiis, In officina Caroli Perier ... 1559. 4°. A-B^4. [63

VAZQUEZ Y MENCHACA, FERDINANDO. D. Ferdinandi Vasquii Menchacensis Pinciani Hispani ... controuersiarum ... libri tres. Venetiis, Apud Franciscum Rampazetum MDLXIIII. (*Colophon.*) fol. A-MM^4 a-ee^4 ff^6 Aa-Mm^4 Nn^6 A-C^4 D^6. ff. 1-140, 1-118, 1-54. [64

VECCHI, ORAZIO. Basso Canzonette di Hoatio [*sic*] Vecchi da Modona libro primo a quattro voci ... Quinta impressione. In Venetia Appresso Angelo Gardano. M. D. LXXXXI. 4°. K-M^4. pp. 1-22. (Music.) [65

VECELLIO, CESARE. Habiti antichi, et moderni di tutto il Mondo. ... Vestitus Antiquorum, recentiorumque ... per Sulstatium Gratilianum Senapolensis Latinè declarati. In Venetia, Appresso i Sessa. (... M. D. XCVIII. ...) 8°. a-g^8 A-3R^8 3S^4. ff. 2-507. (Fine Arts.) [66

VEGETIUS RENATUS, FLAVIUS. Flauij Vegetij Renati vier bucher der Rytterschafft ... (Gedruckt yn ... Erffurt durch Hanssen Knappen/ M.CCCCC.Xi.) fol. A-D^6 E^8 F-O^6 P^4. ¶P4 *defective.* [67

VEGETIUS RENATUS, PUBLIUS. Vegetii Renati artis veterinariae, siue mulomedicinæ libri quatuor ... Basileae (... M. D. XXVIII. excudebat Ioannes Faber Emmeus Iuliacensis.) 4°. [a]-b⁴ A-S⁴. ff. 1-72. [68

VEGIUS, MAPHAEUS. Maphei Vegij patria Landēsis ... de Educatione Liberoꝝ et eorum claris moribus Libri sex. ... Dyalogus veritatis ... & Philalithis ... Venundaẗ Parrhisius A ... Bertholdo Rembolt/ et Iohanne vvaterloes ... (Anno ... Millesimo quingētesimovndecimo. Die vero. XXIII. Martij.) 4°. π² A-L⁸. ff. I-LXXIIII. [69

-- -- Francisci Philelfi ... de educatione liberorum ... opus ... (Tubingæ in ædibus Thomæ Anshelmi Anno M. D. XV. Mense Septembri) 4°. a-b⁴ c⁶ d-f⁴ g⁸ h-i⁴ k⁸ l⁴ m⁶. [70

-- Maphęi Vegij Laudēsis ... De preseruātia religionis libri septē ... (Parisius per ... Bertholdum Rembolt & Iohannem vvaterloes ... Anno dñi millesimo quingentesimo vndecimo. Die vero .xxiij. Octobris.) 4°. A⁸ a-m⁸. ff. I-XCVI. [71

-- Maphei Vegij ... inter inferiora corpora/ scilicet Terram. Aurum/ et superiora/ presertim Solem ... disputatio. Venūdatur Parrhisijs ... Per ... Bertholdum Rembolt. (... per ... Bertholdum Rembolt et Iohānem vvaterloes ... Anno ... millesimo quingētesimovndecimo. Die vero quindecima mensis Decembris.) 4°. a-b⁸. ff. iij-xvj. [72

-- Ein schőn gesprāche/ von einem waldtmann/ Philalethes geheissen/ welchem die Iunckfraw Veritas (die Warheit) ... begegnet ... Newlich durch Iacoben Freien ... aus dem Latein/ in Deutsche sprach gebracht. Anno 1555. Gedruckt zů Strassburg in Knoblochs druckerei. 4°. A-F⁴. [73

VEHE, MICHAEL. Assertio sacrorum quorundam axiomatum ... ... M.D.XXXV. (Excusum Lipsiae, apud Michaelem Blum ... Mense Iunio.) 4°. A-Z⁴ a-n⁴ o². [74

-- Wie/ vnderschydlicher weiss/ Gott vnd seine ausserwelten Heiligen/ von vns Christen sollen geehret werden. ... 1532. ... (Gedruckt zu Leyptzigk durch Michael Blum ...) 4°. A-I⁴. [75

VELENUS, ULRICH. In hoc libello ... racionibus uariis probatur: Apostolū Petrū Rhomam nō uenisse ... (Finit ... viii. kalendas Decembres. ... M.D.XX.) 4°. A-F⁴ G² H⁴. [76

VENICE. *Laws &c.* Videbis Lector: hoc in volumine Statuta veneta emendatissima ... (Stampata in Venetia ꝑ Bernardino benalio ⁊ compagno ... 1537. adi .15. Mazo. ...) 8°. B.L. ✠⁸ A-Dd⁸ ✠¹². ff. 1-192, 1-11. [77

-- Volumen statutorum, legum, ac iurium D. Venetorum ... diligentia D. Iac. Nouello ... in lucem data. ... Venetiis, M D LXIIII. (... Apud Cominum de Tridino Montisferrati, Anno M D LXIII.) 4°. a-d⁸ (-a1, *presumably blank*) A-Cc⁸ Dd⁴. ff. 2-211. (Lea.) [78

-- *History.* Le alegrezze fatte in Venetia per la miracolosa Vittoria attenuta dalla Santissima Liga ... 7 Ottobrio. 1571. 8°. A⁴. ¶*In verse.* [79

-- Ein Summari der Türckischen Botschaft werbung/ an die Herrschafft zu Venedig ... Copia eins brieffs dem Cardinal von Neapolis zugeschickt/ inhaltend die anzal der Türckischen Armada ... Zu Venedig gedrůckt/ vnd yetzt von wort zu wort verteutscht Anno 1537. [Augsburg, Silvan Otmar?] 4°. [a]⁴. [80

VENIER, MAFFIO. Hidalba tragedia ... In Venetia, M. D. XCVI. Appresso Andrea Muschio. 4°. π² A-R⁴. pp. 2-136. [81

VENIERO, FRANCESCO. I discorsi di M. Francesco Veniero, sopra i tre libri dell'anima d'Aristotele ... In Venetia, appresso Andrea Arriuabene. M D LV. 8°. *⁴ A-Q⁸ R-S⁴. ff. 2-134. [82

VENTURA, LORENZO. Laurentii Venturae Veneti ... de ratione conficiendi Lapidis philosophici, liber Vnus. ... Huic accesserunt eiusdem Argumenti Ioan. Garlandij Angli liber Vnus. Et ex Speculo magno Vincentij libri Duo. ... Basileae [Petrus Perna,] M.D.LXXI. 8°.):(⁸ a-o⁸ A-H⁸ a-l⁸. pp. 1-203, 1-121, 1-173. (Smith.) [83

VENTURI, VENTURA. Conclusioni diuerse ... In Perugia, Appresso Pietroiacomo Petrucci. MDXCVII. ... (*Colophon.*) 4°. A-B⁴. [84

VENUSTI, ANTONIO MARIA. Compendio vtilissimo di quelle cose, le quali a nobili e Christiani mercanti appartengono. ... In Milano Appresso di Giouan'Antonio degli Antonij. M D LXI. (... Imprimeuano gli fratelli da Meda ...) 8°. *-**8 A-Q8 a-d8. ff. 2-127, 1-32. [85

VERANZIO, FAUSTO. Dictionarium quinque ... Europæ linguarum, Latinæ, Italicæ, Germanicæ, Dalmatiæ, & Vngaricæ. ... Venetiis, Apud Nicolaum Morettum. 1595. 4°. *4 A-Q4. pp. 9-128. [86

VERCELLI. Hec sunt statuta cōmunis ⁊ Alme ciuitatis Vercellarum. (Impressum Vercellis per Ioannem mariam de Peliparis de Pallestro. ... M.ccccc.xlj. die .xxiij. mensis Iunij.) fol. B.L. ✠-✠✠8 a-z8 ⁊8 ꝯ8 ꝶ8 aa-bb8 cc6. ff. I-CCXXVIII. (Lea.) [87

VERDIZOTTI, GIOVANNI MARIA. Cento fauole morali ... tradotti in ... versi volgari ... In Venetia, appresso Giordano Zileti, & compagni. M D LXX. 4°. a6 A4 B-S8 (-G4) T6 V4. pp. 11-301. [88

VEREEPT, SIMON. Simonis Verrepaei de epistolis Latine scribendis et rescribendis libri V. ... Coloniae, Apud Maternum Cholinum. Anno M. D. LXXXIII. ... 8°. A-N8. pp. 4-206. [89

VERGERIO, PIETRO PAOLO. Petri Pauli Vergerii Iustinopolitani iunioris iuris ciuilis scholastici praelectio. (Venetiis in Aedibus Bernardini Veneti de Vitalibus ... M.DXXIII. Die uero. XXII. Iunii. ...) 4°. a-c4 d2. [90

VERGILIO, POLYDORO. Polydori Vergilii Vrbinatis Anglicae historiae libri XXVI. ... Basileæ, apud Io. Bebelium anno M. D. XXXIIII. fol. a-z6 A-Ii6. pp. 4-610. (Furness.) [91

-- -- ... Accessit Anglorum Regum Chronices Epitome, per Georgium Lilium Britannum. ... Gandaui, Excudebat Cornelius Manilius. ... 8°. A-Z8 a-ee8 ff4 gg-oo8. pp. 1-644. ¶*Part 1 only.* [92

-- Les memoires et histoire de l'origine, inuention & autheurs des choses. ... traduicte par Francoys De Belle-forest Comingeois. ... A Paris, Chez Robert le Mangier ... M. D. LXXVI. ... 8°. *6 ā8 ē8 ī8 ō8 ū8 āā8 ēē2 a-z8 A-HH8. pp. 1-863. [93

-- -- Zwey Capitel Polydori Virgilij vom Namē vnd Stifftern der Mess ... Item/ Widderlegung D. Mart. Luth. des grewels der Stillmesse/ so man den Canō nennet. ... (Gedruckt zu Magdeburg/ bey Christian Rődinger. Anno M.D.L.) 4°. A-E4 F2. ¶*Published by Matthias Flacius Illyricus.* [94

-- Polydori Vergilii Vrbinatis ... Prouerbiorū liber ... (Matthias Schürerius Heluetensis Argentorati ... excudit. Mense Februario ... M. D. X.) 4°. a8 b4 c-h8.4.4 i8 k4 L4. ff. I-L. [95

VERGILIUS MARO, PUBLIUS. P. Virgilii Maronis Opera. Mauri Seruii Honorati ... commentarii ... Castigationes ... per Ioannem Pierium Valerianum. ... Parisiis. Ex officina Roberti Stephani M.D.XXXII. ([3B9v] ... XVII. Cal. Augusti. [o8r] ... M.D.XXIX. IX. Cal. Nouēbris) fol. *4 A-3A8 3B10 a-o8 (-a1). pp. 1-707, 3-205. [96

-- -- [1] P. Virgilii Maronis ... opera ... cum ... commentariis. Seruii, Donati, Mācinelli, Probi, Domitii Calderini, atq; Ascēsii. ... adnotationes ... Christophori Landini, Augustini Dathi & Philippi Beroaldi. ... castigationes ... per ... Ioannem Pierium Valerianum ... Venetiis M. D. XXXIII. Mense Ianuario. fol. ✠8 a-r8. ff. 1-136. [2] ... Aeneis ... addito Maphęi Vegii .xiii. libro ... *Same imprint.* (... in ædibus Lucæantonii Iuntæ Florentini ...) ✠✠6 A-NN8. ff. 1-286. [3] ... opuscula. ... (... M.D.XXXII. Mense Septembris.) aa-ee8 ff4. ff. 1-43. [97

-- -- Publii Virgilii Maronis bucolica georgica Aeneis cum Seruii Probique commentariis ... (Venetiis per Alexandrum Vellutellum ... emendati, & propriis expēsis in ædibus Petri de Nicolinis de Sabbio impressi ... M.D.XXXIIII. mense Septembri.) 8°. AA8 A-Ss8 Tt12 (-Tt12, *blank*). ff. 1-339. [98

-- -- P. Vergilii Maronis bucolicorum, georgicorum, et Aeneidos, Cum ... Seruij Mauri Honorati expositione, pars prima. Basileae apud Ioan. Valderum. Anno, M. D. XXXIIII. 4°. *4 (-*4) a-z4 A-Zzz4 AAA-EEE4. pp. 1-775. [99

-- -- P. Virgilii Maronis vniuersum poema vna cum ... commentariis Seruii, Marii, et Tiberii Donati ... Addita sunt præterea quæ in hoc ab Ascensio ... scripta fuere. Venetiis apud Alouissium de Tortis. M.D. XLI. (*Colophon.*) fol. A-3R^{8}. ff. 2-3, 1-491. [100

-- -- Publii Vergilii Maronis opera, duobus tomis distincta ... Basileae, apud Nicolaum Bryling. Anno M. D. XLIII. 8°. *^{8} a-z^{8} A-Z^{8} Aaa-Ccc^{8} (-Ccc8, *presumably blank*). pp. 1-724. [101

-- -- P. Vergilii Maronis ... bucolica, georgica, et Aeneis, ... Seruij Mauri Honorati, & Aelij Donati ... Commentarijs illustrata ... Basileae per Hieronymum Curionem M. D. XLIIII. (*Colophon.*) fol. A^{4} a-z^{6} A-FF^{6}. pp. 1-621. ¶A1 *defective.* [102

-- -- P. Virgilii Maronis opera Omnia ... ad veterum Petri Bembi cardinalis et Andreæ Naugerii exemplarium fidem ... castigata. Cum XI. Commentarijs ... Venetiis apud Iuntas. MDLII. (*Colophon.*) fol. *^{10} a-e^{8} f-g^{6} h-r^{8} s-t^{6} v^{4} x^{10} y-z^{8} &^{8} ɔ^{8} aa-3v^{8} 3x^{6} 3y-3z^{8} A-D^{8}. ff. 1-588. ¶*Additional t.p.* (v1^{r}): P. Virgilii Maronis Aeneis ... Venetiis M D LII. [102

-- -- Opera P. Vergilii Maronis. D. Philippi Melanchthonis & aliorum ... virorum Scholijs, Annotationibus, & nouis Argumentis illustrata ... versuum prouerbialium ex Erasmi Chiliadibus expilcationem inseruimus. Tiguri apud Christ. Frosch. Impensis Roberti Camberi. 1581. 8°. *^{8} a-z^{8} A-Cc^{8}. pp. 1-740. [104

-- -- Les oeuures de Virgile Maron, Latin et François, traduites ... Par Robert et Antoine le Cheualier d'Agneaux, freres ... A Paris, Chez Guillaume Auuray ... M. D. LXXXIII. ... 8°. ã^{8} A-Ss^{8} 3A-3B^{8} 3C^{4}. ff. 1-328, 1-20. [105

-- P. Virgilii Maronis ... Aeneides Libri Duodecim. ... (Argentorati, Ex Aedibus Matthiæ Schurerij, Mense Iunio. ... M. D. XV.) 4°. A^{10} (-A10, *blank*) B-Z$^{8.4}$ &^{8} Aa^{4} Bb^{8} Cc-Ff$^{8.4}$ Gg^{8}. [106

-- Die twaelf boecken van Aeneas ... beschreuen door ... Vergilius Maro/ Nu eerst in onser duytscher talen door Cornelis van Ghistele Retorijckelijck ouergeset ... Thantwerpen, By Niclaes Soolmans ... M.D.LXXXIII. (Typis Matthæi de Rische.) 8°. A-Qq^{8} Rr^{2}. ff. 2-307. [107

-- -- La Eneide di Virgilio tradotta in terza rima. Per M. Giouanpaulo Vasio. In Vinegia M.D.XXXVIII. di Ottob. (Stampato ... per Bernardino di Vitali Venetiano. ... Octobrio. XXIIII.) 8°. a-z^{8} A-L^{8}. ¶*A revision of the translation of Tommaso Cambiatore.* [108

-- -- L'Eneida in Toscana del ... Caualier Cerretani. ... In Fiorenza, appresso Lorenzo Torrentino ... MDLX. 4°. A-LL^{4}. pp. 2-259. [109

-- -- L'Eneide di Virgilio, del Commendatore Annibal Caro. ... In Venetia, Appresso Bernardo Giunti, & fratelli. M. D. LXXXI. 4°. π^{4} A-LL^{8} MM^{6} ✠^{2}. pp. 2-556. [110

-- -- Los doze libros de la Eneida de Vergilio ... traduzida en octaua rima y verso Castellano. En Anueres En Casa de Iuan Bellero ... [1570?] (En casa de Gerardo Smits, a la costa de Iuan Bellero.) 12°. A-Bb^{12} (-Bb12, *presumably blank*). pp. 3-598. ¶*Translator: Gregorio Hernández de Velasco.* [111

-- -- La Eneida de Virgilio ... traduzida en octaua rima y verso Castellano ... Las dos Eglogas de Virgilio, Primer, y Quarta. El libro tredecimo de Mapheo Veggio ... La moralidad de Virgilio sobre la letra de Pytagoras. ... Impressa en Çaragoça. En casa de Lorenço, y Diego de Robles hermanos, Año. M.D.LXXXVI. (*Colophon.*) 12°. ₵^{10} A-Gg^{12}. ff. 2-321. ¶₵1 *defective. Translator: Gregorio Hernández de Velasco.* [112

-- [Aeneid i-vi.] (Stampata in Vinetia per Comin de Trino. Ad instantia de Nicolo d'Aristotile detto Zopino. ... A di .xij. del mese di Ottobre.) 8°. [1] I sei primi libri del Eneide di Vergilio, Tradotti ... M D XXXX. A-C^{8}. ff. 2-24. ¶*Book i translated by Alessandro Sansedoni.* [2] Il secondo di Vergilio ... tradotto da Hippolito de Medici cardinale. M D XXXIX. A-C^{8}. ff. 2-24. [3] Il terzo di Vergilio tradotto da M. Bernardino Borghesi ... M D XXXX. Aa-Bb^{8} Cc^{4}. ff. 2-20. [4] Il quarto di Vergilio di M. Bartolameo Carli Picholomini ... M D XXXX. A-B^{8} C^{4}. ff. 2-19. [5] Il quinto di Vergilio tradotto da M. Aldobrando ... M D XXXX. 3A-3C^{8} 3D^{4}. ff. 2-27. [6] Il sesto di Vergilio tradotto da M. Alessandro Picholomini ... MDXL. AA-DD^{8} (-DD8, *presumably blank*). ff. 2-25. [113

-- Il primo libro della Eneida di Vergilio, ridotto da Giouanni Andrea dell'Anguillara in ottaua rima ... In Padoua, Appresso di Gratioso Perchacino 1564. 4°. A-M^{4}. ff. 2-47. [114

-- -- Il primo libro dell'Enea di M. Lodouico Dolce. ... In Venetia Presso Giorgio de' Caualli. 1566. 8°. A-E^8. ff. 2-40. [115

-- Il quarto libro dell'Eneide di Virgilio in ottaua rima. Di M. Stephano Ambrosio Schiappalaria. Con alcune annotationi ... In Anuersa, Per Christophoro Plantino. M. D. LXVIII. 8°. *^{4} A-O^8 P^4. pp. 1-212. [116

-- P. Virgilii Maronis bucolica & Georgica, Paraphrasi exposita. Autore Nicodemo Frischlino, Alemanno. Tubingae, Apud Alexandrum Hockium, Anno M. D. LXXX. (... 20. Augusti.) 16°.)(^{8} A-Aa^8. pp. 1-378. [117

-- In Pub. Virgilii Maronis ... bucolica Commentarij Michaelis Barth Annaebergensis. Expressi Lipsiæ a Iohanne Rhamba ... M. D. LXX. 8°.)(^{8} A-Z^8. pp. 1-340. [118

-- -- Bucolica Virgilii in vsum puerorum Germanicè reddita per M. Stephanum Riccium. ... M.D.LXXIII. (Lipsiæ, apud hæredes Iacobi Berualdi. ...) 8°. A-R^8. [119

-- -- P. Virgilii Maronis bucolica, P. Rami ... prælectionibus exposita ... Editio quinta. Francofurdi Apud heredes Andreæ Wecheli, Claudium Marnium & Ioann. Aubrium. CIↃ. IↃ. LXXXX. 8°. A-L^8 (-L8, *blank*). pp. 3-168. [120

-- [1] P. Virgilii Maronis priores duo libri georgicorum in vsum studiosæ Iuuentutis Germanicè redditi, & editi a M. Stephano Riccio seniore. ... M. D. LXXI. (Gorlicii excudebat Ambrosius Fritsch, impensis Iacobi Apelij Bibliopolæ Lipsensis.) 8°. A^8 A-V^8. ff. 1-159. [2] Posteriores duo libri georgicorum ... Anno, M. D. LXXII.)(^{8} A-X^8 Y^6. ff. 1-166. [121

-- -- La Georgica di Vergilio da M. Ant. Mario Nigresoli ... Tradotta in versi volgari sciolti. Alcune rime del medesimo ... In Venetia, M D XLIII. (... per Melchior Sessa. ...) 8°. ✠^{4} A-M^8 (-E8, *without loss of text or break in foliation*). ff. 1-92. [122

-- -- La Georgica di Virgilio Nuouamente di Latina in Thoscana fauella, per Bernardino Daniello tradotta, e commentata. ... In Venetia appresso Ioan. Gryphio. M D XLIX. (*Colophon.*) 4°. a-b^4 A-BB^4 CC^6. ff. 1-105. [123

-- -- La Georgica ... da M. Ant. Mario Nigresoli ... stampata In Vinegia. L'anno MDLII (... per Nicolo de Boscarini ... nel mese di Febraio. ...) 8°. A-R^8 S^{8+2}. ff. 2-140. [124

-- Pub. Virgilii Maronis appendix, Cum supplemento multorum antehac nunquam excusorum Poëmatum veterum Poëtarum. Iosephi Scaligeri ... Castigationes & Commentarii ... curante edenteq̃ue Friderico Lindenbruch ... Lugduni Batauorum, Ex officina Plantiniana, Apud Franciscum Raphelengium, cIↄ. Iↄ. XCV. 8°. *^{4} A-Q^8 R^4 a-z^8. pp. 1-262, 3-348. ¶*Adams V565.* [125

VERLATO, LEONORO. Rodopeia tragedia ... In Venetia. Appresso Francesco Ziletti. 1582. 8°. A-K^8 L^4. ff. 1-75. [126

VERMAHNUNG. Ein getrewe vermanung eins liebhabers der Euangelischen warheyt an gemeyne Pfaffheyt nit zů widderfechten den Ehelichen standt/ so ein Erssamer Priester zů Wormbs ... an sich genōmen hat. ([Speyer, Jakob Schmidt,] M.D.XXIII.) 4°. A^4. ¶*In verse.* [127

VERMEULEN, JAN. D. Ioannis Molani ... liber, de piis testamentis, & quacunq; alia pia vltimæ voluntatis dispositione. ... Coloniae in officina Birckmannica, sumtibus Arnoldi Mylij. ... M. D. LXXXV. 8°. A^8 A-R^8 (-R8, *presumably blank*). pp. 1-246. (Lea.) [128

-- D. Ioannis Molani ... libri quinque. De fide hæreticis seruanda, tres. De fide rebellibus seruanda, liber vnus ... Item vnicus, de fide et iuramento, quæ à Tyrannis exiguntur ... Coloniae, Apud Godefridum Kempensem, Anno cIↄ. Iↄ. LXXXIIII. 8°.)(^{8} A-O^8 P^4. pp. 1-214. (Lea.) [129

VERMIGLI, PIETRO MARTIRE. Melachim Id est, Regum libri duo posteriores cum Commentariis Petri Martyris Vermilii Florentini ... et Ioannis Wolphii Tigurini ... Heidelbergæ, Ex Officina Andreae Cambieri. Anno M. D. XCIX. fol. *^{6} **^{4} a-z^6 A-3B^6 (-3B6, *presumably blank*). ff. 1-424. [130

VERONA. Statuta magnificae ciuitatis Veronae. Additis eiusdem Ciuitatis Priuilegijs ... Venetiis, Apud Andream Carnaciolum, M D LXI. fol. *^{8} A-Z^6 χ^1 A-I^6 K^4. pp. 1-277, 1-110.

¶*Additional t.p.* ($\chi 1^r$): Priuilegia ... ciuitatis Veronae. ... *Same imprint.* ^{2}A-^{2}K, *with the colophon* Veronæ, Excudebat Hieronymus Discipulus sumptibus M. Antonij Palatioli. M D LXXXVIII, *is part of another edition.* [131

-- Statuta ciuilia. Domus mercatorum Veronæ ... Anno. CIↃ. IↃ. IIC. ... (Veronæ, Apud Hieronymum Discipulum. ...) fol. $*^2$ A-O^4 P^6. pp. 1-117. ¶*Engraved t.p.* [132

-- Capitoli formati per facilitare La prattica, & osseruanza delle parti in proposito della regolatione del Palazzo della mag. citta di Verona ... In Verona, Nella Stamperia di Girolamo Discepolo. M D XCVII. fol. A^6. [133

VERONESE DA PISTOIA. Le belle rime ... In Verona M. D. XXXX. Per Antonio Putelleto Portese. (*Colophon.*) 8°. A-E^4. ff. 2-18. [134

VERSTEGAN, RICHARD. Theatrum crudelitatum Hæreticorum Nostri Temporis. Antuerpiæ, Apud Adrianum Huberti, Anno M. D. LXXXVII. ... 4°. A-M^4. pp. 3-95. ¶*T. p. repaired.* (Lea.) [135

-- -- Antuerpiæ. Apud Adrianum Huberti, Anno M. D. XCII. ... 4°. A-M^4. pp. 3-95. (Lea.) [136

VESALIUS, ANDREAS. Andreae Vesalii Bruxellensis ... de Humani corporis fabrica Libri septem. ... Basileae, per Ioannem Oporinum. (... MDLV. Mense Augusto.) fol. a-v^6 x^{2+1} y-z^6 A-Z^6 aa-zz^6 (ff5 + 2 *leaves*) Aa^8 Bb-Ee^6. pp. 2-824. [137

VETTER, CONRAD. M. Conradi Andreæ, &c. Augenscheinliche Beweisung/ wie Philipp Heilbrunner den keuschen Luther, &c. nicht allein vngewaschen in dem Pfeffer stecken lassen/ sonder auch sich selber dermassen in disem Pfeffer vertieffe ... Gedruckt zu Ingolstatt in der Ederischen Turckerey/ durch Andream Angermayer. Anno M. DC. 4°. A-D^4 E^6. pp. 1-40. [138

VETTORI, PIERO. Oratio funebris de laudibus Ioannis Medicis S.R.E. Cardinalis: habita VII. K. Dec. 1562. A' Petro Victorio in æde Diui Laurentij Florentiæ. Brixiae apud Ludouicum Sabiensem. M. D. LXIII. 4°. A^6. (Lea.) [139

-- Petri Victorii oratio habita ad Iulium III. initio pontificatus ipsius ... Florentiae. Apud Laurentium Torrentinum. M.D.L. 4°. A^4 B^6. [140

-- Oratio Petri Victorii habita in funere Cosmi Medicis magni ducis Etruriae ... CIↃ IↃ LXXIIII. ... Florentiæ Ex officina Bartholomæi Sermertellii [1574]. 4°. A^2 B-E^4 F^2. [141

-- -- Orazione ... recitata nell'essequie del sereniss. Cosimo de' Medici Gran Duca di Toscano ... Et poscia da Francesco Bocchi Fiorentino dalla lingua Latina tradotta nella fauella Fiorentina. In Fiorenza, Appresso Giorgio Marescotti. MDLXXIIII. ... (*Colophon.*) 4°. A^2 B-G^4. (Lea.) [142

-- Petri Victorii variarum lectionum libri XXV. ... hæc secunda sedulò castigauit ... Lugduni, Apud Ioannem Temporalem. 1554. (Excudebat Bartholomæus Frein, 4 No. Maias ...) 4°. α^4 β^2 a-z^8 A-G^8 H^4 I-K^8 L^4 M^8 N^2. pp. 2-486. [143

-- Petri Victorii variarum lectionem XIII. noui libri. ... Florentiae. In officina Iuntarum Bernardi Filiorum. 1569. ... (*Colophon.*) 4°. a-c^4 A-Ll^4 Mm^2. pp. 1-254. [144

VIAGGI. Viaggi fatti da Vinetia, alla Tana, in Persia, in India, et in Costantinopoli ... In Vinegia M. D. XLIII. (... nelle case de figliuoli di Aldo.) 8°. A-Y^8 Z^4. ff. 2-180. ¶*Includes:* Viaggio del ... Messer Iosaphat Barbaro Ambasciatore della ... Republica di Venetia alla Tana; Viaggio dello istesso ... in Persia; Viaggio del ... Messer Ambrogio Contarini Ambasciator di Venetia ad Vussuncassan Re di Persia ...; Viaggio di Messer Aluuigi di Giouanni in India; Viaggio del detto in Colocut; Viaggio in Costantinopoli ...; Viaggio et impresa che fece Soleyman Bassà del. 1538 contra Portoghesi ... (Lea.) [145

VICO, ENEA. Discorsi di M. Enea Vico Parmigiano, sopra le medaglie de gli antichi diuisi in due libri. ... In Vinegia appresso Gabriel Giolito de Ferrari, et fratelli. M D LV. (*Colophon.*) 4°. $*^4$ A-P^4. pp. 3-112. [146

-- C. Iulius Caesar dictator perp. 4°. π^1 A^2 B^4 $[C]^4$ D-I^4 K^{2+1} L-Q^4 R^2 α^4 β^2. pp. 9-130. ¶$B1^r$: C. Iuli Caesaris dictatoris vitae epitoma, Ab Aenea Vico Permense scripta. $D1^r$: Commentariorum in C. Iuli Caesaris dictatoris numismata Aenae Vici Parmensis liber primus.

R2v: *device of Aldus. Engraved t.p.; presumably lacks printed t.p.* (Ex libris XXIII commentariorum in vetera imperatorum romanorum numismata Æneae Vici liber primus. Venetiis, 1560). [147

VIDA, GIROLAMO. Filliria fauola boscareccia, di Gieronimo Vida Iustinopolitano. In Vinegia, Presso gli Heredi di Marchiò Sessa, M. D. LXXXVII. (... presso Giorgio Angelieri. ...) 12°. A-D12. ff. 3-48. [148

VIDA, MARCO GIROLAMO. [Marci Hieronymi Vidae opera quae quidem extant omnia.] (Venetijs per Melchiorem Sessam. M. D. XXXVIII. Mense Nouembris.) 8°. A-X8 (-A1) ✠8 ✠✠6. pp. 3-335. [149

-- -- Marci Hieronymi Vidae Cremonensis ... opera. ... Lugduni apud Seb. Gryphium. 1541. 8°. a-y8 z4. pp. 3-359. [150

-- -- Venetiis, M D LXXI. (... Apud Christophorum Zanettum. ...) 16°. A-Mm8. pp. 3-559. [151

-- -- Lugduni, apud Antonium Gryphium. M. D. XCII. 16°. a-nn8. pp. 3-573. [152

-- Marci Hieronymi Vidae Cremonensis ... Christiados libri sex. Lugduni apud Seb. Gryphium, 1536. 8°. a-o8. pp. 3-220. [153

-- -- M. Hieronymi Vidae Cremonensis ... Christias, ... Bartholomaeo Botta ... interprete. Ticini, Apud Hieronymum Bartolum. M. D. LXIX. fol. *4 A-Aa8 Bb6 *-**6. ff. 1-198. [154

-- Cremonensium orationes III. aduersus Papienses in controuersia principatus (Cremonae [Giovanni Muzio & Bernardino Locheta,] MDL. mense Quintil.) 8°. π2 A-R8. ff. 2-136. ¶π1: *blank.* π2r: *woodcut.* A1r: *t.p.* [155

-- -- *Another copy.* [155a

-- -- Parisiis MDLXII. (... Kal. Aug. ...) 8°. *4 A-II4 KK2. ff. 1-130. [156

-- M. Hier. Vidae Cremonen. ... dialogi de rei publicae dignitate. (Cremonae ... apud Vincentium Contem M. D. LVI.) 8°. π2 A-EE4. ff. 1-110. [157

-- [1] Marci Hieronymi Vidae Cremonensis ... poemata omnia ... 8°. A-Dd8. ff. 4-216. [2] ... poemata ... (Cremonae ... M D L. mense Nouembri Io. Mutius et Bernardinus Locheta impr.) a-i8 k4. ff. 2-76. [158

VIELFELD, JAKOB. Eyn hübscher Dialogus oder gesprech vierer personen ... von der Beycht ... (M. D. XXvj.) 4°. a-b4. [159

VIENNA. Der Stat wienn Ordnūg vnd Freyhaiten. ... zw Wieñ gedruckt. 1549 fol. A-F4 (-F4, *presumably blank*). [160

-- Infection Ordnung der Stat Wienn. Gedruckht zů Wienn in Osterreich/ durch Hans Syngriener. (Actum Wienn/ am Achtvndzwayntzigisten tag Octobris. Anno ꝛc. im Ainvndfunfftzigisten.) fol. A6. [161

-- *Ferdinand, Roman emperor.* [Regulations for meatcutters in Vienna, with countersignatures and seal.] Geben in ... Wienn am Funffvndzwaintzigisten Aprilis/ Anno ꝛc. im Neunvndfüntzigisten ... s.sh. 31 × 43 cm. [162

-- *Rudolf II, Roman emperor.* [Mandate on the billeting of soldiers.] Geben in ... Wienn/ den Viertzehenden tag Martij/ Anno/ ꝛc. im ViervndNeuntzigisten ... s.sh. 31 × 42 cm. ¶*With manuscript (proof?) corrections.* [163

-- *History.* Viennæ Austriæ ... a Sultano Saleymano immanissimo Turcarꝫ Tyranno immenso cum exercitu obsesse Historia. ... Anno M.D.XXX. (Siluanus Ottmar excussit. Auguste Vindelicorum. Anno. M.D.XXX. Pridie Idus Augusti.) 4°. A-F4. [164

VIERI, FRANCESCO DE'. Compendio della dottrina di Platone ... conforme con la Fede nostra. ... In Fiorenza Appresso Giorgio Marescotti. 1577. (... M D LXXVI.) 8°. a-b8 c2 A-M8. pp. 1-191. ¶a1 *defective.* [165

-- Discorso della grandezza, et felice fortuna d'vna ... Donna, qual fù M. Laura, ... detto il Verino Secondo ... In Fiorenza, Appresso Giorgio Marescotti. MDLXXXI. 8°. A-D8 E4. pp. 7-69. [166

-- Discorso ... Intorno a' Dimonii ... In Fiorenza, Appresso Bartolomeo Sermartelli, MDLXXVI. 8°. *^{8} A-G^8 (-G8, *presumably blank*). pp. 1-108. [167

-- Lezzione ... doue si ragiona delle idee, Et Delle Bellezze. ... In Fiorenza, Appresso Giorgio Marescotti 1581. ... 8°. A-B^8 C^4. pp. 3-39. [168

-- Trattato di M. Francesco de' Vieri, Cognominato il Verino Secondo ... nel quale si contengono i tre primi libri Delle Metheore. ... In Fiorenza, Appresso Giorgio Marescotti. MDLXXXII. (*Colophon.*) 8°. a^8 A-DD^8 EE^4. pp. 1-424. ¶M6^r: Trattato delle cose appartenenti al quarto libro delle metheore ... [169

-- Trattato della lode, dell'honore, della fama, et della gloria ... In Fiorenza, Appresso Giorgio Marescotti. M.D.LXXX. (*Colophon.*) 8°. A-I^8 K^4. pp. 3-150. [170

VIEXMONT, CLAUDE DE. Methodus confessionis, seu potius, Christiani hominis institutio ... Antuerpiæ, Excudebat Ioannes Latius. An. 1553. 8°. A-E^8 F^4. (Lea.) [171

VIGENERE, BLAISE DE. Traicté des chiffres, ou secretes manieres d'escrire ... A Paris, Chez Abel L'angelier ... M. D. LXXXVI. ... 4°. A-Zz^4 (Zz4 + 2 *folded ll.*) 3A-3D^4 (3D4 + *folded leaf*) 3E-3Q^4 3R^2 3S^2 (*a folded l.*) 3V^2 (*a folded leaf*) 3T^2 3X-4R^4 4S^2 ā^2. ff. 2-343. [172

VIGNALI, ANTONIO. La Floria comedia dell' Arsiccio Intronato. ... In Fiorenza appresso i Giunti, M D LXVII. (*Colophon.*) 8°. A-E^8 (-E8, *presumably blank*). pp. 3-77. [173

VIGNE, PIERO DELLE. Querimonia Friderici II. imp. ... Â ... Petro de Vineis ... Anno M.CC.XXX. conscripta. (Haganoæ, per Iohannem Secerium. Anno M. D. XXIX.) 8°. A-P^8. [174

VIGNIER, NICOLAS. Rerum Burgundionum chronicon ... Ex bibliotheca historia Nicolai Vignierij Barrensis ad Sequanam. Basileæ, per Thomam Guarinum, M. D. LXXV. (*Colophon.*) 4°. α^4 A-Z^4 a-c^4. pp. 2-185. [175

VIGO, JOANNES DE. The vvhole worke of that famous chirurgion Maister Iohn Vigo ... Whereunto are annexed certain works, compiled and published by Thomas Gale ... At London Printed by Thomas East. 1586. (*Colophon.*) B.L. 8°. ¶^{10} A-3L^8. ff. 1-455. *S.T.C.* 24723. ¶*Translator: Bartholomew Traherne. Lacks the works of Gale.* [175a

VIGUERA, JUAN. Institutiones ad Christianam theolog. sacrarum literarum, vniuersaliumque Conciliorum authoritate ... His annecti curauimus eiusdem Viguerii commentaria ... in D. Pauli Epistolam ad Romanos ... Venetiis, Apud Bartholomæum Rubinum. M. D. LXXI. (*Colophon.*) 4°. †^{8} ††^{10} A-4G^8. pp. 1-1216. (Lea.) [176

VILLADIEGO, ALDONSO À. Forus antiquus Gothorum regum Hispaniae olim liber iudicum: hodie fuero iuzgo nuncupatus. XII. libros continens. ... Cui accessit breuis eorundem Historia, Regumq; Hispanorum Catalogus ... Anno 1600. Madriti, Ex officina Petri Madrigal. (*Colophon.*) fol. §^{6} A-E^8 A-3L^8 3M^6 3N-3Q^8. ff. 1-461. (Lea.) [177

VILLALPANDO, GASPAR CARDILLO DE. Commentarius in Aristotelis Topica ... Liber de ratione disputandi. ... Compluti Ex officina Ioannis de Villanoua. 1569. 4°. π^4 A-M^4. ff. 1-47. [178

-- Commentarius in categorias Aristotelis vna cum quaestionibus in easdem ... Compluti. Ex officina Ioannis Brocarij. Anno 1558. (*Colophon.*) 4°. A-CC^4. ff. 2-104. [179

-- De nomine Iesu, oratio. Ad ... Synodum Tridentinam. ... Expensis Philippi de Salis. M. D. LXIII. (Brixiae ...) 4°. [A]-B^4. (Lea.) [180

-- Quod non sit laicis Calix permittendus. Oratio. Ad ... Synodum Tridentinam. ... M. D. LXII. 4°. A-B^4. (Lea.) [181

VILLANI, GIOVANNI. Chroniche di Messer Giouanni Villani cittadino Fiorentino ... (Stampate in Venetia per Bartholomeo Zanetti Castergazense. ... M.D.XXXVII. del mese d'Agosto.) fol. ♣^{10} A-DD^8 EE^4. ff. 1-219. [182

-- [1] [La prima parte delle Historie vniuersali de suoi tempi di Giouan Villani cittadino fiorentino. In Venetia, Ad instantia de Giunti di Fiorenza MDLIX.] (Stampata in Venetia per Nicolo Beuilacqua Trentino, ad instantia delli heredi di Bernardo Giunti di Firenze. M D LIX.) 4°. *^{8} (-*1, *8) **^{10} A-Z^{8} a-o^{8} p^{4}. pp. 2-588. ¶**6 *misbound between* **3 *and* **4, **7 *between* **4 *and* **5. [2] La seconda parte delle historie vniuersali de suoi tempi, ... ricorretta da M. Remigio Fiorentino. ... *Same imprint and colophon.* 4°. *^{6} Aa-Pp^{8}. pp. 1-232. ¶*3-4 *misbound between* **4 *and* **7 *of part 1.* (Lea.) [183

VILLANI, MATTEO. Della historia di Matteo Villani cittadino Fiorentino. Li tre vltimi Libri. ... Con vn' Aggiunta di Filippo Villani suo figliuolo, ch'arriua sino all'anno 1364. ... In Firenze. Nella Stamperia de' Giunti 1577. ... (*Colophon.*) 4°. +^{8} A^{8} B-X^{4} Y^{6}. pp. 1-177. [184

-- La prima parte della cronica vniuersale de suoi tempi ... In Fiorenza appresso Lorenzo Torrentino. MDLIIII. (..., del mese di Nouembre ...) 8°. ❧ -2❧^{8} A-Bb^{8}. pp. 1-395. [185

VILLETANUS, LUDOVICUS JOANNES. Concio de diuino spiritu S. Catholicae ecclesiae et S. Oecum. Concilii, Ad Patres S. Synodi Tridentinæ Habita ... Die Pentecostes. M D LXIII. Patauii, Apud Christophorum Gryphium. 4°. A-B^{4}. (Lea.) [186

VINCENT OF BEAUVAIS. [1] Le second volume de Vincent Miroir Hystorial. [*T.p. border of Jean Petit.*] fol. ^{8} AA-XX^{6} aa-ll^{6}. ff. i-C.xcii *present.* [2] Le tiers volume ... [*T.p. border of Galliot du Pré.*] 3Ψ^{8} 3A-3X^{6} 3a-3o^{6}. ff. i-CC.viii. [3] Le Cinquiesme volume ... [*T.p. border of Jean Petit.*] (... imprime a Paris par Nicolas couteau. Et fut acheue dimprimer le .xvie. iour du moys de mars Lan Mil cinq cēs .xxxi. pour Iehan de la garde ...) 5Ψ^{6} 5A-5X^{6} 5a-5o^{6} 5p^{8}. ff. i-CC.xvii. ¶*Translator: Jean de Vignay.* [187

VINCENT FERRER, S. [Sermonum de tempore Sancti Vincentij. Pars estiualis. Lugduni? c. 1515.] 4°. B.L. Ƀ^{10} (-Ƀ1, Ƀ5-6) A-MM^{8}. ff. I-CCLXXX. [188

VIO, TOMMASO DE, CAJETANUS. Opuscula omnia Thomae de Vio Caietani, ... In tres distincta Tomos ... Item tractatus quidam contra modernos Martini Lutheri sectatores, & eorum præcipuos errores, nunquam antehac impressus. Augustae Taurinorum. Apud hæredes Nicolai Beuilaquæ. 1582. ... (*Colophon.*) fol. A-Ee^{8} Ff^{6}. pp. 5-458. (Lea.) [189

-- Reuerendissimi domini. D. Thomæ de Vio Caietani ... aduersus Lutheranos tractatus ... Venetijs [Joannes Antonius Nicolini da Sabbio & fratres]. MDXXXIIII. (*Colophon.*) 8°. A-B^{8}. [190

-- Commentaria ... in libros Aristotelis de Anima. (Impressum Florentiæ in officina Bartholomei Francisci de Libris: Sumptibus ... Federici Strozæ. Anno ... [nono] supra Millesimum Idibus Martiis.) fol. a-o^{6} (-o6, *presumably blank*). ¶m5^{r}: ... Quæstio singularis de infinitate primi motoris edita a ... Thoma de Vio ... *Colophon defaced.* [191

-- Oratio in secunda seseione [*sic*] concilii Lateranensis. (Romae Impressa ... per Ioannem Beplin̄. Alemanum de Argentina [1512].) 4°. A-B^{4} C^{6}. (Lea.) [192

-- [1] Summa caietana de pctis Et noui testamēti iētacula. ... (Rome per dominum marcellum silber/ ... iacobi de giunta florentini impensis ... impressa: & per ... ioannem danielis ... castigata. ... MDXXV. decimo Kalendas martij. ...) 4°. ✠^{8} A-FF^{8} GG^{12}. ff. 2-242. ¶*Additional t.p.* (A1^{r}): Summula caietana ... [2] Ientacula noui testamēti ... (... M.D.xxv. quinto Kalendas aprilis.) A-N^{8}. ff. 2-104. [193

-- Summula Caietani ... Venetiis, Apud Dominicum Nicolinum. M D LXXXIIII. 16°. a-b^{8} c^{2} A-Yy^{8} Zz^{6}. pp. 1-729. (Lea.) [194

VIPERANO, GIOVANNI ANTONIO. Ioan. Antonii Viperani. De bello Melitensi historia. Perusiae. Ex officina Andreac Brixiani. M. D. LXVII. (*Colophon.*) 4°. A-I^{4} (A4 + *folded leaf*) K^{6}. ff. 1-38. [195

-- Io. Antonii Viperani de scribenda historia liber. Antuerpiae, Ex officina Christophori Plantini. M. D. LXIX. 8°. A-D^{8} E^{4}. pp. 3-69. [196

VIRDUNG, JOHANN. Ioannis Hasfurti ... de cognoscendis, et medendis morbis ex corporum coelestium positione Libri IIII. ... Venetijs, Ex Officina Damiani Zenarij, 1584. 4°. *-3*^{4} A-G^{4} (+ *folding leaf*) H-Yy^{4} 3A-3L^{4}. ff. 1-228. ¶*Includes:* Hermetis Trismegisti Iatromathematica; Galeni Pergameni Prognostica ex ęgroti decubitu; Marsilii Ficini De vita studiosorum tuenda, De vita longa, De vita coelitus comparanda, De peste; Ioannis Paulli

Gallucij De figura coelesti erigenda, De parte fortunæ, & hepatis extrahenda, De Zodiaci diuisione, De planetarum dignitatibus tum essentialibus, tum accidentalibus, De temporibus ad medicandum accommodatis. (Lea.) [197

VIRET, PIERRE. The second part of the demoniacke worlde, or worlde possessed with Diuels, conteining three Dialogues: 1. Of Familiar Diuels. 2. Of Lunaticke Diuels. 3. Of the coniuring of Diuels. Translated out of French into English by T. S[tocker]. Gentleman. Imprinted at London for Iohn Perin ... 1583. (Imprinted ... by Thomas Dawson, for Iohn Perin ...) 8°. B.L. A-I^8 (-I8, *presumably blank*). *S.T.C.* 24786, pt. 2. (Furness.) [198

VISCARDO, GIOVANNI ANDREA. La Coronatione d'Henrico Duca d'Angiò a re di Polonia Con la sua partita in Francia L'Anno 1575. ... In Bergamo. cIↄ. Iↄ XCII. Per Comino Ventura. 4°. [A]^4 B-C^4 A^4. pp. 1-7. [199

-- Delle lettere ... Libro Primo. ... In Bergamo, M D XCI. Per Comino Ventura. 8°. a^4 A-N^8 O^6. ff. 1-110. [200

-- Precetti morali e ciuili, Con ... essempi ... In Venetia, Appresso Sebastian Combi, M D C. 8°. a-b^8 A-Cc^8. ff. 1-206. [201

VISCONTI, GIOVANNI BATTISTA. Arminia egloga di Giambattista Visconte ... Rappresentata ... Luglio 1599. ... Stampata in Milano, per Pandolfo Malatesta. Ad instanza di Pietro Martire Locarni. ... 1599. 4°. A-Q^4 R^2. ff. 2-65. [202

VITALIS, JANUS FRANCISCUS. Imperiae panaegyricus ... [Romae, Joannes Beplin, 1512.] 4°. A^6. [203

-- Panegyris. R. Dñi Mathei Episcopi Gurcēsis ... [Romae, Joannes Beplin, 1512.] 4°. a^6. [204

VITELLIUS, ERASMUS. Oratio ... ad Cesarem Maximilianum nomine ... regis Polonie Sigismundi habita ... .XX. Augusti. ... M.D.XVIII. ... (Impressum Augustæ Vindelicorū in officina Millerana.) 4°. A-B^4. [205

VITRUVIUS POLLIO, MARCUS. M. Vitruuius per Iocundum solito castigatior factus cum figuris ... (Impressum Venetiis ... diligentia Ioannis de Tridino alias Tacuino. ... .M.D.XI. Die .XXII. Maii ...) fol. AA^4 A-N^8 O^6 P^{10} (-P10, *blank*). ff. 1-110. [206

-- -- M. Vitruuii ... de architectura libri decem ... Sexti Iulii Frontini de aquaeductibus vrbis Romae, libellum ... Nicolai Cusani card. de staticis experimentis fragmentum. ... Argentorati in officina Knoblochiana per Georgium Machæropioeum. Anno M. D. XLIII. (... mense Augusto ...) 4°. *^{4} *a-*d^4 *e^6 A-HH^4 II^6 α-ε^4 ζ^6. pp. 2-262. (Fine Arts.) [207

-- -- ... Accesserunt, Gulielmi Philandri Castilionii ... annotationes ... Epitome in omnes Georgij Agricolæ de mensuris & ponderibus libros, eodem autore ... Lugduni, apud Ioan. Tornaesium. M. D. LII. ... (Acheuē d'imprimer le huitieme de Feurier ...) 4°. A^4 A^4 a-z^4 (z4 + *folded leaf*) A-Z^4 aa-rr^4. pp. 1-447. [208

-- -- Architecture ou art de bien bastir, de Marc Vitruue Pollion ... mis de Latin en Françoys, par Ian Martin ... A Paris, De l'Imprimerie de Hierosme de Marnef, & Guillaume Cauellat ... 1572. fol. A^4 B-GG^6 HH^4. pp. 1-351. (Fine Arts.) [209

-- -- M. L. Vitruuio Pollione di Architettura ... nella volgar lingua tradotto ... M D XXXV (In Vinegia per Nicolo de Aristotele detto Zoppino. ... del mese di Marzo.) fol. AA-BB^6 A-N^8 O^6. ff. 1-CX. (Fine Arts.) [210

-- -- *Another copy.* [211

VITTORI, MARIANO. De Sacramento confessionis, seu pœnitentiæ, historia ... Mariano Victorio Reatino auctore. Romae, M. D. LXII. Apud Paulum Manutium, Aldi F. 8°. A-Q^8. pp. 3-244. (Lea.) [212

VIVALDI, GIOVANNI LODOVICO. De contritionis veritate aureum opus ... (... impensis ... Ioannis rynman de Oringau: impressus in ... Hagenau per ... Heinricū Gran ... M.d.xviij. prima die decembris.) 4°. B.L. a-r^8 (-r8, *presumably blank*). ff. III-CXI. [213

VIVES, JUAN LUIS. [1] Io. Lodouici Viuis Valentini opera, in duos distincta tomos ... Basileae anno M D L V. (... per Nic. Episcopium iuniorem ...) fol. α-δ^6 ϵ^8 a-z^6 A-Z^6 aa-ii^6 kk^8. pp. 1-687. [2] Secundus tomus ... Basileæ, anno MDLV. (*Colophon.*) AA-ZZ^6 Aa-Zz^6 aAa-zZz^6 AaA-LlL^6 MmM^4 NnN^6 (-MmM^4, NnN^6). pp. 3-959 *present.* [214

-- De conscribendis epistolis ... libellus ... Des. Erasmi Rot. Compendium ... Conradi Celtis Methodus. Christophori Hegendorphini Methodus. ... Apud Seb. Gryphium Lugduni, 1542. 8°. a-i^8. pp. 3-129. [215

-- -- Coloniae, Excudebat Petrus Horst, Anno 1563. 8°. A-K^8 (-B8). pp. 3-149. [216

-- Ioannis Ludouici Viuis Valentini, De Disciplinis Libri XX. ... Lugduni, Apud Ioannem Frellonium 1551. (*Colophon.*) 8°. Aa-Bb^8 Cc^4 A-PP^8 QQ^4. pp. 1-613. [217

-- *De institutione feminae Christianae.* L'institutiō de la femme Chrestienne. ... traduit en langue Françoyse, par Pierre de Changy ... 1545. De l'Imprimerie de Denys Ianot: pour Galiot du Pré ... 16°. a-y^8. ff. 2-175. [218

-- -- Ioannis Lodouici Viuis Von vnderweysung ayner Christlichen Frauwen ... verteūtscht. Durch Christophorum Brunonem ... M. D. XXXXIIII. (Getruckt ... inn ... Augspurg/ durch Hainrich Stainer/ am j. tag Martij ...) fol. aa^4 A-X^6. ff. I-CXXV. [219

-- *De officio mariti.* [1] Erster Theyl Ioannis Ludouici Viuis ... Von gebürlichem thůn vnd lassen eines Christlichen Ehemanns/ Zu Latein/ De Officio Mariti, genannt ... durch Herrn Christophorum Brunonem ... in vnser Můtterliche Teutsche Spraach gebracht ... Zu Franckfort am Meyn/ Bey Christian Egenolffs seligen Erben/ Im Iar M. D. LXVI. (*Colophon.*) fol.)(^{4} A-G^6 H^4 I^6. ff. I-LI. [2] Ander Theyl ... Von vnderweisung vnd Gottseliger anfürung einer Christlichen Frawen/ im Latein/ De Institutione Christianæ Foeminæ genant ... *Same imprint.* ¢^{6} A-Q^6 R^8. ff. I-CIIII. [220

-- Ioannis Lodouici Viuis Valentini declamationes sex. Syllanae quinque. Sexta, qua respondet Parieti palmato Quintiliani. Eiusdem ... de præsenti statu Europæ, & bello Turcico diuersa opuscula. Item. Isocratis orationes duae, Areopagitica & Nicocles, eodem ... interprete. ... Basileae. (... in officina Roberti VVinter, anno M. D. XXXVIII. mense Martio.) 4°. a-b^4 A-Xx^4. pp. 1-315. (Lea.) [221

-- -- Le declamationi sillane di Gio. Lodouico Viues Valentiano tradotte di Latino in volgare per Gio. Domenico Tarsia Iustinopolitano In Vinegia nelle case di Pietro de Nicolini da Sabbio M. D. XLIX. (*Colophon.*) 8°. A-R^8. ff. 1-143. [222

VIVIEN, JORIS. Compendium de diuersis regulis iuris caesarei seu ciuilis ... Per Georgium Viuiennum Antuerpianum ... Coloniae, Apud Theodorum Baumium. Anno MDLXXI. 8°. *^{8} A-F^8. pp. 1-75. (Lea.) [223

-- De gradibus affinitatis et consanguinitatis, et nominibus eorum: titulus decimus, libri XXXVIII. Pandectarum. ... Coloniae, Apud Theodorum Baumium. Anno D.M.LXXI. 8°. 3A-$3C^8$. pp. 3-48. (Lea.) [224

-- Epitome regularum iuris pontificii seu canonici ... Coloniae, Apud Theodorum Baumium. Anno D.M.LXXI. 8°. Aa-Ee^8. pp. 4-76. (Lea.) [225

VIVOLI, FRANCESCO ANTONIO. Francisci Antonii Viuoli ... quaesitum, an singulare substantiae naturaliter ... an de alio subiecto prædicetur ... Neapoli, Apud Horatium Saluianum. M D LXXXV. fol. a^2 A-B^4. pp. 1-16. [226

-- Francisci Antonii Viuoli Neapolitani ... quaesitum de medio demonstrationis simpliciter, iuxta Aristotelis, & Auerrois doctrinam ... Neapoli, In ædibus Decij Lachęi. M D LXXIII. fol. A-E^4 F^2. ff. 2-22. [227

VIZANI, POMPEO. Di Pompeo Vizani ... Bolognese diece libri delle historie della sua patria. In Bologna, Presso gli Heredi di Gio. Rossi. CIϽIϽXCVI. ... (*Colophon.*) 4°. ✠-✠✠^{8} 3✠^{6} 4✠^{2} A-Mm^8. pp. 1-556. [228

VOCABULA. Ex probatissimis authoribus uariaꝝ rerum uocabula ... collecta. MDXVIII (Impressum Augustę in edibus Siluani Otmar ...) 4°. B.L. A-F^4. ff. II-XXIIII. ¶*Latin and German.* [229

VOCABULARIUS. Vocabularius Latinis Gallicis ꝛ Theutonicis verbis scriptū (Getruckc zu Strassburg durch Martinum. Flach. Anno dñi .M.D:xxj) 4°. A^8 B-C^4 D^8 E^4 F^8 (-F8, *presumably blank*). ¶A1 *defective.* [230

-- Vocabularius variorū terminorū: ex poetis et historiographis congestus. (Impressum per ... Iohannem pruss ciuem Argentinensem. Anno .M.CCCCII. [*sic*] xviij. Kal'. Februarij.) 4°. A^8 $B-C^4$ D^8 E^4 F^6 (-F6, *presumably blank*). [231

VOCABULISTA. Quinque linguarum ... Vocabulista. Latine, Tusche, Gallice, Hyspane, & Alemanice. ... (Venetijs per Melchiorem Sessam. M. D. XXXVII.) 4°. B.L. $✠^4$ $A-H^4$. [232

VOELLUS, JOANNES. De ratione conscribendi epistolas ... Brixiae, Ex Officina Petri Mariæ Marchetti. (... Apud Polycretum Turlinum. 1590. ...) 8°. $A-D^8$. pp. 3-64. [233

-- Generale artificium texendae, seu componendae cuiuscunque orationis longè facillimum. ... Brixiæ, Ex Officina Petri Mariæ Marchetti. (... Apud Polycretum Turlinum. 1590. ...) 8°. $A-K^8$. pp. 3-159. [234

VOGEL, EWALD VAN. De lapidis physici conditionibus liber. Quo ... Gebri & Raimundi Lullii ... continentur explicatio. ... Coloniae Agrippinae, Apud Henricum Falckenburg. Anno cIↄ. Iↄ. XCV. 8°. †-††^{8} 3†^{2} $A-Q^8$. pp. 1-252. (Smith.) [235

VOGTHERR, HEINRICH. Ain Fruchtbar büchlin/ wie ain Christñ mensch in Got widerumb neüw geporen ... werd. ... H .Satrapitanus. P Im. Jar. M.D.XXiij. [Augsburg, Melchior Ramminger.] 4°. $A-B^4$. [236

-- Eyn schône Vnd Gotselige kurtzweil/ eines Christlichen Lossbůchs ... In reimen gestelt. ... Gedicht vnd Getruckt zů Strassburg von Heynrichen Vogtherren. Anno M.D.XXXiX. (Volendet ... den vj Augusti ...) fol. $A-I^4$ $[K]^4$ $[L]^6$. [237

VOIT, DAVID. Eine Predigt Vber das Euangelium Matth. 21. ... Gedruckt zu Ihena/ durch Donat Richtzenhan. Anno M. D. LXXXI. (*Colophon.*) 4°. $A-D^4$. [238

VOLDER, WILLEM DE. Acolastus de filio prodigo comoedia ... authore Guilielmo Gnapheo ... Antuerpiæ, Excudebat Ioannes Loêus, Anno, M.D.LI. 8°. $A-D^8$ (-D8, *presumably blank*). [239

VOLUSENE, FLORENCE. De animi tranquillitate dialogus, Florentio Volusano autore. Lugduni apud Seb. Gryphium, M. D. XLIII. 4°. $A-Zz^4$ $3a-3d^4$. pp. 3-399. [240

VORRILONG, GUILIELMUS. Guillermus vorrillong super quattuor libris sententiarum ... (Venetijs per presbyterum Bonetum Locatellum Bergomensem. Impensis vero .D. Lazari de Soardis quinto Idus Iulias. Anno secundo ꝛ quingentesimo supra millesimum.) 4°. B.L. $a-z^8$ ꝛ^8 ꝯ^8 ꝶ^8 $A-L^8$ M^{12}. ff. 2-308. (Lea.) [241

VREDEMANN, JAN. Architectura Oder Bauung der Antiquen auss dem Vitruuius ... Getruck tzo Antorff by Geerhardt de Iode An°. 1581. Antuerpie Apud gerardus de Iode ... 1577. (... Typis Gerrardi Smits.) fol. *engraved t.p.* + 3 *pp. of letterpress (2d verso blank)* + 6 *plates* + 2 *pp. of letterpress* + 7 *plates* + 1 *p. of letterpress (verso blank)* + 4 *plates* + 2 *pp. of letterpress* + 6 *plates* + 1 *p. of letterpress (verso blank, with 2 mounted engravings)* + 9 *plates*. (Fine Arts.) [242

-- Artis Perspectiuæ ... Formulæ ... Inuentor Ioan. Fridmannus Frisius. Liber primus Excudebat Antuerpæ Gerardus de Iode, Neomagensis. An: 1568. obl. fol. *engraved t.p.* + 16 *plates*. (Fine Arts.) [243

-- Differents pourtraicts de menuiserie ... De l'inuention de Iehan Vredeman dict de Vriese. et mis en lumiere par Philippe Galle [Amsterdam, 1565.] fol. *engraved t.p.* + *16 numbered plates*. (Fine Arts.) [244

VULCANIUS, BONAVENTURA. De Literis & Lingua Getarum, Siue Gothorum. Item de notis Lombardicis. Quibus accesserunt specimina variarum Linguarum ... Lugduni Batauorum, Ex officina Plantiniana, Apud Franciscum Raphelengium. cIↄ. Iↄ. XCVII. 8°. $*^8$ $a-g^8$. pp. 1-109. [245

VULPELLUS, OCTAVIANUS. Octauiani Vulpelli ... tractatus de pace, indutiis, et promissionibus de non offendendo. ... Venetijs, Ex Typographia Guerræa. M D LXXIII. 8°. $a-c^8$ d^4 $A-N^8$. pp. 2-204. [246

VULTEIUS, HERMANNUS. Hermanni Vulteii ... ad titulos codicis, Qui sunt, de iurisdictione & forocompetenti, Commentarius. Francofurti In Bibliopolio Zachariæ Palthenii. M. D. XCIX. 8°.)(^{8} A-Rr^8 Ss^4. pp. 1-648. [247

-- Hermanni Vulteii J.C. disceptationum juris Scholasticarum Liber unus. Editio tertia. Marpurgi, Typis Pauli Egenolphi ... cIↄ IↄC. 8°. A-Z^8 a^8. ff. 2-192. [248

VULTEIUS, JOANNES. Ioannis Vulteii Remensis epigrammatum libri IIII. Eiusdem xenia. Lugduni, ... apud Michaelem Parmanterium, M. D. XXXVII. (... excudebat Ioannes Barbous ...) 8°. a-s^8 (-s8, *presumably blank*). pp. 2-282. (Lea.) [249

W

WAGEMAEKERS, JEAN. Cōtra monachos proprietarios plurimi ... tractatus. Primus magistri Ioannis currificis. Secundus ... Ioannis de bomalia. Tertius ... Petri damiani. Quartus ... Petri cantoris. Quintus cuiusdam alterius docti viri. Item tractatus ... Ioannis tinctoris contra defendentes aperturam claustrorum. ... venundantur Parrhisijs ... (Exaratū ... sumptibus ... Gilberti ⁊ Gaufridi de marnef fratrum ...) 8°. B.L. $a\text{-}e^8$ (-e8, *blank*). [1

WAGNER, BARTHOLOMEUS. Christliche Auslegung der ... Prophecey Esaie ... Gedruckt zu Leipzig durch Wolff Günter. M. D. LI. 4°. $[A]^2$ $B\text{-}D^4$. [2

WAIM, GERVAIS. Tractatus noticiarum Geruasii VVaim Sueui. Eiusdem questiones in libros posteriorum resolutionum philosophi. Venundatur [Parisiis] a Conrado Resch ... (... impressus per Nicolaus de pratis Expensis Conradi Resch alemani ... Anno ... Millesimo quingentesimo decimonono. Die vero xxviij. mensis Martij.) fol. $+^4$ $a\text{-}s^6$ (-s6, *presumably blank*). [3

WALASSER, ADAM. Helm des Hayls. Welche der recht Christlich vnd allain seligmachend Glaub sey. ... Gedruckt zů Ingolstatt/ beym Jungen Alexander Weyssenhorn/ in verwaltung vnd kosten seiner Můter Anne Samuel Weyssenhörnin. Anno M. D. LXXI. 4°. $A\text{-}G^8$ (-G8, *presumably blank*). [4

WALBECK, DITHMAR VON. Chronici Ditmari episcopi Mersepurgii, libri VII. ... Accessere de vita & familia Ditmari ... expositiones: Auctore Reinero Reineccio Steinhemio. Francofurti ad Moenum Ex officina Typographica Andreæ Wecheli, M D LXXX. fol. $\bar{a}^6$ $A\text{-}I^6$ K^8 L^4. pp. 1-123. [5

WALDENSES. Apologia verae doctrinae eorum qui vulgo appellantur VValdenses vel Picardi. Retinuerunt enim Ioannis Hussitae doctrinam, cum scripturis sanctis consencientem. ... Anno 1538. ... (Impressum Viteberge per Georgium Rhavv.) 4°. $A\text{-}Z^4$ $a\text{-}f^4$ g^6. ff. 1-117. (Lea.) [6

-- Confessio VValdensium de plerisque nunc controuersis dogmatibus ante 134. annos contra claudicantes Hussitas scripta ... Basileae per Ioannem Oporinum. Anno M.D.LXVIII. 8°. $A\text{-}Z^8$ $a\text{-}f^8$ g^6. pp. 1-196. ¶*Dedication by Matthias Flacius Illyricus.* (Lea.) [7

-- Memorabilis historia persecutionum, bellorumque in populum vulgo Valdensem appellatum ... ab anno 1555, ad 1561, religionis ergô gestorum. Anno M. D. LXII, Gallicè primùm in lucem ædita, nunc verò à Christophoro Richardo Biturige, Latinitate donata. ... Geneuæ, Excudebat Eustathius Vignon. M.D.LXXXI. 8°. $¶^8$ $A\text{-}K^8$ L^2. pp. 1-151. (Lea.) [8

WALDNER, WOLFGANG. Antwort auff des Osianders Schmeckbier. Wolff Waldner. ... 4°. $A\text{-}D^4$ E^2 (-E2, *presumably blank*). [9

WALSINGHAM, THOMAS. Historia breuis Thomæ Walsingham, ab Edwardo primo, ad Henricum quintum. Londini Excusum apud Henricum Binneman ... 1574. (*Colophon.*) fol. $¶^4$ π^1 $A\text{-}Y^6$ $Aa\text{-}Pp^6$ Qq^8 Rr^4 (-Rr4, *presuambly blank*). pp. 1-458. *S.T.C.* 25004. ¶*Lacks* π^1, *which, however, is found after* π2 *in* Ypodigma Neustriae *(next entry), with which this is bound. Between* ¶1 *and* ¶2 *is bound a copy of Asser's* Alfredi regis res gestae (*S.T.C.* 863) *lacking the t.p.* [10

-- Ypodigma Neustriæ vel Normanniæ ... Ab irruptione Normannorum vsq; ad annum .6. regni Henrici quinti. Londini in ædibus Iohannis Daij. 1574. ... (*Colophon.*) fol. π^2 $A\text{-}H^4$ H^2 $I\text{-}Y^4$ $Aa\text{-}Dd^4$. pp. 3-199. *S.T.C.* 25005. [11

WALTHER, CHRISTOPH. Antwort Auff der Flacianisten Lügen vnd falschem Bericht wider die Hauspostill Doctoris Martini Lutheri. Wittemberg. Gedruckt durch Hans Lufft. 1559. 4°. $A\text{-}B^4$. [12

WANNER, VALENTIN. De missa iudicium Valentini Vannii ... 8°. $A\text{-}L^8$ M^4. ¶A2^v: Datæ 10. Ianuraij ... M.D.LV. [13

WARNUNG. Christliche Warnung vnd Vermanung/ wider das Vnchristlich grewlich flůchen vnnd Gotslästern ... Getruckt zů Passaw/ durch Mattheum Nenninger. 1590. 8°. A-B^8. [14

-- Trewe warnung/ An alle fromme ... Christen/ wie sie sich ... vor Irrthumb ... hüten mögen. ... M. D. LXIII. 4°. A-E^4. [15

WARNUNG GEDICHT. Ein Warnung gedicht/ an alle vnd yede ware liebhaber des heiligen Ewangelions Christi/ vnd freiheit der ... Deudschen Nation ... [1546?] 4°. $[A]^4$. [16

WATSON, THOMAS. Holsome and Catholyke doctryne concerninge the seuen Sacramentes of Chrystes Church ... by ... Thomas byshop of Lincolne. Anno. 1558. Mense Februarij. Excusum Londini in ædibus Roberti Caly ... (... The .x. of February. ...) 4°. B.L. π^4 (-π1, *blank*) A-Aa^8 (-Aa8, *presumably blank*). ff. i-cxc. *S.T.C.* 25112. (Yarnall.) [16a

WATT, JOACHIM VON. Dialogus von der zwitrachtung des heyligen Christenlichen glaubens ... [c. 1522.] 4°. A^4. [17

-- Karsthans. [c. 1521.] 4°. aa-dd^4. [18

-- Ioachimi Vadiani Heluetii mythicum syntagma, cui titulus Gallus pugnans. (Hieronymus Vietor, & Ioannes Singrenius, impresserunt Viennæ Austriæ, ad tertiũ Eidus Ianuarii. Anno. M.D.XIIII. ...) 4°. A-F^4. [19

-- Der schlüssel Dauid. ... (so geschriben ist .M.D.xxiij. jar des drittẽ tags Ianuarij.) 4°. A-C^4. [20

-- Vom alten vnd nüen Gott/ Glauben/ vnd Ler. (Getruckt ... M. D. XXj.) 4°. a-k^4 (-k4, *presumably blank*). [21

-- -- Ein Vnderschyd zů erkennen den almechtigen got ... (Getruckt [zu Wien durch Johann Singriener] ... M D XXj) 4°. A-F^4 G^6. [22

-- Das Wolffgesang. [Basel, Adam Petri, 1522.] 4°. A-D^4 E^6 (-E6, *presumably blank*). [23

WECKER, HANS JAKOB. Practica medicinae generalis ... explicata. Basileae Per Hieron. Froebnium & eius affinem, M. D. XXCV. 16°. *-**^{8} A-Ff^8 (-Ff7-8). pp. 1-337. (Smith.) [24

-- Les secrets et miracles de nature, Recueillis ... par Iean Iacques Vuecker, de Basle ... Traduicts de nouueau en François. ... A Lyon, Par Barthelemi Honorati ... 1584. ... 8°. *^{8} a-z^8 A-$3L^8$ $3M^4$. pp. 1-1208. (Smith.) [25

WEIDENSEE, EBERHARD. Ein grundlich Bericht aus der Schrifft/ Ob der mensch sey ein Herre seiner wercke/ vnd alles thu aus seinem freien willen ... Mit einer Vorrede Iohannis Bugenhagens Pomern D. Wittemberg M.D.XLV. (... durch Ioseph Klug. ...) 4°. A-H^4. [26

WEISMAN, MATHIAS. Canones penitentionales ex varijs sanctorũ pontificum decretis collecti ... (Lipsi impressit Martinus Herbipolensis Anno ... Millesimoquingentesimosextodecimo.) 4°. B.L. a-b^4. (Lea.) [27

WEISSAGUNG. Eine Weissagung/ vnd ein schöner Herrlicher trost/ ... zu diser jetzigen trübseligen zeit/ Aus dem XIIII. Cap. Der offenbarung Iohannis. 1548. 4°. A-B^4. [28

WELBER, JAKOB. Beschreibung der gantzen kriegshandlung ... von anfang des Schmalkhallischen bundes her/ biss auff diss gegenwirtig drei vnnd fünfftzigest jar ... 4°. A-C^4. [29

WELSER, MARCUS. De vita S. Vdalrici Augustanorum Vindelicorum episcopi quæ extant. ... Augustæ Vindelicorum ad insigne pinus. ... MDXCV. 4°. A-Kk^4. pp. 3-263. [30

WERNER, GEORG. De admirandis Hungariae aquis hypomnemation. ... (Viennae Austriae excudebat Egidius Aquila ... M. D. LI. mense Septembri.) 4°. A-E^4 (B1 + 4 *leaves signed* A) F^6. ff. 1-20. [31

WERSTEM, JOHANNES. Ioannis Werstemii Dalemensis aduersus Lutheranæ Sectæ Renatum quendam, de Purgatorio, & alijs quibusdã axiomatis Disputatio ... 8°. A-K^8. ¶A6^v: Coloniæ ad ipsas Iulij kalendas ... M. D. XXVIII. (Lea.) [32

-- -- *Another copy.* (Yarnall.) [32a

WESENBECK, MATTHAEUS. Ænigma timorumenon in lutum sanguine maceratum. ... M.D.LXXIII. 4°. A-M^4. ¶*In verse.* [33

-- Matthæi VVesenbecii commentarius in institutionum iuris libros IIII. ... Basileæ, per Eusebium Episcopium, & Nicolai fr. hæredes, M. D. LXXVI. (... LXXVII.) 8°. α-ι^8 κ^{10} a-z^8 A-Zz^8 AA-DD^8. pp. 7-937. (Biddle.) [34

-- [1] Cl. I.C. Matthaei VVesenbecii responsorum iuris, quæ uulgò concilia appellantur, pars I. ... Basileae, apud Eusebium Episcopium, & Nicolai fratris hæredes, Anno M. D. LXXVII. fol. a-z^6 A-Cc^6 Dd^8 Ee-Ii^6 Kk^8 (-Kk8, *presumably blank*). cols. 3-1204. [2] ... pars II. ... *Same imprint.* fol.):(^{4} a-y^6 (-y6). cols. 3-456. [35

WESENBEECK, PIETER. Academiæ Altorphinæ pius Sive, Carminum Liber. ... Noribergae, Excudebat Paulus Kauffman. M. D. XCVIIII. 8°. A-B^8. pp. 1-28. [36

-- Petri VVesenbecii ... oratio de VValdensibus et Albigensibus Christianis. 1585. Genae, Excudebat Tobias Steinman. 8°. A-D^8 E^4 (-E4, *presumably blank*). (Lea.) [37

WESTERBURG, GERHART. Vom fegefewer vnd standt der verscheydē selen eyn Chrystliche meynung durch Doctor Gerhart westerburch von Coellen Newlich aussgangen. Gedruckt [zu Augsburg durch Heinrich Steiner] jm jar. M.D.xxiij. 4°. A-C^4. [38

WESTPHAL, JOACHIM. Apologetica aliquot scripta ..., quibus & sanam Doctrinam de Eucharistia defendit ... Vrsellis Excudebat Nicolaus Henricus. Anno 1558. 8°. A-H^8. [39

-- Confutatio aliquot enormium mendaciorum Ioannis Caluini ... Vrsellis Excudebat Nicolaus Henricus. Anno 1558. 8°. A-E^8. ¶*Additional t.p.* ($E1^r$): Epistola ... cuiusdam viri; qua maculam Serueticae haeresis aspersam sibi a Caluino abstergit. Anno 1558. [40

WIDMER, JOHANN. Acclamatio heroica. Scripta in honorem ... Ioannis Ertlini Sultzdorffii ... Ingolstadij ex Typographia Vueissenhorniana. Anno M.D.LXVIII. 4°. A-C^4. ¶*In verse.* [41

WIER, JOHANNES. Ioannis VVieri de praestigiis dæmonum, et incantationibus ac ueneficijs Libri sex ... Basileae, ex officina Oporiniana. 1568. 8°. a-z^8 A-Aa^8. pp. 3-697. (Lea.) [42

WIGAND, JOHANN. De Stancarismo, dogmata et argumenta cum solutionibus, quibus præmissa est Methodus de Meditatione Christi ... 1585. Lipsiæ, Georgius Defnerus excudebat. (... Impensis Henningi Grosij ...) 4°.)(^{4} (:)^2 A-V^4. pp. 1-159. (Lea.) [43

-- Συνταγμα, seu corpus doctrinae ... Dei, ex ueteri Testamento tantum ... dispositum ... per Iohannem VVigandum & Matthæum Iudicem. ... Basileae, per Ioannes Oporinum & Heruagium. (... M.D.LXIIII. Mense Martio.) 4°. a-z^4 A-Zz^4 AA-ZZ^4 AAa-ZZz^4 $3A^2$. pp. 4-16, cols. 17-1668. (Lea.) [43a

-- Von den Adiaphoristischen verfelschungen in dem grossen buche/ Actorum Synodicorum ... Nothwendige Erinnerung durch M. Iohannem Wigand/ vnd M. Mattheum Iudicem. Von einem Christen aus dem latein verdeudscht. ... (Gedruckt zu Ihena [c. 1560].) 4°. A-K^4. [44

WILD, JOHANN. Examen ordinandorum. ... Auctoribus, R.D. Ioan. Fero, Ioan. Olthusio, ac Georgio VVicelio. Per F. Nicolaum Aurificum Senensem ... locupletatum ... Dilingæ, Excudebat Ioannes Mayer. M. D. LXXXVII. 16°. A-Z^8 a-q^8. pp. 1-605. [45

WILDENBERG, HIERONYMUS GÜRTLER VON. [1] Totius Philosophiae humanae in tres partes ... digestio ... Basileae, per Ioannem Oporinum. 8°. α^8 β^4 (-β4). [2] Vniuersae philosophiae rationalis in Dialecticam Aristotelis Epitome ... Basileae. aa-gg^8. pp. 3-110. [3] Totius naturalis philosophiae in Physicam Aristotelis Epitome ... Basileae. A-I^8. pp. 4-143. [4] ... Moralis Philosophię Epitome ... Basileae. a-h^8 i^6. pp. 3-139. [46

-- Hieronymi Aurimontani Vuildenbergij, Moralis Philosophiæ Epitome: Ethices, Politices, & Oeconomices principia ... enarrans. ... Parisiis, Apud Thomam Richardum ... 1554. 8°. a-h^8 i^6. pp. 3-138. [47

-- Hieronymi Cingularij Aurimontani tersissima latini eloquij Synonymorum collectanea ... Annexus est Tractatulus ... de vocum proprietatibus ... (Impressum Liptzk per Melchiorem Lotterum Anno dn̄i. Millesimo quingentesimo decimoquinto.) 4°. B.L. A-F^6 G^4. [48

-- -- (Impressum Lipsie per Melchiarem Lottherum Anno dñi Millesimo quingentesimo decimooctauo.) 4°. B.L. A^6 B^4 C^6 D^8 E^4 F^6 G^4. [49

-- Totius naturalis philosophiæ in Physicam Aristotelis Epitome ... Hieronymo VVildenbergio Aurimontano authore. Parisiis, Apud Thomam Richardum ... 1554. 8°. A-I^8. pp. 3-143. [50

-- Vniuersae philosophiae rationalis in Dialecticam Aristotelis Epitome ... Hieronymo Vuildenbergio Aurimontano dissertore. Parisiis, Apud Thomam Richardum ... 1553. 8°. a-g^8. pp. 2-110. [51

WILKE, ANDREAS. De vita & morte ... Iohan. Friderici II. captiui, Ducis Saxoniæ ..., oratio ... M. D. XCV. Excusa Smalcaldiæ, 1597. 4°. A-F^4. [52

WILLER, GEORG. Catalogus nouus nundinarum autumnalium Francofurti ad Moenum, anno M.D.LXXVII. celebratarum, eorum scilicet librorum ... Plerique in ædibus Georgii VVilleri, ... Bibliopolæ Augustani, venales habentur. Verzeichnuss fast aller neuwer Bůcher ... Gedruckt zu Franckfurt am Mayn/ bey Georg Raben. M.D.LXXVII. (*Colophon.*) 4°. A-D^4 E^2. [53

WILLIAM I, prince of Orange. Antorffische Zeitung. Von der Practicirten entleibung/ des Printzen von Oranien ... 10. Iulij/ 1584. Zu singen wie die Schlacht in Franckreich. Das Ander/ Vom Lüfflāndischen Todtengsang. (Getruckt zu Basel von Samuel Apiario.) 8°. A^4. [54

WILLIAM of NEWBURGH. Rerum Anglicarum libri quinque ... Auctore Gulielmo Neubrigensi. ... Antuerpiæ, Ex officina Gulielmi Silvij ... M. D. LXVII. 8°. A-Ll^8 Mm^6. pp. 1-519. [55

WILLICH, JODOCUS. Experimenta P. Virgilii Maronis explicata ... Accessit et commentariolus de verborum copia ... eod. autho. Francofordi ad Viadrum Ioan Eichorn excudebat, anno, M. D. L. Mense octob. 8°. A^4 (+ 2 *folded ll., the second signed* A5) B-I^8 K^4 (-K4, *presumably blank*). ff. 1-68. [56

WILSON, THOMAS. The arte of Rhetorike, for the vse of all suche as are studious of Eloquence, sette foorthe in Englishe, by Thomas Wilson. 1553. And now newly set forth againe, with a Prologue to the Reader. 1567. Imprinted at London, by Ihon Kingston. 1584. 4°. B.L. A-P^8 Q^6. pp. 1-225. *S.T.C.* 25805. (Furness.) [57

-- A Discourse vppon vsurye, by vvaye of Dialogue ... 1572. (Londini in ædibus Rychardi Tottelli. ...) 8°. B.L. ℭ-$ℭℭ^8$ A^2 B-Cc^8 Dd^4. ff. 2-201. *S.T.C.* 25807. [58

-- -- Imprinted at London by Roger Warde ... 1584. 8°. B.L. $¶^8$ $**^8$ B-Cc^8 Dd^4. ff. 2-201. *S.T.C.* 25808. [59

WIMMANN, NICOLAUS. Nauigationis maris Arctoi, id est, Balthici, & sinus Codani, descriptio. ... Basileae [Michael Isengrin]. 4°. A-B^8. ¶*Dedication dated 23 April 1550.* [60

WIMPHELING, JAKOB. Ad Iulium .II. Pōtificē max. Querulosa excusatio Iacobi wimphelingij ad instantiam Fratrū Augustinēsium ad curiam Romanā citati ... [Argentorati, Johannes Knoblauch, 1506?] 4°. A^4. [61

-- -- *Another copy.* (Lea.) [62

-- Appologetica declaratio wymphelingij in libellum suū de integritate: de eo. An sanctus Augustinus fuerit monachus. Cum epistolio Thome Volphij iunioris. Keyserspergij epistola ... de modo predicandi passionem domini. Orō wymphelingij metrica. [Argentinae, Johannes Prūss, 1505.] 4°. A-C^4. [63

-- Auisamentum de concubinariis nō absoluendis quibuscūqȝ. ac eorum periculis q̄ȝplurimis. A theologis Coloniensibus approbatū cum additionibus sacratissimorum canonum. ... (Vale ex Colonia. Anno dñi. M.d.vij.) 4°. B.L. a-b^4 c^6. (Lea.) [64

-- -- Auisamentū de cōcubinarijs nō absoluendis ... (Vale ex Argētina. Anno .M.ccccc.vij.) 4°. B.L. A-B^4. [65

-- Carmina Prose et Rithmi editi in laudem pudicię Sacerdotalis contra Prosam excusare conantem Scandalosissimum concubinatum 4°. π^4. [66

-- Iacobi Wimphelingi De Integritate Libellus ... (Ioannes Knoblouch Ciuis Argentineñ. ex Archytipo imprimebat Anno quingentesimoq̄nto supra millesimū .iij. no. Mar.) 4°. B.L. A-C^8 D^6. [67

-- De vita et miraculis Ioannis Gerson. Defensio wymphelingij ꝑ diuo Ioanne Gerson: ꝛ clero seculari: qui in libro (cui titulus supplemēto celifodine) grauiter taxati sunt et reprehensi. [Argentorati, Johannes Prüss, 1506?] 4°. A-B^4. (Lea.) [68

-- -- *Another copy.* [69

-- De vita et moribus ep̄oꝝ, aliorumqȝ prelatorum & principum Libellus ... Breue seu Epistola Gregorij magni Papę de castiganda incontinentia & impudicitia sacerdotum. (Excussum Argentinæ ... per Renatum Beck. Anno M.D.XII. Decimoquinto Kal'. Aprilis.) 4°. A-D^4 (-D4, *presumably blank*). (Lea.) [70

-- Iacobi wimphelingii schletstattensis Elegantiarū medulla: Oratoriaqȝ precepta ... (Impressus Argentine per Ioannem knoblouch Anno ... Millesimo quingentesimo octauo.) 4°. B.L. A^6 B^4 C^6 D^8 (-D8, *presumably blank*). [71

-- -- Iacobi Vuimphelingii Schletstattensis Elegantie maiores Rhetorica eiusdem ... (Phorce in aedibus Thomae Anshelmi Badensis. Anno ... Millesimo quingentesimo nono Mense Martio.) 4°. A^8 B-D^4 E^8 F^4. [72

-- Epistola Ia. wymphelingi de inepta et superflua verboruȝ resolucione in cancellis? et de abusu exempcionis in fauorem omniū episcoporū et archiepiscoporum. Oratio Ia. wymphelingi ad deum pro pecatorum remissione Epitafium wolfgangi de vtenhem ... (Basileae, Jakob Wolff, c. 1503.) 4°. B.L. π^4. [73

-- Iacobi Vimpfelingij Schletstattensis Theosophi Oratio de sancto spiritu. (Phorce In ædibus Thome Anshelmi Anno .M.D.VII. Mense Maio.) 4°. a-b^4. [74

WIMPINA, CONRAD. Farrago miscellaneorum Conradi VVimpinae à Fagis ... Coloniae, apud Io. Soterem, Anno M. D. XXXI. (... Mense Martio.) fol. Aa^4 a-e^6 f-g^4 h-k^6 l^8 m-z^6 A-G^6 aa-ii^6. ff. 1-177, 2-49. [75

-- Sectarum errorum, hallutinationū, & Schismatum, ab origine ferme Christianæ ecclesiæ, ad hæc usqȝ nostra tempora, concisioris Anacephalæoseos ... Francophordie ad Oderā Anno. M.D.XXVIII. ... fol. A-Pp^6 Qq^8 X^6 3A-$3C^6$ $3D^4$ 3E-$3Z^6$ $4A^8$ 4B-$4D^6$. ff. II-CXXVI, II-XCV, I-CLXI. ¶*Half-titles:* (Aa1) Sectarum errorum ... Anacephalæoseos, ... Pars Secunda ... (n1) Errorum ... Anacephalæoseos, ... Pars Tertia. ... (3X1) De predestinatione. ... (4B1) De fortuna ... (Lea.) [76

WINSHEIM, VEIT. Oratio habita in funere ... Philippi Melanthonis ... Vitebergae excudebat Petrus Seitz. Anno LX. (*Colophon.*) 4°. A-D^4 (-D4, *presumably blank*). [77

WINTZER, THOMAS. Die Historia der vnglückseligen Schlacht/ zwischen/ Hertzog Albrechten Marggraffen zu Brandenburg/ vnd ... Hertzog Moritzen Chůrfürsten/ zu Sachsen etc. sampt seinem tode vnd begrebnis. Auffs new in reim zugericht ... im M. D. LIII. Jar. Durch Thomam Wyntzer von Dresden. (Gedruckt Bey Iacob Berwald/) 4°. A-D^4 E^2. [78

WIRSUNG, CHRISTOPH. Praxis Medicinæ vniuersalis; Or A generall Practise of Physicke: ... Translated into English ... By Iacob Mosan Germane ... Imprinted at London by Edmund Bollifant. 1598. fol. B.L. A^{10} A-$3D^8$ 3E-$3S^4$. pp. 1-790. *S.T.C.* 25862. (Furness.) [79

WIRT, WYGAND. Reuocatio Fratris Vuygādi Vuirt ... Rome & Heydelberge facta. ... Apud Trebotes impressa. 4°. B.L. π^4 (-π4, *presumably blank*). (Lea.) [80

WITTEKIND. VVitichindi Saxonis rerum ab Henrico et Ottone I impp. gestarum Libri III ... Basileae apud Io. Heruagium, mense Martio, anno M.D.XXXII. (*Colophon.*) fol. α^6 β^8 a-z^6 A-K^6 (-K6, *presumably blank*). pp. 1-394. [81

WITTENBERG. Ain lobliche ordnūg der ... stat Wittemberg Im tausent fünfhundert vnd zway vnd zwaintzigsten jar auffgericht. 4°. $[A]^4$. [82

-- *University.* Ernstlich Handlung der Vniuersitet zů Wittenberg an den ... Herr Friderich von Sachsen/ Die Mess betreffende. 4°. a-c^4. [83

-- Gründlicher vnd warhafftiger Bericht aller Rathschleg vnd antwort/ so die Theologen zu Wittemberg ... erforderte/ ... wider die dazumal newen Reformation des Augspurgischen Buchs Interim genant ... Von den Professorn in der Vniuersitet Wittemberg in druck verordnet. [Wittenberg,] Durch Georgen Rhawen seligen Erben. Anno 1559. 4°. A-Z^4 a-3Q^4 3R^2 3S^4. ff. 2-345. [84

-- Kurtzer Bericht/ Wie ... Philippus Melanthon sein Leben ... geendet ... Geschrieben von den Professoribus der Vniuersitet Witteberg ... Witteberg/ Gedruckt durch Hans Krafft. 1560. 4°. A-I^4. [85

-- Leges Academiæ VVitebergensis de studiis et moribus auditorum. Item/ Artickel etlicher notwendiger Ordnung vnd Satzung/ zu erhaltung guter policey ... Wittemberg/ Gedruckt durch Hans Lufft. Anno 1573. 4°. A-P^4. [86

-- Statut Der Vniuersitet Wittenberg/ vom Ausfordern vnd Prouociren. 4°. A^4. ¶A4^r: Geben den xxvj. Tag Septembris/ ... LXX. [87

-- Der Vniuersitet zu Wittemberg/ Ordenung. Von kleidung/ geschmuck/ bekostigung der Hochzeiten/ Gastereien etc. ... Gedruckt zu Wittemberg/ durch Georgen Rhaw. M. D. XLVI. 4°. A-C^4. [88

WITTESTEYN, KARL. Caroli VVitestein seu à Petra Alba ... Disceptatio Philosophica de Quinta Chymicorum Essentia. Accessit Alexandri Carerij Patauini Quæstio, An metalla artis beneficio permutari possunt. ... Basileae, per Sebastianum Henricpetri. [1583?] 8°. α^8 A-O^8. pp. 1-233. (Lea.) [89

WITTGENSTEIN, GEORG VON SAYN, count of. Appellation Instrumenta/ An die Römische Keyserliche ... Mayestat ... M.D. LXXXV. 4°. A-H^4 I^2. pp. 1-62. (Lea.) [90

-- Aussschreiben vnd Gründtlicher/ Warhafftiger/ Beständiger Bericht. ... M.D.LXXXV. ... 4°.)(^{4} A-M^4 a-3c^4. (Lea.) [91

-- Instrumentum requisitionis ac supplicationis ... M.D. LXXXVI. 4°. A-B^4 C^2. (Lea.)[92

WITZEL, GEORG. Antwort auff Martin Luthers letzt bekennete Artickel ... Georgij Wicelij. ... Anno M. D. XXXVIII. XXX. Augusti. (Gedruckt zu Leipzig durch Nicolaum Wolrab.) 4°. A-M^4. [93

-- Apologia: das ist: ein vertedigs rede Georgij Wicelij widder seine affterreder die Luteristen ... (Gedruckt zu Leiptzig/ durch Nickel Schmidt: M. D. XXXIII.) 4°. A-F^4 G^2. [94

-- Auslegũge der Prophetischen vnd aller schönisten Gesenge Marie Iesu mutter/ Zaccharie des Priesters/ vnd Simeonis des gerechten ... Mit dreien Cleynen Psalmen ... Dauids. ... Anno M.D.XXXvij. 8°. A-E^8. [95

-- Catechismus Ecclesie: lere vnnd Handlung des heiligen Christenthůms ... (Gedruckt zů Freyburg in Breyssgaw/ durch Ioannem Fabrum Emmeum Iulisacensem/ ... M. D. XXXVj.) 4°. a-p^4. [96

-- Chorus sanctorum omnium Zwelff Bücher Historien Aller Heiligen Gottes ... Zu Cöln am Rhein/ durch die Erben des Erbarn Iohan Quentels ... 1554. ... (... xi. Calendas Septembris ...) fol. A-B^4 a-3r^6 3s^4. pp. 1-734. [97

-- Geor. Wicelii commentariolus de Arbore bona, Antichristo, Intercessione diuorum, deq; Ieiunio, & mortis Dominicæ die. Coloniæ ex officina Ioannis Quentel, ... M.D.XLVIII. ... 8°. A-F^8 G^4. pp. 3-101. [98

-- Confutatio calumniosissimae responsionis Iusti Ionae, id est, Iodoci Kock, vna cum assertione Bonorum operum ... Coloniæ ex officina Ioannis Quentel, Anno M. D. XLIX. ... 8°. A-L^8. pp. 3-175. [99

-- De moribus veterum haereticorum: & quibus cum illi hac ætate affinitatem habent. ... [Lipsiae, Melchior Lotter,] M.D.XXXVII. 8°. A-I^8. [100

-- De raptu epistolae priuatae, et praefixa illi, criminatione, Contra Ludum Syl. Hessi. Expostulatio cum Hoste Iona. ... Anno M.D.XXXV. 8°. a-e^8. [101

-- De Traditione Apostolica et Ecclesiastica. ... Zu Cöln durch Iohan Quentel/ Anno M. D. XLIX. 4°. A-K^4. [102

-- Defensio doctrinae de bonis operibus, contra sectam Martini Luteri. Tyrocinium Georgii Vicelii Zelotæ. ... Coloniæ ex officina Ioannis Quentell, Anno M. D. XLIX. ... 8°. A-F^8 G^4. pp. 4-101. [103

-- [Das dritte Teil/] Postillen/ vber alle Episteln vnd Euangelien der heiligen Sontage ... Gedruckt zu Leipzig durch Nicolaum Wolrab/ anno M. D. XXXIX. ... fol. π^6 A-Bb^6 Cc^8. ff. II-CLVII. ¶π1 *defective.* [104

-- Ecclesiasticae demegoriae. Postill/ Gemeine Predig/ auff die Episteln/ vnd Euangelien ... Gedruckt zu S. Victor bey Mentz/ Durch Franciscum Behem. Anno M. D. XLII. (*Colophon.*) fol. $*^4$ A-Z^6 a-n^6 Pp^4 Qq-$3A^6$ $3B^8$. ff. II-CCLXXXIX. ¶*Additional t.p.* ($Pp1^r$): Die Allerheiligste Historia der Passion vnsers Herren ... *Same imprint.* [105

-- Epistolarum, quae inter aliquot Centurias uidebantur partim profuturæ Theologicarum literarum studiosis, partim innocentis famam aduersus Sycophantiam defensuræ, libri Quatuor. ... Lipsiae, Excudebat Nicolaus Vuolrab. an. M. D. XXXVII. ... (*Colophon.*) 4°. A-Zz^4 a-t^4. [106

-- [1] Epitome Kurtze Predige der Episteln vnd Euangelien/ ... auss den Postillen D. Georgij Wicelij ... Gedruckt zu Cöln durch die Erben etwass Iohã Quẽtels vñ Gerwinum Calenium. M. D. LVIII. (Gedruckt zů S. Victor bey Mentz/ durch Franciscum Behem/ Im Jar. M.D.LI.) 4°. a^4 A-$3Y^4$. ff. 2-268. [2] Epitome de sanctis. ... Im Jar. M. D. LI. A-Ii^4 (-Ii4). ff. 2-126. [107

-- Exercitamenta syncerae pietatis ..., inter quae lector habes liturgiam seu Missam S. Basilij Mag. recognitam, & Missam Aethiopum Christianorum in Aphrica, unà cum uetustiss. Ecclesie Catholicæ Litanijs. ... Anno M. D. LV. (Moguntiae, apud Franciscum Behem Misnensem, Sumptu Hæredum Iohannis Quentelij Ciuis Coloniensis, ... Mense Februario.) 4°. a-d^4 A-Z^4 Aa^2 (-Aa2, *presumably blank*). (Lea.) [108

-- -- *Another copy.* [109

-- Fragmentum paedagogiae Christianae ... Excusum Moguntiæ, ad diuum Victorem, in officina typographica Francisci Behem. 1541. 8°. A-B^8. ff. 3-16. [110

-- Hagiologium, seu de sanctis ecclesiae. ... Moguntiae Ad diuum Victorem excudebat Franciscus Behem. M.D.XLI. fol. π^6 A-Z^4 a-z^4 Aa-Tt^4. ff. II-CCLIX. [111

-- Homiliae aliquot ab Aduentu usq3 in Quadragesimam, & præterea à Dominica XIII. usque ad Aduentum. Adiecta est comprehensio locorum vtriusque Testamenti de Necessitate pie factorum eius qui fidem habet. Epistola de libero arb. Dissertatio item de arbore bona, de Antichristo, de intercessione diuorum &c̄. ... Lipsiae, In officina Nicol. VVolrab. an. M. D. XXXVIII. ... (*Colophon.*) 4°. A-Z^4 a-z^4 Aa-Hh^4. [112

-- Homiliae duae de ecclesiae mysteriis, Baptismo & Eucharistia. Encomium sanctæ linguæ. ... Lipsiae Excudebat Nicolaus Vuolrab, M.D.XXXVIII. 8°. A-G^8. [113

-- Der Hunderst vnnd zwentzigist Psalm Dauids/ Christlich ausgelegt. ... Anno M. D. xxxv. xxviij. Augusti. (Gedruckt zu Leiptzigk/ Melchior Lotter. ...) 4°. A-E^4. [114

-- Idiomata quaedam linguae sanctæ, in Scripturis Veter. Testament. obseruata. ... Moguntiae Ad Diuum Victorem excudebat Franciscus Behem. Anno M. D. XLII. 8°. A-H^8 I^4. ff. 3-76. [115

-- Inspectio ecclesiarum ... Vna cum nonnullis Alijs Epanorthosin Ecclesiasticam pertinentibus ... Coloniae, Apud hęredes Arnoldi Birckmanni Anno 1564. ... 8°. A-D^8 E^4. ff. 1-35. ¶*Half-title* (B7): Media aliquot, adeoque remedia concordiae, etiamnum rudia. ... (Lea.) [116

-- Onomasticon ecclesiaę. Die Tauffnamen der Christen/ deudsch vñ Christlich ausgelegt. ... M. D. XLI. (Gedrůckt zu S. Victor bey Mentz/ Durch Franciscum Behem.) 4°. a-r^4 (-r4, *presumably blank*). ff. 2-67. [117

-- Dn. Georgii Wicelii postilla, hoc est, enarratio epistolarum et euangeliorum de tempore et de sanctis per totum annum, Latinè reddita per Gerardum Lorichium Hadamariensem ... Cum ... Præfatione, indice ... Latinitate per Barthol. Laurentem donatis. Coloniae Ex Officina Hæredum Iohannis Quentel ... M. D. LVII. fol. A^4 B-D^6 a-$3g^6$ $3h^4$ 3i-$4h^6$ $4i^4$ 4k-$4n^6$ 4o-$4p^4$. pp. 1-991. [118

-- Preseruatiu/ Cur vnnd Seelen-Artzney/ wider die ... Seuch der New Euangelischen Secten ... Erstlich Von ... D. Bonifacio Britanno Germano in Latein angestellt: ... Ins Teutsch gebracht ... Durch M. Ioannem Engerdum Turingum ... Getruckt zu Ingolstatt in der Weissenhornischen Truckerey/ bey Wolffgang Eder. Anno M. D. LXXXI. 4°.)(^{4} (:)^4 A-S^4. pp. 1-143. ¶*Additional t.p.* (Q1^r): Catholischen Bekandtnuss ... Sebastiani Flaschij von Manssfeldt/ in welcher er zweyvndzweyntzig Vrsachen/ warumb er die Lutherische Ketzerey ... verlassen habe ... erzählt Ingolstatt/ Anno 1581. [119

-- -- *Another copy.* [120

-- Psaltes ecclesiasticus. Chorbuch der Heiligen Catholischen Kirchen/ Deudsch/ jtzundt new ausgangen. ... In verlag Iohan. Quentels ... zu Cölen. Gedruckt durch Frantz Behem/ zu S. Victor bey Mentz. ... M. D. L. 4°. *^{4} **^{4} A-Z^4 a-y^4. ff. 1-180. [121

-- Publicum ecclesiae sacrum. Von der Warheit der Altkyrchischen Liturgy vnd Opfferung ... Antwort ... wider den Matthis Illyric. ... Zu Cöln durch Iohan Quentel/ ... M. D. LI. 4°. a-aa^4. [122

-- Quadragesimales VVicelii conciones ... interprete autem M. Gerhardo Lorichio Hadamarien. ... Cum indice ..., opera Barth. Laurentis ... Coloniæ apud Hæredes Ioannis Quentell, & Geruinum Calenium ... M.D.LIX. mense Ianuario. ... fol. A^4 a-aa^6 bb^4 cc^6 (-cc6, *presumably blank*). pp. 1-290. [123

-- Quibus modis credendi verbum accipiatur in Sacris literis, Expositio ... An. M. D. XXXV. Februa. (Lipsiae, Nic. Faber ...) 4°. A-D^4 E^2. [124

-- -- Quibus modis fidei, fidelis, Credulitatis seu Credendi, Fiduciæ, Speiq3 vocabula accipiantur in sacris literis ... Item praedicatio ... authore eodem. Coloniæ ex officina Ioannis Quentel ... M.D.XLVIII. ... 8°. a-g^8 h^4. pp. 2-118. [125

-- Retectio Lutherismi, qui se ueteris & Apostolicæ Ecclesiæ nomine uenditat ... Lipsiae In officina Nicolai VVolrab. M. D. XXXVIII. 8°. A-L^8 (-L1) M^4 (-M2-4). ¶*Additional t.pp.:* (I2^r) Querela euangelii ... (L2^r) Oratio in veterem Adam ... [126

-- Sieben psalmen kurtz vnd gewis ausgelegt ... (Gedruckt zu Leiptzig Melchior Lotter. ... M.D.XXXiiii). 4°. A-I^4. [127

-- Syllabus locorum vtroque testamento de bonis operibus ... [Parisiis,] Apud Reginaldum Chaudiere ... 1534. 4°. A-K^4 L^6. [128

-- -- Coaceruatio locorum vtriusque testamenti de absoluta necessitate bonorum à Fide operum ... Coloniae ex officina Ioannis Quentel, Anno M. D. XLVIII. 8°. A-O^8. pp. 3-221. [129

-- Typus ecclesiae prioris. Anzeigung/ wie die heilig Kyrche Gottes ... gestalt gewesen sey. ... M. D. XL. 4°. A-M^4 N^2. pp. I-LXXXIX. [130

-- Vom Beten: Fastenn: vnnd Almosen: Schrifftlich zeugnis ... Eissleben. Anno 1535. Martij. (Gedruckt zů Fryburg im Brissgaw durch Ioannem Emmeum Iuliacensem. Anno M. D. xxxvj.) 4°. aa-ss^4. [131

-- Von der Püss: Beicht: vnnd Bann: tzwey büchlin auss grund der schrifft. ... Año. M.D.xxxvj. (Gedruckt zů Freyburg im Breissgaw/ durch Ioannem Fabrum Emmeum Iuliacensem. Im M. D. XXXVj. Jar/) 4°. A-H^4. [132

-- Ware trostung: grund vnd vrsach auss Götlichem wort/ dz vns Christen die vnuermeidliche not des Tods/ nie erschrecken sol ... An. 1536. (Gedruckt zů Freyburg im Breyssgaw: durch Ioannem Fabrum Emmeum Iusliacensem: ... M. D. XXXVj.) 4°. Aa-Kk^4. [133

WOLF, ERASMUS. In obitu. Ioan. Eckii ... Epicedion. M. Erasmi VVolphii. Ingolstadii excudebat Alexander Vueissenhorn. M. D. XXXXIII. 4°. A-B^4. [134

WOLF, HIERONYMUS. [Commentarii.] Basileae ex officina Heruagiana per Eusebium Episcopium ... fol. [1] Hieronymi VVolfii in Ciceronis Officia ... Commentarij atque Scholia ... M D XXCIV. a-z^6 A-K^6 L^4 M-N^6. pp. 1-8, cols. 9-740, pp. 741-750. [2] M. T. Ciceronis, Cato Maior ... M. D. XXCIII. Aa-Ll^6 Mm-Nn^4. pp. 1-13, cols. 14-267. [3] M. T. Ciceronis Laelius ... M. D. LXXXIIII. AA-FF^6 GG^4. cols. 1-134. [4] M. T. Ciceronis Paradoxa ... M. D. LXXXIIII. AAa-CCc^6. cols. 1-60. [5] M. T. Ciceronis, Scipionis Somnium ... M. D. LXXXIIII. 3A-3B^6 3C^8 3D^4. cols. 1-62. [135

WOLFSBACH, NICOLAUS. Gründtlicher vnd warhafftiger Bericht/ Ob es wahr sey/ Dass nach vnzeittigem Eolffgang Mertzen/ Lutherischen Predicanten/ ... schreiben/ Sanct Vlrich/

Bischoff zu Augspurg/ vff ein zeit ein Weyer fischen lassen/ vnd im selbigen sechsstausent Menschenkoͤpff gefangen hab ... Zu Würtzburg bey Georgen Fleischmann. 1593. (*Colophon.*) 4°. A-O^{4} P^{2}. pp. 1-107. [136

WONSIDEL, ERASMUS. Exercitium De Anima. tres. et Paruorū naturaliū. quatuor vtpote. de Sensu et sensato. de Memoria et reminiscentia. de Sōno et vigilia. de Longitudine ac breuitate vite. libros. ... cōplectens ... (Impressum Liptzick per ... Vuolfgangum Monacensem. ... 1511.) fol. B.L. a-c^{6}. [137

WOODFORD, WILLIAM. Ob nichts anzůnemen sey/ dañ was klar in der hayligen geschrifft ist auss getruckt. Wilhelmus Widefordus contra Iohannem Wicleff. ([Augsburg, Philipp Ulhart,] 1524.) 4°. A-D^{4}. ¶*Translator: Joannes Cochlaeus.* [138

WORMS. Der Stat Worms Reformacion: statutē. ordenūg ... (... getruckt vnd vollendet in dem Fünffzehenhundertsten vnd Neün jar auff Frytag nach dem Sontag Oculi ...) fol. π^{6} A-H^{6} I^{4} K-Q^{6}. ff. II-XCIIII. [139

WÜRTTEMBERG. *Laws &c.* Ordnung in Eesachen. [Tübingen, Ulrich Morhart? 1536 *or earlier.*] 4°. A^{6}. [140

-- Des Fürstenthumbs Wirtemberg Fleisch vnd Metzgerordnung. M. D. LIIII. fol. A-B^{6} C^{4}. ff. I-XIIII. [141

-- Des Fuͤrstentheumbs Wuͤrtemberg gemeine Landtsordnungen. [Tübingen, Georg Gruppenbach,] 1585. fol.)(^{6} A-X^{6} Y^{4}. pp. I-CCLVIII. [142

-- Des Fuͤrstenthumbs Wuͤrtemberg gemein Landrecht ... 1591. (Gedtruckt zu Tuͤbingen/ bey Georgen Gruppenbach. ...) fol.)(-2)(^{6} 3)(^{4} A-Ii^{6} Kk^{4}. pp. I-CCCXC. [143

-- *Ulrich, duke.* [1] Warhafftig vnderrichtung der vffrurn vnnd hanndlung[en sich] im fürstenthumb Wirtemberg begeben Anno fůnffzehenhundert vnd vi[er]ze[h]en. [Tübingen, Thomas Anshelm.] (... der geben ist zü Stůtgart vff Mitwoch nach vnser liebenfrawē tag Assumptionis. ... tusent fünffhundert vnd vierzehen iar.) s.sh. 109 × 43 cm. ¶*With 3 seals. Caption defective.* [2] Vlrich ... hertzog zu Wirtemperg ... [*Printed letter forwarding copies of the* Unterrichtung *to the imperial cities.*] s.sh. 22.5 × 32.5 cm. [3] Wir schicken euch ... [*Printed letter forwarding it to officials.*] s.sh. 16 × 23 cm. [144

-- Vlrich (von gottes gnaden) hertzog zu Wirtemperg vnd Tegk. ... [Proclamation, with seal.] Datum Stutgarten sampstags nach Assumptionis Marie/ Anno fünffzehen hundert vnnd vierzehen. s.sh. 43 × 32.5 cm. [145

-- [Proclamation against the revolting peasants, forbidding the harboring of fugitives and assemblies of the populace without permission, with seal.] [Tübingen, Thomas Anshelm.] Datum Stutgarten sampstags nach Assumptionis Marie/ Anno fünffzehen hundert vnnd vierzehen. s.sh. 43.5 × 32.5 cm. [146

-- *Charles V, Roman emperor.* [Brief requiring the renewal of feudal grants in Württemberg, with countersignatures.] Geben in ... Stůtgarten am sibenden tag des monats Ianuarij Anno ꝛc. im ain vnnd zwaintzigisten ... s.sh. 29.5 × 21 cm. [147

-- *Statthalter.* Wir Roͤmischer Kaiserlicher vnd Hispanischer koͤnigklicher M. vnsers aller genedigsten herren Stathalter/ ir M. Fürstenthumbs Wirtemberge. [Proclamation.] ... [1521.] fol. π^{4}. [148

-- [Printed letter signed Roͤmischer K. M. Stathalter vnd Regenten ir M. Fürstenthumbs Wirtemberg asking the preachers to preach against swearing and drunkenness.] Datum Stůtgarten am zweintzigisten tag Augusti. Anno domini fünffzehen hundert zweintzig vnnd ains. s.sh. 23.5 × 35 cm. [149

-- [Orders against blasphemy, drunkenness, rumormongering and slander, the sheltering of opponents of the government, etc.] [Tübingen? 1521.] fol. π^{4}. [150

-- *Ulrich, duke.* Ordnung eins gemeinen kasten/ für die armen/ wie der allenthalt im Fürstenthumb Wirtemberg angericht soll werden. Anno M. D. XXXVI. 4°. A-C^{4}. [151

-- *History.* Erschreckliche Nüwe Zytung. Warhafftiger ... bericht/ wie das Wetter im Wirttenberger land so grossen schaden gethan hat ... M. D. Lxij. 4°. A^{4}. [152

WÜRZBURG. *Melchior Zobel von Guttenberg, bishop.* Copia etlicher Vertrege/ So der Bischoff von Wirtzburg mit Marggraff Alberten zu Brandenburg etc. vnd Wilhelmen von Grumbach/ auffgericht. 4°. A-C⁴ (-C4, *presumably blank*). ¶*Dated 1 July 1552.* [153

-- *Friedrich von Wirsberg, bishop.* Copia des Vertrags/ zwischen dem Bischoff zu Wirtzburg/ and Wilhelm von Grumbach. 4°. A⁴ B². ¶*Dated 7 October 1563.* [154

-- Des Hochwurdigen Fürsten vnd Herren/ Herren Friderichen Bischofes zu Würtzburg ... verantwortung vnd ableynung/ des vnwarhafften ... lasterbuchs/ welches ... Wilhelm von Grumbach/ Wilhelm vom Steyn/ vnd Ernst von Mandessloe ... im Truck aussgehen ... lassen. ... M.D. LXIIII. 4°. A-B⁴ A-3D⁴ 3E² (-3E2, *presumably blank*). ff. I-CCI. [155

-- -- *Another copy.* [156

-- -- M. D. LXV. 4°. A-3A⁴ 3B². ff. 1-182. [157

-- *University.* Positiones ex metaphy: et physica, quas in alma Herbipol: Vniueristate ... propugnabunt ... Ioannes Harlacherus Buchensis, Martinus Bechtoldus Holderbachensis, ... Georgius Dafrid Vberlingensis. Præside R. P. Ioanne Deun Buslidio ... Wirceburgi, Excudebat Georgius Fleischmannus, Anno 1592. 4°. A⁴ B². [158

WUJEK, JAKÓB. [1] [Postilla Catholica. ... Przez D. Iákubá Wuyká ... W Krákowie/ W Drukárni Siebeneycherowey: Roku Páńsk: 1584.] fol. †⁶ (*wanting*) ††⁸ (*wanting*) A-Nn⁶ (-A1, Hh2, Hh5) Oo-Pp⁴. pp. 1-448. [2] Postylle Kátholicżney ... *Same imprint.* *⁴ AA-3H⁶ 3I⁴ (-3I4, *presumably blank*). pp. 1-377. ¶*Vol. 3 wanting.* [159

WURM, MATHIS. Balaams eselin Von dem Bann/ das er vmb geldtschuld/ vñ andre geringe sachen nit mag Christlich gefelt werden. ... [Augsburg, Heinrich Steiner,] M. D. XXiij. 4°. a-k⁴. [160

-- Von dem pfründt marckt der Curtisanen vnd Tempelknechten. ([Basel, Adam Petri,] M. D. XXj. Mense Septembri.) 4°. aa⁴ bb⁶. [161

WURSTISEN, CHRISTIAN. [1] Germaniae historicorum illustrium, Quorum pleriq; ab Henrico IIII. Imperatore vsque ad annum Christi M. CCCC, ... Tomus vnus, Christiani Vrstitii Basiliensis ... studio in lucem nunc editus. Francofurdi Apud heredes Andreæ Wecheli, MDLXXXV. fol. (:)⁶ a-z⁶ A-I⁶ K-L⁴ M-Aa⁶ Bb⁴ Cc-Hh⁶ Ii⁴. pp. 3-626. [2] Germaniae historicorum qui post Henrici IIII imperatore ætatem trecentis annis scripserunt, Pars altera. ... *Same imprint.* A-Q⁶. pp. 3-182. ¶*Authors:* Otto von Freising, Otto de S. Blasis, Hermannus Contractus, Bertholdus presbyter Constantiensis, Radevicus canonicus Frisinensis, Conradus monachus S. Justinae Paduanae, Conradus Vecerius, Albertus Argentinensis. (Lea.) [162

WYLE, NICLAS VON. Translation. oder Deütschungen ... Nicolai von Weil ... M.D.XXXVI. (Gedruckt ... inn ... Augspurg/ durch Haynrich Stayner ... Am xviij. tag Februariij ...) fol. a⁶ A-Q⁶ R⁴ (-R4, *presumably blank*). ff. I-XCIX. [163

WYSS, URBAN. [Libellus ... multa et uaria scribendarum literarum genera complectens ... (Tiguri, p̲ Vrb. Wys, 1549.)] obl. 4°. A-P⁴ (-A1, A2, K4, L-P⁴). [164

X

XENOPHON. Ξενοφωντος ἅπαντα τὰ σωζόμηνα βιβλία. Xenophontis omnia quæ extant opera ... annotationes Henrici Stephani ... [Genevae] An. M. D. LXI Excudebat Henricus Stephanus ... fol. ¶^{8} a-nn^{8} oo^{6} A-D^{4} E^{6} *^{8} A-MM^{6} NN-OO^{4} PP^{6} (-PP6, *presumably blank*). pp. 1-587, 1-42, 1-428. [1

-- -- *Another copy.* [2

-- -- ... Ioanne Levvenklaio interprete: ... editio secunda. Basileæ, per Thomam Guarinum, M. D. LXXII. fol.)(^{6} a-z^{6} A-S^{6} T^{8} V-Ss^{6} Tt^{8} Vu-Yy^{6} Zz^{4}. pp. 2-790. ¶*Half-title* (V1^{r}): ... Tomus secundus ... [3

-- -- Le opere di Senofonte ... Tradotte dal Greco da Marc'Antonio Gandini ... In Venetia. Presso Pietro Dusinelli. MDLXXXVIII 4°. aa-cc^{8} A-L^{8} M^{4} N-3A^{8} 3B^{6} A-C^{8}. ff. 2-378. ¶*Engraved t.p.* [4

-- L'opere morali di Xenophonte tradotte per M. Lodoulco [*sic*] Domenichi. ... In Vinegia Appresso Gabriel Giolito de Ferrari. MDXLVII. (*Colophon.*) 8°. A-X^{8}. ff. 5-163. [5

-- La Cyropedie de Xenophon ... Traduite de Græc en langue Françoyse, par Iaques de Vintemille, Rhodien. ... A Paris, De l'imprimerie d'Estienne Groulleau: ... 1547. (imprimé ... par Estienne Groulleau pour luy, Ian Longis, & Vincent Sertenas ...) 4°. aa^{4} +^{4} a-z^{4} A-V^{4}. ff. 1-172. [6

-- -- A Paris. Pour Iean Ruelle ... (Acheué di'imprimer le 25. iour de Iuin, l'an 1572.) 8°. A^{8} A-Ff^{8}. pp. 1-456. [7

-- -- Xenophonte della vita di Cyro re de Persi tradotto in lingua Toscana da Iacopo di Messer Poggio Fiorentino ... (Impresso in Firenze per gli Heredi di Philippo di Giunta. Adi .XXII. Daprile. Nel M.D.XXI. ...) 8°. a-t^{8} u^{4}. ff. 2-156. [8

-- -- (Impresso in Tusculano per Alexandro de Paginini. Adi .9. Agosto. 1527.) *Same collation and foliation.* [9

-- -- ... Tradotto per Messer Lodouico Domenichi. ... In Vinegia appresso Gabriel Giolito de' Ferrari. M D LVIII. (... M D XLIX.) 8°. A-V^{8}. ff. 2-159. [10

-- Xenophontis Socratici liber, qui oeconomicus inscribitur. Bernardinus Donatus Veronensis vertit. M D XXXIX. (Venetiis apud Bernardinum Vitalem. ... Kal. Augusti.) 4°. A^{4} a-i^{4}. ff. 1-36. [11

-- -- ... Io. Antonio Guarnerio interprete. Venetijs, Ex officina Dominici Guerræi, & Io. Baptistæ, fratrum. M D LXXIIII. 4°. A-M^{4}. pp. 2-91. [12

-- -- La economica di Xenofonte, tradotta di lingua Greca in lingua Toscana, dal S. Alessandro Piccolomini ... In Vinegia al segno del pozzo. M D XL. (... per Comin de Tridino de Monferrato ...) 8°. A-I^{4}. ff. 2-36. [13

-- *Hellenica.* I fatti de Greci di Xenophonte tradotti per M. Lodouico Domenichi. ... In Vinegia appresso Gabriel Giolito de Ferrari MDXLVIII. (*Colophon.*) 8°. A-V^{8} X^{4}. ff. 2-153. [14

-- -- In Vinegia appresso Gabriel Giolito de' Ferrari. M D LVIII. (*Colophon.*) 8°. A-V^{8} X^{4}. ff. 2-163. [15

-- -- Le guerre de Greci, scritte da Senophonte ... M D L ... tradotte, dall'idioma Greca, nell' Italiano, per Francesco di Soldo Strozzi. ... (In Venetia. ...) 4°. *^{8} a-z^{4} A-Cc^{4} Dd^{6} Ee^{4}. ff. 1-202. [16

-- Les memoires de Xenofon Athenien en quatre liures, Traduits de Grec en François. A la fin duquels est ajouté le discours de la ... mort de Cyre l'ayné; Extrait ... de sa Cyropedie. Par Ian Doublet de Dieppe. A Paris, De l'imprimerie de Denys du Val ... 1582. ... (... le 8. Septembre. ...) 8°. ã^{8} A-O^{8} P^{4}. ff. 1-109. [17

-- *Selections.* Xenophontis Atheniensis de forma reipublicæ Lacedæmoniorum, eiusdem de forma reipublicæ Atheniensium, eiusdem de praefectura & disciplina equestri liber. Quae omnia ... in latinum sermonem à Ioachimo Camerario Pab. conuersa fuerunt ... Lipsiae ... (In officina recente Valentini Papae. Anno M. D. XLIII. XVI. Calendas Decembris.) 8°. A-I^{8}. pp. 2-126. [18

Y

YŪHANNĀ IBN MĀSAWAIH. Ioannis Mesuae Damasceni, de re medica libri tres. Iacobo Syluio medico interprete. ... Parisiis, Apud AEgidium Gorbinum ... 1561. 8°. $*^8$ a-z^8 A-B^8. ff. 1-200. [1

-- Mesue vulgar. Summario ouer collectorio ... extracto da tutti li uolumi delli antiquissimi medici ... Composto ... per ... Gioanni Mesue ... per lindustria de cesaro Arriuabeno Venitiano ... reuisto ... (Impresso in Venetia per Cesaro arriuabeno uenitiano a di uinti octubrio, mille conquecento e uintiuno.) fol. a^4 (-a2-3) A-N^8 O^{10}. ff. 1-CXIII. (School of Dentistry.) [2

Z

ZABARELLA, FRANCESCO. ... Frãcisci zabarelle Cardinalis Cõmẽtarii in clemẽtinarum volumen. Cum ... additiõibus ... Philippi Franchi de Perusia: ꝛ ... Nicolai Superantii ... (Venetijs ex Edibus Ioannis ꝛ Gregorij de gregorijs fratres. ... M.D.iiij. Die .xxvj. mensis Iunij.) fol. B.L. a-z^8 ꝛ^8 ꝯ^8. ff. 2-200. (Biddle.) [1

-- Consilia ... Lugduni, Apud hæredes Iacobi Iuntæ, M. D. LII. (Excudebat ... Thomas Bertellus ...) fol. B.L. a-y^6 z^4 A^6 B^4. ff. 2-136. (Biddle.) [2

ZABARELLA, GIACOMO. ... Bernardo Naugerio ... Iacobus Zabarella Patauinus foelicitatem. ... Pataui (... Iacobus Fabrianus Excudebat M D LIII.) fol. A^6. ¶*240 propositions for disputation.* [3

ZAMBERTI, BARTOLOMMEO. Bartholamei Zamberti Veneti Comedia Dolotechne. (Impressum Venetiis per Ioannem de Tridino. librarium XII. Kl. Septembres a reconciliata diuinitate. VIII. Elemento. IV. Sumpto. XI. que ac .IV. addito. ... [1504.]) 4°. A^6 B-I^4. [4

ZAMORA, FRANCISCO À. Illustriss. Tridentini concilii cardinalibus legatis ... oratio habita ... Dominica secunda Quadragesimæ. Anno M D LXII. Pataui Apud Laurentium Pasquatum & Socios. 4°. A^4. (Lea.) [5

ZAMOYSKI, JAN SARIUS. Ioannis Sarii Zamoscii de senatu Romano libri duo. ... Venetiis, apud Iordanum Ziletum. M. D. LXIII. (*Colophon.*) 4°. *^{4} A-S^4 T^2. ff. 2-68. [6

-- Ioan. Sarij Zamoscij ... in Galliã Legati, Oratio: Qua Henric. Valesium Regem renunciat. Lutetiæ Parisiorum, Ex Officina Federici Morelli ... M.D.LXXIII. ... 4°. A-E^4. ff. 2-18.
[7

ZAMPINI, MATTEO. De gli stati de Francia, et della lor possanza. ... Impresso in Parigi, appresso Dionisio Duuallo ... 1578. 8°. π^2 A-O^8 P^4 Q^2. pp. 1-234. [8

-- -- De statibus Franciæ, illorum potestate, epitome. ... Parisiis, Apud Dionysium du Val ... 1578. 8°. A-B^8 C^2. pp. 7-35. [9

ZANCHA, GIOVANNI TOMASSO. Solutiones contradictionum in dictis Aristo. in prologo primi Phisicorum dilucidatæ ... 4°. [A]^4 B^6. [10

ZANCHI, BASILIO. Basilii Zanchii hymnus in Christum. Romæ Alexidis Bidelli opera M. D. LVI. Mens. Mart. 8°. A^4. [11

-- Basilii Zanchii poematum editio copiosior. Romae M. D. L. (Apud Valerium, & Loisium Fratres Doricos. ... Mense Ianuario.) 8°. A-L^8 M^4. ff. 2-92. [12

ZANCHI, GIOVANNI CRISOSTOMO. Ad sacratiss. ... principem, Carolum .V. Rom. Imp. ... Panegyricus. [Romae, Antonius Bladus, 1536.] 4°. A-E^4. [13

ZANE, GIACOMO. Rime ... In Venetia, M D LXII. Appresso Domenico, & Gio. Battista Guerra, fratelli. 8°. A^4 B-N^8. pp. 1-183. ¶*Some preliminary leaves may be missing.* [14

ZAPATA, LUIS. Carlo famoso De don Luys C,apata ... Impresso en ... Valencia, en casa de Iuan Mey ... M. D. LXVI. (*Colophon.*) 4°. A^4 (-A1-3) B-Oo^8 (-C8, Cc6, Oo7-8) Pp^2 (-Pp1-2, *the latter presumably blank*). ff. 2-209. [15

ZARA, OTTAVIANO. Hippolito tragedia nuoua ... In Padoa, per Gratioso Perchacino ad instantia d'Innocente Olmo. 1558. 8°. A-G^4. ff. 2-28. [16

ZARLINO, GIUSEPPE. [1] De tutte l'opere del R. M. Gioseffo Zarlino da Chioggia ... Il primo volume. ... In Venetia, MDLXXXIX. Appresso Francesco de Franceschi Senese. fol. a^6 b^{10} A-Ee^8. pp. 2-448. [2] ... il secondo volume. ... *Same imprint.* a^8 A-S^8. pp. 2-287. [3] Sopplimenti musicali ... Terzo Volume. ... In Venetia, appresso Francesco de' Franceschi, Sanese. M D LXXXVIII. a^8 A-R^6 S^4 (S4 + *folded leaf*) T-Dd^6 Ee^4 Ff-Gg^6. pp. 2-

330. [4] De tutte l'opere ... Il Quarto, & Vltimo Volume. ... *Same imprint as* [1]. A^{10} B-H^{8} I^{2}. pp. 2-132. ¶I^{2} *defective.* [17

-- Dimostrationi harmoniche ... In Venetia, Per Francesco de i Franceschi Senese. 1571. fol. $[*]^{4}$ A-F^{6} G^{4} H-Cc^{6} Dd^{8}. pp. 1-312. [18

-- Istitutioni harmoniche ... In Venetia, Appresso Francesco de i Franceschi Senese. M. D. LXXIII. fol. $*^{6}$ A-Mm^{6} Nn^{4} a^{6} b^{4}. pp. 1-428. [19

ZASIUS, UDALRICHUS. Vdalrici Zasii ... apologetica defensio contra Ioannē Eckium ... Defensa magni Erasmi assertio, quàm in ... Scholijs sup̲ septimo Matthei capite docuit. ... (Basilleae apud Ioannem Frobenium mense Martio. Anno M. D. XIX.) 4°. a-i^{4}. pp. 2-71. [20

-- Vdalrici Zasii ... in tit. Instit. de actionibus, enarratio. ... Huic accessit Oratio ... Christophori ab Hochemberg, in funere Zasij dicta. Epitaphium Zasij, per Erasmũ Roterodamum. Lugduni, sub scuto Coloniensi. Anno M. D. XLIIII. (... excudebat Ioannes et Franciscus Frellonii, fratres. ...) 8°. α^{8} β^{4} a-z^{8} A-C^{8}. pp. 1-396. [21

-- Vdalrici Zasii ... in vsus Feudorum epitome ... Eiusdem orationes aliquot ... Lugduni apud Gulielmum de Guelques. 1536. (Excudebant ... Melchior et Gaspar Trechsel fratres. ...) 8°. α-γ^{8} a-u^{8}. pp. 1-314. (Biddle.) [22

-- Vdalrichi Zasii ... oratio, Friburgi in funere D. Maximiliani Imp. Aug. habita. Apud ... Basileam. (... apud Ioannem Frobenium mense Maio, anno M. D. XIX.) 4°. a-b^{4}. pp. 2-14. [23

ZAVA, FRANCESCO. [1] Francisci Zauae Cremonen. orationes IV. epistolarum lib. VIII. carminum lib. III. Cremonae Apud Vincentium Comitem. MDLXVIIII. ... 4°. $*^{4}$ *A-C*^{4} *D*^{2}. ff. 2-14. ¶*Additional t.p.:* (*A*1^{r}) ... Oratio prima ... Cremonae Apud Vincentium Comitem. M D LXVIII. [2] ... Oratio secunda ... M D LXVIII. A-X^{4} YY^{4} Z-$4E^{4}$. ff. 2-295. ¶*Additional t.pp.:* (L1^{r}) Oratio tertia ... M D LXVIII. (FF1^{r}) Epistolarum familiarum ... liber primus. ... M D LXVIII. (3R1^{r}) ... Carminum libri tres ... M D LXVIII. [24

ZEITUNG. Ausszug etlicher Zeitungen/ von der Tuͤrcken Kriegshandlung vor Zigeth ... 1566. Gedruckt zu Nuͤrmberg/ durch Valentin Geyssler. 4°. A^{4}. [25

-- Ausszug Ettlicher Zeitungen/ was sich zuͦm anfang des jetzigen Tuͤrckenkriegs ... in Vngern/ verloffen vnnd zuͦgetragen hat. Im Jar/ M.D.LXVI. Getruckt zuͦ Strassburg bey Peter Hug ... (*Colophon.*) 4°. A^{4}. [26

-- Ausszug/ Newer Zeitungen/ auss der Roͤmischen Kayserlichen Maystat Feldleger in Hungern ... von dem XXX. Augusti: 1566. Getruckt zu Augspurg/ durch Hans Zimmerman. 4°. A^{4}. [27

-- Ausszug/ Newer Zeitungen/ auss der Roͤmischen Kayserlichen Maystat Feldleger in Hungern ... von dem 8. vnd 11. tag September/ Anno 1566. Getruckt zuͦ Augspurg/ durch Hans Zimmerman. 4°. A^{4}. [28

-- Bawrenbeicht. Warhaffte Newe Zeitung von einem Bawrn/ wie er in seiner Kranckheit seinem Pfarrherr gebeichtet hat. 8°. A^{8} (-A8, *presumably blank*). [29

-- Ernstliche newe zeytung/ so sich zwischē Keyserlich vnd Koͤniglichen Mayestaten/ dem Bapst/ Herrschafft zu Venedig an einem/ vnd ander teils dem Türcken zugetragen. Auch wie der Türckisch Keyser Corfun belegert hat. 1537. 4°. $[A]^{4}$. [30

-- Gewise neue zeittung von der statt Münster von den jenigen so bey der Sachen gewesen sind. Was sich auch in kücze zwischen der Ro. Ka. Ma. Vnd des Koͤnigs von Franckreich bottschaft begeben vnnd zugetragen hat. M.L.XXXV [*sic*]. (Gedruckt zu Regenspurg [durch Paul Kohl].) 4°. π^{4}. [31

-- New zeytung. Die Schlacht des Turckischen Keysers mit Ludouico etwan Koͤnig zu Vngern geschehen am tag Iohannis entheuptung .1526. ... Item etzlich naw getzeyten aus Polen. New zeytung vom Babst zu Rome am .xxvij. tag Septembris geschehen .1526. 4°. A-B^{4}. [32

-- Newe zeitung Vnnd Bericht/ Welcher gestalt die Roͤmische Keiserliche Maiestat/ mit ... Ertzhertzog Ferdinanden zu Osterreich ... den 12. Augusti aus Wien/ wider den Tuͤrckischen Feindt/ angezogen/ vnd was sich biss auff den 21. Augusti zugetragen. M. D. LXVI. 4°. A^{4}. [33

-- Newe Zeittung vñ Spiegel aller Gaistlicheit/ wie sie ytzt ist/ vnd sein soll ... Gestellt zuͦ singen auf die Melodey/ Von vppiklichen dingen ꝛc. ... M. D. XXXVIII. 4°. A^{4}. [34

-- Newe zeittung/ vom XXj. Augusti/ auss Wien/ Anno 1566. Getruckt zu Augspurg/ durch Hans Zimmerman. 4°. A^4. [35

-- Newe Zeyttung von dem Tyrannen des Türckischen Keysers Haubtman/ mit sambt einem Muͤnch Pauliner Ordens/ was sie zů Ofen vnd Pescht gehandelt haben. [c. 1541.] 4°. π^4. [36

-- Newe zeitung vō den Wider tauffern zu Münsster. Auff die Newe zeitung von Münster D. Matini [*sic*] Luther Vorhede. Propositiones wider die Leher der Wider tauffer gestelt durch Philip. Melanch. Wider das ... Buch/ so zu Münster im truck neulich ist aussgangen/ etlich artikel gestelt/ durch Philp. [*sic*] Melanch. zu Wittenberg. 1535. (Getruckt zu Nurnberg durch Ieronimum Formschneider 1535.) 4°. A-D^4. [37

-- Newe zeyttung von Kaiserlicher Maiestat Kriegsrüstung/ wider den Barbarossa/ gegen der Statt Thunis in Affrica zů schicken/ Auss Neapolis vnd andern orten geschriben. M.D.XXXV. 4°. A^4. [38

-- Newe zeittungen/ Von dem 5. tag Augusti/ diss 66. Jars/ auss Wien/ Vonn der Veste vn̄ Stat/ Schloss/ Iula in Vngern ... Getruckt zů Augspurg/ Durch Hans Zimmerman. 4°. A^4 (-A4, *presumably blank*). [39

-- -- Newe Zeytung/ von dem 5. Augusti ... Getruckt zů Augspurg/ durch Hans Zimmerman. 4°. A^4. [40

-- Newer zeitungen/ auss der Roͤmischen Kayserlichen Maystat Feldlaͤger in Hungern ... von dem 4. tag September/ Anno 1566. Getruckt zů Augspurg/ durch Hans Zimmerman. 4°. A^4. [41

-- Warhaffte Zeitungen auss der Roͤm. Kay. May. Feldleger zwischen Raab vnd Camora/ vom ersten Septemb. Anno ꝛc. 66. ... Getruckt zů Augspurg/ durch Mattheum Francken. 4°. A-B^4. [42

-- Warhafftige Zeittung/ von Eroͤberung Placentz vnd Parma/ Vnd wie Petrus Farnesius/ des jetzigen Bapsts Sohn/ dis vergangen 1547. Jhar vmbkommen ist. Item: Wie der Hertzog von Mantua Gonzaga/ ... gestrafft hat eine Misshandlung eines Amptmans zu Como ... M.D.XLVIII. 4°. A-B^4 (-B4, *presumably blank*). [43

-- Zeittung/ von einem Erschroͤcklichen grossen wunder Man vnd Weib. Vnglaubliche/ vnnd doch Warhaffte erscheinung/ eines gar grossen Risen vnnd Helden/ welcher ... in Wilde Reussen ersehen/ vnd gefangen worden ... Hierin auch wird gedacht/ eines vberauss erschroͤcklichen grosser Weibsbildes ... M. D. LXXXIX. 4°. A^4. [44

-- Zeittung/ Wie vorbewüst/ so ist der Tuͤrckische Oberst/ von der Statt Iula abgezogen ... 1566. Getruckt zu Augspurg/ durch Hans Zimmerman. 4°. A^4. [45

-- Zeittungen/ Von dem Grossen Christen Sieg/ auff dem Ionischen oder Ausonischen Meer/ wider den Tuͤrcken/ so bey dem Porto Le Pante ... erhalten worden ist/ Den 7. Octobr̄is/ Im 1571. ... Gedruckt zu Nuͤrnberg/ durch Wendelinum Borsch ... 4°. A-B^4. [46

ZELL, KATHARINA. Den leydenden Christglaubigen weybern der gemain zů Rentzingen ... Katharina Schützin M.D.xxiiij. 4°. A^4 B^2. [47

ZENO, GIOVANNI JACOPO. La vita del magnifico. M. Carlo Zeno, ... Capitano della ... Republica Venetiana. Composta del Reuerendo Gianiacomo Feltrense, & tradotta in uulgare, Per Messer Francesco Quirino. ... In Venetia. M. D. XLIIII. (Sampato [*sic*] ... per Francesco Brucioli, & i frategli. ...) 8°. π^4 A-Q^8. ff. 1-128. [48

ZENOBIUS. Ζηνοβιου επιτομη ... Zenobij Compendium ueterū prouerbiorum ex Tarræo et Didymo collectum ... Haganoæ anno. XXXV. (Ετυπωθη ... ὑπὸ Πέτρου Βρουβαχχίου ...) 8°. AA-II^8 KK^4. pp. 4-149. ¶*The Greek text. Editor: Vincentius Obsopoeus.* [49

ZENOPHONTE DA UGUBIO, ANDREA. Formulario nuouo da dittar Lettere amorose messiue & responsiue. ... Opera nuoua intitolata flos amoris. M D XLIIII. (In Vinegia per Francesco Bindoni & Mapheo Pasini compagni. 1549.) 8°. A-C^8. [50

ZEROLA, TOMMASO. Praxis sacramenti poenitentiæ. ... Venetiis, Apud Georgium Variscum. M D XCIX. 8°. A-T^8. ff. 7-130. (Lea.) [51

-- Sancti iubilæi, Ac Indulgentiarum: necnon commentarii Super Bullam Indictionis eiusdem Sancti Anni, tractatus ... Venetiis, Apud Georgium Variscum. M DC. (*Colophon.*) 8°. a-$ç^8$ A-X^8 Y^4. pp. 1-336. (Lea.) [52

ZETTEL, WOLFGANG. Panegyricus dictus Ingolstadii ... Ferdinando Primo Cæsari ... Monaci excudebat Adam Berg. M.D.LXV. ... 4°. A-N⁴. [53

ZIEGLER, CLEMENS. Ain fast schon büchli: In welchem yederman findet ein hellen vnd claren verstandt/ von dē leib vnd blůt Christi. ... 1525. ... 4°. A-G⁴. [54

-- Ain Kurtz Register/ vnd ausszug der Bibel in wölchem man findet was Abgöterey sey ... 1524. 4°. A⁴. [55

ZIEGLER, JAKOB. In hoc volumine haec continentur, Duplex Cōfessio Valdensiū ad Regem Vngarie missa, Augustini de Olomucz ... Epistole cōtra ꝑfidiam Valdensium, Eiusdem Doctoris bine Littera ad Regiam Maiestatē de Heresi Valdensium, Excusacio Valdensium cōtra binas litteras Doctoris Augustini, Iacobi Zigleri ex Landau Bauarie contra Heresim Valdensium Libri quinq3 ... (Henricus Kuna de Chunstat sua pecunia impressioriā officinā redemit. Melchiorq3 Loterus ciuis Lypensis excussit. Anno. M.D.XII, Mense Octobri Die ipsius vltimo,) fol. π¹ (*errata*) A-Dd⁶ Ee⁸. (Lea.) [56

ZIGERIUS, EMERICUS. Ein schrifft/ eines fromen Predigers aus der Türckey an Illyricum geschrieben/ Darinnen angezeiget wird/ wie es dort mit der Kirche vnd dem Euangelio zugehet. ... 1550. (Gedruckt zu Magdeburg durch Michael Lotther ...) 4°. A-B⁴. [57

ZIMARA, MARCO ANTONIO. ... Marci Antonij Zimare ... Questio de primo cognito. Eiusdēq3 Solutiones cōtradictionum in dictis Auerrois. ... Venundantur Lugduni apud Scipionem de Gabiano ... (Impressum ... cura ... Iacobi Myt. ... Anno ... Millesimo q̄ngētesimo trigesimo .xviij. Ianuarij.) 8°. B.L. Aa-Ii⁸ Kk⁴. ff. ij-lxxv. [58

-- -- Lugd. apud Iacobum Giunctam. M. D. XLII. (... apud Theobaldum Paganum. ...) 8°. Aa-Ll⁸. ff. 2-88. [59

-- Marci Antonii Zimarae ... tabula dilucidationum in dictis Aristotelis et Auerrois. ... MDXXXVII. (Venetijs apud Octauianum Scotum.) fol. A-Z⁶ aa-ff⁶. ff. 2-174. [60

-- M. Antonii Zimarae Sanctipetrinatis ... Theoremata, seu Memorabilium Propositionum limitationes ... Venetiis, M D LXIIII. (... Ioan. Gryphius excudebat ...) fol. *⁶ A-O⁶ P⁸. ff. 2-92. [61

ZINANO, GABRIELE. L'Almerigo tragedia ... In Reggio, Appresso Hercoliano Bartholi. ... 8°. A-N⁸ P⁶. pp. 2-191, 2-29. ¶*Additional t.p.* (N6ʳ): Discorso della tragedia. Di Gabriele Zinano. ... In Reggio, Appresso Hercoliano Bartholi. ... 1590. [62

-- L'amante, ouero solleuatioone [*sic*] dalla bellezza dell'amata alla bellezza di Dio. ... In Reggio, Appresso Hercoliano Bartholi [1591]. ... 8°. A-C⁸ D². pp. 2-44. [63

-- L'amata, ouero della virtù heroica. ... In Reggio, Appresso Hercoliano Bartholi [1591]. ... 8°. A-B⁸ (-B8, *presumably blank*). pp. 2-23. [64

-- L'amico, ouer del Sospiro. ... In Reggio, Appresso Hercoliano Bartholi [1591]. ... 8°. A⁸ B⁶. pp. 1-24. [65

-- Le due giornate della ninfa, ouer del diletto, et delle muse. ... In Reggio Appresso Hercoliano Bartholi 1590. ... 8°. A-C⁸ D¹⁰. pp. 3-68. [66

-- Il sogno, ouero della poesia. ... In Reggio, Appresso Hercoliano Bartholi [1590]. ... 8°. A-B⁸ C⁶ (-C6, *presumably blank*). pp. 3-42. [67

-- Il soldato, ouer della Fortezza. ... In Reggio, Appresso Hercoliano Bartholi [1591]. ... 8°. A⁸ B⁶. pp. 1-20. [68

-- Sommarii di varie retoriche Greche, Latine, et volgari ... In Reggio, Appresso Hercoliano Bartholi 1590. ... (*Colophon.*) 8°. A-Q⁸. pp. 1-238. [69

-- Il viandante, ouero della precedenza dell'armi, et delle lettere. ... [Reggio, Hercoliano Bartholi, 1590.] 8°. A-B⁸ C⁶. pp. 3-44. [70

ZOBEL VON GUTTENBERG, MELCHIOR. De caede Melchioris Zobelli Herbipolensis episcopi ... liber. ... 1559. 4°. A-C⁴. [71

ZONARAS, JOANNES. Historia rerum in Oriente gestarum ab exordio mundi ... ad nostra haec vsque tempora. ... Francof. ad Moenum impens. Sigis. Feyrabendij. M. D. LXXXVII.

(Impressum ... apud Petrum Fabricium ...) fol.)(^{4} A-3L^6. ff. 1-297. ¶*Additional authors: Nicetas Choniata, Nicephorus Gregoras, Laonicus Chalcondylas, Johannes Carion, Pietro Bizzari, Henricus Porsius, Lodovice Guicciardini.* [72

-- -- Les histoires et Chroniques du Monde, tirees tant du gros volume de Ian Zonoras ... que de plusieurs autres bons & anciens scripteurs Hebrieus & Grecs, & mises ... en langage François ... par Ian de Maumont ... A Paris, De l'imprimerie de Michel de Vascosan. M. D. LXI. ... (Acheue d'imprimer le XXIX. Decemb. ...) fol. *^{6} **^{4} A-ZZ^6 Aa-Rr^6 Ss^4 α-δ^6 ι^8. pp. 1-756. [73

ZOPPIO, GIROLAMO. Particelle poetiche sopra Dante disputate da Hieronimo Zoppio Bolognese. In Bologna, Per Alessandro Benacci. MDLXXXVII. ... 4°. A-G^4. pp. 3-55. [74

-- Rime et prose ... In Bologna, Appresso Alessandro Benacci. M D LXVII. ... 8°. *^{4} A-K^8 L^4. ff. 1-83. [75

-- Ragionamenti ... in difesa di Dante, et del Petrarca. In Bologna, per Gio. Rossi. MDLXXXIII. ... 4°. A-L^4 M^6 (-M6, *presumably blank*). pp. 3-97. [76

-- Risposta ... Alle Oppositioni Sanesi fatte a' suoi Ragionamenti in Difesa di Dante. A Fermo, Presso Sertorio de'Monti. M.D.LXXXV. 4°. A-C^4 D^6. [77

ZOPPO, MELCHIORE. Il Diogene accusato, Comedia del Caliginoso academico Gelato. ... In Venetia, MDXCVIII. Ad instantia di Gasparo Bindoni. ... 12°. A-L^{12}. ff. 15-132. [78

ZUALLARDO, GIOVANNI. Il deuotissimo viaggio di Gierusalemme. ... Aggiontoui i disegni in Rame di varij Luoghi ... In Roma, Appresso Domenico Basa. M.D.XCV. (... M.D.LXCV.) 8°. A-Z^8 (N7 + *folded leaf*; -Z8, *blank*). pp. 17-351. [79

ZUCCHI, BARTOLOMMEO. [1] L'idea del segretario ... Rappresentata & in vn Trattato de l'imitatione, e ne le lettere di Principi, e d'altri Signori. Parte prima. ... In Venetia, Presso la Compagnia Minima. ... M D C. 4°. a-d^8 e^{10} A-Nn^8 Oo^4. pp. 2-582. [2] ... Parte Seconda. ... *Same imprint.* a^8 A-Z^8 Aa^4. pp. 2-375. ¶*In this set vol. 3 is a 1614 printing.* [80

ZUCCOLO, GREGORIO. I discorsi ... Ne i quali si tratta della nobiltà, honore, amore, fortificationi, et antigaglie. ... In Venetia Apresso Gio. Bariletto. 1575. (*Colophon.*) 8°. A-V^8. pp. 1-286. [81

ZWINGER, THEODOR. Aristotelis ... de moribus ad Nicomachum Libri Decem: Tabulis perpetuis ... illustrati, à Theodoro Zuinggero Basiliense ... Basileae, per Ioan. Oporinum & Eusebium Episcopium. fol. α^6 β-γ^4 δ^6 a-z^6 A-F^6 (-F6, *blank*). pp. 4-40, 2-338. ¶*Dedication dated* XIIII. Calend. Sept. M. D. LXVI. [82

-- Methodus apodemica in eorum gratiam, qui cum fructu ... peregrinari cupiunt ... Basileæ Eusebii Episcopii Opera atque impensa M D LXXVII. (*Colophon.*) 4°. α-γ^4 a-z^4 A-Gg^4. pp. 2-400. [83

-- Theatrum humanae vitae Theodori Zwingeri Bas. Tertiatione ... Basileae per Eusebium Episcopium CIƆ IƆ XXCVI. (... CIƆ IƆ XXCVII.) fol. *-**^{6} 3*^{8} a-z^6 A-Aa^6 Bb^8 Cc-Zz^6 AA-TT^6 VV^{10} XX-ZZ^6 aa-dd^6 ee^8 ff-3s^6 3t^8 3u-3z^6 3A-3Z^6 aAa-tTt^6 uVu^8 xXx-zZz^6 AaA-HhH^6 IiI^8 KkK-YyY^6 ZzZ^8 4a-4y^6 4z^{10} 4A-4D^6 4E^8 4F-4K^6 4L^8 4M-4Z^6 aAAa-mMMm^6 nNNn^8 oOOo-zZZz^6 AaaA-GggG^6 HhhH^8 IiiI-TttT^6 VuuV^{10} XxxX-ZzzZ^6 5a-5s^6 5t^8 5u-5z^6 5A-5D^6 5E^{10} 5F-5H^6 5I^4 5K-5Z^6 aaAaa^6 bbBbb^8 ccCcc-llLll^6 mmMmm^4 nnNnn^6 ooOoo^4 χ^1 ppPpp-ssSss^6 ttTtt-yyYyy^8 zzZzz^{10} AAaAA-BBbBB^6 CCcCC^8 DDdDD-XXxXX^6 YYyYY^8. pp. 4-4373. ¶*Divided into 29 volumes: this set bound in 5 volumes.* [84

ZWINGLI, HULDRICH. Die ander Geschrifft Zuinglins An Doctor Iohansen Faber ... [Zürich, Christopher Froschauer, 1526.] 8°. A^8. [85

D'AILLY, PIERRE. De reformatione ecclesiae Petri de Aliaco ... Item, de squaloribus Curiæ Romanæ. ... Basileæ, apud Nicolaum Bryling. Anno M. D. LI. 8°. A-G^8 H^4. pp. 1-106. (Yarnall.) [A96a

ALBERICO DE ROSATE. Dictionarium do. Alberici de rosate I.V. monarce ... (cum additionibus Ioannis Baptiste de Castelliono. ꝛ cum recognitione ... Bartholomei ab horario patauini. Venetijs a Philippo Pincio Mantuano impressum. ... Mcccccxv. Die primo Augusti.) fol. B.L. ₵^{8} (*wanting*) A-G^8 H^6 I-XX^8. (Yarnall.) [A121a

ALEXANDER OF HALES. [1] Doctoris irrefragabilis Domini Alexandri de ales ... Pars secũda summe theologice. ... (Antonij koburger impensis ... M.cccccxvj. xvij. kal'. maij.) fol. B.L. aa-zz^8 ꝛꝛ^8 ɔɔ^8 ꝝꝝ^8 AA-VV^8 XX-ZZ^{10}. ff. II-CCCXCVII. [2] ... Pars tertia ... (... die ij. Iulij.) 3a-3z^8 3A-3M^8 3N^6 3a^8. ff. II-CCLXXXVI. [3] ... Pars quarta ... (... xxiij. Iunii ...) 4a-4z^8 4ꝛ^8 4ɔ^8 4ꝝ^8 4A^8 4B^{10} 4C-4Z^8 AAaa-EEee^8 FFff^6 4a^{10}. ff. II-CCCCXXXVII. (Yarnall.) [A175a

ANDROUET DU CERCEAU, JACQUES. Liure d'architecture ... A Paris, Pour Iaques Androuet, du Cerceau: M. D. LXXXII. fol. A^4 B-D^6 E^4 + 38 *plates*. (Fine Arts.) [A274a

ARISTOTLE. *Ethica Nicomachea*. Aristotelis ... ethicorum siue moralium Nicomachiorum libri decem, vnà cum Eustratii, Aspasii, Michaelis Ephesii, nonnullorumq́ue aliorum Græcorum Explanationibus: nuper a Ioanne Bernardo Feliciano Latinitate donati. ... Feliciani Præfatio ... Basileae [per Ioannem Oporinum, 1542]. fol. α^6 β^8 a-z^6 A-Q^6. pp. 2-450. [A580a

BRUNFELS, OTTO. [1] Herbarum viuae eicones ... M. D. XXXII. ... Argentorati apud Ioannem Schottũ ... (*Colophon.*) fol. A^4 a^6 b^4 c-z^6 A-F^4 G^6. pp. 1-266. [2] Noui herbarii tomus .II. ... M. D. XXXI. ... *Same imprint*. (... XIIII. Febr. ...) A^8 B-G^6 H^4 A-C^6 D^4 E-Q^6 R^4 S^6 (-S6, *blank*). pp. 11 [=5]-90, 7-199. [B721a

CASTELLO BRANCO, JOÃO RODRIGUES DE. In Dioscoridis Anazarbei de medica materia libros quinque, Amati Lusitani ... enarrationes ... Accesserunt ... Adnotationes R. Constantini, Necnon simplicium picturæ ex [Leonhardo Fuchsio,] Iacobo Dalechampio, atque alijs. Lugsuni, Apud Viduam Balthazaris Arnoleti. 1558. (*Colophon.*) 8°. aa-ee^8 a-zz^8 A-D^8 E^4 F^8. pp. 1-807. ¶*T.p. defaced.* [C230a

COPETI, AGOSTINO. Rime spirituali del ... Fr. Agostino Copeti d'Euoli ... A Fermo, Appresso Sertorio de' Monti. M.D.LXXXVI. 4°. [A]^4 B-F^4. pp. 5-48. [C670a

CORDUS, VALERIUS. In hoc volumine continentur Valerii Cordi Simesusij Annotationes in Pedacij Dioscoridis Anazarbei de Medica materia libros V ... Eiusdem ... historiae stirpium lib. IIII. ... Sylua ... De artificiosis extractionibus Liber. Compositiones medicinales aliquot ... His accedunt Stocc-hornii et Nessi in Bernatium Heluetiorum ditione montium, & nascentium in eis Stirpium, descriptio Benedicti Aretij ... Item Conradi Gesneri de hortis Germaniae liber ... Omnia ... studio ... Conr. Gesneri ... collecta ... M. D. LXI. ([Argentorati excudebat Iosias Rihelius.]) fol. a-b^4 A-O^6 P-Z^4 a-z^4 Aa-Zz^4 AA^6 (-AA6). ff. 1-301. ¶AA3-5 *defective*. [C679a

DAMASUS, GULIELMUS. Damasi ... Burchardica, siue Regulæ Canonice ... A Petro s'Aluno Aquilio recognitæ ... Antuerpiae, Ex officina Christophori Plantini, cIɔ. Iɔ. LXVI. ... 8°. A-E^8 F^4. pp. 3-88. [D1a

DONATUS, AELIUS. [Ars minor. Coloniae? post 1500.] 8°. B.L. ¶*2 uncut ll., part or all of 16 pp. (17 ll. to the page), containing portions of the chapters* De coniunctione, De praepositione, De participio, Declinatio participalis *from an unidentified edition*. [D231a

DUARENUS, FRANCISCUS. De sacris ecclesiæ ministeriis ac beneficiis libri VIII. ... Item, pro libertate ecclesiæ Gallicæ aduersus Romanam aulam Defensio Parisiensis curiæ ... Parisiis, Apud Andream Wechelum ... 1557. ... 8°. ã^8 ẽ^4 A-Y^8 Z^4. ff. 2-180. [D299a

ECK, JOHANN. Replica Io. Eckii aduersus scripta secunda Buceri apostatæ super actis Ratisponæ. ... M. D. XXXXIII. (Ingoldstadij excudebat Alexander Weissenhorn.) 4°. a^4 A-O^4. ff. 1-56. [E37a

ENGLAND, CHURCH OF. Certaine Sermons appointed by the Queenes Maiestie, to be declared and read, by all Parsons, Vicars, and Curates, euery Sunday and Holy day in their Churches ... [London, James Roberts,] 1587. ... 4°. B.L. A-M^{8}. *S.T.C.* 13657. (Furness.) [E276a

-- The seconde Tome of Homilies ... [London, James Roberts,] 1587. ... 4°. B.L. A-Pp^{8} (-Pp8, *blank*). *S.T.C.* 13673. (Furness.) [E276b

FUCHS, LEONHARD. Leonharti Fuchsii medici, primi de stirpium historia cōmentariorum tomi viuæ imagines, in exiguam ... formam contractæ ... Basileae, [Michael Isengrin,] 1549. 8°. A^{8} a-ii^{8} kk^{2}. pp. 1-516. [F513a

GUALTEROTTI, RAFFAELLO. Canzone del Signor Caualier Gualtieri, Aretino. In Fiorenza Appresso Bartolomeo Sermartelli. MDLXXII. 4°. A^{6}. ¶*On the victory over the Turks.* [G358a

HESHUSIUS, TILEMANNUS. Warhafftiger Gegenbericht auff Matthiæ Flacij Illyrici kurtz Bekentnis/ Von Der wesentlichen Erbsünde. ... Gedruckt zu Iena/ durch Gůntherum Hůttich/ Anno M. D. LXXI. 4°. A-D^{4}. [H119a

HITTORP, MELCHIOR. De diuinis catholicae ecclesiae officiis ac ministeriis, varii ... Libri, videlicet B. Isidori Hispaleñ Episcopi, Albini Flacci Alcuini, Amalarii Trevirens. Episcopi, Hrabani Mauri ..., VValafridi Strabonis ..., Bernonis Augiensis Abbatis, B. Iuonis Episcopi Carnotensis, & quorundā aliorum ... editi ... per Melchiorem Hittorpium. ... Coloniae Apud Geruuinum Calenium, & hæredes Iohannis Quentel, ... M. D. LXVIII. ... fol. *a^{4} *b^{6} a-v^{4} A-4L^{4}. pp. 1-160, 1-598. (Yarnall.) [H152a

LANCELOTTO, GIOVANNI PAOLO. Institutionum iuris canonici libri IIII. ... Nunc ... annotatiunculis opera Hieronymi Eleni Balensis illustrati. Antuerpiae, Ex officina Christophori Plantini, cIↄ Iↄ LXVI. ... 8°. A-S^{8}. pp. 3-281. [L23a

NIFO, AGOSTINO. Augustini Niphi ... De Armorum Literarūq3 Comparatione Cōmētariolus. ... Eiusdem de inimicitiarū lucro. ... Eiusdem apologia Socratis & Aristotelis. ... (Neapoli ... M.D.XXVI. Octauo Idus Maii. Per ... Euangelistam Papieñ. Heredem Condam M. Sigismūdi Mayr. ...) 4°. A-M^{4} N^{6}. ff. ii-liii. [N122a

INDEX OF PRINTERS, PUBLISHFRS, AND BOOKSELLERS

(Serial numbers in italics refer to the addenda. Some dates are inferential and approximate.)

INDEX OF PRINTERS

ALPHABETICAL LIST OF TITLES NOT ENTERED UNDER THE NAME OF AUTHOR OR EDITOR
(not including anonymous works entered under the first word of the title and official publications entered under the name of the issuing authority or that of the territory to which they apply)

Abschrifft ains bryeffs von Constantinopel (1539) C642
Ad ... sacri Romani Imperii Electores ... Carmē exhortatoriū [1510] H259
Adagia quaecumque (1570) M109
Adriani Turnebi ... tumulus (1565) T391
Aggiunta di Amadis di Grecia (1592) A205
Agricoltura tratta da diuersi moderni scrittori (1577) H114
Alcune rime de diuersi moderni scrittori (1577) L142
Le alegrezze fatte in Venetia per ... la vittoria (1571) V79
Alle ... Gentildonne Bolognesi B585
Alle vnd yede geschicht vnd handlung/ was anfängklich Heinrich ... von Braunschweyg ... fürbracht haben (1544) B758
Anagraphe de origine Cartusiani ordinis (1578) C184
Anschlag wider die grausamen ... Thiraney des Türcken (1541) T379
Antorffische Zeitung. Von der Practicirten entleibung/ des Printzen von Oranien (1589) W54
Antorffischer Empörūg ... kurtzer Bericht (1567) A34
Apologia verae doctrinae eorum qui vulgo appellantur VValdenses (1538) W6
Apophthegmatum ex optimis ... scriptoribus Libri VIII (1596) M110
Auszug eines Brieffs ... was das Türckisch Regiment vnd wesen sey (1526) T390
Ausszug etlicher Zeitungen/ von der Türcken Kriegshandlung (1566) Z25
Ausszug Ettlicher Zeitungen/ was sich ... in Vngern verloffen ... hat (1566) Z26
Ausszug/ Newer Zeitungen/ aus der ... Kayserlichen Maystat Feldleger (1566) Z27-28

Des Bapsts vnd der Pfaffen Badstub (1546) P532
Bawrenbeicht. Warhaffte Newe Zeitung Z29
Ain beschaidner historischer/ vnschmälicher Bericht B234
Bonne responce a tous propos B162
The booke for a Iustice of peace (1559) J109
Briefue description de ... la reduction du Haure de Grace (1563) H34
Brief recueil de toutes les sortes de ieux, au'auoient les anciens (1542) R53

Carcel de amor C768
Carmina, ad Pasquillum ... posita (1510) P88
Carmina Apposita Pasquillo anno. M.D.xiij P89
Carmina quae ad pasquillum fuerunt posita [1509] P87
Carmina quinque Hetruscorum poetarum (1562) C155
Cento fauola morali (1570) V28
Ein Christenlicher Ratschlag ... Welcher gestalt sich alle Christenliche personen/ von Oben vnnd vnterthanen halten soll (1526) R38
Christlich Gebett zůr zeit der Theurung (1573) G53
Christliche Warnung vnd Vermanung/ wider das ... flůchen vnnd Gotslästern (1590) W14
Chronica. Del gran capitan Goncalo Hernandez de Cordoua y Aguilar (1584) H92
Chronica vnnd beschreibung der Türckey (1530) T381
Clarorum virorum epistolae (1519) E296
Comedia chiamata Aristippia (1524) A396
Commentario de le cose de Turchi (1540) T382
I compassioneuoli auuertimenti di Erasto (1558, 1559) S402-403
Complurium eruditoꝝ uatum carmina (1518) C156
Confessio VValdensium (1568) W7
Conspiratio pontificia Des Cardinals Von Lotaring (1573) C356
Constitutiones Insignis Collegij Sancti Illefonsi (1560) A148
Cõuocatio Generalis Concilij parte Principum (1512) P364
Copia delle stupende ⁊ horribile cose (1517) B233
Coronatio Ferdinandi regis [1527] F50
La cronique du ... Roy Loys vnziesme (1558) L360
Cy commence vne petite instruction ... de viure pour vne femme seculiere I22

Rime et versi in lode della ... duchessa di Novera (1585) M404

Salue Regis mater misericordie M185
Scelta di facetie (1579) M17
Scelta di rime di diuersi moderni autori (1591) S242
Schlusse der Augustiner Veter [1522] A866
Ain schone/ geistliche ... vnderveysung von wegen der gelübten [1522] U32
Ain schoner dialogus oder gesprech (1528) D107
Ain schoner Dialogus zwischen einem Priester vñ Ritter D108
Ein Schöner Gesitlicher Kalender [c. 1540] K1
Sentences selectes de Periander, Publian, Seneque, & Isocrate (1561) M1
Ein sinreicher Pasquillus (1537) P95
Solennitas & actus renunciationis (1581) A188
Somnia Salomonis (1501) S485
Sonetti & canzoni di diuersi antichi autori Toscani (1527) S486
Stanze di diuersi illustri poeti (1556) D262
Ein Summari der Türckischen Botschaft werbung (1537) V80

Tertius libellus Epistolarum M. Eobani Hessi et aliorum (1561) C68
Habes ... textū Paruuli/ qδ aiūt/ p̄hie natural' (1513) P80
Τὸ παρὸν εὐχολόγιον ἐτυπώθη [1580] G310a
Transumptum priuilegiorum ... concessorum ... Comitibus de Campegijs (1587) C82
Treffenlicher ... anschlag ... durch die ... Hertzogen zů Sachsen (1541) A293
Trewe warnung/ an alle fromme ... Christen (1563) W15
Eyn trostliche disputation/ ... den glawben vnd die lieb betreffend (1524) D171
Turckische grosse Niederlag (1579) T387

Vltimo auiso ... venuta dall'armata Christiana (1572) A954
Ein vnterredung zwisschen dem Pasquillen vnd Deudschen (1537) P96
Vrgichten zweyer zu Dresen gerechtfertigten Vbelthater (1567) D297

Varia doctorū piorumque virorum, De corrupto Ecclesiæ statu (1557) F137
Vera et minuto ragguaglio di quanto è successo nella ... Armata (1572) R6
Vera relazione del martirio Di due Reuerendi sacerdoti (1590) O142
Vereynigung der funff Chur vnnd Fürsten (1533) M57
Verteutschte Capitulation des Anstanndts (1532) A948
Vetustissimorum ... comicorum quinquaginta ... sententiae [c. 1560] H116
Viaggi fatti da Venetia (1543) V145
V. ampliss. Christophori Thuani tumulus (1583) T203
Viridarium Illustrium Poetaꝝ (1507) M359
La vita del ... M. Carlo Zeno (1544) Z48
Vom des Herren Nachtmal (1526) L349
Vom eydt: da bissher so lang von gezancket ist (1531) E52
Vom Glauben vnd wercken [1520] G242
Vom tag zu Hagenaw [1546?] H6
Von alten vnd neüwen Got (1522) G249
Von Bruder Iohan Nasen Esel N57
Von Christlichen abschied ... Der ... Fraw Sybillen (1554) S412
Von dem Iubel Iar [1525] J91
Von dem new gebornen Abgott zu Babel (1550) A851
Von geistlich gewalt vnd würdighait G158
Von Kayserliche Maiestat einreytten/ auf dem Reychstag [1530] C355
Le vraye histoire de la vie de M. Iean Hus (1565) H367

Ein warhaffte grawsam̄e Geschicht/ So geschehen ist zu Mechel (1556) M218
Warhaffte Kurtze Beschreibung/ Wie der Newgemacht Religion Fried ... (1576) F440
Warhaffte newe Zeitung Welchermassen die Romische Keys. Maiest. ... von den Polnischen Abgesandten ... zu einem Konig in Poland declarirt ... worden (1576) H263
Warhaffte Zeitungen auss der Rom. Kay. May. Feldleger (1566) Z42
Warhafftig vnd kurtzer Inhalt Eines heimlichen Rahtschlags (1589) F452
Warhafftige Abcontrafactur vnd Bildnus aller Gros Hertzogen/ Chur vnd Fursten (1587) S224
Warhafftige Beschreibung ... des ... Kriegs in Franckreich (1572) F447

Warhafftige Beschreibung/ des ... Vogels M245
Warhafftige Contrafactur Hertzog Heinrichs des Iungern [c. 1541] B750
Warhafftige Historia von Magister Iohan Hussen (1538) H368
Eine Warhafftige History/ von einem vngerahtnen Son [c. 1540] H150
Warhafftige Newe zeytung/ der ... belegerung ... der Stat Rhodiss (1523) R120
Warhaffitge Newe Zeitung/ was sich fuͤr Empoͤrung nach des Bapsta Pauli des iiii. Todt ... zu Rom zugetragen hat [1559] R200
Warhafftige newe Zeittung ... Wie Henricus Konig von Nauarra ... sich zu den Catholischen ... Religion begeben (1593) F453
Warhafftige vnnd Erschrockenlich: Newe Zeittung (1567) B242
Warhafftige vnnd gewise jarzal (1537) J9
Warhafftige vnnd kurtze bericht ... wie es ietzo ... in eroberung der Stat Rom ergangen ist (1527) R199
Warhafftige Zeyttung von einer grossen Niderlage ... In Flandern (1558) F159
Warhafftige Zeittung/ von Eroberung Placentz vnd Parma (1548) Z43
Warhafftiger vnd erschrecklicher Auffruhr zu Leiptzig (1593) L127
Was von dem ietzt ausgeschriebenen Tridentischen Concilio zu halten sey (1551) T330
Eyn wegsprech gen Regenspurg (1525) R56
Wider den Hauptschalck vnd Todtfeünd des menschē gewissen H33
Wie der Heilig Vater Bapst Adrianus eingeritten ist zu Rom (1522) R282
Wie die Babstlich geschichte Botschaft yre werbung getthan/ haben (1520) R281
Wie mā die recht Euangelisch ler pflantzē moͤcht (1521) L119
Wie vnd wass massen Gott der Herz ... gestraffet hab (1560) G250
Der Wucherer Messkram oder Jarmarckt (1544) M320
Ein wunderbarlich erschreckenlich Hanndlung ... in ... Schiltach (1533) H13

Zwey Gebet/ Wider die ... Tuͤrcken (1593) G58

INDEX OF NAMES

(Names preceded by an asterisk also occur as headings in the main list above. Contemporary sovereign rulers and members of their family are entered under the names of their territories; popes under "Rome, Church of"; bishops acting officially under the names of their dioceses.)

INDEX OF NAMES

www.ingramcontent.com/pod-product-compliance
Lightning Source LLC
Chambersburg PA
CBHW081138300726
48982CB00006B/994
* 9 7 8 0 8 1 2 2 7 6 9 8 5 *